HISTORY OF THE AMERICAN WHALE FISHERY

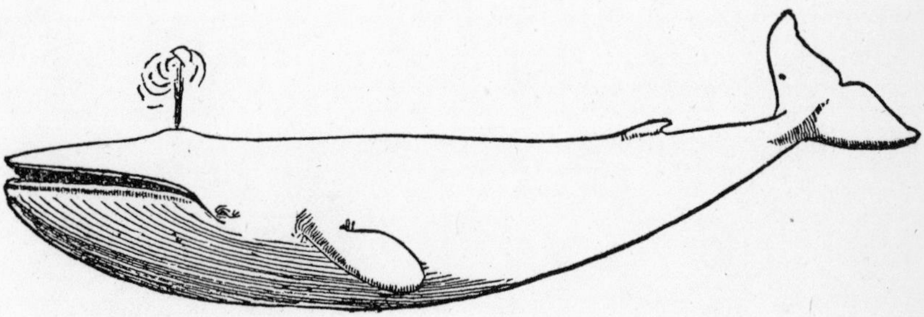

Alexander Starbuck

CASTLE

a division of Book Sales, Inc.
110 Enterprise Avenue
Secaucus, NJ 07094

Printed in the United States of America.
ISBN 1-55521-537-8

CONTENTS

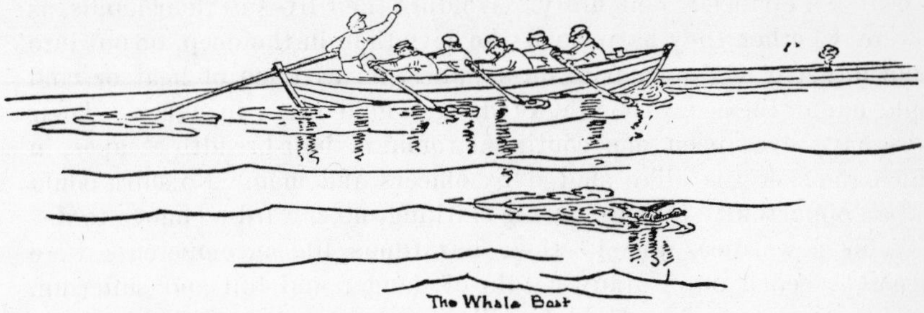

A.—INTRODUCTION.

Few interests have exerted a more marked influence upon the history of the United States than that of the fisheries. Aside from the value they have had in a commercial point of view, they have always been found to be the nurseries of a hardy, daring, and indefatigable race of seamen, such as scarcely any other pursuit could have trained. The pioneers of the sea, whalemen were the advance guard, the forlorn hope of civilization. Exploring expeditions followed after to glean where they had reaped. In the frozen seas of the north and the south, their keels plowed to the extreme limit of navigation, and between the tropics

*More than fifty years ago (in 1825) Samuel H. Jenks, esq., then editor of the Nantucket Inquirer, announced his intention to write the history of whaling, and advertised for material for that purpose, but so little encouragement did he meet, so little material came to hand, that he finally abandoned the design in despair of ever being able to satisfactorily complete it.

In the preface to his admirable Report on the Fisheries, published in 1852, Hon. Lorenzo Sabine says: "More than twenty years have elapsed since I formed the design of writing a work on the American fisheries, and commenced collecting materials for the purpose. My intention embraced the whale-fishery of our flag in distant seas. But increasing cares prevented the consummation of his plans.

The difficulties in the way of collection of historical notes increase greatly with the lapse of years. Newspapers, which must always be considered, where they exist, invaluable aids in the prosecution of such matters, pass from the possession of the very few who, when living, treasured them, and fall into the hands of those who only value them at so many cents per pound. Those who were the actors in the scenes which it is desired to describe die, and with them perishes the source of the information, which ultimately, in the form of tradition, becomes too distorted to be available. In the matter of the whale-fishery still another formidable difficulty is met with, in the absence or destruction of customs-records. During the Revolution many ports were under English control, and very often with the departure of the British also departed the custom-house papers. In other ports, notably New Bedford and Nantucket, these records have been destroyed by fire. Still again in yet other ports, notably Sag Harbor, mildew and decay have obliterated the writing.

About eighteen months ago Prof. Spencer F. Baird, United States Commissioner of Fish and Fisheries, requested the writer to prepare a historical sketch of this indus-

they pursued their prey through regions never before traversed by the vessels of a civilized community. Holding their lives in their hands, as it were, whether they harpooned the leviathan in the deep, or put into some hitherto unknown port for supplies, no extreme of heat or cold could daunt them, no thought of danger hold them in check. Their lives have ever been one continual round of hair-breadth escapes, in which the risk was alike shared by officers and men. No shirk could find an opportunity to indulge his shirking, no coward a chance to display his cowardice, and in their hazardous life incompetents were speedily weeded out. Many a tale of danger and toil and suffering, startling, severe, and horrible, has illumined the pages of the history of this pursuit, and scarce any, even the humblest of these hardy mariners, but can, from his own experience, narrate truths stranger than fiction. In many ports, among hundreds of islands, on many seas the flag of the country from which they sailed was first displayed from the mast-head of a whale ship. Pursuing their avocation wherever a chance presented, the American flag was first unfurled in an English port from the deck of one American whaleman, and the ports of the western coast of South America first beheld the Stars and Stripes shown as the standard of another. It may be safely alleged that but for them the western

---

try, so far as it related to our own country, and append to it, so far as was practicable, a record of every voyage which has been performed. Of the magnitude of this labor only those who have had similar experience can form any idea. In the one item of marine reports, it comprehended the examination of newspapers covering a period of one hundred and seventy years. The limited time allowed for the work performed is not mentioned by the writer in any spirit of self-laudation, but as a statement due to himself for any possible errors of omission or commission that may have occurred.

Fortunately in the collection of material for a work of an entirely different nature much had been gathered which had a bearing upon this subject, and much that was absolutely necessary for use in this connection, and, fortunately, the kindness of many friends lightened still more the labor. Wherever the writer has been in search of material the utmost courtesy has been extended, and, with very rare exceptions, whenever application has been made, books and documents have been freely placed at his command. Especially is he under obligations to Charles Eldridge, esq., of Fairhaven; Dennis Wood, esq., the proprietor of the Shipping-List; and R. C. Ingraham, esq., of New Bedford; the late William R. Sleight, esq., of Sag Harbor, N. Y.; the late Hon. Henry P. Haven, and Haven, Williams & Co., of New London, Conn.; Benjamin F. Cook, esq., of New York; Hon. Lorenzo Sabine, of Boston (who kindly placed all his papers on the subject at the author's disposal); F. C. Sanford, J. S. Barney, and W. H. Macy, esqrs., and Miss R. A. Gardner, of Nantucket; Maj. S. B. Phinney, of Barnstable; R. L. Pease, esq., of Edgartown; Capt. Silas Jones, of Falmouth; Capt. S. W. Macy, of Newport, R. I.; B. Furnald, esq., custodian of historical records of New York (see numerous quotations, the result mainly of his indefatigable researches); and the collectors and assistants of the ports of Boston and New Bedford. He also acknowledges courtesies from those in charge of the libraries of the Massachusetts Historical, Boston Athenæum, and American Antiquarian Societies.

If in the search for facts the historical idols of others have been shattered, it may be a source of satisfaction to them to learn that the writer has been equally iconoclastic with many that he too has reverenced.

ALEXANDER STARBUCK.

WALTHAM, MASS., *March* 1, 1877.

oceans would much longer have been comparatively unknown,* and with equal truth may it be said that whatever of honor or glory the United States may have won in its explorations of these oceans, the necessity for their explorations was a tribute wrung from the Government, though not without earnest and continued effort, to the interests of our mariners, who, for years before, had pursued the whale in these uncharted seas, and threaded their way with extremest care among these undescribed islands, reefs, and shoals. Into the field opened by them flowed the trade of the civilized world. In their footsteps followed Christianity. They introduced the missionary to new spheres of usefulness, and made his presence tenable. Says a writer in the London Quarterly Review: "The whale fishery first opened to Great Britain a beneficial intercourse with the coast of Spanish America; IT LED IN THE SEQUEL TO THE INDEPENDENCE OF THE SPANISH COLONIES." * * * * * "But for our Whalers, *we never might have founded our colonies in Van Dieman's Land and Australia*—or if we had *we could not have maintained them in their early stages of danger and privation.*—Moreover, our intimacy with the Polynesians must be traced to the same source. The Whalers were the first that traded in that quarter—they PREPARED THE FIELD FOR THE MISSIONARIES; and the same thing is now in progress in New Ireland, New Britain, and New Zealand." All that the English fishery has done for Great Britain, the American fishery has done for the United States—and more. In war our Navy has drawn upon it for some of its sturdiest and bravest seamen, and in peace our commercial marine has found in it its choicest and most skilful officers. In connection with the cod-fishery it schooled the sons of America to a knowledge of their own strength, and in its protection developed and intensified that spirit of self-reliance, independence, and national power to which the conflict of from 1775 to 1783 was a natural and necessary resultant. The wars carried on between England and France from 1600

* The North American Review, in 1834, in an article on the Whale Fishery, says, "A few years since, two Russian discovery ships came in sight of a group of cold, inhospitable islands in the Antarctic Ocean. The commander imagined himself a discoverer, and doubtless was prepared with drawn sword and with the flag of his sovereign flying over his head to take possession in the name of the Czar. At this time he was becalmed in a dense fog. Judge of his surprise, when the fog cleared away, to see a little sealing sloop from Connecticut as quietly riding between his ships as if lying in the waters of Long Island Sound. He learned from the captain that the islands were already well known, and that he had just returned from exploring the shores of a new land at the south; upon which the Russian gave vent to an expression too hard to be repeated, but sufficiently significant of his opinion of American enterprise. After the captain of the sloop, he named the discovery 'Palmer's Land,' in which the American acquiesced, and by this name it appears to be designated on all the recently-published Russian and English charts." A similar experience awaited the English ship Caribou, Captain Cubins, who came in sight of Hurd's Island, and, like the Russian, thought it hitherto unknown land. The similarity was carried still further by the appearance of the schooner Oxford, of Fairhaven (tender to the Arab), the captain of which informed him that the island was discovered by them eighteen months before.

to 1760 had, as one of their objective points, a monopoly of these fisheries on the American coast from the plantations in Maine to the northward, and Port Royal, the culminating point of the conflict revealed to America the secret of her own strength. In the final treaty of peace succeeding the war for Independence the protection of these interests, which the colonists had, unaided, maintained, was made one of the ultimati on the part of the Commissioners for the United States, and subsequent events have demonstrated conclusively the wisdom of their statesmanship. At almost every stage of the arrangement of treaties of peace between England and France prior to 1783 and since 1600, and at almost every similar occasion in treaties between England and the United States subsequently to that time, the question of the fisheries has obtruded itself, and demanded a satisfactory solution. Latterly, it is true, the questions have hinged wholly upon the cod-fishery, since the taking of whales is mostly carried on outside of any national jurisdiction, but prior to and immediately after the war of the Revolution, as late indeed as 1818, the question of whaling was quite as much involved.

The development of this industry in the United States, from the period when a few boats first practiced it along the coast to the time when it employed a fleet of seven hundred stanch ships and fifteen thousand hardy seamen, is an interesting chapter in our national history.

B.—FROM 1600 TO 1700.

CAPE COD, CONNECTICUT, LONG ISLAND, NANTUCKET, MARTHA'S VINEYARD, SALEM.

The American whale fishery (limiting that subject entirely to the prosecution of that pursuit from what is now known as the United States,) is cotemporary with the settlement of the New York and New England colonies. Indeed, one of the main ideas in the settlement of Massachusetts was the founding of a fishing colony, and one of the provisions in the charter guaranteed to the colonists their right to unrestrictedly fish.* It was a serious question with the settlers of Eastern Massachusetts whether to adopt Cape Cod for a residence, or select some more propitious site, and the main arguments adduced for that locality were: "1st. That it afforded a good harbor for boats, though not for ships. 2d. That the ground was well adapted to the raising of corn. 3d. It was a place of profitable fishing, *for large whales of the best kind for*

* "Wee have given and graunted * * * all fishes—royal fishes, whales, balan, sturgeons, and other fishes, of what kinde or nature soever that shall at any tyme hereafter be taken in or within the saide seas or waters, or any of them by the said" (here follow the names of the grantees) "their heires and assignes, or by any other person or persons whatsoever there inhabiting, by them, or any of them, to be appointed to fishe therein." (Charter of Massachusetts.)

oil and bone came daily alongside and played about the ship. The master and his mate, and others experienced in fishing, preferred it to the Greenland whale fishery, and asserted that were they provided with the proper implements, £300 or £400 worth of oil might be obtained." 4th. The situation was healthy, secure, and defensible. 5th. It was in the depth of winter and inexpedient to look further.* Coming from England, as the vast majority of the early settlers did, where the value of the fisheries had already assumed considerable importance, it would have been strange if they had failed to have appreciated this important feature of their surroundings.

At this time the whales were very numerous both along the coast and in deep water.† Their habits seem to have been somewhat migratory, as the boat-whaling season usually commenced very regularly early in November and ceased in March or April. According to some writers, the Indians, before the advent of the whites, were accustomed to pursue the whales in their canoes, and occasionally succeeded in harassing them to death. Their weapons consisted of a rude wooden harpoon, to which was attached a line with a wooden float at the end,‡ and the method of attack was to plunge their instruments of torture into the body of the whale whenever he came to the surface of the water to breathe. In Waymouth's journal of his voyage to America in 1605,§ in describing the Indians on the coast, he says: "One especial thing is their manner of killing the whale, which they call powdawe; and will describe his form; how he bloweth up the water; and that he is twelve fathoms long: and that they go in company of their king with a multitude of their boats; and strike him with a bone made in fashion of a harping iron fastened to a rope, which they make great and strong of the bark of trees, which they veer out after him; then all their boats come about him as he riseth above water, with their arrows they shoot him to death; when they have killed him and dragged him to shore, they call all their chief lords together, and sing a song of joy: and those chief lords, whom they call sagamores, divide the spoil and give to every man a share, which pieces so distributed, they hang up about their houses for provisions; and when they boil them they blow off the fat and put to their pease, maize, and other pulse which they eat." Among the Indians of Rhode Island it was the custom when a whale was cast ashore or killed within their jurisdiction, to cut the flesh into pieces and send to the

* Thatcher's Hist. of Plymouth, p. 21.

† Capt. John Smith, in 1614, found whales so plentiful along the coast that he turned aside from the primary object of his voyage to pursue them. Richard Mather, who came over to the Massachusetts Bay in 1635, records in his journal of the voyage seeing near New England "mighty whales spewing up water in the air, like the smoke of a chimney, and making the sea about them white and hoary, as is said in Job, of such incredible bigness that I will never wonder that the body of Jonas could be in the belly of a whale." (Sabine's Report, p. 42.)

‡ "Etchings of a Whaling Cruise," Browne, p. 522.

§ Mass. Hist. Soc. Coll., iii series, viii vol., 156 p.

neighboring tribes as a present of peculiar value.* Scammon says:† "It has been stated by several writers that the American colonists followed up the Indian mode of capturing the whale, by first striking it with a harpoon having a log of wood attached to it by a line, even as late as the commencement of the Sperm Whale fishery." It is quoted that the Hon. Paul Dudley stated: "Our people formerly used to kill the whale near the shore, but now they go off to sea in sloops and *whale-boats*. Sometimes the whale is killed by a single stroke, and yet at other times she will hold the whalemen in play *near half a day together*, with their lances; and sometimes they will get away after they have been lanced and spouted thick blood, with irons in them, and drags (droges) fastened to them, which are thick boards about fourteen inches square." * * * "We are of the opinion, however, that the colonial whalers did not follow the Indian mode of whale-fishing; for it is well known that the British whalers, as early as 1670, used the line attached to the boat, and, so far as the drags or 'droges' are concerned, they are used at the present day in cases of emergency.‡

As early as 1639, Massachusetts, with an eye to the importance of the fisheries, passed an act to encourage them. By its provisions all vessels employed in taking or transporting fish were exempted from all duties and taxes for the term of seven years, and all fishermen were exempted from military service during the fishing season. As important as the pursuit of whaling seemed to have been considered by the first settlers, many years seem to have elapsed before it was followed as a business, though probably something was attempted in that direction prior to any recorded account that we have. The subject of drift-whales appears to have attracted considerable importance both in the Plymouth and the Massachusetts Bay colonies. The colonial government claimed a portion, a portion was allowed to the town, and the finder, if no other

---

* Arnold's Hist. R. I., i, p. 85. Among the Montauk Indians the most savory sacrafice to their deity was the tail or fin of the whale. (Hedge's Address, p. 35.) The Greenlander's idea of Heaven, according to Father Hennepin, was a place where there would be an immense cauldron continually boiling, and each could take as much seal blubber, ready cooked, as he wanted.

† Marine Mammalia and American Whale Fishery, p. 204, note.

‡ It would appear from Purchas' account that lines were used to attach the boat to the whale as early as 1613. He writes: "I might here recreate your wearied eyes with a hunting spectacle of the greatest chase which nature yieldeth; I mean the killing of a whale. When they espy him on the top of the water (which he is forced to for to take breath), they row toward him in a shallop, in which the harponeer stands ready with both his hands to dart his harping iron, *to which is fastened a line of such length that the whale (which suddenly feeling himself hurt, sinketh to the bottom,) may carry it down with him, being before fitted that the shallop be not therewith endangered*; coming up again, they strike him with lances made for that purpose, about twelve feet long, the iron eight thereof, and the blade eighteen inches—*the harping iron principally serving to fasten him to the shallop*, and thus they hold him in such pursuit, till after streams of water, and next of blood, cast up into the air and water, (as angry with both elements, which have brought thither such weak hands for his destruction,) he at length yieldeth up his slain carcass as meed to the conquerors."

claimant appeared to dispute his title, might presume to claim the other third. Evidently at times some disposition to rebel was manifested, for in 1661, the general court of Plymouth Colony sent to Sandwich, Barnstable, Yarmouth, and Eastham the following proposition:

"OCT. 1, 1661.—LOUEING FRINDS: Whereas the Generall Court was pleased to make some proposition to you respecting the drift fish or whales; in case you should refuse theire proffer, they impowered mee, though vnfitt, to farme out what should belonge vnto them on that account; and seeing the time is expired, and it fales into my hands to dispose of, I doe therefore, with the advice of the Court, in answare to your remonstrance, say, that if you will duely and trewly pay to the countrey for euery whale that shall come one hogshead of oyle att Boston, where I shall appoint, and that current and merchantable, without any charge or trouble to the countrey.*—I say, for peace and quietness sake you shall have it for this present season, leaueing you and the Election Court to setle it soe as it may bee to satisfaction on both sides; and in case you accept not of this tender, to send it within fourteen dayes after the date heerof and if I heare not from you, I shall take it for graunted that you will accept of it, and shall expect the accomplishment of the same.

"Youers to vse,

"CONSTANT SOUTHWORTH TREASU."†

The offer was accepted and indorsed as follows:

"THE SIXT OF THE FIRST MONTH 61-62.

"Agreement to give 2 bbls of oyle from each whale according to proposition made for yeare past, to end all troubles.

"ANTHONY THACHER.
"ROBERT DENIS.
"THOMAS BOARDMAN.
"RICHARD TAYLER."

Numerous instances of orders relating to drift-whales occur in the records of Plymouth, Massachusetts, and New York. In 1662, the town of Eastham voted that a part of every whale cast ashore should be appropriated for the support of the ministry.‡ Many were the disputes that the general court was called upon to adjust in regard to stranded whales, but the decisions seem to be, if not generally satisfactory, at least universally acquiesced in.

The earliest account of whale-killing by the people of Cape Cod comes to us in the form of a tradition, and quite an unsatisfactory and improba-

* By an order of court, June 6, 1654, whales cast up on lands of purchasers belonged to said proprietors. (Plym. Col. Rec. iii, p. 53.) This being much more satisfactory than the order compelling tribute to the government, probably caused ill-feeling when the general court preferred a claim.

† Plym. Col. Rec., vol. iv, p. 6.

‡ Freeman's Hist. Cape Cod, ii, p. 362.

ble tradition, too. It is to the effect that one William Hamilton was the first to kill these fish from that region, and he was obliged to remove from that section of country, as his fellow-citizens persecuted him for his skill, attributing his success to undue familiarity with evil spirits. Hamilton is said to have removed to Rhode Island, and from thence to Connecticut, where he died in 1746, aged 103 years. Several things militate against this story. Neither the annals of the Cape* nor genealogical registers contain any record of him. Naturally the courts would take some cognizance of an offense so heinous that the offender was openly persecuted, but we do not find him noted as a criminal. The people who settled on the Cape were too familiar with fishing to attribute success to aught but skill and natural causes, and the Cape was more an asylum for the persecuted than the source of persecution. It is far more probable that at the time of his birth, if he ever existed there, there were people familiar with this art in that region. It had certainly become a pursuit of much importance in other sections of the country long before he was old enough to handle a harpoon, and the product of this fishery had found its way to Boston while he was yet a young man.

In 1688 Secretary Randolph writes home from Massachusetts: "New Plimouth Colony have great profit by whale killing. I believe it will be one of our best returnes, now beaver and peltry fayle us."† In March of the same year there was placed on the colonial records of Massachusetts Bay a memorandum embodying the universally recognized law of whalemen that "craft claims the whale." It specifies: "furst: if aney pursons shall find a Dead whael on the streem And have the opportunity to toss herr on shoure; then ye owners to alow them twenty shillings; 2ly: if thay cast hur out & secure ye blubber & bone then ye owners to pay them for it 30*s* (that is if ye whael ware lickly to be loast;) 3ly, if it proves a floate son not killed by men then ye Admirall to Doe thaire in as he shall please;—4ly; that no persons shall presume to cut up any whael till she be vewed by toe persons not consarned; that so ye Right owners may not be Rongged of such whael or whaels; 5ly, that no whael shall be needlessly or fouellishly lansed behind ye vitall to avoid stroy; 6ly, that each companys harping Iron & lance be Distinckly marked on ye heads & socketts with a poblick mark: to ye prevention of strife; 7ly, that if a whale or whalls be found & no Iron in them: then thay that lay ye neerest claime to them by thaire strokes & ye natoral markes to haue them; 8ly, if 2 or 3 companyes lay equal claimes, then thay equelly to shear."‡

In November, 1690, the colony of New Plymouth appointed "Inspectors of Whale," in order to the "prevention of suits by whalers." The

* It is scarcely probable that so careful a historian as Freeman would have omitted to make mention of Hamilton, if this story of him had any foundation in fact.

† Hutchinson's Coll., p. 558.

‡ Mass. Col. MSS., Treasury, iii, p. 80.

rules governing them were: "1. All whales killed or wounded & left at sea the killers to repaire to the inspectors & give marks, time, place, which shall be recorded. 2. All whales brought or cast ashore to be viewed by inspector or deputy before being cut & marks & wounds recorded with time & place. 3. Any person cutting or defacing whale before being viewed unless necessary shall lose right to it, & pay 10£ to county, & fish to be seized by inspectors for owners' use. Inspectors to have power to make deputy and allow 6*s.* per whale. 4. Those finding whale a mile from shore not appearing to be killed by man shall be first to secure them, pay 1 hogshead of oyle to ye county for each whale." *

In 1647 (May 25) at a meeting of the general court held at Hartford, Conn., the following resolve was passed: "Yf Mr. Whiting, wth any others shall make tryall and p^rsecute a designe for the takeing of whale wth in these libertyes, and if vppon tryall wth in the terme of two yeares, they shall like to goe on, noe others shalbe suffered to interrupt the, for the tearme of seauen yeares." † Whether Mr. Whiting, who seems to have been quite a prominent man and a merchant at Hartford, ever did "prosecute his designe," or not, we are left to conjecture; but so far as we at present know, this is the earliest official document showing any intention in that direction, and many years elapse before Connecticut again claims attention upon this subject.

It is probably safe to assert that the first organized prosecution of the American whale-fishery was made along the shores of Long Island. The town of Southampton, which was settled in 1640 by an offshoot from the Massachusetts Colony at Lynn,‡ was quick to appreciate the value of this source of revenue. In March, 1644, the town ordered the town divided into four wards of eleven persons to each ward, to attend to the drift-whales cast ashore. When such an event took place two persons from each ward (selected by lot) were to be employed to cut it up. "And every Inhabitant with his child or servant that is above sixteen years of age shall have in the Division of the other part," (*i. e.* what remained after the cutters deducted the double share they were, ex officio, entitled to) "an equall proportion provided that such person when yt falls into his ward a sufficient man to be imployed aboute yt." § Among the names of those delegated to each ward are many whose descendants became prominent in the business as masters or owners of vessels—the Coopers, the Sayres, Mulfords, Peirsons, Hedges, Howells, Posts, and others. A few years later the number of "squadrons" was increased to six.

---

* Plym. Col. Rec. vi, pp. 252–3.

† Conn. Col. Rec., i, p. 154.

‡ Southampton was settled under a patent from the Earl of Sterling, and the privileges accorded were essentially those of the Massachusetts Bay Colony. In 1664 the commissioners to adjust the colonial bounds decided this and the adjacent towns to be within the jurisdiction of the Duke of York.

§ Howell's Hist. of Southampton, p. 179.

In February, 1645, the town ordered that if any whale was cast ashore within the limits of the town no man should take or carry away any part thereof without order from a magistrate, under penalty of twenty shillings. Whoever should find any whale or part of a whale, upon giving notice to a magistrate, should have allowed him five shillings, or if the portion found should not be worth five shillings the finder should have the whole. "And yt is further ordered that yf any shall finde a whale or any peece thereof upon the Lord's day then the aforesaid shillings shall not be due or payable."* "This last clause" says Howell, "appears to be a very shrewd thrust at 'mooning' on the beach on Sundays."

It was customary a few years later to fit out expeditions of several boats each for whaling along the coast, the parties engaged camping out on shore during the night. These expeditions were usually gone about one or two weeks.† Indians were usually employed by the English, the whites furnishing all the necessary implements, and the Indians receiving a stipulated proportion of oil in payment.

In Easthampton on the 6th of November, 1651, "It was Ordered that Goodman Mulford shall call out ye Town by succession to loke out for whale."‡ Easthampton, however, like every other town where whales were obtainable, seems to have had its little unpleasantnesses on the subject, for in 1653 the town "Ordered that the share of whale now in controversie between the Widow Talmage and Thomas Talmage" (alas for the old-time Chesterfieldian gallantry) "shall be divided among them as the lot is."§ In the early deeds of the town the Indian grantors were to be allowed the fins and tails of all drift-whales; and in the deed of Montauk Island and Point, the Indians and whites were to be equal sharers in these prizes.‖ In 1672 the towns of Easthampton, Southampton, and Southwold presented a memorial to the court at Whitehall "setting forth that they have spent much time and paines, and the greatest part of their Estates, in settling the trade of whale-fishing in the adjacent seas, *having endeavoured it above these twenty yeares*, but could not bring it to any perfection till within these 2 or 3 yeares last past. And it now being a hopefull trade at New Yorke, in America, the Governor and the Dutch there do require ye Petitioners to come under their patent, and lay very heavy taxes upon them beyond any of his Maties subjects in New England, and will not permit the petitioners to have any deputys in Court,¶ but being chiefe, do impose what Laws they please upon them, and insulting very much over the Petitioners threaten to cut down their timber which is but little they have to Casks for oyle, altho' the Pet^rs^ purchased their landes of the Lord Sterling's deputy, above 30 yeares since, and have till now under the Government and Pat-

* *Ibid.*, p. 184. † *Ibid.*, p. 183.

‡ Bi-Centennial Address at Easthampton, 1850, by Henry P. Hedges, p. 8.

§ *Ibid.*, p. 8. ‖ *Ibid.*

¶ In this petition is an early assertion of the twinship of taxation and representation, for which Massachusetts and her offshoots were ever strenuous.

ent of Mr. Winthrop, belonging to Conitycut Patent, which lyeth far more convenient for ye Petitioners assistance in the aforesaid Trade." They desire, therefore, either to continue under the Connecticut government, or to be made a free corporation. This petition was referred to the "Council on Foreign Plantations."

This would make the commencement of this industry date back not far from the year 1650. In December, 1652, the directors of the Dutch West India Company write to Director General Peter Stuyvesant, of New York: "In regard to the whale fishery we understand that it might be taken in hand during some part of the year. If this could be done with advantage, it would be a very desirable matter, and make the trade there flourish and animate many people to try their good luck in that branch.*" In April, (4th,) 1656, the council of New York "received the request of Hans Jongh, soldier and tanner, asking for a ton of train-oil or *some of the fat of the whale lately captured.*†

In April, 1669, Mr. Samuel Mavericke writes to Colonel Nicolls:‡

"On ye East end of Long Island there were 12 or 13 whales taken before ye end of March, and what since wee heare not; here are dayly some seen in the very harbour, sometimes within Nutt Island. Out of the Pinnace the other week they struck two, but lost both, the iron broke in one, the other broke the warpe.§ The Governor hath encouraged some to follow this designe. Two shallops made for itt, but as yett wee doe not heare of any they have gotten."

In 1672, the town of Southampton passed an order for the regulation of whaling, which, in the latter part of the year, received the following confirmation from Governor Lovelace: "Whereas there was an ordinance made at a Towne-Meeting in South Hampton upon the Second Day of May last relating to the Regulation of the Whale ffishing and Employment of the Indyans therein, wherein particularly it is mentioned. That whosoever shall Hire an Indyan to go a-Whaling, shall not give him for his Hire above one Trucking Cloath Coat, for each whale, hee and his Company shall Kill, or halfe the Blubber, without the Whale Bone under a Penalty therein exprest: Upon Considerac'on had thereupon, I have thought good to Allow of the said Order, And do hereby Confirm the same, untill some inconvenience therein shall bee made appeare, And do also Order that the like Rule shall bee followed at East Hampton and other Places if they shall finde it practicable amongst them.

"Given under my hand in New Yorke, the 28th of Novemb'r, 1672.

[Sign.] "FRAN: LOVELACE."||

---

* N. Y. Col., MSS., vi, p. 75.

† N. Y. Col., MSS., vi, p. 354.

‡ N. Y. Col., Rec. iii, p. 183.

§ It would seem by this that as early as 1669 American whaleman were accustomed to fasten to the whale with their line.

|| N. Y. Col., MSS.

Upon the same day that the people of Southampton passed the foregoing order, Governor Lovelace also issued an order citing that in consequence of great abuse to his Royal Highness in the matter of drift-whales upon Long Island, he had thought fit to appoint Mr. Wm. Osborne and Mr. John Smith, of Hempstead, to make strict inquiries of Indians and English in regard to the matter.*

It was early found to be essential that all important contracts and agreements, especially "between the English and Indians relating to the killing of whales should be entered upon the town books, and signed by the parties in presence of the clerk and certified by him. Boat-whaling was so generally practiced and was considered of so much importance by the whole community, that every man of sufficient abilits in the town was obliged to take his turn in watching for whales from some elevated position on the beach, and to sound the alarm on one being seen near the coast."† In April, (2d,) 1668, an agreement was entered on the records of Easthampton, binding certain Indians of Montauket in the sum of £10 sterling to go to sea, whaling, on account of Jacobus Skallenger and others, of Easthampton, beginning on the 1st of November and ending on the 1st of the ensuing April, they engaging "to attend dilligently with all opportunitie for ye killing of whales or other fish, for ye sum of three shillings a day for every Indian: ye sayd Jacobus Skallenger and partners to furnish all necessarie craft and tackling convenient for ye designe." The laws governing these whaling-companies were based on justice rather than selfishness. Among the provisions was one passed January 4, 1669, whereby a member of one company finding a dead whale killed by the other company was obliged to notify the latter. A prudent proviso in the order was that the person bringing the tidings should be well rewarded. If the whale was found at sea, the killers and finders were to be equal sharers. If irons were found in the whale, they were to be restored to the owners.‡ In 1672, John Cooper desired leave to employ some "strange Indians" to assist him in whaling, which leave was granted;§ but these Indian allies required tender handling, and were quite apt to ignore their contracts when a fair excuse could be found, especially if their hands had already closed over the financial consideration. Two or three petitions relating to cases of this kind are on file at New York. One of them is from "Jacob Skallenger, Stephen Hand, James Loper and other adjoined with them in the Whale Designe at Easthampton," and was presented in 1675. It sets forth that they had associated together for the purpose of whaling, and agreed to hire twelve Indians and man two boats. Having seen the natives yearly employed both by neighbors and those in surrounding towns, they thought there could be no objec-

* N. Y. Col., MSS., General Entries iv, p. 123, Francis Lovelace.

† Howell's Southampton.

‡ This code was very similar to that afterward adopted in the Massachusetts Bay.

§ N. Y. Col. MSS.; General Entries, iv, p. 235.

tion to their doing likewise. Accordingly, they agreed in June with twelve Indians to whale for them during the following season. "But it fell out soe that foure of the said Indians (competent & experienced men) belonged to Shelter-Island whoe with the rest received of your petic̃on^{rs} in pt. of their hire or wages 25*s.* a peece in hand at the time of the contract, as the Indian Custome is and without which they would not engage themselves to goe to Sea as aforesaid for your Petic̃on^{rs}." Soon after this there came an order from the governor requiring, in consequence of the troubles between the English and the aborigines, that all Indians should remain in their own quarters during the winter. "And some of the towne of Easthampton wanteing Indians to make up theire crue for whaleing they take advantage of your hon^{rs} s^{d} Ordre thereby to hinder your petic̃on^{rs} of the said foure Shelter-Island Indians. One of ye Overseers being of the Company that would soe hinder your petic̃on^{rs}. And Mr. Barker warned yor petic̃on^{rs} not to entertaine the said foure Indians without licence from your hon^{r}. And although some of your peticoners opposites in this matter of great weight to them seek to prevent yor petic̃on^{rs} from haveing those foure Indians under pretence of zeal in fullfilling y^{r} hon^{rs} order, yet it is more then apparent that they endeavor to break yor petic̃on^{rs} Company in y^{t} maner that soe they themselves may have opportunity out of the other eight Easthampton Indians to supply theire owne wants." After representing the loss liable to accrue to them from the failure of their design and the inability to hire Easthampton Indians, on account of their being already engaged by other companies, they ask relief in the premises,* which Governer Andross, in an order dated November 18, 1675, grants them, by allowing them to employ the aforesaid Shelter-Island Indians.†

Another case is that of the widow of one Cooper, who in 1677 petitions Andross to compel some Indians who had been hired and paid their advance by her late husband to fulfill to her the contract made with him, they having been hiring out to other parties since his decease.‡

The trade in oil from Long Island early gravitated to Boston and Connecticut, and this was always a source of much uneasiness to the authorities at New York. The people inhabiting Easthampton, Southampton, and vicinity, settling under a patent with different guarantees from those allowed under the Duke of York, had little in sympathy with that government, and always turned toward Connecticut as their natural ally and Massachusetts as their foster mother. Scarcely had what they looked upon as the tyrannies of the New York governors reduced them to a sort of subjection when they were assailed by a fresh enemy. A sudden turn of the wheel of fortune brought them, in 1673, a second time under the control of the Dutch. During this interregnum, which lasted from July, 1673, to November, 1674, they were summoned, by their then

* N. Y. Col. MSS., xxv, Sir Ed. Andross, p. 41.

† Warrants, Orders, Passes, &c., 1674-1679, p. 161.

‡ N. Y. Col. MSS., xxvi, p. 153.

conquerors, to send delegates to an assembly to be convened by the temporary rulers. In reply the inhabitants of Easthampton, Southampton, Southold, Seatoocook, and Huntington returned a memorial setting forth that up to 1664 they had lived quietly and prosperously under the government of Connecticut. Now, however, the Dutch had by force assumed control, and, understanding them to be well disposed, the people of those parts proffer a series of ten requests. The ninth is the particular one of interest in this connection, and is the only one not granted. In it they ask, "That there be ffree liberty granted ye 5 townes aforesd for ye procuring from any of ye united Collonies (without molestation on either side:) warpes, irons or any other necessaries ffor ye comfortable carring on the whale design." To this reply is made that it "cannot in this conjunction of time be allowed." "Why," says Howell,* "the Council of Governor Colve chose thus to snub the English in these five towns in the matter of providing a few whale-irons and necessary tackle for capturing the whales that happened along the coast, is inconceivable;" but it must be remembered that the English and Dutch had long been rivals in this pursuit, even carrying their rivalry to the extreme of personal conflicts. The Dutch assumed to be, and practically were, the factors of Europe in this business at this period, and would naturally be slow to encourage any proficiency in whaling by a people upon whom they probably realized that their lease of authority would be brief. Hence, although they were willing to grant them every other right in common with those of their own nationality, maritime jealousy made this one request impracticable. How the people of Long Island enjoyed this state of affairs is easy to infer from their petition of 1672. The oppressions alike of New York governors and Dutch conquerors could not fail to increase the alienation that difference of habits, associations, interests, and rights had implanted within them. Among other arbitrary laws was one compelling them to carry all the oil they desired to export to New York to be cleared, a measure which produced so much dissatisfaction and inconvenience that it was beyond a doubt "more honored in the breach than in the observance." At times some captain, more scrupulous than the rest, would obey the letter of the law or procure a remission of it. Thus, in April, 1678, Benjamin Alford, of Boston, in New England, merchant, petitioned Governor Brockholds for permission to clear with a considerable quantity of oil that he had bought at Southampton, directly from that port to London, he paying all duties required by law. This he desires to do in order to avoid the hazard of the voyage to New York and the extra danger of leakage thereby incurred. He was accordingly allowed to clear as he desired.†

---

*Hist. of Southampton, p. 62.

†N. Y. Col. MSS., xxvii, pp. 65, 66. Accompanying the order is a blank clearance reading as follows: "Permitt & suffer the good ——— of ——— A. B. Commander, bound for the Port of London in Old England to passe from the Harbo[r] at the North-Sea near South[ton] at the East End of Long Isl. with her loading of Whale Oyl &

In 1684 an act for the "Encouragement of trade and Navigation" within the province of New York was passed, laying a duty of 10 per cent. on all oil and bone exported from New York to any other port or place except directly to England, Jamaica, Barbadoes, or some other of the Caribbean Islands.

In May, 1688, the Duke of York instructs his agent, John Leven, to inquire into the number of whales killed during the past six years within the province of New York, the produce of oil and bone, and "about his share."* To this Leven makes reply that there has been no record kept, and that the oil and bone were shared by the companies killing the fish. To Leven's stâtement, Andross, who is in England defending his colonial government, asserts that all those whales that were driven ashore were killed and claimed by the whalers or Indians.†

In August, 1688, we find the first record of an intention to obtain sperm oil. Among the records in the State archives at Boston is a petition from Timotheus Vanderuen, commander of the brigantine Happy Return, of New Yorke, to Governor Andross, praying for "Licence and Permission, with one Equipage Consisting in twelve mariners, twelve whalemen and six Diuers—from this Port, upon a fishing design about the Bohames Islands, And Cap florida, for sperma Coeti whales and Racks: And so to returne for this Port."‡ Whether this voyage was ever undertaken or not we have no means of knowing, but the petition is conclusive evidence that there were men in the country familiar even then with some of the haunts of the sperm whale and with his capture.

Francis Nicholson, writing from Fort James, December, 1688, says: "Our whalers have had pretty good luck, killing about Graves End three large whales. On the Easte End aboute five or six small ones."§ During this same year the town of Easthampton being short of money, debtors were compelled to pay their obligations in produce, and in order to have some system of exchange the trustees of the town "being Legally met March 6, 1688–9 it was agreed that this year's Towne rate should be held to be good pay if it be paid as Follows:

	£.	s.	d.
"Dry merchantable hides att	0	0	6
"Indian Corn	0	3	0
"Whale Bone 3 feet long and upwards	0	0	8."‖

Whalebone without any manner of Lett Hindrance or Molestacon, shee having beene cleared by order from the Custom house here & given security accordingly. Given under my hand in N. Y. this 20th day of April in the 30th yeare of his Ma[ties] raigne A[o] Dom ini 1678.

"To all his Ma[ties] Offic[rs] whom this may Concerne."

* N. Y. Col. Records, iii, p. 282.

† *Ibid.*, p. 311.

‡ Mass. Col. MSS., Usurpation, vi, p. 126.

§ *Ibid.*, iv, p. 303.

‖ Bi-Centennial Address at Easthampton, p. 41.

The first whaling expedition in Nantucket "was undertaken," says Macy,* "by some of the original purchasers of the island; the circumstances of which are handed down by tradition, and are as follows: A whale, of the kind called 'scragg,' came into the harbor and continued there three days. This excited the curiosity of the people, and led them to devise measures to prevent his return out of the harbor. They accordingly invented and caused to be wrought for them a harpoon, with which they attacked and killed the whale. This first success encouraged them to undertake whaling as a permanent business; whales being at that time numerous in the vicinity of the shores."

In 1672 the islanders, evidently desirous of making further progress in this pursuit, recorded a memorandum of a proposed agreement with one James Loper, in which it is said that the said James "doth Ingage to carrey on a Designe of Whale Catching on the Island of Nantucket that is to say James Ingages to be a third in all Respects, and som of the Town Ingages also to carrey on the other two thirds with him in like manner—the town doth also consent that first one company shall begin, and afterwards the rest of the freeholders or any of them have Liberty to set up another Company provided they make a tender to those freeholders that have no share in the first company and if any refuse the rest may go on themselves, and the town doth engage that no other Company shall be allowed hereafter; also, whoever kill any whales, of the Company or Companies aforesaid, they are to pay to the Town for every such whale five shillings and for the Incoragement of the said James Loper the Town doth grant him ten acres of Land in sume Convenant place that he may chuse in (Wood Land Except) and also liberty for the commonage of three cows and Twenty sheep and one horse with necessary wood and water for his use, on Conditions that he follow the trade of whalling on this Island two years in all seasons thereof beginning the first of March next Insuing; also he is to build upon his Land and when he leaves Inhabiting upon this Island then he is first to offer his Land to the Town at a valuable price and if the Town do not buy it he may sell it to whom he please; the commonage is granted only for the time of his staying here."† At the same meeting John Savidge had a

* Hist. Nantucket, p. 28.

†There are most excellent reasons for concluding that Loper never went to Nantucket. When the parties to whom grants were made settled there, their lots were surveyed and laid out to them and the survey recorded. In Loper's case no after-mention occurs of him in any place or manner, and in the list of proprietors and their grants, made up in 1674, and forwarded to New York, his name is not mentioned. Notwithstanding the islanders, in their desire to honor and perpetuate his name, called two of their ships after him, those who are best judges in the matter concede that he never had a residence there. One James Loper (or Looper) resided at Easthampton and carried on whaling from there prior to 1675 (see petition of Shallenger, Hand & Loper). Undoubtedly this is the man referred to in the Nantucket records. Up to the year 1678, however, he still owned property in Easthampton. In regard to the Loper mentioned by Felt (Annals of Salem, p. 223), and who has been supposed (see Savage's

grant made to him, upon condition that he took up his residence on the island for the space of three years, and also that he should "follow his trade of a cooper upon the island as the Town or whale Company have need to employ him." Loper beyond a doubt never improved this opportunity offered him of immortalizing himself, but Savidge did, and a perverse world has, against his own will, handed down to posterity the name of Loper, who did not come, while it has rather ignored that of Savidge, who did remove to that island.

The history of whaling upon Nantucket from that time until 1690 is rather obscure. There is a tradition among the islanders that in this year several persons were standing upon what was afterward known as Folly House Hill, observing the whales spouting and sporting in the sea. One of these people, pointing to the ocean, said to the others: "There is a green pasture, where our children's grandchildren will go for bread."* It would be a matter of interest to know the name of the individual to whom this prophetic vision was revealed, but tradition is almost always lame somewhere. In 1690 the people of Nantucket, "finding that the people of Cape Cod had made greater proficiency in the art of whale-catching than themselves," sent thither and employed Ichabod Paddock to remove to the island and instruct them in the best method of killing whales and obtaining the oil.† Judging from subsequent events, he must have come and proved himself a good teacher and they most admirable pupils.

The earliest mention of whales at Martha's Vineyard occurs in November, 1652, when Thomas Daggett and William Weeks were appointed "whale cutters for this year." The ensuing April it was "Ordered by the town that the whale is to be cut out freely, four men at one time, and four at another, and so every whale, beginning at the east end of the town." In 1690 Mr. ‡ Sarson and William Vinson were appointed by "the proprietors of the whale" to oversee the cutting and sharing of all whales cast on shore within the bounds of Edgartown, "they to have as much for their care as one cutter."

---

genealogical dictionary) to be the one spoken of, the petition (Mass. Col. MSS., Usurpation, ii, p. 136) gives his name as *Jacobus* Loper, and it is by this name alone he is known. Thus in 1686 the constable of Eastham was ordered to attach *Jacobus* Loper to find sureties for good behavior and appearance at the next court, and at the October term *Jacobus* Loper was acquitted of a criminal charge. In no place does the Latin name undergo a change, and accompanying circumstances would scarcely seem to imply that the appellation was ever intended to be James. On the contrary the Nantucket document plainly says James, as also do the MSS. relating to Easthampton, and in no place is the Latinized form used.

* Macy's Nantucket, p. 33.

† Macy's Nantucket, pp. 29–30. No record exists of this save in the form of tradition, but many circumstances give it an appearance of far greater probability than the story concerning Loper. Among other things, it is related as an historical fact by Zaccheus Macy (Mass. Hist. Soc., Col. iii, p. 155), who died in 1797, aged 83 years, and hence was cotemporary with some of the men living in Paddock's time. He, however, makes no mention of Loper.

‡ Richard L. Pease, esq., in Vineyard Gazette.

In 1692 came the inevitable dispute of proprietorship. A whale was cast on shore at Edgartown by the proprietors, "seized by Benjamin Smith and Mr. Joseph Norton in their behalf," which was also claimed by "John Steel, harpooner, on a whale design, as being killed by him." It was settled by placing the whale in the custody of Richard Sarson, esq., and Mr. Benjamin Smith, as agents of the proprietors, to save by trying out and securing the oil; "and that no distribution be made of the said whale, or effects, till after fifteen days are expired after the date hereof, that so such persons who may pretend an interest or claim, in the whale, may make their challenge; and in case such challenge appear sufficient to them, then they may deliver the said whale or oyl to the challenger; otherwise to give notice to the proprietors, who may do as the matter may require."

Mr. Felt, in his History of Salem,* says that James Loper, of that town, in 1688, petitioned the colonial government of Massachusetts for a patent for making oil. In his petition Loper represents that he has been engaged in whale-fishing for twenty-two years.

On the 12th of March, 1692, John Higginson and Timothy Lindall, of Salem, wrote to Nathaniel Thomas: "We have been jointly concerned in severall whale voyages at Cape Cod, and have sustained greate wrong and injury by the unjust dealing of the inhabitants of those parts, especially in two instances: ye first was when Woodbury and company, in our boates, in the winter of 1690, killed a large whale in Cape Cod harbour. She sank and after rose, went to sea with a harpoon, warp, etc. of ours, which have been in the hands of Nicholas Eldredge. The second case is this last winter, 1691. William Edds and company, in one of our boates, struck a whale, which came ashore dead, and by ye evidence of the people of Cape Cod was the very whale they killed. The whale was taken away by Thomas Smith, of Eastham, and unjustly detained."†

Nor was the art of whaling unknown or unpracticed by our Canadian neighbors in these early years, for M. de Denonville writes to M. de Seignelay, in 1690, that the Canadians are adroit in whaling, and that the "last ships have brought to Quebec, from Bayonne, some harpooners for Sieur Riverin."‡

---

* Vol. ii, p. 224.

† *Ibid.*

‡ Memoir on Acadia, &c., N. Y. Col. Rec., ix, pp. 444-5. Holmes, in his "American Annals" (vol. i, p. 133), says: "Other English ships went this year (1593) to Cape Breton. This is the first mention, that we find, of the whale-fishery by the English. Although they found no whales in this instance, yet they discovered on an island eight hundred whale fins where a Biscay ship had been three years before; and this is the first account we have of whale fins or whale bone by the English." So it appears that for a long term of years Canadian waters were the whaleman's garden.

C.—1700 TO 1750.

NANTUCKET ; LONG ISLAND ; CAPE COD ; SALEM ; BOSTON ; RHODE ISLAND ; MARTHA'S VINEYARD, ETC.

Immediately after the commencement of the eighteenth century the town of Sherburne,* on the island of Nantucket, advanced rapidly to the front rank among whaling ports. So plentiful was their prey almost at their very doors, as it were, that no difficulty was at first experienced by the islanders in obtaining all the oil they desired without going out of sight of land. "The south side of the island," says a writer,† "was divided into four equal parts, and each part was assigned to a company of six, which, though thus separated, still carried on their business in common. In the middle of this distance" (of about three and a half miles to each division) "they erected a mast, provided with a sufficient number of rounds, and near it they built a temporary hut where five of the associates lived, whilst the sixth from his high station carefully looked toward the sea, in order to observe the spouting of whales." When one was seen, the boats were launched and the chase commenced. Sometimes, in pleasant weather, the whalemen would venture nearly out of sight of land. A capture once made, the whale was towed ashore and the blubber "saved" after the manner of cutting in on board a vessel. Try-works were erected on the beach, and the blubber, after being cut up and sliced, was subjected to the process of "trying out." These try-works were used for many years after exclusive shore-fishing had ceased, the blubber of the whales captured at sea being cut up into square pieces and stowed into casks on board of the vessels. On the return home this product was removed to the try-houses and the oil extracted. This was substantially the method of carrying on the fishery all along the coast. As the natural consequence of long-continued practice, the inhabitants of Nantucket soon acquired great dexterity in the pursuit. Says St. John : "These people are become superior to any other whalemen."‡ In this business many Indians were employed, each boat's crew being manned in part, some wholly, by aborigines, the most active among them being promoted to steersmen, and even at times one of them being allowed to command a boat. Under the stimulus of this

* So called prior to 1795 ; since then better known as Nantucket.

† Letters from an American farmer, J. Hector St. John Crevecœur. Within the past twenty five years, when whales were seen off Southampton, the alarm was sounded by means of a horn and boats were hastily manned in pursuit, and to the present day boats and whaling craft are kept in readiness to start in pursuit of whales at a moment's warning.

‡ J. Hector St. John de Crevecœur. "Letters of an American Farmer." (Published 1782.) It is a somewhat disputed question whether St. John ever visited Nantucket or not. If he never did, his description of customs, &c., is remarkably accurate for hearsay evidence.

encouragement they soon became experienced whalemen and conversant with all the details of the business.*

The first sperm whale taken by Nantucket whalemen was captured by Christopher Hussey, about the year 1712, and the capture, destined to effect a radical change in the pursuit of this business, was the result of an accident. "He was cruising," says Macy,† "near the shore for Right whales, and was blown off some distance from the land by a strong northerly wind, where he fell in with a school of that species of whales, and killed one and brought it home. * * * * This event gave new life to the business, for they immediately began with vessels of about thirty tons to whale out in the 'deep,' as it was then called, to distinguish it from shore whaling. They fitted out for cruises of about six weeks, carried a few hogsheads, enough probably to contain the blubber of one whale, with which, after obtaining it, they returned home. The owners then took charge of the blubber, and tried out the oil, and immediately sent the vessels out again."‡ In 1715 Nantucket had six sloops engaged in this fishery, producing oil to the value of £1,100 sterling, the shore fishery being, in the mean time, still continued. There was no perceptible diminution in the number of whales taken from along the coast for quite a number of years after the establishment of the fishery.

In 1720 the inhabitants of Nantucket made a small shipment of oil to London in the ship Hanover, of Boston, William Chadder, master.§

* Macy's Hist., p. 30.

† *Ibid.*, p. 36.

‡ The first sperm whale *known* to Nantucket "was found dead, and ashore, on the southwest part of the island. It caused considerable excitement, some demanding a part of the prize under one pretence, some under another, and all were anxious to behold so strange an animal. There were so many claimants of the prize, that it was difficult to determine to whom it should belong. The natives claimed the whale because they found it" (not a bad reason surely); "the whites, to whom the natives made known their discovery, claimed it by a right comprehended, as they affirmed, in the purchase of the island." (Ah! what lawyers they must have been!) "An officer of the crown" (here steps in the lion) "made his claim, and pretended to seize the fish in the name of His Majesty, as being property without any particular owner. * * * * It was finally settled that the *white* inhabitants who first found the whale, should share the prize equally amongst themselves." (Alas for royalty, and alas for the finders!). The teeth, considered very valuable, had been prudently taken care of by a white man and an Indian before the discovery was made public. The decision in regard to ownership certainly justified their precaution. This compromise made, the whale was cut up and the oil extracted. What the amount of it was is unknown. "The sperm procured from the head was thought to be of great value for medical purpose.s It was used both as an internal and an external application; and such was the credulity of the people, that they considered it a certain cure for all diseases; it was sought with avidity, and, for a while, was esteemed to be worth its weight in silver."—(Macy's Hist.)

§ "Shipped by the grace of God, in good order and well conditioned, by Paul Starbuck, in the good ship called the Hanover, whereof is master under God for the present voyage, William Chadder and now riding in the harbour of Boston, and by God's grace bound for London; to say:—six barrels of

[N. S.]

Whether this was the first adventure of this kind or not we have no means of ascertaining, and we are in a similar state of uncertainty in regard to its success. As the fishery became more important, and vessels were used, it became necessary to select the site where there was the best harbor, and the location where the town of Nantucket now stands was selected.* As the number of vessels increased it was also found necessary to replace the old landing-places, which at best were only temporary, and often destroyed by winter storms, with more substantial wharves, and accordingly, in 1723, the "Straight" wharf was built.† At this time the usual custom in winter was to haul the vessels and boats up on shore, as being safer and less expensive than lying at the wharf. The boats were placed bottom upwards and lashed together to prevent accidents in gales of wind, and the whaling "craft" was carefully stored in the warehouses. In the early days of whaling each vessel carried two boats, one of which seems to have been held in reserve in case of accident to the one lowered for whales.

In 1730 Nantucket employed in the fishery twenty-five vessels of from

---

traine oyle, being on the proper account & risque of Nathaniel Starbuck, of Nantucket, and goes consigned to Richard Patridge merchant in London.

[Prin. Paid.] Being marked & numbered as in the margin & to be delivered in like good order & well conditioned at the aforesaid port of London (The dangers of the sea only excepted) unto Richard Partridge aforesaid or to his assignees, He or they paying Freight for said goods, at the rate of fifty shillings per tonn, with primage & average accustomed.

"In witness whereof the said Master or Purser of said Ship hath affirmed to Two Bills of Lading all of this Tener and date, one of which two Bills being Accomplished, the other to stand void.

"And so God send the Good Ship to her desired Port in safety. Amen!

"Articles & contents unknown to—

"(Signed) WILLIAM CHADDER.

"Dated at Boston the 7th 4th mo. 1720."

(From original bill of lading in possession of F. C. Sanford, esq.)

* The place first settled was at Maddeket, at the west end of the island. According to the records in the state-house at Boston, the following vessels were registered as belonging to Nantucket up to the year 1714: April 28, 1698, Richard Gardner, trader, registers sloop Mary, 25 tons, built in Boston, 1694; August 11, James Coffin, trader, registers sloop Dolphin, 25 tons, built in Boston, 1697; September 1, Richard Gardner, mariner, registers sloop Society, 15 tons, built in Salem, 1695; April 4, 1710, Peter Coffin, registers sloop Hope, 40 tons, built in Boston, 1709; April 24, 1711, Silvanus Hussey, sloop Eagle, 30 tons, built at Scituate, 1711; July 30, 1713, Silvanus Hussey, sloop Bristol, 14 tons, built at Tiverton, 1711; April 27, 1713, Abigail Howse, sloop Thomas, 12 tons, built at Newport, R. I., 1713; May 4, 1714, Ebenezer Coffin, sloop Nonsuch, 25 tons, built at Boston, 1714. (The Nonsuch is registered as of Boston; Coffin, however, was of Nantucket); 1714, Geo. Coffin, sloop Speedwell, 25 tons, built at Charlestown. This, then, was the character of their vessels up to 1715; among them the Hope, of 40 tons, was a very giant.

In 1732, however, the size had very greatly increased, for by a petition (Mass. Col. MSS. Maritime, v, p. 510), it appears that Isaac Myrick built at Nantucket a snow of 118 tons.

† Macy's Hist., p. 37. According to the Boston News Letter, European advices of August 3, 1724, reported that the Emperor of Russia had ordered the directors of the India Company "newly erected there" to get twelve vessels ready against the opening

38 to 50 tons burden each, and the returns were about 3,700 barrels of oil, worth, at £7 per ton, £3,200. Holmes says:* "The whale-fishery on the North American coasts must, at this time" (1730), "have been very considerable; for there arrived in England from these coasts, about the month of July, 154 tons of train and whale oil, and 9,200 of whale bone." At this time there were nearly five hundred ships, manned by four thousand sailors, engaged in foreign traffic from Massachusetts.†

The culminating point of shore-whaling at Nantucket was probably reached in 1726. During that year there were 86 whales taken by boats, and the Coffins and Gardners, the Folgers, the Husseys, the Swains and Paddacks, the progenitors of that race of men who carried the name and fame of the little island of Nantucket to every accessible port on the globe, are chief among those who gathered this harvest.‡

The first recorded loss of a whaling-vessel from the island occurred in 1724, when a sloop, of which Elisha Coffin was master, was lost at sea with all on board.§ The second loss was that of another sloop, Thomas

---

of the spring, to sail for the Greenland whaling-ground, promising to them both protection and monopoly, "by which it will be prohibited, under severe penalties, to bring for the future any Oil or Whalebone into any Part of His Majesty's Dominions from Foreign Countries." Early in 1725 the directors of the English South Sea Company ordered 12 more ships for whaling in these seas. (The inference is that as early at least as the previous year, 1724, the company had vessels there.) Under date of London, July 24, 1725, the ships are reported all returned. The English ships took 25 whales, producing 1,000 puncheons of blubber and oil and 26 tons of fins, worth £450 per ton. In the Dutch fishery, the Hollanders, with 144 ships took 240 whales; the Hamburghers with 43 ships took 463 whales; the Bremenese with 23 ships took 29 whales; the Bergenese with 2 ships took none, and two other ships returned empty. In the spring of 1726, Sweden also looked with longing eyes upon this pursuit, and designed sending twelve ships in the summer of that year to Greenland.

* American Annals, i, p. 126.

† *Ibid.*

‡ The names of the parties (probably captains of boats or vessels), with the number of whales taken by each, may be of interest in this connection: John Swain took 4, Andrew Gardner 4, Jonathan Coffin 4, Paul Paddack 4, Jas. Johnston 5, Clothier Pierce 3, Sylvanus Hussey 2, Nathan Coffin 4, Peter Gardner 4, Wm. Gardner 2, Abishai Folger 6, Nathan Folger 4, John Bunker 1, Shaubael Folger 5, Shubael Coffin 3, Nath'l Allen 3, Edw'd Heath 4, Geo. Hussey 3, Benj. Gardner 3, Geo. Coffin 1, Rich'd Coffin 1, Nath'l Paddack 2, Jos. Gardner 1, Matthew Jenkins 3, Bartlett Coffin 4, Daniel Gould 1, Ebenezer Gardner 4, ——— Staples 1; total 86. The largest number of whales taken in one day was eleven. In the New England Weekly Journal of December 21, 1730, appears an advertisement, informing the public that there has been "Just Reprinted, The Wonderful Providence of God, Exemplified in the Preservation of William Walling who was drove out to Sea from Sandy Hook near New York in a leaky Boat, and was taken up by a Whaling Sloop & brought to Nantucket after he had floated on the Sea eight Days without Victuals or Drink." In 1732, according to a petition in the Mass. Col. MSS. (Maritime, iv, p. 510), a vessel of 118 tons burden was built at Nantucket, the ruling price being then £8 5*s.* per ton.

§ Zaccheus Macy, in a brief sketch of Nantucket, published in vol. iii of the Mass. Hist. Soc.'s Coll., says (p. 157) that up to 1760 no man had been killed or drowned while whaling, and this error Obed Macy, in his History of Nantucket, perpetuates. It must have been intended by the former to include only shore-whaling, since prior to the

Hathaway master, in 1731. These losses were a serious matter for a small whaling-port, where nearly all the inhabitants were related by birth or marriage. In the year 1742 still another sloop, commanded by Daniel Paddack, was lost while on a whaling-voyage, with all on board.

An increase in the business brought with it an increase in the number and size of the vessels employed. Schooners were added, and the size of the vessels increased to between 40 and 50 tons. Whales began to grow scarce in the vicinity of the shore, and still larger vessels were put into the service and sent to the "southward" as it was termed, cruising on that ground till about the first of July, when they returned, refitted, and cruised to the eastward of the Grand Bank during the remainder of the whaling season, unless, as was often the case, they filled sooner. Vessels for this service were generally "sloops of 60 or 70 tons; their crews were made up, in part, of Indians,"* there being generally from four to eight natives to each vessel.

But the time came when Nantucket did not furnish men enough to man the whaling-vessels which the islanders desired to fit out, and Cape Cod, and even Long Island, were called in to supply the deficiency of seamen. It naturally occurred that, with the limited colonial demand, the business became at times overdone, the market glutted, and what oil was sold was disposed of at too low a price to be as remunerative as the islanders thought it should be. The people began to think of another market. For a series of years they had made Boston their factor, selling there their oil and drawing from thence their supplies.† Probably

---

period named at least nine vessels with their crews had been lost, and these facts must have been well known to him. There is on file at the State-house in Boston (Domestic Relations, vol. 1, p. 181), a petition to the general court from Dinah Coffin, of Nantucket, setting forth that "her Husband, Elisha Coffin did on the Twenty Seventh Day of April Annoq Dom: 1722 Sail from sd Island of Nantucket in a sloop: on a whaling trip intending to return in a month or six weeks at most, And Instantly a hard & dismall Storm followed; which in all probability Swallowed him and those with him up: for they were never heard of." She prays that she may now (1724) be allowed to marry again.

* Zaccheus Macy writes (Mass. Hist. Soc. Coll., iii, p. 157), "It happened once, when there were about thirty boats about six miles from the shore, that the wind came round to the northward, and blew with great violence, attended with snow. The men all rowed hard, but made but little headway. In one of the boats were four Indians and two white men. An old Indian in the head of the boat, perceiving that the crew began to be disheartened, spake out loud in his own tongue and said, '*Momadichchator auqua sarshkee sarnkee pinchee eynoo sememoochkee chaquanks wihchee pinchee eynoo;*' which in English is, 'Pull ahead with courage; do not be disheartened; we shall not be lost now; there are too many Englishmen to be lost now.' His speaking in this manner gave the crew new courage. They soon perceived that they made headway; and after long rowing they all got safe on shore." In 1744 a Nantucket Indian struck a blackfish, and was caught by a foul line and carried down and drowned.—(Boston News-Letter.)

† It would be inferred that the shipment made in 1720 did not prove entirely satisfactory. The Boston News-Letter reports that Captain Churchman arrived at Portsmouth, Eng., December 8, 1729, from New England for London, with a cargo of logwood and oil.

had their oil commanded the price which they considered it should have brought, this state of affairs might long have continued, but such was not the case. "It was found," says Macy,* "that Nantucket had in many places become famed for whaling, and particularly so in England, where partial supplies of oil had been received through the medium of the Boston trade. The people, finding that merchants in Boston were making a good profit by first purchasing oil at Nantucket, then ordering it to Boston, and thence shipping it to London, determined to secure the advantages of the trade to themselves, by exporting their oil in their own vessels. They had good prospects of success in this undertaking, yet, it being a new one, they moved with great caution, for they knew that a small disappointment would lead to embarrassments that would, in the end, prove distressing. They, therefore, loaded and sent out one vessel, about the year 1745. The result of this small beginning proved profitable, and encouraged them to increase their shipments by sending out other vessels. They found, in addition to the profits on the sales, that the articles in return were such as their business required, viz, iron, hardware, hemp, sailcloth, and many other goods, and at a much cheaper rate than they had hitherto been subjected to." This naturally gave renewed life to the enterprise, and induced the fitting of new vessels and the development of new adventurers. The sky was not always fair, not every voyage proved remunerative, but the business as a whole steadily increased in importance and profit. At about this time (1746), according to Macy's History, whaling was commenced by our people in Davis's Straits.†

The transfer of the trade of Long Island to Boston and Connecticut was a source of great uneasiness to the early governors of New York. They were repeatedly stirred up on the subject by the lords of trade in England, but with all their trouble and skill and efforts they were unable to alienate the sympathies of the Long Islanders from those who were their friends both by birth and association. They had but little in common with the New York government, which seemed to them only the symbol of wrong, injustice, and oppression. The governors of that

* Page 51. The Boston News-Letter of October 5, 1738, reports from Nantucket that an Indian plot to fire the English houses and kill the inhabitants of the island, had been disclosed by a friendly Indian. In consequence of the warning the plot had been abandoned, but fears were entertained for the safety of several whaling-vessels which sailed in the spring, and of the crews, of which the natives formed an essential part.

† Page 54. Davis's Straits were visited by whalemen as early as 1732, when a Captain Atkins, returning from a whaling voyage thence, brought a Greenland bear. Captain Atkins went as far as 66° north. Among the entries and clearances at the Boston custom-house as recorded in the Boston News-Letter as early as 1737 we find several to and from this locality. Beyond a doubt these vessels are whalemen, and in fact some of the names are common in the annals of this industry at Nantucket. The clearances were usually in March or April, and the arrivals from September to November, varying according to the degree of success, the season, &c. In July, 1737, Capt. Atherton Hough took a whale "in the Straits," and in 1739, under date of August 2, the Boston News-Letter says: "There is good Prospect of Success in the *Whale Fishery to Greenland*

province were numerous and tyrannical, and the people had no redress. The boast of one of them that he would tax them so high that they would have no time to think of anything else but paying these duties, seemed to be resolved into a motto adopted by the majority, and the groanings and writhings of the people only seemed to serve as the excuse for another turn of the screws of executive tyranny.

In June, 1703, Lord Conbury, in a letter to the lords of trade,* speaking of the difficulties the commerce of New York had to contend with from the position of some parts of its territory in relation to Connecticut and Massachusetts, writes that Connecticut fills that part of Long Island with European goods cheaper than New York can, since New York pays a duty which is not assessed by Connecticut; "nor will they" (the inhabitants of the east end of Long Island) "be subject to the Laws of Trade nor to the Acts of Navigation, by which means there has for some time been no Trade between the City of New Yorke and the East end of Long Island, from whence the greater quantity of Whale-oyle comes." He adds that the people are full of New England principles, and would rather trade with Boston, Connecticut, and Rhode Island than with New York.

In 1708, however, under Lord Cornbury, an act was passed for the "Encouragement of Whaling," in which it was provided, 1st, that any Indian, who was bound to go to sea whale-fishing, should not "at any time or times between the First Day of *November* and the Fifteenth Day of *April* following, yearly, be sued arrested, molested, detained or kept out of that Imployment by any person or persons whatsoever, pretending any Contract, Bargain Debt or Dues unto him or them except and only for or concerning any Contract, *Debt* or *Bargain* relating to the Undertaking and Design of the Whale-fishing and not otherwise under the penalty of paying treble Costs to the Master of any such Indian or Indians so to be sued, arrested, molested or detained." Section 2 provided that "if any person or persons shall purchase, take to pawn or anyways get or receive any Cloathing, Gun or other Necessaries that his Master shall let him, from any such Indian or Indians or suffer any such Indian to be drinking or drunk in or about their Houses, when they should be at Sea, or other business belonging to that

this Year, for *several vessels are come in already*, deeply laden, and *others expected.*" This is not mentioned as by any means an extraordinary circumstance, and when it is remembered that the English had already pursued the whale in those seas for fifteen years, and at that time had some forty or fifty ships there engaged in this pursuit, it would scarcely be likely to excite surprise.

In 1744, a whale 40 feet long was found ashore on Nantucket, by three men, who, for lack of more proper instruments, killed it with their jack-knives. (News-Letter October 4.)

* N. Y. Col. Rec. iv, p. 1058. An order was passed in the New York Council, March 2, 1702, directing Thomas Clark and John Crosier, of Suffolk County, to secure three drift whales ashore in said county, they to have one-third of the oil and bone and to deliver the remaining two-thirds to the New York custom-house clear of charge. (Council Minutes, viii, p. 323.)

Design of Whale-fishing or shall carry or cause to be carried any Drink to them, whereby such Indians are made incapable of doing their Labour and Duty in and about their Master's Service," within the date above named, shall be compelled to restore the articles taken, and forfeit to the master the sum of thirty shillings. This act was to be in force seven years after publication, but it did not finally become a law until June 10, 1710. It was renewed in 1716 for four years longer,* and again in 1720 for a further term of six years.†

In July, 1708, Lord Cornbury writes again to the board of trade regarding New York affairs.‡ In his letter he says: "The quantity of Train Oyl made in Long Island is very uncertain, some years they have much more fish than others, for example last year they made four thousand Barrils of Oyl, and this last Season they have not made above Six hundred: About the middle of October they begin to look out for fish, the Season lasts all November, December, January, February, and part of March; a Yearling will make about forty Barils of Oyl, a Stunt or Whale two years old will make sometimes fifty, sometimes sixty Barrils of Oyl, and the largest whale that I have heard of in these Parts, yielded one hundred and ten barrels of Oyl, and twelve hundred Weight of Bone."

In 1709 the fishery had attained such value on Long Island that some parties attempted to reduce it, so far as possible, to a monopoly, and grants of land previously made by Governor Fletcher and others, in a reckless and somewhat questionable manner were improved for personal benefit. Earl Bellomont, in commenting on these irregular practices, writes to the lords of trade, under date of July 2 of that year,§ citing, among others, one Colonel Smith, who, he states, "has got the beach on the sea shore for fourty miles together, after an odd manner as I have been told by some of the inhabitants * * * * * * having forced the town of Southampton to take a poore £10 for the greatest part of the said beach, which is not a valuable consideration in law, for Colonel Smith himself own'd to me that that beach was very profitable to him for whale fishing, and that one year he cleared £500, by whales taken there."

In 1716, Samuel Mulford, of Easthampton, in a petition to the King, gave a sketch of the progress of this industry in that vicinity.‖ In the recital of the grievances of his neighbors and himself, he writes that "the inhabitants of the said Township and parts adjacent did from the first Establishment of the said Colony of New York enjoy the Privilege & Benefit of fishing for whale & applying ye same to their own use as their undoubted right and property."¶ By his petition it appears further that in 1664 Governor Nicolls and council directed that drift-

* Laws of New York, Bradford, p. 72.

† *Ibid.*, pp. 131–198.

‡ N. Y. Col. Rec., v, p. 60.

§ N. Y. Col. Rec., iv, 535.

‖ N. Y. Col. Rec., v, p. 474.

¶ These are undoubtedly what the authorities were pleased to term "Massachusetts notions."

whales should pay a duty of every sixteenth gallon of oil to the government, "exempting the whales that were killed at Sea by persons who went on that design from any duty or imposition." Governor Dongan also claimed duty on drift-whales, and he also exempted those killed at sea. "There was no pretence," under Dongan, "to seize such whales or to exact anything from the fishermen on that account, being their ancient right and property. Thus the inhabitants had the right of fishing preserved to them, and the Crown the benefit of all drift Whales, and everything seemed well established between the Crown and the People, who continued chearfully, and with success, to carry on the said fishing trade." This state of affairs continued until 1696, when Lord Cornbury (afterward Earl of Clarendon) became governor. It was then announced by those in authority that the whale was a "Royal Fish," and belonged to the Crown; consequently all whalers must be licensed "for that purpose which he was sure to make them pay for, and also contribute good part of the fruit of their labour; no less that a neat 14th part of the Oyle and Bone, when cut up, and to bring the same to New York an 100 miles distant from their habitation, an exaction so grievous, that few people did ever comply for it."* The result of this policy was to discourage the fishery, and its importance was sensibly decreased. In 1711 the New York authorities issued a writ to the sheriffs, directing them to seize all whales. This demand created much disturbance, but the people, knowing no remedy, submitted with what grace they could to what they felt was a grievous wrong, and an infringement upon their rights under the patent under which their settlement was founded. Since that time, Mulford continues, a formal prosecution had been commenced against him for hiring Indians to assist him in whaling. He concludes his petition with the assertion that, unless some relief was afforded, the fishery must be ruined, since "the person concerned will not be brought to the hardship of waiting out at sea many months, & the difficulty of bringing into New York the fish, and at last paying so great a share of their profit."

Mulford, during the latter part of his life, was continually at loggerheads with the government at New York. A sturdy representative of that Puritan opposition to injustice and wrong with which the early settlers of Eastern Long Island were so thoroughly imbued, the declining years of his life were continual eras of contention against the tyrannies and exactions of governors, whose only interest seemed to be to suck the life-blood from the bodies of these unfortunate flies caught in their

*It was these outrageously unjust laws that brought the government into the notorious disrepute it attained with its outlying dependencies from 1675 to 1720. In March, 1698, the council of Lord Cornbury declared certain drift-whales the property of the Crown (which apparently meant a minimum amount to the King and a maximum share to the governor), "when the subject can make no just claim of having killed them." One Richard Floyd having offered a reward to any parties bringing him information of such whales, the council ordered an inquiry into the matter in order to prevent such practices in the future. (Council Minutes, viii, p. 6.)

spider's net, and cast the useless remains remorselessly away. He was one of the remonstrants against the annexation of the eastern towns to the New York government, and from 1700 to 1720 was the delegate from these towns to the assembly. In 1715 the opposition of the government to his constituency reached the point of a personal conflict with him. In a speech delivered in the assembly in this year, he boldly and unsparingly denounced the authorities as tyrannical, extravagant, and dishonest. He cited numerous instances of injustices from officers of the customs to the traders of and to his section. While grain was selling in Boston at 6*s.* per bushel, and only commanding one-half of that in New York, his people were compelled by existing laws to lose this difference in value. While the government was complaining of poverty and the lack of disposition on the part of the people to furnish means for its subsistence, the governor had received, says Mulford, during the past three years, three times the combined income of the governors of Massachusetts, Rhode Island, and Connecticut. In 1716 the assembly ordered this speech to be put into the hands of the speaker, but Mulford, without hesitation, caused it to be published and circulated.* From this time forth the war upon him was, so far as the government was concerned, a series of persecutions, but Mulford undauntedly braved them all and in the end was triumphant. Quite a number of letters passed between the governor and himself, and between them both and the lords of trade in London. As an earnest of the feeling his opposition had stirred up, the governor commenced a suit against him in the supreme court, the judges of which owed their appointment to the executive. Shortly after this, Governor Hunter, in a communication to the lords of trade regarding the state of affairs in the province, writes that he is informed that Mulford, who "has continually flown in face of government," and always disputed with the Crown the right of whaling, has gone to London to urge his case.† He states that "that poor, troublesome old man" is the only mutineer in a province otherwise quiet (an assertion that evidenced either a reckless disregard for truth, or a want

* A copy of this speech is bound in an old volume of the Boston News-Letter, in the library of the Boston Athenæum.

† In the address of H. P. Hedges at the Bi-Centennial celebration at Easthampton, in 1850, he says, when Mulford finally repaired to London to present the case to the king, he was obliged to conceal his intention. Leaving Southampton secretly, he landed at Newport, walked to Boston, and from thence embarked for London. Arrived there, he "presented his memorial, which it is said attracted much attention, and was read by him in the House of Commons." He returned home in triumph, having attained the desired end. At this time he was seventy-one years old. "Songs and rejoicings," says J. Lyon Gardiner (*vide* Hedges's Address, p. 21), "took place among the whalemen of Suffolk County upon his arrival, on account of his having succeeded in getting the King's share given up." It is related of him (*Ibid.*, p. 68) that while at the court of St. James, being somewhat verdant, he was much annoyed by pickpockets. As a palliative, he had a tailor sew several fish-hooks on the inside of his pockets, and soon after one of the fraternity was caught. This incident being published at the time won for him an extensive notoriety. He was representative from Easthampton from 1715 to 1720, and died in 1725, aged eighty years.

of knowledge of affairs inexcusably culpable); that the case he pleads has been brought before the supreme court and decided against him, and Mulford is the only man who disputes the Crown's right, and the good governor charitably recommends their lordships to "bluff him."* Still later, Hunter states that it was the custom long before his arrival to take out whaling licenses. Many came voluntarily and did so. If whaling is "decayed," it was not for want of whalemen, for the number increases yearly; "but the truth of the matter is, that the Town of Boston is the Port of Trade of the People inhabiting that end of Long Island of late years, so that the exportation from hence of that commodity must in the Books be less than formerly." The perquisites arising from the sale of these licenses were of no account in themselves, but yielding in this matter would only open a gap for the disputation of ever perquisite of the government.†

To this the lords of trade reply:‡ "You intimate in your letter to our Secretary of 22d November last that the Whale fishery is reserved to the Crown by your Patents: as we can find no such thing in your Commission, you will explain what you mean by it." Mulford is now in London, and desires dispatch in the decision in regard to this matter, pending which the lords desire to know whether dues have been paid by any one; if so, what amount has been paid, and to what purpose this revenue has been applied.§ They close their letter with the following sentence, which would hardly seem open to any danger of misconstruction: "*Upon this occasion we must observe to you, that we hope you will give all due incouragement to that Trade.*" Evidently the case of Mulford *vs.* Hunter looks badly for the governor. Still, Hunter is loth to yield readily, and the discussion is further prolonged.

It is now 1718. Governor Hunter, in his answer to the inquiries of their lordships,‖ says Commission was issued giving power, "Cognoscendi de Flotsam, Jetsom, Lagon, Deodandis, &c.," follows "et de Piscibus Regalibus Sturgeonibus, Balenis Cœtis Porpetüs Delphinis Reggis, &c." In regard to the income, he again writes that it is inconsiderable; that only the danger of being accused of giving up the Crown's right would have led him to write about it. In amount, it was not £20 per annum, (corroboratory of Mulford's assertion of its decline), and as the fish had left this coast, he should not further trouble them about it. Up to the present time all but Mulford had paid and contin-

* N. Y. Col. Rec., v, 480. This assertion must be inexcusably inaccurate, for it was unquestionably on the ground of his sturdy defense of their rights that the people of Easthampton so steadily returned him to the assembly.

† N. Y. Col. Rec., v, p. 484. This admission of Hunter's of the smallness of the revenue is indisputable evidence of his incompetence, and of the truth of Mulford's assertion of the ultimate ruin of the whale-fishery under such restrictions.

‡ N. Y. Col. Rec., v, p. 501.

§ *Ibid.* It looks very much as though Mulford himself was propounding these inquiries, and their lordships' were mere mouth pieces.

‖ N. Y. Col. Rec., v, p. 510.

ued to pay. The subject appears to have been finally referred to the attorney-general, and the governor says (1719), waiting his opinion, he has surceased all demands till it comes. The question must have been left in a state of considerable mistiness, however, for in 1720 Governor Burnett informs the lords,* in a letter which indicates a satisfied feeling of compromise between official dignity and the requirements of the trade, that he remits the five per centum on the whale-fishery, but asserts the King's rights by still requiring licenses, though in "so doing he neglects his own profit," "and this," he adds, "has a good effect on the country." Under his administration the act for the encouragement of the whale-fishery was renewed.

In 1706 some of the inhabitants of Eastham and parts adjacent (including, as one of the names seems to indicate, Nantucket) presented to the general court a petition,† setting forth that the parties "whose names are hereunto subscribed, being Inhabitants of Eastham and other places thereunto adjoining, In regard all or most of us are concerned in fitting out Boats to Catch & take Whales when ye season of ye year Serves: and whereas when wee have taken any whale or whales, our Custom is to cutt them up, and to take away ye fatt and ye Bone of such Whales as are brought in, And afterwards to let ye Rest of ye Boddy of ye Lean of whales Lye on shoar in lowe water to be washt away by ye sea, being of noe vallue nor worth any Thing to us;" therefore they petition for an act of the court to permit Thomas Houghton, of Boston, or his assigns, to take and carry away all this waste, and endeavor, for the space of ten years, to put it to some profitable use, all other persons in New England to be in the mean time "forbidden, discharged, and restrained to make any further use of it than is now usually made, with a penalty on such as presume to doe it during y[t] time without ye Consent and allowance of ye said Thom: Houghton or his Assignes." With an eye to future commercial prosperity, they allege the following reasons why the patent, if granted, will inure to their benefit: "first . . . It will cause more staves to be fetcht and brought in from other places as well as our own, and more Barrells made, and soe more Coopers will be sett at Work, with other hands to build houses for ye use of it. secondly. It will imploy our people to cutt it up, and to order it according to his direction, at such convenient houses and places as he appoints. Thirdly When tis ordered and prepared as hee or his Assignes would have it, it will implye our Sloopes to carry it to Boston, or to such places as hee or they direct, wich will be an advantage to us.

* N. Y. Col. Rec., v, p. 579. There is some discrepancy between the dates of Governor Burnett's concessions, and the triumphant reception of Mulford on his return from England, mentioned by Hedges. "In 1719, February 24," says Hedges, "a whale-boat being alone, the men struck a whale, and she, coming up under ye boat, in part staved it, and tho' ye men were not hurt with the whale, yet, before any help came to them, four men were tired and chilled, and fell off ye boat and oars to which they hung and were drowned, viz: Henry Parsons, William Schellenger, junior, Lewis Mulford, Jeremiah Conkling, junior.

† Mass. Col. MSS., Maritime, iv, pp. 72-3.

Fourthly If any Improvement can be made of it for Exportation, it will not only be of great advantage to Boston, but to many of ye Inhabitants of New England." (This is signed by Simon, Nath[ll] Coffin, John Jones.)

To this is appended a postscript, stipulating that said Houghton employ the inhabitants of the whaling-towns as much as possible for his work; that he shall give the public the benefit of his discovery, if made, at the end of the ten years; and that he shall pay each whale-man "one shilling in money acknowledgment for their several shares in the Lean of the whale fishes that they shall take for the space of ten years." The postcript is signed "Sam[ll] Treat sen[r], David Mc. * * * * *, Jon[a] sparrow, Sam[ll] Knowles, Sam[ll] freeman jr, Richard * * * * , Richard Godfree."

The council granted the patent with the somewhat novel proviso: "That within the space of Four years he shew forth to the Satisfaction of the Govern[r] Council & Assembly That his Projection will take effect, *for the rayseing of Salt Petre to supply the province.*"

During the years 1724 and 1725, in the prosecution of the wars between the Indians and the colonists, some of the friendly Indians from Cape Cod were enlisted, with the express understanding that they were to be discharged in time to take part in the fall and winter whale-fishery. Accordingly, in 1724 Lieutenant-Governor Dummer, of the Massachusetts Bay, writes to Colonel Westbrook: "Upon Sight hereof you must forthwith dismiss Cpt. Bournes Comp[y] of Indians & send them hither in one of the Sloops, That so they may lose no Time for Following the Whale Fishery, w[ch] is agreeable to my Promise made to them at Enlisting."* In a postscript he adds: "Let Capt Bourne come with them to see them safe return'd." And again, in 1725, the secretary writes: "His Hon[r] Having promised the Indians enlisted by Cpt. Bourne (being all those of the County of Barnstable) to dismiss them in the Fall that so they attend their Whale Fishing; directs that you as soon as you have opportunity to send them up to Boston, in Order to their Return Home, & let none of them be detained on any Pretense whatsoever."†

Under date of March 20, 1727, the Boston News-Letter says: "We hear from the Towns on the Cape that the Whale Fishery among them has failed much this Winter, as it has done for several Winters past, but having found out the way of going to Sea Upon that Business, and having had much Success in it, they are now fitting out several Vessels to sail with all Expedition upon that dangerous Design this Spring, more (its tho't) than have ever been sent out from among them."

The same paper, in its issue of February 12, 1730,‡ contains the fol-

* Mass. Col. MSS., Letters, ii, 52.

† Mass. Col. MSS., Letters, ii, 297.

‡ On the 13th of January, 1728, says the News-Letter of February 1, there was a very severe storm at Provincetown. Several vessels were driven ashore; three or four whale boats were also destroyed, one being carried by the force of the wind up a "pretty large steep hill," and thrown upon the roof of a house on top of the hill.

lowing extract from a letter from Chatham, dated "February 6, 1729–30:" "There has been a remarkable Providence in the awful death of some of my neighbors; On the day commonly called New Year's Day, a whaleboat's Crew (which Consists of a Stersman, an Harpineer, and Four Oarmen) coming home from a Place called Hog's-Back, where they had been on a Whaling design, the Boat was overset, and all the Men lost, on a reaf of Sand that lies out against Billingsgate. When the Boat was found bottom upward, and the Stern post broken off, there were two Chests found in it, which were wedged so fast under the Thwards that the water had not washed them out; in which were found the Pocket books of two of the Men, by which it plainly appears what Boat it was; but none of the Bodies are, as yet found, that I can hear of; tho' they found an iron Pot which they had with them, upon the reaf, and discovered the Whaling Irons at the bottom of the Water, where it is about 8 feet deep.

"P. S.—Before I had done writing I had News that two of their Bodies were found."

In March, 1736, the inhabitants of Provincetown captured a large whale at sea, cut him up, and brought the blubber into that port. The estimated quantity of oil that this blubber would produce was 100 barrels.* In the News-Letter of May 27 of the same year a statement is published to the effect that on the 11th of May a whaling-sloop, of which Solomon Kenwick was master, arrived at Chatham, and reported that while on the voyage, "about forty leagues to the eastward of George's Banks, they struck and wounded two Whales, which then lay upon the Water seemingly in a dying Posture: but one of them suddenly rush'd with great Violence over the midst of one of their Boats, and sunk both the Boat and Men into the Sea; one Man was thereby kill'd outright, and two others much wounded: Tis a wonder they were not all destroy'd, for the Whale continued striking and raging in a most furious Manner in the midst of them (now in the Water) for some Time, but the other Boat came and took them all up (except the Man that was kill'd, who sunk immediately) and carried them safe to the Sloop."

The season of 1737–8 must have been an unfortunate one at Provincetown, for up to January 5, 1738, the people of that town had only killed two small whales, and some of the inhabitants took into serious consideration a change of residence.† In July, 1738, Captain Anthony Haugh, master of a whaling-vessel, took "in the Straits" a large whale, and brought him to the vessel's side to cut in. In hoisting the blubber into the hold the runner of the block gave way, by which Benjamin Hamlin, of Eastham, was killed instantly.‡ In February, 1738, the Yarmouth

* Boston News-Letter, April 1, 1736.

† Boston News-Letter. According to the News-Letter of April 21, 1737, a dozen vessels were fitting that spring from Provincetown for the Davis's Straits whale-fishery, some of them of a hundred tons burden each. So many were going on these voyages continues the account, that not more than twelve or fourteen men would be left at home.

‡ Boston News-Letter, August 31.

whalemen had killed but one large whale during the season; the bone of that one was from 8 to 9 feet long.

Nor was the whaling-season of 1738–9 any more successful to the inhabitants of the cape. Up to the 15th of February, 1739—the whaling-season being then over—there had been taken at Provincetown but six small and one large whale, and at Sandwich two more small ones. This was the extent of the catch.* As a result of two successive poor seasons, many of the people of Provincetown were in straitened circumstances and much distressed. Those depending upon the early spring whaling "returned as they went, only more in debt." Many of them were without money or provisions.†

Early in 1741 the French and Spanish privateers commenced their depredations upon the English commerce. Naturally our whaling-vessels came in for their proportion of loss. In May a Spanish privateer, under Don. Francisco Lewis, captured a whaling-vessel from Barnstable, commanded by Capt. Solomon Sturgis, "dismissed the captain and eight Hands, carried away the Sloop and four Hands, and put in John Davis, Mate of said Sloop."‡ The seasons still continued unfavorable for the coast-whaling on the cape,§ but late in the summer and during the early fall of 1741 the inhabitants of that section were cheered by an unexpected success. Great numbers of porpoises and black fish came swarming into the bay, and the hardy fishermen lost no time in attacking them. By the close of October they had killed 150 porpoises and over 1,000 black fish, yielding them about 1,500 barrels of oil, for the most of which they found an immediate sale. "This unexpected Success so late in the Year, put new Life into Some who had spent all the former Season of the Year in Toil and Labour to little or no Purpose."‖

The presence of privateers on the coast appears to have entirely prevented the prosecution of the Davis Strait whaling, for no departures to or arrivals from that region are reported for several years. Whalemen were liable to be overhauled anywhere, but it is to be presumed that the risk became greater as the distance from port increased. Occasionally these privateers would swoop down through Nantucket and Vineyard Sounds

* *Ibid.*, February 15.

† *Ibid.*, April 5.

‡ *Ibid.* The issue of the News-Letter for July 23, 1741, says: "Truro, July 14. On Saturday last Mr. Nath Harding an elderly Man of this Place, being at one of the Fry Houses boiling of Oil, he was taken with a fainting Fit, and fell into a large Vessell of boiling hot Oyl, and was scalded in a most miserable Manner."

§ Whales formerly, for many successive years, set in along shore by Cape Cod. There was good whaling in boats. Proper watchmen ashore, by signals, gave notice when a whale appeared. After some years they left this ground, and passed farther off upon the banks at some distance from the shore. The whalers then used sloops with whale-boats aboard, and this fishery turned to good account. At present (1748) the whales take their course in deep water, where upon a peace our whalers design to follow them. * * * * At present this business is by whaling sloops or schooners, with two whale-boats and 13 men."—(Felt, Salem, ii, 225–6.)

‖ Boston News-Letter.

and bear off whatever came in their way that they were able to take care of. Such a raid was made in the middle of the summer of 1744. One Captain Roach, in a vessel from Cape Cod, arrived in Boston and reported that on the 24th of June, just before night, being in a sloop from Nantucket for Boston, with a cargo of 330 barrels of oil, the weather being calm and his vessel somewhat in advance of the others, another sloop came up showing but few men on deck and hoisting the English flag. Captain Roach, suspecting in spite of her appearance that she was an enemy, and being only about two miles from the shore, took out the most necessary things, and, putting them into his boat, escaped with his crew to the shore. As soon as the pursuer found the sloop was abandoned, he sent a boat of armed men to her, took possession of her, and carried her off. The same vessel, which proved to be a French privateer, took in September several coasting and merchant vessels and one Nantucket whaling-vessel, and landed many of her prisoners on the island of Nantucket.*

The facts in regard to whaling at Salem and vicinity from 1700 to 1750 are very meager. Undoubtedly the business was carried on all through this section in the early part of 1700 in a small way. In 1700 John Higginson writes concerning the business there and at other portions of the coast: "We have a considerable quantitie of whale oil and bone for exportation."† Again, in 1706, he writes to a friend in Ipswich, as one concerned with others in boats engaged in whaling. Here, as elsewhere, there were drift-whales, and in 1722–'23 public‡ notices are given to claimants to prove in courts of admiralty their rights in two such cases.§ In August, 1723, a drift-whale is advertised in the Boston News-Letter as ashore at Marblehead, and the usual notice of court is appended.

Whether Boston was at this period a participant in this pursuit is difficult to determine. Various reasons tended to make that port the factor of the colony in that regard. Vessels from the whole colony cleared from there to go to the northward whaling, while those from Nantucket, the Vineyard, and the south shore of the cape pursued their southern voyages along the edge of the Gulf Stream to the Leeward and Cape de Verde Islands under clearances from Newport, R. I. In the absence of the custom-house records of Boston prior to 1776,‖ it is impossible to determine which of the numerous clearances and entries are whalemen, and equally impossible to determine to what port they belonged. Referring to the files of the colonial gazettes of this period,

---

* Boston News-Letter.

† Felt's Salem, ii, p. 225.

‡ *Ibid.*

§ *Ibid.*

‖ The Boston papers of December 12, 1707, state that a whale 40 feet long entered that harbor and *several whale-boats pursued and killed her* near the back of Noddle's Island. The logical inference is that they had whaling craft and boats ready for instant use and men skilled in handling them.

we find in the News-Letter of September 3, 1722, an advertisement of a court of admiralty to be held to adjudicate on a drift-whale found floating near Brewster's, and towed ashore in August. It was much wasted and decayed, and in cutting it up a ball was found, indicating that it had been attacked by some party, and the advertisement notifies the public that "If any Persons can try any Claim to said Whale so as to make out a property," they should appear at the said court at Boston on the last Wednesday in the month.* On the 5th of December, 1723, "Mr. Peter Butler, of Boston," advertises for sale, "lately Imported from London, extraordinary good Whale Warps at 16*d*. a Pound, which are made of the finest Hemp, either by the Quoile or less Quantity."† In 1730 Samuel Torrey, currier, on Water street, Boston, advertises "Good Blubber by the Barrell or Tun, full Bound."

In 1731 the Rhode Island assembly passed an act for the encouragement of the whale and cod fisheries, giving "a bounty of five shillings for every barrel of whale oil, one penny a pound for bone, and five shillings a quintal for codfish, caught by Rhode Island vessels and brought into this colony * * * to be paid from the interest accruing upon a new bank, or issue bills of credit to the amount of sixty thousand pounds."‡ The whale-fishery had, according to Arnold,§ long been carried on in a small way within that colony, and whales had frequented Narragansett Bay and often been taken with boats. This bounty gave something of a stimulus to the business, and these colonists too began to "whale out into the deep," and in 1733 the first regularly equipped whaleman of which Rhode Island has any record arrived in Newport from her voyage, having on board 114 barrels of oil and 200 pounds of bone. This sloop was the Pelican, of Newport, Benjamin Thurston, owner, and she received the bounty according to the law.‖

By the inhabitants of Martha's Vineyard, in 1702–'3, there appear to have been several whales killed. The following entry occurs under that date in the court records: "The marks of the whales killed by John Butler and Thomas Lothrop. One whale lanced near or over the shoulder blade, near the left shoulder blade only; another killed with an iron forward in the left side, marked W; and upon the right side marked with a pocket-knife T. L.; and the other had an iron hole over

---

* Whalebone is quoted in the News-Letter of April 18, 1723, as bringing from 3*s*. to 3*s*. 6*d*. in Philadelphia.

† B. News-Letter.

‡ Arnold's Hist. of Rhode Island, ii, p. 103.

§ *Ibid.*, p. 110. In point of fact deep-sea whaling had been pursued from Rhode Island some years prior to the time mentioned by Arnold. The News-Letter for May 23, 1723, records the entry of a vessel, commanded by William Bennett, from whaling, which brought the largest sperm whale ever seen, up to that time, in those parts. It produced 18 barrels of head matter and from 40 to 50 barrels of oil, and one-third more head would have been saved had not the weather been stormy. "This spring," the account says, "our Vessels have brought in eight Whales into this port" (Newport).

‖ Arnold's R. I., ii, p. 110.

the right shoulder-blade, with two lance holes in the same side, one in the belly. These whales were all killed about the middle of February last past; all great whales, betwixt six and seven and eight foot bone, which are all gone from us. A true account given by John Butler from us, and recorded Per me, Thomas Trapp, Clerk."*

It is quite probable that deep-sea whaling did not commence at the Vineyard until about the year 1738. In that year Joseph Chase, of Nantucket, removed there, taking with him his sloop, the Diamond, of about 40 tons burden. He purchased a house and about 20 acres of land on the shores of Edgartown Harbor, erected a wharf with a try-house near, and commenced the fishery with his vessel. He followed this pursuit two or three years, till finally his ill success caused him to abandon it.

The year succeeding Chase's immigration James Claghorn purchased a small sloop of 40 tons, called the Leopard, and fitted her for the business. Two or three years' experience served to give him a distaste for it, and he sold out and retired from the contest with a loss of about $500, a large sum for those days.

In 1742 John Harper, of Nantucket, removed to the Vineyard, carrying with him the sloop Humbird, of about 45 tons. For several years he too followed whaling, in his sloop and in other vessels; but the same ill success that attended Chase and Claghorn visited also the standard of Harper, and finding himself running behind-hand year after year, he too sold out his shipping and withdrew.

Undeterred by the misfortunes of the others, John Newman, with partners, in 1744 bought the sloop Susannah, of 55 tons, and they continued nearly one year. In the fall, the corn crop on the Vineyard proving insufficient, Samuel Finley was sent in command of her to the southward for a load of that grain, and on the return passage the vessel was cast away on the Carolina coast, and with her cargo totally lost.

D.—1750 TO 1784.

NANTUCKET; MARTHA'S VINEYARD; CAPE COD; BOSTON; LONG ISLAND; RHODE ISLAND; NEW BEDFORD; WILLIAMSBURGH, &C.

The period from 1750 to 1784 was the most eventful era to the whale-fishery that it has ever passed through. For a large proportion of the time the business was carried on under imminent risk of capture, first by the Spanish and French and after by the English. The colonial Davis Strait fishery seems to have been quite abandoned, and the vessels cruised mostly to the eastward of the Grand Banks, along the edge of the Gulf Stream and in the vicinity of the Bahamas. In 1748 the English Parliament had passed a second act to encourage this fishery. By it the premium on inspection of masts, yards, and bowsprits, tar,

* For all the early information concerning Martha's Vineyard I am indebted to Richard L. Pease, esq., of Edgartown.

pitch, and turpentine, and on British-made sail-cloth were to continue, and the duties on foreign-made sail-cloth were remitted to vessels engaged in this pursuit. A bounty was also granted on all ships engaged in whaling during the then existing war; harpooners and others employed in the Greenland fishery were exempted from impressment. The commissioners of customs were, under the required certificate, to pay the second twenty shillings per ton bounty granted by Parliament over the first twenty previously granted.* The ships which had sailed during the previous March or April were to be equal sharers in this bounty with those whose sailing had been delayed. All ships built or fitted out for this pursuit from the American colonies conforming to this act were to be licensed to whale, and in order to receive the bounties must remain in Davis Straits or vicinity from May (sailing about May 1) until the 20th of August, unless sooner full or obliged to return by accident. Foreign Protestants serving in this fishery for two years, and qualifying themselves for its prosecution, were to be treated as though they were natives.† The cause of this concession to the colonies was a part of Lord Shirley's scheme to rid Acadia of the French. It was his desire that George II should cause them to be removed to some other English colony, and settle Nova Scotia with Protestants,‡ and to this end invitations were sent throughout Europe to induce Protestants to remove thither. "The Moravian Brethren were attracted by the promise of exemption from oaths and military service. The good will of New England was encouraged by care for its fisheries; and American whalemen, stimulated by the promise of enjoying an equal bounty with the British, learned to follow their game among the icebergs of the Greenland seas."§ "The New Englanders of this period," says Bancroft,‖ "were of homogeneous origin, nearly all tracing their descent to the English emigrants of the reigns of Charles the First and Charles the Second. They were a frugal and industrious race. Along the seaside, wherever there was a good harbor, fishermen, familiar with the ocean, gathered in hamlets; and each returning season saw them with an ever-increasing number of mariners and vessels, taking the cod and mackerel, and sometimes pursuing the whale into the icy labyrinths of the Northern seas; yet loving home, and dearly attached to their modest freeholds."

Of this period Hutchinson says: ¶ "The increase of the consumption of oil by lamps as well as by divers manufactures in Europe has been no small encouragement to our whale-fishery. The flourishing state of the island of Nantucket must be attributed to it. The cod and whale

---

* In 6th year of the reign of George II.

† Mass. Col. MSS., Maritime, vi, p. 316.

‡ The carrying out of this scheme and the destruction of the colony of Acadians justly receives execration.

§ Bancroft's Hist. U. S., v, p. 45.

‖ *Ibid.*, iv, p. 149.

¶ Hist. of Massachusetts, ii, p. 400.

fishery, being the principal source of our returns to Great Britain, are therefore worthy not only of provincial but national attention."

A continual succession of foreign wars, in which the hardy fishermen and farmers of New England were constantly called to the aid of England, coupled with a continual succession of intolerant measures adopted by the mother country toward the plantations, which, in common with the colonists at large, they felt impelled to resist, was gradually preparing America for the eventful struggle which was to end in its independence. By the experience of the wars they learned their strength, through the pressure of the tyrannical acts they learned their rights.

Pending the expedition for the reduction of Nova Scotia in 1755 an embargo was laid upon the "bank" fishermen, though the risk of capture was so great that it of itself must have quite effectively embargoed many of them.*

In 1757—the embargo being still continued upon the fishery in these waters—a petition was presented to the general court of Massachusetts from the people of Martha's Vineyard and Nantucket, representing that the memorialists "being Informed that your Honours think it not advisable to Permit the fishermen to Sail on their Voyages untill the time limited by the Embargo is Expired by Reason that their fishing banks where they Usually proceed on said Voyages lyes Eastward not far from Cape breton which may be a means of their falling into the hands of the french which may be of bad Consequence to the Common Cause. Your Memorialists would Humbly observe to Your Honours that that is not the Case with the whalemen their procedure on their Voyages is Westward of the Cape of Virginia and southward of that untill the month of June from which Your Memorialists are of the mind their is nothing like the Danger of their falling into the hands of the Cape breton Privateers as would be If they went Eastward. Your Memorialists would further Observe that the whalemen have almost double the Number of hands that the fishermen Carry which makes Their Charge almost Double to that of fishermen and ye first part of the Whale season is Always Esteemed the Principal time for their making their Voyages which If they lose the greatest part of the People will have nothing to Purchase the Necessaries of life withal they haveing no other way which must make them in miserable Situation.

"Your memorialists would therefore beg that y^r Honours would take Our Miserable Situation under Consideration and grant our Whalemen liberty to Proceed on Our Voyages from this time If it be Consistent with your Great wisdom as in duty bound shall ever pray

"JOHN NORTON (for Martha's Vineyard)
"ABISHAI FOLGER† (for Nantucket)"

---

*A duty was laid upon the colonists in 1756 to support a frigate on the Banks to defend the fishery.

†Mass. Col., MSS., Maritime, vi, p. 371. From this petition it would appear that, having an unfavorable season at the southward, the whalemen would stand for the

In compliance with the foregoing petition the Council passed this resolution (April 8, 1758): "Inasmuch as the Inhabitants of Nantucket most of whom are Quakers are by Law exempted from Impresses for military Service. And their Livelihood intirely depends on the Whale fishery—Advised that his Excelly give permission for all whaling Vessels belong to sd Ild to pursue their Voyages, taking only the Inhts of sd Island in sd Vessells and that upon their taking any other persons whatsoever with them they be subject to all the Penalties of the law in like manner as if they had proceeded without Leave."*

In 1761 the fishery of the Gulf of Saint Lawrence and the Straits of Bellisle was opened to our whalemen, and they speedily availed themselves of its wealth. This was the legitimate result of the conquest of Canada and the cession of territory made by France to England at the conclusion of the war, a result which the colonists had labored hard and spent lives and treasure unstintedly to attain, but of the benefit of which they were destined to be defrauded. A duty was levied on all oil and bone carried to England from the colonies, and by another oppressive act of Parliament they were not allowed to find for this product any other market. The discrimination between the plantations and the mother country was made the more marked since at this time the residents of Great Britain were allowed a bounty from which the provincials were debarred. Against these injustices the merchants of New England, and those of London engaged in colonial trade, respectfully petitioned. They represented that "in the Year 1761 The Province of Massachusetts Bay, fitted out from Boston & other ports† Ten Vessels of from Seventy to Ninety Tons Burden for this Purpose. That the Success of these was such as to encourage the Sending out of fifty Vessels in the Year 1762 for the same trade. That in the Year 1763 more than Eighty Vessels were imploy'd in the same manner.‡ That they

---

Banks, hoping to fill there. If, however, a vessel got home early from the north, they frequently went on another voyage to the south and westward in the same year.

* Mass. Col. MSS., Maritime, vi, p. 371. Martha's Vineyard appears to be ignored in the order.

† As already explained, Boston was the port of entry for many of the Cape towns and its own immediate vicinity.

‡ According to the following doggerel there were seventy-five whaling captains sailing from Nantucket in 1763.

Whale-List, by Thomas Worth, M. 1763.

Out of Nantucket their's Whalemen seventy-five,
But two poor Worths among them doth survive:
Their is two Ramsdills & their's Woodbury's two,
Two *Ways* there is, chuse which one pleaseth you,
Folgers thirteen, & Barnards there are four
Bunkers their is three & Jenkinses no more,
Gardners their is seven, Husseys their are two,
Pinkhams their is five and a poor Delano,
Myricks there is three & Coffins there are six,
Swains their are four and one blue gally Fitch.
One Chadwick, Cogshall, Coleman their's but one,
Brown, Baxter, two & Paddacks there is three,
Wyer, Stanton, Starbuck, Moorse is four you see,
But if for a Voyage I was to choose a Stanton,
I would leave Sammy out & choose Ben Stratton.
And not forget that Bocott is alive,
And that long-crotch makes up the seventy-five.
This is answering to the list, you see,
Made up in seventeen hundred & sixty three.

have already imported to London upwards of 40 Ton of Whale Finn: being the produce of the two first years. That upon Entring of the above Finn, a Duty was required and paid upon it, of thirty one Pound ten shillings ℘ Ton. That the weight of this Duty was render'd much heavier by the great reduction made in the price of Dutch Bone since the commencement of this Trade from £500 to £330 ℘ Ton." They represent further that the reason for the conferring of bounties upon vessels in this pursuit from Great Britain was to rival the Dutch,* but in spite of this encouragement there was not enough oil and bone brought into England by British vessels to supply the demand. They also reasoned that Parliament could not intentionally discriminate between the various subjects of the Crown, granting to one a bounty and requiring of another a duty for the same service. They however ask for no bounty—they are content that Great Britain should alone receive the benefit of that—but they simply desire that they should not be taxed with a duty on these imports.†

The knowledge that the English fishery, even with its bounty, was still unable to fully cope with the Dutch, or even to supply its own home demand, as well as the desire of Earl Grenville to forward certain projects in his American policy, notably the odious stamp-tax, caused some attention to be paid to petitions similar to the foregoing, fortified somewhat by the presence of a special agent from Massachusetts to sustain the position and urge the claims there made. To various sections various tenders were to be made. "The boon that was to mollify New England," says Bancroft,‡ "was concerted with Israel Maudit, acting for his brother, the agent of Massachusetts, and was nothing less than the whale-fishery. Great Britain had sought to compete with the Dutch

* The Dutch from 1759 to 1768 sent to the Greenland fishery 1,324 ships, which took 3,018 whales, producing 146,419 barrels of oil and 8,785,140 pounds of bone. (Scousby.) Great Britain in the same time sent about one-third the number of ships.

† Mass. Col. MSS., Maritime, vol. vii, p. 243. The concluding portion of this petition, including the signatures, is missing, a fact greatly to be regretted, as it would be extremely interesting to know who the prominen t oil-merchants of that time were. The following is the statement of imports of oil and bone from the colonies into England and from Holland to the same country, which accompanied the petition:

Account of Finns & Oil from America to England & Duties from Christmas 1758 *to Christmas* 1763.

Year.	Fins.									Whale-oil.								
				Duty America.			Duty London.						Duty America.			Duty London.		
	T.	*Cwt.*	*Lbs.*	£	*s.*	*d.*	£	*s.*	*d.*	*T.*	*H.*	*G.*	£	*s.*	*d.*	£	*s.*	*d.*
1758 to 1759	17	0	17	11	0	0	10	14	0	3,245	2	28	1,898	13	8	1,436	3	8
1760	18	2	9	28	16	6	27	16	4	2,595	1	14	1,518	5	1	1,148	8	5
1761	27	0	8	42	2	6	40	10	6	3,126	3	31	1,829	4	5	1,383	12	10
1762	335	2	5	522	3	10	502	5	0	2,483	2	39	1,452	18	9	1,090	0	4
1763	1,546	3	13	2,427	5	3	2,315	9	4	5,030	0	12	2,942	11	7	2,225	15	11
Total	1,935	0	24	3,011	10	1	2,896	15	2	16,481	1	16	9,641	13	6	7,293	1	2

‡ Bancroft's United States, v, p. 184.

in that branch of industry; had fostered it by bounties; had relaxed even the act of navigation, so as to invite even the Dutch to engage in it from British ports in British shipping. But it was all in vain. Grenville gave up the unsuccessful attempt, and sought a rival for Holland in British America, which had hitherto lain under the double discouragement of being excluded from the benefit of a bounty,* and of having the products of its whale-fishing taxed unequally. He now adopted the plan of gradually giving up the bounty to the British whale-fishery, which would be a saving of £30,000 a year to the treasury, and of relieving the American fishery from the inequality of the discriminating duty, except the old subsidy, which was scarcely 1 per cent. This is the most liberal act of Grenville's administration, of which the merit is not diminished by the fact that the American whale-fishery was superseding the English under every discouragement. It required liberality to accept this result as inevitable, and to favor it. It was done, too, with a distinct conviction that 'the American whale-fishery, freed from its burden, would soon totally overpower the British.' So this valuable branch of trade, which produced annually three thousand pounds, and which would give employment to many shipwrights and other artificers, and to three thousand seamen, was resigned to America."

With the people of Nantucket every foreign war meant a diminution of their whaling-fleet, for there is scarcely any risk that whalemen have not and will not run in pursuit of their prey. During the years 1755 and 1756, six of their vessels had been lost at sea and six more were taken by the French and burned, together with their cargoes, while the crews were carried away into captivity. In 1760 another vessel was captured by a French privateer of 12 guns and released after the commander of the privateer had put on board of her the crew of a sloop they had previously taken nearly full of oil and burned. The captain of the sloop, ——— Luce, had sailed with three others who were expected on the coast. The day after Luce was taken, the privateer engaged a Bermudian letter of marque and was beaten. During this engagement several whalemen in the vicinity made their escape. In the same month (June) another privateer of 14 guns took several whaling-vessels, one of which was ransomed for $400, all the prisoners put on board of her, and she landed them at Newport.† In 1762 another Nantucket sloop was taken by a privateer from the French West Indies, under one Mons. Palanqua, while she was cruising in the vicinity of the Leeward Islands.

At Martha's Vineyard whaling did not seem to thrive so well as at the sister island of Nantucket. The very situation of Nantucket seemed favorable for the development of this and kindred pursuits; in fact, the situation made them necessities. While the Vineyard was quite fertile and of considerable extent, Nantucket was comparatively sterile and cir-

* The bounty of 1748 had evidently been legislated out of existence.

† These vessels were from several whaling ports.

cumscribed. At the Vineyard a livelihood could be attained from tilling the earth, at Nantucket a large portion of that which sustained life must be wrested from the ocean. A constant struggle with nature, and a constant surmounting of those obstacles incident to their location and surroundings, developed within the Nantucketois a spirit of adventure which was carefully trained into channels of enterprise and usefulness. Hence, the early history of whaling on Martha's Vineyard was not that ultimate success that it was on Nantucket, and while the year 1775 found the latter with a fleet of 150 vessels with a burden of 15,000 tons, the former at the same period could count but 12 vessels and an aggregate of 720 tons.

In 1752 Mr. John Newman and Timothy Coffin built a vessel of 75 tons, but she was also destined to a brief existence. On her second voyage whaling she was captured near the Grand Banks by the French, and Captain Coffin, her commander, lost his life, his vessel, and his cargo. In the same year (1752) John Norton, esq., with others, purchased a vessel of 55 tons for the carrying on of this business, and, like her contemporary, she failed to survive her second voyage, but was cast away on the coast of Carolina, Capt. Christopher Beetle being at the time in command. Mr. Norton immediately chartered a vessel to get his own off, but on their arrival on Carolina, his vessel was gone with her sails, rigging, and appurtenances, and he out of pocket a further sum of $500 to the wrecking party. Eight years later (1760), Esquire Norton, with others, built the sloop Polly, 65 tons burden. On her third whaling trip to the southward she too was lost, and by her destruction perished Nicholas Butler, her captain, and thirteen men. Repeated losses had reduced Norton to somewhat straitened circumstances, and, selling what property he had left, he removed to Connecticut, where he died.

It is impossible to separate in the accounts of whaling at this time the share which Boston took in it from that taken by other ports. The reports which may be found in the current papers rarely gave the name of the port to which entering or clearing vessels belonged. In fact the majority of the reports are merely records of accidents, and it is very rarely indeed that the amount of oil taken by returning whalers is given.

In 1762 a whaling-schooner commanded by ——— Bickford was totally lost on Seil (?) Islands. The crew, fourteen in number, were taken off by a fishing-vessel.*

* Boston News-Letter. It would afford an interesting study to trace the various fashions to their commencement and see if their return is marked by particular eras, or whether it is altogether spasmodic. What particularly called this to mind was reading in the News-Letter some lines addressed to a young lady's wardrobe, of which poem these four lines are appropriate here, and may serve as an illustration of the rest:

"To grace the well shap'd Foot, in Turkey's Soil,
Through Life's short Span laborious Silkworms' toil
The Whale in Zembla's frozen Region found,
That forms the swelling Hoop's capacious Round.

Of the Long Island fishery the only record accessible is the meager one regarding Sag Harbor. Easthampton, Southampton, and their more immediate neighbors seem to have been supplanted by this younger town.* Probably prior to 1760 vessels had been fitted for whaling from this port; if so, their identification is impossible. In 1760, however, three sloops were fitted out by Joseph Conkling, John Foster, and others. They were named Goodluck, Dolphin, and Success, and their cruising ground was in the vicinity of 36° north latitude.

The reports regarding Rhode Island are equally meager. Occasional reports are to be found of the arrivals of whaling-vessels, but no report of where they cruised or what success they met with, and no records exist at the custom-house to help clear up the historical mist. Warren comes into notice at this period as quite a thriving whaling-port. The Boston News-Letter of October 23, 1766, says: "Several Vessels employed in the Whale Fishery, from the industrious Town of Warren in Rhode Island Colony, have lately returned, having met with considerable success. One Vessel, which went as far as the Western Islands, brought home upwards of 300 Barrels of Oil. Some Vessels from Newport have also been tolerably successful. This Business, which seems to be carried on with Spirit, bids fair to be of great Utility to that Government."

Williamsburgh, Va., felt the stimulus caused by success in this business; and in the early spring of 1751 several gentlemen subscribed a sum of money and fitted out a small sloop, called the "Experiment," for whaling along the southern coast. On the 9th of May, 1751, she returned with a valuable whale. This was the first vessel ever fitted for this pursuit from Virginia, and whether she continued for any length of time in the business is unknown. The encouragement of the first success undoubtedly caused another venture.

In the vicinity of New Bedford whaling probably commenced but little prior to 1760. In that year William Wood, of Dartmouth, sold to Elnathan Eldredge, of the same town, a certain tract of land, located within the present town of Fairhaven, and within three-quarters of a mile of the center of the town, on the banks of the Acushnet River, "Always Excepting and reserving * * * * * that part of the same where the Try house and Oyl shed now stands." How long these buildings had been standing at the date of this deed is unknown, but the fact of their being there then is indisputable, and, as it was not the habit in those days to put up useless buildings, they were undoubtedly applied to the purpose for which they were built. That they were considered valuable property is evident from the fact of their being reserved. In 1765, four sloops, the Nancy, Polly, Greyhound, and Hannah, owned by Joseph Russell, Caleb Russell, and William Tallman, and from 40 to 60 tons burden, were employed in the whale-fishery.† In Ricketson's

* Sag Harbor was settled in 1730.

† Ricketson's History of New Bedford, p. 58. Mr. Ricketson says: "To Joseph Russell, the founder of New Bedford, is also attributed the honor of being the pioneer of the

"History of New Bedford" is published a portion of a log-book of the whaling-sloop Betsey, of Dartmouth, in 1761. The early portion is missing, the first date commencing July 27. These small vessels usually sailed in pairs, and, so long as they kept in company, the blubber of the captured whales was divided equally between them. Hence the reports, in which the captains' names are always given instead of the names of the vessels, which rarely occur, often return the vessels in pairs, with the same quantity of oil to each. The following are a few extracts from this journal as published: "August 2d, 1761. Lat. 45.54, long. 53.57. Saw two sperm-whales; killed one.—Aug. 6th. Spoke with John Clasbery; he had got 105 bbls.; told us Seth Folger had got 150 bbls. Spoke with two Nantucket men; they had got one whale between them; they told us that Jenkins & Dunham had got four whales between them, and Allen & Pease had got 2 whales between them. Lat. 42.57.—Sunday, August 9th. Saw sperm-whales; struck two, and killed them between us, (naming their consort.—August 10th. Cut up our blubber into casks; filled 35 hhds.; our partner filled 33 hhds. Judged ourselves to be not far from the Banks. Finished stowing the hold.—August 20. Lat. 44 deg. 2 min. This morning spoke with Thomas Gibbs; had got 110 bbls; told us he had spoke with John Aikin, and Ephraim Delano, and Thomas Nye. They had got no oil at all. Sounded; got no bottom. Thomas Gibbs told us we were but two leagues off the Bank." The Betsey probably arrived home about the middle of September. In 1762 she apparently made another voyage, though the journal up to the 2d of September is missing. On that date they spoke "Shubel Bunker and Benjamin Paddock." On the 3d of September they "Knocked down try-works."* On the 15th they spoke Henry Folger and Nathan Coffin.

About this time a new element entered into antagonism with colonial whaling in the Gulf of St. Lawrence and vicinity. Scarcely had the colonists aided to wrest this fishery from the French, when the English governors, in their turn, strove to keep our vessels from enjoying its benefits. In the News-Letter of August 8, 1765, is the following statement: "Tuesday one of the sloops which has been on the Whaling Business returned here. We hear that the Vessels employed in the Whale

whale-fishery of New Bedford. It is well authenticated by the statements of several cotemporaries, lately deceased, that Joseph Russell had pursued the business as early as the year 1755." From what particular portion of the then town of Dartmouth (which also included what is now known as New Bedford, and Fairhaven) he fitted out his vessels, is uncertain. At that time the land on which stands the city of New Bedford was unpopulated by the whites, and not a single house marked the spot where, within less than a century thereafter, stands the city from which was fitted out more whaling-vessels than from all the other American ports combined.

* In other words, took them down. From this it is evident that some vessels were prepared for trying out their oil on board.

The News-Letter of July 26, 1764, states that one Jonathan Negers, of Dartmouths while whaling, was so injured by a whale's striking the boat that he died a few day, after.

Fishery from this and the neighbouring Maritime Towns,* amounting to near 100 Sail, have been very successful this Season in the Gulph of St. Lawrence and Streights of Belle isle; having, tis said, already made upwards of 9,000 Barrels of Oil." But this rosy-colored report was speedily followed by another of a more somber hue. In August 22 the same paper says: "Accounts received from several of our Whaling Vessels on the Labrador Coast, are, that they meet with Difficulties in regard to their fishing, in Consequence of Orders from the Commanding Officers on that Station, a Copy of which are as follows:

"MEMORANDUM: In Pursuance of the Governor's Directions, all masters of Whaling Vessels, and others whom it may concern, are hereby most strictly required to observe the following Particulars, viz:

"1 To carry the useless Parts of such Whales as they may catch to at least Three Leagues from the Shore, to prevent the Damage that the neighbouring Fishers for Cod and Seal sustain by their being left on the Shore.

"2 Not to carry any Passengers from Newfoundland or the Labradore Coast to any Part of the Plantations.

"3 To leave the Coast by the first of November at farthest.

"4 Not to fish in any of the Ports or Coasts of Newfoundland lying between Point Richi and Cape Bonavista.

"5 Not to carry on any Trade or have any Intercourse with the French on any Pretence.

"6 In all your Dealings with the Indians, to treat them with the greatest Civility: observing not to Impose on their Ignorance, or to take Advantage of their Necessities. You are also on no Account to serve them with spirituous Liquors.

"7 Not to fish for any other than Whale on this Coast.

"Dated on board His Majesty's sloop Zephyr, at the Isle of Bois, on the Labradore Coast, the 21st July, 1765.

"JOHN HAMILTON."

The issue of November 18 reports that on account of this proclamation the vessels "are returning half loaded." It was the custom with many early whalemen, especially from the immediate vicinity of Boston, to go prepared for either cod or whale fishing, and in the event of the failure of the one to have recourse to the other. All restrictions which are sustained by an armed force are liable to be made especially obnoxious by the manner of the enforcement, and this was by no means a contrary case. It was not at all surprising then that the ensuing season's fishing was only a repetition of the failure of that of 1765. "Since our last," says the News-Letter, "several Vessels are returned from the Whaling Business, who have not only had very bad Success, but also have been ill-treated by some of the Cruisers on the Labradore Coast."

*It is impossible to apportion the vessels among their proper ports. The vessels from Cape Cod and the northward cleared at Boston; those from the Vineyard, at Nantucket; those at Dartmouth, sometimes at Nantucket and sometimes at Newport.

Two ships had been fitted out from London, the Pallisser and the Labradore, for the express purpose of trading, fishing, and whaling on the coast of Labrador and in the Straits of Belle-isle. Capt. Charles Penn, who came out in them as pilot, left the Straits on the 9th of July on his way to Newfoundland. On his passage he went on board quite a number of whaling-vessels, and reported that they had met with very poor success, had got only about twenty whales in the entire fleet. In consequence of this failure some of them had, according to the time-honored practice, gone to fishing for cod, but had been interrupted by an armed vessel and by the "company's ships" (the Pallisser and Labradore), and their catch all taken away from them save what their actual necessities required. This was done under the pretence that the whole coast was patented to "the company," and by virtue of orders issued by Hugh Pallisser, "governor of Newfoundland, Anticosti, Magdalenes, and Labradore." Pallisser's proclamation, which bore date of April 3d, 1766, specified that all British subjects whaling in that vicinity should choose places on shore where they should land, cut up their blubber, and make oil as they arrived, but not to select any place which was used in the cod-fishery. Whalemen from the plantations might take whales on those coasts, but were only permitted to land on some unoccupied place within the Gulf of St. Lawrence to cut up and try out their blubber; and it was particularly specified that they were not to make use of any place which was used by the British fishermen for the same or a similar purpose. Complaint having been made of the provincial whalemen in regard to their waste interfering with the cod fishery, they were enjoined that they must carry the carcasses of the whales at least three leagues from the shore. No fishermen from the plantations were to be allowed to winter on Labrador. And then Capt. John Hamilton, "of H. M. sloop of war Merlin, Lieut. Gov. of Labradore," &c., issued his proclamation: "This is to give Notice to all Whalers from the Plantations, that they are allowed to fish for Whales only, on the Coast of Labradore, that if they are found to have any other Fish on Board, the Fish will be seized, and they excluded the Benefit of Whale-fishery this season: and on no Pretence to trade with the Indians; whatever they shall purchase will be confiscated, and after this Notice their Vessels liable to be seized," &c., &c. Capt. Hamilton's decree bore the date of June 25, 1766.

The result of these arbitrary measures was that the whalemen left those seas and went off the banks. The close of the season witnessed the return of the whaling fleet with but indifferent success.* Naturally those interested (and this included the wealthiest merchants and the

* The Boston News-Letter mentions the arrival of Capt. Peter Wells at that port from whaling August 18, 1766. Under date of October 2, the News-Letter says: "Since our last a Number of Vessels have arrived from Whaling. They have not been successful generally. One of them viz: Capt. Clark on Thursday Morning last discovering a Spermaceti Whale near George's Banks, mann'd his Boat, and gave Chase to her.

most skillful mechanics as well as the most indefatigable mariners) felt aggrieved. It seemed scarcely in consonance with the colonial ideas of justice, crude as those notions appeared to the English nobility, that the beneficial results of a conquest which they almost single-handed had made, and for defraying the expense, of which England had declined any remuneration, should be diverted to the sole benefit of those alone who were residents of the British Isles. Merchants in London, too, whose heaviest and most profitable trade was with the provinces, joined their voices in denouncing this wrong. During the early winter the report came that Palliser's regulations were suspended until the ministry and Parliament had time to consider the subject. The matter had already, late in the last whaling season, been brought to the attention of the governor of Newfoundland, and he issued the following supplementary edict, which appeared in the Boston papers of January, 1767:

"By His Excellency Hugh Palliser, Governor and Commander in Chief in and over the Island of Newfoundland, the Coast of Labradore and all the Territories dependent thereupon:

"Whereas a great many Vessels from His Majesty's Plantations employed in the Whale-Fishery resort to that Part of the Gulph of St. Lawrence and the Coast of Labradore which is within this Government. and as I have been informed that some Apprehensions have arisen amongst them that by the Regulations made by me relating to the different Fisheries in those Parts, they are wholly precluded from that Coast:

"Notice is hereby given, That the King's Officers stationed in those Parts have always had my Orders to protect, assist and encourage by every Means in their Power, all Vessels from the Plantations employed in the Whale-Fishery, coming within this Government; and, pursuant to his Majesty's Orders to me, all Vessels from the Plantations will be admitted to that Coast on the same Footing as they have ever been admitted in Newfoundland; the ancient Practices and Customs established in Newfoundland respecting the Cod Fishery, under the Act of Parliament passed in the 10 and 11th Years of William IIId commonly called The Fishing Act, always to be observed.*

"And by my Regulations for the Encouragement of the Whale Fishers, they are also under certain necessary Restrictions therein pre-

& she coming up with her jaws against the Bow of the Boat struck it with such Violence that it threw a Son of the Captain; (who was forward ready with his Lance) a considerable Height from the Boat, and when he fell the Whale turned with her devouring Jaws opened, and caught him. He was heard to scream, when she closed her Jaws, and part of his Body was seen out of her Mouth, when she turned, and went off."

* Duties on oil imported in British ships were remitted, the commander and one-third of each crew being British. Duties were also remitted on fat, furs and tusks of seal, bear, walrus or other marine animal taken in the Greenland Seas. By other acts the imported materials to be used in outfitting were made non-dutiable and bounties were established, amounting in the final aggregate to 40s. per ton.

scribed, permitted to land and cut up their Whales in Labradore; this is a Liberty that has never been allowed them in Newfoundland, because of the Danger of prejudicing the Cod-Fishery carried on by our adventurers' Ships, and by Boat-Keepers from Britain, lawfully qualified with Fishing-Certificates according to the aforementioned Act, who are fitted out at a very great Risque and Expence in complying with said Act, therefore they must not be liable to have their Voyages overthrown, or rendered precarious by any Means, or by any other Vessels whatever. And

"Whereas great Numbers of the Whaling Crews arriving from the Plantations on the Coast of Labradore early in the Spring considering it as a lawless Country are guilty of all Sorts of Outrages before the Arrival of the King's Ships, plundering whoever they find on the Coast too weak to resist them, obstructing our Ship Adventurers from Britain by sundry Ways, banking amongst their Boats along the Coast, which ruins the Coast-Fishery, and is contrary to the most ancient and most strictly observed Rule of the Fishery, and must not be suffered on any Account; also by destroying their Fishing-Works on Shore, stealing their Boats, Tackle and Utensils, firing the Woods all along the Coast, and hunting for and plundering, taking away or murdering the poor Indian Natives of the Country; by these Violences, Barbarities, and other notorious Crimes and Enormities, that Coast is in the utmost Confusion, and with Respect to the Indians is kept in a State of War.

"For preventing these Practices in future Notice is hereby given, That the King's Officers stationed in those Parts, are authorized and strictly directed, to apprehend all such Offenders within this Government, and to bring them to me to be tried for the same at the General Assizes at this Place: And for the better Government of that Country, for regulating the Fisheries, and for protecting His Majesty's Subjects from Insults from the Indians, I have His Majesty's Commands to erect Block Houses, and establish Guards along that Coast.

"This Notification is to be put in the Harbours in Labradore, within my Government, and through the Favour of His Excellency Governour Bernard, Copies thereof will be put up in the Ports within the Province of Massachusetts, where the Whalers mostly belong, for their Information before the next Fishing Season.

"Given under my Hand at St. John's in Newfoundland, this First Day of August, 1766.

"HUGH PALLISER.

"By Order of His Excellency,

"JNO. HORSNAILL."

There can be scarcely a doubt but that the indiscretions of the whalemen were much magnified (if indeed they really existed) in this pronunciamento of Governor Palliser, for the sake of bolstering up the former one. The whalemen of those days were far from being the set of graceless scamps which he represents them to be. Probably there was here and there a renegade. It would be quite impossible to find in so large a number of men that all were strict observers of the laws. Self-preservation, if no more humane motive existed, militated against the acts of which he complained. The whalemen were accustomed to visit the coast for supplies, in many cases several times a year; usually on their arrival in those parts they stood in for some portion of the coast and "wooded;" and it is hardly credible that they should wantonly destroy the stores they so much needed, or make enemies on a coast where they might at any time be compelled to land. The colonial governors quite often made the resources under their control a source of revenue for themselves, and the fact of the modification of Palliser's first proclamation only under pressure of the King and Parliament would seem to indicate personal interest in keeping whalemen from the colonies away from the territory under his control.

It is quite evident that even with this modification the colonial fishermen did not feel that confidence in the St. Lawrence and Belle Isle fishery that they felt when it was first opened to them; for a report from Charleston, S. C., dated June 19, 1767, states that on "the 22d ult. put in here, a sloop belonging to Rhode Island, from a Whaling Voyage in the Southern latitudes, having proved successful about 10 days before. *The master informs us, that near* 50 *New England vessels have been on the whale fishery in the same latitudes, this season, by way of experiment.*"* Over the open sea fortune-seeking governors could exercise no control, and there our seamen probably felt they could pursue their game without let or hinderance. Whales at that time abounded along the edge of the Gulf Stream, and there they continued to be found for some years, shifting their ground gradually as their fierce captors encroached more and more upon them to the vicinity of the Western and Leeward Islands, the Cape de Verdes, the Brazil Banks, and beyond. Some few whalemen, in spite of the restrictions, still visited the newly-opened fishing-ground.

The general results of the various voyages were on the whole good, and other places began to feel the stimulus of a desire to compete. Providence took part, and early in 1768 several vessels were fitted out from that port for this pursuit. New York, too, entered the lists, and Mr. Robert Murray and the Messrs. Franklin fitted a sloop for the same purpose, and she sailed on the 19th of April of that year.† The town of Newport manifested great activity.

It was currently reported in the colonies, during the early part of 1767, that the irksome restrictions upon whaling were to be entirely removed; petitions to that effect had been presented to the home government, and a favorable result was hoped for, and early in 1768 the straits of Davis and Belle Isle were again vexed by the keels of our

* Boston News-Letter.

† There seems to be no accessible report of this vessel's return, and hence the degree of success or failure of her voyage is a matter of doubt. The people of Nantucket were reported to have made £70,000 in 1767.

fishermen, as many as fifty or sixty anchoring in Canso harbor in April of that year, a few of them bound for the former locality, but the majority of them cruising in the vicinity of the Gulf of St. Lawrence and Newfoundland.* Two whaling-sloops from Nantucket, one commanded by ——— Coleman, and the other by ——— Coffin, were lost this season in the straits of Belle Isle, and the crews were saved by Captain Hamilton, of the Merlin sloop of war, who also aided them in saving the sails, rigging, and stores from the wrecks. The fishery in those parts was quite unsuccessful, many vessels, up to the last of August, having taken little or no oil.†

In 1768 there sailed from Nantucket eighty sail of vessels of an average burden of 75 tons, and probably fully as many more from other ports—Cape Cod, Dartmouth, Boston, Providence, Newport, Warren, Falmouth, (Cape Cod,) and perhaps other ports being represented, and the voyages being undertaken to Davis Straits, Straits of Belle Isle, Grand Banks, Gulf of St. Lawrence, and Western Islands. Early in the season the Western Island fleet appears to have done little, but by the middle of September they had obtained an average of about 165 barrels. The northern fleet probably did nearly as well, as numerous instances occur of vessels spoken late in the summer and in the early fall with from 100 to 150 and even as high as 200 barrels. Assuming, then, that 140 vessels returned ‡ with an average produce of 150 barrels (which

---

* From a log-book kept by Isaiah Eldredge, of the sloop Tryall, of Dartmouth, which sailed April 25, 1768, for the straits of Belle Isle. She cleared from Nantucket, as Dartmouth was not then a port of entry. On Friday, April 29, she was at anchor in Canso Harbor, with 50 or 60 other whalemen. Saturday, May 7, left Crow Harbor and at night anchored in Man-of-War Cove, Canso Gut, "with about 60 sail of wailmen." The vessels were continually beset with ice, and on the 23d of May they cleared their decks of snow, which was "almost over shoes deep." They killed their first whale on the 22d of July. The larger number of vessels were spoken in pairs, which was the usual manner of cruising. The sloop returned to Dartmouth on the 5th of November. This log runs to 1775, and commences again in 1785, ending in 1797, with occasional breaks where leaves are cut out.

† In October, 1767, a whaling-sloop, belonging to Nantucket, arrived at the bar off that port, on board of which were four Indians, who had had some dispute at sea and agreed to settle it on their return. As the vessel lay at anchor the officers and crew—except three white men and these Indians—went ashore. The whites being asleep in the cabin, the Indians went on deck, divided into two parties, and, arming themselves with whaling-lances, commenced the affray. The two on one side were killed immediately, the other two were unhurt. The white men, hearing the affray, rushed upon deck, and, seeing what was done, secured the murderers. In November of the same year some Newburyport fishermen were astounded at perceiving their vessel hurried through the water at an alarming rate without the aid of sails. Upon investigating the cause, it was found that the anchor was fast to a whale (or *vice versa*), and the cable was cut, relieving them of their unsolicited propelling power.—(Boston News-Letter.)

‡ Of the 80 vessels sailing from Nantucket but 70 returned, the other 10 being either captured by the French or lost at sea. The same ratio is assumed for the remainder of the fleet. In 1769 a Marblehead brig, the Pitt Packet, Capt. Thos. Power, was boarded by the Rose man-of-war, for the sake of impressing men. Four of the crew, arming themselves with harpoons, retreated to the fore-peak, resolved to resist to the

was the actual average import at Nantucket)* and we have as the result of the season's fishing 21,000 barrels, worth, at £18 per ton, the ruling price, £47,200, or about $236,000.

"Between the years 1770 and 1775," says Macy,† "the whaling business increased to an extent hitherto unparalleled. In 1770 there were a little more than one hundred vessels engaged; and in 1775 the number exceeded one hundred and fifty, some of them large brigs. The employment of so great and such an increasing capital may lead our readers to suppose that a corresponding profit was realized, but a careful examination of the circumstances under which the business was carried on will show the fallacy of such a conclusion. Many branches of labor were conducted by those who were immediately interested in the voyages.‡ The young men, with few exceptions, were brought up to some trade necessary to the business. The rope-maker, the cooper, the blacksmith, the carpenter—in fine, the workmen were either the ship-owners or of their household; so were often the officers and men who navigated the vessels and killed the whales. While a ship was at sea, the owners at home were busily employed in the manufactory of casks, iron-work, cordage, blocks, and other articles for the succeeding voyage. Thus the profits of the labor were enjoyed by those interested in the fishery, and voyages were rendered advantageous even when the oil ob-

extent of their lives. In the *melée* the boarding lieutenant was killed. But three of the men, none of whom, says the News-Letter, were Americans, allowed themselves to become intoxicated, and all were captured.

* Macy's Nantucket, p. 233.

† *Ibid.*, p. 68. In the spring of 1770 three whalemen fitted out from Middletown, Conn. They returned in October of the same year, having met with very poor success.

‡ The almost universal method of settling the voyages of American whalemen was by "lays," each officer and man being shipped to receive a certain proportion of the earnings as his pay. In this way each one was directly interested in the general result. For instance, in settling the voyage of the ship Lion, of Nantucket, in 1807, the account as stated in the Coll. of the Mass. Hist. Soc., ii ser., iii vol., p. 19, is thus:

Dr.		Cr.	
To amount of charge	$362 75	By 37,358 gallons body oil	$19,766 14
To sundry accounts, clearing ship, &c., (no charge against captain, mate, and boy)	43 38	By 16,868 gallons head matter	17,849 73
		By 150½ gallons black oil	45 15
			37,661 02
The share of the captain, $\frac{1}{18}$	$2,072 13	Boy, $\frac{1}{120}$	$310 82
Mate, $\frac{1}{27}$	1,381 41	5 blacks, $\frac{1}{80}$ each	2,331 14
Second mate, $\frac{1}{37}$	1,008 06	1 black, $\frac{1}{80}$ on 400 barrels	108 36
2 ends men, $\frac{1}{48}$ each	1,554 10	1 black, $\frac{1}{90}$	414 42
5 ends men, $\frac{1}{75}$ each	2,486 55	1 black, $\frac{1}{85}$	438 80
Cooper, $\frac{1}{60}$	621 64	1 black, $\frac{1}{90}$ on all but 400 barrels	318 10

Remainder, (coming to owners,) $24,252.74.

Of the interest which those of Nantucket at home had in the success of the ship, Davis says, and with much of truth: "The cooper, while employed in making the casks, took care

tained was barely sufficient to pay the outfits, estimating the labor as a part thereof. This mode of conducting the business was universal, and has continued to a very considerable extent to the present day.* Experience taught the people how to take advantage of the different markets for their oil. Their spermaceti oil was mostly sent to England in its unseparated state, the head matter being generally mixed with the body oil,† for, in the early part of whaling it would bring no more when separated than when mixed. The whale-oil, which is the kind procured from the species called "right-whales," was shipped to Boston

that they were of sound and seasoned wood, lest they might leak his oil in the long voyage; the black-mith forged his choicest iron in the shank of the harpoon, which he knew, perhaps from actual experience, would be put to the severest test in wrenching and twisting, as the whale, in which he had a one hundredth interest, was secured; the rope-maker faithfully tested each yarn of the tow-line, to make certain that it would carry 200 pounds' strain, for he knew that one weak inch in his work might lose to him his share in a fighting monster."—(Nimrod of the Sea, pp. 48, 49.)

* 1835.

† The difference between "head" and "body" matter of the sperm whale can be best understood by reference to the following description of cutting in and diagram copied from Scammon's "Marine Mammalia:" "The first procedure after the animal is fastened to the ship, is to cut a hole through the blubber, between the eye and fin, at A, as seen in the accompanying outline sketch, then, after cutting the scarfs on each side and around the end of the first blanket-piece, a blubber-hook, attached to one of the cutting-tackles, is inserted into the hole at A, and the piece raised by means of the tackle until the whale is rolled on its side; then the line of separation between the upper jaw and junk is cut, as from L to C, and if a large whale, the line of separation is cut between the junk and case, as from B to E, and a cut is made across the root of the case from E to F; a scarf is also made around the root of the lower jaw, from near the corner of the mouth to G. A chain-strap is then put on the jaw near H and hooked or shackled to the second cutting-tackle, and raised by that purchase, while the other tackle attached to the piece is slackened off, if need be, so as to let the whale roll upon its back; when, by means of the tackle attached, and by cutting away the tongue and the adhering flesh, the jaw is wrenched from its socket and placed on deck. This being accomplished, the first tackle, which is attached to the piece, is hove up by means of the windlass, until the whale is rolled over to its opposite side, when the lines of separation are cut to correspond to those made opposite. Holes are then mortised through the head close to the upper jaw-bone, near I, at the end of the junk, near J, and at the root of the case, near K, and through these holes straps are rove, and lines are made fast to those of the junk and case. The second cutting-tackle is then hooked in the strap which is around the upper jaw at I; the fluke-chain is slackened off, and the first tackle fastened to the piece is lowered, when all hands heave on the head-tackle, forcing the whale down again, and thus bringing the creature's head up, and the body nearly to a vertical position. The officers upon the cutting-stage with their keen spades cut away between the bones and junk from L to C, and the enormous weight of the whole fatty mass of the head hanging down opens the gash between it and the skull-bone; then, cutting cross the end of the junk and root of the case, from E to F, completes the process of cutting off the head, which is temporarily made fast to the ship's quarter. The fluke-chain is then hauled in again, and the blubber is rolled from the body in the same manner as that of a baleen-whale, until coming to the region of the small, when it is unjointed just behind the vent, and the remaining posterior portion of the animal is hoisted on board in one mass. The head, as it is termed, is then hauled up to the gangway, and one of the tackles is hooked into the junk-strap at J, and by means of this cutting-tackle purchase, the head is taken in whole, if the

or elsewhere in the colonies, and there sold for country consumption, or sent to the West Indies."*

The seas continued to be infested with French and Spanish privateers and pirates,† and whalemen, especially those frequenting the ocean in the vicinity of the Western Islands, were, from the very nature of their employment, constantly liable to depredations from these corsairs, whether legalized or lawless. In March, 1771, the sloop Neptune, Captain Nixon, arrived in Newport from the mole, bringing with him portions of the crews of three Dartmouth whalemen, who had been taken on the south side of Hispaniola by a Spanish guarda coasta. These vessels were commanded by Captain Silas Butler, William Roberts, and Richard Welding. Another whaling vessel belonging to Martha's Vineyard, commanded by Ephraim Pease, was also taken at about the same time, but released in order to put on board of her the remaining prisoners. At this time Pease had taken 200 barrels of oil, and the Dart-

whale is under forty barrels; but if over that size, it is raised sufficiently out of the water to cut the junk from the case, when it is hoisted on deck. The case is then secured by one or both tackles, hove up to the plank-sheer, and an opening is made at its root, of a suitable size to admit the case-bucket, when the oil is bailed out, or the whole case is hove in on deck before being opened; which finishes the cutting-in of a sperm-whale." The "head" or case oil is, when bailed out, as clear and limpid as water, but after a short time thickens and hardens into a mass as purely white as the newly-fallen snow. The body oil is of a coarser nature. For all practical purposes, the general principles of "cutting-in" the sperm-whale will apply to the same process in regard to the right or bone whale; and for a thorough description of these cetaceans, the implements used in their capture, and the saving of the oil, the work quoted above will be found an excellent authority.

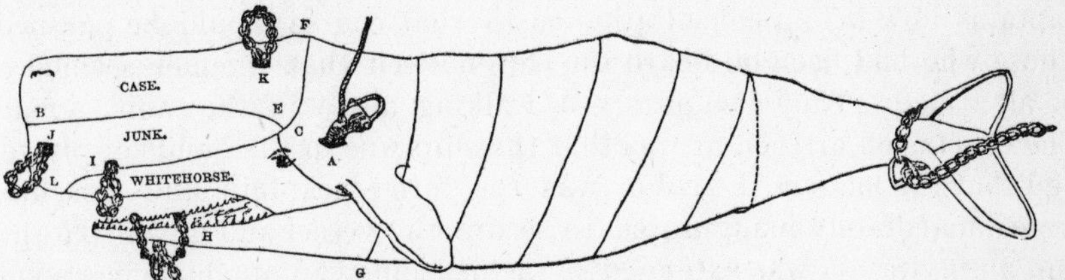

* Bancroft says (Hist. U. S., v, p. 265), in 1765 the colonists were not allowed to export the chief products of their industry, such as sugar, tobacco, cotton, wool, indigo, ginger, dyeing-woods, whalebone, &c., to any place but Great Britain—not even to Ireland. Save in the matter of salt, wines, victuals, horses, and servants, Great Britain was not only the sole market for the products of America, but the only store-house for its supplies.

This stringency must, however, have been somewhat relaxed as regards oil, for the Boston News-Letter of September 8, 1768, gives the report from London, dated July 13, that the whale and cod fisheries of New England "this season promised to turn out extremely advantageous, many ships fully laden having already been sent to the Mediterranean markets." The success of the Americans seems to have again aroused the jealousy of their English brethren, for in this same year an effort was made in Parliament to revive the bounty to English whalemen, with the intent to weaken the American fishery.

† The word "pirate" seems to have been in these days of a somewhat ambiguous signification, and was quite as likely to mean a privateer as a corsair.

mouth vessels, which were carried into St. Domingo, 100 barrels. These captures were made on the 11th of February.*

But it did not always happen that whalemen fell so easy a prey to predatory vessels. A little strategy sometimes availed them when a forcible resistance would have been out of the question, and it may be easily believed that men to whom danger and hairbreadth escapes were part of their every-day life would scarcely submit supinely when there was any chance in their favor. A notable instance of this kind occurred in April, 1771. Two Nantucket whaling-sloops, commanded respectively by Isaiah Chadwick and Obed Bunker, were lying at anchor in the harbor of Abaco, when a ship appeared off the mouth of the harbor with her signals set for assistance. With that readiness to aid distressed shipmates which has ever been a distinguishing trait of American whalemen, one of the captains with a boat's crew made up of men from each sloop hastened to render such help as was in their power. The vessel's side reached, the captain immediately boarded her to find what was desired, and much to his surprise had a pistol presented to his head by the officer in command with a peremptory demand that he should pilot the ship into the harbor. He assured the commander that he was a stranger there, but that there was a man in his boat who was acquainted with the port. The man was called and persuaded in the same manner in which the captain had been. The argument used to demonstrate the prudence of his compliance with the request being so entirely unanswerable the man performed the service, anchoring the ship where a point of land lay between her and the sloops. This being done the boat was dismissed and the men returned to their vessels. The Nantucket captains now held a consultation as to what course should be pursued. Those who had been on board the ship noticed that the men seemed to be all armed. They also observed, walking alone in the cabin, a man. The conclusion arrived at was that the ship was in the hands of pirates and that the man in the cabin was the former captain, and measures were immediately inaugurated to secure the vessel and crew. To this end an invitation was extended to the usurping captain, his officers and passengers to dine on board one of the sloops. The courtesy was accepted, and the pirate captain and his boatswain, with the displaced captain as representative of the passengers, repaired on board the sloop. After a short time he became uneasy and proposed to return to his own vessel, but he was seized by the whalemen and bound fast and his intentions frustrated. The actual captain now explained the situation, which was, that the ship sailed from Bristol (R. I.?) to the coast of Africa, from thence carried a cargo of slaves to the West Indies, and was on her return home with a cargo of sugar when the mutiny occurred, it being the intention of the mutineers to become pirates, a business at that time quite thrifty and promising. Our fishermen now told the boatswain that if he would go on board the ship and bring the former

* The men who came home with Captain Nixon were Oliver Price, Pardon Slocum, and Philip Harkins.—(Boston News-Letter.)

mate, who was in irons, and aid in recapturing the vessel, they would endeavor to have him cleared from the penalties of the law, and they prudently intimated to him that there was a man-of-war within two hours' sail from which they could obtain force enough to overpower his associates. As a further act of prudence they told him they would set a certain signal when they had secured help from the ship of war.

The boatswain not returning according to the agreement made, one sloop weighed anchor and stood toward the pirate-ship as though to pass on one side of her. As she approached the mutineers shifted their guns over to the side which it seemed apparent she would pass and trained them so as to sink her as she sailed by. But those who navigated the sloop were fully alive to these purposes, and as she neared the ship her course was suddenly changed and she swept by on the other side and was out of range of the guns before the buccaneers could recover from their surprise and reshift and retrain their cannon. On the sloop stood upon her course till they were out of sight of the ship, then tacking, the signal agreed with the boatswain was set and she was steered boldly for the corsair. As she hove in sight, the pirates, recognizing the sign, and believing an armed force from the man-of-war was on board the whaling-vessel, fled precipitately to the shore, where they were speedily apprehended on their character being known. The whalemen immediately boarded their prize, released the mate, and carried the ship to New Providence, where a bounty of $2,500 was allowed them for the capture and where the chief of the mutineers was hanged.*

About this time Dr. Benjamin Franklin, being in London, was questioned by the merchants there respecting the difference in time between the voyages of the merchantmen to Rhode Island and the English packets to New York. The variation, which was something like fourteen days, was a source of much annoyance to the English merchants, and believing the place of destination might have something to do with it, they seriously contemplated withdrawing the packets from New York and dispatching them to Rhode Island. In this dilemma they consulted Dr. Franklin. A Nantucket captain named Folger,† who was a relative of the doctor's, being then in London, Franklin sought his opinion. Captain Folger told him that the merchantmen were commanded by men from Rhode Island who were acquainted with the Gulf Stream and the effect of its currents, and in the passage to America made use of this knowledge. Of this the English captains were ignorant, not from lack of repeated warnings, for they had been often told that they were stemming a current which was running at the rate of three miles an hour, and that if the wind was light the stream would set them back faster than the breeze would send them ahead, but they were too wise to be advised by simple American fishermen, and so persevered in their own course at a loss of from two to three weeks on every trip. By

* Boston News-Letter.

† Works of Franklin, iii, p. 353. Probably Capt. Timothy Folger, a man who was prominent for many years in the history of Nantucket.

Franklin's request Captain Folger made a sketch of the stream, with directions how to use or avoid its currents, and this sketch made over a century ago is substantially the same as is found on charts of the present day. "The Nantucket whalemen," says Franklin,* "being extremely well acquainted with the Gulph Stream, its course, strength, and extent, by their constant practice of whaling on the edges of it, from their island quite down to the Bahamas, this draft of that stream was obtained of one of them, Captain Folger, and caused to be engraved on the old chart in London for the benefit of navigators by B. Franklin."

Notwithstanding this information so kindly volunteered to them, and notwithstanding the fact that the Falmouth captains were furnished with the new charts, they still persisted in sailing their old course. There is a point where perseverance degenerates into something more ignoble; it would seem as though at this date these self-sufficient captains had about attained that point.

In 1772 two whaling sloops from Nantucket, with 150 barrels of oil each, were captured by a Spanish brig and sloop off Matanzas.† In December of the same year, the brig Leviathan, Lathrop, sailed from Rhode Island for the Brazil Banks on a whaling voyage. On the 25th of January they lowered for whales, and in the chase the mate's boat (Brotherton Daggett) lost sight of the brig, but the crew were picked up at sea and brought home by another vessel.

In 1773 quite a fleet of American whalers were on the coast of Africa,‡ no less than 14 being reported as coming from that ground, and probably there were as many more of whom no report was made. One brig from Boston, while off the coast of Sierra Leone, sent a boat ashore with six men to procure water. The boat was seized and the crew all massacred by the natives. In the spring of the following year a sloop owned by Gideon Almy of Tiverton, and another belonging to Boston,

* Works of Franklin, iii, p. 364. In a note Franklin says: "The Nantucket captains, who are acquainted with this stream, make their voyages from England to Boston in as short a time generally as others take in going from Boston to England, viz, from twenty to thirty days." Quite a number of Boston packets to and from England were at this time and for many years after commanded by Nantucket men.

† In May, 1870, according to the Boston News-Letter, no less than 19 vessels cleared from Rhode Island, whaling. The Post-Boy for October 14, 1771, is responsible for the following: "We learn from Edgartown, that a vessel lately arrived there from a whaling voyage, and in her voyage, one Marshall Jenkins, with others, being in a boat which struck a whale, she turned and bit the boat in two, took Jenkins in her mouth, and went down with him; but on her rising threw him into one part of the boat, whence he was taken on board the vessel by the crew; being much bruised—and in a fortnight after, he perfectly recovered. This account we have from undoubted authority."

‡ According to Macy, (p. 54,) the following are the dates of the occupation of various fishing-grounds by Nantucket whalemen in addition to the Davis Strait fishery: Island of Disco, 1751; Gulf of Saint Lawrence, 1761; coast of Guinea, 1763; Western Islands, 1765; east of Banks of Newfoundland, 1765; coast of Brazil, 1774. According to a local tradition, the first Nantucket whaleman who "crossed the line," arrived home from his voyage on the day of the battle of Concord and Lexington. This was the brig Amazon, Uriah Bunker, commander.

were seized, while watering at Hispaniola, by a French frigate, carried into Port-au-Prince and there condemned.*

In 1774 a report came by the way of Fayal that a small American whaling brig was lying in the harbor of Rio Janeiro with only her captain and three men on board. It appears that, putting in there for refreshments,† in the summer of 1773, a portion of her crew were, "by fair or foul means," induced to ship on a Portuguese snow ‡ for a three months' whaling voyage. The snow was provided with harpoons and other whaling craft, made after the English models, and was cruising for sperm whales, a business altogether new to the Portuguese, who had been, hitherto, ignorant of any but the right whale, and had never ventured even in the pursuit of them out of sight of land. The brig still lay there in October, 1773, waiting the return of her men.§

In 1774 the whale-fishery in the colonies must have been in the full tide of success. There were probably fitted out annually at this time no less than 360 vessels of various kinds, with an aggregate burden of nearly 33,000 tons, and employing directly about 4,700 men, and indirectly an immensely greater number. Despite the depredations of French and Spanish privateers the fishery continued to flourish. The annual production from 1771 to 1775 was probably at least 45,000 barrels of spermaceti oil, and 8,500 barrels of right whale oil, and of bone nearly or quite 75,000 pounds.‖ In the various seaport towns from

* Boston News-Letter.

† Some vessels never dropped anchor in a port from the day they sailed until their return; but scurvy was very apt to manifest itself where a crew was so long deprived of fresh provisions.

‡ "A snow is a vessel equipped with two masts resembling the main and foremast of a ship, and a third small mast, abaft the mainmast, carrying a trysail. These vessels were much used in the merchant service at the time of the Revolution." (Lossing's Field Book, ii, p. 846, note.)

§ Boston News-Letter.

‖ *State of the whale-fishery in Massachusetts,* 1771 *to* 1775.

Ports.	Vessels fitted annually for northern fishery.		Vessels fitted annually for southern fishery.		Seamen employed.	Sperm-oil taken annually.	Whale-oil taken annually.
	No.	Tonnage.	No.	Tonnage.			
						Barrels.	*Barrels.*
Nantucket	65	4, 875	85	10, 200	2, 025	26, 000	4, 000
Wellfleet	20	1, 600	10	1, 000	420	2, 250	1, 250
Dartmouth	60	4, 500	20	2, 000	1, 040	7, 200	1, 400
Lynn	1	75	1	120	28	200	100
Martha's Vineyard	12	720	.....	....	156	900	300
Barnstable	2	150	.....	....	26	210	....
Boston	15	1, 300	5	700	260	1, 800	600
Falmouth, (Cape Cod)	4	300	.....	....	52	400	....
Swanzey	4	300	.....	....	52	400	....
	183	13, 820	121	14, 020	4, 059	39, 390	7, 650

These statistics are from Jefferson's report, and were gathered for him by governor of Massachusetts.

which this pursuit was carried on, in Nantucket, Wellfleet, Dartmouth, Lynn, Martha's Vineyard, Barnstable, Boston, Falmouth, and Swanzey, in Massachusetts, in Newport, Providence, Warren, and Tiverton, in Rhode Island, in New London, Connecticut, Sag Harbor on Long Island, the merry din of the "yo heave ho" of the sailors was heard; the ring of the blacksmith's hammer and anvil made cheery music; the coopers, with their hammers and drivers, kept time to the tramp of their feet as round and round the casks they marched, tightening more and more the bands that bound together the vessels which should hold the precious oil; and the creaking of the blocks as the vessels unloaded their freight, or the riggers fitted them anew for fresh conquests, and the rattle of the hurrying teams as they carried off the product of the last voyage or brought the necessaries for the future one, lent their portion of animation to the scene. Everywhere was hurry and bustle; everywhere all were employed; none that thirsted for employment went away unsatisfied. If a vessel made a bad voyage, the owners, by no means dispirited, again fitted her out, trusting in the next one to retrieve the loss; if she made a profitable one, the proceeds were treasured up to offset a possible failure in some future cruise. On all sides were thrift and happiness.

But a change was near. "A cloud, at first no bigger than a man's hand," was beginning to overshadow the whole heaven of their commercial prosperity. The colonies, driven to desperation by the heartless cruelty of the mother country, prepared to stay further aggression, and resent at the mouth of the cannon and the point of the bayonet the insults and injuries that for a decade of years had been heaped upon them; and the English ministry, against the earnest entreaty of British merchants on both sides of the Atlantic, prepared also to enforce its desires by a resort to arms.*

The first industry to feel the shock of the approaching storm was the fisheries. Massachusetts, the center of this pursuit, was to the English ministers the very focus of the insurrectionary talk and action, and "the first step," says Bancroft, "toward inspiring terror was, to declare

According to Pitkin, among the exports of the colonies, including Newfoundland, Bahamas, and Bermudas, were, for the year 1770:

	Great Britain.	Ireland.	South of Europe.	West Indies.	Africa.	Total.
Sperm candles ....pounds	4,865	450	14,167	351,625	7,905	379,012
Whale-oil ....tons	5,202	22	175	268	....	5,667
Whalebone ....pounds	112,971	....	....	....	....	112,971

Value sterling: Sperm candles, £23,688 4*s.* 6*d.*; whale-oil, £83,012 15*s.* 9*d.*; bone, £19,121 7*s.* 6*d.*

* The colonial trade had become to many English merchants and manufacturers a matter of great importance, and the loss of it would be a serious misfortune. One of the industries which would feel the deprivation most strongly was the manufacture of cordage, of which the Americans were by far the chiefest purchasers in the English market.

Massachusetts in a state of rebellion, and to pledge the Parliament and the whole force of Great Britain to its reduction; the next, by prohibiting the American fisheries, to starve New England; the next, to excite a servile insurrection."*

Accordingly on the 10th of February, 1775, the ministry introduced into Parliament a bill restricting the trade and commerce of Massachusetts Bay, New Hampshire, Connecticut, and Rhode Island to Great Britain, Ireland, and the British West Indies, and prohibiting the colonies from carrying on any fishery on the Banks of Newfoundland or any other part of the North American coast.† "The best shipbuilders in the world were at Boston, and their yards had been closed; the New England fishermen were now to be restrained from a toil in which they excelled the world. Thus the joint right to the fisheries was made a part of the great American struggle."‡ To this bill there was a small but active and determined opposition, both in the House of Lords and House of Commons. It was urged on the part of the ministry that the fisheries were the property of England, and it was with the English government to do as they pleased with them. To this opinion the minority strenuously demurred. "God and nature," said Johnston, "have given that fishery to New England and not to Old."§ It was also argued by the friends of America that if the American fishery was destroyed the occupation must inevitably fall into the hands of the natural rivals of Great Britain. Despite the efforts of the little band the bill was received by a vote of 261 to 85, and passed through its various stages. As each phase was reached the act was fought determinedly but uselessly and hopelessly. The merchants and traders of London petitioned against it, and the American merchants secured the services of David Barclay to conduct the examination of those who were called to testify by the friends and opponents of the bill.‖ "It was said, that the cruelty of the bill exceeded the examples of hostile rigour with avowed enemies; that

* Bancroft's United States, vii, p. 222, February, 1775.

† Eng. Annual Reg., 1775, p. 78.

‡ Bancroft's United States, vii, p. 239.

§ *Ibid.*

‖ Among the evidence given was much tending to show the importance of the colonial trade. It appeared that in 1764 New England employed in the fisheries 45,880 tons of shipping and 6,002 men, the product amounting to £322,220 16*s*. 3*d*. sterling in *foreign markets;* that all the materials used in the building and equipping of vessels, excepting salt and lumber, were drawn from England, and the net proceeds were also remitted to that country; that neither the whale nor cod fishery could be carried on so successfully from Newfoundland or Great Britain as from North America, for the natural advantages of America could neither be counteracted nor supplied; that, if the fishery was transferred to Nova Scotia or Quebec, government would have to furnish the capital, for they had neither vessels nor men, and these must come from New England; that it must take time to make the change, and the trade would inevitably be lost; and that American fishermen had such an aversion to the military government of Halifax, and "so invincible an aversion to the loose habits and manners of the people, that nothing could induce them to remove thither, even supposing them reduced to the necessity of emigration."—(Eng. Annual Reg.)

in all the violence of our most dangerous wars it was an established rule in the marine service, to spare the coast-fishing craft of our declared enemies; always considering that we waged war with nations, and not with private individuals."*

It was claimed that by the provisions of the bill much hardship must fall upon many people who were already at sea, and who from the very nature of their occupations must be innocent. "The case of the inhabitants of Nantucket was particularly hard. This extraordinary people, amounting to between five and six thousand in number, nine-tenths of whom are Quakers, inhabit a barren island, fifteen miles long by three broad, the products of which were scarcely capable of maintaining twenty families. From the only harbour which this sterile island contains, without natural products of any sort, the inhabitants, by an astonishing industry, keep an 140 vessels in constant employment. Of these, eight were employed in the importation of provisions for the island, and the rest in the whale-fishery." A petition was also presented from the English Quakers in behalf of their brethren at Nantucket, in which they stated the innocence of the inhabitants of that island, "their industry, the utility of their labours both to themselves and the community, the great hazards that attended their occupation, and the uncertainty of their gains; and shewed that if the bill passed into a law, they must in a little time be exposed to all the dreadful miseries of famine. The singular state and circumstances of these people, occasioned some attention to be paid to them. A gentleman on the side of the administration said, that on a principle of humanity he would move, that a clause should be added to the bill, to prevent the operation from extending to any whale-ships, which sailed before the 1st of March, and were at that time the property of the people of Nantucket."†

"The bill," says a reviewer of the time, "was attacked on every ground of policy and government; and with the greatest strength of language and height of colouring. The minority made amends for the smallness of their numbers by their zeal and activity. * * * * Evil principles," they contended, "were prolific; the Boston Port Bill begot this New England Bill; this will beget a Virginia Bill; and that again will become the progenitor of others, until, one by one, parliament has ruined all its colonies, and rooted up all its commerce; until the statute-book becomes nothing but a black and bloody roll of proscriptions; a frightful code of rigour and tyranny; a monstrous digest of acts of penalty and incapacity and general attainder; and that wherever it is opened it will present a title for destroying some trade or ruining some province."‡

It was during the debate upon this bill that Burke made that eloquent defense of the colonies which has rung in the ears of every boy born

---

* Eng. Annual Reg., 1775, p. 80.

† Eng. Annual Reg., 1775, p. 85.

‡ *Ibid.*, p. 85.

or bred in a seaport town since the day it was uttered. "For some time past, Mr. Speaker," said Burke, "has the Old World been fed from the New. The scarcity which you have felt would have been a desolating famine, if this child of your old age,—if America,—with a true filial piety, with a Roman charity, had not put the full breast of its youthful exuberance to the mouth of its exhausted parent. Turning from the agricultural resources of the Colonies, consider the wealth which they have drawn from the sea by their fisheries. The spirit in which that enterprising employment has been exercised ought to raise your esteem and admiration. Pray, Sir, what in the world is equal to it? Pass by the other parts, and look at the manner in which the People of New England have of late carried on the whale fishery. Whilst we follow them among the tumbling mountains of ice, and behold them penetrating into the deepest frozen recesses of Hudson's Bay and Davis' Straits, whilst we are looking for them beneath the Arctic Circle, we hear that they have pierced into the opposite region of Polar cold, that they are at the antipŏdés, and engaged under the frozen serpent of the South. Falkland Island, which seemed too remote and romantic an object for the grasp of national ambition, is but a stage and resting-place in the progress of their victorious industry.* Nor is the equinoctial heat more discouraging to them than the accumulated winter of both the Poles. We know that whilst some of them draw the line and strike the harpoon on the coast of Africa, others run the longitude, and pursue their gigantic game, along the coast of Brazil. No sea but what is vexed by their fisheries. No climate that is not a witness to their toils. Neither the perseverance of Holland, nor the activity of France, nor the dexterous and firm sagacity of English enterprise, ever carried this most perilous mode of hardy industry to the extent to which it has been pushed by this recent People; a People who are still, as it were, but in the gristle, and not yet hardened into the bone, of manhood. When I contemplate these things,—when I know that the Colonies in general owe little or nothing to any care of ours, and that they are not squeezed into this happy form by the constraints of a watchful and suspicious Government, but that, through a wise and salutary neglect, a generous nature has been suffered to take her own way to perfection,—when I reflect upon these effects, when I see how profitable they have been to us, I feel all the pride of power sink, and all presumption in the wisdom of human contrivances melt, and die away within me. My rigor relents. I pardon something to the spirit of liberty."

But eloquence, logic, arguments, facts availed nothing. The bill became a law. In the upper house of Parliament, where a minority fought

* At this time the Falkland Islands were the subject of considerable acrimony between the English, Spanish, and Brazilian governments. According to Freeman (Hist. Cape Cod, ii, p. 539, note), the people of Truro were the first of our American whalemen to go to the Falklands. In 1774 Captains David Smith and Gamaliel Collins, at the suggestion of Admiral Montague, of the British navy, made voyages there on that pursuit, in which they were very successful.

the bill as determinedly as the minor part of the Commons, fifteen lords entered a protest against it. The island of Nantucket was, for the reasons enumerated, relieved somewhat from its extremest features, a fact which did not escape the surveillance of the provincial authorities, who in their turn restricted the exportation of provisions from any portion of the colonies, save the Massachusetts Bay, to that island, and the Provincial Congress of Massachusetts further prohibited any exportation from that colony, save under certain regulations.* But, like the mother country, the colonies yielded to the behests of humanity and relaxed their stringency in regard to this island.

At an early day after the formal opening of the issue of battle between England and the plantations, the general court of Massachusetts passed a resolve, directing "that from and after the fifteenth Day of August instant, no Ship or Vessell should sail out of any port in this Colony, on any whaling Voyage whatever, without leave first had and obtained from the Great and General Court of this Colony, or from some Committee or committees or persons they shall appoint to grant such leave;" and on the 24th of August, the day for adjournment of the court being near at hand, it was further resolved, in view of possible damage liable to accrue to parties for want of these permits, "that the Major part of the Council for this Colony be, and they accordingly are, hereby fully impowered to grant leave for any Vessell or Vessells to sail out of any port in this Colony, on any whaling Voyage whatever, as to them shall seem fit & reasonable for the Benefit of Individuals, and the Good of the Public, provided there be good & sufficient security given that the Oil & Bone, &c., obtained on said Voyage shall be brought into some Port in this Colony, except the port of Boston, & such Permits do not interfere with any Resolve or Recommendations of the Continental Congress:—The power herein given to continue only in the recess of the general court."†

The bells that called the hardy yeomanry of New England to the defense of their imperiled liberties on the ever-memorable morning of the 19th of April rung the death knell of the whale-fishery, save that carried on from Nantucket; the rattle of musketry was the funeral volley over its grave.‡ Save from this solitary island, it was doomed to

* Mass. Col. MSS., Provincial Congress, i, p. 300.

† Mass. Col. MSS. Rev. Council Papers, series i, vol ii, p. 17.

‡ The shipping of Nantucket rendered important ante-revolutionary aid to the colonists in the importation of powder, a service that was continued at intervals during the war. The Earl of Dartmouth, in a letter to Lieutenant-Governor Colden, dated 7th September, 1774, says: "My Information says that the Polly, Captn Benjamin Broadhelp, bound from Amsterdam to Nantucket, has among other Articles received on board, no less a quantity than three Hundred thousand pounds weight of Gunpowder, & I have great reason to believe that considerable quantities of that commodity, as well as other Military Stores, are introduced into the Colonies from Holland, through the Channel of St. Eustatia." (N. Y. Col. Rec., viii, p. 487.) St. Eustatia was captured by the English during the colonial war, the chief grounds of the capture being the alleged supply to the revolting colonies of contraband goods.

annihilation. A few vessels were fitted out early in the war from other ports, but the risk was so great and the necessity so small that the business was soon abandoned. With Nantucket it was simply a case of desperation; the business must be carried on, or the island must be depopulated; starvation or removal were the only alternatives of inaction. The receipt of the news of the battle at Lexington and Concord, glorious as it was to the colonies at large, and glorious as it may have been to the islanders whose religious principles were not rigidly opposed to war in any form and under any circumstances, was to the majority of the inhabitants the announcement of ruined fortunes, annihilated commerce, misery, privation, and suffering. Without the immediate circle of colonial assistance, knowing that they were cut off from aid in case they were attacked, open to and defenseless at all sides from the predatory raids of avowed enemies and treacherous, pretended friends, the only course left open to them to adopt was to be as void of offense as possible and strive to live through the desperate struggle just about to commence. Some of the people removed to New York and eventually established the whale-fishery there. Some removed to North Carolina and there formed a community remarkable for thrift and hospitality; but the vast majority preferred to link their fortunes with those of their island home, and with her sink or swim. Vessels from abroad turned their prows toward home and speeded on their way, hoping to attain their port before English armed vessels could intercept them; those already arrived were most of them stripped of their sails and rigging and moored to the crowded wharves or run high and dry ashore.

The petitions of parties for permission to fit out their vessels for whaling were almost invariably complied with by the general court, bonds being given in about £2,000 that the cargo should be landed at some port in the colony, excepting Boston or Nantucket.*

In 1776 the Continental Congress endeavored to induce France to en-

---

* The following is the form of the bond:

"Know all men by these presents that Nathaniel Macy & Richd Mitchell Jr both of Sherburn in the County of Nantucket, are holden & stand firmly bound unto Henry Gardner Esq of Stowe in the County of Middlesex Treasurer of the Colony of the Massachusetts Bay or his Successors in s^d^ office in the Lawful & Just sum of Two thousand pounds to the which payment well & truly to be made we bind ourselves our Heirs Exec^r^ or Administrators, firmly by these presents sealed wth our seal Dated this fourteenth day of September Anno Dom: 1775.

"The Condition of this obligation is such that whereas the above-said Nathaniel Macy is about to Adventure to sea on a whale Voyage the schooner Dighton Silas Paddack Master—if then the s^d^ Silas Paddack or any other person who may have the Command of s^d^ schooner Dighton, during s^d^ Voyage shall well & truly bring or Cause to be brought into some port or harbour of this Colony except the port of Boston or Nantucket all the oil & whale Bone that shall be taken by s^d^ schooner Dighton in the Course of s^d^ Voyage & produce a Certificate under the hands of the Selectmen of s^d^ Town Adjoining to such port or harbour that he there Landed ye same then the

gage in war against England, but in the proposed negotiations the fisheries on the banks of Newfoundland and the various gulfs and bays of North America were to be understood as not open to a question of division. Spain, too, was applied to. "The Colonies," says Bancroft, "were willing to assure to Spain freedom from molestation in its territories; they renounced in favor of France all eventual conquests in the West Indies; but they claimed the sole right of acquiring British Continental America and all adjacent islands, including the Bermudas, Cape Breton, and Newfoundland. It was America and not France which first applied the maxim of monopoly to the fisheries. The King of France might retain his exclusive rights on the banks of New Foundland, as recognized by England in the treaty of 1763, but his subjects were not to fish 'in the havens, bays, creeks, roads, coasts, or places,' which the United States were to win."*

In the mean time how was England affected by her American policy? The colonial fishery being abolished, it became essential that something should be done to replace it, "and particularly to guard against the ruinous consequences of the foreign markets, either changing the course of consumption or falling into the hands of strangers, and those perhaps inimical to this country. The consumption of fish-oil as a substitute for tallow was now become so extensive as to render that also an object of great national concern; the city of London alone expending about £300,000 annually in that commodity."† The evidence taken on behalf of the ministry in support of their restraining-bill, tending to show that there already existed sufficient capital in ships, men, and money for the immediate and safe transfer of the whale fishery to England, while well enough for partisan purposes, was not considered so reliable by the parties bringing it forward, and the government was not at all desirous or willing to risk a matter of such extreme importance upon the testimony there given.

Measures were accordingly taken to give encouragement to this pursuit to the fishermen and capitalists of Great Britain and Ireland.‡ The committee having the subject in charge were of the opinion that a bounty should extend to the fisheries to the southward of Greenland

above Obligation to be Void & of none Effect otherways to stand and remain in full force & virtue.

"NAT^AL MACY,
"RICH^D MITCHELL, JR."

"Signed, Sealed, & dld in presence of us."
C.

(Mass. Col. MSS. Misc., iii, p. 64.)

The colonial papers of March 28, 1776, mention that the English frigate Renown, on her passage to America, took ten sail of American whalemen, which were sent to England to avoid the danger of recapture.

* Bancroft's U. S., ix, p. 132.

† Eng. Annual Reg. 1775, p. 113.

‡ Speech of the Earl of Harcout to the Irish Parliament, October 10, 1775.

and Davis Straits, and at the same time that the duties on oil, blubber, and bone, imported from Newfoundland, should be taken off. It was found that the restraining bill worked serious damage to the people of Newfoundland, and also to the fisheries from the British islands to that coast, as, in order to prevent absolute famine there, it was necessary that several ships should return light from that vicinity in order to carry cargoes of provisions from Ireland to the sufferers there.*

The English fishery, even under the encouragement given, did not, however, answer the expectations or hopes of its friends. It was not so easily transferred as had been imagined. A few more vessels sailed from Great Britain, employing, of course, a few more men, but the extra supply was a mere trifle in comparison to the deficiency that the restraining bill had caused.

The colonies, in turn, passed a bill cutting off supplies to the English fleet from the plantations, † a course entirely unforeseen by the sage adherents of the British bill. As a natural consequence, the fishery, which promised so well on paper, and upon which the majority in Parliament had founded so many hopes, failed to yield them the solace for the evil done to America that they so fondly anticipated. Many ships, instead of bearing to England supplies, only returned there for provisions to relieve the distress they found on the coast, both on the sea and the land. Indeed, it was estimated that the colonial restraining act caused a loss to England in the fishery in these parts alone of fully half a million of pounds sterling. ‡ To add to the calamities caused by man, the very elements seemed combined against them, for a terrible storm arose, and the center of its fury was the shores and banks of Newfoundland. "This awful wreck of nature," says a chronicler of the time, "was as singular in its circumstances as fatal in its effects. The sea is said to have risen 30 feet almost instantaneously. Above seven hundred boats, with their people, perished, and several ships, with their crews. Nor was the mischief much less on the land, the waves overpassing all mounds, and sweeping everything before them. The shores presented a shocking spectacle for some time after, and the fishing-nets were hauled up loaded with human bodies." § These misfortunes the opposers of the bill attributed to the vengeance of an indignant Providence.

But Parliament went further than this, and added to the atrocity of this measure another none the less barbarous. It was decreed that all those prisoners who should be taken on board of American vessels should be compelled, without distinction of rank, to serve as common

* Annual Reg., 1776, p. 131.

† The "Restraining" bill.

‡ Eng. Annual Reg., 1776, p. 49.

§ English Annual Reg., 1776, p. 43. There was also much distress at the Barbadoes. It was thought at one time to draw supplies for beleaguered Boston from these islands, but cut off as they were from supplies from the colonies, with 80,000 blacks and 20,000 whites to feed, the project was deemed in the highest degree dangerous.

sailors on British ships of war. This proposed measure was received with great indignation by those gentlemen in Parliament whom partisan asperity had not blinded to every feeling of justice to or compassion for the colonies. The clause in the bill which contained this provision was "marked by every possible stigma," and was described by the Lords, in their protest, as "*a refinement in tyranny*" which, "*in a sentence worse than death, obliges the unhappy men who shall be made captives in this predatory war to bear arms against their families, kindred, friends, and country; and after being plundered themselves, to become accomplices in plundering their brethren.*" * And, by the articles of war, these very men were liable to be shot for desertion.

By the action of this measure large numbers of Nantucket whaling captains with their crews and a few from other ports were captured by the English, and given their choice either to enter the service of the King in a man-of-war or sail from an English port in the same pursuit to which they had become accustomed.† In September (13th,) 1779, John Adams, writing from Braintree‡ to the council of Massachusetts, says: "May it please your Honours: § While I resided at Paris I had an opportunity of procuring from London exact Information concerning the British Whale Fishery on the Coast of Brazil, which I beg Leave to communicate to your Honours, that if any advantage can be made of it the opportunity may not be lost.

"The English, the last year and the year before, carried on, this Fishery to very great advantage, off of the River Plate, in South America in the Latitude Thirty five south and from thence to Forty, just on the edge of soundings, off and on, about the Longitude sixty five, from London. They had seventeen vessells in this Fishery, which all sailed from London, in the Months of September and October. All the officers and Men are Americans.

"The Names of the Captains are, Aaron Sheffield of Newport, ———, Goldsmith ‖ and Richard Holmes from Long Island, John Chadwick, Francis May,¶ Reuben May,** John Meader, Jonathan Meader, Elisha

* Annual Reg., 1776, p. 118.

† To his captors Capt. Nathan Coffin, of Nantucket, nobly said, "Hang me, if you will, to the yard-arm of your ship, but do not ask me to be a traitor to my country."—(Bancroft, ix, p. 313.)

‡ Adams, vii, p. 63. This is almost identical with the letter in Mass. Col. MSS., Resolves, vi, p. 216.

§ In 1778 the commissioners (Franklin and Adams) in France wrote to the President of Congress in nearly the same words, urging the destruction of the English whale-fishery on the coast of Brazil and the release of the Americans there, who were practically prisoners of war, compelled to aid in supporting the enemy. In the letter of the commissioners, dated Passy, ———, 1778, Messrs. Franklin and Adams write that three whalemen have been taken by French men-of-war and carried into L'Orient. The crews of these whaling-vessels are Americans. (Works of John Adams, vii, p. 63.)

‖ William Goldsmith, who sailed from Nantucket for London with a cargo of oil in April, 1775.

¶ Francis Macy.

** Reuben Macy.

Clark, Benjamin Clark, William Ray, Paul Pease, Bunker Fitch, Reuben Fitch, Zebbeedee Coffin * and another Coffin, ——— Delano,† Andrew Swain, William Ray, all of Nantucket, John Lock, Cape Cod; ‡ four or five of these vessels went to Greenland. The fleet sails to Greenland, yearly, the last of February or the Beginning of March. There was published, the year before last, in the English Newspapers, and the same Imposture was repeated last year, and no doubt will be renewed this, a Letter from the Lords of Admiralty to Mr. Dennis De Beralt, in Colman street, informing, him that a Convoy should be appointed to the Brazil Fleet. But this, I had certain Information, was a Forgery calcutelad mainly to deceive American Privateers, and that no Convoy was appointed, or did go with that Fleet, either last year, or the year before.

"For the Destruction or Captivity of a Fishery so entirely defenceless, for not one of the Vessells has any arms, a single Frigate or Privateer of Twenty-four, or even of Twenty guns, would be sufficient. The Beginning of December, would be the best Time to proceed from hence, because the Frigate would then find the Whaling Vessells nearly loaded. The Cargoes of these Vessells, consisting of Bone and Oyl, will be very valuable, and at least four hundred and fifty of the best kind of seamen would be taken out of the Hands of the English, and might be gained into the American service to act against the Enemy. Most of the officers and Men wish well to this Country, and would gladly be in its service if they could be delivered, from that they are engaged in. *Whenever an English Man of war, or Privateer, has taken an American Vessell, they have given to the Whalemen among the Crew, by order of Government, their Choice, either to go on Board a Man of war, and fight against their Country or go into the Whale Fishery. Such Numbers have chosen the latter as have made up the Crews of these seventeen Vessells.*§

"I thought it my Duty to communicate this Intelligence to your Honours, that if so profitable a Branch of Commerce, and so valuable a Nursery of Seamen, can be taken from the English it may be done. This State has a peculiar Right and Interest to undertake the Enterprise, as almost the whole fleet belongs to it. I have the Honour to be, with the highest Consideration, your Honours most obedient & most humble servant

"JOHN ADAMS."

This letter was referred to a committee who reported that a copy of it should be sent to the President of the Continental Congress, which report was adopted, and thus Massachusetts let slip through her fingers the identical golden opportunity which the General Government had neglected the year before. The suggestions of Mr. Adams, who of all our revolutionary statesmen seems most to have understood and appre-

* Zebdiel Coffin.

† Abisha Delano (probably.)

‡ From Nantucket. Twenty names are given in this list.

§ Not italicised in the original.

ciated the importance of this industry, were practically disregarded.* It is difficult to calculate how much the American whale-fishery was affected by this failure to act on this suggestion of Mr. Adams. Many of these captains and men, and others captured at other times during the war, had at its close sailed so long from British ports that the extraordinary inducements held out by the English, and the depression in their business in the United States, immediately succeeding the close of the war, operated to transfer to that country their skill and, measurably, their capital.

In the years 1778–'79 the English navy made several forays upon the sea-coast towns of New England, destroying much property at Warren, R. I., Dartmouth, Martha's Vineyard, and Nantucket in Massachusetts.† Indeed, these predatory raids were frequent throughout the war, and liable to occur at any time, consequently the unfortunate inhabitants were kept in a continual ferment. During the same time the government of France was continually intriguing for the exclusive possession of the North American fisheries. On the 6th of February, 1778, a treaty of amity and commerce was arranged between France and the United States. Upon this point each side was to retain the exclusive right to its own. The Americans conceded to the French the rights reserved by the treaties of Utrecht ‡ and Paris, § even to the French interpretation of them, which were the right to fish upon the Banks, and the exclusive use of one-half the shores of Newfoundland upon which to dry their

* An exception to the general apathy in this respect occurred late in the fall or early in the winter of 1776, when boats from the Alfred, man-of-war, were sent ashore at Canso and destroyed the whaling interest there, burning all the materials for that industry, together with all the oil stores with their contents.

† "Return of vessels and stores destroyed on Acushnet River the 5th of September, 1778: 8 sail of large vessels, from 200 to 300 tons, most of them prizes; 6 armed vessels, carrying from 10 to 16 guns; a number of sloops and schooners of inferior size, amounting in all to 70, besides whale-boats and others; amongst the prizes were three taken by Count D'Estaign's fleet; 26 store-houses at Bedford, several at McPherson's Wharf, Crans Mills, and Fairhaven; these were filled with very great quanti ies of rum, sugar, melasses, coffee, tobacco, cotton, tea, medicines, gunpowder, sail-cloth, cordage, &c.; two large rope-walks.

"At Falmouth, in the Vineyard Sound, the 10th of Septembe , 1778: 2 sloops and a schooner taken by the galleys, 1 loaded with staves; 1 sloop burnt.

"In Old Town harbour, Martha's Vineyard: 1 brig of 150 tons burden, burnt by the Scorpion; 1 schooner of 70 tons burden, burnt by ditto; 23 whale-boats taken or destroyed; a quantity of plank taken.

"At Holmes's Hole, Martha's Vineyard: 4 vessels, with several boats, taken or destroyed; a salt-work destroyed, and a considerable quantity of salt taken."—(Ricketson's New Bedford, p. 282.)

At Sag Harbor, L. I., property was taken or destroyed to a large amount; Newport suffered greatly; Nantucket lost twelve or fourteen vessels, oil, stores, &c., to the value of £4,000 sterling. Warren, R. I., suffered during the war to the extent of 1,090 tons of shipping, among them two vessels loaded with oil, and a large amount of other property. Sag Harbor also lost one or more vessels by capture.

‡ April 11, 1713.

§ February 10, 1763.

fish.* In regard to what disposition should be made of that island in case it should be captured, nothing was said; the sentiment of New England, however, upon that point was unmistakable. Later in the same year Samuel Adams, in a letter from Philadelphia, wrote: "I hope we shall secure to the United States, Canada, Nova Scotia, Florida too, and the fishery, by our arms or by treaty." He writes further, and every year of the past century has borne witness to the soundness of his views: "*We shall never be on a solid footing, till Great Britain cedes to us, or we wrest from her, what nature designs we should have.*†

France also sought the aid of Spain, and that power was given to understand that in the final treaty of peace between the United States and England, they, too, would necessarily have some voice. Vergennes, in October (1778) stated, as the only stipulations which France would require, that in the final negotiations the treaty of Utrecht must be either wholly continued or entirely annulled; that she must be allowed to restore the harbor of Dunkirk; and that she must be allowed "the coast of Newfoundland, from Cape Bonavista to Cape St. John, with the exclusive fishery from Cape Bonavista to Point Riche."‡ By a treaty made with Spain, April 12, 1779, France bound herself to attempt the invasion of Great Britain or Ireland, and to share only with Spain the North American fisheries, in case she succeeded in driving the English from Newfoundland.

These discussions (as to the terms to be embraced in the final treaty of peace) were necessary pending the question of an alliance with France and Spain against England. When the subject of frontiers was brought up, France, while yielding all claim to the provinces of Canada and Nova Scotia, which for years had been hers, joined heartily with Spain in opposing the manifest desire of the Americans to secure them. Two States persisted in the right and policy of acquiring them, but Congress, as a body, deferred to the French view of the subject. "With regard to the fisheries, of which the interruption formed one of the elements of the war, public law had not yet been settled. By the treaty of Utrecht, France agreed not to fish within thirty leagues of the coast of Nova Scotia; and by that of Paris, not to fish within fifteen leagues of Cape Breton. Moreover, New England at the beginning of the war had, by act of Parliament, been debarred from fishing on the banks of Newfoundland * * * *. "The fishery on the high seas," so Vergennes expounded the law of nations, "is as free as the sea itself, and it is superfluous to discuss the right of the Americans to it. But the coast-fisheries belong of right to the proprietary of the coast. Therefore the fisheries on the coasts of Newfoundland, of Nova Scotia, of Canada, belong exclusively to the English; and the Americans have no

* Bancroft's U. S., ix, 481. The fact must be kept in mind that whaling and fishing for cod were both carried on on nearly the same waters and often by the same vessels.

† Bancroft's U. S., x, 177.

‡ Bancroft's U. S., x, p. 184.

pretension whatever to share in them.'* In vain the United States urged that the colonies, almost exclusively, had improved the coast-fisheries, and considered that immemorial and sole improvement was practical acquisition. In vain they insisted that New England men, and New England money, and New England brains had effected the first conquest of Cape Breton, and were powerful aids to the subsequent conquest of Nova Scotia and Canada, and hence they had acquired at least a perpetual joint propriety. To their arguments Vergennes replied that the conquests were made not for the colonies but for the crown, and when New England dissolved its allegiance to that crown she renounced her right to the coast-fisheries. In the end the United States were obliged to succumb; they had asked aid from foreign powers, and they must yield so far as was practicable to the demands those powers made. These concessions were a portion of the price of independence.

A committee† was appointed by Congress to definitely arrange upon what terms the future treaty of peace with England should be finally consummated, and in February, 1779, they reported that Spain manifested a disposition to form an alliance with the United States, hence independence was an eventual certainty. On the question of fishing they reported that the right should belong properly to the United States, France, and Great Britain in common. This portion of the report was long under discussion in Congress, and it was finally voted that the common right of the United States to fish "on the coasts, bays, and banks of Newfoundland and Gulf of St. Lawrence, the Straits of Labrador, and Belleisle should in no case be given up."‡ Under a vote to reconsider this subject on the 24th of March, Richard Henry Lee proposed that the United States should have the same rights which they enjoyed when subject to Great Britain, which proposition was carried by the votes of Pennsylvania, Delaware, and the four New England States, New York and the Southern States opposing. New York, under the leadership of Jay and Morris, peremptorily declined to insist on this right by treaty, and Morris moved that independence should be the sole condition of peace. This was declared out of order by the votes of the New England States, New Jersey, and Pennsylvania, against the unanimous vote of New York, Maryland, and North Carolina; Delaware, Virginia, and South Carolina being equally divided.

But France had a vital interest in this matter, and the French minister interposed his influence, and on the 27th of May Congress returned to its original resolve, "that in no case, by any treaty of peace, should the common right of fishing be given up."

On the 19th of June the equanimity of the French minister was suddenly and rudely disturbed by Elbridge Gerry, who, being from Marble-

* Bancroft's U. S., x, pp. 210-11.

† Gouverneur Morris, of New York; Burke, of North Carolina; Witherspoon, of New Jersey; Samuel Adams, of Massachusetts; and Smith, of Virginia. (Bancroft's U. S., x, p. 213.)

‡ Bancroft's U. S., x, p. 213.

head, was the steady and persistent champion of the claims of New England, and who, in the prolonged discussions, always came to the front in defense of those rights. Entirely unexpectedly, Gerry, avoiding "a breach of the rules of Congress by a change in form, moved resolutions, that the United States have a common right with the English to the fisheries on the banks of Newfoundland, and the other fishing-banks and seas of North America. The demand was for no more than Vergennes confessed to belong to them by the law of nations; and Gerry insisted that unless the right received the guarantee of France, on the consent of Great Britain, the American minister should not sign any treaty of peace without first consulting Congress."* A most stormy and bitter debate ensued. The friends of France resisted strenuously. Four States declared if the resolution was adopted they should secede. The matter, however, was somewhat compromised and the common right of fishing on the Grand Banks affirmed; Congress asking for that right the guarantee of France by means of a supplementary article explanatory of former treaties.

The French minister became alarmed, and sought an interview with the President of Congress and two other members known to be equally favorably disposed to the policy he represented. The vigor and zeal with which New England had pressed the matter had disposed them to concede to the desires of this section. He assured them "that disunion from the side of New England was not to be feared, for its people carried their love of independence even to delirium," and continued: "There would seem to be a wish to break the connection of France with Spain; but I think I can say that, if the Americans should have the audacity to force the King of France to choose between the two alliances, his decision would not be in favor of the United States; he will not certainly expose himself to consume the remaining resources of his kingdom for many years, only to secure an increase of fortune to a few shipmasters of New England. I shall greatly regret on account of the Americans, should Spain enter into war without a convention with them." Five hours of discussion failed to induce the members to undertake to change the views of Congress, and a new interview was held on the 12th of July, between Gerard and Congress, in a committee of the whole. As a final result the question was left to be settled, when a treaty of peace was formally arranged with Great Britain.†

In the mean time how fared it with the whale-fishery? The people of Nantucket, with whom alone it was still encouraged, though in the face of the most terrible discouragements, were reduced to the severest straits. To live, they must eat; to eat, they must have provisions; to obtain provisions, they must give in exchange money or its equivalent; to obtain the exchangeable commodity, some business must be pursued. The whale-fishery was the only business available to them. Long prac-

* Bancroft's U. S., x, pp. 216 to 219.

† Bancroft's U. S., x, p. 219.

tice had made them familiar with it, and a singleness of pursuit had kept them comparatively ignorant of any other occupation. But the great problem was how to carry it on, even in the limited way to which, by the destruction of their vessels, they were restricted. If they sailed under American protection, the English captured and destroyed their vessels and imprisoned their men; if they cleared with the sanction of English safeguards, the Americans performed for them the same kindly offices. Between the upper and the nether millstones of war they were quite ground to powder. In their extremity they learned that the English were inclined to be lenient toward them in the matter, and they had quite reliable assurance that the leading men of the American Government looked compassionately upon the distressed situation of the unfortunate islanders.

Influenced by these considerations, the inhabitants sent Timothy Folger, esq., to New York, to represent the condition they were in, and solicit permission to carry on whaling without danger of capture from British cruisers. They asked permits for twenty fishing-boats to fish around the island, for four vessels to be employed in the whale-fishery, for ten small vessels to supply the inhabitants with wood, and for one to go to New York for some few supplies not obtainable elsewhere.* Their petition was not so successful as they had wished.

In 1781 Admiral Digby succeeded Admiral Arbuthnot in the command of the English fleet in these waters, and permission to whale was asked of him,† and permits were issued for twenty-four vessels to pursue the business unmolested by English armed cruisers.‡ "This privi-

* Macy, 113.

† Mr. Macy gives us to understand that no permits were granted, but this must be an error; for Mr. Rotch (*vide* MS.), who was one of the committee the succeeding year to obtain grants from the English, mentions an accusation made by Commodore Affleck, of abuse of confidence in regard to the permits which were granted the year before, and that scarcely a vessel could be found but had one of these documents. To this Mr. Rotch replied: "Commodore Affleck, thou hast been greatly imposed upon in this matter. I defy Capt. ——— to make such a declaration to my face. Those Permits were put into my hands. I delivered them, taking receipts for each, to be returned to me at the end of the voyage, and an obligation that no transfer should be made or copies given. I received back all the Permits except two before I left home, and should probably have received those two on the day that I sailed. Now if any duplicity has been practiced, I am the person who is accountable, and I am here to take the punishment such perfidy deserves." Mr. Rotch's character as a man and a merchant stood too high to be questioned, and the commodore, who a moment before was so violent, became more genial, and replied, "You deserve favor," and assisted Mr. Rotch to obtain it. The termination of this difficulty is but one example of the manner in which all these slanders, from both English and Americans, were disposed of when the accused could have an opportunity of confronting the accusers or those in authority.

‡ The following is a copy of one of these permits, from Macy, p. 115:

"[L. S.] By Robert Digby, Esquire, Rear Admiral of the Red, and Commander-in-chief, &c., &c.

"Permission is hereby given to the Dolphin brig, burthen sixty tons, Walter Folger owner, navigated by Gilbert Folger as master and the twelve seamen named in the

lege," says Macy, "seemed to give new life to the people. It produced a considerable movement in business, but the resources of the island had so diminished, that but a small number of vessels could take the benefit of these permits. Those who had vessels, and were possessed of the means, fitted them out on short voyages, and, had there been no hinderance, it is probable that they would have done well; for the whales, having been unmolested for several years, had become numerous, and were pretty easily caught. To carry on the whale-fishery under permission of the government of Great Britain was a proceeding somewhat novel, and could not pass unnoticed. Although it was not publicly known, yet it was generally believed that some kind of indulgence had been shown by the enemy to the people of Nantucket. This caused some clamor on the continent; but our Government well knew the situation of the place, and its large participation in the calamities of the war, and was, consequently, rather inclined to favor than to condemn he acceptance of favors from the English. Although the Governmentt could not grant an exclusive privilege to any particular part of the Union, yet such encouragement was given by the leading men of the nation, in their individual capacity, as to warrant the proceeding. Several vessels whaling under these permits were taken by American privateers and carried into port, but in every instance they were soon liberated. Whenever it was found that the permits were used for no other purpose than that for which they had been granted, and that the vessels using them had not been engaged in illicit trade, there was no hesitation in releasing them."

Nevertheless a great risk attended this mode of proceeding, and the islanders became satisfied that to make the business reasonably safe permits must be obtained from both contending powers and permission also to make use of each license against the other's vessels of war. Accordingly, a town meeting was convened on the 25th of September, 1782, and a memorial prepared and adopted which was sent to the general court of Massachusetts.* This petition recited the unfortunate situa-

---

James Chase,
Obadiah Folger,
George Coleman
Silvanus Swain
Charles Russell
Peter Pollard
Andrew Coleman
Obed Barnard
Jonathan Briggs

margin, to leave the island of Nantucket and to proceed on a whaling voyage,—to commence the first of January, 1782, and end the last day of ——— following, provided that they have on board the necessary whaling craft and provisions only, and that the master of said brig is possessed of a certificate from the selectmen of the said island, setting forth that she is *bone fide* the property of the inhabitants of the island, with the names of the master and seamen in her; and that she shall not be found proceeding with her cargo to any other port than Nantucket or New York.

"Dated at New York, the first day of December, 1781.

"ROBERT DIGBY.

"To the commissioners of his majesty's ships and vessels of war, as well as of all privateers and letters of marque.

"By command of the Admiral:

"THOMAS M. PALMER."

* By a very disastrous fire at Nantucket, in 1846, the records both of the town and custom-house were destroyed, hence there arises much difficulty in getting many inter-

tion the people were in, exposed to the inroads of English and Americans, with neither side able or willing to protect them against the other, and powerless, because of the defenseless character of the island and the religious convictions of the vast majority of the inhabitants, to suitably guard their own firesides. They urged that people in continental towns, where the broad country opened to them a place for retreat, could have but faint ideas of the suffering of those who were constantly liable to hostile invasion and whose insular position precluded all thoughts of escape, and they indignantly resented the calumnies which had been spread broadcast through the State in regard to alleged actions of theirs. Regarding the prosecution of their business, they said:

"We now beg leave to throw a few hints before you respecting the Whalefishery, as a matter of great importance to this Commonwealth. This place before the War, was the First in that branch of business, & employed more than One Hundred Sail of good Vessels therein, which furnish'd a support not only for Five Thousand Inhabitants here, but for Thousands elsewhere, no place so well adapted for the good of the Community at large as Nantucket, it being destitute of every material necessary in the Business, and the Inhabitants might be called Factors for the Continent rather than Principals; as the war encreased the Fishery ceased, until necessity obliged us to make trial the last Year, with aboutabout seventeen sail of Vessels, Two of which were captured & carried to New York,* & one was burnt the others made saving voyages. The present Year we employed about Twenty Four sail in the same business, which have mostly compleated their Voyages, but with little success; & a great loss will ensue; this we apprehend is greatly owing to the circumscribed situation of the Fishery; we are now fully sensible that it can no longer be pursued by us, unless we have free liberty both from Great Britain & America to fish without interruption; As we now find One of our Vessels is captured & carried to New York, but without any Oil on board, and Two others have lately been taken & carried into Boston & Salem, under pretense of having double papers on board, (Nevertheless we presume the captors will not say that any of our Whalemen have gone into New York during the season as such a charge would have no foundation in Truth). And if due attention is not paid to this valuable branch, which if it was viewed in all its parts, perhaps would appear the most advantageous, of any possess'd by this Government, it will be intirely lost, if the War continues: We view it with regret & mention it with concern, & from the gloomy prospect now before us, we apprehend many of the Inhabitants must quit the Island, not being able even to provide necessaries for the approaching Winter:

esting details. Many of the custom-records of New Bedford were destroyed by fire in 1825; the corresponding documents of Newport, prior to 1779, were carried away by the English, and the vessel containing them being sunk, they were, when recovered, in a very damaged condition; the similar records of Sag Harbor (the older ones) were stored in a damp place, and are mildewed and illegible.

* New York, at this time, was in possession of the English.

some will retreat to the Continent & set down in the Western Governments; and the most active in the Fishery will most probably go to distant Countries, where they can have every encouragement, by Nations who are eagerly wishing to embrace so favourable an opportunity to accomplish their desires; which will be a great loss to the Continent in general, but more to this Government in particular.

"We beg leave to impress the consideration of this important subject, not as the judgment of an insignificant few, but of a Town which a few Years since stood the Third in Rank (if we mistake not) in bearing the Burthens of Government; It was then populous and abounded with plenty, it is yet populous but is covered with poverty. Your Memorialists have made choice of Samuel Starbuck, Josiah Barker, William Rotch, Stephen Hussey and Timothy Folger, as their Committee who can speak more fully to the several matters contain'd in this Memorial, or any other thing that may concern this County, to whom we desire to refer you.

"Signed in behalf of the Town by—

"FREDERICK FOLGER,

"*Town Clerk.*"

This memorial was referred to a committee consisting of George Cabot, esq., on behalf of the Senate, and General Ward and Colonel McCobb on the part of the House, which committee on the 29th of October made the following report: " That altho' the Facts set forth in said Memorial are true and the Memorialists deserve Relief in the premises, yet as no adequate Relief can be given them but by the United States in Congress assembled, therefore it is the opinion of the Committee that the said Memorial be referr'd to the consideration of Congress, and the Delegates of this Commonwealth be required to use their Endeavours to impress Congress with just Ideas of the high worth & Importance of the Whale fishery to the United States in general, & this State in particular."* This report was accepted, and it was ordered

* Mass. Col. MSS., Petitions, i, pp. 124-5-6-7-8-9. A memorandum accompanies this, which various circumstances seem to indicate is the work of Mr. Rotch, and which says: "Perhaps some of those reports may have originated from this—a Committee of our Island in the fore part of the year 1781 applied to some of the Members of the General Court and spread before them the peculiar circumstances wherein the Island was involved, one whereof was that our Vessels whenever they passed in or out were perfectly under the controul of the Britons and it was therefore necessary that permits should be obtained from them for our Vessels to proceed on the Whale fishery—since which time some of them have been taken by the American Privateers for having such Permits—and we are thereby reduced to this difficulty that if we carry our Vessels over the bar without permits from the British Admiral they are made prize to the Britons—if they have such permits they are taken by our own Countrymen—and our harbour is therefore compleatly shut up—and all our prospects terminate in poverty and distress—what gives us great concern is that our people who understand the Whale fishery will be driven to foreign neutral Countries and many years must pass away before we shall again be enabled to pursue a branch of business which hath been in times past our support and hath yielded such large aids to the Commerce of this Country."

that the delegates be furnished with a copy of the memorial, and be required to take the action indicated in the report.

In addition to the action of the general court, the town also sent William Rotch and Samuel Starbuck to Philadelphia to intercede personally in the matter. After conferring with General Lincoln, Samuel Osgood, Nathaniel Gorham, Thomas Fitzsimmons, and James Madison, they approached one of the Massachusetts delegation who was a resident of Boston, and who was greatly prejudiced against Nantucket. After an interview of about two hours with no apparent relaxation of the bitterness of feeling on his part, Mr. Rotch questioned him as to whether the whale-fishery was "worth preserving to this country?" He replied, "Yes." "Can it be preserved in the present state of things by any place except Nantucket?" "No." "Can we preserve it unless you and the British will both give us permits?" "No." "Then, pray," continued Mr. Rotch, "where is the difficulty?" Thus this interview ended. Messrs. Rotch and Starbuck then drew up a memorial and presented it to the consideration of the above-named gentlemen, desiring them to review it, at the same time telling them of the conversation between Mr. Rotch and the delegate from Boston. By advice of these friends they waited again upon the member from Massachusetts, and he accepted the charge of bringing the subject before Congress, where, after deliberation, it was determined to grant permits for thirty-five vessels to sail on whaling voyages, and these were accordingly granted and delivered. The very next day a vessel arrived from Europe bringing the rumor of the signing of a provisional treaty of peace.*

This was early in 1783.† The passage from the provisional to the definitive treaty was long, circuitous, and at times dark. One of the chief sources of difference was the settlement of the question of the fisheries, England with an apparent feeling of magnanimity conceding favors, and America with a sense of justice claiming rights. Against what the United States considered her just dues the diplomacy of the English, their late enemies, and the French, their recent allies, was arrayed, and nothing but firmness, sagacity, and skill on the part of the American commissioners saved the day. The English guarded their assumptions with all possible jealousy; the French sought a loose place in the armor to insert the diplomatic sword, and gain by treaty what they had been unable to sustain with force. The Americans were ever on the alert to overcome the prejudices of a power from whom they had conquered a peace, and to propitiate the supersensitiveness of a power which had rendered them so valuable assistance. They could not, however, depart from certain propositions. The articles which must be inviolate were those guaranteeing to America full and unconditional inde-

* Memoranda of Wm. Rotch—unpublished.

† On the 22d of March, 1783, an order was passed in Congress granting 35 licenses to Nantucket vessels to whale and to secure them from the penalty attached to double papers. (Madison Papers, p. 405.)

pendence, and the withdrawal from the thirteen States of all British troops; the Mississippi as a western, and the Canadian line as it was prior to the Quebec act of 1774, for a northern boundary; and a freedom in the fishery off Newfoundland and elsewhere as it had been enjoyed prior to the commencement of hostilities. In vain Great Britain sought to evade the latter clause; the United States tenaciously, as in a vice, held her to it, and she yielded.

E.—FROM 1784 TO 1816.

But the announcement of peace came to a people whose commerce was sadly devastated. Save such of the interest as had been preserved by what Mr. Jefferson termed the Nantucketois, the business of whaling was practically ruined and required rebuilding. To Nantucket the war had, despite its holy necessity and its glorious conclusion, been a heavy burden. Of the little over 150 vessels owned there in 1775, 134 had fallen into the hands of the English and 15 more were lost by shipwreck; many of the young men had perished through the rigors of war;* in about 800 families on the island there were 202 widows and 342 orphan children; the direct money loss far exceeded $1,000,000 in times when a man's pay was 67 cents per day; one merchant alone lost over $60,000.† And as it was with Nantucket, so it was in a degree with all the whaling ports.‡ With an energy characteristically American, they sought, on the return of peace, to retrieve their losses. Scarcely had the echo of the hostile guns died away, scarcely had the joyful news of peace reached their ports, when the whalemen began to equip anew for their fishery. The Bedford, just returned to Nantucket from a voyage, was immediately loaded with oil and dispatched to London, arriving in the Downs on the 3d of February. Her appearance was thus chronicled by an English magazine of that day: "The ship Bedford, Captain Mooers,§ belonging to the Massachusetts, arrived in the Downs the 3d of February, passed Gravesend the 4th, & was reported at the Custom-House the 6th instant. She was not allowed regular entry until some consultation had taken place between the commissioners of the customs & the lords of council, on account of the many acts of parliament yet in force against the rebels in America. She is loaded with 487 butts of whale oil; is American built;|| manned wholly

* It is estimated that no less than 1,200 seamen, mostly whalemen, were captured by the English or perished at their hands during the Revolution, from Nantucket alone!

† William Rotch, esq.

‡ Warren, R. I., suffered a loss of 12 vessels (about 1,100 tons), of which at least two were whalemen. (Hist. of Warren, p. 101.)

§ Capt. William Mooers, who sailed for many years in the employ of Messrs. Rotch & Co. It is related that one of the crew of the vessel first showing the American flag in the Thames was hump-backed. One day a British sailor meeting him clapped his hand upon the American's shoulder, saying, "Hilloa, Jack, what have you got here?" "Bunker Hill and be d——d to you," replied the Yankee, "will you mount?"

|| The Bedford was built in 1765, by Ichabod Thomas, at North River. She was built a brig.

by American seamen; wears the rebel colors & belongs to the Island of Nantucket in Massachusetts. This is the first vessel which displayed the thirteen rebellious stripes of America in any British Port. The vessel lies at Horseley down a little below the Tower, and is intended immediately to return to New England." Immediately after, almost simultaneously with her, arrived another ship from Nantucket—the Industry, Capt. John Chadwick, while the sloop Speedwell, James Whippey, master, was sent to Aux Cayes.* Those at Nantucket who had capital left resumed the whale-fishery with as many vessels as they could procure. Long comparative immunity from capture had caused the whaling-grounds to become repopulated, and the whales themselves had become less shy and hence more easily killed. Directly succeeding the war the products of the fishery commanded good prices, and soon other ports entered into competition. New London, Sag Harbor, Hudson, N. Y., Boston, Hingham, Wellfleet, Braintree,† Plymouth, Bristol, each sent out one or more whale-hunters. For a brief time the business promised much profit, but the fever was a fitful one. The excessive prices which the commodity commanded immediately after the war‡ rapidly became reduced; Great Britain, the only market for the sperm-oil, had, by an alien duty of £18 sterling per ton, practically precluded its shipment from America. Oil which before the war was worth £30, now scarcely brought £17, while to cover expenses and leave a reasonable margin for profit, £25 were required.§ The situation was indeed desperate—almost hopeless. In the discussion of means for relief many of the people of Nantucket expressed the opinion that if the island could be made neutral, commercial affairs might assume a more healthy tone. A memorial was finally sent to the legislature of Massachusetts praying relief, and the agents presenting it were instructed to have the subject of neutrality acted upon. As may be readily supposed, however, the invidious legislation that Nantucket was unable to obtain during the war, she would scarcely be likely to get on its conclusion, and the subject of neutrality was very properly dismissed. That the depression in the whaling business needed some alleviation was, however, too evident to require discussion, and in 1785 the legislature passed the following preamble and resolution:

"Whereas this court, having a due sense of the high worth and importance of the whale fishery, are desirous of its preservation, not only to this State, but to the United States in general; therefore,

"*Resolved*, That there be paid, out of the treasury of this commonwealth, the following bounties upon whale-oil, of the different qualities hereafter mentioned, viz: For every ton of white spermaceti oil, five pounds; for every ton of brown or yellow spermaceti oil, sixty shillings; for every ton of whale oil, (so called,) forty shillings, that may be taken or caught

* Letter of William Rotch, esq.

† One small schooner of 38 tons burden hailed from Braintree.

‡ Macy's Nantucket, 121.

§ See Mr. Rotch's MS.

by any vessel or vessels, that are or may be owned and manned wholly by the inhabitants of this commonwealth, and landed within the same, from and after the first day of January next, until the further order of the general court."

The selectmen of the various towns were further empowered to appoint sworn inspectors to inspect all oil so landed, and mark on the head of each cask so inspected the initial letters of his name, and a description of the oil by the initials W. B., or Y. W. O., and deliver to the selectmen a sworn certificate thereof. To obtain the bounty, a certificate from the selectmen must be presented to the governor and council,* detailing the kind, quality, and amount of oil, and where landed To this certificate the owners were to make oath or affirmation.

But, although the bounty seemed at first beneficial, the ultimate effect was not so good. The business became unduly stimulated and an overproduction prevented to a great degree the desired advance in profit. The demand was greatly limited. A long suspension in the use of oil had accustomed the people in general to the use of tallow candles, and but little oil was required either for towns or for light-houses.

In the mean time, seeing no chance for any amelioration in their condition, unable to carry on a business at a prospective loss, and accustomed from early childhood only to this pursuit, hence unable and unwilling to adventure another, some of the prominent merchants of Nantucket resolved to transfer their business to some place where the demand for their products and the advantageous bounty offered would make it far more remunerative. Among these was William Rotch. On the 4th of July, 1785, Mr. Rotch sailed from Nantucket in the ship Maria, bound for London, arriving there on the 27th. At as early a day as practicable he opened negotiations with the Chancellor of the Exchequer (William Pitt) for a transfer to England of such of the whale-fishery at Nantucket as he could control.† The subject was laid before the privy council, and Mr. Rotch waited four months for their summons. Finally, in deference to a request of his

* Macy, 129.

† Captain Alexander Coffin was of those who looked upon the whale-fishery as a peculiarly American pursuit, and who denounced any effort looking to a transfer of it to any foreign government. On the 8th of June, 1785, he addressed from Nantucket a vigorous letter to the Hon. Samuel Adams. He wrote in severe terms against the measures being adopted to remove to England, and says Mr. Rotch "is now taking on board a double stock of materials, such as Cedar boards, (commonly called boat-boards,) of which they have none in England, a large quantity of cooper's stuff for casks, &c.—neither does it stop here, the house of Rotch have been endeavoring to engage an acquaintance of mine to go to Bermudas to superintend the business at that place." In a postscript he adds, "Since writing the above I have been favored with the original scheme of establishment of the Fishery at Bermudas, copies of which are here enclosed; one of the company is now at Kennebeck, contracting with some persons for an annual supply of *hoops*, staves, and other lumber necessary for the business." This letter was laid before the senate of Massachusetts, and the result was the passage of an act prohibiting the export to Bermudas of the articles enumerated, and the transfer in this direction was prevented.

that some one be appointed to close the matter, he was referred to Lord Hawksbury, a gentleman not very favorably disposed toward America. Mr. Rotch gave him his estimate of the sum necessary to induce a removal, viz, "£100 sterling transportation for a family of five persons, and £100 settlement; £20,000 for a hundred families." Lord Hawksbury demurred to this as a large sum.* At a subsequent interview Mr. Rotch added to his previous position the demand to bring with him thirty American ships, which demand also met with remonstrance from Lord Hawksbury, who seemed to be of the "penny wise pound foolish" order of statesmen. Mr. Rotch finally took leave of Lord Hawksbury without obtaining any satisfaction, and embarking on board his vessel sailed for France.† Landing at Dunkirk, he drew up proposals to the French government and forwarded them to Paris. These proposals were eagerly entertained, and the preliminaries were speedily arranged for a transfer of the interest of Mr. Rotch and his family and

* "And what," queried Lord Hawksbury, "do you propose to give us in return for this outlay of money?" "I will give you," returned Mr. Rotch proudly, "some of the best blood of the island of Nantucket." At this interview Hawksbury presented his own figures, where, says Mr. Rotch, (see MS.) "he had made his nice calculation of £87 10*s*. for transportation and settlement of a family," and, says he, "I am about a Fishery Bill, and I want to come to something that I may insert it, &c." My answer was, "Thy offer is no object, therefore go on with thy Fishery Bill without any regard to me." I was then taking leave and withdrawing. "Well, Mr. Rotch, You'll call on me again in two or three days." "I see no necessity for it." "But I desire you would." "If it is thy desire perhaps I may call." However, he let me rest but one day before he sent for me. He had the old story over again, but I told him it was unnecessary to enter again into the subject. I then informed him that I had heard a rumor that Nantucket had agreed to furnish France with a quantity of Oil. He stepped to his Bureau, took out one of a file of papers, and pretended to read an entire contradiction, though I was satisfied there was not a line there on the subject. I said, "It was only a vague report that I had heard, and I cannot vouch for the truth of it, but we are like drowning men, catching at every straw that passes by; therefore I am now determined to go to France and see what it is. If there is any such contract, sufficient to retain us at Nantucket, neither you nor any other nation shall have us, and if it is insufficient, I will endeavor to enlarge it." "Ah," says he, "Quakers go to France?" "Yes," I replied, "but with regret." I then parted with Lord Hawksbury for the last time. (Rotch MS.)

† His lordship sent once more for Mr. Rotch to call on him, but Mr. Rotch returned answer: "If Lord Hawksbury desires to see me he will find me on board my vessel up to the hour when she takes her anchor." When Mr. Rotch was once gone, Hawksbury became alarmed and sent to him by letter, informing him that he had made provision in the fishery bill for him, with liberty to bring forty ships instead of thirty, "he having forgotten the number;" but it was too late. This unexpected ending of his hopes was far from pleasing either to his lordship or the government. After the interview with the King of France, Mr. Rotch returned to England, and was importuned to remove to Great Britain. In his memoranda he says he was waited upon by one of the officials, who told him he was "authorized by Mr. Pitt to tell you that you shall make your own terms." "I told him," continues Mr. Rotch, "he was too late. I made very moderate proposals to you, but could obtain nothing worth my notice. I went to France, sent forward my proposals, which were doubly advantageous to what I had offered your Government; they considered them but a short time, and on my arrival in Paris were ready to act. I had a separate interview with all the Ministers of State necessary to the subject, five in number, who all agreed to & granted

friends to Dunkirk, from which port, for several years, a very successful fishery was carried on. Contemporary with the negotiations with Mr. Rotch, a letter was dispatched to the people of Nantucket by Capt. Shubael Gardner, from L—— Coffin, who resided at Dunkirk, stating that his sympathy for the people of that island had led him to apply to the French government in their behalf, and with excellent success. Every request he had made had been granted, and the unlimited freedom, the abundance and cheapness of provisions, the absence of custom-houses, the small taxes, the regularity of the town, the manners and industry of the inhabitants, and its situation, rendered it, in his opinion, "the most eligible place in the universe for the people of Nantucket to remove to.*

What effect this state of affairs may have had in the arrangement of treaties of commerce with Great Britain is somewhat uncertain, but the attempt to a consummation of this plan was intrusted to a man not only

my demands. This was effected in five hours, when I had waited to be called by your Privy Council more than four months." All attempts on the part of the English government to re-open the subject were politely but firmly rejected by Mr. Rotch. "In the beginning of 1793," the account continues, "I became fully aware that war between England & France would soon take place, therefore it was time for me to leave the Country in order to save our vessels if captured by the English. I proceeded to England. Two of them were captured, full of oil, & condemned, but we recovered both by my being in England, where I arrived two weeks before the war took place. My going to France to pursue the whale-fishery so disappointed Lord Hawksbury that he undertook to be revenged on *me* for his own folly, and I have no doubt gave directions to the Cruisers to take any of our vessels that they met with going to France. When the Ospray was taken by a King's ship, the officer sent on board to examine her papers, called to the captain & said, "You'll take this vessel in sir, she belongs to Wm. Rotch." Mr. Rotch returned to the United States with several of his vessels in 1794, and after residing in Nantucket about a year removed to New Bedford, where he lived until his death, in May, 1828.

* The following is a list of advantages secured to Nantucket whalemen by Mr. Coffin:

"1st. An entire free exercise of their religion or worship within themselves.

"2d. The concession of a tract of ground to build their houses and stores.

"3d. All the privileges, exemptions, and advantages promised by the king's declaration in 1662, confirmed by letters-patent of 1784, to all strangers who come to establish there, which are the same as those enjoyed by the natif subjects of his majisty.

"4th. The importation into the kingdom, free from all duties whatever, of the oil proceeding from their fishery, and the same premiums and encouragement granted for the cod and other fisheries to natif subjects.

"5th. A premium per ton on the burthen of the vessels that will carry on the whale fishery, which shall be determined in the course of the negotiation either with Mr. Rotch or with the select men of the island.

"6th. All objects of provisions and victuals for their ships shall be exempted from all duties whatever.

"7th. An additional and heavier duty shall be laid on all foreign oil, as a further encouragement to them, in order to facilitate the sale of their own.

"8th. The expenses of removing those of the inhabitants, who are not capable of defraying themselves, shall be paid by the Government.

"9th. A convenient dock shall be built to repair their ships.

"10th. All trades-people, such as smiths, boat-builders, coopers, and others, shall be admitted to the free exercise of their trade without being liable to the forms and ex-

thoroughly imbued with New England principles, but of sufficient statesmanship to realize of how much national importance this matter was. None knew better than John Adams that the secret of the commercial greatness which should be developed lay in the codevelopment of the fisheries; that herein was the nursery for seamen who would be a source of wealth in peace and of power in war. It was desirable to make duties and courtesies more reciprocal, and one of the first duties intrusted to Mr. Adams on his appointment to the Court of St. James in 1785, was the arrangement of some treaty which should be mutually satisfactory. Naturally one of the principal points was the importation of the products of our fishermen, since that industry perhaps more than any other was in danger of serious injury from the existing condition of things.

In a letter to the Marquis of Carmarthen, dated July 29, 1785, Mr. Adams refers to the trouble accruing from the alien duties laid by England in these words: "The course of commerce, since the peace, between Great Britain and the United States of America, has been such as to have produced many inconveniences to the persons concerned in it on both sides, which become every day more and more sensible. The zeal of Americans to make remittances to British merchants, has been such as to raise the interest of money to double its usual standard, to increase the price of bills of exchange to 8 or 10 per centum above par, and to advance the price of the produce of the country to almost double the

---

pense usually practised and paid by the natif subjects for their admittance to mastership.

"11th. They shall have liberty to command their own vessels, and have the choice of their own people to navigate them.

"12th. They shall be free from all military and naval service, as well in war as in peace, in the same manner and extent as expressed by the king's ordinance of the 16th of February, 1759." (Macy, 257, 258.)

These were probably essentially the same concessions made to Mr. Rotch in person. How many American captains pursued the fishery from the various British and French ports subsequently to the Revolution, it would be difficult to determine. Nantucket alone furnished 83 captains for the French and 149 captains for the English fishery; probably the bulk of the total number came from this one port, though in the course of the prosecution of whaling by these nations, New Bedford furnished a very considerable number. In a "Journal of a Voyage to Greenland" from Dunkirk in the ship Penelope, Capt. Tristram Gardner (a Nantucket man,) he records under the head of Friday, June 6, 1788, in latitude 70° north, "100 *ships in sight.*" On the 22d of the same month he states, as a mere matter of fact not worthy of extended comment, "Wind at South; A Ruged sea; Plenty of Snow. Later Part Saw Ise to ye S. W. of us a 4 ye wind Shifted to ye Northward, but Still thick weather. Saw A Number of ships, but No whale. So ends this 24 hours. Lat. 79. 02." And yet this is within about 175 miles of the highest northern point attained by any of our splendidly equipped expeditions undertaken with the express purpose of pushing as far north as possible in vessels armored and strengthened and equipped in the most complete manner, while the whaling voyages were pursued in small, not uncommonly strong ships, not even having the feeble protection of coppered bottoms. As early as 1753, a schooner was fitted from Boston for the discovery of the northwest passage. She sailed in the spring and returned in October of the same year.

usual rate. Large sums of the circulating cash, and as much produce as could be purchased at almost any rate, have been remitted to England; but much of this produce lies in store here, because it will not fetch, by reason of the duties and restrictions on it, the price given for it in America. No political arrangements having been made, both the British and American merchants expected that the trade would have returned to its old channels, and nearly under the same regulations, found by long experience to be beneficial; but they have been disappointed. The former have made advances, and the latter contracted debts, both depending upon remittances in the usual articles, and upon the ancient terms, but both have found themselves mistaken, and it is much to be feared that the consequences will be numerous failures. Cash and bills have been chiefly remitted; neither rice, tobacco, pitch, tar, turpentine, ships, oil, nor many other articles, the great sources of remittances formerly, can now be sent as heretofore, because of restrictions and imports, which are new in this commerce, and destructive of it; and the trade with the British West India Islands, formerly a vast source of remittance, is at present obstructed. * * * * * * There is a literal impossibility, my lord, that the commerce between the two countries can continue long to the advantage of either upon the present footing."* He continues, that these evils will increase, and asserts that it is the desire of the United States to be on good terms commercially with England, and not be driven to other markets with their goods, and he closes by proposing the arrangement of a treaty of commerce between the two countries.

It would be interesting, though not necessary in this connection, to follow the negotiations through each step; to see how the English administration felt compelled to cater to those who upheld the British navigation laws; to see how jealousy of our incipient naval power procrastinated the treaty which it was inevitable must come; to see how self-confident and secure the English felt that our trade must unavoidably come to them; to see, how, an attempt was made to throw the influence of Ireland against America by ostentatious concessions, and how the attempt failed; to see how, finally, the fear of American reciprocity in restrictions led to English reciprocity in concessions; but those things can be more satisfactorily learned from the diplomatic correspondence of the day.†

On the 24th of August Mr. Adams had a conference with Mr. Pitt for the first time in this connection. Passing by the matter of the interview, so far as it relates to the other portions of the proposed treaty, we find that when the treaty of commerce was proposed, Mr. Pitt inquired what were the lowest terms that might be satisfactory to America. Mr. Adams replied that he might not think himself competent to decide that question; that, because of the rapidly increasing feeling in America,

* Works of John Adams, viii, p. 288.

† Works of John Adams, viii, p. 307.

affairs had already culminated in Massachusetts in the passage of an act of navigation by that State, showing the tendency of the times, and that the action of England would have much to do in arresting that prejudice; that the five hundred ships employed in the commerce of the United States in 1784 might easily be compelled to become the property of American citizens and navigated wholly by American seamen; that the simple passage of an old English statute, "that none of the King's liege people should ship any merchandise out of, or into the realm, but only in ships of the King's liegance, on pain of forfeiture," modified to suit the American form of government, would effect this; that the nation had the legal right to govern its own commerce; that the ability of the Americans to build ships and the abundance of material they had for that purpose could not be doubted; and that whatever laws England might make, she would be glad to receive and consume considerable American produce, even though imported through France or Holland, and sell us as many of her manufactures as we could pay for, through the same channels. The conversation finally introduced the subject of ships and oil, and Mr. Pitt said to Mr. Adams the Americans "could not think hard of the English for encouraging their own shipwrights, their manufactures of ships, and their own whale-fishery." To which Mr. Adams replied, "By no means, but it appeared unaccountable to the people of America, that this country should sacrifice the general interests of the nation to the private interests of a few individuals interested in the manufacture of ships and in the whale-fishery, so far as to refuse these remittances from America in payment of debts, and for manufactures which would employ so many more people, augment the revenue so considerably, as well as the national wealth, which would, even in other ways, so much augment the shipping and seamen of the nation. It was looked upon in America as reconciling themselves to a diminution of their own shipping and seamen, in a great degree, for the sake of diminishing ours in a small one, besides keeping many of their manufacturers out of employ, who would otherwise have enough to do; and besides greatly diminishing the revenue, and, consequently, contrary to the maxim which he had just acknowledged, that one nation should not hurt itself for the sake of hurting another, nor take measures to deprive another of any advantage without benefitting itself."* From the questions of comparative gains or losses to either power, and the relations in which France would stand to both, Mr. Pitt led Mr. Adams into a lengthy and useless conversation on the whale-fisheries of the three countries, referring specially to the efforts of M. de Calonne to introduce this pursuit into France, asking suddenly the question "whether we had taken any measures to find a market for our oil anywhere but in France." To this Mr. Adams replied: "I believed we had, and I have been told that some of our oil had found a good market at Bremen; but there could

5th Richard, ii, ch. 3.

not be a doubt that spermaceti oil might find a market in most of the great cities in Europe which were illuminated in the night, as it is so much better and cheaper than the vegetable oil that is commonly used. The fat of the spermaceti-whale gives the clearest and most beautiful flame of any substance that is known in nature, and we are all surprised that you prefer darkness, and consequent robberies, burglaries, and murders in your streets, to the receiving, as a remittance, our spermaceti oil. The lamps around Grosvenor Square, I know, and in Downing Street, too, I suppose, are dim by midnight, and extinguished by two o'clock; whereas our oil would burn bright till 9 o'clock in the morning, and chase away, before the watchmen, all the villains, and save you the trouble and danger of introducing a new police into the city."*

But despite the fact that Mr. Pitt appeared more favorable than was anticipated, Mr. Adams did not expect any immediate response to his propositions. The English ministers in their individual capacity seemed singularly timorous, and manifested much fear of committing themselves before joint cabinet action. Adams inclined to the opinion that nothing short of the convincing eloquence of dire necessity would drive the English ministry from the position they had assumed in regard to the navigation act, and that an answer to his propositions, even at a late day, was doubtful, without Congress authorized similar acts with the United States, and these counter-irritants were actually put in force, to determine on which side the inconvenience was greatest. The great cry in the United Kingdom was: "Shall the United States be our ship-carpenters? Shall we depend upon a foreign nation for our navagation? In case of a war with them, shall we be without ships, or obliged to our enemies for them?" How much this nightmare of inability to cope with their late colonies in anything like a fair field was stimulated by the government is uncertain, but the authorities evidently used no efforts to allay it.†

The effort to bring about the desired compromise continued, as Mr. Adams had judged it would, all the succeeding fall and winter. In January, 1786, Bowdoin wrote to Adams, in reply to a letter from him, that the navigation act of Massachusetts had been so modified as to be only operative against Great Britain, and copies of the repealing act had been sent to the executives of the other States in order to secure

* Works of John Adams, viii, pp. 308–309.

† In negotiation with the Portuguese ministers in November, 1785, Mr. Adams asked (viii, p. 340) if they did not want our sperm-oil. He replied that they had olives and made oil from them; they had no use for their own sperm-oil and sold it to Spain. "They had now," he said, "a very pretty spermaceti-whale fishery, which they had learned of the New Englanders, and carried on upon the coast of Brazil." According to the Boston News-Letter of April 21, 1774, the method of obtaining their knowledge was somewhat open to objections. (See p. 57.) In 1805, the Portuguese attempted to carry on the whaling business from Mozambique, and Timothy Folger, Francis Paddack, William Hull, and John Hillman, of Nantucket, went there to take charge of the fishery; but early in 1810 accounts were received at Nantucket stating that they had all been taken sick and died there.

harmony of action upon this point. In regard to the effect the existing English laws would have upon the interest which is under consideration here, he wrote: "It is very true, their encouragement of their whale-fishery, by suffering the alien duty on oil to depress ours, will increase their shipping in this branch, increase their seamen, and, in several other ways, be advantageous to them. To a person that looks no farther, it would appear that this was good policy; and the goodness of it would be inferred from the advantages arising. But when he should extend his view, and see how that stoppage of the American whale-fishery, by depriving the Americans of so much capital a means of paying for the woolen goods they used to take of Britain, must, at the same time, occasion the American demand to cease, or be proportionately diminished, not to mention the risk of a change or deviation of the trade from the old channel, he will calculate the national profit and loss that arises from that stoppage.

"Three thousand tons of oil was the usual annual quantity produced by the whalemen at Nantucket; all of which was shipped to England, at an average price of £35 per ton, making about £105,500. The whole of which went to pay for and purchase a like amount of woolens and other British goods; nine-tenths of the value of which are computed to arise from the labor of the manufacturer, and to be so much clear gain to the nation. The other tenth, therefore, being deducted, gives the national gain arising from the industry of the Nantucket whalemen, and the capital employed in that business, namely £94,500, without the nation's paying a shilling for the risk of insurance, or any other risk whatever.

"On the change of trade, pursuant to the new regulations, the British merchants must employ a large capital in the whale-fishery, whose products we will suppose equal to that of the Nantucket, £105,000. They will have made an exceeding good voyage, if the whole of that sum should be equal to one half of the cost of the outfits; though, from many of the vessels not meeting with fish, and from a variety of accidents to which such a voyage is subject, it probably would not be a quarter. The whole of the product goes towards payment of the outfits and charges of the voyage, and a large sum must be advanced for the second voyage, &c.

"Now, although this mode of commerce would be productive of some national benefits, yet, considered in a comparative view with the benefits arising from the former mode, they would be found of little importance. A like comparison may be made with other branches of commerce, particularly the British West Indian, and the result will be found the same. For the sake, then, of gaining pence and farthings, Britain is sacrificing pounds by her new regulations of trade. She has a right to see for herself; but, unhappily, resentment and the consequent prejudices have so disordered her powers of vision, that it requires the skilful hand of a good political optician to remove the obstructing films

If she will not permit the application of your couching instruments, or, if applied, they can work no effect, the old lady must be left to her fate, and abandoned as incurable."*

On the 21st of January, 1786, Mr. Adams, in a letter to Secretary Jay, writes: "It will take eighteen months more to settle all matters, *exclusive of the treaty of commerce.*"† And thus it continued. Argument and persuasion had no effect. Convinced in spite of themselves, they still clung fondly, obstinately, perhaps foolishly, to their obnoxious laws. As late as November, 1787, Mr. Adams writes to Mr. Jay: "They are at present, both at court and in the nation at large, much more respectful to me, and much more tender of the United States, than they ever have been before; but, depend upon it, this will not last; they will aim at recovering back the western lands, at taking away our fisheries, and at the total ruin of our navigation, at least."‡ Mr. Adams's position at the court of St. James was terminated, by his urgent request, soon after this, and the question of commercial relations between the two countries was still unsettled.§

This state of affairs was scarcely such as would occasion the utmost harmony. The United States naturally resented this frigid manner of treating our overtures for friendship. In August, 1786, Mr. Jefferson, in a letter from Paris to Mr. Carmichael, writes: "But as to every other nation of Europe, || I am persuaded Congress will never offer a treaty. If any of them should desire one hereafter, I suppose they will make the first overtures." ¶

But while America was exerting herself so unsuccessfully to be allowed to live on terms of civility with England, the whale-fishery carried on from within her borders was languishing.

Like the effect of the heat of the sun on the iceberg, so was the effect of foreign bounties upon the American fishery, dissolving it, breaking off a fragment here and a fragment there. Lured by the promise of English bounties, discouraged with the prospect in America, where the price for oil would scarely repay the cost of procuring it and where there was no

* Adams, viii, 363-4, In his reply to Mr. Bowdoin, under date of May 9, 1786, Mr. Adams, after expressing surprise that such reasoning as his (Bowdoin's) has no effect on the English cabinet, writes: "Mr. Jenkinson, an old friend of the British empire, is still at his labors. He is about establishing a bounty upon fifteen ships to the southward, and upon two to double Cape Horn, for spermaceti whales. Americans are to take an oath that they mean to settle in England, before they are entitled to the bounty." In September, 1786, Mr. Adams writes to Mr. Jefferson from London, (viii, 414): "The whalemen, both at Greenland and the southward, have been unsuccessful, and the price of spermaceti-oil has risen above £50 per ton."

† Adams, viii, 363-4, 389.

‡ *Ibid.*, 463.

§ Works of Jefferson, ii, 18. See also article on Jefferson, by Parton, in Atlantic Monthly for February, 1873.

|| Referring to Russia, Portugal, Spain, France, Sweden, Tuscany, and the Netherlands.

¶ Jefferson, ii, 18.

market for their chief staple, several of the people of Nantucket removed to the vicinity of Halifax, in Nova Scotia. There, in 1786 and 1787, they settled, building dwellings, wharves, stores, manufactories for sperm-candles and such other structures as were connected with their fishery, and calling their new settlement Dartmouth.* There they carried on the pursuit for several years prosperously, and gave promise of considerable commercial importance. But the disintegration which commenced at Nantucket continued at Dartmouth, and just as the settlement seemed about to become thrifty and important it began to become divided, pieces again split off, and the village, as a whaling-port, soon became a thing of the past. Those who were the earliest to remove from Nantucket soon grew uneasy of their new location, and having greater inducements offered them if they removed to England, again migrated, and settled in Milford Haven, from whence for many years they carried on the business with very considerable success. The parent died in giving birth to the child; Milford Haven flourished, but at the expense of Dartmouth's existence.

France did not view this transfer with indifference. The scheme for the building up of the fishery at Dunkirk by emigration from Nantucket having proven only partially successful,† it was desirable to inaugurate some other measures to prevent further increase of the business in England. A committee of gentlemen well informed in such matters was instructed to investigate and report on the subject of encouragement of a general commerce with the United States. It was evident that the American whalemen could not be induced to leave their native country if they could support themselves there. The natural inference was, if a market could be opened to their products which would replace the one closed, they would not emigrate. Accordingly upon this point the committee reported in favor of an immediate abatement of the duty upon oil and a promise of a further abatement after the year 1790. The letter of M. de Calonnes

* Works of Jefferson, ii, 518. Mr. Jefferson says, referring to a further hegira of the islanders: "A vessel was already arrived from Halifax to Nantucket, to take off some of those who proposed to remove; two families had gone on board, and others were going, when a letter was received there which had been written by Monsieur le Marquis de Lafayette to a gentleman in Boston, and transmitted by him to Nantucket. The purport of the letter was, to dissuade their accepting the British proposals, and to assure them that their friends in France would endeavor to do something for them. This instantly suspended their design; not another went on board, and the vessel returned to Halifax with only the families." In 1796 Wm. Rotch & Son petitioned Congress to remit the excess of duties and tonnage charged then on two whale-ships by the collector of New Bedford, in consequence of their not being provided with United States registers. These were ships which sailed from Nantucket in 1787 and 1789, under registers from the State of Massachusetts, and were used in the Dunkirk fishery, returning to the United States in 1794, some years after the National Government had been in operation. The committee which was appointed to consider the petition reported favorably upon it, and the prayer was granted. (State Papers, vii, p. 411.)

† "Nine families only, of thirty-three persons in the whole, came to Dunkirk."—(Jefferson, ii, 519.)

(who was in treaty with the Nantucket whalemen), recommending this, was immediately sent to America, and after careful investigation of the subject, the *arret* of the 29th of December, 1787, ratifying the abatement and promising a further one if the French King found such a proceeding of mutual benefit, was passed.

But the measure in this form had a contrary effect from what was intended. "The English," says Jefferson,* "had now begun to deluge the markets of France with their whale oils; and they were enabled by the great premiums given by their government, to undersell the French fisherman, aided by feebler premiums, and the American, aided by his poverty alone. Nor is it certain, that these speculations were not made at the risk of the British government, to suppress the French and American fishermen in their only market. Some remedy seemed necessary. Perhaps it would not have been a bad one, to subject, by a general law, the merchandise of every nation, and of every nature, to pay additional duties in the ports of France, exactly equal to the premiums and drawbacks given on the same merchandise, by their own government. This might not only counteract the effect of premiums in the instance of whale oils, but attack the whole British system of bounties and drawbacks, by the aid of which, they make London the centre of commerce for the whole earth. A less general remedy, but an effectual one, was, to prohibit the oils of all *European* nations; the treaty with England requiring only, that she should be treated as well as the most favored *European* nation. But the remedy adopted was to prohibit all oils, without exception."† And this on the 20th of September, 1788, only nine months from the passage of the former law.‡

Through the exertions of Jefferson this error, political as well as commercial, was remedied, and in December, 1788, the abatement of duties on oils was so arranged as to make the American and the French on the same footing, and cut off all danger of overstocking from European

* Jefferson ii, 520.

† Jefferson, ii, 521. "The annual consumption of France, as stated by a person who has good opportunities of knowing it, is as follows:

	Tons.
"Paris, according to the registers of 1786	1,750
"Twenty-seven other cities, lighted by M. Sangrain	500
"Rouen	312½
"Bordeaux	375
"Lyons	187½
"Other cities, for leather and light	1,875
	5,000"

‡ Jefferson states (ii, 523) that before the war Great Britain had less than 100 vessels engaged in whaling, while America employed 309. (This does not take into account Sag Harbor, New York, nor the very important fishery from Newport, Providence, and Warren, in Rhode Island, which Mr. Jefferson seems to have overlooked in his report.) In 1788 these circumstances were reversed, America employing 80, and Great Britain 314.

rivals, and in January, 1789, this arrangement received its legal ratification.*

The revival of the business in the United States, and the growing scarcity of whales in the waters heretofore mostly frequented, made the equipping of larger vessels a necessity, and from the sloops and schooners which formerly composed the greater portion of the whaling fleet an advance was made to brigs and ships, and the field still farther extended.† The sperm-whale being of the most value, the effort to encompass his capture was greater; and he was pursued, as he fled from his old haunts, till the Pacific Ocean was attained.‡ At Nantucket the number of vessels soon increased to such an extent that it became necessary to go abroad for men to man them, and some Indians and a large number of negroes were brought from the mainland to aid in filling the crew-lists. Ups and downs the business had then, as it ever has since. A presumed prosperity induced competition, the markets became glutted, and oil was sold at less than the cost of production. The price of whalebone became reduced to 10 cents per pound and less, instead of commanding a dollar as it did prior to the Revolution. The disturb ances between England and France, and the internal commotions to which the latter country was subjected, effectually annulled the effect of the French *arret* of 1789. So disastrously did these things affect whaling that the quarrels of France and England forced many Nantucket men to sell their vessels, others to dismantle and lay theirs up, while a few still held on, some making a little profit, the majority suffering a severe loss.

* Jefferson, ii, 539. When the Arret of 29th December, 1787, was drawn up, the first draught was so made as to exclude *all European oils*, but at the very moment of passing it, they struck out the word "European," so that our oils became involved. "This, I believe," says he, "was the effect of a single person in the ministry."

† Sag Harbor re-entered the business in 1785; New Bedford in 1787 or 1788. (See Returns of the Fleets.)

‡ In the Pacific the Americans had been preceded by the Amelia, Captain Shields, an English fitted ship, manned by the Nantucket colony of whalemen; and sailing for that ocean from London in 1787, her first mate, Archelus Hammond, killing the first sperm whale known to have been taken in that ocean.

In Jefferson's Report he enumerates three qualities of oil: 1, the sperm; 2, that from the ordinary right whales; 3, that from the right whales on the Brazil Banks, which was darker in color and of a more offensive odor when burned than from No. 2.

In 1791 six ships sailed for the Pacific fishery from Nantucket and one from New Bedford. In the mean time ships from Dunkirk, among them the Falkland, Canton, and the Harmony, had already performed their voyages, and in February, 1792, arrived at Dunkirk with full cargoes. It was the custom in those days to nearly fill with sperm, then return to the Atlantic Ocean and complete their load on the coast of Patagonia or on Brazil Banks, commanders preferring to round Cape Horn with a snugly loaded ship. The brig Sea Horse, Captain Mayo, which arrived at Cape Ann, October 4, 1789, from a whaling voyage to Woolwich Bay, reported a very singular sinking of a point of land there, in sight of quite a large fleet both English and American, the water having a depth of six fathoms where just before was apparently solid land.

In 1798* came the threats of disturbance between France and the United States. French privateers in the excess of their zeal preyed upon American commerce as well as upon that of the powers with whom they were in direct conflict. A large number of vessels fell victims to these depredators, and the friendly relations existing somewhat precariously between France and the United States became nearly supplanted by a state of actual warfare. The whaling interest, as usual, was among the earliest sufferers. Early in 1799 many parties in Nantucket sold their ships rather than fit them out at the risk of capture. News began to reach the island that vessels were already captured, and the business of the islanders both in fishing and trading almost ceased. Instead of fitting out a dozen ships for whaling but two or three were fitted, and sadness and gloom shrouded every face. The difficulties were finally adjusted and business resumed its old channels, but the losses which the unfortunate Nantucketers sustained by the unjustifiable, piratical depredations, though settled to the satisfaction of our Government and duly receipted for, with others, by the United States, have never been remunerated, while some of the unlucky owners, officers, and underwriters, in comfortable circumstances at the commencement of these troubles, lost their little property, the accumulations of years, and died in poverty.† These unauthorized captures were not

* The Boston papers of 1796 reported that the Carisford frigate had arrived at the Cape of Good Hope from England with credentials constituting General Graig governor of the colony, the limits of which were to be so arranged as to cut off other nations from participation in the Delago Bay fishery.

† The subject of the French spoliations is one to which the people of Nantucket have been particularly sensitive. Isolated communities are more liable to feel that the injustice done to one is an injustice to all; hence, although comparatively few of the islanders suffered from the depredations of the French, or rather from the apparent breach of faith on the part of a government bound to protect them and their interests, all felt that seeming injustice as a personal matter. In a letter to the Hon. George McDuffie, giving an account of the claims of Nantucket in this behalf, published in the Warder of May 20, 1846, the following is described as the actual condition of the claimants and character of the demands:

"Ship Joanna, Coffin, taken with 2,000 barrels of oil on board; value of ship and cargo $40,000; one of the original owners still living—seventy-five years old and *poor;* one of the crew also living, *poor;* the master and mate died recently, *poor;* children still surviving; *claim never sold.* Ship Minerva, Fitch, 1,500 barrels of oil on board; value $30,000; one of the original owners living, sixty-eight years old, *poor;* master still alive, seventy-eight years old, with small means and many dependants; one of the crew alive, *poor; claims never sold.* Ship Active, Gardner, 3,000 barrels of oil on board; value $50,000; same owners as Minerva with captain; Captain Gardner died two years ago at the age of eighty-five, leaving a large family and grandchildren; *claims never sold.* Ship Ann, Coffin, (in merchant service); loss of ship $10,000; the captain left a large family in slender circumstances; one of the underwriters died a few years since, in the almshouse, who, at the time of the capture, stood high among Nantucket merchants; *claims never sold.*"

Speaking in the interest of the whale-fishery, it may be safely asserted that the people of Nantucket view with regret and disappointment what they consider the gross injustice showed to them (with others) in putting off, upon untenable pretexts, the settlement of these demands. The stern logic of poverty and the almshouse is keener

confined exclusively to the French, for in 1800 the Spanish authorities at Valparaiso, emulating the hostility to a power ostensibly at peace with them, which the French had shown, seized and condemned the whale-ships Miantonomah, of Norwich, and Tryal, of Nantucket.*

From this time till the opening of the second war with England, whaling was pursued with a gradually-augmenting fleet. And this in the face of the uncertainties which the increasingly critical state of affairs between the United States and England occasioned. In 1802 Nantucket added five ships to her fleet, and New London sent her first large vessel,† and in 1806 the quantity of oil imported into the country was considerably in excess of the consumption.

The embargo act, of 1807, almost suspended the pursuit, not so much by actual proscription as because of the impossibility of effecting insurance upon the vessels, but it soon received another impetus on account of the prospect of a general peace throughout Europe.

The commencement of the war of 1812 found a large portion of the whaling-fleet at sea. Trusting that the causes of contention between England and America would be removed without the necessity of a final appeal to arms, many owners had fitted out their ships. This was particularly the case at Nantucket, from which port a large proportion of the fleet had sailed for the Pacific Ocean on voyages varying from about two years to two years and a half.‡ With the reception of the news of the declaration of war a large portion of the vessels in the North and South Atlantic, and some of those in the Pacific, turned their prows homeward, hoping to make the home port before the seas swarmed with letters-of-marque and national vessels of war. Many of these vessels from Nantucket on arriving home sailed thence immediately for Boston, Newport, New Bedford, or some other fortified port, where they could ride out the storm of war in security. After the month of July, 1812, was ushered in, reports of the capture of whaling-vessels came thick and fast to Nantucket. § First came the news of the taking and burning of the schooner Mount Hope, David Cottle master. In quick succession they learned of the capture of the Alligator, Hope, Manilla,

---

than the sophistries of politicians. The Fox, of New Bedford, Captain Coffin Whippey, captured in 1796 with 1,500 whale and 500 sperm, was another case. In 1853 Captain Whippey—captured a second time in 1798—was living, but dependent upon charity.

* The Miantonomah was a new ship, on her first voyage.

† In 1794 the ship Commerce, of East Haddam, was fitted for a whaling voyage, and sailed from New London on February 6 of that year. In 1770 Capt. Isaiah Eldridge, of the sloop Tryall, of Dartmouth, spoke, among other whalemen on the Davis' Strait ground, Thomas Wiccum, (Wiggin?) of New London.

‡ See Macy, 161-2-3.

§ When war seemed inevitable the ship-owners of Nantucket held a meeting to take into consideration the subject of how to best secure the fleet from capture. It was proposed to request the British minister at Washington to use his influence with his government to obtain from them immunity from capture of whale-ships belonging to the island. This plan was ultimately abandoned, the majority of the owners being of the opinion that "the prospect of success was too faint to warrant the attempt." (Macy, 165.)

Ocean (brig), Ranger, Fame,* Rose, Renown,* Sterling, Edward, Gardner, Monticello, Chili, Rebecca, and others, and it may be easily imagined that the prospect for the islanders had but little in it that appeared encouraging. New Bedford, too, although at this time her interest in this business was far less than that of Nantucket, suffered from the capture of her whaling-vessels.†

Again did war put an effectual stop to the pursuit of whaling from every port of the United States save Nantucket, and again were the inhabitants of that town, knowing no business except through their shipping, compelled to strive to carry their commercial marine through the tempest of fire as free from complete destruction as possible. A new source of danger presented itself. Prior to the declaration of war between Great Britain and America our whalemen on the coast of Peru ‡ had often suffered from piratical acts of the Peruvian privateers, being continually plundered and cut out from Chilian ports whither they had gone to recruit. The chronic state of affairs on this coast being one of war, the Government of the United States had sent the Hon. Joel R. Poinsett, of South Carolina, to those parts to see that American commerce was suitably protected, but for several months his remonstrances had been worse than useless. The declaration of war between England and the United States gave the Peruvian corsairs a fresh pretext for the exercise of their plundering propensities. They claimed that they were the allies of England, and as such were entitled to capture the vessels of any power with which she was at war. An expedition was equipped by the authorities of Lima and sent on its marauding way. This army succeeded in capturing the towns of Conception and Talcahuano. In the latter port was a large number of American ships, many of them whalemen, who, having obtained their cargoes of oil, had put in to recruit with provisions and water before making the homeward voyage. Among these were the ships Criterion, Mary Ann, Monticello, Chili, John and James, Lima, Lion, Sukey, Gardner, President, Perseverance, and Atlas, of Nantucket.

This was in April, 1813. These vessels were detained in the harbor by the Limian armament, which consisted of two men-of-war, with about

* The Fame was used in the English fishery, and the Renown under the name of "Adam," while engaged in the same pursuit under the same flag, went ashore on Deal beach and bilged in 1824 or 1825.

In 1812 the brig Nanina, Capt. Valentine Barnard, of New York, sailed to the Falkland Islands on a sealing and elephant-oil cruise. The British ship Isabella having become wrecked, her crew were rescued by the Nanina, and showed their gratitude to Captain Barnard by seizing his vessel and setting him, with Barzillai Pease, Andrew Hunter, and E. Pease, of his crew, ashore on New Island, one of the group. A protest signed by the four was published in the Hudson Bee, and also in the supplement of Niles' Register for 1814.

† The ship Sally, Clark master, was captured while homeward bound with 1,200 barrels of sperm-oil on board. Value of vessel and cargo $40,000. The Triton also was captured, involving a loss of $16,000.

‡ These vessels belonged almost exclusively to New Bedford and Nantucket.

1,500 troops. Having found a bag containing about $800 on board the President, they carried her captain, Solomon Folger, ashore under a guard and imprisoned the remaining officers and crew, excepting the mate, one boat-steerer, and the cook.

Learning of this condition of affairs, Poinsett immediately joined the Chilian army and directed its movements. On the 15th of May a battle was fought between the contending forces near the town of San Carlos, but when the day had closed neither side could claim the victory. Taking advantage of the cover of the night, Poinsett put himself at the head of 400 picked men, with three pieces of light artillery, and, leaving the main body, marched directly to Talcahuano, whither the enemy had withdrawn. The town was immediately carried by storm and the detained whalemen were released.* Some of the ships having had their papers destroyed, Poinsett furnished them with consular certificates. The friendly regard for the United States which diplomatic address and persuasion had been unable to obtain, were secured in a much shorter time and probably far more efficaciously by force of arms, and Lima yielded to muskets and cannon the respect she had been unwilling to concede to the seal of the Department of State. Her depredations on American commerce did not, however, entirely cease until the advent of Captain Porter in those waters.† Soon after this the United States Government, realizing the defenseless condition of our commerce in the Pacific, dispatched Porter to that locality to protect our interests. Up to the time of the capture of his vessel he had not only done all in his power in this direction, but had effectually destroyed the English whale-fishery in those seas, and so turned the tables upon the enemy who had sent out his whale-ships well armed and manned to perform the same kindly office toward our whalemen.‡

Up to the latter part of the year 1813 the people of Nantucket had fished unmolested both for cod-fish and for humpback whales on the shoals at the eastward of the island, and by this means eked out a livelihood which was beginning to be quite precarious, but this resort was now taken from them. An English privateer, during the fall, appeared among

* See Nantucket Inquirer, August 9, 1824; also Inquirer and Mirror, September 14, 1872. In the latter paper is an account of the affair written by Captain Nathaniel Fitzgerald, one of the crew on one of the detained whalers.

† The Walker, of New Bedford, was captured by an English armed whale-ship, but recaptured by Porter. The Barclay, of New Bedford, also was captured by the Peruvians, and recaptured by Porter.

‡ So far as operations in the Pacific were concerned, the English went out to shear but "returned shorn." Wherever our sailors went ashore in foreign ports and met English seamen, a melee was a frequent occurrence. An amusing instance is related of the officer of a whaling-vessel incurring the displeasure of an English naval officer in one of the South American Pacific ports, by his zeal in behalf of his country. A challenge was the result. The American being the challneged party, had, of course, the right to a choice of weapons, and being most familiar with the harpoon, chose that. They met according to the preliminaries and took their positions. For a moment the English officer stood before the poised harpoon of our whaleman, then gave in, and the proposed combat was deferred.

the fleet, capturing one Nantucket vessel, and driving away the remainder. In this dilemma a town-meeting was assembled and a petition prepared and forwarded to Congress representing the situation there, and praying that some arrangement might be entered into "whereby the fisheries may be prosecuted, without being subject to losses by war."* But no adequate relief was afforded, and the people found the history of their sufferings during the Revolution repeating itself with a distressing pertinacity and fidelity, and they bade fair to perish of starvation and cold. They eventually succeeded in obtaining permission to import provisions, but attempts to get leave to sail on whaling voyages, coupled with immunity from capture, were unsuccessful.

The return of peace effected for them the protection that all negotiations had failed to secure. Early in February, 1815, news came to Nantucket that the war was over, and immediately all was hurry and bustle. The wharves, lately so deserted, teemed with life; the ships, lately dismantled, put on their new dress; the faces of the people, lately so disconsolate, were radiant with hope. In May two ships fitted and sailed on their voyages; by the last of June this number was increased to nine; by the 1st of August eighteen had gone, and by the 31st of December over thirty ships, brigs, schooners, and sloops were pursuing the leviathans in the North and South Atlantic, the Indian and Pacific Oceans. On the 9th of July, 1815, the first returning whaling-vessel arrived at Nantucket; in all probability this was the first arrival at any port in the United States after the war. This vessel was the sloop Mason's Daughter, which, after a six weeks' voyage, returned with 100 barrels of oil.

From this period the business rapidly increased in extent. Nantucket, which, during the war of 1812, had had its fleet of whale-ships reduced from forty-six to twenty-three, by the last of December, 1820, possessed seventy-two whale-ships, (with an aggregate of 20,449 tons,) besides several brigs, schooners, and sloops.† The same success which had

*November 26, 1813. Macy, 177. In an official report Captain Porter gives the following list of his captures, chiefly vessels, as he says, engaged in the British sperm-whale fishery:

	Tons.	Men.	Guns.
Montezuma	270	21	2
Policy	175	26	10
Georgiana	280	25	6
Greenwich	388	25	10
Atlantic	355	24	8
Rose	220	21	8
Hector	270	25	11
Catharine	270	29	8
Seringapatam	357	31	14
Charlton	274	21	10
New Zealander	259	23	8
Sir A. Hammond	301	31	12

†Journal of Obed Macy. See also Degrand's report. Degrand said: "When we consider the numerous other vessels engaged in the coasting and other commercial

advanced Nantucket so rapidly served to stimulate other ports, and New York, Long Island, New London, Cape Cod, Boston, and more particularly New Bedford, entered more vigorously into competition,* and but a few years elapsed before the latter port, which was an offshoot, a child as it were of Nantucket, had far outstripped the extremest growth of the parent. In the mean time the same love of adventure, the same longing to explore new fields, the same yearning to more speedily return home with a full cargo, that sent our whalemen from home to the West Indies and the Cape de Verdes, from the Cape de Verdes to the shores of Africa and Brazil, to the Falklands and the coast of Patagonia, from Patagonia to the Pacific coast of South America, urged them still further.† In 1818 Capt. George W. Gardner, in the ship Globe of Nantucket, steering west from the old track, found, in latitude 5° to 10° south and longitude 105° to 125° west, a cruising ground where the objects of his search seemed to exist in almost countless numbers. This he termed the "Off-shore Ground," and, within two years, more than fifty ships were whaling in the same locality.

The next cruising ground was off the coast of Japan. Having received word from Captain Winship, of Brighton, Mass., who had friends at Nantucket, that on a recent voyage from China to the Sandwich Islands he had seen large numbers of sperm-whales on that coast, Captain Joseph Allen, in the ship Maro, was dispatched there in the fall of 1819. In 1821 six or seven ships were cruising in this vicinity, and in the following year ‡ more than thirty visited that field.

The grouping of whalemen upon the various grounds as they were discovered soon caused the slaughter or dispersion of the whales, and as a necessary consequence new fields must be opened up to supply the demand that had become rapacious. Since the close of the war of 1812, not only had the number of vessels in the various recognized whaling ports become greatly augmented, but every year witnessed the creation of new ports from whence this crusade against the whale was relentlessly pursued. Our vessels spread in their courses rapidly to all parts of the Pacific, and hundreds of islands received their first visit from

---

trade of the island; the small number of inhabitants it contains, and that the island itself is but a *speck* upon the bordering waters of our republic; and moreover, that almost the whole of their shipping was captured or destroyed so lately as the last war; we are struck with admiration at the invincible hardihood and industry of this little active, enterprising and friendly community, whose harpoons have penetrated with success every nook and corner of every ocean."—(Niles' Register, December 2, 1820.)

* This competition was also entered into by France and England, more particularly by the latter. (Macy, 214.)

† Capt. George Swain, 2d, of the ship Independence, which sailed from Nantucket in 1817, asserted, on the return from his voyage in 1819, that no ship would ever fill with sperm-oil again. A similar assertion had been made in 1789, when the ship Ranger, Captain William Swain, returned to Nantucket with a cargo of over 1,000 barrels of whale-oil. Her captain thought no other vessel would ever succeed in obtaining so large a cargo.

‡ The Maro returned in March, 1822, with 2,425 barrels of sperm-oil.

white men from the adventurous captors of these cetaceans.* The navigation of those waters was then a far different thing from what it at present is. The sea was comparatively unknown; what charts there were in existence were full of inaccuracies, and the first intimation that many a vessel had that she was sailing on dangerous ground was the splash of the breakers close at hand, or the grinding of her keel upon the treacherous rocks. Nor were the dangers of the seas the only risks which they experienced. The natives of many of the numerous groups of islands, with which the Pacific is so thickly studded, were more relentless than the waves, more treacherous than the reefs, and after the first emotions of surprise and awe the firing of a gun caused among them were over, woe to the ill-fated crew which fell into their clutches. It must be acknowledged that, in far too many cases, their barbarities were perpetrated in revenge for injuries received at the hands of some preceding ship's crew, † but they were not punctillious as to whether the actual culprit was punished or one of his kind—they warred against the race and not individuals. Many vessels carried with them the various gewgaws which would please the savage eye for the purpose of trading among the islands, and these, in cases where the natives were not sadly overreached, served to excite their cupidity and invite attack.

So large a portion of our fishing-fleet visited the Pacific that the United States was finally forced, when petition after petition had been sent to Congress, to send an exploring expedition to those seas, the ostensible purpose of which was to render the navigation of that ocean more secure as well in respect to the dangers of the land as in regard to those of the sea.

In 1828 four ships were sent from Nantucket to the coast of Zanzibar

---

*Hundreds of islands in the Pacific Ocean were first made known to civilization and first located upon charts by whalemen, and the captains of whale-ships were eagerly consulted when exploring expeditions to these seas were to be undertaken. Wilkes and Perry both were indebted to these hardy, adventurous mariners, and in the compilation of his great work on "Ocean Currents," Maury was in constant communication with them. That these favors reacted to the benefit of our whalemen is true; thus in December, 1858, Professor Agassiz, in a letter to the American Geographical Society, encouraged the Polar expedition then agitated in the following words: "I beg to add a word with regard to Dr. Hayes' Expedition,—I consider it as highly important, not only in a scientific point of view, but particularly so for the interests of the whale fisheries." He considered the habits of the whale as sure evidence of an open sea, "and the discovery of a passage into that open water which would render whale-fishing possible during the winter, would be one of the most important results for the improvement of whale-fishing."

†Thus Davis mentions (Nimrod of the Sea, p. 343) speaking a ship from London which had put in to the Marquesas Islands. While there three of the crew deserted. The captain of the English ship demanded of the chief that he return the deserters under reprisal, which demand was refused. Thereupon the master of the whaleman double-shotted his nine-pound guns, fired a round into the midst of the crowded grass huts composing the village, and carried off three of the Marquesans. "We Christians," continues Davis, "must not be unduly shocked when we hear of retaliation by

for sperm whales, and they cruised in the vicinity of the Seychelle Islands, and off the mouth of the Red Sea. Indeed, such was the vigor with which the new haunts were sought for that one adventurous captain even invaded the Red Sea itself in the pursuit of his occupation.*

In the year 1835 commenced that period of whaling which might be termed its Golden Age, for during the next decade the whale-fishery assumed its greatest importance and reached the zenith of its commercial value. In this year (1835) the ship Ganges of Nantucket, Barzillai T. Folger, master, took the first right whale ever taken on the Kodiah ground. This was the commencement of this fishery on the northwest coast. From this period the fleet rapidly augmented in size to the year 1846, when there belonged to the various ports of the United States 678 ships and barks, 35 brigs, and 22 schooners, with an aggregate capacity of 233,189 tons, and valued at $21,075,000.†

In 1843, the first bow-head whales taken in the North Pacific were captured on the coast of Kamschatka by the ships Hercules, Captain Ricketson, and Janus, Captain Turner, both of New Bedford.‡

In 1848, Captain Royce, in the bark Superior, of Sag Harbor, passed through Behring's Straits, and performed a good season's work. Being the first whaler in those seas he found the whales comparatively tame and easy to strike. In this high latitude,§ at the season of his whaling

---

the savages on the next ship's crew that falls into their power." And this atrocious treatment of the unoffending South Sea Islanders was by no means limited to English captains. Many seamen were eventually to be found upon these various Pacific islands who had deserted or been discharged from their ships. Some of them, scoundrels under any circumstances, became leaders of the natives in their attacks upon trading and whaling vessels; some of them became influential men upon the islands, both by means of their superior civilization and through marriage with dusky maidens—daughters of the chief men of the islanders. One of the most marked cases of this latter kind was that of David Whippey, who left a Nantucket whaling-vessel while at the Feejee Islands, about the year 1839, and, making himself friendly and useful to the chiefs, soon became a most important man among them. According to the custom there he acquired several wives, (albeit he is said to have left one behind him in Nantucket,) and became father of a numerous family. He was appointed one of the United States vice-consuls, and for many years was of great service to our Government.

* The ship Columbus. (Scammon's Marine Mammalia, p. 212.)

† The foreign whaling-fleet at this time numbered 230 vessels. (Scammon, 213.)

‡ Scammon, p. 213. Davis says (p. 388) the value of the "bow-head" whale was not at first recognized. According to his account Capt. George A. Covill, of New Bedford, first learned their value, and his discovery was somewhat accidental. For lack of sperm whales they struck one of this species in the Ochotsk, and killed him with but little trouble. Before cutting in they judged he would make about seventy barrels of oil, but to their surprise he turned out one hundred and fifty, with bone in proportion. There is some question as to this priority of Captain Covill's. Capt. J. H. Swift credits the French ship Asia with being the first, and Captain Royce advances the same claim for the American ship Huntsville. (See Scammon, note, p. 60.)

§ The following extract from the log of the Saratoga, of New Bedford, Capt. Harding, will serve to show to how high a northerly point whaling was pushed: "September 1, 1851, latitude 71° 40′ N., longitude 150° 40′ W.; 71 N., the depth of water was 6 fathoms.

there, the pursuit could be made at any hour of the twenty-four; in fact, the first whale taken was captured at 12 o'clock at night. The field thus opened was speedily vexed with the keels of our adventurous whalemen, and within the next three years two hundred and fifty ships had obtained cargoes of oil there. The season for Arctic whaling is short, and the pursuit of the whale at times extremely dangerous. Often, when struck, the wounded animal makes for the ice, and, unless killed before that barrier is gained, escapes with the harpoons and lines. Fogs are frequent and dense, and while these last the ringing of bells, firing of guns, blowing of horns, and pounding on empty casks, as the ships pierce through the mists, indicate their position as well to avoid collision with each other as to recall the missing boats, if any are out. It frequently happens that the crew of such a boat will fail to find their own ship, and will meet with some other; in which case they have no hesitation in repairing on board the stranger, there to remain until the fog lifts and they can find their own vessel.*

The fishery continued with varying success until the year 1847. Fluctuations in the business were constant, and with many ports the tide of success seemed to ebb and flow with quite as measured a rythm as the alternating rise and fall of old ocean. A few years of success overstimulated the business, new ships were added, and the natural result of overstocking the market and a fall in prices ensued. This was quite as much the case in 1830, when the imports of oil amounted

Proceeding to the northward and eastward the depth of water gradually increased to thirty fathoms. Experienced here severe gales, with a beat of 15 miles between packed ice, to the northward and eastward. In the bite saw whales in great numbers, gradually working north." Captain Beechey, in the Blossom, in 1826 reached 70° 30', and explored with boats to 71° 25'. The Saratoga, therefore, went 15 miles farther north than the Blossom's boats. The following table taken from the Honolulu Friend of October 15, 1849, gives a record of thirteen Arctic whalers in the year, showing the amount of oil taken, the number of whales captured, the highest latitude attained, and the dates when the first and last whales were obtained:

Ship.	Barrels of oil.	Number of whales.	Highest latitude.	First whale.	Last whale.
Junior	1,900	11	66°	June 5	July 15
Jeannette	1,200	8	67° 40'	July 13	Aug. 14
Two Brothers	1,000	6	68° 10'	July 14	Aug. 26
Marengo	2,000	14	69°	June 25	Aug. 26
Metacom	1,600	13	67°	June 1	Aug. 15
Isaac Hicks	800	4	69° 50'	July 19	Aug. 14
Electra	350	2	67°	July 7	Aug. 10
Margaret	1,350	9	69° 30'	July 21	Aug. 3
J. Maury	1,000	7	68°	July 14	Aug. 23
Catharine	1,450	9	67° 30'	July 2	Aug. 17
Washington	1,800	16	68° 30'	June 28	Aug. 10
Omega	1,550	12	70° 12'	July 1	Aug. 25
Tiger	1,650	9	68° 40'	July 18	Aug. 30
Total	17,650	120			

*Scammon, p. 63. See, also, a very interesting series of articles by William H. Macy, esq., entitled "My Cruise in the Arctic," published in the Nant. Inq. and Mir., 1876.

to 106,829 barrels of sperm and 86,274 barrels of whale, as in 1845, when 157,917 barrels of sperm and 272,730 barrels of whale were brought in.* Then came losses, and as whales became more scarce and voyages were more prolonged and far more expensive, these reverses became more and more serious, until individual owners dropped out of the corporations, corporations became extinct in the ports, and finally the ports themselves became disconnected with the business.†

The war of the rebellion came with a suddenness that was entirely unexpected to the larger portion of the people of the North. The *ignis fatuus* of compromise beguiled them on with illusory hopes of peace, and when the storm finally burst it found them wholly unprepared. No special commercial interest was in a poorer state to withstand war than the whale-fishery. Ships were in various portions of the Pacific, on voyages averaging nearly four years, and were gone from port months at a time. If they were communicated with, the remedy was scarcely better than the disease. To go into port and there lay idle was quite as disastrous—even more so—to the owners than to continue their perilous calling at the hazard of capture by southern privateers.

But whalemen in the Pacific continued for several years unmolested. Those engaged in rebellion were unable to fit out the throng of privateers which their disposition prompted them to do. The first vessels of

* A similar and somewhat ludicrous case (as viewed in our present light) occurred in the early history of the cotton factory of the Boston Manufacturing Company. Not many years after its establishment, at one of the corporation dinners, a prominent director expressed great alarm arising from a dread that the mill at Waltham would prove an unfortunate speculation, because of its prospectively *overstocking the market* Then there were probably not half a dozen cotton factories in the country. The time is within the memory of people who are not yet what would be called old when the little town of Weston, in Massachusetts, could overstock the boot and shoe market of Boston.

In 1849, the English made an effort to revive the southern whale-fishery. Some merchants were incorporated under the name of "The British Southern Whale Fishery Company," and an attempt was made to establish a colony at the Auckland Islands, having in this company its recognized head, but dissensions arose as to jurisdictions, and the design fell through.

† In 1850, San Francisco became a whaling port. On the 13th of December of that year the Popmunnett (an old whaler) sailed from there on a whaling voyage to the Gallipagos Islands and coasts of Peru and Chili. The bark Sarah soon followed her on a sperm whaling voyage, intending to obtain a cargo and carry it to the Eastern States. In 1855, two stock companies were formed at Monterey and Crescent City for the prosecution of shore whaling. Boats were kept in constant readiness to put out in chase when a school of whales appeared. Quite a successful business was pursued in this way.

In January, 1858, the freighter, John Gilpin, with a large cargo of oil, was wrecked and sunk off Cape Horn. On the 1st of January, 1861, the Congress, of New Bedford, while cruising between Cape Leurwin and Bull Head, picked up a cask of oil, covered with barnacles, a relic of the wreck of the John Gilpin. In three years this cask had drifted east by north 7,780 miles. In February of the same year, 150 miles from New Holland, two other casks from the same cargo were picked up, having, in their three years of wandering, drifted from longitude 70° west to longitude 111° 15′ east.

the fleet to suffer from the depredations of such letters-of-marque as they were able to equip were three Atlantic whalers from Provincetown, the John Adams, Mermaid, and Parana, the first two schooners and the last a brig. They were captured when about 90 miles south of Balize, within the period of two hours, by the privateer Calhoun, formerly the tug-boat W. H. Webb, of New York. The vessels with their cargoes, about 215 barrels of sperm oil, were burned, and the sixty-three men composing their crews were taken to New Orleans and there left to shift for themselves.*

Several rebel privateers were soon cruising on the Atlantic whaling-grounds, and in the track of outward and homeward bound Pacific whalers. They adopted a device to ensnare their victims, which can but be severely reprobated as inhuman. Capturing a vessel they waited until night had fallen upon the scene, and then, firing her, they pounced upon the unfortunates who, obeying the natural impulses of humanity, bore down for the burning craft to save the lives they believed to be endangered. In this way several whale-ships fell victims to this atrocious device.†

Naturally, with these risks staring them in the face, the owners were in no haste to refit such of their returning vessels as evaded rebel cruisers. Ships were sold, transferred to the merchant service, or laid up to await a change in affairs. Some in the Pacific were put under the Hawaiian flag. Of those sold, forty were purchased by the United States and formed the larger portion of the two famous stone fleets, which, in 1861, were sunk off the harbors of Charleston and Savannah to prevent the entrance of blockade-runners and the ingress and escape of privateers.‡

---

* In 1861.

† Thus were captured and burned by the Alabama the ships Benjamin Tucker, Osceola, Virginia, and Elisha Dunbar, of New Bedford, Ocean of Sandwich, Alert of New London, and schooners Altamaha of Sippican and Weather Gage of Provincetown, all of whom, attracted by the burning of the Ocean Rover of Mattapoisett, hastened to rescue the shipmates whose lives they believed to be imperilled.

‡ Among these vessels were several famous China and European merchantmen. The Herald, formerly of Boston, was nearly one hundred years old. (F. C. S., in Boston Advertiser, December 20, 1871.) Another famous ship was the Corea, which was formerly an armed store-ship belonging to the English navy, and came to this country during the Revolution loaded with stores. A storm arising, she sought shelter in Long Island Sound. This fact soon became known to our Yankee fishermen, and they determined to capture her, and accordingly about a hundred of them, well armed, left New Bedford in a small vessel for that purpose. Coming within sight of the Corea all hands, except four men and a boy, were sent below, the vessel soon reached the fishing-ground, and, to all appearance, the five on deck were soon engaged in innocent piscatorial employments. The Corea ran down toward them and fired a gun, at which summons our fishermen stood for the storeship, and coming within hail were ordered alongside. Grumblingly they obeyed and were despoiled of their fish, while the Corea's crew crowded around curious to see the prize. At this juncture one of the captive fishermen threw some fish out of one of the ports upon the schooner's deck and at the signal the secreted men swarmed up from below. Before the astonished

In 1865 the privateer steamer Shenandoah entered the Pacific Ocean, and on the 26th of June she captured and burned five ships and barks in Behring's Straits.* On the 27th of June the ship Brunswick, of New Bedford, having got jammed in the ice, those of the fleet that were near went to her assistance. The wind dying away, they anchored close to each other. The next morning the Shenandoah appeared upon the scene and captured and destroyed nine of them. Among these was the bark Favorite, of Fairhaven, Capt. Thos. G. Young, a man between sixty and seventy years of age, but full of courage and determination. It was no part of his creed to see his ship (in which he was part owner) given up without a struggle, however great the odds or however hopeless the resistance. Accordingly he loaded all his bomb-guns and fire-arms and took a position on the cabin roof. As the Shenandoah's boat came alongside he ordered her officer to "stand off," an order which, when he saw the look of mischief in the captain's eye, he prudently obeyed, and lost no time in returning to his vessel to report his lack of progress. The commander of the privateer had perceived the action of the boat, and ordered a gun trained upon the whaler and that his gunner should fire low. In the mean time the officers of the Favorite, deeming resistance as worse than useless, urged Captain Young to desist, assuring him that it was only a fruitless sacrifice of his life, to which the captain replied that he would die willingly if he could but shoot Waddell, who commanded the Shenandoah. Finding remonstrance useless, the officers secretly removed the caps from the loaded arms, removed the ammunition not already in the guns, and took to the boats, leaving the heroic old captain to defend the castle, in which his entire property was invested, alone.

The gun from the Shenandoah was not discharged, as the returning boat was in range; and when it had reached the steamer Waddell had changed his mind, and ordered another boat to capture the obdurate skipper. As she came alongside, the officer in charge ordered Captain Young to haul down his colors. In language more forcible than polite

---

Englishmen could recover their senses their vessel was a prize. She was taken to New Bedford and discharged, and some years after the war she was added to the whaling fleet. The first "stone fleet" consisted of the Archer, Courier, Cossack, Frances, Henrietta, Garland, Herald, Kensington, Leonidas, L. C. Richmond, Maria Theresa, and South America of New Bedford, Amazon, Harvest, and Rebecca Sims of Fairhaven, Potomac of Nantucket, American of Edgartown, Corea, Fortune, Lewis, Phœnix, and Tenedos of New London, Meteor and Robin Hood of Mystic, and Timor of Sag Harbor. In the second fleet were the following whalers: America, Edward, India, Valparaiso, and Majestic of New Bedford, Montezuma, New England, and Dove of New London, Mechanic and William Lee of Newport, Emerald and Noble of Sag Harbor, Messenger of Salem, and Newburyport of Gloucester. Many of these had been noted ships in their prime; some of them European packets, others in the China trade, &c.

* The Isabella, Gypsey, Catharine, General Williams, and Wm. C. Nye. Those captured on the 27th were the Hillman, Isaac Howland, Nassau, Brunswick, Waverly, Martha 2d, Congress, Favorite, and Covington.

he replied, "I'll see you d——d first." "If you don't," said the officer of the boat, "I'll shoot you." "Shoot and be d——d," returned the imperturbable Young. The crew of the boat were now ordered to board the Favorite; and as the captain pulled the trigger to his gun and ineffectually endeavored to explode the charge, he saw the defenceless condition in which he had been left, and realized that he had nothing to do but to surrender. His inhuman captors, who were unable to appreciate bravery, put him in irons in the topgallant forecastle, and robbed him of his money, his watch, and even of his shirt-studs.

Capt. Ebenezer F. Nye, of the ship Abigail, of New Bedford, which ship was also captured and burned in the Ochotsk Sea by the Shenandoah in June, manned two boats before his ship was in the privateer's possession, and started for the rest of the fleet to warn them of the impending danger.

In all, the Shenandoah captured and burned thirty-four ships and barks, and captured and bonded the Milo, the General Pike, and the James Maury, of New Bedford, and the Nile, of New London.

During the war for the maintenance of our national integrity, the seaport towns responded with the utmost alacrity to the calls for men and for money. Our gallant whalemen hastened to defend the flag, and enlisted in large numbers in the Navy as more congenial with their inclinations. A large portion of the officers in this branch of our service had gathered their experience on the deck of a whaler, and tested their courage in a whale-boat; and it is safe to assert that no braver men defended and no more experienced seamen navigated those castles of oak and of iron that sustained in these later years the renown our Navy won in the war of 1812.*

The rebellion over, renewed activity took place in the whaling world. Ships that had been laid up were rigged and sent away, and new ships were again added to the fleet. The business was carried on with caution, for the inroads made upon the trade by the general use of coal-oils were becoming matters of serious consideration.

In the fall of 1871 came news of a terrible disaster to the Arctic fleet, rivaling in its extent the depredations of the rebel cruiser. Off Point Belcher thirty-four vessels lay crushed and mangled in the ice; in Honolulu were over twelve hundred seamen who by this catastrophe were shipwrecked.

Early in May the fleet arrived south of Cape Thaddeus, where they found the ice closely packed, and the wind blowing strong from the northeast.† This state of affairs continued during the most of the

* A meeting of the whaling-agents in Payta was held, at which they offered both money and personal service in support of the Union. The whalemen were at this time advised to cruise in companies.

† Harper's Weekly, December 2, 1871.

The following table, copied from the New Bedford Shipping List, will show the number of vessels in the North Pacific each year, and the rise and decline of the fishery in

month. June came in with light and variable winds and foggy weather; but the ice opening somewhat, the ships pushed through in sight of Cape Navarine, where they took five or six whales, and for a short time heard many more spouting among the ice. About the middle of June the ice opened still more, and the fleet passed on through Anadir Sea, taking a few whales as they went. By the 30th of June the vessels had passed through Behring's Straits, preceded by the whales. Waiting the further breaking up of the ice, they commenced catching walruses, but with comparatively poor success. During the latter part of July, the ice disappearing from the east shore south of Cape Lisburne, the fleet pushed on to the eastward, following the ice, the principal portion of which was in latitude 69° 10′. A clear strip of water appearing on the east shore, leading along the land to the northeast, they worked along through it to within a few miles of Icy Cape. Here some of the vessels anchored, unable to proceed farther on account of the ice lying on Blossom Shoals.

About the 6th of August the ice on the shoals started, and several ships got under way. In a few days most of the fleet was north of the shoals, and, aided by favorable weather, they worked to the northeast as far as Wainwright Inlet, eight vessels reaching there on the 7th. Here the ships either anchored or made fast to the ice, which was very heavy and densely packed, and whaling was carried on briskly for several days, and every encouragement was given for a favorable catch. On the 11th of August a sudden change of wind set the ice inshore, catching a large number of boats which were cruising for whales in the open ice, and forcing the ships to get under way to avoid being crushed. The vessels worked inshore under the lee of the ground ice, and succeeded, despite the difficulties of the situation, in saving their boats by hauling them for long distances over the ice, some of them, however, being badly stoven. On the 13th the ice grounded, leaving a narrow strip of water along the land up to Point Belcher. In this open water lay the fleet anchored or fast to the ice, waiting for the expected northeast wind that

those seas. The locality includes the water between the Asiatic and American coasts north of 50° north latitude:

Year.	No. of ships.	Average barrels.	Total barrels.	Year.	No. of ships.	Average barrels.	Total barrels.
1839	2	1, 400	2, 800	1858	196	620	121, 650
1840	3	587	1, 760	1859	176	535	94, 160
1841	20	1, 412	28, 200	1860	121	518	62, 678
1842	29	1, 627	47, 200	1861	76	724	55, 024
1843	108	1, 349	146, 800	1862	32	610	19, 525
1844	170	1, 528	259, 570	1863	42	857	36, 010
1845	263	953	250, 600	1864	68	522	35, 490
1846	292	869	253, 800	1865	59	617	36, 415
1847	177	1, 059	187, 443	1866	95	598	56, 925
1848	159	1, 164	185, 256	1867	90	640	57, 620
1849	155	1, 334	206, 850	1868	61	708	43, 230
1850	144	1, 692	243, 648	1869	43	890	38, 275
1851	138	626	86, 360	1870	46	1, 069	49, 205
1852	278	1, 343	373, 450	1871	40	....	15, 000
1853	238	912	217, 056	1872	27	729	19, 680
1854	232	794	184, 063	1873	29	665	19, 300
1855	217	873	189, 579	1874	22	915	20, 120
1856	178	822	146, 410	1875	16	1, 374	21, 980
1857	143	796½	113, 900	1876	8	656	5, 250

was to relieve them of their icy barrier, whaling constantly being carried on by the boats, though necessarily under many adversities.

On the 15th of August the wind came around to the westward, driving the ice still closer to the shore and compelling the vessels to work close in to the land. The drift of the ice inland was so rapid that some of the vessels were compelled to slip their cables, there being no time to weigh anchor. By this event the fleet was driven into a narrow strip of water not over half a mile in width at its widest part. Here, scattered along the coast for 20 miles, they lay, the water from 14 to 24 feet deep, and ice as far as the lookouts at the mastheads could see. Whaling was still carried on with the boats off Sea-Horse Island and Point Franklin, although the men were obliged to cut up the whales on the ice and tow the blubber to the ships.

On the 25th a strong northeast gale set in and drove the ice to a distance of from four to eight miles off shore, and renewed attention was given to the pursuit of the whale. Up to this time no immediate danger had been anticipated by the captains beyond that incidental to their usual sojourn in these seas. The Esquimaux, nevertheless, with the utmost friendliness, advised them to get away with all possible speed as the sea would not again open, but this was contrary to the Arctic experience of the whalemen, and they resolved to hold their position.

On the 29th began the series of conflicting circumstances resulting in the destruction of the fleet. A southwest wind sprang up, light in the morning, but freshening so toward evening that the ice returned inshore with such rapidity as to catch some of the ships in the pack. The rest of the fleet retreated ahead of the ice, and anchored in from three to four fathoms of water, the ice still coming in and small ice packing around them. The heavy floe-ice grounded in shoal-water and between it and the shore lay the ships, with scarcely room to swing at their anchors.

On the 2d of September the big Comet was caught by the heavy ice and completely crushed, her crew barely making their escape to the other vessels. She was pinched until her timbers all snapped and the stern was forced out, and hung suspended for three or four days, being in the mean time thoroughly wrecked by the other vessels; then the ice relaxed its iron grip and she sunk. Still our hardy whalemen hoped that the looked-for northeasterly gale would come, and felt greater uneasiness on account of the loss of time than because of their present peril. Their experience could not point to the time when the favoring gale had failed to assure their egress. Nothing but ice was visible offshore, however, the only clear water being where they lay, and that narrowed to a strip from 200 yards to half a mile in width, and extending from Point Belcher to two or three miles south of Wainright Inlet. The southeast and southwest winds still continued, light from the former and fresh from the latter direction, and every day the ice packed more and more closely around the doomed vessels.

On the 7th of September the bark Roman, while cutting-in a whale, was caught between two immense floes of ice off Sea-Horse Islands, whence she had helplessly drifted, and crushed to atoms, the officers and crew escaping over the ice, saving scarcely anything but their lives.

The next day beheld the bark Awashonks meet a similar fate, and a third fugitive crew was distributed among the remaining ships. The peril was now apparent to all; the season was rapidly approaching the end; the ice showed no signs of starting, but on the contrary the little clear water that remained was rapidly filling with ice and closing around them. Frequent and serious were the consultations held by the captains of the beleagured vessels. One thing at least was evident without discussion; if the vessels could not be extricated the crews must be got away before winter set in, or the scanty stock of provisions they had could only postpone an inevitable starvation. As a precautionary measure, pending a decision on the best course to adopt, men were set to work to build up the boats, that is, to raise the gunwales so as to enable them the better to surmount the waves. Shoes* were also put on them to prevent, as far as possible, injury from the ice. The brig Kohola was lightened in order to get her over the bar at Wainwright Inlet, upon which there were only 5 or 6 feet of water. Her oil and stores were transferred to the deck of the Charlotte, of San Francisco, but when discharged it was found that she still drew 9 feet of water, and the attempt to get her over the shoal water was abandoned.† An expedition of three boats, under the command of Capt. D. R. Frazer, was now sent down the coast to ascertain how far the ice extended; what chances there were of getting through the barrier; what vessels, if any, were outside, and what relief could be relied upon. Captain Frazer returned on the 12th, and reported that it was utterly impracticable to get any of the main body of the fleet out; that the Arctic and another vessel were in clear water below the field, which extended to the south of Blossom Shoals, 80 miles from the imprisoned crafts; and that five more vessels, then fast in the lower edge of the ice, were likely to get out soon. He also reported, what every man then probably took for granted, that these free vessels would lay by to aid their distressed comrades. It is a part of the whaleman's creed to stand by his mates. On hearing this reported, it was decided to abandon the fleet and make the best of their way, while they could, to the rescuing vessels. It was merely a question whether they should leave their ships and save their lives, or stand by their ships and perish with them.

The morning of the 14th of September came, and a sad day it was to the crews of the ice-bound crafts. At noon the signals, flags at the mast-heads, union down, were set, which told them the time had come

* A sheathing—in this case copper—being used.

† The same experiment, with the same result, was tried by Captain Redfield, of the brig Victoria. The Kohola and Victoria are rated as barks in a succeeeding page.

when they must sever themselves from their vessels.* As a stricken family feels when the devouring flames destroy the home which was their shelter, and with it the little souvenirs and priceless memorials which had been so carefully collected and so earnestly treasured, so feels the mariner when compelled to tear himself from the ship which seems to him at once parent, friend, and shelter. In these vessels lay the result of all the toil and danger encountered by them since leaving home. Their chests contained those little tokens received from or reserved for friends thousands of miles away, and nothing could be taken with them save certain prescribed and indispensable articles. With heavy hearts they entered their boats and pulled away, a mournful, almost funereal, flotilla, toward where the vessels lay that were to prove their salvation. Tender women and children were there who, by their presence, sought to relieve the tedium of a long voyage to their husbands and fathers, and the cold north wind blew pitilessly over the frozen sea, chilling to the marrow the unfortunate fugitives.

The first night out the wanderers encamped on the beach behind the sand hills. A scanty supply of fire-wood they had with them and such drift-wood as they could collect sufficed to make a fire to protect them somewhat from the chilling frost. The sailors dragged boats over the hills, and by turning them bottom upward and covering them with

---

*The following protest was written on the 12th of September, and signed by all the captains on the following day before abandoning their vessels:

"POINT BELCHER, *Arctic Ocean, Sept.* 12, 1871.

"Know all men by these presents, that we, the undersigned, masters of whale-ships now lying at Point Belcher, after holding a meeting concerning our dreadful situation, have all come to the conclusion that our ships cannot be got out this year, and there being no harbor that we can get our vessels into, and not having provisions enough to feed our crews to exceed three months, and being in a barren country, where there is neither food nor fuel to be obtained, we feel ourselves under the painful necessity of abandoning our vessels, and trying to work our way south with our boats, and, if possible, get on board of ships that are south of the ice. We think it would not be prudent to leave a single soul to look after our vessels, as the first westerly gale will crowd the ice ashore, and either crush the ships or drive them high upon the beach. Three of the fleet have already been crushed, and two are now lying hove out, which have been crushed by the ice, and are leaking badly. We have now five wrecked crews distributed among us. We have barely room to swing at anchor between the pack of ice and the beach, and we are lying in three fathoms of water. Should we be cast on the beach it would be at least eleven months before we could look for assistance, and in all probability nine out of ten would die of starvation or scurvy before the opening of spring.

"Therefore, we have arrived at these conclusions: After the return of our expedition under command of Capt. D. R. Frazer, of the Florida, he having with whale-boats worked to the southward as far as Blossom Shoals, and found that the ice pressed ashore the entire distance from our position to the shoals, leaving in several places only sufficient water for our boats to pass through, and this liable at any moment to be frozen over during the twenty-four hours, which would cut off our retreat, even by the boats, as Captain Frazer had to work through a considerable quantity of young ice during his expedition, which cut up his boats badly."

(Signed by the masters.)

sails, made quite comfortable habitations for the women and children. The rest made themselves comfortable as best they could.

"On the second day out," says Captain Preble, "the boats reached Blossom Shoals, and there spied the refuge-vessels lying five miles out from shore, and behind a tongue of ice that stretched like a great peninsula ten miles farther down the coast, and around the point of which the weary crews were obliged to pull before they could get aboard. The weather here was very bad, the wind blowing fresh from the southwest, causing a sea that threatened the little craft with annihilation. Still the hazardous journey had to be performed, and there was no time to be lost in setting about it. * * * * All submitted to this new danger with becoming cheerfulness, and the little boats started on their almost hopeless voyage, even the women and children smothering their apprehensions as best they could. On the voyage along the inside of the icy point of the peninsula everything went moderately well; but on rounding it, they encountered the full force of a tremendous southwest gale and a sea that would have made the stoutest ship tremble. In this fearful sea the whale-boats were tossed about like pieces of cork. They shipped quantities of water from every wave which struck them, requiring the utmost diligence of all hands at bailing to keep them afloat. Everybody's clothing was thoroughly saturated with the freezing brine, while all the bread and flour in the boats was completely spoiled. The strength of the gale was such that the ship Arctic, after getting her portion of the refugees on board, parted her chain-cable and lost her port anchor, but brought up again with her starboard anchor, which held until the little fleet was ready to sail."

By four o'clock in the afternoon of the second day all were distributed among the seven vessels that formed the remnant of the fleet that sailed for the Arctic Ocean the previous spring. Not a person was lost to add to the grief already felt or to increase the gloom of their situation. To the Europa was assigned 280; to the Arctic, 250; to the Progress, 221; to the Lagoda, 195; to the Daniel Webster, 113; to the Midas, 100; and to the Chance, 60: in all 1,219 souls in addition to their regular crews. On the 24th of October the larger portion of these vessels reached Honolulu, and the remaining ones of the seven speedily followed.*

* The names of the beleaguered fleet were: from New Bedford, barks Awashonks, value, $58,000; Concordia, $75,000; Contest, $40,000; Elizabeth, $60,000; Emily Morgan, $60,000; Eugenia, $56,000; Fanny, $58,000; Gay Head, $40,000; George, $40,000; Henry Taber, $52,000; John Wells, $40,000; Massachusetts, $46,000; Minerva, $50,000; Navy, $48,000; Oliver Crocker, $48,000; Seneca, $70,000; William Rotch, $43,000; ships George Howland, $43,000; Reindeer, $40,000; Roman, $60,000; Thomas Dickason, $50,000. From New London, bark J. D. Thompson, value $45,000, and ship Monticello, $45,000. From San Francisco, barks Carlotta, value $52,000; Florida, $51,000; and Victoria, $30,000. From Edgartown, ships Champion, value $40,000, and Mary, $57,000. And from Honolulu, Sandwich Islands, barks Paira Kohola, $20,000; Comet, $20,000; and Victoria 2d and ship Julian, $40,000. The Honolulu vessels had generally American owners, having been placed under the Hawaiian flag to protect them from rebel cruisers.

Capt. William H. Kelley, who commanded the Gay Head, visited the locality the

On the receipt of the news of this disaster, more particularly in New Bedford, great excitement was occasioned. The value of the wrecked vessels sailing from that port alone exceeded, with their cargoes, one million of dollars. But the owners of whaling-vessels were not the men to yield supinely to a single misfortune, however overpowering it might seem, and the ensuing year twenty-seven ships were busy in the Arctic, and in 1873 twenty-nine visited that precarious sea.

Still whaling in general continued to decline. The sun of its destiny was moving toward its western horizon. Whether some modern Joshua shall command it to stand still, or whether it shall move still nearer its full setting, is yet uncertain. Some oil will still be used until its perfect substitute is produced at so low a rate that the expenses of whaling will entirely absorb its profits.

On the 1st of January, 1877, the entire fleet was reduced to 112 ships and barks, and 51 brigs and schooners, having a total capacity of 37,828 tons.*

Before closing this chapter it would be well to see to what causes this decline is attributable. Many circumstances have operated to bring this about. The alternate stimulus and rebuff which the fishery received as a short supply and good prices led to additions to the fleet and an overstock and decline in values, were natural, and in themselves probably

---

following year, and wrote home the condition of such of the vessels as still remained. The Minerva lay at the entrance to Wainwright Inlet, as good in hull as when abandoned. The T. Dickason lay on her beam-ends on the bank, bilged and full of water The Seneca was dragged by the ice up the coast some distance; her bowsprit was gone bulwarks stove, and rudder carried away, and she was frozen in solid. The Reindeer sank, and the Florida was ashore on Sea-Horse Islands, burned to the water's edge. The rest of the fleet were either carried away by the ice, crushed to pieces, or burned by the natives. The Gay Head and Concordia were burned where they lay. "The bark Massachusetts went around Point Barrow. There was one white man on board her who staid up here last winter. He made his escape over the ice this summer, and was five days getting back to the ships. He was about used up when they found him this summer. The natives set out to kill him, but the women saved him, and afterward the old chief took care of him. He saved a large quantity of bone, but the natives took it away from him, except a small quantity. He said $150,000 would not tempt him to try another winter in the Arctic. He said that four days after we left the ships last year the water froze over and the natives walked off to the ships; and fourteen days after there came on a heavy northeast gale and drove all but the ground-ice away, (that never moved.) Shortly after there blew another northeast gale, and he said that of all the butting and smashing he ever saw, the worst was among those ships driving into each other during those gales. Some were ground to atoms, and what the ice spared the natives soon destroyed, after pillaging them of everything they pleased."

Since writing the account of the disaster of 1871, the reports have been received of another of less pecuniary extent but more appalling in its effect on human life. The fleet for 1876 consisted of twenty ships and barks. Of these, twelve are reported lost or abandoned in the Arctic. Much of the melancholy story seems a duplicate description of that of 1871. Again the fleet had entered that fatal ocean early in August, and again commenced the season's whaling with prospect of fair success; again the ice com-

---

* The lowest ebb was reached on the 1st of January, 1875, when the fleet consisted of 119 ships and barks, and 44 brigs and schooners, with a capacity of 37,733 tons.

formed no positive impediment. The increase in population would have caused an increase in consumption beyond the power of the fishery to supply, for even at the necessarily high prices people would have had light. But other things occurred. The expense of procuring oil was yearly increasing when the oil-wells of Pennsylvania were opened, and a source of illumination opened at once plentiful, cheap, and good. Its dangerous qualities at first greatly checked its general use, but, these removed, it entered into active, relentless competition with whale-oil, and it proved the more powerful of the antagonistic forces.

The length of voyages increased from two years for a cargo of sperm and from nine to fifteen months for a cargo of whale oil to four years to fill with the latter, while the former was practically abandoned as a separate business * after it became necessary to make voyages of four, five, and even six years, and then seldom return with a full cargo. As a matter of necessity the fitting of ships became far more expensive,†

menced closing around them; again they cherished delusive hopes that a strong gale would drive it off-shore and afford them a means of escape, and again these hopes were doomed to a bitter disappointment. Again the masters decided it was necessary to abandon their vessels, and again the abandonment was accomplished. Here the parallel ceases. Several men perished from exposure in journeying from one beleaguered vessel to another apparently more safe, and many died on the toilsome, perilous march and voyage to the rescuing ships. Many more preferred to stay by the ships and risk their chances of surviving during the terrible Arctic winter to assuming the nearer and, to them, apparently no less dangerous alternative of an immediate escape. These men are still there, and there seems no feasible way to communicate with them until the summer of 1877. Judging by the experience of Arctic navigators and by the condition of several of the former abandoned fleet when found in the ensuing season, their chance for a comfortable survival seems good, unless attacked by the avaricious natives. Provisions and fuel are reported amply sufficient for them, and with the first clear water of 1877 ready hands and willing hearts will hasten to their assistance. Fifty-three men remained, and three hundred made their escape. The names of the lost and abandoned vessels with their approximate values, not including cargoes, are as follows: (Of these the Arctic is reported lost; the others abandoned.) From New Bedford, the Acors Barns, $36,000; Camilla, $36,000; Cornelius Howland, $40,000; James Allen, $36,000; Java 2d, $26,000; Josephine, $40,000; Marengo, $40,000; Mount Wollaston, $32,000; Onward, $40,000; and St. George, $36,000. From San Francisco, the Clara Bell, $24,000. And from Honolulu, the Arctic, $32,000, and Desmond, $24,000. A total loss of $442,000. The estimated value of reported cargoes is about $375,000 more.

* Always excepting, of course, Atlantic whalers. Sperm-whaling in the Atlantic has always been pursued by the bulk of the Provincetown vessels and by quite a fleet of schooners and brigs from other ports. There is an occasional revival of this pursuit in larger vessels at intervals of a few years, at present some of the most successful voyages being made by ships and barks cruising for sperm whales in this ocean.

† The cost of fitting of late years has grown out of all proportion to the value of the return. Thus, in 1790, a ship carrying 1,900 barrels of oil would be fitted for a two-years' sperm whaling voyage to the Pacific Ocean for $12,000, while in 1858, with a doubled capacity, the length of the average voyage was more than doubled, and the cost of fitting had increased to about $65,000. But few people have an idea of the amount and variety of occupations to which the fitter-out of a whale-ship pays tribute. In 1765 the schooner Lydia, of Edgartown, Capt. Peter Pease, used the following articles in fitting for her whaling-cruise: 5 barrels beef, 6 barrels pork, 1,200 pounds bread, 60 pounds butter, 3 small cheeses, 500 pump-nails, 2 wine-glasses, 600 board-nails, 1,500 shingle-nails, 24 deck-nails, 30 spikes, 1 mallet, 1 dipsy-line, 2 scrapers, 1 adze, 2

a rivalry in the furnishing adding perhaps considerably to the outlay. Vessels were obliged to refit each season at the various islands in the Pacific, usually at the port of Honolulu when passing in its vicinity, and the bills drawn upon the owners on these occasions were so enor-

---

axes, 5 spades, 1 tunnel, 4 barrels flour, 12 bushels corn, 14 bushels meal, 100 pounds rice, 2 barrels rum, 55 gallons molasses, 20 pounds candles, 314 feet boards, 230 feet boat-boards, 600 fathoms tow-line, 130 fathoms main-warp, 28 guns, 12 lances, 3 cod-lines, 2 log-lines, 6 gimlets, 3 skeins twine, 6 bowls, 6 knives and forks, 6 plates, 4 pounds tea, 5 pounds chocolate, 15 pounds coffee, 100 pounds sugar, 50 pounds hog's-fat, 5 bushels beans, 1 platter, 2 brooms, 2 hour-glasses, 1 lantern, 50 pounds spun yarn, 4 pump-bolts, 3 pump-brakes, 6 upper boxes, 4 lower boxes, 1 pump-hook, 1 draw-bucket, 2 cedar pails, 1 hand-pump, 2 finishing-planes, 1 pound pepper, 1 speaking-trumpet, 2 half-minute glasses, 1 punch-bowl, 6 tea-cups and saucers, 1½ pounds powder and shot, 1 drawingknife, 1 candlestick, 3 skeins marling, 3 skeins housing, 8 spare blocks, 1 cat-block, 40 fathoms spare rigging, 1 sounding-lead, 1 boat-hook, 12 sail-needles, 18 yards mending-cloth, 1 penknife, 1 jackknife, 10 pounds chalk, 1 bung-borer, 3 chisels, 1 handsaw, 1 large hammer, 1 pump-hammer.

The ship Beaver, of Nantucket, which sailed for a Pacific sperm whaling voyage in 1791, cost, with her outfit, $10,212. She was a ship of 240 tons, carried 17 men, and required in outfitting, among other articles, 400 iron-hooped casks (this was before iron came into general use for this purpose, and the remainder of her casks, to the capacity of 1,400 barrels, were wooden-hooped), 40 barrels of salt provisions, 3½ tons bread, 30 bushels beans and peas, 1,000 pounds of rice, 40 gallons molasses, 24 barrels of flour. All the additional provisions used were 200 pounds of bread. She made a seventeen-months' voyage.—(Macy.)

The whaling-fleet in 1831 consisted of about 290 ships and barks, (170 sperm and 120 right whalers.) This fleet required in outfitting, among other things, 36,000 barrels of flour, 30,000 barrels of beef and pork, 18,000 bolts of duck, 3,000 tons of hoop-iron, 6,000,000 staves, 2,000 tons cordage, besides large quantities of iron, (for harpoons, lances, spades, blubber-hooks, and camboose-grates,) molasses, rice, beans, peas, corn, tea, coffee, sugar, &c. The annual consumption of copper amounted to 700,000 pounds.

It has been said, and probably with a very great degree of truth, that the "whaling-fleet made Honolulu," and when one considers for how many years large fleets of whalemen (formerly English, French, and American, but latterly exclusively from the latter country,) rendezvoused there, the known prodigality of the sailor, and the increasingly heavy bills for refitting, of all of which Honolulu reaped the benefit, it is easy to believe the statement. Several merchants removed thence also from the United States and purchased and fitted whaling-vessels from that port, the first whaler belonging to Honolulu being fitted in 1832 by Henry A. Pierce, of New Bedford.

The principal articles used in fitting out the whaling-fleet sailing from New Bedford alone in 1858, 65 ships, amounted in gross to $1,950,000, and included 13,650 barrels flour, 260 of meal, 10,400 of beef, 7,150 of pork, 19,500 bushels of salt, 97,500 gallons molasses, 39,000 pounds rice, 1,300 bushels beans, 39,000 pounds dried apples, 78,000 of sugar, 78,000 of butter, 19,500 of cheese, 16,300 of ham, 32,500 of cod-fish, 18,000 of coffee, 14,300 of tea, 13,300 of raisins, 1,950 bushels corn, 2,600 of potatoes, 1,300 of onions, 400 barrels vinegar, 2,000 pounds sperm-candles, 32,500 barrels fresh water, 1,200 cords oak wood, 260 of pine, 1,000,000 staves, 260,000 feet heading, 1,000 tons iron hoops, 33,000 pounds rivets, 520,000 pounds sheathing-copper and yellow-metal, 15,000 of sheath-nails, 52,000 of coppering nails, 400 barrels tar, 739,000 pounds cordage, 450 whale-boats, 32,500 feet boat-boards, 65,000 feet pine boards, 36,000 feet oars, 8,500 iron poles, 22,500 pounds flags, 23,000 bricks, 200 casks lime, 205,000 yards canvas, 13,000 pounds cotton-twine, 234,000 yards assorted cotton-cloth, 130,000 pounds tobacco, 39,000 gallons white lead, 5,200 pounds linseed-oil, 400 gallons turpentine, 13,000 pounds paints, 2,600 gallons new rum, 1,000 gallons other liquors, 120 casks powder, besides clothing, &c. The advance-wages alone amounted to $130,000.

mous as to call forth loud and frequent complaints;* and in later years the only available western fishery was in the North Pacific and Arctic Oceans, where disasters were the rule and immunity from them the exception, thereby incurring, when the vessels were not lost, heavy bills for repairs, besides the ordinary ones of refitting.

Again, during the later days of whaling, more particularly immediately after the discovery of the gold mines in California, desertions from the ships were numerous and often causeless, generally in such numbers as to seriously cripple the efficiency of the ship. In this way large numbers of voyages were broken up and hundreds of thousands of dollars were sunk by the owners. During a portion of the time many ships were fired by their refractory and mutinous crews, some of them completely destroyed, others damaged in amounts varying from a few hundred to several thousand dollars. Crews would apparently ship simply as a cheap manner of reaching the gold mines, and a ship's company often embraced among its number desperadoes from various nations, fit for any rascality which might best serve them to attain their end. They took no interest in the voyage, nor cared aught for the profit or loss that might accrue to the owners. In order to recruit, it became necessary, particularly during the ten years next succeeding the opening of the gold mines, to offer heavy advance-wages, and too often these were paid to a set of bounty-jumpers, as such men were termed in the Army during the late war, who only waited the time when the ship made another port to clandestinely dissolve connection with her and hold themselves in readiness for the next ship. Unquestionably there were times when men were forced to desert to save their lives from the impositions and severity of brutal captains, but such cases were undoubtedly very rare. Formerly the crews were composed almost wholly of Americans, but latterly they were largely made up of Portuguese shipped at the Azores, a mongrel set shipped anywhere along the western coast of South America, and Kanakas shipped at the Pacific islands. There were times, when the California fever was at its highest, that the desertions did not stop with the men, but officers and even captains seem to vie with the crew in defrauding the men from whose hands they had received the property to hold in charge and increase in value.

Another source of loss was, strangely enough, to be found in the

* The increased cost of refitting has for years been a source of serious concern to ship-owners. A meeting of agents was held in New Bedford, in February, 1860, to take some action in regard to this evil. Among the things complained of, besides the enormous charges, were the extortions of consuls, the decisions of the courts of admiralty, the inducements offered to sailors to desert, &c. The New London Star, in 1859, said that in order to make whaling profitable business must be done where the vessel is owned, not one-fourth in New London and three-fourths in Honolulu; however poorly a ship did in the aggregate, Honolulu fared just as well. "All the business must be done in the home port to make it profitable, and the sooner whaling-merchants withdraw their ships from the Sandwich Islands the better it will be for all concerned. The deluge of oil that is thrown into the eastern market by holding it at the islands until some freighter wants a cargo, and then sending it home, operates with great detriment to the holders of oil at the home ports."

course of the consular agents sent out by our Government to protect the interests of our whalemen. Many and bitter were the complaints at the extortionate charges and percentages demanded by many of these men.*

As another important source of the decline in this business must be regarded the scarcity and shyness of whales. Prior to the year 1830, a ship with a capacity for 2,000 barrels would cruise in the Pacific Ocean and return in two years with a cargo of sperm-oil. The same ship might go to Delago or Woolwich Bay and fill with whale-oil in about fifteen months, or to the coast of Brazil and return in nine months full of the oil peculiar to the whales of those seas; but, as has been previously remarked, this has all changed, and the length of the voyage has become entirely disproportioned to the quantity of oil returned.

Briefly, then, this is the case. Whaling as a business has declined; 1st, from the scarcity and shyness of whales, requiring longer and more expensive voyages; 2d, extravagance in fitting out and in refitting; 3d, the character of the men engaged; 4th, the introduction of coal-oils.

Of late years sperm whaling in the Atlantic Ocean has been revived with some success, but the persistency with which any field is followed up, makes its yield at least but temporary. It may perhaps be a question worthy of serious consideration whether it is policy for the United States Government to introduce the use of coal-oils into its light-house and similar departments, to replace the sperm-oil now furnished from our whaling ports, and thus still further hasten the ultimate abandonment of a pursuit upon the resources of which it draws so heavily in the day of its trouble,† or whether this market—the only aid asked from the Government—may still continue at the expense of a few dollars more per year.

* In many cases justice (?) seems to have been meted more in accordance with the requirements of the income of our representatives than with those of abstract right, and it has happened that the case of an arbitrary, cruel captain against some unfortunately weak and impecunious sailor has been decided on the time-honored (among barbarians) maxims that "might makes right," and "the king can do no wrong."

† The London Mercantile Gazette, of October 22, 1852, said: "The number of American ships engaged in the Southern whale-fishery alone would of themselves be nearly sufficient to man any ordinary fleet of ships-of-war which that country might require to send to sea." Instances are not wanting, indeed, where whalemen have undertaken yeoman's service for their country. Thus, in November, 1846, Captain Simmons, of the Magnolia, and Capt. John S. Barker, of the Edward, both of New Bedford, hearing that the garrison at San José, Lower California, was in imminent danger, landed their crews and marched to its relief. Nor were their good services toward foreign governments in peace less honorable to the country than in war, for when the government buildings at Honolulu were burning some years ago, and entire and disastrous destruction threatened, American whalemen rushed to the rescue and quenched the flames already beyond the control of the natives. During the rebellion, of 5,956 naval officers, Massachusetts furnished 1,226, Maine 449, Connecticut 264, New Hampshire 175, Rhode Island 102, and Vermont 81.

F.—THE DANGERS OF THE WHALE-FISHERY.

Notwithstanding the many perils encountered in this pursuit, perils arising from the necessary exploration of new fields to replenish the supply which constantly fails in the old, perils arising from the nature of the cruising-grounds themselves which include the stormiest, most labyrinthine, and most treacherous of seas, and those most subject to typhoons, perils arising too from the very nature of their calling to the men themselves, the casualties are no more at least than fall to the lot of those who follow the sea in other pursuits. Shipwrecks there are, dreary boat-voyages for hundreds of miles, with the terrible accompaniments of death from hunger and thirst, and men fall victims to the strength and ferocity of the gigantic object of their pursuit. Ships sail from port and are never heard of more, or if heard of, it is the casual report of some passing vessel, ships to which the beautiful language of Irving is most appropriate, that have too truly "gone down amidst the roar of the tempest; their bones lie whitening among the caverns of the deep. Silence, oblivion, like the waves, have closed over them and no one can tell the story of their end." But with a greater risk there seems to be no greater mortality than may be found in the lists of the merchant service.

No nobler class of men, no more skillful navigators, ever trod any deck than those who have shipped upon our whalemen. Those in command are brave and daring without recklessness, quick to act in an emergency, but prudently guarding the lives of their men and the safety of their ship; self-reliant but self-possessed.* Every ship is fully manned, and discipline is intended to be fully enforced; hence when immediate action is required by the exigencies of the storm or other threatening circumstances, there is no lack of ready hands to execute any order which may issue from those in authority.†

It is appropriate, however, in a work of this nature, to notice some of the many incidents and accidents which have occurred, and of which an account has been transmitted.

Classifying these somewhat chronologically, one of the earliest re-

* "The highest testimony to the seamanship of our whalemen is that the rate of insurance on the American is just one-half of that on the British vessels engaged in the service."—(Nimrod of the Sea, p. 56.)

† Says the New York Journal of Commerce, in August, 1857: "There lives in affluence at Nantucket, in the eightieth year of his age, and in full possession of a sound intellect, and the enjoyment of all the respect and affection which a well-spent life commands, a retired whaling captain, the keel of whose ship never touched the bottom—who was never at sea a day without going aloft except in a gale of wind—who never lost a man by abandonment or otherwise, or had one off duty more than a week by sickness—who never lost but one spar, though distinguished for many short passages—who never returned from a voyage without a full cargo of sperm-oil. He had sixteen apprentices, mostly uneducated boys from the lower walks of life, whom he instructed and trained to his own calling, and every one of these he has lived to see in respectable standing, and several of them holding high rank as shipmasters."

corded accidents (not previously mentioned in this work) was the one which befel the ship Union, of Nantucket, Capt. Edmund Gardner, master, which sailed from Nantucket on the 19th of September, 1807, for Brazil Banks. When twelve days out, running along at the rate of about seven miles an hour, she struck on a sperm whale with sufficient force to break two timbers on the starboard bow.* The pumps were immediately manned, but the water came in through the break so rapidly that it became evident that the certain destruction of the ship was only being briefly postponed, and preparations were made by Captain Gardner, who was a young man and this his first voyage as commander, to leave her. The boats were lowered, and provisions, water, fireworks, books, and nautical instruments, whatever, in fact, they could safely carry, and which would be of use, were stowed away in them. By midnight—only two brief hours after the accident—the water was up between decks, and an immediate departure was inevitable. This was accomplished, though with much difficulty and danger, as a heavy swell was running. The crew, sixteen in number, left the ship in three boats, but the increased risk of separation led them to divide themselves between two boats and abandon the third. The course of the prevailing wind, which was northwest, and the lateness of the season, made it imperative upon them to steer, not for Newfoundland, which was perhaps the nearest, but for one of the Azores, which was the most easily accessible land.

On the morning of the 2d of October the men rigged sails for the boats, and thus not only progressed with greater speed, but relieved themselves of the fatigue of rowing. During the nights of the 2d and 3d the wind blew a gale, and during a portion of the time they were compelled to lash the boats together and let them drift. By the 4th of October they were obliged to allowance themselves to three quarts of water and sixteen cakes for the whole company for twenty-four hours.

* Quite a number of similar instances are upon record. Marco Paulo mentions, as long ago as 1298, that many of the Chinese junks have as many as thirteen compartments in the hold "to guard against accidents which may cause the vessel to leak, such as striking a rock, or being attacked by a whale. This last circumstance is not unusual; for during the night the motion of the ship through the waves raises a foam that invites the hungry animal, which, hoping to find food, rushes violently against the hull, and often forces out a part of the bottom." Sir William Monson also says the same kind of accident happened to the ship in which he was taken prisoner off the Burlings in 1791, a week before his capture, "the ship giving stem to a whale that lay asleep on her back above the water. The accident was so strange and rare that it amazed the company, who gave a sudden shriek, thinking the ship had foundered upon a rock; but looking overboard they beheld the sea all bloody, which comforted them, conceiving it to be, as they found it was, a stem upon a whale." He also mentions the foundering of a ship from the same cause. Winthrop (ii, p. 7) says, "One of the ships, which came this summer (1640), struck upon a whale with a full gale, which put the ship a stays; the whale struck the ship on her bow, with her tail a little above water, & brake the planks and six timbers and a beam, and staved two hogsheads of vinegar." In March, 1796, the ship Harmony, of Rochester, Capt. George Blankenship, ran upon a whale off the coast of Brazil, and was stove and sunk. The crew were saved, but

When at length they landed, on the morning of October 9, on the island of Flores, their stock of water was already exhausted. They had been at sea seven days and eight nights, and in that time had rowed and sailed nearly 600 miles.*

The accidents resulting from belligerent whales are numerous and well authenticated. At times it has happened that in their rage they have attacked even ships, apparently treating the boats as beneath their notice. Two of the most remarkable instances of this kind are the attacking and sinking of the ships Essex, of Nantucket, and Ann Alexander, of New Bedford.

The former ship, under the command of Capt. George Pollard, jr., sailed from Nantucket on the 12th of August, 1819, for the Pacific Ocean. Nothing out of the ordinary course of events occurred until the 20th of November, 1819. On the morning of that day, the ship being in latitude 0° 40′ south, longitude 119° west, whales were discovered, and all three boats were lowered in pursuit, the ship being brought to the wind and lying with her maintop sail hove aback waiting the issue of the contest. The mate's boat soon struck a whale, but a blow of his tail opening a bad hole in the boat, they were obliged to cut from him, and devote their entire attention to keeping afloat. By stuffing jackets into the hole, and keeping one man constantly bailing, they were enabled to check the flow of the water and reach the ship in safety. In the mean time the captain's and second mate's boats had fastened to another whale, and the mate, heading the ship for them, set about overhauling his boat preparatory to lowering again. While doing this he

---

the vessel and cargo were lost. In March, 1855, the British schooner Waterloo was attacked and sunk by a whale in the North Sea. In 1859 the ship Herald of the Morning arrived at Hampton Roads leaking badly, having been struck by a large sperm-whale off Cape Horn. She was found to have started seven feet of her stem as far as the wood ends, and to have carried away both bobstays. The whale spouted a large quantity of blood. In 1865 the British schooner Forest Oak, on her passage from Boston to Yarmouth, N. S., struck a whale with such force as to nearly knock her foremast out. She was going at the time at the rate of seven knots an hour. In 1873 the three-masted schooner Watauga, of Washington, N. C., was wrecked on a reef off one of the West Indies. She was originally a side-wheel steamer, and was of 200 tons register. "While running along with a fine six or seven knot breeze, a sudden and heavy shock and jar was felt, and all supposed that the vessel had scudded into a sea with violence. The next moment a pair of whales were seen close alongside to leeward. One of them seemed frisky enough, and made off rapidly, but the other seemed loggy, moved with apparent difficulty, and presently disclosed a huge gash in his side, from which the blood was issuing and coloring the sea about him. The Watauga passed on, and soon lost sight of the whale, when it was discovered that the false stem was torn off, her main stem split, and the wood ends started. The bobstay had, of course, parted, and the bowsprit was adrift. * * * She was with difficulty kept free until she had made Point Peter, where temporary repairs were made to enable her to reach home. Upon her arrival at Washington she was repaired, and the damage found to exceed $700."—(Preble's Notes on Whales and Whaling.) In 1860 the steamer Eastern City, *en route* for St. John, ran into a humpback whale 60 feet long, displacing her cutwater.

* Macy, pp. 237 to 242.

observed a large sperm-whale* break water about twenty rods from the ship. After lying there a few moments he disappeared, but immediately came up again about a ship's length off, and made directly for the vessel, going at a velocity of about three miles an hour, and the Essex advancing at about the same rate of speed. Scarcely had the mate ordered the boy at the helm to put it hard up, when the whale with a greatly accelerated speed struck the ship with his head just forward of the fore-chains. "The ship," says the mate, from whose account this is condensed, "brought up as suddenly and violently as if she had struck a rock, and trembled for a few seconds like a leaf." The whale passed under the vessel, scraping her keel as he went, came up on the leeward side of her, and lay on the surface of the water, apparently stunned, for about a moment; he then started suddenly off to leeward. Mr. Chase immediately had the pumps rigged and set going. At this time the vessel was beginning to settle at the head, and the whale, about 100 yards off, was thrashing the water violently with his tail, and opening and closing his jaws with great fury. Signals had been set for the return of the other boats, for the ship had already settled quite rapidly, and Mr. Chase had given her up as lost. "I, however," writes he, "ordered the pumps to be kept constantly going, and endeavored to collect my thoughts for the occasion. I turned to the boats, two of which we then had with the ship, with an intention of clearing them away, and getting all things ready to embark in them, if there should be no other resource left; and while my attention was thus engaged for a moment, I was aroused with the cry of a man at the hatchway, 'Here he is—he is making for us again.' I turned around and saw him about 100 rods directly ahead of us, coming down apparently with twice his ordinary speed, and to me at that moment it appeared with tenfold fury and vengeance in his aspect." A line of foam about a rod in width, made with his tail, which he continually thrashed from side to side, marked his oncoming. Mr. Chase hoped, by putting the helm hard up, the vessel might cross the line of the whale's approach, and the second shock be avoided, and instantly gave orders to that effect; but scarcely had the course of the ship, already somewhat waterlogged probably, been changed a single point, when the head of the whale crashed into her bows, staving them completely in directly under the cat-head. The speed of the whale at this time was about six miles an hour, the Essex moving at about one-half of that rate. After the second assault the whale passed under the ship as before, and out of sight to the leeward.

Whatever was to be done now, must be done with the utmost despatch. They were in mid ocean, more than a thousand miles from the nearest land, their ship rapidly settling beneath them, and nothing to save them but frail open boats, each of which must of necessity be heavily loaded. The lashings of the spare boat were cut, and she was

* In the account given by the mate, Mr. Owen Chase, the length of this whale is estimated at about 85 feet, (p. 26.)

carried from the quarter-deck to the waist; two quadrants, two practical navigators, and the captain's and mate's trunks had been hurriedly secured from below by the steward; and the mate had saved the two binnacle compasses. Then, as the ship fell over on her beam-ends, the boat, into which these articles had been placed, was launched. Not more than ten minutes had elapsed since the whale had first attacked the ship, and now she lay full of water, her deck scarcely above the surface of the waves, and her crew abroad on the ocean. As the captain and second mate came up in their boats, their amazement and horror on seeing the condition of their late home cannot be described. By order of Captain Pollard the masts were cut away and the decks were scuttled, and about 600 pounds of bread, some 200 gallons of water, a musket, a small canister of powder, two files, two rasps, two pounds of boat nails, and some turtle were secured. Each boat was fitted with two masts, and a flying-jib and two sprit-sails constructed for each out of the lighter canvas of the ship. The boats were also strengthened and built up about 6 inches above the gunwales as an additional measure for safety. These preparations occupied the larger portion of three days. The ship was now rapidly breaking up, and the captain called a council of the officers to determine what should be done. By an observation taken at noon on the 22d of November they found they were in latitude 0° 13′ north, longitude 120° west. The nearest land was the Marquesas Islands, next to them the Society Islands, but at this time the Pacific was but little explored, and these islands were presumably inhabited by savages than whom the very elements were more kind and hospitable. The final conclusion then was to make for the coast of Chili or Peru. The men were accordingly apportioned among the boats; the mate's boat being the weakest, having been stove several times and being old and patched, was assigned six, while the other two carried seven each. The record of the passage is full of melancholy interest, but too long for insertion here. It tells at length how, in spite of the utmost care, a portion of their miserable pittance of bread was damaged by the breaking of heavy seas into their boats; how their boats were damaged and leaking by the repeated blows of the water; how in the night of November the 28th Captain Pollard's boat was attacked by some kind of a fish and nearly wrecked; how thirst, consuming, raving thirst began its terrible assault; how on the 20th of December they landed on Ducie's Island;* how, unable to find subsistence there, they again set sail, after leaving three of their number, by their own desire, on the island, and commenced, on the 27th of December, to make the perilous voyage toward the island of Juan Fernandez, distant 2,500 miles. The sad recital tells us that on the 10th of January the second mate, Matthew P. Joy, died and was buried at sea, if indeed the simple launching of his body into the deep by his feeble, saddened companions could be called a burial; that on the night of the 12th of January the

* Latitude 24° 40′ south, longitude 124° 40′ west.

boats became separated; that one and then another of the mate's crew became enfeebled and died; that the body of the second unfortunate was dismembered, the flesh cut from his bones, and served out like that of an animal to his starving, raving comrades; that when the darkness of despair had settled upon their clouded, tottering minds the welcome cry of "A sail" was given, and the poor wrecks of humanity still surviving in the mate's boat were picked up, on the 17th of February, by the English brig Indian, Capt. William Crozier, and treated with a brotherly tenderness and humanity.

The captain's and late second mate's boats kept together until the night of the 29th of January, 1820; during the interval between the separation from the mate and this time four men had died out of the two boats, and their bodies furnished their comrades with their only food. The captain's crew became at last reduced to the alternative of drawing lots to see which should be killed to furnish sustenance to the survivors. On the 23d of February, three months from the time when they left their shattered ship, Captain Pollard and Charles Ramsdale, the sole survivors of the boat's crew, were picked up by the ship Daughin, of Nantucket, Capt. Zimri Coffin. The third boat was never heard from. The three men left on Ducie's Island were afterward rescued. The number surviving in the mate's boat was three.*

The fate of the Ann Alexander, Capt. John S. Deblois, which belonged to and sailed from New Bedford June 1, 1850, was not less sudden than that of the Essex, and had her crew been as far from helping hands as was that of the latter ship, not even so favorable a record as the melancholy one of Captain Pollard and his men would have been left of them, and the Ann Alexander would have been set down as one of those missing ships the fate of which will be forever unknown.

On the 20th of August Captain Deblois, having reached that whaling locality known as the "Off-shore Ground,"† discovered whales at about 9 o'clock in the morning. The boats were immediately lowered, and by noon the mate's boat was fast to one. The whale ran a short distance, and then turning rushed at the boat, seized it in his jaws, and in an instant had smashed it to fragments no larger than a common chair. Captain Deblois immediately hastened to the rescue, and took the mate's crew into his boat, which, this being done, contained eighteen men. In the mean time, the disaster having been observed from the ship, the waist-boat was dispatched to assist. When she arrived the crews were divided; the mate taking command of the waist and the captain continuing with his own (or the starboard) boat, and the attack was recom-

*Captain Pollard never cared to allude to the terrible privations and sufferings undergone on this occasion, and would always avoid reference to it if possible. His next voyage was as captain of the ship Two Brothers, which was lost on a coral reef in the Pacific while under his command. For many years Captain Pollard was on the night police in Nantucket, having abandoned the sea. He was employed as a deck hand on board Fulton's first steamboat on the Hudson, on some of its earliest trips.

†Latitude 5° 50′ south, longitude 102° west.

menced, the mate's boat being in the advance. No sooner had the whale perceived this demonstration than he again turned upon the mate, and before anything could be done to avoid the assault the second boat had shared the fate of the first. Again Captain Deblois picked up the swimming crew, and ordered his men to pull for the ship. The situation had become exceedingly critical, for the whale still maintained his hostile demonstrations toward the now greatly overloaded boat. They had proceeded but little distance on their return when he was discovered, with jaws widely open, in hot pursuit. Situated as they were, six or seven miles from their ship, with an enraged whale in pursuit, and no rescuing boat at hand, destruction seemed inevitable, but, to their surprise and joy, the monster passed without harming them, and they soon regained their vessel. Again on board, a spare boat was sent to pick up the oars of the demolished ones, and on her return the attack was renewed upon the cetacean from the ship. As she passed him a lance was thrown into his head. This but served to still more infuriate him, and he again resumed the offensive, making for the ship. As he came near, the vessel was hauled on the wind, and the whale allowed to go past, after which Captain Deblois again advanced his ship to the attack, but when within about fifty rods of the whale it was discovered that he had settled some distance below the surface of the water. It being about sundown, the attack, so far as the sailors were concerned, was given up. Not so, however, with the whale.

Captain Deblois had been standing on the knight-heads, iron in hand, ready to strike when the ship had got near enough, the vessel moving through the water at the rate of five knots per hour. Before time enough had elapsed for him to change his position he discovered the monster rushing toward the ship at a speed of fifteen knots, and in an instant he struck her a terrible blow about two feet from the keel and just abreast of the foremast, shaking her with as much violence as though she had struck a rock, and breaking a large hole through her bottom, through which the water poured in a rushing stream. As soon as the extent of the damage was discovered by Captain Deblois, he ordered the anchors cut away and the cables got overboard, that the ship might be lightened as much as possible. One anchor and cable was cleared, but the other chain, being made fast around the foremast, was not cast off. He also hastily secured his chronometer, sextant, and charts, though the water had invaded the cabin to a depth of three feet. The boats were cleared away, and such articles of necessity as it was possible to get were put into them. The captain made another, but ineffectual, attempt to get into the cabin, and then ordered the boats to shove off, he being the last man to leave the ship, which was already on her beam-ends, with her topgallant yards under water, and being obliged to throw himself into the water and swim to the nearest boat.

When clear of the vessel, and beyond the influence that her sudden sinking would have on the surrounding water, an examination was made of their stores, which were found to consist of but three gallons of water, not a mouthful of provisions of any kind having been saved! Their boats each contained eleven men, and such was the condition of them that it required unremitting bailing to keep them afloat.

The next morning at daylight, the vessel being still above water, the captain, who alone dared venture on board, succeeded in cutting away her masts with a hatchet. This being done, she righted. The crew then went on board, and, with the aid of their whale-spades, cut away the cable which still hung around the foremast, and when that went overboard the ship sat nearly upright. Holes were now cut in the decks, in the hope of saving some provisions, but all that could be got was five gallons of vinegar and twenty pounds of bread.

It must have been with indescribably heavy hearts that these wrecked mariners set off from the so lately gallant ship that had been for many months their home, and to which they must have become attached, as every true sailor does to his vessel. On the wide waste of waters, in boats which, at their best, are but frail shells, but which now were in poor condition, and leaking, with but twelve quarts of water, and *not one full day's stock of food*, their situation was, indeed, appalling. The terrible alternative was forced upon them, that unless a speedy rescue could be effected, the time was near at hand when the life of one or more of their number must be sacrificed that the others might survive. With what horror must they have recalled the terrible tale of the loss of the Essex, and remembered how, one by one, her crew wasted away and died, or how, when the fearful lottery of death was drawn, a miserable wreck of a man, a merely animate mass of skin and bones, yielded up his life to prolong that of his comrades!

Happily their story was to be no further the counterpart of that of Captain Pollard and his men. Steering northerly, hoping to reach a rainy latitude, and thereby prolong with water that life which they had no food to sustain, on the 22d of August they sighted a sail, signalled it, and to their indescribable joy were seen, and soon they trod the deck of the ship Nantucket, of Nantucket, Capt. Richard C. Gibbs.*

---

* The Honolulu Friend, dated May 6, 1854, reports that about five months after this disaster, this pugnacious whale was taken by the Rebecca Simms, of New Bedford. Two of the Ann Alexander's harpoons were found in him, and his head had sustained serious injuries, pieces of the ships's timbers being embedded in it. Disease had robbed him of his propensity to resist attack or of any further "carrying of the war into Africa." He yielded to his captors from 70 to 80 barrels of oil. Among other cases of the attack by whales upon a ship may be mentioned one where the Pocahontas of Holmes's Hole was assailed. Two boats had been lowerd, and one had fastened to a whale. In attempting to lance the whale, he turned upon the boat and crushed it to atoms. The other boat picked up the crew and returned to the vessel, which was run down toward the victor in the previous contest. When within two boat's length, the whale turned upon the ship, striking her bow with such violence as to start one or two planks and break one or two timbers on the starboard side. The Pocahontas was obliged to put into Rio Janeiro, leaking 250 strokes per hour. The merchant-ship Cuban, of and for Greenock, from Demerara, in 1857 was attacked by a whale, which struck her with such force as to completely stop

How many instances of the destruction of ships by whales the catalogue of "missing" vessels may furnish can never be known, but it may be safely presumed that some of those ships from which widows, fatherless children, and sorrowing relatives have sought for some tidings or some memento in vain, would help to swell the list. A few briet days, and had not the crew of the Ann Alexander so providentially met a rescuer, their doom must have been sealed, and their vessel would have appeared on the marine lists simply as a "missing" ship. The landsman would glance casually at the expression, and think no more of it. The mariner and the relatives and friends of those who followed the sea would read the word with a shudder as they thought of the probable sufferings, privations, and possibly horrible, lingering death the unfortunate crew might have encountered. Those to whom the word meant far more than an empty sound would think—"What sighs have been wafted after that ship! What prayers have been offered up at the deserted fireside of home! How often has the mistress, the wife, the mother pored over the daily news, to catch some casual intelligence of this rover of the deep! How has expectation darkened into anxiety,—anxiety into dread,—and dread into despair! Alas, not one memento remains for love to cherish. All that shall ever be known is, that she sailed from her port and was never heard of more."

But the pugnacity of the whale is rarely directed against the ships themselves, so rarely that when the account of the loss of the Essex reached England, some of the prominent British journals scouted the tale as preposterous. Scarcely a whaleman, however, but can tell some story of the attacking of boats by these monsters, and the attacks and parryings require on the part of those having charge of the boats the utmost nerve, adroitness and precision. A few instances of this kind it may be well to briefly mention.

In October, 1832, the ship Hector, of New Bedford, Capt. John O. Morse, then ninety days from port, "raised" a whale, and lowered for him. But while the crews were proposing offensive operations, the whale himself took the initiative, and just as the harpoon struck him he struck the mate's boat, staving it badly. By drawing sails under her and bailing, the boat was kept afloat, and the attack resumed. In the mean time Captain Morse came to his assistance, and the mate warned him of the character of his antagonist, but Captain Morse told him he had a long lance and he wanted to try it. Accordingly the Captain advanced to the whale, which immediately turned, and, taking the Cap-

her headway. As she was a ship of 500 tons, deeply laden, and running at the rate of nearly ten knots an hour, some idea can be gained of the tremendous momentum of her assailant.—(Ricketson's Hist. of New Bedford, p. 101.) The London Punch of December 6, 1851, contained a humorous description of the attack on the Ann Alexander. A similar, though not so disastrous an experience befel the Pocahontas, of Holmes's Hole, in 1850. She was attacked by a large bull sperm whale, and put into Rio Janeiro for repairs, leaking 250 strokes per hour.

tain's boat in his mouth,* held it on end and shook it in pieces in a moment. Not satisfied with this he chewed up the boat-kegs and whatever appurtenances to, or pieces of the boat came in his way. The mate now offered to pick a crew and boat, and renew the fight, to which suggestion the captain assented, and with the best and most experienced men of the crew, Mr. Norton again essayed to capture the wrecker of boats. As the mate's boat again approached, the whale again assumed the offensive, and the order was given to "stern all" for their lives. For half a mile or more the chase was continued, the crew striving, as only men in a desperate situation can strive, to keep clear of the enraged whale, which followed them so closely as several times to bring his jaws together within 6 or 8 inches of the head of the boat. By watching his chance, as the monster became exhausted and turned to spout, Mr. Norton succeeded in burying his lance in the whale's vitals, killing him almost instantly.

On cutting him in, two irons were found belonging to the ship Barclay, and it was afterward ascertained that about three months before the first mate of the Barclay had lost his life in an encounter with him. He made ninety barrels of oil. Mr. (afterward captain) Norton mentioned this as the first instance within his knowledge where a whale attacked a boat before being struck.

In 1850, Captain Cook, of the bark Parker Cook, of Provincetown, lowered two boats for a bull sperm whale. The nearest boat met him

---

* In attacking a boat the sperm whale will sometimes turn upon his back, resuming his natural position to breathe.

In 1859, Captain Pierce, of the Emerald of New Bedford, wrote home that he had had an encounter with a "digger" whale, and after nine hours of hard fighting, had killed and sunk him. They had had three boats stoven, lost five irons and seven bombs, and broken several oars in the melee, and in trying to haul the whale up, both lines had parted, and he had again gone down in forty fathoms of water.

Captain Davis thus describes the whale-boat and its fittings. (See Nimrod of the Sea, p. 157): "It is the fruit of a century's experience, and the sharpened sense and ingenuity of an inventive people, urged by the peril of the chase and the value of the prize. For lightness and form; for carrying capacity as compared with its weight and sea-going qualities; for speed and facility of movement at the word of command; for the placing of the men at the best advantage in the exercise of their power; by the nicest adaptation of the varying length of the oar, to its position in the boat; and lastly, for a simplicity of construction, which renders repairs practicable on board the ship, the whale-boat is simply as perfect as the combined skill of the million men who have risked life and limb in service could make it. This paragon of a boat is 28 feet long, sharp, and clean cut as a dolphin, bow and stern swelling amidships to 6 feet, with a bottom round and buoyant. The gunwale amidships, 22 inches above the keel, rises with an accelerated curve to 37 inches at each end, and this rise of bow and stern, with the clipper-like upper form, gives it a duck-like capacity to top the oncoming waves, so that it will dryly ride where ordinary boats would fill. The gunwales and keel, of the best timber, are her heaviest parts, and gives stiffness to the whole; the timbers, sprung to shape, are a half-inch or three-quarters in depth, and the planking is half-inch white cedar. Her thwarts are inch pine, supported by knees of greater strength than the other timbers. The bow-oar thwart is pierced by a 3-inch hole for the mast, and is double-kneed. Through the cuddy-board projects a silk-hat-shaped

head on, and, when abreast of the hump, the boat-steerer put two irons into him. Before the boat could be brought head on, the whale broached half out of water and capsized her, the line fouling the boat-steerer's leg, almost severing it from the body. With great presence of mind he cut the line, and the other boat picked up the upset crew, and returned to the bark. But the whale was not satisfied with his victory over the boat. Like his fellow-destroyers of the Essex and Ann Alexander, he aimed at a larger prey. Making for the bark, he struck her a tremendous blow, prostrating the men on deck and burying the cutwater and stern up to the planking in his head. A second time he struck the vessel, but with much less force. In the mean time Captain Cook got his bomb-lance ready and lowered another boat. Three times, within eight yards of him, the captain fired the lance into his body, and eventually made him spout blood, though with every piercing of the lance he rushed open-mouthed at the boat, requiring the utmost skill and coolness to avoid him. One hundred and three barrels of oil was

---

loggerhead, for subbing and managing the running line; the stem of the boat is deeply grooved on top, the bottom of the groove being bushed with a block of lead, or sometimes a bronze roller, and over this the line passes from the boat. Four feet of the length of the bow is covered in by a depressed box, in which the spear-line, attached to harpoons, lies in carefully adjusted coils. Immediately back of the box is a thick pine plank, in which the "clumsy cleet," or knee-brace, is cut. The gunwale is pierced at proper distances for thole-pins, of wood, and all sound of the working oars is muffled by well-thrummed mats, kept carefully greased, so that we can steal on our prey silent as the cavalry of the poor badgered Lear. The planking is carefully smoothed with sand-paper, and painted. Here we have a boat which two men may lift, and which will make ten miles an hour in dead chase by the oars alone.

"The equipment of the boat consists of a line-tub, in which are coiled 300 fathoms of hemp line, with every possible precaution against kinking in the outrun; a mast and sprit-sail; five oars; the harpoon and after-oar, 14 feet; the tub and bow-oar, 16 feet; and the midship, 18 feet long; so placed that the two shortest and one longest pull against the two 16 feet oars, which arrangement preserves the balance in the encounter, when the boat is worked by four oars, the harpoon-oar being apeak. The boat is steered by an oar 22 feet long, which works through a grummet on the stern-post. The gear of the boat consists of two live harpoons, or those in use, and two or three spare irons, *i. e.*, harpoons secured to the side of the boat above the thwarts, and two or three lances, secured by cords in like position, the sharp heads of all these being guarded by well-fitted, soft wood sheaths. The harpoon is a barbed, triangular iron, very sharp on the edges, or it is a long, narrow piece of iron, sharpened only on one end, and affixed on the shank by a rivet, so placed that before use the cutting edge is on a line with the shank, but after penetrating the whale, and on being drawn back, the movable piece drops at right angles to the shank, and forms a square *toggle* about six inches across the narrow wound caused by its entrance. The porpoise iron is preferred among the Arctic whalemen, as, owing to the softness of their blubber, the fluked iron is apt to cut its way out. The upper end of a shank, 30 inches long, terminates in a socket, into which a heavy oak or hickory sapling pole 6 feet long is introduced. A short piece of whale-line with an eye-splice at one end is then wrapped twice around the shank below the socket and close spliced. This line is stretched with great strain, and secured to the pole with a slight seizing of rope-yarn, intended to pay away and loose the pole in a long fight. The tub-line is secured to the eye of the short line, after the boat is lowered. The lance is simply an oval-headed instrument, with a cutting edge, a shank 5 or 6 feet long, and a handle as long,

the reward of the captors, who were obliged to put into Fayal for medical advice for the boat-steerer, and to repair their damaged vessel.*

Captain Davis, in his "Nimrod of the Sea,"† mentions two instances of fighting whales. The first was encountered by Captain Huntting, off the river De la Plata, and was, as is usually the case with these aquatic warriors, a bull sperm. "When the monster was struck," says Captain Davis, "he did not attempt to escape, but turned at once on the boat with his jaw, cut her in two, and continued thrashing the wreck until it was completely broken up. One of the loose boats picked up the swimmers and took them to the ship; the other two boats went on, and each planted two irons in the irate animal. This aroused him, and he turned his full fury on them, crushing in their bottoms with the jaw, and not leaving them while a promising mouthful held together. Twelve demoralized men were in the water, anxious observers of his majestic anger. Two men who could not swim had, in their terror, climbed on his back, and seated themselves astride forward of the hump, as perhaps the safest place from that terrible ivory-mounted war-club which he had brandished with such awful effect. At one time another man was clinging to the hump with his hands. The boat which had gone to the ship with the crew of the first stove boat now returned and took the swimmers on board.

The whale had now six harpoons in him, and to these were attached three tow-lines of 300 fathoms each. He manifested no disposition to escape, but sought to reduce still further the wreck about him. Boats, masts, and sails were entangled in his teeth; and if an oar or anything touched him, he struck madly at it with his jaw. This was entirely satisfactory to Captain Huntting, who was preparing other boats to renew the fight. At length two spare boats were rigged, and these, with the saved boat, put off again. The captain pulled on, but the whale saw the boat and tried his old trick of sweeping his jaw through the bottom of it. She was thrown out of his sweep, however, and the captain fired a bomb-lance, charged with six ounces of powder, which entered behind the fin and exploded in his vitals. Before the crew could get out of his way "he tore right through my boat like a hurricane, scattering all

with a light warp to recover it. A hatchet and a sharp knife are placed in the bow-box, convenient for cutting the line, and a water-keg, fire apparatus, candles, lantern, compass, and bandages for wounds, with waif-flags on poles, a fluke-spade, a boat-hook, and a "drug," or dragging float, complete the equipment of a whale-boat. Among this crowd of dangerous lines and threatening cutting gear are six pair of legs, belonging to six skilled boatmen. Such a whale-boat is ours, as she floats two miles from the ship, each man in the crew watching under the blade of his peaked oar for the rising whale, and the captain and boat-steerer standing on the highest point, carefully sweeping the horizon with trained eye, to catch the first spout, and secure the chance of 'getting on.'"

*Luckily the whale struck the Parker Cook directly on the stem. Had the blow been delivered on almost any other part of her hull, she undoubtedly would have shared the fate of the Essex and Ann Alexander.

†Pages 357–'8–'9, 385–'6–'7.

hands right and left." So said Captain Huntting. Now four boats were utterly lost, some twelve hundred fathoms of line, and all the gear. The remaining two boats were hastily and poorly provided, the men were gallied,* the sun was going down, and the captain, when he was fished out, consented to give up the day and cry beat.

All hands went to work to fit other boats. Through the night, under shortened sail, the ship lay near the scene of conflict, and while the weather was calm it was possible to keep track of the whale as he occasionally beat around. But the breaking day brought rough weather, and the captain proceeded to Buenos Ayres, as much to allow his men, who were mostly green, to run away, as for the purpose of refitting, as he knew they would be useless thereafter. In this design he was not thwarted. Most of them promptly deserted, having had enough of wrestling with "the fighting whale of the La Plata."

The second instance mentioned by Captain Davis, is the more rare case of vicious pugnacity in the right whale. The name of the captain who was the chief actor in the scenes is not given, but after premising that he is not an old man, and his residence is upon Long Island, he plunges directly into the narration thus, using the language of his informant: "My second mate had fastened to a large whale that seemed disposed to be ugly; so I pulled up and fastened to her also. I went into the bow and darted my lance, but the whale rolled so that I missed the life and struck into the shoulder-blade. It pierced so deep into the bone (perhaps through it) that I could not draw it out; the whole body of the whale shivered and squirmed as though in great pain. Then, turning a little, she cut her flukes, taking the boat amidships.† The broadside was stove in, and the boat rolled over, the crew having jumped into the sea. I cut the line in the chocks at the same moment, to save being run under with a kink. The crew were soon safely housed on the bottom of the upturned boat, or swimming and clinging to the keel. The second mate wanted to cut his line and pick us up, but I foolishly told him to hold on and kill the whale; that we were doing quite as well as could be expected. But I had bragged too soon. Just then the whale came up on the full breach, and striking the boat, he went right through it, knocking men and wreck high in the air. Next the great bulk fell over sideways, like a small avalanche, right in our midst; and spitefully cut the corners of her flukes right and left. In the surge and confusion two

* That is, frightened.

† The tail is the chief weapon of the right whale, offensively and defensively, and such is the ability with which it can wield this terrific weapon that it can sweep an arc from eye to eye clear of its foes. The sperm whale, on the contrary, relies mainly on its jaw. In the attack on these monsters, then, the tactics must be varied to avoid more particularly the flukes of the right and the equally formidable lower jaw of the spermaceti whale. Not that the opposite extremes of these brutes are by any means harmless, but they are secondary to these chief agents. When it is possible to haul alongside the running whale, the officer of the boat will sometimes with his fluke-spade succeed in "hamstringing" the brute by severing the tendons at the "small."

poor fellows went down; we saw no sign of them afterward, and the water was so dark, stained with blood, that we could not see into it.

"As the whale came feeling around with her nose, she passed close by me. I was afraid of the flukes, and got hold of the warp, or iron pole, or her small, or something, and towed a little way till she slacked speed a little. Then I dove under, so as to clear the flukes, and came up astern of them. I was in good time; for having felt the boat she turned over and threshed the spot with a number of blows in quick succession, pounding the wreck into splinters. She must have caught sight of me, for she came up on a half breach, and dropped her head on me, and drove me, half stunned, deep under water. Again I came up near the small, and again dove under the flukes. From this time she seemed to keep me in sight. Again and again—the mate told me afterward—she would run her head in the air and fall on my back, bruising and half drowning me as I was driven down in the water.

"Sometimes I caught hold of the line, or something attached to the mad brute, and would hold until a sweep of the flukes would take my long legs and break my hold. The second mate's boat had cut long ago, and watched her chance to pick up the surviving crew, but had not been able to reach me; for when the whale's eye caught the boat, she would dash for it so wickedly that the whole crew became demoralized, owing to the loss of the two men, and the sight, to them more terrible than to me perhaps, of the peril the captain was in. To husband my strength, I gave over swimming, and, treading water, I faced the danger, and several times by sinking avoided the blow from her head. As a desperate resource, I strove with my pointed sheath-knife to prick her nose;* I did all a strong man was in duty bound to do to save his life. The cooper, who was ship-keeper, ran down with the ship, intending to cut between the whale and myself, but we were at too close quarters. He was afraid to run me down lest he might tear me with the ragged copper. Thus for three-quarters of an hour that whale and I were fighting; the act of breathing became labored and painful; my head and shoulders were sore from bruises, and my legs had been pounded by his flukes; but it was not until I found myself swimming with my arms

* Says Captain Davis: "Had the right whale the habit of 'jawing back,' as the sperm whale has, it would be next to impossible to secure him by the present weapons and methods of our whalemen. * * * Read Scoresby, Jardin, and Beale, the fathers of whaling literature, and they will not reveal the secret of the weakness of the right whale. Whalemen and naturalists, they have failed to record the important fact, that on the tip of the upper jaw there is a spot of very limited extent, seemingly as sensitive in feeling as the antennæ of an insect; as keenly alive to the prick of lance or harpoon as a gentleman's nose is to the tweak of finger and thumb. However swiftly a right whale may be advancing on the boat, a slight prick on this point will arrest his forward motion at once. I think it safe to say that he will not advance a single yard after the prick is given. He will either pitch his head, and round down, like a great wheel turning on a fixed axis, or he will turn shortly to the right or left, according to the part of the nose which is pricked. Sometimes he will throw his enormous head straight in the air, and settle backward tail first, by this motion exposing his

alone and that my legs were hanging paralyzed, that I felt actually scared. Then it looked as if I couldn't hold out much longer; I had seen the ship close beside me, and the second mate's boat trying to get in to me, and throwing me lines, or something to float on, but I had failed to reach them. Now these things seemed very far off; that was the last I remembered until I came to on board the ship.

"I was afterwards told that the first mate, in answer to a signal from the ship,* had come up, and seeing me feebly paddling with my hands and not answering to his hail, he put straight into the fight. The whale saw them coming and made for them. The men sprang to their oars, and the mate had only time to seize my collar, while they pulled their best to escape from the furious whale. They thus gained time to take me into the boat, seemingly a drowned man. The mate had true pluck. Leaving me to the care of the crew on board, he put back for the whale. As he afterwards said, "She was too dangerous a cuss to run at large in that pasture-field." Watching a chance, he got a "set" on her over the shoulder-blade, and sent the red flag into the air. This tamed her; she lagged around for a time, and settled away dead. The mate then

---

whole throat to the thrust of the harpoon or lance; he may take any course, save the one directly forward. It seems almost as though this sensibility to touch was a guard against the collision of parts so important to existence with other objects, and which are beyond the line of vision. And it is also endowed with a backing power which is simply marvelous, when we consider the enormous weight moving forward with great speed. This very marked peculiarity of the right whale is constantly taken advantage of by the whaleman, who, working about its head completely out of the reach of its active flukes, parries the charge of the enraged monster as deftly as the fencer glances the thrust of his antagonist's sword. If an advancing whale glides under the boat, and the back, or 'small,' touches the keel, then, quick as the lightning flash, the responsive flukes will whip up, and send boat and crew into the air, amidst a perilous tangle of kinking line, sharp harpoons, lances, spades, hatchets, knives, and boat-gear generally. An accursed attribute of such sharp company is to travel point or edge first, and form closer acquaintance than is agreeable." (Nimrod of the Sea, p. 376.)

*Each whale-ship has a private code of signals for her absent boats to signify when to return, where to find whales, &c., so when two ships, not cruising in company, lower for whales, the men on board of one ship can recall the boats, change their course, or convey any other similar intelligence without the nature of the tidings being known to the crew of the rival vessel until it is too late to be available. Captain Preble, in his "Notes on Whales and Whaling" (No. 37), illustrates this fact by giving the following, which was the code used by Capt. Elisha Dexter, of the whaling brig William & Joseph: "Whales ahead—Down jib. Whales astern—Haul up spanker. Whales between the ship and boats—Flag half mast. Whales on the weather bow—Haul up the weather clew of the foresail. Whales on lee bow—Lee clew of foresail. More whales and a better chance—Flags on the fore-top-gallant-mast head and peak of the spanker. Whales on the weather beam—Mizzen topsail aback. Whales on the lee beam—Keep the ship off and luff her up again. Whales too near to keep off—Signal to come on board. This signal is made by standing on the top-gallant yards and holding flags in your hands." Signaling is sometimes done with the mast-head waif, which is a light pole 6 or 8 feet long, with a hoop fastened on the end and covered with canvas. (This is sometimes called a "yonder" by English whalemen.) Scammon, 230.

came on board and reported sunk whale;* and I was put to bed, a mass of bruised flesh. It was several weeks before I was able to take my place in the head of my boat again."†

In the early days of Pacific whaling, not only did our sailors have to seek and encounter their gigantic antagonist amid the dangers of hidden reefs and an unexplored and unknown ocean, but frequently, when putting into some of the numerous islands for supplies, they were compelled to fight the wily and treacherous savages inhabiting some of those groups. Many a vessel had been "cut out," and not a man survived to tell the story of the massacre. How far their brother whalemen had been instrumental in thus bringing upon their heads this vengeance for real or fancied wrongs it is difficult to determine. Beyond a question the natives in some localities, disposed to be peaceable at first, had been enraged by the thoughtless, contemptible, or villainous conduct of some of their white visitors, and upon the heads of the next unguarded comers descended the blow now aimed rather at a race than at any particular set of men. Instances are not wanting of cruel, dastardly, treacherous conduct on the part of sailors towards the inhabitants of these sunny islands, and, smarting under their wrongs, their spirit of revenge made no discriminating divisions between the innocent and the guilty; the only thing cared for was the fact that they were whites.

An instance of this dangerous element in the whaleman's life occurred to the crew of the ship Awashonks, of Falmouth, Prince Coffin master.

* Captain Davis says, (p. 238,) "A peculiar feature in right-whaling is the considerable number which sink on being killed. This rarely occurs with the sperm whale. With the hump-back it is the rule, and therefore this fishing is carried on in shallow sounds and bays. On putting the question, 'Why do right whales sink?' scarcely two men will give the same reason in reply. Captain West, when master of the Adeline Gibbs, in conversation with two Arctic whalemen, at Maui, gave the following answer: 'To lance a right whale over the shoulder-blade, directing the lance downward, will kill it in the shortest time; but he will be almost certain to sink. Such a wound will be followed by a rushing escape of air, manifesting itself in large and continuous bubbles rising through the water. When this occurs the whale is certain to sink.' Therefore, he holds to the theory that whales are furnished with a sound, or air bladder, like fish, and that through no other cause than injury to this bladder could the whale settle instantly as it does. The two captains above mentioned stated that on their last cruises one had taken nine whales, without one sinking. The other had sunk eight whales, and prided himself on the fatal thrust of his lance over the shoulder." Capt. S. P. Winegar, of the Julian, expressed himself in 1860 (see N. B. Shipping List) of a decidedly different opinion. He believed it was owing to the whales themselves and not to the manner of killing them. He further states that whales sink more often on some ground than on others, and some kinds on the same ground more than others. The right whale is more liable to sink than the bow-head, and bow-heads sink oftener in the Ochotsk than in the Arctic. He had whaled six seasons in the Arctic and never knew of whales sinking there.

† Different captains have different opinions about the captain's place. Some of the most successful say they can do better by remaining on board the ship and directing the movements of the boats; others equally fortunate prefer to be "where the battle rages" strongest.

On the 5th of October, 1835, the ship touched at Namarik Island * to recruit. The natives came on board the ship, as was usually their custom, but in no extraordinary numbers, and they manifested only the ordinary curiosity common to all these islanders in those days. At noon the captain, mate, and second mate went down to dinner, leaving the third mate, Silas Jones, in charge of the deck. Having finished, they returned, and Mr. (afterward Captain) Jones went below, coming back in about fifteen minutes. The ship's company at this time were scattered about the vessel; three of them were aloft on the lookout for whales, and one watch was below. Just after the return of Mr. Jones to the deck the attack commenced. The natives, who had, unnoticed, grouped themselves, suddenly made a rush for the whale-spades, which were in their accustomed places in the spade-rack under the spare boats. Captain Coffin was the first one to fall, being beheaded with a broad-edged spade, and almost simultaneously the man at the helm was killed. The first mate was butchered as he leaped down the fore hatch, while the second mate, who had run out on the jib-boom, was struck with some missile, and, falling, was clubbed to death by the savages. In the mean time the third mate had seized a spade, and after a struggle secured it. This he threw at a native, but, the wily savage dodging, it fastened firmly into the wood-work. Before Mr. Jones could loosen it, two natives had hold of the pole behind him. Unable to secure it, and the inequality of the conflict becoming each moment greater, Mr. Jones made a run for his life. At this time he was the only white man on deck abaft the try-works, and so closely was he beset that he was unable to escape until he reached the fore hatchway, down which he jumped. The deck was now in the possession of the natives, who proceeded to fasten down the hatches and close the companion-way so as to imprison the crew. The leader then took the wheel and headed the ship for the shore. The men who were aloft and were the horrified spectators of this butchery, feeling that their only safety lay in thwarting the plans of the savages, went as far down the rigging as they safely could and cut the braces. The yards now swinging freely the ship lost her steerage-way and slowly drifted toward open water.

During this time the third mate and the remaining survivors of the ship's company were by no means idle. Knowing that in the cabin were the ship's muskets, and realizing that it was necessary to secure them before they fell into the hands of the natives, they worked their way aft, and managed to gain possession of them unseen by their foe. From this castle they fired upon the savages wherever a mark was offered, now at the faces as they peered through the skylights, now through the cabin windows at the assembling canoes. But now a new idea occurred to the prisoners. By order of the third mate a keg of powder was got up from the run, a quantity of it was placed on the upper step of the companion-way and a train laid to the cabin. Direct-

* Latitude 5½° north, longitude 168° east. One of the Marshall group.

ing his men to be ready to rush on deck the instant the explosion had taken place, regardless of him if he was injured by it, he fired the train. The crash of the timbers and the screams and yells of the wounded and terrified savages told of the success of the plot. Rushing on deck the crew speedily drove overboard those natives who had not already found refuge there, and the terrible conflict was over. From first to last the fight occupied about an hour. The captain, mate, and second mate were killed, and four men had received fearful gashes from the murderous spades; one man died a few days afterward, the rest recovered. Mr. Jones took charge of the ship and brought her home.*

One of the most fruitful sources of peril to the whaleman is the danger of his boat being taken down by the whale through the line fouling, or of being taken out of sight from the ship in his desire to hold to his whale to the last moment. Numerous cases have occurred where a boat's crew has been lost under one or the other of these circumstances, and though occasionally in the latter case they may have recovered their own ship, or have been rescued by another, the danger arising from this cause has always been formidable. Occasionally the boat

---

*This account is gathered from that of the third mate, Captain Silas Jones, of Falmouth (who, with the characteristic modesty of whalemen, refers but little to his own actions in the struggle), and from that given by Captain Davis in the "Nimrod of the Sea." The annals of whaling afford many instances of a similar nature to this, both in the English and American South Sea fishery.

In April, 1825, the ship Oeno, of Nantucket, struck on a reef near Turtle Island, one of the Fejee group, and speedily showed signs of breaking up. The crew, twenty-one in number, took to the boats and landed upon the island, lured thither by the friendly motions of the natives, but when ashore about two weeks a tribe from a larger island visited the one upon which they were, and finding them unarmed massacred all but one of them. He escaped by hiding until they returned to their own island, and subsequently got away from the island.

In 1834, or '5, the brig Waverly, Capt. William Cathcart, of Woahoo, was cut off at Strong's Island and all on board massacred, and in 1842 the English whaler Harriet, of London, Capt. Charles Bunker, shared the same fate.

In 1842 or '3, seventeen of the crew of the whale-ship Offly, of London, were massacred by the natives of Solomon Islands, in revenge for the murder of a thief by the mate of another vessel.

In 1845 the captain, second mate, and two boats' crews of the French whaler Angeline were reported massacred at the Mulgrave Islands.

In 1847 the ship Triton, of New Bedford, put into Sydenham's Island (one of the King's Mill group), to recruit. While the captain with his boat's crew were ashore purchasing a fluke-chain, the natives, incited by a renegade Spaniard, attacked and captured the ship, killing one of the mates and several of the crew. The second mate with his men escaped in a boat. The ship worked off shore and the natives left her. She was afterwards carried into Papiete, (one of the Society Islands). The United States and Alabama, both of Nantucket, touched at the King's Mill group and succeeded in rescuing the survivors. In all, five were killed and seven wounded.

In 1852 the brig Inga was cut off at Pleasant Island, and all on board were murdered. One of the original crew, left on the island about a year before to recruit, was spared.

These are only a few of numerous instances. The crews of English ship Syren, the Boy, of Warren, R. I., the Twilight, of New Bedford, and many others suffered at the hands of the natives of the Pacific and Indian Oceans.

gains a rescuing ship or port only after intense suffering on the part of the crew. One of the most notable instances of this kind is recounted in "The Whale and his Captors"* of Captain Hosmer and his boat's crew from the bark Janet of Westport.

While off the coast of Peru, on the 23d of June, 1849, three boats were lowered for a school of sperm whales. Each boat made fast, and Captain Hosmer soon "turned up" his. In putting about to tow him to the ship the boat was capsized, and boat-keg, lantern-keg, boat-bucket, compass, paddles, &c., were lost. She was righted and the oars lashed across her to prevent another overturn, as she was full of water, and the sea continually breaking over her. Signals of distress were set, the other boats being about a mile and a half off. Captain Hosmer saw the other boats take their whales alongside the bark, which was still heading toward his own, but to his amazement, when within about a mile, she stood off on another course and continued so until the coming on of night hid her from the anxious eyes of the horror-stricken crew. They now got up alongside the whale and tried unsuccessfully to free their boat of water. Relinquishing this hope they cut from the whale, and, rigging some pieces of the boat-sail, they steered toward the vessel's light, which at intervals became visible, but in the morning the distance had apparently not lessened. They could behold their shipmates cutting in their whales, but all efforts to attract their attention were unavailing. Again they made a futile attempt to bail the water from their boat. Finding it impossible to make their situation known to their comrades and the distance between them constantly increasing, they put about before the wind. On the second morning the wind, which from the time they lowered had blown freshly, being less strong, they threw overboard their whaling craft and a third time tried to bail their boat, but they lost one of their companions without accomplishing their purpose. Again in the afternoon they essayed, and this time they were successful, but another man was sacrificed in the attempt. For forty-eight hours they had been up to their arms in water, without a morsel of food or a drop of drink, and they were suffering painfully from thirst. Two of the survivors already were delirious. The nearest known land was Cocus Island, on the coast of Peru, a thousand miles away; not a man on board was capable of handling an oar, and their only means of propulsion was a small fragment of sail.

For Cocus Island then it was determined to head, and tearing up the ceiling of the boat they fashioned from it a sort of wooden sail.

Nothing out of the ordinary course of starvation, thirst, and a rapid decline of their energies, occurred until seven days had elapsed, during which time not a morsel of food nor a drop of water had lent them strength, nor a reviving shower fallen to aid in prolonging their existence. It was now agreed to cast the terrible lot to see which of their number should die that the rest might live, and the unfortunate man

*Page 311.

upon whom the choice fell met his fate without a murmur. Toward the close of the day a shower fell.

Being without compass or other instrument to determine their course or situation Captain Hosmer was obliged to steer as best he could with such aid as was afforded by the north star and the rolling swell of the sea from the south. On the eighth day another of their number died from exhaustion, and it was deemed necessary to steer a more northerly course in hopes to again be blessed with rain.

On the ninth day another shower fell, and this blessing was followed by the remarkable circumstance of a dolphin leaping directly into their boat. Several birds also approached so near as to be killed by the wanderers, and great relief was afforded them by these happy events.

On the 13th of July, land was seen, which proved to be Cocus Island (uninhabited),* and this land the shattered remnant of a strong and hardy crew succeeded in reaching. They succeeded in catching a pig, and, drinking its blood, were reinvigorated. A plentiful supply of birds and fresh water aided their recuperation. On the second day after landing they were overjoyed to see a boat approach, which proved to belong to the Leonidas, Captain Swift, of New Bedford, a brother whaleman, then recruiting in Chatham Bay, and it is needless to say that all that could be done for the survivors was done.†

Revolts among the crew, occasioned sometimes by the brutality of the officers, and fully as often by a spirit of lawlessness in a very small minority of the men, and spreading from them like an infection to their shipmates, are at times met with. Two of the most notable of these, coming entirely within the latter category, are given.

Scarcely had the horrors of the loss of the Essex ceased to appal the minds of the people of Nantucket, when news of another and a more

---

* Latitude 5° 27′ north, longitude 87° 15′ west. Of the crew of six, but two survived.

† In a letter from the mate of the Janet to her owners he says that after his boat returned to the ship, he run down for that of the second mate, the only one then in sight from the ship. They then proceeded in the direction in which the captain's boat was last seen going, and lay to all night with all sail set and lights burning. They cruised three days, but were unable to get any trace of the captain's boat and were forced to the melancholy conclusion that it had been carried down by a foul line, more particularly as he had a new line with him coiled but two days before. (See "The Whale and His Captors.")

In January, 1860, the Massachusetts, of New Bedford, lowered four boats for a school of whales. One was killed and the mate was sent to bring the ship. She was not out of sight and the mate did not succeed in regaining her until 10 o'clock in the evening. The other three boats lay by the whale all night, and the next day, having seen nothing of the vessel, cut from him, and started for Brazil, 330 miles distant, reaching land in five days. Cheever, in "The Whale and His Captors," p. 219, instances another thrilling adventure of this kind.

"Foul lines" have been the death of many a whaleman. A kink in the line, as it runs from the tub, catches an arm, or a leg, and in an instant the unfortunate man is overboard and too often never seen again alive. On page 138 of "The Whale and His Captors" may be found an example of this form of peril.

shocking calamity was brought to the island. The most diabolical, cold-blooded mutiny ever perpetrated upon the deck of any whaleship was that on board the Globe, of Nantucket, in the month of January, 1824, and this it was that thrilled the minds of the islanders and eclipsed the terrible details of the loss of the Essex.

The Globe, Thomas Worth commander, sailed from Nantucket in the latter part of December, 1822, and when she again entered that port in November, 1824, her decks were stained with the life-blood of her captain and her three mates. On the night of January 25, 1824, four of the crew, headed by Samuel B. Comstock, a boat-steerer, mutinied, and killing their superior officers, took the ship into the Mulgrave Islands, intending to destroy her. Arrived there, they proceeded to strip the vessel, and while doing so a quarrel arose among themselves, and it culminated in the death of Comstock. Soon after this, before the work of demolition had further progressed, six of the men, most of whom had taken no part in the mutiny, and simply remained quiet to avoid the fate that had overtaken the captain and mates, having been sent to guard the ship, cut the cable and escaped from the islands, arriving at Valparaiso after a long and boisterous passage. Here the vessel was taken in charge by the American consul, and the men confined pending their examination, after which they were restored to the Globe, which was put in charge of Captain ——— King and sent to Nantucket. Ten men had been left at the Mulgraves,* but repeated injuries to the natives on the part of Silas Payne (the second in command of the mutineers at the time of the outbreak, and the murderer of his associate conspirator, Comstock), so incensed them that one after another of the crew were slain, the innocent perishing with the guilty, until on the arrival of a United States vessel, which had been sent there to rescue the survivors, but two remained alive.†

In an account of this sad affair, published by Messrs. Lay and Hussey immediately after their rescue, is related the following incident as showing the gross brutality of Comstock, the chief of the mutineers, and the miserably slight pretexts by which they justified to themselves their diabolical plot and its carrying out. Some time previously to the mutiny Comstock, who was a boat-steerer, had desired a friendly wrestle with the third mate, Nathaniel Fisher. Mr. Fisher, being the more athletic, handled him with so much ease that Comstock, enraged at Fisher's superiority, struck him, whereupon the third mate laid him on deck several times quite severely. Comstock at the time made threats of vengeance upon Mr. Fisher, to which he paid no attention.

After murdering the captain and first mate, who were both asleep at the time of the assault, the mutineers proceeded to attack the second and third mates, who were in the cabin. Comstock had loaded two muskets, and on reaching the cabin-door he fired one of them in the

*One man was hung by the mutineers.

†William Lay, of New London, and Cyrus Hussey, of Nantucket.

direction in which he judged the officers were, shooting Fisher in the mouth. "They now," continues the account, "opened the door, and Comstock making a pass at Mr. Lumbert (the second mate), missed him, and fell into the state-room. Mr. Lumbert collared him, but he escaped from his hands. Mr. Fisher had got the gun, and actually presented the bayonet to the monster's heart, but Comstock assuring him that his life should be spared if he gave it up, he did so; when Comstock immediately ran Mr. Lumbert through the body several times. He then turned to Mr. Fisher and told him there was no hope for *him!* 'You have got to die,' said he, and he alluded to the wrestling affair between them, and the full force of the threats made at the time became apparent to the mind of the unfortunate second mate. Finding his cruel enemy deaf to his remonstrances and entreaties, he said, 'If there is no hope, I will at least die like a man!' and having, by order of Comstock, turned back to, said in a firm voice, '*I am ready.*' Comstock then put the muzzle of the gun to his head and fired, which instantly put an end to his existence." The body of the captain was brutally mutilated, and with those of the mates was thrown overboard, the first and second officers being, in spite of their terrible wounds, still alive.

Similar in diabolical atrocity, both in the lack of provocation and in the carrying out of the plot, was the outbreak on the ship Junior, of New Bedford, in 1857. The ship sailed in July of that year on a voyage to the Indian and Pacific Oceans. Christmas came, the day of hallowed associations to the natives of civilized countries, whether their place of sojourning be on the land or on the sea. The day passed tranquilly on board the ship, Captain Mellen serving to each of the crew in the evening a small glass of spirits to commemorate the return of the Christian holiday. To all outward appearance, this kindly act on the part of the captain, an act which has a specially friendly significance to the mariner, was appreciated and reciprocated in sentiment by the crew. This being accomplished, Captain Mellen retired to his cabin, and soon he and his officers were calmly slumbering in their berths, little dreaming that hands that had but just received the token of hospitality and good-feeling from them would, ere another sun had dawned, be reeking with their blood. The major portion of the crew, who also had no suspicion of the cold-blooded schemes of their comrades, also "turned in" to their berths and slept.

At about 1 o'clock in the morning of the 26th of December, the ring-leader in the mutiny, Cyrus Plummer, with four of his associates, all armed with guns cocked and extra-loaded, entered the cabin, having first stationed five others outside to prevent aid reaching the officers in case they gave the alarm. With the muzzles of their guns almost touching the bodies of their victims, the conspirators, at the word from Plummer, fired. Three bullets pierced the body of the captain, who was almost instantly killed. The first mate, shot by six balls, survived, The third mate was killed with a whaling-spade or lance as he rose.

wounded by the murderous muskets. Alarmed by the discharge of the fire-arms, the remainder of the crew rushed to the deck, where they were confronted by the whole force of the mutineers, those who had assaulted the officers hurrying up to aid those left on guard. In the confusion the first and second mate hid themselves from their would-be murderers. The loyal men of the crew, finding themselves completely in the power of the revolting ones, had no recourse but to submit. After the first burst of passion was over, the second mate made his appearance and his life was spared. The chief mate had secreted himself in the hold, where, in spite of the torture from his wounds, he remained for five days undiscovered, and when at last he was found, the mutineers required his services to navigate the vessel.

When within about twenty miles of the coast of Australia, Plummer and his accomplices, taking two whale-boats and rifling the ship of everything they could find of value, left the vessel and landed upon those shores, where eight of them were subsequently captured.*

With the opening of navigation in high latitudes came increased perils. Not sufficient were the dangers from their gigantic prey, or furious gales, or the losing sight of the ship; to these must be added the risk of being ground between two mighty ice-bergs, of being caught in some field of ice and forced ashore, of having the stout timbers of their vessel pierced by the glittering spear of some stray berg as it was driven by the force of the polar currents. The season in either northern sea lasts but two or three months, and the temptation to incur many risks for the sake of rapidly filling the ship is too great to be withstood. The life of the whale-hunter is a life of risks—this only adds a little more to his repertoire of exciting scenes.

Captain Pease, of the ship Champion, of Edgartown, in a letter published in the New Bedford "Shipping List," of November 29, 1870, thus describes some of the incidents of Arctic whaling: "We made and entered the ice on the 17th day of May, about 40 miles South of Cape Navarin, weather thick and snowing; on the 20th the weather cleared up, showing about a dozen ships in the ice. The weather having every appearance of a gale, I worked out of the ice, and soon found myself surrounded by fifty ships. Saw but one whale in the ice. On the 23d, weather pleasant, two or three ships worked a short distance in the ice; the next day the fleet commenced following, and in a few hours fifty ships were on a race to Cape Thaddeus; it was oak against ice, and like all heavy moving bodies which come in collision, 'the weakest structure always gives way;' so with the ships, they *all* came out more or less damaged in copper and sheathing—the Champion four days ahead to Cape Thaddeus, and in clear water.

*In 1853 the crew of the brig William Penn, of San Francisco, consisting of five whites and fifteen natives of the Pacific Islands, mutinied, killing the captain, Isaac B. Hussey, and one man, and badly wounding the first and second mates and another man. The second man died a few days after the outbreak.

"Unfortunately, for the first time since whaling, there were no whales. On the 13th of June, we lowered for a whale going quick into the ice, Cape Agchen bearing southwest 90 miles, and before getting the boats clear, the ice packed around us. From that time until the 26th, so close and heavy was the ice packed around us, that we found it impossible to move the ship. With our sails furled, we drifted with the ice about 12 miles per day toward Cape Agchen, the ship lying as quiet as in a dock, but on the 22d, when close under the cape, a gale set in from the southward, producing a heavy swell and causing the ship to strike heavily against the ice. We saved our rudder by hooking our blubber-hooks to it and heaving them well taut with hawsers to our quarters. Had the current not taken an easterly shore course, the ship must have gone on shore. The wind blowing on shore, which was distant less than half a mile, 5 to 6 fathoms of water under us, ship rolling and pounding heavily against the ice, weather so thick we could not see 50 yards, made it rather an anxious time. For 36 hours I was expecting some sharp-pointed rock would crash through her sides. On the 24th, finding only 4½ fathoms water, little current, with the larger pieces of ice around, we let go an anchor and held her to a large floe of ice. Here we broke our sampson-post off in the deck. On the morning of the 25th the weather cleared up, showing our position to be at the head of a small bay about 15 miles east of Cape Agchen. Here for two days we lay becalmed and ice-bound. On the second day the ice loosened, when we took our anchor and by 18 hours' hard work succeeded in kedging about 4 miles seaward; a breeze then springing up from off shore, we spread sail and passed into clear water. We spent a short time in the straits, but saw nothing of the bowhead kind. Passed into the Arctic July —, and found most of the fleet catching walrus; about a dozen ships (this one among the number) went cruising along the northern ice for bowheads. After prospecting from Icy Cape to near Herald Island, and seeing not a whale, I returned to the walrus fleet. The first ship I saw was the Vineyard, with 175 walrus; since then I have not seen or heard from her. This walrusing is quite a new business, and ships which had engaged in it the previous season and came up prepared were very successful. While at it, we drove business as hard as the best of them, but soon became convinced that the ship's company (taken collectively) were much inferior to many others; they could not endure the cold and exposure expected of them. I have seen boats' crews that were properly rigged, kill and strip a boat-load of walrus in the same length of time another (not rigged) would be in killing one and hauling him on the ice. We took some 400, making about 230 barrels. About August 5, all the ships went in pursuit of bowheads, (most of them to Point Barrow). When off the Sea Horse Islands we saw a few whales working to the westward, just enough to detain us; we took two making 200 barrels; the weather cold, and a gale all the time. In September I worked up about 70 miles from Point Barrow; saw quite a show of small whales in the sea; took four which made about 100 barrels. As that was a fair sample, and not having the right boys to whale in that ice, where the thermometer stood only 8 above zero, I went back to the westward. Ships that had from 40 to 50 men, (clad in skins), and officers accustomed to that particular kind of whaling, did well. In going back, the fourth mate struck a whale which made about 70 barrels. From the 28th of September to the 4th of October we saw a good chance to get oil, had the weather been good and a well, hardy crew. We could not cut and whale at the same time. We took four whales which would have made 500 barrels had we had good weather to boil them. On the 4th of October we put away for the straits, in company with the Seneca, John Howland and John Wells—a gale from northeast, and snowing. On the evening of the 7th it blew almost a hurricane; hove the ship to south of Point Hope, with main-topsail furled; lost starboard bow boat, with davits—ship covered with ice and oil. On the 10th, entered the straits in a heavy gale; when about 8 miles south of the Diomedes, had to heave to under bare poles, blowing furiously, and the heaviest sea I ever saw; ship making bad weather of it; we had about 125 barrels of oil on deck, and all our fresh water; our blubber between decks in horse-pieces, and going from the forecastle to the mainmast every time she pitched, and impossible to stop it; ship covered with ice and oil; could only muster four men in a watch, decks flooded with water all the time; no fire to cook with or to warm by, made it the most anxious and miserable time I ever experienced in all my sea-service. During the night shipped a heavy sea, which took off bow and waist boats, davits, slide-boards, and everything attacked, staving about 20 barrels of oil. At daylight on the second day we found ourselves in 17 fathoms of water, and about 6 miles from the center cape of St. Lawrence Island. Fortunately the gale moderated a little, so that we got two close-reefed topsails and reefed courses on her, and by sundown were clear of the west end of the island. Had it not moderated as soon as it did, we should, by 10 a. m., have been shaking hands with our departed friends."

Another difficulty of North Pacific navigation is mentioned in a letter from Capt. William H. Kelley, of the bark James Allen, of New Bedford, to the Hawaiian Gazette, in 1874.* He says: "One of the perplexities of the navigator cruising in the Arctic Ocean is the singular effect northerly and southerly winds seem to have upon the mariner's compass. Captains have noticed this singularity for years, and no solution of the matter, as far as I have learned, has yet been arrived at. Navigators have noticed that with a north or northeast wind they can tack in eight points, while with the wind south or southwest in from fourteen to sixteen points. All navigators know that for a square-rigged vessel to lie within four points of the wind is an utter impossibility, the

*See New Bedford "Shipping List," January 5, 1875.

average with square-rigged vessels being six points. This peculiar action of the compass renders the navigation of the Arctic difficult and at times dangerous, especially in thick, foggy weather. Navigators in these regions have proved to their satisfaction that on the American coast, north and east of Point Barrow, to steer a land course by the compass and allow the variations given by the chart, 44° 15′ east, with the wind at north or northeast, *would run the ship ashore, steering either east or west.* * * * * Experience, therefore, has obliged navigators to ignore the variations marked upon the charts, and lay the ship's course by the compass alone to make a land-course safe in thick weather. * * * * With an east or west wind the effect on the compass is not so great as with other winds. I have said this much to show the working of the compass in the Arctic Ocean during different winds, not that I admit that the wind has any effect whatever upon the compass. I give the facts as they came under my observation, and corroborative testimony will be borne by any shipmaster who has cruised in the Arctic Ocean."

Although in the earlier, and at times in the later years of Arctic whaling the yield of oil has been large, yet the extra expense of obtaining it has been a formidable element entering into the calculation on the profits of the voyage. The anchorage was found to be of that character that the ground-tackle in use in other oceans availed but little, and heavier anchors and cables had to be furnished to prevent the almost inevitable drifting upon a lee shore, which, in a heavy gale, lighter anchors and lighter cables could only postpone. Again, but few ships returned from these regions without showing heavy scars and wounds as the result of their contest with the ice, while many vessels laid their bones in these desolate seas and on the rock-bound coasts. The most memorable instance of loss from shipwreck in the Arctic is that of the season of 1871, when thirty-four vessels out of a fleet of forty-one were abandoned in the ice as hopelessly lost.

More particular stress has been laid upon the North Pacific fishery because the bulk of the Arctic whaling was carried on on the western coast, but the pursuit was carried on in Hudson's Bay* and the surrounding seas with no less danger and with no less loss when we consider the number of vessels engaged. Scurvy, that dread of the sailor, was more to be feared in the North Atlantic than in the North Pacific Ocean.† Vessels usually fitted for shorter voyages, and the sudden closure of the ice around them, cutting them off from all communication with the outside world, attended as it was with a distressing uncertainty as to when their imprisonment would terminate, was an event that was positively appalling. The long catalogue of whale-ships crushed by the ice, which

* Malte Brun says (v, p. 76, ed. 1826,) "All attempts at whaling in Hudson's Bay are unsuccessful."

† The Ansel Gibbs, of New Bedford, was lost in the ice in Hudson's Bay, October 19, 1872. Fifteen of her crew died of scurvy before they were freed from their icy prison.

is an accompaniment to the history of the English fishery in the Greenland seas, is ample attestation to the perils North Atlantic mariners were obliged to encounter, and ample testimony to the bravery and hardihood of those men, English, Dutch, and American, who pursued their prey amid so much of danger, privation, and suffering.*

The American Greenland sea-fishery affords but few examples of these perils, simply because the fleet in these waters was of late years very small. Vessels have sailed on their voyages to Hudson's Bay and Davis Straits and never returned, and the fate of the gallant men who composed their crews has been and must ever remain a mystery.

Mention has been made more particularly of those sources of disaster more peculiar to the business, but it must not be inferred that these are the only trials which beset the life of the whaleman. In common with, but probably not in proportion to, the merchant service, the scenes of shipwreck and suffering are alike the shadows darkening the sunshine of their lives; shipwrecks, resulting not from the nature of their avocation, but the result of gales, of fire, and of sudden calamity.

On the 4th of March, 1854, the ship Canton, of New Bedford, was wrecked on a reef in the Pacific Ocean situated in 2° 45′ south latitude, and 173° west longitude. The crew gained the shore of a small barren island, and there subsisted as best they could for four weeks. During this time, in the best procurable shade, the thermometer denoted a temperature of 135° by day and 94° by night. Long existence there was out of the question, since their only source of supplies was the wreck of their vessel, and it was determined to endeavor to reach the King's Mill group of islands, some eight hundred miles distant. Having procured a very limited stock of bread and water, they started in four boats, reducing themselves to an allowance of one-half a pint of water and half a biscuit per day to each man. During the night the boats

* One of the most horrible tales of suffering in the annals of the whale-fishery is that of the English whaleship Diana, which left the Shetlands in 1866 for an Arctic (Davis Strait) voyage, with a crew of fifty officers and men. The time for her return came and passed, and nothing was heard of her whereabouts or fate. A premium was offered for tidings from the missing vessel, and at last she brought her own intelligence. On the 2d of April, 1867, the people living near Rona's Voe were startled by seeing the ghastly wreck of a ship sailing into the harbor. Battered, ice-crushed, her sails and cordage cut away and dismantled by the rigors of her terrible imprisonment, her boats and spars cut up to feed the fires which kept the wretched crew from freezing, her decks strewed with the dead and dying, the long lost Diana returned. The fifty who sailed were all brought back, but how? Ten bodies, one of them the captain's, lay on the deck carefully arranged for that burial which their comrades could not bring themselves to give to them. Thirty-five lay helplessly sick, some of them dying. Two still retained strength enough to go aloft, and three more were able to crawl around on deck. The man at the wheel fainted with excitement when help was at hand. One of the sick died in his berth after the rescuers had boarded the ship. The surgeon had worked untiringly, but cold, hunger, scurvy, and dysentery had done their work as unceasingly. The captain was the first to succumb, and one by one the others followed him. Another night and the ship which had been for all a common home would have proved to all a common tomb.

were kept together, but in the day-time they separated as widely as was prudent, to increase their chances of seeing a sail. On their perilous voyage they encountered considerable severe weather, and passed the islands where they intended to stop. When at length, after a voyage of forty-five days, they landed at Sypan (one of the Ladrones), not one of their number was able to stand. Here they caught birds and fish, and obtained cocoanuts, but no water, and they again started, this time for Tinian, distant about thirty miles. Arrived off there, the commander refused to allow them to land, thinking they were pirates. He even ordered his soldiers to fire upon them, but they finally convinced him who they were, and he supplied them with bread and water. Four days after they landed at Guam, having sailed in their boats about thirty-five hundred miles.

On the 21st October, 1851, the ship Junius, of New Bedford, was lost on a reef in Mozambique channel. The crew left the ship, unable to secure any provisions save four salt hams. All but one boat's crew landed at Saint Augustine Bay, about two hundred miles from the scene of their shipwreck, having been in their boats six days and nights without water and with no food except the hams, which to men in their situation were worse or but little better than no food. The missing ones were subsequently rescued.

The ship Logan, of New Bedford, was lost January 26, 1855, on Sandy Island Reef. A boat-steerer and three men were drowned at the time. The survivors landed at the Feejee Islands after enduring much suffering.

In 1846 the ship Lawrence, of ———, was lost off the coast of Japan, and of the entire crew only the second mate and seven men reached the shore alive. They were immediately seized by the Japanese and kept for seventeen months in the most rigorous and barbarous custody, in cages, dungeons, holds of junks, &c., and passed from port to port until they reached Nangaski. On their journey they were exposed to all sorts of ill-treatment, were threatened, insulted, and sometimes cruelly beaten. One poor fellow who endeavored to escape these brutal captors was cruelly put to death. At Nangaski the wretched remnant were compelled to go through the ceremony of trampling on the cross or a representation of it, in accordance with an edict adopted at the time of the expulsion of the Portuguese some two hundred years before.* At the

* The ship Manhattan, Budd, of Sag Harbor, had visited Jeddo less than twelve months before to restore to their home 22 Japanese seamen whom they had rescued from a wreck. They had been hospitably received, but warned not to come there again. Vessels which have been classed as missing—as for instance the Lady Adams of Nantucket in 1823—have been last seen off that coast. If dire necessity drove their crews upon that inhospitable shore, what scenes of barbarity may have been enacted in which they were the struggling and helpless victims! (NOTE.—Although these accounts of the Lawrence and Lagoda are current in the newspapers of the time and even remembered indistinctly by whalemen who were near Japan, it has been impossible to find these vessels among the whaling-lists before the alleged accidents.—THE AUTHOR.)

very time these atrocities were being perpetrated the squadron of Commodore Biddle lay in the harbor of Yeddo, and our Government fondly imagined that it had made a favorable impression on the people of those islands in respect to American dignity, moderation, and power.

Similar to the experience of the Lawrence was that of the Lagoda, of New Bedford, also wrecked on these, then inhospitable, islands. Those of the crew who survived the wreck were so inhumanly treated by the Japanese into whose power they were so unfortunate as to fall that one of their number in sheer despair relieved himself of further torture by taking his own life.*

Another class of accidents to which whalemen seem peculiarly liable, but which, because of the care and vigilance exercised by the officers and crew, is of rare occurrence, is destruction by fire.† When indeed this casualty does occur, it is usually the result of some circumstance which might occur in any vessel. The case of the Cassander, of Providence, R. I., Henry Winslow commander, was one of this kind, and its narration is given, not so much in illustration of perils incidental to this pursuit, as to record the sufferings of her crew on account of that disaster.

Vessels in the merchant service have, as a general rule, a certain series of courses to steer. They usually make the shortest distance from port to port. Hence in case of accident to the vessel they are in, the crew have only to continue in their course in order to insure most speedy relief. Not so with the whaler. Her cruising ground may be hundreds of miles from the tracks of merchantmen, and she may be a solitary cruiser on that station. Hence the destruction of the vessel involves far greater risk and possibly privation and suffering to the crew.

The Cassander sailed from Providence on the 19th of November, 1847. Nothing worthy of special mention occurred until, on the morning of the 1st of May, 1848, between 4 and 5 o'clock, the cry of fire was raised.‡ The wind at the time was blowing a moderate gale from the northwest. All hands were instantly on deck, and search for the source and cause of the fire was made. It was found that it was raging most severely in the lower hold, apparently near the foremast, where four barrels of tar

---

* Fifteen of the crew of the Lagoda reached the shore alive; one subsequently died, a victim to the barbarities of his captors; the thirteen survivors were rescued by the United States ship of war Preble in 1849. The Preble also took on board a sailor named Ronald MacDonald, formerly of the whale-ship Plymouth of Sag Harbor. MacDonald received his discharge and was given a whale-boat furnished with books, provisions, &c., and left the ship off Japan in June, 1848, with the expressly avowed purpose of visiting the Japanese islands. He landed upon one of them and was immediately captured, deprived of his books, and imprisoned. Having nothing to occupy his time he turned his attention to teaching his captors the English language, and soon had quite a class receiving instruction. But his presence was a thorn in the side of the Japanese, and they availed themselves of the first opportunity to get rid of him.

† Incendiary fires, which became of disastrous frequencey in later years, are not meant when we speak of this immunity.

‡ This account is taken from that of the captain, published in the Baltimore Sun.

were known to have been stored. Simultaneously with this discovery it was found that two of the crew—negroes from the coast of Africa—had jumped overboard. One of them, refusing to take the rope thrown to him by Captain Winslow, soon sank, the other was subsequently picked up by the second mate's boat.*

Orders were given, and every exertion was made to save the ship, but the position of the fire, the rapidity with which it increased, and the density of the smoke, rendered all their efforts unavailing, and the means of escape became the chief consideration. Attempts were made to procure bread and water, but the smoke in the steerage was so dense that it was impossible to do so. This circumstance led to the belief that the ship had been fired at both ends. Three boats were now lowered, and in them were placed such stores as the crew could get at, the nautical instruments and some clothing, and the burning wreck was abandoned, the entire crew, save the drowned African, numbering in all 23 souls, escaping in safety.

With the dawning of the day they took an inventory of their supplies and found them to consist of about ten gallons of water, fifteen pounds of bread, and a small amount of raw meat taken from the harness-cask. By the previous day's reckoning their position was found to be in latitude 34° 30′ south, longitude 45° 50′ west—400 miles from the nearest land. The crew were immediately allowanced to one gill of water and a very small amount of bread per day. The weather was bad, and during the earlier portion of their voyage they were obliged to depend upon their oars to make progress against the head winds. Of course they soon became exhausted, and rowing had to be given up and the sails alone were used, the boats being kept as nearly as possible in the direction of land.

At about 10 o'clock on the morning of the 5th of May, the boats being then in latitude 32°, longitude 47°, a sail was discovered. All hands immediately took to the oars, and after five hours of hard rowing, signals of distress being also repeatedly made, the mate's boat came up with the vessel and found her to be a Spanish brig, 100 days from Barcelona, bound to Montevideo. The captain of the brig made every effort to get away from the shipwrecked mariners, and when the mate's boat came up would not allow it alongside, but passed the crew a rope and towed them some distance astern. When Captain Winslow's boat came up he stated to the Spaniard, through an interpreter, their condition and circumstances, and asked permission for his officers and crew to go on board, but this was peremptorily refused. Equally futile were the endeavors to get him to take them to Montevideo or St. Catharine's, or even one or two days' sail toward land. The stony-hearted man, with a refinement of cruelty entirely foreign to maritime men, paid no heed

*The rescued negro confessed that the ship had been fired by his drowned companion and himself. Their fears of being sold into slavery had been excited, and this desperate act was performed as a means of escaping, through death, that more miserable fate. Before leaping into the sea his companion had stabbed himself.

to their entreaties, nor would he even permit them the solace they could derive from one night's rest and sleep on board his vessel, that they might the better withstand the further fatigues and hardships in store for them. Against the express wishes of this monster, Captain Winslow sprang into the main chains and aboard of the vessel, but the aid which the unfortunates wanted the Spanish captain could not be induced to give, and the crews of toil-worn, famishing, abandoned men proceeded on their voyage. Who would not say that if the sea, which proved more hospitable than man, had swallowed up these miserable men, their blood would have been on the head of Captain Dominick, of the brig Alercidita?*

The night of the 6th was the most perilous of their voyage, as the wind blew in a succession of heavy squalls. The boats were hove to by making a line fast to the oars and paying them out ahead. In this situation they lay until the dawn. From daylight until 11 o'clock they used their sails, but the wind blowing a heavy gale from a northeasterly direction they were again compelled to heave to. At about 4 o'clock in the afternoon the captain's boat was swamped, but the occupants were all rescued and divided between the other two boats. By this accident the water and the nautical instruments it contained were lost, and the two remaining boats were so loaded that their gunwales were not more than 6 or 8 inches out of water. "In this situation," says the captain, "we passed the night; nothing was heard save the awful roaring of the tempest and occasionally the voices of some of the officers and crew offering up a prayer to the Almighty Ruler of wind and wave for their safety. He heard our prayers. In the morning the wind moderated and the sea was beaten down by a heavy shower of rain." From this time they were favored with pleasant weather, and on the 10th of May they landed near Conventus, in the province of St. Catharine, in Brazil, without water and utterly exhausted. So much reduced had they become that a boat-steerer was drowned by the capsizing of the mate's boat, he being too weak to extricate himself from the surf.

It would be easy to greatly extend the mournful lists, but those enumerated are types of each class of casualties. Still another class appears, however, and with this we will pass to the consideration of other subjects.

Among the dangers encountered by our whalemen in the Pacific Ocean is the serious and insidious one of the attacks of boring-worms upon the bottoms of their ships. The least exposed place upon their planking where the copper may have become chafed off by contact with sunken rocks and reefs, without a thought of danger incurred or damage done presenting itself to the mariner, serves as a rallying point for the teredo, and soon the vicinity of the break becomes honey-combed with its habitations, and fortunate is it for the seamen if a warning leak drives them into some haven for repairs while yet the damage is repar-

*On his arrival in port Captain Dominick reported that he had *tendered them help, which they refused.* As though drowning men ever refused substantial aid!

able. This may be still another plausible solution of that terrible problem of "missing vessels." A noteworthy instance of the havoc made by these "toilers of the sea" occurred to the ship Minerva 2d, of New Bedford, Captain Swain, in 1857.

In August, 1856, while off the King's Mill group, she touched on a reef, the water being at the time perfectly smooth and but little wind blowing. So trifling was the sensation of the contact that Captain Swain gave himself no thought that any damage was sustained, and the voyage was continued as usual until February, 1857, when, in a heavy gale, the vessel was found to leak 250 strokes per hour. She reached Norfolk Island on the 19th of March, but was blown off by heavy gales which continued for three days, the leak meanwhile increasing to 1,000 strokes, and Captain Swain bore away for Sydney. On the 29th of March she was leaking 2,400 strokes (or about 16 inches) per hour, and Captain Swain had the forehold cleared to examine for the cause of the trouble. Upon cutting through the ceiling several holes were found in the bottom through which the water rushed furiously. These the men, though standing in the water up to their middles, succeeded in plugging up and covering with canvas and blankets well tarred. Over these a stream-chain was coiled to prevent the plugs from bursting in from the force of the water, and the pumps were kept going day and night. The ship reached Sydney on the 7th of April and was taken upon the marine railway. Upon examination it was found that two sheets of copper had been rubbed off (probably while off the King's Mill Islands) about six feet from the keel, and a little abaft the bluff of the bow on the starboard side. When this place was laid bare the planks were completely eaten to a shell by the worms. No person not an eye-witness, said the captain, would have believed the planks would have held together, and it was certainly wonderful that in plugging the whole plank was not driven out, in which case every soul on board must have been drowned before the boats could have been lowered.*

G.—A MISCELLANEOUS CHAPTER.

While some vessels on their voyages have made but poor returns, even bringing, in numerous cases, positive and at times damaging loss to their owners, others have done extraordinarily well, and brought in fortunes to those investing in them. The ups and downs of the business made it alternately profitable and, if not positively losing, at least hazardous. This was the fact when no unusual accident occurred, but in case of a disaster it changed the beam of the balance from the speculative to the unmistakably negative side of the account. To illustrate the two phases of the owners' business experience, the following examples are given:

The Wilmington and Liverpool packet, Captain Richmond, sailed from

*The new ship Niphon, of Nantucket, on her first voyage, sunk at sea on her passage home, January 12, 1849, in consequence of the depredations of ship-worms.

New Bedford in June, 1820, for the Pacific Ocean, returning on the 27th of December, 1823, with 2,600 barrels of sperm-oil—the largest amount procured by any one New Bedford ship to that date, and worth, at the average price of oil in 1823, about $65,000.

The ship Uncas, of Falmouth, Capt. Henry C. Bunker, sailed in 1828 and returned in 1831, having been absent two years and eight months, bringing a cargo of 3,468 barrels of sperm-oil, worth about $88,000.

The Loper, of Nantucket, Capt. Obed Starbuck, returned in September, 1830, after an absence of only fourteen months and fourteen days, with 2,280 barrels of sperm-oil, worth, at the average price of oil, $50,000. On her next voyage, under the command of John Cotton, she took 2,170 barrels of sperm-oil in less than eighteen months, and on the voyage immediately preceding that of 1829–'30, under the command of Captain Starbuck, she brought in 2,131 barrels of sperm-oil in less than seventeen months. In less than sixty-two months she had performed three Pacific Ocean voyages and landed 6,581 barrels of sperm-oil.

The ship Sarah, of Nantucket, Capt. Frederick Arthur, sailed for the Pacific Ocean on the 26th of May, 1827, returning April 19, 1830, with 3,497 barrels of sperm-oil, valued at $89,000. This is the largest quantity of sperm-oil ever brought into Nantucket from a single voyage.

In 1830 the ship America, Capt. Shubael Cottle, sailed from Hudson, N. Y., for the Pacific Ocean. She returned in 1823, after a voyage of thirty-one months, bringing 3,180 barrels of sperm-oil. The value of her cargo was about $80,000.

The Magnolia, of New Bedford, Capt. George B. Worth, obtained a cargo of 3,451 barrels of sperm-oil on a voyage of forty-one months, the value of which was $85,000.

In 1838 there arrived at New Bedford the ship William Hamilton, Capt. William Swain, with 4,060 barrels of sperm oil, having sent home from the Western Islands on her passage out 121 barrels more, making a total of 4,181 barrels, worth $109,269.

In 1842 the America, Captain Fisher, brought into New Bedford 400 barrels of sperm and 4,300 barrels of whale oil, and 45,000 pounds of bone, after a voyage of 26 months, the entire cargo being worth $66,478. In the same year the Maria, of Nantucket, Capt. Elisha H. Fisher, returned from a 22 months' voyage with 2,413 barrels of sperm-oil, bringing to the owners the sum of $70,000.

In 1843 the Silas Richards, of Sag Harbor, returned with 3,600 barrels of whale-oil, 220 of sperm, and 30,000 pounds of bone, having been gone 28 months. The value of her cargo was $54,722. In the same year the Bowditch, of Providence, carried into that port 3,500 barrels of whale-oil and $10,000 worth of bone, the value of which cargo was $47,485; she was gone 20 months. The schooner Cordelia. of Provincetown, also returned in 1843 from a *four days' voyage* with 120 barrels of whale-oil and $100 of bone, worth $1,385

In 1845 the Lowell, Captain Benjamin, and the General Williams, Captain Holt, arrived at New London, the former having been gone 21 and the latter 22 months, each bringing about 4,500 barrels of whale-oil and 43,000 pounds of bone, each cargo being valued at about $61,400. The Lowell was said to have had alongside *at one time sixteen whales.*

In 1849 the South America, of Providence, Capt. R. N. Sowle, returned from a voyage of 26 months, with 5,300 barrels of whale and 200 barrels of sperm oil, and 50,000 pounds of bone, worth $89,000. As she fitted at $40,000, it will be seen that she paid her cost and a dividend of about 125 per cent. The Russell, of New Bedford, Captain Morse, also brought to her investors, in the same year, a cargo valued at $92,000, (2,650 barrels of sperm-oil.) She was absent three years and four months. The cargo of the Plymouth, of Sag Harbor, Capt. L. B. Edwards, which also returned in 1849, was worth $71,000. She brought 4,873 barrels of whale-oil, and was gone 41 months.

In 1850 the Coral, of New Bedford, Captain Seabury, returned from a three years' voyage with 3,350 barrels of sperm-oil, worth $126,630.

Probably the most extraordinary voyage ever made was that of the Envoy, of New Bedford, which sailed in 1848. She returned to Providence in 1847 from a whaling voyage, and was there condemned and sold to William C. Brownell, esq., of New Bedford, to be broken up. Mr. Brownell, however, concluded to fit her for another voyage, and did so, sending her to sea under the command of Capt. W. T. Walker.* She sailed immediately to Wytootacke, and took on board 1,000 barrels of oil that Captain Walker had purchased from a wreck on a previous voyage at a merely nominal price,† and stored there; thence he proceeded to Manila and shipped this oil to London. From Manila he cruised in the North Pacific Ocean, and in fifty-five days took 2,800 barrels of whale-oil. Of this he shipped to London from Manila 1,800 barrels, and also 40,000 pounds of bone. Cruising again he took 2,500 barrels of whale-oil and 35,000 pounds of bone. Captain Walker now put into San Francisco, sold 25,000 gallons of oil at $1 per gallon, and the remainder (85,000 gallons) at 51 cents per gallon, and shipped $12,500 worth of bone to New Bedford. While at San Francisco an offer of $6,000 was made for the vessel. The gross amount of oil obtained was 5,300 barrels, and of bone 75,000 pounds. Summing up, then, the entire result of the voyage, we find:

Net profit on 1,000 barrels first shipped to London	$9,000
Net profit on catchings for first season	37,500
Sales at San Francisco	73,450
Value of bone shipped home	12,500
Value of vessel at San Francisco	6,000
	138,450

The Envoy was fitted at about $8,000.

* The underwriters declined to insure her.

† Wrecked oil was sometimes purchased at from fifty cents to one dollar a barrel.

The year after the cruise of the Superior in the Arctic, 154 ships were whaling in that sea. These vessels took during that season (1849) 206,850 barrels of right-whale oil and 2,481,600 pounds of whalebone. The value of the ships and outfits was $4,650,000, and the value of that season's catchings was $3,419,622.

In 1853 the following more than ordinarily good voyages were reported at New Bedford: Bark Favorite, of Fairhaven, Captain Pierce, gone three years, with 300 barrels of sperm and 4,300 barrels of whale oil and 72,000 pounds of bone,* worth in the aggregate $116,000; ship Montreal, of New Bedford, Capt. Frederick Fish, absent 32 months and 15 days, with 195 barrels sperm, 3,823 barrels whale-oil, and 31,700 pounds of bone, worth $136,023.19; ship Sheffield, also of New Bedford, gone four years, with 7,000 barrels of whale-oil and 115,000 pounds of bone, worth $124,000.

The Pioneer, of New London, Capt. Ebenezer Morgan, sailed from that port June 4, 1864, for the Davis Straits and Hudson's Bay fishery, valued, with her outfits, at $35,800. On the 18th of September, 1865, she returned with 1,391 barrels of whale-oil and 22,650 pounds of bone, worth, at the current prices, $150,060.† This voyage the people of New London claim to be the best ever made by an American whaler.

But success has not been confined to large vessels or to expensive voyages. In addition to the cruise of the Cordelia, of Provincetown, there are reported as making extraordinary voyages the following small vessels: The schooner Admiral Blake, of Sippican, Capt. B. B. Handy, in a voyage of two months and nine days (in 1854) took 250 barrels of sperm and 10 barrels of blackfish oil, worth, in all, $11,000. The schooner Altamaha, of the same port, Capt. Consider Fisher, sailed in 1855, was gone six months and nine days, and returned with a cargo of 240 barrels of sperm and 8 barrels of blackfish oil, valued at $13,500. She was worth, with her outfits, $2,200, and after paying off her crew and refitting for another voyage the owners divided $8,000. The schooner James, also of Sippican, Capt. B. B. Handy, sailed in 1856, and in a cruise of three months and a half obtained $10,000 of oil (220 barrels sperm.)

Occasionally some piece of good fortune, out of the ordinary course of whaling success, is met with. Thus, in September, 1857, the schooner Watchman, of Nantucket, Capt. Chas. W. Hussey, sailed for an Atlantic Ocean cruise. She returned in August, 1858, having obtained 41 barrels of sperm and 386 barrels of whale oil, and 4 barrels of ambergris.‡ This last was sold for $10,000, making the entire value of the voyage $19,125.

So much for the cheering, sunny side of the picture. There is, however, a shadowy side, on which may be found heavy and disastrous

* Prior to the commencement of Polar whaling, the amount of bone taken bore to the number of barrels of whale-oil the proportion of 8 or 10 to 1. A vessel taking 2,000 barrels of whale-oil would be reasonably supposed to bring home (when they saved it) from 16,000 to 20,000 pounds of bone. But Arctic whaling destroyed all these calculations, for the bone was larger and the proportion yielded much greater.

† This was at a time when oil and bone commanded a good price.

‡ Ambergris is generally considered as a product of the rectum of a diseased whale.

losses, and financial ruin for many a merchant. Thus, of the 81 whalers expected to arrive in 1837, 53 made paying voyages, 8 made saving ones, 11 lost money, and 9 involved their owners in severe losses. A mutiny among the crew of the Clifford Wayne, of Fairhaven, necessitating her return to port, occasioned a loss of $10,000 to those who invested in her.

The brig Emeline, of New Bedford, Captain Wood, sailed from port on the 11th of July, 1841. The captain was killed by a whale in July, 1842, and in September, 1843, the brig returned, bringing home only 10 barrels of oil as the result of a 26 months' cruise.

The Benjamin Rush, of Warren, Captain Munroe, sailed in October, 1852, for the Pacific Ocean. On the coast of Japan the captain and his boat's crew were lost by a whale. This, combined with the extremely poor success that had attended the vessel, had so discouraging an effect upon the crew that it was considered useless to prolong the voyage, and she returned to port under charge of the cooper in 1853, having obtained but 50 barrels of sperm-oil and 40 of whale. On her voyage she had circumnavigated the globe, and during the entire period sighted land but twice, the Cape de Verde Islands, outward-bound, and Trinidad on the passage home.

Of the 68 whalers expected to arrive in New Bedford and Fairhaven in 1858, 44 were calculated as making losing voyages, and the same proportion would apply to other ports. The estimated loss to owners during this year was at least $1,000,000.

The net loss on 12 whaling schooners of the Provincetown fleet, which arrived in 1870, was $36,000.

These are cases taken somewhat at random. Almost every year witnessed some misfortune, saw some persons impoverished by an unsuccessful termination of the venture in which their little all was invested.

Among the pursuits which grew out of the prosecution of the sperm-whale fishery was the manufacture of candles, which was at one time an important industry both home and commercial.

"The first manufactory of sperm candles in this country," says Macy,* "was established in Rhode Island, a little previous to 1750, by Benjamin Crabb, an Englishman. His candle-house was burnt in 1750 or 1751." In 1750 the general court of Massachusetts granted to Benjamin Crabb, of Rehoboth, the sole right to make sperm candles in that colony for a term of years, on the ground that he and no other person had a knowledge of the art and he agreeing to instruct five of the inhabitants therein.† In 1753 Obadiah Brown built candle-works at Tockwotten, now

*Macy's Hist. Nant., p. 69. Mr. Macy must, for reasons enumerated in the succeeding note, be slightly in error in this date.

†Mass. Col. MSS., Manufactures, p. 369. The memorial does not seem to be on file. The documents relating to it are as follows:

"ANNO REGNI REGIS GEORGII SECUNDI VICESSIMO QUARTO: *An Act for Granting unto Benjamin Crabb the Sole priviledge of making Candles of Coarse Sperma Cœti Oyle:*

"Whereas Benjamin Crabb of Rehoboth in the County of Bristol has Represented

known as India Point, in Providence, and engaged Crabb to superintend the business. Brown manufactured that year about 300 barrels of spermaceti, which was nearly all that was saved separately from the body-oil, and not sent to England. Crabb proved less capable than Brown supposed, and the secret of refining was only acquired by Brown as the result of his own experiments.

In 1754 or '55, Moses Lopez engaged in the business in a small way, at Newport, followed soon after by Collins & Reveria, Aaron Lopez, John Maunsley & Co., Thomas Robinson, and others. In 1761 there were eight manufactories in New England and one in Philadelphia. These were: in Providence, Obadiah Brown & Co., the firm consisting of

---

to this Court that he (A) *has the Art of making Candles of Coarse Sperma Cœti Oyle* and has been at Great Expense in providing himself with proper Implements therefor and s Willing on due encouragment to undertake and Carry on that Business here and to Teach and Instruct Some of the Inhabitants of this province his Art Aforesaid, and this Court being Willing to Encourage an undertaking so likely to prove Beneficial to the province:—

"Therefore Be it Enacted by the Lieut-Governour, Council And House of Representatives—That the said Benjamin Crabb and his Heirs shall and may have and enjoy the Sole use, Exercise and Benefit of making Candles of Course Sperma Cæti Oyle (B) *Within this province for Sale for the Term of Fourteen years next ensuing the publication of this Act provided he forthwith engage in and Carry on the Business Aforesaid within this province During that Term and Do Instruct Five of the Inhabitants of this province the Art Aforesaid Within Ten years after the publication of this Act*—.

"And be it further Enacted by the Authority Aforesaid that no person or persons saving such only as shall first obtaine the Consent of the said Crabb or his Heirs signified under his or their hands shall Sell Within this province or Export out of it any Candles made of the Oyle (C) Aforesaid during the time the said Cobb And his Heirs are Entitled to the priviledge Aforesaid other than Such as are made by the said Crabb his Heirs or Assigns on pain of Forfeiting Ten pounds For each offence."

This bill passed its three readings on January 25, 1750, and was sent to the council for concurrence. On the 6th of February the council returned it with these amendments, viz: "Insert at A:—And no other Person in the Province has the Art of pressing, fluxing & chrystalizing of Sperma Ceti & course Sperma Ceti Oyle, and of making Candles of the same as so prepared. Insert at B:—So prepared untill the 31 day of May which shall be in the year of our Lord 1759 Provided that He do forthwith engage in & carry on the business aforesaid within this Province: and shall some time before the 31 day of May 1752 remove to some place within seven Miles of the Town of Boston & there set up Works suitable for carrying on the said Business; and shall then & there manufacture all such quantities of Oyl as can be procured fit for the purpose; and shall likewise within five years from the publication of this Act well & fully instruct five of the Inhabitants of this Province (two of whom shall be appointed by General Court if they see cause) in the Art aforesaid. Insert at C:—prepared as."

(The amendments A and B would strike out the words italicized.)

The house concurred with amendment A, and returned the bill to the council, who, though first non-concurring, finally, on the 12th of Feb., 1750, agreed with the amended house bill.

It will seem evident that this Benjamin Crabb and the one mentioned by Macy must be the same party, in which case he must have presented his petition late in 1749; and there is scarcely a chance that he was manufacturing in Rhode Island prior to 1750. There seems no means of knowing whether he ever pursued his occupation in Massachusetts or not. According to Macy it would appear that for some reason he did not accept the terms of the act.

Obadiah, Nicholas, Joseph, John and Moses Brown."* In Boston, Joseph Palmer & Co., consisting of Thomas Fluekar, Nathaniel Gorham, Joseph Palmer, Richard Cranch, and William Belcher. In Newport, which monopolized by far the largest share of this pursuit, were Thomas Robinson & Co., (William, Thomas, and Joseph Robinson, and William Richardson), Riveria & Co., (Henry Collins and Jacob Rod Reveria), Isaac Stelle & Co., (John Marodsley,† Isaac Stelle and John Slocum), Naphthali Hart & Co., (Naphthali, Samuel, Abraham, and Isaac Hart), Aaron Lopez and Moses Lopez. There was also, besides the Philadelphia firm, the name of which is not now accessible, one more manufactory, that of Edward Langdon & Son, which was probably located in Boston.‡

In 1761 Richard Cranch & Co. endeavored to associate the manufacturers for mutual protection in regard to the purchase of "head-matter" and the sale of manufactured stock. Such was the success of the project that the union was formed and articles drawn up and signed by all the above parties save Moses Lopez and the Philadelphians. The signers formed a general association under the name of "United Company of Spermaceti Chandlers." It was agreed to give positive orders to their agents not to give for head matter more than £6 sterling per ton above the price of "common merchantable Spermaceti body brown oil," the price of the oil to be determined in all cases by the current prices paid by Boston merchants for the London market, and the members were debarred giving, either directly or indirectly, more than the above rate, or to receive any head-matter acknowledged by the seller to be pre-engaged. No commission exceeding 2½ per cent. was to be allowed to any factor; and if the price of head-matter should continue above the agreed price of the association, the members of the company agreed to fit out at least twelve vessels for whaling, each house furnishing and owning in the fleet equally; the number of vessels was to be increased from time to time as occasion required. No house was to manufacture for any parties not belonging to the association, and new partners could only be admitted by unanimous consent. Candles were not to be sold in New England at a less price than 1*s.* 10½*d.* sterling per pound, an additional shilling to be charged for each box made to contain 25 pounds.

The quantity of head-matter brought into New England was found insufficient to supply the number of factories already at work; and each member of the company was under obligation to do all in his power by fair and honorable means to prevent any increase of competition.

* The name of this firm was changed in 1763 to Nicholas Brown & Co. This account of the early sperm-candle factories is compiled from Macy's History of Nantucket, from a communication to the Providence Journal signed "M.," and from newspapers and memoranda of the time.

† Probably the same name as Macy spells Mausley.

‡ "M." says: "We cannot give the locality of this house." It is judged by the writer, however, to be located in Boston, from the fact that a few years later (in 1769) one John Langdon carried on the sale of sperm oil and the manufacture of candles in that town "in Fleet street, near the Old North Meeting House." In the same year candles of this kind are advertised as made by Russell & Howard, of Boston, and Daniel Jenckes & Co., of Providence.

Obadiah Brown & Co., with one or two others, were empowered to call a special meeting at Taunton if the influence of the whole company was required. Two general meetings were ordered, one for the first Tuesday in November, 1762, and the second for the first Tuesday in March, 1763. Expenses were to be apportioned *pro rata*, and at least one member from each firm was required to be present under a penalty of $8 for neglect to attend. The absentees were to be bound by the unanimous vote of the company's representatives, and the association could be dissolved upon evidence under the hand of one credible witness that one or more members of the copartnership had broken the agreement.

At a meeting held in Providence on the 13th of April, 1763, some slight alterations were made in the agreement. Ten pounds sterling was the price to be paid for head matter, and the members agreed to receive it only of following parties who were appointed the factors of the company: John & William Rotch, Sylvanus Hussey & Co., Folger & Gardner, Robert & Josiah Barker, Obed Hussey, Richard Mitchell, and Jonathan Burnell, of Nantucket; Benjamin Mason, of Newport; George Jackson, of Providence; and Henry Lloyd, of Boston. All such matter was, after the date of these revised articles, to be common stock, whether obtained by the company's or other vessels, and to be divided in the following proportion of parts to the hundred: Nicholas Brown & Co., 20 barrels; Joseph Palmer & Co., 14; Thomas Robinson & Co., 13; Aaron Lopez, 11; Rivera & Co., 11; Isaac Stelle & Co., 9; Naphthali Hart & Co., 9; the Philadelphians, 7;* Edward Langdon & Son, 4; Moses Lopez, 2.* The factors were to divide their purchases according to the above rule, and dishonorable conduct by any member in endeavoring to obtain an advantage over his fellow-partners entailed a forfeiture of the whole share.

John Slocum, Jacob Rod Rivera, Thomas Robinson, and Moses Brown were appointed to treat with the factors at Newport and Nantucket, John Brown with the one in Providence, and Joseph Palmer with the one in Boston. These gentlemen were to report to Nicholas Brown & Co., who were in turn to report to the other manufacturers.

There is no means at hand of arriving at the results of the partnership and manufacture; those enumerated were by far the principal parties engaged, though there were subsequently many others in Newport, Nantucket, and other towns with a large aggregate capital. The expense, says "M.,"† of a manufactory was trifling. The building was of wood, usually about 60 feet by 30 feet, one half formed with 14-feet posts and used as a work-room, the other half with 8 feet posts and used as a shed. Building and utensils cost about $1,000, and about 600 barrels of head matter would be used up each year in such a factory.‡

The process of manufacture was so carefully kept a secret that it was not until 1772 that the people of Nantucket acquired sufficient knowl-

* By this agreement it would seem that the arrangement had become unanimous.

† See New Bedford Shipping-List, January 23, 1855.

‡ At the last report Newport did not have a candle factory worthy of the name.

edge to enable them to carry on the business there. In that year one of the most enterprising men of the island obtained the desired information and established a manufactory there, acquiring in the pursuit a large property. Others experimented and succeeded, and the business finally became one of very considerable importance. In 1792 ten such factories were in existence on the island.*

Probably the first candle-house in New Bedford was built very nearly cotemporaneously with that in Nantucket. According to Ricketson,† Joseph Russell erected the first one, previously to the Revolution, near the corner of Center and Front streets, employing one Captain Chaffee, who had engaged in the manufacture of spermaceti in Lisbon, to take charge of the establishment, at the extravagant salary (for the times) of $500. This building was destroyed by the British in their raid in September, 1778.

Among the exports of the colonies, including Newfoundland, Bahama, and Bermudas, in 1770 were sperm candles to the extent of 379,012 pounds, distributed as follows: To Great Britain, 4,865 pounds; to Ireland, 450 pounds; to the south of Europe, 14,167 pounds; to the West Indies, 351,625 pounds; and to Africa, 7,905 pounds. The total value of this branch of exports for that year was £23,688 4*s.* 6*d.*, sterling.

The following table from Pitkin's Statistics‡ will show the exports of sperm candles from the United States from 1791 to 1815:

Year.	Pounds.	Year.	Pounds.
1791	182,400	1803	238,034
1792	157,520	1804	127,602
1793	235,600	1805	180,535
1794	214,960	1806	294,789
1795	240,720	1807	172,132
1796	221,903	1808	45,130
1797	§130,438	1809	214,444
1798	144,149	1810	187,190
1799	240,301	1811	257,094
1800	181,321	1812	157,596
1801	290,666	1813	26,522
1802	135,627	1814	21,154

*The New Bedford Medley has, under date of Nantucket, November 30, 1792, an item to the following effect: "This day was cut from the loom the first piece of sail-cloth manufactured at the new duck factory. It employs more hands than the five rope-walks and ten sperm-candle works, 'which number there is here.'" The papers in January, 1793, reported canvas as being manufactured at Salem, Boston, and Nantucket, and another factory being about to be started at Newport, R. I. In the Mass. Col. MSS., Manufactures, pp. 295–6–7, are papers relating to the encouragement to be given by the general court to the manufacture of duck as carried on by John Powell of Boston (in 1727), and affidavits of captains of vessels the sails of which were made from canvas of Powell's make.

†Hist. New Bedford, p. 77.

‡Tables of Exports, Pitkin.

§ The falling off of exports occurs chiefly in those years when European wars or national troubles make shippers cautious. In 1797 Hudson, N. Y., possessed one or more sperm-candle factories.

There are some incidents connected with this pursuit which may, perhaps, not inaptly be called the curiosities of whaling. Many of these are incorporated already in this work, and it may not be inappropriate to add a few more.

The Honolulu Commercial Advertiser in December, 1870, contained an account of a harpoon which was found in a whale captured by the ship Cornelius Howland, of New Bedford, then cruising in the North Pacific Ocean. It is the custom among whalemen to have each iron stamped with initials designating the ship to which it belongs. This is done to prevent dispute in case it is necessary to waif the whale, or in case boats from two different ships lay claim to one which has been killed. While off Point Barrow the Cornelius Howland took a large polar whale, in the blubber of which was imbedded the head of a harpoon marked "A. G.," the wound made by it having healed over. This was presumed to have belonged to the bark Ansel Gibbs, also of New Bedford. But she was known to have been pursuing the fishery in Cumberland Inlet and its vicinity for some ten or eleven years previously. The obvious inference was that this whale must have found his way from ocean to ocean by some channel unknown to navigators, and that at some seasons of the year there must be an inter-ocean communication. The Advertiser adds, "We have heard before of instances where whales have been caught at Cumberland Inlet with harpoons in them, with which they have been struck in the Arctic Ocean, but we believe this is the first authenticated instance of a whale having been caught in the Arctic Ocean with a harpoon in it from the Davis Straits side."

Quite a number of instances are on record where irons have been recovered, several years after they had been carried off by escaping whales, by parties who were in the ships to which the harpoons belonged. Thus Cheever mentions the case* of Captain Bunker, commanding the ship Howard, of New Bedford, who struck a large whale in latitude 30° 30′ north, longitude 154° east. The whale escaped, taking the iron with him. About five years after, while in the same latitude, but 14° farther west, he made fast to and succeeded in securing a noble whale. Upon cutting him up, the identical iron lost five years before proved the whale also the same.

A more singular case yet was one reported to the editors of the New Bedford Standard, in 1865, when they were shown the head of an iron thrown into a whale in the Pacific Ocean, in 1802, from a boat from the ship Lion, of Nantucket, Peter Paddack commander. In 1815, Captain Paddack, then in command of the Lady Adams, also of Nantucket, captured the same whale, and recovered his long-lost harpoon.

The Milton, of New Bedford, in 1865 or 1866 took a whale that in spouting made a shrill sound like a steam-whistle. In cutting off the head the man who put his feet into the spout-holes got one of them cut.

* The Whale and his Captors, p. 157.

Upon examination it was found that a harpoon blade was run transversely through the breathing-holes, and the whistling sound was caused by the action of the escaping air against its edge. The iron was marked with the name of the Central America, which performed her last voyage fifteen years before the capture of this whale by the Milton.*

The amount of oil obtained is not always in proportion to the size of the whale. The conditions of leanness or corpulence are quite as applicable to them as to land animals. Sperm whales which yield 100 barrels are considered very large, but this yield is occasionally exceeded. Captain Davis, in his "Nimrod of the Sea,"† says: "The largest whale we took made 107 barrels. Its length was 79 feet; from the nose to the bunch of the neck 26 feet; thence to the hump 29 feet; from hump to tail 17 feet; length of tail 7 feet; breadth of tail 16 feet 6 inches; height at forehead 11 feet; width 9 feet 6 inches; girt at fin 41 feet 6 inches; at junction of tail 7 feet 9 inches; lower jaw 16 feet long and 41 inches in circumference at thick part. It had 51 teeth, the heaviest weighing 25 ounces. Blubber on back 18 inches; on side 12 to 15 inches; and belly 9 to 10 inches. The hump was 2 feet above the level. The case made 19 barrels; body 73½ barrels; junk 14½ barrels. Captain Sullivan, of the James Arnold, of New Bedford, off New Zealand, took in one voyage 8 whales that made over 100 barrels each, the largest yielding 137 barrels. The head of this made 52 barrels, and the case baled 27 barrels. It was 90 feet long; the flukes 18 feet in length, jaw 18 feet, case 22 feet, and the forehead 13½ feet high. During the same season and on the same ground, Captain Vincent, ship Oneida, of New Bedford, took ten sperm-whales, which stowed 1,140 barrels. Captain Norton, ship Monka,‡ of New Bedford, took on the off-shore ground a sperm-whale that stowed 145 barrels."

In 1853 it is said that the ship Harvest, of Nantucket, took a sperm whale which made 156 barrels of oil, exclusive of the jaw, which was lost by bad weather.§ In 1862 the Ocmulgee, of Edgartown, reported having taken a 130-barrel sperm whale, with a jaw measuring 28 feet in length. Captain Briggs, of the bark Wave, of New Bedford, reported that on the 2d of August, 1876, he took a sperm whale which made 162 barrels and 5 gallons of oil.‖

The right whale is often taken with a much larger yield of oil, though its length of body is considerably less than that of the sperm whale. Another valuable product obtained from the right whale is the lining of the jaw, or bone.¶ This, as it usually runs, will average from 8 to 10

*New Bedford Shipping List. Captain Hamblen, of the Andrew Hicks, of Westport, took, in 1871, from a sperm whale captured near the Gallipagos Islands an iron which belonged to the ship Catawba, of Nantucket, and had been lost 20 years previously. This was the second time Captain Hamblen had recovered a harpoon lost from the same ship—the first time the interval between loss and recovery being about 7 years.

†Page 188.

‡Menkar.

§ New Bedford Shipping-List, 1871.

‖ *Ibid.*, October 10, 1876.

¶ The use of bone was unknown in 1578. At present its uses are multifarious. Mr. John K. Andrews, a whalebone-worker in Boston, kindly furnishes the following list

pounds for each barrel of oil yielded. Thus, if a ship hails 3,000 barrels of right-whale oil, the probability is that she has also obtained from 25,000 to 30,000 pounds of bone. For quite a number of years the price of whalebone was so low that but few whalemen would encumber their vessels with it, the space being of much greater value to fill with oil. When brought home it was worth but about 6 cents per pound. But the price of this commodity has been greatly enhanced. So varied and important are the uses to which it is put that it is extremely sensitive to the fluctuations caused by abundance or scarcity. Thus in the latter part of July, 1876, the price quoted was $2.05 per pound. This was already high; but by the last of October news of disaster to the Arctic fleet sent the price up to $2.50, and by the 1st of December it was quoted at $3.* "Captain Sullivan and Captain Taber, both of New Bedford," says Davis, "speak of bone of the bow-head which measured 17 feet." As whales producing such length of bone yield usually about 3,000 pounds of it, besides their proportionate supply of oil, it is apparent that one such monster is a valuable prize.

"I should like," says the author of The Nimrod of the Sea, a veteran whaleman, "to convey to the reader some idea of the dimensions of the creature from which such bone is taken. To do so is only possible by entering into the details of the various parts, with their sizes, and by comparison with objects familiar to the mind. The blubber, or blanket, of such a whale would carpet a room 22 yards long and 9 yards wide, averaging half a yard in thickness. * * * Set up a saw-log 2 feet in diameter and 20 feet in length for the ridge-pole of the room we propose to build; then raise it in the air 15 feet, and support it with pieces of timber 17 feet long, spread, say, 9 feet. This will make a room 9 feet

---

of the principal purposes to which it is put, viz: in the manufacture of whips, parasols, umbrellas, dresses, corsets, supporters of various kinds, caps, hats, suspenders, neck-stocks, canes, rosettes, cushions to billiard-tables, fishing-rods, divining-rods, bows, busks, fore-arm bows, probangs, tongue-scrapers, pen-holders, paper folders and cutters, graining-combs for painters, boot-shanks, shoe-horns, brushes, mattresses, &c.

* Page 380. Captain Davis, on p. 368, gives another description of the head of the right whale. The mouth, unlike that of his spermaceti relative, has no teeth, but instead is lined with some five or six hundred horny plates (better known as whalebone) attached to the upper jaw and extending from the throat to the end of the narrow roof. These plates are parallel, running transversely with the sides, about one-fourth of an inch apart, and terminating on the inner edge in a hairy fringe. It is these fringes that, interlacing, form the sieve or strainer through which the animal forces the water retaining within the meshes the minute food gathered as it swims along. The gullet is small; by some it is said to be too contracted to admit even a herring; but this statement Captain Davis, for obvious reasons, is not inclined to fully credit. The cavity of the mouth, when the lips are closed, exclusive of the tongue, is equal in capacity to 300 barrels, and the mass of the tongue may occupy 250 barrels, leaving about 50 barrels' capacity for a single mouthful of food-charged water. The ship Sarah Sheafe took a bow-head whale in 1857 that produced 100 barrels of oil and 3,000 pounds of bone; so it will be seen that the old formula of 10 pounds of bone to the barrel of oil does not apply to Arctic whaling. Small amounts of cut bone were sold in February, 1877, as high as $6 per pound.

wide at the bottom, 2 feet wide at the peak, and 20 feet long, and will convey an idea of the upper jaw, the saw-log and slanting supports representing the bone. * * * These walls of bone are clasped by the white, blubbery lips, which at the bottom are 4 feet thick, tapering to a blunt edge, where they fit into a rebate sunk in the upper jaw. The throat is 4 feet thick, and is mainly blubber, interpenetrated by fibrous, muscular flesh. The lips and throat of a 250-barrel whale should yield 60 barrels of oil, and, with the supporting jaw-bones, will weigh as much as twenty-five oxen of 1,000 pounds each. Attached to the throat by a broad base is the enormous tongue,* the size of which can be better conceived by the fact that 25 barrels of oil have been taken from one. Such a tongue would equal in weight ten oxen. The spread of lips, as the whale plows through the fields of 'brit,'† is about 30 feet. Sometimes in feeding the whale turns on its side, so as to lay the longer axis of the cavity of the mouth horizontally. Keeping the lower lip closed, and the upper one thrown off, and standing perpendicularly, it scoops along just under the surface, where the 'brit' is always most densely packed. After thus sifting a track of the sea 15 feet wide and a quarter of a mile in length, the water foaming through the slatted bone, and packing the mollusks upon the hair-sieve, the whale raises the lower jaw; but still keeping the lips apart, it forces the spongy tongue into the cavity of the sieve, driving the water with great force through the spaces between the bone. Then, closing the lips, it disposes of the catch, and repeats the operation until satiated. * * * The tail of such a whale is about 25 feet broad and 6 feet deep, and is considerably more forked than that of the spermaceti. The point of juncture with the body is about 4 feet in diameter, the vertebra about 15 inches; the remainder of the small being packed with rope-like tendons from the size of a finger to that of a man's leg. The great rounded joint at the base of the skull gleams like an ivory sphere, nearly as large round as a carriage-wheel. Through the greatest blood-vessels, more than a foot in diameter, surges, at each pulsation of a heart as large as a hogshead, a torrent of barrels of blood heated to 104°. The respiratory canal is over 12 inches in diameter, through which the rush of air is as noisy as the exhaust-pipe of a thousand-horse-power steam-engine; and when the fatal wound is given, torrents of clotted blood are sputtered into the air over the nauseated hunters. In conclusion, the right whale has an eye scarcely larger than a cow's, and an ear that would scarcely admit a knitting-needle."

* This tongue and throat afford the most vulnerable point of attack to the killer-whales and sharks.

† This "brit" consists of little reddish, shrimp-shaped medusæ, which occur in prodigious numbers in various parts of the ocean, where they are carried by the currents. So numerous are they that Scoresby estimates that an area of two square miles contains 23,888,000,000,000,000 individuals. These being dependent upon the action of currents for their means of locomotion, Commodore Wilkes was led to locate upon his charts those places which would necessarily become the natural feeding-grounds of the whales, and hence the localities where they would be more certainly captured.

The Boston News-Letter for March 18, 1736, mentions a whale that was "lately killed near Cape Cod," which would make its owners £1,500. This must be either a very remarkable whale, or an equally surprising inaccuracy, for it necessitates a yield of at least 2,500 pounds of bone, worth £800 per ton, and about 290 barrels of oil, worth £14 per ton. Now in 1730 oil was worth £7 per ton, and in 1748 £14 per ton, while about 1760 bone was worth in England £500 per ton. It would seem probable that the whale was very large, and that the price during that year must have run extraordinarily high, for the News-Letter appears to be usually careful in its statements.*

Capt. John Howland, in a whaling-sloop from New Bedford, while cruising in the Straits of Belleisle just previously to the Revolution, took two whales which produced 400 barrels of oil, one of them producing 212 barrels.

In 1861 the General Pike, of New Bedford, took a whale on the Kodiah ground which stowed down 274 barrels of oil. In 1855 the ship Adeline, of New Bedford, took a whale in the Ochotsk which produced 250 barrels; the result of that day's work was worth $5,000.

Naturally such immense creatures are possessed of strength; they likewise are endowed with speed and endurance. When struck they have been known, according to the Rev. Dr. Scoresby,† to descend *perpendicularly* from 4,200 to 4,800 feet, or nearly a mile. Captain Royce, who commanded the Superior in her first voyage into the Arctic, states that he has known a whale to take out 6,300 feet of line in sounding. He does not, however, mean that the whale sounded to that depth, since the line continues to be drawn from the boat even while the whale is rising, so that two-thirds of this number of feet for the perpendicular descent would probably be making a liberal estimate. The time usually occupied by whales in sounding varies from about half an hour for the right to about an hour and a half for the sperm whale.‡ A frightened whale will, according to the judgment of old whalemen, go from 10 to 12 miles an hour; indeed, when first struck they frequently rush at the rate of from 20 to 25 miles an hour for a short time. Though often killed without extraordinary difficulty, yet their tenacity of life at times

* In an editorial in the Nantucket Inquirer & Mirror of February 17, 1877, the difficulty of correctly ascertaining the yield of a single whale is commented on. In a busy season it is no uncommon thing for a ship to "boil out" a thousand or even two thousand barrels of oil without "cooling down," and unless the most extraordinary care was exercised it would be hard to tell where one whale's yield ended and another began. The Honolulu Friend, in 1849, reported a whale taken by the Junior, of New Bedford, which produced 316 barrels of oil, and the same paper is the authority for the story of a whale seen by Captain Royce of the Superior, of Sag Harbor, that was so large they would not attempt his capture, because the strain on the mast in cutting in (if he was taken) would be so great. How well authenticated this story is, is not known, but unless the authority was above suspicion, the strain on one's imagination must be as disastrous as that on the mast would have been.

† Notes on Whales and Whaling, xviii.

‡ Nimrod of the Sea, Appendix A.

is surprising. Captain Malloy, of the bark Osceola, of New Bedford, mentions an instance,* where one of his boats struck a large sperm-whale from the waist-boat. Soon after the starboard boat fastened to him and got stove; a bomb-lance was then fired into him from the waist-boat, whereupon he turned upon her and stove her, knocking the bottom completely out. The ship picked up the swimming crews, and was then steered for the whale. On seeing his new antagonist he rushed at her, striking her on the bow, knocking off the cut-water with his head, and tearing the copper and sheathing from the bow with his jaw. The ship was again put into position and run for him. As she ranged alongside two bomb and two whale lances were fired into him. A boat was then lowered and two more bomb-lances were discharged into him without effect. It was night by this time, so the boat was called aboard and arrangements were made to hold the position of the ship during the night. Occasionally the infuriated monster could be heard fighting the fragments of boats, oars, &c. "Thus through the night," continues the journal, "he held his ground, although he had two lines (600 fathoms) towing on to the harpoons, five bombs exploded in him, and other wounds from lances." The next morning the attack was renewed with bomb-lances, and *thirty-one were fired into him before he was killed.* Many similar anecdotes could be related.†

A most singular trait of the sperm-whale is what is termed by whalemen "settling." At times when suddenly alarmed it will sink bodily in the water with the apparent rapidity of a lump of lead; so rapidly, in fact, that the mortified boat-steerer hauls in the harpoon which he has thrown but which failed to hit the object thrown at. This sudden sinking is unaccompanied by any change in the horizontal position, or any motion of the tail or fins, and seems to be adopted as a means of securing safety when there seems to be no time to round out and sound.‡

Another singular feature connected with the whale-fishery is the sudden coming and going of the objects of pursuit. According to Davis,§ their appearance and disappearance would seem somewhat periodical, as though perhaps certain phases of the moon were better than others for the prosecution of the fishery. At such times whales suddenly ap-

* *Ibid.*, p. 233.

† Scoresby (ii, p. 276) relates an instance in the experience of the English whaleship Resolution, where a whale was finally killed after a chase of nine miles, and after having carried off one boat (which was lost) and 10,440 yards or nearly six miles of line.

‡ P. 187. The thorough descriptions of whales, their habits, haunts, &c., given by Scammon and Davis, make extended comments unnecessary in this work.

§ P. 177. Schools of whales containing many individuals have, even within a comparatively late period, been seen and attacked in the Indian Ocean. The fishery there extends from Cape Leeurvin to Java Head, a distance of 1,600 miles. In 1838 the American and French whalemen took at one capture off Cape Leeurvin 10,000 barrels; in 1845 the Americans in one onslaught in Champion Bay took 6,000 barrels; in 1857 the American and French fleets, while off King George's Sound, took at one time 12,000 barrels.

pear and are plenty, and this season will be followed by a pèriod in which none will be in sight.

In 1868 there appeared in the Flag of our Union a series of sketches entitled "Leaves from the Arethusa's Log," by William H. Macy, esq., a veteran whaleman. Among them was one detailing the "raising," pursuit, and capture of a sperm-whale.* Being a life-like description of this event as it ordinarily occurs, it is, with the author's permission, transferred to this work:

"The next morning, having the first mast-head, I was in the foretop-gallant cross-trees at sunrise, thinking, of course, of the five-dollars' bounty all the way up the rigging.† The him outline of the peak was still visible, and the topsails of the Pandora just in sight, astern, the wind still continuing moderate at west-northwest, both ships steering south by west. As I looked astern, when I *first* got my footing aloft I caught sight of something like a small puff of steam or white smoke, rising a little and blowing off on the water. Looking intently at the same spot, after a short interval another puff rose like the former, satisfying me, from the descriptions I had heard, that some sort of whale was there, and I instinctively shouted, 'There she blows!'

"Where away?" hailed Mr. Johnson, who was just climbing the main-topmast rigging; "O, yes, I see him! sperm whale, I believe—hold on a bit till he blows again—yes—thar 'sh' blo-o-ows! large sperm whale! two points off the larboard! Blo-o-ows! headed to windward!"

"How far off?" shouted Mr. Grafton from the deck.

"Three miles! 'ere sh' blows!"

By this time the old man‡ was on deck and ready for action. "Call all hands out, Mr. Grafton! Hard a starboard there! Stand by to brace round the yards. Cook! get your breakfast down as fast as you can. Keep the run of him, there, aloft! Maintop bowline, boat-steerers! Sure it's a sperm whale, eh, Mr. Johnson? Steward! give me up the glass—I must make a cleet in the gangway for that glass soon. Muster 'em all up, Mr. Grafton, and get the lines in as fast as you can (mounting the shearpole). Sing out when we head right, Mr. Johnson! Mr. Grafton, you'll have to brace sharp up, I guess (just going over the maintop). See the Pandora, there? O, yes, I see her (half-way up the topmast-rigging). Confound him! he's heading just right to see the whale, too! ("There goes flukes!" shouted the mulatto.) Yes! yes! I see him—just in time to see him (swinging his leg over the topmast cross-trees), a noble fan, too! a buster! Haul aboard that maintack! We must have that fellow, Mr. Johnson. Steady-y! Keep her along just full and by. *We mustn't let the Pandora get him, either!*"

The Arethusa bent gracefully to the breeze, as, braced sharp on the port tack, she darted through the water as though instinctively snuffing

* "The First Whale." The series is soon to be published in book-form.

† It is sometimes the custom on whalemen for the captain to offer some reward to the man who first "raised" or discovered whales.

‡ The term applied by the sailors to the captain.

her prey. The whale was one of those patriarchal old bulls, who are often found alone, and would probably stay down more than an hour before he would be seen again. Meantime, the two ships were rapidly nearing each other; and the Pandora's lookouts were not long in discovering that "something was up," as was evinced by her setting the main royal and foretopmast studding-sail, though they could not possibly have seen the whale yet. But the whale was apparently working slowly to windward, and the Pandora coming with a flowing sheet, all of which was much in her favor. The old man remained aloft, anxiously waiting the next rising, from time to time hailing the deck to know "what time it was?" and satisfying himself that the boats were in readiness, and breakfast served out to those who wanted it. As three-quarters of an hour passed, he grew more anxious and fidgety, shifting his legs about in the cross-trees and clutching the spy-glass in his nervous grasp.

"Are you all ready, Mr. Grafton?"

"Ay, ay, sir," answered the mate from the maintop, where he had mounted to get a look at the whale when he should rise again.

"Let them hoist and swing the boats."

"Ay, ay, sir."

"I think I saw a ripple then," said the second mate, from the topsail yard directly beneath him.

"Where?" demanded the captain.

"Four points off the lee bow."

"O! no, you didn't, he won't come there. He'll rise right ahead or a little on the weather bow. I don't think he'll go to windward—Good gracious! see that Pandora come down! She'll be right in the suds here directly! I think we've run far enough, eh, Mr. Grafton? Haul the mainsail up, then! and square the main-yard!"

Silence for a few minutes after this evolution was performed.

"He can't be far off when he comes up again. Look at the men old Worth has got aloft there, his cross-trees swarming, and every rattlin manned. Look sharp! all of ye! We must see that whale when he first breaks water. That helm eased down? Haul the foresail up! and let the jib-sheets flow a little more. It can't be possible that the whale has been up—no, we couldn't help seeing him, some of us—I *know* 'twas a sperm whale. I saw his fan; besides, there's Mr. Johnson—best eyes in the ship. What time is it there? An hour and ten minutes that whale has been down—a long-winded old dog! We shall have to wear around, I'm afraid we shall forge. Blo-o-ows! right ahead, not one mile off! Down, there, and lower away! Now, Mr. Grafton, work carefully—Mr. Dunham, too; if you don't strike this rising, spread your chances well, and don't crowd each other—*but don't you let the Pandora get him!*" The captain was by this time in the stern of his own boat. "All ready, Mr. Johnson? Where's Old Jeff.* at my midship oar? O, here you are, eh?

* Every man has his place.

You ain't turned white yet—lower away! Cooper! Where's Cooper?* As soon as we are clear, wear round—*let run that davit fall!*—wear round and make a short board—haul up your tackle, boy. Keep to windward all you can, Cooper! Pull a little off the weather bow, Mr. Grafton, and then set your sail! Haul in these gripes towing over the quarter. By thunder, there's Worth's boats all down! coming with a fair wind, too! Out oars, lads."

The Pandora had luffed to, and dropped her boats a mile to windward, and they were coming down before the breeze, wing-and-wing, with their paddles flashing in the sunlight, and their immense jibs guyed out on the bow-oar as studding-sails, promising to stand about an equal chance for the whale with ourselves. The larboard boat, to which I belonged, proved the fastest of the three, and had a little the lead. After pulling a few quiet strokes to windward, Father Grafton set his sails, and, as he gave the order to "peak the oars and take the paddles," seemed as cool and calm as when engaged in the most ordinary duty on board. There was no confusion or bustle in his boat, but, with his practiced eye fixed upon the huge spermaceti, he kept encouraging us in a low, dry tone, as he conned the steering-oar with such skill that he seemed to do it without effort.†

---

* Usually the cooper is also head ship-keeper while the boats are down, if the captain is in one.

† Exciting scenes have often occurred where boats from rival ships contended for the prize, which by the law of whaling belongs to the first "fast" boat. Many years ago an English, a French, a Portuguese, and an American ship lay becalmed within a radius of a mile of each other in the South Pacific, when a whale was "raised." With a celerity peculiar to whaling, a boat from each ship was down and in pursuit. The American whaleman is the only man who attends exclusively to his own duty; the oarsmen leave it to their officers to watch the whale and only attend to getting the boat through the water. Says the boat-steerer of the American boat in his account of the race: "Placing the palm of my left hand under the abaft oar, while with my right I guided the boat, and at each stroke threw a part of my weight against it, our boat would 'skim the water like a thing of life.' A few moments from the start brought us up with the Portuguese. The crews of the different ships witnessing the chase, the excitement was tremendous. Our shipmates cheered us as we came up with the first boat, and as we passed, the whale again made its appearance. Singing out to the men, 'There she blows! She's an eighty-barrel—right ahead. Give way, my boys!' &c., we were soon alongside the Frenchman. The Frenchman was too polite to oppose us, and we passed him with ease. The English boat was now about ten rods in advance, and the whale about one and three-fourths of a mile. Now came the trial. The English boat was manned by the same number of stout, active hands as our own, and, seeing us pass the other boats, their whole strength and force was put to the oar. We gained on them but slowly, and such was the excitement of the race that we were in danger of passing over where the whale had last 'blowed.' At this moment the English boat-steerer noticed the manner in which I had placed my left hand and weight against the oar. Instantly laying hold of his own in a like manner, his first effort broke it short at the lock. Thus disabled, he gave us a hearty curse as we shot past him like a meteor. We had been so excited with the race that we had lost sight of the whale. As luck would have it, at this instant she 'blowed' but a few rods ahead. In a moment we were fast, and 'all hands stern.' * * * That whale stowed us down

"Now, lads, you face round to paddle, you can all see him. I declare, he's a noble fellow—ninety barrels under his hide if there's a drop. Bunker, do you see that fellow? he's got a back like a ten-acre lot—paddle hard, lads,—if you miss him, go right overboard yourself, and don't come up again—long and strong stroke, boys, on your paddles. See that boat coming—that's Ray, the second-mate of the Pandora—three or four more spouts, and we'll have him—he's ours, sure! they can't get here in time—scratch hard, boys! don't hit your paddles on the gunwale. Stand up, Bunker, and get your jib-tack clear! Don't let them gally* you, if they shout in that boat."

"All right!" said his boat-steerer, with his eager hand resting on the iron pole, "Never fear, sir."

"Paddle hard, lads, a stroke or two. That's right, Bunker. Keep cool, my boy, keep cool, and make sure of him."

A wild and prolonged shout rang on the air from six sturdy pairs of lungs in the Pandora's waist-boat, as Mr. Ray, seeing that he was baffled, let fly his sheets and rounded to, a ship's length to windward. It was too late, however.

"All right," said Father Grafton, in the same dry, quiet tone, as before. "Hold your hand, Bunker. Hold your hand, boy, till you're past his hump—another shoot, lads—way enough, in paddles. Now, Bunker, give it to him. Down to your oars, the rest. Give him t'other one, boy! Well done! both irons to the hitches.† Hold water, all. Bear a hand, now, and roll up that sail. Wet line, Tom! wet line! Where's your bucket? All ready with your sail, Bunker? Let her come, then—all right. Come aft here, now, and let me get a dig at him."

The line was spinning round the loggerhead with a whizzing noise, and a smoking heat, as the huge leviathan, stung to the quick, darted down into the depths of the ocean. Bunker threw on the second round turn to check him, and jamming the bight of the line over the stern-

---

eighty-five barrels of oil, and shortened our voyage two months." (See The Whale and his Captors, p. 196.)

Another international race took place once in Delago Bay. A large whale was "raised" at the same moment by an English and an American ship, about equidistant from each, and immediately the boats were down. The English, having the lead, finding the American gaining, bore wide from the whale to throw their rivals on the outside. When, however, they both came, side by side, abreast of the whale, the English inside, of course, one of the American sailors sprang from his seat and darted his harpoon directly over the English boat, planting it clear to the socket in the whale's life, and the Englishmen, hastily releasing themselves from their perilous position, left the field to their American cousins, while the shores of Delago Bay echoed with the cheers of the comrades of the victors. (N. A. Review, 1834.)

*Mr. Macy thinks this word may be a corruption of the obsolete verb *gallow*, to be found in old writers. Thus Shakespeare says, in King Lear, "The wrathful skies gallow the deep wanderers of the dark."

†It sometimes happens that as the iron is thrown, the whale "bows," and the harpoon striking in the concave against what is called "slack blubber" fails to penetrate. (See Nimrod of the Sea, p. 378.)

sheets, watched it carefully as it flew through his grasp; while the mate cleared his lance, and got ready to renew the attack. Every moment his anxiety increased as he kept turning his head, and looking at the tub of line, rapidly settling, as the whale ran it out, "I declare, I believe he'll take all my line. Blacksmith! pass along the drug!* Check him hard, Bunker!" then, seeing the other boats near at hand, he opened his throat, and, for the first time, we learned the power of Father Grafton's lungs.

"Spring hard, Mr. Dunham! I want your line! Cast off your craft, and stand by to throw your line to me! Spring hard! *Do!*"

The ash sticks in the waist-boat were doing their best, as the loud "Ay, ay!" was borne back o'er the water from Dunham, while the old man could be seen in the rear of the picture wildly straining every nerve to be "in at the death," and heaving desperately at the after oar, with his hat off, his hair flying loosely in the breeze, and his whole frame writhing with eager excitement. Our line was going, going; already there was but one flake in the tub, when the waist-boat ranged up on our quarter, and Fisher, with the coil gathered in his hand, whirled it over his head, making ready for a cast.† At this instant his strain was suddenly relieved, and the line slacked up.

"Never mind!" roared Mr. Grafton. "Hold on, Fisher. All right, he's coming. Never mind your line, Mr. Dunham, he's coming up! Pull ahead and get fast! Get a lance at him if you can! Haul line, *us!* Face round here all of ye, and haul line! Careful, Bunker, about coiling down.‡ He'll be up now, in a minute; haul lively!"

The waist-boat had shot ahead under a fresh impulse of her own, and the captain came drawing up abreast of the fast boat.

"Are you well fast, Mr. Grafton?" "Ay, ay, sir; both irons chock to the socket." "That's the talk. Got 'most all your line, hasn't he?" "Yes, sir." "Well, gather in as fast as you can. Spring hard, *us!* Spring! I want to grease a lance in that fish. There he is; up," he shouted, as the tortured monster broke water, showing his whole head out in his agony, and started to windward.

Fisher had bent on his craft again, and was about two ship's lengths from the whale when he rose.

"Haul quick, my lads," said the mate, "and get this stray line in. There's Mr. Dunham going on, and the old man will be with him in a minute. There he brings to!" as the whale suddenly stopped short in his mad career, and lay swashing up and down, as if rallying his strength for a fresh effort.

---

*Drag.

†In taking the second boat's line the upper end is made fast to the lower end of the line of the "fast" boat, which then becomes the "loose" one, and the second boat takes the place of the first.

‡In hauling in the line from a fast whale it is not recoiled in the tub, but in the boat. The utmost care is, however, necessary in this coiling, for if occasion demands it must run out as freely the second time as from the tub.

"There 's 'stand up' in the waist-boat! There he darts! Hurrah! two boats fast. Haul lively, *us*, and get this line in!"

His whaleship seemed staggered by this accumulation of cold iron in his system, and lay wallowing in the trough of the waves. It was a critical moment for him; for Mr. Dunham was getting his lance on the half-cock, ready for darting, and as the whale suddenly "milled short round" to pass across the head of his boat, the young man saw his advantage, and cried, "Pull ahead! Pull ahead,* and we'll get a 'set' on him! Lay forward, Fisher! Lay forward hard, my lad! right on for his fin! Pull ahead! So, way enough—hold water, all;" and, driven by a strong arm, the sharp lance entered his "life," its bright shank disappearing till the pole brought it up.

"Hold her so!" said the second mate. "Way enough! just hold her so till he rises again!" as the whale hollowed his back under the sea, now crimsoned with his life-tide, and again rising, received the lance anew in his vitals; but the first "set" was enough, and the gush of clotted blood from his spiracle told how effectually it had done its work.

"There," said Father Grafton, who had just got his line gathered in and was ready to renew the assault, "there's the red flag flying at his nose. Blacksmith, we may as well put up our lance, we sha'n't want it to-day. Well done, Mr. Dunham. Thick as tar the first lance. Hold on line, Bunker! heave on a turn!" as the whale, making a dying effort, started up to windward, passing among the Pandora's boats within easy hail.

"Give us your warp, Pitman, if you want a tow," said Bunker, in passing, to Mr. Ray's boat-steerer.

"Every dog has his day," growled Pitman in reply.

---

* It sometimes happens that it is desirable to draw up alongside the whale while fast to him, the more effectually to use the lance. This operation is thus described: "Having hauled as well forward as the position of the harpoon will admit, the boat-header reaches over the bows, and, taking hold of the line forward of the *chocks*, brings it around outside the boat, then giving it into the hands of the bow-oarsman, who has faced forward on his thwart. Now, as the man hauls on the line, the direction of strain is oblique, well back on the bow, and the course of the boat becomes parallel with that of the whale a few feet distance from him. The boat-header then has his chance to ply the lance with deadly effect. If the harpoon is well forward of the hump of the whale, the boat will run in comparative safety, as the strokes of the tail will be behind the boat, and the swing of the jaw in front. As long as the whale continues running in a straight course on the surface, the persistent boat will cling behind his fin as a bull-dog will to the nose of an ox. His only escape is to run deep, or, by suddenly *milling* or turning, to bring the boat in reach of jaws or flukes. The duty of the bow-oarsman is arduous when the whale is running fast, or there is a high sea. By his own strength he must keep the boat in its position, though drenched with the flying spray from the bow. Should the strain wrench the wet line through his burned hands, the blessings of the excited boat-header are poured on his head with a vigor heard only in the rushing hiss of this 'Nantucket sleigh-ride.'" (Nimrod of the Sea, p. 142.)

"Yes. Come aboard to-morrow; I'll give you a scrap for luck."

The whale went in his flurry* and turned up nearly under the stern of the Pandora, as she luffed to for her boats; but Captain Worth could not afford to lose the breeze long, and, by the time the last boat was on the cranes, his helm was up and his mizzen-topsail shivering. The old ship fell off to her former course, and, setting her royal and studding sails, left her more fortunate consort "alone in her glory."

H.—INTRODUCTORY TO RETURNS.

In making up these reports many difficulties occur.

1st. In the earlier years, in fact down to about the years 1844–'45, the reports of the amount of bone taken were only occasional. Most of that commodity was imported prior to 1840 in New London and Sag Harbor ships, its value being so low that captains of vessels from many of the other ports did not care to be encumbered with it. For this reason a large amount of bone was brought home which it is impossible to properly accredit.

2d. Oil and bone were frequently sold by vessels in foreign ports to pay for repairs, of which no account appears.

3d. Much oil and bone came home as freight which was not recorded in the shipping journals, and hence does not appear in the record. In many cases where it was recorded the return was made in the name of some shipping agent and not of the vessel. Where one man or one firm acted as agent for from two to ten ships proper credit was impossible. Again, many cases occur where two and occasional cases where even three vessels of the same name sail from the same port. Where a credit to them is made, it must be made, unless the vessel is carefully specified, according to the best judgment of the compiler.

4th. Oil is sent home in casks and bone in bundles, and in many cases is returned in that form. Now casks hold from two to eight barrels, and bundles of bone are of various sizes. The estimate in such cases has been founded on 4½ barrels to the cask, and 90 pounds to the bundle.

Abbreviations used: A. O. or Atl., Atlantic Ocean; C. G. H., Cape of Good Hope; P. or P. O., Pacific Ocean; Brazil, B. B., or B. Banks, Brazil Banks; Woolwich, Woolwich Bay; Falk., Falkland Islands; W. I., W. Ind. or West Ind., West Indies; Peru or Chili, coast of Peru or coast

* The head rises and falls, and the flukes strike the surface in rapid succession. With great force it will rapidly swim in a large circle, sometimes passing two or three times around, and then closing the circuit by rolling on its side, dead. This is termed the "flurry," and the ending of the tragedy is "fin out." (Nimrod of the Sea, p. 177.) The food of the sperm whale consists principally of squid, and in the agonies of his "flurry" he often throws up immense pieces of undigested food, pieces half as large as a whale-boat are frequently seen, and these seem to be mere fragments of the immense marine monster to which they formerly belonged. Mr. Joseph Swain, of Nantucket, relates an instance where a piece of shark several feet long was similarly vomited up in the death-struggle of a sperm whale.

of Chili; S. A. or S. Atl., South Atlantic; Africa, coast of Africa; S. S. or S. Seas, South Seas; Pat., coast of Patagonia; South Coast, along the edge of the Gulf Stream; Delago, Delago Bay; W. Ilds., West. Ilds., or C. de V., Cape de Verdes or Western Islands; East coast or East shore, that part of the African coast; Shoals, Nantucket Shoals; Guinea or Japan, the coasts of those countries; N. W., Northwest coast of America; N. P., North Pacific; S. P., South Pacific; Ind., Indian Ocean; N. Z., New Zealand; Des., Desolation Islands; Cum. In., Cumberland Inlet; Hud. Bay, Hudson Bay.

I.—RETURNS OF WHALING-VESSELS, SAILING FROM AMERICAN PORTS, SINCE THE YEAR 1715.

1715.

Six sloops sailed from Nantucket of from 30 to 40 tons burden each, returning with cargoes amounting to 600 barrels of oil and 11,000 pounds of bone, and valued at £1,100 sterling. This number was probably for some years pretty constant.*

1722.

In 1722, the sloop ——, of Nantucket, Elisha Coffin master, was lost at sea with all on board.

1723.

Among the vessels sailing this year was one from Rhode Island, commanded by William Bennett, and a sloop from Nantucket, commanded by Nathan Skiff. Bennett brought into Rhode Island the largest sperm whale ever seen in Rhode Island up to that date (May, 1723). He obtained from it 18 barrels of head matter and from 40 to 50 barrels of body oil, and reported that he might have obtained one-third more from the head if the weather had been favorable. The account concludes: "This spring our vessels have brought eight whales into this port."† The sloop reported from Nantucket was captured by the pirate Low, her captain killed, two Indians carried away, and the balance of the crew sent adrift in the two boats with no sustenance save water. They arrived safely in Nantucket, however.‡

1730.

Twenty-five vessels, from 38 to 50 tons burden each, sailed from Nantucket and obtained 3,700 barrels of oil, valued at £7 per ton, £3,200.

1731.

Among the vessels sailing this year was a sloop from Nantucket, of which Thomas Hathaway was commander, and which was lost with all on board. The sloop Pelican, of Newport, Benjamin Thurston, owner, made a voyage, returning with 114 barrels oil, 200 pounds bone.

1732.

A vessel, commanded by a Captain Atkins, made a whaling-voyage to Davis's Straits, going as far as 66° north. This was probably the first voyage to this locality from the Colonies.

* It must be remembered that these lists, up to the year 1815, are entirely made up from newspaper reports and sundry scraps of information gathered here and there.

† Boston News-Letter.

‡ *Ibid.*

1733.

Lot Thatcher, son of Major Thatcher, of Barnstable, was drowned while on a whaling-voyage, probably in a Barnstable vessel. A whale was taken in the Bay of Fundy by a Captain Hussey, and brought into Boston in August.

1736.

In March whaling-vessels commanded by the following men cleared from the port of Boston:* James Smalley and Daniel Smalley (for Greenland). In April, Doty, Doane & Mayo (for Greenland); Jenkins, Myrick, Doane, Langstaff, Lombard, Dimock, Rider, Doane, and Davis (Davis's Straits). In May, Yeates (Davis's Straits). In August, a whaling-schooner arrived at Nantucket from the northward with three large whales, one of them "twelve-foot bone."† In the same month Captain Langstaff returned from Davis's Straits to Cape Cod. While in the straits he struck a large whale which stove his boat, breaking an arm and a leg (in two places) of one of the crew, and injuring less seriously four others. A day or two after they fell in with a Dutch ship which had a surgeon on board, who set the broken bones and dressed the wounds. Captain Langstaff took two whales besides this troublesome one, one before, and the other after the accident. In September, Dimock, Barker, Dimock (No. 2), Myrick, Jenkins, Lombard, and Langstaff (No. 2), arrived home.

1737.

In February there cleared from the port of Boston for Davis's Straits, Rider & Webster. In March, Rider (No. 2), Adams, Doane, Lombard, Mayo, Crowell, Davis, Strout, Crawford, Glargon, Smalley, Doty, Freeman, and Mayo (No. 2). In April, Dimock, Bangs, Taylor, Gorham, Somes, Daniel Gorham, West, Doane, (No. 2), Paddock, Snow, White, Under wood, Smith, Small, Vickery, Small (No. 2), Higgins, Vickery (No. 2), Bickford, and Smith (No. 2)‡. In May, Black, Rust, Cudworth, and Oakley—in all 40.

Captain Atherton Hough arrived at Eastham from a whaling-voyage to Davis's Straits in August. There also entered at Boston from the same locality—in August, Captains Paddock, Smalley, Isaac Smalley, Somes, and Smith; in September, Clift, Mayo, Lombard, Watts, Doty, Robert Mayo, Vickery, Bickford, Bayly,§ Haugh, Mayo, Gorum, Bacon, Snow, Russell, Oakley, Taylor, and Dimock; in October, Hussey and White. (The Davis's Straits fleet from Massachusetts alone in this year must have consisted of between 50 and 60 vessels.)

---

* Boston was the port of entry for nearly the whole State. Vessels from Dartmouth and vicinity usually cleared from and entered at Newport, and Nantucket vessels, before that port was made one of entry, cleared sometimes from Newport and sometimes from Boston. The names of captains and not of vessels are given.

† Referring to the length of the slabs.

‡ A dozen whaling-vessels, says the Boston News-Letter, are fitting for Davis Straits from Provincetown (1737). "So many people are going that not over a dozen or fourteen men will be left."

§ The spelling is as per report.

1738.

Cleared from Boston for Davis's Straits in March, Stephen Snow, Prince Snow, John Gorham, Benjamin Gorham, Strout, Elisha Mayo, Robert Mayo, John Smalley, Elisha Smalley, Doane, and Hatch; in April, White and Howland.

Entered at Boston from Davis's Straits, in August, Mayo, White, and Smalley; in September, Smalley (No. 2); in November, Bennett and Gorham. The Davis's Straits fishery yielded excellent returns.

Joseph Chase also made a whaling voyage from Martha's Vineyard in the sloop Diamond, 40 tons burden.

1739.

Cleared at Boston in April for Davis's Straits, Captain White. Entered at Boston from Davis's Straits, Small, Robbins, Doty, Mayo, White, and Smalley (August), Sears (September), and Gorham (November).* James Claghorn in the sloop Leopard (40 tons), and Jos. Chase in the sloop Diamond, also made whaling-voyages from Martha's Vineyard.

1740.

Cleared at Boston in March for Davis's Straits, Mayo. Sailed from Martha's Vineyard, sloop Leopard, Claghorn master. A whaleman on the Banks having lowered for whales, his boat was attacked by a sperm whale and stove into kindling-wood. The crew were rescued unharmed, by another boat, to which also the whale immediately gave chase, but by dint of hard rowing the fate of its predecessor was avoided.

1741.

The sloop ——, Capt. Solomon Sturgis, sailed from Barnstable, whaling. The sloop was captured by a Spanish privateer under command of Don Francisco Lewis. Sturgis and eight of his men were allowed to leave, and the vessel with four men was carried away. The sloop Leopard, Claghorn, made another voyage from Martha's Vineyard.

1742.

Sloop Humbird, John Harper master, made a voyage from Martha's Vineyard. Sloop ——, Daniel Paddack master, sailed from Nantucket and was lost.

1744.

A whaleman from Nantucket was captured by a French privateer. Sloop Susannah, 55 tons burden, made a voyage from Martha's Vineyard.

---

* At this very time the English papers were remarking the success of the Dutch in the Greenland fishery, and saying, "It is surprising that such Instances of the prodigious Advantage of the Greenland Fishery should not push the English to more vigorously pursue it." See item in Boston News-Letter, dated Newcastle, July 23.

1746.

A whaling-vessel, presumably from Martha's Vineyard, was taken by a French man-of-war near Newfoundland,* and a sloop from Nantucket was taken by a French privateer, released and subsequently captured by a Spanish privateer and put in charge of a prize crew, who being unable to navigate her, turned her over to the prisoners and by them she was carried into Philadelphia.

1747.

Among the whaling-fleet of this year there sailed a schooner from Boston, ———, Mayo master, and a sloop from Nantucket, Peter Bunker master. These two vessels were captured by a Spanish privateer off the Capes of Virginia. The sloop was ransomed for $800 and a brother of the captain was detained by the Spaniard as security.

1748.

Sixty vessels, of from 50 to 75 tons burden each, sailed from Nantucket, returning with 11,250 barrels of oil, valued at £14 per ton, £19,684.

1750.

In August Captain Atkins entered at Boston from Davis's Straits.

1751.

Sloop Experiment made a whaling voyage from Williamsburg, Va., along the coast, returning early in May with a valuable whale.

1752.

A vessel of 75 tons burden, owned by John Newman and Timothy Coffin, of Martha's Vineyard, made a whaling voyage; also one of 55 tons owned by John Norton, esq., and others of the same place, made another.

1753.

The two vessels which sailed from Martha's Vineyard last year sailed again this. The former, which was commanded by Coffin himself, was captured off the Grand Banks by a French vessel and Coffin was killed. The latter, under the command of Christopher Beette, was lost on the coast of Carolina.

1754.

Two whalemen off the Capes of Virginia were struck by lightning, and two men killed on board one of them.

1755.

Three sloops from Nantucket, commanded respectively by John Starbuck, Jonathan Coffin, and Peter Bunker, were lost while whaling.

* The Boston News-Letter of February 26, 1746, says: Two men arrived at Martinico who were whaling near Newfoundland, and were taken by a French man-of-war and carried to Chebueta, thence sent to Canada.

1756.

Eighty vessels, of an average of 75 tons burden, pursued the business from Nantucket this year. Of these, three, commanded respectively by Christopher Coffin, Peleg Coffin 2d, and Nathan Daggett, were lost, and six others, under Captains Henry Coffin, Jonathan Coffin 2d, Seth Hussey, Nathaniel Coleman 2d, William Barnard, and Josiah Gorham, were captured by the French. (One of those captured was said to have had 600 barrels of oil on board.) The returning vessels brought in 12,000 barrels of oil, valued at £18 per ton, £27,600. In September, Captain Smith entered at Boston from Davis Straits.

1757.

Capt. Nathaniel Woodbury, in a whaling-sloop from Nantucket, was captured by the French privateer Revenge, about the middle of August, east of the Grand Bank. He had no oil on board at the time, and his vessel was restored to him with the warning that another privateer was cruising in that vicinity. Woodbury immediately made the best of his way to Nantucket, arriving there early in September.

1758.

Two whaling-sloops were captured this year by a privateer brig from Mississippi, and the sloop Industry, Isaiah Eldredge, master,* was captured by a French privateer.

1760.

A whaling-vessel from Nantucket was captured by a French privateer sloop of 12 guns, but released after the Frenchman had put on board of her the crew of sloop ———, Luce master, which they had taken full of oil a few days before, and burned. Another privateer, mounting 14 guns, took several whalemen; one of them was ransomed for $400, and the crews of all put on board of her and landed at Newport. Sloop Polly (65 tons), of Martha's Vineyard, owned by John Norton, esq. and others, made a voyage from that port. The sloops Goodluck, Dolphin, and Success, owned by Jos. Conkling, John Foster, and others, are said to have sailed from Sag Harbor, in this pursuit, to Disco Island.

1761.

Ten vessels, of from 70 to 90 tons burden each, cleared from Massachusetts for the St. Lawrence fishery. Names of captains engaged in the fishery, so far as are now known,† John Clasby, Seth Folger, ——— Jenkins, ——— Dunham, ——— Allen, ——— Pease, Thomas Gibbs, John Akin, Ephraim Delano, Thomas Nye, ——— Shearman.

* Probably from Dartmouth.

† From the log of the Betsey. See Ricketson's History of New Bedford.

1762.

Seventy-eight vessels cleared this year for the whaling-grounds. Of these 50 went to the Gulf of St. Lawrence. The produce of the fishery was 9,440 barrels of oil, valued at $102,518.40. A schooner, ——— Bickford master, was lost on Seal Islands. The sloop Polly, from Martha's Vineyard, was lost while whaling at the southward, and her crew of thirteen men perished with her. A sloop from Nantucket was taken by a privateer while whaling near the Gulf Stream. Among the captains who sailed were, Shubael Bunker, Benjamin Paddock, Henry Folger, and Nathan Coffin.

1763.

More than 80 vessels sailed this year from Massachusetts for the Gulf of St. Lawrence.

1764.

Seventy-two vessels sailed this year, returning with 11,983 barrels of oil, valued at $131,135.38. One of these vessels was commanded by Jonathan Negers, of Dartmouth. While fast to one whale the boat which Captain Negers headed was struck by a second, and the captain received injuries from which he died a few days after. A brig from Nantucket, Solomon Gardner, master, was lost.

1765.

One hundred and one vessels sailed in 1765, and the produce was 11,512 barrels of oil, valued at $125,020.32. A new whaling-sloop from Dartmouth was run down and sunk by another whaleman from the same port. The majority of the vessels fished in the Gulf of St. Lawrence and Straits of Belleisle.

1766.

One hundred and eighteen vessels, of an average of 75 tons each, went whaling from Nantucket, producing 11,969 barrels of oil, valued at $129,983.24. Captain Peter Wells arrived at Boston, August 18, and between September 25 and October 2 quite a number of whalemen arrived at the same port. From one of them the son of the captain (Clark) was lost while striking a sperm-whale off George's Banks. Several vessels also sailed from Warren, R. I., most of them going southward, and one of them from the Western Islands, bringing in over 300 barrels of oil. Newport sent some vessels too.

1767.

Nantucket sent 108 vessels, averaging 75 tons each, producing 16,561 barrels of oil, worth $179,852.46. Two sloops, one commanded by Captain Coleman and the other by Captain Coffin, both of Nantucket, were lost in the Straits of Belleisle.

1768.

The fleet from Nantucket consisted of 125 vessels, of an average of 75 tons, returning with 15,439 barrels of oil, worth $167,667.54.* (In addition to these a large number of vessels sailed from Boston, Cape Cod, Dartmouth, Providence, Warren, Newport, and other ports.) One sloop sailed from New York in April. The names of the captains of vessels in the northern fishery, so far as can be ascertained, are as follows: Joseph Tripp, Benjamin Jenney, Salathiel Eldridge, Isaiah Eldridge, and Fortunatus Sherman, of Dartmouth; Phineas Fish and Nathaniel Allen, of Falmouth; ——— White, of Cape Cod; Dillingham and Peter Welding, of Boston; and Louis Taber, Gamaliel Spooner, Thomas Paine, Jeguthan Hammond, Benjamin Young, John Howland, Daniel Hussey, ——— Nye, ——— Meader, Nathaniel Delano, Ephraim Delano, William Russell, Elisha Cushman, Christopher Hopkins, David Snow, Elijah Crocker, John Akin, Daniel Ricketson, John Howland, Seth Folger, Abishai Folger, Shubael Weeks, Alexander Gardner, ——— Butler, ——— Luce, ——— Batty, ——— Clarke, John Clasby, ——— Anthony, George Smith, Solomon Hatch, and Benjamin Barnard.

1769.

One hundred and nineteen vessels engaged in whaling from Nantucket, producing 19,140 barrels of oil, valued at $462,996.60. The names of the captains commanding in the northern fleet, so far as can be ascertained, are Isaiah Eldridge, ——— Delano, Joseph Tripp, James Coffin, Melatiah Pease, Lemuel Jenkins, Benjamin Dillingham, Fortunatus Sherman, and Thomas Marshall, of Dartmouth; Joseph Coleman, Nathaniel Coleman, Seth Coleman, William Long, Benjamin Chase, Jonathan Coffin, Solomon Folger, Benjamin Jenkins, John Woodbury, Matthew Barnard, and Joseph Gardner, of Nantucket; Edmund Conkling, Joseph Conkling, and John Squires, Long Island; Richard Whelden, Rufus Fish, Barachian Bassett, and Shubael Weeks, Falmouth; Samuel Whippey, New York; Gilbert Nash and Thomas White, Boston; Silas Snow and Joshua Harding, Cape Cod; and Benjamin Stratton, of Sandwich. In addition to the foregoing, Captains Butler, Wass, Strange, Sears, Pease, Coffin, Norton, Edmonds, Wheldon, and Daggett sailed from Providence, most of them sailing to the southward; Captain Grinnell sailed from Warren; and Capt. William Reade made a voyage in sloop Hampton, from Newport to the Western Islands grounds, obtaining 130 barrels of oil.†

1770.

Nantucket sent 125 vessels, of an average of 93 tons each, to both the northern and southern whaling-grounds; the produce being 14,331 barrels of oil, valued at $358,200. Probably fully as many more sailed from

* The Boston News-Letter, in its dispatches from New York, under date of April 20, 1768, says, "it is understood that the people of the island of Nantucket alone took oil and bone last season to the value of £70,000."

† Captain Strange took 200 barrels. Probably the total yield *exclusive of Nantucke* would exceed 6,000 barrels.

all the other ports combined, and probably the yield was about the same. Among the captains were the following, sailing most of them to Davis Straits and the Straits of Belleisle: Isaiah Eldredge (in sloop Tryall), ——— Delano, Seth Hamblin, Lazarus Spooner, Fortunatus Sherman, ——— Dillingham, and Joseph Tripp, of Dartmouth; James Fitch, Abishai Folger, Benjamin Jenkins, George Smith, Jethro Myrick, George Russell, Samuel Long, Abraham Pease, William Worth, Richard Coffin, and Benjamin Hussey, of Nantucket; Joshua Harding, of Cape Cod; Thomas Wiccum,* of New London; and Nailer Hatch, Cornelius Jenney, Francis Chase, Nymphas Price, Robert Gardner, and Zadock Lewis, unknown.

From 1770 to 1775 the state of the whale-fishery from Massachusetts was nearly as follows:†

Ports from which vessels sailed.	Number of vessels fitted annually for the northern fishery.	Tonnage.	Vessels fitted annually for southern fishery.	Tonnage.	Total number of seamen employed.	Barrels of sperm-oil taken annually.	Barrels of right-whale oil taken annually.
Nantucket	65	4,875	85	10,200	2,025	26,000	4,000
Wellfleet	20	1,600	10	1,000	420	2,250	1,250
Dartmouth	60	4,500	20	2,000	1,040	7,200	1,400
Lynn	1	75	1	120	28	200	100
Martha's Vineyard	12	720	......	......	156	900	300
Barnstable	2	150	......	......	26	240	......
Boston	15	1,300	5	700	260	1,800	600
Falmouth, Cape Cod	4	300	......	......	52	400	......
Swanzey	4	300	......	......	52	400	......
Total	183	13,820	121	14,020	4,059	39,390	7,650

To this estimate must be added for Providence, Newport, Warren, Sag Harbor, New London, New York, about 50 vessels more, and the proportion carried through would add 4,600 tons of shipping, 450 men to the number of seamen, 6,500 barrels of sperm and 1,200 of whale oil to the above total.

The names of such of the captains as are known are as follows:

For 1771: Joshua Delano (sloop Defiance of Rochester), Eldridge, Jenney, Peter Fitch, Uriah Bunker, Caleb Lombard, Richard Whelden,

* Wiggin.

† "No less than 19 Sail of Vessels were cleared for a Whaling Voyage from Rhode Island the week before last."—Boston News-Letter, May 21, 1770. The sloop Marquis of Granby, Pelatiah Russell, master, is reported in February, 1770, at Cape St. Nicholas Mole with 170 barrels of oil, her crew of Indians having run off with one boat and craft. The sloop Deliverance, Marchant, of Dartmouth, in two voyages this year took 360 barrels. John Claghorn, mate of a Dartmouth brig, was taken out of his boat by a foul line and drowned—the fourth brother in a family of six who had lost his life in this way. A Providence brig, a Newport schooner, and a Rhode Island sloop (these accounts all seem to make a distinction between Rhode Island vessels and those from Newport), all whalers, went ashore at Tarpaulin Cove, and a Warren schooner was lost on Chatham bar.

Richard Coffin, Paul Rawson, Benjamin Church, John Squires, Tristram Gardner, Francis Barnard, Thomas Manter, Benjamin Paperdy (?), George Russell, David Swain, Cornelius Marchant, William Pease, Robert Wyer, Jonathan Barnard, David Clark, and John Winslow.

For 1772: ———, (sloop Defiance, of Rochester), Peter Wells, John Howland, Thomas Pain, Thatcher Rich, Elisha Doane, Jonathan Doane (Dartmouth), Thomas Ryder (Cape Cod), Jeremiah Bickford, William Moores, Benjamin Coffin (Nantucket), Joseph Smith, Elisha Cobb, S—— Swett, Thomas Groose, Jonathan Moores, David Swain, Stephen Sears, Obed Bunker, ——— Bunker (of Nantucket, in sloop Fancy), Paul Cook, Barnabas Atwood, ——— Jenney, Obed Nye. Two vessels from Marblehead were whaling during part of the season. Two sloops from Nantucket, with about 150 barrels of oil each, were captured by a Spanish brig and sloop off Matanzas. The sloops Pluto, of Acushnet, John Winslow master, and King of Prussia, of Nantucket, Paul Rawson master, were found in September bottom up, and it is supposed that the crews had perished. Brig Leviathan, Lathrop master, sailed from Rhode Island for Brazil Banks.

For 1773: John Delano (in sloop Neptune, of Dartmouth), Obed Nye, Matthew Price, Hugh Cathcart, Joseph Gardner, William Roberts, Francis Chase, ——— Wyatt, ——— Barlow, Paul Cook, Joseph Cartwright, Edmund Cottle, Nathaniel Coleman, Samuel Manter, Oliver Price, Matthew Price (in sloop Dolphin), Ephraim Pease, Marshall Jenkins, Benjamin Starbuck, Richard Coffin, Benjamin Foswick, Obed Hussey, Jonathan Doane, George Shockley, Isaiah Eldridge, Silas Butler. In August a schooner, ——— Worth master, arrived in New York, having taken with her consort (name or port not given) 380 barrels of whale-oil and between 7,000 and 8,000 pounds of bone. Sloop A, of Providence, Abishai Luce master, was damaged in a gale December 4, and lost two men.

For 1774 and 1775* (in brig No Duty on Tea, of Dartmouth): ——— Swain, Jonathan Mitchell, William Swain, Robert Wyer, George Allen (in command, the captain having been caught by a foul line while fast to a whale and drowned), Benjamin Jenney, Abishai Luce (see 1773), Michael Hathaway, Caleb Lombard, Benjamin Hussey, Benjamin Berry, Eleazer Hopkins, Luther Burgess, John Bassett, Francis Butler, John Squires, Benjamin Allen (Nantucket), Daniel Snow, Edward Wing, Abel Easterbrooks (Warren), Benjamin Coffin (Nantucket), William Ramsdell (ditto), ——— Meader (ditto). A whaling-sloop, owned by Gideon Almy, of Tiverton, and another, owned in Boston, were captured by a French frigate off Hispaniola, carried into Port au Prince and condemned.

* From the "No Duty on Tea's" log of a voyage to the Western Islands. On June 10, 1774, the sloop Rochester, commanded by David Squires, and owned by Nathaniel Macy, and the schooner Lowden, commanded by Peleg Swain, and owned by John Ramsdell, sailed from Nantucket on a whaling-voyage. They struck on Great Point Rip and were lost, the crews very narrowly escaping drowning.

1775 to 1783.

Between these years the fishery produced but little. Nantucket was the only port which attempted to carry it on, and the fleet from there suffered a rapid diminution in numbers, until at the close of the war 134 vessels had fallen into the hands of the English, and 15 had been lost at sea. Many of these had cargoes varying from a few barrels to the entire capacity of the vessel. A more complete account will be gained by reference to the historical portion of this work.

It appears from the records of Massachusetts that bonds were filed with the State treasurer for the following whaling-vessels:

George Hussey, jr., and Paul Hussey, sloop Harlequin, of Nantucket; Daniel Paddack, master.

George Hussey, jr., and Paul Hussey, brigantine Warren, of Nantucket; Benjamin Whippey, master.

George Hussey, jr., and Paul Hussey, brigantine Brittania, of Nantucket; Silas Jones, master.

George Hussey, jr., and Paul Hussey, brigantine Lark, of Nantucket; Paul Hussey, master.

Reuben and Elisha Swain, brig Speedwell, of Nantucket; Elisha Swain, master.

Joseph Hussey, of Nantucket, and Shubael Cottle, of Tisbury, sloop Fame; Stephen Skinner, master. (This vessel did not sail.)

Joseph Hussey, of Nantucket, and Shubael Cottle, of Tisbury, brig Donoho (?); Nathaniel Coleman, master.

Joseph Barnard and Stephen Hussey, both of Nantucket, schooner Delight; Timothy Coleman, master.

Same parties, brigantine Britannia; Zebulon Whippey, master.

Nathaniel Macy and Richard Mitchell, jr., of Nantucket, schooner Dighton; Silas Paddack, master.

Josiah Coffin and Richard Mitchell, jr., of Nantucket, schooner Mermaid; Josiah Coffin, jr., master.

Same parties, brigantine Ann, of Dartmouth; Simeon Coffin, master.

Reuben Gardner and Paul Bunker, of Nantucket, brigantine Enterprize; Jonathan Fitch, master.

Same parties, schooner Harrison; Peter Fitch, jr., master.

Richard Coffin and Stephen Hussey, of Nantucket, brig Mayflower; George Lawrence, master.

Ebenezer Calef and Stephen Hussey, of Nantucket, sloop Nightingale; Elisha Folger, master.

Richard Mitchell, jr., and Stephen Hussey, of Nantucket, schooner Roebuck; William Chadwick, master.

Same parties, brig Sherburne; Jonathan Burnell, jr., master.

Same parties, brigantine Pembroke; Obed Bunker, master.

Same parties, brig Mercury; George Bunker, master.

Francis Brown and Richard Gardner, of Nantucket, brigantine Warwick; Peleg Gardner, master.

Thomas Jenkins and Andrew Myrick, of Nantucket, brigantine Windsor; Stephen Kidder, master.

Thomas Jenkins and Stephen Hussey, of Nantucket, brigantine Polly; John Barnard, master.

Thomas Jenkins and Andrew Myrick, of Nantucket, sloop Mary; Barzillai Swain, master.

Josiah Coffin, esq., Richard Mitchell, jr., Thomas Jenkins, and Andrew Myrick, of Nantucket, brigantine Donahoe, brigantine Dover, sloop Nightingale, schooner Delight, brigantine Brittania, sloop Success, sloop Conway,* brigantine Monmouth, sloop Dove, brigantine Mayflower, brigantine Polly, brigantine Bedford, schooner Dighton, schooner Harrison, and brigantine Enterprise.

Thomas Jenkins and Andrew Myrick, of Nantucket, brigantine Hawk; George Clark, master.

Same parties, schooner Raven; Seth Mayo, master.

Same parties, schooner Adventure; James Coffin, master.

Same parties, brigantine Hannah; Nathan Folger, master.

Francis Rotch and Leonard Jarvis, of Dartmouth, brigantine Falkland; William Covell, master.

Same parties, sloop Defiance; Jonathan Mitchell, master.

Same parties, brigantine Fox; Silas Butler, master.

Same parties, brigantine George; Thomas Banning, master.

Same parties, brigantine Enterprise; James Whippey, master.

Aaron Lopez, of Newport, and Leonard Jarvis, of Dartmouth, ship Africa; Joseph Ripley, master.

Same parties, brig Minerva; John Locke, master.

Joseph Russell, Isaac Howland, Barnabas Russell, and Caleb Greene, of Dartmouth, schooner Juno; George Shockley, master.

David Shepherd, Seth Russell, David Sowle, Abraham Smith, brigantine Kezia; David Sowle, master.

John Alden and Walter Spooner, of Dartmouth, schooner Grampus; Job Springer, master.

Samuel Smith, jr., and Marshall Jenkins, of Edgartown, brigantine Frederick; Edmund Cottle, master.

Shubael Cottle and John Pease, jr., of Edgartown, sloop Hannah; Jesse Luce, master.

Jonathan Allen and Thomas Cooke, of Edgartown, schooner Spermaceti; John Pease, master.

Joseph Nye, jr., and Nathaniel Freeman, of Sandwich, schooner Catharine; Jonathan Coffin, master.

Same parties, schooner Elizabeth; Henry Folger, master.

*According to the certificates, the sloop Conway, Bartlett Coffin commander, landed 200 barrels of oil at Falmouth; the brig Donahue, Nathaniel Coleman, 201 barrels (from coast of Brazil); brig Polly, John Barnard, 220 barrels (from Brazil); sloop Mary, Barzillai Swain, 200 barrels and 1,000 pounds bone (brought by brig Liberty, Henry Folger); brig Hawk, George Clark, 200 barrels (from Brazil); schooner Raven, Seth Mayo 200 barrels (from Brazil); Mayflower, Charles Coleman, 200 barrels; all 1776.

David Nye, of Wareham, and Ebenezer White, of Rochester, schooner Desire; George Smith, master.

Francis Rotch and Leonard Jarvis, of Dartmouth, brigantine Ann; Simeon Coffin, master.

Same parties, brig Royal Charlotte; William Roberts, master.

Lemuel Williams and William Tallman, of Dartmouth, sloop Neptune; Luther Burgess, master.

Nathaniel Curtis, of Stoughton, Caleb Davis, late of Boston, now of Dedham, schooner Betsey; Nathaniel Curtis, master.

These bonds are all filed from August, 1775, to early in January, 1776, none appearing after the latter date.

The Bedford, of Nantucket, sailed in 1776 for Brazil Banks, and arrived March 13, 1777, full.

Table showing returns of whaling-

NOTE.—Where the tables are incomplete it is because

Name of vessel.	Class.	Tonnage.	Captain.	Managing owner or agent.
1784.				
District of Boston, Mass.				
Chance	Schooner		—— Cook	
Friendship	Sloop		—— House	
Fortune	Brig		—— Kendrick	
Nancy	do	70	John Rich	
Nancy	Schooner	60	Elisha Cobb	
Peace and Plenty	do	60	Peter Well	
——			—— Collins	
Two or three small whaling-vessels arrived in Boston in June, 1784, clean.				
Sag Harbor, N. Y.				
A ship and a brig sailed in 1784 for the Atlantic whale-fishery, but made poor voyages, returning the same year or early in 1785.				
New London, Conn.				
Rising Sun	Sloop		—— Squires	
Providence, R. I.				
Industry	Brig		—— Swain	
1785.				
Sag Harbor, N. Y.				
America	Brig			
Lucy	do			B. Huntting
Port of Boston, Mass.				
Betsy	Schooner	40	Parnal Cook	
Constance	Brig	90	John Wetherell	
Industry	Schooner	55	Hezekiah Doane	
Lucy	do	25	Solomon Clark	
Nancy	Sloop	45	David Foster	
Nancy	Brig	70	John Rich	
Peacock	do	90	Jacob Higgins	
Polly	Sloop		—— Cottle	
Speedwell	Schooner	30	Stephen Sears	
Wellfleet, Mass.				
Ranger	Schooner	85	Stephen King	
Sculpion	do	40	Daniel Covel	
Hingham, Mass.				
Nancy	do	60	Elisha Cobb	
Plymouth, Mass.				
Hannah	do	50	Winslow Lewis	
Newburyport, Mass.				
Chance	Brig	70	Barnabas Clark	
Dartmouth, Mass.				
Hero	Sloop		Joshua Delano	
1786.				
Boston, Mass.				
Betsy	Schooner	40	Solomon Cook	
Constance	Brig	90	John Witherell	

vessels sailing from American ports.

the data cannot be obtained to fill them out.

Whaling-ground.	Date— Of sailing.	Date— Of arrival.	Result of voyage. Sperm-oil.	Result of voyage. Whale-oil.	Result of voyage. Whalebone.	Remarks.
			Bbls.	*Bbls.*	*Lbs.*	
Atlantic		Oct. 9, 1784				No report of oil.
...do		Sept. 18, 1784				Do.
...do		Oct. 9, 1784				Do.
...do	 Oct. 16	Oct. 16, 1784 				Do.
...do		Oct. 9, 1784				Do.
...do	Oct. 14					No further report.
...do						Do.
...do	May 20					
...do		July —, 1784	300	100		
		June 4, 1785		300		
Brazil Banks		May 15, 1785		360		Bought from Middletown, Conn., 1785.
	Nov. 7					No report.
	Apr. 27					Do.
	Apr. 9					Do.
	Apr. 5					Do.
	Apr. 30					Do.
	Aug. 27	May 24, 1786				Do.
	May 9	June 14, 1786				Do.
		Oct. —, 1785				Do.
	Apr. 14					Do.
	Apr. 14 Sept. 30	 Apr. 15, 1786				Do.
	Oct. 26					Do.
	Apr. 6					Do.
	Apr. 15 Sept. 30	 Apr. 15, 1786				Do.
	Apr. 27					Do.
Atlantic	July 4					
	Mar. 30					
	May 22					

Table showing returns of whaling-vessels

Name of vessel.	Class.	Tonnage.	Captain.	Managing owner or agent.
1786.				
Boston, Mass.—Continued.				
Friendship	Sloop	60	Jonathan Snow	
Nancy	Schooner	90	Richard Rich	
Nancy	Brig	70	do	
Penelope	do	70	Hezekiah Doane	
Hingham, Mass.				
Nancy	Schooner	60	Elisha Cobb	
Braintree, Mass.				
Fortune	do	38	Jonathan Howes	
Wellfleet, Mass.				
Ranger	do	85	Stephen King	
Sculpion	do	40	Daniel Covell	
Wellfleet	do	40	Barnabas Atwood	
Plymouth, Mass.				
Hannah	do	50	Winslow Lewis Shubael Sweat	
Bristol.				
Dispatch	Sloop	48	John Collins	
There were a few vessels belonging to Hudson, N. Y., engaged in whaling and sealing at this time.				
1787.				
There is no report of vessels from Nantucket or New Bedford for 1784, 1785, 1786, and 1787, though beyond a doubt several sailed each year.				
Dartmouth, Mass.				
Rainbow	Sloop	....	Joshua Delano	
Boston, Mass.				
Nancy	Brig	....	—— Snow	
A Boston schooner from a South Atlantic voyage was wrecked off Cape Hatteras; lost captain, mate, and five men, and considerable oil, (had taken 180 barrels;) was towed into some Rhode Island port by a sloop.				
1788.				
Nantucket, Mass.				
Fox	Brig	....	Barzillai Folger	
Harmony	Ship	....	Seth Folger	
Industry	do	172	Gilbert Folger	
Sally	do	194	Joseph Chase	
Spy	do	....	William Fitch	
——	do	....	Barzillai Coleman	
——	do	....	Benjamin Clark	
Gloucester, Mass.				
Sea Horse	Brig	....	Elkanah Mayo —— Rich	
Hudson, N. Y.				
Liberty	do	....	—— Bunker	

sailing from American ports—Continued.

Whaling-ground.	Date.		Result of voyage.			Remarks.
	Of sailing.	Of arrival.	Sperm-oil.	Whale-oil.	Whalebone.	
			Bbls.	*Bbls.*	*Lbs.*	
....	Apr. 15	....	......	......	......	
....	June 6	....	......	......	......	Must have arrived prior to September 2.
West Indies ..	Sept. 2	....	......	......	......	
....	Apr. 15	....	......	......	......	
....	Mar. 30	....	......	......	......	
....	Apr. 13	....	......	......	......	
{	Apr. 17	....	......	......	......	
{ West Indies .	Sept. 23	....	......	......	......	
....	May 13	....	......	......	......	
....	Apr. 15	....	......	......	......	
....	Apr. 17	....	......	......	......	
West Indies ..	Sept. 23	....	......	......	......	
....	Apr. 20	....	......	......	......	
Atlantic	....	....	......	......	......	
....do	Aug. 16	....	......		......	
....	....	—— —, 1789	......	......	......	
....	....	....	......	......	......	
....	....	—— —, 1789	......	......	......	
....	....	....	......	......	......	
....	....	....	......	......	......	
....	....	....	......	......	......	
....	....	....	......	......	......	
} Coast Africa.	....	Oct. 4, 1789	......	800	......	Reported the sudden sinking of part of the shores of Woolwich Bay to a depth of six fathoms.
Brazil	....	July —, 1789	......	350	......	

Table showing returns of whaling-vessels

Name of vessel.	Class.	Tonnage.	Captain.	Managing owner or agent.
1788.				
The sloop Rainbow, Capt. Joshua Delano, made a whaling-voyage from Dartmouth, sailing in company with vessels commanded by Elnathan and Nathaniel Delano. On the voyage the following captains were spoken—the oil reported at the date of hailing being given in brackets: —— Stott [from the West Indies, 100 barrels], Cornelius Butler, Benjamin Dillingham, George Allen, Amos Kelley, Robert Neader [from the West Indies, 100 barrels], Rufus Fish [40], —— Squires [30], Seth Folger [from Brazil, 500], Walter Brock [from Brazil, 500], Benjamin Hillman [40], Reuben Clark, Joseph Russell, [Nantucket], James Coffin, John Bassett [from Brazil, 600], Robert Hathaway [20], Abishai Luce, Joseph Russell [Dartmouth]. The larger number of these are unquestionably from Nantucket; others from the vicinity of Dartmouth, Cape Cod, &c. The Rainbow arrived July 25, and sailed again for a Gulf-Stream voyage August 5. On the second cruise she spoke Thomas Allen [4], Benjamin Hillman [4], George Allen [80], Edy Coffin, Benjamin Dillingham, Robert Hathaway [15], Rufus Fish, Jonathan Cushman, Daniel Bennett [70], Prince Shearman, Prince Hatch, and Ebenezer Allen. She arrived the second time September 17.				
1789.				
Gloucester, Mass.				
Polly	Ship	....	J. Coffin	
Sea Horse	Brig	....	Elkanah Mayo	
Sag Harbor, N. Y.				
Lucy	Brig	....	D. Squires	Benjamin Huntting
Boston, Mass.				
Sarah	Ship	....	C. Gardner	
New Bedford, Mass.				
———	Brig	....	—— Brock	
Rhode Island.				
L	Schooner	25	Solomon Lewis	Sylvanus Hussey
N	do	25	Caleb Lombard	do
Hudson, N. Y.				
———	Brig	..		
The sloop Rainbow, of Dartmouth, Joshua Delano commander, sailed from that port June 3, 1789, arriving August 7, of the same year. On her voyage she spoke Benjamin Hillman [70], Obed Cushman [1 whale], Jesse Luce, Tristram Coffin, Cornelius Butler [60], Thomas Bates, John Carver, Obed Nye, Rufus Fish, Seth Tobey, Robert Hathaway, Samuel Shockley, Thomas Cook, Thomas Snow, [in a brig, 200], Nathaniel Delano, Shubael Swain, Amos Kelley, Samuel Crosby, and Salvanus Luce.				

sailing from American ports—Continued.

Whaling-ground.	Date.		Result of voyage.			Remarks.
	Of sailing.	Of arrival.	Sperm-oil.	Whale-oil.	Whalebone.	
			Bbls.	*Bbls.*	*Lbs.*	
C. Good Hope..	....	Jan. —, 1791	......	1,600	15,000	
....do	....	—— —, 1790	......	800	10,000	
Brazil.........	....	July —, 1790	......	800	......	
Woolwich Bay.	....	—— —, 1790	......	900	......	
....	....	....	......	......	......	
Atlantic	....	Sept. 21, 1789	40	54	......	
....	....	Sept. 21, 1789	61	90	......	
Brazil	Oct. —	....	......	......	......	Probably the brig Liberty.

Table showing returns of whaling-vessels

Name of vessel.	Class.	Tonnage.	Captain.	Managing owner or agent.
1789.				
Nantucket, Mass.				
Asia	Ship		Elijah Coffin	
Africa	do		William Barnard	
Amazon	Brig		David Giles	
Britannia	do		Peter Fosdick	
Columbia	Ship		Obed Barnard	
Fox	Brig		Barzillai Folger	
Favourite	Ship		Silas Jones	
Harlequin	Brig		Benjamin Whippy	
Industry	Ship	172	Gilbert Folger	
Leo	Brig	217	William Clisby	
Minerva	Ship	200	S. Coffin	
Mary Ann	do		T. Folger	
Manilla	Brig		David Barnard	
Nantucket	Ship		B. Folger	
Ranger	do		William Swain	
Rebecca	do		Seth Folger	
Trial	Brig		George Chase	
Venus	Brig		Obed Eldridge	
Warren	Ship		Robert Meader	
——	do		—— Baxter	
Cape Cod, Mass.				
Codfish	Schooner		John Collins	
Endeavour	do		Paul Cook	
Patty	do		Benjamin Hopkins	
——	Ship		—— Cobb	
——	do		Pardon Cook	
——	do		J. Cook	
——	do		—— Ryder	
——	do		—— Alcott	
——	do		Solomon Cook	
1790.				
*Nantucket, Mass.**				
The sloop Industry, Capt. Joshua Delano, sailed from New Bedford May 28, 1790, returned July 9, and sailed a second time July 20. She spoke Cornelius Marchant [70], —— Covell [New Bedford], James Banning [Wareham], Thomas Cook [50], Joseph Kersey [130], John Carver, and Henry Fish [24].				
1791.				
Nantucket, Mass.				
Alliance	Ship		Bartlett Coffin	
Beaver	do		Paul Worth	
Diana	do		Timothy Long	
Favourite	do		Obed Barnard	
Hector	do		Thomas Brock	
Rebecca	do		Seth Folger	
Washington	do		George Bunker	
Warren	do		Robert Meader	
New Bedford, Mass.				
Rebecca	Ship	175	Joseph Kersey	
Boston district, Mass.				
Charlotte	Schooner		John Collins	John Collins
Enoch	Ship	46	Zaccheus Higgins	Enoch Rust

* No report of arrivals or

sailing from American ports—Continued.

Whaling-ground.	Date—Of sailing.	Date—Of arrival.	Result of voyage.—Sperm-oil.	Result of voyage.—Whale-oil.	Result of voyage.—Whalebone.	Remarks.
			Bbls.	*Bbls.*	*Lbs.*	
	Aug. 27					
	Aug. 27					
	Aug. 27	June 16, 1790				
	Sept. 1					
Woolwich Bay	Sept. 11	— —, 1790		770		
	Sept. 1					
	Sept. 14					
Woolwich Bay	Sept. 11	— —, 1790		750		
....do	Sept. 1	— —, 1790		951		
	Aug. 27	June 15, 1790				
Woolwich Bay		— —, 1790		1,160		
....do		— —, 1790		1,140		
....do	Aug. 27	— —, 1790				
....do		— —, 1790		920		
....do	Sept. 1	— —, 1790		1,160		
	Sept. 1					
	Sept. 11	May 17, 1790				
	Sept. 20	June 17, 1790				
	Sept. 3	— —, 1791				
Brazil	Oct. —					
Straits Belleisle		Oct. 6, 1789	80	125	1,300	
Africa		— —, 1790	64			
Straits Belleisle		Oct. —, 1789	80	125	1,300	
....do		Aug. —, 1789	50	125	1,300	About.
....do		Oct. —, 1789	50	125	1,300	
....do			80	125	1,300	About.
....do			50	125	1,300	Do.
....do			50	125	1,300	Do.
....do			50	125	1,300	
Dalago Bay	Oct. —	Feb. 15, 1794				Captain Coffin died; the ship made a poor voyage.
Pacific Ocean	Aug. —	Mar. 25, 1793	1,100	200		Built 1791; the first American whaler in the Pacific. She was ordered out of Lima without supplies, and ordered off the coast by the Spaniards.
Brazil						
....do						
Pacific Ocean		Apr. 8, 1793	700	500		Hector built 1791.
....do		Apr. 30, 1793	800	240		
....do		Apr. 8, 1793	800	400		The Washington was the first vessel to hoist the American flag in a Spanish Pacific port. Built 1791.
		— —, 1793				
Pacific Ocean		Feb. 21, 1793	750	1[illegible]0		The first New Bedford whaler in the Pacific.
Atlantic		Sept. 15, 1791		60	1,000	
....do						Probably sailed one or two voyages each year to 1794, when she surrendered her enrollment.

departures for 1790 is accessible.

Table showing returns of whaling-vessels

Name of vessel.	Class.	Tonnage.	Captain.	Managing owner or agent.
1791.				
Boston district, Mass.—Continued.				
Mars	Schooner		Matthias Rich	Matthias Rich
Rising Sun	...do		——— ———	——— ———
Union	...do	161	John Rich	
Gloucester, Mass.				
Two Friends	Brig		——— Mayo	
1792.				
Nantucket, Mass.				
Amazon	Brig		David Giles	
Fox	Ship		Daniel Kelley	
Hero	...do		Obed Eldridge	
Harmony	...do		James Chase	
Harlequin	...do		Benjamin Whippey	
Industry	...do	172	Gilbert Folger	
Juno	...do		George Clark	
Leo	Brig	217	William Clisby	
Minerva	Ship		Seth Coffin	
Maria	...do		——— Hillman	
Mary Ann	...do		Tristram Folger	
Ranger	...do		William Swain	
Sally	Brig	194		
Sea Fox	Ship			
Venus	Brig		James Brown	
New Bedford district, Mass.				
Betsey	Sloop		——— Blankenship	
Columbia	Ship		Joseph Bennett	
Eliza	...do		B. Coleman	
Lively	Schooner		Rowland Gibbs	
Polly	Brig		——— Cottle	
Polly and Betsey	Schooner		T. Nye	
Tryall	Sloop		——— Gibbs	
Union	Brig		——— Hammatt	
Boston, Mass.				
———	Ship		——— Lee	
New York, N. Y.				
Josephus and tender	Ship		——— Youte	
1793.				
Nantucket, Mass.				
Amazon	Brig		David Giles	
Beaver	Ship		Paul Worth	
Britannia	Brig		Joseph Wyer	
Columbia	Ship		Alpheus Coffin	
Favourite	...do		Obed Barnard	
Favorite	...do		David Folger	
Hector	...do		Thomas Brock	
Hero	...do	313	Obed Aldridge	
Industry	...do	172	William Fosdick	
Lydia	...do	160	Zenas Coffin	
Leo	Brig	217	William Clisby	
Maria	...do		——— Cash	
Minerva	Ship	200	Peter Myrick	
Manilla	...do		Andrew Barnard	
Mary Ann	...do		Tristram Folger	
Polly	Brig		{ ——— Pinkham ——— Starbuck	
Ranger	Ship		Gilbert Folger	
Rebecca	...do		Seth Folger	
Ruby	...do		Isaiah Clark	
Swallow	Schooner		Latham Gardner	

sailing from American ports—Continued.

Whaling-ground.	Date— Of sailing.	Date— Of arrival.	Result of voyage. Sperm-oil.	Result of voyage. Whale-oil.	Result of voyage. Whalebone.	Remarks.
			Bbls.	*Bbls.*	*Lbs.*	
Atlantic		Sept. 8, 1791		60	900	
do						
do	Nov. 10					
Brazil		June 19, 1792	100	900		
Brazil		July 23, 1793		650		
Woolwich		Nov. 1, 1793		800		
do		Oct. 16, 1793		1,300		
do		Oct. 16, 1793		800		
do		Nov. 1, 1793		800		
Brazil		May 3, 1793		900		
Africa		Nov. —, 1793		600		
Brazil		July 23, 1793		550		
do		June 6, 1793		1,200		
Pacific Ocean		Mar. 27, 1794	730	90		
Brazil		Aug. —, 1793		1,100		
do		June 6, 1793		1,100		Built 1792.
Woolwich		Oct. 16, 1793		700		
Woolwich		Nov. —, 1793		500		
Atlantic		Dec. —, 1792				
Brazil		July 26, 1793		900		
Woolwich		Dec. —, 1793		1,800		
Atlantic	Nov. —					
do }						
		Dec. —, 1792				
	Dec. —					
do	Dec. —					
do	Dec. —					
do	Dec. —					
Falkland and Pacific.	June 1					Whaling and sealing.
Pacific Ocean						
	Oct. 16	June 30, 1794				
Brazil	Aug. 5	May 16, 1794				
Woolwich	Aug. 5	Sept. 16, 1794				
Brazil	Sept. 15	June 22, 1794				
Coast Peru	July 13					
	Dec. 16					
	Aug. 17	—— —, 1794				
	Dec. 6	—— —, 1795				
Brazil	Aug. 3	May 16, 1794				
do	Oct. 10	July 6, 1794				
do	Sept. 14	June 21, 1794				
Atlantic		July —, 1793	100			
Brazil	Aug. 9	July 14, 1794		900		
	Aug. 9	May 21, 1794				
	Dec. 12					
Bahamas		—— —, 1793 }	Clean			
Cape Good Hope	Oct. —	—— —, 1794 }				
	Aug. 5					
Brazil	Aug. 17	June 19, 1794				
	Sept. 14					
Falkland		May 17, 1794				Whaling and sealing.

Table showing returns of whaling-vessels

Name of vessel.	Class.	Tonnage.	Captain.	Managing owner or agent.
1793.				
Nantucket, Mass.				
Swan	Ship		—— Swain	
Union	do		Grafton Gardner	
Washington	do		Solomon Smith	
Warren	do		Matthew Starbuck	
New Bedford district, Mass.				
Atlantic	Brig		L. Stott	
Beaver	do		Isaiah Burgess	
Columbia	do		P. Fish	
Friendship	Schooner		—— Butler	
Keziah	Sloop		Oliver Adams	
Mary	Brig		B. Pease	
Nancy	do		S. Cunningham	
Russell	do		F. Butler	
Rebecca	Ship	175	Joseph Kersey	
Swan	Schooner		—— Eldredge	
Providence, R. I.				
Ranger	Snow		—— Bradley	
Gloucester, Mass.				
——	Ship		Jona. Coffin	
1794.				
Nantucket, Mass.				
Boston Packet	Ship		—— Easty	
Cato	do		—— Swain	
Commerce	do		A. Gardner	
Fox	do		—— Joy	
Hector	do		Thomas Brock	
Hudson	do		Grafton Gardner	
Joanna	do		—— Fosdick	
Minerva	do	200	William Myrick	
Ranger	do		William Swain	
Uniba	do		—— Gardner	
New Bedford district, Mass.				
Atlantic	Brig	120	J. Parker	John Alden
Beaver	do		I. Burgess	
Eliza	do		B. Coleman	
Hero	Sloop		B. Summerton	
Industry	do	60	William Taber	John Alden
Keziah	do		Oliver Adams	
Rebecca	Ship	175	—— Gardner	
Swan	Schooner	70	N. Mayhew	John Alden
Sally	do	180	Step. Cunningham	do
Wareham, Mass.				
Nabby	Schooner		Thomas Gibbs	
Sag Harbor, N. Y.				
Lucy	Brig		—— Rogers	
Gloucester, Mass.				
Polly	Ship		E. Mayo	
Boston district, Mass.				
Betsey	Schooner	52	Joseph Hatch	Enoch Rust
Hope	do	55	Stephen King	Daniel Sargent
Nancy	do	61	John Collins	Joseph Russell

sailing from American ports—Continued.

Whaling-ground.	Date—Of sailing.	Date—Of arrival.	Result of voyage.—Sperm-oil.	Result of voyage.—Whale-oil.	Result of voyage.—Whalebone.	Remarks.
			Bbls.	*Bbls.*	*Lbs.*	
Brazil		July 14, 1794		400		
	Aug. 18	June —, 1794		1, 280		The Union did not anchor once on the voyage, and the only land she sighted was Cape Augustine on the way home.
Peru and Chili	July 10	May 16, 1795	700			About.
	Sept. 15					
	Jan. —					
Atlantic	Sept. 29	Nov. 3, 1793	100			
Delago Bay		Oct. 11, 1794	550	500		
	Jan. 5					
Atlantic		Nov. 8, 1793				Lost a man overboard and returned clean.
Cape Good Hope	Jan. 11					
	Jan. —					
	Jan. —					
Brazil		Apr. 26, 1794		1, 000		
	Jan. —					
		— —, 1794				Had 350 barrels at last report.
Brazil						Had 900 barrels at last report.
Woolwich		Oct. —, 1795		Full		
Delago Bay		Jan. —, 1796				
Woolwich		Oct. —, 1795		Full		
do		Oct. 3, 1795		Full		
Pacific Ocean				Full		
Delago Bay		Feb. —, 1796				
Pacific Ocean		Aug. —, 1796	1, 100	400		
Woolwich		Oct. 3, 1795		Full		
Brazil				1, 200		
Woolwich		Oct. 3, 1795		Full		
Atlantic	May 17	Sept. 17, 1794	60			
do		Oct. 30, 1794	80			
Woolwich	Jan. 11					
Atlantic		Aug. 19, 1794		Clean		
do	June 21	Oct. 14, 1794		Clean		
West Indies	Jan. 25	Aug 22, 1794		Clean		
Brazil	July —					
Atlantic		Sept. 17, 1794	40			
Cape Good Hope	Feb. 8	Apr. —, 1795		900		Was built on wreck of brig Fame, burned at Fairhaven 1792.
Atlantic						Last reported with 16 barrels.
Brazil						Last reported with 750 barrels.
Woolwich				1, 400		Put into the West Indies in November or December, 1795, in distress. Probably arrived home early in 1796.
Atlantic						Surrendered her license 1795. Find no other report.
do						Find no other report.
do						Do.

Table showing returns of whaling-vessels

Name of vessel.	Class.	Tonnage.	Captain.	Managing owner or agent.
1794.				
Boston district, Mass.				
Polly	Schooner	69	Pardon C. Cook	Solomon Cook
Paulina	...do	74	Richard Atwood	Naaman Holbrook
East Haddam, Conn.				
Commerce	Ship			
1795.				
Nantucket, Mass.				
Alliance	Ship		V. Pease	
Beaver	...do		—— Long	
——	...do		Paul Worth	
Cæsar	...do		S. Smith	
——	...do		W. Easton	
Harlequin	...do		—— Clark	
Union	...do		—— Barney	
New Bedford district, Mass.				
Ann	Ship		—— Coleman	
Berkeley	...do			
Commerce	...do		—— Handy	
Delaware	...do		—— Tuckerman	
Industry	Sloop	60	John Carver	John Alden
Janus	Ship		Obed Folger	
Lydia	...do		Obed Fitch	
Rebecca	Ship	175	—— Gardner	
Suzy	...do		Barzillai Hussey	
Union	...do		J. Barney	
Providence, R. I.				
Ranger	Snow		Edward Cole	
Hudson, N. Y.				
American Hero	Ship		Solomon Bunker	
1796.				
Nantucket, Mass.				
Alliance	Ship		—— Pease	
Brothers	...do	256	L. Coffin	
Beaver	...do		—— Long	
Cato	...do		V. Swain	
——	...do		—— Folger	
——	...do		David Giles	
Hero	...do	313	—— Aldridge	
Leo	...do	217	William Cash	
Lion	...do		A. Barnard	
Mars	...do		D. Folger	
Rebecca	...do		S. Long	
——	...do		Uriah Bunker	
Providence, R. I.				
Ranger	Snow		Edward Cole	
Hudson, N. Y.				
——	Ship		—— Clark	

sailing from American ports—Continued.

Whaling-ground.	Date— Of sailing.	Date— Of arrival.	Result of voyage. Sperm-oil.	Result of voyage. Whale-oil.	Result of voyage. Whalebone.	Remarks.
			Bbls.	*Bbls.*	*Lbs.*	
Atlantic						Find no other report. Surrendered enrolment 1795.
....do						Find no other report. Belonged in Barnstable.
	Feb. 6					Cleared from New London.
Woolwich		Dec. 15, 1796		1,100		
Brazil		— —, 1796		1,100		Returned dismasted in October. Arrived early in 1797.
Pacific Ocean						Last reported with 1,200 sperm.
Cape G'd Hope	Aug. -	Jan. —, 1797				Put into Charleston, S. C., with loss of mainmast, cross-trees, quarter-rails and boards, and boat's stove. Took 36 whales; saved 25.
Pacific Ocean						Last reported with 700 sperm.
Brazil	Dec. —	May —, 1797		1,100		
Woolwich		— —, 1796		900	7,000	At Charleston, S. C., in distress in October, 1796.
Pacific Ocean		Jan. 11, 1798	1,750			
Woolwich		June 21, 1797		1,400		
	Aug. 22					Built at North River, 1795.
Woolwich		June 21, 1797		700		
Atlantic		{ Aug. 20, 1795 { Oct. 17, 1795	} 20	Clean		Lost both boats first voyage.
Woolwich	July 7	— —, 1796		1,250		Last reported with 1,250 whale.
....do	Aug. 11	— —, 1797				Last reported January 29, 1797, at Antigua, in distress.
	July 28					
Woolwich	July 7					
Brazil	July 31					
Woolwich		— —, 1796		470		
Pacific Ocean		— —, 1797				
Woolwich Bay		Dec. 15, 1796		1,100		
Brazil						Last reported with 600 sperm.
... do		— —, 1797		1,100		
....do						Last reported with 1,000 whale.
Woolwich Bay	Feb. 4					
						Captain Cash was killed by the first whale struck.
Woolwich Bay						Last reported with 700 whale.
		July —, 1797				
Brazil						Last reported with 850 whale.
St. Helena		Dec. —, 1796		470		
Delago Bay						

Table showing returns of whaling-vessels

Name of vessel.	Class.	Tonnage.	Captain.	Managing owner or agent.
1796.				
Boston, Mass.				
Polly	Schooner	69	Pardon C. Cook	Enoch Rust.
Sarah	Ship		George Pollard	
1797.				
Nantucket, Mass.				
Alliance	Ship		Hezekiah Barnard	
Beaver	do		Nathan Long	
Commerce	do		Amaziah Gardner	
Cæsar	do		Solomon Swain	
Diana	do		—— Swain	
Eagle	do		—— Clasby	
Fortitude	do		Obed Paddock	
——	do		Obed Aldridge *	
——	do		Alpheus Coffin	
Hope	do		David Giles	
Hector	do		Benjamin Worth	
Mars	do		D. Folger	
Ruby	do	221	Andrew Myrick	
Renown	do			
Trial	do		Simeon Starbuck	
New Bedford district, Mass.				
Barclay	Ship		Griffin Barney	
Bedford	do		Jonathan Barney	
Betsey	Schooner		N. Mayhew	
Commerce	Brig			John Alden
Fox	Ship			
Industry	Sloop			John Alden
Juno	Ship		W. Clark	
——	Sloop		W. Easton	
Lydia	Ship		Obed Fitch	
Maria	do		—— Paddock	
Nancy	Sloop			Samuel Proctor
Polly	Brig		G. Whippey	
President	Ship		—— Pinkham	
Swan	Schooner			John Alden
Warren	Ship		—— Tobey	
Wareham	do		—— Clark	
New York, N. Y.				
Maryland	Ship		—— Liscomb	
Hudson, N. Y.				
American Hero	Ship		William Pitts	
Oswego	do		George Clark	
Boston district, Mass.				
Betsey	Schooner	52	Joseph Hatch	Enoch Rust.
Enoch	do	46	Zaccheus Higgins	do
1798.				
Nantucket, Mass.				
Favourite	Ship		Thaddeus Folger	
Leo	do	217	Joseph Allen	
Phebe	do		Edward Coffin	
Ruby	do	221	Andrew Myrick	

* So many Nantucket captains commanded French and English whalers that one may occasionally be from the marine lists of the papers of the time.

sailing from American ports—Continued.

Whaling-ground.	Date—Of sailing.	Date—Of arrival.	Result of voyage.—Sperm-oil.	Result of voyage.—Whale-oil.	Result of voyage.—Whalebone.	Remarks.
			Bbls.	*Bbls.*	*Lbs.*	
Atlantic						No report.
Brazil	May 30	Dec. 9, 1797				Last reported with 1,100 whale.
Pacific Ocean		Oct. 18, 1799				Nearly full.
Woolwich		Dec. 30, 1798		1,200		
Pacific Ocean	July 5	Sept. 26, 1799	1,000	200		Captain Gardner, mate, and boats' crew barbarously treated by the Spaniards at Saint Mary's, January, 1799.
....do		Oct. —, 1799	1,000			Nearly full.
....do						
Delago Bay		Mar. 8, 1799		Full.		
....do		Mar. 4, 1799		Full.		
....do		Mar. 18, 1799				Nearly full.
		Dec. 29, 1799				
Peru		Nov. —, 1799	Full.			
		Dec. 25, 1798				
Pacific Ocean		Feb. 5, 1800	1,000	50		
....do		—— —, 1799	1,250	150		
....do		Nov. —, 1799	800			
....do	Aug. 25	June 26, 1799	700	500		Also 21,000 seal-skins.
....do	July 5	Sept. 26, 1799	1,000	200		
Atlantic	May 31	Oct. 14, 1797		Clean		
....do						
	Jan. 9					
Atlantic						
Pacific Ocean	Jan. —	Apr. 12, 1799	1,200	50		
Atlantic	July —	July —, 1797	90			From Dartmouth; out 15 days.
Pacific Ocean	July 8	Feb. —, 1799	950	400		
....do		Mar. 15, 1798				
Atlantic		—— —, 1797				
Africa	June 26					
Pacific Ocean		Apr. 1, 1799	1,200	50		
Grand Banks		—— —, 1797				
South Atlantic		Dec. —, 1798	150	850		
Pacific Ocean	July 5	Sept. 24, 1798	Full.			Built 1797.
Pacific Ocean	Aug. 25	—— —, 1799	800			Fitted from New Bedford. Captain Liscomb, mate, and boats' crew captured and abused by Spaniards at Saint Mary's, but released. The vessel was captured homeward bound by a French privateer, but released, after losing 2,000 seal-skins. Brought home 20,000 skins.
Pacific Ocean						
....do		—— —, 1799	1,100	100		
						No report.
						Do.
Pacific Ocean		Aug. 20, 1800	1,200			
....do		Dec. 9, 1800	800	300		
South Seas		Dec. 14, 1800		Full.		
Pacific Ocean		Feb. 5, 1800	1,000	50		

found in these returns, particularly where a large part of the work is made up prior to about 1835

Table showing returns of whaling-vessels

Name of vessel.	Class.	Tonnage.	Captain.	Managing owner or agent.
1798.				
New Bedford district, Mass.				
Maria	Ship		Benjamin Paddock	
Nancy	do		——— Swain	
Rebecca	do	175	Andrew Gardner	
Wareham	do		——— Clark	
1799.				
Nantucket, Mass.				
Industry	Ship	172		
———	do		William Easton	
———	do		Uriah Bunker	
———	do		Levi Starbuck	
———	do		Simeon Long	
Phebe	do			
Prudence	Sloop		Jonathan Paddack	
Ranger	Ship		William Joy	
New Bedford district, Mass.				
Barclay	Ship		Griffin Barney	
Edward	do		Jonathan Perry	
Franklin	do		——— Tuckerman	
1800.				
Nantucket, Mass.				
Alliance	Ship		Amaziah Gardner	
Betsey	Sloop		——— Clasby	
Bluebell	Schooner		——— Long	
Cato	Ship		John Brown	
Fame	do		Thomas Barnard	
Hope	do		David Giles	
Julianna	Sloop		——— Marshall	
Lydia	Ship	160	William Clark	
———	do		Paul Worth	
———	do		William Clisby	
———	do		Simeon Long	
———	do		David Harris	
Mary Ann	do		Tristram Folger	
Ruby	do		——— Swain	
Ranger	do		William Joy	
———	do		——— Perkins	
Tryal	do		——— Coffin	
New Bedford district, Mass.				
Ann	Ship		——— Coleman	
Dolphin	do		——— Bennett	
Edward	do		Jonathan Perry	
Maria	do		——— Paddack	
Swan	Schooner		William Taber	
Union	Sloop		{——— Swift ——— Coleman}	
Wareham	Ship		——— Gwinn	
Norwich, Conn.				
Miantonomah	Ship		——— Swain	

sailing from American ports—Continued.

Whaling-ground.	Date— Of sailing.	Date— Of arrival.	Result of voyage. Sperm-oil.	Result of voyage. Whale-oil.	Result of voyage. Whalebone.	Remarks.
			Bbls.	*Bbls.*	*Lbs.*	
Pacific Ocean	Dec. 25	Mar. 15, 1800	Full.			Fourth voyage of the Maria in five years.
Desolation	Feb. 12					The first American whaler at Desolation, only one English vessel there before her; was captured, homeward bound, by the French privateer Reliance, and recaptured by United States brig Eagle; value of cargo, $50,000.
Pacific Ocean						The Rebecca was captured by a French privateer 1799; retaken by an English vessel and sent into Nova Scotia; half of the value of vessel and cargo claimed as salvage.
		— —, 1800				
Brazil		— —, 1800		900		Capt. ——— was killed by a whale.
Pacific Ocean		June 28, 1801		Full.		Crew badly troubled with scurvy.
....do		June 28, 1801		Full.		Do.
....do		June 28, 1801		Full.		
Brazil		July 3, 1800	60	Full.		Full; 60 barrels sperm.
	Apr. —					
Patagonia		July 17, 1802				On a whaling and sealing voyage; no report.
Pacific Ocean		Oct. 27, 1801	Full.			
Pacific Ocean	Oct. 23	— —, 1801				Copper-bottomed.
....do		Dec. 15, 1800	Full.			
South Seas		Sept. 19, 1800	1,300			
Woolwich	Aug. 18	Nov. —, 1801		Full.		
Atlantic		Aug. 18, 1800				Took one whale.
....do		Aug. 16, 1800				Took two whales.
Woolwich		Nov. —, 1801		Full.		
Brazil	Sept. 8	June 28, 1801		Full.		
South Seas	Aug. 27	June 28, 1801		Full.		
		Aug. 17, 1800				Took one whale.
Brazil		May 28, 1801		1,000		One of the crew a disguised female; had been two voyages undetected.
....do		Apr. 29, 1801		Full.		
Bahamas		May 27, 1801		64		
Brazil		June 28, 1801		Full.		
....do		June 28, 1801		Full.		
Woolwich		Nov. 16, 1801		Full.		
Pacific Ocean						Ruby last reported with 900 sperm.
		Oct. 27, 1801		Full.		
Pacific Ocean		July —, 1802	1,500			
....do						Condemned by the Spanish at Valparaiso 1801.
Pacific Ocean						Last reported with 1,300 sperm.
		Aug. —, 1801				Made a poor voyage.
Pacific Ocean	Aug. 14	Dec. 4, 1802				
....do		June 15, 1802	Full.			
South Coast		Aug. 24, 1800 Sept. 27, 1800	40 40			
South Coast		Aug. 9, 1800 Sept. 27, 1800	65 Clean			
Pacific Ocean						Last reported with 1,100 sperm.
Pacific Ocean	Sept. 5					Seized by the Spanish and condemned at Valparaiso 1801.

Table showing returns of whaling-vessels

Name of vessel.	Class.	Tonnage.	Captain.	Managing owner or agent.
1801.				
Nantucket, Mass.				
Brothers	Ship	256	—— Folger	
Diana	do			
Fame	do		—— Barnard	
Industry	do	172	Obed Fitch	
John Jay	do	217	William Clark	
Leo	do	217	—— Allen	
Lydia	do	160	—— Starbuck	
Mars	do		—— Swain	
Renown	do		—— Coffin	
Union	do		Grafton Gardner	
Small vessels brought from 500 to 600 barrels of humpback oil into Nantucket in 1801.				
New Bedford district, Mass.				
Abby	Brig		—— Coffin	
Barclay	Ship		—— Randall	
Diana	do		—— Waterman	
Dolphin	do		—— West	
Exchange	do		—— Wyer	
Herald	do		—— Gibbs	
Hunter	do		—— Butler	
Hannah and Eliza	do			
Lydia	Schooner		—— Pinkham	
Oxford	Sloop		—— Taber	
Swan	Schooner		—— Paddock	
Boston, Mass.				
Jenney	Schooner		—— Leatherbee	
1802.				
Nantucket, Mass.				
Alliance	Ship		Amaziah Gardner	
Atlas	do	249	William Easton	
Boston	do	187	David Harris	
Betsey	Schooner		—— Coffin	
Belvidere	Ship		Hezekiah Barnard	
Commerce	do			
Cato	do		Solomon Folger, jr	
Criterion	do	229	—— Joy	
Hope	do		Obed Joy	
Hazard	Sloop		—— ——	
Harriet	Ship		Philip Fosdick	
Hudson	do		Uriah Bunker	
Industry	do	172	George Russell, jr	
John Jay	do	217	William Clark	
Lady Adams	do	230	—— Fitch	
Mary Ann	do		Tristram Folger	
Minerva	do	200	—— Jones	
Rebecca	do		George Chase	
—— ——	do		—— Coffin	
Ranger	do		William Joy	
Sukey	do		David Whippey	
Union	do			
The Eliza, Captain —— Bunker, also sailed in July, on a sealing voyage.				

*Vessels sailing for the Pacific rarely filled in that ocean, preferring to round Cape Horn on the whalers brought some right-whale oil, and, *per contra*, some right-whalers picked up a sperm-whale, returns.

sailing from American ports—Continued.

Whaling-ground.	Date—Of sailing.	Date—Of arrival.	Result of voyage.—Sperm-oil.	Result of voyage.—Whale-oil.	Result of voyage.—Whalebone.	Remarks.
			Bbls.	*Bbls.*	*Lbs.*	
South Atlantic		Aug. 12, 1802				
Woolwich		Nov. 5, 1802				
Brazil		Aug. 12, 1802				Full; probably about 1,500 whale.
....do		July 17, 1802				Full; probably about 1,800 whale.
Pacific Ocean	Aug. —	Feb. —, 1803	1,000	500		
Woolwich		Nov. 5, 1802				
		Aug. 12, 1802				
		Nov. 26, 1802				
Brazil		July 17, 1802		1,400		
	Aug. 7					
Delago	Oct. 3	Nov. 14, 1802				Returned in November in consequence of some accident.
Cape G'd Hope	May —	—— —, 1802				
	Oct. —	—— —, 1802				
	Nov. —					
Brazil		May 2, 1803				
Woolwich	Mar. —	May 20, 1803				
Pacific Ocean		—— —, 1802				
Atlantic	Mar. 15	Aug. 11, 1801	100			
						Sailed in August for Atlantic; no further report.
Atlantic	Dec. 10	Oct. —, 1801	60			
		July —, 1802	110			
Atlantic	Dec. 7					
Brazil		June 31, 1803				"Most full."
Pacific Ocean	Sept. 16	Mar. 30, 1805	1,800			Had, also, some whale-oil.*
Cape G'd Hope		Jan. 2, 1804	600	300		
Cape de Verde		Aug. 12, 1802		No report.		Sailed again October 19, 1802.
Pacific Ocean		Jan. 2, 1804	800			
		May 25, 1804				
Pacific Ocean		Nov. 12, 1804				Nearly full.
Brazil	Aug. 20	Mar. 15, 1804				
South Atlantic		Aug. 11, 1803		1,000		
Atlantic	Dec. —					Last reported with 40 sperm.
Woolwich		Dec. 3, 1803		1,000		
Pacific Ocean	July —					
Brazil		Sept. 13, 1803		450		
Woolwich		Nov. 5, 1803		900		
	Aug. 24					Last reported with 32,000 skins, bound for China.
Woolwich		Nov. 9, 1803		900		
Pacific Ocean		Aug. —, 1804				Whaling and sealing; reported with 23,000 skins.
Brazil		Apr. —, 1803				Full.
Pacific Ocean	July —					
Brazil		Sept. 13, 1803		900		
Pacific Ocean		Sept. 1, 1804	900			Bought from Boston, 1802.
		Apr. 20, 1804				

homeward trip with a well trimmed ship and fill with right-whale oil on Brazil; hence many sperm-
outward or homeward bound. Probably the gross amounts would not, however, vary much from the

Table showing returns of whaling-vessels

Name of vessel.	Class.	Tonnage.	Captain.	Managing owner or agent.
1802.				
New Bedford district, Mass.				
Abby	Brig		Solomon Coffin	
Diana	Ship		—— Waterman	
Dolphin	do		—— West	William Rotch
Hannah and Eliza	do			
Hunter	do		—— Butler	
Herald	do		—— Hathaway	
Lucy	Schooner		—— Pinkham	
Maria	Ship		—— Brightman	
Susan	Sloop			
Triton	Brig		Lot Clasby	
Wareham	Ship		—— Baxter	
Winslow	do		—— Paddock	
——	do		—— Tobey	
New London, Conn.				
Dispatch	Ship			
Sag Harbor, N. Y.				
Abigail	Ship		—— Barnard	
Minerva	do		—— Fowler	
1803.				
Nantucket, Mass.				
Alligator	Ship		—— Swain	
Aurora	Brig		—— Coffin	
Alliance	Ship		Amaziah Gardner	
Betsey	Schooner		—— Gardner	
Dove	Sloop			
Eliza	Brig		—— Paddack	
Henry	Ship		Peter Myrick	
Hope	do		Obed Joy	
Harlequin	do		—— Starbuck	
Leo	Brig	217	Uriah Bunker	
Lydia	Ship	160	—— Ray	
Margaret	do		Reuben Starbuck	
Neutrality	do			
Perseverance	do		—— Coffin	
Renown	do		Alpheus Coffin	
Ruby	do	221	Tristram Barnard	
Rebecca	do		George Chase	
Swallow	Brig		—— Bunker	
——	Ship		Barzillai Hussey	
Three Nantucket whaling-schooners (one commanded by David Folger) are reported to have been seized by the French armed schooner Telegraphe, off Aux Cayes, carried into Jacmel, and condemned; the crews were imprisoned in the fort, and six of them are said to have died. The ship Favorite, Captain Coffin, sailed in 1802 or 1803, arrived May 6, 1804.				
New Bedford district, Mass.				
Abby	Brig		—— Taber	Joseph Tripp
Ann	Ship		—— Gwinn	
Barclay	do		—— Randall	
Commerce	Brig		—— Paddock	
Dolphin	Ship		—— West	
Diana	do		—— Waterman	
Exchange	do		—— Wyer	J. Allen
Herald	do		—— Hathaway	
Hero	Bark		Barzillai Hussey	

sailing from American ports—Continued.

Whaling-ground.	Date— Of sailing.	Date— Of arrival.	Result of voyage. Sperm-oil.	Result of voyage. Whale-oil.	Result of voyage. Whale bone.	Remarks.
			Bbls.	*Bbls.*	*Lbs.*	
Atlantic		June —, 1803				Last reported with 100 sperm.
Woolwich		Oct. 13, 1803		Full		
Delago	Nov. —	Feb. 16, 1804		1,200		Probable yield.
		Aug. 11, 1803				No report from Hannah and Eliza.
Brazil		June 25, 1804				No report. Had, at last accounts, 900 whale.
....do		May 2, 1803				No report.
Atlantic		July 1, 1803				Last reported with 100 sperm.
Delago		—— —, 1804		800		
Atlantic		Oct. 22, 1803	Clean			
Delago		Feb. 2, 1804				
		Dec. 11, 1803				
Pacific Ocean		Sept. —, 1804				Last reported with 950 sperm.
Woolwich						Last reported with 200 sperm, 1,200 whale.
						Withdrawn on her return.
Brazil	Aug. —	—— —, 1803				Last reported with 900 whale.
....do	Aug. —	—— —, 1803				Do.
Delago		Mar. —, 1804		1,600		
Cape G'd Hope						
Patagonia		Apr. 14, 1804		Full		Mostly elephant oil.
						Reported at Barbadoes, February 17, 1804, with 400 sperm.
Patagonia		June —, 1804				
Pacific Ocean		Oct. 31, 1805	1,000			
Brazil		July 20, 1804				
		Aug. 3, 1804				
Patagonia		Feb. 24, 1804				
		Nov. 23, 1804				
Pacific Ocean		Dec. 13, 1805	1,100			
Brazil		Apr. 20, 1804				
		Nov. 23, 1804				
Pacific Ocean		Nov. 3, 1805	1,250			
....do			Full			
Brazil		Sept. —, 1804		800		
Patagonia	Oct. 15					
Brazil		May 5, 1804		1,000		
Atlantic	July —	June 22, 1804	280			
	Nov. 11					
Delago	May 13	Nov. 23, 1804				
	Dec. —	Dec. 9, 1803		Clean		
		Feb. 16, 1804				
	Dec. 30					
		Apr. 27, 1804				Captain Wyer died on the voyage. No report of oil.
Brazil	Aug. 5	Sept. 21, 1804				Owned in Fairhaven. Last reported with 1,000 whale.
....do		June 15, 1804				

Table showing returns of whaling-vessels

Name of vessel.	Class.	Tonnage.	Captain.	Managing owner or agent.
1803.				
New Bedford district, Mass.—Cont'd.				
Hannah and Eliza	Ship			
Hunter	do		—— Butler	
Lucy	do		Obed Pinkham —— Cheeley	
Oxford	Sloop		—— Hillman	
Swan	Schooner		—— Smith —— Smith	John Alden
Rover	Ship		—— Ray	
Sarah	do			
Triton	do			
The ship Edward sailed 1801 or 1802; arrived December 23, 1803.				
Hudson, N. Y.				
Juno	Ship		—— Bunker	
Thomas	do		—— Folger	
Uncle Toby	do		—— Swain	
Volunteer	Brig		—— Jenkins	
Sag Harbor, N. Y.				
Abigail				
Minerva				
1804.				
Nantucket, Mass.				
Alliance	Ship		Amaziah Gardner	
Alligator	do		David Swain	
Aurora	do	340	—— Hussey	
Boston	do	187	William Perkins	
Belvidere	do		Richard G. Swain	
Commerce	do		—— Eldridge	
Criterion	Ship	229	—— Joy	
Dove	Sloop		—— White	
Essex	Ship	238	David Harris	
Eliza	Brig		—— Chase	
Eagle	Brig		David Folger	
Fame	Schooner		Timothy Folger	
Fame	Ship		Obed Wyer	
Harriet	do		David Worth	
Henry	do		Peter Myrick	
Industry	do	172	George Russell, jr	
John Jay	do	217	William Clark	
Lima	do	160	Solomon Swain	
Lydia	do		Paul Ray	
Mars	do		Jonathan Barney	
Manilla	do		George Barrett	
Mary Ann	do		Tristram Folger	
President	Schooner			
Sally	Sloop			
Sterling	Ship		Simeon Starbuck	
Union	do		—— Folger	
New Bedford, Mass.				
Abby	Brig		—— Taber	
Betsey	Schooner			
Charles	Ship		—— Baxter	
Drucilla	Sloop		—— Hammond	
Exchange	Ship		—— Smith	
Hannah and Eliza	do		—— Gardner	
Hunter	do		—— Butler	

sailing from American ports—Continued.

Whaling-ground.	Date—Of sailing.	Date—Of arrival.	Result of voyage.—Sperm-oil.	Result of voyage.—Whale-oil.	Result of voyage.—Whalebone.	Remarks.
			Bbls.	*Bbls.*	*Lbs.*	
	Aug. 12	May 4, 1804				
	Aug. 12	June 25, 1804				
Atlantic		July 1, 1803	100			
	July —	May 6, 1804	80			
South Coast		Mar. 25, 1803	40			
		Sept. —, 1803	25			
Atlantic		Sept. 6, 1803	16			
	Nov. 25	June 7, 1804	80			
Cape G'd Hope	Nov. —	Jan. —, 1805	900			
Delago		Apr. —, 1804		1,600		
....do						
Pacific Ocean						
South Seas		— —, 1804		900		
Pacific Ocean						
Patagonia						Last reported with 300 whale and some seal-skins.
		— —, 1804				
		— —, 1804				
Patagonia	Mar. 21	Apr. —, 1805		Full.		Elephant-oil.
Cape G'd Hope	Aug. —	Feb. 4, 1806	750	317		
New Holland	Aug. 24					
Cape G'd Hope		Nov. —, 1806		Full.		
Pacific Ocean		— —, 1806				
....do		Feb. 15, 1806		Full.		Elephant-oil. Captain Eldridge died on the voyage, 1804.
	Jan. —					
Atlantic	July 23					
Cape G'd Hope	Aug. —	Jan. 23, 1806		Full.		
Patagonia						
Cape de Verde	June 7	Apr. —, 1805	90			Brought also the crew and cargo (70 sperm) of schooner Fame, lost on Isle of Sol.
....do	May 29					Lost on Isle of Sol, 1804; crew and cargo saved.
Pacific Ocean		Feb. 15, 1806	Full.			
South Seas	June 1	— —, 1806				
Pacific Ocean		— —, 1806				
Cape G'd Hope		Dec. 24, 1805	450	Full.		Full, 450 barrels of which were sperm.
Pacific Ocean		Feb. 28, 1806	1,400			
						Lima, built 1804.
Brazil						
Pacific Ocean		— —, 1806				
Patagonia		Feb. —, 1806		Full.		
South Seas	July —	— —, 1806		1,230		
Patagonia						
Cape de Verde	Jan. 8					Last reported with two whales, May 8.
Pacific Ocean		— —, 1806				
South Seas	Nov. —					
	July —					
Atlantic		June 29, 1804	120			
	Oct. —					
Atlantic		Sept. —, 1804				No report.
Cape G'd Hope	July —					
	May 1					Returned May 12, the English man-of-war Leander having taken out of her twelve English sailors; sailed again, 1804.
	Sept. —					

Table showing returns of whaling-vessels

Name of vessel.	Class.	Tonnage.	Captain.	Managing owner or agent.
1804.				
New Bedford district, Mass.				
Lucy	Brig		—— Brock	
Maria	Ship		—— Brightman	
Maria	do		—— Coffin	
Phebe Ann	do		—— Barnard	
Rhoda	Schooner		—— Sanford	
Sally	Ship		—— Clasby	
Sarah	do			
Swan	Schooner		—— Simmons	John Alden
Triton	Brig			
Walker	Ship		—— Coleman	
Winslow	do		—— Cross	
	Brig		Sylvanus Russell	
Sag Harbor, N. Y.				
Alknomac	Ship		John Hildreth	Benjamin Huntting
A sloop commanded by —— Wickham (?) was spoken July 5, 1804, six months out, with 60 barrels. Port not ascertained.				
1805.				
Nantucket, Mass.				
Commerce	Ship		Jesse Bunker	
Cato	Ship		Solomon Folger, jr	
Chili	do	293	—— Bunker	
Eliza	Brig		—— Chase	
Edward	Ship		Isaiah Ray	
Fame 2	do		Richard Folger	
Hope	do		Obed Joy	
Hudson	do		Uriah Bunker	
Lydia	do	160	Paul Ray	
Mary	do		—— Barney	
Rebecca	do		George Chase	
Sukey	do			
Union	do		Silas Swain	
New Bedford district, Mass.				
Herald	Ship		—— Coffin	
	do		—— Hathaway	
Russell	do		—— Allen	
Sag Harbor, N. Y.				
Minerva	Ship			
New London, Conn.				
Dauphin	Ship	240		
1806.				
Nantucket, Mass.				
Alliance	Ship		—— Pinkham	
Essex	do	238	David Harris	
Fame	do		—— Folger	
Hope	do			
Henry	do		—— Myrick	
John Jay	do	217	William Clark	
Mars	do			
Neutrality	do		—— Folger	
Ranger	do			
Rebecca	do			
Ruby	do	221	—— Barnard	
Sukey	do		—— Gardner	
Union	do			

sailing from American ports—Continued.

Whaling-ground.	Date— Of sailing.	Of arrival.	Result of voyage. Sperm-oil.	Whale-oil.	Whalebone.	Remarks.
			Bbls.	*Bbls.*	*Lbs.*	
	June —					
Delago	Jan. —					
Pacific Ocean	June —					
South Seas	July —					
West Indies {	Jan. —					
	Aug. 17					
	Aug. —					
	May 5					
	June 1					
Pacific Ocean	Feb. 4					
South Seas	Dec. —					
Atlantic	June 7					
Patagonia	Aug. —	May 20, 1805		1,350		
						A missing ship; last seen near the line, homeward bound, with a cargo of oil.
Brazil		—— —, 1806		Full.		
		Aug. 25, 1807				
Brazil		—— —, 1806		Full.		
do		—— —, 1806		Full.		
do		—— —, 1806		1,200		
Patagonia		—— —, 1806		Full.		
Brazil		Apr. 14, 1806		Full.		
Patagonia		Mar. —, 1806				
Brazil		———, 1806		Full.		
	Jan. —					
Brazil		Aug. —, 1806		1.400		
	Feb. 8					
South Seas		Aug. —, 1806		1,200		
	Jan. 8					Built 1804.
Brazil		May —, 1806				
Brazil	Sept. 6	June 14, 1806				
East Cape		Apr. 21, 1808				
Delago		Jan. 9, 1808		1,300		
Brazil		Aug. 31, 1807				Last reported with 1,000 whale.
						Last reported with 800 whale.
Pacific Ocean		Aug. 8, 1808	Full.			
do		Jan. 9, 1808	1,400			
do		June 21, 1808				
do						Lost on coast of Brazil, February, 1807; oil (1,000 sperm) saved.
Pacific Ocean		June 21, 1808				
Pacific Ocean		Sept. 11, 1808				
do		Dec. 2, 1808	1,000			
						Last reported with 1,000 whale.

Table showing returns of whaling-vessels

Name of vessel.	Class.	Tonnage.	Captain.	Managing owner or agent.
1806.				
New Bedford district, Mass.				
Acushnet	Ship		—— Tobey	
Hero	do		—— Tobey	
Jefferson	do		—— Brock	
Maria	do		—— Coffin	
Phebe Ann	do		—— Russell	
Sally	do		—— Clasby	
Triton	do		—— Clark	
Winslow	do		—— Coleman	
New London, Conn.				
Dolphin	Ship	240	—— Sayer	
Lydia	do		—— Douglass	
Leonidas	do	282	—— Barns	
1807.				
Nantucket, Mass.				
Alert	Brig		—— Worth	
Brothers	Ship	256	—— Perkins	
Boston	do	187	—— Clasby	
Criterion	do	229	—— Starbuck	
Chili	do	29[illegible]	—— Bunker	
Gardner	do		—— Briggs	
Hope	do			
Leo	do	217	—— Gardner	
Lydia	do	160	—— Allen	
Lion	do		—— Paddack	
Olive	do		—— Swain	
Samuel	do	287	—— Gardner	
Union	Brig		—— Hussey	
Union	Ship		Edmund Gardner	
Greenwich, R. I.				
Dauphin	Ship		—— Sayre	
New Bedford district, Mass.				
Ann	Ship		—— Gwinn	
Barclay	do		Gideon Randall	
Charles	do		—— Baxter	
Diana	do		—— Paddack	
Swan	Schooner		—— West	
New London, Conn.				
Dolphin	Ship	240	—— Sayre	
Leonidas	do	282	—— Barns	
Lydia	do		—— Douglass	
Sag Harbor, N. Y.				
Alknomac	Ship		—— Jones	
Brazil	do		—— Fowler	
1808.				
Nantucket, Mass.				
Alliance	Ship		—— Pinkham	
Adolphus	Sloop			
Atlas	Ship		—— Joy	
Alligator	do			
Belvidere	do		—— Nichols	
Brothers	do		—— Worth	
Criterion	do		—— Starbuck	
Eliza	Brig		—— Chase	

sailing from American ports—Continued.

Whaling-ground.	Date— Of sailing.	Date— Of arrival.	Result of voyage. Sperm-oil.	Result of voyage. Whale-oil.	Result of voyage. Whalebone.	Remarks.
			Bbls.	*Bbls.*	*Lbs.*	
Cape G'd Hope		Mar. 11, 1808		1,500		
Delago		Dec. 5, 1807				Of Westport.
South Seas						Jefferson carried her oil to Milford Haven.
Pacific Ocean		Nov. 27, 1808				
....do		June 22, 1808	1,200			
East Coast		Jan. 13, 1808		800		
Cape G'd Hope		Oct. 17, 1807		Full.		
Pacific Ocean						
Patagonia		——, 1807				
....do						
....do		June 23, 1807				Built 1806.
	Nov. —					
	Dec. 12					
East Cape		Sept. 18, 1808		Full.		
Pacific Ocean	Aug. 27					
....do	Dec. 12	Aug. —, 1809	1,500			
Cape G'd Hope		Oct. 31, 1808				
	Sept. 19					Boarded and badly damaged by a waterspout, 1808.
Pacific Ocean		May 17, 1809	Full.			
	Aug. 27					
	July 6					
Pacific Ocean		May 5, 1809	1,700			
Patagonia		Mar. 12, 1808				Brought oil and seal-skins.
	Sept. 19					Struck on a whale and sunk October 1. The crew landed at Flores October 8, after a voyage of 600 miles in open boats.
	Oct. —	May 13, 1809		1,700		
Pacific Ocean						Last reported with 1,200 sperm.
	Oct. —			Full.		Carried her cargo to England.
Pacific Ocean	Aug. —	Feb. 28, 1809	Full.			
Atlantic	Sept. 9	Sept. 24, 1807				
Patagonia						
....do		——, 1808				Crew of Leonidas sick with scurvy; sent boat ashore at Trinidad for supplies, and were unable to return for her. The men were rescued by schooner Experiment, sent by the United States Government for that purpose.
....do						
Brazil		May —, 1808				
Cape G'd Hope		Apr. 12, 1810		700		
Atlantic	Apr. 27					
	Apr. —	——, 1810				
Pacific Ocean						
	Apr. —					
Brazil						

Table showing the returns of whaling-vessels

Name of vessel.	Class.	Tonnage.	Captain.	Managing owner or agent.
1808.				
Nantucket, Mass.—Continued.				
Hope	Ship		—— Clark	
Harlequin	do		—— Starbuck	
John and James	do		—— Clark	
John Jay	do			
Leo	Brig		Owen Swain	
Lady Adams	Ship		—— Folger	
Lydia	do		—— Swain	
Mars	do			
Ranger	do		—— Joy	
Reliance	do		—— Pinkham	
Union	Brig		—— Luce	
New Bedford district, Mass.				
Cornelia	Schooner		—— Hathaway	
Danube	Ship		—— Mosher	
Edward	do		—— Ray	
Herald	do		—— Coffin	
Hero	do		—— Paddack	
Lucy	Brig		—— Lewis	
Maria	Ship	202	—— Coffin	
Martha	do		—— Tobey	
Phebe Ann	do		—— Russell	
Sally	do		—— Clark	William Rotch, jr
Thacher	Schooner		—— Mosher	
Triton	Ship		—— Swain	
Walker	do		—— West	
Winslow	do		—— Coleman	
New London, Conn.				
Dolphin	Ship	240	—— Sayre	
Lydia	do		—— Douglass	
Leonidas	do	282		
Sag Harbor, N. Y.				
Alknomac	Ship		—— Jones	
Brazil	do		—— Fowler	
Warren	do		—— Post	
Washington	do		—— Fowler	
Greenwich, R. I.				
Dauphin	Ship		—— Sawyer	
Schooner Thacher sailed from Dartmouth on a whaling-cruise in 1808, but there is no further report.				
1809.				
Nantucket, Mass.				
Atlas	Ship	249	Reuben Joy	
Brothers	do	256	Benjamin Worth	
Criterion	do	229	William Clasby	
Chili	do	293	James Bunker	
Delight	Schooner		—— Coffin	
Eliza	Ship			
Essex	do	238	Daniel Russell	
Fame	do		Job Coffin	
Gardner	do		Isaiah Ray	
Golden Farmer	do	295	George Swain, 2d	
Hope	do		—— Clark	
Henry	do		Isaac Gardner	
Hunter	Sloop		—— Luce	
Industry	Ship	172	G. Russell	
John and James	do		—— Perkins	
Lydia	do	160	Silas Swain	
Lima	do	280	Solomon Swain	
Lion	do		Peter Paddack	
Leo	do	217	Robert Gardner, jr	
Mount Hope	Schooner			
Monticello	Ship		Barzillai Coffin	

sailing from American ports—Continued.

Whaling-ground.	Date—		Result of voyage.			Remarks.
	Of sailing.	Of arrival.	Sperm-oil.	Whale-oil.	Whalebone.	
			Bbls.	*Bbls.*	*Lbs.*	
		May 17, 1809		Full.		Last reported with 1,200 whale.
Pacific Ocean						Condemned at Payta, 1809.
Brazil		June 27, 1809				
Pacific Ocean		June 3, 1810	1,400			
....do		Aug. —, 1810	500			Brought some whale-oil.
Brazil	Apr. —	Apr. —, 1809				
Pacific Ocean		May 1, 1810				
....do		June 3, 1810	1,800			
Cape G'd Hope		Apr. 11, 1810				
....do		Mar. 5, 1810				
Atlantic	May —					
Pacific Ocean	Sept. —	June 12, 1810				No report.
						Last reported with 1,200 sperm.
Cape G'd Hope	Sept. —	Apr. 13, 1810		400		
....do	Oct. —	—— —, 1810		850		Belonged to Westport.
	May —					
Pacific Ocean	July —	May 8, 1810	1,120	500		
Pacific Ocean	Sept. —	July 22, 1810	1,200			
....do		Aug. 16, 1810				
Atlantic	Apr. — July —	—— —, 1808 —— —, 1809				Belonged to Dartmouth.
Cape G'd Hope		Jan. 7, 1810		750		
Pacific Ocean	July —	June 13, 1810	1,700			
....do	Oct. —	June —, 1810				
Brazil		—— —, 1809				
....do		—— —, 1809				
....do		—— —, 1809				Sold, 1809.
Brazil		—— —, 1809		1,600		
....do						Last reported with 1,000 whale.
....do						Probably obtained about 1,600 barrels.
....do		May 13, 1809		1,700		
Pacific Ocean						
....do	June 27	Nov. 18, 1810				
....do		July 2, 1811	Full.			
....do	Nov. 5	Nov. —, 1811	Full.			Some whale.
Atlantic	Dec. —					
	June 20					
Pacific Ocean						
East Shore		Apr. 26, 1811				Full, lacking 100 barrels.
Pacific Ocean	Oct. —	July 16, 1811	Full.			
....do	Oct. —	June 22, 1811	Full.			
Brazil		Nov. —, 1810	200	1,000		
Pacific Ocean		Feb. 9, 1811	1,200			
Atlantic	May 7					Last reported 30 days out, clean.
Brazil		Nov. —, 1810		900		
....do		Nov. —, 1810		1,200		Captain Swain was killed by a whale.
....do		July 1, 1810				
Pacific Ocean	July 11	July 1, 1811	1,900			
....do		Jan. 13, 1811	1,600			
....do	Aug. 2	Nov. —, 1811	Full.			Mostly sperm.
Atlantic	Feb. —					Last reported June 10, 90 barrels.
Pacific Ocean		Jan. 13, 1811	1,350			

Table showing the returns of whaling-vessels

Name of vessel.	Class.	Tonnage.	Captain.	Managing owner or agent.
1809.				
Nantucket, Mass.—Continued.				
Perseveranda	Ship		Absalom Coffin	
Rebecca	do		George Chase	
Ruby	do	221	Christopher Wyer	
Ranger	do		—— Joy	
Sterling	do		Richard Folger	
Sukey	do		George W. Gardner	
Samuel	do	287	Jonathan Swain	
Thomas	do	269	Davis Whippey	
New Bedford district, Mass.				
Barclay	Ship		Gideon Randall	
Charles	do		—— Baxter	
Diana	do		—— Paddock	Wm. Rotch, jr., & Sons
Herald	do		—— Coffin	
Martha	do		—— Tobey	
Swan	Schooner			J. Alden
Thacher	do		—— Tobey	
Sag Harbor, N. Y.				
Abigail	Ship		—— Bunker	
Aiknomac	do		—— Jones	
Jefferson	do		—— Post	
Lavinia	do		—— Fowler	
Warren	do		—— Sayre	
Washington	do		—— Fowler	
Greenwich, R. I.				
Dauphin	Ship		—— Sawyer	
1810.				
Nantucket, Mass.				
Alligator	Ship		Owen Swain	
Alliance	do		Hezekiah Pinkham	
Boston	do	187		
Dove	Sloop		—— Wood	
John Jay	Ship	217	William B Coffin	
——	do			
Lady Adams	do	230	Elisha Folger, jr	
Lydia	do	160	David Swain, 2d	
Leo	Brig	217	Obed Luce	
Mars	Ship	315	John Fitch	
Minerva	do	200	Brown Chase	
Mary Ann	do		—— Folger	
Renown	do			
Rebecca	do		—— Coffin	
Ranger	do		William Joy	
Sukey	do			
Union	Brig		—— Bunker	
New Bedford, Mass.				
Diana	Ship		—— Hathaway	Samuel Rodman
Maria	do		—— Coffin	do
Martha	do		—— Dillingham	Seth Russell & Sons
Phebe Ann	do		—— Russell	Samuel Rodman
Sally	do		Obed Clark	Rotch & Hazard
Walker	Ship		—— West	
Winslow	do		—— Gardner	Samuel Rodman
Greenwich, R. I.				
Dauphin	Ship		—— Coffin	
Sag Harbor, N. Y.				
Abigail	Ship		—— Bunker	

sailing from American ports—Continued.

Whaling-ground.	Date—Of sailing.	Date—Of arrival.	Result of voyage.—Sperm-oil.	Result of voyage.—Whale-oil.	Result of voyage.—Whalebone.	Remarks.
			Bbls.	*Bbls.*	*Lbs.*	
....do		Nov. 18, 1810	Full.			
Brazil		Aug. 4, 1810	Full.			
Pacific Ocean	Aug. 2	Oct. 17, 1811	Full.			
Woolwich						
Pacific Ocean		June 22, 1811	Full.			
....do	July 11	June 6, 1811	Full.			
....do	July 26	June 22, 1811	Full.			
....do	Oct. —	Sept. 27, 1811	Full.			Built 1809.
Pacific Ocean		May 9, 1811	2,000			
	Nov. —					
Pacific Ocean	Aug. —	June 13, 1811				
Cape G'd Hope						
Brazil	Aug. —	June 12, 1810		1,000		
Atlantic	May 5					
Brazil						
....do						
....do						
....do		June —, 1810				
Patagonia		June 16, 1810		700		
Brazil						
Brazil						
Pacific Ocean						Captured by the English, 1812, full of sperm-oil and sent into St. Thomas.
....do	July 8	Dec. 8, 1812				Arrived at Newport.
....do		July 16, 1812				
West Indies		——— 1811				No report.
Pacific Ocean	Sept. 16	Sept. 4, 1812	Full.			Arrived at Newport.
....do		Dec. 4, 1812				Arrived at New Bedford.
....do		Jan. 29, 1812	1,150			
....do		July 21, 1812	Full.			Captain Swain was killed by a whale.
....do		Apr. 8, 1813	Full.			Also 60 barrels on deck.
....do	Aug. 21	Oct. 26, 1812	1,100			Arrived at Norfolk, Va.
....do		Dec. 7, 1812	1,400			
Coast Africa		Mar. 16, 1811		Full.		
South Seas		Mar. —, 1811				
Woolwich						Last reported with 600 whale.
Pacific Ocean						Captured with 1,300 sperm and sent into Bermudas, 1812.
....do						
South Coast		Jan. 11, 1811				
	Apr. 13	July 3, 1812				
Pacific Ocean		May 8, 1812				
Brazil		July 15, 1811				
Pacific Ocean	Nov. —	June 2, 1812				
....do						Captured July 20, 1812, by the English sloop-of-war Recruit, and sent into Bermudas; had 1,250 sperm; value of vessel and cargo, $40,000.
....do						Captured by the English with a cargo of sperm-oil.
....do	Aug. —	Feb. 5, 1812	1,200			
Patagonia	Sept. 20	Oct. 8, 1811				
Brazil		Aug. 12, 1811		800		

Table showing returns of whaling-vessels

Name of vessel.	Class.	Tonnage.	Captain.	Managing owner or agent.
1810.				
Nantucket, Mass.—Continued.				
Alliance	Ship		Hezekiah Pinkham	
Boston	do	187		
Dove	Sloop		—— Wood	
——	Ship			
John Jay	do	217	William B. Coffin	
Lady Adams	do	230	Elisha Folger, jr	
Leo	Brig	217	Obed Luce	
Lydia	Ship	160	David Swain, 2d	
Mars	do		John Fitch	
Minerva	do	200	Brown Chase	
Rebecca	do		—— Coffin	
Ranger	do		William Joy	
Sukey	do			
New Bedford, Mass.				
Diana	Ship		—— Hathaway	Samuel Rodman
Sally	do		Obed Clark	Rotch & Hazard
Walker	do		—— West	
Greenwich, R. I.				
Dauphin	Ship		—— Coffin	
1811.				
Nantucket, Mass.				
Atlas	Ship	249	Obed Joy	
Brothers	do	256	Benjamin Whippey, jr	
Betsey	Schooner		—— Gardner	
Criterion	Ship	229	William Clark	
Chili	do	293	Robert Gardner, jr	
Dove	Sloop		—— Luce	
Essex	Ship	238	—— Russell	
Fame	do		Job Coffin	
Golden Farmer	do	295	George Swain, 2d	
Gardner	do		Isaiah Ray	
George	do		Benjamin Worth	
Hope	do		Reuben Weeks	
Hunter	Sloop		—— Luce	
Industry	Ship	17[illegible]	—— Russell	
Lion	do		—— Paddack	
Leo	do	217	Tristram Folger	
Lima	do	286	—— Swain	
Monticello	do		Barzillai Coffin	
Mary Ann	do		George Russell, jr	
Manilla	do		Joseph McCleave	
Mount Hope	Schooner			
Ocean	Brig		Absalom Coffin	
Orange	Sloop		William Perkins	
Perseveranda	Ship		Thomas Paddock	
Renown	do		Zaccheus Barnard	
Rebecca	do		Jethro Coffin	
Sterling	do		Jonathan Swain	

sailing from American ports—Continued.

Whaling-ground.	Date— Of sailing.	Date— Of arrival.	Result of voyage. Sperm-oil.	Result of voyage. Whale-oil.	Result of voyage. Whalebone.	Remarks.
			Bbls.	*Bbls.*	*Lbs.*	
Pacific Ocean	July 8	Dec. 8, 1812				Arrived at Newport.
....do		Dec. 16, 1-12				
West Indies		—— —, 1811				No report.
Pacific Ocean		Dec. 4, 1812				Arrived at New Bedford.
....do	Sept. 16	Sept. 4, 1812	Full.			Arrived at Newport.
		Jan. 29, 1812	1,150			
Pacific Ocean		Apr. 8, 1813	Full.			Also 60 barrels on deck.
....do		July 11, 1812	Full.			
	Aug. 21	Nov. 27, 1812	Full.			Arrived at Norfolk, Va.
		Dec. 7, 1812	1,400			
Woolwich						Last reported with 600 whale.
Pacific Ocean						Captured with 1,300 sperm, and sent into Bermudas, 1812.
....do						
	Apr. 13	July 3, 1812				
Pacific Ocean						Captured July 20, 1812, by English sloop-of-war Recruit; sent into Bermudas; had 1,250 sperm. Value of vessel and cargo, $40,000.
....do						Captured by the English with a cargo of sperm-oil.
Patagonia	Sept. 20	Oct. 8, 1811				
Pacific Ocean	Nov. —	Dec. —, 1813	850			
....do		Dec. 7, 1812	1,800			
Atlantic	Jan. —		50			
Pacific Ocean		Dec. —, 1813	Full.			Arrived in Rhode Island.
Atlantic	July 20	—— —, 1812	60			
Pacific Ocean						
....do	Aug. —					Captured in 1813 with 1,200 sperm; sent to England.
....do	Oct. 3	Dec. —, 1812	1,800			Arrived at New Bedford.
....do	Dec. 12					Captured by the Loire December 4, 1813; had 400 sperm.
....do	Nov. 23					Captured in 1813 with 1,300 sperm, and sent into Halifax.
Woolwich	Aug. 4					Captured with a cargo of oil, by the Tribune, September 27, 1812; sent into Barbadoes.
Atlantic	May 7					No report.
Patagonia	June 4					
Pacific Ocean						
Coast Africa		May —, 1813		Full.		Captain Folger was 61 years old; had 60 barrels on deck.
Pacific Ocean	Sept. 28					Captured by the Albion December 7, 1813; sent into Bermudas.
....do	Oct. 3					Captured by the English brig Sophie, off Delaware; had 580 sperm.
Patagonia						Captured within five days' sail of Nantucket, by English letter-of-marque Tiger, in 1812; full of elephant-oil.
Atlantic	Feb. —					No report.
South Seas						Sent home 83 sperm; captured and sent into Cape of Good Hope 1812.
Atlantic		Aug. 17, 1811	Full.			
Pacific Ocean	July 21					Captured on Tuckanuck Shoals, 1814, by an English 74; had 350 sperm.
....do	Aug. 4					Sent home 37 casks sperm; captured by an English armed whaler; had 1,600 sperm.
Brazil						Captured by an English brig; sent into Rio Janeiro.
Pacific Ocean						Captured and sent into Barbadoes, 1813.

Table showing returns of whaling-vessels

Name of vessel.	Class.	Tonnage.	Captain.	Managing owner or agent.
1811.				
Nantucket, Mass.—Continued.				
Sukey	Ship	..	John Macy	
Stanhope	Schooner	..	—— Gamble	
Samuel	Ship	287	Prince Coleman	
William Penn	do	15[illegible]	George W. Gardner	
Sag Harbor, N. Y.				
Abby	Ship	..		
New Bedford, Mass.				
Ann	Ship	..	James Gwinn	
Barclay	do	..	Gideon Randall	
Diana	do	..	—— Paddock	
Maria	do	..	—— Coffin	
Westport, Mass.				
Hero	Bark	..	—— Barns	
1812.				
Nantucket, Mass.				
Brothers	Ship	250	—— Worth	
Charles	do	274	Grafton Gardner	
Diana	Brig	80	Calvin Bunker	
Dove	Sloop	..	David Swain	
Lima	Ship	280	—— Swain	
Mount Hope	Schooner	..	David Cottle	
Nancy	Sloop	..	Marshall Crosby	
President	Schooner	..	William Brown	
President	Ship	293	Solomon Folger	
Thetis	Schooner	..	William Perkins	

Two Nantucket schooners, with from 50 to 60 barrels of oil each, put into Boston, October 19, 1812; names not ascertained.

The brig Nanina, of Hudson, Capt. Valentine Barnard, sailed from New York April 4, 1812, for the Falkland Islands, whaling and sealing. Arrived there, the English brig Isabella, with a number of passengers, was found wrecked. The English officers offered Captain Barnard all of the Isabella's cargo which could be saved, if he would rescue them, to which he replied that his sense of duty commanded him to relieve them without reference to compensation; nevertheless, if they so desired, he would take the remnant of the wrecked cargo as some repayment for a spoiled voyage. Captain Barnard received the officers, crew, and passengers of the Isabella on board his vessel, and to reward him for his exertions and loss, his vessel and crew were infamously betrayed into the hands of English authorities, and he and his crew brutally treated. Tidings of the affair coming to the ears of the English naval commander in those waters, he dispatched a vessel to release the American captives. Captain Barnard's protest appears in the Hudson Bee in 1814.

sailing from American ports—Continued.

Whaling-ground.	Date— Of sailing.	Date— Of arrival.	Result of voyage. Sperm-oil.	Result of voyage. Whale-oil.	Result of voyage. Whalebone.	Remarks.
			Bbls.	*Bbls.*	*Lbs.*	
Pacific Ocean	Oct. 9					Returned October 12, having sprung foremast; sailed again 1811.
Atlantic	July 11					No report.
Pacific Ocean	Oct. —	—— —, 1813	1,100			Arrived at New Bedford.
....do	Nov. 9					Captured December 4, 1813, and sent into Cape of Good Hope; had 1,300 sperm.
Brazil	Sept. —	July —, 1812		1,100		
Pacific Ocean						
....do	Nov. 23	Mar. —, 1814	1,800			
....do	Nov. 7					
....do		May 15, 1812				
Pacific Ocean	June 28					
....do		Feb. 28, 1814	1,750			
Atlantic		July —, 1812	170			Heard of the war and came home.
....do		July —, 1812	120			Came home, hearing of the war.
Pacific Ocean	Mar. —					
Atlantic	Mar. 7					The first whaler to fall a victim to the English; captured and burned with 170 barrels sperm on board, July 9, 1812.
....do		Aug. 2, 1812		80		
....do		July —, 1812	50			Heard of the war and came home.
Pacific Ocean		Dec. 8, 1813	1,000			Built at Rochester, 1811.
Atlantic		Aug. —, 1812	90			

Table showing returns of whaling-vessels

Name of vessel.	Class.	Tonnage.	Captain.	Managing owner or agent.
1813.				
Nantucket, Mass.				
Juno	Ship		Obed Ray	
Nancy	Sloop			
There were about 10 small vessels from Nantucket, humpback-whaling on the shoals in 1813.				
1814.				
Several small vessels from Nantucket were whaling on the shoals in 1814.				
1815.				
Nantucket, Mass.				
Atlas	Ship	249	William Easton	
Alert	Brig		Seth Folger	
Boston	Ship	187	Reuben Clasby	
Brothers	do	256	Benjamin Whippey	
Belvidere	Brig		Reuben Baxter	
Charles	Ship	274	Benjamin Worth	
Charles	Schooner		—— Cottle	
Criterion	Ship	329	Shubael Brown	
Diana	Brig		—— Bunker	
Dauphin	Ship	216	Seth Pinkham	
Dove	Sloop		—— Swain	
Essex	Ship	238	Daniel Russell	
Experiment	Sloop		—— Randall	
Edward	Brig		Charles Coleman	
Golden Farmer	Ship	294	George Swain, 2d	
Ganges	do	265	Isaiah Ray	
Globe	do	293	George W. Gardner	
Gen. Jackson	Brig	174	Stephen Skinner	
Hannah	Sloop		—— Coffin	
Industry	Ship	172	George Russell, jr	
John Adams	do	296	Elisha Folger	
John	Sloop		—— Brown	
John Jay	Ship	217	David Swain	
Lydia	do	160	Joseph McCleave	
Lima	do	286	Christopher Wyer	
Leo	do	217	William Joy	
Lady Adams	do	230	Peter Paddack	
Martha	do	273	Reuben Weeks	
Maria	Schooner		—— Worth	
Minerva	Ship	200	George B. Chase	
Mason's Daughter	Sloop		William Perkins	
Nancy	do		—— Swain	
New Packet	do		—— Paddock	
Olive	do		—— ——	
President	Ship	293	Jonathan Swain, 2d	
President	Schooner		—— Luce	
Parnel	do		—— Chadwick	

sailing from American ports—Continued.

Whaling-ground.	Date— Of sailing.	Date— Of arrival.	Result of voyage. Sperm-oil.	Result of voyage. Whale-oil.	Result of voyage. Whalebone.	Remarks.
			Bbls.	*Bbls.*	*Lbs.*	
Shoals						Captured by an English brig; never heard of afterward.
....do	July 7					Captured by an English brig, July 8, 1813.
Pacific Ocean	June 29	June 6, 1817	1,372			
Cape Good Hope	Nov. 16	Dec. 20, 1816	130	480		Captain Folger died on the voyage.
Pacific Ocean	May 16	Aug. 25, 1816	974			
...do	June 29	Mar. 19, 1817	1,552			
Patagonia	May 18	Mar. 1, 1816		840		Elephant oil.
Pacific Ocean	June 4	Nov. 4, 1817	1,872			Detained 45 days in Valparaiso, then sent to Lima for adjudication for having no "sea-letter."
{ Atlantic { Coast Africa.	May — Nov. —	Sept. —, 1815	60			
Pacific Ocean	July 20	Apr. 10, 1817	1,410			
Atlantic {	May —	Aug. 28, 1815	60			
	Sept. —	Oct. —, 1815		Clean		
Pacific Ocean	July 28	Jan. 17, 1817	1,020	60		
Atlantic						Last report, July, 1815, with 25 barrels sperm.
Pacific Ocean	July 13	Nov. 19, 1816	1,431			
Atlantic {		Sept. —, 1815	15			
	Sept. —	Oct. —, 1815		Clean		
	Dec. 30	Jan. 26, 1817	173			
Pacific Ocean	June 29	Dec. 29, 1816	1,115	420		Alexander Coffin, first mate, killed by falling from aloft.
....do	Aug. 17	Oct. 17, 1817	1,785	139		Built at Haverhill, 1809.
....do	Oct. 24	Jan. 1, 1818	1,890	125		Built 1815; the first ship bringing over 2,000 barrels.
Cape Good Hope	Dec. 30	Dec. 28, 1816	170	570		
{						Last reported with 34 barrels on board and a 30-barrel whale alongside.
{ Atlantic		Sept. —, 1815		Clean		Lost both boats.
{ Cape de Verde	Oct. 31					Last reported with 60 barrels.
Brazil	July 2	Oct. 6, 1816		734		
Pacific Ocean	July 31	Nov. 7, 1817	1,473	346		Built at Rochester, 1812.
Atlantic		Aug. 23, 1815	150			
Pacific Ocean	Sept. 6	June 7, 1817	1,410			
Patagonia	May 16	Mar. 10, 1816		1,012		Elephant oil.
Pacific Ocean	June 25	Dec. 24, 1817	1,824			
Brazil	July 2	Oct. 21, 1816	38	1,310		
Pacific Ocean	Aug. 14	May 11, 1817	1,168			
....do	July 2	Oct. 20, 1817	1,654			Built at Pembroke, 1810; detained 20 days in Valparaiso, and part of her crew pressed on a patriot armed vessel for a short cruise.
Patagonia		Apr. 2, 1816		700		Elephant-oil.
Pacific Ocean	July 17	Sept. 18, 1817	1,460			
Atlantic {	May —	July 9, 1815	100			} The first whaler to arrive after the war.
	July —	Sept. 3, 1815	120			
....do		Sept. 3, 1815	70			
....do {		July 27, 1815				} Took three whales.
		Sept. —, 1815	15			
....do		Sept. —, 1815	90			
Pacific Ocean	June 25	July 1, 1817	1,778	111		
Atlantic	May —	Sept. —, 1815	250			
....do		Sept. —, 1815		Clean		Lost one boat.

Table showing returns of whaling-vessels

Name of vessel.	Class.	Tonnage.	Captain.	Managing owner or agent.
1815.				
Nantucket, Mass.—Continued.				
Rover	Sloop		—— ——	
Ruby	Ship	221	Albert Clark	
Statira	Brig		—— Barney	
Samuel	Ship	287	Ariel Coffin	
			—— Davis	
Success	Sloop		—— Chase	
Tarquin*	Ship	301	James Bunker	
Thomas	do	270	John Macy	
Three Sons	Brig		Obed Joy	
Union	do		—— Bunker	
Weymouth	Ship	329	David Harris	
William Penn	Brig		Matthew Norton	
——	Sloop		—— Randall	
——	Ship		—— Sedgewick	
New Bedford, Mass.				
Barclay	Ship		—— Coffin	William Rotch, jr., & Sons
Diana	do		—— Paddock	Thomas Hazard
Elizabeth	Sloop		—— Clark	Samuel Rodman
Maria	Ship		—— Swain	do
Mary	Brig		—— Howland	William Rotch, jr., & Sons
Martha	Ship		—— West	
Phebe Ann	do		—— Coffin	Samuel Rodman
Sally	Brig		—— Coleman	
Winslow	Ship		—— Gardner	Samuel Rodman
William Thacher	Schooner		—— Howland	William Rotch, jr., & Sons
Fairhaven, Mass.				
Herald	Ship		—— Bunker	
			—— Hathaway	
Liberty	Schooner		—— Hathaway	John Alden
			—— Butler	
Hudson, N. Y.				
Gen. Scott	Ship		Robert Jenkins	
——	do		David Paddock	
Westport, Mass.				
Industry	Brig		—— Clark	
Sag Harbor, N. Y.				
Argonaut	Ship		—— Halsey	
Martha	do			
Warren	do		—— Fowler	
1816.				
Nantucket, Mass.				
Amphibious	Schooner		—— Ray	
Antoinette	Ship		—— Folger	
Boston	Ship	187	Reuben Clasby	
Betsy	Brig		William Brown	
Belvidere	do		Reuben Baxter	
Boniff	do		John H. Pease	
Charles	do		—— Meader (?)	
Diana	do		—— Bunker	
Dispatch	do		William Brown	
Dove	Sloop		—— Swain	

* On the voyage the Tarquin fell in with a disabled Portuguese frigate and towed her into port. As a rec

sailing from American ports—Continued.

Whaling-ground.	Date— Of sailing.	Date— Of arrival.	Result of voyage. Sperm-oil.	Result of voyage. Whale-oil.	Result of voyage. Whalebone.	Remarks.
			Bbls.	*Bbls.*	*Lbs.*	
Atlantic	Sept. 27	Sept. 29, 1815				Got two humpbacks, in company with sloop Success.
Brazil	June 4	Oct. 4, 1816		1,512		
....do	May —					Sold at Pernambuco 1815.
Pacific Ocean	July 17	May 9, 1817	1,646			
Atlantic		July 18, 1815	60			
....do	July 26	Sept. —, 1815	60			Got two humpbacks in company with sloop Rover.
....do	Sept. 27	Sept. 29, 1815				
Brazil	Aug. 19	June 5, 1817	80	1,390		Sailed June 28; returned in August, in distress, with 50 sperm.
Pacific Ocean	Oct. 9	May 11, 1817	1,009			Heard that the country was at war, and returned.
Patagonia	May 24					Lost on the coast of Patagonia August 30, 1815.
Atlantic		Oct. 20, 1815		Clean		Was thrown on her beam-ends and damaged in a gale.
Pacific Ocean	Nov. 22	Apr. 17, 1818	1,980			
Cape Good Hope	Dec. 30	Jan. 11, 1817	185	485		Built 1815.
Atlantic	Aug. 12					Reported August 22; 30 sperm.
....do	July —					Reported September 12; clean.
Pacific Ocean	July —	Nov. 8, 1817	1,950			
....do	Aug. —	Mar. 7, 1817				Full
Cape de Verdes	June —	Dec. 3, 1815	420			
Pacific Ocean	May —	May 13, 1817	1,200			
Patagonia	May —	Mar. 19, 1817		1,300		
Brazil	June 20	May 8, 1816				
Pacific Ocean	July —	Mar. 19, 1817	1,400			
Atlantic	May 26	Oct. —, 1815				No report of cargo.
Pacific Ocean	July —	June 6, 1817	1,350			
Patagonia		Mar. 7, 1817		950		
Patagonia	July 18	June 22, 1816		1,400		
Atlantic	July 1	Sept. 7, 1815	100			Lost boats and received other damage in a gale.
	Sept. 1	Oct. —, 1815		Clean		
	Nov. —	May 6, 1816	35			
Pacific Ocean		Aug. 16, 1817	450			Went sealing and whaling; made a poor voyage because of inexperience.
....do		Mar. —, 1817	Full.			
Brazil		June 2, 1816		1,500		
....do						
....do		July —, 1816		900		Returned, leaking badly.
West Indies		July 16, 1816	80			The Amphibious sailed again; arrived September 26 with 10 whale.
Patagonia						Last reported at Rio Janeiro May 6; 9,000 skins, and full of oil.
Pacific Ocean	Nov. 10	May 12, 1818	989			
	Nov. 19	July 1, 1817	170			
Patagonia	May 7	June 5, 1817		777		
	May 21	June 7, 1817		450		Lost at St. Michael's Sept. 4, 1817
Africa		Oct. 13, 1817	150			
Atlantic		Aug. 12, 1816		8		
	Aug. 15	Nov. 19, 1817	70	420		
Atlantic		Aug. 6, 1815	80			

ompense she was allowed 900 barrels of oil and permission to whale in Portuguese waters for three years

Table showing returns of whaling-vessels

Name of vessel.	Class.	Tonnage.	Captain.	Managing owner or agent.
1816.				
Nantucket, Mass.—Continued.				
Experiment	Sloop	...	—— Randall	
Francis	Ship	291	Barzillai Coffin	
Fanny	Brig	...		
Franklin	Ship	309	Grafton Gardner	
George	do	359	John Fitch	Obed Mitchell
Hope	Sloop	...		
Hero	Ship	313	James Russell	
Hannah	Sloop	...	—— Coffin	
Hycso	Ship	290	William B. Coffin	
Hazard	Sloop	...	—— West	
Indus	Brig	262	Obed Joy	
Juno	Schooner	...	—— Paddock	
John	Sloop	...	—— Coffin	
Liberty	Brig	...	—— Gardner	
Lydia	Ship	160	Shubael Hussey	
Morning Star	Schooner	...		
Mason's Daughter	Sloop	...	William Perkins	
Maro	Ship	315	Joseph Allen	
New Packet	Sloop	...	—— Coffin	
North America	Ship	351	Absalom Coffin	
President	Schooner	...	Obed Luce	
Phœnix	do	...	—— Paddock	
Ruby	Ship	221	Albert Clark	
Success	Sloop	...	—— Davis	
South America	Ship	397	George Clark	
Sally	Sloop	...	George Luce	
William and Nancy	Brig	...	Coffin Whippey	
Vulture	Ship	299	Jesse Coffin	
A galliot, Captain —— Coleman, made an unsuccessful cruise. Schooner Charles, Cottle, arrived November 19 from the Cape de Verdes with 230 sperm; probably sailed early in 1816.				
New Bedford, Mass.				
Caroline	Schooner	...	—— Chase	
Experiment	Sloop	...	—— Bourne	
Elizabeth	do	...	—— Chase	
Industry	Brig	...	—— Clark	
Martha	Ship	...	—— West	Seth Russell & Sons
Orion	Brig	...	—— Randall	
Ocean	do	...	—— Randall	
Ospray	do	...	—— Hathaway	Thaddeus Swain
President	Schooner	...	—— Clark	
Russell	Ship	...	—— Delano	Samuel Rodman
Richmond	do	...	—— Earle	
Sally	Brig	...	—— Arthur	T. Swain & Son
Swift	Ship	...	—— Price	Humphrey Hathaway
Rochester, Mass.				
Sally	Schooner	...	—— Smith	
Holmes's Hole, Mass.				
Harmony	Schooner	...	—— Chase	
Newport, R. I.				
Liberty	Brig	...	Amaziah Gardner	

sailing from American ports—Continued.

Whaling-ground.	Date—		Result of voyage.			Remarks.
	Of sailing.	Of arrival.	Sperm-oil.	Whale-oil.	Whalebone.	
			Bbls.	*Bbls.*	*Lbs.*	
Atlantic	......	June 19, 1816	60	15	......	The Experiment (Brown) sailed again; arrived September 26 with 100 sperm.
Pacific Ocean	July 15	Sept. 1, 1818	1, 805	......	......	Built 1816.
......	Jan. —	......	......	......	......	
Pacific Ocean	Oct. 6	Nov. 22, 1818	1, 831	21	......	Do.
....do	Feb. 25	July 24, 1818	2, 106	5	......	Built 1815 at Rochester.
......	......	......	......	......	......	
Pacific Ocean	Oct. 18	Feb. 27, 1819	2, 025	33	......	Built 1816 at Rochester.
Atlantic	......	July 16, 1816	50	......	......	
Pacific Ocean	Nov. 7	Sept. 8, 1818	1, 545	55	......	Built 1816.
Cape de Verdes	June 1	Dec. 28, 1816	120	......	......	
Patagonia	May 19	July 1, 1817	......	1, 490	......	Elephant-oil.
South Coast	......	Oct —, 1816	70	......	......	
West Indies	July 16	Oct. 4, 1816	60	......	......	The John sailed once before in 1816, returning June 19 with 120 sperm.
Guinea	Oct. 14	Oct. 16, 1817	200	......	......	
Brazil	July 27	July 21, 1817	......	700	......	
Atlantic	Apr. 19	......	......	......	......	
....do	......	June 21, 1816	150	......	......	The Mason's Daughter sailed again; arrived September 16 with 60 sperm.
Pacific Ocean	Nov. 10	July 9, 1819	2, 363	......	......	Built 1816.
Atlantic	May —	Aug. 11, 1816	25	......	......	The New Packet sailed again; arrived September 24 with one small whale.
Pacific Ocean	Nov. 30	Nov. 8, 1818	234	942	......	
Atlantic	Aug. 21	Sept. 5, 1816	70	......	......	
Cape de Verdes	......	Sept. 22, 1816	70	......	......	
Brazil	Nov. 21	Apr. 17, 1818	82	1, 235	......	
Atlantic	......	May 22, 1816	90	......	......	The Success sailed again, and arrived August 15 with 30 sperm.
Brazil	June 19	May 26, 1818	......	1, 955	......	
Atlantic	Apr. 2	Aug. 2, 1816	160	......	......	The sloop Sally sailed again August 8; arrived September 2, clean.
Guinea	Oct. 9	Oct. 13, 1817	170	......	......	The William and Nancy is reported as having arrived September 6, 1816, with 120 sperm; probably sailed late in 1815 or early in 1816.
Pacific Ocean	Aug. 19	June 3, 1819	1, 532	172	......	
Atlantic	Apr. 18	......	......	......	......	
....do	Dec. —	June —, 1817	90	......	......	
....do	June —	......	......	......	......	
Cape de Verdes	Feb. —	Nov. 12, 1816	200	......	......	
Brazil	......	June 18, 1817	......	1, 600	......	
Cape de Verdes	......	Nov. 1, 1816	500	......	......	
Woolwich	......	......	......	......	......	Last reported with 400 sperm.
Africa	Oct. —	Jan. 1, 1818	......	1, 000	......	
Cape de Verdes	......	Dec. 29, 1816	450	......	......	
South Seas	June 14	Nov. 5, 1817	......	Full.	......	
Brazil	July 18	May 26, 1817	......	1, 700	......	
Africa	Sept. —	June 13, 1817	......	250	......	
Pacific Ocean	......	Nov. 8, 1818	1, 800	......	......	
......	......	......	......	......	......	Last reported in July with 50 sperm.
Cape de Verdes	Apr. 23	Dec. 31, 1816	250	......	......	
Africa	......	July 17, 1817	......	......	......	

Table showing returns of whaling-vessels

Name of vessel.	Class.	Tonnage.	Captain.	Managing owner or agent.
1816.				
Wareham, Mass.				
Enterprize	Ship			
Fairhaven, Mass.				
Liberty	Schooner		—— Brock	
Resident	do		—— Burtch	N. Stoddard
Edgartown, Mass.				
Apollo	Ship		—— Daggett	
Boston, Mass.				
John	Brig		—— Randall	
Potomack	Ship		—— Alley	
1817.				
Nantucket, Mass.				
Atlas	Ship	247	Robert M. Joy	
Alert	Brig		David Cottle	
Brothers	Ship	256	Alexander D. Bunker	
Betsey	Brig		William Brown	
Criterion	Ship	229	Shubael Brown	
Charles	Brig		Obed Luce	
Dauphin	Ship	216	Seth Pinkham	
Dove	Sloop		—— Swain	
Diana	Brig		Calvin Bunker	
Essex	Ship	238	Daniel Russell	
Experiment	Sloop		—— Randall	
Edward	Brig		William Paddack	
Factor	Ship	299	Reuben Swain	
Golden Farmer	do	294	Matthew Norton	
Gov. Strong	do	270	Obed Fitch	
Gen. Jackson	Brig	174	Stephen Skinner	
Gen. Lincoln	Ship	285	Shubael Chase	
Industry	do	172	Jethro Coffin	
Independence	do	311	George Swain, 2d	
Improvement	Ship	256	Obadiah Coffin	
Indus	Brig		Obed Joy	
Leo	Ship	217	William Joy	
Lydia	do	160	Elias Ceeley	
Lady Adams	do	230	Shubael Hussey	
Mason's Daughter	Sloop		William Perkins	
President	Ship	293	Jonathan Swain, 2d	
Success	Sloop		—— Crosby	
Samuel	Ship	287	Ariel Coffin	
Tarquin	do	301	George Barrett	
Thomas	do	270	John Brown	
William	Sloop			
William	Ship	208	Thomas Paddack	
William Penn	Brig		Benjamin Folger	
New Bedford, Mass.				
Elizabeth	Sloop		—— Whippey	
George and Susan	Ship	320	—— Randall	G. & J. J. Howland
Mary	Brig		—— Howland	Wm. Rotch, jr., & Sons
Martha	Ship		—— West	Seth Russell & Sons
Milwood	do		—— Wilcox	do
Maria	do		—— Swain	Samuel Rodman
Orion	Brig		—— Tobey	
President	do		—— Clark	Samuel Rodman, jr
Phebe Ann	Ship		—— Covill	
Richmond	do		—— Earl	I. Howland, jr., & Co.
William and Eliza	do		—— Randall	

sailing from American ports—Continued.

Whaling-ground.	Date—Of sailing.	Date—Of arrival.	Result of voyage.—Sperm-oil.	Result of voyage.—Whale-oil.	Result of voyage.—Whalebone.	Remarks.
			Bbls.	*Bbls.*	*Lbs.*	
....	....	....	......	......	......	Last reported Aug. 29 with 70 sperm.
....						
Africa	Aug. —	July —, 1817	350	......	......	
Pacific Ocean ..	June 19	....	......	......	......	Last reported with 1,100 sperm.
Brazil	....	....	......	......	......	Captain Randall either died or left the ship Last reported with 800 whale.
Patagonia	June —	....	......	......	......	Stopped off Nantucket June 17, 1816; crew (11 blacks) mutinied; the mutiny was quelled by men from Nantucket; blacks stole a boat soon after and part of them ran away.
Pacific Ocean ..	Nov. 19	Nov. 11, 1819	1,222	331	......	
....do	Apr. 19	Nov. 9, 1818	329	333	......	
....do	Aug. 8	Nov. 5, 1819	1,505	110	......	
....	July 20	Oct. 18, 1817	......	Clean	......	
Pacific Ocean ..	Aug. 18	Dec. 10, 1819	1,315	......	......	
Cape de Verdes.	Mar. 13	....	......	......	......	Condemned at Bonavista, 1817. Captain Luce chartered schooner Jane Marsh, and finished his voyage.
Pacific Ocean .	May 31	Nov. 16, 1819	1,041	148	......	
Atlantic	....	July 7, 1817	60	......	......	Sixty barrels at last report. The Dove sailed again September 3.
Iceland	May 14	Sept. 25, 1817	......	100	......	
Pacific Ocean ..	June 11	Apr. 14, 1819	1,284	154	......	
West Indies ...	June 19	July 6, 1817	......	......	......	Sailed again July 7 under Captain Brown.
Iceland	May 14	Jan. 1, 1818	30	......	......	
Pacific Ocean ..	Oct. 8	July 8, 1819	420	1,183	......	
Brazil..........	June 1	Apr. 20, 1818	......	1,417	......	
Pacific Ocean ..	July 12	Oct. 30, 1819	733	1,075	......	Built 1817.
....do	Apr. 5	Jan. 27, 1819	318	97	......	
Brazil..........	Sept. 20	Aug 12, 1818	......	665	......	
....do	May 31	July 25, 1818	......	890	......	
Pacific Ocean ..	July 26	Nov. 12, 1819	1,388	568	......	Built 1817. Captain Swain said no ship would fill again with sperm oil.
....do	Sept. 7	Dec. 8, 1819	1,527	50	......	
Brazil	Aug. 15	Sept. 17, 1818	......	1,132	......	
....do	June 11	Sept. 8, 1818	......	804	......	
....do	Sept. 5	Aug. 15, 1818	......	665	......	Broken up at Nantucket 1818.
Pacific Ocean ..	Oct. 25	Oct. 2, 1819	1,246	23	......	
Atlantic	....	....	......	......	......	Last reported with 60 barrels sperm.
Pacific Ocean ..	Nov. 19	May 7, 1820	1,577	374	......	
Newfoundland .	....	Aug. 28, 1817	176	......	......	
Brazil..........	Aug. 4	July 22, 1818	65	1,595	......	
....do	Aug. 10	Apr. 5, 1819	......	1,930	......	
Pacific Ocean ..	Aug. 13	Jan. 12, 1820	1,000	500	......	
Atlantic	Sept. 3	....	......	......	......	
Brazil..........	July 3	Sept. 14, 1819	21	695	......	
South Atlantic.	Mar. 6	Mar. 11, 1818	170	324	......	
Cape de Verdes.	May —	....	150	......	......	
Patagonia......	May —	June 1, 1818	......	1,950	......	
....do	May —	Feb. 7, 1818	......	1,300	......	Elephant oil.
Brazil..........	Aug. —	June 7, 1818	......	1,650	......	
South Atlantic.	Aug. —	July 19, 1818	......	1,200	......	
Pacific Ocean ..	Sept. —	May 18, 1819	1,250	......	......	
Delago	Jan. —	Jan. 29, 1818	......	Full	......	
Cape de Verdes.	May —	May 11, 1818	450	......	......	
Pacific Ocean .	June —	Feb. 6, 1820	1,050	......	......	Arrived at Newport.
Patagonia	July —	May 24, 1818	100	1,900	14,000	
Pacific Ocean ..	July 18	Feb. 4, 1820	2,500			Returned July 31 with loss of bowsprit; sailed again August 5.

Table showing returns of whaling-vessels

Name of vessel.	Class.	Tonnage.	Captain.	Managing owner or agent.
1817.				
New Bedford, Mass.—Continued.				
Winslow	Ship		—— Chase	Samuel Rodman
Wm. Thacher	do		—— Tucker	Wm. Rotch, jr., & Sons
Fairhaven, Mass.				
Agenora	Brig		—— Burtch	Delano, Tripp & Terry
Herald	Ship		—— Bunker	S. Borden
Westport, Mass.				
Industry	Brig		—— Mayhew	
Sag Harbor, N. Y.				
Abigail	Ship		—— Post	
Andes	do		—— Skinner	
Charlotte	do			
Fair Helen	do			
Gov. ——	do		—— Fowler	
Octavia	do		—— Post	
Hudson, N. Y.				
Diana	Ship		—— Coffin	
Eliza Barker	do		—— Paddock	
Boston, Mass.				
John	Brig			
1818.				
Nantucket, Mass.				
Boston	Ship	187	Frederick Barnard	
Betsey	Brig		William Brown	
Charles	Ship	274	Abraham Swain	
Cordelia	Sloop		—— Cook	
Diana	Brig		Calvin Bunker	
Dispatch	do		William Brown	
Dove	Sloop			
Eagle	Ship	335	William H. Coffin	
Equator	do	262	Elisha Folger	
Eagle	Brig		Joseph McCleave	
Edward	do		Latham Paddack	
Francis	Ship	291	Tim. Fitzgerald	
Fortunate Farmer	do			
Globe	do	293	George W. Gardner	
Ganges	do	265	Isaiah Ray	
Golden Farmer	do	294	Peter Coffin	
Gen. Lincoln	do	285	Shubael Chase	
George	do	359	John Fitch	
Hannah	Sloop		—— Alley	
Hycso	Ship	290	Ammiel Coffin	
Industry	do	172	Amaziah Gardner	
John Adams	do	296	Peter Paddack	
Juno	Schooner		Abraham Pollard	
John Jay	Ship	217	{ William H. Coffin { John Bunker	
Lima	do	286	Albert Clark	

sailing from American ports—Continued.

Whaling-ground.	Date—Of sailing.	Date—Of arrival.	Result of voyage.—Sperm-oil.	Result of voyage.—Whale-oil.	Result of voyage.—Whalebone.	Remarks.
			Bbls.	*Bbls.*	*Lbs.*	
Pacific Ocean	Oct. —	Jan. 12, 1820	1,400	......	.....	
Patagonia	May —	Feb. 7, 1818	......	Full	.....	Elephant-oil.
Brazil	Aug. 5	June 8, 1818	......	1,200	.....	Withdrawn for merchant service, and sunk off Bermudas 1818.
....do	Jan. —	May 26, 1818	130	700	.....	
Atlantic	June 1	May —, 1818	250	......	.....	
Brazil	......	......	......	......	.....	Last reported with 500 whale.
....do	......	......	......	......	.....	Last reported with 900 whale.
....do	......	......	......	......	.....	No report.
....do	......	......	......	......	.....	Last reported with 800 whale.
....do	......	......	......	......	.....	Last reported with 700 whale.
......	......	......	......	......	.....	Last reported with 1,200 whale.
Pacific Ocean	......	......	......	......	.....	Last reported with 760 sperm, 140 whale.
....do	Aug. 29	Nov. 27, 1819	1,950	150	.....	Boarded by a privateer, and the officers and crew robbed of all their clothing, 1818.
Brazil	......	......	......	......	.....	Last reported with about 800 whale.
Brazil	Aug. 12	Nov. 25, 1819	......	812	.....	
......	Jan. 18	Sept. 10, 1818	70	12	.....	
Pacific Ocean	Jan. 15	Aug. 13, 1820	1,782	......	.....	
Atlantic	......	Aug. —, 1818	......	......	.....	No report.
......	{May 2	Oct. 6, 1818	......	40	.....	
	{Oct. 31	May 27, 1819	72	198	.....	
Atlantic	July 8	Aug. 20, 1819	......	371	.....	
Gulf of Mexico	Jan. —	—— —, 1818	......	......	.....	Boarded twice in Gulf of Mexico, and robbed of provisions and boats. Came home leaky.
Pacific Ocean	Oct. 17	June 12, 1821	2,142	......	.....	
....do	Oct. 31	Dec. 1, 1820	709	611	.....	The Equator and the Balaena of New Bedford were the first whalers to visit the Sandwich Islands, arriving there September 17, 1819. Equator built 1818.
Patagonia	June 4	May 18, 1819	......	806	.....	
Atlantic	Apr. 26	June 3, 1819	......	420	.....	
Pacific Ocean	Nov. 10	Nov. 28, 1821	784	611	.....	
......	July 13					
Pacific Ocean	Mar. 3	May 29, 1820	2,090	......	.....	
... do	June 22	June 2, 1821	1,616	......	.....	
Brazil	July 19	June 20, 1819	40	1,389	.....	
....do	Sept. 21	......	......	......	.....	Dismasted in a gale September 27, 1818; abandoned October 29; one man lost.
Pacific Ocean	Nov. 10	May 19, 1821	2,135	25	.....	
Banks	......	Sept. 12, 1818	170	......	.....	The Hannah was captured by an English cruiser, a prize crew put on board, and her own crew taken away. Was recaptured by Captain Alley and one of his mates two days after.
Pacific Ocean	Dec. 13	June 11, 1821	1,560	....	.....	
Brazil	Oct. 6	Aug. 21, 1819	66	574	.....	
Pacific Ocean	Jan. 15	Dec. 5, 1820	788	862	.....	
Banks	......	Oct. 6, 1818	......	100	.....	Was taken by an English cruiser and carried into Saint John's, where she was released. Brought rest of Hannah's crew.
Pacific Ocean	Feb. 6	May 6, 1818	......	......	.....	{Got ashore at Bonavista and returned leaking.
....do	Aug. 29	May 16, 1821	369	100	.....	{
....do	July 13	Sept. 10, 1820	1,762	177	.....	

Table showing returns of whaling-vessels

Name of vessel.	Class.	Tonnage.	Captain.	Managing owner or agent.
1818.				
Nantucket, Mass.—Continued.				
Leo	Ship	217	William Joy	
Minerva	do	200	Sylvanus Coffin	
Martha	do	273	Reuben Weeks	
Peru	do	257	David Harris	
Pacific	do	314	Benjamin Whippey	
Peruvian	do	334	Christopher Wyer	
Planter	do	340	George B. Chase	
Ruby	do	221	Obed Ray	
Rambler	do	318	Benjamin Worth	
States	do	290	David Swain, 2d	
Samuel	do	287	Hezekiah Pinkham	
Success	Sloop	...		
South America	Ship	397	Joseph Earle	
Two Brothers	do	217	George B. Worth	
Weymouth	do	329	William Chadwick	
William	do	208	Obed Luce	
William and Nancy	Brig	...	Coffin Whippey	
William Penn	Ship	...	Benjamin Folger	
New Bedford, Mass.				
Augustus	Ship	380	—— Butler	
Barclay	do	...	—— Coffin	
Balaena	do	..	Edmund Gardner	
Commodore Decatur	Brig	...	—— Tucker	J. & J. Howland
Charles	Ship	...	—— Coffin	Samuel Rodman, jr
George and Susan	do	320	—— Randall	George Howland
Gleaner	Brig	...	David Leslie	J. A. Parker
Golconda	Ship	...	—— Bennett	George Howland
Independence	do	...	—— Perry	
Juno	Brig	...	—— Spooner	
Martha	Ship	...	—— Whitfield	Seth Russell & Sons
Minerva	do	...	—— Williams	J. & J. Howland
Midas	do	326	—— Tobey	John Coggeshall & William R. Rotch.
Milwood	Ship	...	—— Wilcox	
Mary	Brig	...	—— Howland	William Rotch, jr., & Sons
Mercator	Ship	...	—— Swain	
Ospray	Brig	...	James Drew	
Persia	Ship	...	—— Cross	
Pindus	do	...	—— Barrett	
President	Brig	...	—— Clark	
Richmond	Ship	...	—— Dillingham	
Russell	do	...	—— Arthur	
Triton	do	...	Zephaniah Wood	
Victory	do	...	—— Bunker	
William Thacher	do	...	—— Howland	William Rotch, jr. & Sons
Fairhaven, Mass.				
Herald	Ship	...	—— Burtch	
Stanton	do	...	—— Burtch	
Westport, Mass.				
Industry	Brig	...	—— Mayhew	
Salem, Mass.				
Britannia	Ship	...		
Sag Harbor, N. Y.				
Argonaut	Ship	...	—— Halsey	
Martha	do	...		
Octavia	do	...	—— Post	
Thomas Nelson	do	...	—— Gardner	

sailing from American ports—Continued.

Whaling-ground.	Date— Of sailing.	Date— Of arrival.	Result of voyage. Sperm-oil.	Result of voyage. Whale-oil.	Result of voyage. Whalebone.	Remarks.
			Bbls.	*Bbls.*	*Lbs.*	
Brazil..........	Dec. 13	July 15, 1820	.....	600	.....	
Pacific Ocean..	Feb. 6	July 25, 1819	.....	704	.....	Broken up at Nantucket 1819.
....do..........	June 28	July 29, 1821	1,620	.....	.....	
....do..........	Aug. 29	Dec. 5, 1820	1,146	463	.....	Built 1818 at Hanover.
....do..........	Aug. 29	Oct. 8, 1820	1,764	543	.....	Built 1818.
....do..........	Sept. 25	Nov. 3, 1821	1,966	60	.....	Built 1818 at Scituate.
...do..........	Sept. 25	Sept. 15, 1820	1,890	391	.....	Built 1818 at Middletown, Conn.
Brazil..........	Aug. 22	Feb. 24, 1820	.....	1,306	.....	
Pacific Ocean..	Nov. 21	Oct. 31, 1821	2,040	.....	.....	Built 1818 at Kingston.
....do..........	July 8	June 27, 1820	1,698	.....	.....	Built 1818.
Brazil..........	Sept. 16	May 1, 1820	.....	1,700	.....	
Shoals..........	July 25	.....	.....	.....	.....	Last reported August 1 with two whales.
Pacific Ocean..	Sept. 25	Oct. 20, 1820	378	1,836	.....	
....do..........	Nov. 21	Aug. 5, 1821	1,231	158	.....	
....do..........	July 20	Dec. 27, 1820	1,597	433	.....	
Brazil..........	Oct. 30	Feb. 28, 1820	113	540	.....	
	May 4	Sept. 25, 1818	.....	Clean	.....	
Cape G'd Hope	May 29	Feb. 12, 1819	38	639	.....	
Patagonia......	June 7	June 4, 1819	.....	1,800	.....	Bought 1810.
Pacific Ocean..	Jan. —	Oct. 12, 1820	.....	.....	.....	Last reported with 1,600 sperm.
....do..........	Nov. —	June 10, 1821	.....	.....	.....	Last reported with 1,500 sperm. See Equator, Nantucket.
Patagonia......	May —	Feb. 25, 1819	.....	Full.	.....	
Pacific Ocean..	Jan. 25	July 21, 1820	1,900	.....	.....	
Brazil..........	July —	June 24, 1819	.....	2,000	.....	George and Susan built at Dartmouth 1810. Captain Randall came home sick 1819.
Patagonia......	May —	Jan. 10, 1819	.....	1,030	.....	Elephant-oil.
....do..........		July 14, 1819	.....	1,700	.....	
Pacific Ocean..	Jan. 9	Feb. 18, 1821	1,900	100	.....	
Brazil..........	May —	June 3, 1819	.....	400	.....	
....do..........	July 23	June 30, 1819	.....	1,700	.....	
Patagonia......	May —	Feb. 3, 1819	.....	900	.....	
Brazil..........	May 26	June 18, 1819	.....	1,750	.....	Midas built at New Bedford 1810.
Patagonia......	Sept. —	Feb. 14, 1820	.....	1,600	.....	
....do..........	May —	.....	.....	.....	.....	Lost May 28 on Cape Blanco. Robbed by the Arabs; one man killed, one wounded, and one captured; driven from the shore and wreck. The survivors reached the Isle of Sal in their boats June 5.
Pacific Ocean..	Jan. —	.....	.....	.....	.....	
....do..........	Feb. —	July 25, 1820	800	.....	.....	
... do..........	Jan. —	May 1, 1820	1,800	.....	.....	
Africa..........	Jan. —	.....	.....	.....	.....	
Cape de Verde	July —	.....	.....	.....	.....	
Brazil..........	July —	June 3, 1819	.....	1,800	.....	
Pacific Ocean..	.....	May 30, 1820	1,100	700	.....	
....do..........	Nov. 12	June 7, 1821	1,980	50	.....	
Patagonia......	July —	—— —, 1820	.....	.....	.....	Last reported with 1,600 whale.
....do..........	May —	Jan. 10, 1819	.....	900	.....	
....do..........	July —	.....	.....	.....	.....	
Pacific Ocean..	.....	Nov. 11, 1821	2,100	.....	.....	
Cape de Verde	July —	May —, 1819	300	.....	.....	
.....	Dec. 5	.....	.....	.....	.....	Wrecked on Pickard's rocks going out. No further report.
Brazil..........	.....	July 2, 1819	.....	.....	.....	
....do..........			.....	.....	.....	
....do..........	.....	June —, 1819	.....	1,800	.....	
....do..........	.....	July —, 1819	.....	1,300	.....	

Table showing returns of whaling vessels

Name of vessel.	Class.	Tonnage.	Captain.	Managing owner or agent.
1818.				
Boston, Mass.				
John	Brig		—— Alley	W. Lewis & Co
* ——, *N. Y.*				
Harriot	Brig		Nathan Hildreth	
Edgartown, Mass.				
Apollo	Ship		—— McKenzie	
Loan	do		—— Norton	
Philadelphia, Pa.				
Governor Hawkins	do		T. Coffin	
1819.				
Nantucket, Mass.				
Aurora	Ship	346	Daniel Russell	Gideon Folger & Co
Ark	do	372	Reuben Clasby	Jethro Mitchell
Atlantic	do	321	Barzillai Coffin	Gardner Macy & Co
Barclay	do	301	Peter Coffin	J. J. Barney & Co
Chili	do	291	Absalom Coffin	Jethro Mitchell
Diana	Brig		Calvin Bunker	
Eagle, 2d	Ship	233	Tristram C. Swain	Baxter & Ewer
Essex	do	238	George Pollard, jr	Gideon Folger & Co
Franklin	do	309	Elihu Coffin	Uriah Folger & Co
Foster	do	317	Shubael Chase	P. Mitchell & Sons
Gideon	Bark	204	John R. Caswell	J. & B. Burnell
George Porter	Ship	285	David Cottle	David Pease & Co
General Jackson	Brig	174	Henry Cottle	F. G. Macy & Co
Hero	Ship	313	James Russell	J. Starbuck & Co
Huntress	Schooner			T. Starbuck & Co
Indus	Ship	262	Obed Joy	Aaron Mitchell
Independence, 2d	do	352	George Barrett	Valentine Swain
Industry	do	172	Amaziah Gardner	
John Adams, 2d	do	268	David Easton	G. Easton & Co
Juno	Schooner			
Leander	Ship	313	Ariel Coffin	Gardner, Macy & Co
Maro	do	315	Joseph Allen	E. Mitchell & Co
Paragon	do	309	William Perkins	J. Jenkins & Co
Prince George	Brig	155	George Luce	Mitchell & Cary
Roxana	Ship	237	Francis Coffin, 2d	Peter Myrick & Co
Reaper	do	338	Jedediah Fitch	P. Gardner & Sons
Sally	do	195	Thomas Paddock	B. & P. Gardner
Sea Lion	do	307	Benjamin Folger	John Jenkins & Co
Thomas, 2d	do	206	Laban Cottle	P. Chase & Co
Tarquin	do	301	Micajah Gardner	R. Mitchell & Co
Vulture	do	299	Jesse Coffin	M. Barney & Co
Washington	do	308	Reuben Swain, 2d	Z. Coffin
NOTE.—A sloop sailed from Nantucket, whaling, in December, 1819.				

*Probably

sailing from American ports—Continued.

Whaling-ground.	Date—		Result of voyage.			Remarks.
	Of sailing.	Of arrival.	Sperm-oil.	Whale-oil.	Whalebone.	
			Bbls.	*Bbls.*	*Lbs.*	
Patagonia	....	July 28, 1819	....	1,150	.....	
Brazil	....	....	.....	.....	.....	Lost on coast of Brazil May 23, 1819, with 600 whale.
Pacific Ocean	....	Aug. —, 1820	1,250	.....	.....	
....do	....	....	.....	.....	.....	Last reported with 1,350 sperm.
....	....	....	.....	.....	.....	Last reported with 350 elephant-oil and 4,000 skins. Captain Coffin died in 1819.
Pacific Ocean	Dec. 26	Dec. —, 1822	1,630	130	.....	Built at Haddam, Conn., 1819.
....do	Feb. 12	Mar. 27, 1822	612	1,200	.....	Broken up at Nantucket 1822.
....do	July 4	Jan. 18, 1822	1,530	120	.....	Built at Haddam 1819.
....do	Oct. 15	Nov. 22, 1821	1,940	.....	.....	Built at Rochester, Mass., 1819.
....do	Aug. 12	Nov. 12, 1822	560	370	.....	Built 1819.
Brazil	July 17	....	.....	.....	.....	
Cape G'd Hope	July 18	....	.....	.....	.....	Condemned at St. Domingo after obtaining some oil.
Pacific Ocean	Aug. 12	....	.....	.....	.....	Stove by a whale November, 1820; captain, mate, and three men saved in the boats; three men left on Disco Island.
....do	Jan. 25	Nov. 23, 1821	1,254	15	.....	
....do	July 22	Apr. 12, 1822	1,624	.....	.....	The bottom of the Foster was pierced by a horn-fish and the horn left there. On sawing it off in the hold the water rushed through the opening 1,000 strokes por hour. Built 1819.
Brazil	May 21	July 25, 1820	50	920	.....	
....do	June 17	Mar. 28, 1821	.....	684	.....	
South Atlantic	May 14	May 15, 1820	25	534	.....	The General Jackson took her oil on the afterward celebrated "Tristan" ground.
Pacific Ocean	July 17	Aug. 5, 1821	1,070	63	.....	Taken off St. Mary's by the pirate Beneveder, carried to Aranco, where Captain Russell and a boy were shot. The mate, Obed Starbuck, brought the ship home.
....	....	....	.....	.....	.....	Last reported with 30 sperm.
Pacific Ocean	Jan. 25	Oct. 29, 1821	735	565	.....	Altered from a brig, 1818.
New Zealand	July 23	June 16, 1822	2,150	18	.....	Captain Barrett died on the voyage.
Brazil	Dec. 20	....	.....	.....	.....	Condemned at St. Domingo, 1820; had 339 barrels of oil.
... do	June 23	Feb. 1, 1821	51	1,260	.....	
Gulf Mexico	....	June 15, 1820	90	.....	.....	
Pacific Ocean	July 20	Oct. —, 1822	1,370	200	.....	Built 1819.
....do	Oct. 26	Mar. 10, 1822	2,425	.....	.....	Took his oil off the Japan coast.
....do	Jan. 7	Dec. 26, 1821	1,690	.....	.....	
....	Jan. 7	May 8, 1822	.....	800	.....	Filled once and sold her oil at San Salvador, 1820. Captured from the English in the war of 1812.
Brazil	June 5	Feb. 10, 1821	19	1,195	.....	
Pacific Ocean	Nov. 30	....	1,250	300	.....	Captain Fitch died on the voyage. Built 1819.
Brazil	Mar. 22	Aug. 26, 1820	22	487	.....	
Cape G'd Hope	July 8	Mar. 26, 1821	.....	1,087	.....	
Pacific Ocean	May 9	Mar. 2, 1821	.....	1,005	.....	
Brazil	July 20	Apr. 4, 1821	.....	500	.....	Reported at Charleston, S. C., November 21, 1820, with 500 whale, 40 hogsheads sperm, and 1,600 pounds bone.
Pacific Ocean	Sept. 14	Dec. —, 1822	1,354	122	.....	
....do	Dec. 26	Feb. 14, 1822	1,920	.....	.....	Washington built at Hanover, 1819.

Hudson.

Table showing returns of whaling-vessels

Name of vessel.	Class.	Tonnage.	Captain.	Managing owner or agent.
1819.				
New Bedford, Mass.				
Augustus	Ship	..	—— Butler	
Alliance	Brig	..	—— Ashley	
Cornelia	do	..	—— Gardner	
Commodore Decatur	do	..	—— Tucker	
Dragon	do	..	—— Chadwick	
Francis	Ship	..	—— Howland	
George and Susan	do	32	—— Whitteus	
Golconda	do	..	—— Bennett	
Gleaner	Brig	..	—— Leslie	
Iris	Ship	..	—— Hathaway	
Mercator	do	..	—— Swain	
Minerva	do	..	—— Pease	
Martha	do	..	—— Whitfield	S. & C. Russell
Maria	do	..	—— Chase	
Minerva	Brig	..	—— Williams	
Midas	Ship	32	—— Smith	
Pacific	do	..	—— West	
Richmond	do	..	Timothy Daggett	I. Howland, jr., & Co
Swift	do	..	—— Price	
Timoleon	do	34	George Randall	I. Howland, jr., & Co
Westport, Mass.				
Industry	Brig		—— Emery	
Sag Harbor, N. Y.				
Abigail	Ship	..		
Argonaut	do	25		
Fair Helen	do			
Hannibal	do	30		
Octavia	do			
Thomas Nelson	do		—— Coffin	
Union	do	26	—— Osborne	
New York, N. Y.				
Diana	Ship	..	—— Coffin	
H——	Brig	..		
New London, Conn.				
Carrier	Ship	..		
Fairhaven, Mass.				
Herald	Ship	..	—— Spooner	
Pindus	do	..	—— Barrett	
Stanton	do	..	—— Burtch	
Boston, Mass.				
John	Ship	17	Prince B. Mooers	
Dartmouth, Mass.				
William Thacher	Brig	...	—— Chase	
1820.				
Nantucket, Mass.				
Atlas	Ship	24	Robert M. Joy	F. Joy & Son
Alert	Brig		Peleg Brock	
Boston	Ship	18	Frederick Barnard	Jethro Mitchell
Brothers	do	25	David Brayton	Samuel Mitchell & Bros
Criterion	do	22	Seth Coffin, jr	John Cartwright & Son.
Crown Prince	Schooner			
Charles	Ship	274	Abraham Swain	John Cartwright & Son
Columbus	do	344	Daniel Folger	Uriah Folger & Co
Dauphin	do	27	Zimri Coffin	Gilbert Coffin & Sons
Dispatch	Sloop	..	—— Bunker	
Diana	Brig	....	Calvin Bunker	

sailing from American ports—Continued.

Whaling-ground.	Date—Of sailing.	Date—Of arrival.	Result of voyage.—Sperm-oil.	Result of voyage.—Whale-oil.	Result of voyage.—Whalebone.	Remarks.
			Bbls.	*Bbls.*	*Lbs.*	
Patagonia	....	July 25, 1820	.....	1,300	....	
Brazil	July 17	June 2[illegible], 1820	....	1,500	....	Crew sick with scurvy.
Patagonia	May —	June 20, 1820	....	90	....	
....do	May —	Apr. 21, 1820	....	....	....	Last reported with 580 whale.
....do	May —	June 7, 1820	....	500	....	
....do	May —	June 21, 1820	....	1,900	....	
Brazil	....	May 24, 1820	....	1,900	....	
Pacific Ocean..	Oct. 15	....	....	....	....	
Patagonia	May —	Mar. 19, 1820	....	....	....	Returned with a cargo of elephant-oil and sugar.
Pacific Ocean..	....	July 19, 1821	....	....	.....	Last reported with 1,600 sperm.
....	....	....	....	....	....	Last reported with 1,300 barrels.
Pacific Ocean..	Jan. —	June 7, 1822	1,200	....	....	
Patagonia	....	July 23, 1820	.....	1,500	....	
Pacific Ocean..	Sept. —	....	....	....	....	
Patagonia	May —	May 3, 1820	....	....	....	Last reported with 550 whale.
Brazil	....	June 17, 1820	....	2,200	....	
Patagonia	June 18	Mar. 25, 1820	....	2,200	....	
....do	Aug. —	July 25, 1820	180	1,300	6,940	
Pacific Ocean..	May —	June 5, 1822	2,150	....	....	
Brazil	July —	Feb. 13, 1820	....	2,030	10,105	Arrived at Newport; bought for New Bedford 1810.
Atlantic	Aug. —	May 10, 1820	12	.....	....	
Brazil	July —	....	....	....	....	Last reported with 600 whale.
....	....	....	....	....	....	Last reported with 1,260 whale.
Brazil	July 5	....	....	....	....	Last reported with 800 whale.
....do	....	June —, ——	....	1,600	....	
....do	July —	....	....	....	....	Last reported with 1,400 whale.
....do	....	June —, ——	....	2,500	....	
....	....	....	....	....	....	Last reported with 900 whale.
Patagonia	....	Apr. 12, 1820	....	1,100	....	
....	July —	....	....	....	....	
....	Aug. 1	....	....	....	....	
Patagonia	....	June 5, 1820	....	1,200	....	
....do	....	July 25, 1820	....	900	....	
Pacific Ocean..	....	....	....	....	....	Last reported with 1,300 sperm.
Patagonia	Oct. 30	June —, 1820	....	....	....	Last reported with 850 whale.
....	....	....	....	....	....	Last reported with 100 sperm.
Pacific Ocean..	July 16	Apr. 4, 1823	1,600	......	.....	Sold 1823.
Atlantic	....	Mar. 24, 1822	255	100	.....	
Pacific Ocean.	Jan. 20	Mar. 17, 1822	1,100	......	.....	
....do	June 14	June 5, 1823	1,40[illegible]	.....	.....	
... do	May 14	Apr. 13, 1823	1,400	.....	.....	
Atlantic	....	....	....	.....	.....	Last reported in August with 60 sperm.
Pacific Ocean.	Dec. 20	....	....	.....	.....	Lost at Valparaiso. Had 1,600 sperm. Saved 775 sperm and shipped it home.
....do	July 23	Apr. 1, 1823	1,903	.....	.....	Built 1820; sold 1823.
....do	Sept. 4	July —, 1823	1,272	.....	.....	
Atlantic	....	....	....	.....	.....	Last reported with 25 sperm.
South Atlantic	....	....	....	.....	.....	Skinning voyage.

Table showing returns of whaling-vessels

Name of vessel.	Class.	Tonnage.	Captain.	Managing owner or agent.
1820.				
Nantucket, Mass.—Continued.				
Factor	Ship	299	John Maxcy	Baxter, Ewer & Co
Falcon	do	297	Shubael Brown	E. Mitchell & Co.
Golden Farmer	do	294	Alfred Alley	John Jenkins & Co
Gov. Strong	do	27[illegible]	Moses Smith	P. Chase & Co
Globe	do	293	George W. Gardner	P. & C. Mitchell
Gen. Jackson	do	174	John Fisher	F. G. Macy
Galen	do	365	Seth Pinkham	Gilbert Coffin & Sons
Hesper	do	247	Reuben Joy, jr	G. & J. J. Barney
Huntress	Schooner		Chris. Burdick	
Improvement	Ship	25[illegible]	Obadiah Coffin	G. Coffin & Sons
Independence	do	311	Jona. Swain, 2d	Zenas Coffin
Lucy	Brig			
Lady Adams	Ship	230	Shubael Hussey	O. Mitchell & Sons
Liberty	Schooner		—— Coffin	
Leo	Ship	217	Henry Cottle	F. Joy
Lively	Schooner		—— Coffin	
Lima	Ship	286	Nathaniel Gorham	Chris. Mitchell & Co
Mason's Daughter	do		—— Brown	
North America	do	351	Obed Wyer	T. Hussey & Sons.
Ontario	do	354	Alexander D. Bunker	Samuel Mitchell & Bros.
Oliver H. Perry	Schooner		—— Coffin	
President	Ship	293	Shubael Cottle	J. Starbuck & Co
Phœnix	Schooner			
Pacific	Ship	314	Franklin Chase	Paul Mitchell & Sons
Planter	do	240	Job Coffin	Jared Coffin
Ruby	do	22[illegible]	Obed Ray	Jethro Mitchell
Spermo	do	296	James Bunker	A. Mitchell
States	do	290	Isaac Chase	Zenas Coffin
Samuel	do	287	Robert Inott	
Sally	do	194	Samuel Barrett	James Barker
Thomas	do	27[illegible]	John Brown	S. & O. Macy
Urchin	Brig			
Vesta	Schooner		—— Holmes	
William and Nancy	Brig		Tristram Folger	
New Bedford, Mass.				
Alliance	Brig		—— Ashley	
Ann Alexander	Ship		—— Cowell	
Com. Decatur	Brig		—— Handy	
Charles	Ship		—— Coffin	Samuel Rodman, jr
Cornelia	Brig		—— Gardner	
Dragon	do		—— Wood	
Eliza Barker	Schooner		—— Howland	
Elizabeth	do		—— Rotch	
Francis	Ship		—— Swain	
George and Susan	do	32[illegible]	—— Whitteus	
Independence	do		—— Hammond	
Juno	Brig		—— Long	
Laura	Schooner		—— Davis	
Lorenzo	Ship		—— Coffin	
Maria	do		—— Chase	
Minerva	Brig		Daniel Wood	
Milwood	Ship		—— Wilcox	
Midas	do		—— Smith	
Martha	do		—— Whitfield	
Minerva Smyth	do		Daniel McKenzie	
Ospray	Brig		—— Howland	
President	do		—— Covell	Samuel Rodman, jr
Phebe Ann	Ship		—— Chase	
Persia	do		—— Cross	
Pacific	do		—— West	
Parnassa	do		—— Covell	
Russell	do		—— Arthur	
Sophia	do		—— Cathcart	
Timoleon	do	346	Charles Starbuck	I. Howland, jr., & Co
Traveler	Brig		—— Howland	
Victory	Ship		—— Bunker	
Winslow	do		—— Clark	

sailing from American ports—Continued.

Whaling-ground.	Date—		Result of voyage.			Remarks.
	Of sailing.	Of arrival.	Sperm-oil.	Whale-oil.	Whalebone.	
			Bbls.	*Bbls.*	*Lbs.*	
Pacific Ocean	Aug. 9	Aug. 16, 1823	1,707			
....do	Oct. 8	Nov. 8, 1822	1,600			Built 1820. Captain Brown was accidentally killed on the voyage.
....do	Feb. 5	Jan. 12, 1822	200	800		Benjamin Swain, mate, died on the voyage.
....do	Feb. 21	Jan. 12, 1822	917	350		Sold out 1822.
....do	Aug. 9	May 3, 1822	2,025			
....do	Oct. 8	July 6, 1823	860			Altered from a brig 1820; sold 1823.
....do	Dec. 31	Sept. 6, 1823	2,210	70		Built 1820; sold out 1823.
....do	June 5	Sept. 12, 1822	900			
South Atlantic						Skinning voyage.
Pacific Ocean	June 20	Apr. 2, 1823	805	467		
....do	July 20	Apr. 8, 1823	2,023			
						Last reported with 100 sperm.
Pacific Ocean	Feb. 28	Oct. 17, 1821	1,136	80		
Atlantic		Nov. 27, 1820				Last reported with 200 sperm.
Pacific Ocean	Oct. 20	June 7, 1823	1,108			Broken up at Nantucket 1823.
Atlantic						
Pacific Ocean	Dec. 6	July 6, 1823	1,225			
Atlantic	Dec. —	July 19, 1821	170			Boarded and plundered by pirates.
Pacific Ocean	May 17	July 8, 1823	660			Captain Wyer died on the voyage.
....do	Nov. 29	Nov. 14, 1823	1,948			Built 1820 at Rochester.
Atlantic						
Pacific Ocean	Aug. 9	Nov. 17, 1822	1,383	400		
Atlantic	July 1					
Pacific Ocean	Dec. 16	Aug. —, 1823	1,639			
....do	Dec. 20	Nov. 17, 1823	1,465	201		
....do	Dec. 20					Condemned at Oahu, 1822; oil shipped home.
....do	Aug. 27	Mar. 24, 1823	1,920			Built 1820; sold 1823.
....do	Sept. 4	Apr. 8, 1823	1,100			
....do	Oct. 25					Condemned at Rio Janeiro 1822; oil (1,800 sperm) shipped home; sold 139 sperm.
....do	Nov. 22	July 9, 1823	970			Broken up at Nantucket 1823.
....do	Aug. 4	Sept. —, 1822	1,515			
Atlantic						
....do		Oct. 19, 1821	90			
South Atlantic						The William and Nancy returned from a whaling voyage November 27, 1820, clean. Skinning voyage.
Patagonia		July 20, 1821				
....do	June —					
South Seas	May 27	Aug. 7, 1821	900			
Pacific Ocean	Sept. 19	Aug. 5, 1823	Full.			
Patagonia		July 7, 1821				
... do		July 1, 1821				
Atlantic		Dec. 27, 1821				
....do	July 25	Sept. 18, 1820	Clean			
Pacific Ocean	Dec. 9	Dec. 12, 1823	1,900			
Patagonia		June 12, 1821				
Pacific Ocean		Dec. 6, 1823	2,000			
Brazil	May —	Jan. 19, 1821	400			
						Laura last reported with 130 sperm.
						Lorenzo was lost on the coast of Peru.
West'n Islands	June —	Aug 7, 1821	300	54	466	
Pacific Ocean	June —					Last reported with 1,200 sperm.
Brazil	July 25					
South Seas	Aug. —	Apr. 9, 1821		1,400		
Pacific Ocean	Dec. —	Nov. 13, 1823	1,625			
....do	Aug. —					
....do	May —	Apr. 12, 1821	470			
....do	July 25	May 4, 1823	Full.			Captain Chase died on the voyage.
Japan		Feb. 20, 1823	Full			
Brazil		Mar. 10, 1821	280	1,920		
Pacific Ocean	Dec. 8	July 5, 1823	Full.			
... do	Aug. —	Oct. 7, 1822	1,900			
....do	July 25	Dec. 8, 1822	1,500			
Brazil	May —	Apr. 5, 1822	300	2,200	9,943	
Cape de Verdes	May —					
Patagonia		May 28, 1821		2,000		
Brazil	May —					

Table showing returns of whaling-vessels

Name of vessel.	Class.	Tonnage.	Captain.	Managing owner or agent.
1820.				
New Bedford, Mass.—Continued.				
Wilmington and Liverpool Packet	Ship	....	—— Richmond	
William and Eliza	do	....	—— Paddock	
William Thacher	Brig	....	—— Chase	
William Rotch	Ship	....	do	
Fairhaven, Mass.				
Leonidas	Ship	....	—— Potter	
Pindus	do	....	—— Bennett	
Westport, Mass.				
Almy	Brig	....	—— Allen	
Industry	do	....	—— Cory	
Polly and Eliza	do	....	—— Mayhew	
Susan	Sloop	....	—— Warner	
Traveler	Brig	....	—— Howland	
Rochester, Mass.				
Orion	Brig	....	—— Luce	
Falmouth, Mass.				
Sarah Herrick	Brig	150		Elijah Swift
New York, N. Y.				
Caroline Ann	Ship	....		
Combine	Schooner	....	—— Jenkins	
Diana	Ship	....	—— Paddock	
Eliza Barker	do	....	—— Alley	
Neptune	do	....	—— Coffin	
Trident	do	....	Reuben Coffin	
Salem, Mass.				
Gen. Knox	Ship	....	—— Orne	
Polly	Brig	....		
Newport, R. I.				
Courier	Ship	....	William Fitzgerald	S. and J. Whitehorn
Robinson Potter	do	....	Reuben Swain	Robinson Potter
New London, Conn.				
Mary	Brig	....	—— Davis	
Mary Ann	do	....	—— Coffin	
Pizarro	do	....	—— Coit	
Sag Harbor, N. Y.				
Abigail	Ship	....		
Argonaut	do	254	—— Sayre	
Fair Helen	do	....		
Julius Cæsar	Ship	....	Oliver Fowler	
Marcus	do	283		
Ontario	do	....	—— Smith	
—— ——	do	....	—— Post	
Union	do	262	—— Osborne	
Boston, Mass.				
Beverly	Ship	498	Elias Ceeley	Israel Thorndike
George	do	....	—— Cary	
Edgartown, Mass.				
Apollo	Ship	....	—— Daggett	
John	do	....	—— Norton	

sailing from American ports—Continued.

Whaling-ground.	Date— Of sailing.	Date— Of arrival.	Result of voyage. Sperm-oil.	Result of voyage. Whale-oil.	Result of voyage. Whalebone.	Remarks.
			Bbls.	*Bbls.*	*Lbs.*	
Patagonia	June —	Dec. 27, 1823	2,600			The largest quantity to date.
Pacific Ocean	June —					Last reported December, 1821, with 1,500 sperm.
Brazil	June —					
Pacific Ocean	June 11					Reported June, 1821, with 1,850 sperm.
Pacific Ocean	Aug. 9	Feb. 26, 1823				Full of sperm.
Brazil	Aug. —	July 3, 1821		800		Crew sick with scurvy.
Sts. Belleisle		Sept. 1, 1820	40			Went cod-fishing and whaling; brought 91,000 cod-fish.
West'n Islands	June —					
do		Oct. 17, 1820	120			
Atlantic	June —					
do		May —, 1821				Last reported with 200 sperm.
Cape de Verdes	June 25					Last reported with 150 sperm.
Atlantic	June 17	——, 1822	300			Withdrawn.
Pacific Ocean						Last reported with 130 sperm.
West'n Islands	June —	Sept. 24, 1820				
Pacific Ocean	Aug. 22					
Japan		June 6, 1823	1,550			
Pacific Ocean	Sept. 7	Mar. —, 1822		1,300		
do		Aug. 13, 1823	2,000			
Falkland		June 6, 1821		600		On a sealing-voyage principally. Brought home 5,000 skins.
	Aug. —					
Pacific Ocean	Nov. 3	July 9, 1823	1,900	300		
do	July —	Dec. 31, 1822	2,100			Second mate killed by a whale.
	July 22	Apr. 9, 1821		827		
		June —, 1821		406		
	Aug. 1	June 1, 1821	105	1,145	2,375	
Patagonia						Last reported with 1,200 whale.
Brazil	Aug. 22					Returned in September with a sprung mainmast; sailed again in 1820.
Pacific Ocean						
Brazil						
Patagonia	July —					
Brazil	July —	Mar. —, 1821		2,000		
Pacific Ocean	Dec. 13	Mar. —, 1824	2,400			
Brazil						Reported nine months out with 1,400 whale. Not on the custom-house clearances.
Pacific Ocean		June 13, 1823	1,250			
do		Oct. 15, 1823				Last reported with 1,800 sperm.

Table showing returns of whaling-vessels

Name of vessel.	Class.	Tonnage.	Captain.	Managing owner or agent.
1820.				
Provincetown, Mass.				
Laurel	Brig		—— Cook	
Margaret	Schooner		—— Atwood	
Minerva	do		—— Soper	
Nero	do		—— Smalley	
Neptune	do		—— Cook	
Sophronia	do		—— Smith	
New Haven, Conn.				
Henry	Ship		Uriah Coffin	Forbes & Goodrich
——, N. Y.				
Caroline Ann	Ship		—— Coffin	
Eliza Barker	do		—— Alley	
1821.				
Nantucket, Mass.				
Ann	Schooner		—— Perry	
Alexander	Ship	421	George B. Chase	Gardner & Swift
Constitution	do	318	David Swain, 2d	Zenas Coffin
Cyrus	do	348	Elisha Folger, jr	
———	Sloop			
Equator	Ship	262	Joseph Barney	Myrick, Folger & Co
Eagle	do	335	George Kelley	J. & L. Starbuck
Francis	Schooner			
Ganges	Ship	265	Joshua Coffin	Gideon Gardner
Gideon	do	204	Obed Clark	J. & B. Burnell
George	do	359	John Fitch	
George Porter	do	285	Prince B. Moores	Robert Coggeshall
Harmony	Schooner		—— Hodges	
Hycso	Ship	290	Ammiel Coffin	Zenas Coffin
Industry	Schooner		—— Macy	
Iris	Sloop		—— Luce	
John Adams	Ship	296	George Bunker, 2d	Barnard & Macy
John Adams	do	268	Ammiel Joy	Peleg Macy, jr
Lion	do	326	Albert Clark	
Loper	do	316	William Henry Coffin	
Mason's Daughter	Sloop		—— Brown	
Martha	Ship	273	John H. Pease	
Oeno	do	328	George B. Worth	Aaron Mitchell
Oliver H. Perry	Schooner			
Peru	Ship	257	Peter Veeder	
Ploughboy	do	301	William Chadwick	
Phenix	do	323	David Harris	
Roxana	do	237	Alexander Ray	Reuben Starbuck
Spartan	do	333	George Swain. 2d	
Sea Lion	do	307	Alexander Russell	
Thomas	do	209	Laban Cottle	K. Starbuck
Two Brothers	do	217	George Pollard, jr	
Urchin	Brig		—— Chadwick	
Weymouth	Ship	329	Moses Harris	
Salem, Mass.				
Nancy	Brig		—— Upton	S. White
New Bedford, Mass.				
Ann Alexander	Ship		—— Covell	

sailing from American ports—Continued.

Whaling-ground.	Date—Of sailing.	Date—Of arrival.	Result of voyage.—Sperm-oil.	Result of voyage.—Whale-oil.	Result of voyage.—Whalebone.	Remarks.
			Bbls.	*Bbls.*	*Lbs.*	
Western Isl'ds	....	Nov. —, 1821	210	.....	.....	
....do	....	Oct. 17, 1821	160	.....	.....	
....do	....	Oct. —, 1821	220	.....	.....	
....do	....	Oct. —, 1821	260	.....	.....	
....do	....	Oct. —, 1821	260	.....	.....	
....do	....	Oct. —, 1821	80	.....	.....	
Pacific Ocean	Dec. 16	Nov. 18, 1823	1,800	200	.....	Made a losing voyage. Sold 1824.
Pacific Ocean	Dec. 21	....	1,050	.....	.....	
Atlantic	Oct. 3	....	.....	.....	.....	
Pacific Ocean	Aug. 18	May 2, 1824	2,836	.....	.....	
....do	June 24	July —, 1823	2,01[illegible]	.....	.....	Built 1821 at Hanover.
....do	Nov. 8	Mar. 10, 1825	2,111	.....	.....	
....	....	....	.....	.....	.....	Last reported with 100 sperm.
Pacific Ocean	Feb. 28	July 6, 1823	1,443	.....	.....	
....do	Nov. 13	Aug. 4, 1824	1,566	.....	.....	
Atlantic	July 16	....	.....	.....	.....	Last reported Aug. 26 with 60 sperm.
Pacific Ocean	Aug. 15	Mar. 31, 1824	1,823	.....	.....	
....do	Aug. 21	....	.....	.....	.....	Condemned at Saint Bartholomew's; had 444 sperm, 214 whale.
....do	Oct. 3	Dec. 10, 1824	1,414	287	.....	
....do	....	Dec. 10, 1824	1,531	.....	.....	Sold to New Bedford 1824.
N. S. Shetland	....	June 10, 1822	.....	250	.....	Brought also 1,000 seal-skins.
Pacific Ocean	Aug. 18	May 6, 1824	1,528	.....	.....	
Brazil	....	Dec. 30, 1821	.....	250	.....	
South	Apr. 29	....	.....	.....	.....	
Pacific Ocean	June 23	Aug. 22, 1823	1,109	.....	.....	Captain Bunker died; the mate and boat's crew were lost. Sold to New Bedford 1824.
....do	Dec. 12	Feb. 28, 1825	1,176	.....	.....	
....do	June 24	....	.....	.....	.....	Built 1821. Lost on rocks going into Fanning's Island. Had 1,400 sperm; saved 250.
....do	Aug. 20	May 6, 1824	1,071	.....	.....	
....	....	....	.....	.....	.....	Condemned at Port Royal March, 1822.
Pacific Ocean	Dec. 3	Apr. 27, 1825	1,583	.....	.....	
....do	Dec. 19	July 24, 1824	1,883	60	.....	
Mexico	....	....	.....	.....	.....	Reported August 13, 1821, homeward bound, with "80 or 180 sperm."
Pacific Ocean	Mar. 4	Apr. 26, 1824	1,525	238	.....	
....do	July 31	May 11, 1824	2,49[illegible]	.....	.....	Built 1821.
....do	Sept. 10	Apr. 30, 1824	1,935	.....	.....	Built 1821 at Rochester. Temporarily withdrawn 1824.
....do	July 25	June 4, 1824	1,175	34	.....	Sold out 1824. Condemned at Saint Bartholomew's subsequently.
....do	Aug. 18	Nov. 5, 1823	2,090	.....	.....	Built 1821 at Rochester.
....do	Aug. 29	Apr. 30, 1824	1,567	.....	.....	Second mate, Ensign Rogers, drowned by a foul line. Sold out 1825.
....do	June 13	Feb. 12, 1824	716	529	.....	
....do	....	....	.....	.....	.....	Lost on a coral reef, lat. 24° N, long. 168° W. Crew saved by the Martha, Captain Pease.
Atlantic	Apr. —	....	.....	.....	.....	Last of 1821 reported on Brazil, with 500 whale.
Pacific Ocean	June 23	Mar. 25, 1824	1,970			
Falkland and N. S. Shetl'd.	....	May 27, 1822	.....	100	.....	Brought also 1,800 seal-skins.
South Seas	May —	Apr. 25, 1822	.....	1,500	.....	

Table showing returns of whaling-vessels

Name of vessel.	Class.	Tonnage.	Captain.	Managing owner or agent.
1821.				
New Bedford, Mass.				
Alliance	Brig	..	—— Ashley	
Abigail	Ship	..	—— Covell	
Barclay	do	..	—— Glover	
Balœna	do	..	—— Gardner	
Camillus	do	..	—— Gardner	
Com. Decatur	do	..	—— Tilton	
Elizabeth	Brig	..	—— Blackmer	
Eliza Barker	Schooner	..	—— Howland	
Florida	Ship	..	—— Rice	
Good Return	do	..	—— Terry	
George and Susan	do	..	—— Upham	George Howland
George and Martha	do	..	—— Randall	
Indian Chief	Brig	..	—— Nye	
Independence	Ship	..	—— Hammond	
Iris	do	..	—— Hathaway	
Juno	do	..	—— Long	
Laura	Schooner	..	—— Long	
Loring	Ship	..	—— Coffin	
Midas	do	..	—— Spooner	
Minerva	do	..	—— Swain	
Martha	do	..	—— Perry	
Maria Theresa	do	..	—— Wilcox	
Mercator	do	..	—— Wood	
Milwood	do	..	—— Burgess	
Maryland	do	..	—— Folger	Samuel Rodman
Pacific	do	..	—— Whitfield	
President	Brig	..	—— Howland	
Planter	do	..	—— Long	
Protection	do	..	—— Wainer	
Portia	Ship	..	—— Ray	
Richmond	do	..	Richard Williams	
Roscoe	do	..	—— Swain	
Swift	do	..	John Pinkham	T. S. & N. Hathaway
Timoleon	do	..	Charles Starbuck	I. Howland, jr., & Co.
Triton	do	..	Zephaniah Wood	do
Victory	do	..	—— Bunker	
Winslow	do	..	—— Clark	
Wilmington and Liverpool Packet	do	..	—— Briggs	
Fairhaven, Mass.				
Arab	Ship	..	—— Gibbs	
Amazon	do	..		
Columbus	do	..	—— Brock	
Herald	do	..	—— Shearman	
Pindus	do	..	—— Eldridge	
Telamachus	Schooner	..	—— Hitch	
Westport, Mass.				
Almy	Brig	..	—— Mayhew	
Amstead	do	..	—— Seabury	
Industry	do	..	—— Cory	
Polly and Eliza	do	..	—— Webber	
Traveller	do	..	—— Dyer	
Edgartown, Mass.				
Hope	Schooner	..		
Loan	Ship	..	—— Tilton	
Planter	Brig	..	—— Pease	
Palmer	Schooner	..	—— Osborn	
Boston, Mass.				
Hope	Ship	309	Jethro Coffin	
John	Ship	172	Charles Coleman	
Palladium	do	..	—— Macy	Israel Thorndike

sailing from American ports—Continued.

Whaling-ground.	Date— Of sailing.	Date— Of arrival.	Result of voyage. Sperm-oil.	Result of voyage. Whale-oil.	Result of voyage. Whalebone.	Remarks.
			Bbls.	*Bbls.*	*Lbs.*	
	June 1					
Pacific Ocean	July —	Sept. 6, 1823	Full			
Japan	Apr. 14	Apr. 14, 1824	1,600			
Pacific Ocean						Balœna last reported with 1,500 sperm.
Brazil		June —, 1822		1,200		
Pacific Ocean	Oct. —	Apr. 25, 1824	1,600			
Cape de Verdes	June —	— —, 1821				
Pacific Ocean	Dec. —					
South Seas	May —	May 4, 1823		2,000		
Pacific Ocean	Sept. 23	Apr. 23, 1824	1,900			
South Seas	Apr. 12	Mar. 24, 1822	100	2,200		
Cape de Verdes	Apr. —	Mar. 13, 1822		550		
Pacific Ocean	May —					
....do		Feb. 2, 1824	2,000			
Brazil	May —	Apr. 23, 1822		800		
West Indies	Apr. —					
Pacific Ocean						Lost on Peru.
South Seas	June 3					Reported November 8, 1821, with 1,100 whale.
Pacific Ocean	Sept. 8	Aug. 20, 1823	1,100			
South Seas	July —	Mar. 30, 1822		1,750		
....do		June 5, 1823		2,000		
....do	Dec. 31					
Brazil	May —	Apr. 26, 1822		1,700		
Pacific Ocean		Nov. 11, 1824	2,300			Belonged to Havre, probably.
Brazil	May —					Last reported with 1,400 whale.
....do	May —	May 5, 1822	220	120		
Cape de Verdes		Aug. —, 1822	150			
Brazil	May —	Apr. 29, 1822		500		
Pacific Ocean	Dec. —					
....do	June 3	Mar. 3, 1823	140	1,811		
....do	Oct. —	June 28, 1824	1,400			
....do	Oct. —	May 26, 1824				
Brazil	May —	Apr. 13, 1822	85	2,485	3,231	
Pacific Ocean	Aug. 5	May 3, 1824	1,000			Captain Wood died at sea.
Brazil	June —	Apr. 26, 1822		1,300		
South Atlantic		Sept. —, 1822		1,000		Second mate, Prince Look, killed by a whale.
Pacific Ocean	Apr. 12	Dec. 27, 1823	2,600			
New Zealand						Arab last reported with 350 barrels.
Brazil		May 20, 1822		1,100		
Pacific Ocean	June —	June 5, 1823	1,800			
Brazil	May —	May 17, 1822		1,500		
....do	Aug. —	May 23, 1820		600		Reported Feb., 1822, with 600 whale.
West Indies	Apr. —	May 20, 1821				Last reported with 80 sperm.
Mexico		July 26, 1822				
C. de Verdes		Mar. 24, 1822				
		Apr. —, 1822				Last reported with 70 sperm.
C. de Verdes	June 3	Dec. 24, 1821	70			
Pacific Ocean		Aug. 7, 1823	1,700			
	July 1					
Atlantic	July 1					Last reported with 38 barrels.
Pacific Ocean	Jan. 6	Nov. 4, 1823	1,100	300		The Hope was condemned at Fayal in 18—; sailed whaling from there several years under the name of Perseverance; finally lost at sea.
Brazil	May 19	Sept. 6, 1822	30	220		
Pacific Ocean		Oct. 18, 1824	2,000			

Table showing returns of whaling-vessels

Name of vessel.	Class.	Tonnage.	Captain.	Managing owner or agent.
1821.				
Provincetown, Mass.*				
Cora	Brig			
Charles	Schooner		—— Grozier	
Laurel	Ship		—— Cook	
Minerva	Schooner		—— Soper	
Margaret	Ship		—— Atwood	
Neptune	Schooner		—— Cook	
Nero	do		—— Smalley	
President	do		—— Soper	
Sophronia	do		—— Smith	
Unitaro	do			
Vesta	do		—— Holmes	
New York, N. Y.				
Charity	Brig		—— Barnard	
Dawn	Ship		—— Gardner	
Diana	do		Aaron Paddock	
Hesper	do			
Neptune	do		—— Brown	
Newport, R. I.				
Frederick Augustus	Ship		Joseph Earl	Whitton & Ruggles
George and Mary	do		James Townsend	Bowen & Ennis
James Munroe	Sloop		—— Palmer	
Stonington, Conn.				
Essex	Sloop		—— Chester	
New Haven, Conn.				
Huron	Ship		—— Davis	
Dartmouth, Mass.				
William Thacher	Brig		—— Chase	
——, R. I.				
Emily	Brig		—— Mayhew	
New London, Conn.				
Carrier	Ship		—— Swain	
Com. Perry	do		—— Davis	
Gen. Scott	Brig			
Mary Ann	do		—— Coffin	
Mary	do		—— Smith	
Pizarro	do		—— Coit	
Stonington	Ship		—— Ray	
Thames	do		—— Coffin	
Sag Harbor, N. Y.				
Andes	Ship			
Abigail	do		—— Green	
Fair Helen	do			
Hannibal	do			
Julius Cæsar	do			
Octavia	do		—— Green	
Thorn	do		—— Gardner	
Warren, R. I.				
Rosalie	Ship			
Plymouth, Mass.				
Mayflower	Ship	?50	—— Harris	
Falmouth, Mass.				
Pocahontas	Ship	350	Frederick Chase	Elijah Swift

* Some of these vessels

sailing from American ports—Continued.

Whaling-ground.	Date—		Result of voyage.			Remarks.
	Of sailing.	Of arrival.	Sperm-oil.	Whale-oil.	Whalebone.	
			Bbls.	*Bbls.*	*Lbs.*	
....	....	....	......	......	......	
Atlantic				.. ..	......	
....do	Apr. 10	Nov. 16, 1821	220	......	......	
....do	Apr. 23	Nov. 16, 1821	220	......	......	
....do	....	....	......	......	......	Last reported, Aug. 12, with 1[illegible]0 sperm.
....do	....	....	......	......	......	Neptune last reported with 70 sperm.
....do	....	....	......	......	......	Nero last reported with 60 sperm.
....do	....	....	......	......	......	President last reported with 120 sperm.
....do	....	....	......	......	......	Sophronia last reported with 35 sperm.
....do	May —	Sept. —, 1821	260	......	......	
....do	May 1	Oct. 18, 1821	90	......	......	
N. S. Shetland .	....	May —, 1822	......	......	......	Brought 8,000 seal-skins and some oil.
Pacific Ocean ..	....	Apr. 13, 1824	2, 200	......	......	
....do	....	June 8, 1823	1, 250	......	......	
....do	....	....	......	......	......	
Brazil..........	....	—— —, 1822	......	......	......	Last reported 1,300 whale.
Pacific Ocean ..	....	Feb. 28, 1824	2, 000	......	......	
Brazil	....	May 24, 1822	......	1, 000	......	
N. S. Shetland .	....	Apr. 20, 1822	......	......	......	Full of oil and furs.
N. S. Shetland .	....	Apr. —, 1822	......	200	......	Brought also furs.
....	....	....	......	......	......	Last reported at "Yankee Harbor" with 12,000 skins and 700 barrels oil.
Brazil	....	....	......	......	......	
....	....	....	......	......	......	
Pacific Ocean ..	Feb. 28	July 12, 1823	2, 074	......	......	
Brazil	July 22	Mar. 26, 1822	81	1, 544	2, 260	
N. S. Shetland .	....	May —, 1822	......	300	......	Also 1,200 fur-skins.
Brazil	July —	Mar. —, 1822	50	381	......	
....do	June 6	Apr. 7, 1822	......	777	......	
....do	July 15	Mar. 24, 1822	63	1, 288	......	
Pacific Ocean ..	Nov. 18	May 8, 1823	1, 880	......	......	Built 1821.
Brazil	....	Apr. —, 1822	......	538	......	
Brazil	Oct. 29	—— —, 1822	......	......	......	Reported Feb., 1822, with 1,700 whale.
....do	....	—— —, 1822	......	......	......	
....do	....	Mar. —, 1822	......	1, 700	......	
....do	....	....	......	......	......	
Pacific Ocean ..	....	....	......	......	......	Last reported with 1,350 sperm.
Brazil	July —	....	......	......	......	Last reported with 1,400 whale.
Patagonia	....	Apr. —, 1822	......	1, 850	......	
Pacific Ocean ..	July —	Dec. 7, 1824	......	......	......	
Pacific Ocean ..	Sept. —	June 3, 1824	2, 000	......	......	Built 1821.
Pacific Ocean ..	Dec. —	Oct. —, 1824	2, 000	......	......	Built at Wareham, 1821.

also hail from Boston.

Table showing returns of whaling-vessels

Name of vessel.	Class.	Tonnage.	Captain.	Managing owner or agent.
1822.				
Nantucket, Mass.				
Atlantic	Ship	321	Sylvanus Russell	John B. Macy
Alert	Brig		Charles Ray	
Barclay	Ship	301	Peter Coffin	Griffin Barney
Belvidere	Schooner		—— Cobb	
Boston	Ship	187	George Joy	
Dove	Brig		William Collins	Joseph Winslow
Diana	do		—— Bunker	
Dolphin	do		Charles Macy	
Dispatch	Sloop		—— Bunker	
Enterprise	Ship	413	Reuben Weeks	
Franklin	do	309	Elihu Coffin	John Cartwright
Foster	do	317	Shubael Chase	Paul Mitchell & Sons
Francis	do	291	Josiah B. Whippey	Daniel Jones
Franklin	Schooner		—— Coffin	
Friendship	do			
Golden Farmer	Ship	294	Alfred Alley	
Globe	do	293	Thomas Worth	
Hero	Ship	313	Obed Starbuck	S. L. and J. Starbuck
Indus	do	262	Obed. Fitch	Val. Hussey & Bros
Industry	do		—— Boston	
Independence	do	352	William Plaskett	Aaron Mitchell
John Jay	do	217	Alexander Drew	Z. and G. Coffin
Japan	do	332	Shubael Hussey	
Kingston	do	312	Alexander Perry	
Lady Adams	do	230	Charles Tobey	
Lydia	do	325	Joseph Allen	Zenas Coffin
Maro	do	315	Richard Macy	
Maria	do	365	George W. Gardner	
Nancy	Sloop		—— Luce	
Ocean	Ship	349	Tim. Fitzgerald	
O. H. Perry	Schooner			
Peruvian	Ship	334	Edward Clark	C. Mitchell & Co.
Paragon	do	309	Henry Bunker	
Rambler	do	318	William Worth, 2d	Aaron Mitchell
South America	do	397	Stephen West	
Syren	Sloop		—— Gardner	
Thetis	Schooner		—— Brown	
Tarquin	Ship	301	Daniel Bunker	
Thomas	do	270	Benjamin F. Coffin	K. Starbuck
Washington	do	308	Reuben Swain, 2d	Zenas Coffin
New Bedford, Mass.				
Ann Alexander	Ship		—— Bates	
Alliance	do		—— Coffin	
Bourbon	Ship		—— Paddock	
Commodore Rodgers	do		—— Smith	William C. Nye
Dragon	Brig		—— Aikin	
Elizabeth	do		—— Blackmer	
Eliza Barker	Schooner		—— Howland	
Elizabeth	Ship		Eber Clark	
Florida	Ship		—— Price	
Golconda	do		—— Brock	George Howland
George and Martha	do		—— Randall	
Indian Chief	Brig			
Juno	do		—— Lawrence	
Martha	Ship		—— Reed	
Maria	do		—— Sprague	

sailing from American ports—Continued.

Whaling-ground.	Date—		Result of voyage.			Remarks.
	Of sailing.	Of arrival.	Sperm-oil.	Whale-oil.	Whalebone.	
			Bbls.	*Bbls.*	*Lbs.*	
Pacific Ocean	June 23	Mar. 19, 1825	1,990			
....do	June 23	Dec. 23, 1824	444	214		
....do	Jan. 16	Dec. —, 1823	1,810			
Mexico		Aug. 2, 1822	150			
Pacific Ocean	Dec. 18		1,144			The Boston was probably transferred to New York and arrived there May 9, 1825.
Bay of Mexico	Jan. 24	—— —, 1823	190			Returned September 15, 1822, with 290 sperm, and sailed again November 12.
C. de Verdes	Oct. 31					No report.
Brazil	June 3	Dec. 23, 1824	444	214		Sold 650 barrels at River Francisco, at 75c. per gallon, and refitted. Samuel Merry, second mate, lost overboard, 1824.
C. de Verdes	May 28	July 1, 1823				
Pacific Ocean	Sept. 3	Jan. 27, 1826	2,425	95		Built 1822 at Haddam, Conn.
....do	June 11	—— —, 1824	1,969			
....do	June 24	Dec. 27, 1824	2,167			
....do	Aug. 17	Aug. 9, 1825	1,134			Sold out 1825.
Bay of Mexico		Nov. 15, 1822		Clean		
	May 7					
Pacific Ocean	June 3	—— —, 1824	1,563			
....do	Dec. 20	Nov. 14, 1824	372			On this voyage and on this ship occurred the most horrible mutiny that is recounted in the annals of the whale-fishery from any port or nation. (See History.)
....do	Jan. 4	Feb. 9, 1824	2,173			
Brazil	June 23	May 4, 1823		1,050		Barzillai Luce, first mate, drowned 1822.
C. de Verdes		Nov. —, 1822	70			Manned wholly by blacks.
Pacific Ocean	Sept. 3	July 24, 1825	1,954			
....do	Jan. 4	—— —, 1824	1,250			
....do	July 18	Oct. 20, 1825	1,915	127		Built 1822 at Scituate.
....do	July 14	Dec. 8, 1824	1,807			Built 1822.
....do	Mar. 11					A missing ship, supposed to have been burned at sea off Japan; all on board lost.
....do	Aug. 22	July 3, 1825	2,318			Built 1822. Sent home 70 sperm.
....do	Aug. 2	Apr. 17, 1825	2,350			
....do	Nov. 17	Apr. 27, 1825	2,343			Built 1822 at Haddam, Conn.
Atlantic	Aug. 9	Oct. 16, 1822		8		
Pacific Ocean	Aug. 17	Apr. 16, 1825	1,99			
Pacific Ocean	Jan. 9	Apr. 2, 1824	2,161			
....do	June 11	Jan. 18, 1825	1,85			
....do	Jan. 9	Mar. 22, 1824	1,880			
Brazil	May 13	July 5, 1823	120	1,734		
Atlantic						
....do		Sept. 13, 1822	16			Returned leaking 300 strokes an hour.
Pacific Ocean	Jan. 9					Abandoned at sea off Barbadoes.
....do	Dec. 18					Condemned at Oahu 1825.
....do	June 23	Feb. 26, 1825	2,054			
South Seas	May —	Apr. —, 1823		1,540		
Pacific Ocean	May —					Condemned at Buenos Ayres December 15, 1825.
Brazil	Dec. —					Belonged to Havre, France.
South Seas	May —	Feb. 22, 1823		1,800		
Patagonia	May —	May 30, 1823				Brought a cargo of elephant-oil.
Cape de Verde	Jan. 16					
Mexico	Jan. 16	June 14, 1823	125			
Pacific Ocean	Apr. 30	Apr. —, 1824				Captain Clark died on the voyage. Returned full. Probably owned in Westport.
South Seas		Nov. 26, 1823		2,000		
Pacific Ocean	Sept. 3	Dec. 8, 1824	2,000			
South Seas	June —	Apr. 27, 1823		2,050	9,000	First mate killed by a whale.
Pacific Ocean		Dec. —, 1825	1,900			At Newport December 19.
Brazil		June 23, 1823	550	150		
....do	May —					Probably belonged in Fairhaven.
Pacific Ocean	May 9	Apr. 21, 1825	Full			

Table showing returns of whaling-vessels

Name of vessel.	Class.	Tonnage.	Captain.	Managing owner or agent.
1822.				
New Bedford, Mass.—Continued.				
Mercury	Ship		William Austin	I. Howland, jr., & Co
Midas	do		—— Spooner	
Minerva	Brig		Daniel Wood	
Mercator	Ship		—— Wood	
Massachusetts	do		—— Cathcart	
Milwood	do		—— Burgess	
Nautilus	Brig		—— Covill	
Planter	do		—— Hussey	
Phœnix	Ship		—— Worth	
Packet	do		—— Delano	
Pacific	do		—— Whitfield	
Portia	do		—— Ray	
Roscoe	do		—— Swain	Andrew Robeson
Russell	do		—— Coleman	
Telemachus	Schooner		—— Long	
Timoleon	Ship		Charles Starbuck	
Victory	do		—— Adams	
William Rotch	do		—— Tobey	
Fairhaven, Mass.				
Amazon	Ship		—— Eldredge	
Herald	do		—— Neil	
Pindus	do		—— Townsend	
Stanton	do		—— Burtch	
Westport, Mass.				
Almy	Brig		—— Mayhew	
Columbus	do		—— Seabury	
Industry	do		—— Parker	
Polly and Eliza	do		—— Wilbur	
Traveller	do		—— Phelps	
Boston, Mass.				
Ardent*	Brig		Samuel Soper	
Cadmus	Ship		—— Cary	
Charles	do		B. Coffin	Bridge & Brown
Fair Lady*	Schooner			
Hannah and Eliza	Ship		—— Grozier	
Laurel*	Brig		—— Cook	
President*	Schooner		—— Paine	J. Russell
Edgartown, Mass.				
Almira	Ship		—— Daggett	
Plymouth, Mass.				
Fortune	Ship	280	Peter C. Myrick	
Marblehead, Mass.				
Lavalette	Schooner		—— Colby	Benjamin Knight
New Haven, Conn.				
Thames	Brig		Reuben Clasby	N. H. Whaling Co
New London, Conn.				
Ann Maria	Ship		—— Smith	
Commodore Perry	do		—— Davis	
Connecticut	do		—— Bunker	
Jones	do		—— Coit	
Pizarro	Brig		—— Rice	
Thames	do		—— Miller	

* Many small vessels clearing from Boston

sailing from American ports—Continued.

Whaling-ground.	Date— Of sailing.	Date— Of arrival.	Result of voyage. Sperm-oil.	Result of voyage. Whale-oil.	Result of voyage. Whalebone.	Remarks.
			Bbls.	*Bbls.*	*Lbs.*	
Pacific Ocean		Mar. 11, 1825	2,205	71	572	
Brazil		May 4, 1823		2,100		
Africa		Mar. 3, 1823	837	31		
Pacific Ocean	Jan. —	Aug. 7, 1824	1,500			
do	Jan. 25					Belonged to Havre.
South Seas	June —	May 5, 1823		1,800		
do	May 16	June 14, 1823	380			
Africa		Nov. 4, 1823	500			
Pacific Ocean	May —	Sept. 13, 1824	2,900			
Atlantic	June —	June 17, 1823	160			
South Seas	May —	Apr. —, 1823		2,000		
Pacific Ocean		June 7, 1824	1,400			
do						
do	Dec. 5	Mar. 19, 1825	Full			
Africa		June 15, 1823	280			
South Seas	June —	Apr. 9, 1823	245	2,265	5,068	Bought for New Bedford 1810.
Brazil	June —	June 8, 1823		1,700		
Pacific Ocean	May —	June 2, 1824	1,700			
Brazil		June 16, 1823		1,650		
do		May 21, 1823		1,300		Crew badly troubled with scurvy.
Pacific Ocean		Mar. 19, 1825	1,200			
do	Jan. 31	Apr. 25, 1824	1,850			
West Indies		July 13, 1823	280			
Mexico		Aug. 21, 1823	320			
W. Islands	May —	July 9, 1823	400			
						Lost; her crew were taken off by an English brig.
W. Islands	Aug. 5	———, 1822	70			Manned by blacks.
Atlantic	Mar. 4	Oct. —, 1822	200			On the next voyage of the Ardent she was wrecked at sea, and nine of the crew lost. The captain and four men were rescued by a New York packet.
Pacific Ocean		Dec. 7, 1825	Full			
Brazil	July 6	Dec. 27, 1823		1,600		
Atlantic		Mar. —, 1823				Last reported with 170 sperm.
do		Oct. 9, 4822	150			
West Indies		Mar. —, 1823	50			
do	Mar. 6	Oct. —, 1822	100			
Pacific Ocean	Feb. 6	May 8, 1824	2,300			
Pacific Ocean	Sept. 10	Sept. 20, 1825	2,000			Built 1822.
Atlantic	Apr. 8					
Pacific Ocean	Oct. 10	Oct. 29, 1825				
Brazil	July 1	Mar. 23, 1823	145	1,919	7,000	
do	June 16	May 19, 1823		1,445	6,900	
Pacific Ocean	Oct. 17	Apr. 30, 1825	2,154			Built 1822.
Brazil	June 16	Mar. 23, 1823		1,761	6,000	
do	June 9	May 20, 1823	99	779		
do		June 16, 1823		808	3,393	

belonging, undoubtedly, to Provincetown.

Table showing returns of whaling-vessels

Name of vessel.	Class.	Tonnage.	Captain.	Managing owner or agent.
1822.				
Sag Harbor, N. Y.				
Andes	Ship		—— Griffing	
Argonaut	do		Isaac Sayre	
Fair Helen	do		—— Sayre	
Gen. Scott	Brig			
Hannibal	Ship		G. Post	
Ocean	Sloop			
Octavia	Ship		H. Green	
Thorn	do		—— Gardner	
Eight ships sailed from Sag Harbor in 1822, returning in 1823 with 1,842 sperm, 9,731 whale, 45,800 pounds bone.				
Stonington, Conn.				
Hydaspe	Ship	318	Peter Paddack	B. Pendleton
Hersilia	do			
Falmouth, Mass.				
Salome	Schooner			
New York, N. Y.				
Dawn	Ship		—— Gardner	
Neptune	do		—— Brown	
Provincetown, Mass.				
Several Provincetown vessels are placed under the head of Boston.				
Four Brothers	Schooner			
Gen. Jackson	do		—— Atkins	
Hannah & Eliza	do			
Mary	do		—— Cook	
Neptune	do		do	
Olive Branch	do			
Seventh Son	do		—— Cook	
Sophronia	do		—— Rider	
Vesta	do		—— Holmes	
Tiverton, R. I.				
Amstel	Brig	116	—— Almy	
Rochester, Mass.				
Pocahontas	Brig		—— Johnson	
Newport, R. I.				
Alliance	Ship		James C. Swain	Clark & Fowler
George and Mary	do		Frederick Winslow	Bowen & Ennis
Boston, Mass.				
Charles	Ship	216	Barna Coffin	
1823.				
Nantucket, Mass.				
Aurora	Ship	346	Seth Coffin, jr	Paul Macy
Brothers	do	256	James Britton	Samuel Mitchell & Bros
Chili	do	291	Frederick Barnard	
Dove	Sloop		—— Collins	J. Winslow
Dauphin	Ship	273	Obed Swain	Gilbert Coffin & Sons
Diana	Brig		—— Bunker	
Equator	Ship	262	Joseph Barney	
Falcon	do	297	Benjamin C. Chase	

sailing from American ports—Continued.

Whaling-ground.	Date—		Result of voyage.			Remarks.
	Of sailing.	Of arrivals.	Sperm-oil.	Whale-oil.	Whalebone.	
			Bbls.	*Bbls.*	*Lbs.*	
Brazil		Mar. 5, 1823		1,400		
....do		Jan. 29, 1823	100	1,500	11,000	
....do		June —, 1823		1,450		
Brazil						
Brazil						
....do		May 31, 1823		1,600		
Pacific Ocean		Sept. —, ——	1,600	200	1,400	Built 1822.
....do						
Pacific Ocean		Apr. 13, 1824	2,200			
Patagonia		Aug. 21, 1823	70	750		
Atlantic	Jan. —	Oct. —, 1822	50			
....do	May —	Oct. —, 1822	200			
....do	Jan. —	Oct. —, 1822	180			
....do		Oct. —, 1822	100			
....do		Oct. —, 1822	100			
Atlantic		Oct. —, 1822	90			
....do		Oct. —, 1822	60			
....do		Oct. —, 1822	90			
West Indies		June 19, 1823	75			
Atlantic	Oct. —					Last reported with 35 sperm.
Pacific Ocean		May 21, 1824	2,200			
Brazil		Mar. 13, 1823		1,000		
....do	July 6					
Pacific Ocean	Oct. 2	Dec. 22, 1826	1,556			
Brazil	Aug. 24					Condemned at Rio Janeiro 1823 or 1824.
Pacific Ocean	Apr. 15	May 17, 1826	1,72			Sold to New Bedford 1826.
Mexico		Sept. 9, 1823	200			The Dove sailed again in 1823; arrived at Philadelphia August 27, 1824, with 130 sperm and 2 live sea-elephants.
Pacific Ocean	Dec. 6	Jan. 28, 1826	1,560			Thomas Clark, 2d mate, killed by a whale, May, 1824.
Atlantic		Oct. 7, 1824		Clean		
Pacific Ocean	Oct. 2	Feb. 5, 1826	1,424			Sold to New Bedford 1826.
....do	Feb. 21					Lost on the island of Ohiteroa.

Table showing returns of whaling-vessels

Name of vessel.	Class.	Tonnage.	Captain.	Managing owner or agent.
1823.				
Nantucket, Mass.—Continued.				
Factor	Ship	299	John Maxcy	
Hesper	do	247	William Chase	J. J. Barney
Indus	do	26[illegible]	Samuel Joy	V. Hussey & Bros.
Independence	do	311	William Whippey	Aaron Mitchell
Improvement	do	256	Reuben Kelley	
Pacific	do	314	Albert Clark	Paul Mitchell & Sons
Rose	do	350	Shubael Cottle	L. & J. Starbuck
Reaper	do	338	Alexander Ramsdell	
Swift	do	456	Frederick Arthur	Gardner & Swift
South America	do	397	Edmund Gardner	
Urchin	Brig		—— Chadwick	
New Bedford, Mass.				
Ann Alexander	Ship		—— Bowen	
Bourbon	do			
Benezet	Brig		—— Covell	
Charles	Ship		—— Joy	
Com. Rodgers	do		—— Smith	
Dragon	Brig		—— Bates	
Elizabeth	do		—— Blackmer	
Enterprise	Ship		—— Gardner	
George and Martha	do		—— Chase	
Good Return	do		—— Terry	
Lyra	do		—— Joy	J. & J. Howland
Mary	Brig		—— Mayhew	
Martha	Ship		—— Reed	
Milwood	do		—— Burgess	
Maria Thersea	do		—— Hillman	
Midas	do		—— Spooner	
Pacific	do		—— Whitfield	
Parnasso	do		—— Covell	
Phebe Ann	do		—— Rawson	
President	Brig		—— Tilton	
Packet	Schooner		—— Delano	
Richmond	Ship		—— Covell	I. Howland, jr., & Co
Sophia	do		—— Cathcart	Joseph Rotch
Timoleon	do		Charles Starbuck	
Victory	do		—— Adams	
William and Eliza	do		—— Sprague	
Westport, Mass.				
Columbus	Brig		—— Seabury	
Industry	do		—— Bennett	
Fairhaven, Mass.				
Amazon	Ship		—— Adams	
Columbus	do		—— Brock	
Herald	do		—— Neil	
Sag Harbor, N. Y.				
Andes	Ship			
Argonaut	do		—— Sayre	
Fair Helen	do		do	
Gen. Scott	Brig		do	
Hannibal	Ship		—— Green	
Marcus	do		—— Sayre	
Octavia	do		—— Griffin	
Ocean	Sloop		—— Smith	
Thorn	Ship		—— Gardner	
Union	do		—— Griffin	
New London, Conn.				
Com. Perry	Ship		—— Davis	

sailing from American ports—Continued.

Whaling-ground.	Date— Of sailing.	Date— Of arrivals.	Result of voyage. Sperm-oil.	Result of voyage. Whale-oil.	Result of voyage. Whalebone.	Remarks.
			Bbls.	*Bbls.*	*Lbs.*	
Pacific Ocean	Dec. 20					Took a full cargo (1,816 sperm); sprung a leak off Cape Horn and threw overboard 800 barrels. Put into Rio Janeiro and was condemned; balance of oil shipped home.
....do	Feb. 21	Apr. 11, 1825	1,087			Sold to New Bedford 1825.
Brazil	June 23	May 21, 1824		1,500		Broken up 1824.
Pacific Ocean	Aug. 5	Aug. 7, 1826	1,875			
Brazil	Aug. 8	Mar. 17, 1825		1,100		Lost on Eel Point, Nantucket, 1825.
Pacific Ocean	Nov. 25	July 23, 1826	1,766	456		
....do	Aug. 12	Nov. 9, 1825	2,160	116		Built 1823, at Rochester.
....do	Oct. 2	Mar. 10, 1826	1,854			
....do	June 5	Oct. 28, 1825	3,120			Built 1823.
Brazil	Aug. 21	May 14, 1824	54	1,427		
....do	June 2					
....do	June 10	Apr. 10, 1824		1,600		
		July 28, 1824		1,600		Of Havre.
Pacific Ocean	Dec. 30					
Brazil	Aug. 27	Apr. 11, 1824		1,900		
....do	July —	May 29, 1824		Full.		
....do	July —					
Cape de Verdes	Aug. 27					
Brazil	Dec. 14					
....do	June —	June 6, 1824		1,000		
....do		Apr. 25, 1824		2,500		
South Seas		Apr. —, ——				Last reported with 2,000 whale.
Brazil	May 29	Apr. 23, 1824		1,900		
....do		Apr. 25, 1824		1,700		
....do	July 26	July 25, 1824		2,200		
....do	Aug. 1	June 4, 1824		2,000		
....do	May —	May 21, 1824		2,000		
....do		May 18, 1824		1,500		
....do	June 23	Aug. 27, 1824				
Cape de Verdes		Dec. 14, 1823	280			
Africa	Sept. 3					
South Seas	June —	Mar. 22, 1824		2,200		
Brazil	Dec. 14	Apr. 10, 1825	120	1,380		
....do	June —	May 10, 1824		2,519	9,314	
....do	July —	June 6, 1824		1,150		
Pacific Ocean	Jan. 8	Aug. 6, 1825	2,200			
Mexico	Oct. 20					
Africa		Nov. 11, 1824	230			
Brazil		May 2, 1824		2,000		
....do	July 20	May 14, 1824		Full.		
Patagonia		May 22, 1824		1,300		
Brazil	June 3	Apr. 30, 1824	150	1,450		
	May 31					
	May 31	May 31, 1824	50	350		Sold a large part of her cargo, and returned with coffee, sugar, and specie.
Pacific Ocean		Jan. 29, 1825	1,800			Brought home some bone.
Patagonia		June 5, 1825		1,700		Lost her mast off Sandy Hook; was towed into New York.
Atlantic						
Brazil		May 31, 1824		1,400		
....do	May 31					
	July 9	Apr. 25, 1824	44	1,504	12,000	

Table showing returns of whaling-vessels

Name of vessel.	Class.	Tonnage.	Captain.	Managing owner or agent.
1823.				
New London, Conn.—Continued.				
Jones	Ship		R. Smith	
Pizarro	Brig		—— Rice	
Thames	do		—— Young	
Provincetown, Mass.				
Ardent	Brig		—— Soper	
Four Brothers	Schooner			
Sophronia	do			
Boston, Mass.				
Onslow	Brig		—— Holmes	
Newport, R. I.				
Atlas	Ship		Abraham Gardner	Caleb Greene
Providence, R. I.				
Hampton	Sloop		—— Smith	
Neptune	Brig			
New York, N. Y.				
Diana	Ship		Aaron Paddack	
Edgartown, Mass.				
Apollo	Ship			
Loan	do		—— Tilton	
1824.				
Nantucket, Mass.				
Alexander	Ship	421	Samuel Bunker	
Barclay	do	301	Peter Coffin	Griffin Barney
Criterion	do	229	Alvan Ewer	
Constitution	do	318	Isaac Chase	
Hycso	do	290	Reuben Coffin	
Hero	do	313	Nathaniel Fitzgerald	
John Adams	do	296	Daniel Folger	
Lima	do	286	Abraham Swain	Chris. Mitchell & Co
Loper	do	316	Obed Starbuck	J. & L. Starbuck
North America	do	351	Franklin Chase	Val. Hussey & Bro
Oeno	do	328	Samuel Riddell	
Ontario	do	354	Alex. D. Bunker	S. Mitchell & Bro
Ploughboy	do	391	William Chadwick	
Peru	do	257	Samuel Joy	
Planter	do	340	Clement Norton	
Sea Lion	do	307	Alexander Russell	John B. Macy
Spartan	do	333	Prince B. Mooers	
South America	do	397	Job Coffin	
Thomas 2d	do	205	Frederick Swain	
New Bedford, Mass.				
Ann Alexander	Ship		—— Brown	
Barclay	do		—— Coffin	Wm. R. Rotch & Co
Balæna	do		—— Russell	J. & J. Howland
Com. Rodgers	do		—— Wilcox	

sailing from American ports—Continued.

Whaling-ground.	Date— Of sailing.	Date— Of arrival.	Result of voyage. Sperm-oil.	Result of voyage. Whale-oil.	Result of voyage. Whalebone.	Remarks.
			Bbls.	*Bbls.*	*Lbs.*	
	June 15	Apr. 11, 1824		1,828		
	July 13	June 25, 1824		1,011	4,656	
		—— —, 1824		653	2,379	
Africa						Wrecked at sea; Captain Soper and four men survived.
Africa	Jan. —	Feb. 8, 1824	160			
Brazil	Jan. 16	May 31, 1824		1,450		
Atlantic						Fell in with sloop Ocean, of Sag Harbor, dismasted, and towed her into New York.
Pacific Ocean		—— —, 1824				Captain Paddack was drowned in March, 1824.
Pacific Ocean						Last reported with 1,250 sperm.
....do		Dec. 26, 1825	Full			Last reported with 1,650 sperm.
Pacific Ocean	July 24	June 17, 1827	2,844			
Brazil	June 14	Apr. 29, 1825	160	1,600		
Pacific Ocean	July 4	Aug. 8, 1826	1,420			Captain Ewer was killed while cutting in the last whale.
....do	July 24	May 15, 1826	2,015			
....do	Nov. 15					Lost on Huakeine Island, 1825 or 1826.
....do	Nov. 22	Apr. 16, 1827	2,222			
....do	June 30	May 25, 1827	1,617			
....do	July 11	Apr. 26, 1827	1,477			
....do	Dec. 7	Oct. 19, 1826	2,006			
....do	Sept. 3	Nov. —, 1827	2,080	230		Captain Chase died, outward bound. Sold 1828.
....do	Nov. 4					Lost on Feejee Islands, 182–; crew all murdered by the natives, except William S. Cary, who escaped after several years' imprisonment among them.
....do	Sept. 1	Mar. 12, 1827	2,250			
....do	Sept. 17	Mar. 3, 1827	2,615			
....do	Sept. 17	Dec. 11, 1827	1,332	84		
Brazil	Nov. 22	—— —, 1825		1,400		
....do	Aug. 8	Aug. 12, 1825		1,084		Ensign Rogers, second mate, taken out of boat by a line. Sold to Buenos Ayres, 1825.
Pacific Ocean	Nov. 22	Jan. 14, 1827	2,116			
Brazil	Nov. 22					Sold her oil at Pernambuco; took freight to New York; was lost on Long Island Sound on her way thence to Nantucket, 1825.
....do	June 25	Aug. 8, 1825		1,000		Sold, 1825.
Brazil	June 6	June 21, 1825	100	1,550		
Pacific Ocean		Apr. 19, 1827	2,000			
....do		Dec. 3, 1827	2,000			
Brazil		July —, 1825		1,700		

Table showing returns of whaling-vessels

Name of vessel.	Class.	Tonnage.	Captain.	Managing owner or agent.
1824.				
New Bedford, Mass.—Continued.				
Charles	Ship		—— Brayton	
Dragon	Brig		—— Shearman	J. A. Parker
Elizabeth	do		—— Blackmer	
Francis	Ship		—— Paddock	
George and Martha	do		—— Randall	
George and Susan	do		—— Upham	G. Howland
Good Return	do		—— Terry	
Independence	do		—— Ray	T. S. & N. Hathaway
Indian Chief	Brig		—— Hathaway	
Martha	do		—— Reed	Seth Russell & Sons
Minerva	Brig		—— Gifford	Cornelius Grinnell
Milwood	Ship		—— Burgess	S. Russell & Sons
Minerva Smyth	do		Daniel McKenzie	I. Howland, jr., & Co
Midas	do		—— Spooner	
Pacific	do		—— Potter	S. Russell & Sons
Phœnix	do		—— Stetson	
Parnasso	do		—— Covell	
President	Brig		—— Tilton	
Roscoe	Ship		—— Worth	Andrew Robeson
Richmond	do		Charles Covell	I. Howland, jr., & Co
Russell	do		—— Coleman	
Swift	do		—— Allen	T. S. & N. Hathaway
Triton	Ship		James Swain	I. Howland, jr., & Co
Timoleon	do		Charles Starbuck	I. Howland, jr., & Co
Victory	do		—— Taber	
William Rotch	do		—— Adams	W. R. Rotch & Co
Winslow	do		—— Clark	Charles W. Morgan
Wilmington and Liverpool Packet	do		—— Briggs	John A. Parker
Edgartown, Mass.				
Apollo	Ship		—— Daggett	
Almira	do		—— Osborne	
Fairhaven, Mass.				
Amazon	Ship		—— Adams	
Columbus	do		—— Brock	
Plymouth, Mass.				
Mayflower	Ship		—— Harris	
New London, Conn.				
Com. Perry	Ship	270	I. Smith	
Jones	do	338	R. Smith	
Neptune	do	285	—— Coit	
Stonington	do	351	—— Gardiner	
Sag Harbor, N. Y.				
Argonaut	Ship			
Fair Helen	do		—— Howland	
Hannibal	do			
Octavia	do			
Thorn	do		—— Sayre	
Union	do			
New York, N. Y.				
Dawn	Ship		—— Gardner	Thomas Hazard
Diana	do		George Drew	
Perth Amboy, N. Y.				
Susquehannah	Ship		—— Joy	Commercial Bank

*It will be observed that it is only occasionally that the "take" of bone is given; generally in these agents. For several years the price of this article was so low that many masters would not encumber

sailing from American ports—Continued.

Whaling-ground.	Date—		Result of voyage.			Remarks.
	Of sailing.	Of arrival.	Sperm-oil.	Whale-oil.	Whalebone.	
			Bbls.	*Bbls.*	*Lbs.*	
Pacific Ocean		July 2, 1827	1, 900			
Brazil		May 19, 1826	350	650		
Cape de Verdes		Apr. 5, 1825				
Pacific Ocean	May 4					Reported June, 1825, with 1,600 sperm.
Brazil		June 2, 1825	150	2, 150	13, 000	
Pacific Ocean		Feb. 8, 1827	2, 200			
Brazil	Oct. —	June 27, 1825		2, 400		
Pacific Ocean		Dec. 2, 1827	2, 200			
Coast of Africa						Last reported 310 sperm.
Brazil		May 27, 1825		1, 900		
Cape de Verdes		Sept. 4, 1825	800			
Brazil	June 26	May 9, 1825		Full		Last reported 1,500 whale.
Pacific Ocean		Apr. 3, 1827	2, 070			
Brazil	July 30	Apr. 25, 1825		2, 300		
	Aug. —	Mar. 9, 1827	2, 400			Returned in October, damaged by a gale.
Pacific Ocean		Aug. 6, 1827	3, 000			
Brazil	June 25	June 9, 1825		1, 650		
Africa	May 7	Apr. 5, 1825	Full.			
Pacific Ocean		Feb. 10, 1827	2, 200			
Brazil	June 6	Apr. 11, 1825	330	1, 750	*10487	
Pacific Ocean		Dec. —, 1827				Last reported with 2,150 sperm.
....do		Feb. 13, 1827	2, 000			The ship sailed under command of Capt. John Pinkham, who, with two of this crew, was killed by a whale in August, 1824. The voyage was continued under Mr. Allen.
Brazil		June 27, 1825	222	1, 465	5, 418	
....do	July —	June 27, 1825	72	1, 862	8, 888	Captain Starbuck died on the voyage.
....do	July 30	—— —, 1825				Last reported May 25, 1824, 1,500 whale.
Pacific Ocean	Dec. 1	Feb. —, 1827	1, 950			
....do		Apr. 12, 1825	1, 350			
....do	Dec. 1	Mar. 8, 1827	2, 700			
Pacific Ocean	Dec. 7	Mar. 31, 1827	Full.			
....do	Sept. 13	Dec. 14, 1826	2, 300			
Brazil	June 27					Last reported 1,600 whale.
....do		May 8, 1825		Full		
Pacific Ocean	Dec. 10	May 27, 1827	2, 300			
South Seas	July 1	May 11, 1825	53	1, 767		
....do	June 27	May 1, 1825	69	2, 141		
....do	June 7	June 29, 1825		1, 575		
Pacific Ocean	Sept. 9	Feb. 15, 1827	2, 093			
						Last reported 1,100 whale.
Brazil		June —, 1825		1, 700		
....do		June 22, 1825		2, 060		
....do						Last reported 1,800 whale.
....do		June 6, 1825		2, 000		
						Last reported 1,400 whale.
Pacific Ocean		Aug. 31, 1827	2, 300			
....do	Nov. —					Lost on Peru, December 1, 1827. Captain Drew died at sea July 2, 1825.
....do	Mar. 13	Sept. —, 1825				

early times no report of bone occurs in the papers, and the record is obtained through the courtesy of their ships with it.

Table showing returns of whaling-vessels

Name of vessel.	Class.	Tonnage.	Captain.	Managing owner or agent.
1824.				
Philadelphia, Pa.				
George and Albert	Ship			
Newport, R. I.				
Atlas	Ship		—— Gardner	Caleb Greene
Frederick Augustus	do		Joseph Earl	Whitton & Ruggles
Westport, Mass.				
Almy	Brig		—— Mahew	
1825.				
Nantucket, Mass.				
Atlantic	Ship	321	John J. Gardner	
Barclay	do	301	Peter Coffin	
Cyrus	do	328	David Harris	
Eagle	do	335	Benj. A. Coleman	Simeon Starbuck
Foster	do	317	Edy Coffin	Paul Mitchell & Sons
Franklin	do	309	Thaddeus Coffin	
George	do	359	Charles Lawrence	
Ganges	do	265	Joshua Coffin	Gideon Gardner
Globe	do	293	Reuben Swain, 2d	
Golden Farmer	do	294	George Joy	
Harvest	do	360	Richard Macy	V. Hussey & P. H. Folger
Independence	do	352	William Plasket	
John Jay	do	217	Alexander Drew	
Japan	do	332	Shubael Chase	Paul Mitchell & Sons
Kingston	do	312	Alexander Perry	
Lydia	do	325	David Swain, 2d	Zenas Coffin
Maria	do	365	George W. Gardner	
Maro	do	315	Barzillai Swain	
Ocean	do	349	Timothy Fitzgerald	
Peruvian	do	334	Alexander Macy	
President	do	293	Henry Winslow	
Planter	do	340	Henry Bunker	
Paragon	do	309	David N. Edwards	
Rambler	do	318	William Worth, 2d	Aaron Mitchell
Sarah Porter	Sloop		{ —— Cathcart { —— McCleave	}
Weymouth	Ship	329	Moses Harris	
Washington	do	308	George Kelley	
Falmouth, Mass.				
Pocahontas	Ship	350	Frederick Chase	Elijah Swift
New Bedford, Mass.				
Ann Alexander	Ship	211	—— Hillman	
Amazon	Brig		—— Tilton	
America	do		do	
Abigail	Ship		—— Potter	Benjamin Rodman
Balæna	do		—— Russell	J. & J. Howland
Com. Decatur	do	247	—— Wood	do
Com. Rodgers	do		—— Nye	William C. Nye
Canton	do	408		
Golconda	do		—— Brock	George Howland
George and Martha	do	275	—— Covell	
Hesper	do	247	—— Smith	Peter Barney
Iris	do		—— Weeks	
Independence	do		—— Perry	T. S. & N. Hathaway
Lyra	do		—— Joy	J. & J. Howland
Maria Theresa	do		—— Tobey	S. & C. Russell
Martha	do	271	Sheffield Reed	S. Russell & Sons
Mercury	do		William Austin	I. Howland, jr., & Co

sailing from American ports—Continued.

Whaling-ground.	Date—		Result of voyage.			Remarks.
	Of sailing.	Of arrival.	Sperm-oil.	Whale-oil.	Whalebone.	
			Bbls.	*Bbls.*	*Lbs.*	
Brazil	July —					Probably a Havre ship. Reported, 1825, as of Philadelphia, with 1,400 barrels whale.
Brazil		May 17, 1825		Full.		Last reported with 1,800 whale.
Pacific Ocean		Dec. 11, 1826	2,000			Second Mate Robert Collins and boat's crew lost while fast to a whale, January 18, 1825.
Mexico		July 17, 1825	200			
Pacific Ocean	June 27	Mar. 21, 1828	2,165			
Brazil	July 2	June 17, 1826		1,946		
Pacific Ocean	July 9	June 2, 1828	2,037			
....do	Dec. 5	May 14, 1828	2,269			
....do	June 7	Oct. 16, 1827	2,291	39		Partly sheathed with leather.
....do	July 17	Nov. 17, 1827	2,037	12		Built at Duxbury, 1825.
....do	June 10	Dec. 13, 1827	1,562	69		
....do	June 16	Nov. 20, 1827	1,665			Partly sheathed with leather.
....do	June 13	May —, 1828	2,105			Sold out and went to Buenos Ayres. 1828; broken up there.
....do	Aug. 14	Apr. 4, 1828	1,685			
....do	Oct. 7	May 8, 1828	2,158			Built, 1825, at Middletown, Conn.
....do	Oct. 30	Aug. 8, 1828	1,850			
....do	Dec. 3	Mar. 21, 1828	910			Lost mate; second mate died of injuries received from the captain.
....do	Dec. 20	Mar. 18, 1829	2,134			
....do	June 7	Mar. 11, 1828	2,117			Partly sheathed with leather.
....do	Sept. 28	Aug. 13, 1828	2,281	88		
....do	July 17	June 2, 1828	2,269			
....do	Aug. 4	Feb. 22, 1828	2,437			John Hackleton, second mate, killed by a whale, 1826.
....do	Aug. 2	May 18, 1828	1,807			
....do	June 8	Dec. 14, 1827	2,285			Lost first mate, Paul Bunker.
....do	June 27	Apr. 22, 1828	1,597			
....do	Sept. 30	Mar. 21, 1828	2,322			
....do	Nov. 16					Sunk at sea a few days after leaving Oahu, 1828; crew taken off by the Rosalie, of Newport; had 2,100 sperm.
....do	July 18	Nov. 20, 1828	1,875			
Shoals {		Aug. 19, 1825		25		
	Sept. 6	Sept. 10, 1825				
Pacific Ocean	July 10	July 6, 1825	2,048			
....do	July 17	Apr. 5, 1825	2,027			Lost first mate, David Starbuck.
....do	May —	— —, 1827	2,100			
Brazil	Aug. —	— —, 1826				
Africa	June 19					
Atlantic	July 27	Sept. —, 1826		700		Dismasted in a gale, Sept. 7, 1826.
Pacific Ocean	Dec. 19	Dec. 13, 1828	Full.			
....do	Oct. 30	Dec. 3, 1827	2,000			
South Seas	June 22	Feb. 12, 1829	1,300			
Pacific Ocean	Sept. —	Mar. 21, 1828	2,000			
....do		— —, 1829				Last reported with 2,100 sperm.
....do	May —	Apr. 26, 1827	2,000			
Brazil	July —	— —, 1826				
Pacific Ocean	Sept. —	July 9, 1826	350	200		
....do	June —	Jan. 17, 1828	2,000			
....do	July —	Nov. 30, 1827	2,200			
....do		Apr. 16, 1828	2,200			
....do	Jan. 3	May 5, 1828	1,700			Captain Taber died April, 1825; Tobey took command.
Brazil		June 2, 1826		1,900		
Pacific Ocean	May —	Dec. 30, 1827	2,485			

Table showing returns of whaling-vessels

Name of vessel.	Class.	Tonnage.	Captain.	Managing owner or agent.
1825.				
New Bedford, Mass.—Continued.				
Milwood	Ship	253	—— Sampson	S. Russell & Sons
Missouri	do		—— Whitfield	
Minerva	Brig		—— Gifford	Cornelius Grinnell
Maria	Ship	202	—— Joy	Samuel Rodman
Midas	Ship	326		
Mercator	do		—— Lawrence	John A. Parker
Parnasso	do	236	—— Covell	
Persia	do		—— Barnard	G. Grinnell, jr.
Phœnix	do		—— Stetson	
Pocahontas	Brig		—— Johnson	J. A. Hawes
Pocahontas	Ship		—— Chase	
Richmond	do		Abraham Gardner	I. Howland, jr., & Co.
Triton	do		Ivory C. Albert	do
Victory	do	268	—— Taber	
Winslow	do		—— Chase	
Wilmington and Liverpool Packet	do			
Fairhaven, Mass.				
Amazon	Ship		—— Whittens	
Charleston Packet	Brig		Jabez Delano	W. Delano
Herald	Ship		—— Burtch	
Pindus	do		—— Neal	
Stanton	do			
Edgartown, Mass.				
John	Ship		—— Daggett	
Loan	do		—— Daggett	
President	Brig		—— Pease	
Warren, R. I.				
Rosalie	Ship		—— Gardner	
Sag Harbor, N. Y.				
Fair Helen	Ship		—— Howell	
Hannibal	do		—— Green	
Marcus	do		—— Sayre	
Octavia	do		—— Griffin	
Union	do		—— Griffin	
New London, Conn.				
Connecticut	Ship		—— Chester	
Com. Perry	do		I. Smith	
Jones	do		R. Smith	
Neptune	do		C. Holmes	
Dartmouth, Mass.				
By Chance	Brig		—— Chase	
Westport, Mass.				
Industry	Brig		—— Parker	B. Rodman
President	Brig		—— Tilton	D. Coffin
Boston, Mass.				
Hope	Ship			
Newport, R. I.				
Alliance	Ship		James C. Swain	Clarke & Bush
Plymouth, Mass.				
Fortune	Ship		—— Swain	

sailing from American ports—Continued.

Whaling-ground.	Date— Of sailing.	Date— Of arrival.	Result of voyage. Sperm-oil.	Result of voyage. Whale-oil.	Result of voyage. Whalebone.	Remarks.
			Bbls.	*Bbls.*	*Lbs.*	
Brazil		June 7, 1826		1,800		
....do	July —					
Africa		Apr. 14, 1827	800			
Pacific Ocean	Sept. —	Mar. 21, 1828	1,300			This is the "old" Maria which has already performed (1828) four voyages to London, three to Brazil Banks, one to Indian Ocean, one to Falkland Islands, and fifteen to the Pacific since 1783.
Pacific Ocean	Nov. 17	Mar. 21, 1828	1,700			
Brazil	Aug. —					
South Seas	Aug. —	Mar. 7, 1828	1,900			Captain Barnard was left at Oahu sick.
Pacific Ocean	Jan. 6					Last reported with 1,200 sperm.
Cape de Verdes		Aug. 21, 1826	670			
Pacific Ocean	Jan. 22					
Brazil	July —	Aug. —, 1826	153	1,870	11,389	
Pacific Ocean	Sept. 1	Aug. 23, 1827	2,062			
South Seas	Aug. —					
....do	Aug. —	July 20, 1827		1,400		
Pacific Ocean						Reported in 1826 with 1,350 sperm.
South Seas	Aug. —					
Guinea	May 19	Aug. 25, 1826	450			
Brazil	June 6					
....do	June —					
Pacific Ocean						Last reported with 1,400 sperm.
....do	Sept. —	Oct. 6, 1828	2,100			
....do						
Guinea	May 26	June 1, 1826	400			
Pacific Ocean		Apr. 22, 1828	2,211			
Brazil	Aug. —	June 25, 1826		1,585	9,000	
....do	Aug. —					
South Seas	Aug. –					
Brazil	Aug. —	May —, 1826		400		
....do		May —, 1826		600		
Pacific Ocean	June 29	May 26, 1827	2,110	54		
....do	July 24	June 30, 1827	1,731			
Brazil	June 29	May 14, 1826	60	2,107		
....do	July 24	May 28, 1826	28	697		
Africa		Sept. 16, 1826	350			
C. de Verdes	Aug. 29	Oct. 19, 1826	340			
Africa		May 1, 1826	590			
Pacific Ocean	Jan. —	June 11, 1828	2,300			Six of the crew died on the voyage.
....do	Dec. 31	Mar. 12, 1829	Full.			

Table showing returns of whaling-vessels

Name of vessel.	Class.	Tonnage.	Captain.	Managing owner or agent.
1826.				
Nantucket, Mass.				
Barclay	Ship	301	Joseph Barney	
Constitution	do	318	Isaac Chase	
Clarkson	do	380	Joseph Allen	
Congress	do	339	Benjamin Worth, 2d	Philip H. Folger
Dauphin	do	273	Benjamin F. Hussey	Gilbert Coffin & Sons
Enterprise	do	413	Obed Swain	do
Independence	do	311	William Whippey	
John Adams	do	268	Seth Cathcart	
Martha	do	273	Benj. Gardner	
Otter	Brig	165	Rob't S. Cathcart	
Orion	do	354	Alfred Alley	T. Hussey & Sons
Omega	do	363	Allen Tilton	
Phebe	do	379	Micajah Swain	Chris. Mitchell & Co
Pacific	do	314	David Baker	Paul Mitchell & Sons
Phenix	do	323	William Fitzgerald	
Rose	do	350	Shubael Cottle	
Reaper	do	338	Benjamin F. Coffin	Paul Gardner & Sons
Swift	do	450	Jona. Swain, 2d	
Susan	do	349	Frederick Swain	Aaron Mitchell
Statira	do	346	Peter Coffin	
New Bedford, Mass.				
Ann Alexander	Ship	211	Walter Hillman	George Howland
America	Brig	149	Ebenezer Hathaway	T. S. & N. Hathaway
Canton	Ship	40[illegible]	Isaiah Burgess	
Columbus	do	....	—— Brock	Samuel Rodman
Equator	do	262	Stephen Howland, jr	I. Howland, jr., & Co
Emily	Brig	87	Leonard West	Coombs & Crocker
Elizabeth	Brig	83	Lloyd Covell	David Coffin
George and Martha	Ship	275	Caleb Kempton	
Hector	do	380	Clement Norton	
Hydaspe	do	312	George Ramsdell	John C. Haskell
Hope	do	316	Ezra Smith, jr	George Howland
Hesper	do	247	Henry Pease	Charles W. Morgan
Juno	Brig	165	William Hussey	J. A. Parker
Logan	Ship	302	Reuben F. Coffin	
Milwood	do	25[illegible]	Ellis C. Eldridge	Seth Russell & Sons
Martha	do	271	Sheffield Read	do
Midas	do	326	Joseph Spooner	J. Coggeshall, jr
Missouri	do	370	Moses Samson	
Parnasso	do	236	Hiram Covell	
Phebe Ann	do	210	Joseph Barnard	
Richmond	do	291	Abraham Gardner	I. Howland, jr., & Co
Sophia	do	295	Reuben Creasy	Joseph Rotch
Sally Anne	do	31[illegible]	Clement P. Covell	D. R. Greene
Timoleon	do	346	Latham Cross	I. Howland, jr., & Co
Victory	do	268	Obed Cathcart	J. A. Parker
William and Eliza	do	321	George Crocker	Joseph Rotch
Young Phœnix	do	376	Simeon Price	John A. Parker
Fairhaven, Mass.				
Amazon	Ship	318	Martin Bowen	
Charleston Packet	Brig	144	Jabez Delano, jr	Warren Delano
Herald	Ship	26[illegible]	James Wood	
Leonidas	do	243	Barzillai S. Adams	
Oregon	do	...	—— Bunker	Asa Swift
Pindus	do	193	Peter M. Coffin	
Quito	Brig	138	—— Burtch	
Dartmouth, Mass.				
By Chance	Brig	107	John E. Coggeshall	P. Gray
William Thacher	do	147	David Collins	William T. Hawes
New London, Conn.				
Ann Maria	Ship	368	R. Smith	
Jones	do	338	—— Davis	
Neptune	do	285	C. Holme	

sailing from American ports—Continued.

Whaling-ground.	Date— Of sailing.	Date— Of arrival.	Result of voyage. Sperm-oil.	Result of voyage. Whale-oil.	Result of voyage. Whalebone.	Remarks.
			Bbls.	*Bbls.*	*Lbs.*	
Pacific Ocean ..	Sept. 29	Nov. 19, 1829	1,6[illegible]0	115	......	
....do	Aug. 1	Apr. 13, 1827	....	601	......	Captain Chase would not go around Cape Horn. Went to the "Banks" and returned, accusing his crew of mutiny.
....do	Sept. 29	June 14, 1830	2,800	....	......	Built 1826.
....do	Sept. 29	May 2, 1829	2,507	......	......	Built at Mattapoisett, 1823.
....do	July 10	Mar. 14, 1829	1,517	......	......	
....do	Aug. 1	Mar. 7, 1829	2,902	......	......	
....do	Nov. 8	May 19, 1829	2,043	......	......	
....do	Sept. 30	Oct. 15, 1828	1,356	......	......	
....do	Jan. 13	Apr. 22, 1828	1,843	......	......	
Africa	June 27	Aug. 20, 1827	400	......	......	
Pacific Ocean ..	Aug. 24	June 15, 1829	2,627	......	......	Built 1826.
....do	Aug. 28	Dec. 26, 1829	2,189	40	......	Built 1826, at Rochester.
....do	Sept. 6	Feb. 4, 1830	2,597	......	......	Built 1826.
....do	Nov. 4	Mar. 8, 1829	2,182	......	......	
....do	Dec. 27	June 22, 1829	2,234	......	......	
....do	June 4	Mar. 30, 1828	2,261	....	......	
....do	Nov. 8	June 23, 1829	1,985	......	......	An excellent voyage.
....do	Jan. 6	Apr. 21, 1828	3,245	...	....	Built 1826 at Rochester.
....do	Aug. 21	Oct. 27, 1829	2,582	121	......	Built 1826. Third mate died 1827.
....do	Sept. 6	June 9, 1829	2,526	....	....	
Brazil	July 25	June 21, 1827	.....	1,650	....	
Atlantic	Nov. 18	May 4, 1828	400	......	......	
Brazil	May 12	June 29, 1827	......	2,500	20,000	
Pacific Ocean ..	....	Jan. 7, 1829	Full	......	...	
Atlantic	June 12	Apr. 22, 1828	333	768	5,142	Bought from Nantucket 1826.
....do	Aug. 9	Dec. 24, 1827	120	....	....	
Africa	Aug. 26	Aug. 4, 1827	250	......	......	
Brazil	July 18	—— —, 1827	.....	.....	......	
Pacific Ocean .	Aug. 18	Apr. 13, 1829	2,512	......	..	
Brazil	June 3	Apr. 25, 1827	120	1,850	13,000	
Pacific Ocean .	June 29	May 11, 1829	Full	.....	.....	
....do	Aug. 19	July 7, 1828	1,100	....	......	Bought from Nantucket 1825.
Atlantic	June 10	Oct. 29, 1827	150	......	......	
....	Dec. 7	....	.....	......	......	Cleared first for Rotterdam, thence for whaling.
Brazil	July 6	May 26, 1827	170	1,630	......	
....do	July 19	May 27, 1827	......	1,900	......	
....do	July 27	June 21, 1827	......	2,100	......	
Pacific Ocean ..	Sept. 16	....	......	......	......	
Brazil.	July 24	June 2, 1828	350	1,200	......	
Pacific Ocean ..	Oct. 9	June 15, 1829	1,400	......	......	
Patagonia	June 22	June 25, 1827	......	1,756	14,785	
Pacific Ocean ..	Feb. 4	Apr. 18, 1829	1,900	......	......	
Brazil	May 6	June 18, 1827	......	1,600	......	
....do	May 20	June 19, 1828	230	......	......	Sold 2,600 whale at Rio Janerio.
Pacific Ocean .	Sept. 22	July 9, 1829	1,950	......	......	
....do	May 12	Nov. 16, 1828	2,400	......	......	
....do	Nov. 14	Dec. 26, 1829	3,000	......	......	
Brazil	July 29	July 1, 1827	......	2,250	....	
Guinea	Dec. 30	June 20, 1828	500	......	......	
Brazil	July 31	....	......	......	......	Had 1,300 whale at last report.
....do	June 24	Aug. 4, 1827	......	1,600	......	
Pacific Ocean ..	....	May 31, 1829	1,900	......	......	
....do	Sept. 15	Nov. 20, 1829	1,150	50	......	Lost third mate.
Atlantic	Sept. —	Sept. 13, 1827	270	......	......	
Africa	Oct. 14	Mar. 30, 1828	160	......	......	
South Seas	July 27	May 22, 1827	450	......	......	
Brazil	Dec. 11	Apr. 22, 1828	63	2,258	......	
South America	June 29	May 27, 1827	140	1,687	......	
....do	July 2	Apr. 28, 1827	82	1,634	......	

Table showing returns of whaling-vessels

Name of vessel.	Class.	Tonnage.	Captain.	Managing owner or agent.
1826.				
Sag Harbor, N. Y.				
Argonaut	Ship		—— Griffin	
Fair Helen	...do			
Hannibal	...do		—— Green	
Marcus	...do		—— Sayre	
Thamas	...do		—— Cooper	
Thorn	...do		—— Howell	
Union	...do		—— Griffin	
New York, N. Y.				
Atlas	Ship	260	—— Townsend	
Diana	...do		—— Russell	
Westport, Mass.				
Almy	Brig	91	Jonathan Mayhew	
President	...do	132	Samuel Tilton, jr	
Polly and Eliza	...do	111	Job Davis	
Rochester, Mass.				
Magnolia	Schooner	9[illegible]	—— Randall	
Boston, Mass.				
Beverly	Ship	498	—— Moore	
Telemachus	..do		—— Atkins	
Edgartown, Mass.				
Resident	Brig			
Rising Sun	Schooner			
1827.				
Nantucket, Mass.				
Alexander	Ship	421	Samuel Bunker	
Aurora	...do	346	Frederick B. Chase	
Ann	...do	361	Prince B. Mooers	
Constitution	..do	318	Alexander Coffin	
Diana	Brig			
Edward	...do		—— Coleman	
Hero	Ship	31[illegible]	George Alley	L. & J. Starbuck
Iris	Sloop		—— Luce	
John Adams	Ship	29[illegible]	George Clark	Silvanus Ewer
Loper	...do	316	Obed Starbuck	L. & J. Starbuck
Lima	...do	286	Charles G. Andrews	
Lydia	...do	325	Peter F. Chase	
Mary Mitchell	...do	354	Timothy Upham	Aaron Mitchell
Otter	Brig	165	Robert S. Cathcart	
Ontario	Ship	354	John G. Coffin	
Ploughboy	...do	391	Nathan Chase	
Rapid	Sloop		—— Myrick	
Sarah	Ship	495	Frederick Arthur	
Spartan	...do	333	William Pitman	P & B. Gardner
William	Schooner		—— Whitteus	
Zone	...do	365	Alex. D. Bunker	S. & J. Mitchell
New Bedford, Mass.				
Ann Alexander	Ship	211	Walter Hillman	George Howland
Ann	...do	361	Prince B. Mooers	
Barclay	...do	241	Samuel Barrett	
Columbus	Brig	152	Nehemiah West	P. Gray
Clitus	Ship	191	George Almy	
Com. Decatur	...do	247	Daniel Wood	J. & J. Howland

sailing from American ports—Continued.

Whaling-ground.	Date— Of sailing.	Date— Of arrival.	Result of voyage. Sperm-oil.	Result of voyage. Whale-oil.	Result of voyage. Whalebone.	Remarks.
			Bbls.	*Bbls.*	*Lbs.*	
Pacific Ocean						
		June 27, 1827		1,2[illegible]0		
Patagonia	July 22	July —, 1827	50[illegible]	1,150		
....do		June 26, 1827		1,660		
Brazil	June 25	June 22, 1827		[illegible],450		
....do	July 22	May —, 1827		1,900		
Patagonia	July 22	July —, 1827		1,250		Reported February 5, 1827, with 1650 whale.
Brazil	Sept. 10					Sheathed with leather.
Pacific Ocean						Reported lost at Tumbez, 1828.
Cape de Verdes	Sept. 22	July 14, 1827	2[illegible]0			
Atlantic	June 8					
Cape de Verdes	Sept. 9					Wrecked and abandoned at sea September 26, 1826. Crew rescued by an English brig.
Atlantic		Aug. 23, 1827	15[illegible]	15		
	Oct. —					Burned on Brazil, 1826.
Atlantic						Lost at sea September 26, 1826. Crew rescued by an English brig.
	Aug. 21					Sold part of her oil and took freight home.
Belleisle	May 21					
Pacific Ocean	Sept. 13	Mar. 12, 1831	2,225			
....do	Dec. 6	Dec. 22, 1829	2,02[illegible]			Built 1827, at Mattapoisett.
....do	Dec. 13	Mar. 28, 1830	2,66[illegible]			
....do	June 19	Oct. 13, 1830	1,91[illegible]			
		May 27, 1828	30[illegible]			
		June 3, 1828		500		
Pacific Ocean	Sept. 18	May 1, 1830	2,35[illegible]			
Atlantic		Sept. 1, 1827	4[illegible]			
Brazil	Sept. 18	Mar. 13, 1829		1,517		
Pacific Ocean	June 22	Jan. 10, 1829	2,131			
....do	Aug. 8	Nov. 3, 1830	1,420			
....do	Oct. 13	Sept. 3, 1830	2,367			
....do	Dec. 13	May 1, 1831	2,43[illegible]			Do.
Africa	Sept. —					Took some oil. Went into St. Catharines and was sold.
Brazil	July 23	June 19, 1828		1,100		
Pacific Ocean	June 23	July 15, 1830	2,52[illegible]			
Atlantic	June 30	Oct. 21, 1827				Between these dates of departure and arrival the Rapid made 7 trips on Nantucket Shoals, taking in all 40 to 50 barrels whale.
Pacific Ocean	May 26	Apr. 19, 1827	3,49[illegible]			Built 1827. An excellent voyage; the largest quantity of sperm oil ever brought into Nantucket on one voyage.
....do	May 30	July 1, 1829	2,32[illegible]			
Atlantic	June 3	Sept. 14, 1827		Clean		Run into by another vessel and lost boats.
Pacific Ocean	Dec. 13	Feb. 12, 1830	2,614			Built at Rochester 1827; lost first mate, Nicholas Easton.
Brazil	July 17	May 4, 1828		1,600		
Pacific Ocean	Dec. 15					
....do	Aug. 18	Oct. 21, 1830	1,858			
Western Isl'ds	Apr. 23	Aug. 24, 1828	250			
	June 13					Cleared for "Bremen and whaling."
Pacific Ocean	June 15	Feb. 12, 1829	Full			

Table showing returns of whaling-vessels

Name of vessel.	Class.	Tonnage.	Captain.	Managing owner or agent.
1827.				
New Bedford, Mass.—Continued.				
Canton	Ship	408	Shubael Hawes	
Charles	do	290	David Brayton	
Dwight	Brig	139	Abner P. Norton	
Empire	do	125	Joseph Bates, jr	
Euphrates	Ship	364	Henry B. Gifford	C. Grinnell, jr
Eagle	do	336	Isaiah Burgess	
Frances	do	347	Obed Alley	William R. Rotch & Co
George and Susan	do	287	Edward Gardner	George Howland
George Porter	do	285	Seth Samson	
Gallatea	do	310	Abraham Russell	S. Russell & Sons
Good Return	do	376	Job Terry, jr	J. Tripp
George and Martha	do	275	Caleb Kempton	John C. Haskell
Golconda	do	330	Gustavus A. Bayliss	George Howland
Grand Turk	do	323	Robert Taber	
Hydaspe	Ship	312	Charles Covell	
Hercules	do	334	Moses Samson	S. Russell & Sons
India	do	366	Isaac S. Maxfield	William T. Russell
Juno	Brig	165	William Hussey	
Martha	Ship	271	Richard Weeden	
Milwood	do	...	Ellis C. Eldridge	
Minerva Smyth	do	335	Daniel McKenzie	I. Howland, jr., & Co
Midas	do	326	Joseph Spooner	John Coggeshall, jr
Minerva	Brig	195	Cornelius Howland, jr.	
Mary Mitchell	Ship	354	Timothy Upham	
Pocahontas	Brig	141	Benjamin Ellis	
Pacific	Ship	384	Stephen N. Potter	S. Russell & Sons
Pocahontas	do	341	Charles D. Swift	
Parthian	Brig	119	John J. Parker	Abraham Barker
Roscoe		362	George B. Worth	
Richmond	Ship	...	Abr. Gardner	I. Howland, jr., & Co
Rodman	do	371	Robert M. Joy	Charles W. Morgan
Swift	do	320	John M. Russell	
Sally Anne	do	312	Clement T. Covell	David R. Greene
Triton	do	300	William Swain	I. Howland, jr., & Co
William Rotch	do	289	Robert Tuckerman	William R. Rotch & Co
Winslow	do	222	Owen Chase	
William Thacher	Brig	147	David Collins	
Wilmington and Liverpool Packet	Ship	384	John Briggs	
Fairhaven, Mass.				
Amazon	Ship	318	Martin Bowen	Nathan Church
Herald	do	262	J. Wood	Samuel Borden & Co
Leonidas	do	243	Barz. S. Adams	
Mentor	Brig	89	Charles Dyer	L. Wilson & Son
Quito	Brig	138	Stanton Burtch	
Westport, Mass.				
Industry	Brig	94	Owen Wilber	
Mexico	do	130	Job Davis	
Regulator	Schooner	...		
Boston, Mass.				
John	Brig	...	—— Alley	
Washington	Schooner	84	John Dickenson	
Rochester, Mass.				
Magnolia	Schooner	...	—— Randall	
Sophronia	do			
Plymouth, Mass.				
Mayflower	Ship	...	—— Harris	

sailing from American ports—Continued.

Whaling-ground.	Date—Of sailing.	Date—Of arrival.	Result of voyage.—Sperm-oil.	Result of voyage.—Whale-oil.	Result of voyage.—Whalebone.	Remarks.
			Bbls.	*Bbls.*	*Lbs.*	
Brazil	July 28	June 19, 1828	.....	1,700	.....	
....do	July 28	June 20, 1828	.....	1,000	.....	
Pacific Ocean	Sept. 29	May 2, 1829	750	.....	.....	
Brazil	Aug. 9	.....	.....	.....	.....	
Pacific Ocean	Dec. 10	June 5, 1830	2,840	.....	.....	
Brazil	Oct. 26	Apr. 22, 1829	.....	1,700	22,000	
Pacific Ocean	Jan. 6	Nov. 4, 1829	2,500	.....	.....	Built at Mattapoisett 1826.
....do	Apr. 16	Sept. 17, 1829	Full	.....	.....	
Brazil	Apr. 21	June 20, 1828	.....	1,600	.....	
... do	June 2	July 6, 1828	260	1,340	.....	
....do	June 29	June 8, 1828	.....	2,400	.....	
....do	July 11	June 6, 1828	100	2,100	.....	
Pacific Ocean	July 17	July 13, 1829	2,300	.....	.....	
Brazil	Aug. 4	June 20, 1828	.....	800	.....	Phillip Russell, first mate, and one man killed by a whale January 9, 1828; bought from Boston, 1827.
....do	June 15	June 16, 1828	.....	1,300	.....	
....do	Aug. 10	July 4, 1828	200	1,300	.....	
Pacific Ocean	Dec. 21	July 17, 1830	2,561	.....	.....	
Africa	Dec. 4	.....	.....	.....	.....	
Brazil	July 20	June 18, 1828	.....	1,500	.....	
....do	June 29	June 30, 1828	120	1,880	.....	
Pacific Ocean	Sept. 25	Mar. 12, 1830	2,153	.....	.....	
Brazil	Oct. 3	Apr. 18, 1829	120	2,580	.....	
Pacific Ocean	Nov. 21	June 9, 1830	1,148	.....	.....	
....do	Dec. 1	.....	.....	.....	.....	
Western Islands.	May 7	— —, 1828	325	.....	.....	
Pacific Ocean	May 25	Aug. 4, 1829	2,800	.....	.....	
....do	Aug. 15	.....	.....	.....	.....	
Western Islands.	Apr. 21	June 8, 1828	460	.....	.....	
Pacific Ocean	June 19	May 5, 1830	2,714	.....	.....	
Brazil	July 21	June 19, 1828	10	1,800	12,295	
Pacific Ocean	Nov. 20	June 8, 1830	2,875	.....	.....	Built at New Bedford 1827.
....do	May 19	Nov. 20, 1829	2,100	.....	.....	
Brazil	July 28	June 7, 1828	30	1,770	.....	
....do	Sept. 5	June 7, 1828	90	1,880	14,754	
Pacific Ocean	May 19	Apr. 23, 1830	1,871	.....	.....	
Brazil	Aug. 15	July 7, 1830	1,906	.....	.....	Returned October 19 damaged by a gale; sailed again 1827.
Africa	June 12	Apr. 22, 1828	250	.....	.....	
Pacific Ocean	Aug. 25	June 24, 1830	2,830	.....	.....	
Brazil	Aug. 21	June 8, 1828	130	1,450	.....	
....do	Aug. 8	June 18, 1828	.....	1,600	.....	
....do	Aug. 20	June 21, 1828	.....	600	.....	
Western Islands.	May 9	Oct. 9, 1828	200	.....	.....	Captain Dyer was taken out of his boat by a foul line August 29, 1828.
South Seas	Oct. 17	Oct. 31, 1828	450	.....	.....	
West Indies	Jan. 16	Sept. 13, 1827	.....	.....	.....	Last reported with 200 sperm.
Guinea	July 21	Aug. —, 1828	320	.....	.....	
.....	.....	.....	.....	.....	.....	Last reported with 155 sperm.
Brazil	.....	.....	.....	.....	.....	Reported early in 1828 with 700 whales.
South Seas	Nov. 10	.....	.....	.....	.....	Went sealing and whaling; no report of arrival.
Atlantic	Oct. —	June 2, 1828	.....	.....	.....	Last reported with 300 sperm.
....do	.....	.....	.....	.....	.....	Last reported with 120 sperm.
Pacific Ocean	Oct. 8	June 5, 1830	2,350	.....	.....	

Table showing returns of whaling-vessels

Name of vessel.	Class.	Tonnage.	Captain.	Managing owner or agent.
1827.				
Edgartown, Mass.				
Almira	Ship		—— Fisher	
Planter	Brig			
New York, N. Y.				
Atlas	Ship		—— Townsend	
Chili	do			
Portsmouth, R. I.				
Sarah Atkins	Ship	44	—— Kenney	
Bristol, Mass.				
Frances	Brig		—— Doty	
Leonidas	Ship		—— Lawton	
Falmouth, Mass.				
Pocahontas	Ship	350	Charles Swift	Elijah Swift
New London, Conn.				
Chelsea	Ship	396	—— Davis	
Caledonia	do	445	—— Young	
Com. Perry	do	270	L. Allyn	
Connecticut	do	390	—— Smith	
Friends	do	403	—— Chester	
Jones	do	338	—— Davis	
Neptune	do	285	C. Holmes	
Phenix	do	404	J. Smith	
Stonington	do	351	—— Gardiner	
Superior	do	405	—— Rice	
Newport, R. I.				
Frederick Augustus	Ship		Joseph Earl	Whitthorn & Ruggles
Francis	Brig			
Sag Harbor, N. Y.				
Andes	Ship		—— Tupper	
Arabella	do	366	Matthew Sayre	S. & L. Howell
American	do	282	—— Post	
Argonaut	do	254	—— Sayre	
Cadmus	do	310		
Fair Helen	do	..	—— Harris	
Hannibal	do	309	—— Green	
Marcus	do	283	—— Halsey	
Neptune	do			
Thorn	do	333	—— Hand	
Thames	do	350		
Union	do		—— Sayre	
1828.				
Nantucket, Mass.				
American	Ship	340	David Paddack	
Atlantic	do	321	John J. Gardner	
Baltic	do	410	William Chadwick	
Criterion	do	229	Ambrose Whiteous	
Cyrus	do	328	Benjamin R. Hussey	
Eagle	do	335	Benjamin A. Coleman	
Foster	do	317	Job C. Clark	Paul Mitchell & Sons
Fame	do	374	John Ramsdell	

sailing from American ports—Continued.

Whaling-ground.	Date—		Result of voyage.			Remarks.
	Of sailing.	Of arrival.	Sperm-oil.	Whale-oil.	Whalebone.	
			Bbls.	*Bbls.*	*Lbs.*	
Pacific Ocean	July 1	Feb. 27, 1830	2,550			
....do	June 28	Mar. 23, 1829	Full.			
Brazil						Last reported at Rio Janeiro March 5, 1828, with 1,100 whale.
....do						Last reported at Pernambuco, March 5, 1828, with 1,200 whale.
Falkland		June —, 1828				Arrived at Stonington, Portsmouth's first sealer; had 4,000 seal and some other skins, and some oil.
						Last reported November 30, 1827, clean.
Pacific Ocean	Dec. 10	July 3, 1830	2,292			
Pacific Ocean		Oct. —, 1830	1,700			
Pacific Ocean	Aug. 23	Apr. 24, 1831	2,471			
....do	Aug. 2	Apr. 27, 1831	1,497	146		Captain Robert Smith who went out in command was killed by a whale February, 1829.
Brazil	Dec. 1	June 10, 1829		1,775		
Pacific Ocean	Sept. 9	Mar. 22, 1830	2,131			
....do	Oct. 31	May 19, 1830	2,388			
South Atlantic	July 21	May 23, 1828	26	1,477		
Brazil	June 15	May 23, 1828	79	1,700		
Pacific Ocean	Oct. 7	May 1, 1830	2,653			
....do	May 2	June 25, 1829	1,753			
....do	June 18	May 1, 1830	2,451			
South Seas	Aug. 3	Aug. 30, 1830	2,800			
Africa	Aug. 3					
Brazil		— —, 1828				Reported with 1,600 whale.
Pacific Ocean	Aug. 24	July 3, 1830	2,853			
Patagonia		June 9, 1828		1,600		
Brazil		May —, 1828		1,400		The Argonaut is reported in another place as having 1,750 whale.
Brazil	July 28					
....do		May —, 1828		Full		
....do		June 12, 1828		1,200	8,000	
....do						
Patagonia		June 7, 1828	170	1,500	1,000	
....do	Sept. --	May 24, 1828		2,000		
....do						Last reported March, 1828, with 1,000 whale.
Pacific Ocean	Apr. 19	July 18, 1830	2,189	88		Formerly a merchantman; added 1828 from New York; built at New York 1822.
Pacific Ocean	Jan. 14	May 12, 1831	3,173			Formerly a merchantman; added 1828.
Brazil	Apr. 19 June 22	Apr. 29, 1828 July 4, 1829		491		Out ten days; returned leaking 1,200 strokes an hour.
Pacific Ocean	Sept. 6	May 12, 1832	2,055			Captain Hussey came home sick, but rejoined the ship again; Mr. Clasby, first mate, drowned.
....do	Oct. 5	May 10, 1831	1,904			
Brazil	Apr. 19	June 30, 1829		935		
Pacific Ocean	June 13	May 9, 1831	1,995			Formerly a merchantman; added 1828.

Table showing returns of whaling-vessels

Name of vessel.	Class.	Tonnage.	Captain.	Managing owner or agent.
1828.				
Nantucket, Mass.—Continued.				
Franklin	Ship	309	Joseph M. Chase	
George	do	359	Edwin Barnard	S. & J. Mitchell
Ganges	do	265	Joshua Coffin	
Howard	do	364	Peleg Brock	
Harvest	do	360	David N. Edwards	
John Jay	do	217	Abraham Swain	
Kingston	do	312	William E. Sherman	
Maro	do	315	Elihu Fisher	
McDonough	Sloop	....	Imbert	
Martha	Ship	273	Sylvanus Swain	
Maria	do	365	Benjamin Ray	
Ontario	do	354	John G. Coffin	
Ocean	do	349	Edwin Coffin	
Peruvian	do	334	Alexander Macy	
Peru	do	257	Joseph Pease	
Planter	do	340	Isaac Brayton	
President	do	293	Charles Robbins	
Rose	do	350	George Russell	
Richard Mitchell	do	380	Edy Coffin	
Swift	do	456	Barzillai Coffin	
Washington	do	308	Barzillai Swain	
Weymouth	do	329	Moses Harris	
Zenas Coffin	do	338	George Joy	
New Bedford, Mass.				
Almy	Brig	91	Benjamin Seabury; Samuel Lake	
America	do	149	Avery F. Parker	
Ann Alexander	Ship	211	Josiah Howland	George Howland
Averick	do	384	George Lawrence	
Balaena	do	300	Thomas Russell	J. & J. Howland
Cortes	do	382	Ebenezer Coleman	George Howland
Com. Rodgers	do	298	Nathaniel H. Nye	
Courier	do	381	Seth Wood	
Canton	do	408	Abram Gardner	William C. Nye
Columbus	Brig	152	Edwin Russell	
Charles	Ship	290	David Brayton	Samuel Rodman, jr
Ceres	do	328	William P. Haskins	Seth Russell
Emily	Brig	87	Leonard West	
Equator	Ship	262	John Smith	I. Howland, jr., & Co
Enterprise	do	291	Samuel Tilton	Alfred Gibbs
Favorite	do	293	Brad. Hathaway	
Fanny	Brig	....	——— West	
George and Martha	Ship	275	Austin Cox	John C. Haskell
Grand Turk	do	323	Robert Taber	Abraham Barker
Good Return	do	376	Job Terry, jr	
George Porter	do	285	Seth Samson	Thomas Riddell
Galatea	do	310	Abr'm Russell 2d	Seth Russell
Hydaspe	do	312	Shubael Hawes	John C. Haskell
Hercules	do	334	Moses Samson	Seth Russell
Hesper	Bark	261	George F. Brown	
Iris	Ship	311	Constant Norton, jr	
Independence	do	318	Reuben Joy, jr	
Isaac Howland	do	399	William Austin	I. Howland, jr., & Co
Lyra	do	304	Edward Howland	J. & J. Howland
Lancaster	do	382	Hiram Weeks	
Mercury	do	339	I. C. Albert	I. Howland, jr., & Co
Mercator	do	246	Richard Holley	
Martha	do	271	Richard Weeden	Charles Russell
Milwood	do	....	Ellis C. Eldredge	Seth Russell & Sons
Maria	do	202	Ammiel H. Joy	
Maria Theresa	do	330	Cranston Wilcox	
Phenix	do	423	Elihu Coffin	
Persia	do	240	Elisha Luce	
Parthian	Brig	119	Daniel Flanders	

sailing from American ports—Continued.

Whaling-ground.	Date— Of sailing.	Date— Of arrival.	Result of voyage. Sperm-oil.	Result of voyage. Whale-oil.	Result of voyage. Whalebone.	Remarks.
			Bbls.	*Bbls.*	*Lbs.*	
Pacific Ocean ..	June 20	June 28, 1830	2, 058	......	......	
Brazil..........	July 10	June 17, 1829	......	1, 337	......	
Pacific Ocean ..	Aug. 8	May 8, 1832	1, 660	......	......	
....do	Oct. 5	May 8, 1832	1, 860	......	......	Built 1828.
....do	Nov. 17	Nov. 13, 1831	2, 685	......	......	
Brazil..........	July 20	July 5, 1829	329	472	......	Broken up at Nantucket 1830.
Pacific Ocean ..	July 31	May 24, 1832	1, 515	......	......	First mate died.
Brazil..........	June 10	....	......	......	......	Run into by French ship Archimedes; put into Rio Janeiro December 20, and was condemned.
....	....	....	......	......	......	Damaged by collision with a Salem brig.
Brazil..........	July 13	Dec. 28, 1830	......	324	......	
Pacific Ocean ..	Sept. 6	June 10, 1832	1, 980	21	......	
....do	Dec. 5	Apr. 24, 1832	2, 106	......	......	Captain Coffin died June 15, 1831.
....do	Dec. 15	Nov. 14, 1831	2, 270	......	......	
....do	June 8	Oct. 21, 1831	1, 960	79	......	
Brazil..........	June 18	June 14, 1829	......	718	......	
....do	June 22	Oct. 21, 1830	99	1, 769	......	
Pacific Ocean ..	Oct. 5	July 16, 1831	1, 766	......	......	
....do	June 22	June 17, 1829	2, 079	......	......	
....do	Aug. 16	....	......	......	......	Built 1828; lost at Fayal September 3, 1828.
....do	July 13	June 17, 1829	2, 828	......	......	
....do	July 24	May 24, 1832	1, 774	......	......	
....do	Dec. 23	June 12, 1831	2, 288	......	......	
....do	Sept. 1	Nov. 15, 1831	2, 732	......	......	Built, 1828, at Hanover.
West Indies .	Mar. 20 Nov. 14	....	....	......	......	
Atlantic	July 21	....	......	......	......	
Pacific Ocean ..	Oct. 16	May 14, 1832	1, 900	......	......	
....do	Nov. 26	Sept. 2, 1831	3, 150	......	......	
....do	Jan. 12	Aug. 16, 1830	2, 190	......	......	
....do	Apr. 3	Nov. 6, 1830	2, 750	......	......	
Patagonia	May 26	May 28, 1829	......	900	......	
Brazil..........	June 18	June 8, 1829	......	1, 600	......	Second mate, Jeremiah Borden, and boats crew taken down by a whale and lost.
Pacific Ocean ..	Aug. 23	May 26, 1831	2, 800	......	......	
....do	Oct. 13	June 6, 1830	440	......	......	
....do	Oct. 31	Aug. 28, 1830	2, 050	......	......	
Brazil..........	June 7	Mar. 18, 1830	62	1, 250	9, 000	
Cape de Verdes	Feb. 9	....	......	......	......	
Pacific Ocean ..	June 17	May 20, 1831	1, 400	......	......	
Brazil..........	July 14	June 19, 1829	230	1, 270	......	
....do	Aug. 5	....	......	......	......	
Mexico	Feb. 11	....	......	......	......	
Brazil..........	July 19	June 20, 1829	......	1, 600	......	Lost first mate.
....do	July 26	June 20, 1829	160	890	......	
....do	July 26	....	......	......	......	
....do	July 26	July 7, 1829	......	1, 350	11, 000	
....do	Aug. 4	Apr. 20, 1829	400	1, 500	......	
....do	July 12	May 16, 1829	......	1, 950	20, 000	
....do	Aug. 16	Mar. 10, 1830	120	1, 730	16, 500	Sold some oil at Rio Janeiro.
Pacific Ocean ..	Dec. 27	Dec. 28, 1830	1, 700	......	......	
....do	Apr. 28	Aug. 26, 1831	1, 700	......	......	
....do	June 25	July 6, 1831	Full	......	......	
....do	Nov. 21	Oct. 6, 1831	3, 174	6	......	
....do	July 1	....	......	......	......	Ship and cargo totally lost on a reef near Oahu, August, 1830; valued $60,000.
....do	July 19	Apr. 22, 1831	......	......	......	
....do	Apr. 16	June 16, 1831	2, 325	......	......	
Brazil..........	June 26	June 5, 1829	300	750	......	
....do	July 15	Jan. 21, 1830	......	1, 900	21, 000	
....do	July 28	July 7, 1829	60	940	7, 000	
Pacific Ocean ..	Sept. 24	Apr. 19, 1831	......	......	......	
....do	Oct. 15	July 17, 1831	2, 600	......	......	
....do	Jan. 7	Dec. 27, 1830	2, 800	......	......	
....do	June 9	May 6, 1831	2, 800	......	......	
Atlantic	June 19	July 14, 1829	395	......	......	

Table showing returns of whaling-vessels

Name of vessel.	Class.	Tonnage.	Captain.	Managing owner or agent.
1828.				
New Bedford, Mass.—Continued.				
Pocahontas	Brig	141	Benjamin Ellis	
Russell	Ship	301	Shubael Worth	Benjamin Rodman
Richmond	do	291	William Swain	
Rebecca Sims	do	400	Barna Coffin	
Stephania	do	315	David Collins	John Coggeshall
Sally Anne	do	312	C. T. Covell	
Trident	do	448	Peleg H. Stetson	
Triton	do	300	Reuben Chase 2d	I. Howland, jr., & Co.
Timoleon	do	346	Eben Clark	do
Winslow	do	263	Owen Chase	Samuel Rodman, jr
Fairhaven, Mass.				
Amazon	Ship	318	Benjamin Manter	Nathan Church
Albion	do	326	Sheffel Read	
Charleston Packet	Brig		George Tobey	
Herald	Ship		Stephen Grinnell	
Java	do	291	Barz. Adams	
Leonidas	do		Hawes Norris	Ansel Gibbs
Mentor	Brig	89	{ Charles Dyer Francis Neil }	
Staunton	Ship	304	Isaac Daggett	
Rochester, Mass.				
Magnolia	Schooner	98	George Lewis	
Sophronia	do		—— Daggett	
Westport, Mass.				
Industry	Brig	94	Matthew Mayhew	
Mexico	do		Job Davis	
President	Bark	166	Charles Lawrence	
Regulator	Schooner	74	{ William Austin Beriah Tilton, jr }	
Thos. Winslow	Brig	135	Benjamin Seabury	
Dartmouth, Mass.				
By Chance	Brig	107	—— Howland	
Falmouth, Mass.				
Uncas	Ship	400	Henry C. Bunker	Elijah Swift
Sag Harbor, N. Y.				
American	Ship	282	George Post	
Argonaut	do	254	Uriah Sayre	
Claudio	Brig	136	A. K. Griffin	
Cadmus	Ship	310	George Howell	
Henry	do			
Hannibal	do	309	Henry Green	
Marcus	do	283	Andrew Halsey	
Thames	do	350	Huntting Cooper	
Thorn	do	333	Sylv. Griffing	
Union	do		Edward Halsey	
Edgartown, Mass.				
Gleaner Packet	Schooner		—— Bunting	
Loan	Ship		—— Marchout	
Meridian	do		—— Osborn	
New York, N. Y.				
Atlas	Ship		—— Gardner	
Louisa	do		—— Townsend	
Logan	do		—— Coffin	F. Gebhard

sailing from American ports—Continued.

Whaling-ground.	Date— Of sailing.	Date— Of arrival.	Result of voyage. Sperm-oil.	Result of voyage. Whale-oil.	Result of voyage. Whalebone.	Remarks.
			Bbls.	*Bbls.*	*Lbs.*	
Africa	Oct. 16					
Pacific Ocean	May 2	May 19, 1831	Full			
....do	Sept. 2	Apr. 25, 1831	2, 274			
....do	Nov. 22	Apr. 7, 1832	2, 600			
Brazil	June 16	July 7, 1829		1, 700	14, 500	
....do	July 14	June 6, 1829		1, 800		
Pacific Ocean	June 12	Mar. 2, 1831	Full			
....do	July 31	Feb. 27, 1831	2, 120			
....do	Sept. 11	Sept. 4, 1831	300	2, 900		Returned September 29 badly damaged by a gale; sailed again October 19.
....do	July 2	July 7, 1830	1, 800			
Brazil	Sept. 12	May 7, 1830	190	1, 473	12, 700	
Patagonia	May 21	June 8, 1829		1, 500		
Atlantic	Aug. 23	Aug. 24, 1829	350			
Brazil	Aug. 5					
....do	Nov. 5	Apr. 19, 1830	120	1, 920	16, 000	
....do	July 23	July 8, 1829		1, 700	25, 000	
West'rn Islands	June 12					
Atlantic	Oct. 30					
Pacific Ocean	Jan. 8	Feb. 4, 1830	2, 202			
West Indies	June — / Dec. 15	Aug. —, 1829	90	40		
Atlantic	May 18					Last reported with 190 sperm.
West Indies	Jan. 4	July 14, 1829	160			
....do	Dec. 2	Aug. 24, 1829	220	50		
Pacific Ocean	July 2	Feb. —, 1830	820			
Atlantic	May 28					
	Oct. 7	Aug. 28, 1829	100			
Cape de Verdes	Oct. 31	Aug. 24, 1829	650	25		
West Indies	June 16	July —, 1829	300			
Pacific Ocean	Nov. 17	July 15, 1831	3, 468			Built at Falmouth, 1828.
South Seas	July 10	May 30, 1829		1, 687	16, 773	
Brazil	July 17	Apr. 24, 1829		1, 490	13, 328	
Africa	Oct. —	Nov. 19, 1829		300		Brought also 300 furs.
Brazil	June 19	Apr. 8, 1829	25	1, 927	17, 012	
....do						Reported December, 1828, with 1,700 whale.
....do	July 18	Apr. 15, 1829		1, 906	18, 641	
....do	July 23	June 1, 1829	24	1, 406	11, 466	
Patagonia	July 7	June 1, 1829		1, 986	16, 700	
Brazil	July 18	Apr. 27, 1829	68	2, 170	21, 195	
....do	July 26	Apr. 9, 1829	28	1, 449	12, 368	
Straits Belleisle		Sept. 13, 1828	15			
Pacific Ocean	Jan. 1	Dec. 6, 1830	1, 430			
....do	Oct. 5	Apr. 23, 1831	Full			Built at Rochester, 1828. Returned to Tarpaulin Cove twice, with Captain Osborn, sick. Sailed finally under command of the mate, ——— Fisher.
Brazil						Sold to Lynn, 1830.
....do	Nov. 13					Last reported at Tarpaulin Cove, November 15, in distress.
Pacific Ocean		July —, 1830	1, 200			

Table showing returns of whaling-vessels

Name of vessel.	Class.	Tonnage.	Captain.	Managing owner or agent.
1828.				
Bristol, R. I.				
Ann	Ship		—— Wilcox	
Essex	Bark			
Ganges	Ship		—— Gardner	
Stonington, Conn.				
Acasta	Ship			
Newport, R. I.				
Alliance	Ship		Hiram Covell	Bush & Gibbs
Warren, R. I.				
Magnet	Ship		—— Gardner	
Rosalie	do		—— Brown	
New London, Conn.				
Ann Maria	Ship	368	C. Holmes	
Flora	do	338	—— Coit	
Jones	do	338	I. Sayre	
John and Edward	do	318	—— Pearson	
M. Packet	do	170	M. Griffing	
Neptune	do	285	—— Starks	
Wabash	do	250	I. Butler	
1829.				
Nantucket, Mass.				
Atlantic	Ship	321	Elihu Fisher	
Congress	do	339	Thomas Brock	
Criterion	do	229	Barzillai Folger	
Dauphin	do	273	Benjamin F. Hussey	
Enterprise	do	413	John Stetson	
Fabius	do	432	Thaddeus Coffin	
Foster	do	317	Job C. Clark	
George	do	359	Edwin Barnard	L. & J. Mitchell
Independence	do	311	William Whippey	
John Adams, 2d	do	268	Seth Cathcart	
Japan	do	332	John Lincoln	
John Adams	do	296	George Clark	
Loper	do	316	Obed Starbuck	
Montano	do	380	Benjamin Worth	
Martha	do	273	Alexander Whippey	
Orion	do	354	Shadrack Freeman	
Pacific	do	314	William Plaskett	Paul Mitchell & Sons
Peru	do	257	Joseph Pease	David Joy, jr
Planter	do	340	Charles Fisher	Gilbert Coffin
Phœnix	do	323	John J. Gardner	
Rambler	do	318	William Worth, 2d	
Richard Mitchell	do	386	David Baker	
Reaper	do	338	Benjamin F. Coffin	
Spartan	do	333	William Pitman	
Susan	do	349	Frederick Swain	
Westport, Mass.				
Almy	Ship		Jonathan Mayhew	
Industry	Brig		Thomas C. Hammond John A. Cornell	
Mexico	do		Job Davis	
Thos. Winslow	do		Benjamin Seabury	
New Bedford, Mass.				
Abigail	Ship	309	Benjamin Clark	
Aurora	Brig		Leonard West	George Tyson
Com. Rodgers	Ship	298	Joshua Grinnell	William C. Nye

sailing from American ports—Continued.

Whaling-ground.	Date.		Result of voyage.			Remarks.
	Of sailing.	Of arrival.	Sperm-oil.	Whale-oil.	Whalebone.	
			Bbls.	*Bbls.*	*Lbs.*	
Brazil	....	July 8, 1829	......	1, 100	......	A grand complimentary banquet was given by the owners to the officers and crews of these two vessels, on account of the success of Bristol's first real venture in this pursuit.
....do	....	June 20, 1829	......	1, 000	700	
Pacific Ocean	Oct. 10	Oct. —, 1831	2, 700	......	......	
Brazil	....	....	......	......	......	Reported in December, 1828, with 12 whales.
Pacific Ocean	Oct. 25	Sept. 10, 1832	2, 700	......	......	
Pacific Ocean	Nov. —	May 28, 1831	2, 900	......	......	
....do	June —	Feb. 20, 1831	Full	......	......	
....	July 2	June —, 1829	60	1, 848	......	
....	May 16	June 8, 1829	......	1, 061	......	
....	July 2	June — 1829	59	1, 617	......	
....	July 9	June 20, 1829	133	1, 077	......	
....	May 21	June —, 1829	......	1, 343	......	
....	July 26	June —, 1829	......	1, 204	......	
....	....	June 8, 1829	200	1, 400	......	
Pacific Ocean	Dec. 26	Jan. 26, 1832	2, 153	......	......	
....do	June 26	June 1, 1830	7	1, 299	......	Formerly a merchantman; added 1829.
Brazil	July 26	....	......	......	......	Condemned at Halifax, 1829.
....do	Aug. 14	....	......	......	......	Lost in Saldanha Bay, Cape of Good Hope, 1830.
Pacific Ocean	June 30	Aug. 4, 1832	2, 955	......	......	Sent home 79 sperm.
....do	Aug. 14	Mar. 23, 1833	2, 162	......	......	Formerly a merchantman; added 1829.
....do	Nov. 15	Jan. 27, 1833	2, 260	......	......	
Brazil	July 22	June 9, 1830	155	1, 217	......	
Pacific Ocean	Oct. 29	June 6, 1833	1, 506	21	......	
....do	June 26	Feb. 28, 1831	626	......	......	
Brazil	June 21	Mar. 29, 1832	7	1, 299	......	
....do	Aug. 1	June 7, 1830	......	198	......	
Pacific Ocean	June 21	Sept. 7, 1830	2, 280	......	......	An excellent voyage—gone 14 months 14 days.
....do	July 24	Dec. 18, 1832	2, 816	......	......	Formerly a merchantman; added 1829; built at New York, 1822.
....do	Nov. 27	July 15, 1833	1, 680	......	......	
....do	Sept. 20	Oct. 10, 1832	2, 620	......	......	
Brazil	June 12	June 8, 1830	80	1, 607	......	
....do	July 13	June 2, 1830	64	1, 152	......	
....do	Aug. 1	June 9, 1830	159	1, 469	......	
Pacific Ocean	Oct. 7	Aug. 10, 1831	2, 340	......	......	
....do	June 26	Feb. 28, 1832	2, 240	......	......	
....do	July 21	Sept. 3, 1831	3, 012	......	......	Built at Mattapoisett, 1829.
....do	Oct. 23	Apr. 21, 1832	1, 808	......	......	Captain Coffin died on the voyage.
....do	Aug. 31	Sept. 2, 1831	2, 361	......	......	
....do	Dec. 10	Aug. 9, 1833	2, 180	......	......	
Cape de Verdes	Oct. 9	Aug. 23, 1830	170	......	......	
Espirito Santo	Aug. 17	....	......	......	......	
Cape de Verdes	Oct. 5	July 26, 1830	240	......	......	
....do	Oct. 9	Aug. —, 1830	340	24	......	
....do	Oct. 5	Aug. 19, 1830	350	......	......	
Pacific Ocean	May 23	June 16, 1831	2, 500	......	......	
Atlantic	May 30	Aug. 28, 1830	430	......	......	
Brazil	June 19	June 28, 1830	122	1, 042	8, 125	

Table showing returns of whaling-vessels

Name of vessel.	Class.	Tonnage.	Captain.	Managing owner or agent.
1829.				
New Bedford, Mass.—Continued.				
Com. Decatur	Ship	247	Warren Howland	J. & J. Howland
Chili	do	291	Grafton Luce	
Condor	do	348	Edward Merrill	
Courier	do	381	Joseph Barnard	
Eagle	do	336	Shubael Hawes	William C. Nye
Emerald	do	359	Clement Norton	Thomas Riddell
Enterprise	do	291	Samuel Tilton	Alfred Gibbs
Frances Henrietta	do	407	Abm. Russell	
Galatea	do	310	Elihu Russell	
Grand Turk	do	323	Robert Taber	
Good Return	do	376	Job Terry, jr	James Tripp
George and Martha	do	275	Arthur Cox	John C. Haskell
George Porter	do	285	Charles Weeks	Thomas Riddell
Golconda	do	330	J. D. Samson	George Howland
Hector	do	...	John C. Morse	Charles W. Morgan
Hydaspe	do	312	Joseph Spooner	
Herald	do	262	Ezra Smith	
Hope	do	316	Joseph Paddock, jr	
Java	do	295	Walter Hillman	George Howland
Juno	Brig	165	John J. Parker	John A. Parker
Midas	Ship	326	Richard G. Luce	John Coggeshall
Mercator	do	246	Jonathan Fisher	John A. Parker & Son
Milwood	do	...	Ellis C. Eldredge	
Ospray	Bark	169	H. N. Howland	
Parthian	Brig	119	Granville Manter	
Pocahontas	do	141	George Lewis	
Pacific	Ship	384	Paul Chase	J. Perry
Sophia	do	295	Charles Rawson	Joseph Rotch
Sally Anne	do	312	Andrew Almy	
Stephania	do	315	David Collins	John Coggeshall, jr
Victory	do	268	A. P. Norton	
William & Eliza	do	321	George Crocker	J. Rotch & Co
Fairhaven, Mass.				
Albion	Ship	...	Sheffel Read	E. Sawin
Columbus	do	313	David Osborn	Gibbs & Jenney
Favorite	Bark	...	Bradford Hathaway	F. R. Whitwell
Heroine	Ship	337	Charles Smith	Nathan Church
Herald	do	274	Caleb Kempton	Alexander Gibbs
Leonidas	do	...	Howes Norris	
Mentor	Brig	...	—— Neil	Luther Wilson
Maine	Ship	294	Benjamin Manter	E. Sawin
Oregon	do	307	Jabez Delano, jr	Lemuel Tripp
Quito	Brig	...	Stanton Burtch	Alfred Gibbs
Dartmouth, Mass.				
By Chance	Brig	...	Stephen Howland, jr	
New London, Conn.				
Ann Maria	Ship	368	C. Holme	
Com. Perry	do	270	—— Sayre	
Electra	do	348	—— Griffing	W. Williams & Co
Flora	do	338	L. Allyn	
John and Edward	do	318	—— Pearson	
Jones	do	338	—— Cararly	
Manchester Packet	do	170	—— Fordham	
Neptune	do	285	—— Starks	
Stonington	do	351	—— Blydeburg	
Wabash	do	250	C Butler	
Edgartown, Mass.				
John	Ship	...	—— Pease	Jethro Daggett
Mary Ann	do	240	—— Worth	
Planter	Brig	...	—— Pease	

sailing from American ports—Continued.

Whaling-ground.	Date—Of sailing.	Date—Of arrival.	Result of voyage.—Sperm-oil.	Result of voyage.—Whale-oil.	Result of voyage.—Whalebone.	Remarks.
			Bbls.	*Bbls.*	*Lbs.*	
Brazil	May 21	Mar. 15, 1830	140	1, 350	9, 000	
....do	May 22	June 8, 1830	180	227	750	Returned leaking badly.
....do	July 18	June 22, 1830	267	1, 870	14, 000	
Pacific Ocean	Aug. 19	Feb. 11, 1832	2, 750	......	......	
Brazil	June 6	June 2, 1830	....	1, 820	17, 500	Captain Hawes and his mate, with their boats' crews, were accidentally left at Novowha. The ship was navigated home by the mate of the Euphrates. Captain Hawes and his men started for Pernambuco in open boats, but were picked up by the Rodman.
Atlantic	June 23	Mar. 8, 1830	......	2, 500	28, 900	
South Atlantic	July 17	May 21, 1831	230	1, 270	......	
Pacific Ocean	Nov. 9	Feb. 23, 1833	2, 300	......	......	
Brazil	May 30	....	......	......	......	
... do	July 23	May 6, 1830	50	1, 236	1, 800	
....do	July 17	July 17, 1830	100	2, 100	19, 600	
....do	July 18	June 9, 1830	28	1, 85[illegible]	16, 000	
....do	July 29	May 31, 1830	90	1, 472	12, 020	
Pacific Ocean	Oct. 7	Sept. 24, 1832	2, 300	......	......	
....do	June 20	Oct. 13, 1831	2, 600	......	......	
Brazil	June 20	June 8, 1830	......	1, 567	12, 200	
....do	July 24	June 19, 1830	55	500	2, 800	
Pacific Ocean	July 28	May 24, 1832	Full.	......	......	
Brazil	June 8	Mar. 19, 1830	70	2, 100	19, 000	
Cape Good Hope	May 14	May 20, 1830	220	......	......	
Brazil	June 13	Mar. 19, 1830	68	1, 964	14, 41[illegible]	
....do	June 26	June 3, 1830	70	1, 220	10, 300	
....do	Oct. 5	June 1, 1831	.....	.....	.....	
Pacific Ocean	July 20	Feb. 25, 1832	1, 070	......	......	
Cape de Verdes	Aug. 6	....	.....	.....	.....	
Atlantic	Oct. 5	May 7, 1830	90	......	......	Reported arrived September 12, 1830, 150 sperm.
Pacific Ocean	Nov. 16	Oct. 4, 1832	Full.	......	......	
Patagonia	June 2	June 2, 1830	......	1, 365	13, 000	
Atlantic	July 10	June 10, 1830	25	1, 800	16, 527	
Brazil	July 30	June 2, 1830	......	1, 900	18, 000	
Pacific Ocean	Sept. 11	Apr. 7, 1832	1, 750	......	......	Captain Norton killed by a whale.
....do	Apr. 28	Aug. 22, 1831	2, 100	......	......	
Brazil	July 18	Apr. 3, 1830	......	2, 000	16, 600	
Pacific Ocean	May 13	Jan. 28, 1832	Full.	......	......	
Brazil	July 18	June 19, 1830	......	......	......	
... do	June 23	....	......	......	......	
....do	July 18	June 6, 1830	200	1, 600	12, 000	
....do	Aug. 8	....	......	......	......	
Atlantic	......	Dec. 30, 1829	......	......	......	Belongs to Fairhaven or Westport.
Brazil	June 10	May 31, 1830	......	600	......	
Pacific Ocean	July 29	Oct. 8, 1831	2, 300	......	......	
Atlantic	Jan. 22	Apr. 23, 1830	200	......	......	
Guinea	Sept. 30	Aug. 23, 1830	250	......	......	
South Atlantic	June 18	Mar. 22, 1830	65	2, 008	......	
....do	June 12	June 1, 1830	......	1, 500	......	
....do	June 27	May 31, 1830	......	1, 896	......	Built 1829.
....do	July 5	Apr. 15, 1830	62	1, 900	......	
....do	July 22	May 31, 1830	......	1, 403	......	
....do	July 2	Mar. 22, 1830	......	1, 407	......	
....do	June 20	June 6, 1830	......	1, 194	......	
....do	June 10	Apr. 20, 1830	......	1, 596	......	
....do	July 30	May 31, 1830	42	975	......	
....do	July 23	May 31, 1830	......	1, 358	......	
Brazil	......	July —, 1830	160	1, 640	12, 000	
....do	......	June 1, 1830	100	600	......	Sold 1830.
......	May 24	....	......	......	......	

Table showing returns of whaling-vessels

Name of vessel.	Class.	Tonnage.	Captain.	Managing owner or agent.
1829.				
Stonington, Conn.				
Acasta	Ship		—— Wood	
Sag Harbor, N. Y.				
Argonaut	Ship	254	Uriah Sayre	S. & L. Howell
American	do	282	William A. Jones	S. & B. Huntting & Co.
Cadmus	do	310	George Howell	Mulford & Sleight
Columbia	do	285	Robert F. Hand	Luther D. Cook
Henry	do	333	Sylvester Griffing	Charles T. Dering
Hannibal	do	369	Henry Green	S. & B. Huntting & Co.
Marcus	do	283	Barney Green	S. & N. Howell
Thames	do	350	Hunttling Cooper	Mulford & Sleight
Thorn	do	299	Hervey Harris	do
New York, N. Y.				
Cincinnatus	Ship		—— Howland	Barker & Co
William Tell	do	362	Nathaniel Gardner	Jacob Barker
Plymouth, Mass.				
Fortune	Ship		—— Swain	
Bristol, R. I.				
Ann	Ship			
Balance	do	321	—— Daggett	
Essex	Bark		—— Mayhew	
Warren, R. I.				
Magnet	Ship		—— Gardner	
North America	do		—— Pickens	
Bristol, R. I.				
Ann	Ship		—— Wood	
Rochester, Mass.				
Magnolia	Schooner		—— Lewis	
Sophronia	do		—— Daggett	
Newport, R. I.				
Erie	Ship		—— Adams	Engs & Bush
The Potosi was fitted from Greenport, N. Y., in 1828 or 1829; sailed under Captain Charles Griffin; John Brown, managing owner. She made a good voyage; sailed again in 1829 or 1830, and was lost on the Falklands.				
1830.				
New Bedford, Mass.				
Augusta	Ship	344	Charles Lawrence	William R. Rodman
Amanda	Bark	217	John E. Coggeshall	Phillips, Russell & Co.
Braganza	Ship	470	Daniel Wood	William T. Russell
Brandt	do	310	Warren Howland	N. Leonard
Balæna	do	300	Obed Fosdick	J. & J. Howland
Com. Decatur	do	247	J. H. Howland	do
Ceres	do	328	Timothy Russell	
Chili	do	291	David Collins	
Condor	do	349	Edward Merrill	Charles W. Morgan
Com. Rodgers	do	298	Joshua Grinnell	Jireh Perry
China	do	370	Russell Maxfield	
Charles	do	290	George Cannon, jr	
Cortes	do	382	Daniel Holway	George Howland

sailing from American ports—Continued.

Whaling-ground.	Date— Of sailing.	Date— Of arrival.	Result of voyage. Sperm-oil.	Result of voyage. Whale-oil.	Result of voyage. Whalebone.	Remarks.
			Bbls.	*Bbls.*	*Lbs.*	
Brazil	......	May 29, 1830	......	1, 600	......	
Brazil	June 24	June 12, 1830	110	590	4, 250	
....do	June 24	June 5, 1830	163	1, 359	13, 055	
....do	June 22	May 27, 1830	107	1, 468	12, 622	
....do	July 27	June 5, 1830	......	1, 533	11, 585	Added 1829.
....do	July 30	May 27, 1830	65	1, 890	17, 050	
....do	June 30	Apr. 20, 1830	......	1, 877	14, 686	
....do	June 30	June 5, 1830	104	1, 218	9, 896	
....do	July 22	May 27, 1830	62	1, 660	13, 726	
....do	June 22	June 3, 1830	......	1, 594	12, 875	
Brazil	Oct. 11	......	......	......	......	Reported at Rio Janeiro, September, 1831 with 800 sperm, 1,500 whale.
Pacific Ocean	Nov. 23	Feb. —, 1833	1, 700	......	......	
Pacific Ocean	Aug. 3	Dec. 15, 1832	Full.	......	......	
......	Aug. —	......	......	......	......	
......	Dec. 16	......	......	......	......	
Brazil	......	July —, 1830	......	1, 200	......	
Pacific Ocean	May 11	......	......	......	......	
Brazil	......	June 9, 1830	......	1, 000	......	
Brazil	......	June 10, 1830	......	600	......	
Atlantic	Jan. —	......	......	......	......	Reported in May with 40 sperm.
....do	Apr. 30 Sept. 3	Aug. —, 1829 Sept. 17, 1829	50	......	......	Reported with 90 sperm.
Pacific Ocean	Nov. 26	Apr. 24, 1832	2, 200	......	......	Built at Newport, 1828.
Pacific Ocean	Dec. 8	Jan. 15, 1834	2, 536	......	......	
Brazil Banks	June 28	Mar. 26, 1831	......	950	......	
Pacific Ocean	June 26	Nov. 29, 1833	3, 985	......	......	
South Atlantic	June 11	Feb. 26, 1831	......	Full.	......	
Pacific Ocean	Oct. 14	Jan. 15, 1834	1, 800	......	......	
South Atlantic	May 11	Mar. 10, 1831	140	960	......	
Indian Ocean	May 12	—— —, 1831	......	......	......	
Atlantic	July 17	June 15, 1831	......	......	......	
....do	Aug. 2	May 9, 1831	170	2, 630	......	
Pacific Ocean	Oct. 19	Mar. 14, 1833	2, 100	......	......	
Indian Ocean	Oct. 20	Feb. 29, 1832	750	2, 300	23, 000	
Pacific Ocean	Dec. 14	Sept. 29, 1833	......	......	......	
....do	Dec. 25	Apr. 11, 1834	2, 470	......	......	

Table showing returns of whaling-vessels

Name of vessel.	Class.	Tonnage.	Captain.	Managing owner or agent.
1830.				
New Bedford, Mass.—Continued.				
Dwight	Brig	140	James Wood, 2d	
Endeavour	Ship	234	Joseph B. Leonard	
Emerald	do	359	Clement Norton	
Euphrates	do	364	Cornelius Howland, jr	J. Grinnell
Eagle	do	336	Shubael Hawes	
Frances	do	348	Obed Alley	
Franklin	do	333	James Davis	C. Russell
Falcon	do	273	Joseph Barker	
George and Susan	do	356	Edward Gardner	George Howland
Grand Turk	do	324	Stanton Burtch	
George Porter	do	285	Jared Fisher	
George and Martha	do	275	Thomas Barnard	
Good Return	do	376	Job Terry, jr	Job Eddy
Hercules	do	290	Clement P. Covell Peter F. Chase	
Hope	do	283	David Flanders	
Hercules	do	335	Moses Samson	Seth Russell
Hydaspe	do	313	Joseph Spooner	
Herald	do	262	Isaiah West	
Hibernia	do	327	Henry Pease, 2d	
Herald	do	303	N. H. Nye	
India	do	366	Grafton Luce	William T. Russell
Jasper	do	360	Martin Bowen	Atkins Adams
Java	do	295	Walter Hillman	
Juno	Brig	166	John J. Parker	
John	Ship	308	Andrew Almy	
John Howland	do	377	Henry B. Gifford	
Logan	do	302	Stanton C. Fisher	I. Howland, jr., & Co
Leader	Bark	170	David F. Case	
Martha	Ship	271	Richard Weeden	
Midas	do	326	Richard G. Luce	John Coggeshall, jr
Minerva Smyth	do	335	Gideon H. Smith	I. Howland, jr., & Co
Mentor	do	213	E. C. Barnard	
Mercator	do	246	Jonathan Fisher	
Minerva	Bark	195	Simeon Price	J. & J. Howland
Martha	Ship	349	Edwin Russell	
Mary Ann	do	240	Abraham Swain	
Milo	do	398	Leonard West	
New England	do	375	A. F. Parker	
Nautilus	do	340	Isaiah Burgess	William C. Nye
Octavia	Bark	257	Granville Manter	
Pacific	Ship	332	D. McKenzie	
Parthian	Brig	119	James Maxfield	Alexander Gibbs
Roscoe	Ship	362	George G. Chase	Charles W. Morgan
Rodman	do	371	Robert M. Joy	do
Swift	do	321	Lewis Tobey	T. S. & N. Hathaway
Sophia	do	296	Robert Tuckerman	
Stephania	do	315	Elisha Dexter	
Sally Anne	do	312	A. T. Eddy	
William Rotch	do	290	Elihu Russell	John Coggeshall, jr
Wilmington and Liverpool Packet	do	384	Alexander Russell	
Winslow	do	263	Edward G. Coffin	Samuel Rodman
William Thompson	do	495	Stephen N. Potter	
Young Phenix	do	377	Obed Cathcart	John A. Parker & Son
Fairhaven, Mass.				
Albion	Ship	326	Sheffield Reade	
Amazon	do	319	Arthur Cox	
Herald	do	274	Caleb Kempton	Alexander Gibbs
Java	do	292	Barz. S. Adams	
Marcus	do	286	N. S. Bassett	Lemuel Tripp
Maine	do	294	Benjamin Manter	

sailing from American ports—Continued.

Whaling-ground.	Date— Of sailing.	Date— Of arrival.	Result of voyage. Sperm-oil.	Result of voyage. Whale-oil.	Result of voyage. Whalebone.	Remarks.
			Bbls.	*Bbls.*	*Lbs.*	
Cape G'd Hope.	Nov. 9					Probably returned in 1831, and was withdrawn.
South Atlantic.	June 19	Mar. 2, 1831				
....do	July 16	Mar. 1, 1831	80	2, 420		
Pacific Ocean ..	Sept. 3	July 13, 1833	2, 950			
Brazil Banks...	Sept. 25	Jan. 25, 1832		Full.		
Pacific Ocean ..	Jan. 8	June 10, 1832	2, 600			
South Seas.....	Jan. 9	Mar. 14, 1833	800	1, 600		
Brazil Banks...	Aug. 17	Apr. 24, 1832				
Pacific Ocean ..	Jan. 23	July 15, 1833	2, 150			
South Atlantic.	May 28	Mar. 4, 1831	200	1, 700		
....do	July 3	Feb. 26, 1831	30	1, 820		
Patagonia	Aug. 4	Mar. 22, 1832				
Pacific Ocean ..	Sept. 4	Mar. 10, 1833	450	2, 500	20, 000	Mate lost, 1831. Detained at Talcahuano 5 months on a frivolous charge. Chilian government paid $20,000 in 1875 as indemnification.
South Seas.....	Jan. 5	Nov. 27, 1830	450 (both voyages)	1, 450		
Indian Ocean ..	Dec. 28	Jan. 31, 1832				
Brazil..........	Jan. 30	Feb. 19, 1831		Full.		
....do	June 29	Mar. 26, 1831		2, 000	20, 000	
Patagonia......	July 24	Mar. 9, 1832	150	1, 450		
Brazil..........	Aug. 13	June 17, 1831		1, 200		
South Atlantic.	Aug. 16	June 14, 1831	200	1, 000		
Pacific Ocean ..	Nov. 20	May 11, 1834				
....do	Sept. 20	Jan. 2, 1834	2, 000			
South Atlantic.	May 4					Owned in Marblehead. Returned to Boston in July, 1830. Damaged by running on a reef at Bonavista.
....do	June 7	Mar. —, 1831		2, 000		
Atlantic.......	June 16					Probably returned late in 1830.
Brazil..........	Aug. 10	Jan. 20, 1832				
Pacific Ocean ..	Dec. 30	—— —, 1832				Reported with 2,300 barrels.
....do	Oct. 21	Nov. 29, 1833				
....do	Dec. 18	Sept. 11, 1833	950			
South Atlantic.	Apr. 14	Feb. 13, 1831				Probably of Fairhaven.
....do	May 22	May 26, 1831		2, 300		
Pacific Ocean ..	May 25	Apr. 22, 1833				
South Atlantic.	June 4					
Brazil..........	July 12	May 7, 1831		1, 450		
Pacific Ocean ..	July 23	Jan. 7, 1833				
South Atlantic.	Aug. 16					Lost at Delago Bay, June, 1831.
Brazil..........	Sept. 17	June —, 1831		1, 000		Belonged to Rochester. Wrecked on Gay Head, homeward bound.
Pacific Ocean ..	Nov. 8	May 9, 1834	1, 400	400		
....do	Dec. 23	Mar. 10, 1834				
South Atlantic.	Mar. 13	Mar. 8, 1831		1, 900		
....do	July 16	July 5, 1831	100	800		
South Seas.....	May 12	Nov. 21, 1831		Full.		
Guinea	July 17	May 24, 1831	240	180	1, 200	
Pacific Ocean ..	Aug. 23	Jan. 4, 1833	2, 500			
....do	Sept. 29	Apr. 10, 1833	3, 000			
....do	Jan. 7	Oct. 1, 1832	2, 100			
Brazil	June 28	May 9, 1831		1, 100		
....do	July 20	Feb. 24, 1832	100	2, 100		
Indian Ocean ..	Nov. 18	Feb. 27, 1832				
Brazil..........	July 17	June 17, 1831	100	1, 600		
Pacific Ocean ..	Aug. 27	Apr. 30, 1833	3, 000			
....do	Sept. 2	Aug. 27, 1833	1, 300			George Adlington, second mate, killed by a whale March 6, 1833.
....do	Oct. 13	Aug. 12, 1834	2, 600			
....do	Feb. 5	May 14, 1833	Full			
South Atlantic	June 14	Feb. 17, 1831		2, 300		
Brazil..........	July 22	Jan. 29, 1832		1, 600		
South Seas.....	July 4	May 30, 1831	70	1, 630		
South Atlantic	June 17					
Pacific Ocean ..	Aug. 5	Aug. 7, 1833	1, 600			
South Atlantic.	July 28	Feb. 14, 1832		1, 550	1, 300	Pardon Devol, first mate, died December, 1830.

Table showing returns of whaling-vessels

Name of vessel.	Class.	Tonnage.	Captain.	Managing owner or agent.
1830.				
Fairhaven, Mass.—Continued.				
Pindus	Bark	193	John Bunker	
Quito	Brig	138	George H. Richmond	
Stanton	Ship	304	Isaac Daggett	Lemuel Tripp
Westport, Mass.				
Mentor	Brig	89	Samuel Lake	
President	Bark	167	Charles Downs	
Thomas Winslow	Brig	130	John A. Cornell	
Falmouth, Mass.				
Awashonks	Ship	355	Obed Swain	Elijah Swift
Rochester, Mass.				
Franklin	Bark	252	Nathaniel C. Cary	Gideon Barstow & Son
Lexington	Schooner		—— Daggett	
Sopronia	do			
Nantucket, Mass.				
Aurora	Ship	340	John Hussey	
Ann	do	361	Isaac Brayton	
American	do	340	William Wyer	
Barclay	do	304	William Barney, jr	
Columbus	do	344	Peter Coffin	
Congress	do	339	Thomas Brock	
Clarkson	do	380	Alexander D. Bunker	
George	do	359	Edwin Barnard	
Hero	do	313	George Alley	
John Adams	do	290	Shubael Clark	
Loper	do	310	John Cotton	
Lydia	do	325	David Swain, 2d	
Omega	do	363	Frederick B. Chase	
Planter	do	340	Charles Fisher	
Phebe	do	379	William C. Briggs	
Pacific	do	314	William Plaskett	
Peru	do	257	Joseph Pease	
Ploughboy	do	391	Nathan Chase	
Statira	do	340	Prince Coffin, 2d	
Sarah	do	495	Benjamin Barney	
Zone	do	365	John M. Russell	
Lynn, Mass.				
Atlas	Ship	260	S. H. Gardner	
Plymouth, Mass.				
Arabella	Ship		—— Harris	
Newport, R. I.				
Frederick Augustus	Ship		William Kurn	Ruggles & Bush
George Champlin	do		Fordin Haskell	H. Ruggles & Son
Warren, R. I.				
Miles	Ship		—— Tobey	
North America	do		—— Pickens	
Providence, R. I.				
C. Burdick	Brig		—— Kelley	
Hudson, N. Y.				
America	Ship		—— Cottle	S. G. Macey
Alexander Mansfield	do		—— Bennett	do
Meteor	do		—— Clasby	
Sag Harbor, N. Y.				
Argonaut	Ship			
American	do	282	—— Jones	

sailing from American ports—Continued.

Whaling-ground.	Date— Of sailing.	Of arrival.	Result of voyage. Sperm-oil.	Whale-oil.	Whalebone.	Remarks.
			Bbls.	*Bbls.*	*Lbs.*	
South Atlantic.	June 5	May 1, 1831	......	......	......	
....do	May 22		......	......	......	Probably returned late in 1830.
....do	May 15	Nov. 23, 1832	2,200	......	......	
Cape de Verdes	May 13	Nov. 5, 1830	335	......	......	
Pacific Ocean ..	Apr. 22	May 7, 1832	......	......	......	
Cape de Verdes	Oct. 21	June 29, 1831	......	......	......	
Pacific Ocean ..	Nov. 6	Nov. 1, 1833	2,000	......	......	Built in Falmouth 1830.
Brazil.........	July 3	May 21, 1831	......	1,750	......	
Atlantic	....	Sept. 24, 1830	70	......	......	
....	....	....	....	......	......	Sailed 1830; was lost at sea Aug. 17.
Pacific Ocean ..	May 7	Apr. 25, 1833	2,135	......	......	
....do	June 13	Apr. 28, 1833	2,824	......	......	
....do	Sept. 15	Oct. 29, 1833	1,474	220	......	Built at New York.
Brazil.........	May 27	May 9, 1831	40	1,190	......	
....do	Apr. 19	Apr. 18, 1831	220	1,550	......	
....do	June 22	Oct. 5, 1831	546	1,363	......	
Pacific Ocean ..	Aug. 23	Apr. 13, 1834	2,962	......	......	
Brazil.........	July 29	Mar. 1, 1832	......	2,140	......	
Pacific Ocean ..	Oct. 27	Apr. 26, 1833	2,240	......	......	
Brazil	July 18	Mar. —, 1831	87	1,185	......	
Pacific Ocean .	Dec. 30	Aug. 19, 1832	2,170	......	......	
....do	Dec. 5	Jan. 20, 1833	2,120	106	......	
....do	June 27	Jan. 6, 1833	2,575	27	......	
Brazil.........	Nov. 1	Feb. 8, 1832	......	2,600	24,000	Captain Briggs died on the voyage.
Pacific Ocean ..	May 28	Nov. 5, 1833	2,131	......	......	
Brazil.........	July 11	May 27, 1831	25	1,786	......	
....do	July 18	Apr. 2, 1831	134	1,423	......	
Pacific Ocean ..	Oct. 16	Mar. 5, 1834	1,741	......	......	
....do	May 7	Oct. 27, 1833	1,104	....	......	
....do	Aug. 11	Jan. 14, 1834	2,093	....	......	
....do	June 27	Sept. 29, 1833	2,430	....	......	
Brazil.........	June 26	'30 or early '31	....	......	......	Bought from New York, 1830.
Pacific Ocean ..	Sept. 3	Apr. —, 1834	200	2,100	......	
Pacific Ocean ..	....	Oct. 12, 1833	1,600	......	....	
....do	Aug. —	July 24, 1833	1,800	....	....	
South Atlantic	....	Mar. 24, 1831	......	1,200	....	
South Seas	July 16	Feb. 7, 1832	......	Full.	....	
Pacific Ocean ..	Dec. 2	....	....	....	....	
Pacific Ocean ..	Aug. 3	Apr. 23, 1833	3,200	....	....	
South Atlantic	June —	Mar. 31, 1831	123	2,200	1,600	
....	....	....	....	......	......	Probably sold 1830. Captain Clasby killed by a whale 1832.
....	July 24	....	....	....	....	Returned in August leaky and condemned.
Patagonia......	....	June 16, 1831	....	1,800	......	

Table showing returns of whaling-vessels

Name of vessel.	Class.	Tonnage.	Captain.	Managing owner or agent.
1830.				
Sag Harbor, N. Y.—Continued.				
Henry	Ship	333		
Hannibal	do	309	—— Parker	
Nimrod	do		—— Halsey	
Neptune	do		—— Post	
Phenix	do			
Potosi	do			
Thames	do	350	—— Cooper	
Thorn	do	299	—— Howell	
Stonington, Conn.				
Francis	Ship	236	—— Burdick	
New London, Conn.				
Ann Maria	Ship	368	—— Chester	
Connecticut	do	390	—— Smith	
Com. Perry	do	270	C. Holmes	
Electra	do	348	—— Griffing	
Flora	do	338	F. Smith	
Friends	do	403	—— Blydenburg	
Jones	do	338	—— Cararly	
John & Edward	do	318	—— Allyn	
Mentor	do	460	—— Butler	
Manchester Packet	do	170	—— Fordham	
Neptune	do	285	—— Richards	
Phenix	do	404	J. Smith	
Superior	do	405	—— Fitch	N. & W. W. Billings
Stonington	do	351	—— Pearson	
Wabash	do	250	C. Butler	
Bristol, R. I.				
America	Ship		—— Grinnell	
Ann	do		—— Wilcox	
Essex	do	200	—— Mayhew	
Leonidas	do		—— Cleaveland	
Edgartown, Mass.				
Almira	Ship		—— Eldredge	
Planter	Brig		—— Pease	
1831.				
New Bedford, Mass.				
Amanda	Ship			
Abigail	do	309	Benjamin Clark	C. W. Morgan
Averick	do		Edward Swain	
Barclay	do	241	Alex. Coffin, 2d	William R. Rotch & Co
Bramin	Bark	245	W. P. Haskins	
Brighton	Ship	354	Robert Tuckerman	W. T. Russell & Co
Brandt	do	310	Warren Howland	
Courier	do	293	Thomas Severance	
Com. Decatur	do	247	Seth D. Fisher	
Condor	do	349	Richard G. Luce	
Cicero	do	251	William Hussey	
Chili	do	291	David Collins	
Canton	do	408	Abram Gardner	Jireh Perry
Ceres	do	373	Moses Samson	Phillips & Russell
Corinthian	do	401	Timothy Upham	George Howland
Dragon	do		Isaac Thacher	
Emerald	do	359	Clement Norton	
Equator	Bark	262	Benjamin F. Riddell	L. Standish & Son
Endeavour	Ship	234	Richard Flanders	
Enterprise	do	291	Samuel Tilton, jr	Alfred Gibbs
Forrester	Bark		Charles B. Ray	
Frances	Ship	367	John Briggs	

* Vessels from Dartmouth, Westport, Rochester, Fairhaven, and

sailing from American ports—Continued.

Whaling-ground.	Date— Of sailing.	Date— Of arrival.	Result of voyage. Sperm-oil.	Result of voyage. Whale-oil.	Result of voyage. Whalebone.	Remarks.
			Bbls.	*Bbls.*	*Lbs.*	
Brazil	....	May 14, 1831	300	1, 800	.....	
South Atlantic	....	Feb. 25, 1831	.....	1, 900	.....	
Tristan	....	Mar. 23, 1831	90	1, 600	.....	
Brazil	....	May 14, 1831	300	1, 200	.....	
....do	....	—— —, 1831	.....	2, 400	.....	
....do	....	May 14, 1831	.....	1, 500	.....	
....do	....	Apr. 16, 1831	.....	1, 760	.....	
Patagonia	....	May 20, 1831	.....	1, 450	.....	
Brazil	....	May —, 1831	20	185	1, 200	
South Seas	June 26	Nov. 9, 1831	291	1, 982	.....	
....do	June 9	May 10, 1831	252	1, 483	.....	
....do	July 9	May 21, 1831	186	937	8, 000	
....do	July 15	May 9, 1831	.....	927	.....	
Tristan	June 24	Feb. 16, 1831	65	2, 025	22, 000	
Pacific Ocean	Aug. 25	Jan. 17, 1834	1, 393	20	.....	
South Seas	June 5	Mar. 23, 1831	.....	1, 702	.....	
....do	July 1	Aug. 20, 1831	127	2, 064	15, 000	
....do	June —	Feb. 27, 1821	248	2, 607	.....	
....do	July 1	June 12, 1831	23	947	.....	
....do	June 9	Feb. 26, 1831	85	1, 821	.....	
Pacific Ocean	Aug. 8	Nov. 25, 1833	2, 971	.....	.....	
....do	Aug. 12	July 26, 1833	2, 950	.....	.....	
South Seas	July 6	June 20, 1831	239	1, 271	11, 000	
....do	July 15	Apr. 25, 1831	....	1, 488	.....	
Tristan	....	Mar. 25, 1831	.....	1, 500	.....	Anson Grinnell, first mate, lost overboard March 1830.
Brazil	....	May —, 1831	100	800	.....	
Patagonia	....	June 20, 1831	.....	1, 100	.....	
Pacific Ocean	....	Aug. 8, 1833	2, 500	....	.....	
Pacific Ocean	....	Aug. 8, 1833	1, 600	....	.....	Captain Eldredge was left at Oahu, sick.
Atlantic	....	....	.....	....	.....	Captured by Don Miguel's squadron, carried into Lisbon and condemned.
....	....	Feb. 26, 1832	.....	....	.....	
Pacific Ocean	Nov. 19	June 12, 1835	2, 254	....	.....	
....do	Nov. 23	....	....	....	.....	Captain Swain died at Payta June 21, 1833. Ship chartered as a freighter from Valparaiso to New York.
....do	Apr. 26	June 22, 1834	1, 200	.....	.....	Mate taken out of boat by a foul line, 1832.
Cape Good Hope	Jan. 7	....	.....	....	.....	
Pacific Ocean	Nov. 25	Mar. 20, 1835	2, 560	....	.....	Bought from New York, 1831.
South Atlantic	July 16	Feb. 25, 1832	.....	Full.	.....	
....do	Apr. 15	Mar. 8, 1832	100	1, 500	.....	
....do	May 2	Mar. 13, 1832	.....	.....	.....	
Brazil	July 1	Apr. 22, 1832	150	2, 550	.....	
South Atlantic	Aug. 15	Jan. 7, 1833	.....	.....	.....	
....do	Aug. 1	Mar. 25, 1832	500	1, 700	1, 200	
Pacific Ocean	Aug. 19	May 31, 1834	2, 800	.....	.....	
South Atlantic	Oct. 4	Feb. 25, 1832	.....	1, 400	.....	Bought from New York, 1831.
Pacific Ocean	Nov. 7	Apr. 29, 1835	1, 900	.....	.....	Captain Upham and his boat's crew were seized by the natives of the Friendly Islands; only released by giving up ship's cannon.
Atlantic	Feb. 5	....	....	....	.....	
South Atlantic	June 25	Feb. 27, 1832	....	....	.....	
Pacific Ocean	July 10	Apr. 23, 1833	1, 500	....	.....	
Tristan	July 30	Mar. 31, 1832	....	1, 200	.....	
Pacific Ocean	Aug. 2	July 17, 1834	2, 300	....	.....	
....do	Mar. 5	Aug. 2, 1833	1, 850	....	.....	Probably of Dartmouth. * See Dartmouth
South Atlantic	July 30	Apr. 21, 1832	....	1, 400	.....	

New Bedford all cleared at the New Bedford custom-house.

Table showing returns of whaling-vessels

Name of vessel.	Class.	Tonnage.	Captain.	Managing owner or agent.
1831.				
New Bedford, Mass.—Continued.				
George Porter	Ship	285	Clement Hammond	
Grand Turk	do	323	Stanton Burtch	
General Pike	do	313	William Adams	
Gratitude	do	336	—— Fisher	
Gideon Howland	do	378	Jireh Shearman, jr	
Hercules	do	334	Albert G. Goodwin	
Hesper	Bark	261	George F. Brown	Charles W. Morgan
Herald	Ship	303	Frederick Ricketson	
Hibernia	do	327	Henry Pease, 2d	
Hope	do	262	Benjamin Price	
Honqua	do	339	Valentine Pease, jr	
Isabella	do	410	Joseph Taber, jr	
Independence	do	318	Frederick A. Chase	
Isaac Howland	do	399	William Austin	J. & J. Howland
Iris	do	311	Edward W. Coffin	
Java	do	295	Henry Colt	
John Adams	do	268	Thomas B. Swain	
Lancaster	do	382	Obed N. Swift	Jireh Perry
Liverpool	do	305	Elihu Russell	
Mayflower	do	....	Isaac Swain	John C. Haskell
Mercator	do	246	Jonathan Fisher	
Magnolia	do	396	George B. Worth	Andrew Robeson
Mentor	Brig	89	Peleg Cornell	
Minerva	Ship	....	Joseph B. Leonard	
Maria Theresa	do	....	—— Fisher	
Midas	do	326	Alexander Waggoner	
Mentor	do	213	Edward C. Barnard	William R. Rodman
Mercury	do	339	William Swain	I. Howland, jr., & Co
Maria	do	202	Isaac G. Hedge	S. Rodman, jr
Nautilus	do	340	Hiram Weeks	
Nye	do	....	Isaiah Burgess	
Octavia	Bark	257	Granville Manter	
Phenix	Ship	323	Charles Stetson	J. A. Parker & Son
Parthian	Brig	119	Charles B. Hammond	A. & N. B. Gibbs
Pioneer	Bark	..	Benjamin Ellis	Coggeshall & Russell
Phocion	Ship	265	James C. Swain	
Persia	do	240	William Handy, jr	
Parker	do	406	Charles F. Brown	John A. Parker & Son
Pocahontas	Brig	141	Step. Howland, jr	
Richmond	Ship	291	John Tucker	I. Howland, jr., & Co
Russell	Bark	301	Shubael Worth	Benjamin Rodman
Robert Edwards	Ship	355	Edward Howland	
Rajah	Bark	249	Joseph Bennett, jr	
South Carolina	Ship	....	James Maxfield	
Two Brothers	do	288	Clement P. Covell	
Triton	do	300	Reuben Chase, 2d	
Tobacco Plant	do	270	Henry Tracy	
Trident	do	448	Peleg H. Stetson	J. A. Parker & Sons
Timoleon	do	340	Joshua Bunker	William T. Russell
William Rotch	do	289	Charles E. Waterman	
William & Eliza	do	321	Frederick H. Barnard	
Zephyr	do	361	David L. Adams	
Fairhaven, Mass.				
Albion	Ship	326	John E. Coggeshall	
Arab	Bark	276	Samuel Bunker	Alden D. Stoddard
Charles Drew	Ship	344	Robert F. Fosdick	Lemuel Tripp
Columbus	do	381	Gustavus A. Baylies	
Cadmus	do	320	Frederick C. Taber	Atkins Adams
Friendship	do	360	George R. Merchant	Gibbs & Jenney
Favorite	Bark	293	Bradford Hathaway	
Heroine	Ship	....	Benjamin R. C. Wilson	
Herald	do	262	Isaiah West	
Isabella	do	242	Ivory C. Albert	E. Sawin
Java	do	291	William Ritchie	

sailing from American ports—Continued.

Whaling-ground.	Date—		Result of voyage.			Remarks.
	Of sailing.	Of arrival.	Sperm-oil.	Whale-oil.	Whalebone.	
			Bbls.	*Bbls.*	*Lbs.*	
South Atlantic	Apr. 6	Feb. 28, 1832	80	1,800		
....do	Apr. 8	Mar. 13, 1832				
Tristan	Mar. 11	Mar. 7, 1832				
Pacific Ocean	Aug. 30	May 28, 1835				
....do	Nov. 9	Dec. 4, 1834	3,100			
South Atlantic	May 2	Feb. 25, 1832		2,500		
Pacific Ocean	May 9	Sept. 5, 1834	1,400			
South Atlantic	July 5	Mar. 3, 1832		1,000		
....do	July 9	Mar. 8, 1832		1,800		
....do	July 12	May 17, 1832				
Pacific Ocean	Dec. 13	May 11, 1835				Lost a man overboard, and in saving him lost second and third mates, two boat-steerers, and two men.
....do	Apr. 13	Apr. 29, 1835	1,300			
....do	Aug. 29	Apr. 27, 1835	100	1,750		
....do	Nov. 28	Jan. 25, 1835				
....do	Dec. 17	May 11, 1835	1,500			
South Atlantic	June 10	Mar. 14, 1832		1,900		
Pacific Ocean	Aug. 19	Apr. 6, 1835	900			
....do	June 18	May 27, 1834	2,200			
South Atlantic	Aug. 26	Feb. 10, 1833				
Pacific Ocean	May 2	July 13, 1834	2,000			
Tristan	May 31	Feb. 26, 1832	100	1,300		
Pacific Ocean	Jan. 1	June 15, 1834	3,400			
Bahamas	Mar. 28					Capsized in a squall in 1831; two men lost. The crew took to the boats and were picked up by a Kennebec vessel.
Tristan	July 4	Mar. 26, 1832	90	2,510		
Pacific Ocean	Oct. 27	Apr. 5, 1835	1,400			
South Atlantic	July 8	Mar. 8, 1832				
....do	July 20					Lost on Pelew Islands May 21, 1832; first mate and ten men lost.
Pacific Ocean	Aug. 28	Sept. 25, 1833	2,600			
....do	Aug. 25	May 11, 1834	800			
....do	July 29	July 28, 1834	2,600			
	Nov. 12					
Pacific Ocean	Aug. 14	Mar. 24, 1835	1,600			
....do	June 17	June 19, 1834	2,000			
Guinea	June 28	July 27, 1832	150			
Atlantic	Jan. 20	Mar. 15, 1832	200	1,500		
Brazil	Mar. 1	May 14, 1832	100	2,100		Captain Swain died January 3, 1832.
Pacific Ocean	July 29	Oct. 8, 1834	1,700			
....do	Oct. 6	Feb. 24, 1835	3,150			Built, 1831, at Fairhaven.
Africa	Oct. 12	Aug. 3, 1832				
Pacific Ocean	Aug. 13	Jan. 21, 1835	2,000			
....do	Nov. 9	July 20, 1834	2,300			
....do	Nov. 25	May 3, 1835	2,200			H. H. Howland, 3d mate, killed 1831.
....do	Dec. 19	May 11, 1834				
South Atlantic	July 12	Feb. 22, 1832		2,000		
....do	June 15	Feb. 7, 1832	65	2,035		
Pacific Ocean	June 17	Aug. 11, 1834	2,000			
South Atlantic	Feb. 5	Mar. 9, 1832		Full.		
Pacific Ocean	July 23	June 12, 1834	2,400			
....do	Dec. 17	July 5, 1835	1,700			
....do	Aug. 10	May 11, 1835	1,500	150		
....do	Nov. 22	Feb. 25, 1835				
South Atlantic	Mar. 3	Mar. 14, 1832	150	1,750		
East Cape	July 18	Feb. 12, 1832		2,000		
Pacific Ocean	Oct. 14	Dec. 17, 1834	1,343			
....do	Apr. 30	Aug. 21, 1834	2,044			
South Atlantic	June 1	Mar. 8, 1832		2,000		
Pacific Ocean	May 23	Apr. 1, 1834	2,313			
....do	Dec. 8	Apr, 29, 1835	1,889			Bought from Salem, 1831.
South Atlantic	July 30	Sept. 26, 1832	150	1,600		
....do	June 9	Feb. 27, 1832		Full.		
....do	July 20	Feb. 22, 1832				
Pacific Ocean	Dec. 2	July 15, 1834	2,000			
East Cape	June 10					

Table showing returns of whaling vessels

Name of vessel.	Class.	Tonnage.	Captain.	Managing owner or agent.
1831.				
Fairhaven, Mass.—Continued.				
Leonidas	Ship		John H. Pease	
Oregon	do	307	Nathan F. Delano	L. Tripp
Pindus	Bark	193	John C. Daggett	
South Boston	Ship		Sheffel Reed	
Nantucket, Mass.				
Alexander	Ship	421	Jonathan Swain, 2d	
Barclay	do	301	William Barney, jr	Griffin Barney
Baltic	do	410	William Chadwick	P. H. Folger
Columbus	do	344	Peter Coffin	Richard Mitchell
Constitution	do	318	Frederick Arthur	C. G. & H. Coffin
Catharine	do		Joseph M. Chase	Jared Coffin
Eagle	do	335	Joseph Pease	David Joy
Franklin	do	309	George Prince	
Fame	do	374	Seth Worth	
John Adams	do	296	Shubael Clark	Griffin Barney
Lima	do	286	Oliver P. Winslow	
Mary	do		David Paddack	
Mary Mitchell	do	354	Elihu Coffin	
Peru	do	257	William Brooks, jr	David Joy, jr
Pacific	do	314	William Plasket	Paul Mitchell
Phenix	do	323	Sanford Wilber	T. & P. Macy
President	do	293	Seth Cathcart	Joseph Starbuck
Rose	do	350	Obed Starbuck	do
Richard Mitchell	do	386	James Gwinn	P. Mitchell & Sons
Spartan	do	333	David U. Coffin	Daniel Jones
Swift	do	456	Barzillai Coffin	
Weymouth	do	329	Moses Harris	
Stonington, Conn.				
Charles Adams	Ship		—— Palmer	
Courier	Schooner		—— Barnard	
Francis	Ship		—— Brewster	
Edenton, N. C.				
Robert	Sloop			
Provincetown, Mass.				
Fair Play	Schooner			
Dartmouth, Mass.				
Forrester	Bark		Charles B. Ray	Sears & Howland
Westport, Mass.				
Elizabeth	Bark		Peter Hussey, 3d	
Industry	Brig		—— Soule	
Mexico	do	130	Job Davis	
Thomas Winslow	do	135	Samuel Lake	
Rochester, Mass.				
Dryade	Bark		Nathaniel C. Carey	
Franklin	do	251	Priam P. Brock	
Lexington	Schooner		—— Daggett	
Laurel	do		—— Taber	Gideon Barstow
Providence, R. I.				
Olive Branch	Ship		—— Cook	
Lynn, Mass.				
Atlas	Ship	242	S. H. Gardner	Hezekiah Chase
Louisa	do	382	I. Townsend	do

sailing from American ports—Continued.

Whaling-ground.	Date— Of sailing.	Of arrival.	Result of voyage. Sperm-oil.	Whale-oil.	Whalebone.	Remarks.
			Bbls.	*Bbls.*	*Lbs.*	
South Atlantic	July 6	Feb. 27, 1832		1,700		
Pacific Ocean	Dec. 20	July 10, 1834	2,000			
South Atlantic	June 15	Mar. 28, 1832		1,200		
....do	July 16	Feb. 12, 1832		2,000		
Pacific Ocean	Oct. 20	Sept. —, 1834	1,416			Sold to New Bedford.
South Atlantic	July 1	May 8, 1832		1,390		
Pacific Ocean	Sept. 20	Apr. 29, 1835	2,322			
Atlantic	May 26	Mar. 26, 1832	15	1,896		
....do	June 9	Apr. 11, 1832	131	1,492		
Pacific Ocean	July 21	Jan. 17, 1835	2,690			Built at Mattapoisett 1832.
Atlantic	July 20	Mar. 30, 1832	90	1,510		
Pacific Ocean	June 27					Captain Prince, the mate, and five men died of scurvy; Matthew Clark, a boat-steerer, took command Lost on the coast of Brazil. Saved 400 barrels sperm.
Atlantic	July 24	Apr. 22, 1832	74	1,731		Third mate, F. W. Ramsdell, drowned by a foul line, 1831.
Pacific Ocean	June 9	Apr. 22, 1832	105	1,148		
....do	May 21	May 11, 1834	1,637			
....do	July 20	Mar. 21, 1835	2,612	19		Built, 1831, at Rochester.
....do	July 25	Jan. 22, 1835	1,897			Third mate died of scurvy, 1834.
Atlantic	May 26	Mar. 27, 1832	109	1,405		
....do	Aug. 17	May 8, 1832	107	1,588		
Pacific Ocean	Oct. 10	Jan. —, 1834	2,205			
....do	Nov. 20	Apr. 14, 1834	1,630			
....do						Stranded on the bar going out; got off and taken into the harbor July 31, 1832; refitted and sailed 1833.
....do	Nov. 12	Nov. 16, 1834	1,950			
....do	Dec. 4	Dec. 31, 1834	2,140			
....do	Aug. 3	Oct. 28, 1834	1,868			
....do	Sept. 30	Feb. 15, 1835	1,552			Broken up at Nantucket, 1835.
South Atlantic	Sept. 1					
....do	Sept. 1					Tender to C. Adams.
Brazil	July 6					
Atlantic	Apr. 19	— —, 1831				Took one large whale.
						Reported with 130 sperm.
Pacific Ocean	Mar. 5	Aug. 2, 1833	1,850			
Brazil	July 2	Apr. 24, 1832		1,200		
Cape de Verdes		Nov. 4, 1831	220			
....do	Apr. 5	Nov. 1, 1831				
Cape Good Hope	Aug. 30					
South Atlantic	July 13	Mar. 28, 1832		1,550		
....do	July 20	Apr. 23, 1832		1,400		
Atlantic		July 15, 1831	20			
....do		Aug. 4, 1831	90	40		
Cape de Verdes		Nov. 3, 1831	140			Credited to Providence, R. I., but probably belongs to Provincetown, Mass.
South Atlantic	May 25	1831 or 1832				
....do	June 23	Feb. 25, 1832		1,200		

Table showing returns of whaling-vessels

Name of vessel.	Class.	Tonnage.	Captain.	Managing owner or agent.
1831.				
Falmouth, Mass.				
Brunette	Bark	200	—— Cottle	Elijah Swift
Pocahontas	Ship	350	Joseph Swift	do
Uncas	do	400	Henry C. Bunker	do
Newport, R. I.				
John Coggeshall	Ship		S. W. Macy	Bush & Clarke
Boston, Mass.				
Jasper	Ship	359	B. S. Adams	Atkins Adams
Bristol, R. I.				
America	Ship		—— Grinnell	
Ann	do		—— Lambert	
Essex	do		—— Mayhew	
Gov. Fenner	do		—— Swain	W. E. Norris
New London, Conn.				
Com. Perry	Ship	270	—— Hobron	
Chelsea	do		—— Davis	
Caledonia	do		—— Smith	
Connecticut	do	390	Paul Burgess	
Electra	do	348	—— Caverly	
Flora	do	338	—— Allen	
Julius Cæsar	do		—— Smith	
Jones	do	338	—— Fish	
Mentor	do		—— Flanders	
Neptune	do	285	do	
Do	Schooner		Richards	
Stonington	Ship	351		
Wabash	do	250	—— Sayer	
The Jason, Captain Coit, (E. M. Frink & Co.,) arrived May 31, 1835, from Pacific Ocean, full. Probably sailed 1831-'32.				
Sag Harbor, N. Y.				
Acasta	Ship		—— Allen	
Arabella	do	366	—— Pearson	
Argonaut	do			
Columbia	do	285	—— Hand	
Cadmus	do	310	—— Howell	
Hannibal	do	309		
Henry	do	333		
Marcus	do	283	—— Greene	
Neptune	do			
Nimrod	do			
Potosi	do		—— Griffin	
Phenix	do		—— Greene	
Thames	do		—— Hand	
Thorn	do		—— Howell	
Telegraph	do		—— Sayer	
Triad	do		N. Case	H. & N. Corwin
Xenophon	do		—— Griffin	
Warren, R. I.				
Benjamin Rush	Ship	384		Child & Driscol
Magnet	do		—— Brown	Joseph Smith
Miles	do		—— Champlin	
Rosalie	do		—— Stillwell	
Warren	do		—— Mayhew	J. Smith, jr
Salem, Mass.				
Izette	Bark		—— Hoit	

sailing from American ports—Continued.

Whaling-ground.	Date— Of sailing.	Of arrival.	Result of voyage. Sperm-oil.	Whale-oil.	Whalebone.	Remarks.
			Bbls.	*Bbls.*	*Lbs.*	
Pacific Ocean	Jan. —	Mar. 20, 1834	800			
....do	July 10	Apr. 23, 1835	1,700			
....do	Nov. 9	—— —, 1835	2,900			
....do		Mar. 29, 1835	1,500			Built 1834.
South Atlantic	June 29					
South Atlantic		Mar. 23, 1832		1,900	15,800	
Tristan	Aug. 19	June 8, 1832		1,050		
....do	Aug. 7					
Pacific Ocean	Jan. —	Apr. 3, 1834	1,800			
	June 20					
Pacific Ocean	June 20	Sept. 5, 1834	2,150			
....do	May —	June 16, 1835	2,800			
....do						Captain Burgess killed while fast to a whale, September, 1831.
	June 20					
East Cape	Apr. —	Feb. 21, 1832	50	2,300	20,000	
South Atlantic		Feb. 6, 1832	300	2,000		
	May 23					
South Atlantic		Mar. 13, 1832	100	1,200		
....do	Apr. –	Dec. —, 1832		Full		
	May 25					
Brazil		Apr. 8, 1832		2,000		
	June 23	Mar. 26, 1832		1,800		
South Atlantic	July 24					
Pacific Ocean		Apr. 28, 1833	2,800			
South Atlantic		Mar. 21, 1832		2,000		
Brazil	July 30					
South Atlantic		Mar. 3, 1832		Full		
....do	May 23	Feb. 24, 1832		1,950		
Brazil	July 30	Apr. 1, 1832		2,300		
....do	July 30	Feb. 21, 1832		1,800	16,000	
Africa		Apr. 1, 1832		2,450		
South Atlantic		Feb. 24, 1832				
Brazil	Aug. 13					Belonged to Greenport; lost at Falklands, March, 1832. Had 1,400 whale; saved 800.
....do	July 30	Apr. 1, 1832		2,500		
South Atlantic		Mar. 3, 1832		2,000		
Brazil	July 9	Mar. 27, 1832		1,950		
Pacific Ocean		June 19, 1834	2,900			
Brazil	July 30	June 8, 1832		3,000		Belonged to Greenport.
Pacific Ocean		Oct. 17, 1834				
Tristan		Jan. 3, 1833	400	2,000		Formerly in Canton trade; built at Philadelphia, 1814.
Pacific Ocean	Sept. 3	Feb. 20, 1835	1,700			
Tristan	June 2	Apr. 2, 1832	150	1,200		
Pacific Ocean	June 2	Sept. 6, 1834	1,750			
....do		June 12, 1834	2,300			
South Atlantic	Mar. 13	Mar. 24, 1832	100	1,500		Built at Newmarket, N. H.

Table showing returns of whaling-vessels

Name of vessel.	Class.	Tonnage.	Captain.	Managing owner or agent.
1831.				
Hudson, N. Y.				
Alexander Mansfield	Ship		—— Neils	
Henry Astor	do		—— Rawson	
Martha	do			
Washington	do		—— Barrett	
Edgartown, Mass.				
George and Martha	Ship		—— Lawrence	
Loan	do		—— Luce	
Meridian	do		—— Fisher	
Robert	Sloop		—— Osborne	
1832.				
New Bedford, Mass.				
Amanda	Bark	217	Latham Cross, jr	
Ann Alexander	Ship	253	James Shepherd	George Howland
Amethyst	do	359	Jonathan Fisher	John A. Parker & Son
Bramin	Bark	245	Herman N. Stuart	Gideon Allen
Brandt	Ship	310	Francis Neil	
Com. Decatur	do	247	Seth D. Fisher	N. Leonard & Co
Coral	do	370	William Whitten, jr	Gideon Allen
China	do	370	Russell Maxfield	
Cambria	do	362	George Crocker	William T. Russell
Columbus	do	313	Tristram D. Pease	William R. Rodman
Ceres	do	328	Elihu Gifford	do
Courier	do	293	Thomas Severance	A. & N. B. Gibbs
Do	do	381	William B. Cash	
Chili	do	291	David Collins	
Condor	do	349	Richard G. Luce	Charles W. Morgan
Endeavour	do	234	Edward Soule	
Eagle	do	336	Jonathan Nye	T. & A. R. Nye
Emerald	do	359	Clement Norton	T. Riddell
Francis	do	367	John Briggs	
Falcon	do	273	Joseph Barker	
Frances	do	348	Obed Alley	William R. Rotch & Co
George and Martha	Bark	275	Francis Sayer	
Grand Turk	Ship	324	Abraham T. Eddy	
Gen. Pike	do	313	William Adams	Oliver Crocker
George Porter	do	285	Clement Hammond	T. Riddell
Golconda	do	330	Joseph Covell	George Howland
George	do		Nehemiah West	
Hercules	do	290	Peter F. Chase	D. R. Greene
Hydaspe	do	313	Owen Hillman	
Hector	do	380	John C. Morse	
Hope	do	282	Benjamin Price	
Herald	do	274	Frederick Ricketson	
Hercules	do	334	Albert G. Goodwin	
Huntress	do	391	Francis Post	Alfred Gibbs & Co
Hibernia	do	327	Henry Pease, 2d	
Hope	do	316	Charles G. Smith	George Howland
Java	do	295	Henry Colt	do
John	do	308	Andrew Almy	
John Howland	do	376	Jonathan Haffards	
London Packet	do	280	Howes Norris	
Milton	do	387	John A. Howland	
Milwood	do	254	Charles H. Taber	Gideon Allen
Mercator	do	246	Anson Churchill	J. A. Parker & Son
Midas	do	326	Alexander Waggoner	
Messenger	do	277	Peter Hussey	
Mary Ann	Brig	171	Joseph Crocker	William P. Grinnell
Mercury	Ship	339	Joseph B. Leonard	
Mary	do		Richard Weeden	
Norfolk	do	275	John H. Pease	J. A. Parker & Son
Nye	do	211	Ezra Smith	T. & A. R. Nye
Ospray	Bark	169	William Calder	
Orozimbo	Ship	588	Caleb Kempton	
Pioneer	Bark	231	Benjamin Ellis	

sailing from American ports—Continued.

Whaling-ground.	Date—		Result of voyage.			Remarks
	Of sailing.	Of arrival.	Sperm-oil.	Whale-oil.	Whalebone.	
			Bbls.	*Bbls.*	*Lbs.*	
South Atlantic	June 20	Feb. 26, 1832		2,000		
Pacific Ocean		Jan. 18, 1835	2,200			Built at New York, 1820.
	Nov. 25					
Pacific Ocean	May 16	Jan. —, 1834				
....do		Apr. 28, 1835	3,100			
....do	Apr. 23	May 25, 1834	Full			
....do		June 18, 1834	2,800			
Atlantic		June 16, 1831	35			
South Atlantic	Apr. 25					Condemned at Mahe, 1834; had 600 sperm.
Pacific Ocean	Aug. 2	Dec. 24, 1835	1,880	17		
....do	Sept. 6	Dec. 24, 1835	1,835			Captain Fisher died 1834.
South Atlantic	Apr. 10	Feb. 4, 1834		2,000		
....do	May 26	Apr. 14, 1833		1,450		
....do	May 16	Mar. 7, 1833		1,350		
Pacific Ocean	May 26	May 31, 1835	2,450			Second mate lost overboard, 1832.
South Atlantic	May 30	Apr. 29, 1833	90	2,100		
Pacific Ocean	June 2	Oct. 3, 1835	1,904			
South Atlantic	Apr. 18	Sept. 21, 1835	1,625			
....do	Aug. 3	Jan. 27, 1833	800	2,200	22,000	
....do	June 17	Apr. 7, 1833	70	1,830		
Pacific Ocean	June 30					
South Atlantic	July 3	May 6, 1833		1,500		
....do	July 14	May 27, 1833	70	2,100		
....do	May 23	Mar. 22, 1833		1,200		
....do	June 18	Feb. 10, 1833		2,200		
....do	July 5	Mar. 12, 1833		1,200		
....do	June 23	Apr. 22, 1833		2,000		
....do	July 18	Apr. 22, 1833		1,800		
Pacific Ocean	Dec. 2	Oct. 19, 1835	2,500			
South Atlantic	May 19					
....do	June 2	Jan. 19, 1834				
....do	June 17	Mar. 14, 1834				Davis Luce, second mate, died 1832.
....do	July 25	Mar. 13, 1833				
Pacific Ocean	Dec. 1	Nov. 5, 1835				
....do	Dec. 17	Dec. 28, 1835	2,300			Belongs to Dartmouth; brought from Providence, 1831.
South Atlantic	Apr. 26	May 6, 1833				Second mate died, 1832.
Tristan	June 12	Apr. 14, 1833				
Pacific Ocean	June 24	Oct. 2, 1834	2,500			
South Atlantic	July 2	Apr. 29, 1833		1,700		
....do	July 9	May 19, 1833	170	1,030		
....do	July 14	May 7, 1833				
Pacific Ocean	Aug. 13	Mar. 13, 1836	1,538			
South Atlantic	Aug. 14	June 17, 1833				
Pacific Ocean	Sept. 16	July 24, 1835	2,712			
South Atlantic	June 21	Apr. 28, 1833	90	2,000		
....do	June 26	May 9, 1833				
Pacific Ocean	Dec. 2	July 3, 1836	1,400			Owen Cottle died from injuries caused by a whale, 1833.
....do	Nov. 24	Aug. 31, 1835				
....do	May 2	July 24, 1835	1,300	100		
South Atlantic	May 3	Apr. 2, 1833	20	1,180		Returned with crew sick with scurvy.
....do	May 16	Mar. 18, 1833		850		Returned leaking 500 strokes per hour.
....do	May 26	Mar. 29, 1833		2,100		
Pacific Ocean	June 23	July 17, 1835	1,200			
South Atlantic	July 2	Aug. 6, 1833	500			
....do	July 16					
Pacific Ocean	Dec. 1					Lost on Juan Fernandez, 1833.
South Atlantic	July 13	May 13, 1833		1,400		
Pacific Ocean	Nov. 23	Mar. 7, 1836	1,250			
....do	May 3	Apr. 22, 1835				
South Atlantic	July 17	Jan. 2, 1833	400	700		
....do	May 22	May 12, 1833	150	1,050		

Table showing returns of whaling-vessels

Name of vessel.	Class.	Tonnage.	Captain.	Managing owner or agent.
1832.				
New Bedford, Mass.—Continued.				
Phocion	Ship	265	Joseph Spooner	
Parthian	Brig	119	Lemuel Drew	
Pocahontas	...do	141	Peter M. Coffin	
Quito	...do	138	James Maxfield	
Rousseau	Ship	305	Walter Hillman	
Rebecca Sims	...do	400	Barna Coffin	William R. Rodman
Sally Anne	...do	312	William H. Cox	
Stephania	...do	315	Elisha Dexter	
South Carolina	...do	302	Edmund Maxfield	
Tobacco Plant	...do	270	Henry Tracy	
Two Brothers	...do	288	Clement P. Covell	
Victory	...do	268	Matthew Mayhew	
Zephyr	...do	361	James B. Wood	
Fairhaven, Mass.				
Amazon	Ship	....	Arthur Cox	Sawin & Church
Albion	...do	....	John E. Coggeshall	E. Sawin
Charles Drew	...do	....	——— Fosdick	
Columbus	...do	....	David Osborn	Gibbs & Jenney
Herald	...do	....	Isaiah West	
Heroine	...do	....	Benj. R. C. Wilson	N. Church
Java	...do	291	William Ritchie	Atkins Adams
Jasper	...do	....	Barz. T. Adams	
Leonidas	...do	....	Charles Fisher	Jenney & Tripp
Maine	...do	....	Jared Worth	E. Sawin
Marcia	...do	....	Peter Butler, jr	
Oscar	...do	....	Charles Downs	E. Sawin
Pindus	Bark	....	Prince Russell	
Pactolus	Ship	....	——— Grinnell	I. F. & J. Terry
South Boston	...do	....	——— Read	E. Sawin
Nantucket, Mass.				
Alexander Coffin	Ship	381	David Baker	
Atlantic	...do	321	Elihu Fisher	P. & B. Gardner
Barclay	...do	301	William Barney, jr	Griffin Barney
Congress	...do	339	Charles Abrahams	
Constitution	...do	318	James G. Coffin	C. G. & H. Coffin
Columbus	...do	344	Reuben Russell, 2d	Paul Mitchell & Sons
Charles Carroll	...do	376	Owen Chase	
Charles and Henry	...do	336	George Joy	C. G. & H. Coffin
Cyrus	...do	328	Benj. R. Hussey	
Eagle	...do	335	Charles Smith	David Joy
Enterprise	...do	413	John Stetson	
Franklin	...do	246	Joshua Coffin, 2d	
Factor	Schooner	....	——— Macy	
Fame	Ship	374	Seth Worth	Philip H. Folger
Ganges	...do	265	Russell S. Bodfish	W. H. & G. L. Gardner
George	...do	359	John C. Congdon	S. & J. Mitchell
Hazard	Sloop	....	——— Swain	
Harvest	Ship	360	Alex'r Pollard	Samuel B. Folger
Howard	...do	364	William Worth, 2d	T. Hussey & Son
John Adams	...do	296	Shubael Clark	Griffin Barney
Japan	...do	332	William Plaskett	James Athearn
Kingston	...do	312	William E. Sherman	Frederick Hussey & Co.
Lexington	Schooner	....	——— Cash	
Loper	Ship	316	John Cotton	
Mariner	...do	349	Eben Coleman	
Mount Vernon	...do	384	Edwin Coffin	
Maria	...do	365	Alexander Macy	
Ocean	...do	349	Elijah Parker	T. & P. Macy
Orbit	...do	351	John J. Gardner	
Ontario	...do	354	Edwin Barnard	
Peruvian	...do	334	Benj. Coggeshall	C. Mitchell & Co.
Planter	...do	340	Reuben Manter	Gilbert Coffin

sailing from American ports—Continued.

Whaling-ground.	Date— Of sailing.	Of arrival.	Result of voyage. Sperm-oil.	Whale-oil.	Whalebone.	Remarks.
			Bbls.	*Bbls.*	*Lbs.*	
South Atlantic.	June 25	Mar. 22, 1833		1,400		
....do	Aug. 26	Aug. 7, 1834				
....do	Sept. 8	May 22, 1833	180			
Cape de Verdes	Aug. 13					Sold part of her cargo at St. Michaels.
South Atlantic.	July 3	Jan. 26, 1834				
Pacific Ocean.	Aug. 26	Dec. 9, 1835	2,300			
....do	May 24	May 22, 1833		1,650		
....do	June 28	July 18, 1835	1,500			
South Atlantic.	July 23	Mar. 24, 1833				
....do	June 16	Apr. 11, 1834	700	1,000		
....do	June 30	Mar. 22, 1832		1,900		
....do	June 17	Aug. 3, 1835	1,800			
South Atlantic	June 17	Sept. 19, 1833				Full; 350 sperm.
South Atlantic.	July 12	Mar. 20, 1833	200	2,100		
....do	June 20	Mar. 17, 1833		1,600		
Pacific Ocean..	Apr. —	Aug. 22, 1834	2,200			
South Atlantic.	Aug. 5	Mar. 7, 1833	360	2,000	20,000	
....do	June 4	Apr. 14, 1833		1,300		
....do	July 21	Mar. 14, 1833	100	900		
Atlantic	June 15	Apr. 22, 1833	350	1,550		
South Atlantic.	July 1					
....do	June 6	Mar. 12, 1833	40	2,060		
....do	May 13	Jan. 19, 1834		1,050		
....do	July 3	Apr. 29, 1833	75	2,000		
Pacific Ocean..	Nov. 24	Mar. 7, 1836	2,250			
South Atlantic.	June 20					
Pacific Ocean..		Dec. 29, 1835	1,000			
South Atlantic.		Feb. 14, 1833	408	2,400		
Pacific Ocean..	Dec. 25	May 19, 1836	1,946			Built 1832.
....do	Oct. 9	Sept. 14, 1835	1,845			
....do	Sept. 3	July 21, 1835	1,006	4		
....do	Jan. 13	Apr. 29, 1835	988			
Indian Ocean..	June 29	Apr. 21, 1833		1,230		
Atlantic	July 7	May 21, 1834		900		
Pacific Ocean..	Oct. 10	Mar. 3, 1836	2,610			Built 1832 at Nantucket.
....do	Nov. 25	July 7, 1836	2,546			Built 1832.
....do	Oct. 3	Apr. 21, 1836	1,810			
Atlantic	July 8	May 7, 1833	203	723		
Pacific Ocean..	Dec. 30	June 12, 1836	1,896			Captain Stetson left the ship and came home sick.
Atlantic	May 8	Apr. 12, 1834	921			
Nant. Shoals		Sept. 29, 1832				Schooner Factor made two cruises; returned September 12 with 9 blackfish, and again September 29 with a large (humpback?) whale.
Atlantic	June 10	Mar. 20, 1833		910		
Pacific Ocean..	June 5	Aug. 24, 1835	1,467			
Atlantic	July 31	May 7, 1834		2,100		
Gulf of Mexico.	Nov. 22	July 17, 1833	90			
Pacific Ocean..	June 11	Dec. 21, 1835	2,280			
....do	Sept. 22	May 11, 1835	2,070			First mate, Ammiel Joy, died on the voyage.
Atlantic	July 6	Mar. 14, 1833	224	1,456		
Indian Ocean..	June 17	May 6, 1834	632	678		
Pacific Ocean..	Oct. 19	Oct. 3, 1835	484			
South Atlantic.		Sept. 6, 1833	130			
Pacific Ocean..	Nov. 25					Sunk at sea 1835, homeward bound, with 1,800 sperm.
....do	Aug. 12	—— —, 1836	2,429			Built 1832 at Rochester.
....do	Sept. 15	July 25, 1835	3,071			Built 1332 at Mattapoisett.
....do	Oct. 10	Mar. 11, 1836	1,665			
....do	June 16	Nov. 13, 1835	1,490			
....do	Aug. 3	Feb. 9, 1836	2,011	783		Built 1832.
....do	Dec. 1	Aug. 4, 1836	1,345			
....do	June 10	Sept. 28, 1835	1,854			
....do	June 11	July —, 1834	909	996		

Table showing returns of whaling-vessels

Name of vessel.	Class.	Tonnage.	Captain.	Managing owner or agent.
1832.				
Nantucket, Mass.—Continued.				
Pacific	Ship	314	Joseph Congdon	Paul Mitchell & Sons
Peru	Bark	257	William Brooks, jr	David Joy
Rambler	Ship	318	Thomas Derrick	Aaron Mitchell
Reaper	do	338	Tristram P. Swain	Jared Coffin
Thule	do	285	Josiah Smith	
Washington	do	308	Thomas W. Hussey	
Young Eagle	do	377	Benj. A. Coleman	Simeon Starbuck
Zenas Coffin	do	338	John B. Coleman	C. G. & H. Coffin
Westport, Mass.				
Elizabeth	Bark		Ray G. Sanford	
Industry	Brig		—— Soule	
Mexico	do		—— Davis	
Falmouth, Mass.				
Bartholomew Gosnold	Ship	360	John C. Daggett	Ward M. Parker
Hobomok	do	412	—— Barnard	Elijah Swift
Fall River, Mass.				
Edward Quesnal	Ship		—— Barnard	John Eddy
Gold Hunter	do		—— Brock	
Wareham, Mass.				
George Washington	Ship	373	George Gibbs	Nye & Thompson
Edgartown, Mass.				
Vineyard	Ship		—— Tobey	G. Norton
Rochester, Mass.				
Dryade	Bark		George H. Richmond	
Franklin	do		Priam P. Brock	
Gideon Barstow	Ship	379	Nathaniel C. Carey	Gideon Barstow & Son
Laurel	Schooner		—— Mayhew	
Orion	Brig			
Salem, Mass.				
Bengal	Ship		—— Russell	
Catharine	do		—— Paddock	
Izette	do		—— Kempton	
Pallas	Bark		—— Archer	
Lynn, Mass.				
Atlas	Ship	260	—— Wooley	H. Chase & Co
Louisa	do	383	—— Gardner	do
Portsmouth, N. H.				
Ann Parry	Ship	348	—— Ray	James Kennard
Pocahontas	do		—— Barnard	
Bristol, R. I.				
Ann	Ship		—— Littlefield	
America	Bark		—— Chase	
Balæna	Ship	321	—— Daggett	W. H. DeWolf
Bowditch	do	398	—— Gardner	William R. Taylor
Canton Packet	do	312	—— Bradford	Fitz Henry Homer
Corinthian	do	503	—— Grinnell	W. H. DeWolf
Essex	do	200	—— Wilcox	William R. Taylor
General Jackson	do	329	—— Smith	William H. De Wolf
Ganges	do	380	—— Clark	do
Newport, R. I.				
Erie	Ship		A. W. Dennis	Engs & Bush

sailing from American ports—Continued.

Whaling-ground.	Date— Of sailing.	Of arrival.	Result of voyage. Sperm-oil.	Whale-oil.	Whalebone.	Remarks.
			Bbls.	*Bbls.*	*Lbs.*	
Indian Ocean	June 28	Apr. 1, 1834		1,450		
Atlantic	July 28	May 22, 1833	126	722		
Pacific Ocean	June 17	Apr. 3, 1835	1,697			
do	Sept. 5	Mar. 18, 1835	1,950	48		
do	Dec. 21	May 30, 1835	270			Added 1832; formerly a merchantman; Captain Smith left at Talcahuano.
do	Nov. 5	Dec. 30, 1835	1,538			
do	July 11	Oct. 18, 1835	2,625			Built 1832 at Rochester.
do	June 24	Oct. 21, 1835	1,720			
Pacific Ocean	June 20	July 27, 1835	900			
Atlantic		Oct. 19, 1832	130			
Cape de Verdes		Nov. 2, 1832	450			
Pacific Ocean	Nov. 29	Aug. 5, 1836	2,200			Built at Falmouth 1832.
do	Dec. 24	July 6, 1836	1,700			Built 1832.
Pacific Ocean		Nov. 13, 1835	2,000			
Brazil	June 23	—— —, 1833				
Pacific Ocean	Oct. 31	Oct. 19, 1835	2,950			Built 1832.
Pacific Ocean	Sept. 15	Mar. 24, 1836	2,100			
South Atlantic	May 3	Mar. 22, 1833		1,300		
do	May 31	May 12, 1833		700		Captain Brock and his boat's crew were lost while fast to a whale, September 23 1832.
Pacific Ocean	Aug. 16	Dec. 29, 1835	2,100			
Atlantic		Oct. 22, 1832	230			
	July —					
Pacific Ocean	Mar. 24					
do	Mar. 24					
South Atlantic	June 9					
Pacific Ocean	July 21					
South Atlantic	June 8	Apr. 12, 1833		800	5,000	
do	July —	Apr. 21, 1833		1,000		
Pacific Ocean	Dec. 31	Sept. 9, 1836	1,900			
do		Apr. 26, 1836	1,050			
South Atlantic		May 3, 1833		1,000	10,000	
Pacific Ocean	July 25					
South Atlantic		July 27, 1833		2,600		
Pacific Ocean	Aug. 2	Nov. 18, 1835	2,600			
do	Nov. 16	Dec. 28, 1835	1,600			
do	Dec. 14	June 9, 1836	1,200			
South Atlantic	June 29	Mar. —, 1833		900		
Pacific Ocean	June 29	Octr 11, 1835	1,400			
do	Mar. 17	July 30, 1835	2,700			
New Zealand	Apr. —	June 11, 1835	200	1,800		Sailed under command of Capt. F. Spooner, who left her at New Zealand.

Table showing returns of whaling-vessels

Name of vessel.	Class.	Tonnage.	Captain.	Managing owner or agent.
1832.				
Warren, R. I.				
Atlantic	Ship		—— Pickens	
Chariot	do		—— Luther	N. M. Wheaton
Miles	do		—— Champlin	
North America	do		—— Borden	
New London, Conn.				
Ann Maria	Ship			
Armata	do	414	—— Butler	Abner Bassett
Betsy	Brig			
Boston	Ship		—— Sayer	
Com. Perry	do	270	—— Hobron	
Connecticut	do	390	—— Tate	
Electra	do	348	—— Chester	
Flora	do	338	—— Allen	
Georgia	do		—— Brewster	
Jones	do		—— Fisher	
Julius Cæsar	do		—— Hebron	N. & W. W. Billings
Montgomery	Schooner		—— Cliff	E. M. Frink & Co
McDonough	Ship			
Manchester Packet	do		—— Read	
Mentor	do		—— Rice	
Neptune	do		—— Middleton	
North America	do		—— Richards	
Palladium	do		—— Wood	
Tuscarora	do		—— Smith	
Wabash	do		—— Fuller	
Sag Harbor, N. Y.				
Acasta	Ship		—— Harris	
American	do	282	—— Jones	
Ann	do		—— Howell	
Cadmus	do	310		
Columbia	do	285	—— Hand	
Franklin	do		—— Fordham	
Gov. Clinton	do		—— Rogers	
Hannibal	do	309	—— Parker	
Marcus	do	283	—— Cartwright	
Nimrod	do		—— Halsey	
Neptune	do		—— Cooper	S. & B. Huntting & Co
Phenix	do		—— Cooper	
Thorn	do	299	—— Havens	
Washington	do		—— Loper	
Greenport, N. Y.				
Delta	Ship		Isaac Sayer	H. & N. Corwin
Hudson, N. Y.				
Alexander Mansfield	Ship	320	—— Taber	Barnard, Curtis & Co
America	do	464		do
Beaver	do		—— Gardner	
Huron	do	290	B. Lawrence	Robert A. Barnard
Boston, Mass.				
Wave	Brig	124	E. Tillson	Lombard & Whitmore
Stonington, Conn.				
Acasta	Ship		—— Allen	C. B. Williams
Charles Adams	do		A. Palmer	
Frances	do		—— Pendleton	
Uxor	Brig		—— Burrows	
Mystic, Conn.				
Bingham	Ship		—— Churchill	
New York, N. Y.				
Martha	Ship		William H. Young	
Mobile	do		—— Rawson	

NOTE.—The Helvetius, Brewster, of New London, is reported, in 1835, as stranded

sailing from American ports—Continued.

Whaling-ground.	Date— Of sailing.	Date— Of arrival.	Result of voyage. Sperm-oil.	Result of voyage. Whale-oil.	Result of voyage. Whalebone.	Remarks.
			Bbls.	*Bbls.*	*Lbs.*	
South Atlantic.	June 26					
Pacific Ocean	Oct. —	Oct. 19, 1835	1,400			
South Atlantic.	June 3	Apr. 11, 1833		1,450		
do	June 8	Apr. 14, 1833		1,420		
South Atlantic.		Apr. 10, 1833		2,100		
Pacific Ocean	Aug. 13	Dec. 22, 1835	2,400			
South Atlantic.						
do	July 20	Feb. —, 1833		1,900	16,000	Of Norwich, probably.
do		Mar. 31, 1833	90	1,410		
do		Mar. 31, 1833	180	1,320		
do		Mar. 23, 1833		1,800		
do	July —	Feb. 27, 1833		2,200		
do		Feb. 28, 1833	400	1,900		
East Cape		Apr. 15, 1833		1,700		
South Atlantic.		Feb. 13, 1833		2,300		
do		Sept. —, ——				
	Sept. 12					
South Atlantic.		Oct. 3, 1833	230	1,436		
Pacific Ocean		Aug. 15, 1836				Mentor took out several missionaries.
	Apr. 26	Apr. 19, 1834	100	1,800		
Pacific Ocean		May 30, 1835	1,200	100		
East Cape		Feb. 6, 1833		Full.		
South Atlantic.		Mar. 5, 1833	700	2,200		
do	June 20	Apr. 11, 1833		1,600		
South Atlantic.	June 12	May 13, 1833	250	1,350		
do	June —	May 23, 1833		1,100		
do	Nov. 28					
do	June 12	Apr. 15, 1833		1,150		
do	June —	Apr. 14, 1833		2,300		
do		Apr. 2, 1833	170	2,130		
do		Apr. 28, 1833		1,600		
do		May 14, 1833	250	1,650		
do		May 13, 1833		1,600		
do	June 12	Apr. 27, 1833		1,400		
East Cape	June —	Apr. 28, 1833	60	2,100	18,500	
	June —					
South Atlantic.		May 30, 1833	110	1,640		
do	Nov. 24					
South Atlantic.	June —	Apr. 15, 1833		1,400		
South Atlantic.	June 5	Apr. 22, 1833	120	1,480		
do		Apr. 23, 1833				
Pacific Ocean		Aug. 3, 1836	1,900			
do	June 7	May 1, 1836	1,250			
Atlantic	Mar. 28	Jan. —, 1833	300			
South Atlantic.		Feb. 19, 1833				Full, (200 sperm.)
do		Sept. 2, 1833	100	2,200		
do		Sept. 2, 1833	100	2,300		
do		Sept. 2, 1833				
South Atlantic.		Feb. 21, 1833		550		Returned leaking 500 strokes per hour.
South Atlantic.		Mar. 18, 1833		2,200	18,900	
Pacific Ocean		Mar. 5, 1836	1,450			

at Woahoo with 1,450 sperm, (900 saved.) If so, she probably sailed 1832.

Table showing returns of whaling-vessels

Name of vessel.	Class.	Tonnage.	Captain.	Managing owner or agent.
1832.				
Newburgh, N. Y.				
Portland	Ship	....	—— Cook	Newburgh Whaling Co.
Plymouth, Mass.				
Levant	Ship	....	—— Russell	
Salem, Mass.				
Bengal	Ship	....	—— Russell	
Poughkeepsie, N. Y.				
Vermont	Bark	....	—— Davis	Poughkeepsie Whal. Co.
Lynn, Mass.				
Atlas	Ship	260	I. Woolley	Hezekiah Chase
Clay	do	299	I. Townsend	do
Louisa	do	382	T. H. Gardner	do
Falmouth, Mass.				
Bartholemew Gosnold	Ship	356	—— Daggett	Ward M. Parker
1833.				
New Bedford, Mass.				
Adeline	Ship	329	—— Buckley	I. Howland, jr., & Co
Brandt	do	310	James Maxfield	Alexander Gibbs
Benezet	Bark	192	Charles Pitman, jr	C. W. Morgan
Com. Rogers	Ship	298	Asaph Taber	T. & A. R. Nye
Com. Decatur	do	247	George Tobey	
Chili	do	291	Lot Luce	B. B. Howard
Charles	do	290	Barz. Morselander	Samuel Rodman
Courier	do	293	Thomas Severance	
Condor	do	349	Richard G. Luce	Charles W. Morgan
China	do	370	Russell Maxfield	William H. Stowell
Cicero	do	252	William Hussey	Kollock & Grinnell
Ceres	do	373	John J. Parker	G. R. Thornton
Columbus	Bark	313	—— Osborn	William R. Rodman
Cora	do	220	Ebenezer M. Hinckley	I. H. Bartlett
Dartmouth	Ship	....	Thomas Brock	I. Howland, jr., & Co
Eagle	Ship	336	Joshua Grinnell	Jireh Perry
Endeavour	do	252	Edward G. Soule	C. C. Gilbert
Euphrates	do	365	Shubael Norton	Lawrence Grinnell
Emerald	do	359	Clement Norton	Thomas Riddell & Sons
Emily Morgan	do	368	George C. Ray	Charles W. Morgan
Equator	Bark	262	Peter M. Coffin	Levi Standish
Franklin	Ship	333	Elijah Davis	Abm. H. Howland
Frances, 2d	do	368	John Briggs	Gideon Allen
Fenelon	do	328	Jeptha Jenney, jr	David Coffin
Frances Henrietta	do	407	Timothy Russell	
Falcon	do	273	George A. Hatch	
Grand Turk	do	323	—— Eddy	A. Barker
George and Susan	do	356	Edward Gardner	George Howland
George Porter	do	285	Alfred K. Fisher	Thomas Riddell & Sons
Good Return	do	376	Warren Howland	
Hydaspe	do	313	David Randall	
Herald	do	274	Frederick Ricketson	Tobey & Ricketson
Hibernia	do	....	John Cole	
Hope	do	282	Robert Brown	Sullings & Collins
Hercules	do	334	Albert G. Goodwin	Jireh Perry
James	do	278	Joseph B. Taber	T. & A. R. Nye
Java	do	295	Owen Hillman, jr	George Howland
John	do	308	Wilmot Luce	
London Packet	do	280	George W. Bennett	
Lucas	do	281	Caleb Kempton	

sailing from American ports—Continued.

Whaling-ground.	Date— Of sailing.	Date— Of arrival.	Result of voyage. Sperm-oil.	Result of voyage. Whale-oil.	Result of voyage. Whalebone.	Remarks.
			Bbls.	*Bbls.*	*Lbs.*	
Cape G'd Hope.	June 20	Apr. 29, 1833	140	1,060	......	Newburgh Whaling Company incorporated 1832.
Pacific Ocean..	July —	Dec. —, 1834	2,700	......	......	
Pacific Ocean..	....	Feb. 23, 1835	1,200	......	......	
Pacific Ocean..	Dec. —	Feb. 22, 1835	500	......	......	Sailed under Capt. Constant Norton, who died in 1835. Brought also $16,000 cash, proceeds from sale of oil.
South Atlantic.	June 8	....	......	......	......	
....do	May 8	1832 or 1833	......	......	......	
....do	July 2	....	......	......	......	
Pacific Ocean..	Nov. 29	Aug. 5, 1836	2,200	......	......	
Pacific Ocean..	Nov. 13	June 25, 1837	1,600	......	......	
South Atlantic	Aug. 25	Mar. 17, 1835	76	1,490	13,000	
Pacific Ocean..	Sept. 5	Jan. 27, 1836	1,400	......	......	
....do	Apr. 28	Mar. 5, 1836	2,230	......	......	
Atlantic & Ind.	May 20	Apr. 6, 1835	111	612	......	
South Atlantic.	June 28	Mar. 27, 1834	......	1,293	......	
....do	Dec. 20	Feb. 20, 1837	2,200	......	......	
....do	June 7	Apr. 13, 1834	60	1,300	......	
....do	July 16	July 27, 1834	277	1,807	......	
....do	July 4	Apr. 4, 1835	391	2,542	......	
Indian Ocean..	Apr. 18	Mar. 12, 1835	275	760	......	
....do	Apr. 13	Jan. 30, 1834	718	882	......	The Ceres must have sailed again in 1834, for she is entered at the custom-house March 2, 1835.
Pacific Ocean..	Aug. 2	Sept. 21, 1835	1,625	......	......	
....do	Sept. 26	Feb. 17, 1837	1,720	......	......	
....do	Sept. 1	Apr. 7, 1836	1,100	......	......	Built, 1833. Captain Brock died November 22, 1835.
....do	Aug. 14	Nov. 11, 1836	1,596	......	......	
South Atlantic	Oct. 9	Mar. 18, 1835	286	367	4,000	
Pacific Ocean..	Nov. 14	May 14, 1837	2,330	......	......	
Atlantic	May 29	Mar. 21, 1834	77	2,224	......	
Pacific Ocean..	July 8	July 27, 1837	1,438	17	......	Built at Portland, Me., 1833.
....do	July 31	Feb. 28, 1836	1,100	......	......	
....do	June 12	Nov. 11, 1836	2,425	......	......	
S. A. and P.....	June 6	Aug. 14, 1836	643	1,443	......	
South Atlantic	July 17	Apr. 6, 1835	......	1,014	......	
Pacific Ocean..	June 6	Sept. 6, 1834	2,200	......	......	Returned with captain sick; sailed again June 13.
South Atlantic	June 3	Apr. 13, 1834	......	......	......	
....do	....	Jan. 20, 1834	365	2,235	......	
Pacific Ocean..	Oct. 3	June 1, 1837	2,402	......	......	
South Atlantic.	May 6	May 4, 1834	......	1,703	......	
Pacific Ocean..	May 30	Apr. 13, 1834	140	2,460	......	
....do	June 3	....	......	......	......	
South Atlantic	July 1	Mar. 8, 1834	......	......	......	
....do	July 8	Feb. 22, 1834	......	......	......	
....do	June 11	May 7, 1834	......	1,700	16,000	
....do	June 18	Mar. 8, 1834	1,000	900	......	
....do	July 17	Feb. 20, 1835	330	2,000	......	
....do	June 11	Mar. 14, 1835	50	1,450	......	
... do	June 17	May 1, 1834	......	1,300	......	
Indian Ocean..	Jan. 7	Apr. 13, 1834	500	1,100	......	
South Atlantic.	Aug. 5	....	......	......	......	

Table showing returns of whaling-vessels

Name of vessel.	Class.	Tonnage.	Captain.	Managing owner or agent.
1833.				
New Bedford, Mass.—Continued.				
Liverpool	Ship		Albert Daggett	
Midas	do	326	Joseph Spooner	John Coggeshall
Minerva	Bark	195	Lewis Fish	
Milwood	do	254	Charles H. Taber	
Moss	do	334	Shubael Clark	
Martha	do		Oliver Potter	
Mercator	do	246	David Sprague	John A. Parker & Sons
Minerva Smyth	do	335	Gideon H. Smith	
Mary Ann	Bark	171	Joseph Crocker	
Mercury	Ship	339	Fordyce D. Haskell	I. Howland, jr., & Co
Nile	do	321	James Townsend	
Norfolk	do	275	Alex. Waggoner	
Nassau	do	408	John D. Samson	Isaiah Burgess
Orozimbo	do	588	Lewis Adams	William T. Russell
Pocahontas	Brig	141	Bartlett Allen	
Pioneer	Bark	231	Benjamin Ellis	
Pacific	Ship	331	David Collins	Andrew Robeson
Pacific	do	384	Paul Chase	
Phocion	do	265	Warren N. Bourne	
Pactolus	do	288	Isaac Grinnell	
Quito	Brig	138	James Maxfield	
Roscoe	Bark	235	George H. Richmond	
Roscoe	Ship	362	George B. Chase	A. Robeson
Rodman	do	371	Henry Lewis	
South Carolina	do	302	Edmund Maxfield	
Sally Anne	do	312	Henry Colt	D. R. Greene & Co
Swift	do	456	Lewis Tobey	
Selma	do	268	Benjamin Price	
Two Brothers	do	288	Jonathan Nye	
Wilmington and Liverpool Packet	do	384	Alexander Russell	J. A. Parker & Son
William C. Nye	do	389	Benjamin F. Riddell	
William Wirt	do	386	Isaac Daggett	
Winslow	Bark	263	Edward C. Barnard	S. Rodmon, jr
Young Phenix	Ship	377	James Bassett	John A. Parker & Son
Fall River, Mass.				
Gold Hunter	Ship	281	—— Coffin	Henry Slade
Fairhaven, Mass.				
Addison	Ship	426	Gus. A. Bayliss	Gibbs & Jenney
Albion	do	326	John E. Coggeshall	E. Sawin
Amazon	do	318	Reuben Creasey	do
Arab	do	336	Arthur Cox	do
Columbus	do	382	Tristram D. Pease	Gibbs & Jenney
Favorite	Bark	293	Brad. Hathaway	E. Sawin
Heroine	Ship		Charles Fisher	Sawin & Church
Herald	do	262	Isaiah West	
Java	do	291	William Ritchie	Atkins Adams
Jasper	do		—— Adams	do
Joseph Maxwell	do	301	Joseph Sampson	
Leonidas	do		Benjamin J. Crapo	
Marcia	do		Peter Butler	
Marcus	do	286	Obed Shearman	
Pindus	do		—— Russell	
South America	do		—— Maxfield	
Stanton	do		John Church	Lemuel Tripp
South Boston	do		John D. Taber	
William Wirt	do	387	—— Doggett	Warren Delano
Nantucket, Mass.				
Ann	Ship	361	Peter Brock	Jared Coffin
Aurora	do	346	John Hussey, jr	T. & P. Macy
Constitution	do	318	James G. Coffin	C. G. & H. Coffin
Eagle	do	335	Joseph Pease	David Joy

sailing from American ports—Continued.

Whaling-ground.	Date—		Result of voyage.			Remarks.
	Of sailing.	Of arrival.	Sperm-oil.	Whale-oil.	Whalebone.	
			Bbls.	*Bbls.*	*Lbs.*	
South Atlantic	Aug. 6	Mar. 15, 1835				
Pacific Ocean	Nov. 19	Aug. 2, 1837	2,453			
....do	Apr. 14	May 25, 1836				The Minerva, Capt. Jos. Barker, cleared June 19; whether the two clearances are the same vessel or not is uncertain.
South Atlantic	May 15	Apr. 24, 1834		1,250		
Pacific Ocean	June 1	Sept. 21, 1836	2,400			
South Atlantic	Oct. 22					
Pacific Ocean	July 19	July 9, 1836	1,100			Mate lost when three days out.
....do	Aug. 19	June 8, 1836	1,100			
Indian Ocean	Sept. 5	Apr. 6, 1835				
Pacific Ocean	Dec. —	Dec. 8, 1836	2,250			
South Atlantic	Aug. 20	June 16, 1835	700	1,300	18,000	
....do	June 11	Jan. 17, 1835		1,500		
Pacific Ocean	Dec. 20	June 22, 1837	2,533			
....do	Jan. 26	July 9, 1836	2,200			
South Atlantic	June 18	June 3, 1834	130			
....do	July 8	Aug. 4, 1834	80	630		
....do	July 30	Mar. 2, 1835	230	2,370	21,000	
Pacific Ocean	Mar. 22	Aug. 19, 1836	2,500			
Indian Ocean	Sept. 19	Apr. 29, 1835				Bought from New York, 1833.
Pacific Ocean	Jan. 12	Dec. 28, 1835				Probably of Fairhaven.
West'n Islands	Feb. 14					
South Atlantic	Aug. 7	Mar. 12, 1836	200	1,000		
Pacific Ocean	June 11	Jan. 26, 1836	2,200			
....do	July 6					
South Atlantic	May 1	Mar. 2, 1834	80	920		Returned because Captain Maxfield's shoulder was broken by a whale.
....do	June 26	Feb. 20, 1835	370	1,950	19,000	
Pacific Ocean	June 18	Nov. 22, 1836	1,200			
....do	Oct. 8	Nov. 12, 1836	2,200			Bought from New York, 1833.
South Atlantic	May 6	Mar. 24, 1834				
Pacific Ocean	Nov. 14	May 13, 1837	2,725			Captain Russell left the ship and came home sick.
....do	Aug. 4	May 11, 1837	1,836			Added, 1833.
....do	Dec. 19					
....do	Dec. 20	July 7, 1837	1,001			
....do	Aug. 17	Aug. 16, 1836	2,700			
South Atlantic	July 7					
South Atlantic	Apr. 13	Mar. 4, 1834	24	2,236	19,100	
....do	May 6	Apr. 13, 1834	125	1,065		Captain Coggeshall left the ship; sick.
Pacific Ocean	June 12	Jan. 9, 1837	1,927			
South Atlantic	Sept. 22	Mar. 12, 1835		2,076		Bought from Philadelphia, 1833.
S. A. and Ind.	May 18	Mar. 15, 1835	783	565		
Indian Ocean	Feb. 1	Nov. 22, 1834	54			Sold 1,500 whale at Bahia.
South Atlantic	May 17	Mar. 16, 1834	200	2,200	20,000	
....do	July 10	May 9, 1834		1,300	11,000	
....do	June 24	Mar. 12, 1835	130	1,300		
....do		Mar. 12, 1834	600	1,800		
Indian Ocean	Aug. 28	Feb. 18, 1836	200	1,200		
South Atlantic	June 3	Apr. 12, 1834		1,400		
....do	June 6	Mar. 12, 1835				
Pacific Ocean	Sept. 20					
South Atlantic		Feb. 3, 1834	50	50		
....do	Apr. 27					
Pacific Ocean	June 1	Mar. 12, 1836	Full.			
South Atlantic	July 2	Feb. 25, 1835				
Pacific Ocean	Dec. 20	Sept. 5, 1837	2,582			Built, 1833, at Fairhaven. Third mate killed by a whale, 1834.
Pacific Ocean	Aug. 6	Oct. 15, 1837	1,845			
....do	Oct. 18	May 13, 1837	1,713			
Atlantic	July 13	Apr. 22, 1835	140	775		
....do	Aug. 18	Apr. 7, 1835	604	580		James Gibson, first mate, died, 1835.

Table showing returns of whaling-vessels

Name of vessel.	Class.	Tonnage.	Captain.	Managing owner or agent.
1833.				
Nantucket, Mass.—Continued.				
Fame	Ship	376	Isaac Gardner	
Fame	Sloop		Peter C. Myrick	
Foster	Ship	317	Josiah C. Long	
Fabius	do	432	Benjamin C. Chase	Val. Hussey & Bro
Hazard	Sloop		—— Swain	
Harmony	Schooner		—— Chadwick —— Burdick	
Hero	Ship	313	Peter Smith	Joseph Starbuck
Independence	do	311	Isaac Brayton	
John Adams	do	296	Obed Luce, jr	Griffin Barney
Levi Starbuck	do	376	Shadrach Freeman	Levi Starbuck
Lexington	Schooner		—— Cash	
Lydia	Ship	325	Edward C. Joy	
Montano	do	365	David N. Edwards	Samuel B. Folger
Martha	do	273	Tristram Pinkham	do
Orion	do	354	Moses Brown	F. W. Hussey
Omega	do	363	Henry Phelon	Joseph Starbuck
Ohio	do	381	Charles W. Coffin	Jared Coffin
Peru	Bark	257	William Brooks, jr	David Joy
Pilot	Schooner		—— Pinkham	
Rose	do	350	James Davis	Joseph Starbuck
Robert	Sloop		—— Luce	
Susan	Ship	349	Frederick Swain	Aaron Mitchell
Three Brothers	do	384	George Alley	Joseph Starbuck
Dartmouth, Mass.				
By Chance	Brig		Hiram Covell	
Wade	Bark	261	Charles B. Ray	
Edgartown, Mass.				
Almira	Ship	362	—— Merchant	Abraham Osborn
Champion	do	396	—— Worth	Grafton Norton
Rochester, Mass.				
Dryade	Bark		Joseph R. Taber	
Franklin	do		Calvin C. Adams	Gideon Barstow & Son
Laurel	Schooner		—— Mayhew	
Shylock	Ship	277	Clement Hammond	
Westport, Mass.				
Industry	Brig		George Soule	
Mexico	do	130	Alden Wilkey	
Thomas Winslow	do	136	Benjamin Seabury	
Plymouth, Mass.				
Fortune	Bark	278	—— Upham	Isaac L. Hedge
Triton	Ship		—— Tilton	
Marblehead, Mass.				
Atlas	Ship		—— Gardner	
Gloucester, Mass.				
Lewis	Ship		—— Wood	
Mount Wollaston	do		—— Adams	

*Experiments had been made in the English fishery in 1831 with killing whales by the injection of such consternation that they refused to have more to do with it. At what time this weapon was English discovery; but, resting the matter upon the published record of actual use alone, England
The harpoon-gun is described by Scoresby as having been in use in the English service as early as

sailing from American ports—Continued.

Whaling-ground.	Date— Of sailing.	Of arrival.	Result of voyage. Sperm-oil.	Whale-oil.	Whalebone.	Remarks.
			Bbls.	*Bbls.*	*Lbs.*	
Atlantic	May 23	Mar. 3, 1835	280	1,040		Came home leaky; broken up at Nantucket, 1835.
....do	July 27					Sailed in search of whales, *sea-serpents*, &c.; was armed with a patent harpoon charged with poison.*
Pacific Ocean	June 27	Nov. 16, 1836	1,408			
....do	Aug. 31	July 31, 1837	863			
Mexico	May —					The Hazard probably arrived in September; sailed again in October; returned again September 9, 1834, with 225 sperm.
Atlantic {	June 12		}			15 whale.
	Nov. 14	Sept. 17, 1833	}			
Pacific Ocean	Oct. 4	Aug. 15, 1836	1,177			
....do	Nov. 17					Lost on Starbuck's Island, with 1,800 sperm.
Atlantic	July 20	Mar. 13, 1835	149	1,335		
Pacific Ocean	July 27	Oct. 13, 1836	1,885			Built at Mattapoisett, 1833.
West Indies	Oct. 6	Sept. 14, 1834	100			Second mate died.
Pacific Ocean	Nov. 18					Burned at sea January 31, 1835; supposed to have been fired by one of the crew.
....do	June 1	Apr. 10, 1836	3,097			First mate, E. Burditt, taken down by a foul line November, 1833.
....do	Nov. 24	Apr. 19, 1837	666			
....do	Jan. 15	Mar. 3, 1836	980			Captain Brown came home sick.
....do	June 11	June 8, 1836	2,904			
....do	Aug. 15	Jan. 8, 1837	2,615	176		Built at Mattapoisett, 1833.
Atlantic	July 4	—— —, 1835	43	696		
South Coast	Aug. 10	Aug. 29, 1833		20		
Pacific Ocean	Aug. 21	Jan. 26, 1837	1,180			
South Coast	May 17	July 20, 1833	20			Sailed again July 26; returned September 1, clean.
Pacific Ocean	Nov. 17	May 14, 1837	1,406			
....do	Aug. 25	Nov. 2, 1836	2,212			
Pacific Ocean	Sept. 5					Condemned and sold at Bayta, August, 1835.
....do	Dec. 27	Dec. 18, 1836	1,850	250		Took 50 barrels ambergris; third mate killed by a whale, 1834; bought from New York, 1833.
Pacific Ocean	Dec. 12	Feb. 2, 1837				
....do	Dec. 22	Sept. 13, 1837	2,100			Built at Mattapoisett, 1833.
South Atlantic	May 29	Apr. 21, 1834	350	850		
....do	June 27	Apr. —, 1835	200	1,300		
West'n Islands	Apr. 2	Nov. 12, 1833	275			
Indian Ocean		June 11, 1834		650		
West'n Islands	Apr. 19	Oct. 10, 1833	250			
South Atlantic	May 9	Nov. 12, 1833	90			
West'n Islands	Apr. 19	Oct. 10, 1833	250			
Pacific Ocean	July 19	Dec. 14, 1836	1,000			
South Atlantic		Apr. —, 1835		700		Sailed under Captain Taber, who came home sick, 1834; added from Boston, 1833.
South Atlantic	June —					
Brazil	Jan. 26					
South Atlantic	Jan. 11	May 14, 1834		1,500		

poison into them from the barb of the harpoon, with such an effect as, it is said, filled the men with invented in Nantucket is somewhat uncertain. The islanders have claimed that it was prior to the leads by two years.

1733 (vol. ii, p. 70).

Table showing returns of whaling-vessels

Name of vessel.	Class.	Tonnage.	Captain.	Managing owner or agent.
1833.				
Salem, Mass.				
Charles Doggett	Brig		—— Goodwin	
Catharine	Ship			
Clay	..do		—— Church	
Emerald	Bark	271	—— Eggleston	John B. Pierce
Eliza	..do	262		James W. Cheever
James Maury	Ship	355	—— Bigelow	John B. Osgood
Reaper	Bark	230	J. T. Worth	
Samuel Wright	Ship	372	—— Pitman	J. B. Osgood
Newburyport, Mass.				
Adeline	Ship		—— Buckley	
Merrimac	..do	414	—— Pease	Lunt & Titcomb
Dorchester, Mass.				
Charles Carroll	Ship	386	R. Weeks	
Boston, Mass.				
Wave	Bark	124	G. L. Nickerson	Lombard & Whitmore
Falmouth, Mass.				
Awashonks	Ship	355	Prince Coffin	Elijah Swift
William Penn	..do	370	John C. Lincoln	Stephen Dillingham
Warren, R. I.				
Atlantic	Ship		—— Pickens	
Benjamin Rush	..do	374	—— Coffin	Driscol & Child
Boy	..do	251	—— Champlin	William Collins
Galen	..do	365	—— Borden	Driscol & Child
Luminary	..do		—— Gardner	
Miles	..do		—— Luce	
North America	..do	288	—— Grinnell	Driscol & Child
Philip Tabb	..do	405		..do
Rose	..do		—— Coffin	
Providence, R. I.				
Envoy	Ship	392	J. C. Clark	Amherst Everett
Bristol, R. I.				
Anne	Ship	222	—— Swain	William H. De Wolf
Balance	..do	321	—— Davis	..do
Fama	..do	362	—— Littlefield	Fitzhenry Homer
Leonidas	..do	353	—— Cleveland	William H. De Wolf
Roger Williams	..do	285	—— Mayhew	Robert Rogers
Newport, R. I.				
Audley Clarke	Ship		Joseph Paddack	Bush & Clarke
Constitution	..do		E. Gifford	N. Ruggles
George Champlin	..do		J. A. Brown	Ruggles & Lee
Martha	..do		Oliver Potter	Lee, Norton & Stevens
New London, Conn.				
Aeronaut	Ship		—— Mallory	
Ann Maria	..do		—— Chester	
Boston	..do	291	—— Fitch	I. Lawrence
Com. Perry	..do		—— Hobron	
Connecticut	..do	398		
Flora	..do		—— McLane	
Georgia	..do	343	—— Brewster	Thomas W. Williams
Halcyon	..do		—— Thompson	
Manchester Packet	..do		—— Reed	

sailing from American ports—Continued.

Whaling-ground.	Date— Of sailing.	Of arrival.	Result of voyage. Sperm-oil.	Whale-oil.	Whalebone.	Remarks.
			Bbls.	*Bbls.*	*Lbs.*	
Pacific Ocean	Jan. 11					
....do						Burned off Oahu, 1834.
South Atlantic	June 19					
Pacific Ocean	Nov. 23					
....do	May 26					
....do	May 15					Bought from Boston, 1833.
Indian Ocean	Sept. 7	July 5, 1835		900		
Pacific Ocean	June 15	Aug. 27, 1836	2,000			
Pacific Ocean	Nov. 13					
....do	Sept. 24	Apr. 20, 1837	1,800	1,900		Built, 1833, at Newburyport.
Pacific Ocean	Oct. 31	Aug. 29, 1857	2,000			Sold 1837.
South Atlantic	Feb. 25	Oct. 27, 1833	20	2		
Pacific Ocean	Dec. 28	May 20, 1836	600			Was attacked in October, 1835, by the natives of Namarik; Captain Coffin, first and second mates, and four men killed.
....do	Jan. —	Apr. 29, 1836	1,200			Built at Falmouth, 1832; Mr. Eldredge, first mate, killed, and two boats' crews captured by the natives of Navigator Islands; Captain Lincoln came home sick.
South Atlantic		Apr. 12, 1834	350	1,650		
Pacific Ocean	May 25	Feb. 11, 1837	1,820	120		
....do	July 28	Mar. 4, 1836	1,700			
....do	July 30	May 23, 1834		1,050		
....do		Sept. 19, 1836	1,380			
South Atlantic		May 10, 1834	130	1,050		
....do	July 12					
....do		May 10, 1834	400	800		
Pacific Ocean						
Pacific Ocean	Dec. 26	Jan. 1, 1838	2,100			
Pacific Ocean	July 16	Dec. 9, 1836	800			
....do	Dec. 3	June 4, 1837	1,200			Sold to Providence, 1837.
Indian Ocean	Dec. 3	Mar. 11, 1836	450	1,450		
Pacific Ocean	Nov. 19	Sept. 11, 1837	1,400			Sold to Salem 1837 and withdrawn.
....do	Aug. 2					Condemned at Pernambuco 1837; had 1,200 sperm, 500 whale.
Pacific Ocean	Dec. 4	June 19, 1837	1,700			Built 1833.
	June 11	May 23, 1836	1,900			
	Dec. —	Aug. 2, 1837				
South Atlantic		May 29, 1835	225	1,100	9,000	
South Atlantic		May 20, 1834	150	1,650		
Indian Ocean	June 4					
....do	Nov. 25	Mar. 12, 1835	150	1,750	11,000	
South Atlantic		Apr. 9, 1834	200	1,200		
....do	May 19					
....do		Mar. 19, 1831		2,200		
....do	Apr. —	Feb. 21, 1835	600	1,100		
Indian Ocean	Nov. —					
South Atlantic	Nov. —					Wrecked and condemned at Gambia 183[illegible], had 500 whale.

Table showing returns of whaling-vessels

Name of vessel.	Class.	Tonnage.	Captain.	Managing owner or agent.
1833.				
New London, Conn.—Continued.				
Montgomery	Schooner	...	—— Cliff	E. M. Frink & Co
Ospray	Brig	...	—— Sleight	
Ruth and Mary	Ship	290	—— Chester	
Stonington	...do	351	—— Lawton	Williams & Barns
Sun	Schooner	...	—— Trott	
Superior	Ship	406	—— Fitch	N. & W. W. Billings
Tuscarora	...do	379	—— Smith	...do
Wabash	...do	...	—— Fuller	E. M. Frink
Stonington, Conn.				
Acasta	Ship	330		
Charles Adams	...do			
Thomas Williams	...do	340	—— Allen	C. P. Williams
Uxor	Brig	...		
Bridgeport, Conn.				
Atlantic	Ship	291	Samuel H. Ford	
Sag Harbor, N. Y.				
Ann	Ship	...	—— Howell	
Arabella	...do	367	—— Pierson	N. & G. Howell
Acasta	...do	...	—— Hand	
Columbia	...do	285	—— Hedges	Luther D. Cook
Cadmus	...do	307	—— Hand	Mulford & Sleight
Daniel Webster	...do	397	—— Pierson	E. Mulford
Franklin	...do	391	C. Griffin	C. T. Dering
Gov. Clinton	...do	...	—— Ludlow	
Hannibal	...do	311	—— Cooper	S. & B. Huntting & Co
Henry	...do	...	E. D. Topping	C. T. Dering & Co
Hudson	...do	368	—— Greene	Luther D. Cook
Marcus	...do	283	—— Cartwright	S. & N. Howell
Nimrod	...do	280	—— Barns	C. T. Dering & Co
Neptune	...do	338	—— Parker	S. & B. Huntting & Co
Phenix	...do	...	—— Cooper	
Thames	...do	...		
Washington	...do	...		
Greenport, N. Y.				
Delta	Ship	314	—— Sayre	H. & N. Corwin
Triad	...do	...	—— Case	
Hudson, N. Y.				
America	Ship	464	—— Folger	Barnard, Curtis & Co
Alexander Mansfield	...do	320	—— Starbuck	...do
Beaver	...do	427	—— Gardner	...do
Edward	...do	274	—— Ray	Seth G. Macy
Helvetia	...do	333	—— Cottle	Robert A. Barnard
James Munroe	...do	...	—— Coffin	
Martha	...do	369	—— Riddell	Alexander Jenkins
Poughkeepsie, N. Y.				
Elbe	Ship	333	—— Whippey	David S. Sherman
Siroc	...do	...	—— Swain	
Newburgh, N. Y.				
Illinois	Ship	414	—— Leonard	Charles Ludlow
Portland	...do	...	—— Cook	
Russell	...do	387		Charles Ludlow
New York, N. Y.				
Com. Barry	Ship	...	—— Braddock	
Cornelia	Schooner	...	—— Storer	
Desdemona	Ship	...	—— Smith	
Hamilton	...do	...	—— Pendleton	S. Hicks & Sons

sailing from American ports—Continued.

Whaling-ground.	Date—		Result of voyage.			Remarks.
	Of sailing.	Of arrival.	Sperm-oil.	Whale-oil.	Whalebone.	
			Bbls.	*Bbls.*	*Lbs.*	
South Atlantic		Sept. 1, 1834		400	3,200	Brought also 700 seal-skins.
Indian Ocean	May 19	May 10, 1834		500		
....do	May 18					Bought from New York 1833; lost on Block Island going out, May 18, 1833.
Pacific Ocean	Sept. 2	May 11, 1837	1,200			
Falkland		Sept. 27, 1833				Brought oil and skins.
Pacific Ocean	Oct. 15	Apr. 23, 1837	2,650			Captain Fitch and third mate accidentally killed March —, 1835.
South Atlantic	June 4	Mar. 12, 1834	80	2,800		
....do	June 16					Lost on Montauk Point April 19, 1834, with 1,100 whale.
			97	1,797	13,960	
Falkland		Dec. 22, 1834				
Pacific Ocean	July 6					
Patagonia		Dec. —, 1834		650		
South Atlantic	Nov. 2	—— —, 18				Bought from New York 1833.
South Atlantic		Apr. 15, 1834		1,050		
Pacific Ocean	Aug. 19	Apr. 18, 1837	1,900	100		
South Atlantic		June 12, 1834	250	1,400	12,000	
....do	June 10	May 22, 1834	75	1,685	15,000	
Indian Ocean	June 6	Mar. 18, 1834		1,850		
Pacific Ocean	Aug. 20	May 12, 1837	2,500			Built 1833.
....do	Aug. 7	May 18, 1837	2,550			
....do	Aug. 9					Lost in a typhoon 1834.
South Atlantic	July 10	May 21, 1834	23	1,350	9,000	
....do		Jan. 18, 1834	400	2,100		
....do	July 12					Formerly a London packet; added 1833.
....do	June 19					
....do	June 19	June 12, 1834	130	1,220	11,500	
....do	June 4	May 21, 1834		1,800	15,000	
....do		May 20, 1834	150	1,850		
....do		Mar. —, 1834	400	2,000	18,000	
East Cape		Apr. 19, 1834		1,900		
South Atlantic	June 4	May 11, 1834		1,600		
		Feb. 3, 1834	500	2,200	1,800	
Pacific Ocean	Sept. 11	Jan. 27, 1837	800			
Chili	July 5	July 21, 1835		1,500		
Pacific Ocean	June 8	Aug. 3, 1836	1,900			
South Atlantic	Jan. 10	Mar. 12, 1835	900	120		Added 1832.
Pacific Ocean	Sept. 28	Mar. 18, 1837	2,400	150		
Africa	June —	Sept. 1, 1834	150	1,000		Added 1832.
Pacific Ocean	Sept. 25	Apr. 17, 1837	1,400			Built 1833.
Pacific Ocean	Aug. 14	Mar. 31, 1837	900	400	3,000	Added 1833.
....do	Apr. 11					Sold at Simons Town, Cape Good Hope, 1833.
South Atlantic	Aug. 15	Feb. 22, 1835	30	500	11,000	
Indian Ocean		Mar. 24, 1835		1,600		
Falkland	Aug. 19					
	Jan. 9					
South Atlantic		May 25, 1834		1,200		
Falkland	Jan. 9	Oct. 9, 1834		4,350	30,000	Also 1,150 seal-skins.

Table showing returns of whaling-vessels

Name of vessel.	Class.	Tonnage.	Captain.	Managing owner or agent.
1833.				
New York, N. Y.—Continued.				
Meteor	Ship		—— Coffin	
White Oak	Bark	291	—— Lawrence	Pell, Zabieskie & Pell
Portsmouth, N. H.				
Ann Parry	Ship		—— Ray	Portsmouth Pier Company.
Triton	do		—— Flanders	
Lynn, Mass.				
Atlas	Ship	2[illegible]2	—— Gardner	Hezekiah Chase
Clay	do	299	C. Church	do
Louisa	do	382	I. Woolley	do
Gloucester, Mass.				
Lewis	Ship		—— Wood	
Schooner Monticello, —— Lindell, sailed August 20, 1833, from Baltimore for the Atlantic and Pacific Oceans, but whether for sealing, whaling, or trading is not known.				
1834.				
New Bedford, Mass.				
Averick	Ship	385	Humphrey Shearman	John A. Parker & Son
Augusta	do	344	Charles Lawrence	W. R. Rodman
Balaena	do	301	Thomas D. Lucas	J. & J. Howland
Barclay	do	281	Henry Cottle	William R. Rotch & Co
Braganza	do	469	Michael Baker	William T. Russell
Cortes	do	382	Alexander Bunker	George Howland
Canton	do	409	Abraham Gardner	Jireh Perry
Chili	do	291	Lot Luce	B. B. Howard
Condor	do	349	George H. Dexter	Charles W. Morgan
Enterprize	do	291	Oliver P. Winslow	Alfred Gibbs & Co
Emerald	do	359	Clement Norton	Thomas Riddell & Sons
Falcon	do	273	Charles D. Harding	Briggs & Bartlett
George Howland	do	374	Joseph Taber, jr	George Howland
Grand Turk	do		David H. Bartlett	A. Barker & Co
George Porter	do	285	Alfred K. Fisher	Thomas Riddell & Sons
Gen. Pike	do		William Adams	
Good Return	do	376	Warren Howland	Henry Taber
George and Martha	Bark	275	Abraham T. Eddy	George Randall
Hercules, 2d	Ship	290	Peter F. Chase	D. R. Greene
Herald, 2d	do	303	Nathaniel H. Nye	T. & A. R. Nye
Hector	do	380	Thomas A. Norton	Charles W. Morgan
Hope	do		Robert Brown	Sullings & Collins
India	do	366	Joshua Coffin	William T. Russell
John	do		Andrew Almy	
Lancaster	do	383	Rudolphus N. Swift	T. & A. R. Nye
Logan	do	302	Benjamin Ray	I. Howland, jr., & Co
Maria	do	202	Isaac G. Hedge	C. W. Morgan
Mayflower	do	350	Joseph T. Chase	Randall & Haskell
Martha	do		Charles Fisher	
Magnolia	do	396	Cornelius Howland, jr	C. W. Morgan
Nautilus	do	340	Obed N. Swift	Jireh Perry
Pocahontas	Brig		Bartlett Allen	
Persia	Bark	240	Holder Almy	Lawrence Grinnell
Pioneer	do	231	Reuben Russell, 2d	C. W. Morgan
Russell	do	301	Henry B. Gifford	J. & J. Howland
Rousseau	Ship	306	Edward A. Luce	George Howland
Triton	do	300	Obed S. Carr	I. Howland, jr., & Co
Trident	do	449	Charles Stetson	J. A. Parker & Son
Two Brothers	do	288	Henry Pease, 2d	
Tobacco Plant	do	271	Silvanus Swain	William R. Rodman

sailing from American ports—Continued.

Whaling-ground.	Date— Of sailing.	Date— Of arrival.	Result of voyage. Sperm-oil.	Result of voyage. Whale-oil.	Result of voyage. Whalebone.	Remarks.
			Bbls.	*Bbls.*	*Lbs.*	
Cape G'd Hope		Mar. 30, 1834	300	1,800		
Indian Ocean	Apr. 18	Apr. 27, 1834	140	600		Captain Lawrence came home sick.
Pacific Ocean		Sept. 7, 1836	1,950			Built 1833.
South Atlantic		Feb. 23, 1834	450	1,550		First ship at Portsmouth.
South Atlantic		Mar. —, 1835	150	850		
....do	June 17					
....do	May 25	May 11, 1834		1,400		
Indian Ocean		Dec. 11, 1834	400			
South Atlantic and Indian.	Mar. 16	Apr. 17, 1836	264	1,489		
Pacific Ocean	June 30	Dec. 30, 1837	2,155	14		
....do	May 18	Apr. 28, 1837	2,331			
....do	Sept. 13	Sept. 26, 1837	1,362			
....do	May 18	Nov. 2, 1837	2,578			
....do	July 20	Nov. 5, 1837	2,320			
....do	Oct. 25	May 20, 1838	2,627			
South Atlantic	May 18	Mar. 15, 1836	34	1,275		
Brazil	Aug. 27	Aug. 6, 1835	171	1,295		
Pacific Ocean	Nov. 23	June 7, 1838	1,484			
South Atlantic	June 22	Apr. 21, 1835	149	2,248		
....do	June 14	Mar. 9, 1836	133	1,061		
Pacific Ocean	Dec. 5	Jan. 13, 1838	2,833			Built 1834.
South Atlantic	May 13	Jan. 23, 1836	150	2,400		
....do	July 3	June 7, 1835	52	963		
....do	June 17	Apr. 6, 1835				
....do	June 17	Mar. 8, 1836	395	2,954		
....do	July 24	Mar. 11, 1836	500	1,400		The George and Martha came home in charge of —— Allen. Captain Eddy died from injuries received from a whale, July, 1835.
Indian Ocean	June 3	Sept. 17, 1836	408	1,123		
South Atlantic	July 3	May 1, 1836	290	1,009		
Pacific Ocean	Dec. 21	Aug. 23, 1837	2,650			
South Atlantic	June 27	Mar. 13, 1836	500	1,350		
....do	Oct. 25	Apr. 30, 1836	2,241			
....do	July 14	Apr. 18, 1836	360	1,240		
Pacific Ocean	Nov. 1	May 20, 1838	2,385			
....do	May 28	Nov. 21, 1837	2,040			
Atlantic	July 15	Jan. 19, 1836	400			
Pacific Ocean	Oct. 14	Apr. 28, 1838	2,254			
South Atlantic	June 26	Apr. 15, 1836	60	1,840		
Pacific Ocean	Sept. 28	Aug. 5, 1838	3,004			
....do	Nov. 2	May 27, 1838	2,412			
South Atlantic	June 29	Nov. 29, 1834	320			The Pocahontas sailed again, arriving June 24, 1835.
Pacific Ocean	Dec. 19	Apr. 9, 1838	1,665			
....do	Nov. 2	Apr. 28, 1837	937	896		
....do	Oct. 8	Dec. 8, 1836	2,200			
....do	May 1	May 13, 1837	1,820			
....do	Nov. 17	Apr. 8, 1838	1,447	40		
....do	Dec. 4	Jan. 21, 1838	2,932	7		
South Atlantic	May 9	May 11, 1835	230	1,400	15,000	
Pacific Ocean	Aug. 21	Sept. 27, 1837	1,594			

Table showing returns of whaling-vessels

Name of vessel.	Class.	Tonnage.	Captain.	Managing owner or agent.
1834.				
New Bedford, Mass.—Continued.				
William Hamilton	Ship	463	William Swain	I. Howland, jr., & Co.
Zephyr	do	361	Thomas Severance	Alexander Gibbs
Fairhaven, Mass.				
Addison	Ship	426	Avory Parker	Gibbs & Jenney
Albion	do	326	Sheffel Read	E. Sawin
Charles Drew	do	344	Robert F. Fosdick	Lemuel Tripp
Cadmus	do	320	William Crowell	Atkins Adams
Herald	do	262	Isaiah West	
Heroine	do		Daniel Borden	
Hesper	Bark	261	Obed Fosdick	Charles W. Morgan
Isabella	Ship	410	Frederick C. Taber	James H. Howland
Jasper	do	359	Elihu Gifford	
Leonidas	do		Benjamin J. Crapo	
London Packet	do	280	Gilbert Jenney	Gibbs & Jenney
Maine	do	294	Jared Worth	
Oregon	do		Edward Harding	
Pindus	Bark	193	George W. Nye	Lemuel Tripp
Rochester, Mass.				
Dryade	Bark	263	Joseph R. Taber	G. Barstow & Son
Laurel	Schooner		—— Mayhew	do
Shylock	Ship		Clement Hammond	
Edgartown, Mass.				
Loan	Ship	262	—— Luce	Abraham Osborne
Meridian	do	381	—— Fisher	G. Norton
Newburgh, N. Y.				
Russell	Ship	387	—— Brock	Charles Ludlow
Falmouth, Mass.				
Brunette	Bark		—— Fisher	Elijah Swift
Dartmouth, Mass.				
Forester	Bark	243	Edward G. Clark	Prince Sears
South Carolina	Ship	302	Edmund Maxfield	James Rider
Washington	do	344	Elihu Russell	B. & J. W. Howland
Westport, Mass.				
Industry	Brig	94	George Soule	
Thos. Winslow	do		Benjamin Seabury, jr	
Nantucket, Mass.				
American	Ship	340	Aaron Coffin	Matthew Crosby
Alpha	do	345	Frederick B. Chase	Hadwen & Barney
Amazon	Sloop		—— Riddell	
Christopher Mitchell	Ship	387	Sanford Wilber	Chris. Mitchell & Co.
Clarkson	do	380	William Plasket	James Athearn
Elizabeth Starbuck	do	381	Obed Cathcart	Levi Starbuck
Franklin	do	246	Edward H. Morton	James Athearn
George	do	359	John C. Congdon	
Harmony	Schooner		{ —— Chadwick { —— Swain	} Rand & Coffin
Jones Hale	Sloop		—— Kuhn	
Japan	Ship	332	Edwin Hiller	James Athearn
Lima	do	286	William Wyer	William B. Coffin
Lexington	Schooner		—— Drew	Philip H. Folger
Neptune	do		{ —— Farris { —— Coon	}
Phebe	Ship	379	Shubael S. Russell	Chris. Mitchell & Co.
Phenix	do	323	Isaac B. Hussey	T. & P. Macy

sailing from American ports—Continued.

Whaling-ground.	Date—		Result of voyage.			Remarks.
	Of sailing.	Of arrival.	Sperm-oil.	Whale-oil.	Whalebone.	
			Bbls.	*Bbls.*	*Lbs.*	
Pacific Ocean..	May 28	Aug. 23, 1837	4,008	......	......	
South Atlantic.	June 6	Mar. 15, 1836	40	1,960	......	
Pacific Ocean..	June 10	Dec. 21, 1837	2,090		......	Sold to New Bedford, 1838.
South Atlantic	May 30	Mar. 11, 1835	375	2,119	......	
Pacific Ocean..	Nov. 24	Apr. 28, 1838	2,422	......	......	
....do	Oct. 16	Nov. 21, 1837	2,063	......	......	
South Atlantic	June 26	June 12, 1835	70	950	8,000	
....do	May 22	Apr. 21, 1835	......	1,780	......	
Pacific Ocean..	Dec. 5	Sept. 13, 1838	1,063	20	......	
....do	Nov. 2	Aug. 30, 1838	2,546	......	......	Sold to New Bedford.
Indian Ocean ..	May 22	July 25, 1835	350	1,800	21,000	
South Atlantic.	June 11	Apr. 15, 1836	......	1,000	......	
Indian Ocean ..	May 17	Mar. 18, 1836	200	2,000	......	
South Atlantic.	May 25	Jan. 2, 1836	160	1,950	......	
Pacific Ocean..	Oct. 14	....	......	......	......	Oregon lost May, 1837, on a reef near Tahiti; had 2,300 sperm; saved 1,400.
....do	Oct. 14	Apr. 28, 1836	454	104	......	
Atlantic	July 3	Dec. 14, 1835	140	1,630	......	
....do	....	Nov. 5, 1834	200	......	......	
....do	July 15	May 24, 1835	200	900	6,000	
Pacific Ocean..	Aug. 10	Nov. 26, 1837	1,000	......	......	
....do	Nov. 4	....	......	......	......	Lost in the Pacific, 1836, with all on board had about 2,300 sperm.
....do	Aug. —	Jan. 7, 1838	1,400	......	......	Sold to Dartmouth, 1838.
....	May 3	Nov. 4, 1834	60	......	......	
Pacific Ocean ..	Mar. 13	Apr. 28, 1837	529	......	......	
South Atlantic	July 14	Mar. 19, 1835	40	1,400	......	
Pacific Ocean ..	Feb. 2	Mar. —, 1836	200	2,100	......	
Atlantic	Apr. 4	Nov. 14, 1834	210	......	......	
Cape de Verdes.	Apr. 4	Dec. 15, 1834	170	......	......	
Pacific Ocean ..	June 3	Nov. 21, 1837	1,288	......	......	
....do	July 25	Dec. 31, 1837	1,660	......	......	Built, 1834, at Mattapoisett.
Atlantic	Aug. 13	Aug. 15, 1834	......	......	......	Returned with boat stove.
	Aug. 15	Aug. 19, 1834	......	......	......	No report.
	Sept. 23	Oct. 7, 1834	......	35	......	
	Oct. —	May 7, 1835	......	......	......	
Pacific Ocean..	July 15	Aug. 21, 1837	2,843	......	......	Built at Mattapoisett, 1834.
....do	Aug. 9	Dec. 20, 1837	2,523	......	......	
....do	July 27	May 5, 1837	2,708	......	......	Do.
....do	June 15	June 12, 1837	160	452	......	
Atlantic Ocean.	Aug. 4	May 12, 1836	396	1,255	......	Sold to New Bedford, 1836.
Gulf Mexico .	....	Sept. 25, 1834	360	......	......	
	Dec. 5	July 20, 1835	150	......	......	
Atlantic	Aug. 11	Aug. 14, 1834	......	......	......	Lost mainsail.
	Aug. —	Aug. 19, 1834	......	......	......	No report.
Indian Ocean ..	Sept. 3	Nov. 22, 1837	2,115	......	......	
Pacific Ocean ..	Dec. 9	Apr. 7, 1838	1,173	......	......	
Gulf Mexico ...	Nov. 10	Sept. 22, 1835	130	......	......	
Atlantic	Aug. 23	Aug. 30, 1834	......	......	......	Do.
	Sept. 11	Sept. 26, 1834	......	Clean	......	
Pacific Ocean ..	May 25	Nov. 21, 1837	1,009	......	......	Sent home 115 sperm.
....do	July 6	Feb. 3, 1837	2,345	......	......	

Table showing returns of whaling-vessels

Name of vessel.	Class.	Tonnage.	Captain.	Managing owner or agent.
1834.				
Nantucket, Mass.—Continued.				
Ploughboy	Ship	391	Moses Brown	Philip H. Folger
Pacific	do	314	Joseph Congdon	Paul Mitchell & Sons
Planter	do	340	Reuben Manter	William B. Coffin
Primrose	Schooner		—— Fisher	David Joy
Reliance	Schooner		P. C. Myrick —— Farris P. C. Myrick	
Statira	Ship	346	George Cannon, jr	Samuel B. Tuck
Sarah	do	495	Joseph Holley	Jared Coffin
Warren	Sloop		—— Baker	
Zone	Ship	365	John M. Russell	S & J. Mitchell
Salem, Mass.				
Izette	Ship	275	—— Sistare	John B. Osgood
Lynn, Mass.				
Clay	Ship	299	C. Church	H. Chase & Co
Com. Preble	do	323	—— Loper	S. H. Gardner
Louisa	do	383	I. Woolley	H. Chase & Co
Dorchester, Mass.				
Courier	Ship	293	W. Luce	Josiah Stickney
Herald	do	242	J. C. Lincoln	do
Gloucester, Mass.				
Mt. Wallaston	Ship		—— Adams	
Newburyport, Mass.				
Newburyport	Ship	341	—— Starbuck	Hunt & Titcomb
Navy	do	356	F. Neil	
Plymouth, Mass.				
Arabella	Ship	404	—— Eldridge	James Bartlett, jr
Bristol, R. I.				
Essex	Ship	200	—— Coleman	William R. Taylor
Fama	do		—— Littlefield	
Gov. Fenner	do	375	—— Swain	William H. DeWolf
Gov. Hopkins	Brig	111	—— Bly	William R. Taylor
Lemuel C. Richmond	Ship		Joseph Sherman	
Warren, R. I.				
Atlantic	Ship	323	—— Mason	Driscol & Child
Galen	do	365	—— Borden	do
Miles	do		—— Luce	
North America	do		—— Grinnell	Driscol & Child
Philip Tabb	do	405	—— Bowen	do
William Baker	do	224	—— Wilcox	do
Warren	do	382	—— Mayhew	Joseph Smith, jr., & Co
Providence, R. I.				
Brunswick	Ship	295	—— Stuart	Amherst & Everett
Newport, R. I.				
Harvest	Bark		Andrew Pickens	Devins & Clark
Mechanic	Ship		Edward Harding	Bush & Lee
New London, Conn.				
Ann Maria	Ship		—— Chester	
Bingham	do	375	—— Smith	Benjamin Brown
Com. Perry	do	270	—— Hobron	C. Chew & Co

sailing from American ports—Continued.

Whaling-ground.	Date— Of sailing.	Date— Of arrival.	Result of voyage. Sperm-oil.	Result of voyage. Whale-oil.	Result of voyage. Whalebone.	Remarks.
			Bbls.	*Bbls.*	*Lbs.*	
Pacific Ocean	July 22	Apr. 9, 1838	1, 811	471		
do	July 29	Nov. 13, 1837	2, 035			
do	Oct. 31	Aug. 6, 1837	1, 054	828		
Mexico		Aug, 25, 1834	70			Returned leaky.
Guinea	Sept. 25	Sept. 21, 1835	30			
Atlantic	Aug. 15					No report.
	Sept. 30	Sept. 30, 1834				Do.
	Oct, 4	Oct. 9, 1834		Clean		
Pacific Ocean	Aug. 14	June 14, 1838	1, 201	333		
do	Dec. 31	Nov. 3, 1837	2, 326			Went to New York, freighting, 1837; returned 1839.
Atlantic	Aug. 7	Aug. 10, 1834		18		
	Aug. 10	Aug. 19, 1834				No report.
	Aug. 23	Aug. 30, 1834				Returned with one small whale.
Pacific Ocean	Apr. 12	Sept. 7, 1837	1, 475			Captain Russell and one man lost overboard in a gale off New Zealand.
South Atlantic	May 21	Apr. 21, 1835		1, 400		
South Atlantic	June 2	Apr. 27, 1835		1, 450		
Pacific Ocean	Nov, 8	Apr. 25, 1836	450	1, 400		
South Atlantic	July 1					
South Atlantic	June 24	Mar. 24, 1836	500	1, 250		
Indian	Sept. 30	Mar. 17, 1837	1, 200	450		
South Atlantic	June —	Mar. 10, 1836	550	1, 600		
Pacific Ocean	Aug. 15	June 9, 1837	2, 700			Built 1834; sold 1837.
South Atlantic	Nov. 7	Apr. —, 1835		2, 100		
South Atlantic	July 9	May 14, 1836	300	1, 300		
Pacific Ocean	Jan. —	June 1, 1837	500			
South Atlantic		Mar. 11, 1836	460	1, 450		
Pacific Ocean	Aug. 22	Mar. 25, 1838	1, 350	300		Withdrawn for freighting, 1838
Africa	Nov. 24					
Pacific Ocean	Jan. 17					Built 1834 at Bristol.
South Atlantic	June 14	Mar. 2, 1836	40	460		
Pacific Ocean	Aug. 31	Jan. 8, 1838	1, 600			
South Atlantic		May 18, 1835	50	1, 150	9, 000	
do		Apr. 7, 1835	100	1, 500		
do		Apr. 8, 1836	300	2, 300		
do	Aug. 19					
Pacific Ocean	Sept. 28					
South Atlantic	Apr. 15	Apr. 7, 1836	60	1, 440		Bought from New York, 1833.
Indian Ocean	Dec. 12	May 14, 1836	370	1, 130	14, 000	
Pacific Ocean	Sept. 22	July 6, 1838	1, 740			Built 1834.
South Atlantic	May —	Apr. 21, 1835	600	1, 200		
do	June 2	Feb. 17, 1836	350	1, 650		
do	July 1	Mar. 12, 1836	370	1, 470		

Table showing returns of whaling-vessels

Name of vessel.	Class.	Tonnage.	Captain.	Managing owner or agent.
1834.				
New London, Conn.—Continued.				
Connecticut	Ship	398	—— Middleton	Thomas W. Williams
Chelsea	do	396	—— Butler	Havens & Smith
Emily	Schooner			
Electra	Ship	347	—— Payne	William Williams, jr
Flora	do		—— McLean	
Friends	do	403	—— Butler	Benjamin Brown
George	do	290	—— Tate	L. Allen
Indian Chief	do	401	—— Douglass	E. M. Frink & Co
Julius Cæsar	do		—— Hobron	
John and Edward	do		—— Bailey	
Jones	do		—— Fish	
Neptune	do	285	—— Andrews	Thomas W. Williams
Ospray	Brig		—— Fordham	
Phenix	Ship	404	—— Allen	N. & W. W. Billings
Tuscarora	do		Smith	
Stonington, Conn.				
Acasta	Ship	330	—— Peabody	Charles P. Williams
Eveline	Schooner			
Mystic, Conn.				
Aeronaut	Ship	265	—— Mallory	Charles Mallory
Bingham	do	375	—— Smith	do
Blackstone	Bark		—— Andrews	
Meteor	Ship		—— Bailey	
Norwich, Conn.				
Atlas	Ship	261	—— Fuller	
Sag Harbor, N. Y.				
Ann	Ship	299	—— Howell	Marcus B. Osborn
American	do		—— Jones	
Acasta	do	286	—— Howell	Mulford & Sleight
Cadmus	do	307	—— Hand	do
Columbia	do	285	—— Hedges	Luther D. Cook
Gem	do		—— Rogers	
Henry	do	333	—— Cartwright	Charles T. Dering
Hudson	do		—— Greene	L. D. Cook
Hannibal	do	311	—— Harris	S. & B. Huntting & Co
Marcus	do	283	—— Eldridge	S. & N. Howell
Neptune	do	338	—— Sayre	S. & B. Huntting & Co
Nimrod	do	280	—— Barns	C. T. Dering & Co
Ontario	do	368	—— Parker	S. & B. Huntting & Co
Phenix	do	314	—— Cooper	Luther D. Cook
Thames	do		—— Green	
Telegraph	do		—— Howett	
Thorn	do	299	—— Havens	Mulford & Sleight
Washington	do		—— Topping	
Greenport, N. Y.				
Delta	Ship	314	—— Payne	H. & N. Corwin
Triad	do	336	—— Case	do
Hudson, N. Y.				
George Clinton	Ship	427	—— Barrett	Robert A. Barnard
James Munroe	do	425	—— Plaskett	Barnard, Curtis & Co
New York, N. Y.				
Desdemona	Ship	295	—— Smith	Pell, Zabieski & Pell
Elizabeth Jane	Schooner		—— Alberton	
Washington	Ship		—— Clark	
White Oak	Bark		—— Fordham	
Poughkeepsie, N. Y.				
New England	Ship	375	—— Terry	David S. Shearman

sailing from American ports—Continued.

Whaling-ground.	Date—		Result of voyage.			Remarks.
	Of sailing.	Of arrival.	Sperm-oil.	Whale-oil.	Whalebone.	
			Bbls.	*Bbls.*	*Lbs.*	
South Atlantic	June 2	Jan. 19, 1836	150	2,050		
Pacific Ocean	Nov. 5	Mar. 25, 1838	1,800			
South Atlantic	Aug. 15					On a whaling and sealing voyage.
....do	June 10	May 16, 1835	150	1,600		
....do		Apr. 14, 1835	250	1,600	14,000	
....do	May 4	Mar. 11, 1836	200	2,800		
....do	June 2	Feb. 22, 1836	100	2,000		Bought from Dartmouth, 1834.
Indian Ocean	Feb. 18	Mar. 1, 1836	700	700		Added 1833.
South Atlantic		Apr. 21, 1835		2,000	16,000	
East Cape		Jan. 31, 1835	160	2,300		R. J. Bailey, first mate John and Edward, died, 1834.
South Atlantic		Mar. 12, 1835	200	1,600		
... do	June 10	Apr. 16, 1836		1,650		
....do		June 12, 1835		220		
Pacific Ocean	Mar. 25	May 20, 1837	2,900			
South Atlantic		Apr. 21, 1835		2,700	25,000	
South Atlantic	June 2	Apr. 10, 1835	100	1,600		Returned with skins, oil, and bone.
....do		May 3, 1835				
South Atlantic	June 2	Mar. 19, 1836	180	2,200		
....do	May 24	Feb. 17, 1836				
....do		Jan. —, 1835	170	130		
....do		Feb. 7, 1836	300	2,600		
South Atlantic	July 27	Oct. 4, 1835	270	700		Returned leaky.
South Atlantic	June 4	May 11, 1835	65	975		
....do		May 8, 1835	300	2,000	18,000	
....do	July 10	May 11, 1835	140	1,550		
....do	June 4	May 3, 1835		1,200		
....do	July 14	May 12, 1835	200	1,600	1,300	
....do		Apr. 21, 1835	300	1,200		
....do	May 12	May 2, 1835				
Indian Ocean		Jan. 29, 1835	350	2,350	2,500	
South Atlantic	July 1	May 11, 1835		1,500		
....do	July 14	June —, 1835	70	1,000		
....do	June 26	May 7, 1835	200	1,950	15,000	
....do	July 25	May 16, 1835	130	220		Also reported with 1,400 whale, 150 sperm.
....do	July 17	May 11, 1836		1,700		Built at Wareham 1834.
....do	July 25	May 16, 1835	500	1,900		
....do	June 4	May 24, 1835		1,300		
Pacific Ocean						Lost at the Marquesas, 1835; had 2,000 barrels.
South Atlantic	July 26	Apr. —, 1835		1,200		
Tristan		May 12, 1835	30	1,820	1,400	
South Atlantic	July 8	May —, 1835		1,800		
....do	June 4	May —, 1835		1,900		
Pacific Ocean	Aug. 16					Lost on New Jersey, homeward bound, January 18, 1838; saved 1,459 sperm.
....do	Nov. 19	July 3, 1838	1,650			
South Atlantic	May 20	Apr. 28, 1835		1,550		
South Pacific		Nov. 5, 1834		125	1,400	Also 800 seal-skins.
Pacific Ocean	May 25					
South Atlantic		Apr. —, 1835	57	943		
South Atlantic	June 7	Aug. 3, 1836	800	2,000		Built 1834.

Table showing returns of whaling-vessels

Name of vessel.	Class.	Tonnage.	Captain.	Managing owner or agent.
1834.				
Newburgh, N. Y.				
Russell	Ship	387	—— Brock	Charles Ludlow
Portland, Me.				
Science	Ship	388	—— Whippey	Chadwick & Davis
Wiscasset, Me.				
Wiscasset	Ship	380	Richard Macy	Jothan Parsons
Portsmouth, N. H.				
Plato	Ship		—— Manter	
Triton	do		—— Flanders	
Provincetown, Mass.				
Imogene	Brig		—— Smalley	
Fall River, Mass.				
Gold Hunter	Ship		—— Coffin	
Bridgeport, Conn.				
Atlantic	Ship		—— Young	
Wilmington, Del.				
Ceres	Ship	328	—— Weeden	William Wheeler
1835.				
New Bedford, Mass.				
Abigail	Ship	310	William H. Reynard	C. W. Morgan
Alexander	do	421	Simeon Price	J. A. Parker & Son
America	do	418	Elihu Gifford	I. Howland, jr., & Co
Brandt	do	310	James Maxfield	Alexander Gibbs
Brighton	do	354	Ebenezer Smith, jr	Charles R. Tucker
Corinthian	do	401	Leonard Crowell	George Howland
Com. Decatur	do	247	Joseph H. Trapp	Jireh Perry
Condor	do	349	George H. Dexter	C. W. Morgan
Clarice	Bark	237	Edward Merrill	do
China	do	370	William E. Tower	William H. Stowell
Coral	do	370	Hervey Sherman	Gideon Allen
Cicero	do	252	Owen Hillman, jr	Kollock & Grinnell
Ceres	do	373	John S. Barker	G. R. Thornton
Charleston Packet	Brig	184	Ebenezer Ellis, jr	Crane & French
Delight	do	102	Ray G. Sanford	Jona. Mosher
Endeavor	Ship	251	Ebenezer I. Stetson	C. C. Gilbert
Eliza Adams	do	402	John O. Morse	
Elizabeth	Bark	200	Elisha Dexter	
Emerald	Ship	359	Clement Norton	Thomas Riddell & Sons
Frances Henrietta	do	407	Richard G. Luce	Charles W. Morgan
Fenelon	do	3[illegible]8	John R. L. Smith	David Coffin
Friendship	do	360	Isaiah West	
George Porter	do	285	Ephraim Poole	Thomas Riddell & Sons
Gratitude	do	337	Alfred H. Fisher	do
General Pike	do	313	Thomas Dexter	Oliver Crocker
Gideon Howland	do	379	Jireh Shearman, jr	I. Howland, jr., & Co
Hercules	do	335	Albert G. Goodwin	Jireh Perry
Herald	do	274	Frederick Ricketson	Tobey & Ricketson
Hibernia	do	327	John Cole	Alfred Gibbs & Co
Honqua	do	339	Edward P. Mosher	Alexander Gibbs
Iris	do	311	Edward W. Coffin	E. Dunbar & Co
Independence	do	317	Loudon Fisher	Thomas S. Hathaway
Isaac Howland	do	399	Tristram P. Swain	I. Howland, jr., & Co
Julian	do	356	—— Trapp	Thomas Riddell & Sons
Java	do	295	Otis Smith	George Howland
John Adams	do	268	Abraham Russell, 2d	Jireh Perry
Janus	do	278	Ellery T. Taber	T. & A. R. Nye
Lucas	do	281	Richard Flanders	

sailing from American ports—Continued.

Whaling-ground.	Date— Of sailing.	Date— Of arrival.	Result of voyage. Sperm-oil.	Result of voyage. Whale-oil.	Result of voyage. Whalebone.	Remarks.
			Bbls.	*Bbls.*	*Lbs.*	
Pacific Ocean..	Aug. —	Jan. 7, 1837	1, 400	......	......	
Pacific Ocean..	Jan. 25	May 4, 1838	2, 100	......	......	
Pacific Ocean..	May 13	Sept. 10, 1837	2, 800	......	......	
South Atlantic.	Jan. 1	Feb. —, 1835	250	700	7, 000	
....do	May —	Apr. —, 1835	......	1, 400	......	
Cape G'd Hope.	....	Dec. 16, 1834	400	......	......	
South Atlantic	....	Mar. 6, 1835	......	1, 850	......	
South Atlantic.	....	Mar. —, 1835	......	800	......	
Pacific Ocean..	May 5	Oct. 5, 1837	1, 000	......	......	
Pacific Ocean..	Oct. 24	Oct. 26, 1838	2, 400	9	......	
....do	Apr. 27	July 25, 1838	1, 200	......	......	
Indian Ocean ..	Oct. 25	Apr. 19, 1838	911	2, 205	......	Bought from Boston 1835.
South Atlantic	May 24	Dec. 18, 1836	265	855	......	
Pacific Ocean ..	June 14	Oct. 26, 1838	1, 580	......	......	
....do	Nov. 8	Feb. 20, 1839	3, 025	33	......	
South Atlantic	June 14	Apr. 10, 1836	......	712	7, 000	
Brazil	Oct. 29	Feb. 25, 1837	29	2, 241	......	
Atlantic	May 13	Aug. 4, 1836	474	612	......	
South Atlantic	July 2	Apr. 10, 1837	......	2, 985	28, 800	
Pacific Ocean ..	Aug. 24	Nov. 13, 1838	2, 400	14	......	
South Atlantic	June 2	Mar. 11, 1837	325	1, 164	8, 808	
South Atlantic and Ind.	May 28	Apr. 15, 1837	341	2, 178	21, 100	
South Atlantic	Nov. 21	Mar. 15, 1837	40	874	8, 000	
Atlantic	Nov. 1	Aug. 30, 1836	143	11	.....	
Pacific Ocean ..	May 13	....	......	......	......	
....do	Nov. 1	Apr. 29, 1837	261	1, 597	....	
South Atlantic.	Sept. 7	....	......	.....	......	Wrecked at Pico September, 1836.
....do	July 15	Apr. 13, 1837	......	2, 890	28, 100	
Brazil Banks ..	Apr. 23	June 19, 1836	148	2, 198	......	Took off Brazil a 200-barrel whale.
South Atlantic	June 21	Feb. 25, 1837	270	2, 760	......	
New Zealand ..	July 9	....	......	......	......	
South Atlantic	July 26	May 1, 1836	......	707	......	
New Zealand ..	Sept. 11	Aug. 19, 1837	300	3, 100	......	
South Atlantic	May 21	Mar. 9, 1837	565	1, 970	20, 800	
Pacific Ocean ..	May 27	Sept. 13, 1838	1, 746	...	......	
South Atlantic	July 12	Mar. 29, 1837	457	1, 875	15, 600	
Indian Ocean ..	Aug. 5	Sept. 15, 1837	1, 400	350	......	
South Atlantic and Ind.	May 13	Mar. 16, 1836	......	2, 397	25, 000	
South Atlantic	Aug. 9	Apr. 9, 1837	176	1, 728	15, 400	
Pacific Ocean ..	Oct. 14	May 4, 1839	1, 305	230	......	
....do	Sept. 1	....	......	......	......	Lost at Vauvoo, 1837.
....do	July 1	Oct. 4, 1838	2, 620	......	......	
South Atlantic	July 1	July 25, 1838	......	3, 217	......	
....do	July 11	Apr. 26, 1837	270	1, 553	......	
Coast Chili	June 28	Apr. 19, 1837	272	1, 515	......	
South Atlantic.	May 21	Apr. 15, 1837	148	1, 941	16, 475	
New Zealand ..	July 9	Apr. 15, 1836	......	......	......	

Table showing returns of whaling-vessels

Name of vessel.	Class.	Tonnage.	Captain.	Managing owner or agent.
1835.				
New Bedford, Mass.—Continued.				
Lalla Rookh	Ship	323	Edward W. Howland	J. A. Parker & Son
Liverpool	do	305	Francis Fisher	Abraham Barker
Leader	Bark	169	Alexander P. Weeks	David Coffin
Mary Ann	do	171	William Handy, jr	
Milo	Ship	398	Shubael Worth	Andrew Robeson
Maria Theresa	do	330	Joseph B. Taber	
Messenger	do	277	John G. Chase	
Nile	do	371	James Townsend	
Ospray	Bark	169	Cornelius Noyes	T. & A. R. Nye
Octavia	do	257	James Alley	
Phenix	Ship	423	Squire Sandford	J. A. Parker & Son
Pocahontas	Brig	141	Isaac J. Sanford	Alexander Gibbs
Pacific, 2d	Ship	331	David Collins	Andrew Robeson
Parachute	do	330	Edmund Maxfield	
Phocion	do	265	Warren N. Bourne	Palmer & Coggeshall
Parker	do	406	William Austin	J. A. Parker & Son
Parthian	Brig	119	John Adams	Crane & French
Roman	Ship	375	Robert M. Joy	E. Dunbar & Co
Richmond	do	291	John Tucker	I. Howland, jr., & Co
Robert Edwards	do	356	Edward Howland	J. & J. Howland
Rajah	Bark	250	George W. Bennett	Isaiah Burgess
Stephania	Ship	315	Stephen H. Hathaway	Palmer & Coggeshall
Sally Anne	do	311	David Flanders	
Samuel Robertson	do	421	Daniel McKenzie	Andrew Robeson
——— Swift	do	456	Alexander M. Chase	
St. George	do	408	Jared Fisher	Abraham Barker
Tuscaloosa	do	284	William Hussey	Howland & Hussey
Timoleon	do	346	John Bunker	William T. Russell
Two Brothers	do	288	Henry F. Eastham	D. R. Greene & Co
Victory	do	268	John N. Cotton	Gideon Allen
William and Eliza	do	321	Job Collins	George Randall
William Rotch	do	290	David B. Delano	John Coggeshall
William Thompson	do	495	Hiram Weeks	Jireh Perry
Waverly	do	327	Reuben Russel, 2d	I. Howland, jr., & Co
Fairhaven, Mass.				
Ansell Gibbs	Ship	319	Tristram D. Pease	Gibbs & Jenney
Arab	Bark	275	Charles C. Russell	
Arab	Ship	336	Arthur Cox	E. Sawin
Columbus	do	382	Benjamin Ellis	Gibbs & Jenney
Eliza Adams	do	403	John O. Morse	Atkins Adams
Friendship	do	366	Isaiah West	Gibbs & Jenney
Favorite	Bark	293	John Bunting	E. Sawin
Herald	do	262	Zenas Dillingham	Samuel Borden
Heroine	do	337	Daniel Borden	E. Sawin
Isabella	Bark	243	John D. Taber	do
Java	Ship	292	Randall Kelley	A. Adams
Jasper	do	360	Stephen Raymond	do
Marcia	do	314	Benjamin Cushman	E. Sawin & Co
South Boston	do	339	Peter Butler	E. Sawin
Edgartown, Mass.				
George and Mary	Ship	356	——— Coffin	Abraham Osborne
Gold Hunter	Brig	202	——— Allen	Coffin & Darrow
Splendid	Ship	392	——— Luce	Abraham Osborne
Holmes s Hole, Mass.				
Delphos	Ship	338	Merry	Thomas Bradley

sailing from American ports—Continued.

Whaling-ground.	Date— Of sailing.	Date— Of arrival.	Result of voyage. Sperm-oil.	Result of voyage. Whale-oil.	Result of voyage. Whalebone.	Remarks.
			Bbls.	*Bbls.*	*Lbs.*	
Indian Ocean	Dec. 13	Apr. 26, 1837	276	1,038		Captain Howland and boat's crew lost.
South Atlantic	May 26	May 3, 1836	150	1,350		
Pacific Ocean	May 28	Apr. 9, 1838	480	138		Sold to Westport 1838.
Atlantic	July 2					Returned September 15 with Captain Handy, sick; sailed again September 23; upset and abandoned September 29, 1835.
Pacific Ocean	Mar. 12	Oct. 26, 1838	2,586			Sailed January 22; returned, leaking 1,000 strokes per hour, and sailed again.
South Atlantic	July 30	June 12, 1836	100	1,900		
....do	Aug. 19					
....do	Aug. 14					
Pacific Ocean	June 20					Condemned at Tahiti April 7, 1837; had 800 barrels oil; sold at Tahiti.
South Atlantic	June 7					
Pacific Ocean	Jan. 18	Oct. 26, 1838	2,901			
West'n Islands	July 12	Jan. 1, 1836	80			Sailed first March 5, 1835, Allen Wilkey, captain.
Atlantic	July 14	Apr. 9, 1837	52	2,533		
South Atlantic	July 8					
....do	Aug. 14	Apr. 16, 1837	437	1,760		
Pacific Ocean	May 30	May 3, 1839	1,523	1,539	15,200	
Atlantic	Aug. 27					Condemned and sold at Rio Janeiro August, 1836.
Pacific Ocean	Nov. 28	Apr. 7, 1839	2,993			
....do	May 27		1,400			Lost 2d and 3d mates and 9 men. Condemned at Bay of Islands August, 1839. Oil sold.
....do	Sept. 4	May 21, 1838	2,530			
South Atlantic	June 30	Apr. 10, 1837	108	1,389		Captain Bennett came home sick 1836.
South Atlantic and Ind.	Oct. 16	May 18, 1837	318	939		
South Atlantic	May 13	Apr. 15, 1836	190	1,750		
South Atlantic and Ind.	Aug. 23	June 24, 1837	185	3,351		Bought from New York 1835.
Pacific Ocean	Nov. 6					
....do	Nov. 6	June 19, 1839	2,485			Bought from New York 1835.
South Atlantic	July 12	Dec. 16, 1837	132	1,868		Bought from New York 1835.
Pacific Ocean	Nov. 13	June 24, 1839	1,209	244		
Indian Ocean	Oct. 9	Apr. 10, 1837	99	1,487		
Pacific Ocean	Dec. 7		1,600			Condemned at Otaheite July 12, 1838.
....do	Aug. 22	May 3, 1839	1,641	75		
....do	Nov. 17	Mar. 1, 1839	1,925			
....do	June 18	Aug. 31, 1838	1,352	2,854		
....do	July 8	Oct. 4, 1838	1,450	626		
Indian & Pacific	Dec. 10	Aug. 1, 1839	1,840			Built 1835.
Pacific Ocean	June 23	Mar. 11, 1836	360	2,400		
South Atlantic	June 14	Aug. 5, 1836	225	2,252		
Indian & Pacific	June 7	Feb. 26, 1837	605	2,047		
Pacific Ocean	Nov. 21	July 15, 1838	3,230			
New Zealand	July 9	Apr. 15, 1837	706	2,164		
S. A. and Indian	Jan. 27	Mar. 16, 1837	158	595	5,500	
South Atlantic	July 30	Apr. 12, 1836		599		
....do	July 7	Apr. 17, 1836	146	689		
Pacific Ocean	Aug. 22	Sept. 25, 1837	1,803			
New Zealand	Oct. 31	Feb. 11, 1838	1,165	778		
....do	Sept. 13	June 24, 1837	232	1,755		
Pacific Ocean	June 17	Nov. 22, 1836	180	2,120		
South Atlantic	July 13	Aug. 9, 1837	378	2,594		
Pacific Ocean	Aug. 2	May 10, 1839	3,000			
Atlantic	Apr. 19	May 14, 1836	430	60		
Pacific Ocean	Aug. 14	Sept. 19, 1839	1,600	500		Built at Mattapoisett 1835.
Brazil	Nov. 1	July 11, 1837	180	1,920		Bought from Boston 1835.

Table showing returns of whaling-vessels

Name of vessel.	Class.	Tonnage.	Captain.	Managing owner or agent.
1835.				
Nantucket, Mass.				
Barclay	Ship	301	Reuben Barney	Griffin Barney
Baltic	do	410	William Keene	P. H. Folger
Columbus	do	344	Peter Coffin	Paul Mitchell's Sons
Congress	do	339	William Upham	P. H. Folger
Catharine	do	384	Joseph M. Chase	Jared Coffin
Constitution	do	318	Edward C. Joy	C. G. & H. Coffin
Eagle	do	335	Isaac Gardner	David Joy
Ganges	do	265	Barzillai T. Folger	William H. Gardner
Harmony	Schooner	....	A. Swain	Thomas Coffin
Howard	Ship	365	William Worth, 2d	S. & T. Hussey
John Adams	do	296	Obed Luce, jr	Griffin Barney
Mary Mitchell	do	354	Samuel Joy	S. B. Tuck
Mary	do	369	Thomas Coffin, 2d	Daniel Jones
Mount Vernon	do	384	Lewis B. Imbert	William Folger
President	do	293	Seth Cathcart	Joseph Starbuck
Peru	do	257	William Brown, jr	David Joy
Richard Mitchell	do	385	Henry C. Cleveland	P. Mitchell & Sons
Rambler	do	318	Robert M. McCleave	Aaron Mitchell
Reaper	do	338	Timothy R. Coffin	P. H. Folger
Spartan	do	333	David W. Coffin	Daniel Jones
Lynn, Mass.				
Atlas	Ship	260	——— Gardner	H. Chase & Co
Clay	do	....	——— Church	
Ninus	do	260	——— Fordham	S. H. Gardner
Plymouth, Mass.				
Mary and Martha	Ship	317	John B. Coffin	James Bartlett, jr
Triton	do	315	{ ——— Ritchie { ——— Abrams	do do
Salem, Mass.				
Bengal	Ship	304	George Netcher	John B. Osgood
Cavalier	Bark	295	——— Russell	James King
Lydia	Ship	293	——— Ramsdell	John B. Osgood
Izette	do	....	——— Sistare	
Palestine	Bark	249	——— Cartwright	Nathaniel Weston
Reaper	do	230	——— Jackson	John B. Osgood
Richard	do	252	——— Dewing	Joseph Hodges
Westport, Mass.				
Elizabeth	Brig	107	George Sowle	Abner B. Coffin
Industry	do	94	Hiram Francis	
Mexico	do	....	——— Davis	
Dartmouth, Mass.				
South Carolina	Ship	306	William B. Perry	James Rider
Sag Harbor, N. Y.				
Ann	Ship	299	——— Howell	Marcus B. Osborne
American	do	283	——— Jones	S. & B. Huntting & Co
Acasta	do	286	——— Glover	Mulford & Sleight
Camillus	do	345	——— Topping	Charles T. Dering
Columbia	do	285	——— Hedges	Luther D. Cork
Cadmus	do	307	——— Hand	Mulford & Sleight
Gem	do	326	——— Halsey	Huntting Cooper
Hudson	do	....	——— Green	Luther D. Cook
Henry	do	333	——— Cartwright	Charles T. Dering
Hannibal	do	311	——— Harris	S. & B. Huntting & Co
Marcus	do	283	——— Eldridge	S. & N. Howell
Neptune	do	338	——— Sayre	S. & B. Huntting & Co
Nimrod	do	280	——— Barns	C. T. Dering & Co
Panama	do	464	——— Howell	N. G. Howell

sailing from American ports—Continued.

Whaling-ground.	Date—		Result of voyage.			Remarks.
	Of sailing.	Of arrival.	Sperm-oil.	Whale-oil.	Whalebone.	
			Bbls.	*Bbls.*	*Lbs.*	
Pacific Ocean	Nov. 13	——, 1839	1,550			
do	Sept. 8	Mar. 18, 1839	1,420	1,694		
do	June 29	Nov. 12, 1838	1,398	16		
do	July 23	Nov. 20, 1838	1,902			
do	July 29	Oct. 26, 1838	3,016			
do	Oct. 25	Apr. 7, 1839	1,630			
Atlantic	July 29	Apr. 17, 1837	625	1,293		Broken up at Nantncket 1837.
Pacific Ocean	Oct. 26	May 10, 1839	1,644			
Gulf of Mexico	Aug. 2	Aug. 20, 1836	260	150		
Pacific Ocean	Sept. 21	Apr. 21, 1838	2,312			
Atlantic & Ind.	July 15	July 9, 1837	302	1,570		
Pacific Ocean	July 14	May 17, 1838	596	1,974		
do	July 30	May 12, 1839	1,866	515		
do	Oct. 5	July 17, 1839	2,456			
do	June 24	June 1, 1838	1,670			
do	Oct. 4	Apr. 13, 1839	676	149		
do	July 20	Dec. 27, 1838	1,172	937		
do	Sept. 8	Aug. 23, 1838	2,246			
do	Oct. 12					Supposed to have foundered in a gale off New Zealand, and all on board lost.
do	Oct. 4	May 4, 1839	1,790			
South Atlantic	July 19					Condemned at Isle of France, September, 1836.
S. A. and Indian	June —	Apr. 29, 1836		1,100		
South Atlantic	Sept. 2	Apr. 18, 1837	120	600		Bought from New York, 1835.
South Atlantic	Sept. 17	Sept. 26, 1837	150	2,250		
do	July 23	——, 1834				Returned leaky.
do	Nov. 29	Dec. 31, 1835				Arrived at Holmes' Hole leaky.
South Atlantic	July 11	Mar. 28, 1837	140	1,600		
do	Oct. 25	May 22, 1737	75			Sold 980 whale at Rio Janeiro.
do	Sept. 22	Nov. 5, 1837	1,500	300		Bought from Portsmouth 1835.
do	May 31					
Pacific Ocean	Nov. 8	Apr. 10, 1839	1,600			Bought from Boston 1835.
S. A. and Indian	Aug. 5	July 12, 1837	1,100			
South Atlantic	Oct. 12	——, 1837				
Atlantic	June 14	June 17, 1836	330	7		
do	Apr. 17					The Industry sailed again late in 1835, or early in 1836, under Captain Soule, and was lost in the Gulf of Mexico with 310 sperm.
{ South Atlantic	Apr. —	Nov. 22, 1835	370			
{ Cape de Verde		Nov. 3, 1835	300			
South Atlantic	Aug. 14	Apr. 23, 1837	30	1,670		
South Atlantic	July 13	May 3, 1836		1,850		
do	June 29	July 1, 1836		1,000		
do	June 17	Apr. 23, 1836	150	1,650		Captain Glover was killed by a whale.
do	Aug. 2	May 10, 1836	160	1,100		Bought from New York 1835.
do	July 16	May 11, 1836	400	1,000		
do	July 17	May 19, 1836	380	820		
do	June 9	Mar. 6, 1836	100	900		
do		July 1, 1836	520	1,400		
do	July 20	Apr. 18, 1836		2,500		
do	May 16	June 5, 1836		1,000		
do	June 29	June 17, 1836	100	500		
do	July 2					
do	July 13					
do	Aug. 6	Apr. 10, 1838	700	3,400		

Table showing returns of whaling-vessels

Name of vessel.	Class.	Tonnage.	Captain.	Managing owner or agent.
1835.				
Sag Harbor, N. Y.—Continued.				
Thames	Ship	....	—— Green	
Thorn	...do	299	—— Havens	Mulford & Sleight
Washington	...do	340	—— Topping	Josiah Douglass
Xenophon	...do	389	—— Hand	Mulford & Sleight
Wilmington, Del.				
Lucy Anne	Ship	309	John J. Parker	William Wheeler
Bristol, R. I.				
Golconda	Ship	359	—— Chase	Fitzhenry Homer
Sarah Lee	...do	235	—— Weeks	W. H. De Wolf
Troy	Brig	156	—— Lake	Thomas Church
William Baker	Ship	...		
New London, Conn.				
Atlas	Ship	299	—— Barnum	Joseph Lawrence
Ann Maria	...do	368	—— Chester	Thomas W. Williams
Boston	...do	291	—— Fitch	Joseph Lawrence
Com. Perry	...do	270	—— Hobron	C. Chew & Co
Caledonia	...do	446	—— Hall	Thomas W. Williams
Electra	...do	347	—— Lax	William Williams, jr
Flora	...do	338	—— Smith	N. & W. W. Billings
Georgia	...do	343	—— Peabody	Thomas W. Williams
Jason	Bark	335	—— Fuller	E. M. Frink & Co
John and Edward	Ship	318	—— Bailey	N. & W. W. Billings
Julius Cæsar	...do	...	—— McLean	
Jones	...do	336		Thomas W. Williams
North America	...do	385	—— Richards	...do
Ospray	Brig	...	—— Clift	
Palladium	Ship	342	—— Prentiss	E. M. Frink & Co
Philetus	Bark		—— Brewster	
Tuscarora	Ship	379	—— Smith	N. & W. W. Billings
Warren, R. I.				
Atlas	Brig	126	—— Smith	William Carr, jr
Hoogley	Ship	292	—— Luce	William Collins & Co
Magnet	...do	355	—— Brown	Joseph Smith, jr., & Co
Miles	...do	...	—— Adams	
North America	...do	288	—— Grinnell	Driscoll & Child
Rosalie	...do	323	—— Stillwell	Joseph Smith, jr., & Co
Hudson, N. Y.				
Alexander Mansfield	Ship	320	B. E. Starbuck	Barnard, Curtis & Co
Edward	...do	274	—— Coffin	Seth G. Macy
Henry Astor	...do	375	—— Rawson	Robert A. Barnard
Poughkeepsie, N. Y.				
Newark	Ship	323	—— Whitfield	David S. Shearman
Vermont	Bark	292	—— Topham	...do
Newburgh, N. Y.				
Illinois	Ship	414	Henry H. Merchant	Charles Ludlow
New York, N. Y.				
Desdemona	Ship	295	—— Smith	Pell, Zabieskie & Pell
Hesper	Bark	...	—— Heyer	S. E. Burrows
Julia	Brig	...	—— Nash	
Medina	...do	...	—— Albertson	S. E. Burrows
Portland	Ship	...	—— Cook	
White Oak	Bark	291	—— Post	Pell, Zabieskie & Pell
Fall River, Mass.				
Gold Hunter	Ship	281	—— Coffin	Henry Slade
Pantheon	...do	284	Jabez J. Pell	John Eddy

sailing from American ports—Continued.

Whaling-ground.	Date—		Result of voyage.			Remarks.
	Of sailing.	Of arrival.	Sperm-oil.	Whale-oil.	Whalebone.	
			Bbls.	*Bbls.*	*Lbs.*	
South Atlantic.	July 20	....	....	......	......	
....do	July 20	May 12, 1836	190	1,210	......	
...do	July 11	....	......	......	......	
....do	May 25	Apr. 12, 1837	400	2,400	......	
South Atlantic.	Sept. 12	Apr. 27, 1837	300	1,400	......	
Indian Ocean ..	Dec. 7	Mar. 25, 1838	200	1,400	......	Bought from Boston 1835; sold to New Bedford 1838.
....do	Feb. 2	Apr. 26, 1837	......	1,700	......	
West. Islands ..	May 14	....	......	......	......	
....	....	Mar. 8, 1836	220	900	......	
Indian Ocean ..	May 17	....	......	......	......	
South Atlantic.	June 26	Apr. 10, 1837	100	2,150	......	2d mate lost.
....do	June 9	Mar. 18, 1837	140	2,000	......	
Indian Ocean ..	May 18	Mar. 12, 1836	370	1,470	......	
Falkland	Sept. 28	Mar. 17, 1837	200	3,400	......	Sold to Stonington 1837.
South Atlantic	June 27	Apr. 28, 1836	......	1,000	......	
....do	May 30	Apr. 16, 1836	80	1,570	......	
....do	June 9	Feb. 12, 1837	300	2,100	......	
....do	May 14	....	......	......	......	
....do	May 21	....	......	......	......	
....do	Apr. 7	Apr. 7, 1836	30	1,900	......	
Falkland	May 30	....	......	......	......	
Pacific Ocean ..	Aug. 11	July 16, 1839	2,200	......	......	
South Atlantic	Aug. 11	Aug. 4, 1836	......	900	......	
....do	June 30	....	......	......	......	
....do	Nov. 10	....	......	......	......	
Indian Ocean ..	May 15	Mar. 28, 1836	......	2,825	......	
West. Islands ..	July 27	June 10, 1836	50	......	......	
Indian Ocean ..	Nov. 10	Apr. 18, 1837	150	1,000	......	Bought from Boston 1835.
Pacific Ocean ..	Nov. 21	Mar. 3, 1839	1,600	......	......	
South Atlantic.	....	Apr. 18, 1836	170	350	......	
....do	June 14	May 5, 1837	......	2,000	......	
Pacific Ocean ..	June 29	....	......	......	......	Crew mutinied; ship carried into Rio by an English schooner.
Pacific Ocean ..	Nov. 5	Apr. 29, 1837	25	975	......	
South Atlantic.	June 14	Aug. 3, 1836	140	700	......	
Pacific Ocean ..	July 25	Aug. 5, 1839	1,000	700	......	Sold to Nantucket 1839.
Pacific Ocean ..	July 22	May 15, 1839	1,800	......	......	
South Atlantic.	June 6	May 12, 1837	400	2,500	......	
Pacific Ocean ..	Aug. 22	Apr. 7, 1839	2,200	100	......	
South Atlantic	June 18	May 4, 1837	50	1,850	......	
Falkland	Apr. —	....	......	......	......	
South Atlantic.	May —	....	......	......	......	
Patagonia	Mar. 8	....	......	......	......	Last reported at Rio Janeiro, Nov. 30, 1839.
South Atlantic	June 19	....	......	......	......	
....do	June 14	May 10, 1837	300	......	......	Sold 1,400 whale at Rio Janeiro.
South Atlantic.	June 6	Apr. 7, 1837	90	1,240	......	
Pacific Ocean ..	Sept. 13	May 4, 1839	1,000	1,400	......	Added 1835.

Table showing returns of whaling-vessels

Name of vessel.	Class.	Tonnage.	Captain.	Managing owner or agent.
1835.				
Dorchester, Mass.				
Lewis	Bark	280	W. Reed	C. O. Whitmore
Rochester, Mass.				
Laurel	Schooner		—— Mayhew	
Orion	Brig		—— Snow	
Shylock	Ship	277	Hallett Swift	
Newburyport, Mass.				
Navy	Ship	356	—— Neil	Lunt & Titcomb
Stonington, Conn.				
Acasta	Ship	330	—— Pendleton	C. P. Williams
Charles Adams	do	268	—— Beck	B. & F. Pendleton
George	Bark	251	—— Brewster	C. P. Williams
Henry	Brig			
Mercury	Ship		—— Stanton	
Philetus	do	278	—— Brewster	E. Faxon, jr., & Co
Greenport, N. Y.				
Bayard	Ship	339	—— Miller	H. & N. Corwin
Delta	do	314	—— Payne	do
Falmouth, Mass.				
Brunette	Bark	200	—— Cottle	Elijah Swift
George Washington	do	180	Consider Fisher	Sanford Herendeen
Pocahontas	Ship	350	Joseph Swift	Elijah Swift
Uncas	do	400	Uriah Clark	do
Newport, R. I.				
Erie	Ship		A. W. Dennis	Engs & Bush
Frederick	Bark		J. D. Dornin	N. Ruggles
John Coggeshall	Ship		S. W. Macy	Bush, Macy & Clark
Martha	do		Oliver Potter	Lee, Newton & Stevens
Bridgeport, Conn.				
Atlantic	Ship	291	—— Cooper	Samuel H. Ford
Hamilton	do		—— Harris	do
Provincetown, Mass.				
Imogene	Brig			
Imogene	do		—— Atkins	
Newark, N. J.				
John Wells	Ship			
Mystic, Conn.				
Blackstone	Ship	258	—— Chester	Silas Beebe
Portsmouth, N. H.				
Triton	Ship		—— Ritchie	
1836.				
New Bedford, Mass.				
Ann Alexander	Ship	253	—— Bailey	George Howland
Amethyst	do	359	—— Howland	John A. Parker & Son
Averick	do	385	—— Lawrence	do
America	Brig	150	{ —— Hawes —— Hutchins }	Lawrence Grinnell
Agate	do		{ A. H. Seabury —— Cornell }	

sailing from American ports—Continued.

Whaling-ground.	Date—		Result of voyage.			Remarks.
	Of sailing.	Of arrival.	Sperm-oil.	Whale-oil.	Whalebone.	
			Bbls.	*Bbls.*	*Lbs.*	
South Atlantic.	July 7	....	.....	......	......	Bought from Gloucester; altered from a ship, 1835.
Cape de Verde	....	Nov. 27, 1835	300	15	......	Probably sailed twice; arrived June 7, 1835, 110 sperm.
Atlantic	Apr. 22	July 1, 1835	275	......	......	
South Atlantic	July 13	....	.....	......	....	
S. A. and Pacific	July 2	July 15, 1837	200	2, 600	....	
Falkland	....	Feb. 3, 1837	50	2, 000	.....	
Pat. and Falk..	....	June 15, 1836	.....	1, 800	......	Tender brought home 500 whale besides.
Brazil	....	Apr. 28, 1837	120	1, 900	....	
Falkland	....	Aug. 27, 1836	.....	600	......	
....do	....	Sept. 2, 1836	.....	2, 400	24, 000	
South Atlantic	Nov. 10	—— —, 1837	300	700	.....	About.
South Atlantic	....	May 7, 1837	....	1, 950	......	Bought from New York 1835.
....do	July 23	May 3, 1836	150	1, 650	......	
....	May 10	Feb. 25, 1837	700	...	......	
South Atlantic	Nov. 24	Apr. 15, 1837	60	400	......	Bought from New York 1835.
Pacific Ocean ..	Oct. 31	Jan. —, 1838	1, 200	..	......	Sold to Holmes's Hole 1838.
....do	Aug. 2	Apr. 9, 1839	1, 800	1, 000	.....	
PScific Ocean ..	Sept. 6	July 23, 1838	300	2, 600	....	
....do	Aug. 2	Mar. 26, 1838	1, 400	600	......	Sold to Boston, 1838, for a merchantman.
....do	Oct. 2	Apr. 13, 1839	1, 500	850	11, 000	
....do	Sept. 8	June 1, 1837	250	1, 700	....	Lost second mate.
South Atlantic	May 27	Apr. 28, 1837	250	1, 500	....	
Brazil	....	June 4, 1836	.....	1, 800	....	
Cape de Verde.	Apr. —	Nov. 9, 1835	470	......	....	
Atlantic	Apr. —	....	.....	......	.....	Reported, middle of July, 200 sperm.
....	....	No report	.....	......	......	Bought from Philadelphia 1834.
South Atlantic	July —	Mar. 17, 1837	400	1, 200	......	
South Atlantic	July 25	Apr. 21, 1837	170	1, 830	......	
South Atlantic.	May 19	Apr. 7, 1837	131	1, 406	12, 230	
....do	Aug. 15	Mar. 24, 1838	733	1, 482	......	
Pacific Ocean ..	July 31	Apr. 10, 1840	2, 350	......	......	
Atlantic	....	Nov. 5, 1836	.....	......	......	Crew sick. Withdrawn for freighting. Condemned at Rio Janeiro 1838. Bought from Boston 1836.
	Dec. 15	Oct. 20, 1837	50	......	......	
....	Apr. 7	Nov. 13, 1837	175	......	......	
	Dec. 22	....	.....	......	......	

Table showing returns of whaling-vessels

Name of vessel.	Class.	Tonnage.	Captain.	Managing owner or agent.
1836.				
New Bedford, Mass.—Continued.				
Bramin	Bark	245	—— Russell	Gideon Allen
Com. Rogers	Ship	298	—— Howland	T. & A. R. Nye
Com. Decatur	do	247	—— Luce	
Chili	do	291	Elihu Russell	B. B. Howard
Courier	do	381	Jared Worth	Randall & Haskell
Clarice	Bark	237	Benjamin Clark	Charles W. Morgan
Cambria	Ship	362	—— Cary	William T. Russell
Charles Frederick	do	317	Charles F. Brown	J. A. Parker & Son
Cherokee	Bark	261	Caleb Howland	David Coffin
Columbus	do	313	—— Cary	William R. Rodman
Delight	Brig	102	—— Sanford	Jona. Mosher
Equator	Bark	262	—— Coffin	—— Standish
Frances	Ship	347	—— Christian	Wm. R. Rotch & Co
Frances, 2d	do	368	—— Briggs	Gideon Allen
Falcon	do	273	—— Taber	Briggs & Bartlett
Florida	do	330	Russell Maxfield	E. Dunbar & Co
Golconda	do	330	—— Adams	George Howland
George Porter	do	285	Jos. B. Leonard	Thomas Riddell & Sons.
Good Return	do	376	Warren Howland	Henry Taber
George	do	273	Thomas Hammond	J. A. Parker & Son
George and Martha	Bark	275	—— Allen	Haskell & Randall
Hope	Ship	316	—— Gifford	George Howland
Herald, 2d	do	303	—— Manchester	T. and A. R. Nye
Hibernia	do	327	—— Brown	Alfred Gibbs & Co
Huntress	do	391	John Cole	do
John	do	308	—— Howland	Frederick Parker
John Howland	do	376	William Whitton	J. & J. Howland
Jasper	Bark	223	William Flanders	Alexander Gibbs
Juno	Brig	123	P. G. Macomber	A. H. Seabury & Bro
Liverpool	Ship	306	—— Fisher	Abm. Barker
London Packet	do	280	—— Jenney	A. H. Howland
Lucas	do	281	George Tobey	Tobey & Ricketson
Mercator	do	246	—— Mayhew	J. A. Parker & Son
Maria Theresa	do	330	—— Taber	T. & A. R. Nye
Maria	do	202	—— Prince	C. W. Morgan
Minerva Smyth	do	335	—— Brownell	I. Howland, jr., & Co
Mary	do	287	—— Luce	do
Minerva	do	407	Moses Samson	William Gifford
Milton	do	387	—— Tuckerman	Henry Taber & Co
Mobile	do	263	—— Rawson	William R. Rodman
Mount Vernon	do	352	C. P. Covell	D. R. Greene & Co
Massachusetts	do	364	—— Brown	O. Crocker & Co
Marcella	Bark	210	—— Derrick	David Coffin
Milwood	do	254	—— Russell	Gideon Allen
Minerva	do	195	—— Starbuck	Charles R. Tucker
Nye	Ship	211	—— Shearman	T. & A. R. Nye
Newton	Bark	283	—— Hathaway	Isaiah Burgess
Orozimbo	Ship	588	—— Shearman	William T. Russell
Pacific	do	385	—— Palmer	Jireh Perry
Pocahontas	Brig	141	—— West	
Parachute	Ship	331	—— Maxfield	A. H. Seabury & Bro
Roman, 2d	do	350	—— Bartlett	Abm. Barker
Roscoe	do	362	—— Pitman	And. Robeson
Rebecca Sims	do	400	—— Ray	William R. Rodman
Roscoe	Bark	235	—— Brown	Jona. Bourne, jr
Rising States	Brig	134	—— Pompey	Richard Johnson
Sally Anne	Ship	312	Henry Colt	D. R. Greene & Co
Sarah Louisa	Brig	144	Ray G. Sanford	William R. Rodman
Virginia	Ship	346	R. Luce	William H. Stowell
Young Phenix	do	377	—— Shearman	J. A. Parker & Son
Zephyr	do	361	—— Perry	Alexander Gibbs
Fairhaven, Mass.				
Alto	Bark	197	—— Calder	Alden D. Stoddard

sailing from American ports—Continued.

Whaling-ground.	Date—Of sailing.	Date—Of arrival.	Result of voyage.—Sperm-oil.	Result of voyage.—Whale-oil.	Result of voyage.—Whalebone.	Remarks.
			Bbls.	*Bbls.*	*Lbs.*	
Pacific Ocean ..	Mar. 15	Sept. 29, 1839	1,443	......	......	
....do	June 1	....	......	......	......	Lost at Monterey, Cal. Had 800 sperm, mostly saved.
Atlantic	May 13	Nov. 22, 1836	259	7	......	
South Atlantic.	July 29	May 3, 1837	110	1,366	......	
....do	July 1	Jan. 12, 1838	......	2,550	26,000	Captain Worth died at sea Oct. 14, 1837.
Brazil Banks...	Sept. 14	July 23, 1838	72	934	......	
South Atlantic.	June 2	Mar. 24, 1838	500	2,094	......	
Pacific Ocean ..	Jan. 7	Mar. 4, 1838	2,630	......	......	Built 1836. Bought 466 barrels sperm from wreck of Swift.
South Atlantic.	July 14	Apr. 28, 1837	50	1,233	......	Captain Howland and two men were lost 1836.
Pacific Ocean ..	May 20	July 15, 1839	556	......	......	Moses Morse, second mate, died June 23, 1837.
Atlantic	Nov. 26	Oct. 7, 1837	221	......	......	Sailed September 30; returned October 15; lost both masts and boats in a gale Oct. 4.
Pacific Ocean ..	May 13	June 20, 1839	1,137	......	......	
....do	May 19	June 14, 1839	2,837	9	......	
....do	Dec. 6	June 26, 1840	1,071	409	......	
South Atlantic.	May 21	Apr. 26, 1838	604	1,583	......	
....do	July 13	June 9, 1838	219	1,830	......	Bought from New York 1836.
Pacific Ocean ..	May 9	Mar. 27, 1839	1,509	4	......	
South Atlantic.	May 30	May 18, 1838	42	633	......	
....do	May 21	Apr. 12, 1838	367	2,168	......	
Pacific Ocean ..	June 4	Oct. 3, 1839	1,500	......	......	
South Atlantic.	May 10	Apr. 30, 1838	154	1,745	......	
Pacific Ocean ..	July 27	Dec. 11, 1839	1,940	50	......	
South Atlantic.	June 15	Apr. 20, 1838	158	1,835	......	
Indian Ocean ..	May 5	Apr. 9, 1837	......	1,776	20,458	
....do	May 14	Nov. 5, 1837	100	1,450	......	Sold 50 sperm, 1,700 whale, at Bahia.
South Atlantic.	June 16	Mar. 25, 1838	184	2,066	......	
Pacific Ocean ..	Aug. 16	July 30, 1839	2,550	160	......	
South Atlantic	July 31	Apr. 27, 1837	170	490	......	
Atlantic	Dec. 28	Mar. 10, 1838	120	10	......	Bought from Providence 1836.
South Atlantic	July 6	Mar. 15, 1838	275	1,092	......	Captain Fisher left ship and came home sick.
....do	June 5	Mar. 10, 1838	363	1,987	19,500	
....do	June 9	May 7, 1838	166	2,166	......	
Pacific Ocean ..	Dec. 28	Feb. 21, 1840	1,235	......	......	
South Atlantic.	July 31	Mar. 30, 1838	539	1,600	......	
....do	July 17	Oct. 21, 1837	343	87	......	Sailed once and returned, having been struck by lightning.
Pacific Ocean ..	Oct. 7	July 7, 1839	1,386	213	......	
Brazil Banks...	Sept. 14	Mar. 6, 1838	162	2,066	......	
South Atlantic.	July 4	Apr. 9, 1837	116	1,865	14,500	
Chili	Nov. 16	Apr. 9, 1839	542	2,076	16,411	
Pacific Ocean ..	Aug. 15	Sept. 18, 1839	1,427	4	......	
Indian Ocean ..	June 10	July 10, 1837	244	1,938	20,271	
Pacific Ocean ..	Dec. 7	July 29, 1840	1,924	......	......	Built 1836.
....do	May 26	Feb. 29, 1840	837	43	......	
South Atlantic.	June 29	Mar. 24, 1838	175	550	......	
Pacific Ocean ..	July 21	Mar. 26, 1839	233	207	......	
....do	May 19	Oct. 2, 1839	1,076	....	......	
South Atlantic.	May 21	Apr. 20, 1838	130	2,445	......	
....do	Sept. 29	Oct. 3, 1838	305	3,297	......	
Pacific Ocean ..	Nov. 2	May 25, 1840	1,378	......	......	
Cape de Verdes	Apr. 11	Nov. 5, 1836	100	.....	......	Returned, the crew having mutinied.
South Atlantic.	June 5	Apr. 21, 1837	83	1,890	......	
Indian Ocean ..	June 10	May 8, 1838	233	2,972	......	Bought from New York 1836.
Pacific Ocean ..	July 27	Nov. 7, 1839	2,481	26	......	
....do	July 11	Sept. 19, 1839	2,490	93	......	
South Atlantic	May 26	Apr. 9, 1837	92	1,035	11,674	
Atlantic	Nov. 6	June 29, 1837	78	9	......	
Indian Ocean ..	June 1	Apr. 3, 1838	106	2,183	......	
Atlantic	Nov. 25	June 10, 1838	287	40	......	
Brazil Banks...	Dec. 1	Mar. 24, 1838	240	2,260	......	Built at Mattapoisett 1836.
Pacific Ocean ..	Dec. 11	Mar. 28, 1840	2,397	......	......	
South Atlantic	May 19	Mar. 26, 1838	422	1,461	......	
Atl'c & Ind'n ..	June 9	Nov. 21, 1837	530	......	......	

Table showing returns of whaling-vessels

Name of vessel.	Class.	Tonnage.	Captain.	Managing owner or agent.
1836.				
Fairhaven, Mass.—Continued.				
Albion	Ship	326	—— Hathaway	E. Sawin
Arab	do	336	—— Jenney	do
Clifford Wayne	do	305	—— Downs	E. Sawin & Co.
George	do	360	—— Chase	Fish & Huttlestone
Herald	do	262	—— Dillingham	Samuel Borden
Heroine	do	337	—— Harding	E. Sawin
Joseph Maxwell	do	302	—— Hathaway	F. R. Whitwell
Leonidas	do	243	—— Mayhew	Jenney & Tripp
London Packet	do	335	—— Norris	Gibbs & Jenney
Martha	do	298	—— Fisher	Nathan Church
Martha, 2d	do	301	—— Borden	Atkins Adams
Maine	do	294	—— Magee	E. Sawin
Pactolus	do	288	—— Grinnell	I. F. Terry
Staunton	do	304	John Delano	Lemuel Tripp
Rochester, Mass.				
Annawan	Brig	148	{ —— Snow —— Hammond }	G. Barstow & Son
Caduceus	do	109	—— Southworth	Joseph Meigs
Dryade	Bark	263	—— Smalley	G. Barstow & Son
Gideon Barstow	Ship	379	—— Severance	do
Laurel	Schooner		—— Luce	
Mattapoisett	Ship		—— Southworth	
Orion	Brig		—— Daggett	
Sarah	Ship		—— Mayhew	
Nantucket, Mass.				
Atlantic	Ship	321	Thomas Russell	James Athearn
Alexander Coffin	do	381	John C. Congdon	Richard Mitchell
Catawba	do	335	John B. Coleman	Charles G. Coffin
Charles Carroll	do	376	Owen Chase	David Joy
Cyrus	do	328	Benj. R. Hussey	George Myrick, jr
Charles and Henry	do	336	George Joy	Charles G. Coffin
Dromo	Brig		—— Chadwick	
Enterprise	Ship	413	George Haggarty	Gilbert Coffin
Harvest	do	360	William B. Cash	Samuel B. Folger
Henry	do	346	George G. Chase	Daniel Jones
Harmony	Schooner		—— Gifford	
Jefferson	Ship	377	Obed. Swain	William Folger
Kingston	do	312	Thaddeus Coffin	Timothy Hussey
Lexington	do	399	Alexander Pollard	Franklin Macy
Lexington	Schooner		—— Hamblin	
Mariner	Ship	349	Geo. W. Gardner, jr	Matthew Crosby
Maria	do	365	Elisha H. Fisher	Gorham Coffin
Orbit	do	351	Benj. B. Raymond	Thomas Macy
Ocean	do	349	Elijah Parker	Peter Macy
Orion	do	354	Elihu Coffin	Timothy Hussey
Omega	do	363	Albert C. Gardner	Joseph Starbuck
Ontario	do	354	George G. Cathcart	Samuel Mitchell
Panama	do	253	Alexander D. Bunker	George B. Upton
Primrose	Schooner		—— Fisher	
Peruvian	Ship	334	David Osborne	Gorham Coffin
Thule	do	285	James Coleman	Samuel B. Tuck
Washington	do	308	Charles F. Coffin	Matthew Crosby
Walter Scott	do	339	Benj. Coggeshall	Gorham Coffin
Young Eagle	do	377	George Crocker	Simon Starbuck
Zenas Coffin	do	338	Hiram Bailey	Charles G. Coffin
Edgartown, Mass.				
Gold Hunter	Brig	202	—— Allen	Coffin & Darrow
Mary	Ship	348	Henry Pease	do
Vineyard	do	381	—— Tilton	G. Norton

sailing from American ports—Continued.

Whaling-ground.	Date—Of sailing.	Date—Of arrival.	Result of voyage.—Sperm-oil.	Result of voyage.—Whale-oil.	Result of voyage.—Whalebone.	Remarks.
			Bbls.	*Bbls.*	*Lbs.*	
South Atlantic.	Aug. 20	Apr. 6, 1838	180	1, 438	.....	
Falklands......	Sept. 20	Apr. 29, 1838	162	1, 372	.....	Captain Jenney left the ship and came home sick.
Pacific Ocean ..	Dec. 28	Sept. 10, 1837	50	.....	.....	Bought from Boston 1836. Returned on account of mutiny with crew.
South Atlantic.	Oct. 3	May 15, 1838	158	1, 126	.....	
....do	Aug. 12	Apr. 11, 1838	180	426	.....	
....do	Sept. 14	June 22, 1837	150	1, 650	.....	
.. do	June 5	May 5, 1837	115	1, 334	....	
.. do	July 17	June 5, 1837	67	1, 426	.....	
Indian Ocean ..	June 5	Aug. 16, 1839	2, 325	.....	.....	
South Atlantic	July 6	Mar. 24, 1838	276	2, 074	.....	
....do	Sept. 15	Apr. 28, 1838	656	586	.....	
....do	July 3	May 16, 1838	96	1, 517	.....	
Pacific Ocean ..	May 18	....	.....	.....	.....	Burned at sea November 3, 1838, in Pacific. Had 700 sperm, 700 whale.
....do	Aug. 15	....	1, 900	.....	.....	Condemned at Talcahuano September 5, 1840; oil shipped home.
Atlantic ..... {	Apr. 8	Nov. 20, 1836	250	50	.....	
	Dec. 16	June 19, 1837	178	20	.....	
....do	Apr. 30	....	.....	.....	.....	Supposed to have foundered at sea and all hands lost.
South Atlantic	July 1	Mar. 6, 1838	23	1, 813	.....	
Cape de Verdes	June 15	Mar. 25, 1838	158	2, 527	.....	
....do	Apr. 24	Dec. 5, 1836	60	.....	.....	
....do	Apr. 23	....	...	.....	.....	Spoken, with 140 sperm.
....do	Apr. 8	Oct. 14, 1836	400	.....	.....	
....do	May 4	....	.....	.....	.....	Spoken, with 250 sperm in September.
Pacific Ocean ..	Jan. 27	Dec. 4, 1838	1, 701	.....	.....	
....do	Aug. 25	July 10, 1840	1, 884	.....	.....	
....do	Jan. 14	Sept. 20, 1839	1, 698	139	.....	Built at Mattapoisett 1836.
....do	Aug. 30	Feb. 14, 1840	2, 678	.....	.....	
....do	Sept. 9	May 1, 1840	1, 697	.....	.....	
....do	Dec. 1	Oct. 12, 1840	1, 920	.....	.....	
Mexico	....	July 1, 1836	.....	.....	.....	
Pacific Ocean ..	Nov. 22	June 29, 1840	1, 395	.....	.....	
....do	July 21	Apr. 6, 1840	2, 299	.....	.....	
....do	Oct 23	Jan. 16, 1840	2, 436	.....	.....	Built, 1836, at Rochester.
Gulf Mexico ...	Oct. 8	July 2, 1837	200	200	.....	Fell in with wreck of Industry and got about 200 barrels.
Pacific Oeean ..	Aug. 11	Mar. 14, 1840	2, 309	.....	.....	Built 1838.
....do	July 22	Oct. 27, 1839	753	.....	.....	
....do	Nov. 27	June 10, 1840	2, 185	.....	.....	Built at Nantucket 1836. Captain Pollard died on the voyage.
Mexico	Apr. 18	....	.....	.....	.....	
Pacific Ocean ..	Sept. 14	June 20, 1840	1, 925	.....	.....	
....do	Oct. 22	Oct. 14, 1839	2, 069	47	.....	
....do	May 1	May 12, 1839	395	2, 146	.....	
....do	Sept. 5	July 8, 1840	1, 847	.....	.....	
....do	Oct. 2	Feb. 21, 1840	1, 652	.....	.....	
....do	Nov. 5	Apr. 22, 1840	2, 452	13	.....	Captain Gardner died on the voyage.
....do	Dec. 19	Nov. 19, 1839	1, 480	30	.....	
....do	Jan. 3	Aug. 4, 1839	1, 330	.....	.....	Formerly a merchantman; bought 1836; sold to Sag Harbor, 1839.
Atlantic	Apr. 28	Nov. 6, 1836	Clean	.....	.....	
Pacific Ocean ..	July 31	Apr. 24, 1840	1, 590	.....	.....	
Atlantic	July 19	July 19, 1839	68	2, 085	.....	
Pacific Ocean ..	July 14	Dec. —, 1839	1, 780	.....	.....	
....do	Aug. 11	Sept. 2, 1840	2, 227	.....	.....	Built 1836.
....do	July 8	May 1, 1840	2, 440	.....	.....	
....do	Sept. 3	Jan. 14, 1840	2, 259	.....	.....	
South Atlantic	Aug. 10	Aug. 31, 1837	400	.....	.....	Sold to Rochester.
....do	June 30	May 16, 1838	....	2, 200	.....	Bought from New York, 1836.
Pacific Ocean ..	July 31	July 7, 1840	2, 200	.....	.....	

Table showing returns of whaling-vessels

Name of vessel.	Class.	Tonnage.	Captain.	Managing owner or agent.
1836.				
Portsmouth, N. H.				
Pocahontas	Ship	300	—— Manter	
Stonington, Conn.				
Charles Adams	Ship	268	—— Carew	B. & F. Pendleton
Corvo	do	349	—— Beck	C. P. Williams
Mercury	do	305	—— Smith	C. T. Stanton
New London, Conn.				
Armata	Ship	414	—— Butler	Abner Bassett
Bingham	do	375	—— Smith	Benjamin Brown
Com. Perry	do	270	—— Hobron	C. Chew & Co
Connecticut	do	398	—— Stetson	Thomas W. Williams
Clematis	do	311	—— Bailey	Williams & Barns
Columbia	do	492	—— Smith	Havens & Smith
Candace	do	310	—— Reed	do
Columbus	Brig	153	—— White	Williams & Barns
Electra	Ship	347	—— Lax	William Williams, jr
Friends	do	403	—— Brown	Benjamin Brown
Flora	do	338	—— Keeney	N. & W. W. Billings
George	do	290	—— Baker	L. Allen
Gen. Williams	do	440	—— Holdridge	Williams & Barns
Indian Chief	do	401	—— Smith	E. M. Frink & Co.
Iris	do	245	—— Cleft	Frink, Chew & Co
Julius Cæsar	do	347	—— Hobron	N. & W. W. Billings
Jason	do	337	—— Fuller	E. M. Frink & Co.
John and Elizabeth	do	290	—— Halsey	Havens & Smith
Mentor	do	460	—— Butler	Benjamin Brown
Neptune	do	283	—— Andrews	Thomas W. Williams
Tuscarora	do	379	—— Smith	N. & W. W. Billings
Sag Harbor, N. Y.				
Ann	Ship	299	—— Bishop	Marcus B. Osborn
American	do	283	—— Jennings	S. & B. Huntting & Co
Acasta	do	286	—— Dennison	Mulford & Sleight
Camillus	do	343	—— Topping	Charles T. Dering
Columbia	do	287	—— Hedges	Luther D. Cook
Cadmus	do	307	—— Hand	Mulford & Sleight
Fanny	do	39	—— Payne	N. & G. Howell
Gem	do	320	—— Halsey	Huntting Cooper
Henry	do	333	—— Cartwright	Charles T. Dering
Hudson	do	368	—— Green	Luther D. Cook
Hannibal	do	311	—— Douglass	S. & B. Huntting & Co.
Hamilton	do	32	—— Jones	Charles T. Dering
Marcus	do	283	—— Sweeney	S. & N. Howell
Monmouth	do	273	—— Topping	
Neptune	do	333	—— Slate	S. & B. Huntting & Co.
Nimrod	do	280	—— Parker	C. T. Dering & Co
Ontario	do	368	—— Green	S. & B. Huntting & Co.
Phenix	do	314	—— Cooper	Luther D. Cook
Romulus	do	23	—— Rodgers	Mulford & Howell
Thorn	do	299	—— Havens	Mulford & Sleight
Thames	do	...	—— Nickerson	
Washington	do	340	—— Topping	Josiah Douglass
Salem, Mass.				
Elizabeth	Ship	397	—— Hedge	Stephen C. Phillips
Emerald	Bark	271	—— Dexter	do
Emeline	Brig	93	—— Lombard	John B. Pierce
Franklin	Schooner	89	—— Newcomb	James King
Mount Wollaston	Ship	325	—— Jewett	John B. Osgood
Mac	Schooner	80	—— Winslow	do
Samuel Wright	Ship	372	—— Coffin	do
Sapphire	do	360	—— Mayhew	S. C. Phillips
Statesman	Bark	258	—— Coffin	Timothy Bryant, jr

sailing from American ports—Continued.

Whaling-ground.	Date— Of sailing.	Date— Of arrival.	Result of voyage. Sperm-oil.	Result of voyage. Whale-oil.	Result of voyage. Whalebone.	Remarks.
			Bbls.	*Bbls.*	*Lbs.*	
South Atlantic.	Aug. 13	May 4, 1838	250	......	......	Withdrawn for merchant-service, 1838.
Falkland Islds.	Oct. 15	....	......	......	......	Burned at Falkland Islands, 1837.
....do	Oct. —	Nov. 13, 1837	......	2,700	......	Had for tenders schooners La Grange and Bolton.
....do	....	Aug. —, 1838	......	2,100	21,000	
Indian Ocean...	July —	Apr. 30, 1838	300	1,200	......	Mate and boat's crew taken down by a whale, 1837.
South Atlantic.	Aug. 2	Apr. 20, 1838	......	1,700	......	
....do	May 18	Apr. 6, 1838	85	1,600	......	
....do	May 9	Apr. 5, 1837	300	1,500	......	
....do	May 24	Apr. 27, 1837	140	1, 4 0	......	
....do	July 5	May 9, 1838	150	3,350	......	
....do	June 14	Mar. 10, 1838	200	1,800	......	
Falkland Islds	Aug. 20	Jan. 23, 1839	......	600	......	Tender to Gen. Williams.
South Atlantic	June 7	Apr. 11, 1838	300	1,500	......	
Falkland Islds	Aug. 31	Apr. 9, 1839	100	2,100	......	
South Atlantic.	June 21	—— —, 1837	160	1,300	......	
....do	Apr. 23	June 2, 1837	230	1,770	......	
Falkland Islds.	Sept. 7	Aug. 5, 1838	200	3,300	......	
South Atlantic.	June 7	Apr. 3, 1838	200	2,500	......	
Falkland Islds	Nov. 9	....	......	......	......	
South Atlantic	June —	Apr. 7, 1837	200	2,000	......	
....do	May 14	Apr. 23, 1837	30	2,150	......	
....do	Oct. 1	Mar. 29, 1838	200	2,300	......	
Falkland Islds.	Dec. 12	May 19, 1839	70	2,600	......	
South Atlantic.	June 6	May 11, 1837	250	1,300	......	
....do	May 16	May 6, 1837	200	2,500	......	Sold to Cold Spring, 1837.
South Atlantic.	July 6	May 18, 1837	......	1,350	......	
....do	July 29	Apr. 8, 1838	250	2,150	......	
....do	June 9	Apr. 28, 1837	......	......	......	
....do	July 18	Apr. 19, 1837	......	2,000	......	
....do	July 7	Apr. 27, 1837	100	2,100	......	
....do	July 18	Mar. 15, 1837	90	1,800	......	
....do	July 28	May 3, 1837	100	2,100	......	
....do	July 20	May 18, 1837	......	......	......	
....do	June 16	Apr. 27, 1837	85	1,800	......	
....do	Aug. 27	Apr. 9, 1837	100	2,300	......	
....do	July 8	Apr. 15, 1837	......	1,500	......	
....do	Sept. 26	May 7, 1838	......	1,300	......	
....do	July 18	May 4, 1837	......	1,350	......	
....do	July 18	Apr. 10, 1837	......	1,700	......	
....do	July 1	May 3, 1837	......	2,300	......	
....do	Sept. 26	May 9, 1837	......	1,300	......	Returned once with 60 sperm.
....do	June 29	Apr. 30, 1838	......	3,500	......	
....do	Aug. 10	June 10, 1838	170	1,600	......	
....do	June 15	May 5, 1837	100	1,250	......	
....do	June 29	Apr. 10, 1837	......	1,950	......	
....do	July 7	Apr. 18, 1837	50	1,350	......	
....do	July 18	Apr. 28, 1838	......	1,500	......	
Pacific Ocean..	Nov. 5	May 1, 1840	2,400	......	......	Bought from Boston 1836.
S. A. and Ind...	July 10	Apr. 5, 1838	300	1,450	......	Built 1824.
Atlantic.......	Mar. 28	June 8, 1837	75	20	......	Built 1832.
....do	Apr. 6	May 9, 1837	40	......	......	Built 1828.
South Atlantic	June 28	Apr. 12, 1838	450	1,250	......	Built 1822.
Atlantic.......	Apr. 21	Apr. 23, 1837	......	Clean	......	Built 1831.
Pacific Ocean..	Nov. 24	Mar. 1, 1839	300	2,200	......	Built 1831.
....do	June 19	Sept. 9, 1839	1,000	500	......	Built 1828.
....do	Dec. 22	Sept. 23, 1838	[illegible], 100	......	......	

Table showing returns of whaling-vessels

Name of vessel.	Class.	Tonnage.	Captain.	Managing owner or agent.
1836.				
Bristol, R. I.				
America	Bark	257	—— Browning	Robert Rodgers
Bowditch	Ship	398	—— Ramsdell	W. R. Taylor
Canton Packet	do	312	—— Downs	Fitzhenry Homer
Fama	do	362	—— Littlefield	do
Gov. Hopkins	Brig		—— King	
Gen. Jackson	Ship	392	—— Crocker	William H. De Wolf
Ganges	do	380	—— Harris	do
Falmouth, Mass.				
Awashonks	Ship	355	Rufus Pease	Elijah Swift
Bartholemew Gosnold	do	360	Elihu Fish	Ward M. Parker
Hobomok	do	412	Henry C. Bunker	Elijah Swift
Popmunnett	Bark	200	Stanton Fish	John Robinson
William Penn	Ship	370	Russell Bodfish	Stephen Dillingham
Dartmouth, Mass.				
Grand Turk	Ship	324	Luther Little	James Rider
Washington	do	344	—— Whelden	B. & J. W. Howland
Plymouth, Mass.				
Arabella	Ship	404	—— Eldridge	James Bartlett, jr
Triton	do	315	—— Abrams	do
Warren, R. I.				
Atlantic	Ship	323	—— Howland	Driscol & Child
Atlas	Brig	126	—— Smith	William Carr, jr
Boy	Ship	251	—— Barton	William Collins & Co
Chariot	do	355	—— Champlin	do
Crawford	Brig	126	—— Luther	J. & D. K. Luther
Franklin	Bark	219	—— Worth	do
Miles	Ship	240	—— Davoll	William Collins & Co
Philip Tabb	do	405	—— Bowen	Driscol & Child
Rosalie	do	323	—— Pickens	Joseph Smith, jr., & Co.
William Baker	do	224	—— Sanford	Driscol & Child
Mystic, Conn.				
Aeronaut	Ship	265	—— Mallory	Charles Mallory
Meteor	do	325	—— Lester	I. & W. P. Randall
Fall River, Mass.				
Ann Maria	Brig	196	—— Swain	John Eddy
Edward Quesnal	Ship	388	—— Wood	do
William	Brig	107	—— Brownell	J. S. Barnard
Lynn, Mass.				
Commodore Preble	Ship	323	—— Eldridge	S. H. Gardner
Louisa	do	383	—— Woolley	H. Chase & Co
Nahant	do	303	Charles Church	do
New York, N. Y.				
Athenian	Brig	...	—— Hallett	
G. Browne	Bark	200	—— Spencer	Silas E. Barnard
Shibboleth	do	219	—— Dickins	S. E. Burrows
Bridgeport, Conn.				
Hamilton	Ship	359	—— Rose	Samuel F. Hurd
Wareham, Mass.				
George Washington	Ship	374	—— Gibbs	E. Thompson

sailing from American ports—Continued.

Whaling-ground.	Date—		Result of voyage.			Remarks.
	Of sailing.	Of arrival.	Sperm-oil.	Whale-oil.	Whalebone.	
			Bbls.	*Bbls.*	*Lbs.*	
North Atlantic	July 20	May 20, 1838	......	300	......	Captain Browning left the ship, sick.
Pacific Ocean	July 6	Jan. 12, 1838	300	2,400	......	Sold to Providence 1838.
South Atlantic	June 23	Apr. 3, 1838	300	1,200	......	Sailed in May, 1838, for Europe.
....do	July 7	Apr. 1, 1838	120	2,680	......	Sold to Boston 1838.
Atlantic	May 5	......	......	......	......	
Pacific Ocean	July 31	Dec. 1, 1839	2,000	......	......	
....do	Feb. 29	May 10, 1839	750	1,750	......	Captain Harris and boat's crew lost fast to a whale; sold to Fall River 1839.
Pacific Ocean	Aug. 22	Jan. 24, 1840	2,500	......	......	
....do	Nov. 17	Sept. 19, 1839	700	1,900	......	
....do	Oct. 25	Nov. 7, 1839	2,000	1,200	......	
Atlantic	July 6	Nov. 29, 1836	90	......	......	Built 1836; returned with Captain Fish, sick.
Pacific Ocean	Oct. 8	May 28, 1841	1,300	370	......	
South Atlantic	June 15	Apr. 20, 1838	160	2,365	......	
....do	June 22	June 4, 1837	......	1,700	......	Sold to New Bedford 1837.
South Atlantic	Aug. 25	May 12, 1838	80	2,220	......	Withdrawn for freighting 1838.
Indian Ocean	July 13	Apr. 13, 1838	......	500	......	
South Atlantic	June 21	Apr. 16, 1838	80	1,920	......	
West'n Islands	July 16	Apr. 9, 1837	150	......	......	
Pacific Ocean	Sept. 10	Nov. 6, 1839	800	......	......	
....do	Aug. 20	Sept. 20, 1838	Full	......	......	About 3,000 barrels sperm.
West'n Islands	June 22	Feb. 7, 1837	150	......	......	
South Atlantic	June 19	Mar. 10, 1838	......	1,300	......	
....do	June 7	Apr. 14, 1837	1,200	......	......	
Pacific Ocean	July 25	Apr. 7, 1838	800	2,200	......	
South Atlantic	July 16	May 2, 1839	120	......	10,000	Sold 2,000 whale at Rio Janeiro and loaded with coffee for home.
....do	June 9	Mar. 27, 1838	35	1,330	......	
South Atlantic	June 18	Apr. 21, 1838	60	1,940	......	First mate killed by a whale.
....do	June 13	Mar. 12, 1838	40	2,340	......	
Atlantic	Aug. 16	Oct. 23, 1837	190	......	......	
Pacific Ocean	May 2	......	......	......	......	Lost on Long Island May 15, 1839; had 1,400 sperm, 800 whale; saved 870 sperm, 570 whale.
West Islands	July 23	June 18, 1837	230	......	......	Sailed once and returned, having a rotten mainmast.
South Atlantic	July 28	Apr. 28, 1837	150	2,000	......	
....do	July 8	May 8, 1837	200	1,200	......	
....do	Oct. 8	Mar. 17, 1838	230	2,100	......	Built at Portland 1836.
South Atlantic	......	......	......	......	......	Arrived July, 1839, under the Brazilian flag and renamed Flaminense; lost on Crozettes 1841.
Falk. Islands	Feb. 26	......	......	......	......	Returned to Rio Janeiro, full, and was sold there.
....do	Jan. —	Nov. 20, 1837	......	......	......	Sold cargo at Rio Janeiro and returned in ballast.
South Atlantic	July 18	May 10, 1837	......	2,300	......	
Pacific Ocean	Jan. 20	Sept. 27, 1839	2,400	......	......	

Table showing returns of whaling-vessels

Name of vessel.	Class.	Tonnage.	Captain.	Managing owner or agent.
1836.				
Poughkeepsie, N. Y.				
Nath'l P. Tallmadge	Ship	370	—— Post	David S. Shearman
New England	do	375	Job Terry	do
Providence, R. I.				
Brunswick	Ship	295	—— Stuart	Amherst & Everett
Newark, N. J.				
Columbia	Ship	390	—— Hussey	J. H. Stephens
Wilmington, Del.				
North America	Ship	270	William H. Cox	William Wheeler
Superior	Bark	275	—— Crocker	do
East Haddam, Conn.				
Bruce	Bark	148	—— Purrington	
Greenport, N. Y.				
Delta	Ship	314	—— Griffin	H. & N. Corwin
Roanoke	do	251	—— Harris	Wiggins & Parsons
Triad	do	336	—— Loper	H. & N. Corwin
Hudson, N. Y.				
Beaver	Ship	427	—— Rogers	Barnard, Curtis & Co
Edward	do	274	—— Daggett	Seth G. Macy
Huron	do	290	—— Nye	Robert A. Barnard
Dorchester, Mass.				
Courier	Ship	293	—— Crapo	Josiah Stickney
Julia	Bark		—— Nash	
Westport, Mass.				
Elizabeth	Brig	107	—— Francis	Abner B. Coffin
Dr. Franklin	Bark	171	Job Davis	
Mexico	Brig		—— Davis	Job Davis
President	Bark		—— Sowle	Andrew Hicks
Thomas Winslow	do		—— Cary	
Newport, R. I.				
Constitution	Ship		E. Gifford	N. Ruggles
Geneva	Schooner	112	—— Paddock	do
Harvest	Bark		John H. Stackpole	Devins & Clarke
Margaret	Ship	375	A. Wilcox	
William Lee	do		F. W. Hussey	R. P. Lee
Provincetown, Mass.				
Flora	Schooner			
Imogene	Brig		—— Atkins	
Louisa	Schooner		—— Tilson	
Mystic, Conn.				
Meteor (see p. 330)	Ship		—— Lester	
Norwich, Conn.				
Atlas	Ship	261	—— Barnum	
1837.				
New Bedford, Mass.				
Adeline	Ship	329	—— Brown	I. Howland, jr., & Co
Ann Alexander	do	253	—— Bailey	George Howland
Alexander Barclay	do	465	—— Norton	J. A. Parker & Son
Balaena	do	301	—— Lucas	I. & I. Howland
Brandt	do	310	Seth D. Fisher	Alexander Gibbs
Com. Decatur	do	247	—— Luce	
Chili	do	291	Elihu Russell	B. B. Howard

sailing from American ports—Continued.

Whaling-ground.	Date— Of sailing.	Date— Of arrival.	Result of voyage. Sperm-oil.	Result of voyage. Whale-oil.	Result of voyage. Whalebone.	Remarks.
			Bbls.	*Bbls.*	*Lbs.*	
Pacific Ocean ..	Aug. 16	Apr. 14, 1840	.....	.....	.....	
....do	Dec. 3	Apr. 11, 1839	280	1, 120	.....	Captain Terry left the ship and came home sick.
Brazil Banks...	July 6	July 4, 1837	200	1, 200	.....	
Pacific Ocean ..	Sept. 15	....	.....	.....	.....	Bought from Boston 1836; lost on coast of Chili December 5, 1835.
South Atlantic.	Aug. 12	Apr. 12, 1838	300	2, 100	.....	
Pacific Ocean ..	Jan. 9	May 3, 1839	1, 500	.....	.....	
Atlantic	June 17	June 24, 1837	450	.....	.....	
South Atlantic.	July —	Apr. 20, 1838	.....	1, 950	.....	
....do	Aug. —	May 3, 1837	100	700	.....	
....do	July —	Apr. 28, 1837	.....	1, 800	.....	
Pacific Ocean ..	Nov. 15	May 1, 1840	1, 100	1. 400	.....	
South Atlantic.	Sept. 21	Apr. 10, 1838	100	1, 600	.....	
....do	July 2	Jan. 21, 1838	.....	800	.....	
Indian Ocean ..	June 11	Apr. 13, 1838	150	1, 850	.....	Sold 1838.
South Atlantic.	May 18	....	.....	.....	.....	
Atlantic	Aug. 1	May 7, 1837	212	13	.....	
....do	June 28	June 5, 1837	661	24	.....	
Cape de Verdes.	....	Nov. 7, 1836	450	.....	.....	
South Atlantic.	May 14	Apr. 16, 1837	644	6	.....	
Cape de Verdes.	Mar. 25	Nov. —, 1836	.....	.....	.....	
South Seas.....	Oct. 15	May 6, 1839	800	1, 000	.....	
Falkland Islds	June 25	Oct. 2, 1837	.....	900	.....	
Indian Ocean ..	July 20	Mar. 4, 1837	82	812	.....	Sold to Fairhaven 1839.
East Cape	....	Apr. 4, 1838	.....	.....	.....	
Pacific Ocean ..	Sept. 29	Apr. 28, 1840	1, 000	.....	.....	
Cape de Verdes.	....	....	.....	.....	.....	
....do	July 5	Oct. 25, 1836	560	.....	.....	
....do	....	Nov. 5, 1836	175	.....	.....	
Indian Ocean ..	....	Mar. 12, 1838	60	2, 400	.....	
South Atlantic.	May 17	Apr. 9, 1837	.....	1, 650	.....	Sailed from New London; mostly elephant-oil.
Ind. and N. Z...	Nov. 27	May 16, 1840	100	2, 400	.....	
Indian Ocean ..	July 1	Apr. 22, 1838	69	1, 446	.....	
....do	Dec. 16	Nov. 26, 1839	.....	4, 500	.....	Unloaded at Bremen July 25, 1839.
Pacific Ocean ..	Nov. 2	Aug. 4, 1841	1, 581	9	.....	
Indian Ocean ..	Mar. 14	Apr. 19, 1838	131	1, 460	.....	
Atlantic	Apr. 10	Apr. 1, 1838	51	565	.....	
South Atlantic.	July 5	May 11, 1839	206	1, 597	.....	

Table showing returns of whaling-vessels

Name of vessel.	Class.	Tonnage.	Captain.	Managing owner or agent.
1837.				
New Bedford, Mass.—Continued.				
Charles	Ship	290	—— Morselander	Samuel Rodman
Condor	do	349	—— Harding	Charles W. Morgan
China	do	370	—— Tower	William H. Stowell
Cicero	do	252	—— Snow	Kollock & Grinnell
Cherokee	Bark	261	—— Cook	David Coffin
Cora	do	220	—— Shearman	I. H. Bartlett
Charleston Packet	Brig	184	—— Ellis	Crane & French
Cornelia	Bark	216	—— Flanders	L. Kollock
Delight	Brig	102	—— Sanford	Jonathan Mosher
Eagle	Ship	336	—— Coffin	Jireh Perry
Endeavour	do	252	—— Stetson	W. H. Stowel (?)
Euphrates	do	365	—— Lewis	Lawrence Grinnell
Emily Morgan	do	368	—— Clark	Charles W. Morgan
Frances Henrietta	do	407	—— Hawes	do
Franklin	do	333	William H. Mosher	Abm. H. Howland
Francis, 2d	do			
Fenelon	do	328	—— Smith	David Coffin
George and Susan	do	356	—— Cushman	George Howland
Gratitude	do	337	—— Fisher	Thomas Riddell & Sons
Gen. Pike	do	313	—— Townsend	Oliver Crocker
Hope	do	295	—— Grinnell	William T. Russell
Hercules	do	335	—— Phinney	Jireh Perry
Hercules, 2d	do	290	Peter F. Chase	D. R. Greene
Herald	do	274	—— Ricketson	Tobey & Ricketson
Hydaspe	do	313	—— Price	Randall & Haskell
Hibernia	do	327	—— Dexter	Alfred Gibbs & Co
Honqua	do	339	Edward Mosher	Alexander Gibbs
Java	do	295	—— Taber	George Howland
John Adams	do	268	—— Baker	Jireh Perry
Janus	do	278	—— Taber	T. & A. R. Nye
Jasper	Bark	223	Joseph Shockley	Alexander Gibbs
Lalla Rookh	Ship	323	—— Bassett	J. A. Parker & Son
L. C. Richmond	do	341	James B. Wood	Daniel Wood
Laurel	Schooner	119	—— Manter	I. H. Bartlett
Messenger	Ship	277	—— Kendrick	J. R. Thornton
Mercury	do	340	—— Haskell	I. Howland, jr., & Co
Midas	do	326	S. B. Coggeshall	John Coggeshall
Minerva	do	407	Moses Samson	William Gifford
Moss	do	334	—— Gibbs	William R. Rodman
Mount Vernon	do	352	E. T. Shearman	D. R. Greene & Co
Nile	do	322	—— Hall	David Coffin
Nassau	do	408	—— Chase	Isaiah Burgess
Octavia	do	257	—— Gifford	Gideon Allen
Pacific, 2d	do	331	—— Collins	Andrew Robeson
Parachute	do	331	—— Durfee	A. H. Seabury & Bro
Pioneer	Bark	231	—— Adams	C. W. Morgan
Rousseau	Ship	306	—— Luce	Abm. Barker
Rodman	do	371	—— Dexter	Charles W. Morgan
Russell	do	302	—— Long	J. & J. Howland
Rajah	Bark	250	—— Nickerson	Isaiah Burgess
Roscoe	do	235	—— Brown	Jonathan Bourne, jr
Rising States	Brig	134	—— Caff	Richard Johnson
Swift	Ship	321	Lewis Tobey	Thomas S. Hathaway
Stephania	do	315	Warren N. Bourne	Palmer & Coggeshall
Selma	do	269	—— Howland	A. H. Seabury & Bro
Samuel Robertson	do	421	Daniel McKenzie	Andrew Robeson
St. Peter	do	267	—— Hussey	Frederick Bryant
Seine	Bark	281	D. Flanders	Crane & French
Two Brothers	Ship	288	H. F. Eastham	D. R. Greene & Co
W. & L. Packet	do	384	—— Foster	J. A. Parker & Son
Winslow	do	263	—— Gifford	S. Rodman, jr
Fairhaven, Mass.				
Amazon	Ship	318	—— Macomber	E. Sawin
Arab	Bark	276	—— Russell	do
Columbus	Ship	382	—— Ellis	Gibbs & Jenney

sailing from American ports—Continued.

Whaling-ground.	Date—		Result of voyage.			Remarks.
	Of sailing.	Of arrival.	Sperm-oil.	Whale-oil.	Whalebone.	
			Bbls.	*Bbls.*	*Lbs.*	
South Atlantic.	Nov. 30	Dec. 26, 1840	1, 972	21	......	Captain Morselander died Sept. 2, 1839.
....do	July 14	Apr. 7, 1839	50	2, 037	......	
S. A. and Ind...	June 28	Aug. 29, 1838	90	1, 461	......	
South Atlantic	June 4	Apr. 30, 1838	20	430	......	
....do	June 7	Sept. 2, 1838	158	1, 490	......	
....do	May 4	Mar. 20, 1839	251	1, 036	6, 400	
Atlantic	May 7	May 29, 1839	185	47	......	
South Atlantic.	Sept. 21	Feb. 23, 1838	......	200	......	
Atlantic	Dec. 25	July 19, 1838	301	1	......	
Pacific Ocean ..	Apr. 19	Apr. 14, 1840	2, 214	......	......	
....do	Aug. 10	Apr. 10, 1841	390	1, C90	......	Lost fourteen men by African fever.
....do	Dec. 20	Oct. 17, 1841	1, 661	46	......	
....do	Dec. 11	Sept. 26, 1841	2, 882	109	......	
Brazil Banks ..	Apr. 23	Apr. 8, 1839	860	1, 852	16, 000	
South Atlantic.	May 7	Mar. 1, 1839	500	1, 600	......	
Pacific Ocean ..	Mar. —	June —, 1840	950	360	......	
South Atlantic.	July 11	June 28, 1838	40	2, 300	......	
Pacific Ocean ..	Nov. 8	May 28, 1841	2, 906	......	......	
Ind. and N. Z...	Dec. 31	Oct. 27, 1839	260	2, 490	......	Second mate killed by a whale December, 1838. Sold 950 whale at Pernambuco.
Indian Ocean ..	June 27	Jan. 10, 1839	164	546	......	Captain died at sea 1838.
South Atlantic	May 5	May 4, 1839	982	295	......	
....do	July 2	June 18, 1839	555	1, 921	......	
Indian Ocean ..	Apr. 11	Apr. 28, 1840	796	1, 022	......	
....do	Dec. 22	Sept. 29, 1840	1, 788	......	......	
New Zealand ..	June 15	Feb 25, 1839	......	1, 825	......	
South Atlantic.	July 2	Apr. 28, 1838	308	1, 085	......	
....do	July 23	May 8, 1839	......	2, 741	25, 000	
Ind. and N. Z ..	July 6	Mar. 22, 1839	431	2, 019	......	
New Zealand ..	June 19	Mar. 19, 1839	702	1, 147	......	
S. A. and Ind...	June 28	Mar. 27, 1839	108	1, 278	......	
South Atlantic.	June 8	Apr. 12, 1838	77	671	......	
New Zealand ..	June 15	Mar. 27, 1840	1, 538	996	......	
Pacific Ocean.	Nov. 26	Feb. 1, 1841	2, 618	102	......	
Atlantic	Apr. 19	Mar. 24, 1838	417	......	......	
South Atlantic.	May 21	Mar. 18, 1839	500	1, 527	......	
Pacific Ocean ..	June 11	Oct. 12, 1840	2, 538	......	......	
....do	Dec. 7	Jan. 1, 1842	1, 389	210	......	
South Atlantic.	July 23	Mar. 22, 1839	372	1, 474	......	Captain Samson left ship and came home sick.
Pacific Ocean ..	Apr. 7	July 3, 1840	1, 227	523	......	Captain Gibbs died September 13, 1837.
P. O. and N. Z..	Nov. 1	Mar. 17, 1840	909	2, 285	31, 586	
Ind. and P. O...	Aug. 24	Jan. 6, 1841	1, 619	......	......	
Pacific Ocean ..	Nov. 6	May 13, 1841	2, 470	......	......	
Indian Ocean ..	Aug. 6	Apr. 11, 1839	104	441	......	Captain Gifford left ship and came home sick.
Chili	Aug. 7	July 10, 1839	704	622	......	
South Atlantic.	July 5	Oct. 14, 1838	240	1, 715	......	
Chili	Aug. 15	Apr. 9, 1839	510	528	......	
Pacific Ocean ..	Nov. 8	Dec. 10, 1840	2, 010	......	......	
Chili	Aug. 6	Apr. 13, 1840	1, 445	1, 204	......	
South Atlantic.	July 2	Oct. 27, 1840	1, 818	......	......	
Indian Ocean ..	June 11	Jan. 28, 1839	310	1, 649	......	Captain Nickerson died at Bay of Islands, March, 1838.
South Atlantic	June 4	June 21, 1839	315	1, 271	......	Sold 150 sperm at Swan River.
Atlantic	July 20	....	143	......	......	Condemned at Cape de Verdes Dec., 1837.
Pacific Ocean ..	Feb. 22	Aug. 31, 1841	1, 610	735	......	
Indian Ocean ..	July 19	Mar. 24, 1839	270	1, 895	......	
....do	Mar. 26	May 15, 1839	338	1, 438	......	
New Zealand ..	Nov. 8	Jan. 24, 1840	306	2, 441	......	
Indian Ocean ..	Mar. 19	Apr. 1, 1839	......	1, 660	......	Bought from New York, 1836.
South Atlantic.	Aug. 10	Sept. 1, 1838	226	1, 084	......	
....do	June 6	Aug. 30, 1838	78	933	......	
Pacific Ocean ..	Nov. 19	Aug. 21, 1841	2, 300	......	......	
Atlantic	Aug. 7	July 8, 1838	1, 207	......	......	
South Atlantic.	June 26	Mar. 7, 1839	256	2, 245	......	
Chili	Sept. 3	Sept. 27, 1839	417	1, 773	......	
New Zealand ..	July 30	Feb. 21, 1839	135	3, 065	......	

Table showing returns of whaling-vessels

Name of vessel.	Class.	Tonnage.	Captain.	Managing owner or agent.
1837.				
Fairhaven, Mass.—Continued.				
Clifford Wayne	Ship	305	—— Downs	E. Sawin & Co
Friendship	do	366	—— West	Gibbs & Jenney
Favorite	do	293	—— Swift	E. Sawin
Heroine	do	337	—— Harding	do
Joseph Maxwell	do	302	—— Stewart	F. R. Whitwell
Jasper	do	360	—— Adams	Atkins Adams
Leonidas	do	243	—— Stewart	Jenney & Tripp
Marcia	do	315	—— Cushman	E. Sawin
Marcus	do	286	—— Shearman	Lemuel Tripp
Sharon	do	354	—— Church	Gibbs & Jenney
Sarah Frances	do	301	—— Cox	E. Sawin
Rochester, Mass.				
Annawan	Brig	148	—— Snow	G. Barstow & Son
Lagrange	do	170	—— Daggett	Elijah Willis
Le Barron	do	170	—— Rogers	G. Barstow & Son
Mattapoisett	do	150	—— Southworth	Jos. Meigs
Orion	do	99	{ —— Wing { —— Purrington }	Elijah Willis
Shylock	Ship	278	—— Taber	S. C. Luce
Sarah	Brig	171	—— Mayhew	G. Barstow & Son
Nantucket, Mass.				
Ann	Ship	361	Peter C. Brock	Jared Coffin
Aurora	do	346	John Hussey, jr	Thomas Macy
Elizabeth Starbuck	do	381	Alexander M. Chase	Levi Starbuck
Foster	do	317	Josiah C. Long	Richard Mitchell
Franklin	do	246	Benjamin F. Riddell	James Athearn
Harmony	Schooner		—— Coleman	
Hero	Ship	313	Reuben Joy, jr	Joseph Starbuck
John Adams	do	296	Asa Coleman	Griffin Barney
Levi Starbuck	do	376	John C. Lincoln	Levi Starbuck
Montano	do	365	Benjamin C. Sayer	Samuel B. Folger
Maria	Sloop		—— Hiller	
Martha	Ship	273	James Alley	James N. Bassett
Nantucket	do	350	David N. Edwards	H. G. O. Dunham
Ohio	do	383	Charles W. Coffin	Jared Coffin
Obed Mitchell	do	354	Reuben Ray, jr	Joseph Mitchell
Phœnix	do	323	Isaac B. Hussey	Thomas Macy
Primrose	Schooner	90	—— Swain	William Bartlett
Planter	Ship	340	Eben M. Hinckley	William B. Coffin
Rose	do	356	Benjamin A. Coleman	Simeon Starbuck
Susan	do	348	Reuben Russell	Aaron Mitchell
Three Brothers	do	384	Henry Phelon	Matthew Starbuck
Edgartown, Mass.				
Almira	Ship	362	Richard Flanders	Abraham Osborn
Holmes's Hole, Mass.				
Delphos	Ship	338	—— Merry	Thomas Bradley
William and Joseph	Brig	143	—— Cleveland	John Holmes
Falmouth, Mass.				
Brunette	Bark	200	—— Pool	Elijah Swift
George Washington	do	180	Consider Fisher	Sanford Herendeen
Popmunnett	do	200	—— Nickerson	John Robinson
Dartmouth, Mass.				
Elizabeth	Ship	329		
Westport, Mass.				
Champion	Bark	209		Andrew Hicks
Dr. Franklin	do	171	Job Davis	Job Davis
Elizabeth	Brig	107	—— Sowle	Abner B. Coffin
Juno	do	165	do	Abner B. Gifford
President	Bark	187	—— Hathaway	Andrew Hicks
Thomas Winslow	Brig	136	—— Seabury	P. W. Peckham

sailing from American ports—Continued.

Whaling-ground.	Date— Of sailing.	Date— Of arrival.	Result of voyage. Sperm-oil.	Result of voyage. Whale-oil.	Result of voyage. Whalebone.	Remarks.
			Bbls.	*Bbls.*	*Lbs.*	
Ind. and Pacific	Nov. 26	Oct. 18, 1840	2,060			
New Zealand	Aug. 12	Jan. 22, 1838	119	2,615		
South Atlantic	July 12	Aug. 25, 1838		2,412		
....do	Aug. 15	Apr. 19, 1839	450	1,700		
....do	July 2	Aug. 2, 1838	138	1,504		
New Zealand	Oct. 3	July 2, 1839	740	1,890		
South Atlantic	July 25	June 2, 1839	381	1,411		
Indian Ocean	Feb. 3	Apr. 20, 1838	57	2,534		
Pacific Ocean	Aug. 1	Sept. 5, 1840	2,366			
... do	June 14	Dec. 10, 1840	2,640	48		
Falkland Il'ds	July 16	Oct. 3, 1839	150	2,036		
Atlantic	July 20	June 27, 1838	308	35		
....do	Apr. —	Mar. 17, 1838	240	660		
....do	July 29	Sept. 5, 1838	601			
....do	Mar. 25	Mar. 22, 1838	483	25		
....do {	Apr. 21	Oct. 5, 1837	80	15		
		June 26, 1836	60			
South Atlantic	July 2	Dec. 6, 1838	41	2,444		
Atlantic	Mar. 25	June 7, 1838	416	25		
Pacific Ocean	July 5	June 22, 1841	2,427			Sold to New Bedford 1841.
....do	Nov. 5	Dec. 2, 1840	2,036			
....do	Nov. 16	May 2, 1841	1,359	7		
....do	Sept. 1	Apr. 28, 1841	2,101			
....do	Oct. 12	Feb. 13, 1841	1,711	37		
Atlantic	Aug. 30	Aug. 9, 1838	130			
Pacific Ocean	Aug. 16	May 18, 1841	1,992			
....do	Nov. 27	Oct. 4, 1840	1,050	650		
....do	Aug. 27	Nov. 29, 1840	2,375	25		
....do	Aug. 4	May 30, 1839	53	2,716		
Atlantic	Aug. 2	— —, 1837	Clean			
Pacific Ocean	Sept. 6	Mar. 31, 1840	308	1,112		
....do	June 12	Feb. 1, 1841	2,036	465		Built at Nantucket 1837.
....do	July 12	Apr. 19, 1841	2,520			
....do	Sept. 22	June 27, 1841	870			Built 1837.
....do	Nov. 4	Feb. 14, 1840	2,419			
Mexico	Feb. 27	Aug. 9, 1837	100	50		The Primrose sailed again Oct. 23, 1837, and June 13, 1838, with 25 sperm, 75 whale.
Pacific Ocean	Nov. 14	May 28, 1841	1,460	24		
....do	Oct. 3	May 29, 1841	1,987			
....do	Dec. —	May 28, 1841	1,892	477		
....do	June 12	Apr. 28, 1841	2,719			
New Zealand	June 2	Apr. 4, 1839	200	1,100		Sold 1,100 whale at Bahia.
Ind. and Pacific	Aug. 26	May 30, 1839	250	2,250		
Atlantic	Dec. 12	— —, 1838				
Atlantic	May 4	May 23, 1838	400			
....do		Apr. —, 1838	80	300		
....do	Jan. 13	— —, 1838	300			
Pacific Ocean	Dec. —	Mar. —, 1840	2,200			
Atlantic	Sept. 20	Apr. 6, 1839	335			
....do	Sept. 1	July 23, 1838	595	5		
....do	Aug. 22	June 9, 1838	188	6		
....do	May 10	July 21, 1838	254	8		
....do	June 28	June 23, 1838	617			
....do	June 5	Mar. 26, 1838	370	10		

22

Table showing returns of whaling-vessels

Name of vessel.	Class.	Tonnage.	Captain.	Managing owner or agent.
1837.				
Fall River, Mass.				
Ann Maria	Brig	196	—— Browning	John Eddy
Gold Hunter	Ship	231	—— Estes	Henry Slade
Taunton	Brig	103	—— Collins	William Coggeshall
William	do	107	—— Cudworth	J. S. Barnard
Lynn, Mass.				
Com. Prebble	Ship	323	—— Eldridge	S. H. Gardner
Louisa	do	383	—— Woolley	H. Chase & Co
Ninus	do	260	—— Smith	S. H. Gardner
Newburyport, Mass.				
Merrimac	Ship	414	—— Starbuck	Lunt & Titcomb
Navy	do	356	—— Brock	do
Salem, Mass.				
Bengal	Ship	304	—— Jackson	John B. Osgood
Cavalier	Bark	295	—— Francis	James King
Derby	do	....	—— Radcliff	
Emeline	Brig	98	—— Lombard	John B. Pierce
Franklin	Schooner	89	—— Tracy	James King
Izette	Ship	275	—— Hall	J. B. Osgood
James Maury	do	395	—— Bigelow	do
Lydia	do	293	—— Ramsdell	do
Malay	Bark	268	—— Barnard	Stephen G. Phillips
Mac	Schooner	80	—— Emmons	J. B. Osgood
Reaper	Bark	230	—— Neal	do
Richard	do	252	—— Dewing	Joseph Hodges
Warren, R. I.				
Atlas	Brig	126	—— Russell	Jos. Smith, jr., & Co
Benjamin Rush	Ship	374	—— Coffin	Driscol & Child
Crawford	Brig	126	—— Sowle	J. & D. K. Luther
Hoogley	Ship	292	—— Luce	William Collins & Co
Jane	do	371	—— Eddy	S. P. Child
Luminary	do	432	—— Mayhew	J. Smith, jr., & Co
Miles	do	240	—— Davol	William Collins & Co
North America	do	288	—— Grinnell	Driscoll & Child
Warren	do	382	—— Lewis	J. Smith, jr., & Co
Providence, R. I.				
Brunswick	Ship	295	—— Gardner	Amherst & Everett
Bristol, R. I.				
Anne	Ship	222	—— Richmond	William H. De Wolf
Corinthian	do	503	—— Gardner	do
Essex	do	200		William R. Taylor
Gov. Hopkins	Brig	111	—— King —— Simmons	do
Metacom	Ship	360	—— Grinnell	William H. De Wolf
Sarah Lee	do	235		do
Troy	Brig	156	—— Hart	Thomas Church
Newport, R. I.				
Audley Clarke	Ship	....	Joseph Sherman	Bush & Clarke
Martha	do	....	Oliver Potter	Charles Devans & Lee
Pocahontas	Schooner	....	Alden Wilkey	George Knowles
New London, Conn.				
Ann Maria	Ship	368	—— Middleton	Thomas W. Williams
Boston	do	291	—— Pendleton	J. Lawrence

sailing from American ports—Continued.

Whaling-ground.	Date— Of sailing	Date— Of arrival.	Result of voyage. Sperm-oil.	Result of voyage. Whale-oil.	Result of voyage. Whalebone.	Remarks.
			Bbls.	*Bbls.*	*Lbs.*	
Atlantic	Dec. 7	July 25, 1838	110	......	......	
South Atlantic	Aug. 4	Apr. 10, 1839	......	2,200	......	
Atlantic	May 20	Feb. 16, 1838	......	Clean	......	
....do	July 24	June 6, 1838	280	......	......	
South Atlantic	July 11	May 8, 1838	125	1,875	......	
S. A. and Ind	July 27	Apr. 29, 1838	......	1,350	......	
....do	Aug. 13	May 11, 1838	......	1,500	......	
N. Z. and Ind	Nov. 27	Sept. 19, 1839	350	3,350	......	
Pacific Ocean	Nov. 27	Sept. 11, 1839	200	2,500	......	
S. A. and Ind	Nov. 6	May 29, 1840	1,800	......	......	Built 1816.
....do	July 8	Mar. 24, 1839	180	820	8,000	Sold out, 1839; built 1828.
Indian Ocean	July 15	....	......	......	......	Lost at Falkland Islands April 15, 1838; shipped oil home.
Atlantic	Sept. 5	July 1, 1838	110	5	......	Sold out, 1838.
....do	May 27	Dec. 8, 1837	......	Clean	......	Sold out, 1837.
S. A. and Ind	Oct. 16	Dec. 20, 1839	250	2,050	......	Built 1825.
S. A. and P. O	July 5	Dec. 11, 1840	400	2,600	......	Built 1832.
S. A. and Ind	Dec. 20	Mar. 25, 1840	380	1,450	......	Built 1822.
Indian Ocean	May 21	May 5, 1839	500	1,000	......	
Atlantic	May 24	Nov. 17, 1837	70	......	......	
S. A. and P	Aug. 21	May 28, 1839	500	100	......	Built 1825.
South Atlantic	Apr. 19	Mar. 1, 1839	......	300	......	Brig Eagle, Williams, sailed as tender. The Richard's oil was sold at Pernambuco, and she was lost in July or August off Montevideo in the merchant service.
New Zealand	July 9	....	......	......	......	Tender to Luminary; made a trading voyage; no report.
Pacific Ocean	Sept. 29	Mar. 21, 1841	1,425	450	......	Mate and boat's crew lost, 1839; fast to a whale.
Atlantic	Apr. 12	Nov. 18, 1837	80	......	......	
Pacific Ocean	Oct. 19	Aug. 29, 1840	700	1,500	......	
....do	Sept. 2	Oct. 1, 1839	600	900	......	
New Zealand	July 9	Oct. 2, 1839	600	3,200	......	
South Atlantic	July 13	Mar. 14, 1839	130	1,170	......	
....do	Aug. 20	May 14, 1839	500	800	......	
New Zealand	July 9	Jan. 16, 1840	235	3,065	......	
South Atlantic	Aug. 10	Apr. 10, 1839	80	1,320	......	
Pacific Ocean	Dec. 2	June 5, 1840	1,300	......	......	
....do	Jan. 7	Mar. 23, 1839	300	3,000	......	
....	....	....	......	......	......	
Mexico	Feb. 16	July 25, 1837	250	20	......	
Atlantic	Aug. 13	June 11, 1838	100	......	......	
Pacific Ocean	Dec. 21	May 28, 1841	1,700	100	......	Built at Bristol, 1836; sold at New Bedford, 1841.
....	....	....	......	......	......	
Mexico	Feb. 23	Nov. 25, 1837	3	100	......	The sperm was picked up.
Pacific Ocean	Oct. 25	Aug. 6, 1840	2,350	......	......	
....do	Oct. 2	Apr. 19, 1841	1,950	......	......	
North Atlantic	Sept. 27	July 30, 1838	190	40	......	
South Atlantic	July 25	Feb. 28, 1839	180	2,070	......	
....do	May 3	Feb. 3, 1839	160	2,400	15,000	

Table showing returns of whaling-vessels

Name of vessel.	Class.	Tonnage.	Captain.	Managing owner or agent.
1837.				
New London, Conn.—Continued.				
Connecticut	Ship	398	—— Crocker	T. W. Williams
Clematis	do	311	—— Bailey	Williams & Barns
Flora	do	3[illegible]8	—— Fitch	N. & W. W. Billings
Georgia	do	343	—— Peabody	T. W. Williams
George	do	290	—— Baker	L. Allen
John and Edward	do	318	—— Bailey	N. & W. W. Billings
Julius Cæsar	do	347	—— McLean	do
Jones	do	336	—— Hobron	T. W. Williams
Jason	do	335	—— Fuller	E. M. Frink & Co
Neptune	do	285	—— Andrews	T. W. Williams
Palladium	do	342	—— Prentiss	E. M. Frink & Co
Phenix	do	404	—— Allen	N. & W. W. Billings
Pembroke	do	199	—— Chester	Jos. Lawrence
Superior	do	406	—— Allen	N. & W. W. Billings
Stonington	do	351	—— Rice	Williams & Barns
Stonington, Conn.				
Acasta	Ship	330	—— Pendleton	C. P. Williams
Bolton	Schooner			
Corvo	Ship	349	—— Beck	C. P. Williams
Caledonia	do	446	—— Pendleton	do
Philetus	do	278	—— Brewster	E. Faxon, jr., & Co
Mystic, Conn.				
Atlas	Ship	261	—— Bailey	
Blackstone	do	258	—— Chester	Silas Beebe
Sag Harbor, N. Y.				
Ann	Ship	299	—— Bishop	Marcus B. Osborn
Acasta	do	286	—— Hand	Mulford & Sleight
Arabella	do	367	—— Pearson	N. & G. Howell
Camillus	do	345	A. Rogers	Charles T. Dering
Columbia	do	285	—— Hedges	Luther D. Cook
Concordia	Bark	265	—— Woodward	Thomas Brown
Cadmus	Ship	307	—— Hand	Mulford & Sleight
Daniel Webster	do	397	—— Harlow	E. Mulford
Franklin	do	391	—— Griffin	Charles T. Dering
Fanny	do	391	—— Payne	N. and G. Howell
France	do	411	—— Howell	do
Gem	do	326	—— Ludlow	Huntting Cooper
Henry	do	333	—— Cartwright	C. T. Dering
Hudson	do	36[illegible]	—— Green	Luther D. Cook
Marcus	do	283	—— Payne	S. & N. Howell
Monmouth	do	273	—— Smith	
Neptune	do	338	—— Slate	S. & B. Huntting & Co
Noble	do	274	—— Sayer	Ira B. Tuthill
Nimrod	do	280	—— Parker	C. T. Dering & Co
Romulus	do	233	—— Rodgers	Mulford & Howell
Thorn	do	299	—— Topping	Mulford & Sleight
Thomas Dickason	do	454	—— Havens	do
Thames	do		—— Nickerson	
Xenophon	do	384	—— Halsey	Mulford & Sleight
Greenport, N. Y.				
Bayard	Ship	339	—— Miller	H. & N. Corwin
Roanoke	do	251	—— Case	Wiggins & Parsons
Seraph	Brig	174	—— Shearman	Samuel Lamson
Triad	Ship	336	—— Loper	H. & N. Corwin
Washington	do	236	—— Wilber	James Tuthill
Dartmouth, Mass.				
Elizabeth	Ship	329	—— Wood	James Rider
Forester	Bark	243	—— Ray	Prince Sears
South Carolina	Ship	302	—— Smith	James Rider

sailing from American ports—Continued.

Whaling-ground.	Date— Of sailing.	Date— Of arrival.	Result of voyage. Sperm-oil.	Result of voyage. Whale-oil.	Result of voyage. Whalebone.	Remarks.
			Bbls.	*Bbls.*	*Lbs.*	
South Atlantic.	June 6	Mar. 17, 1839	220	1,880	......	
....do	June 14	Mar. 7, 1839	50	2,750	......	
Patagonia	Dec. 8	Apr. 21, 1839	300	1,200	......	
South Atlantic.	Apr. 19	Apr. 7, 1838	200	1,600	......	
....do	July 20	Mar. 2, 1839	.....	2,000	......	
....do	May 28	Aug 29, 1838	......	1,500	......	Crew mutinied.
....do	June 6	June 1, 1838	200	1,600	......	
Falk. Islands ..	Apr. 2	Dec. 29, 1838	130	2,300	......	
South Atlantic.	July 1	Apr. 9, 1839	120	2,100	......	
....do	June 21	Mar. 28, 1839	200	1,650	......	
... do	Aug. 4	Apr. 24, 1839	120	1,580	16,000	
Pacific Ocean..	Nov. 12	Feb. 5, 1841	1,900	600	......	
....	Oct. 14	Apr. 4, 1840	500	1,000	......	
South Atlantic.	Nov. 21	Aug. 4, 1840	120	2,880	......	
....	July 1	Feb. 28, 1839	340	1,760	......	
Patagonia	....	Dec. 6, 1838	50	2,200	......	
Falk. Islands ..	....	Sept. 1, 1838	......	Full.	......	
Falk. Islands .	Dec. 27	Oct. 13, 1839	......	3,600	....	Bought from Boston, 1836.
....	June —	Mar. 8, 1839	250	1,650	......	
South Atlantic.	....	Apr. 21, 1839	70	1,430	......	Lost third mate and boat's crew by a whale, 1838.
South Atlantic.	June 14	....	......	......	......	Belonged to Norwich; lost on Crozettes, with her tender, (Colossus,) 1837 or 1838.
....do	July 8	Mar. 16, 1839	100	1,800	......	
South Atlantic.	Aug. 3	May 20, 1838	.....	1,350	......	
....do	July 11	May 19, 1838	130	570	......	
....do	July 22	May 20, 1839	60	740	......	
....do	July 8	Apr. 28, 1838	130	1,620	......	
....do	July 14	May 7, 1838	......	1,750	......	
....do	May 20	May 10, 1838	.....	1,100	......	
....do	....	May 19, 1838	90	1,800	......	
....do	Aug. 17	Apr. 13, 1839	280	2,020	......	Captain Harlow was killed by a whale, November 6, 1838.
....do	Aug. 17	May 4, 1839	220	1,100	......	
....do	July 8	May 7, 1838	60	1,450	......	Captain Payne was killed by a whale, January 2, 1838.
....do	June 21	May 7, 1838	.....	2,300	......	
....do	July 18	May 8, 1838	180	1,350	......	
....do	June 27	Apr. 27, 1838	130	1,620	......	
....do	Aug. 3	May 26, 1839	700	2,000	......	
....do	July 8	Apr. 30, 1838	......	750	......	
....do	July —	May 8, 1838	......	1,300	......	
....do	June 27	Apr. 24, 1839	180	2,000	......	
....do	July 22	May 8, 1838	......	1,100	......	
....do	July 25	May 20, 1838	......	500	......	
....do	July 8	Mar. 18, 1839	......	1,500	......	
....do	July 10	Apr. 7, 1838	......	1,000	......	
....do	July 18	Apr. 27, 1839	120	3,880	40,000	
....do	June 27	May 10, 1838	.....	1,100	......	Condemned at Sag Harbor, 1838.
....	June 27	June 23, 1838	......	1,475	......	
South Atlantic.	July —	Apr. 22, 1839	300	1,600	......	
....do	June —	Apr. —, 1838	.....	1,650	......	
Atlantic.	July —	May 21, 1838	140	100	......	Hailed from Greenport; probably owned in Southold.
South Atlantic.	June —	Apr. 24, 1839	165	1,700	......	
....do	June —	Apr. 19, 1838	150	1,300	......	
Pacific Ocean..	Nov. 30	Mar. 26, 1841	2,240	......	......	Sold to New Bedford, 1841.
....do	Dec. 5	....	......	......	......	Lost on Montauk Point, April 17, 1841.
South Atlantic.	June 28	May 20, 1838	50	1,150	......	

Table showing returns of whaling-vessels

Name of vessel.	Class.	Tonnage.	Captain.	Managing owner or agent.
1837.				
Westport, Mass.				
Champion	Bark	209		Andrew Hicks
Juno	Brig	165	—— Sowle	Abner B. Gifford
Mexico	do	130	—— Davis	Gideon Davis
Boston, Mass.				
Margaret	Brig	125	—— Dwight	S. J. Bridge
Dorchester, Mass.				
Herald	Ship	242	—— Reynolds	Josiah Stickney
Lewis	Bark	281	—— Cunningham	C. O. Whitmore & Co
Hudson, N. Y.				
Alexander Mansfield	Ship	320	—— Douglass	Barnard Curtis & Co
America	do	464	—— Topham	do
Helvetia	do	333	—— Cottle	Robert A. Barnard
New York, N. Y.				
Ocollo	Schooner	...	—— Hallett	
Scituate	do	..	—— Thaine	R. A. Barnard
White Oak	Bark	291	—— Barney	Pell, Zabieskie & Pell
Bridgeport, Conn.				
Atlantic	Ship	291	—— Post	Samuel F. Hurd
Hamilton	do	359	—— Rose	do
Harvest	Bark	263	—— Halsey	do
Cold Spring, N. Y.				
Tuscarora	Ship	379	—— Dennison	
East Haddam, Conn.				
Bruce	Ship	148	—— Bradford	
Newark, N. J.				
John Wells	Ship	366	Uriah Russell	J. H. Stephens
Newburgh, N. Y.				
Portland	Ship	292	—— Cook	Charles Ludlow
Plymouth, Mass.				
Fortune	Bark	278	—— Goodwin	Isaac L. Hedge
James Munroe	Brig	115	—— Chase	Northam & Fearing
Mary and Martha	do	317	John B. Coffin	James Bartlett, jr
Portsmouth, N. H.				
Ann Parry	Ship	348	—— Swain	James Kennard
Poughkeepsie, N. Y.				
Vermont	Bark	292	—— Howland	David S. Shearman
Wilmington, Del.				
Ceres	Ship	328	—— Ayres	William Wheeler
Lucy Anne	do	309	John J. Parker	do
Provincetown, Mass.				
Imogene	Brig	172	—— Smalley	James Smalley
Louisa	Schooner	...	—— Tillson	
1838.				
New Bedford, Mass.				
Ann Alexander	Ship	253	—— Dornin	George Howland
Amethyst	do	359	—— Reynard	John A. Parker & Son

sailing from American ports—Continued.

Whaling-ground.	Date— Of sailing.	Date— Of arrival.	Result of voyage. Sperm-oil.	Result of voyage. Whale-oil.	Result of voyage. Whalebone.	Remarks.
			Bbls.	*Bbls.*	*Lbs.*	
Atlantic	Sept. 20	Apr. 6, 1839	335	....	......	
....do	May 10	July 21, 1838	254	8	......	
....do	Apr. 21	Apr. 26, 1838	555	20	......	
N. & S. Atlantic	Sept. 20	....	......	....	.....	Dropped out of the lists in November, 1840, with no report from her from date of sailing.
Pacific Ocean ..	Nov. 5	May 29, 1841	1,800	....	......	Sold to Stonington, 1841.
South Seas....	July 27	Sept. 5, 1839	200	1,600	......	
South Atlantic	June 25	Mar. 21, 1839	200	900	......	Sailed in 1839, and was condemned at Tahiti, 1840; oil (1,000 sperm) shipped home.
Indian Ocean ..	Aug. 14	May 2, 1839	200	3,300	......	
Pacific Ocean ..	Oct. 19	June 16, 1839	350	2,350	21,000	
Falk. Islands ..	....	....	......	....	......	Lost in 1839.
Atlantic	Nov. 27	Sept. 26, 1838	45	....	......	Sold, 1838.
....	Dec. 9	June 11, 1840	350	1,700	......	First mate taken out of boat by a line and lost; sold to New London, 1840.
South Atlantic.	July —	Apr. 10, 1839	......	1,900	......	
....do	July 8	May 1, 1838	......	1,900	......	
....	June —	June 21, 1838	150	......	......	Sold the whale-oil on the voyage.
South Atlantic	Sept. 9	Apr. 23, 1839	120	1,280	......	Bought from New London, 1837.
Atlantic	Aug. 20	July 5, 1838	110	....	.....	
S. A. and P. O ..	May 20	Apr. 9, 1839	300	1,900	......	
Indian Ocean ..	June 10	Apr. 10, 1839	230	2,160	20,000	Sold to Sag Harbor, 1839.
South Atlantic	June 30	Oct. 31, 1839	......	2,300	......	
Atlantic	Aug. 6	Nov. 1, 1839	55	4	......	
South Atlantic	Dec. 19	Dec. 3, 1840	450	2,000	.....	
Indian Ocean ..	Jan. 6	Apr. 9, 1839	500	1,250	......	
....	July 20	Oct. 2, 1838	200	2,600	......	
Pacific Ocean ..	Dec. 10	Mar. 18, 1841	1,800	....	.....	
South Atlantic	July 24	Apr. 24, 1839	100	2,400	24,000	
Atlantic	Mar. 29	Nov. 5, 1837	450	....	......	
....do	....	Nov. 10, 1837	100	....	......	
Pacific Ocean ..	Aug. 22	Aug. 21, 1841	1,900	....	......	
Indian Ocean ..	Mar. 23	Mar. 3, 1840	18	2,734	......	

Table showing returns of whaling-vessels

Name of vessel.	Class.	Tonnage.	Captain.	Managing owner or agent.
1838.				
New Bedford, Mass.—Continued.				
Alexander	Ship	421	Charles Stetson	John A. Parker & Son
Augusta	do	344	—— Lawrence	W. R. Rodman
Averick	do	470	—— Stetson	John A. Parker & Son
America	do	418	John Cole	I. Howland, jr. & Co
Agate	Brig	81	—— Landry	
Addison	Ship	426	—— Tower	A. H. Seabury
Barclay	do	281	—— Swain	Wm. R. Rotch & Co
Brandt	do	310	—— Delano	Alexander Gibbs
Cortes	do	382	Edward Gardner	George Howland
Canton	do	409	—— Leary	Jireh Perry
Com. Decatur	do	247	Elihu Wood	
Courier	do	381	—— Harding	Randall & Haskell
Clarice	Bark	237	Benjamin Clark	C. W. Morgan
China	Ship	370	—— Potter	William H. Stowell
Cicero	do	252	—— Hillman	
Ceres	do	373	George Tobey	Alexander Gibbs
Charles Frederick	do	317	—— Brown	J. A. Parker & Son
Cherokee	Bark	261	—— Cook	
Charleston Packet	Brig	184	—— Daggett	Crane & French
Cornelia	Bark	216	—— Netchen	L. Kollock
Delight	Brig	102	—— Howland	Jona. Mosher
Enterprize	Ship	291	—— Downs	Alfred Gibbs & Co
Falcon	do	273	Abm. Russell	Briggs & Bartlett
Fenelon	do	328	—— Smith	David Coffin
Florida	do	330	Edward Maxfield	E. Dunbar & Co
George Howland	do	374	—— Weeks	George Howland
Gideon Howland	do	379	—— Baker	I. Howland, jr., & Co
George and Martha	Bark	275	—— Willcox	Haskell & Randall
Garland	do	234	Elihu Gifford	Jas. D. Thompson
Herald, 2d	Ship	303	Nathaniel H. Nye	T. & A. R. Nye
Hector	do	380	Thomas A. Norton	Charles W. Morgan
Hibernia	do	327	—— Gray	Alfred Gibbs & Co
Huntress	do	391	—— Hull	do
India	do	366	—— Luce	William T. Russell
John	do	308	Isaac Thatcher	Frederick Parker
Jasper	Bark	223	Jos. Shockley	Alexander Gibbs
Juno	Brig	123	—— Brownell	A. H. Seabury & Bro
Lancaster	Ship	383	R. N. Swift	T. & A. R. Nye
Logan	do	302	Luther J. Briggs	I. Howland, jr., & Co
Liverpool	do	306	—— Thomas	Abm. B rker
London Packet	do	280	John Samson	A. H. Howland
Lucas	do	281	—— Taber	Tobey & Ricketson
Laurel	Schooner	119	{ —— Manter —— Worth }	I. H. Bartlett
Maria Theresa	Ship	330	—— Turner	T. & A. R. Nye
Maria	do	202	—— Raymond	C. W. Morgan
Mary	do	287	—— Black	I. Howland, jr., & Co
Milo	do	398	—— Gardner	Andrew Robeson
Magnolia	do	396	David Barnard	C. W. Morgan
Milwood	Bark	254	Joseph Spooner	Gideon Allen
Nautilus	Ship	340	Alden G. Ellis	Jireh Perry
Newton	Bark	283	—— Hathaway	Isaiah Burgess
Parachute	Ship	331	—— Eastham	A. H. Seabury & Bro
Persia	Bark	240	—— Norton	Lawrence Grinnell
Roman 2d	Ship	350	—— Bartlett	Abm. Barker
Robert Edwards	do	356	—— Howland	J. & J. Howland
Sally Anne	do	312	Robert E. Borden	D. R. Greene & Co
Seine	Bark	281	—— Adams	Crane & French
Sarah Louisa	Brig	144	Ray G. Sanford	William R. Rodman
Tuscaloosa	Ship	284	William Hussey	Howland & Hussey
Triton	do	300	Avery F. Parker	I. Howland, jr., & Co
Trident	do	449	John H. Ricketson	J. A. Parker & Co
Two Brothers	do	288	I. C. Howland	D. R. Greene & Co
Tobacco Plant	do	271	—— Swain	W. R. Rodman
Virginia	do	346	—— Luce	William H. Stowell
William Hamilton	do	463	William Swain	I. Howland, jr., & Co
Waverly	ds	327	William Monroe	do

sailing from American ports—Continued.

Whaling-ground.	Date—Of sailing.	Date—Of arrival.	Result of voyage.—Sperm-oil.	Result of voyage.—Whale-oil.	Result of voyage.—Whalebone.	Remarks.
			Bb'ls.	*Bbls.*	*Lbs.*	
Pacific Ocean ..	Dec. 30	June 11, 1842	2, 200	......	......	Mate killed by natives at the Marquesas Islands.
....do	June 26	Jan. 6, 1842	2, 071	67	......	
New Zealand ..	Feb. 2	Oct. 3, 1839	......	4, 200	......	Arrived at Bremen.
Indian Ocean ..	July 9	May 27, 1840	530	3, 879	......	
Atlantic	Dec. —	July —, 1840	90	210	......	
New Zealand ..	Dec. 19	Apr. 1, 1841	392	2, 450	......	
Indian Ocean ..	Apr. 29	Apr. 24, 1840	165	1, 939	......	
South Atlantic.	June 19	June 28, 1839	189	847	......	
Pacific Ocean ..	Apr. 24	Apr. 22, 1842	2, 230	......	......	
....do	Nov. 22	Aug. 26, 1842	2, 634	40	......	
South Atlantic	May 25	....	.....	......	......	Condemned at Bermudas, January 4, 1840. Had 500 whale.
Pacific Ocean ..	June 8	July 18, 1842	2, 283	......	......	
....do	Nov. 15	Aug. 12, 1841	1, 206	......	......	
New Zealand ..	Oct. 2	May 2, 1840	751	1, 934	......	
South Atlantic.	June 12	June 1, 1840	310	1, 012	......	
Indian Ocean ..	Oct. 13	....	.....	......	......	Condemned at Isle of France, April, 1839.
Pacific Ocean ..	Dec. 1	Nov. 22, 1841	2, 656	......	......	
New Zealand ..	Nov. 7	Oct. 14, 1840	532	1, 922	......	
South Atlantic.	June 19	May 31, 1839	256	8	......	
S. A. and Ind ...	Apr. 3	July 9, 1840	583	230	......	
Atlantic	Aug. 20	May 18, 1839	65	......	......	Voyage spoiled by mutiny of crew.
Pacific Ocean ..	Sept. 2	June 19, 1844	407	2, 001	......	
P. O. and N. Z ..	Aug. 2	June 3, 1840	265	1, 895	......	
South Atlantic	Aug. 29	June 22, 1840	782	1, 750	......	
....do	July 24	Feb. 22, 1840	539	2, 250	......	
Pacific Ocean ..	Apr. 24	Oct. 21, 1841	1, 994	27	......	
....do	Dec. 6	June 23, 1842	2, 765	......	......	
S. A. and Ind...	June 18	May 15, 1840	287	2, 006	......	
Indian Ocean ..	Sept. 15	May 25, 1840	212	1, 000	......	
Pacific Ocean ..	Nov. 20	Nov. 27, 1842	1, 550	......	......	
....do	May 27	Aug. 16, 1840	2, 675	7	......	
Indian Ocean ..	June 30	Nov. 7, 1839	706	1, 445	......	
....do	Apr. 9	June 10, 1839	141	2, 898	27, 000	Sold 114 sperm at Hobart Town.
....do	Aug. 12	Mar. 14, 1840	750	1, 975	......	
....do	June 4	Feb. 21, 1840	233	2, 025	......	
....do	June 3	May 13, 1839	111	574	......	
Atlantic	Apr. 14	May 29, 1839	404	14	......	
Pacific Ocean ..	Nov. 15	Mar. 26, 1842	2, 744	......	......	
....do	May 1	Dec. 13, 1841	1, 339	946	......	
South Atlantic.	June 8	Apr. 7, 1840	224	1, 916	......	
Indian Ocean ..	May 12	May 18, 1840	330	1, 470	......	
....do	July 1	Aug. 9, 1839	......	2, 608	......	
Atlantic ..... {	Apr. 28	June 25, 1838	71	3	......	
	July 19	June 27, 1839	200	......	......	
Indian Ocean ..	July 6	Mar. 21, 1840	800	1, 912	......	
....do	May 18	Sept. 7, 1840	750	......	......	
....do	June 3	Oct. 27, 18 9	910	1, 318	......	
Pacific Ocean ..	Dec. 24	Aug. 10, 1842	2, 693	89	......	First mate and boat's crew reported lost, October, 1841.
...do	Dec. 2	Aug. 4, 1842	1, 944	1, 065	......	
South Atlantic.	May 25	Mar. 31, 1840	86	1, 324	......	
Pacific Ocean ..	Nov. 20	Mar. 3, 1842	2, 688	......	......	
New Zealand ..	Dec. 31	Mar. 9, 1841	586	2, 033	......	
....do	Nov. 15	Sept. 8, 1840	485	2, 285	......	
Pacific Ocean ..	Sept. 30	Dec. 12, 1842	1, 593	......	......	
Indian Ocean ..	July 11	July 9, 1840	278	3, 115	......	
Pacific Ocean ..	Aug. 24	Mar. 26, 1841	2, 663	......	......	
South Atlantic.	June 6	May 6, 1840	292	1, 976	......	
....do	Oct. 3	Aug. 9, 1840	600	600	......	
Atlantic	Aug. 8	June 26, 1840	396	3	......	
Indian Ocean ..	May 2	Apr. 3, 1840	253	1, 852	......	Ordered away from Two People's Bay by Her Britannic Majesty's ship Harold.
Pacific Ocean ..	Sept. 3	Nov. 3, 1841	1, 459	453	......	
....do	Aug. 8	Nov. 9, 1842	1, 590	40	......	
S. A. and Ind ..	Oct. 16	May 6, 1840	600	212	......	
Pacific Ocean ..	May 12	Nov. 5, 1841	1, 085	99	......	
Chili	May 21	Mar. 31, 1840	575	2, 090	......	
Pacific Ocean ..	May 1	May 31, 1842	2, 156	......	......	
....do	Dec. 7	May 25, 1842	1, 921	......	......	

Table showing returns of whaling-vessels

Name of vessel.	Class.	Tonnage.	Captain.	Managing owner or agent.
1838.				
New Bedford, Mass.—Continued.				
Winslow	Ship	263	—— Pease	S. Rodman, jr
Washington	do	344	C. P. Covell	Jona. Bourne, jr
Fairhaven, Mass.				
Alto	Bark	197	—— Caldwell	Alden D. Stoddard
Albion	Ship	328	—— Smith	E. Sawin
Arab	do	336	—— Cushman	do
Benezett	Bark	192	—— Stetson	Jabez Delano, jr
Charles Drew	Ship	344	—— Bonney	Lemuel Tripp
Cadmus	do	320	—— Mayhew	Atkins Adams
Eliza Adams	do	403	—— Holley	do
Favorite	do	293	—— Swift	E. Sawin
George	do	360	—— Chase	Fish & Huttlestone
Hesper	Bark	262	Holder Almy	I. Hitch
Herald	Ship	262	—— Devoll	Samuel Borden
Isabella	Bark	243	—— Davis	E. Sawin
Joseph Maxwell	Ship	302	—— Stewart	F R. Whitwell
Java	do	292	—— Crowell	Atkins Adams
Martha	do	298	John D. Taber	Nathan Church
Martha, 2d	do	301	—— Kelley	Atkins Adams
Maine	do	294	—— Magee	E. Sawin
Marcia	do	315	Edward Mosher	do
Mary Ann	do	335	—— Chase	L. Tripp, jr
Pindus	Bark	193	—— Perry	Lemuel Tripp
Pacific	Ship	314	—— Butler	Asa Swift
Quito	Brig	138	—— Webb	E. Sawin
South Boston	Ship	338	—— Butler	do
William Wirt	do	387	—— Daggett	Warren Delano
Rochester, Mass.				
Annawan	Brig	148	Charles Bates	G. Barstow & Son
Dryade	Bark	263	—— Smalley	do
Gideon Barstow	Ship	379	—— Cary	do
Lagrange	Brig	170	—— Daggett	Elijah Willis
Le Barron	do	170	—— Rogers	G. Barstow & Son
Mattapoisett	do	150	—— Southworth	Joseph Meigs
Orion	do	99	—— Purrington	Elijah Willis
Sarah	do	171	—— Purrington	G. Barstow & Son
Solon	do	129	—— Hammond	Noble E. Bates
Nantucket, Mass.				
American	Ship	340	David Barker	Matthew Crosby
Alpha	do	345	Joseph Congdon	Nathaniel Barney
Christopher Mitchell	do	387	Charles A. Veeder	Gorham Coffin
Clarkson	do	380	Joseph C. Chase	James Athearn
Daniel Webster	do	336	Joseph N. Plasket	Jared Coffin
Harmony	Schooner		—— Tracy	
Howard	Ship	364	William Worth, 2d	Timothy Hussey
Iris	Sloop		—— Weeks	
Japan	Ship	332	John Tobey	James Athearn
James Loper	do	348	Obed Cathcart	Levi Starbuck
Joseph Starbuck	do	416	Sanford Wilbur	George Starbuck
Lima	do	286	Obed Luce, jr	William B. Coffin
Mary Mitchell	do	354	Joseph McCleave	Samuel B. Tuck
Napoleon	do	360	William Plasket	George B. Upton
Phebe	do	379	George Allen, 2d	Gorham Coffin
Primrose	Schooner		—— Coleman	
President	Ship	293	Reuben Starbuck	Joseph Starbuck
Robert	Sloop		—— Meader	
Rambler	Ship	318	Robert McCleave	Frederick C. Sanford
Thule	do	285	James Coleman	S. B. Tuck
Young Hero	do	339	George Alley	Joseph Starbuck
Edgartown, Mass.				
Champion	Ship	396	—— Lawrence	Grafton Norton
Loan	do	262	—— Merchant	Abm. Osborne
Mary	do	348	—— Fisher	Coffin & Darrow

sailing from American ports—Continued.

Whaling-ground.	Date—		Result of voyage.			Remarks.
	Of sailing.	Of arrival.	Sperm-oil.	Whale-oil.	Whalebone.	
			Bbls.	*Bbls.*	*Lbs.*	
Atlantic	Aug. 1	June 20, 1839	280	......	......	
New Zealand	Dec. 15	July 1, 1840	457	2,030	......	Bought from Dartmouth, 1838.
S. A. and Ind.	Mar. 3	May 15, 1840	602	......	......	
Indian Ocean	July 9	Feb. 24, 1840	600	2,241	......	
....do	July 26	Mar. 19, 1840	26	2,374	......	
Pacific Ocean	June 8	Oct. 12, 1840	1,045	......	......	
....do	Aug. 9	Apr. 15, 1842	1,960	......	......	Sold to New Bedford, 1842.
....do	June 3	Mar. 16, 1841	2,002	......	......	
....do	Oct. 22	Jan. 23, 1842	2,771	......	......	
New Zealand	Dec. 2	Aug. 7, 1840	240	2,293	......	
Indian Ocean	July 17	Aug. 6, 1840	48	2,076	......	
Ind. and P. O	Nov. 25	May 9, 1841	1,822	......	......	Bought from New Bedford, 1838.
South Atlantic	July 19	Apr. 2, 1840	112	1,360	......	
Pacific Ocean	Jan. 9	June 14, 1841	991	694	......	
Indian Ocean	Sept. 19	July 10, 1840	491	1,353	......	
Pacific Ocean	May 27	May 30, 1841	590	800	......	
Indian Ocean	June 25	July 6, 1841	625	1,330	......	
....do	July 21	June 4, 1840	670	1,555	......	
....do	Aug. 12	Mar. 31, 1840	188	1,982	......	
....do	Feb. 3	Nov. 4, 1841	657	1,435	......	
Pacific Ocean	Sept. 13	May 31, 1842	2,306	......	......	
South Atlantic	Aug. 4	May 29, 1840	375	725	......	
....do	Aug. 28	Feb. 13, 1840	114	1,971	......	Bought from Nantucket 1838.
Indian Ocean	July 26	Nov. 7, 1839	45	597	......	Tender to ship Arab.
South Atlantic	Apr. 30	Sept. 19, 1839	......	2,960	......	
Indian Ocean	June 23	June 4, 1842	2,760	......	......	
Atlantic	July —	....	......	......	......	Lost at sea, in a gale, March, 1839. Captain, 1st and 2d mates, and 12 men lost.
Indian Ocean	July 3	Oct. 23, 1839	242	1,350	......	
....do	June 20	....	......	......	......	Lost at Cocos Islands March, 1839.
Atlantic	Apr. 30	May 10, 1839	431	5	......	
South Atlantic	Oct. 20	Nov. 7, 1839	646	......	......	
Atlantic	Apr. 3	June 4, 1839	220	......	......	
....do	Sept. 13	May 27, 1839	120	......	......	
....do	July 22	May 16, 1839	563	......	......	
....do	June 6	Apr. 16, 1839	440	......	......	
Pacific Ocean	July 4	Oct. 21, 1841	2,181	9	......	Sent home 90 barrels sperm.
....do	June 3	Dec. 2, 1841	2,265	......	......	
....do	Apr. 28	Apr. 5, 1841	2,714	52	......	
....do	July 16	Apr. 17, 1841	1,580	310	......	
....do	Dec. 16	Oct. 15, 1842	1,832	......	......	Built at Mattapoisett 1838.
Indian Ocean	Sept. 22	....	......	......	......	Lost in the Indian Ocean February 8, 1839.
Pacific Ocean	Oct. 19	Jan. 1, 1841	2,209	......	......	
Shoals	......	....	......	......	......	Made three trips; took one small whale.
Pacific Ocean	June 10	Dec. 12, 1841	2,176	27	......	
....do	June 26	May 11, 1842	1,842	......	......	Built 1837, at Rochester.
....do	Nov. 15	Apr. 3, 1842	3,321	......	......	Built 1838, at Nantucket.
....do	Aug. 29	Feb. 7, 1842	1,660	......	......	
....do	Aug. 26	Apr. 27, 1842	1,370	96	......	David O. Bearse, 2d mate, died Sept. 13, 1841.
....do	Sept. 9	Sept. 13, 1842	1,676	512	......	Built 1838, at Rochester.
....do	July 18	Apr. 2, 1842	1,387	......	......	
Atlantic	....	Nov. 14, 1838	Clean	......	......	
Pacific Ocean	Nov. 15	July 18, 1842	1,840	......	......	
Shoals	....	....	......	......	......	Made several voyages; took 60 bbls. humpback.
Pacific Ocean	Dec. 12	Nov. 10, 1842	1,548	......	......	
....do	Oct. 19	Dec. 29, 1841	1,526	52	......	
....do	June 27	Oct. 21, 1841	2,504	....	......	Built 1838, at Rochester.
New Zealand	May 12	May 12, 1841	3,100	......	......	
Pacific Ocean	May 30	....	....	......	......	Sent home 900 sperm; lost at Talcahuano August 19, 1841.
New Zealand	Aug. 8	Sept. 20, 1840	700	2,200	......	

Table showing returns of whaling-vessels

Name of vessel.	Class.	Tonnage.	Captain.	Managing owner or agent.
1838.				
Stonington, Conn.				
George	Ship	251	—— Brewster	Charles P. Williams
Mercury	do	305	—— Smith	C. T. Stanton
Thomas Williams	do	340	—— Hall	C. P. Williams
Wareham, Mass.				
Pleiades	Bark	261	—— Allen	M. S. F. Tobey
Holmes's Hole, Mass.				
Pocahontas	Ship	341	—— Dillingham	Thomas Bradley
William and Joseph	Brig		—— Cleveland	
Provincetown, Mass.				
Imogene	Brig		—— Smalley	James Smalley
Fall River, Mass.				
Ann Maria	Brig	196	—— Snell	J. S. Barnard
Taunton	do	103	—— Cummings	William Coggeshall
William	do	107	—— Cudworth	J. S. Barnard
Lynn, Mass.				
Com. Preble	Ship	323	—— Eldridge	Andrew Breed
Louisa	do	383	—— Wooley	Hezekiah Chase & Co
Ninus	do	260	—— Ludlow	Isaiah Breed
Falmouth, Mass.				
Brunette	Bark	200	—— Pool	Elijah Swift
Geo. Washington	Brig	180	—— Whitehouse	Sanford Herendeen
Popmunnett	Bark	200	—— Nickerson	John Robinson
New London, Conn.				
Armata	Ship	414	—— Peabody	Abner Bassett
Bingham	do	375	—— Barnum	Benjamin Brown
Com. Perry	do	270	—— Hobron	C. Chew & Co
Columbia	do	492	—— Smith	Havens & Smith
Candace	do	310	—— Reed	do
Chelsea	do	396	—— Smith	do
Electra	do	347	—— Lax	William Williams, jr
Georgia	do	343	—— Hall	Thomas W. Williams
Gen. Williams	do	446	—— Holdridge	Williams & Barns
Hand	Schooner	86	—— Randall	Havens & Smith
Indian Chief	Ship	401	—— Skinner	Frink, Chew & Co
John and Elizabeth	do	296	—— Halsey	Havens & Smith
John and Edward	do	318	—— Bailey	N. & W. W. Billings
Julius Cæsar	do	347	—— McLean	do
McDonough	Schooner	125	—— Lawton	Benjamin Brown
Phenix	Ship			
Superior	do			
Sag Harbor, N. Y.				
Ann	Ship	299	—— Bishop	Marcus B. Osborn
American	do	283	—— Jennings	S. & B. Huntting & Co
Acasta	do	286	—— Smith	Mulford & Sleight
Camillus	do	345	—— Rogers	Charles T. Dering
Concordia	Bark	265	—— Woodward	Thomas Brown
Columbian	Ship	285	—— Pierson	Luther D. Cook
Cadmus	do	307	—— Babcock	Mulford & Sleight
France	do	411	—— Howell	N. & G. Howell
Fanny	do	391	—— Payne	do
Gem	do	326	—— Ludlow	Huntting Cooper
Henry	do	333	—— Sweeney	S. L. Hommedien
Hannibal	do	311	—— Bennett	S. & B. Huntting & Co
Hamilton	do	322	—— Jones	C. T. Dering
Marcus	do	283	—— Glover	S. & N. Howell
Monmouth	do	273	—— Smith	

sailing from American ports—Continued.

Whaling-ground.	Date— Of sailing.	Date— Of arrival.	Result of voyage. Sperm-oil.	Result of voyage. Whale-oil.	Result of voyage. Whalebone.	Remarks.
			Bbls.	*Bbls.*	*Lbs.*	
Pacific Ocean	Oct. 24	Feb. 28, 1841	900	1,200	......	Sold 600 whale at Pernambuco.
....do	Nov. 1	Sept. 6, 1840	600	2,000	......	
South Atlantic	May 19	June 27, 1840	600	2,450	......	
South Atlantic	Oct. 2	June 18, 1840	303	1,420	......	
Indian Ocean	June 16	....	......	......	......	
Atlantic	....	Sept. 22, 1838	60	......	......	
Bay of Mexico	Jan. 10	July 24, 1838	400	200	......	
South Atlantic	Aug. 20	Oct. 24, 1839	250	......	......	
Atlantic	Mar. 23	Aug. 30, 1838	65	......	......	Sailed again October 30, 1838; arrived August 19, 1839.
....do	June 25	Dec. 19, 1838	400	......	......	
Indian Ocean	July 14	May 26, 1840	380	1,900	......	
....do	July 11	....	......	......	......	Condemned at Mauritius December, 1839; had 1,100 whale.
....do	July 14	Aug. 7, 1840	......	1,650	10,000	
Atlantic	July 12	Dec. 11, 1839	400	......	......	
....do	June 20	Mar. 6, 1840	200	......	......	
....do	....	—— —, 1838	200	......	......	
South Atlantic	July 6	Mar. 31, 1840	200	1,900	......	
....do	June 18	May 13, 1839	80	1,720	......	Sold to Mystic.
....do	June 1	—— —, 1839	470	530	......	
....do	July 25	May 1, 1839	......	3,700	......	
....do	May 22	Feb. 14, 1839	300	1,900	......	
....do	June 26	Oct. 10, 1839	30	2,800	......	
....do	July 6	Apr. 10, 1840	100	1,800	......	
....do	Oct. 28	July 1, 1839	......	90	......	Had schooner Amazon for tender; crew mutinied.
Falk. Islands	Nov. 28	Oct. 14, 1840	400	2,300	......	Had Brig Magellan, Lax, for tender.
Indian Ocean	July 28	May 23, 1840	......	300	7,000	
....do	Oct. 1	Apr. 5, 1841	150	2,600	......	
South Atlantic	July 6	May 14, 1840	650	800	......	
....do	Nov. 28	Jan. 11, 1840	100	2,300	......	Sold to New Bedford.
....do	Nov. 14	—— —, 1839	......	......	......	Probably arrived in June or July, full.
Indian Ocean	Aug. 1	....	......	......	......	
Pacific Ocean	Nov. —	Feb. —, 1841	1,900	600	......	
South Atlantic	Oct. —	July —, 1840	120	2,880	......	
South Atlantic	July 11	May 9, 1839	30	970	......	
....do	May 28	July 10, 1840	400	1,100	......	
....do	July 6	Aug. 31, 1840	200	1,700	......	
....do	Aug. 1	June 13, 1839	......	1,600	......	
....do	July 11	Oct. —, 1840	300	1,800	......	
....do	June 14	May 15, 1839	......	300	......	
....do	June 14	May 15, 1839	......	500	......	
....do	July 16	Aug. 17, 1841	700	3,500	26,730	
....do	July —	May 9, 1839	......	1,000	......	
....do	July 11	July 30, 1839	600	1,000	......	
....do	June 23	May 29, 1839	......	900	......	
....do	July 26	July 8, 1840	100	1,550	......	
....do	Aug. 9	May 7, 1840	160	2,200	......	
....do	June 9	Apr. 30, 1839	50	1,100	......	
....do	July 17	May 24, 1839	75	825	......	

Table showing returns of whaling-vessels

Name of vessel.	Class.	Tonnage.	Captain.	Managing owner or agent.
1838.				
Sag Harbor, N. Y.—Continued.				
Nimrod	Ship	280	—— Parker	C. T. Dering & Co.
Ontario	do	368	—— Green	S. & B. Huntting & Co.
Phenix	do	314	—— Topping	L. D. Cook
Panama	do	464	Thomas E. Crowell	N. & G. Howell
Thorn	do	299	—— Tuttle	Mulford & Sleight
Washington	do	340	—— Sayer	Josiah Douglass
Xenophon	do	384	—— Halsey	Mulford & Sleight
Westport, Mass.				
Dr. Franklin	Bark	171	—— Francis	Job Davis
Elizabeth	Brig	107	—— Sowle	Abner B. Coffin
Juno	do	165	—— Sowle	Abner B. Gifford
Mexico	do	130	—— Macomber	Gideon Davis
President	Bark	187	—— Sowle	Andrew Hicks
Mystic, Conn.				
Aeronaut	Ship	265	—— Mallory	Charles Mallory
Gov. Endicott	do	298	—— Holmes	J. & W. P. Randall
Meteor	do	325	—— Lester	do
Tampico	Brig	99	—— Bailey	C. Mallory
Uxor	do	96	—— McKinstry	do
Bridgeport, Conn.				
Hamilton	Ship	359	—— Brown	Samuel F. Hurd
Harvest	Bark	....	—— Godbee	do
East Haddam, Conn.				
Bruce	Bark	148	—— Bradford	
Dartmouth, Mass.				
Grand Turk	Ship	324	—— Dexter	James Rider
South Carolina	do	302	—— Bailey	do
Wade	Bark	261	—— Swift	
Wilmington, Del.				
North America	Ship	270	—— Simmons	William Wheeler
Greenport, N. Y.				
Delta	Ship	314	—— Griffin	H. & N. Corwin
Roanoke	do	251	—— Case	Wiggins & Parsons
Seraph	Brig	174	—— Barns	Samuel Lamson
Washington	Ship	236	—— Wilbur	James Tuthill
Hudson, N. Y.				
Edward	Ship	274	—— Daggett	Seth G. Macy
Huron	do	290	—— Barrett	Robert A. Barnard
Martha	do	369	—— Whelden	Alexander Jenkins
New York, N. Y.				
Elizabeth	Brig	..	—— Nash	S. E. Burrows
Shibboleth	Bark	219	—— Smith	do
Providence, R. I.				
Envoy	Ship	392	—— Pease	Amherst & Everett
Salem, Mass.				
Eliza	Bark	362	—— Radcliffe	James W. Cheever
Emerald	Ship	271	—— Dexter	S. C. Phillips
Mt. Wollaston	do	325	—— Jewett	John B. Osgood
Statesman	Bark	258	—— Coffin	do

sailing from American ports—Continued

Whaling-ground.	Date— Of sailing.	Of arrival.	Result of voyage. Sperm-oil.	Whale-oil.	Whalebone.	Remarks.
			Bbls.	*Bbls.*	*Lbs.*	
South Atlantic	July 11	May 9, 1839		1,400		
do	July —	July 18, 1839				
do	July 25	May 8, 1840	120	2,380		Captain Topping left the ship and came home sick.
do	June 12	Apr. 11, 1841	400	3,300	29,000	
Pacific Ocean	Oct. 18					Condemned at Bay of Islands, July, 1840; had 50 sperm, 1,600 whale.
South Atlantic	July 26	Apr. 24, 1839	58	350		
do	July 26	July 10, 1840	240	2,710		
Atlantic	Sept. 5	May 13, 1839	401			
do	Aug. 28	May 27, 1839	212			
do	Aug. 24	June 24, 1839	433	2		
do	June —	June 12, 1839	360			
do	Aug. 26	Sept. 19, 1839	383			
South Seas	June 18	Mar. 31, 1840	80	2,200		
do	July 11	Sept. 5, 1839		1,300		Had for tender schooner Plutarch, 81 tons Captain Stevens.
do	June 1	—— —, 1839	150	1,800		
Crozettes	June —	Apr. 8, 1839		100		Elephant-oil.
South Atlantic	May 15	Mar. 9, 1839		300		Do.
South Atlantic	July 6	May 30, 1839		1,350		
do	July 28	June 6, 1840	140	1,860		
Atlantic	Sept. 13	Sept. 20, 1838				Put into Newport badly damaged by a gale; sold to Fairhaven 1839.
Indian Ocean	July 11	Dec. 10, 1839	130	2,470		
Pacific Ocean	Dec. 15	Apr. 15, 1842	1,150	800		
South Seas	Apr. 18	May 7, 1840	708	1,280		
South Atlantic	June 1	Aug. 6, 1839		2,400		Sailed for the Indian Ocean December 6, 1839, and was lost at Geographé Bay, July 6, 1840.
South Atlantic	July —	—— —, 1839				
do	July —	May 4, 1839	200	1,250		
do	July —	Feb. 26, 1839	190	720		
do	July —	May 2, 1839	200	1,000		
South Atlantic	July 10	Sept. 1, 1840	200	1,300		
do	Sept. 26	May 28, 1840		900		Sold to Sag Harbor.
Indian Ocean		Apr. 23, 1839	150	1,150	13,000	
Falk. Islands	Feb. 14	Aug. 18, 1839		1,450		
South Atlantic	Jan. 26					Sold at Rio Janeiro.
Pacific Ocean	June 18	Mar. 18, 1841	1,000	2,500		
Indian Ocean	Nov. 21	May 9, 1841	275	1,300		
do	May 24	Feb. 27, 1840	250	1,750		Sold 100 sperm at Hobart Town.
do	June 2	Apr. 17, 1840	600	1,100		
New Zealand	Oct. 26	Mar. 9, 1842	1,800			

Table showing returns of whaling-vessels

Name of vessel.	Class.	Tonnage.	Captain.	Managing owner or agent.
1838.				
Portland, Me.				
Science	Ship	388	—— Whippey	Caleb Adams
Wiscasset, Me.				
Wiscasset	Ship	380	S. B. Horton	John Brooks
Newport, R. I.				
Erie	Ship	375	A. W. Dennis	Samuel Whitehorne
Margaret	do	375	T. Wimpenny	John Stevens & Co
Mechanic	do	335	Spencer Pratt	Thomas Bush
Pocahontas	Brig	....	William Barker	Samuel Barker
Sailor's Return	Schooner	....	—— Smiley	N. S. Ruggles
Bristol, R. I.				
America	Bark	257	—— Simmons	Robert Rogers
America	Ship	....	....	....
Gov. Hopkins	Brig	111	—— Simmons	William R. Taylor
Troy	do	156	—— King	Thomas Church
Warren, R. I.				
Brilliant	Brig	....	—— Smith	....
Chariot	Ship	355	—— Littlefield	N. M. Wheaton & Co
Crawford	Brig	121	—— Luther	J. & D. K. Luther
Franklin	Bark	219	—— Barton	do
Galen	Ship	365	—— Borden	Driscol & Child
Philip Tabb	do	405	—— Jenney	do
William Baker	do	224	Sanford	do
Poughkeepsie, N. Y.				
Elbe	Ship	333	Charles Waterman	David S. Shearman
Vermont	do	292	—— Kendrick	do
Plymouth, Mass.				
James Munroe	Brig	115	—— Randall	Northam & Fearing
New Suffolk, N. Y.				
Noble	Bark	274	—— Sayer	Ira B. Tuthill
Portsmouth, N. H.				
Ann Parry	Ship	348	—— Youngs	James Kennard
1839.				
New Bedford, Mass.				
Abigail	Ship	310	James V. Cox	C. W. Morgan
Alexander Barclay	do	465	—— Norton	J. A. Parker & Son
Benjamin Tucker	do	349	—— Worth	Charles R. Tucker
Brandt	do	310	Hezekiab Adams	N. Leonard & Co
Brighton	do	354	—— Sherman	William T. Russell
Cambria	do	362	—— Ray	James Arnold
Chili	do	291	D. B. Delano	N. Leonard & Co
Coral	do	370	James H. Shearman	Gideon Allen
Corinthian	do	401	—— Paddock	George Howland
Condor	do	349	—— Harding	C. W. Morgan
Copia	do	315	John Worth	Lemuel Kollock
Cora	Bark	220	—— Shearman	I. H. Bartlett
Charleston Packet	Brig	184	—— Tripp	Crane & French
Delight	do	102	—— West	Jona. Mosher
Draper	Ship	291	—— Howland	Jos. Dunbar & Co
Desdemonia	Bark	295	—— Phinney	T. & A. R. Nye
Emerald	Ship	359	—— Merchant	Riddell & Dix

sailing from American ports—Continued.

Whaling-ground.	Date— Of sailing.	Date— Of arrival.	Result of voyage. Sperm-oil.	Result of voyage. Whale-oil.	Result of voyage. Whalebone.	Remarks.
			Bbls.	*Bbls.*	*Lbs.*	
Pacific Ocean ..	Sept. 8	June 4, 1841	300	2, 800	......	
Pacific Ocean ..	Jan. 27	July 22, 1841	900	1, 200	......	Sold 600 whale at Bahia; sold to Sag Harbor.
South Atlantic.	May 20	....	......	......	......	Lost at Chatham Island, 1841; oil saved, (1,100 whale.)
Pacific Ocean ..	June 13	Oct. 17, 1840	1, 600	200	......	
....do	July 21	Jan. 4, 1842	2, 400	......	......	
North Atlantic.	....	July 10, 1840	80	18	......	
....	Aug. —	....	......	......	......	Lost October 11, 1838, on Cape Saint Roque.
South Atlantic.	Aug. 26	Apr. 26, 1840	75	1, 225	......	
Indian Ocean...	Jan. —	June —, 1840	1, 300	......	......	
Atlantic	July 14	July 1, 1839	60	......	......	
....do	Apr. 6	July 2, 1839	680	......	......	
New Zealand ..	Oct. 16	....	......	......	......	Lost in Poverty Bay, New Zealand.
....do	Dec. 6	Oct. 12, 1840	180	1, 920	......	Sailed first, March 10; struck by lightning; returned the second time in July, damaged in a gale.
Atlantic	Apr. 4	Dec. 11, 1839	350	......	......	
Indian Ocean ..	July 24	Aug. 7, 1840	750	250	......	
Pacific Ocean ..	Oct. 5	June 24, 1842	1, 700	......	......	
....do	July 10	Apr. 14, 1840	200	2, 450	......	
South Atlantic.	July 11	Apr. 19, 1839	180	620	......	
South Atlantic.	June—	May 20, 1840	850	1, 850	......	
....do	Dec. 5	Oct. 12, 1840	450	2, 100	......	
Atlantic	Dec. 2	Dec. 29, 1839	313	......	......	
South Atlantic.	....	May 9, 1839	195	450	......	
Indian Ocean ..	Aug. 3	June 1, 1842	472	2, 030	15, 000	
Pacific Ocean ..	Apr. 2	Apr. 6, 1843	1, 640	......	......	Returned July 6, 1839, leaky, having landed 60 sperm at Western Islands. Sailed again July 28.
New Zealand ..	Oct. 8	Sept. 27, 1841	......	4, 500	......	Unloaded at Bremen.
Pacific Ocean ..	Nov. 16	Sept. —, 1843	2, 035	35	......	
....do	Dec. 20	Feb. 12, 1843	500	110	800	
Indian Ocean ..	May 18	Nov. 24, 1841	1, 260	1, 144	......	
New Zealand ..	May 4	Oct. 1, 1842	2, 021	......	......	
Pacific Ocean ..	Oct. 14	Apr. 21, 1843	2, 000	......	......	
....do	June 15	Sept. 11, 1842	3, 118	......	......	
....do	Aug. 11	Aug. 7, 1843	2, 600	100	......	
Indian Ocean...	July 11	June 27, 1841	910	1, 764	......	
New Zealand ..	Oct. 9	July 17, 1840	500	......	......	Returned in consequence of a mutiny.
....do	May 10	May 12, 1841	351	1, 514	......	
Atlantic	July 12	June 14, 1840	122	8	......	
....do	June 12	May 26, 1840	281	......	......	
Indian Ocean ..	Aug. 13	Jan. 23, 1842	782	1, 304	......	
Pacific Ocean ..	Oct. 7	May —, 1843	800	400	2, 400	
....do	Dec. 25	May —, 1843	1, 746	......	......	

Table showing returns of whaling-vessels

Name of vessel.	Class.	Tonnage.	Captain.	Managing owner or agent.
1839.				
New Bedford, Mass.—Continued.				
Emma	Bark	246	—— Davis	Lawrence Grinnell
Equator	do	263	—— Fisher	John A. Standish
Frs. Henrietta	Ship	407	William H. Reynard	C. W. Morgan
Frances	do	348	Stephen C. Christian	James Arnold
Franklin	Bark	218	William E. Butle	John A. Parker & Son
Franklin	Ship	333	—— Howland	Abm. H. Howland
Golconda	do	331	Edward Howland, 2d	George Howland
George	do	273	—— Lake	J. A. Parker & Son
George Porter	do	285	—— Luce	Riddell & Dix
Good Return	do	376	—— Taber	Henry Taber
Gen. Pike	do	313	—— Little	Oliver Crocker
Golconda, 2d	do	359	—— Smith	William H. Stowell
Hope	do	295	—— Robinson	William T. Russell
Hope, 2d	Bark	186	—— Davis	E. Dunbar & Co.
Hercules	Ship	335	H. H. Ricketson	Jireh Perry
Hydaspe	do	313	—— Hathaway	Randall & Haskell
Huntress	do	391	—— Hull	Alfred Gibbs & Co
Honqua	do	339	—— West	Alexander Gibbs
Iris	do	311	Gideon B. Spooner	Edward C. Jones
Isaac Howland	do	399	—— Swain	I. Howland, jr., & Co
Julian	do	356	—— Hawes	Hathaway & Luce
Java	do	295	—— Holt	George Howland
John Howland	do	377	—— Whitfield	J. & J. Howland
John Adams	do	268	—— Baker	Jireh Perry
James	do	278	—— Taber	T. & A. R. Nye
Jasper	Bark	223	—— Sanford	Alexander Gibbs
Juno	Brig	123	—— Pease	A. H. Seabury & Bro
Lucas	Ship	281	—— Severance	Tobey & Ricketson
Laurel	Brig	119	—— Smith	I. H. Bartlett
Messenger	Ship	277	—— Kendrick	J. R. Thornton
Mary	do	287	Hiram Nickerson	I. Howland, jr., & Co
Minerva	do	408	Moses Samson	William Gifford
Mayflower	do	350	Henry Colt	Randall & Haskell
Milton	do	388	Robert Tuckerman	Henry Taber & Co
Minerva	Bark	195	Warren Howland	Charles R. Tucker
Montpelier	Ship	320	—— Cary	Walter Spooner
Nye	do	211	Ezra Smith	T. & A. R. Nye
Octavia	do	257	—— Manchester	Gideon Allen
Phenix	do	423	Squire Sanford	J. A. Parker
Pacific, 2d	do	332	—— Collins	Andrew Robeson
Parker	do	406	Prince Sherman	J. A. Parker & Son
Pioneer	Bark	231	—— Hillman	C. W. Morgan
Phocion	Ship	265	—— Smith	Palmer & Coggeshall
Roman	do	375	—— Smith	Edward C. Jones
Rajah	Bark	250	—— West	Isaiah Burgess
Roscoe	do	235	George H. Clark	Jona. Bourne, jr
Stephania	Ship	315	Warren N. Bourne	Richard A. Palmer
Selma	do	269	—— Willcox	A. H. Seabury & Bro
St. George	do	408	—— Fisher	George O. Crocker & Co
St. Peter	do	267	William H. Mosher	Bryant & Perry
Timoleon	do	346	—— Baylies	J. Dunbar & Co
William and Eliza	do	321	Samuel F. Rogers	James Arnold
William Thompson	do	495	—— Doane	Jireh Perry
William Botch	do	290	Rudolphus Toby	John Coggeshall
Winslow	do	263	—— Grinnell	S. Rodman, jr
Zoroaster	Brig	159	—— King	A. H. Seabury
Zephyr	Ship	361	Abraham Gardner	Alexander Gibbs
Fairhaven, Mass.				
Ansell Gibbs	Ship	319	—— West	Gibbs & Jenney
Amazon	do	318	—— Smith	Nathan Church
Bruce	Bark	148	—— Reynolds	M. O. Bradford
Columbus	Ship	382	—— Fish	Gibbs & Jenney

sailing from American ports—Continued.

Whaling-ground.	Date— Of sailing.	Date— Of arrival.	Result of voyage. Sperm-oil.	Result of voyage. Whale-oil.	Result of voyage. Whalebone.	Remarks.
			Bbls.	*Bbls.*	*Lbs.*	
Atlantic	Aug. 18	Oct. 18, 1840	334	......	......	
Pacific Ocean ..	Nov. 2	Apr. —, 1840	871	......	......	
....do	Aug. 4	Feb. 16, 1843	1,700	1,420	11,500	
....do	Dec. 22	Aug. 2, 1843	1,771	15	......	
....do	July 9	May 13, 1843	779	......	......	
New Zealand ..	Apr. 16	Feb. 28, 1841	427	1,860	......	
Pacific Ocean ..	Dec. 5	June 17, 1843	1,288	......	......	
....do	Dec. 26	May 2, 1843	1,387	......	......	First mate, Samuel Waggoner, died November, 1841.
....do	Nov. 8	July 3, 1843	1,408	......	......	
New Zealand ..	May 30	Aug. 16, 1841	215	3,130	......	
....do	May 4	Mar. 1, 1841	653	2,156	......	
....do	May 4	Apr. 9, 1841	180	3,120	......	Bought from Bristol.
Indian Ocean ..	July 11	May 28, 1841	800	1,300	......	
Atlantic	July 11	Nov. 29, 1840	910	16	......	
New Zealand ..	Aug. 14	Dec. 15, 1841	805	1,813	8,400	
South Atlantic	Mar. 24	Sept. 18, 1840	444	......	......	
Indian Ocean .	Oct. 25	June 26, 1841	551	2,804	......	
....do	July 8	Apr. 6, 1841	689	2,293	......	
Pacific Ocean ..	Aug. 15	May 27, 1843	1,595	55	......	
... do	May 30	Apr. 23, 1843	2,481	19	......	
Indian Ocean ..	Sept. 28	Oct. 21, 1841	635	2,295	......	
New Zealand ..	May 31	Mar. 28, 1841	330	2,172	......	
Pacific Ocean ..	Oct. 31	May 7, 1843	2,761	......	......	
New Zealand ..	June 2	Apr. 27, 1841	1,221	603	......	
....do	May 15	Apr. 21, 1841	332	1,602	......	
New Holland ..	June 17	June 3, 1840	191	1,123	......	
Atlantic	June 22	June 24, 1840	40	20	......	
New Zealand ..	Sept. 17	Apr. 15, 1842	250	1,550	16,000	
Atlantic	Aug. 3	Aug. 31, 1840	215	10	......	
South Atlantic	Sept. 17	May 1, 1841	425	65	......	Captain, mate, and four men died on voyage.
Indian Ocean ..	Dec. 24	Apr. 5, 1842	530	1,840	18,000	
... do	Oct. —	Sept. 10, 1842	150	1,050	......	
New Zealand ..	July 10	May 23, 1841	965	1,460	......	
Pacific Ocean ..	Dec. 11	Mar. 26, 1842	804	1,740	......	
Atlantic	May 11	May 5, 1840	607	2	......	
New Zealand ..	Sept. 21	Oct. 19, 1841	750	1,550	......	
Pacific Ocean ..	Dec. 18	May 14, 1844	30	983	......	
South Atlantic	May 30	May 28, 1841	49	2,126	......	
Pacific Ocean ..	Apr. 29	May 29, 1842	3,039	31	......	
....do	Nov. 3	May 31, 1842	897	934	......	
....do	Aug. 26	....	......	......	......	Captain Sherman's boat was stove by a whale and he was drowned, 1841. Ship lost on Ocean Island September 24, 1842; mate, H. Kelly, and three men lost. Had 2,000 sperm and 1,000 whale; all lost.
Indian Ocean ..	June 6	May 26, 1842	491	827	8,000	
South Atlantic and Ind.	June 13	June 27, 1841	295	1,300	......	Returned August 10, 1839, leaky. Sailed again September 8, Collins, master.
Pacific Ocean ..	July 2	Dec. 22, 1842	2,702	......	......	
New Zealand ..	June 8	May 28, 1841	502	1,672	......	
Indian Ocean ..	Sept. 6	Mar. 28, 1842	426	830	7,500	
....do	July 18	Oct. 9, 1841	916	1,390	......	
New Zealand ..	June 4	Apr. 19, 1841	196	1,376	......	
Pacific Ocean ..	Sept. 3	Mar. 31, 1843	2,322	......	......	
Indian Ocean ..	May 19	May 27, 1842	341	1,634	......	
Pacific Ocean ..	Dec. 17	July 29, 1843	1,902	......	......	Marshall B. Caldwell, third mate, died November, 1842.
....do	Oct. 21	June 24, 1844	800	682	31,643	Shipped home about 2,300 whale.
....do	Apr. 21	Feb. 25, 1842	1,685	2,060	......	
....do	June 30	Nov. 27, 1842	1,185	......	......	
Indian Ocean ..	July 14	May 5, 1840	420	3	......	
Atlantic	Oct. 10	Oct. 28, 1840	378	6	......	
Pacific Ocean ..	June 29	Mar. 19, 1843	2,200	......	......	
Pacific Ocean ..	Sept. 17	Sept. 10, 1842	2,530	......	......	
Indian Ocean ..	June 10	May 28, 1841	343	1,876	......	
Atlantic	Apr. 7	Aug. 6, 1840	302	16	......	Bought from East Haddam, 1839.
New Zealand ..	May 7	June 9, 1841	900	2,600	......	

Table showing returns of whaling-vessels

Name of vessel.	Class.	Tonnage.	Captain.	Managing owner or agent.
1839.				
Fairhaven, Mass.—Continued.				
Draco	Bark	257	—— Ray	A. D. Stoddard
Friendship	Ship	366	—— Taber	Gibbs & Jenney
Gen. Scott	..do	333	—— Fosdick	L. C. Tripp
Heroine	..do	337	—— Smith	Nathan Church
Harvest	Bark	314	—— Fisher	Jabez Delano, jr
Jasper	Ship	360	—— Leavitt	Atkins Adams
Leonidas	..do	243	—— Stewart	Jenney & Tripp
London Packet	..do	335	Moses Howland	Gibbs & Jenney
Lagrange	Bark	280	—— Taber	Atkins Adams
Marcia	Ship	315	Edward P. Mosher	E. Sawin
Sarah Francis	..do	301	—— Daggett	..do
Rochester, Mass.				
Chase	Brig	153	—— Mayhew	G. Barstow & Son
Lagrange	..do	170	—— Riddell	Elijah Willis
Mattapoisett	..do	150	—— Southworth	Jos. Meigs
Orion	..do	99	—— Snow	Elijah Willis
Pearl	..do	157	—— Purrington	J. S. Bates
Richard Henry	Bark	173	—— Ellis	G. Barstow & Son
Shylock	Ship	278	—— Taber	S. C. Luce
Sarah	Brig	171	—— Purrington	G. Barstow & Son
Solon	..do	129	—— Wing	Noble E. Bates
Two Sisters	..do	122	—— Hammond	..do
Volant	Bark	210	—— Hammond	J. S. Bates
Willis	Brig	164	—— Boodry	R. L. Barstow
Nantucket, Mass.				
Atlantic	Ship	321	George C. Hoeg	Daniel Jones
Baltic	..do	410	John J. Gardner	John H. Shaw
Barclay	..do	301	Reuben Barney	Griffin Barney
Catharine	..do	384	John Brown	Chris. Wyer
Comet	Schooner	....	—— Coffin	
Columbus	Ship	344	William B. Gardner	R. Mitchell & Sons
Constitution	..do	318	Obed Ramsdell	C. G. & H. Coffin
Congress	..do	339	John Pitman	Philip H. Folger
Dromo	Brig	....	—— Lawrence	
Henry Clay	Ship	385	Benjamin C. Sayer	Chris. Wyer
Montano	..do	365	Reuben Chase	Barker & Athearn
Mary	..do	369	Thomas Coffin, 2d	Daniel Jones
Mount Vernon	..do	384	Lewis B. Imbert	J. H. Shaw
Orbit	..do	351	Isaac Gardner	P. H. Folger
Ploughboy	..do	391	Moses Brown	Val. Hussey & Bro
Primrose	Schooner	90	—— Carr	
Peru	Ship	257	Joshua Coffin	David Joy
Richard Mitchell	..do	385	William H. Gardner	R. Mitchell & Sons
Sarah	..do	495	William Upham	George B. Elkins
Spartan	..do	333	David U. Coffin	Daniel Jones
Statira	..do	346	Barzillai T. Folger	Samuel B. Tuck
Tyleston	Schooner	111	—— Swain	David Thain
Telescope	..do	70	—— Manter	Fred. A. Chase
Zone	Ship	365	Edwin Hiller	James Athearn

*The "camels" were practically a floating dock, with a very light draught, propelled by steam. They with water. The vessel to be transported over the "bar" was received within the suitably-formed together, the water pumped out, and the loaded ship carried into or out of the harbor, as was desired. the south beach of the harbor, until time and the elements left nothing to show that it had ever

sailing from American ports—Continued.

Whaling-ground.	Date—Of sailing.	Date—Of arrival.	Result of voyage.—Sperm-oil.	Result of voyage.—Whale-oil.	Result of voyage.—Whalebone.	Remarks.
			Bbls.	*Bbls.*	*Lbs.*	
Pacific Ocean	Aug. 28	June 12, 1843	1,000			Sold to New Bedford, 1843.
Indian Ocean	June 29	Nov. 3, 1841	519	2,152		
Pacific Ocean	May 22	June 18, 1843	910			
New Zealand	June 25	Feb. 14, 1841	93	2,483		
...do	June 23	July 2, 1841	811	1,330		Bought from Newport.
....do	Sept. 17					Condemned at Talcahuano May, 1841. Bought from Newburyport.
....do	Nov. 21	Nov. 8, 1842	1,530	157		
Indian Ocean	Nov. 16	July 4, 1843	1,850			
....do	July 31	Mar. 23, 1841	290	1,845		
New Zealand	Aug. 4	—— —, 1841				
Pacific Ocean	Dec. 13	Oct. 18, 1843	1,613			
Atlantic	Aug. 21	Oct. 23, 1840	430			Abandoned at sea, 1841.
....do	June 30	June 21, 1840	52			
....do	July 14	Dec. 14, 1840	300			
....do	June 23					Lost at Porto Rico, March 22, 1840.
....do	July 4	June 24, 1840	130	30		
....do	Aug. 17	Aug. 18, 1840	300			Captain Ellis was killed by a whale July 24, 1840.
New Zealand	May 26					Lost at Feejee Islands, 1840.
Atlantic	July 7	July 13, 1840	500			
....do	May 17	June 2, 1840	200			
....do	July 30	Mar. 27, 1840	500			Bought from Boston 1839.
South Atlantic	Oct. 18		120	200		Condemned at St. Helena February, 1841.
Atlantic	June 16	Aug. 28, 1840	475			
Pacific Ocean	May 12	May 11, 1843	1,255	95		
....do	Aug. 17	Apr. 6, 1843	2,007	323		Sold to Fairhaven, 1843.
....do	Dec. 10	Aug. 12, 1843	818	2		
....do	May 8	June 23, 1843	650	270		Captain Brown died in his boat, fast to a whale. Sold to New London.
Atlantic	Aug. 3	Aug. 29, 1839	Clean			
Pacific Ocean	May 25	Apr. 28, 1843	1,180			Sold to New London.
....do	July 21	May 31, 1842	2,167	20		
....do	Aug. 27	June 18, 1843	1,298	50		Sold to New Bedford.
Atlantic		Dec. 29, 1839				Reported late in 1839 with 200 sperm; condemned, 1840.
Pacific Ocean	Dec. 17	Feb. 27, 1844	1,946	5		Built 1839, at Rochester.
....do	July 20	July 7, 1841	236	2,156		
....do	Sept. 10	July 14, 1843	1,443			Second mate, Thomas M. Gardner, lost April, 1843.
... do	Oct. 31	June 23, 1844	2,877			
....do	Aug. 10					Lost near Payta; had 1,200 sperm; saved 600 sperm, and sold it for $3,900.
....do	June 27	May 15, 1843	747	700		Sold to New Bedford 1843.
Atlantic	Apr. 17	June 4, 1840	200	25		
Pacific Ocean	July 11	Oct. 13, 1842	1,340			The first ship brought over the bar by the "camels."* Bells were rung, guns fired, and a great concourse of citizens greeted her arrival.
....do	July 17	May 11, 1843	1,078			
....do	July 14	July 15, 1843	2,646			The Sarah arrived at New York and sailed from there in 1843.
....do	Oct. 17	Mar. 23, 1843	1,903			
....do	Nov. 10	May 29, 1843	2,703			Sold to New Bedford 1843.
Atlantic	May 9	June 7, 1839		18		Tyleston built at Nobleborough, Me., 1836; sailed again July 24, 1839; arrived June 10, 1840, with 200 sperm.
....do	June 6	Sept. 4, 1839		100		Telescope sailed again December 10, 1839; arrived June 17, 1840, with 90 whale.
Pacific Ocean	May 19	May 8, 1843	2,061			

were made in two sections, which opened and were sunk by means of chambers which were flooded space of this dock, and securely fastened to prevent any strain on her hull. The sections were brought The timbers of this structure that at one time promised so much for Nantucket lay for some years on existed.

Table showing returns of whaling-vessels

Name of vessel.	Class.	Tonnage.	Captain.	Managing owner or agent.
1839.				
Edgartown, Mass.				
Athalia	Ship	162	—— Sprague	Joseph Mayhew
Almira	do	362	—— Tobey	Abraham Osborne
George and Mary	do	356	—— Coffin	do
Splendid	do	392	—— Coffin	do
Plymouth, Mass.				
Triton	Ship	315	—— Russell	James Bartlett
Fall River, Mass.				
Gold Hunter	Ship	281	—— Estes	Nathan Durfee
Ganges	do	380	—— Wood	John Eddy
Pantheon	Bark	284	—— Pell	do
Panama	Ship	253	—— Cummings	J. S. Barnard
William	Brig	107	—— Sanford	Hiram Bliss
Salem, Mass.				
Malay	Bark	268	—— Barnard	S. C. Phillips
Palestine	do	249	—— Crimblish	Nathaniel Weston
Reaper	do	230	—— Neal	John B. Osgood
Samuel Wright	Ship	372	—— Coffin	do
Sapphire	do	366	—— Cartwright	S. C. Phillips
Warren, R. I.				
Canova	Ship	343	—— Saunders	Child & Mauran
Magnet	do	355	—— Champlin	Joseph Smith
Miles	do	242	—— Downes	John R. Wheaton
North America	do	288	—— Mosher	Driscol & Child
Rosalie	do	323	—— Eddy	Joseph Smith, jr., & Co
Triton	do	345	—— Bowen	S. P. Child
Wm. Baker	do	224	—— Bowen	Driscol & Child
Bristol, R. I.				
Corinthian	Ship	503	—— Heath	William H. D'Wolf
Gov. Hopkins	do	111	—— Davis	W. R. Taylor
Troy	Brig	156	—— Lake	Thomas Church
New London, Conn.				
Ann Maria	Ship	368	—— Middleton	Thomas W. Williams
Amazon	Schooner	71	—— Beebe	Havens & Smith
Boston	Ship	291	—— Pendleton	I. Lawrence
Connecticut	do	398	—— Crocker	T. W. Williams
Com. Perry	do			
Columbus	Brig	153	—— Holt	Williams & Barns
Clematis	Ship	311	—— Bailey	do
Chelsea	do	396	—— Smith	Havens & Smith
Flora	do	338	—— Fitch	N. & W. W. Billings
Friends	do	403	—— Brown	Benjamin Brown
Georgia	do	343	—— Peabody	T. W. Williams
George	do	290	—— Dustan	L. Allen
Jones	do	336	—— Green	T. W. Williams
Jason	do	335	—— Chester	E. M. Frink & Co
Julius Cæsar	do	347		
Mentor	do	460	—— Baker	Benjamin Brown
North America	do	388	—— Richards	T. W. Williams
Neptune	do	285	—— Green	do
Pacific	Schooner	96	—— Havens	Havens & Smith
Palladium	Ship	342	—— Prentiss	E. M. Frink & Co
Stonington	do	351	—— Rice	Williams & Barns
Stonington, Conn.				
Acasta	Ship	330	—— Swain	C. P. Williams
Corvo	do	349	—— Pendleton	do

sailing from American ports—Continued.

Whaling-ground.	Date— Of sailing.	Date— Of arrival.	Result of voyage. Sperm-oil.	Result of voyage. Whale-oil.	Result of voyage. Whalebone.	Remarks.
			Bbls.	*Bbls.*	*Lbs.*	
Atlantic	May 8	Mar. 11, 1840	450	......	......	
Pacific Ocean ..	Nov. 9	Jan. 1, 1843	2, 200	......	......	
....do	Aug. 31	Apr. —, 1843	1, 900	60	......	Sold to New London.
....do	Dec. 24	July 24, 1843	2, 300	......	......	
Pacific Ocean ..	Aug. 27	Nov. 12, 1842	2, 100	......	......	
New Zealand ..	June 5	Sept. 11, 1840	340	1, 560	......	
Pacific Ocean ..	Nov. 9	....	......	......	......	Burned at Talcahuano April, 1840.
....do	Aug. 7	July 12, 1842	1, 450	1, 100	......	
South Atlantic	Dec. 19	Sept. 11, 1841	450	190	......	Bought from Nantucket.
Atlantic	Jan. 28	....	.....	......	......	Sold 150 sperm; condemned at St. Thomas January 15, 1840.
Indian Ocean ..	July 3	Jan. 20, 1842	1, 300	......	......	
....do	May 18	Oct. 16, 1842	1, 700	......	......	Captain and first mate (George Coffin) died 1841; wrecked after this voyage; built 1835.
....do	Aug. 17	Sept. 13, 1842	1, 000	......	......	
....do	May 4	....	......	......	......	Lost on New Holland July 8, 1840.
Pacific Ocean ..	Nov. 28	Dec. 17, 1842	800	1, 200	......	Foundered at sea after this voyage; bound to Mobile.
New Zealand ..	Oct. 20	....	......	......	......	Condemned at Rio September, 1841; had 2,650 whale.
Pacific Ocean ..	Dec. 27	Mar. —, 1843	1, 200	1, 160	12, 800	Returned in December, damaged by a gale.
Indian Ocean ..	June 1	....	......	......	......	Condemned at Mozambique September, 1841.
South Atlantic	July 22	June 17, 1841	700	300	......	Lost several of the crew by scurvy.
Pacific Ocean ..	Sept. 6	Apr. 1, 1841	300	1, 700	......	
....do	Nov. 5	Nov. 2, 1841	200	2, 000	......	
South Atlantic	July 5	May 28, 1841	450	800	......	
Indian Ocean ..	Sept. 23	May 13, 1842	300	2, 400	22, 000	
Atlantic	Aug. 26	Sept. 1, 1830	160	......	......	
....do	Nov. 12	June 22, 1840	600	......	......	
South Atlantic	May 29	Mar. 5, 1841	70	2, 130	......	
Indian Ocean ..	Oct. 31	....	......	......	......	Captain Beebe and boat's crew lost at the Aucklands 1840; tender to the Chelsea; no report of return.
South Seas.....	May 22	May 23, 1840	160	1, 600	......	
....do	June 10	May 5, 1840	175	1, 750	......	
Indian Ocean ..	June —	June —, 1840	500	2, 000	......	
South Atlantic	Apr. 16	May 26, 1840	450	......	......	
Indian Ocean ..	June 26	July 6, 1840	150	2, 450	......	
South Atlantic	Nov. 28	Aug. 21, 1840	......	2, 700	....	Returned once; sailed again December 10.
Patagonia	May 19	July 9, 1840	1, 250	2, 000	14, 000	
New Zealand ..	July 22	Feb. 14, 1841	50	2, 800	......	
....do	Aug. 25	May 12, 1841	240	700	......	
South Atlantic	May 11	....	......	......	......	Lost on Amsterdam Island August, 1839.
Patagonia......	Mar. 4	Jan. 10, 1841	.....	1, 200	......	
South Pacific ..	Aug. 10	May 28, 1841	200	2, 300	......	
South Atlantic	Sept. —	June 22, 1840	400	2, 000	......	
Indian Ocean ..	Aug. 19	Mar. 28, 1841	140	3, 160	......	
Pacific Ocean ..	Oct. 20	June 20, 1842	......	......	......	
South Seas.....	May 29	July 9, 1840	130	2, 000	......	
....do	Nov. 8	Feb. 4, 1841	25	550	......	
....do	July 13	Apr. 19, 1841	600	1, 600	......	
Indian Ocean ..	May 4	July 9, 1840	130	2, 000	18, 000	
South Seas.....	May 10	....	......	......	......	Foundered at sea September, 1840; crew picked up by the Java, F. H.; had 700 sperm and 1,600 whale on board.
....do	Dec. 11	Feb. 6, 1842	300	1, 700	......	

Table showing returns of whaling-vessels

Name of vessel.	Class.	Tonnage.	Captain.	Managing owner or agent.
1839.				
Stonington, Conn.—Continued.				
Caledonia	Ship	446	—— Hancox	C. P. Williams
Henry	Brig	98	—— Pendleton	C. T. Stanton
Philetus	Ship	278	—— Brewster	E. Faxon, jr., & Co
Rebecca Groves	Brig	129	—— Barnum	C. P. Williams
Wilmington, Del.				
Jefferson	Ship	396	—— Baker	William Wheeler
Lucy Ann	do	309	—— Cox	do
Superior	do	275	—— Crocker	do
Hudson, N. Y.				
America	Ship	464	—— Topham	Barnard, Curtis & Co
Alex. Mansfield	do	320	—— Douglass	do
Helvetia	do	333	—— Gardner	do
Martha	do	369	—— Whelden	Alexander Jenkins
Sag Harbor, N. Y.				
Ann	Ship	299	E. H. Curry	Marcus B. Osborn
Arabella	do	367	John Bishop, jr	N. & G. Howell
Camillus	do	345	—— Howes	Charles T. Dering
Columbia	do	285	L. B. Edwards	Luther D. Cook
Cadmus	do	307	Henry Nickerson, jr	Mulford & Sleight
Daniel Webster	do	397	Edw'd M. Baker	E. Mulford
Franklin	do	391	David Youngs	C. T. Dering
Fanny	do	391	S. W. Edwards	N. & G. Howell
Gem	do	326	—— Worth	Huntting Cooper
Hamilton, 2d	do	455	D. Hand	Mulford & Sleight
Hudson	do	368	Samuel Dennison	L. D. Cook
Marcus	do	283	—— Glover	S. & N. Howell
Monmouth	do	273	—— Bennett	
Neptune	do	338	S. H. Sleight	S. & B. Huntting & Co
Nimrod	do	280	—— Parker	C. T. Dering & Co
Ontario	do	368	—— Green	S. & B. Huntting & Co
Portland	do	292	William H. Payne	do
Romulus	do	233	—— Fordham	Mulford & Howell
Thos. Dickason	do	454	W. S. Havens	Mulford & Sleight
Thames	do	414	Jere. W. Hedges	Thomas Brown
Washington	do	340	William Osborn	Josiah Douglass
New Suffolk, N. Y.				
Noble	Bark	274	—— Sayer	Ira B. Tuthill
Wareham, Mass.				
Inga	Brig	169	—— Cudworth	M. S. F. Tobey
Meridian	do	73	—— Ricketson	do
Somerset, Mass.				
Pilgrim	do	137	—— Collins	Wheaton Luther
Bridgeport, Conn.				
Atlantic	Ship	291	—— Rose	Samuel H. Ford
Hamilton	do	359	—— Brown	Samuel F. Hurd
Harvest	do			
Mystic, Conn.				
Bingham	Ship	375	—— Bailey	Charles Mallory
Blackstone	do	258	—— Baker	Silas Beebe
Gov. Endicott	do	298	—— McKinstry	J. & W. P. Randall
Meteor	do	325	—— Lester	do
Tampico	Brig	99	—— Pendleton	C. Mallory
Uxor	do	96	—— Mitchell	do
Greenport, N. Y.				
Bayard	Ship	339		H. & N. Corwin
Delta	do	314	—— Payne	H. & N. Corwin
Roanoke	Bark	251	—— Case	Wiggins & Parsons

sailing from American ports—Continued.

Whaling-ground.	Date—		Result of voyage.			Remarks.
	Of sailing.	Of arrival.	Sperm-oil.	Whale-oil.	Whalebone.	
			Bbls.	*Bbls.*	*Lbs.*	
Indian Ocean ..	July 6	Mar. 23, 1841	300	2, 900	......	
Atlantic	July 6	May 8, 1840	......	300	......	Elephant-oil.
South Atlantic.	July 10	Feb. 28, 1841	......	1, 800	......	
Indian Ocean ..	July 15	June 7, 1840	......	650	......	Do.
New Zealand ..	Sept. 17	Oct. 23, 1841	1, 700	1, 100	......	Bought from Baltimore, 1839.
....do	July 20	June 24, 1841	400	1, 200	......	
Pacific Ocean ..	Oct. 7	Dec. 21, 1841	600	....	......	Captain died at Cocus Island September 4, 1841; sold to Sag Harbor.
Pacific Ocean ..	Sept. 19	Jan. 5, 1842	1, 000	2, 600	......	Sold to Stonington, 1842.
....do	July 24	....	......	......	......	Condemned at Tahita, August, 1840. Sent oil home; had about 75 sperm, 800 whale.
....do	Oct. 4	Apr. 26, 1842	460	2, 000	......	Sold to New London, 1842.
Indian Ocean ..	July 30	Mar. 5, 1841	300	2, 800	......	
South Seas.....	Aug. 25	May 12, 1841	450	1, 750	14, 640	
....do	July 30	June 14, 1841	200	2, 200	16, 200	
....do	Aug. 7	July 9, 1840	200	1, 450	......	
....do	July 14	Apr. 2, 1841	60	2, 350	25, 207	
Pacific Ocean ..	June 24	Sept. 24, 1841	553	1, 473	12, 000	
South Seas.....	May 30	Apr. 19, 1841	400	2, 700	26, 271	
....do	July 17	Apr. 14, 1841	250	2, 800	20, 246	
Pacific Ocean ..	July 14	Mar. 8, 1841	100	3, 100	25, 500	
South Seas.....	Sept. 9	July 15, 1840	280	1, 970	......	
....do	June 17	Oct. 11, 1840	300	2, 600	......	
South Atlantic.	Aug. 1	July 23, 1841	330	......	15, 858	Sold 1,750 whale.
....do	July 1	May 3, 1840	370	850	......	
....do	July 27	May 3, 1840	90	1, 200	......	
....do	Aug. 1	Apr. 6, 1841	......	2, 700	22, 206	
....do	Aug. 7	May 29, 1840	200	1, 200	......	
....do	Sept. 17	May 15, 1840	......	2, 350	......	
New Zealand ..	June 13	May 14, 1841	350	2, 100	16, 200	Bought from Newburgh.
South Atlantic.	May 30	May 26, 1840	130	1, 170	......	
....do	July 26	Mar. 26, 1841	360	4, 000	38, 000	
South Seas.....	May 30	Apr. 3, 1841	150	3, 140	26, 884	Bought from Newport.
....do	July 6	Mar. 5, 1841	85	2, 500	22, 214	
South Atlantic.	June 12	May 14, 1840	70	530	......	
Atlantic	June 17	Jan. 9, 1840	720	......	......	
....do	Oct. 1	July 27, 1840	60	40	......	
Atlantic ..... {	....	Dec. 11, 1839	......	......	......	Returned, having lost her boats.
	Dec. 19	Oct. 24, 1840	300	20	......	
South Seas.....	June 19	July 2, 1840	450	1, 050	......	
South Atlantic.	Sept. 26	May 28, 1841	300	2, 000	......	
....	July —	June —, 1840	140	1, 860	......	
South Atlantic.	June 26	May 14, 1840	488	1, 075	......	
....do	May 21	Jan. 3, 1841	200	1, 600	......	
....do	Dec. 1	....	......	......	......	Lost on New Holland, July 8, 1840.
....do	Aug. 7	June 22, 1840	200	1, 500	......	
....do	June 22	Mar. 6, 1840	......	550	......	Elephant-oil.
....do	July 10	—— —, 1840	......	600	......	Do.
South Atlantic	July —	June —, 1840	......	1, 100	......	
....do	July 15	May 29, 1841	375	1, 650	12, 484	
....do	July 12	June 15, 1840	140	960	......	

Table showing returns of whaling-vessels

Name of vessel.	Class.	Tonnage.	Captain.	Managing owner or agent.
1839.				
Greenport, N. Y.—Continued.				
Seraph	Brig	174	—— Barns	Samuel Lawson
Triad	Ship	336	Isaac M. Case	H. & N. Corwin
Washington	..do	236	—— Wilbur	James Tuthill
Holmes' Hole, Mass.				
Delphos	Ship	338	—— Lambert	Thomas Bradley
Macon	..do	358	—— Merry	..do
William and Joseph	Brig	143	—— Dexter	John Holmes
Falmouth, Mass.				
Popmunnett	Bark	200	—— Nickerson	John Robinson
Uncas	Ship	400	Ephraim Eldridge	Elijah Swift
Newport, R. I.				
Benjamin D'Wolf	Schooner	66	—— Smiley	William Varo
George Champlain	Bark	361	J. A. Brown	Ruggles & Lee
John Coggeshall	Ship	338	S. W. Macy	Macy & Clarke
Pocahontas	Brig	113	—— Barker	Samuel Barker
Poughkeepsie, N. Y.				
Factor	Ship	333	—— Howland	David S. Shearman
New England	..do	375	..do	..do
Newark	..do	223	—— Winslow	..do
New York, N. Y.				
Desdemona	Ship	295	—— Phinney	Pell, Zabiescke & Pell
Westport, Mass.				
Champion	Bark	209	Edward G. Sowle	Andrew Hicks
Dr. Franklin	Bark	171	—— Francis	Job Davis
Elizabeth	Brig	107	—— Cook	Abner B. Coffin
Juno	Brig	165	—— Simmons	Abner B. Gifford
Mexico	Brig	130	—— Baker	Gideon Davis
President	Bark	187	—— Sowle	Andrew Hicks
Thomas Winslow	Brig	136	—— Seabury	P. W. Peckham
Cold Spring, N. Y.				
Barclay	Bark	167	—— Macomber	T. Macomber
Tuscarora	Ship	379	—— Halsey	
Providence, R. I.				
Bowditch	Ship	399	—— Sowle	Thomas Fletcher
Brunswick	..do	295	—— Manchester	Amherst & Everett
Newark, N. J.				
John Wells	Ship	366	—— Russell	J. H. Stephens
Provincetown, Mass.				
Imogene	Brig	172	—— Smalley	James Smalley
1840.				
New Bedford, Mass.				
Amethyst	Ship	359	—— Black	John A. Parker & Son
America	..do	418	—— Fisher	I. Howland, jr., & Co
Agate	Brig	81	Joseph Spooner	A. H. Seabury
Adeline	Ship	329	—— Gray	I. Howland, jr., & Co
Averick	..do	385	Thomas Mickell	J. A. Parker & Son
Barclay	..do	281	—— Briggs	James Arnold
Braganza	..do	470	Chas. C. Waterman	Pope & Morgan
Bramin	Bark	245	Joseph H. Allen	Gideon Allen
Bogota	Brig	155	—— Manter	I. H. Bartlett
China	Ship	370	William R Potter	William H. Stowell

sailing from American ports—Continued.

Whaling-ground.	Date— Of sailing.	Date— Of arrival.	Result of voyage. Sperm-oil.	Result of voyage. Whale-oil.	Result of voyage. Whalebone.	Remarks.
			Bbls.	*Bbls.*	*Lbs.*	
South Atlantic.	June 11	May 12, 1840	100	300	......	
....do	July 15	Apr. 18, 1841	275	1, 525	11, 291	
....do	July 8	May 3, 1840	200	1, 200	.....	
Indian Ocean ..	Aug. 1	Mar. 22, 1841	500	1, 200	.....	
....do	Oct. 25	May 15, 1842	800	2, 200	......	
Atlantic Ocean.	June 4	June 17, 1840	100	......	......	
Atlantic Ocean	July 11	....	......	......	......	Sold to Newport.
Pacific Ocean ..	Aug. 10	May 11, 1843	2, 200	300	2, 400	Sold to New Bedford, 1843.
South Atlantic.	Mar. 30	....	......	......	......	Went sealing; no report of return.
Pacific Ocean ..	Oct. 1	May 5, 1843	1, 700	......	......	
....do	Oct. 20	Oct. 11, 1842	1, 500	600	......	
South Atlantic.	Aug. 21	July —, 1840	80	......	......	
New Zealand ..	June 1	Sept. 8, 1840	250	2, 950	30, 000	Bought from Boston, 1839.
Pacific Ocean ..	Dec. 27	May —, 1843	1, 300	700	700	Sold to New London.
....do	July 29	June 22, 1841	600	2, 000	......	Sold to Stonington.
Pacific Ocean ..	Oct. 5	May 15, 1843	776	400	......	
Atlantic	July 8	Oct. 11, 1840	640	......	......	
....do	July 20	June 29, 1840	663	......	......	
....do	July 17	June 6, 1840	220	......	......	
....do	July 2[illegible]	July 6, 1840	370	9	......	
....do	Aug. 27	Nov. 4, 1840	400	......	......	
....do	Dec. 14	July 6, 1841	350	......	......	
....do	June 5	June 8, 1840	80	20	......	
Atlantic	....	May 18, 1841	664	10	......	
South Atlantic.	July 27	May 25, 1841	......	2, 400	......	
New Zealand ..	July 13	Apr. 5, 1841	250	3, 100	27, 000	Bought from Bristol.
South Atlantic.	Aug. 1	Apr. 29, 1841	280	2, 500	......	Including 340 whale bought of condemned brig Volant.
New Zealand ..	July 23	Mar. 18, 1841	40	2, 460	......	
Atlantic	....	Sept. 27, 1839	350	250	......	Probably broken up at home, 1839.
Indian Ocean...	May 19	Apr. 22, 1842	769	2, 185	15, 000	
....do	July 19	Sept. 17, 1842	330	4, 484	45, 000	
Atlantic	Oct. 31	Mar. 25, 1841	Clean	......	......	Returned in consequence of losing men and boats by desertion.
Indian Ocean...	Oct. 13	Nov. 3, 1842	1, 000	2, 000	......	
Pacific Ocean...	Aug. 1	May 5, 1844	2, 350	250	2, 000	James Winslow, first mate, died January 2, 1842.
Indian Ocean...	July 12	Mar. —, 1843	191	1, 685	13, 200	
Pacific Ocean...	Dec. 1	Feb. 25, 1843	400	3, 600	42, 000	
South Atlantic.	Apr. 21	Aug. 16, 1841	542	122	......	
Atlantic	Sept. 10	Feb. 21, 1842	356	......	......	Bought from Boston.
New Zealand ..	Oct. 6	Nov. 26, 1842	1, 575	1, 300	......	

Table showing returns of whaling-vessels

Name of vessel.	Class.	Tonnage.	Captain.	Managing owner or agent.
1840.				
New Bedford, Mass.—Continued.				
Cicero	Ship	252	—— Simmons.	Lemuel Kollock
Copia	...do	315	John A. Macomber	...do
Cherokee	Bark	261	—— Adams	Hathaway & Luce
Columbus	Bark	313	Pease	William R. Rodman
Cornelia	Bark	216	—— Grinnell	L. Kollock
Charleston Packet	Brig	184	—— Flanders	Levi L. Crane
Dragon	Bark	190	—— Taber	Tobey & Ricketson
Delight	Brig	102	—— Swain	Jonathan Mosher
Eagle	Ship	336	—— Coffin	Jireh Perry
Falcon	...do	273	Freeman Richmond	Wilcox & Richmond
Fenelon	...do	328	—— Hathaway	William H. Stowell
Frances, 2d	...do	368	—— Hussey	Gideon Allen
Florida	...do	330	—— Jenney	E. Dunbar & Co
Garland	Bark	234	—— Day	J. D. Thompson
Grand Turk	...do	324	—— Taylor	Barton Ricketson
George and Martha	Bark	275	Ezra Smalley	Randall & Haskell
Hope	Ship	316	—— Stewart	George Howland
Hercules, 2d	...do	290	William C. Swain.	D. R. Greene & Co
Herald	...do	274	—— Sanford	Tobey & Ricketson
Hector	...do	380	James Gray	Charles W. Morgan
Hibernia	...do	327	—— Cook	Alfred Gibbs
India	...do	366	—— Gelett	Abraham H. Howland
John	...do	308	Isaac Thacher	Frederick Parker
Jasper	Bark	223	Isaac J. Sanford	Alexander Gibbs
Juno	Brig	123	—— Howland	A. H. Seabury & Brother
Liverpool	Ship	306	—— Thomas	Abraham Barker
Laurel	Schooner	119	—— Smith	I. H. Bartlett
Lafayette	Ship	260	Cornelius Howland	Charles R. Tucker
Lalla Rookh	...do	323	Owen Raymond	J. A. Parker & Son
London Packet	Bark	280	—— Sampson	A. H. Howland
Maria Theresa	Ship	330	—— Turner	T. & A. R. Nye
Massachusetts	...do	364	—— Barnard	G. O. Crocker & Co
Mercator	...do	246	—— Delano	John A. Parker
Minerva Smyth	...do	335	—— Brownell	I. Howland, jr., & Co
Mobile	...do	263	Henry B. Gifford	Edward C. Jones
Moss	...do	334	—— Austin	William R. Rodman
Mount Vernon	...do	352	E. T. Shearman	D. R. Greene & Co
Marcella	Bark	210	—— Ellis	C. R. Tucker
Milwood	Bark	254	Charles Church	Gideon Allen
Minerva	Bark	195	—— Gifford	Charles R. Tucker
New Bedford	Ship	351	Leonard Crowell	I. Howland, jr., & Co
Orozimbo	...do	588	—— Bartlett	Barton Ricketson
Peri	Brig	191	Joseph Shockley, jr	Rodney French
Pacific	Ship	385	—— Taber	Jireh Perry
Parachute	...do	331	Joseph Willcox, jr	Walter S. Spooner
Plato	Bark	240	—— Butler	Daniel Perry
Parker	Ship	406	Prince Shearman	J. A. Parker & Son
Roman, 2	...do	350	Alex. R. Barker	Abraham Barker
Roscoe	...do	362	—— McCleave	Andrew Robeson
Rodman	...do	371	William Whitten, jr	C. W. Morgan
Rebecca Simms	...do	400	—— Ray	William R. Rodman
Sally Anne	...do	312	Rob. E. Borden	D. R. Greene & Co
Seine	Bark	281	—— Adams	Rodney French
Sarah Louisa	Brig	144	Ray G. Sanford	William R. Rodman
Two Brothers	Ship	288	—— Shockley	D. R. Greene & Co
Tuscaloosa	...do	284	—— Taber	Howland & Hussey
Virginia	...do	346	—— Luce	Hathaway & Luce
Winslow	...do	263	Richard Pease	Samuel Rodman
Wade	Bark	261	John Swift	A. H. Howland
Washington	Ship	344	James G. Coffin	Jonathan Bourne, jr
Young Phenix	...do	377	—— Sherman	J. A. Parker & Son

sailing from American ports—Continued.

Whaling-ground.	Date—		Result of voyage.			Remarks.
	Of sailing.	Of arrival.	Sperm-oil.	Whale-oil.	Whalebone.	
			Bbls.	*Bbls.*	*Lbs.*	
Indian Ocean...	July 20	July 9, 1842	908	......	......	Sold 50 sperm 860 whale oil at Bahia.
....do	Aug. 2	Sept. 12, 1842	442	2,460	......	
Pacific Ocean ..	Dec. 14	May 9, 1843	500	1,900	22,800	
....do	May 21	Dec. 11, 1843	1,350	......	......	
South Atlantic	Sept. 1	Apr. 12, 1842	330	281	......	Sailed July 14, 1840, and returned leaky.
Atlantic	Sept. 12	Nov. 8, 1841	......	......	......	
Indian Ocean..	Apr. 19	Apr. 28, 1842	750	870	......	
Atlantic	June 24	June 28, 1841	130	......	......	Broken up at New Bedford 1841.
Pacific Ocean..	Sept. 3	Sept. 6, 1844	1,700	......	......	Bought from Boston.
Indian Ocean ..	July 22	Oct. 25, 1842	800	1,100	......	
....do	Aug. 6	June 26, 1842	205	2,765	......	
Pacific Ocean...	Sept. 1	Feb. 24, 1845	300	1,200	28,036	
South Atlantic	Apr. 19	Aug. 3, 1841	259	2,621	......	
Indian Ocean ..	July 12	Apr. 21, 1842	421	642	......	
Atlantic	Apr. 13	Dec. 16, 1841	612	68	......	Sailed again, under Captain Taylor, April 23, 1842, for the South Seas; returned September 10, 1842. Condemned 1843 and broken up.
....do	Aug. 8	Oct. 4, 1842	430	1,757	......	
Pacific Ocean ..	Apr. 24	Oct. 30, 1843	1,786	30	......	
Indian Ocean ..	July 19	June 17, 1843	735	1,126	......	
Pacific Ocean ..	Dec. 14	Nov. 27, 1844	1,381	70	......	
....do	Nov. 21	Sept. 6, 1843	2,717	......	......	
Indian Ocean ..	Jan. 6	Apr. 6, 1842	1,010	765	......	H. H. Maxfield, first mate, lost 1840.
Pacific Ocean ..	July 19	Feb. 14, 1843	679	2,541	30,000	
....do	Sept. 29	Feb. 20, 184[illegible]	483	1,003	9,500	
Indian Ocean ..	July 21	Jan. 2, 1842	173	1,253	......	
Atlantic	Sept. 15	Oct. 29, 1841	254	......	......	
Indian Ocean ..	June 15	May 25, 1842	263	2,265	......	
Atlantic	Oct. 7	Mar. 1, 1841	......	Clean	......	Returned on account of mutiny of crew.
Pacific Ocean ..	Oct. 22	June 17, 1844	1,800	......	......	Henry Loveland, second mate, died January, 1843.
....do	Oct. 22	Aug. 8, 1844	2,000	......	......	
....do	Nov. 23	June 27, 1844	2,150	......	......	
Indian Ocean ..	July 31	May 25, 1842	576	2,119	......	
Pacific Ocean ..	Oct. 6	June 23, 1844	1,600	......	......	
....do	May 22	Mar. 20, 1843	655	640	......	
....do	Jan. 10	Dec. 5, 1843	1,743	17	......	
Atlantic	July 5	Dec. 5, 1842	1,217	......	......	
Pacific Ocean ..	Dec. 24	....	......	......	......	Sold 600 sperm at Talcahuano; condemned at Valparaiso, March, 1845.
Indian Ocean ..	Dec. 18	Aug. —, 1843	305	2,947	24,000	
Atlantic	Apr. 27	Oct. 12, 1841	869	5	......	
....do	May 2	May 16, 1842	274	1,500	......	
....do	June 2	Nov. 1, 1841	373	53	......	
Pacific Ocean ..	Apr. 3	June 2, 1844	1,673	4	......	
....do	Dec. 8	Apr. —, 1843	528	3,346	34,223	Sold 1,500 whale at Bahia.
Atlantic	May 16	Sept. 25, 1841	390	58	......	
Pacific Ocean ..	Aug. 15	May 1, 1844	2,441	......	......	Sailed once, was out three months, and returned with 280 sperm.
New Zealand ..	Nov. 3	Mar. 15, 1843	541	2,644	29,228	
Indian Ocean ..	Sept. 14	....	......	......	......	Bought from New York; last reported March 12, 1842, off New Holland, 1,400 whale.
Pacific Ocean ..	Aug. 26	....	......	......	......	Lost on Ocean Island, September 23, 1842; December 4, 1841; Captain Shearman taken out of his boat by a line.
New Zealand ..	Aug. 15	Feb. 16, 1842	210	2,959	29,864	
Pacific Ocean ..	Apr. 18	May 13, 1843	2,447	......	......	
....do	Aug. 17	Apr. 30, 1843	3,018	16	......	
....do	June 6	Oct. 30, 1844	1,156	240	1,500	Sold 700 barrels; sent home 700 more.
Indian Ocean ..	June 24	July 9, 1842	276	1,461	......	
South Atlantic	Oct. 6	July 30, 1842	812	......	......	
Atlantic	Sept. 29	Apr. 29, 1842	141	20	......	Captain Sanford died November, 1841.
Indian Ocean .	June 13	Sept. 25, 1841	268	1,664	......	
Pacific Ocean ..	July 15	July 21, 1844	1,590	127	......	
....do.	Aug. 23	Sept. 4, 1843	2,200	......	......	
Indian Ocean ..	Aug. 26	Oct. 23, 1844	1,208	125	1,500	
Pacific Ocean ..	July 19	Apr. 9, 1844	890	1,400	11,500	Sent home 230 whale.
Indian Ocean ..	Aug. 18	May 17, 1842	94	1,718	......	
Pacific Ocean ..	Dec. 11	Aug. 4, 1844	2,750	......	......	F. W. Gardner, second mate, died at Timor July 26, 1841.

Table showing returns of whaling-vessels

Name of vessel.	Class.	Tonnage.	Captain.	Managing owner or agent.
1840.				
Fairhaven, Mass.				
Arab	Bark	276	—— Writhington	I. F. Terry
Alto	do	197	—— Coffin	A. D. Stoddard
Amazon	Ship	318	—— Smith	E. Sawin
Albion	do	326	—— Smith	do
Arab	do	336	—— Cox	do
Bruce	Bark	148	—— Alden	Bradford, Fuller & Co
Benezett	do	192	—— Parker	Jabez Delano, jr
Erie	Ship	451	—— Luce	Nathan Church
Eagle	do	283	—— Perry	H. H. Stackpole
Favorite	Bark	293	—— Adams	F. R. Whitwell
Herald	Ship	262	William Devol	Samuel Borden
Joseph Maxwell	do	302	—— Harding	F. R. Whitwell
James Munroe	do	424	Benjamin Cushman	E. Sawin
Maine	do	294	—— Magee	do
Martha, 2d	do	301	—— Hammond	Atkins Adams
Marcus	do	286	—— Wood	Lemuel Tripp
Omega	do	365	Henry D. Gardner	Nathan Church
Pindus	Bark	193	—— Wady	Jenney & Tripp
Pacific	do	314	—— Webb	I. F. Terry
South Boston	Ship	339	—— Crowell	E. Sawin
Rochester, Mass.				
Cossack	Bark	256	—— Delano	Stephen C. Luce
Dryade	do	263	—— Rogers	G. Barstow & Co
Lagrange	Brig	170	—— Daggett	Elijah Willis
Le Barron	do	170	—— Cushing	G. Barstow & Son
Pearl	do	157	—— Blankenship	J. S. Bates
Richard Henry	do	134	—— Dexter	G. Barstow & Son
Sarah	do	171	—— Purrington	do
Solon	do	129	—— Wing	Noble E. Bates
Two Sisters	do	122	—— Bolles	do
Willis	do	164	—— Boodry	R. L. Barstow
Nantucket, Mass.				
Alexander Coffin	Ship	381	Samual C. Wyer	R. Mitchell & Sons
Catawba	do	335	Henry Pease	C. G. & H. Coffin
Charles Carroll	do	376	Thomas S. Andrews	W. C. Swain
Cyrus	do	328	Daniel Emmons	George Myrick, jr
Charles and Henry	do	336	John B. Coleman	C. G. & H. Coffin
Enterprise	do	413	George Cannon	Gilbert Coffin
Fabius	do	432	Frederick B. Chase	G. & M. Starbuck & Co
Henry Astor	do	375	Seth Pinkham	William R. Easton
Henry	do	346	William Brown	Daniel Jones
Harvest	do	360	John Gardner, 2d	Edward Field
Jefferson	do	377	William B. Cash	John H. Shaw
Kingston	do	312	William Rawson	Frederick Hussey
Lexington	do	399	Henry W. Davis	F. C. Sanford
Lydia	do	351	George G. Cathcart	James Athearn
Maria	do	365	Elisha H. Fisher	Barrett & Upton
Mariner	do	348	George Palmer	Matthew Crosby
Ontario	do	354	Stephen B. Gibbs	Barrett & Upton
Omega	do	365	George Haggerty	Joseph Starbuck
Ocean	do	349	Elijah Parker	T. & P. Macy
Phenix	do	323	Josiah Hamblen	do
Peruvian	do	334	Frederick Arthur	W. B. Coffin
Washington	do	308	Stephen Bailey	Matthew Crosby
Walter Scott	do	339	Cromwell Bunker	Barrett & Upton
Young Eagle	do	377	Edward C. Austin	Simeon Starbuck
Zenas Coffin	do	323	Hiram Bailey	C. G. & H. Coffin
Falmouth, Mass.				
Awashonks	Ship	355	Rufus Pease	Elijah Swift
Brunette	do	200	—— Luce	do

sailing from American ports—Continued.

Whaling-ground.	Date— Of sailing.	Date— Of arrival.	Result of voyage. Sperm-oil.	Result of voyage. Whale-oil.	Result of voyage. Whalebone.	Remarks.
			Bbls.	*Bbls.*	*Lbs.*	
Indian Ocean ..	Apr. 30	June 2, 1843	428	1,755	13,600	
Pacific Ocean ..	Aug. 2	Apr. 7, 1843	482	......	......	Sold to New Bedford 1844.
South Atlantic.	June 10	May 28, 1841	343	1,876	......	
Indian Ocean ..	May 28	May 16, 1842	569	2,043	18,000	
....do	June 10	Apr. 22, 1842	......	1,120	......	
....do	Sept. 10	May 26, 1842	430	......	......	
Pacific Ocean ..	Dec. 1	....	......	......	......	Lost August 9, 1842, on Feejee Islands, with 700 sperm.
....do	Dec. 14	Feb. —, 1844	1,125	1,719	18,000	Bought from New York.
....do	Dec. 18	Apr. 22, 1843	291	1,618	18,000	
....do	Nov. 4	June 10, 1843	848	1,000	8,000	
Indian Ocean ..	July 16	May 21, 1842	200	1,400	......	
Pacific Ocean ..	Aug. 21	Oct. 18, 1843	1,600	......	......	
....do	Dec. 4	Nov. 25, 1843	1,624	1,206	14,000	Bought from Hudson 1840.
Indian Ocean ..	July 6	June 18, 1842	266	1,456	......	
Pacific Ocean ..	Aug. 16	Mar. 18, 1844	1,050	1,250	12,000	
....do	Nov. 22	July 13, 1844	1,517	130	......	Samuel Pitman, first mate, died 1843.
....do	Jan. 6	Oct. 20, 1843	2,591	96	......	
Indian Ocean ..	Sept. 3	July 17, 1842	519	744	......	Condemned and broken up 1842.
....do	Aug. 11	Dec. 4, 1842	21	1,720	......	Sailed May 17, 1840; returned August 3, with 300 sperm; first and third mates sick; sailed again as given.
New Zealand...	Mar. 8	Aug. 24, 1842	543	1,989	......	
Indian Ocean ..	July 9	May 10, 1843	350	1,356	11,600	
....do	Apr. 13	June 17, 1842	725	95	......	
Atlantic	Sept. —	May 9, 1841	600	......	......	
South Atlantic.	Apr. 2	Nov. 2, 1841	350	......	......	
Atlantic	Aug. 20	Oct. 15, 1841	200	......	......	Lost a boat's crew by a whale, 1841.
....do	Sept. 15	Sept. 29, 1841	70	......	......	
....do	Oct. 10	Apr. 17, 1842	624	......	......	
....do	July 30	Oct. 17, 1841	220	......	......	
....do	May 11	June 7, 1841	30	......	......	
....do	Oct. 4	Jan. 1, 1842	260	......	......	
Pacific Ocean ..	Sept. 8	June 23, 1844	1,953	......	......	Sold to New Bedford.
....do	Feb. 2	Oct. 21, 1843	2,009	40	......	
....do	May 29	Dec. 6, 1843	1,926	......	......	Sent home 250 bbls. sperm.
....do	Nov. 1	Oct. 14, 1844	1,458	......	......	
....do	Dec. 20	Mar. 8, 1845	689	146	.....	
....do	Dec. 18	June 17, 1844	1,094	1,014	.....	
....do	July 12	Apr. 6, 1844	2,140	......	......	Sold to New Bedford.
....do	Jan. 24	May 23, 1844	1,277	980	......	Bought from Hudson, 1839; mate, Alexander Swain, killed by a whale; Capt. Pinkham died at Pernambuco, April 17, 1844.
....do	June 1	Apr. 16, 1844	1,641	60	......	
....do	Sept. 17	Aug. 5, 1844	1,636	......	......	
....do	July 28	....	......	......	......	Lost on Atooi, Sandwich Islands, June 22, 1842, with 2,480 bbls. sperm, 80 bbls. whale.
....do	June 12	May 14, 1844	1.067	342	......	Sold to Fairhaven, 1844.
....do	Aug. 29	Mar. 14, 1844	1,336	1,334	......	Sent home 125 bbls. sperm; Capt. Davis left the ship at Rio Janeiro, sick.
....do	Sept. 2	Feb. 17, 1845	1,225	......	......	Built in 1840; sold to Fairhaven 1845.
....do	Apr. 22	Feb. 20, 1842	2,413	......	......	
....do	Oct. 6	May 13, 1844	1,632	7	......	
....do	May 28	Nov. 20, 1842	2,073	......	......	Sent home 40 bbls. sperm.
....do	Sept. 8	Aug. 9, 1844	1,397	......	......	
....do	Oct. 18	Oct. 3, 1844	1,662	......	......	Sold to New Bedford 1844.
....do	June 21	Feb. 17, 1844	2,241	24	......	
....do	July 31	June 23, 1844	1,212	508	......	Sent home 300 bbls. sperm.
....do	May 14	Sept. 24, 1843	1,095	58	......	
....do	Oct. 31	July 8, 1844	1,296	......	......	
....do	Sept. 1	July 19, 1843	2,544	......	......	Sailed Aug. 20, but returned with mate sick.
....do	July 12	May 25, 1843	3,049	177	......	
....do	July —	—— —, 1843	1,800	......	......	
Atlantic	Aug. 11	May 28, 1842	300	20	......	Sold to Col. Colt, the revolver manufacturer, taken to Washington, and blown to atoms with a torpedo of his invention.

Table showing returns of whaling-vessels

Name of vessel.	Class.	Tonnage.	Captain.	Managing owner or agent.
1840.				
Falmouth, Mass.—Continued.				
Bartholomew Gosnold	Ship	360	Abraham Russell	Ward M. Parker
George Washington	Bark	180	Lemuel Eldredge	Sanford Herendeen
Hobomok	Ship	412	Silas Jones	Oliver C. Swift
Lynn, Mass.				
Com. Preble	Ship	323	—— Eldridge	F. S. Newhall
Ninus	...do	260	—— Ludlow	Isaiah Breed
Newport, R. I.				
Audley Clarke	Ship	....	H. Griswold	Bush & Clarke
Helen	Brig	....	James Price	William Price
Pocahontas	...do	....	William Barker	Samuel Barker
William Lee	Ship	....	E. Gifford	J. S. Munroe
Edgartown, Mass.				
Athalia	Bark	162	—— Sprague	Joseph Mayhew
Deborah	Brig	145	—— Worth	......do
Vineyard	Ship	381	—— Crocker	Grafton Norton
Holmes' Hole, Mass.				
Pocahontas	Ship	341	—— Smith	Thomas Bradley
William and Joseph	Brig	143	—— Dexter	John Holmes
Newburyport, Mass.				
Merrimac	Ship	414	—— Starbuck	Micajah Lunt
Navy	...do	356	—— Brock	Thomas Buntin
Boston, Mass.				
Creole	Bark	222	—— Cook	Charles A. Brown
Cambrian	Brig	197	—— Holmes	P. & S. Sprague & Co
Hudson, N. Y.				
Beaver	Ship	320	—— Rogers	Barnard, Curtis & Co
Edward	...do	274	—— Daggett	......do
New London, Conn.				
Armata	Ship	414	—— Hull	Abner Bassett
Betsey	Schooner	113	—— Noyes	Joseph Lawrence
Boston	Ship	291	—— Pendleton	......do
Com. Perry	...do	270	—— McLane	C. Chew & Co
Connecticut	...do	398	—— Crocker	Thomas W. Williams
Clematis	...do	311	—— Bailey	Williams & Barns
Columbia	...do	492	—— Smith	Havens & Smith
Candace	...do	310	—— Reed	......do
Columbus	Brig	153	—— Holt	Williams & Barns
Charles Henry	Ship	265	—— Halsey	Havens & Smith
Ceres	Bark	176	—— Bailey	William Tate
Electra	Ship	347	—— Lax	William Williams, jr
Francis	Schooner	....		
Gen. Williams	Ship	446	—— Bailey	Williams & Barns
Hand	Schooner	86	—— Long	Havens & Smith
Julius Cæsar	Ship	347	—— Gibson	N. & W. W. Billings
John and Elizabeth	...do	296	—— Miller	Havens & Smith
Neptune	...do	285	—— Green	T. W. Williams
Pembroke	...do	199	—— Peabody	Joseph Lawrence
Shaw Perkins	Sloop	55	—— Stroud	Havens & Smith
Superior	Ship	406	—— McLane	N. & W. W. Billings
Stonington	...do	351	—— Rice	Williams & Barns
Tenedos	Bark	245	—— Chester	Joseph Lawrence

sailing from American ports—Continued.

Whaling-ground.	Date— Of sailing.	Of arrival.	Result of voyage. Sperm-oil.	Whale-oil.	Whalebone.	Remarks.
			Bbls.	*Bbls.*	*Lbs.*	
Pacific Ocean	Jan. 1	— —, 1843	1,800	600		Sold to New Bedford, 1843.
Atlantic		— —, 1840				Gone two months; returned clean, leaky and was sold to New Bedford, 1840.
Pacific Ocean	May 29	Mar. 14, 1844	2,200			
Indian Ocean	July 20	June 2, 1842	260	2,600		
....do	Sept. 23	June 9, 1842	150	1,300	8,000	
Pacific Ocean	Nov. 16	Aug. 30, 1844	1,400			Captain Griswold died, 1843.
North Atlantic	Aug. 22	Nov. 15, 1841	210	15		
....do	July 30	July 23, 1841	137			
Pacific Ocean	July 12	Feb. 23, 1844	600	1,100	11,000	
Atlantic	May 18	Apr. 2, 1841	190			Came home leaky.
....do	Oct. 17	Dec. 8, 1841	65	20		Bought from Salem.
Pacific Ocean	Oct. 24	June 23, 1844	1,000			
....do	Sept. 23	Dec. —, 1843	1,400			
Atlantic	Aug. 18					Lost at sea Oct. 21, 1841; four men lost.
Pacific Ocean	July 28	Apr. 15, 1844	260	2,750	22,000	Captain Starbuck died, 1841.
....do	May 20	June 12, 1843	600	1,300	10,400	Sold to New Bedford.
South Seas	Dec. 10	Sept. 21, 1841	550			
South Atlantic	Dec. 1	Apr. 23, 1842	420			
Pacific Ocean	Jan. 31	May 16, 1842	270	1,930		
....do	Dec. 4	Apr. 3, 1845	800	800	8,000	Sold to New Bedford, 1845.
Indian Ocean	July 31	July 12, 1842	260	2,000	28,000	
Pacific Ocean	Aug. 14	June 8, 1842		115	1,100	Also a large number of fur-skins.
Indian Ocean	June 22	May 28, 1841		1,700		
South Seas	June 8	May 24, 1842	200	1,000		
....do	June 29	May 23, 1841		1,600		
Indian Ocean	Aug. —	July 4, 1841		2,800		
South Atlantic	July 9	May 6, 1842	100	4,000		
....do	Apr. 20	Apr. 30, 1842		2,200		S cond mate, William Lacky, killed by a whale June, 1843.
Atlantic		May 23, 1841	650			
South Atlantic	Aug. 8	May 25, 1842	350	650		
....do	Oct. 12	July 2, 1842	80	1,220		
....do	June 1	June 1, 1841	240	1,460		Sent home 60 sperm.
....do	Mar. —	Feb. —, 1841		500		
... do	Dec. 7	Mar. 16, 1843	100	4,200	46,200	Encountered a heavy gale off Black Point L. I.; cut away masts and anchored Captain Bailey and five men drowned going ashore in a boat for help.
Indian Ocean	June 6	Apr. 30, 1842	150			Tender to the Columbia.
....do	July 25	June 21, 1841	40	1,900		
....do	June 22	Apr. 27, 1842	75	2,550		
South Atlantic	Oct. 13	Apr. 15, 1842	650	1,450		
....do	May 23	June 26, 1841		400		Captain Peabody left the ship at Madagascar.
Indian Ocean	June 6	Apr. 16, 1842	120			Tender to Columbia.
South Atlantic	Sept. 29	July 3, 1842	150	2,750		
....do	Sept. 1	May 5, 1842	250	2,000	20,000	
....do	Oct. 12	Aug. 9, 1842	200	1,300		Bought from Boston.

Table showing returns of whaling-vessels

Name of vessel.	Class.	Tonnage.	Captain.	Managing owner or agent.
1840.				
Sag Harbor, N. Y.				
Acasta	Ship	280	Sylvester P. Smith	Mu'ford & Sleight
American	do	28	—— Cooper	S. & B. Huntting & Co.
Camillus	Bark	34	Ezekiel H. Howes	Charles T. Dering
Concordia	do	26	—— Woodward	Thomas Brown
Gem	Ship	32	T. B. Worth	Huntting Cooper
Huron	do	29	—— Greene	Luther D. Cook
Henry	do	33	John Sweeney	Samuel L'Hommedieu
Hannibal	do	31	Lewis L. Bennett	S. & B. Huntting & Co.
Hamilton	do	32	—— Ludlow	Charles T. Dering
Hamilton, 2d	do	45	D. Hand	Mulford & Sleight
Monmouth	do	27	—— Sayre	
Marcus	do	28	David Loper	N. & G. Howell
Nimrod	do	280	—— Barnes	C. T. Dering
Ontario	do	36	—— Green	S. & B. Huntting & Co.
Phenix	do	314	—— Briggs	L. D. Cook
Romulus	do	23	—— Rogers	Mulford & Howell
Xenophon	do	38	—— Halsey	Mulford & Sleight
New Suffolk, N. Y.				
Noble	Bark	274	James Sayer	Ira B. Tuthill
Warren, R. I.				
Boy	Ship	25	—— Barton	N. M. Wheaton
Crawford	Brig	1[illegible]	—— Huttlestone	J. & D. K. Luther
Franklin	Bark	240	—— Barton	Samuel Barton
Hoogley	Ship	29	—— Nye	John R. Wheaton
Jane	do	371	—— Eddy	S. P. Child
Luminary	do	43	—— Price	Joseph Smith, jr., & Co.
Magnet	do	35	—— Champlin	do
Philip Tabb	do	40	—— Jenney	Driscol & Child
Warren	do	38	—— Cleaveland	J. Smith, jr., & Co.
Salem, Mass.				
Bengal	Ship	30	—— Jackson	John B. Osgood
Emerald	Bark	271	—— Brown	S. C. Phillips
Izette	Ship	27	—— Hall	J. B. Osgood
Mount Wollaston	do	32	—— Rose	do
Stonington, Conn.				
Bolton	Bark	220	—— Pendleton	Charles P. Williams
Enterprize	Brig	9	—— Greene	do
Henry	do	9	—— Pendleton	William Pendleton
Mercury	do	30	—— Gray	C. T. Stanton
Rebecca Groves	Brig	12	—— Hubbard	G. Trumbull
Thomas Williams	Ship	340	—— Manwaring	C. P. Williams
Bridgeport, Conn.				
Atlantic	Ship	291	—— Jennings	Samuel H. Ford
Harvest	Bark	26	—— Godbee	do
Westport, Mass.				
Dr. Franklin	Bark	171	—— Francis	Job Davis
Emma	do	24	—— Davis	Abner Tripp
Elizabeth	Brig	10	—— Cook	David Coffin
Juno	do	16	—— Sowle	A. B. Gifford
Leader	Bark	170	—— Ball	Job Davis
Thos. Winslow	Brig	136	Elihu Russell, jr	Thomas W. Mayhew
United States	Bark	217	—— Hicks	Andrew Hicks
Bristol, R. I.				
America	Bark	257	—— Richmond	Henry Wardwell
Essex	do	200	—— Devol	Lemuel C. Richmond
Gov. Hopkins	Brig	111	—— Waldron	William R. Taylor
Sarah Lee	Ship	235	—— Bly	W. H. D'Wolf
Troy	Brig	156	—— Morris	Thomas Church

sailing from American ports—Continued.

Whaling-ground.	Date— Of sailing.	Date— Of arrival.	Result of voyage. Sperm-oil.	Result of voyage. Whale-oil.	Result of voyage. Whalebone.	Remarks.
			Bbls.	*Bbls.*	*Lbs.*	
South Seas.....	Oct. 11	Aug. 13, 1841	.....	2,000	14,900	
New Zealand...	Aug. 11	May 16, 1842	200	2,250	.....	
Atlantic.......	Oct. 15	Dec. 6, 1841	201	1,400	11,377	
Indian Ocean..	Nov. 28	Apr. 9, 1842	250	1,100	800	
South Atlantic.	Aug. 28	July 19, 1841	50	2,250	14,990	
....do.........	Sept. 1	June 11, 1842	550	450	......	Bought from Hudson.
....do.........	.....	....	154	1,903	14,358	
Indian Ocean..	Aug. 25	June 26, 1841	60	1,65[illegible]	9,459	
Pacific Ocean..	July 2	July —, 1843	700	1,000	.....	
South Seas.....	Dec. 3	July 14, 1843	340	3,700	.....	Returned once; damaged in a gale.
South Atlantic.	Aug. 4	June 19, 1841	......	1,850	.....	
....do.........	June 15	Sept. 24, 1841	83	904	4,070	
....do.........	July 9	July 19, 1841	110	1,550	3,419	
....do.........	Sept. 1	May 22, 1842	500	2,200	......	
New Zealand...	July 10	May 26, 1842	500	2,100	17,000	
South Atlantic.	July 8	May 9, 1842	500	1,203	8,000	
....do.........	Aug. 12	Nov. 24, 1842	100	2,003	.....	Broken up after this voyage.
South Atlantic.	Mar. 15	June 2, 1841	260	1,200	6,945	
Pacific Ocean..	Apr. 28	Aug. 12, 1843	1,450	.....	.....	
Western Isl'ds	Apr. 13	May 28, 1841	Clean	.....	.....	
Indian Ocean..	Oct. 25	May 10, 1843	803	.....	.....	
....do.........	Nov. 13	Oct. —, 1843	1,300	65	.....	Captain Nye died November 24, 1841.
Pacific Ocean..	Mar. 8	May —, 1843	400	1,6[illegible]	12,800	
....do.........	Jan. 7	June —, 1843	300	2,200	20,000	
....do.........	Jan. 1	Mar. 1, 1843	1,200	1,600	.....	
....do.........	July 23	Apr. 30, 1843	500	1,100	16,000	Sold 100 sperm, 800 whale, at Valparaiso.
....do.........	Aug. 26	Apr. 6, 1843	600	2,050	33,000	Sold 1,350 whale at Rio Janeiro.
Indian Ocean..	July 24	Mar. 26, 1844	1,800	.....	.....	Sold to New London, 1844.
....do.........	May 2	Feb. 26, 1843	400	1,100	8,800	
....do.........	May 2	June 19, 1842	900	1,100	.....	
....do.........	June 24	June 11, 1843	400	700	5,600	Sold 1,200 whale at Rio Janeiro. Sold to ———, 1843.
Pacific Ocean..	June 8	May 10, 1843	1,000	450	3,600	
....do.........	Sept. 3	....	.....	.....	.....	
South Atlantic	July 6	....	.....	.....	.....	Probably sold at Rio Janeiro in 1841.
...do..........	Dec. 3	Apr. 13, 1842	300	1,900	17,000	
....do.........	Aug. 21	....	.....	.....	.....	
South Seas.....	Aug. 25	Mar. 19, 1842	280	2,720	.....	
South Seas.....	Sept. —	July 23, 1841	......	1,700		
....do.........	Aug. 4	May 25, 1842	150	2,050	.....	
Atlantic.......	Sept. 6	June 19, 1841	732	......	.....	
....do.........	Dec. 23	May 13, 1842	568	53	.....	
....do.........	June —	Nov. 1, 1840	150	......	.....	
....do.........	Aug. 9	Nov. 5, 1841	390	14	.....	
....do.........	May 2	Nov. 25, 1841	500	......	.....	
....do.........	Aug. 7	July 30, 1841	585	7	.....	
Pacific Ocean..	Oct. 10	June —, 1843	700	.....	.....	
Pacific Ocean..	Oct. 7	July 2, 1844	500	900	9,000	Sold to New Bedford, 1844.
Atlantic.......	July 4	Nov. 5, 1841	450	15	.....	Returned once, having lost her mainmast; Captain Daggett left the ship, sick, and Devol took charge.
...do..........	Sept. 23	May 28, 1841	240			
....do.........	Oct. 31	Oct. 21, 1841	80	40		
....do.........	July 25	Sept. —, 1841	420	......	.....	

Table showing returns of whaling-vessels

Name of vessel.	Class.	Tonnage.	Captain.	Managing owner or agent.
1840.				
Poughkeepsie, N. Y.				
Elbe	Ship	333	—— Merrihew	David S. Sherman
N. P. Tallmadge	do	370	—— Coffin	do
New England	do	375	—— Howland	do
Vermont	Bark	292	—— Almy	do
Mystic, Conn.				
Aeronaut	Ship	265	—— Mallory	Charles Mallory
Bingham	do	375	—— Destin	do
Meteor	do	325	—— Lester	J. & W. P. Randall
Tampico	Brig	99	—— Clift	C. Mallory
Uxor	do	96	—— Mitchell	do
Sippican, Mass.				
Popmunnett	do	184	—— Flanders	do
Quito	do	140	do	do
Solon	do	129	—— Wing	N. E. Bates
Fall River, Mass.				
Ann Maria	do	196	—— Carr	John Eddy
Montezuma	do	190	—— Randall	M. S. F. Tobey
Pleiades	Bark	26	—— Allen	do
Taunton	Brig	105	—— Cummings	William Coggeshall
Wareham, Mass.				
George Washington	Ship	374		E. Thompson
Inga	Brig	169	—— Cudworth	M. S. F. Tobey
Meridian	do	73	—— Derrick	do
Plymouth, Mass.				
Exchange	Schooner	99	—— Dexter	R. W. Holmes
Fortune	Bark	278		Isaac L. Hedge
James Munroe	Brig	115	—— Dyke	Northam & Fearing
Mercury	Schooner	74	—— Luce	Isaac Barnes, jr.
Maria	do			
Greenport, N. Y.				
Bayard	Ship	339	Francis Sayre	H. & N. Corwin
Magellan	Brig	9	—— Lax	
Roanoke	Ship	251	Benjamin Glover, jr.	Wiggins & Parsons
Seraph	Brig	174	George W. Corwin	Samuel Lamson
Washington	Ship	230	Robert N. Wilbur	Wiggins & Parsons
Provincetown, Mass.				
Fairy	Brig	180	—— Ginn	Abraham Small
Franklin	do	173	—— Soper	Robert Soper
Phenix	do	150	—— Small	Leonard Small
1841.				
New Bedford, Mass.				
Addison	Ship	429	Thomas West	Isaac B. Richmond
Ann	do	361	—— Almy	Howland & Hussey
Alex. Barclay	do	46	—— Fish	J. A. Parker & Son
Archer	Ship	322	—— Ricketson	Tobey & Ricketson
Agate	Brig	8	—— Landre	Pope & Morgan
Ann Alexander	Ship	253	—— Taber	George Howland
Balæna	do	30	Richmond Manchester	J. & J. Howland
Bramin	Bark	24	—— Taber	Gideon Allen
Charles	Ship	290	—— Gardner	Samuel Rodman
Charles W. Morgan	do	351	—— Norton	Charles W. Morgan
Chase	Bark	153	—— West	Barton Ricketson
Cora	do	220	—— Baker	Ivory H. Bartlett
Canton	Ship	459	—— Lucas	Charles R. Tucker
Canton Packet	Bark	274	—— Shearman	I. H. Bartlett

sailing from American ports—Continued.

Whaling-ground.	Date— Of sailing.	Date— Of arrival.	Result of voyage. Sperm-oil.	Result of voyage. Whale-oil.	Result of voyage. Whalebone.	Remarks.
			Bbls.	*Bbls.*	*Lbs.*	
Pacific Ocean ..	July 10	....	.....	.....	.....	Lost in Cook's Straits, December 13, 1841.
....do	Oct. 22	Mar. 22, 1843	120	2,500	25,000	
....do	Jan. 1	May —, 1843	1,300	700	700	
Indian Ocean ..	Dec. 10	July —, 1843	350	2,500	20,000	Sold to Mystic.
South Atlantic	June 6	Mar. 5, 1842	225	2,075	......	
....do	July 10	June —, 1842	450	1,550	......	Sold 400 whale at Pernambuco.
... do	Aug. 10	May 9, 1842	100	2,300	......	
....do	June 22	....	......	......	......	Condemned at Saint Catharines, March, 1841. Sent home 100 sperm.
....do	July 22	Jan. 1, 1841	......	400	......	Elephant-oil.
....do	May 11	Oct. 20, 1841	400	......	......	
....do	July 8	Nov. 3, 1841	350	......	......	
....do	July 30	Sept. —, 1842	40	20	......	
Indian Ocean ..	May 11	June 9, 1841	500	700	......	Returned once leaky.
....	June 1	Oct. 3, 1840	413	224	......	
Indian Ocean ..	Aug. 15	Sept. 11, 1842	......	2,032	......	Belongs to Wareham.
Atlantic	Nov. 30	....	......	......	......	Condemned 1840.
Pacific Ocean ..	Apr. 21	—— —, 1844	......	......	......	Probably full.
Atlantic	Apr. —	Apr. 7, 1841	669	12	......	
....do	Aug. 27	June 22, 1841	60	......	......	
Atlantic Ocean	....	June 7, 1841	19	150	......	
....	Sept. 22	—— —, 1841	.....	......	......	
Atlantic.......	Feb. 21	June 27, 1841	160	......	......	
....do	Apr. 30	Nov. 25, 1840	Clean	......	......	
....do	Apr. 28	....	......	......	......	
South Atlantic	Aug. 5	Aug. 6, 1841	200	1,400	7,432	
....do	June 5	....	.....	.....	......	Condemned at Pernambuco.
....do	Aug. 3	Apr. 18, 1841	150	1,650	12,028	
Atlantic	July 10	June 4, 1841	180	315	3,000	
South Atlantic	Aug. 6	Aug. 19, 1841	130	1,125	9,500	
Atlantic	Apr. —	Sept. 23, 1840	580	......	......	
....do	Mar. 3	Sept. 15, 1840	700	......	......	
....do	Mar. 27	Sept. 23, 1840	670	......	......	
Indian Ocean ..	June 3	Aug. 31, 1845	750	1,000	10,000	
Pacific Ocean ..	Sept. 29	....	.....	.....	......	Built 1829. Lost on Timor 1842.
....do	....	—— —, 1845	......	4,200	......	A. Barclay landed her oil at Bremen. Sold to Bremen 1845.
....do	July 26	Feb. 17, 1845	1,400	1,100	11,000	Bought from Philadelphia 1841.
Atlantic	May 1	Jan. 30, 1842	150	......	.....	
Pacific Ocean ..	Oct. 25	June 12, 1845	1,700	.....	.....	
....do	Nov. 12	May 20, 1845	1,700	68	500	
....do	Dec. 25	Aug. 9, 1845	200	800	3,000	Captain Taber left the ship in 1842, sick. Sent home 650 pounds bone.
....do	May 21	Nov. 16, 1844	1,900	.....	.....	
....do	Sept. 4	Jan. 1, 1845	1,600	800	10,000	
Atlantic	June 12	Oct. 12, 1842	492	[illegible]	.....	Formerly a brig. Altered 1841.
Pacific Ocean ..	Sept. 2	Nov. 29, 1845	500	500	4,000	Withdrawn from the service 1845.
....do	Nov. 9	Aug. 26, 1842	2,500	.....	.....	
....do	Dec. 12	Feb. 17, 1845	2,100	......	......	

Table showing returns of whaling-vessels

Name of vessel.	Class.	Tonnage.	Captain.	Managing owner or agent.
1841.				
New Bedford, Mass—Continued.				
Clarice	Bark	237	—— Dexter	C. W. Morgan
Condor	Ship	349	—— Norton	do
Dartmouth	do	326	—— Whimpeney	I. Howland, jr., & Co
Elizabeth	do	339	H. F. Eastham	T. & A. R. Nye
Emeline	Brig	98	—— Wood	Barton Ricketson
Endeavour	Bark	252	—— Weeks	William H. Stowell
Franklin	Ship	333	Washington Walker	Ab'm H. Howland
Florida	do	330	—— Cunningham	Edw. C. Jones
General Pike	do	313	—— Tobey	William Gifford
George and Susan	do	316	—— Howland	George Howland
George Washington	Bark	230	Alex. Hathaway	Levi L. Crane
Golconda, 2d	Ship	359	—— Smith	William H. Stowell
Gratitude	do	337	—— Stetson	Ireneus Gooding
Good Return	do	376	—— Taber	H. Taber & Co
Gov. Troup	do	430	G. H. Jenney	E. C. Jones
Harrison	do	371	J. R. L. Smith	William H. Stowell
Houqua	do	339	—— Holley	Alexander Gibbs
Hydaspe	do	313	Francis Post	Daniel Wood
Huntress	do	391	—— Taber	Alfred Gibbs
Hope 2d	do	295	—— Robinson	Wilcox & Richmond
Hope	Bark	186	—— Brownell	William Watkins
Isabella	Ship	411	—— Howland	Jas. H. Howland
Israel	do	357	—— Little	Walter S. Spooner
Java	do	295	William Shockley	George Howland
John Adams	do	268	—— Bradford	Jireh Perry
John and Edward	do	318	Barz. N. Hudson	Wilcox & Richmond
Junior	do	378	—— Hathaway	D. R. Greene & Co
Julian	do	356	—— Mayhew	Hathaway & Luce
Kutusoff	do	415		
Lagoda	do	341	—— Maxfield	Jona. Bourne, jr
Lewis	Bark	231	—— Tallman	J. D. Thompson
L. C. Richmond	Ship	341	—— Luce	Daniel Wood
Laurel	Brig	119	—— Smith	I. H. Bartlett
Margaret Scott	Ship	307	—— Smith	S. & W. Ingalls
Mars	Bark	270	—— Brownell	Charles R. Tucker
Mayflower	Ship	350	—— Gifford	John C. Haskell
Mercury	do	340	Dennis F. Haskell	I. Howland, jr., & Co
Messenger	do	291	Peter Butler	John R. Thornton
Montezuma	do	430	—— Tower	West & Paine
Maria	Bark	202	—— Raymond	Samuel W. Rodman
Metacom	Ship	300	—— Reynolds	J. B. Wood & Co
Nassau	do	408	—— Weeks	Jireh Perry
Nile	do	322	Edwin F. Cook	Hathaway & Luce
Newton	Bark	283	—— Sawyer	Isaiah Burgess
Octavia	do	257	Isaac C. Howland	Gideon Allen
Pantheon	do	271	—— Taber	Jona. Bourne, jr
Peri	do	191	—— Russell	Rodney French
Phocion	Ship	266	—— Corey	Richard A. Palmer
Robert Edwards	do	356	—— Burgess	J. & J. Howland
Rousseau	do	306	John E. Brayton	George Howland
Rajah	Bark	250	—— West	Isaiah Burgess
Russell	do	302	Frederick A. Stall	Howland & Hussey
Selma	Ship	269	—— Luce	George O. Crocker & Co
Susan	do	261	Weston Howland	Ab'm H. Howland
Sam. Robertson	do	421	—— Warner	Andrew Robeson
Swift	do	321	—— Fisher	Thomas S. Hathaway
Smyrna	Bark	219	—— Miller	Barton Ricketson
Stephania	Ship	315	—— Collins	R. A. Palmer
Two Brothers	do	288	—— Tinkham	D. R. Greene & Co
Wilmington and Liverpool Packet	do	384	Gilbert Place	J. A. Parker, & Co
Zoroaster	Brig	159	—— Seabury	Pardon G. Seabury

sailing from American ports—Continued.

Whaling-ground.	Date— Of sailing.	Date— Of arrival.	Result of voyage. Sperm-oil.	Result of voyage. Whale-oil.	Result of voyage. Whalebone.	Remarks.
			Bbls.	*Bbls.*	*Lbs.*	
South Atlantic	Dec. 7	Aug. 13, 1845	.....	633	.....	Sold 220 sperm.
New Holland ..	Oct. 9	Mar. 10, 1844	150	2,450	14,000	
Pacific Ocean ..	Feb. 20	June 17, 1844	1,30	600	6,000	
Indian Ocean ...	June 7	May 6, 1844	600	500	12,000	Sold 1,000 barrels whale at Bahia.
Atlantic	July 12	Sept. 28, 1843	10	5	.....	Captain Wood's boat was stove by a whale, and he died from exhaustion before help reached them. Brig Emeline withdrawn from the service 1843.
Indian Ocean ...	June 22	June —, 1843	1,300	600	4,800	
Pacific Ocean ..	June 23	Nov. 23, 1842	22	2,314	.....	
Indian Ocean ...	Sept. 14	July —, 1843	60	2,300	18,400	
....do	July 1	Feb. 26, 1843	60	900	7,000	
Pacific Ocean ..	Oct. 17	July 12, 1845	1,60	......	......	
Atlantic	Mar. 25	Dec. 8, 1842	35	......	......	
Pacific Ocean ..	June 30	July 21, 1844	750	2,300	17,000	
....do	Apr. 25	Apr. 7, 1845	1,15	1,030	9,000	Bought from Boston 1841.
New Holland ..	Oct. 21	May 3, 1844	10	3,00	......	
....do	Nov. 4	Apr. 25, 1844	17	3,250	30,000	First mate, Edward Harris, died April, 1843, from effects of a fall down after-hatchway.
Pacific Ocean ..	July 28	Feb. 23, 1845	.....	......	......	Built at Mattapoisett, 1841.
....do	July 12	June 29, 1843	450	2,40	28,800	
....do	Apr. 24	Apr. 14, 1845	850	850	8,000	
Indian Ocean ..	Aug. 20	Mar. 6, 1844	40	2,500	20,000	First mate, Eben. Peck, taken out of his boat by a line and lost. Sold 100 barrels whale at Hobart Town.
....do	Sept. 14	Mar. 5, 1844	300	1,500	15,000	
Atlantic	Mar. 16	Nov. 14, 1842	5	......	......	
Pacific Ocean ..	July 22	May 19, 1845	2,700	6	......	
Atlantic	June 29	Sept. 9, 1843	30	1,900	22,000	Bought from Boston 1841.
Indian Ocean ..	June 10	Apr. 22, 1843	18	2,250	22,500	
....do	July 1	May —, 1844	1,000	300	2,500	
....do	May 19	July 19, 1844	40	830	6,000	
Pacific Ocean ..	Sept. 18	Mar. 11, 1844	1,15	1,600	16,000	
New Holland ..	Dec. 12	May 31, 1844	3,00	250	27,000	
....	Nov. 11	....	......	......	......	Sent home 10,000 pounds bone.
New Holland ..	Oct. 9	Sept. —, 1843	600	2,100	17,000	
Indian Ocean ..	Nov. 6	July 9, 1844	450	350	3,200	
Pacific Ocean ..	June 6	Oct. 31, 1844	2,200	......	......	Samuel Pent, second mate, died on passage home.
Atlantic	Mar. 12	Nov. 8, 1841	17	7	.....	Withdrawn, 1843.
Pacific Ocean ..	Jan. 9	Apr. 15, 1844	850	1,350	18,000	Bought from Portsmouth.
....do	June 6	Aug. 12, 1845	1,50	340	......	Formerly a brig; bought from New York, 1841.
Atlantic	July 11	Apr. 11, 1844	50	2,400	18,000	Second mate, Thomas Dunham, fell overboard and was drowned November 4, as the ship was leaving Lahaina.
Pacific Ocean ..	May 25	Aug. 1, 1844	1,600	......	.....	
Indian Ocean ..	June 2	May 10, 1843	35	1,650	13,200	
Pacific Ocean ..	Aug. 29	May 5, 1844	45	3,150	.....	
Atlantic	Jan. 1	Oct. —, 1843	500	......	......	
Pacific Ocean ..	Nov. 6	Sept. 20, 1845	2,00	......	.....	
....do	Sept. 6	Sept. 16, 1845	1,100	1,700	20,000	
....do	May 30	June 23, 1844	1,500	60	6,000	
Indian Ocean ..	June 20	Oct. 10, 1843	300	1,500	12,000	
....do	June 25	June 30, 1843	300	1,000	8,000	
Pacific Ocean ..	June 9	Feb. 25, 1845	80	600	6,000	Bought from New York 1841.
....do	Dec. 12	July 19, 1843	850	......	......	
Indian Ocean ..	Aug. 4	July 24, 1843	80	1,120	8,960	
Pacific Ocean ..	July 2	Dec. 14, 1844	2,250	......	.....	
....do	Apr. 24	Feb. 17, 1845	1,300	1,000	10,000	
....do	Aug. 8	July 7, 1844	750	800	8,000	Sold to Westport 1844.
....do	May 19	May 19, 1845	800	700	7,000	
....do	July 31	....	......	......	......	Burned at sea, September 9, 1841.
....do	May 6	Apr. 3, 1845	900	1,000	10,000	Bought from Boston 1841.
....do	Oct. 22	Mar. 13, 1846	1,200	......	......	Sold to Fairhaven 1846.
....do	Dec. 22	May 11, 1845	1,000	1,300	13,000	
....do	Dec. 29	June 23, 1845	1,00	......	......	Captain Miller fell overboard and died from exhaustion after his rescue.
Indian Ocean ..	Nov. 18	Mar. —, 1844	200	2,100	21,000	
....do	Nov. 18	Feb. 27, 1844	1,250	800	6,400	
Pacific Ocean ..	Dec. 22	....	300	1,500	.....	Condemned at Sandwich Islands, 1845; oil shipped home. Sent home 5,850.
Atlantic	Mar. 4	Nov. 12, 1841	380	14	......	

Table showing returns of whaling-vessels

Name of vessel.	Class.	Tonnage.	Captain.	Managing owner or agent.
1841.				
Nantucket, Mass.				
Aurora	Ship	346	Frederick S. Coffin	T. & P. Macy
American	do	339	Alexander Coffin	Daniel Jones
Columbia	do	329	George Joy	C. G. & H. Coffin
Christopher Mitchell	do	387	William Keene	C. Mitchell & Co
David Paddack	do	352	John Hussey, jr	Daniel Jones
Edward Cary	do	353	John Tobey	Jas. Athearn
Elizabeth Starbuck	do	381	Henry Bigelow	Levi Starbuck
Foster	do	317	John C. Congdon	R. Mitchell & Sons
Franklin	do	246	Shubael Ray	Jas. Athearn
Ganges	do	315	George Pitman	David Joy
Hero	do	313	William S. Chase	Jos. Starbuck
Howard	do	364	Alexander Bunker	Timothy Hussey
John Adams	do	296	Isaac Stockman	David Joy
Japan	do	332	Benjamin F. Riddell	Barker & Athearn
Levi Starbuck	do	376	Jos P. Nye	Levi Starbuck
Martha	do	273	William Baxter	William R. Easton
Monticello	do	358	Benjamin Coggeshall	John H. Shaw
Massachusetts	do	360	Seth Nickerson	George C. Gardner
Montano	do	365	Roswell M. Coon	Barker & Athearn
Nantucket	do	350	George W. Gardner	H. G. O. Dunham
Navigator	do	333	Elihu Fisher	Matthew Crosby
Narraganset	do	398	Charles W Coffin	Christopher Wyer
Orion	do	354	James Nichols	Frederick Hussey
Ohio	do	381	Varamus Smith	Chris. Wyer
Obed. Mitchell	do	354	Elihu Coffin	Aaron Mitchell
Primrose	Schooner	....	—— Narbeth	William Bartlett
Potomac	Ship	356	Isaac B. Hussey	T. & P. Macy
Penobscot	Brig	138	—— Carr	A. W. Starbuck
Susan	Ship	348	Reuben Russell	Aaron Mitchell
Three Brothers	do	384	Jos. Mitchell, 2d	G. & M. Starbuck & Co.
Tylston	Brig	111	—— Brown	David Thain
United States	Ship	372	Calvin B. Worth	Barrett & Upton
Fairhaven, Mass.				
Acushnet	Ship	359	—— Pease	Bradford, Fuller & Co
Adeline Gibbs	do	381	—— Baylies	Gibbs & Jenny
Amazon	do	318	—— Clarke	Nathan Church
Clifford Wayne	do	305	—— Crowell	E. Sawin
Cadmus	do	320	—— Mayhew	Atkins Adams
Columbus	do	382	—— Fish	Gibbs & Jenny
Friendship	do	366	—— Taber	do
George	do	360	—— Swift	Fish & Huttlestone
Harvest	Bark	314	—— Hale	Jabez Delano, jr
Heroine	Ship	337	—— Smith	Nathan Church
Hesper	Bark	26[illegible]	—— Handy	L. Jenny and J. Tripp
Isabella	do	243	—— Netcher	E. Sawin
Java	Ship	294	—— Lane	Atkins Adams
Lagrange	Bark	280	—— Stetson	do
Marcia	Ship	315	—— Mosher	E. Sawin
Martha	do	298	—— Sayer	Nathan Church
Oregon	do	339	—— Shearman	L. C. Tripp
Sharon	do	354	—— Norris	Gibbs & Jenney
William & Henry	do	261	—— Benjamin	I. F. Terry
New London, Conn.				
Ann Maria	Ship	368	—— Middletown	Havens & Smith
Atlas	do	299	—— Pendleton	Joseph Lawrence

sailing from American ports—Continued.

Whaling-ground.	Date— Of sailing.	Date— Of arrival.	Result of voyage. Sperm-oil.	Result of voyage. Whale-oil.	Result of voyage. Whalebone.	Remarks.
			Bbls.	*Bbls.*	*Lbs.*	
Pacific Ocean ..	May 13	Dec. 9, 1844	1, 801	.....	.....	
....do	Dec. 1	July 10, 1845	1, 890	.....	.....	
....do	Sept. 4	Dec. 2, 1845	1, 660	.....	.....	New this voyage; built at East Boston.
....do	Oct. 25	June 24, 1845	1, 250	.....	.....	First and second mates, boat-steerers, and nearly all the crew left the ship at Bay of Islands.
....do	Oct. 7	Oct. 16, 1845	88	17	.....	New this voyage; built at Rochester.
....do	Sept. 26	July 22, 1845	1, 559	32	.....	Built at Rochester 1841.
....do	Aug. 21	Aug. 10, 1845	1, 10	.....	.....	Sent home 116 sperm.
....do	July 28	Sept. 1, 1845	1, 430	.....	.....	
....do	Aug. 11	Apr. 3, 1845	1, 440	16	.....	Captain Ray died on the voyage. Henry Starbuck took command.
....do	July 28	May 20, 1845	73	470	.....	Rebuilt and enlarged at Brant Point.
....do	Sept. 29	Feb. 22, 1846	830	.....	.....	
....do	Nov. 1	June 8, 1845	1, 96	2	.....	
....do	Aug. 31	June 24, 1845	540	.....	.....	Captain Stockman died; ——— Thompson took command.
....do	Sept. 17	June 10, 1845	1, 890	.....	.....	
....do	May 26	Mar. 31, 1845	85	865	.....	
....do	July 28	June 17, 1845	1, 057	276	.....	Captain Baxter left the ship at Zanzibar and came home; Richard C. Gibbs took command.
....do	Aug. 2	July 15, 1845	2, 430	.....	.....	New this voyage; built at Mattapoisett.
....do	Aug. 26	Mar. 24, 1845	1, 25	1, 388	12, 000	Do.
....do	Dec. 25	Apr. 10, 1845	1, 48	442	.....	
....do	June 16	May 12, 1845	1, 27	1, 326	.....	Peter F. Swain, 2d mate, taken out of his boat by a foul line January 21, 1842.
....do	Aug. 21	May 7, 1845	1, 737	246	.....	New this voyage; built at Medford.
....do	Nov. 7	Oct. 25, 1845	2, 25	.....	.....	New this voyage; built at Rochester.
....do	July 5	Nov. 14, 1844	2, 040	169	1, 000	
....do	July 18	May 3, 1845	2, 804	80	.....	Sold to New Bedford.
....do	Sept. 4	May 10, 1845	1, 18	2	.....	
Atlantic	July 8	....	.....	.....	.....	Lost near Trinidad, May, 1842; had 280 sperm.
Pacific Ocean ..	Nov. 12	May 4, 1845	2, 354	.....	.....	Built at Mattapoisett; new this voyage.
Atlantic	Sept. 26	May 17, 1843	100	.....	.....	
Pacific Ocean ..	Dec. 9	May 27, 1846	63	1, 405	12, 000	
....do	July 12	Nov. 6, 1845	2, 15	22	.....	
Atlantic	June 17	Sept. 5, 1842	230	.....	.....	
Pacific Ocean ..	Nov. 12	Oct. 16, 1845	1, 42	10	.....	
Pacific Ocean ..	Jan. 3	May 13, 1845	850	1, 350	13, 500	Built 1840.
....do	Sept. 6	July 29, 1845	2, 100	.....	.....	
....do	Sept. 21	June 17, 1845	60	1, 300	8, 000	
Indian Ocean ..	Mar. 25	July 23, 1845	1, 400	.....	.....	
Pacific Ocean ..	Nov. 11	....	.....	.....	.....	Lost on Cadmus Island August 3, 1842.
Indian Ocean ..	Aug. 16	Sept. —, 1843	50	2, 000	20, 000	
Pacific Ocean ..	Dec. 6	Apr. 9, 1844	30	2, 500	24, 000	
....do	Jan. 3	July 9, 1844	1, 70	.....	.....	
....do	Sept. 1	Aug. 15, 1843	50	1, 750	.....	Sold 210 sperm on voyage.
New Holland .	May 30	Mar. 23, 1843	350	2, 200	17, 60	
New Zealand ..	July 15	June 16, 1844	1, 90	.....	.....	
Pacific Ocean ..	Nov. 7	Aug. —, 1845	1, 150	.....	.....	Withdrawn 1847.
....do	Aug. 14	May 8, 1845	2, 10	.....	.....	
Indian Ocean ..	June 12	Apr. 16, 1845	50	.....	.....	
....do	Dec. 22	Apr. 19, 1844	100	2, 800	26, 000	Sold to New Bedford 1844.
Pacific Ocean ..	Oct. 10	Aug. 4, 1845	60	1, 0[illegible]0	10, 0[illegible]	
....do	July 12	Mar. 31, 1845	1, 30	1, 200	12, 000	
....do	May 25	Feb. 10, 1845	900	1, 050	9, 000	Put into Sydney December 22, 1842, the crew having mutinied and killed Captain Norris.
	Apr. 14	Oct. 29, 1841	5	2	.....	Returned in consequence of sickness among the officers.
....do	Nov. 15	—— —, 1845	.....	.....	.....	Bought from Salem.
Indian Ocean ..	May 18	....	.....	.....	.....	Lost off Saint Paul's August 30, 1842; run into by French ship Ajax.
South Atlantic.	Aug. 23	....	.....	.....	.....	Lost at Two People's Bay August 29, 1842.

Table showing returns of whaling-vessels

Name of vessel.	Class.	Tonnage.	Captain.	Managing owner or agent.
1841.				
New London, Conn.—Continued.				
Avis	Ship	299	—— Pendleton	Joseph Lawrence
Boston	Bark	291	—— Hamsted	do
Chelsea	Ship	399	—— Potts	Havens & Smith
Clematis	do	311	—— Benjamin	Williams & Barnes
Clement	Bark	279	—— Pendleton	Jos. Lawrence
Cervantes	do	232	—— Brown	Benjamin Brown
Connecticut	do	398	—— Crocker	Frink, Chew & Co
Columbus	Brig	159	—— Holt	Williams & Barnes
Electra	Ship	348	—— Ward	do
Flora	do	33	—— Mayhew	N. & W. W. Billings
Friends	do	403	—— Brown	Benjamin Brown
Francis	Brig	98	—— Holland	Havens & Smith
Georgia	Ship	344	—— Hull	Lyman Allyn
Iris	Bark	245	—— Douglass	Frink, Chew & Co
Jones	do	336	—— Sisson	Havens & Smith
Julius Cæsar	Ship	347	—— Gibson	N. & W. W. Billings
Jason	do	335	—— Skinner	Frink, Chew & Co
Mentor	do	460	—— Chester	Benjamin Brown
Montezuma	do	424	—— Baker	Williams & Barnes
Phœnix	do	404	—— Slate	N. & W. W. Billings
Palladium	do	342	—— Prentiss	Frink, Chew & Co
Pembroke	Bark	199	—— Church	Jos. Lawrence
Peruvian	Ship	388	—— Brown	Fitch & Leonard
Pacific	Schooner	96	—— Harris	Havens & Smith
Somerset	Brig	134	—— Beck	William Beck
White Oak	Bark	292	—— Fitch	Daniel Fitch
William C. Nye	Ship	389	—— Buddington	N. & W. W. Billings
Westport, Mass.				
Barclay	Bark	167	—— Macomber	Davis & Corey
Champion	do	209	—— Sowle	Andrew Hicks
Dr. Franklin	do	171	—— Francis	Job Davis
Elizabeth	Brig	107	—— Cook	A. B. Gifford
Mexico	do	130	—— Smith	Davis & Corey
President	Bark	167	—— Southworth	Andrew Hicks
Theophilus Chase	do	168	—— Baker	Henry Wilcox
Thos. Winslow	Brig	136	—— Manchester	Thos. W. Mayhew
Provincetown, Mass.				
Belle Isle	Schooner	104	—— Cook	Eben Cook
Fairy	Brig	186	—— Ginn	Abraham Small
Franklin	do	172	—— Soper	Robert Soper
Gem	do	162	—— Fluker	Timothy P. Johnson
John B. Dods	do	163	—— Prior	E. S. Smith
Phœnix	do	150	—— Small	Leonard Small
Spartan	Bark	188	James Small	Step. Nickerson
Samuel and Thomas	Brig	191	—— Soper	Samuel Soper
William Henry	do	111	—— Ryder	G. Ryder
Mattapoisett, Mass.				
Annawana	Brig	159	—— Pool	Seth Freeman
Edward	do	133	—— Mayhew	Wilson Barstow
Elizabeth	Bark	219	—— Bates	R. L. Barstow
Lagrange	Brig	170	—— Dexter	E. Willis
Le Baron	do	170	—— Parker	G. Barstow & Son
Mattapoisett	do	150	—— Brightman	Leonard Hammond
Richard Henry	Bark	173	—— Snow	G. Barstow & Son
Solon	Brig	129	—— Wing	N. E. Bates
Two Sisters	do	122	—— Bolles	do

NOTE.—Brig Chase, Lumbert, sailed April 5; was abandoned at sea April 12.

sailing from American ports—Continued.

Whaling-ground.	Date—Of sailing.	Date—Of arrival.	Result of voyage.—Sperm-oil.	Result of voyage.—Whale-oil.	Result of voyage.—Whalebone.	Remarks.
			Bbls.	*Bbls.*	*Lbs.*	
Indian Ocean ..	Aug. 21	....	......	......	......	Wrecked in King George's Sound, New Holland, with 800 barrels whale-oil.
New Zealand ..	June 28	....	......	......	......	Condemned at Bay of Islands; oil (1,400 whale) shipped home.
Indian Ocean ..	Sept. 14	July 1, 1843	100	2, 200	17, 600	
....do	Aug. 7	Feb. 28, 1843	500	2, 200	17, 600	
....do	May 8	July —, 1843	300	1, 800	6, 000	
South Seas.....	June 12	May —, 1843	300	700	5, 000	
.. do	Aug. 18	June 16, 1843	200	1, 600	12, 800	
South Atlantic	June 25	Oct. 16, 1842	600	......	......	
Indian Ocean ..	July 21	May 9, 1843	400	2, 000	16, 000	Sold 470 whale at Rio.
New Zealand ..	Jan. 19	Apr. 7, 1843	500	2, 200	17, 600	
Indian Ocean ..	July 12	Mar. 11, 1843	300	2, 800	22, 400	
South Atlantic	Mar. 6	....	......	......	......	Lost at the Falklands 1842.
Indian Ocean ..	July 17	June 1, 1843	50	2, 000	16, 000	
South Seas....	Nov. 8	May 9, 1844	180	2, 120	17, 000	
Indian Ocean ..	Feb. 18	Aug. 30, 1842	140	1, 200	......	Sold 250 sperm; broken up at home after this voyage.
....do	Aug. 2	Mar. 15, 1843	......	2, 200	17, 600	
....do	July 10	June 17, 1842	150	1, 950	......	
....do	Aug. 12	Apr. 7, 1843	100	2, 900	23, 200	
....do	Sept. 22	Apr. 6, 1844	......	3, 300	26, 400	
South Atlantic	June 10	June 10, 1842	130	2, 570	23, 000	
Crozette Island	July 30	May 15, 1843	......	1, 300	10, 400	
South Atlantic	July 13	May 24, 1842	40	1, 000	......	
Crozette Island	Oct. 15	July —, 1843	100	2, 400	19, 200	
South Atlantic	Mar. 19	Apr. 29, 1842	......	500	......	Condemned at Cape Town 1844.
South Seas....	Apr. 10	....	......	......	......	Sold with her cargo at Rio Janeiro.
....do	Apr. 10	Mar. 15, 1843	100	......	22, 000	Bought from New York. Sold whale-oil at Rio; brought 500 seal-skins.
Pacific Ocean ..	Oct. 19	Sept. —, 1843	800	2, 400	30, 000	
Atlantic	July 8	Nov. 10, 1842	457	......	......	
....do	May 18	Oct. 7, 1842	314	30	......	
....do	July 27	Jan. 28, 1842	273	......	......	
....do	May 18	May 6, 1842	260	120	......	Broken up at Westport 1842.
....do	May 13	July 19, 1842	230	......	......	
....do	Sept. 10	Apr. 17, 1843	270	35	......	
....do	May 18	Oct. 11, 1842	370	......	......	
....do	Nov. 12	Sept. 30, 1842	130	7	......	
Atlantic	Mar. 10	Nov. 2, 1841	120	40	......	
....do	Feb. 11	Nov. 1, 1841	220	......	......	
....do	Jan. 30	Nov. 1, 1841	220	......	......	
....do .... }	Feb. —	June 18, 1841	33	......	......	} Bought from Boston 1841.
	July 3	Sept. 14, 1842	240	......	......	
....do	Feb. 6	Nov. 9, 1841	150	30	......	
....do	Jan. 18	Oct. 14, 1841	340	......	......	
....do	Mar. 31	May 22, 1842	350	......	......	
....do	Mar. 19	Jan. 2[illegible], 1842	300	......	......	Built 1841.
....do	Mar. —	Sept. 21, 1841	160	......	......	
Atlantic	July 8	Nov. 23, 1842	200	......	......	Built at Mattapoisett 1841.
....do	Apr. 10	Feb. 7, 1842	260	......	......	Edward bought from Boston 1841.
Indian Ocean ..	May 29	Apr. 4, 1844	400	750	7, 000	
Atlantic	June 12	Oct. 12, 1842	450	......	......	
....do	Dec. 22	....	......	......	......	Sold to Newport 1844.
....do	Mar. 26	Sept. 5, 1842	439	......	......	
....do	Nov. 18	Apr. —, 1843	300	......	......	Sold to Stonington.
....do	Dec. 25	Sept. 7, 1841	40	20	......	
....do	July 24	Oct. 11, 1842	200	......	......	Sold to New Bedford.

Table showing returns of whaling-vessels

Name of vessel.	Class.	Tonnage.	Captain.	Managing owner or agent.
1841.				
Wareham, Mass.				
America	Brig	148	—— Lumbard	M. S. F. Tobey
Inga	do	169	—— Cudworth	do
Montezuma	do	195	—— Shiverick	do
Meridian	do	73	—— Russell	do
Plymouth, Mass.				
Exchange	Schooner	99	—— King	Richard W. Holmes
Maracaibo	Brig	9	—— Pope	Atwood L. Drew
James Munroe	do	11	—— Dike	Isaac L. Hedge
Mary and Martha	Ship	31	—— Coffin	James Bartlett
Mercury	Schooner	74	—— Nickerson	Isaac Barnes, jr
Vesper	do	95	—— Ellis	Bradford Barner, jr
Somerset, Mass.				
Jane	Bark	23	—— Manchester	Wheaton Luther
Pilgrim	Brig	137	—— Collins	do
Duxbury, Mass.				
Sophia and Eliza	Bark	20	—— Coffin	George Frazier
Fall River, Mass.				
Ann Maria	Bark	19	—— Carr	J. S. Barnard
Gold Hunter	Ship	28	—— Wood	Nathan Durfee
Leonidas	Brig	12	—— Baker	Noah Hathaway
Otranto	Bark	15	—— Cook	Cranston Wilcox
Panama	Ship	25	—— Cummings	J. S. Barnard
Rowena	do	40	—— Estes	Nathan Durfee
Freetown, Mass.				
Elizabeth	Bark	34	—— Winslow	
Providence, R. I.				
Balance	Ship	32	—— Reed	W. Humphrey
Bowditch	do	39	—— Sowle	Thomas Fletcher
Brunswick	do	29	—— Champlin	Amherst Everett
Cassander	do	29	—— Dennis	Nathaniel Potter
Envoy	do	3	—— Fisher	Amherst Everett
Lexington	do	20	—— Jayne	William Earle
Lion	do	29	—— Howland	Edward Carrington, jr
Bristol, R. I.				
Anna	Bark	22	—— Moores	Bryon Diman
Emigrant	do	18	—— Lake	Samuel Church
Gov. Hopkins	Brig	11	—— Wilcox	William R. Taylor
Leonidas	Ship	35	—— King	do
Troy	Brig	15	—— Sherman	Samuel Church
NOTE.—The Sarah Lee, of Bristol, sailed in November, 1841, but returned, damaged by a gale, in two weeks after. She was then withdrawn, and soon after lost in the merchant service.				
Newport, R. I.				
Margaret	Ship	37	T. Wimpenney	J. Stevens and J. S. Munroe.
Martha	do	271	—— Davenport	Devins & Tisdale
Menkar	do	35	Joseph Shearman	R. Coggeshall
Ohio	Schooner	12	—— Smyley	Gilbert Chase
Pocahontas	Brig	...	William Barker	Samuel Barker
Sea Bird	do	14	—— Tripp	Gilbert Chase

sailing from American ports—Continued.

Whaling-ground.	Date— Of sailing.	Date— Of arrival.	Result of voyage. Sperm-oil.	Result of voyage. Whale-oil.	Result of voyage. Whalebone.	Remarks.
			Bbls.	*Bbls.*	*Lbs.*	
Atlantic	July 13	Oct. 1, 1842	450	30		Bought from New York 1841. Took 18 pounds ambergris.
....do	June 1	Apr. 11, 1842	810			
....do	Nov. 27	July —, 1843	400			
....do	July 23	July 4, 1842	40			Withdrawn.
Atlantic	Aug. 5	Oct. 17, 1842	100	60		
....do	Sept. 25	May —, 1843	100			
....do	July 28	June 18, 1842	170			
Indian Ocean	June 16	Dec. 25, 1845				Sold to New Bedford 1846.
Atlantic	Jan. 12	Sept. 12, 1841	150			
	Sept. 12	Oct. 10, 1841		13		
....do	July 31	July 28, 1842	26	8		
Indian Ocean	Sept. 16	Apr. 22, 1843	162	567	4,330	
Atlantic	May 27	June 1, 1842	230			
Indian Ocean	Aug. 1	Apr. 26, 1844	200	1,300	7,000	Sold to Stonington 1844.
South Atlantic	Aug. 9	Dec. 10, 1842	550			
Indian Ocean	May 22	July —, 1843	200	1,300	10,400	
Atlantic	May 4	May 3, 1842	350			Bought from New York 1841.
....do	Sept. 16	June 10, 1842	110	20		Lost part of her officers and crew by African fever.
Indian Ocean	Nov. 21	Dec. 20, 1841				Returned leaking.
....do	July 1	July —, 1843	330	2,700	21,600	
Indian Ocean	Nov. 15	Mar. 1, 1844	150	850	8,500	Captain Winslow and his boat's crew carried down by a whale.
Indian Ocean	Oct. 18	Mar. 9, 1844	150	2,500	25,000	
Pacific Ocean	July 20	Mar. —, 1843	190	2,410	36,000	Sold 600 whale at Bahia.
Indian Ocean	Aug. 2	July 4, 1843	150	850		Sold to New Bedford.
Pacific Ocean	Nov. 15	July 9, 1844	400	1,300	14,000	
....do	June 29	Feb. —, 1844	300	3,200	32,000	
Indian Ocean	Dec. 4	Apr. 3, 1845	500			
Pacific Ocean	June 16	Sept. 18, 1844	2,200			
Indian Ocean	Aug. 14	Aug. 8, 1844	600	300	3,000	
Atlantic	Aug. 20	June 7, 1842	130	15		Sailed in June, 1842, and returned in January, 1843; clean.
....do	June 20	Nov. 3, 1841	40			
Indian Ocean	Mar. 4	Jan. 14, 1843	550			
Atlantic	Oct. 6	Oct. 7, 1842	172	12		
Pacific Ocean	Aug. 28	Feb. 25, 1845	1,100	1,100	10,000	Withdrawn 1846; lost at Society Islands 1847.
....do	Nov. 4	Oct. 30, 1844	1,650			
....do	Nov. 23	Apr. 10, 1845	1,400	1,200	13,000	
Atlantic	July 14					
....do	Sept. —	Oct. 4, 1842	280	20		
....do	June 24					Returned in August, 1842, with 30 sperm; sailed in August, 1842, and was condemned in Patagonia, September 8, 1843.

Table showing returns of whaling-vessels

Name of vessel.	Class.	Tonnage.	Captain.	Managing owner or agent.
1841.				
Mystic, Conn.				
Blackstone	Bark	258	—— Baker	Charles Mallory
Leander	..do	213	—— Bailey	..do
Uxor	Brig	96	—— Stephens	..do
New Suffolk, Conn.				
Noble	Bark	274	—— Brown	Ira B. Tuthill
Bridgeport, Conn.				
Atlantic	Ship	291	—— Howell	Samuel H. Ford
Hamilton	..do	359	—— Bishop	Sherwood Sterling
Cold Spring, N. Y.				
Monmouth	Bark	255?	—— Hedges	
Tuscarora	Ship	379	—— White	
Greenport, N. Y.				
Bayard	Ship	339	—— Fordham	H. & N. Corwin
Delta	..do	314	—— Glover	..do
Roanoke	Bark	251	—— Case	Wiggins & Parsons
Seraph	Brig	174	—— Corwin	Samuel Landon
Triad	Ship	336	—— Case	H. & N. Corwin
Washington	..do	236	—— Griffin	..do
Sag Harbor, N. Y.				
Acasta	Bark	286	—— Havens	Mulford & Sleight
Ann	Ship	299	—— Curry	Mulford & Howell
Arabella	..do	357	—— Babcock	N. & G. Howell
Cadmus	..do	307	—— Smith	Mulford & Sleight
Camillus	..do	345	—— Jennings	Charles T. Dering
Columbia	..do	385	—— Edwards	Luther D. Cook
Crescent	..do	340	—— Royce	Post & Sherry
Daniel Webster	..do	397	—— Baker	Mulford & Howell
Fanny	..do	391	—— Fordham	N. & G. Howell
France	..do	411	—— Edwards	..do
Franklin	Bark	391	—— Halsey	Hunting Cooper
Gem	..do	326	—— Worth	..do
Henry	Ship	333	—— Young	S. L'Hommidieu
Hannibal	..do	311	—— Bennett	S. & B. Hunting & Co
Marcus	..do	203	—— Loper	N. & G. Howell
Monmouth	..do	273	—— Hedges	
Neptune	..do	338	—— Ludlow	S. & B. Hunting & Co.
Nimrod	..do	280	—— Rogers	C. T. Dering & Co.
O. C. Raymond	..do	..	—— Dennison	
Panama	..do	465	—— Crowell	N. & G. Howell
Portland	..do	292	—— Payne	S. & B. Hunting & Co.
S. Richards	..do	454	—— Dering	Mulford & Sleight
Thames	..do	414	—— Hedges	Thomas Brown
Thomas Dickinson	..do	451	—— Havens	Mulford & Sleight
Washington	..do	340	—— Osborn	Hunting Cooper
Wickford	Brig	115	Davis Miller	D. T. Vail
Wiscasset	Ship	380	—— Smith	
Warren, R. I.				
Benj. Rush	Ship	385	—— Gifford	S. Child and Jas. Coffin
Crawford	Brig	126	—— Pickens	Charles Luther
Chariot	Ship	360	—— Littlefield	N. M. Wheaton
Exchange	Bark	180	—— Luce	John R. Wheaton
Rosalia	Ship	323	—— Eddy	Joseph Smith
Vermont	Brig	154	—— Martin	Stephen Martin
Wm. Baker	Ship	225	—— Gifford	Child & Fessenden
Salem, Mass.				
Eliza	Bark	262	—— Chase	James W. Cheever
Elizabeth	Ship	398	—— Hedge	S. C. Phillips

sailing from American ports—Continued.

Whaling-ground.	Date—		Result of voyage.			Remarks.
	Of sailing.	Of arrival.	Sperm-oil.	Whale-oil.	Whalebone.	
			Bbls.	*Bbls.*	*Lbs.*	
Indian Ocean ..	May 17	Apr. 25, 1843	300	1,600	12,800	
Crozette Island	Aug. 16	May 23, 1843	......	1,600	13,000	
South Atlantic	July 12	....	......	......	......	Lost on the Crozettes, October 28, 1841.
New Zealand ..	July 19	May 1, 1843	200	2,000	16,000	
Crozette Island	Sept. —	July 2, 1842	100	1,400	10,000	
....do	July 27	June —, 1843	800	2,100	16,800	
South Atlantic	Sept. 12	June 27, 1842	......	1,850	14,000	
Indian Ocean ..	Aug. 3	June —, 1843	75	1,77.	11,000	
Crozette Island	Sept. 26	May 7, 1843	250	1,900	15,200	
South Seas.....	Dec. 4	June —, 1843	300	1,40.	11,200	Returned once damaged in a collision.
South Atlantic	June 2	July 23, 1842	580	60.	......	
Atlantic	July 8	....	......	......	......	Had 150 sperm, 75 whale; condemned and sold at Rio Janeiro, January, 1842.
New Zealand ..	July 7	May —, 1843	110	2,100	16,800	
South Atlantic	Sept. 30	May 22, 1843	......	1,700	13,600	
South Atlantic	Sept. 12	July 31, 1842	50	1,750	13,000	
New Zealand ..	July 19	May 10, 1843	60	2,340	18,720	
Crozette Island	Sept. 26	Mar. 17, 1844	500	2,200	22,000	
South Atlantic	Oct. 19	June 28, 1843	70	2,080	......	
... do	Dec. 9	Aug. —, 1843	300	1,000	......	
New Zealand ..	June 26	Mar. 16, 1843	400	2,200	21,000	
Crozette Island	Sept. 27	Aug. —, 1843	300	1,200	18,000	Sold 1,500 whale, at Rio Janeiro.
N. W. Coast	July 8	June 1, 1843	......	3,30.	33,000	
New Zealand ..	May 21	Oct. —, 1843	350	2,550	22,000	
Indian Ocean ..	Oct. 1	June 10, 1843	220	2,450	19,600	
New Zealand ..	July 12	Apr. 9, 1844	200	2,800	28,000	
South Atlantic	Sept. 26	Aug. 5, 1843	......	2,200	18,000	
New Zealand ..	June 16	May 10, 1843	100	2,25.	18,000	
Indian Ocean ..	Aug. 4	June 7, 1842	......	1,900	......	
South Atlantic	Nov. 17	July —, 1843	700	700	5,000	
....do	Sept. 11	June 25, 1842	......	1,850	......	Belongs to Cold Spring.
New Zealand ..	June 1	May 7, 1843	40	2,650	21,200	
South Atlantic	Oct. —	July 11, 1842	300	1,200	......	
New Holland ..	Sept. 21	....	......	......	......	Sold at Valparaiso, 1843.
New Zealand ..	July 6	Oct. —, 1842	130	3,570	30,000	
Indian Ocean ..	June 28	June 23, 1842	80	2,270	......	
New Zealand ..	July 10	Nov. —, 1843	220	3,600	30,000	
....do	July 6	Apr. 4, 1843	8.	3,230	38,600	
....do	July 14	June 18, 1844	50	2,950	12,000	
... do	June 2	Apr. 22, 1843	......	2,300	18,240	Captain Osborne died July, 1842.
Atlantic ..... {	....	—— —, 1841	100	......	......	} Withdrawn, 1843.
	Dec. 22	Apr. —, 1843	50	......	......	
New Zealand ..	Dec. 6	June 7, 1844	250	2,600	27,000	
Pacific Ocean ..	July 31	May 13, 1845	1,000	60.	6,000	
South Atlantic	July 17	Oct. 17, 1842	100	......	......	Condemned, 1843.
Pacific Ocean ..	May 7	Jan. —, 1844	400	2,600	26,000	Lost first and second mate; 7 months out.
Indian Ocean ..	Sept. 17	Nov. —, 1843	1,050	......	......	
New Zealand ..	July 16	Apr. 15, 1842	....	250	......	Returned leaking.
South Atlantic	Apr. 30	Jan. 4, 1842	50	......	......	
Indian Ocean ..	Aug. 24	Aug. —, 1843	100	1,300	12,000	
Indian Ocean ..	July 3	....	200	......	......	Condemned at Tahiti, July, 1843; had 200 sperm.
Pacific Ocean ..	Jan. 12	Oct. 20, 1844	1,500	......	......	

Table showing returns of whaling-vessels

Name of vessel.	Class.	Tonnage.	Captain.	Managing owner or agent.
1841.				
Salem, Mass.—Continued.				
Henry	Bark	..	—— Manchester	
James Maury	Ship	395	Benjamin R. Hussey	John B. Osgood
Edgartown, Mass.				
Athalia	Bark	162	—— Mayhew	Jos. Mayhew
Champion	Ship	399	—— Pease	Grafton Norton
Mary	do	348	—— Atkins	Benjamin Worth
Pavillion	Brig	150	—— Adams	Calvin C. Adams
Rhine	Bark	174	—— Morse	John O. Morse
Vesta	Brig	156	—— Smith	Benjamin Worth
York	Ship	434	—— Pease	John O. Morse
Stonington, Conn.				
Caledonia	Ship	446	—— Hancox	Charles P. Williams
Eugene	do	297	—— Pendleton	do
George	do	251	—— Forsyth	do
Herald	do	241	—— Brewster	do
Newark	do	323	—— Pendleton	John F. Trumbull
Philetus	Bark	278	—— Brewster	do
Rebecca Groves	Brig	129	—— Barnum	C. P. Williams
Tybee	Ship	299	—— Swan	John F. Trumbull
Falmouth, Mass.				
Commodore Morris	Ship	350	Charles Downs	Oliver C. Swift
Wm. Penn	do	364	John C. Lincoln	Obed Goodspeed
Holmes's Hole, Mass.				
Delphos	Ship	338	—— West	Thomas Bradley
Sippican, Mass.				
Drymo	Bark	262	—— Hammond	Elisha Luce
Hecla	do	207	—— Crapo	J. S. Bates
Two Sisters	Brig	122	—— Bolles	N. E. Bates
Hudson, N. Y.				
Martha	Ship	369	—— Whelden	Barnard Curtis & Co.
Poughkeepsie, N. Y.				
Factor	Ship	343	—— Howland	David S. Shearman
New York, N. Y.				
Autumn	Bark	181	—— Lansing	D. & A. Kingsland
Caledonia	Schooner	100	—— Davis	do
Sabina	Ship	416	—— Slate	Slate, Gardner & Howell
Newark, N. J.				
John Wells	Ship	366	—— Russell	J. H. Stephens
Wilmington, Del.				
Ceres	Ship	328	—— Ayres	Stephen Bonsal
Jefferson	do	306	—— Howland	do
Lucy Ann	do	309	—— Cox —— King	do
Boston, Mass.				
Creole	Bark	222	—— Cook	Charles A. Brown
Carib	Brig	162	—— Woolley	William V. Kent
Fama	Bark			

sailing from American ports—Continued.

Whaling-ground.	Date— Of sailing.	Of arrival.	Result of voyage. Sperm-oil.	Whale-oil.	Whalebone.	Remarks.
			Bbls.	*Bbls.*	*Lbs.*	
Indian Ocean	Oct. 14	Apr. 15, 1845	140	300	2,400	
....do	Mar. 11	Feb. 19, 1845	1,400	500	3,600	Sold to New Bedford, 1845. Captain Hussey died June 15, 1844; Charles F. Pinkham, first mate, died September, 1844.
Atlantic	June 3	Dec. 6, 1842	420	.....	......	Withdrawn for merchant service.
Pacific Ocean	Aug. 19	Apr. 3, 1845	1,300	1,400	14,000	
....do	Jan. 5	July 24, 1844	700	1,500	15,000	
Atlantic	May 8	Dec. 16, 1842	350	......	......	Bought from New York 1841.
....do	Apr. 6	Sept. 2, 1842	175	......	......	Do.
....do	May 17	Oct. 2, 1842	400	......	......	Bought from Woods Hole 1841.
N. W. Coast	Sept. 15	Jan. —, 1844	400	4,200	30,000	
New Zealand	June 16	Apr. 25, 1843	80	3,120	24,900	
... do	Nov. —	Mar. 18, 1844	150	2,200	18,000	
Pacific Ocean	June 1	Mar. 15, 1843	500	1,500	12,000	
Crozette Island	Oct. —	May 4, 1843	250	1,700	13,600	Bought from Dorchester.
....do	Nov. —	Mar. 14, 1844	100	2,200	22,000	
New Zealand	July 1	May —, 1844	125	1,875	15,000	
Atlantic	July —	....	......	......	......	Condemned at Madeira 1841.
New Zealand	July 15	Oct. —, 1844	400	1,700	16,000	
Pacific Ocean	Nov. 30	May 3, 1845	1,450	40	.....	Built 1841.
....do	Oct. 25	Apr. 2, 1845	1,300	100	22,000	21,000 pounds bone on freight from ship Stonington, of New London.
New Holland	June 30	Aug. —, 1843	400	1,700	13,600	
Pacific Ocean	Aug. 5	May 21, 1844	600	......	.....	Bought from Boston 1841; sold to Fairhaven, 1844.
Indian Ocean	Aug. 16	Mar. —, 1845	900	......	....	Bought from New York 1841.
Atlantic	July 24	....	......	......	......	
Indian Ocean	July 30	Apr. 5, 1844	400	2,400	24,000	Sold, in 1845, to Sag Harbor; Hudson's last whaler.
Indian Ocean	July 30	June 24, 1844	700	1,600	13,000	Sold to New Bedford 1844.
Atlantic	Jan. 17	Oct. 14, 1842	150	150	.....	
....do	Jan. 6	....	......	......	......	Condemned and sold at Saint Thomas, March, 1842.
Crozette Island	Sept. 6	Dec. 10, 1843	100	2,900	30,000	Sold to Sag Harbor 1844.
N. W. Coast	July 20	May 9, 1844	......	......	.....	
Pacific Ocean	Aug. 1	—— —, 1845	......	......	.....	Sold; Wilmington's last whaler.
Indian Ocean	Dec. 18	June 4, 1844	1,300	900	31,000	
....do	Oct. 6 Nov. 28	Oct. 25, 1841 June 14, 1844	400	1,600	12,800	Returned once, small-pox having broken out among the crew. Sold to Greenport 1844.
South Atlantic	Dec. 7	Dec. 8, 1842	250	......	......	Withdrawn 1843.
Atlantic	Apr. 19	May 19, 1842	200	20	......	
Pacific Ocean	....	....	......	......	......	Fama sold on the voyage; had 600 sperm and 1,000 whale.

Table showing returns of whaling-vessels

Name of vessel.	Class.	Tonnage.	Captain.	Managing owner or agent.
1841.				
Boston, Mass.—Continued.				
Imogene	Brig	179	—— Atkins	G. & N. Sturtevant & Co.
Maine	do		S. Genn, jr	do
Dartmouth, Mass.				
Russell	Ship	387	—— Ray	Prince Sears
Bucksport, Me.				
Warwick	Schooner		—— Grogin	
Gloucester, Mass.				
Thorn	Schooner	114	—— Jewett	
1842.				
New Bedford, Mass.				
Agate	Brig	81	—— Cornell	Pope & Morgan
Alexander	Ship	421	—— Dornin	J. A. Parker
Amethyst	do	359	—— Reynard	J. A. Parker & Son
Augusta	do	344	—— Davis	William R. Rodman
Bogota	Brig	155	L. N. Fuller	I. H. Bartlett
Brighton	Ship	354	—— Cox	C. R. Tucker
Callao	do	324	—— Norton	Henry Tabor & Co
Cambria	do	362	—— Harding	James Arnold
California	do	398	George Lawrence, jr	I. Howland, jr., & Co
Caroline	do	364	—— McKenzie	Pardon G. Seabury
Charles Drew	do	344	—— Carey	William Gifford
Canton	do	409	—— Leary	J. Perry & Tillinghast
Chase	Bark	153	—— West	Barton Ricketson
Chas. Frederick	Ship	317	—— Allen	J. A. Parker & Son
Cicero	do	252	—— Taber	Lemuel Kollock
Copia	do	315	—— Taber	do
Cortes	do	382	—— Hammond	George Howland
Courier	do	381	—— Marchant	Randall & Haskell
Cornelia	Bark	216	—— Devoll	Lemuel Kollock
Charlestown Packet	do	184	—— Randall	Levi L. Crane
Coral	Ship	370	—— Seabury	Gideon Allen
Draper	do	291	—— Lawton	Joseph Dunbar & Co
Dragon	Bark	190	—— Clark	Tobey & Ricketson
Emily Morgan	Ship	368	P. W. Ewer	C. W. Morgan
Emma	Bark	246	—— Ball	Daniel Tripp
Enterprise	Ship	291	—— Bailey	Alfred Gibbs
Euphrates	do	365	—— Post	Lawrence Grinnell
Fenelon	do	328	—— Hathaway	B. B. Howard
Garland	Bark	234	—— Scranton	J. D. Thompson
Geo. Howland	Ship	374	—— Cushman	George Howland
Grand Turk	do	325	—— Taylor	Barton Ricketson
George and Martha	Bark	275	—— Smalley	Randall & Haskell
Hercules	Ship	335	—— Ricketson	Jireh Perry
Hibernia	do	327	—— Sanford	Alfred Gibbs
James	do	321	J. K. Turner	T. & A. R. Nye
Junius	Bark	198	Charles Church	Andrew Robeson
Jasper	do	223	—— Bennett	Alexander Gibbs
Jeannette	Ship	340	—— Mayhew	I. B. Richmond
June	Brig	123	—— Spooner	Barton Ricketson
Lancaster	Ship	383	—— Barker	T. & A. R. Nye
Leonidas	do	231	—— Nye	F. S. Hathaway

sailing from American ports—Continued.

Whaling-ground.	Date—Of sailing.	Date—Of arrival.	Result of voyage.—Sperm-oil.	Result of voyage.—Whale-oil.	Result of voyage.—Whalebone.	Remarks.
			Bbls.	*Bbls.*	*Lbs.*	
Atlantic	Jan. 25	May 3, 1842	400	80	......	
....do	Jan. 25	Apr. 26, 1842	400	......	......	
Pacific Ocean ..	Nov. 27	....	......	......	......	Bought from Newburgh.
West'n Islands	June 18	Sept. 10, 1842	110	......	......	Withdrawn.
Atlantic	Mar. 4	....	......	......	......	Bought from Boston; last reported December 28, 1841, at Havana.
Atlantic	Mar. 27	June —, 1843	300	50	......	
Pacific Ocean ..	Aug. 22	Jan. 26, 1846	2, 250	......	......	
Indian Ocean ..	Oct. 20	Feb. 18, 1844	55	2, 800	34, 000	
Pacific Ocean ..	July 11	....	......	......	......	Put into Rio Janeiro October, 1845, leaky. Condemned; oil (1,600 sperm) sent home.
Atlantic	June 7	....	120	......	......	Wrecked April 14, 1842, off the coast of Africa, and condemned at Zanzibar; oil sent home.
Indian Ocean ..	Aug. 2	July 28, 1844	115	2, 285	24, 000	
Pacific Ocean ..	Nov. 1	June 14, 1845	730	1, 750	......	Built at Mattapoisett 1842; sent home about 20,000 pounds bone.
....do	Dec. 23	June 26, 1846	2, 100	600	4, 000	
....do	May 21	Mar. 13, 1846	3, 000	......	......	Built 1842.
North W. Coast	Dec. 17	June 2, 1846	660	1, 340	12, 000	Built at Dartmouth 1842.
Pacific Ocean ..	July 14	Mar. 11, 1844	265	2, 885	28, 000	
Pacific Ocean ..	Nov. 23	Apr. 27, 1846	750	2, 000	6, 000	Captain Ripley died September, 1844.
Atlantic	Dec. 31	July 7, 1844	650	30	......	
Pacific Ocean ..	June 20	Apr. 18, 1846	2, 150	......	......	Sailed under Captain Smith April 12; returned May 28, and left him sick.
Indian Ocean ..	Aug. 20	May 18, 1844	......	1, 800	14, 500	
North W. Coast	Nov. 1	Feb. 25, 1845	200	3, 100	15, 000	Sent home 22,000 pounds bone
Pacific Ocean ..	June 30	July 21, 1846	1, 500	......	......	
....do	Oct. 4	June 20, 1846	700	800	......	
South Atlantic	May 17	Oct. 25, 1843	450	......	......	
Atlantic	Feb. 8	Apr. 15, 1844	300	500	4, 000	
Pacific Ocean ..	Nov. 16	Mar. 9, 1846	1, 900	1, 000	11, 000	
Indian Ocean ..	May 1	June 13, 1844	190	2, 050	20, 000	
....do	June 23	Apr. 25, 1844	140	1, 300	9, 000	
Pacific Ocean ..	Apr. 12	Apr. 27, 1846	1, 600	300	3, 000	
Atlantic	July 4	Apr. 4, 1844	50	1, 000	8, 000	
Pacific Ocean ..	Oct. 20	June 19, 1844	400	1, 950	16, 000	
....do	May 20	May 1, 1846	500	500	1, 400	Captain Post left ship at Valparaiso and returned home sick.
Indian Ocean ..	Sept. 1	Oct. 1, 1844	150	2, 550	19, 000	
Pacific Ocean ..	June 21	July 6, 1845	350	750	7, 000	
...do	May 20	Nov. 29, 1845	2, 500	......	......	
South Atlantic	Apr. 23	Sept. 10, 1842	......	80	......	Condemned and broken up at home, 1843.
Indian Ocean ..	Dec. 14	Apr. 3, 1845	200	1, 900	12, 000	
....do	Apr. 21	May 10, 1845	450	900	16, 000	
....do	June 21	Jan. 14, 1844	550	1, 400	14, 000	Returned lacking 500 barrels of being full, in consequence of a mutiny among her crew.
....do	Oct. 22	June 9, 1845	270	1, 600	20, 000	Captain Taber, of James, came home sick; built at Mattapoisett 1842; sold 400 whale at Rio Janeiro; shipped home 371 barrels sperm and 16,000 pounds bone.
Pacific Ocean ..	Dec. 6	May 19, 1845	750	......	......	Captain Church died at Callao January 30, 1845; formerly a brig; bought from Fall River and rerigged 1842.
Indian Ocean ..	June 1	Apr. 9, 1844	260	1, 000	10, 000	
....do	Apr. 29	May 19, 1845	1, 600	60	......	Bought from New York 1842.
Atlantic	Jan. 5	June 10, 1843	300	......	......	
Indian Ocean ..	July 7	Jan. 22, 1845	700	2, 000	20, 000	
Pacific Ocean ..	Jan. 11	May 28, 1845	700	25	......	

Table showing returns of whaling-vessels

Name of vessel.	Class.	Tonnage.	Captain.	Managing owner or agent.
1842.				
New Bedford, Mass.—Continued.				
Laurel	Brig	119	—— Smith	I. H. Bartlett
Liverpool	Ship	306	—— Slocum	Abraham Barker
Logan	do	302	—— Stott	I. Howland, jr., & Co
Lucas	do	281	—— Shockley	Tobey & Ricketson
Majestic	do	297	—— Hawes	Eddy & Thomas
Maria Theresa	do	330	—— Taber	T. & A. R. Nye
Mary Frazier	Bark	288	—— Smith	Abraham H. Howland
Mary	Ship	287	—— Nickerson	I. Howland, jr., & Co
Milton	do	388	—— Lewis	H. Taber & Co
Marcella	Bark	210	—— Ellis	C. R. Tucker
Milwood	do	254	—— Luce	Gideon Allen
Magnolia	Ship	396	—— Simmons	C. W. Morgan
Midas	do	326	—— Parker	John Coggeshall
Minerva	do	408	—— Macomber	William Gifford
Minerva	Bark	197	—— Horton	C. R. Tucker
Montpelier	Ship	320	—— Taber	John R. Thornton
Nautilus	do	340	—— Mason	Jireh Perry
Nimrod	do	346	—— Shearman	Barton Ricketson
Otranto	Bark	150	—— Coggeshall	Cranston Willcox
Phœnix	Ship	423	—— Bassett	John A. Parker
Pioneer	do	231	—— Tallman	J. D. Thompson
Pacific, 2d	do	332	—— Leavitt	Andrew Robeson
Roscoe	Bark	235	—— Bourne	Jona. Bourne, jr
Roman, 2d	Ship	350	Alexander Barker	Abraham Barker
Sally Ann	do	315	—— Borden	D. R. Greene & Co
Seine	do	281	—— Smith	Rodney French
St. Peter	do	267	—— Foster	J. B. Wood & Co
South Carolina	do	302	—— Stewart	Barton Ricketson
Tobacco Plant	do	371	Samuel P. Skinner	William R. Rodman
Triton	do	300	Reuben Chase, 2d	I. Howland, jr., & Co
Waverly	do	327	—— Munroe	do
Wm. Hamilton	do	463	—— Cole	do
W. Thompson	do	495	—— Ellis	Jireh Perry
Washington	do	344	James G. Coffin	Jona. Bourne, jr
Zoroaster	Brig	159	—— Seabury	Pardon G. Seabury
Fairhaven, Mass.				
Albion	Ship	328	—— Smith	E. Sawin
Arab	do	330	—— Harding	do
Bruce	Bark	148	—— Alden	Bradford, Fuller & Co
E. L. B. Jenney	Ship	386	John Church	Gibbs & Jenney
Eliza Adams	do	403	William Holley	Atkins Adams
Herald	do	262	—— Hathaway	Samuel Borden
Maine	do	294	—— Magee	E. Sawin
Mary Ann	do	335	—— Bonney	L. C. Tripp
South Boston	do	339	—— Crowell	E. Sawin
Wm. Wirt	do	387	—— Morse	Warren Delano
Falmouth, Mass.				
Brunette	Bark	187	—— Luce	Elijah Swift
Edgartown, Mass.				
Deborah	Brig	145	—— Worth	Joseph Mayhew
Gournet	Schooner	64	Samuel Tilton	Samuel Tilton
Rhine	Bark	174	—— Morse	John O. Morse
Sarah and Esther	do	159	—— Lambert	
Vesta	Brig	156	—— Smith	Benjamin Worth
Holmes' Hole, Mass.				
Macon	Ship	358	—— Merry	Thomas Bradley

sailing from American ports—Continued.

Whaling-ground.	Date— Of sailing.	Of arrival.	Result of voyage. Sperm-oil.	Whale-oil.	Whalebone.	Remarks.
			Bbls.	*Bbls.*	*Lbs.*	
Atlantic	Feb. 12	Oct. 27, 1842	266	8	....	
Indian Ocean	July 20	June 10, 1844	100	1,700	17,000	Second mate, George Coffin, killed by a whale July 5, 1843.
....do	May 14	Feb. 18, 1844	25	2,500	22,000	
....do	July 25	June —, 1843	150	2,000	16,000	
....do	July 22	June 2, 1844	350	2,650	24.000	Bought from Boston 1842.
....do	July 26	Dec. 10, 1844	100	2,650	9,000	Shipped home 20,000 pounds bone; lost third mate and three men in a gale May 14, 1845.
Pacific Ocean	Apr. 17	Apr. 14, 1846	800	1,900	19,000	Bought from Boston, 1842.
Indian Ocean	June 13	Apr. 4, 1844	480	1,920	19,000	
Pacific Ocean	May 28	May 8, 1844	120	2,780	7,000	Shipped home 15,700 pounds bone.
Indian Ocean	Apr. 15	Aug. 9, 1844	950	......	......	
....do	June 25	June 2, 1844	150	1,650	12,000	
North W. Coast	Nov. 9	Dec. 29, 1844	500	3,400	13,000	
Indian Ocean	May 26	Apr. 16, 1844	125	2,200	20,000	
North W. Coast	Nov. 2	May 19, 1844	280	2,420	8,000	
Indian Ocean	Apr. 6	Sept. —, 1843	150	270	......	
....do	Jan. 23	July 3, 1844	100	2,650	23,000	
Pacific Ocean	Oct. 4	....	......	......	......	Lost on Tumbez Bar October 9, 1843; cargo saved.
....do	Nov. 15	Jan. 5, 1845	150	2,500	10,000	Built at Dartmouth 1842; sent home 120 sperm, 15,500 bone.
Indian Ocean	Oct. 4	Sept. 10, 1844	707	......	......	
New Holland	Dec. 10	Apr. 10, 1847	900	1,800	900	Capt Bassett came home sick 1846.
Pacific Ocean	Oct. 4	May 19, 1844	240	1,560	7,000	Sent home 8,000 pounds bone.
Indian Ocean	Aug. 16	July 6, 1844	575	1,400	15,000	
... do	May 26	Mar. 18, 1844	150	1,950	20,000	Sent home 153 barrels sperm.
North W. Coast	June 25	June 28, 1844	260	2,200	28,000	
Indian Ocean	Sept. 3	June 2, 1844	100	1,600	12,800	
....do	Sept. 12	July 28, 1844	350	1,450	13,000	
Pacific Ocean	Oct. 4	July 22, 1846	700	1,000	10,000	
....do	June 30	Apr. 4, 1844	......	2,400	20,000	
....do	June 9	Mar. 15, 1846	1,250	......	......	
....do	Apr. 29	Apr. 26, 1846	700	......	......	
....do	Sept. 23	July 4, 1846	1,100	900	8,000	
North W. Coast	Aug. 29	Apr. 3, 1845	70	4,000	23,000	Sent home 8,000 pounds bone.
Pacific Ocean	Oct. 19	Apr. 8, 1846	1,050	3,150	14,000	Sent home 9,000 pounds bone.
Indian Ocean	Sept. 16	Oct. 14, 1844	180	1,900	18,000	Hiram H. Ashley, fourth mate, died at sea August 11, 1844.
Atlantic	Jan. 8	May 16, 1843	150	30	......	
Indian Ocean	Sept. 8	June 16, 1844	130	2,370	20,000	Captain Jenney killed by a whale March, 1844.
....do	Sept. 15	Oct. 2, 1845	1,400	700	6,000	
....do	July 17	Sept. 12, 1844	450	......	......	
Pacific Ocean	Nov. 23	June 28, 1846	2,400	......	......	Built at Fairhaven 1842.
....do	July 12	Dec. 23, 1845	2,100	200	......	
South Atlantic	Aug. 11	June 23, 1844	90	1,510	12,000	
Indian Ocean	Nov. 20	May 6, 1846	230	1,500	16,000	
Pacific Ocean	Oct. 10	July 30, 1846	1,800	......	......	
....do	Nov. 3	Feb. 10, 1845	175	2,725	26,000	
....do	Oct. 8	July 4, 1846	2,900	......	......	
Atlantic	July 11	Aug. —, 1843	300	20	......	Sold 1843 to United States.
Atlantic	May 11	July 17, 1843	60	......	......	Withdrawn 1844.
....do	Jan. 12	July 1, 1842	40	......	......	Withdrawn.
....do	Dec. 3	Sept. 21, 1845	400	......	......	Sold to New Bedford 1845.
New Holland	Jan. 1	Dec. 16, 1842	Clean	......	......	Sold to Greenport; built at Salisbury 1823.
Atlantic	Dec. 25	Sept. 9, 1844	350	......	......	
New Holland	Aug. 12	....	......	......	......	Wrecked February 22, 1844, on a reef off Fort George, Isle of France; oil mostly saved.

Table showing returns of whaling-vessels

Name of vessel.	Class.	Tonnage.	Captain.	Managing owner or agent.
1842.				
Nantucket, Mass.				
Alpha	Ship	345	John B. Rodgers	Hadwen & Barney
Clarkson	do	380	Jos. C. Chase	James Athearn
Constitution	do	318	Obed R. Bunker	C. G. & H. Coffin
Geo. Washington	Schooner		—— Pinkham	
James Loper	Ship	348	Jos. Congdon	Levi Starbuck
Jos. Starbuck	do	416	Charles A. Veeder	G. & M. Starbuck & Co
Lima	do	286	Obed Luce	William B. Coffin
Maria	do	365	Edward Jennings	Barrett & Upton
Mary Mitchell	do	354	Charles Lawrence	Aaron Mitchell
Napoleon	do	360	Elisha H. Fisher	Barrett & Upton
Phebe	do	379	Samuel W. Harris	C. Mitchell & Co
President	do	293	John C. Brock	Jos. Starbuck
Rose	do	349	William B. Swain	Simon Starbuck
Tyleston	Brig	111	—— Carr	A. W. Starbuck
Thule	do	286	Charles W. Coffin	Samuel B. Tuck
Young Hero	do	340	Peter Brock	Jos. Starbuck
Westport, Mass.				
Champion	Bark	209	—— Cook	Andrew Hicks
Catherwood	Brig	199	—— Boodry	Thomas W. Mayhew
Dr. Franklin	Bark	171	—— Francis	Job Davis
Harbinger	Ship	262	—— Gifford	Gideon Davis, jr
Juno	Brig	166	—— Sandford	A. B. Gifford
Mexico	do	130	—— Smith	Davis & Corey
Th. Winslow	do	126	—— Root	Thomas W. Mayhew
Theop. Chase	Bark	168	—— Baker	Henry Wilcox
Sippican, Mass.				
Pearl	Bark	157	—— Blankenship	J. S. Bates
Popmunnet	do	184	—— Flanders	do
Quito	Brig	140	—— Chase	do
Solon	do	129	—— Brightman	N. E. Bates
Mattapoisett, Mass.				
Dryade	Bark	263	—— Rogers	G. Barstow & Son
Edward	Brig	134	—— Tabor	Wilson Barstow
Joseph Meigs	Ship	338	Joseph R. Taber	Joseph Meigs
Mattapoisett	Brig	150	—— Purrington	Leonard Hammond
Sarah	Bark	171	—— Cushing	G. Barstow & Son
Willis	do	164	—— Daggett	R. L. Barstow
Wareham, Mass.				
America	Brig	148	—— Bellows	M. S. F. Tobey
Inga	do	169	—— Cudworth	do
Levant	Bark	219	—— Allen	do
Pleiades	do	261	—— Russell	do
Provincetown, Mass.				
Amazon	Schooner		—— Cook	
Belle Isle	do	104	{ —— Cook —— Smith }	Eben Cook
Carter Braxton	Ship	132	—— Sparks	Joseph Atkins
Franklin	Brig	172	—— Soper	Robert Soper

sailing from American ports—Continued.

Whaling-ground.	Date—		Result of voyage.			Remarks.
	Of sailing.	Of arrival.	Sperm-oil.	Whale-oil.	Whalebone.	
			Bbls.	*Bbls.*	*Lbs.*	
Pacific Ocean	May 15	Nov. 19, 1845	2,413	19		Third mate, Richard Ennis, killed by a whale.
....do	Sept. 18		1,825	12		Comdemned at Talcahuano; oil shipped home.
....do	Sept. 23	Feb. 12, 1847	1,842	41		First ship taken out by the "camels."
Atlantic		Aug. 17, 1842				No report.
Pacific Ocean	Oct. 30	May 6, 1846	2,358			
....do						Lost on Nantucket Bar; sold and broken up.
....do	May 31					Asa Gardner, third mate, lost 1842; condemned at Rio 1842, outward bound.
....do	May 11	May 20, 1846	1,706			
....do	Aug. 25	June 24, 1847	1,176	587		Sold to San Francisco. Lost in the Arctic 1851.
....do	Oct. 24	Nov. 25, 1845	2,495	19		
....do	Sept. 19		1,175	500		Put into Pernambuco December 24, 1846, leaking 290 strokes per hour, and was condemned. Shipped sperm-oil home by Bark Carolina of Boston. Sold 500 barrels whale-oil at Sydney and Pernambuco.
....do	Dec. 20	Apr. 8, 1847	1,170			
....do	Feb. 8	Mar. 10, 1846	1,650	250	2,500	
Atlantic	Oct. 2	Sept. 2, 1843	130	40		
Pacific Ocean	June 17					Lost on Booby Shoal, latitude 21½ south, longitude 159 east; mate and boat's crew lost.
....do	Apr. 17	Apr. 8, 1846	1,429			
Atlantic	Dec. 27	Aug. 1, 1844	350			
....do	June 6	Oct. 25, 1843	800			Bought from New York.
....do	July 18	July 28, 1843	630			
Indian Ocean	Aug. 3	Oct. 20, 1844	300	700	6,000	Bought from New York 1842.
Atlantic	Jan. 8	May 2, 1843	208	15		
....do	Aug. 31	June 30, 1843	236			
Indian Ocean	Dec. 17	Feb. 26, 1845				Sent home 100 sperm.
Atlantic	Dec. 26	Aug. 26, 1844	550			
Pacific Ocean	Jan. 12					Lost on Japan ground August 11, 1843; 6 of her crew lost with her.
Atlantic	Feb. 20	Sept. 23, 1843	350	60		
....do	May 17	Oct. —, 1842	270	30		
....do	Oct. 26	Nov. —, 1843	250			Sold to Mattapoisett 1844.
Indian Ocean	Aug. 13	July 24, 1844	450	1,450	14,000	Sold to New Bedford 1844.
Atlantic	Mar. 28	Aug. —, 1843	420			
Indian Ocean	Oct. 8	June 20, 1844	600	2,500	600	Built at Mattapoisett 1842; sent home 160 whale, 18,000 pounds bone.
Atlantic	Oct. 26	May 30, 1844	50	70		
....do	May 21	Nov. —, 1843	330	270		
....do	Apr. 24	Aug. —, 1843	650	50		First mate killed by a whale 1844.
Atlantic	Nov. 23	May 19, 1844	150			
....do	June 21	Apr. 9, 1843	750			
Pacific Ocean	Oct. 6					Condemned at Honolulu 1847.
....do	Dec. 14	Feb. 18, 1845	300	2,000	16,000	
Atlantic	June 20	Aug. 4, 1842		50		
....do {	Jan. 7	Aug. 4, 1842	380			
	Oct. 4	Sept. —, 1843	340	20		
....do	Feb. 10	Apr. 29, 1843	250			
....do	Mar. 8	Jan. 24, 1843	500			

Table showing returns of whaling-vessels

Name of vessel.	Class.	Tonnage.	Captain.	Managing owner or agent.
1842.				
Provincetown, Mass.—Continued.				
Fairy	Bark	186	—— Genn	Abraham Small
Joshua Brown	Schooner	113	—— Small	Seth Nickerson
John B. Dods	Brig	163	—— Prior	E. S. Smith
Louisa	Schooner	98	—— Cook	Samuel Cook
Phenix	Brig	150	—— Small	Leonard Small
Pacific	do	130	—— Cook	Stephen Cook, jr
Spartan	Bark	188	—— Small	Stephen Nickerson
Samuel and Thomas	Brig	191	—— Soper	Samuel Soper
Wm. Henry	Schooner	111	{ —— Ryder —— Cook }	Godfrey Ryder
Plymouth, Mass.				
Exchange	Schooner	99	—— King	Richard W. Holmes
Jas. Munroe	Brig	114	—— Strickland	Isaac L. Hedge
Mercury	Schooner	74	—— Winslow	Isaac Barnes, jr
Vesper	do	95	—— Hammond	Bradford Barnes, jr
Newburyport, Mass.				
Merrimack	Ship	414	—— Howe	Micajah Lunt
Boston, Mass.				
Cambrian	Bark	197	—— Holmes	P. & S. Sprague & Co
Carib	Brig	162	—— James	William V. Kent
Byron	do	....	—— Cook	do
Imogene	Bark	180	—— Russell	E. Atkins
Maine	Brig	174	—— Genn	N. Sturtevant
Lynn, Mass.				
Com. Preble	Ship	323	—— Ludlow	F. S. Newhall
Ninus	do	260	—— Woolley	Isaiah Breed
Salem, Mass.				
Malay	Bark	268	—— Lakeman	Stephen C. Phillips
Statesman	do	258	Elisha Doane	John B. Osgood
Somerset, Mass.				
Pilgrim	Brig	137	—— Collins	Wheaton Luther
Fall River, Mass.				
Holder Borden	Ship	442	—— Pell	Nathan Durfee
Leonidas	Brig	128	—— Baker	Noah Hathaway
Panama	Ship	253	—— Cummings	William Coggeshall
Pantheon	Bark	284	—— Borden	John Eddy
Portsmouth, N. H.				
Ann Parry	Bark	348	—— Bennett	James Kennard
Providence, R. I.				
Hope	Ship	471	—— Heath	Pearce & Bullock
Bristol, R. I.				
Corinthian	Ship	503	—— Easterbrook	William H. D'Wolf
Essex	do	200	—— Devoll	William R. Taylor
Gen. Jackson	do	329	—— Ramsdell	William H. D'Wolf
Gov. Hopkins	Brig	111	—— Morris	William R. Taylor
Moro Castle	do	....	—— Waldron	

sailing from American ports—Continued.

Whaling-ground.	Date—		Result of voyage.			Remarks.
	Of sailing.	Of arrival.	Sperm-oil.	Whale-oil.	Whalebone.	
			Bbls.	*Bbls.*	*Lbs.*	
Atlantic	Mar. 18	June 12, 1843	300	30	......	Formerly a brig; rerigged 1842.
....do	Mar. 29	June 2, 1843	220	40	......	
....do	Mar. 23	Aug. 1, 1843	200	100	......	
....do	June 19	Oct. —, 1843	......	300	......	
....do	Mar. 6	Feb. 26, 1843	320	......	......	
....do	Apr. 12	June 26, 1843	235	50	......	Built 1842.
....do	July 20	Oct. —, 1843	700	80	......	Built 1841.
....do	Feb. 10	Mar. 8, 1843	700	......	......	
... do	Feb. 28	Sept. 19, 1842	300	50	......	
	Dec. 14	July —, 1843	340	......	......	
Atlantic	Dec. 15	Sept. 25, 1843	160	......	......	Dismasted in a gale September 2; lost a 100-barrel whale from alongside, and 50 barrels of oil from on deck.
... do	July 11	....	80	......	......	Condemned at Bahia December 10, 1843; oil shipped home.
....do	Jan. 26	Sept. 13, 1842	150	......	...	Lost; capsized at sea June 21, 1843.
	Nov. 26	....	......	......	...	
....do	Sept. 6	Aug. 9, 1843	130	......	......	Withdrawn 1843.
Pacific Ocean	Jan. 25	Apr. 15, 1844	260	2, 750	22, 000	Sold to New London 1844.
Atlantic	June 3	June 14, 1843	120	70	560	Withdrawn from the service 1844.
....do	June 10	Nov. 1, 1843	250	......	......	Withdrawn from the service 1842.
....do	Jan. 8	Apr. —, 1843	200	......	......	Sold to Stonington.
....do	June 30	Nov. —, 1843	350	......	......	Withdrawn 1844.
....do	June 15	Sept. 19, 1843	420	80	......	Returned having lost two boats and received other damage in gale of September 2.
Indian Ocean	Aug. 29	....	......	......	......	
....do	July 28	July 12, 1844	100	1, 400	11, 000	
Indian Ocean	Mar. 26	....	......	......	......	Lost in Mozambique Channel July, 1842.
Pacific Ocean	June 12	....	500	......	......	Comdemned at Talcahuano November, 1844.
Atlantic	July 7	July —, 1843	280	......	......	
Indian Ocean	Nov. 10	....	......	......	......	Lost April 13, 1844, about latitude 24°. 57′ north, longitude 174°. 09′ west; fourth mate killed by a blackfish September, 1843.
Atlantic	June 23	Aug. —, 1843	250	15	......	
Indian Ocean	Apr. 11	....	......	......	......	Wrecked on Island of Dominica (Marquesas) 1844; vessel and cargo (900 barrels oil) a total loss.
....do	Nov. 26	May 25, 1845	100	2, 400	23, 000	
South Atlantic	Oct. 21	July 13, 1845	2, 000	......	......	Rerigged 1842.
Indian Ocean	Sept. 15	May 20, 1845	150	3, 450	30, 000	Lost early in 1847.
Pacific Ocean	Nov. 9	Apr. 13, 1846	700	2, 000	6, 000	
Atlantic	Feb. 1	....	......	......	......	Comdemned at Montevideo January, 1843.
Pacific Ocean	Jan. 23	Oct. 24, 1845	1, 000	......	......	Sold 1847.
Atlantic	Apr. 11	June 2, 1842	70	......	......	
....do	July 7	....	......	......	......	Dismasted; carried into Rio December, 1842, by an English man-of-war, and condemned there; had 100 sperm.

Table showing returns of whaling-vessels

Name of vessel.	Class.	Tonnage.	Captain.	Managing owner or agent.
1842.				
Warren, R. I.				
Galen	Ship	365	—— Bowers	Driscol & Child
Hector	Bark	225	William Martin	R. B. Johnson
Lafayette	Ship	341	—— Bowen	Coffin & G. T. Gardner
Montgomery	do	135	—— Martin	Stephen Martin
North America	do	285	—— Grinnell	Driscol & Child
Rosalie	do	323	—— Mosher	Jos. Smith
Triton	do	345	—— Saunders	S. P. Child
Newport, R. I.				
Damon	Bark	...	Oliver Potter	Silas H. Cotterell
Helen	Brig	120	—— Price	William Price
Mechanic	Ship	335	—— Pratt	Thomas Bush
Sea Bird	Brig	143	—— Barney	Gilbert Chase
Stonington, Conn.				
America	Ship	464	—— Hubbard	Charles P. Williams
Charles Phelps	do	362	—— Hall	do
Corvo	do	349	—— Pendleton	do
Enterprise, (sealer)	Brig	95	—— Fish	do
Fellowes	Ship	268	—— Brewster	do
Mercury	do	305	—— Gray	Joseph E. Smith
Thomas Williams	do	340	—— Manwarring	Charles P. Williams
United States	do	244	—— Barnum	John F. Trumbull
Mystic, Conn.				
Aeronaut	Ship	265	—— Mallory	Charles Mallory
Bingham	do	375	—— Destin	do
Congress	Bark	280	—— Lester	J. & William P. Randall
Meteor	Ship	325	—— Burrows	do
Romulus	do	233	—— Rogers	
Shepherdess	do	274	—— Clift	J. & William P. Randall
New London, Conn.				
Armata	Ship	299	—— Pendleton	Abner Bassett
Betsey	Schooner	125	—— Perkins	Joseph Lawrence
Black Warrior	Ship	231	—— Sisson	Havens & Smith
Candace	do	310	—— Reed	do
Columbia	do	492	—— Smith	do
Commodore Perry	Bark	270	—— Hampsted	Frink, Chew & Co
Columbus	Brig	159	—— Avery	Williams & Barnes
Charles Henry	Ship	265	—— Jeffrey	Havens & Smith
Ceres	Bark	176	—— Bailey	William Tate
Dove	do	145	—— Peabody	Havens & Smith
Franklin	Schooner	119	—— Allen	Perkins & Smith
Halcyon	Bark	258	—— Lee	Havens & Smith
Hand	Schooner	86	—— Long	do
Helvetia	Ship	332	—— Rice	Joseph Lawrence
Indian Chief	do	401	—— Skinner	Frink, Chew & Co
Jason	do	235	—— Harris	do
John and Elizabeth	do	296	—— Miller	Havens & Smith
Mogul	do	395	—— Mallory	Williams & Barnes
Neptune	do	285	—— Green	Havens & Smith
North America	do	388	—— Destin	do
Pembroke	Bark	199	—— Tate	Joseph Lawrence
Phœnix	Ship	404	—— Slate	N. & W. W. Billings
Robert Bourne	do	505	—— Fitch	do
Stonington	do	351	—— Harnley	Williams & Barnes

*Seal and

sailing from American ports—Continued.

Whaling-ground.	Date—Of sailing.	Date—Of arrival.	Result of voyage.—Sperm-oil.	Result of voyage.—Whale-oil.	Result of voyage.—Whalebone.	Remarks.
			Bbls.	*Bbls.*	*Lbs.*	
Pacific Ocean ..	Dec. 8	....	......	......	......	Wrecked at Fox Bay, Falkland Islands, February 20, 1846, with 1,800 barrels of oil; vessel a total loss; cargo partly saved.
... do	Aug. 3	Apr. 6, 1845	900	......	......	Built 1842.
Indian Ocean ..	Jan. 14	Dec. 10, 1844	1,500	......	......	
....do	July 13	Sept. —, 1843	40	......	......	
... do	June 12	....	......	......	......	Lost at Swan River, New South Wales, April 15, 1842; oil, 400 barrels, saved.
Pacific Ocean ..	Aug. 2	Apr. —, 1845	500	1,600	16,000	Sailed in 1846, and was condemned 1850; had sold 350 sperm at Maui, and sent 132 sperm home.
New Zealand ..	Jan. 23	Nov. 1, 1844	150	2,250	18,000	Brought home 2,000 pounds of bone; had sent 16,000 pounds home.
South Seas	Oct. 20	Apr. 25, 1846	200	......	......	Shipped home 631 barrels sperm.
Atlantic	Mar. 15	June 2, 1843	350	50	......	
Pacific Ocean ..	Sept. 22	July 3, 1846	1,200	200	2,000	
Atlantic	Oct. 9	....	......	......	......	Condemned in Patagonia September, 1843.
Pacific Ocean ..	Aug. 23	May 8, 1844	150	2,600	20,800	Bought from Hudson 1842.
N. W. Coast....	Aug. 29	Mar. 30, 1844	160	2,540	25,000	
South Seas.....	June 20	Feb. 26, 1845	460	3,040	25,000	
Coast of Chili..	Aug. —	May 30, 1844	(*)	(*)	(*)	
Pacific Ocean ..	Jan. 18	Mar. 31, 1845	1,000	500	4,000	Sent home 400 barrels sperm.
South Atlantic	July 11	Apr. 8, 1844	200	2,100	18,000	
South Seas....	June 20	Feb. —, 1845	200	2,800	10,000	Sent home 20,000 pounds bone.
....do	Apr. 27	Apr. —, 1843	60	2,000	......	
South Seas.....	July —	July 13, 1843	60	1,340	10,700	
...do	Aug. —	Feb. 17, 1844	175	2,150	21,500	
South Atlantic	Aug. 13	July 19, 1844	......	1,900	15,000	
....do	July 14	June 19, 1844	......	2,000	17,000	
South Seas	July 14	Apr. —, 1845	70	2,930	25,000	
South Atlantic.	Apr. 30	July 12, 1844	230	1,460	12,000	Second mate, Thomas Scanell, died July 17, 1843.
Indian Ocean...	Sept. 7	Mar. 7, 1844	200	2,750	28,000	
Sealing	July 18	....	......	120	......	
South Seas.....	Oct. 26	Mar. 3, 1845	490	1,330	11,000	Bought from Salem 1842.
Indian Ocean ..	Oct. 1	Mar. 30, 1845	53	1,450	4,700	Second mate killed by a whale.
South Atlantic.	July 13	Apr. 8, 1844	......	4,200	7,000	Mostly elephant-oil.
South Seas.....	July 13	May 25, 1844	......	1,800	14,400	
Atlantic	Nov. 12	Apr. 5, 1844	......	450	.....	
South Atlantic.	July 2	July 16, 1843	200	1,600	15,000	
....do	Aug. 15	Sept. 1, 1844	170	800	8,000	
South Seas.....	Apr. 20	Mar. 18, 1844	100	1,000	8,000	Bought from Boston 1842.
Crozettes	Aug. 13	Apr. 8, 1844	......	600	......	The Franklin was a tender and brought elephant-oil.
South Atlantic	Feb. 18	June —, 1843	......	350	2,800	Returned June 15, 1843, crew having mutinied. Formerly a brig; rerigged 1842. Bought from Boston.
South Seas.....	June 29	Apr. 10, 1844	......	300	......	
N. W. Coast ...	July 13	Apr. 5, 1844	300	2,600	26,000	Bought from Hudson 1842.
Indian Ocean ..	Oct. 1	Apr. 5, 1844	150	2,650	28,000	
South Atlantic.	Aug. 12	May 31, 1844	......	1,900	15,000	
Indian Ocean ..	June 20	May 23, 1844	......	2,450	19,600	
N. W. Coast....	Oct. 3	July 22, 1844	400	2,800	26,000	
Indian Ocean ..	June 20	June 23, 1844	170	1,830	18,000	
New Zealand...	Aug. 13	Apr. 4, 1844	100	2,600	26,000	
South Seas.....	June 15	June 24, 1843	200	950	6,000	
South Atlantic.	July 20	Feb. 28, 1844	350	2,350	18,800	
Pacific Ocean ..	Oct. 5	Feb. 25, 1845	200	4,600	40,000	
Indian Ocean ..	June 11	June 29, 1843	......	1,950	......	

other skins.

Table showing returns of whaling-vessels

Name of vessel.	Class.	Tonnage.	Captain.	Managing owner or agent.
1842.				
New London, Conn.—Continued.				
Superior	Ship	406	—— Hart	N. & W. W. Billings
Shaw Perkins	Sloop	55	—— Stroud	Havens & Smith
Tenedos	Bark	245	—— Chester	Joseph Lawrence
Bridgeport, Conn.				
Atlantic	Ship	291	—— Youngs	Sherwood Sterling
Harvest	Bark	263	do	do
Sag Harbor, N. Y.				
Acasta	Ship	286	—— Havens	Mulford & Sleight
Alciope	do	377	—— Paine	Post & Sherry
American	do	284	—— Cooper	S. & B. Hunting & Co
Ann Mary Ann	do	380	—— Winters	Mulford & Sleight
Barbara	Bark	260	—— Howes	Charles T. Dering
Gem	Ship	326	—— Worth	Hunting Cooper
Hamilton	do	322	—— Ludlow	Charles T. Dering
Hannibal	do	311	—— Bennett	S. & B. Hunting & Co
Henry Lee	do	409	—— Bennett	do
Hudson	do	368	—— Nickerson	Luther D. Cook
Huron	do	290	—— Green	do
John Jay	do	494	—— Rogers	N. & G. Howell
Nimrod	do	280	—— Howes	Charles T. Dering
Ontario	do	368	—— Greene	S. & B. Hunting & Co.
Phenix	do	314	—— Briggs	L. D. Cook
Portland	do	292	—— Paine	S. & B. Hunting & Co
Romulus	do	233	—— Case	Mulford & Howell
Superior	Bark	275	—— Cartwright	Post & Sherry
Timor	Ship	289	—— Eldridge	Hunting Cooper
Tuscany	do	299	—— Godbey	John Budd
Cold Spring, N. Y.				
Monmouth	Bark	250	—— Hedges	John H. Jones
Greenport, N. Y.				
Roanoke	Bark	252	—— Case	Wiggins & Parsons
1843.				
New Bedford, Mass.				
Abigail	Ship	310	D. Barnard	C. W. Morgan
Adeline	do	329	—— Cole	I. Howland, jr., & Co
Agate	Brig	81	—— Vincent	Barton Ricketson
America	Ship	418	—— Fisher	I. Howland, jr., & Co
Benjamin Tucker	do	349	—— Sands	Charles R. Tucker
Brandt	do	310	—— Sampson	Alexander Gibbs
Barclay	do	281	—— Grinnell	James Arnold
Braganza	do	470	—— Waterman	Pope & Morgan
Brunswick	do	295	—— Almy	Barton Ricketson
Canada	do	545	—— Topham	do
China	do	370	—— Potter	William Phillips
Corinthian	do	401	J. Munckley	George Howland
Cherokee	Bark	261	—— Devoll	Hathaway & Luce
Cornelia	do	216	—— Flanders	Lemuel Kollock
Chili	Ship	291	R. W. Dexter	B. B. Howard
Congress	do	339	—— Weeks	Edward C. Jones
Draco	Bark	257	J. V. Cox	Jona. Bourne, jr
Desdemona	Ship	295	M. Baker	T. & A. R. Nye
Endeavour	Bark	252	—— Taber	C. R. Tucker
Emerald	Ship	359	—— Cathcart	Riddell & Dix
Equator	Bark	263	T. Mathews	John A. Standish

sailing from American ports—Continued.

Whaling-ground.	Date— Of sailing.	Of arrival.	Result of voyage. Sperm-oil.	Whale-oil.	Whalebone.	Remarks.
			Bbls.	*Bbls.*	*Lbs.*	
Pacific Ocean ..	Sept. 28	Apr. 10, 1844	.....	......	......	
South Seas. ..	June 29	Apr. 10, 1844	.....	115	.....	
Crozette Island.	Sept. 6	July 8, 1844	100	1,000	9,000	
South Seas....	Aug. —	May 4, 1844	180	1,520	15,000	Sold to Mystic 1844.
....do	July —	Apr. 24, 1844	.....	2,300	18,000	
South Seas....	Aug. 29	June 20, 1844	......	1,600	13,000	
Crozette Island.	Sept. 11	May 19, 1844	170	2,830	25,000	Bought from Boston 1842.
... do	July 18	—— —, 1843	50	1,000	6,000	
South Seas....	Nov. 25	May 27, 1845	75	2,600	23,000	
...do	May 31	July 6, 1843	400	900	7,200	Formerly a brig; rerigged 1842.
Crozette Island.	Sept. 1	Aug. 5, 1843	......	2,200	22,000	
South Seas ...	July 14	May 24, 1844	350	2,050	18,000	
Crozette Island.	Aug. 4	—— —, 1843	50	1,000	6,000	
....do	Sept. 2	Feb. 17, 1845	100	2,800	28,000	
South Seas....	Oct. 11	Apr. 14, 1844	......	2,450	23,000	
South Atlantic	Aug. 20	Aug. —, 1843	......	1,200	......	
Crozette Island	Oct. 7	Feb. 10, 1845	500	4,000	40,000	Third mate, Johiel Penny, killed by a whale June 28, 1843; bought from Portsmouth 1842.
South Seas.....	Aug. 28	July —, 1843	100	1,000	8,000	
Indian Ocean ..	June 30	July 8, 1844	80	3,220	27,000	
....do	July 30	July 28, 1844	.....	2,500	18,000	
Crozette Island	Aug. 4	Apr. 14, 1844	.....	2,500	25,000	
South Seas....	June 22	Aug. —, 1843	130	950	......	
....do	July —	June 10, 1843	.....	1,100	8,600	
Crozette Island	Sept. 27	Apr. 26, 1844	......	2,500	25,000	Bought from Boston 1842.
... do	Oct. 7	Feb. 26, 1845	......	3,300	30,000	Bought from Philadelphia 1842.
South Atlantic	Aug. 13	July —, 1843	75	1,550	12,400	
South Seas....	Oct. 1	Apr. 18, 1844	100	1,800	15,000	
Pacific Ocean ..	Nov. 27	July 26, 1847	1,400	250	2,000	
N. W. Coast...	May 25	Apr. 27, 1846	140	2,800	......	Sent home 600 whale.
Atlantic	July 20	....	60	......	......	Lost on Isle of Sal, Cape de Verdes, December 29, 1844; oil shipped home.
Ind. and Pacific	June 13	July 13, 1845	400	4,200	43,000	
Pacific Ocean ..	Nov. 20	Feb. 22, 1846	150	2,500	10,000	Sent home 750 sperm and 23,000 pounds bone.
South Seas ...	May 20	June 22, 1846	500	500	......	
Pacific Ocean ..	Dec. 12	July 9, 1844	.....	......	......	Returned July 9, 1844, with captain sick; sold again; Captain Mann took Captain Grinnell's place July 20, 1844.
P. and N. W ...	Aug. 1	May 6, 1846	400	3,400	14,000	Sailed under Captain Edward Gardner, who came home sick, 1846; sent home about 40 barrels whale.
Indian Ocean .	Nov. 6	June 3, 1846	250	2,350	7,000	Sent home some bone.
N. W. Coast .	Jan. 1	Apr. 8, 1846	350	2,800	3,000	
Ind. and Pacific	June 15	Oct. 30, 1845	800	1,600	15,000	
Pacific Ocean .	Nov. 12	May 21, 1847	2,70[illegible]	.....	......	
Indian Ocean ..	June 8	June 7, 1846	550	2,100	6,000	
....do	Dec. 12	Apr. 27, 1846	600	400	3,000	
....do	June 28	May 19, 1845	400	1,900	23,000	
Pacific and Ind	Dec. 8	Feb. 22, 1846	50[illegible]	1,950	16,000	Bought from Nantucket, 1843; sent home 600 sperm and 8,000 pounds bone.
Pacific Ocean ..	Dec. 18	Apr. 16, 1847	1,650	......	......	Bought from Fairhaven 1843.
....do	Oct. 18	July 21, 1846	1,800	......	......	
Indian Ocean ..	Aug. 10	May 24, 1847	100	1,600	15,000	
Pacific Ocean ..	Nov. 28	July 9, 1847	1,400	100	......	
....do	Oct. 10	May 19, 1847	1,400	......	......	

Table showing returns of whaling-vessels

Name of vessel.	Class.	Tonnage.	Captain.	Managing owner or agent.
1843.				
New Bedford, Mass.—Continued.				
Falcon	Ship	273	—— Richmond	Wilcox & Richmond
Florida	...do	330	—— Cunningham	E. C. Jones
Frances	...do	348	E. Gardner	J. Arnold
Frances Henrietta	...do	407	—— Dexter	C. W. Morgan
Franklin	Bark	218	—— Winslow	West & Paine
Franklin	Ship	333	—— Chadwick	Abm. H. Howland
Gen. Pike	...do	313	—— Pierce	William Gifford
George	...do	273	—— M'Cleeve	J. A. Parker & Son
George Porter	...do	285	E. A. Arthur	Riddell & Dix
G. Washington	Bark	230	—— Taylor	Charles Hitch
Golconda	Ship	331	—— Howland	George Howland
Herald, 2d	...do	303	—— Mayhew	T. & A. R. Nye
Hector	...do	380	George Manter	C. W. Morgan
Hercules, 2d	...do	290	—— Marvell	D. R. Greene & Co
Hope	...do	316	—— Tucker	George Howland
Hope	Bark	186	—— Taylor	William Watkins
Honqua	Ship	339	—— Brown	Alex. Gibbs
India	...do	366	—— Walker	A. H. Howland
Iris	...do	311	G. B. Spooner	E. C. Jones
Isaac Howland	...do	399	—— Fisher	I. Howland, jr., & Co
Israel	...do	357	—— Finch	B. B. Howard
Java	...do	278	—— Shockley	George Howland
John Howland	...do	377	—— Leary	J. & J. Howland
Juno	Brig	103	—— Spooner	B. Ricketson
Lagoda	Ship	341	Henry Colt	Jona. Bourne, jr
Lucas	...do	281	—— Borden	Edward W. Howland
Mercator	...do	246	—— Cook	John A. Parker
Maria	Bark	203	—— Coffin	Samuel W. Rodman
Milo	Ship	398	—— Gardner	And. Robeson
Minerva	Bark	195	—— King	C. R. Tucker
Messenger	Ship	291	—— Downs	John R. Thornton
Mount Vernon	...do	352	G. A. Covell	D. R. Greene & Co
Newton	...do	28[illegible]	—— Sawyer	J. Bourne, jr
Navy	...do	356	—— Smith	J. B. Wood & Co
Octavia	...do	257	—— Barker	Gideon Allen
Orozimbo	...do	588	—— Bartlett	B. Ricketson
Peri	Bark	191	—— Jose	Rodney French
Phocion	Ship	260	P. Butler	J. R. Thornton
Ploughboy	...do	391	S. Clark	T. & A. R. Nye
Parachute	...do	331	—— Cole	B. B. Howard
Persia	Bark	240	—— Whippey	Lemuel Kollock
Roscoe	Ship	362	—— McCleeve	A. Robeson
Rodman	...do	371	—— Newcomb	C. W. Morgan
Roman	...do	375	—— Shockley	Edw. C. Jones
Roscius	Bark	306	—— Hazard	William P. Howland
St. George	Ship	408	—— Thomas	Abraham Barker
Statira	...do	34[illegible]	—— Adams	Hathaway & Luce
Sarah Louisa	Brig	144	—— Plaskett	William R. Rodman
Trident	Ship	449	—— Black	J. A. Parker & Son
Timoleon	...do	340	W. Plasket	J. Dunbar & Co.
Two Sisters	Brig	12[illegible]	—— Maxfield	Frederick P. Shaw
Uncas	Ship	413	—— Gelett	A. H. Howland
Virginia	...do	340	Jos. T. Chase	Hathaway & Luce

sailing from American ports—Continued.

Whaling-ground.	Date—		Result of voyage.			Remarks.
	Of sailing.	Of arrival.	Sperm-oil.	Whale-oil.	Whalebone.	
			Bbls.	*Bbls.*	*Lbs.*	
Ind. and N. W	July 17	May 23, 1846	200	1,400	8,000	
Indian Ocean ..	Aug. 16	Mar. 13, 1846	350	1,850	17,000	Captain Cunningham and one man drowned October, 1844.
Pacific Ocean ..	Nov. 1	July 20, 1847	1,300	......	......	Captain Gardner returned sick, 1846; sent home 830 sperm.
P. and N. W ...	Aug. 12	May 20, 1845	600	2,000	20,000	Third mate and two men lost; boat stove by a whale, 1844.
Pacific Ocean ..	Aug. 29	Sept. 25, 1845	1,340	......	......	
Ind. and Pacific	Apr. 20	May 26, 1846	300	1,850	15,000	
N. W. Coast	Sept. 9	Sept. 20, 1845	300	2,300	22,000	
Pacific Ocean ..	Aug. 21	May 28, 1847	1,500	300	2,000	
....do	Sept. 19	Mar. 3, 1847	1,400	......	......	Temporarily withdrawn, 1847; sent home 200 sperm.
Indian Ocean ..	June 6	July 2, 1845	750	450	......	
Pacific Ocean ..	Sept. 2	June 6, 1847	1,400	200	......	
....do	July 5	June 5, 1847	900	100	......	
....do	Dec. 18	Oct. 28, 1847	1,700	......	......	
South Seas	Aug. 1	Mar. 1, 1845	400	400	3,200	
Pacific Ocean ..	Dec. 18	....	......	......	......	Wrecked and condemned at Bay of Islands September, 1848; had 1,600 sperm, 300 whale, which was saved.
Indian Ocean ..	Jan. 17	July 31, 1847	1,300	......	......	Mr. Williams, first mate, died at sea January, 1846.
N. W. Coast	Sept. 1	Apr. 13, 1846	75	2,925	13,000	
Ind. and Pacific	May 11	Apr. 9, 1845	......	3,200	30,000	
Pacific Ocean ..	Nov. 7	Feb. 26, 1847	1,100	700	......	
Indian Ocean ..	July 11	Feb. 4, 1845	120	3,280	32,000	Dismasted in a gale off Elizabeth Islands February 4, 1845, on passage home.
....do	Dec. 5	May 12, 1846	185	2,700	28,000	
Ind. and Pacific	June 24	Apr. 3, 1845	60	2,240	25,000	
Pacific Ocean ..	Aug. 23	Apr. 22, 1847	2,200	70	......	
Atlantic	July 24	....	......	......	......	Condemned and sold at St. Catharines April, 1845; bought by parties in Sippican.
N. W. Coast	Nov. 8	May 26, 1846	120	3,080	14,000	
Crozettes	July 10	....	......	......	......	Lost at Fort Dauphin, Madagascar, March 9, 1845; had 1,700 barrels whale-oil; saved 900.
Indian Ocean ..	June 20	Sept. 11, 1845	750	850	5,000	
....do	Nov. 12	May 20, 1846	900	......	......	
Pacific Ocean ..	May 11	May 19, 1846	369	2,500	7,000	Sold 150 whale at Callao. Sent home 600 whale.
Indian Ocean ..	Dec. 18	May 6, 1846	1,000	......	......	Sent home 36 sperm.
Pacific Ocean ..	July 29	Apr. 7, 1847	1,400	300	2,500	
N. W. Coast	Nov. 23	May 21, 1846	270	2,230	20,000	
....do	Nov. 25	May 22, 1846	60	2,300	7,500	Crew mutinied at Oahu; new crew shipped; Captain Sawyer died at San Diego December, 1844.
Ind. and N. W .	Sept. 12	May 28, 1845	300	2,800	25,000	
Ind. and Pacific	Aug. 1	Sept. 11, 1845	550	850	6,500	
Indian Ocean ..	July 13	May 15, 1845	100	3,640	37,000	
....do	Aug. 22	Dec. 19, 1845	650	......	......	
....do	Sept. 19	Apr. 24, 1846	80	1,400	......	
Pacific Ocean ..	Oct. 19	Nov. 28, 1847	2,200	50	.....	Bought from Nantucket.
N. W. Coast	May 24	July 9, 1845	100	2,400	26,000	
Ind. and Pacific	July 20	Apr. 27, 1846	100	1,600	9,000	
Pacific Ocean ..	Sept. 14	Apr. 4, 1847	1,900	250	2,000	
....do	Aug. 15	May 11, 1847	2,400	......	......	
Ind. and N. W	July 19	Apr. 27, 1847	100	2,550	24,000	Sold 760 whale at Bahia; sent home 65 sperm, 9,866 pounds bone.
Pacific Ocean ..	Nov. 23	May 6, 1846	975	800	7,000	Bought from Boston 1843.
N. W. Coast	July 11	July 9, 1847	150	2,950	6,000	Added 1843; sent home 23,932 pounds bone.
....do	Aug. 24	July 31, 1845	250	2,750	26,000	Bought from Nantucket.
South Atlantic	Sept. 21	Mar. —, 1846	130	......	......	
Pacific Ocean ..	June 8	Sept. 13, 1846	120	......	......	
N. W. Coast	Oct. 9	July 12, 1845	500	30	8,800	
....	May 7	....	......	......	......	Lost in Union Bay, Patagonia, September 21, 1843.
Ind. and N. W .	Aug. 5	Apr. 13, 1846	50	3,950	16,000	
Pacific Ocean ..	Nov. 7	June 5, 1847	2,050	......	......	

Table showing returns of whaling-vessels

Name of vessel.	Class.	Tonnage.	Captain.	Managing owner or agent.
1843.				
New Bedford, Mass.—Continued.				
William Rotch	Ship	290	—— Tobey	John Coggeshall
Zephyr	do	361	—— Smith	Alex. Gibbs
Zoroaster	Brig	159	—— Seabury	Pardon G. Seabury
Fairhaven, Mass.				
Ansel Gibbs	Ship	319	—— West	Gibbs & Jenney
Arab	Bark	276	—— Wrightington	I. F. Terry
Baltic	Ship	409	Charles Butler	Asa Swift
Columbus	do	382	—— Fish	Gibbs & Jenney
Eagle	do	283	—— Perry	Reuben Fish
Favorite	Bark	293	—— Young	F. R. Whitwell
General Scott	Ship	333	—— Daggett	L. C. Tripp
Harvest	Bark	314	J. D. Taber	Jabez Delano, jr
Heroine	Ship	337	—— West	Nathan Church
Jos. Maxwell	do	302	—— Perry	F. R. Whitwell
Leonidas	do	243	—— Tobey	L. Jenney & J. Tripp
London Packet	do	335	J. Howland	Gibbs & Jenney
Omega	do	305	—— Gardner	Nathan Church
Pacific	Bark	314	—— Merrihew	Charles Butler
Sarah Frances	Ship	301	—— Hiller	E. Sawin
Holmes's Hole, Mass.				
Delphos	Ship	338	—— West	Thomas Bradley
Nantucket, Mass.				
Atlantic	Ship	321	James Coleman	R. Gardner
Barclay	do	301	Eben Baker	John H. Shaw
Catawba	do	355	William Coleman	C. G. & H. Coffin
Dan'l Webster	do	336	Reuben F. Starbuck	French & Coffin
Empire	do	403	Charles A. Veeder	G. & M. Starbuck & Co.
Mary	do	369	Charles Pitman, jr	Daniel Jones
Ontario	do	354	Stephen B. Gibbs	Barrett & Upton
Penobscot	Brig	138	—— Kelley	Justin Lawrence
Peru	Bark	254	Edwin Barnard	David Joy
Rambler	Ship	318	Robert McCleave	F. C. Sanford
Richard Mitchell	do	386	Josiah C. Long	R. Mitchell & Sons
Spartan	do	333	Nehemiah C. Fisher	Daniel Jones
Tyleston	Brig	300	—— Luce	David Thain
Washington	Ship	308	Stephen Bailey	Matthew Crosby
Young Eagle	do	377	Benjamin Lathrop	Simeon Starbuck
Zenas Coffin	do	338	Obed Ramsdell	C. G. & H. Coffin
Zone	do	365	Obed Starbuck	Levi Starbuck
Edgartown, Mass.				
Almira	Ship	36[illegible]	—— Alley	Abm. Osborne
Pavillion	Brig	150	—— Adams	Calvin C. Adams
Splendid	Ship	392	—— Smith	Abm. Osborne
Westport, Mass.				
Barclay	Bark	167	—— Macomber	Davis & Corey
Dr. Franklin	do	171	—— Francis	Job Davis
Juno	Brig	166	—— Cook	A. B. Gifford
President	Bark	167	—— Simons	Andrew Hicks
United States	do	217	—— Gifford	do

sailing from American ports—Continued.

Whaling-ground.	Date— Of sailing.	Date— Of arrival.	Result of voyage. Sperm-oil.	Result of voyage. Whale-oil.	Result of voyage. Whalebone.	Remarks.
			Bbls.	*Bbls.*	*Lbs.*	
Pacific Ocean ..	June 13	May 24, 1847	1,200	......	......	
....do	June 15	Feb. 28, 1847	2,200	......	......	Withdrawn 1847; sold to Fairhaven.
Indian Ocean ..	July 6	May 19, 1845	70	......	.....	
Indian Ocean ..	June 15	Feb. 12, 1845	350	2,100	23,000	
Ind. and Pacific	Aug. 16	Sept. 17, 1846	80	1,000	17,000	
Pacific Ocean ..	Dec. 10	....	......	......	......	Bought from Nantucket; sent home 15,589 pounds bone; transferred to New Bedford September, 1845; wrecked on Behring Island June 15, 1846, with 2,000 barrels oil.
N. W. Coast ..	Nov. 23	Apr. 13, 1846	800	2,400	14,000	First mate, Harvey Cole, died 1844.
Pacific Ocean ..	June 12	....	......	......	......	Second mate, Pearce A. Stillman, killed by the falling of a whale-fin while cutting in, April 17, 1844; condemned at Rio Janeiro February, 1846.
Ind. and N. W .	Aug. 27	Feb. 22, 1846	900	1,600	6,000	Sent home 340 barrels whale and 100 barrels sperm oil and 9,000 pounds bone.
Pacific Ocean ..	Aug. 14	Apr. 6, 1847	1,900	300	2,000	
Indian Ocean ..	Oct. 4	Apr. 20, 1846	55	1,900	20,000	
....do	June 14	Feb. 24, 1845	60	2,650	22,000	
Pacific and Ind	Dec. 12	Nov. 26, 1847	1,400	......	......	
New Holland ..	July 1	Jan. 27, 1846	1,050	750	7,000	
Pacific Ocean ..	Nov. 9	May 20, 1847	2,050	250	2,000	
....do	Dec. 19	Oct. 27, 1846	800	1,400	14,000	
Ind. and Pacific	Aug. 1	Mar. 30, 1845	90	2,060	19,000	
Pacific Ocean ..	Dec. 13	Oct. 14, 1847	1,200	.....	......	Captain Hiller lost by upsetting of his boat while fast to a whale May 31, 1844.
N. W. Coast .	Oct. 3	Apr. 28, 1845	200	2,300	25,000	
Pacific Ocean ..	Oct. 28	June 22, 1846	1,965	......	......	
....do	Oct. 20	June 16, 1847	1,280	3	......	
....do	Dec. 24	Sept. 23, 1847	1,853	41	......	
....do	May 18	Nov. —, 1847	1,264	264	......	
....do	May 18	Nov. 27, 1847	2,076	35	......	Sold 100 barrels whale-oil; new this voyage; built at Mattapoisett.
....do	Oct. 1	Apr. 16, 1847	862	82	1,500	
....do	May 24	May 2, 1846	2,213	......	......	—— mate, —— Brooks, shot by a mutineer 1844.
Indian Ocean ..	July 24	....	230	140	......	Condemned at Simon's Bay, Cape of Good Hope, February, 1845.
Pacific Ocean ..	May 10	Sept. 19, 1846	966	......	......	
....do	July 13	May 25, 1847	1,578	52	......	Sent home 63 barrels sperm; second mate, —— ——, killed by a whale January, 1844.
....do	Oct. 14	Sept. 30, 1847	1,808	......	......	
....do	Nov. 19	July —, 1847	1,387	......	......	
Atlantic	Oct. 21	Oct. 15, 1845	......	......	......	
Pacific Ocean ..	Dec. 2	June 12, 1847	1,613	20	......	
....do	Dec. 5	....	......	......	......	Sunk at sea 1847 homeward bound.
....do	Sept. 17	May 28, 1848	1,820	320	3,000	
....do	Oct. 13	Nov. 10, 1846	1,226	......	......	Third mate, Manuel Valado, knocked overboard and drowned April 20, 1844. Sold to Fairhaven 1847.
Pacific Ocean ..	June 12	Apr. 6, 1847	1,200	300	2,500	
Atlantic	May 10	Sept. 16, 1845	50	50	......	
Pacific Ocean ..	Oct. 15	Apr. 25, 1846	450	1,900	19,000	First mate, James Brice, died at Lahaina, April 20, 1845.
Atlantic	May 29	Oct. 20, 1844	550	......	......	
....do	Sept. 19	Apr. 6, 1844	370	......	......	
....do	June 20	Aug. 27, 1844	100	70	760	
South Atlantic	May 31	May 31, 1844	230	120	960	
Indian Ocean ..	Sept. 13	Mar. 5, 1846	1,150	......	......	

Table showing returns of whaling-vessels

Name of vessel.	Class.	Tonnage.	Captain.	Managing owner or agent.
1843.				
Sippican, Mass.				
Cossack	Bark	256	—— Delano	S. C. Luce
Popmunnet	do	184	—— Flanders	Henry M. Allen
Quito	Brig	140	—— Chase	J. S. Bates
Mattapoisett, Mass.				
Annawan	Brig	159	—— Dexter	Seth Freeman
Edward	do	134	—— Taber	Wilson Barstow
Lagrange	do	170	—— Lumbert	E. Willis
Wareham, Mass.				
Inga	Brig	169	—— Cudworth	M. S. F. Tobey
Montezuma	Bark	195	—— Allen	do
		172		
Provincetown, Mass.				
Carter Braxton	Ship	132	—— Sparks	Joseph Atkins
Fairy	Bark	186	—— Cook	Abraham Small
Franklin	Brig	172	—— Soper	Robert Soper
Gem	do	162	—— Nickerson	Timothy P. Johnson
John B. Dods	do	163	—— Genn	E. S. Smith
Pacific	do	130	—— Tilson	Stephen Cook, jr
Phenix	do	150	—— Small	Leonard Small
Samuel and Thomas	do	191	—— Nickerson	Samuel Soper
Wm. Henry	Schooner	111	—— Chase	Godfrey Ryder
Plymouth, Mass.				
Maracaibo	Brig	93	—— Nickerson	Atwood L. Drew
Triton	Ship	315	—— Russell	James Bartlett
Yeoman	Brig	175	—— Gooding	
Boston, Mass.				
Maine	Brig	174	—— Tobey	N. Sturtevant
Fall River, Mass.				
Ann Maria	Brig	196	—— Carr	J. S. Barnard
Gold Hunter	Ship	281	—— Wood	Nathan Durfee
Leonidas	Brig	128	—— Marvel	do
Rowena	Ship	404	—— Estes	do
Providence, R. I.				
Bowditch	Ship	399	—— Sowle	Thomas Fletcher
South America	do	616	—— Sowle	do
Bristol, R. I.				
Emigrant	Bark	180	—— Shearman	Samuel Church
Leonidas	Ship	353	—— Waldron	William R. Taylor
Warren, R. I.				
Boy	Ship	252	—— Barton	N. M. Wheaton
Covington	do	351	—— Devoll	Mauran & Fessenden
Franklin	Bark	240	—— Barton	Samuel Barton
Jane	Ship	371	—— Eddy	S. P. Child
Montgomery	do	135	—— Champlin	Stephen Martin
Magnet	do	355	—— Munro	Joseph Smith
Philip Tabb	do	405	—— Webb	Driscol & Child
Warren	do	383	—— Gardner	Joseph Smith
Wm. Baker	do	225	—— Bordon	Child & Fessenden
Newport, R. I.				
Helen	Brig	120	—— Peabody	William Price

sailing from American ports—Continued.

Whaling-ground.	Date— Of sailing.	Of arrival.	Result of voyage. Sperm-oil.	Whale-oil.	Whalebone.	Remarks.
			Bbls.	*Bbls.*	*Lbs.*	
N. W. Coast	Oct. 24	May 21, 1846	80	1, 620	14, 000	
Indian Ocean	Dec. 2	July 3, 1845	170	550	3, 000	
Atlantic	Jan. 9	Sept. 21, 1845	280	40	......	
Atlantic	Apr. 28	Oct. 3, 1844	530	......	......	
....do	Oct. 19	Sept. 7, 1844	630	......	......	
....do	Apr. 28	July 1, 1845	300	......	......	
Atlantic	June 26	Nov. 24, 1844	830	......	......	
South Atlantic	Aug. 29	Oct. 25, 1845	500	100	800	Sold to New Bedford 1846.
Atlantic	July 6	Aug. 13, 1844	280	......	......	
Indian Ocean	Sept. 8	Oct. 25, 1844	490	......	......	
Atlantic	July 9	Oct. 5, 1844	90	......	......	
....do	Mar. 27	June 30, 1844	250	......	......	
South Atlantic	Oct. 20	Aug. 27, 1844	190	15	......	
..do	Aug. 25	Sept. 12, 1844	220	......	......	
Atlantic	July 14	Oct. —, 1844	460	......	......	
....do	July 15	Oct. 10, 1844	290	......	......	
....do	Dec. 30	Aug. 12, 1844	30	......	......	
Atlantic {	....	July 12, 1844	......	55	500	
	July 16	Apr. 10, 1844	55	10	......	
Pacific Ocean	Jan. 13	July 24, 1846	1, 400	......	......	Sold to New Bedford 1846.
Atlantic	Oct. 20	Apr. 14, 1845	650	......	......	Bought 1843.
Indian Ocean	Nov. 18	May —, 1846	......	......	......	Withdrawn 1846.
Indian Ocean	June 11	Mar. 30, 1845	900	200	1, 600	
Pacific Ocean	Oct. 31	May 4, 1846	120	1, 200	4, 000	Sent home about 7,500 pounds bone.
....	Nov. 7	June 6, 1845	260	......	......	
Pacific Ocean	Oct. 12	May 1, 1846	250	2, 850	22, 000	
Pacific Ocean	June 9	May 8, 1846	......	1, 600	14, 000	Captain Sowle drowned May 10, 1844, while fast to a whale; sold 1846.
N. W. Coast	Nov. 14	Mar. 5, 1846	170	4, 100	22, 000	Formerly of the New York and Liverpool line of packets; bought for a whaler 1843; sent home 800 barrels whale, 100 barrels sperm, 36,000 pounds bone; sold at Bahia 1,000 barrels whale; largest voyage on record up to date.
Pacific Ocean	Feb. 8	Sept. 9, 1844	300	200	2, 000	
....do	June 11	Apr. 9, 1846	170	4, 100	22, 000	Sold 1847.
Pacific Ocean	Dec. 17	Dec. 16, 1846	650	1, 100	11, 000	Sent home 14,700 pounds bone.
N. W. Coast	Dec. 8	Apr. 25, 1846	150	2, 400	14, 000	Bought from Baltimore 1843.
Pacific Ocean	Sept. 10	Dec. 21, 1846	650	1, 100	......	
N. W. Coast	July 30					
Indian Ocean	Oct. 28	Nov. 9, 1844	......	......	......	Withdrawn 1844.
Pacific Ocean	June 4	Apr. 12, 1845	......	2, 500	25, 000	
Ind. & N. W	Aug. 4	Apr. 30, 1845	......	2, 800	28, 000	
N. W. Coast	Aug. 4	June 9, 1846	30	2, 100	3, 000	
....do	Oct. 29	Apr. 18, 1846	100	1, 300	4, 000	Sold 1846.
South Atlantic	Aug. 31	May 5, 1844	130	......	......	

Table showing returns of whaling-vessels

Name of vessel.	Class.	Tonnage.	Captain.	Managing owner or agent.
1843.				
Newport, R. I.—Continued.				
Jno. Coggeshall	Ship	338	—— Macy	Peleg Clarke
Pocahontas	Brig	114	—— Barker	Samuel Barker
Salem, Mass.				
Emerald	Bark	270	—— Lakeman	S. C. Phillips
Somerset, Mass.				
Jane	Bark	231	—— Manchester	Wheaton Luther
Pilgrim	do	137	—— Collins	George B. Hood
New Suffolk.				
Noble	Bark	274	—— Sweeny	Ira B. Tuthill
Greenport, N. Y.				
Bayard	Ship	339	—— Fordham	Corwins & Howell
Caroline	do	252	—— Rose	Wiggins & Parsons
Delta	do	314	—— Weeks	Corwins & Howell
Triad	do	336	—— Case	do
Washington	do	236	—— Brown	Wiggins & Parsons
Sarah and Esther	do	157	—— Harlow	Ireland Wells & Carpenter.
New York, N. Y.				
Autumn	Bark	181	—— Wady	D. & A. Kingsland & Co.
Sarah	Ship	495	Frederick W. Myrick	George B. Elkins
New London, Conn.				
Alert	Ship	398	—— Middleton	Havens & Smith
Benj. Morgan	do	407	—— Pendleton	Perkins & Smith
Clematis	do	311	Edwin J. Ames	Williams & Barnes
Chelsea	do	390	—— Potts	Perkins & Smith
Clement	Bark	279	—— Fuller	Joseph Lawrence
Cervantes	do	232	—— Gibson	Benjamin Brown
Connecticut	do	398	Benjamin Hempsted	Frink, Chew & Co
Charles Henry	Ship	265	—— Jeffrey	Perkins & Smith
Catharine	do	384	—— Smith	Thomas Fitch, 2d
Columbus	do	344	—— Crocker	Lyman Allyn
Electra	do	348	—— Ward	Williams & Barnes
Flora	do	338	—— Allen	N. & W. W. Billings
Friends	do	403	—— Jeffrey	Benjamin Brown
Gen. Williams	do	446	—— Holt	Williams & Barnes
Georgia	do	344	—— Hull	Thomas Fitch, 2d
George and Mary	do	356	—— Baker	Lyman Allyn
Halcyon	Bark	258	—— Bailey	Havens & Smith
Hannibal	Ship	441	—— Brown	Benjamin Brown
Julius Cæsar	do	347	—— Green	N. & W. W. Billings
Lowell	do	414	—— Benjamin	Williams & Barnes
Mentor	do	460	—— Sweet	Benjamin Brown
Nantasket	do	434	—— Smith	Havens & Smith
New England	do	368	—— Pendleton	Joseph Lawrence
Palladium	do	342	—— McLane	Frink, Chew & Co
Pembroke	Bark	199	—— Tate	Joseph Lawrence.
Peruvian	Ship	388	—— Brown	E. H. Learned
Superior	Bark	275	—— Bishop	Post & Sherry
Stonington	Ship	351	—— Hamley	Williams & Barnes

sailing from American ports—Continued.

Whaling-ground.	Date— Of sailing.	Date— Of arrival.	Result of voyage. Sperm-oil.	Result of voyage. Whale-oil.	Result of voyage. Whalebone.	Remarks.
			Bbls.	*Bbls.*	*Lbs.*	
Pacific Ocean ..	Nov. 14	July 24, 1847	1,300	......	.....	Sent home 11,160 pounds bone; sold to New Bedford 1847.
Atlantic	Apr. 6	Mar. 18, 1844	100	......	......	Withdrawn 1844.
Indian Ocean ..	Sept. 3	....	1,100	......	......	Wrecked off Fort Daughin, Madagascar, March 10, 1845; oil saved.
New Zealand ..	July 11	....	100	900	9,000	Condemned at Valparaiso March, 1845; cargo sent home.
South Atlantic.	Aug. 25	Oct. 9, 1844	350	......	......	
South Seas.....	July 17	....	......	1,450	......	Put into Auckland May 29, 1846, badly damaged in a gale; condemed; cargo saved.
N. W. Coast...	Sept. 27	July 31, 1845	44	2,160	20,000	
South Seas.....	Mar. 25	Apr. 22, 1845	60	1,540	12,000	
Crozette Island	Aug. 17	July 3, 1845	200	1,300	11,000	
South Seas.....	July —	Feb. 26, 1845	100	2,500	25,000	
....	July 15	July 19, 1844	......	1,400	11,000	
South Seas.....	June 16	June 23, 1844	......	600	4,500	
Indian Ocean ..	Feb. 8	Mar. 30, 1845	130	1,650	15,000	
Pacific Ocean ..	Dec. 31	....	......	3,000	......	Owned in Nantucket; condemned at Tahiti July, 1846; oil shipped to Bremen.
Ind. & N. W ...	July 1	Mar. 17, 1845	30	3,270	30,000	Bought ——, 1843.
N. W. Coast....	Nov. 2	Apr. 14, 1846	40	3,300	13,000	Bought from New York 1843.
Indian Ocean ..	May 9	Apr. 15, 1845	......	2,500	22,000	Captain Ames and one man killed by a blow from a whale's flukes Nov. 21, 1843.
N. W. Coast....	Sept. 13	....				Second mate, John Massey, died at Honolulu October, 1844; lost on Chatham Island; vessel and cargo a total loss.
Pacific Ocean ..	Aug. 19	May 21, 1846	......	2,000	......	
South Atlantic.	June 23	....				Lost June 29, 1844, on coast of New Holland.
Indian Ocean ..	Sept. 5	July 5, 1845	80	1,800	17,000	
....do	Aug. 24	May 10, 1845	......	1,850	15,000	
....do	Sept. 26	Aug. 4, 1845	35	2,465	5,000	Bought from Nantucket; third mate, Erastus T. Weaver, taken out of his boat by a line and lost; sent home 17,000 pounds bone.
N. W. Coast ..	Oct. 14	May 19, 1846	100	2,100	22,000	Bought from Nantucket 1843.
South Atlantic.	June 8	Mar. 7, 1845	150	1,950	18,000	
Indian Ocean ..	May 29	Jan. 28, 1845	180	2,200	22,000	
Chili & N. W ..	May 17	Apr. 4, 1845	......	3,000	27,000	
N. W. Coast....	May 23	Mar. 20, 1845	......	4,000	40,000	
....do	Aug. 30	Apr. 25, 1846	40	2,260	10,000	
Ind. & N. W ...	July 19	Feb. 25, 1845	70	3,000	30,000	
Indian Ocean ..	Aug. 2	....	......	......	......	Lost August 5, 1844, in Geographe Bay; oil (500 barrels whale) saved.
N. W. Coast...	Oct. 12	June 9, 1846	60	3,040	20,000	Hannibal new 1843; Captain Brown left the ship and came home in the Daniel Webster, sick.
Indian Ocean ..	May 9	June 17, 1844	......	1,500	12,000	
N. W. Coast....	July 18	Apr. 27, 1845	300	4,000	37,500	Added 1843.
Indian Ocean ..	July 6	Apr. 2, 1845	90	2,800	29,000	
Chili & N. W ..	June 22	May 4, 1847	350	4,350	20,000	Added 1843; sold to New York 1847.
N. W. Coast....	Aug. 8	May 1, 1845	80	2,920	22,000	
Indian Ocean ..	June 22	Feb. 23, 1845	......	2,300	26,000	Sent home 230 sperm, 2,000 pounds bone.
South Atlantic.	July 25	Apr. 6, 1845	......	700	9,000	
N. W. Coast....	Oct. 9	May 26, 1845	......	3,000	30,000	
Indian Ocean ..	July 24	June 21, 1844	190	2,560	7,000	Sent home 21,000 pounds bone.
N. W. Coast....	Sept. 9	Sept. 29, 1847	......	500	500	Sent home 80 barrels sperm; sold 2,020 barrels whale at Rio Janeiro.

Table showing returns of whaling-vessels

Name of vessel.	Class.	Tonnage.	Captain.	Managing owner or agent.
1843.				
New London, Conn.—Continued.				
White Oak	Ship	292	—— Nory	Joseph Lawrence
William C. Nye	do	389	—— Buddington	N. & W. W. Billings
Stonington, Conn.				
Bolton	Bark	220	—— Nash	Charles P. Williams
Byron	do	170	—— Willcox	John F. Trumbull
Cabinet	Ship	305	—— Noyes	do
Caledonia	do	446	—— Forsyth	C. P. Williams
Calumet	do	317	—— Hancox	do
George	do	251	—— Williams	do
Herald	do	241	—— Morgan	do
Philetus	Bark	278	—— Brewster	J. F. Trumbull
Richard Henry	do	137	—— Peck	do
Tybee	Ship	299	—— Swan	do
United States	do	244	—— Barnum	do
Cold Spring, ——.				
Monmouth	Bark	250	—— Hedges	John H. Jones
N. P. Tallmadge	Ship	370	—— Hedges	do
Richmond	do	437	—— Ludlow	do
Tuscarora	do	379	—— White	do
Sag Harbor, N. Y.				
Alexander	Ship	370	—— Jones	William A. Jones
American	Bark	284	—— Havens	S. & B. Hunting & Co.
Ann	Ship	299	—— Leek	Mulford & Howell
Barbara	Bark	268	—— Howes	Charles T. Dering
Cadmus	do	307	—— Smith	Mulford & Sleight
Columbia	Ship	285	—— Edwards	Luther D. Cook
Concordia	Bark	365	—— Cartwright	Thomas Brown
Crescent	Ship	340	—— Miller	Post & Sherry
Citizen	Bark	464	—— Lansing	Mulford & Sleight
Daniel Webster	Ship	397	—— Curry	Mulford & Howell
Fanny	do	391	—— Edwards	N. & G. Howell
France	do	411	—— Edwards	do
Gem	Bark	326	—— Worth	Hunting Cooper
Hamilton, 2d	Ship	455	—— Loper	Mulford & Sleight
Hannibal	do	311	—— Canning	S. & B. Hunting & Co.
Henry	do	333	—— Brown	S. L'Hommedieu
Huron	do	292	—— Green	L. D. Cook
Helen	do	424	—— Cartwright	Charles T. Dering & Co.
Illinois	do	413	—— Jagger	John Budd
Josephine	do	397	—— Royce	Post & Sherry
Marcus	do	283	—— Shearman	N. & G. Howell
Manhattan	do	440	—— Cooper	John Budd
Neptune	do	388	—— Pierson	S. & B. Hunting & Co
Nimrod	Bark	280	—— Rogers	C. T. Dering
Ontario, 2d	Ship	489	—— Green	Post & Sherry
Romulus	do	233	—— Rogers	Mulford & Howell
Superior	Bark	275	—— Bishop	Post & Sherry
Thames	Ship	414	—— Bishop	Thomas Brown
Washington	do	340	—— Sanford	Hunting Cooper
Wm. Tell	do	370	—— Glover	Thomas Brown
Mystic, Conn.				
Aeronaut	Ship	265	—— West	Charles Mallory
Blackstone	Bark	258	—— Pendleton	do
Leander	do	213	—— Avery	do
Vermont	do	292	—— Nash	do
Bridgeport, Conn.				
Hamilton	Ship	359	—— Peck	Sherwood Sterling

sailing from American ports—Continued.

Whaling-ground.	Date—		Result of voyage.			Remarks.
	Of sailing.	Of arrival.	Sperm-oil.	Whale-oil.	Whalebone.	
			Bbls.	*Bbls.*	*Lbs.*	
South Atlantic.	July 13	Feb. 17, 1845	......	1,900	13,000	Withdrawn 1847.
N. W. Coast....	Oct. 30	Feb. 5, 1846	......	3,100	12,000	
....	July 30	May 24, 1844	......	1,400	......	
....	July 20	May 26, 1845	......	1,300	2,400	
N. W. Coast....	Apr. 28	Feb. 21, 1845	25	2,500	25,000	Bought from Boston 1842.
South Seas.....	Aug. 10	Apr. 15, 1846	104	2,100	6,000	
New Zealand ..	Nov. 8	June 4, 1846	400	2,100	22,000	Bought 1843.
....	June 7	Mar. 6, 1845	130	2,000	16,000	
Crozette Island	June 24	Aug. 11, 1845	170	1,530	11,000	
....	July 12	Apr. 3, 1845	......	1,900	19,000	
....	July 20	....	......	......	......	Lost at South Shetland Islands Feb., 1845.
Indian Ocean ..	Dec. 29	July 4, 1846	200	1,300	12,000	
Crozettes	June 19	May 30, 1844	110	1,800	......	
Indian Ocean .	Oct. 11	Jan. 1, 1846	150	2,000	5,000	Sent home 10,000 pounds bone.
South Seas....	June 14	Feb. 19, 1845	200	2,500	22,000	
N. W. Coast...	Dec. 2	Mar. 13, 1846	100	3,800	12,000	Added 1843.
....do	Sept. 23	May 26, 1845	......	2,400	23,000	
N. W. Coast....	Sept. 15	July —, 1848	......	......	......	Bought 1843; second mate died 1845.
Crozettes	Sept. 18	Aug. 11, 1845	100	1,500	14,000	
South Atlantic.	July 7	May 6, 1856	200	1,800	5,000	
....do	Aug. 26	July 10, 1844	130	1,000	8,000	
Crozettes	Aug. 24	June 9, 1845	300	1,100	8,000	
South Atlantic.	June 20	Apr. 2, 1845	250	2,250	28,000	Sold 500 barrels whale at Pernambuco.
South Seas.....	June 30	May 31, 1845	160	1,500	14,000	
N. W. Coast....	Oct. 11	May 6, 1846	......	1,500	5,000	Withdrawn 1847.
....do	Apr. 21	July 22, 1846	130	3,000	9,000	Bought 1843.
....do	Aug. 17	Apr. 2, 1845	25	3,225	33,000	
....do	Dec. 4	Mar. 12, 1846	40	3,100	13,000	
New Holland ..	July 21	May 23, 1846	90	2,710	10,000	Sent home 400 barrels whale and 11,432 pounds bone; withdrawn from the service.
Crozettes	Sept. 15	May 11, 1845	200	2,500	25,000	
N. W. Coast....	Aug. 28	....	......	......	......	Lost near Rio Grande, February, 1845; vessel total loss; saved 2,300 barrels whale-oil.
South Atlantic.	Aug. 29	Sept. 2, 1845	100	1,500	10,000	
....do	July 5	May 14, 1845	100	2,250	22,000	Bought from Boston 1842.
N. W. Coast....	Sept. 21	May 19, 1845	......	2,400	24,000	
....do	Oct. 18	Apr. 6, 1846	20	3,980	12,000	Bought from New York 1843.
....do	Oct. 25	Apr. 5, 1845	30	2,900	26,000	Do.
....do	Oct. 29	Sept. 14, 1846	60	3,000	6,000	Do.
Crozettes	Aug. 31	May 13, 1845	75	1,000	6,000	Sold for merchant-service.
N. W. Coast....	Nov. 8	Oct. 14, 1846	......	......	......	Bought from New York 1843; sold 1847.
....do	June 10	May 10, 1845	90	2,160	18,009	
South Atlantic.	Aug. 26	July 28, 1844	200	300	2,400	
N. W. Coast....	Aug. 31	May 11, 1845	265	3,400	36,000	Bought 1843.
Crozettes	Sept. 25	June 8, 1845	70	1,120	9,000	
Indian Ocean ..	July 24	May 10, 1845	120	1,400	19,000	
N. W. Coast....	July 7	June 2, 1846	......	2,000	4,000	Sold 400 barrels whale at Rio Janeiro.
South Atlantic	June 19	Mar. 30, 1845	25	2,675	25,000	
N. W. Coast....	Oct. 4	July 21, 1846	......	2,750	22,500	Bought 1843.
....	Sept. 6	June 23, 1845	100	1,400	11,200	
Indian Ocean ..	June 18	Apr. —, 1845	100	1,900	18,000	
....do	July 3	May 30, 1845	350	1,150	12,000	
N. W. Coast....	Nov. 20	Apr. 14, 1846	......	2,100	18,000	
N. W. Coast....	Oct. 23	Apr. 20, 1846	135	6,520	20,000	Captain Peck died at Lahaina May 3, 1845.

Table showing returns of whaling-vessels

Name of vessel.	Class.	Tonnage.	Captain.	Managing owner or agent.
1844.				
New Bedford, Mass.				
Alto	Bark	197	Nehemiah West	Richmond & Wood
Alex. Coffin	Ship	381	J. S. Hathaway	Jonathan Bourne, jr
America	Bark	257	H. F. Eastham	Barton Ricketson
Amethyst	Ship	359	J. A. Baylies	J. A. Parker & Son
Averick	do	385	Robert Reynard	do
Arnolda	do	350	D. U. Coffin	James Arnold
Barclay	do	281	—— Mann	do
Brighton	do	354	—— Cox	C. R. Tucker
Barth. Gosnold	do	356	Edw. P. Mosher	I. Howland, jr., & Co
Chas. Drew	do	344	N. C. Carey	William Gifford
Chandler Price	do	441	—— Pease	Pope & Morgan
Chase	Bark	153	—— West	B. Ricketson
Cicero	Ship	252	—— Howland	Lemuel Kollock
Condor	do	349	Jacob Taber	C. W. Morgan
Charleston Packet	Bark	184	W. Howland	Thos. Knowles & Co
Columbus	do	313	—— Hutchins	William R. Rodman
Champion	Ship	336	Isaac J. Sanford	J. D. Thompson
Dartmouth	do	336	W. Upham	I. Howland, jr., & Co
Draper	do	261	G. T. Lawton	Jos. Dunbar & Co
Dragon	Bark	190	Joseph Bennett, jr	Tobey & Ricketson
Drymo	do	262	John Taber	Jas. H. Howland
Dryade	do	263	J. S. Bolles	Thomas & Dow
Emma	do	246	Elihu Russel	J. D. Thompson
Elizabeth	Ship	339	—— Barker	T. & A. R. Nye
Enterprise	do	291	S. Brayton	Robert Gibbs
Eagle	do	336	—— Wood	Jireh Perry
Factor	do	343	S. Hawes	Chs. R. Tucker & Co
Fenelon	do	328	Luke Baker	B. B. Howard
Formosa	do	450	L. Briggs	O. N. Swift
Fortune	Bark	291	—— Bailey	Gilbert Hathaway
Fabius	Ship	432	H. Nickerson	C. R. Tucker & Co
Gid'n Howland	do	379	—— Mayhew	I. Howland, jr., & Co
Golconda, 2d	do	359	—— Studley	E. W. Howland
Good Return	do	376	—— Swift	H. Taber & Co
Gov. Troup	do	430	G. H. Jenney	E. C. Jones
Hibernia	do	327	N. P. Simmons	Robert Gibbs
Hope, 2d	do	295	A. Willcox	Wilcox & Richmond
Huntress	do	391	Edw. T. Shearman	Robert Gibbs
James Allen	do	355	Harvey Shearman	Gideon Allen
Jasper	Bark	223	Ancel Pope	Alexander Gibbs
John Adams	Ship	268	F. A. Mason	Jireh Perry
John	do	308	Squire Sanford	Frederick Parker
John & Edward	do	318	—— Christian	Wilcox & Richmond
Julian	do	356	S. M. Blackmer	Hathaway & Luce

sailing from American ports—Continued.

Whaling-ground.	Date— Of sailing.	Date— Of arrival.	Result of voyage. Sperm-oil.	Result of voyage. Whale-oil.	Result of voyage. Whalebone.	Remarks.
			Bbls.	*Bbls.*	*Lbs.*	
Atlantic	Sept. 3	Apr. 26, 1847	230	320	2,600	Bought from Fairhaven 1844.
N. W. Coast....	Oct. 20	Apr. 19, 1849	452	908	......	Bought from Nantucket 1844; sold to go to California 1849.
South Atlantic.	Dec. 12	May 19, 1847	200	800	6,000	Bought from Bristol 1844.
N. W. Coast....	Oct. 12	June 22, 1846	85	1,815	16,000	Sailed June 10; returned October 3; captain sick.
Pacific Ocean ..	Aug. 15	....	......	......	......	Lost on island of Ulitea February 15, 1845; got off; sailed under Chilian flag in whaling business; renamed Recovery.
....do	July 13	Mar. 29, 1848	1,550	......	......	Added 1844.
....do	July 20	Jan. 5, 1850	415	......	......	Sold 400 sperm.
Ind. and N. W	Oct. 31	Apr. 22, 1847	160	2,500	9,000	Sailed October 1, returned October 6, damaged by a gale; sent home 20,382 pounds bone.
N. W. Coast ...	July 24	Apr. 2, 1847	150	......	13,000	Bought from Falmouth 1844; sold 2,765 whale at Rio Janeiro.
....do	Aug. 5	May 15, 1846	190	2,570	26,000	
....do	Sept. 12	May 18, 1847	400	3,100	15,000	Bought 1844 from Philadelphia; sent home 15,862 pounds bone; withdrawn, 1847, for merchant-service.
Atlantic	Nov. 8	Sept. 9, 1846	350	......	......	
Indian Ocean ..	July 2	July 3, 1846	70	1,730	3,500	Sent home 145 barrels oil.
Pacific Ocean ..	May 29	Apr. 13, 1846	180	2,500	20,000	Second mate, James Ashley, died March 19, 1846.
Indian Ocean ..	June 20	Aug. 14, 1846	700	......	......	
Pacific Ocean ..	Apr. 1	Apr. 9, 1847	150	750	2,000	
N. W. Coast....	June 13	Mar. 3, 1847	115	3,100	14,000	Added 1843, from Boston; Captain Sandford was injured by the breaking of a tackle-fall, and died from the effect 1845; sent home 14,000 pounds bone.
Pacific Ocean ..	Aug. 7	Aug. 6, 1847	500	2,100	10,000	
Indian Ocean ..	Sept. 15	Aug. 19, 1847	500	1,750	10,000	
....do	June 20	Apr. 17, 1847	50	300	2,000	
....do	Aug. 28	....	......	......	......	Bought 1844 from Sippican; lost on a reef at Lahaina October 17, 1845; oil saved 350 barrels.
....do	Sept. 20	May 20, 1847	300	1,200	500	Bought from Mattapoisett 1844.
... do	July 29	Jan. 9, 1847	1,000	......	......	
....do	July 25	May 24, 1847	700	1,800	4,000	Captain Taber, who went out in command, returned sick, 1844.
....do	Aug. 21	Apr. 30, 1847	70	1,300	13,000	
Pacific Ocean ..	Dec. 3	Jan. 15, 1849	1,700	50	......	Sent home 350 sperm.
Ind. and Pacific	Oct. 1	....	500	2,200	......	Added 1844 from Poughkeepsie; sent home 85 sperm, 1,936 whale; condemned at Tahiti July 8, 1847.
South Seas.....	Nov. 21	Apr. 22, 1847	100	650	5,000	Captain Baker died at sea 1846.
N. W. Coast....	Nov. 7	May 11, 1849	1,483	1,652	52,200	Bought from New York 1844; fourth mate killed by a whale June 1845.
....do	Nov. 17	May 19, 1847	180	2,020	10,000	Bought from Plymouth 1844. Sent home 9,080 pounds bone.
Ind. and Pacific	July 7	Feb. 14, 1846	......	2,600	28,000	Bought from Nantucket 1844.
N. W. Coast....	Dec. 20	Apr. 8, 1847	165	2,950	27,000	Isaac C. Howland, first mate, died at sea January, 1845.
....do	Oct. 24	Oct. 25, 1848	640	1,400	16,000	Sold to go to California 1849.
....do	July 25	Oct. 12, 1847	150	2,850	15,000	Sold 12,000 pounds bone at Sidney.
....do	July 10	Feb. 5, 1847	120	3,400	14,000	Captain Jenney died at Honolulu May 3, 1845.
South Seas.....	June 15	May 20, 1846	25	2,000	......	
Indian Ocean ..	May 23	May 4, 1847	350	1,000	1,500	
South Seas.....	June 25	May 27, 1847	75	1,800	61,197	
Pacific Ocean ..	Oct. 12	May 20, 1848	2,700	......	......	Built 1844 at Fairhaven.
Atl. and Ind ...	June 8	Apr. 14, 1846	200	1,250	10,000	
Pacific Ocean ..	July 23	May 30, 1848	2,700	......	......	Sent home 20 sperm. Captain Mason died at sea 1844. The John Adams is reported condemned in 1848 or '49, having sent home 1,019 sperm.
Atl. and Pacific	June 20	May 28, 1848	1,800	50	......	
Ind. and Pacific	Sept. 17	Mar. 25, 1847	750	300	......	Second mate, —— Jenney, died at Talcahuano, January, 1845.
Indian Ocean ..	Aug. 13	Mar. 25, 1847	300	2,700	14,000	Sent home 14,000 pounds bone.

Table showing returns of whaling-vessels

Name of vessel.	Class.	Tonnage.	Captain.	Managing owner or agent.
1844.				
New Bedford, Mass.—Continued.				
Junior	Ship	378	Silas Tinkham	D. R. Greene & Co
Juno	Brig	166	—— Howland	Benj. F. Howland
Lafayette	Ship	260	—— Smith	Edw. W. Howland
Lalla Rookh	...do	323	O. Reynard	J. A. Parker & Son
Lewis	...do	308	J. R. Tallman	J. D. Thompson
Liverpool	...do	300	—— Devoll	Abraham Barker
Logan	...do	302	Chandler Gardner	I. Howland, jr., & Co
London Packet	Bark	280	Tim. J. Howland	A. H. Howland
L. C. Richmond	Ship	341	—— Wood	Daniel Wood
Liverpool, 2d	...do	428	J. Willcox	Thomas Willcox
Morea	...do	330	—— Cushman	B. B. Howard
Majestic	...do	297	—— Smith	Thomas & Dow
Mary	...do	287	Thomas Corey	I. Howland, jr., & Co
Mayflower	...do	350	—— Gifford	John C. Haskell
Milton	...do	388	—— Cash	H. Taber & Co
Minerva Smyth	...do	335	—— Fisher	I. Howland, jr., & Co
Marcella	Bark	210	—— Smith	C. R. Tucker
Milwood	...do	254	R. W. Hathaway	G. Allen
Margaret Scott	Ship	307	Benjamin Price	S. H. & W. Ingalls
Mercury	...do	340	F. D. Haskell	I. Howland, jr., & Co
Massachusetts	...do	364	William B. Cash	O. & G. O. Crocker
Midas	...do	326	E. W. Collins	John Coggeshall
Minerva	...do	408	J. S. Macomber	William Gifford
Mobile	...do	263	Charles G. Smith	E. C. Jones
Montpelier	...do	320	—— Taber	J. R. Thornton
Moctezuma	...do	436	William E. Tower	West & Paine
Marcia	...do	315	H. Howland	E. W. Howland
Niger	...do	437	James Gray	Hathaway & Luce
New Bedford	...do	351	T. C. Swain	I. Howland, jr., & Co
Nile	...do	322	—— Hamlin	Hathaway & Luce
Nye	...do	211	R. F. Pease	T. & A. R. Nye
Olympia	...do	296	—— Taber	Ashley & Philips
Otranto	Bark	150	—— Coggeshall	Cranston Willcox
Pioneer	...do	231	—— Wolverton	J. D. Thompson
Pacific	Ship	385	Asa Hoxie	Jireh Perry
Pacific, 2d	...do	332	L. Little	A. Robeson
Roscoe	Bark	235	W. N. Bourne	Jona. Bourne, jr
Roman, 2d	Ship	350	A. R. Barker	Abm. Barker
Sallie Anne	...do	312	G. H. Clark	D. R. Greene & Co
Seine	...do	281	—— Smith	Rodney French
Stephania	...do	315	Samuel Coggeshall	John Coggeshall
South Carolina	...do	302	—— Gardner	J. D. Thompson
Science	...do	388	William Wood	J. B. Wood & Co
Tacitus	...do	414	S. S. Hathaway	Swift & Allen
Two Brothers	...do	288	Isaac H. Jenny	D. R. Greene & Co
Tuscaloosa	Bark	284	—— Goodwin	Swift & Allen
William and Eliza	Ship	321	W. H. Whitfield	Henry Taber & Co
Wade	Bark	261	George W. Downs	A. H. Howland
Washington	Ship	344	—— Whelden	Jona. Bourne, jr
Young Phenix	...do	377	—— Mickell	J. A. Parker & Son
Fairhaven, Mass.				
Albion	Ship	326	—— Hathaway	E. Sawin

***sailing from American ports*—Continued.**

Whaling-ground.	Date— Of sailing.	Date— Of arrival.	Result of voyage. Sperm-oil.	Result of voyage. Whale-oil.	Result of voyage. Whalebone.	Remarks.
			Bbls.	*Bbls.*	*Lbs.*	
South Seas	June 6	May 21, 1847	400	2, 200	25, 000	
Atlantic	Oct. 10	....	......	......	......	Bought 1844; condemned at Saint Catherines February, 1845.
Pacific Ocean	Sept. 7	Aug. 21, 1847	950	800	7, 000	
....do	Nov. 14	July 6, 1848	1, 200	200	1, 200	
N. W. Coast	Nov. 5	May 18, 1848	250	1, 600	6, 000	Sold 190 barrels whale at Saint Catherines.
Indian Ocean	July 25	Mar. 5, 1847	500	1, 800	18, 000	Sent home 14,000 pounds bone.
Pacific Ocean	May 21	May 25, 1847	200	1, 600	15, 000	Third mate, John Francis, killed by a whale July, 1846.
....do	Oct. 12	Sept. 30, 1848	1, 300	120	......	
N. W. Coast	Dec. 16	Mar. 20, 1848	2, 000	500	4, 000	
....do	June 27	June 23, 1847	90	1, 910	6, 000	Bought from New York 1844.
Pac. and N. W	July 10	Feb. 13, 1847	7	2, 643	......	Bought from Boston 1844; withdrawn 1847.
N. W. Coast	July 20	May 5, 1848	400	1, 200	2, 000	Sent home 10,685 pounds bone; sold 200 sperm and 200 whale on voyage.
Indian Ocean	June 10	Apr. 10, 1847	500	1, 500	7, 000	
N. W. Coast	July 9	Oct. 24, 1847	125	1, 775	12, 000	Went into California trade 1849.
Ind. and N. W	July 1	Apr. 1, 1847	350	2, 700	14, 000	Sent home 32,700 pounds bone.
Pacific Ocean	Jan. 4	Sept. 19, 1845	150	2, 150	24, 000	
Indian Ocean	Nov. 26	Jan. 5, 1847	800	......	......	
....do	July 25	July 3, 1846	200	1, 300	10, 000	Second mate, Barney Merrick, drowned by capsizing of a boat, November 8, 1844.
Indian and Pac	Sept. 11	Aug. 19, 1847	115	1, 800	14, 000	Sent home 44 sperm.
Pacific Ocean	Nov. 19	Feb. 11, 1848	590	800	600	Sent home 8,838 pounds bone.
....do	Sept. 5	June 2, 1848	2, 300	......	......	First mate killed by a whale, October, 1845; sent home 150 sperm.
Indian & N. W	June 19	Apr. 30, 1847	100	1, 400	......	Captain Collins died February 4, 1845.
N. W. Coast	Oct. 30	Mar. 3, 1847	800	2, 100	4, 000	Added 1844; sent home 40 sperm.
Pacific Ocean	Aug. 2	June 26, 1848	900	200	......	
N. W. Coast	Sept. 22	July 29, 1847	400	2, 100	16, 000	
....do	July 10	Apr. 28, 1847	600	2, 200	10, 000	
....do	July 12	May 25, 1847	......	2, 200	7, 000	Bought from Fairhaven, 1844; sent home 7,200 pounds bone.
Pacific Ocean	July 30	Nov. 28, 1847	1, 450	1, 450	5, 000	Built at Mattapoisett, 1844; sent home 95 sperm.
....do	July 17	Feb. 28, 1848	300	2, 000	1, 500	Sent home 13,221 pounds bone.
....do	Sept. 19	....	......	......	......	Sold to parties in San Francisco for whaling thence; shipped 1,050 sperm and 250 whale to London.
....do	Oct. 24	May 12, 1848	750	50	1, 150	Sailed October 1; returned October 15th, damaged by a gale.
N. W. Coast	Oct. 21	May 25, 1847	250	2, 250	23, 000	Bought from Boston, 1844.
Indian Ocean	Dec. 3	Nov. 22, 1846	720	......	......	
....do	Aug. 12	Mar. 8, 1847	130	1, 850	18, 000	
Pacific Ocean	Oct. 21	July 5, 1848	2, 500	......	......	
South Seas	Aug. 29	....	......	......	......	Lost on a reef off Pernambuco, March 23, 1848; had 200 sperm and 2,000 whale; saved about 900 barrels
Indian Ocean	June 18	Mar. 13, 1846	140	1, 900	18, 000	
N. W. Coast	Nov. 2	July 28, 1847	850	2, 150	1, 500	
Indian Ocean	July 7	Apr. 14, 1847	500	1, 500	10, 500	Sent home 9,500 bone.
....do	Nov. 4	May 1, 1846	200	1, 600	12, 000	
N. W. Coast	Aug. 3	June 29, 1847	2[illegible]0	1, 650	11, 000	
Indian & N. W	July 2	May 10, 1848	300	1, 100	3, 500	Sent home 40 whale.
N. W. Coast	July 3	May 27, 1847	100	2, 500	14, 000	Bought from Portland, Me., 1844; sold, 1847.
New Zealand	June 27	....	......	......	......	Bought from Boston, 1844; lost on Island of Roratonga, March 11, 1845.
Indian Ocean	May 8	June 4, 1847	1, 000	400	3, 000	
Pacific Ocean	Nov. 7	....	......	......	......	Lost in St. Matthew's Bay, Patagonia, Oct. 5, 1845; saved 500 barrels oil.
....do	Oct. 6	July 4, 1848	1, 700	......	......	
Indian Ocean	June 28	Apr. 15, 1846	200	1, 800	20, 000	
N. W. Coast	Dec. 2	May 29, 1847	100	2, 100	1, 500	Sent home 21,622 pounds bone.
Pacific Ocean	Nov. 13	Oct. 17, 1848	1, 800	......	......	
Indian Ocean	Aug. 6	Mar. 31, 1847	80	1, 720	15, 000	New 1844; was absent 7 years and 9 months; brought 400 barrels cocoa-nut oil; shipped to England on voyage 2,600 barrels sperm, 950 whale, 1,450 cocoa-nut; sent home 324 whale, 19,000 bone.

Table showing returns of whaling-vessels

Name of vessel.	Class.	Tonnage.	Captain.	Managing owner or agent.
1844.				
Fairhaven, Mass.—Continued.				
Belle	Bark	320	—— Handy	Edmund Allen
Bruce	do	148	—— Cochran	M. O. Bradford
Clifford Wayne	Ship	305	—— Howland	E. Sawin
Erie	do	451	—— Holly	Nathan Church
Friendship	do	366	W. J. Stott	Gibbs & Jenney
George	do	360	—— Swift	Fish & Huttlestone
Herald	do	262	—— Luce	Samuel Borden
Hesper	Bark	262	—— Pease	L. Jenney & J. Tripp
James Munroe	Ship	424	—— Harding	F. R. Whitwell
Kingston	do	312	T. Ellis, jr	Nathan Church
Marcus	do	286	S. H. Taber	Lemuel Tripp
Martha, 2d	do	301	H. Stewart	Atkins Adams
Holmes' Hole, Mass.				
Ocmulgee	Ship	458	—— Manter	Thomas Bradley
Pocahontas	do	341	do	do
Nantucket, Mass.				
Charles Carroll	Ship	376	Thomas L. Andrews	W. C. Swain
Citizen	do	360	Hiram Bailey	C. G. and H. Coffin
Harvest	do	360	George D. Coffin	Edward Field
Henry	do	346	William Brown	Daniel Jones
Henry Clay	do	385	Edward C. Austin	Christopher Wyer
Henry Astor	do	375	Thomas Coffin, 2d	William R. Easton
Lexington	do	399	Edward Weeks	F. C. Sanford
Mariner	do	349	Albert Ray	Matthew Crosby
Mount Vernon	do	383	Henry Coleman	John H. Shaw
Niphon	do	340	John Gardner, 2d	J. H. Shaw & W. Folger
Omega	do	363	Charles H. Morton	Joseph Starbuck
Peruvian	do	334	George B. Folger	William B. Coffin
Phœnix	do	323	Perry Winslow	T. & P. Macy
Planter	do	340	Barzillai T. Folger	Gilbert Coffin
Two Brothers	Schooner			
Walter Scott	Ship	339	Charles Grant	Barret & Upton
Falmouth, Mass.				
Awashonks	Ship	342	Ephraim Eldridge	Thomas Swift
Hobomok	do	414	Roland R. Jones	Elijah Swift
Harriet	Schooner	100	—— Gifford	S. Dillingham
Edgartown, Mass.				
Alfred Tyler	Bark	225	—— Luce	Alex. P. Weeks
Mary	Ship	343	—— Pease	Abraham Osborne
Milton	Bark	175	—— Sprague	Thomas Milton
Vineyard	Ship	381	—— Coffin	Benjamin Worth
York	do	434	do	John O. Morse
Westport, Mass.				
Champion	Bark	209	—— Sowle	Andrew Hicks
Catherwood	Brig	199	—— Boodry	Thomas W. Mayhew
Dr. Franklin	Bark	171	—— Francis	Job Davis
Mexico	Brig	130	—— Wing	Davis & Corey
President	Bark	167	—— Simonds	A. Hicks
Rajah	do	250	—— West	Henry Willcox
Theo. Chase	do	168	—— Ball	do

sailing from American ports—Continued.

Whaling-ground.	Date— Of sailing.	Of arrival.	Result of voyage. Sperm-oil.	Whale-oil.	Whalebone.	Remarks.
			Bbls.	*Bbls.*	*Lbs.*	
Pacific Ocean..	Dec. 10	Sept. 10, 1852	350	......	......	
Atlantic Ocean	Nov. 22	May 25, 1847	570	......	......	
Indian and Pac	Oct. 22	July 26, 1847	1, 800	70	......	
....do	June 8	Feb. 27, 1847	330	3, 370	33, 000	
Indian & N. W	July 9	Feb. 24, 1846	350	2, 400	12, 000	Sent home 13,279 pounds bone.
Pacific & N. W.	Sept. 16	Feb. 12, 1846	230	2, 200	4, 000	Sent home 22,335 pounds bone, 1846.
Indian Ocean ..	Sept. 14	Apr. 6, 1847	100	1, 000	8, 500	
Pacific Ocean..	Sept. 11	Apr. 26, 1848	1, 300	......	......	
Indian and Pac	May 5	July —, 1847	1, 250	1, 050	12, 000	
Pacific Ocean..	Sept. 14	May 26, 1848	59	......	......	Added 1844, from Nantucket.
..do	Oct. 22	July 20, 1847	300	800	4, 000	Captain Taber left the ship at Paita, sick.
Indian Ocean .	Aug. 5	Nov. 27, 1847	1, 100	800	7, 000	
N. W. Coast....	Nov. 21	May 25, 1847	280	2, 520	24, 000	Added 1844, from New York.
Pacific Ocean..	May 15	July 20, 1846	1, 100	950	9, 000	
Pacific Ocean..	May 16	May 29, 1848	1, 261	473	9, 000	
....do	Aug. 25	July 17, 1849	1, 302	1, 175	5, 000	Built 1844, at Boston; sold 150 sperm, 425 whale.
....do	Oct. 18	....	......	......	......	Lost second mate, ten men, spars, boats, &c., by shipping a sea; returned January 6, 1845, and sailed again in 1845.
....do	July 1	Apr. 24, 1848	1, 150	482	4, 000	Sold 70 barrels whale.
....do	June 10	Aug. 15, 1847	2, 756	......	......	Sold 91 barrels sperm.
....do	Oct. 14	Oct. 19, 1848	1, 796	......	......	Sold 120 barrels sperm.
....do	June 26	July 7, 1848	1, 560	1, 374	......	Sold 220 sperm, 30 whale.
....do	July 31	Sept. 15, 1848	1, 236	407	3, 000	
....do	Oct. 3	Oct. 2, 1848	2, 607	10	......	Lost boats, spars, &c., in a gale, October 6; returned and sailed again November 8; sold to Mattapoisett 1848.
....do	Nov. 29	....	......	......	......	Built 1844; Captain Gardner left the ship at Sandwich Islands, sick; sunk at sea, homeward bound, January 12, 1849, bottom bored by worms.
....do	Oct. 26	July 4, 1848	1, 095	......	......	
....do	Oct. 1	Jan. 29, 1848	1, 515	......	......	
....do	Sept. 17	June 3, 1848	1, 648	24	......	
....do	Sept. 15	Apr. 26, 1847	1, 276	914	7, 500	Lost second mate, Andrew Brock, and two men by boat capsizing.
Atlantic	....	June —, 1844	......	20	......	
Pacific Ocean..	Aug. 31	Mar. 10, 1849	1, 868	55	......	Sold to Edgartown.
South Seas.....	June 7	July 22, 1848	1, 400	1, 190	10, 000	
Pacific Ocean..	June 14	Apr. 29, 1848	1, 000	1, 000	......	
Atlantic	May 16	Mar. 18, 1845	50	......	......	Added 1844.
Pacific Ocean..	Oct. 30	July 22, 1848	950	500	......	Bought from New York 1844; sent home 85 bundles bone.
....do	Dec. 1	Apr. 20, 1848	400	1, 300	10, 000	First mate, Peter West, died at Valparaiso, May, 1847; sent home 109 sperm.
Atlantic	May 11	Dec. 21, 1845	60	340	......	Bark Milton added 1844; withdrawn in 1846; Captain Sprague left the ship and came home sick.
Pacific Ocean..	Sept. 16	May 22, 1847	400	2, 000	20, 000	
....do	Apr. 28	Mar 2, 1847	500	2, 100	20, 000	Sold 1847.
Atlantic	Sept. 18	June 11, 1845	200	40	......	
....do	Jan. 25	July 2, 1845	750	......	......	Captain Boodry died November 14, 1844; first mate, —— Leonard, took command.
....do	May 13	June 1, 1845	550	20	......	
....do	Apr. 12	Aug. 9, 1845	320	......	......	
....do	Aug. 3	June 2, 1845	350	450	1, 800	
Pacific Ocean..	Sept. 27	May 24, 1847	300	1, 550	16, 000	Added 1844.
Atlantic	Oct. 26	Dec. 8, 1845	800	......	......	

Table showing returns of whaling-vessels

Name of vessel.	Class.	Tonnage.	Captain.	Managing owner or agent.
1844.				
Mattapoisett, Mass.				
Annawan	Brig	159	—— Dexter	Seth Freeman
Elizabeth	Bark	219	—— Jenny	R. L. Barstow
Edward	Brig	134	—— Southworth	Wilson Barstow
Joseph Meigs	Ship	338	—— Taber	Jos. Meigs
Mattapoisett	Bark	150	—— Brightman	Leonard Hammond
Sarah	do	171	—— Mayhew	C. Barstow & Son
Solon	Brig	129	—— Dillingham	A. Daggett
Willis	Bark	164	—— Higgins	R. L. Barstow
Wareham, Mass.				
America	Brig	148	—— Delano	M. S. F. Tobey
Geo. Washington	Ship	374	—— Russell	S. C. Gibbs
Provincetown, Mass.				
Belle Isle	Schooner	104	—— Smith	Eben Cook
Edwin	do			
Esquimaux	do	100	—— Cook	Parker Cook
Gem	Brig	162	—— Nickerson	Timothy P. Johnson
Joshua Brown	Schooner	113	—— Genn	Seth Nickerson
John B. Dods	Brig	163	—— Winslow	E. S. Smith
Louisa	Schooner	98	—— Cook	Samuel Cook
Medford	do	125	—— Cook	
Pacific	Brig	130	—— Tillson	D. Small
Rienzi	Schooner		—— Cook	
Rienzi	Brig		—— Small	
Spartan	Bark	188	—— Cook	Abraham Small
Stranger	Schooner			
Samuel and Thomas	Bark	191	—— Swift	Samuel Soper
Sippican, Mass.				
Quito	Brig	140	—— Chase	J. S. Bates
Plymouth, Mass.				
Exchange	Schooner	99	—— Hopkins	Richard W. Holmes
Maracaibo	Brig	93	—— Nickerson	Atwood L. Drew
Freetown, Mass.				
Elizabeth	Bark	349	Elihu Gifford	E. P. Hathaway
Harriet	do	285	—— Durfee	
Providence, R. I.				
Balance	Ship	322	—— Reed	W. Humphrey
Cassander	do	299	—— King	Nathaniel Potter
Envoy	do	392	—— Fisher	Amherst Everett
Richmond	Bark		—— Swift	Pearce & Bullock
Bristol, R. I.				
Emigrant	Bark	180	—— Shearman	Samuel Church
Troy	Brig	156	—— Grinnell	do
Warren, R. I.				
Chariot	Ship	360	—— Luce	N. M. Wheaton
Exchange	Bark	180	—— Merry	John R. Wheaton
Hoogley	Ship	292	—— Townsend	do
Henry Tuke	do	365	—— Champlin	Joseph Smith
Hopewell	do	413	—— Littlefield	Burr & Smith
Luminary	do	432	—— Cleveland	Joseph Smith
Newport, R. I.				
Geo. Champlin	Ship	361	—— Swain	N. S. Ruggles

sailing from American ports—Continued.

Whaling-ground.	Date— Of sailing.	Of arrival.	Result of voyage. Sperm-oil.	Whale-oil.	Whalebone.	Remarks.
			Bbls.	*Bbls.*	*Lbs.*	
Atlantic	Nov. 28	June 3, 1846	470	......	......	
Indian Ocean	July 17	May 16, 1846	340	120	1, 000	Sent home 500 barrels sperm.
Atlantic	Oct. 23	Oct. 30, 1845	320	240	......	Withdrawn 1846.
Indian and Pac.	Sept. 25	June 19, 1846	240	2, 360	......	Burned at anchor at Mattapoisett, June 27, 1846.
Atlantic	July 7	Aug. 5, 1846	350	......	......	Sold to Westport 1846.
....do	Apr. 10	Feb. 14, 1846	550	......	......	Sent home 200 barrels oil.
....do	Nov. 12	Aug. 28, 1846	90	......	......	Added 1844; bought from Sippican.
....do	June 6	Aug. 11, 1845	250	......	......	Added 1844; first mate killed by a whale December, 1844.
....do	July 9	Sept. 20, 1845	230	......	......	Sold to Mattapoisett 1846.
Pacific Ocean	July 26	Aug. 3, 1847	400	1, 600	6, 000	
Atlantic	Jan. 26	Oct. 5, 1844	160	......	......	
....do	....	July —, 1844	300	20	......	
....do	Jan. 26	Sept. 29, 1844	70	......	......	
....do	July 20	Oct. 20, 1845	200	......	......	
....do	Apr. 9	June 18, 1845	170	80	......	Withdrawn 1845.
River Plate	Nov. 13	Mar. 15, 1846	50	50	......	Withdrawn 1846.
Atlantic	May 15	Oct. 16, 1844	......	250	......	
....do	May 15	Sept. 29, 1844	210	60	......	Added 1844.
....do	Nov. 30	May 14, 1846	440	......	......	
Bay Mexico	Mar. 7	July 30, 1844	220	......	......	
Atlantic	May 1	Oct. 31, 1844	300	......	......	Added 1843 from Boston.
Brazil Banks	Jan. 26	Apr. 6, 1845	750	......	......	
....	....	Sept. —, 1844	......	245	......	
Atlantic	Dec. 17	May 29, 1846	470	10	......	
Atlantic	Jan. 9	Sept. 21, 1845	280	40	......	
Atlantic	Dec. 14	Oct. 10, 1844	200	......	......	
....do	Apr. 29	Dec. 27, 1844	30	25	......	
Indian Ocean	July 14	....	......	1, 100	......	Burned at Feejee Islands, February, 1846; cargo saved; added 1844; sent home 10,000 pounds bone and 128 barrels sperm.
....do	July 11	....	......	1, 250	......	Condemned at Pernambuco, August, 1848.
N. W. Coast	June 7	May 19, 1847	150	1, 100	12, 000	A portion of the bone was on freight; sold 1847.
....do	Oct. 7	Aug. 26, 1847	200	1, 800	2, 500	
Indian and N.W	July 7	Feb. —, 1847	150	2, 850	56, 000	Withdrawn 1847; sold to New Bedford.
N. W. Coast	Oct. 19	Apr. 7, 1847	110	3, 200	17, 000	Added 1844; sent home 19,654 pounds bone.
Indian Ocean	Nov. 11	Feb. 2, 1847	272	130	......	Sold to New Bedford 1848.
South Atlantic	Oct. 19	July 4, 1846	250	......	......	
N. W. Coast	June 20	June 7, 1847	350	2, 350	23, 000	Sold for California 1848.
Indian Ocean	May 12	Oct. 7, 1846	350	......	......	Sold to New Bedford, 1847.
Pacific Ocean	Sept. 4	Sept. 15, 1848	860	140	......	
N. W. Coast	May 28	June 14, 1848	400	2, 600	44, 000	Added 1844; sent home 2,033 pounds bone; withdrawn 1849.
....do	Aug. 1	Mar. 8, 1848	170	3, 000	10, 000	Added 1844 from New York.
Indian Ocean	May 21	Sept. 29, 1847	70	2, 730	8, 000	Sold for California 1848; sent home 23,931 pounds bone.
N. W. Coast	Nov. 3	....	......	......	......	Shipped 500 sperm, 21,000 pounds bone to London; from Sidney; changed her name to Sacramento and went into the California trado 1851; sent home 1,750 whale.

Table showing returns of whaling-vessels

Name of vessel.	Class.	Tonnage.	Captain.	Managing owner or agent.
1844.				
Newport, R. I.—Continued.				
Helen	Brig	120	T. B. Peabody	William Price
Le Baron	Bark	170	James Price	do
Pocahontas	Brig	114	—— Barker	Samuel Barker
William Lee	Ship	311	—— Wimpenney	J. S. Monroe
Lynn, Mass.				
Ninus	Ship	260	—— Wyatt	Andrews Breed
Salem, Mass.				
Elizabeth	Ship	398	—— Hall	S. C. Phillips
Somerset, Mass.				
Pilgrim	Bark	137	—— Clark	George B. Hood
Cold Spring, Mass.				
Alice	Bark	281	—— Smith	John H. Jones
Huntsville	Ship	523	—— Howe	do
Splendid	do	473	—— Fordham	do
Stonington, Conn.				
America	Ship	464	—— Nash	Charles P. Williams
Bolton	Bark	220	—— Barber	do
Charles Phelps	Ship	362	—— Pendleton	do
Eugene	do	297	—— Pendleton	do
Mercury	do	305	—— Pendleton	Pendleton & Trumbull
Mary and Susan	do	392	—— Hubbard	C. P. Williams
Newark	do	323	—— Pendleton	John F. Trumbull
Newburyport	Bark	341	—— Gray	Pendleton & Trumbull
Prudent	do	398	—— Brewster	C. P. Williams
Sophia and Eliza	Ship	206	—— Stevens	J. F. Trumbull
United States	do	244	—— Stevens	do
Warsaw	do	332	—— Barnum	Pendleton & Stant
New London, Conn.				
Armata	Ship	413	—— Hull	Abner Bassett
Bengal	Schooner	304	—— Frink	Thomas Fitch, 2d
Betsey	do	125	—— Perkins	Joseph Lawrence
Chas. Carroll	Ship	404	—— Long	Perkins & Smith
Charleston	do	373	—— Chester	N. & W. W. Billings
Columbia	do	492	—— Kelley	Perkins & Smith
Com. Perry	Bark	270	—— Bailey	Frink, Chew & Co
Columbus	Brig	159	—— Huntley	Williams & Barnes
Ceres	Bark	176	—— Harris	Weaver & Rogers
Dove	Bark	145	—— Douglass	Havens & Smith
Dromo	Ship	306	—— Steel	Thomas Fitch, 2d
Exile	Schooner	70	—— Bolls	Learned & Stoddard
Fame	Bark	258	—— Mitchell	William Tate
Franklin	Schooner	119	—— Stroud	Perkins & Smith
Garland	do	60	—— Marks	William Tate
Hibernia	Ship	551	—— Smith	Thomas Fitch, 2d

sailing from American ports—Continued.

Whaling-ground.	Date—		Result of voyage.			Remarks.
	Of sailing.	Of arrival.	Sperm-oil.	Whale-oil.	Whalebone.	
			Bbls.	*Bbls.*	*Lbs.*	
Atlantic	May 26	Aug. 22, 1845	80	15	......	Sold 1847.
....do	Oct. 10	Aug. 23, 1846	320	20	......	Added 1844 from Mattapoisett; sold to New Bedford 1846.
South Atlantic.	May 10	Aug. 29, 1844	......	15	......	Returned in consequence of a mutiny among the crew; withdrawn 1844.
Pacific Ocean ..	July 10	Oct. 12, 1847	500	1,300	12,000	
N. W. Coast....	Aug. 30	May 23, 1847	150	1,850	19,000	Sent home 8,604 pounds bone; sold 1847.
Pacific Ocean ..	Dec. 17	May 15, 1848	620	1,580	14,000	
Atlantic	Dec. 19	June 4, 1846	117	30	......	
....	Sept. 18	June 17, 1846	150	2,000	19,000	Added 1844.
N. W. Coast...	Oct. 23	June 29, 1847	200	2,900	31,000	Added 1844; third mate, —— Weeks, killed by a whale, December, 1845.
....do	June 28	Apr. 26, 1848	......	2,400	12,000	Added 1844; sent home 12,016 pounds bone; second mate, John Drury, died at Honolulu, March, 1845.
N. W. Coast...	Dec. 16	June 17, 1847	150	2,650	25,000	Sold to New Bedford for California trade 1848.
Crozette Island	July 1	Mar. 30, 1845	......	600	......	
Indian Ocean ..	June 25	Apr. 15, 1847	50	1,750	16,000	
....do	July 15	May 20, 1847	50	1,750	16,000	
Chili and N. W.	July 30	Apr. 13, 1846	70	2,000	17,000	
Indian Ocean ..	July 30	May 23, 1847	100	2,050	20,000	Sent home 11,000 pounds bone; added 1844.
Chili and N. W.	June 20	Apr. 30, 1846	250	2,000	20,000	
....do	July 8	Mar. 5, 1847	100	2,900	16,000	Added 1844.
N. W. Coast....	Sept. 11	Mar. 1, 1847	25	2,300	20,000	Added 1844.
Indian Ocean ..	July 22	....	......	......	......	Run into by British bark Wellington, latitude 18° south, longitude 17° west, and abandoned in a sinking condition; added 1844 from Duxbury.
N. W. Coast....	Sept. 27	July 20, 1847	60	1,540	7,000	
....do	Dec. 1	May 12, 1847	100	800	......	Added 1844; withdrawn 1847.
Indian and N. W.	Aug. 1	Apr. 13, 1846	120	2,775	22,000	
South Atlantic.	May 21	Mar. 9, 1847	......	2,100	......	Added 1844 from Salem; sent home 68 barrels sperm and 14,000 pounds bone.
Sealing	July 19	....	......	......	......	Lost in Straits of Magellan, January 3, 1845.
Desolat'n Isl'd.	June 26	July 30, 1845	......	3,200	17,000	Added 1844.
Indian and N. W.	June 26	Mar. 10, 1847	50	3,150	30,000	Added 1844 from Boston; sold 1847.
....do	June 18	....	......	......	......	Lost January 6, 1846, on Sydenham's Island with 2,700 barrels oil.
....do	Aug. 20	May 24, 1847	250	1,750	6,000	Sent home 9,380 pounds bone; sold 200 barrels oil at Sidney; sold 1847 to be broken up.
Atlantic	May 28	Mar. 16, 1846	200	60	......	
N. W. Coast....	Oct. 12	....	100	1,000	......	Condemned at Rio Janeiro 1847; sold whale oil; shipped sperm home.
Indian Ocean ..	June 14	Aug. 16, 1846	550	......	......	
Chili and N. W.	June 20	Mar. 10, 1847	600	2,200	9,000	Added 1844 from Boston; sent home —— pounds bone.
Desolat'n Isl'd.	July 17	Jan. 8, 1846	......	322	8,500	Added 1844.
....do	June 18	....	......	......	......	First mate, ——, Penny killed by a whale; added 1844 from Boston; went into the slave trade 1847.
... do	June 5	Apr. 7, 1846	......	500	......	
....do	June 17	....	......	......	......	Added 1844; lost on Desolation Island 1848.
Ind. and N. W.	Aug. 13	Aug. 11, 1847	......	4,000	10,000	Added 1844; sent home 16,000 pounds bone.

Table showing returns of whaling-vessels

Name of vessel.	Class.	Tonnage.	Captain.	Managing owner or agent.
1844.				
New London, Conn.—Continued.				
Hand	Schooner	80	—— Butler	Perkins & Smith
Helvetia	Ship	339	—— Porter	Joseph Lawrence
Henry Thompson	do	315	—— Andrews	Frink, Chew & Co
India	do	433	—— Miller	Havens & Smith
Indian Chief	do	401	—— Hemsted	Frink, Chew & Co
Iris	Bark	245	—— Haynes	do
Isaac Hicks	Ship	495	—— Rice	Jos. Lawrence
Izaak Walton	do	440	—— Fitch	N. & W. W. Billings
Jason	do	335	—— Slate	Learned & Stoddard
Jefferson	do	390	—— Harris	William P. Benjamin
John and Elizabeth	do	290	—— Walker	Havens & Smith
Julius Cæsar	do	347	—— Lyons	Learned & Stoddard
Louvre	do	370	—— Green	Lyman Allen
Mogul	do	395	—— Andrews	Williams & Barnes
Montezuma	do	424	—— Baker	do
Merrimack	do	414	—— Destin	Havens & Smith
Morrison	do	563	—— Greene	do
Neptune	do	285	—— Oat	do
North America	do	388	—— Richards	do
Phœnix	do	404	—— Skinner	N. & W. W. Billings
Superior	do	406	—— Hart	do
Shaw Perkins	Sloop	55	—— Carr	Perkins & Smith
Tenedos	Bark	245	—— Comstock	Jos. Lawrence
Venice	do	353	—— Lester	Weaver & Rogers
Vesper	do	321	—— Clark	Williams & Barnes
Greenport, N. Y.				
Lucy Ann	Ship	309	—— Brown	Wiggins, Parsons & Cook
Neva	do	362	—— Case	Ireland, Wells & Carpenter.
Philip, 1st	do	293	—— Case	do
Roanoke	Bark	252	—— Baldwin	Wiggins & Parsons
Washington	Ship	336	—— Corwin	do
New Suffolk, N. Y.				
Gentleman	Bark	227	—— Payne	Ira B. Tuthill
Sag Harbor, N. Y.				
Acasta	Bark	286	—— Harlow	John Budd
Alciope	Ship	377	—— Halsey	Post & Sherry
Arabella	do	367	—— Babcock	N. & G. Howell
Barbara	Bark	268	—— French	Charles T. Dering
Franklin	Ship	391	—— Halsey	Hunting Cooper
Hamilton	do	329	—— Babcock	C. T. Dering
Hudson	do	368	—— Nickerson	L. D. Cook & H. Green
Italy	do	299	—— Weld	David G. Floyd
John Wells	do	366	—— Hedges	Thomas Brown
Levant	do	382	—— Havens	Tiffany & Bennett
Martha	do	369	—— Drake	L. D. Cook & H. Green
Niantic	do	452	—— Slate	C. T. Dering
Nimrod	Bark	280	—— Fowler	do
Noble	do	273	—— Howes	do
Ontario	Ship	368	—— Greene	S. & B. Hunting & Co
Ohio	do	297	—— Lowen	Post & Sherry

sailing from American ports—Continued.

Whaling-ground.	Date—		Result of voyage.			Remarks.
	Of sailing.	Of arrival.	Sperm-oil.	Whale-oil.	Whalebone.	
			Bbls.	*Bbls.*	*Lbs.*	
Desolat'n Isl'd.	June 5	....	......	....	....	Lost on No Man's Land May 23, 1847, homeward bound; sent home 60 barrels oil saved; had on board 100 whale and 200 elephant.
N. W. Coast....	June 1	....	......	....	....	Burned at Honolulu January 25, 1846; had a cargo of 1,350 sperm and 150 whale; saved about 750 barrels.
Ind. and N. W.	Sept. 11	May 24, 1847	370	2,030	12,000	Added 1844 from New York; sent home 8,000 pounds bone.
....do	Aug. 21	Apr. 6, 1847	200	4,100	15,000	Added 1844 from Boston; sent home 21,600 pounds bone 1846.
Chili and N. W	July 1	Mar. 7, 1847	130	3,070	......	Sent home 19,549 pounds bone.
Indian Ocean ..	July 17	May 5, 1848	....	1,300	10,000	
N. W. Coast....	Sept. 26	May 27, 1848	270	4,230	14,000	Added 1843; sent home 28,796 pounds bone.
....do	Oct. 8	May 20, 1847	30	3,070	31,000	New; built at Mattapoisett 1844; withdrawn 1847.
South Atlantic.	July 2	Jan. 23, 1846	......	2,650	......	
Ind. and N. W.	Aug. 15	May 24, 1847	30	1,600	16,000	Added 1844 from Wilmington.
....do	July 11	May 25, 1847	140	1,910	1,600	Sent home 12,133 pounds bone 1846.
N. W. Coast...	Sept. 20	July 14, 1847	130	1,400	12,000	
Ind. and N. W.	Aug. 1	Apr. 6, 1847	140	2,960	12,000	Added 1844; sent home 20,191 pounds bone 1846; withdrawn 1847.
....do	Sept. 17	Apr. 8, 1847	150	2,150	22,000	
....do	June 4	May 24, 1847	60	3,350	34,000	Sold 1847.
....do	July 17	May 29, 1847	25	2,975	5,000	Added 1844 from Newburyport.
....do	Sept. 16	May 5, 1848	1[illegible]	3,982	15,000	Added 1844; bought from New York; built at Philadelphia 1832; sent home 23,712 pounds bone.
....do	Aug. 3	May 19, 1847	100	1,300	12,000	Sent home 9,598 pounds bone 1846.
Chili and N. W.	July 1	June 19, 1847	250	750	2,000	Sent home 5,593 pounds bone 1846.
Indian Ocean ..	June 5	July 4, 1846	110	1,590	15,000	
Ind. and N. W.	Aug. 10	Nov. 12, 1847	150	1,5[illegible]0	80	Sent home 12,967 pounds bone 1846.
Desolat'n Isl'd.	June 5	....	......	.....	......	Lost at Desolation Island with all on board, 8 souls, 1847.
Indian Ocean ..	Aug. 5	June 9, 1847	75	1,725	1,400	First mate, ——— Churchill, injured by falling off a water-cask and died Dec., 1847.
Ind. and N. W.	July 17	Apr. 28, 1847	350	2,550	16,000	Added 1844.
N. W. Coast....	Sept. 27	July 22, 1846	160	2,640	26,000	Added 1844 from New York.
Ind. and N. W.	Nov. 7	May —, 1847	.....	2,400	24,000	Added 1844 from Wilmington.
N. W. Coast....	Sept. 4	May 1, 1847	220	2,380	20,000	Added 1844 from New York.
Ind. and N. W.	May 13	Apr. 13, 1846	2[illegible]	1,700	17,000	Bought from New York 1843.
South Seas.....	July —	July 15, 1845	....	900	7,200	
....do	Aug. 31	June 4, 1846	125	1,675	15,000	
Crozettes	June 4	Sept. 25, 1845	.....	450	......	Added 1844 from New York.
Tristan	Aug. 23	July 23, 1847	300	1,500	13,000	
New Zealand ..	July 23	July 1, 1847	175	2,650	15,000	Sent home 7,868 pounds bone; sold out of the business.
N. W. Coast...	May 28	May 24, 1847	330	1,870	16,000	
Crozettes	Aug. 30	....	......	......	......	Condemned at Valparaiso January, 1846.
N. W. Coast....	June 5	Apr. 6, 1847	160	1,640	3,000	Sent home 11,888 pounds bone.
Crozettes	July 22	June 8, 1845	160	290	2,300	
Pacific Ocean..	July 8	May 22, 1847	100	1,830	4,000	Third mate, Isaac Platt, drowned February 6, 1845; sold to Mystic 1848.
N. W. Coast....	Oct. —	May 25, 1847	300	2,700	28,000	Added 1844 from New York.
....do	July 30	June 7, 1846	60	2,340	20,000	Added 1844; bought from Newark.
....do	Sept. 19	June 5, 1847	70	1,830	18,000	Added 1844.
....do	Sept. 18	Apr. 8, 1847	180	2,550	24,000	Added 1844 from Hudson; sold 1847.
New Zealand ..	June 4	Feb. 1, 1847	120	2,400	10,000	Added 1844; sold 1847 to Warren.
Crozettes	Aug. 31	July 26, 1846	160	940	7,000	
N. W. Coast....	Sept. 19	June 22, 1846	120	1,480	6,000	Added 1844.
....do	Aug. 29	June 9, 1847	40	2,260	10,000	Withdrawn 1847.
New Zealand ..	May 28	Apr. 29, 1848	....	1,150	5,000	Added 1844 from Boston.

Table showing returns of whaling-vessels

Name of vessel.	Class.	Tonnage.	Captain.	Managing owner or agent.
1844.				
Sag Harbor, N. Y.—Continued.				
Oscar	Ship	369	—— Ludlow	Hunting Cooper
Panama	do	465	—— Crowell	N. & G. Howell
Phenix	do	314	—— Braggs	Cook & Green
Portland	do	292	—— Wade	S. & B. Hunting & Co.
Salem	do	470	—— Hand	Mulford & Sleight
S. Richards	do	454	—— Dering	do
St. Lawrence	do	523	—— Baker	Cook & Green
Sabina	do	416	—— Vail	C. T. Dering
Thos. Dickason	do	454	—— Lowen	Mulford & Sleight
Timor	do	289	—— Edwards	H. Cooper
Wiscasset	do	380	—— Paine	S. & B. Hunting & Co.
Mystic, Conn.				
Atlantic	Ship	291	—— Keeny	Charles Mallory
Alibree	Bark	378	—— Burrows	I. & W. P. Randall
Bingham	Ship	375	—— Eldredge	C. Mallory
Congress	Bark	280	—— Lester	I. & W. P. Randall
Coriolanus	Ship	268	—— Appleton	C. Mallory
Meteor	do	325	—— Lester	I. & W. P. Randall
Shepherdess	do	274	—— Clift	do
Bridgeport, Conn.				
Harvest	Bark	263	—— Brooks	Sherwood Sterling
Stieglitz	Ship	350	—— Youngs	do
1845.				
New Bedford, Mass.				
Abm. H. Howland	Ship	414	Washington Walker	Abm. H. Howland
Abm. Barker	do	400	—— Brayton	Abraham Barker
Addison	do	426	—— West	Isaac B. Richmond
Alfred	Schooner	180	J. P. Davenport	Pope & Morgan
America	Ship	418	—— Crowell	I. Howland, jr., & Co.
Ann Alexander	do	253	—— Sawtelle	Geo. Howland
Archer	do	322	M. Snell	Tobey & Ricketson
Balæna	do	301	—— Dexter	J. & J. Howland
Bramin	Bark	245	—— Macomber	Gideon Allen
Callao	Ship	324	—— Sisson	Henry Taber & Co.
Ceres	do	328	—— Adams	Thomas Knowles & Co.
Canton, 2d	do	280	—— Taber	Charles R. Tucker & Co.
Canton Packet	do	274	H. Shearman	I. H. Bartlett
C. W. Morgan	do	351	J. D. Sampson	C. W. Morgan
Charles	do	296	E. Coan	Samuel Rodman
Copia	do	315	D. H. Taber	Lemuel Kollock
Clarice	Bark	237	—— Wady	Pope & Morgan
Chili	Ship	291	H. H. Ricketson	B. B. Howard
Cowper	do	391	J. R. Hatheway	do
Dimon	Bark	220	Abner Smith	Ingalls & Lucas
Dragon	do	190	—— Bennett	Tobey & Ricketson
Edward	Ship	339	J. S. Barker	Pope & Morgan

sailing from American ports—Continued.

Whaling-ground.	Date— Of sailing.	Date— Of arrival.	Result of voyage. Sperm-oil.	Result of voyage. Whale-oil.	Result of voyage. Whalebone.	Remarks.
			Bbls.	*Bbls.*	*Lbs.*	
Crozettes	Oct. 31	Nov. 13, 1845	.....	700	5,600	Bought from New York 1844; returned in consequence of a mutiny among the crew.
N. W. Coast....	May 23	May 26, 1847	80	2,920	10,000	
....do	Oct. 10	June 5, 1847	......	1,800	8,000	
New Zealand ..	June 1	June 5, 1846	100	1,300	12,000	
N. Z. and N. W.	Oct. 14	Apr. 29, 1848	300	1,400	12,000	Added 1844 from New York.
New Zealand ..	May 2	July 28, 1847	70	1,800	......	Sold 1847.
N. W. Coast....	July 29	May 20, 1848	300	4,500	11,000	Added 1844; sent home 29,688 pounds bone.
....do	June 24	May 24, 1847	60	1,940	18,000	Added 1844 from New York; sold 1847.
....do	Aug. 12	Apr. 14, 1847	.....	3,800	10,000	Sold 1847.
....do	July 1	May 1, 1846	140	2,310	20,000	
....do	Sept. 27	Feb. 19, 1847	.....	3,700	34,000	Withdrawn 1847.
N. W. Coast....	July 15	May 25, 1847	.....	2,300	9,000	Added 1844 from Bridgeport; lost 1847.
....do	July 22	Apr. 8, 1847	150	2,100	20,000	Added 1844 from New York; Captain Burrows came home sick; Captain Avery took command; Captain Avery was killed by a whale 1846; withdrawn 1847.
....do	May 23	Mar. 12, 1846	80	2,350	22,000	
Ind. and N. W.	Oct. 12	Apr. 6, 1847	150	2,150	20,000	Sent home 150 sperm, 2,150 whale, and 20,000 pounds bone.
N. W. Coast....	Oct. 3	July 7, 1847	70	1,000	5,000	Added 1844 from Boston.
Ind. and N. W.	Sept. 15	Apr. 8, 1847	200	1,800	20,000	
....do	Sept. 3	June 5, 1847	150	1,700	16,000	Sent home 10,000 pounds bone.
South Seas.....	June 27	May 26, 1847	400	1,400	5,000	Sold to New Bedford 1847.
N. W. Coast....	Aug. 7	June 20, 1849	300	2,200	22,000	Added 1844; sold 1,200 barrels whale at Hobart Town; sold to New Bedford and withdrawn for California.
Ind. and N. W.	Sept. 2	Apr. 2, 1848	125	3,475	......	Built at New Bedford 1845.
Pac. and N. W.	Sept. 25	May 4, 1848	500	2,400	15,000	Built at Fairhaven 1845.
N. W. Coast....	Oct. 13	Apr. 4, 1848	150	2,650	11,000	First mate, Daniel Borden, died at sea June 13, 1847; sent home 15,877 pounds bone and 100 sperm.
Pacific Ocean..	Aug. 28	Apr. 28, 1852	53	......	......	Built at Baltimore 1845; sold and sent home 2,147 barrels sperm.
N. W. Coast....	Oct. 21	Apr. 24, 1848	80	1,800	2,000	Went into the California trade 1849; sent home 17,300 pounds of bone.
Pacific Ocean..	Nov. 11	Nov. 4, 1849	1,243	12	......	
Pac. and N. W.	May 27	Oct. 9, 1847	400	1,150	11,800	
Pacific Ocean..	Oct. 23	May 7, 1849	1,860	180	1,000	
Atl. and Ind ...	Aug. 31	Sept. 5, 1847	370	100	4,000	
Pacific Ocean..	Aug. 19	July 1, 1849	2,007	81	......	Sent home 110 sperm.
Ind. and N. W.	July 28	....	......	......	......	Bought from Wilmington 1845; lost in Torres Straits 1849.
Indian Ocean ..	July 29	June 15, 1847	150	1,850	......	Sent home 9,679 pounds bone.
Pacific Ocean..	Oct. 15	Oct. 12, 1849	1,747	87	500	Badly burned at Fejee Islands by crew June, 1846; repaired at Sydney.
....do	June 10	Dec. 9, 1848	2,100	100	......	Sent home 70 sperm.
....do	July 8	May 6, 1849	1,759	......	......	
Ind. and N. W	June 17	May 5, 1848	290	2,100	6,000	
Pacific Ocean..	Oct. 13	July 21, 1846	40	30	......	
Indian Ocean ..	July 10	June 29, 1848	150	1,550	10,000	Sent home 36 sperm.
Ind. and N. W.	June 3	Sept. 24, 1848	150	2,756	23,000	Bought from Newburyport 1845; withdrawn 1848.
Atlantic	June 18	Sept. 2, 1848	700	.....	......	Formerly a brig; bought from New York 1845; sent home 125 sperm; sold for California 1848.
South Atlantic.	Aug. 13	....	.....	......	......	Sailed; returned July 12 leaking badly; lost 1847.
Ind. and N. W.	July 15	Apr. 5, 1849	179	2,050	7,400	Bought from Hudson 1845; Captain B. marched with his crew to relief of garrison at San José 1846. Captain B. left ship afterward and came home sick; sold to go to California 1849; sold to Nantucket 1851.

Table showing returns of whaling-vessels

Name of vessel.	Class.	Tonnage.	Captain.	Managing owner or agent.
1845.				
New Bedford, Mass.—Continued.				
Endeavour	Bark	253	—— West	C. R. Tucker & Co
Florida, 2d	Ship	524	Arthur Cox	Samuel W. Rodman
Frances	Bark	368	Reuben Taber, jr	G. Allen
Frances Henrietta	Ship	407	—— Poole	S. W. Rodman
Gen. Pike	...do	313	—— Pierce	William Gifford
Geo. and Susan	...do	350	—— Taber	G. Howland
George and Martha	Bark	277	—— Beard	Randall & Haskall
Globe	Ship	479	—— Daggett	George Hussey
Geo. Washington	Ship	230	—— Baker	Charles Hitch
Gratitude	...do	337	—— Wilcox	Swift & Allen
Harrison	...do	371	—— Shearman	Abraham Ashley, 2d
Herald	...do	274	George Stewart	Tobey & Ricketson
Henry Kneeland	...do	304	A. Fish	Gilbert Hatheway
Hercules	...do	335	H. Beette	Jireh Perry
Hercules, 2d	...do	290	—— Marvel	D. R. Greene & Co
Hope	Bark	180	B. Ellis	William Watkins
Hydaspe	Ship	313	—— Taylor	J. B. Wood & Co
India	...do	360	—— Fisher	A. H. Howland
Inez	...do	350	—— Jackson	B. B. Howard
Isaac Howland	...do	399	Andrew Corey	I. Howland, jr., & Co
Isabella	...do	411	—— Stewart	James H. Howland
Java	...do	278	L. B. Bronson	George Howland
Janus	...do	321	—— Hammond	T. & A. R. Nye
James Maury	...do	397	—— Whelden	C. R. Tucker & Co
Junius	Bark	198	—— Smith	A. Robeson
Jeannette	Ship	340	—— Atkins	I. R. Richmond
J. E. Donnell	Bark	343	William A. Hussey	Swift & Allen
Kutusoff	Ship	415	William Shockley	J. Dunbar & Co
Lancaster	...do	383	James Cornell	T. & A. R. Nye
Leonidas	...do	231	R. Swift	F. S. Hathaway
Marengo	...do	420	T. Cole	Jona. Bourne, jr
Maria Theresa	...do	330	S. D. Fisher, jr	T. & A. R. Nye
Mars	Bark	270	—— Borden	C. R. Tucker & Co
Mercator	Ship	246	—— Sanford	John A. Parker
Metacom	...do	360	—— Smith	J. B. Wood & Co
Menkar	...do	371	—— Norton	Philip Anthony
Minerva Smyth	Ship	335	—— Crocker	I. Howland, jr., & Co
Magnolia	...do	396	B. Simmons	C. W. Morgan
Minerva, 2d	...do	291	O. Smalley	Thomas Knowles & Co.
Mt. Wollaston	...do	325	M. Bowen	Dwight R. Perry
Nimrod	...do	340	W. H. Shearman	B. Ricketson
Navy	...do	356	J. Norton	J. B. Wood & Co.
Obed Mitchell	...do	355	P. S. Wing	Haskell & Randall
Ocean	...do	349	—— Almy	J. R. Thornton
Ohio	...do	383	O. Webb	E. W. Howland

sailing from American ports—Continued.

Whaling-ground.	Date— Of sailing.	Date— Of arrival.	Result of voyage. Sperm-oil.	Result of voyage. Whale-oil.	Result of voyage. Whalebone.	Remarks.
			Bbls.	*Bbls.*	*Lbs.*	
Ind. and N. W	July 4	May 21, 1847	100	1,600	15,000	
....do........	Aug. 4	May 2, 1849	35	3,553	19,200	Formerly in guano trade; sold to go to California 1849; sent home 328 sperm and 12,000 pounds bone.
....do........	Aug. 2	....	......	......	......	Burnt at Mauritius April 24, 1846; sent home 80 sperm.
....do........	Aug. 12	June 3, 1848	160	2,840	28,000	Sent home 40 sperm.
N. W. Coast...	Nov. 21	Oct. 5, 1849	1,260	178	......	
Pac. and N. W.	Oct. 16	July 14, 1848	150	2,600	12,000	
Indian Ocean..	Aug. 27	Apr. 29, 1848	70	700	10,700	Sold to go to California 1849; sailed June 17; returned August 16, captain sick.
N. W. Coast....	Sept. 13	Aug. 22, 1850	76	4,394	17,200	Bought from Philadelphia 1845; sent home 13,411 pounds bone.
Indian Ocean..	Nov. 6	Apr. 4, 1848	1,050	......	......	
Ind. and N. W	June 14	June 12, 1848	. 120	2,800	10,000	Sent home 275 sperm, 20,897 pounds bone.
....do........	May 21	Oct. 13, 1850	63	39	......	Sold some oil at Sydney; shipped some thence to London; sent home 11,148 pounds bone.
Pacific Ocean.	May 23	Nov. 25, 1848	1,500	......	......	Sent home 117 sperm.
N. W. Coast...	Oct. 30	May 22, 1848	100	1,400	11,000	Added 1845 from New York.
Indian Ocean..	July 18	May 15, 1849	243	1,407	14,100	Sent home 240 sperm.
Atlantic	May 18	Mar. 25, 1847	250	......	......	Sent home 200 sperm.
Atl. and Ind...	May 22	July 31, 1847	1,300	......	......	
Indian Ocean..	June 2	Sept. 30, 1848	1,400	200	......	Sent home 110 sperm.
Ind. and N. W	July 1	Mar. 23, 1848	250	2,650	10,000	Sent home 21,688 pounds bone.
N. W. Coast...	Oct. 30	....	......	3,000	......	Bought from Boston 1845; shipped oil to London and went into California trade; sent home 5,757 pounds bone.
Ind. and N. W..	June 10	Apr. 29, 1848	150	2,650	24,000	
....do........	July 26	June 8, 1848	1,050	1,650	8,000	
Pac. and N. W	Aug. 26	June 18, 1848	40	1,510	8,000	Sent home 7,172 pounds bone.
Pacific Ocean..	Oct. 4	May 8, 1848	50	1,600	8,000	Sailed under Capt. W. Taber, but he left the ship and came home sick.
Pac. and N. W	June 5	May 14, 1848	......	3,600	38,000	Bought from Salem 1845; sent home 100 sperm.
Indian Ocean..	July 14	Apr. 8, 1850	126	34	......	
N. W. Coast...	July 31	June 21, 1848	500	1,300	13,000	Third mate, George S. Daniels, killed by a whale 1846; sent home 45 sperm.
Pac. and N. W	Dec. 3	Apr. 5, 1849	49	3,066	17,660	Bought from Boston 1845; sent home 340 sperm, 22,000 pounds bone.
N. W. Coast...	July 26	Mar. 23, 1848	400	2,900	14,000	
Pac. and N. W	May 10	Jan. 18, 1847	425	2,225	14,000	Sent home 9,148 pounds bone.
Pacific Ocean..	Nov. 21	May 22, 1850	665	8	......	
N. W. Coast...	Oct. 5	Apr. 22, 1848	400	3,400	32,000	Bought from New Orleans 1845; sent home 16,672 pounds bone.
Ind. and N. W	July 1	July 4, 1847	260	2,200	2,500	Sailed May 1st; May 14th lost first mate, Benjamin Golden, one boat-steerer and three men in a gale; returned June 9th; sent home 16,000 pounds bone.
Indian Ocean..	Sept. 24	May 27, 1848	350	1,350	6,000	
....do........	Nov. 7	May 9, 1850	572	271	1,000	
N. W. Coast..	Nov. 29	Mar. 12, 1848	100	2,700	1,200	Sent home 70 whale, 29,000 pounds bone.
Ind. and N. W..	Aug. 20	May 4, 1848	250	2,250	14,000	Bought from Newport 1845; sent home 140 sperm, 12,203 pounds bone.
South Seas....	Oct. 23	Apr. 4, 1848	200	2,700	29,000	
Ind. and N. W.	June 25	Oct. 16, 1848	450	3,250	17,000	Captain Simmons and Captain Barker of the Edward landed their crews and marched to the relief of the garrison at San José 1846; withdrawn 1848; sent home 50 sperm.
Indian Ocean..	May 2	Apr. 5, 1848	320	2,080	19,000	
Ind. and N. W..	July 10	Apr. 24, 1849	726	140	......	Added 1845 from Fairhaven; bought from Salem; shipped oil to London; return of bone not given; sent home 150 whale, 1,400 pounds bone.
....do........	May 27	Apr. 6, 1848	300	2,300	500	Sent home 12,805 pounds bone.
....do........	Aug. 22	Mar. 11, 1848	25	2,500	15,000	
N. W. Coast....	Oct. 27	May 10, 1848	350	2,000	8,000	Bought from Nantucket 1845.
Indian Ocean..	Jan. 2	Nov. 7, 1848	1,380	2[illegible]	......	Added 1844 from Nantucket.
Ind. and N. W..	Sept. 2	Apr. 28, 1848	130	2,770	10,00	Bought from Nantucket 1845; sent home 21,877 pounds bone.

Table showing returns of whaling-vessels

Name of vessel.	Class.	Tonnage.	Captain.	Managing owner or agent.
1845.				
New Bedford, Mass.—Continued.				
Olive Branch	Ship	366	G. J. Place	James D. Thompson
Orozimbo	do	588	—— Norton	B. Ricketson
Pantheon	Bark	271	W. Jenney	J. Bourne, jr
Parachute	Ship	331	—— Devoll	B. B. Howard
Rebecca Sims	do	400	—— Taber	William R. Rodman
Robert Edwards	do	356	N. Burgess	J. & J. Howland
Rodman	Brig	83	—— Sowle	B. Ricketson
Roman	Ship	375	H. Shockley	E. C. Jones
Rousseau	do	300	—— Smith	George Howland
Russell	Bark	302	J. O. Morse	Edward Munroe
Saratoga	Ship	543	J. R. L. Smith	Abm. Ashley
Swift	do	321	—— Jenkins	Thomas S. Hathaway
Statira	do	340	—— Adams	Hathaway & Luce
Smyrna	Bark	219	—— Hillman	B. Ricketson
Susan	Ship	261	—— Manchester	A. H. Howland
Timolean	do	340	—— Luscomb	J. Dunbar & Co.
Valparaiso	Bark	402	Richard Luce	Hathaway & Luce
W. Hamilton	Ship	463	—— Fisher	I. Howland, jr., & Co.
Winslow	Bark	263	—— Simons	Samuel Rodman
Zoroaster	Brig	159	—— Hammond	Pardon G. Seabury
Fairhaven, Mass.				
Acushnet	Ship	359	—— Rogers	Bradford, Fuller & Co
Adeline Gibbs	do	354	—— West	Gibbs & Jenney
Amazon	do	348	—— Smith	Nathan Church
Ansel Gibbs	do	319	—— Merrihew	Gibbs & Jenney
Arab	do	336	—— Braley	E. Sawin
Heroine	do	337	—— West	N. Church
Java	do	294	—— Lucas	Atkins Adams
John A. Robb	do	273	—— Winslow	L. C. Tripp
Lagrange	Bark	280	—— Dexter	Atkins Adams
Lydia	Ship	358	—— Robinson	Sheffield Reed
Martha	do	298	R. N. Smith	N. Church
Oregon	do	339	—— Wimpenny	L. C. Tripp
Pacific	Bark	314	—— Alden	Asa Swift
Sharon	Ship	354	Benjamin Clough	Gibbs & Jenney
South Boston	do	339	—— Hoxie	E. Sawin
Wm. & Henry	do	261	—— Benjamin	I. F. Terry
Dartmouth, Mass.				
Russell	Ship	387	—— Sowle	Prince Sears
Falmouth, Mass.				
Com. Morris	Ship	350	Silas Jones	Oliver C. Swift
Wm. Penn	do	364	—— Wimpenny	do
Mattapoisett, Mass.				
Cachalot	Ship	230	—— Taber	Wilson Barstow
Willis	Bark	164	—— Higgins	R. L. Barstow
Sippican, Mass.				
Hecla	Bark	207	—— Hedge	J. S. Bates
Juno	Brig	123	—— Bates	Elisha Luce
Popmunnet	Bark	184	—— Tilton	Henry M. Allen
Wareham, Mass.				
Inga	Brig	169	—— Cudworth	M. S. F. Tobey
Pleiades	Bark	261	—— Russell	do

sailing from American ports—Continued.

Whaling-ground.	Date— Of sailing.	Date— Of arrival.	Result of voyage. Sperm-oil.	Result of voyage. Whale-oil.	Result of voyage. Whalebone.	Remarks.
			Bbls.	*Bbls.*	*Lbs.*	
Pac. and N. W.	Oct. 21	May 4, 1849	224	2,670	21,200	Added 1845; sold 1,300 whale on voyage. Sold to go to California 1849.
N. W. Coast....	Oct. 30	Apr. 6, 1848	100	3,100	11,100	
Ind. and N. W.	May 15	May 13, 1849	501	1,140	2,500	
....do	Sept. 2	Mar. 12, 1848	130	3,000	16,000	
New Zealand ..	May 24	June 1, 1849	1,495	9	......	Third mate and boats' crew lost; supposed to have been carried down by a whale.
Pacific Ocean ..	June 14	Nov. 17, 1848	2,200	70	......	
Atlantic	Oct. 28	May 20, 1846	14	2	....	Added, 1845.
Ind. and N. W..	May 12	Apr. 27, 1847	100	2,550	24,000	Sent home 75 sperm, 9,866 pounds bone.
Pacific Ocean..	Aug. 7	Feb. 4, 1849	1,700	550	7,000	
....do	Aug. 31	Jan. 17, 1849	2,300	......	.....	Went into California trade 1849; sent home 200 sperm.
Pac. and N. W.	Oct. 22	May 5, 1849	222	4,37[illegible]	7,700	Bought from New York 1845; sent home 32,502 pounds bone.
Pacific Ocean..	Aug. 31	Apr. 5, 1849	1,290	17[illegible]	200	
N. W. Coast....	Oct. 21	May 15, 1848	210	2,400	15,000	Sent home 9,075 pounds bone.
Pacific Ocean..	Oct. 21	June 5, 1849	777	......	.....	Second mate, Mr. Fisher, died at sea 1848.
Ind. and N. W.	July 28	Nov. 17, 1848	500	750	.....	Sent home 106 sperm.
N. W. Coast....	Aug. 21	Apr. 23, 1848	70	1,650	11,000	Condemned and broken up at New Bedford 1849.
Pac. and N. W.	July 28	Mar. 11, 1848	500	2,500	1,000	Bought from New York 1845; sent home 50 sperm.
Ind. and N. W.	July 10	Jan. 14, 1848	120	4,000	15,000	Sent home 25,740 bone.
South Atlantic.	Apr. 11	Sept. 7, 1849	371	23[illegible]	......	Withdrawn for California trade 1849.
Atlantic	July 19	Oct. 15, 1846	260	.....	......	Sold 1847.
N. W. Coast....	July 18	June 7, 1848	500	800	6,000	Had boat stove by a whale December, 1847. John Taber, third mate, and 4 men killed.
Pac. and N. W	Oct. 16	July 1, 1848	400	2,100	7,000	Sent home 20,070 pounds bone.
Ind. and N. W..	Aug. 2	May 5, 1848	70	2,230	10,000	Sent home 9,665 pounds bone.
...do	June 5	July 9, 1849	25	2,300	14,000	
South Atlantic.	Nov. 22	June 2, 1849	1,800	......	.....	
Ind. and N. W..	June 4	Sept. 14, 1847	190	2,000	10,000	
Pac. and N. W	Oct. 20	June 14, 1849	1,000	300	2,000	
Pacific Ocean..	Nov. 28	July 16, 1849	900	500	5,000	Bought from Baltimore 1845.
Ind. and N. W..	July 19	July 11, 1850	340	990	......	Sent home 2,272 pounds bone.
Pacific Ocean..	May 8	Apr. 25, 1848	500	1,900	4,000	Bought from Nantucket.
Pac. and N. W.	Oct. 21	July 31, 1848	14	1,800	15,000	
....do	June 12	Mar. 10, 1849	1,750	700	6,000	
Ind. and N. W..	July 13	June 14, 1849	300	1,100	5,000	
....do	May 20	Apr. 23, 1848	200	2,000	15,000	Sent home 6,000 pounds bone.
....do	May 24	Apr. 30, 1848	300	2,000	23,000	
....do	Sept. 30	Dec. 4, 1848	850	......	.....	Sold for California 1848.
Ind. and N. W..	June 17	....	....	....	.....	Struck on a sunken rock off Feejee Islands, August 8, 1847; a total loss.
Pacific Ocean..	July 9	Apr. 1, 1849	2,450	100	.....	Sent home 90 barrels sperm 1845; third mate, E. Chadwick, and his boats' crew capsized and lost on coast of Chili, 1846.
Ind. and N. W..	July 19	....	....	.....	.....	Sent home 9,798 pounds bone; totally lost on the Island of Whytootacke, November 26, 1847; had 100 sperm and 1,700 whale; saved 1,200 barrels and sold it at 50 cents per barrel.
Atlantic	Apr. 28	Apr. 10, 1847	850	450	3,000	New 1845.
....do	Nov. 20	Aug. 13, 1847	70	140	......	
Indian Ocean ..	Sept. 26	Nov. 10, 1848	450	......	......	
Atlantic	June 18	Aug. 21, 1846	300	......	......	Withdrawn 1847.
Atl. and Ind ..	Aug. 22	Sept. 10, 1847	300	......	......	Sent home 85 barrels sperm 1845; sold to Fairhaven 1847; first mate, ——— Lumbert, and one man drowned 1846.
Atlantic	Mar. 25	June 3, 1846	750	......	......	
Indian Ocean ..	June 1	Mar. 4, 1848	900	60	......	

Table showing returns of whaling-vessels

Name of vessel.	Class.	Tonnage.	Captain.	Managing owner or agent.
1845.				
Westport, Mass.				
Barclay	Bark	167	—— Grinnell	Davis & Corey
Champion	do	209	—— Gifford	Andrew Hicks
Catherwood	Brig	199	—— Cushing	Thomas W. Mayhew
Dr. Franklin	Bark	171	—— Hazard	Job Davis
Harbinger	Ship	262	—— Brownell	Davis & Corey
Mexico	Brig	130	—— Wing	do
President	Bark	167	—— Little	Andrew Hicks
Th. Winslow	do	126	—— Baker	T. W. Mayhew
Nantucket, Mass.				
American	Ship	340	Frederick W. Luce	Daniel Jones
Aurora	do	346	Frederick W. Coffin	T. & P. Macy
Chris. Mitchell	do	387	Enoch Ackley	C. Mitchell & Co
Charles & Henry	do	336	Benjamin C. Sayer	
Cyrus	do	328	Alex. M. Myrick	George Myrick, jr
David Paddack	do	352	Charles B. Swain, 2d	D. Jones
Edward Cary	do	353	Benjamin C. Sayer	C. G. & H. Coffin
Elizabeth Starbuck	do	381	Elijah Parker	Levi Starbuck
Enterprise	do	413	Samuel C. Wyer	E. W. Gardner
Foster	do	317	Francis C. Coffin	Edward H. Barker
Franklin	do	246	Henry Starbuck	do
Ganges	do	315	James Nichols	Barker Burnell
Harvest	do	360	George D. Coffin	E. Swain & N. Rand
Howard	do	364	Alexander Bunker	Timothy Hussey
Japan	do	33[illegible]	Valentine S. Riddell	Barker & Athearn
John Adams	do	296	William Rawson	Francis B. Folger
Levi Starbuck	do	376	Joseph P. Nye	Levi Starbuck
Martha	do	27[illegible]	Henry B. Folger	Peter Folger
Massachusetts	do	360	James Codd	George C. Gardner
Montano	do	365	Uriah Russell	Edward Field
Monticello	do	368	John M. Folger	John H. Shaw
Nantucket	do	350	Benjamin C. Gardner	H. G. O. Dunham
Navigator	do	33[illegible]	George Palmer	Matt. Crosby
Norman	do	338	Richard Gardner	G. & M. Starbuck
Orion	do	354	Edward S. Ray	Frederick Hussey
Potomac	do	356	Oliver C. Swain	T. & P. Macy
Sarah Parker	do	387	Thomas Russell	David Thain
Scotland	do	384	Veranus Smith	French & Coffin
Tyleston	Brig	...	...	David Thain
United States	Ship	37[illegible]	Calvin G. Worth	Barrett & Upton
Edgartown, Mass.				
Champion	Ship	399	—— Merry	Grafton Norton
Pavillion	Brig	150	—— Adams	Calvin C. Adams
Vesta	do	156	—— Mayhew	Benjamin Worth
Holmes' Hole, Mass.				
Delphos	Ship	338	—— West	Thomas [illegible]radley
Malta	Brig	150	—— Smith	Thomas Barrows

sailing from American ports—Continued.

Whaling-ground.	Date—		Result of voyage.			Remarks.
	Of sailing.	Of arrival.	Sperm-oil.	Whale-oil.	Whalebone.	
			Bbls.	*Bbls.*	*Lbs.*	
Atlantic	June 5	Nov. 22, 1846	200	.....	.....	
....do	Sept. 10	Nov. 5, 1846	450	50	.....	
....do	Oct. 14	Jan. —, 1848	450	.....	.....	
....do	July 26	Oct. 11, 1846	320	17	.....	
Indian Ocean	Jan. 2	Oct. 1, 1847	450	.....	.....	
Atlantic	Oct. 8	Oct. 11, 1846	400	.....	.....	
....do	Aug. 22	Apr. 8, 1846	65	.....	.....	Returned in consequence of the death of Captain Little; sailed again in 1846.
....do	June 22	May 22, 1846	280	.....	.....	
Pacific Ocean	Nov. 5	July 22, 1849	1,270	390	.....	Sold 100 barrels sperm.
....do	May 19	June 25, 1848	1,980	34	.....	
....do	June 29	July 4, 1848	1,936	66	.....	Sent home 161 barrels sperm 1845; sold 118 barrels sperm; struck on the "Hedge Fence" going out; returned and sailed July 18.
....do	June 4	.....	.....	.....	.....	Lost on Corvo June, 1845.
....do	May 9	.....	.....	.....	.....	Sent home 12 casks sperm 1845; condemned at Rio Janeiro December, 1845.
....do	Dec. 8	.....	.....	.....	.....	Lost in La Perouse Straits with a full cargo, mostly whale.
....do	Oct. 9	Mar. 28, 1848	175	2,232	11,000	Sent home 11,578 pounds of bone.
....do	Dec. 29	.....	.....	.....	.....	Condemned at Monterey.
....do	Dec. 28	Jan. 2, 1850	2,108	.....	.....	
....do	Nov. 18	.....	.....	.....	.....	Shipped 8,000 gallons oil to London; condemned at Seychelle Islands 1847.
....do	July 13	May 1, 1849	1,463	.....	.....	
....do	July 15	June 28, 1849	1,9[illegible]0	.....	.....	
....do	Feb 17	July —, ——	385	.....	.....	
....do	Nov. 29	.....	.....	.....	.....	Condemned and sold at Sydney.
....do	Sept. 25	May 3, 1849	1,199	456	5,000	
....do	Aug. 12	June 30, 1849	1,080	290	.....	
....do	July 16	Apr. 19, 1850	1,448	136	.....	Sold to New Bedford 1850.
....do	Sept. 21	June 8, 1849	1,667	10	.....	
....do	May 31	Aug. 6, 1848	541	1,945	5,000	Sold 20 sperm and 40 whale.
....do	Aug. 1[illegible]	Mar. 9, 1849	294	1,3[illegible]0	.....	Third mate, —— Fuller, and three men drowned by the staving of a boat by a whale; sold in California; sold 290 whale.
....do	Oct. 13	May 7, 1850	1,671	.....	.....	
....do	Aug. 17	Jan. 7, 1[illegible]50	2,0[illegible]1	.....	.....	
....do	July 3	June 5, 1849	1,82[illegible]	30	.....	
....do	May 31	July 4, 1848	1,77[illegible]	30	.....	Sent home 25 casks sperm 1845; sold 250 sperm, 50 hump; built 1845 at Mattapoisett.
....do	July 15	.....	.....	.....	.....	Condemned at New Zealand; repaired and sold by Captain Ray, in California.
....do	Sept. 4	May 31, 1849	2,017	26	.....	Jos. T. Upham, first mate, killed by a whale.
....do	June 15	May 10, 1849	59	2,700	24,000	Bought 1845; sold for California 1849; formerly a merchantman; built at Portsmouth, N. H., 1827.
....do	Oct. 31	Feb. 8, 1851	2,660	226	.....	Built 1845; fitted from Boston; sold 70 sperm; sold to New Bedford 1851.
Pacific Ocean	Dec. 8	.....	.....	.....	.....	Lost in December, 1849, near Tongataboo.
Pacific Ocean	July 9	Mar. 10, 1848	140	2,150	14,000	
South Atlantic	Dec 27	Aug. 27, 1847	320	.....	.....	
Atlantic	Mar. —	Oct. 14, 1846	300	.....	.....	
N. W. Coast	Aug. 18	.....	.....	.....	.....	Sent home 75 barrels sperm 1845; struck on a reef near Palmerston's Island, S. P., and sunk in 15 minutes, with cargo of 1,400 barrels whale, 250 barrels sperm; two of the crew lost.
Atlantic	Apr. 28	June 5, 1847	350	10[illegible]	600	Added 1843 from Boston.

Table showing returns of whaling-vessels

Name of vessel.	Class.	Tonnage.	Captain.	Managing owner or agent.
1845.				
Plymouth, Mass.				
Maracaibo	Brig	93	—— Nickerson	Atwood L. Drew
Yeoman	Bark	175	—— Gooding	Bradford Barnes, jr
Provincetown, Mass.				
Belle Isle	Schooner	104	—— Howard	Parker Cook
Cadmus	Brig	130	—— Soper	Samuel Soper
Carter Braxton	Ship	132	—— Martin	J. Adams
Council	Schooner	100	—— Genn	Samuel Cook
Edwin	do	100	—— Cook	Lemuel Cook
Fairy	Bark	186	—— Cook	Ebenezer Cook
Franklin	Brig	172	—— Nickerson	S. Soper
Gem	do	162	—— Nickerson	Timothy P. Johnson
Grand Island	Schooner	100	—— Cook	S. Cook
Jane Howe	Brig	130	—— Bowley	
Joshua Brown	Schooner	113	—— Genn	Abraham Small, jr
John Adams	do		—— Higgins	
Louisa	do	98	—— Cook	Samuel Cook
Medford	do	105	—— Cook	P. Cook
Outesie	do	110	—— Chapman	C. A. Crozier
Parker Cook	Brig	135	—— Smith	
Phenix	do	150	—— Small	Abraham Small
Rienzi	do	101	—— Small	
Rienzi	Schooner	115	—— Cook	A. Cook
Spartan	Bark	188	—— Cook	A. Small
Stranger	Schooner	100	—— Sparks	S. Hillyard
Tarquin	do	100	—— Sparks	H. Sparks
Fall River, Mass.				
Ann Maria	Bark	196	—— Jefferson	Jesse Eddy
Caravan	Ship	330	—— Manchester	J. W. Lindsey
Leonidas	Brig	128	—— Cornell	Nathan Durfee
Pantheon	Bark	284	—— Dimon	do
Sol. Saltus	Ship	316	—— Fales	do
Providence, R. I.				
Lexington	Bark	291	—— Saunders	J. L. Joslin
Lion	Ship	298	—— Howland	Lloyd Bowers
Bristol, R. I.				
Anna	Ship	22[illegible]	—— Moore	Byron Diman
Warren, R. I.				
Benj. Rush	Ship	385	—— Smith	Child & Coffin
Dromo	Bark	267	—— Grinnell	C. F. Child
Hector	do	225	—— Martin	R. B. Johnson
Harvest	do	300	—— Bowen	Child & Johnson
Lafayette	Ship	341	—— Bowen	Coffin & Gardner
Magnet	do	355	—— Wilbur	Joseph Smith
Philip Tabb	do	405	—— Jolls	Driscol & Child
Sarah	Bark	286	—— Rice	John R. Wheaton
Triton	Ship	345	—— Jolls	S. P. Child
Newport, R. I.				
America	Bark	217	—— Smiley	W. H. Smiley & C. E. Bell
Audley Clark	Ship	331	—— Griswold	P. Clarke & T. Bush
Catharine	Schooner	75	—— Smiley	W. H. Smiley
Helen	Brig	120	—— Davis	William Price
Martha	Ship	271	E. Gifford	R. P. Lee
Lynn, Mass.				
Com. Preble	Ship	323	—— Lamphier	Andrews Breed
Wm. Badger	do	397	—— Perkins	do

sailing from American ports—Continued.

Whaling-ground.	Date— Of sailing.	Of arrival.	Result of voyage. Sperm-oil.	Whale-oil.	Whalebone.	Remarks.
			Bbls.	*Bbls.*	*Lbs.*	
Atlantic	Mar. 12	July 7, 1846	260	30		
Indian Ocean	July 2	Sept. 22, 1846	500			Sent home 170 barrels sperm 1845; withdrawn 1849.
Atlantic	Jan. 29	Sept. —, 1845	125			
....do	Mar. 12	Oct. 31, 1845	110			Bought from Marblehead 1844.
....do	Feb. 24	Aug. 8, 1846	300	70		Withdrawn 1846.
Sts. Belleisle	May 13	Oct. —, 1845	60	70		
	Apr. 2	Sept. —, 1845	170			
Atlantic	Mar. 28	Aug. 11, 1846	610	40		
....do	Feb. 26	Apr. —, 1846	340			
....do	Mar. 17	Oct. 20, 1845	200			
....do	Apr. 2	June 7, 1846	17			
....do	Apr. 23	Sept. —, 1845	60			New 1845; withdrawn 1846.
....do	July 24	Nov. 22, 1845		6		Blackfish-oil; withdrawn 1845.
....do	Apr. 12	Sept. —, 1845	170			
....do	Mar. 12	Aug. 12, 1845	250	90		
....do	Apr. 23	June 6, 1846	230	30		Added 1844.
....do	Apr. 12	Oct. —, 1845		200		Withdrawn 1846.
....do	May 21	Aug. —, 1846	180			
....do	Mar. 22	May 9, 1846	430			
....do	May 15	Oct. 31, 1845	180			
....do	Mar. 4	Sept. —, 1845	310	10		
....do	July 22	Apr. 12, 1847	350			Withdrawn 1847.
....do	May 4	Oct. —, 1845	20	120		Added 1844; withdrawn 1846.
....do	Mar. 17	Aug. 14, 1845	70	100		Added 1844.
Atlantic	June 2					Lost 1847.
Pacific Ocean	Nov. 11	May 5, 1849	250	2, 850	49, 000	Bought from Newburyport 1845.
Atlantic	Aug. 17	Apr. 2, 1847	200	30		Sold to Westport 1848.
N. W. Coast	Oct. 25	Apr. 28, 1849	50	1, 350	13, 000	Seized at St. Carlos, Chili, for alleged violation of the revenue laws, detained five months and released; sold for California 1849.
Pacific Ocean	Oct. 3	Mar. 12, 1848	150	2, 000	20, 000	
Indian Ocean	July 17	Nov. 18, 1850	40			Sold to New Bedford 1850.
Pacific Ocean	Aug. 28	July 8, 1849	2, 100	60		
Pacific Ocean	Jan. 2	Dec. 10, 1848	700	100		Sold for California 1848.
N. W. Coast	Oct. 13	Mar. 1, 1848	35	2, 500	7, 000	
Indian Ocean	July —	June 26, 1848	900	300		Bought from Salem 1845.
Pacific Ocean	July 8	Dec. 4, 1847	1, 000			Sent home 60 barrels sperm 1845.
N. W. Coast		May 17, 1849	100	1, 000		Added 1845; withdrawn 1849.
Indian Ocean	July 22	July 4, 1848	550	850		
N. W. Coast	Aug. 8					Condemned at Callao March, 1848.
....do	Sept. 8		500	25		Condemned at Honolulu May, 1847.
Pacific Ocean	July 22	Feb. 9, 1849	1, 300			Bought from Boston 1845; sold to New Bedford 1849.
N. W. Coast	Jan. 14	May 18, 1848	1, 119	790	44, 000	Sold 190 sperm.
South Atlantic	Aug. 31	Sept. 9, 1847		1, 400		
N. W. Coast	Jan. 14	Aug. 1, 1848	950			Sold for California 1848.
Patagonia	Sept. —					Tender to bark America; lost at South Shetland 1847.
Atlantic	Nov. 29	Sept. 6, 1846	150			Sold to New Bedford 1849.
Pacific Ocean	Apr. 21	June 11, 1849	1, 100			
Ind. and N.W.	July 19	June 23, 1848	180	1, 800		Sent home 13,114 pounds of bone.
Indian Ocean	Oct. 17	Feb. 11, 1849	900	1, 600		Bought from Boston 1845; withdrawn 1849.

Table showing the returns of whaling-vessels

Name of vessel.	Class.	Tonnage.	Captain.	Managing owner or agent.
1845.				
Salem, Mass.				
Henry	Bark	262	—— Lind	James W. Cheever
Stonington, Conn.				
Autumn	Bark	181	—— Perry	Elisha Faxon, jr
Bolton	...do	220	—— Lewis	Charles P. Williams
Byron	...do	170	—— Reed	John F. Trumbull
Cincinnati	Ship	457	F. Stanton Williams	F. Pendleton & Co
Cabinet	...do	305	—— Bottum	J. F. Trumbull
Cynosure	Bark	230	—— Simonds	...do
Cavalier	...do	295	—— Marchant	Charles P. Williams
Corvo	Ship	349	—— Burell	...do
Fellowes	...do	268	—— Babcock	...do
George	...do	251	—— Taber	...do
Herald	...do	241	—— Barker	...do
Philetus	Bark	278		J. F. Trumbull
Tiger	Ship	311	—— Brewster	...do
Thos. Williams	...do	340	—— Williams	C. P. Williams
New London, Conn.				
Alert	Ship	398	—— Middleton	Havens & Smith
Atlantic	...do	700	William Peck	Miner, Lawrence & Co
Black Warrior	Bark	231	—— Chappell	Havens & Smith
Brooklyn	Ship	360	—— Jeffrey	Perkins & Smith
Candace	...do	310	—— Bolles	Havens & Smith
Catharine	...do	384	—— Smith	Thomas Fitch, 2d
Clematis	...do	311	—— Bailey	Williams & Barnes
Connecticut	Bark	398	—— Towne	Frink, Chew & Co
Charles Carroll	Ship	412	—— Long	Perkins & Smith
Charles Henry	...do	265	—— Allen	...do
Corea	...do			
Carolina	...do	395	Charles Prentiss	Stoddard & Learned
	...do	385	Benjamin Hempstead	Frink, Chew & Co
Dover	...do	430	—— Jeffrey	Benjamin Brown
Electra	...do	348	—— Ward	Williams & Barnes
Emma	Schooner	181	—— Bailey	William Tate
Flora	Bark	338	—— Baker	N. & W. W. Billings
Friends	Ship	403	—— Howard	B. Brown
Gen. Williams	...do	446	—— Ward	Williams & Barnes
Gen. Scott	...do	360	—— Sistaire	Weaver & Rogers
G. Washington	...do	620	—— Holt	Williams & Barnes
George & Mary	...do	356	—— Bailey	Lyman Allyn
Leader	Schooner	130	—— Pray	Abner Bassett
Lowell	Ship	414	—— Benjamin	Williams & Barnes
Mentor	...do	460	—— Sweet	B. Brown
New England	Ship	368	—— Wilber	Miner, Lawrence & Co
Palladium	...do	342	—— McLane	Frink, Chew & Co
Pembroke	Bark	199	—— Lax	Miner, Lawrence & Co
Peruvian	Ship	388	—— Brown	Stoddard & Learned
Robert Boune	...do	505	—— Baker	N. & W. W. Billings

sailing from American ports—Continued.

Whaling-ground.	Date—Of sailing.	Date—Of arrival.	Result of voyage.—Sperm-oil.	Result of voyage.—Whale-oil.	Result of voyage.—Whalebone.	Remarks.
			Bbls.	*Bbls.*	*Lbs.*	
Pacific Ocean ..	June 12	....	300	600	.....	Wrecked on the Marquesas Islands; got off and was taken to Tahiti and sold; 800 barrels oil saved.
Pacific Ocean ..	Nov. 13	June 17, 1849	950	.....	.....	Bought from New York 1845; sold for California 1849.
....do	June 25	Mar. 8, 1848	700	.....	.....	Sold to Boston 1849.
Falkland Islds .	Aug. 12	Feb. 15, 1850	......	900	8,000	
N. W. Coast....	Nov. 24	Mar. 9, 1849	300	2,500	6,000	Added 1845.
New Holland ..	May 29	Apr. 30, 1848	40	1,950	13,000	
Indian Ocean ..	Aug. 17	....	.....	.....	.....	Bought from Boston 1845; sent home 110 barrels sperm 1845; the Cynosure was sold in Bahia 1847.
N. Z. & N. W ...	Aug. 5	May 27, 1848	30	1,470	14,000	Bought from Salem 1845.
Coast of Chili ..	May 31	Mar. 2, 1847	70	3,400	20,000	Withdrawn 1847.
Pacific Ocean ..	June 7	June 18, 1850	400	1,200	16,000	
N. Z. & N. W ...	July 31	June 20, 1849	70	1,400	6,000	
Indian Ocean ..	Dec. 6	....	......	.....	.....	Sold at Rio Janeiro (?) 1848 by the captain; also 600 sperm.
....	June —	May 4, 1848	430	1,100	6,000	Sent home 30 barrels sperm 1845.
Ind. and N. W ..	Nov. 4	Mar. 8, 1848	100	2,700	8,000	Bought from New York 1845; sent home 15,380 pounds of bone.
N. W. Coast....	May 24	....	.....	.....	.....	Burned at sea July 11, 1845, outward bound.
Ind. and N. W ..	June 16	May 24, 1847	50	2,800	2,800	Sent home 27,120 pounds of bone.
....do	Aug. 4	Apr. 24, 1848	50	5,500	23,000	Formerly the Westchester of New York; added 1845; Captain Beck died at sea October, 1846; sent home 26,607 pounds of bone.
Indian Ocean ..	May 3	Apr. 21, 1847	70	1,700	15,000	
Ind. and N. W ..	July 7	Apr. 6, 1848	160	3,840	3,000	Sent home 14,495 pounds of bone.
Indian Ocean ..	June 2	Apr. 26, 1847	100	2,100	23,000	Sent home 21,135 pounds of bone.
Ind. and N. W ..	Sept. 3	Apr. 29, 1848	150	1,650	11,000	
....do	Sept. 17	June 3, 1848	120	1,480	14,000	
Indian Ocean ..	Aug. 21	....	.....	.....	.....	Condemned and sold at Honolulu 1849; had 40 sperm, 900 whale; sent home 5,000 pounds of bone.
Desolation Isld.	Aug. 26	May 24, 1847	......	3,500	14,000	
Ind. and N. W ..	July 15	....	50	1,600	18,000	Struck on a bar near Montauk Point, homeward bound, and was lost; cargo mostly saved; had sold 200 barrels whale at Hobart Town.
....	......	June 1, 1849	250	2,450	.....	
Ind. and N. W ..	July 1	May 20, 1847	100	2,100	1,500	Bought from New York 1845; sent home 20,237 pounds of bone; sold 1847.
N. W. Coast....	Oct. 21	....	.....	.....	.....	
....do	Aug. 10	Apr. 7, 1848	260	3,400	3,500	Bought from New York 1845.
Ind. and N. W ..	Apr. 22	Mar. 5, 1847	250	1,150	12,000	
Falkland Islds .	July 2	....	.....	.....	.....	Added 1845; lost on coast of Patagonia October 26, 1845.
N. W. Coast....	Apr. 24	Apr. 25, 1846	......	2,200	20,000	Second mate, D. W. Chappell, taken out of his boat by a whale-line.
....do	June 18	May 2, 1847	75	3,025	3,500	Sent home 28,784 pounds of bone.
Ind. and N. W ..	June 2	May 5, 1848	300	2,700	18,000	Sent home 20,020 pounds of bone.
....do	June 21	Mar. 27, 1848	200	1,150	2,000	Bought from Boston 1845.
....do	July 29	May 19, 1848	500	4,000	15,000	Formerly a New York packet; built at New Bedford 1832; added 1845 sent home 28,059 pounds of bone. ;
....do	June 2	May 26, 1847	250	2,350	1,600	
Whaling and sealing.	July 6	....	.....	.....	.....	Seized in Chiloe, 1846, for infringement on the laws; released November, 1847, and sold at Valparaiso.
Ind. and N. W ..	July 1	May 27, 1847	150	3,850	40,000	Sold to Boston for a merchantman 1848.
....do	July 10	Mar. 13, 1848	250	2,700	10,000	Withdrawn for California trade 1848; sent home 25,938 pounds of bone.
N. W. Coast....	Aug. 4	June 29, 1848	150	3,100	31,000	
....do	June 16	May 24, 1847	150	2,250	10,000	
Indian Ocean ..	May 18	May 4, 1847	240	1,400	14,000	
Indian and N. W	July 24	Apr. 13, 1848	600	1,100	1,000	
....do	June 10	May 8, 1848	180	4,400	22,000	Sent home 21,990 pounds bone. Built at Stonington, 1832.

Table showing returns of whaling-vessels

Name of vessel.	Class.	Tonnage.	Captain.	Managing owner or agent.
1845.				
Sag Harbor, N. Y.				
American	Bark	284	William Pierson	S. & B. Hunting & Co
Ann Mary Ann	Ship	380	I. Winters	Mulford & Sleight
Cadmus	Bark	307	—— Smith	do
Columbia	do	285	S. B. Pierson	Cook & Green
Concordia	do	365	—— Loper	Thomas Brown
Daniel Webster	Ship	397	—— Curry	Ezekiel Mulford
Eliz. Frith	Bark	355	John Bishop	Post & Sherry
Gem	do	320	—— Worth	Huntting Cooper
Hamilton	Ship	322	—— Babcock	Charles T. Dering
Hannibal	do	311	—— Canning	S. & B. Huntting & Co
Henry	do	333	—— Brown	S. L'Hommedieu
Henry Lee	do	409	B. C. Payne	S. & B. Huntting & Co
Huron	do	292	—— Woodruff	Cook & Green
Illinois	do	415	—— Jagger	John Budd
Jefferson	do	435	—— Smith	T. Brown
John Jay	do	494	—— Harwood	N. & G. Howell
Konohassett	do	426	T. B. Worth	Huntting Cooper
Laurens	Bark	420	—— Eldredge	Tiffany & Halsey
Marcus	do	283	—— Ryder	N. & G. Howell
Neptune	Ship	388	—— Nichols	S. & B. Huntting & Co
Ontario, 2d	do	489	B. R. Green	Post & Sherry
Oscar	do	369	—— Green	Huntting Cooper
Plymouth	do	425	L. B. Edwards	Cook & Green
Romulus	do	233	P. Winters	Ezekiel Mulford
Superior	Bark	275	—— Mulford	Post & Sherry
Tuscany	Ship	299	—— Goodale	John Budd
Washington	do	340	—— Sandford	Huntting Cooper
Greenport, N. Y.				
Bayard	Ship	339	J. W. Fordham	H. & N. Corwin
Caroline	do	252	—— Halsey	Wiggins & Parsons
Delta	do	314	D. Weeks	H. & N. Corwin
Nile	do	403	—— Case	Ireland, Wells & Carpenter.
Roanoke	Bark	252	—— Baldwin	Wiggins & Parsons
Sarah and Esther	Ship	157	—— Bennett	Ireland, Wells & Carpenter.
Triad	do	336	—— Horton	H. & N. Corwin
New Suffolk, Mass.				
Gentleman	Bark	227	A. G. Post	Ira B. Tuthill
Cold Spring, N. Y.				
N. P. Tallmadge	Ship	370	—— Mumford	John H. Jones
Sheffield	do	579	—— White	do
Tuscarora	do	379	—— Doan	do
Mystic, Conn.				
Aeronaut	Ship	265	—— Holmes	Charles Mallory
Blackstone	Bark	258	—— Bellows	do
Eleanor	Ship	301	—— Pendleton	George W. Ashbey & Co
Globe	do	316	—— West	Joseph Avery
Hellespont	do	346	—— Manwarring	I. & W. P. Randall
Highlander	do	238	—— Cleaveland	G. W. Ashbey & Co
Leander	Bark	213	—— Brereton	C. Mallory
Robin Hood	Ship	395	—— Pendleton	do

sailing from American ports—Continued.

Whaling-ground.	Date— Of sailing.	Date— Of arrival.	Result of voyage. Sperm-oil.	Result of voyage. Whale-oil.	Result of voyage. Whalebone.	Remarks.
			Bbls.	*Bbls.*	*Lbs.*	
N. W. Coast....	Sept. 25	....	......	......	......	Captain and three men lost by a whale running over their boat, June, 1846; the American was condemned at St. Thomas, August, 1848.
South Seas.....	July 21	Apr. 29, 1848	......	3,100	10,000	Sent home 21,381 pounds bone.
N. W. Coast....	Sept. 2	May 12, 1847	150	1,850	8,000	
....do	July 11	June 5, 1848	200	2,100	11,000	Sent home 7,000 pounds bone.
....do	Aug. 24	May 20, 1847	25	700	8,000	Returned home in consequence of mutiny among the crew.
....do	July 21	July 4, 1848	200	2,450	15,000	Sold for California 1848.
....do	Oct. 30	May 20, 1848	100	2,000	10,000	
....do	Aug. 9	July 8, 1847	400	1,250	12,000	Sent home 90 barrels sperm 1845.
....do	Sept. 5	Apr. 29, 1848	55	1,300	12,000	
South Seas.....	Oct. 16	....	......	......	......	Condemned at Rio Janeiro 1849; sent home 2,000 whale, 9,360 pounds bone.
N. W. Coast....	Aug. 22	May 24, 1847	130	1,900	......	Sent home 17,610 pounds bone; sold 1847.
....do	June 17	May 24, 1847	35	2,800	27,000	
....do	Sept. 15	May 8, 1848	......	2,300	......	Sent home 18,839 pounds bone; withdrawn.
....do	July 4	July 27, 1847	200	2,100	20,000	
Indian and N.W	July 15	May 24, 1847	55	2,600	23,000	
N. W. Coast....	June 13	Mar. 11, 1849	60	4,300	13,000	Sent home 33,060 pounds bone.
....do	Dec. 6	....	......	......	......	Bought from Boston 1845; wrecked at Pell's Island, May 24, 1846.
....do	Aug. 21	Jan. —, 1848	......	1,400		Bought from Kennebunk 1845.
Indian and N.W	July 4	May 24, 1847	80	1,470	12,000	
N. W. Coast....	July 23	July 2, 1849	......	2,700	17,000	Sold for California 1849.
N. Z. and N. W.	Aug. 13	Apr. 22, 1848	80	3,600	17,000	Sent home 23,196 pounds bone.
N. W. Coast....	Dec. 9	May 9, 1849	......	2,800	30,000	Sold to Mattapoisett 1849.
....do	Dec. 2	Apr. 30, 1849	......	4,800	13,000	Bought from Boston 1845; sent home 16,000 pounds bone.
South Atlantic.	Sept. 24	Aug. 18, 1846	......	......	......	Captain Winters returned home sick 1846. No report.
N. W. Coast....	July 9	June 6, 1847	75	1,125	9,000	
....do	June 18	Apr. 26, 1847	180	1,300	13,000	Sent home 13,553 pounds bone.
....do	July 7	May 24, 1847	200	1,400	13,000	
N. W. Coast....	Dec. 9	May 13, 1849	......	2,700	17,000	
....do	July 12	July 26, 1847	......	950	9,000	
....do	Sept. 9	June 4, 1848	70	2,380	15,000	
....do	Oct. 15	June 7, 1848	170	2,400	14,000	Bought from New York 1845; second mate, F. Ackley, died January 1846.
South Seas....	Sept. —	May 21, 1847	100	1,500	15,000	
South Atlantic	Oct. 15	....	......	......	......	
N. W. Coast...	June 22	Apr. 7, 1848	180	1,700	5,000	
S. A. and Indian	Nov. 13	May 10, 1848	300	200	1,500	
N. W. Coast ...	June 5	May 1, 1848	45	1,775	......	
....do	Nov. 11	Feb. 7, 1849	200	4,000	22,000	Bought from New York 1845; sent home some oil and bone.
....do	Aug. 12	Mar. 24, 1848	300	150	1,000	
N. W. Coast....	Oct. 13	Aug. 14, 1848	370	1,050	......	
Indian and N.W	July 7	....	......	......	......	Condemned at Cape Town 1846.
N. W. Coast....	Aug. 12	Apr. 5, 1849	150	1,850	5,000	Sent home 13,500 pounds bone; sold for California 1849.
....do	Oct. 28	....	......	......	......	Added 1845; sent home 5,191 pounds bone; condemned at Valparaiso 1849; had 100 sperm; 3,000 whale.
Indian and N.W	July 3	Apr. 30, 1848	50	2,800	12,000	Sent home 13,552 pounds bone; bought from New York 1845.
Pacific Ocean ..	July 21	....	......	......	......	Added 1845; condemned at Talcahuano 1849; sent home 600 sperm.
Crozette Islands	Aug. 15	July 7, 1847	70	1,030	8,000	
N. W. Coast....	Oct. 8	June 26, 1848	200	3,400	34,000	Bought from Boston 1845.

Table showing returns of whaling-vessels

Name of vessel.	Class.	Tonnage.	Captain.	Managing owner or agent.
1845.				
Mystic, Conn.—Continued.				
Romulus	Ship	365	—— Montgomery	C. Mallory
Trescott	do	341	—— Mallory	do
Boston, Mass.				
Ontario	Schooner	100		
Portsmouth, N. H.				
Ann Parry	Ship	348	—— Dennett	James Kennard
1846.				
New Bedford, Mass.				
Adeline	Ship	329	—— Jernegan	I. Howland, jr., & Co
Alexander	do	421	—— Reynard	J. A. Parker
Amethyst	do	359	—— Howes	J. A. Parker & Son
Brandt	do	310	—— Sampson	Alexander Gibbs
Benj. Tucker	do	349	J. R. Sands	Charles R. Tucker & Co.
Braganza	do	470	—— Devol	Pope & Morgan
Brunswick	do	295	—— Almy	B. Ricketson
California	do	398	—— Fisher	I. Howland, jr., & Co
Canada	do	545	W. H. Reynard	B. Ricketson
Caroline	do	364	—— Carey	William Gifford
Chas. Drew	do	344	—— Coffin	do
Canton	do	409	—— Fisher	Perry & Tillinghast
Chase	Bark	153	—— Brownell	B. Ricketson
Charles Frederick	Ship	317	H. P. Barnes	J. A. Parker & Son
China	do	370	—— Fisher	William Phillips
Cicero	do	252	Jacob Howland	Lemuel Kollock
Cortes	do	382	—— Swift	George Howland
Courier	do	381	—— Holley	Randall & Haskell
Cherokee	Bark	261	—— Cleaveland	Hathaway & Luce
Clarice	do	237	—— Gifford	Edward C. Jones
Condor	Ship	349	J. Taber	C. W. Morgan
Cornelia	Bark	216	—— Flanders	L. Kollock
Chas'tn Packet	do	184	—— Besse	Thomas Knowles & Co.
Coral	Ship	370	—— Seabury	Gideon Allen
Congress	do	339	Charles Little	E. C. Jones
Congaree	do	324	—— Cushman	Thomas Wilcox
Desdemona	do	295	Walter Taber	T. & A. R. Nye
Edward	Bark	274	—— Luce	T. Knowles & Co
Emily Morgan	Ship	368	—— Ewer	William J. Rotch
Euphrates	do	365	—— Edwards	Edw. W. Howland
Falcon	do	273	—— Kirby	Wilcox & Richmond
Florida	do	330	—— Gray	E. C. Jones
Franklin	Bark	273	I. Davis	West & Paine
Franklin	Ship	333	—— Hazard	W. P. Howland
Fabius	do	432	—— Smith	C. R. Tucker & Co
Garland	do	243	—— Crowell	Rodney French
Geo. Howland	do	374	Owen Fisher	George Howland
Hibernia	do	327	—— Shearman	Robert Gibbs
Honqua	do	339	—— Brown	Alex. Gibbs
Israel	do	357	—— Dexter	B. B. Howard
Jasper	Bark	223	—— Pope	Alexander Gibbs
Lagoda	Ship	341	—— Finch	Jona. Bourne, jr
Mary Frazier	do	288	James Smith	A. H. Howland
Milwood	Bark	254	F. W. Deane	G. Allen
Maria	do	202	—— Coffin	Samuel W. Rodman
Milo	Ship	398	—— Plaskett	Thomas R. Robeson
Montezuma	Bark	195	—— Allen	Ingalls & Lucas
Mount Vernon	Ship	352	A. Covell	D. R. Greene & Co

sailing from American ports—Continued.

Whaling-ground.	Date—		Result of voyage.			Remarks.
	Of sailing.	Of arrival.	Sperm-oil.	Whale-oil.	Whalebone.	
			Bbls.	*Bbls.*	*Lbs.*	
N. W. Coast...	June 13	July —, 1848	......	1,750	......	
Indian and N. W	Aug. 25	Sept. 29, 1848	50	3,450	18,000	Withdrawn for California 1848.
Atlantic	Dec. —	Sept. 21, 1846	115	65	......	
Indian Ocean ..	Oct. 23	July 23, 1848	650	......	......	Captain Dennett left the ship sick at Zanzibar; first mate, Abial P. Perry, took command; sold to Salem 1848.
Pacific Ocean..	July 28	Mar. 23, 1850	359	2,861	19,300	Sent home 402 barrels whale, 27,000 pounds bone.
....do	June 22	Feb. 24, 1848	400	2,400	25,000	
....do	Nov. 5	Apr. 24, 1850	1,806	632	7,100	
Indian Ocean ..	Oct. 10	Sept. 17, 1849	266	1,540	1,000	
Pacific Ocean ..	July 6	Apr. 1, 1849	188	2,509	23,800	Sent home 800 whale and some bone.
Pacific and N. W	Sept. 8	Mar. 15, 1850	169	3,661	25,300	Sent home 35 barrels sperm.
South Seas	Sept. 18	Sept. 30, 1848	250	2,250	22,000	
Indian and N. W	Aug. 17	Jan. 13, 1849	400	2,600	12,000	
N. W. Coast....	July 11	Apr. 2, 1849	650	3,400	......	Went into California trade 1849; sent home 28,799 pounds bone.
Indian and N. W	Aug. 22	Mar. 8, 1849	410	2,080	3,600	
Pacific and N. W	Sept. 1	May 5, 1849	156	2,462	21,500	
Pacific Ocean ..	Aug. 17	Mar. 24, 1850	732	1,830	4,200	Third mate, Hiram Gifford, died at Cape Town, May, 1848; sent home 9,679 pounds bone.
South Atlantic	Oct. 10	Aug. 14, 1848	420	20	......	Went into the California trade 1849.
Pacific Ocean ..	Sept. 19	May 12, 1850	1,790	26	......	
....do	July 2	June 2, 1850	2,138	38	......	Second mate, Obed H. Coleman, taken out of boat by a line, 1846.
Indian Ocean ..	Sept. 10	June 11, 1849	350	400	......	
Pacific Ocean ..	Nov. 15	Jan. 14, 1849	125	2,675	15,000	Third mate, George Bailey, killed by a whale 1847.
....do	Oct. 10	Aug. 6, 1850	1,800	366	......	
Indian and N. W	Aug. 6	Apr. 7, 1849	288	2,341	16,000	
Indian Ocean ..	Sept. 5	July 11, 1849	837	10		
....do	July 7	Mar. 7, 1848	320	2,600	24,000	
....do	June 23	July 31, 1848	630	70	4,600	Sent home 100 sperm.
South Seas....	Oct. 7	May 27, 1848	420	180	1,500	
Pacific Ocean ..	Nov. 17	June 11, 1850	3,350	......	......	Cargo sold for $123,000.
N. W. Coast...	June 21	Nov. 24, 1848	850	1,400	13,000	
Pacific Ocean ..	Nov. 22	Oct. 27, 1850	2,325	......	......	Added 1846, from Boston.
....do	Oct. 28	June 2, 1849	1,884	......	......	
Indian Ocean ..	June 7	Apr. 1, 1849	1,750	......	......	
Pacific and N. W	Sept. 12	July 10, 1849	403	2,230	19,900	
....do	Aug. 5	Mar. 11, 1849	93	2,405	6,200	Sent home 40 sperm, 12,200 bone.
Indian and N. W	July 22	May 6, 1849	40	1,010	7,000	
Ind. and N. W	Aug. 2	Sept. 7, 1848	750	1,900	17,000	Third mate, G. Thing, drowned by staving of boat by a whale, December 25, 1846.
Indian Ocean ..	May 16	Sept. 23, 1849	815	......	......	Captain Davis came home sick 1848.
N. W. Coast ...	Nov. 3	Apr. 30, 1850	1,563	459	500	
Pacific Ocean ..	Aug. 10	Jan. 8, 1849	200	2,400	6,000	
....do	Jan. 19	Apr. 30, 1849	954	20	......	
....do	June 25	Dec. 27, 1849	1,450	50	......	
Ind. and N. W.	Aug. 10	June 25, 1849	1,085	620	......	
....do	Aug. 1	May 23, 1849	30	3,022	40,000	
Indian and Pac.	Aug. 15	....	175	70	......	Lost in Table Bay, Cape Good Hope, April, 1847; oil saved.
Indian Ocean ..	Sept. 7	June 13, 1849	552	543	......	
Pac. and N. W.	Aug. 25	Apr. 24, 1850	68	2,734	5,400	Sent home about 23,000 pounds bone.
Ind. and N. W..	Aug 6	July 7, 1849	632	1,780	8,000	
Indian Ocean ..	July 29	Nov. 21, 1850	77	......	......	
....do	July 25	Sept. 1, 1849	1,013	......	......	
Pacific Ocean ..	July 21	Apr. 5, 1849	308	2,869	19,900	
Indian Ocean ..	Oct. 10	Aug. 14, 1849	790			Added 1846, from Wareham.
N. W. Coast ...	Aug. 6	July 11, 1849	140	3,140	32,000	First mate, John L. Spooner, killed by a whale.

Table showing returns of whaling-vessels

Name of vessel.	Class.	Tonnage.	Captain.	Managing owner or agent.
1846.				
New Bedford, Mass.—Continued.				
Nassau	Ship	408	—— Weeks	Jireh Perry
Newton	do	283	—— Hale	J. Bourne, jr
Octavia	do	257	J. J. Pell	G. Allen
Peri	Bark	191	—— Mayhew	Rodney French
Phocion	Ship	266	—— Worth	J. R. Thornton
Persia	Bark	240	—— Manchester	L. Kollock
Rhine	do	174	—— Francis	E. C. Jones
Roscoe	do	235	—— A. S. Tobey	J. Bourne, jr
Rodman	Brig	83	—— Flanders	B. Ricketson
Roscius	Bark	303	—— Winslow	W. P. Howland
Sarah Louisa	Brig	144		William R. Rodman
Seine	Ship	281	—— Slocumb	Rodney French
St. Peter	do	267	—— Simmons	J. B. Wood & Co
Tobacco Plant	do	271	A. Allen	W. P. Rodman
Trident	do	449	—— Stetson	J. A. Parker & Son
Triton	do	300	—— Spencer	I. Howland, jr., & Co
Triton, 2d	Ship	315	—— King	C. R. Tucker & Co
Uncas	do	413	C. W. Gelett	A. H. Howland
Waverly	do	327	—— Crowell	I. Howland, jr. & Co
W. Thompson	do	495	—— Ellis	Jireh Perry
Wade	Bark	261	—— Bradbury	A. H. Howland
Fairhaven, Mass.				
Arab	Bark	276	—— Terry	I. F. Terry
Atkins Adams	Ship	330	—— Lane	Atkins Adams
Columbus	do	382	—— Fish	Gibbs & Jenney
E. L. B. Jenney	do	380	—— Allen	do
Eliza Adams	do	403	E. Harding	Atkins Adams
Favorite	Bark	293	—— Young	F. R. Whitwell
Friendship	Ship	366	William Stott	Gibbs & Jenney
George	do	360	—— Marston	Fish & Huttlestone
Harvest	Bark	314	—— Lakey	Jabez Delano, jr
Leonidas	Ship	243	J. N. Tatch	Jenney & Tripp
Maine	do	294	—— Netcher	E. Sawin
Mary Ann	do	335	—— Taber	L. C. Tripp
Sam Robertson	do	421	J. K. Turner	I. F. Terry
Wm. Wirt	do	387	Jesse Luce	Warren Delano
Wolga	Bark	285	—— Luce	James Tripp
Dartmouth, Mass.				
Gov. Hopkins	Brig	111	—— Pease	D. H. Bartlett
Mattapoisett, Mass.				
America	Brig	148	—— Lambert	R. L. Barstow
Annawan	do	159	—— Mayhew	Seth Freeman
Dumbarton	Bark	199	—— Handy	Wilson Barstow
Elizabeth	do	219	—— Flanders	R. L. Barstow
Lagrange	do	170	—— Southworth	E. Willis
Sarah	do	171	—— Snow	Wilson Barstow
Solon	Brig	129	—— Hammond	Samuel Sturtevant, jr
Sarah	Ship	370	—— Purrington	Joseph Meigs

* When two ships of the same name sail from the same port it is extremely difficult at times to tell

sailing from American ports—Continued.

Whaling-ground.	Date— Of sailing.	Of arrival.	Result of voyage. Sperm-oil.	Whale-oil.	Whalebone.	Remarks.
			Bbls.	*Bbls.*	*Lbs.*	
Pacific Ocean ..	June 22	May 8, 1850	442	2, 664	15, 000	Sent home 504 sperm, 15,000 pounds bone.
Ind. and Pac...	Sept. 15	Apr. 30, 1849	434	2, 020	20, 500	
Pacific Ocean ..	July 2	....	......	......	......	
Atl. and Ind ...	June 16	Nov. 9, 1848	500	70	......	
Pacific Ocean ..	July 21	Aug. 29, 1849	815	216	12, 600	
....do	July 29	Apr. 2, 1849	1, 065	73	300	
South Atlantic	Mar. 30	May 13, 1848	800	25	......	Bought from Edgartown 1845.
Indian Ocean ..	July 2	Jan. 30, 1849	740	1, 100	4, 500	Sent home 60 sperm.
South Atlantic	June 16	June 4, 1847	......	70	......	Sent home 80 sperm; sold 1847; lost in Straits of Magellan 1850.
Ind. and N. W..	Aug. 1	Feb. 18, 1850	2, 020	......	......	
Atlantic	......	....	......	......	......	Abandoned at sea 1846.
Pacific Ocean ..	July 9	Mar. 14, 1848	100	1, 800	4, 000	
Indian Ocean ..	Sept. 10	Aug. 14, 1849	1, 115	541	3, 700	
Pacific Ocean ..	Sept. 14	....	......	......	......	Burned at Honolulu 1849; total loss; sent home 67 sperm.
....do	Nov. 21	June 2, 1850	22	2, 327	27, 000	Captain Stetson came home sick 1848.
... do	July 21	May 31, 1850	185	1, 746	......	Added 1846 from Plymouth. Attacked by natives at Sydenham's Island; 5 of the crew killed, 7 wounded; Captain Spencer rescued by the ships United States and Alabama, of Nantucket. Sent home 600 sperm, 40,000 pounds bone (?)*
Pacific Ocean ..	Nov. 15	Sept. 26, 1849	980	......	......	
Pac. and N. W..	Aug. 27	May 11, 1849	460	2, 940	19, 000	
....do	Sept. 1	Apr. 6, 1849	289	2, 190	3, 800	
Pacific Ocean ..	Nov. 5	Apr. 30, 1850	76	3, 378	15, 700	Was set on fire three times on the voyage by the crew; sent home 12,500 lbs. bone.
Indian Ocean ..	Aug. 12	....	......	......	......	Condemned at Bermudas, January, 1851.
Indian Ocean ..	Dec. 5	Feb. 12, 1850	450	1, 450	2, 000	
Pacific Ocean ..	Aug. 22	June 16, 1850	2, 200	......	......	Added 1846; 500 barrels were on freight.
Ind. and Pac ...	Sept. 8	Apr. 25, 1849	950	2, 250	4, 000	
Ind. and Japan	Nov. 30	May 15, 1851	2, 570	......	......	
Ind. and Pac ...	June 12	Apr. 25, 1849	150	2, 950	26, 000	Sent home 15,660 pounds bone; sold to N. Bedford 1849.
Ind. and N. W..	Aug. 1	Nov. 25, 1849	1, 550	250	1, 400	
Ind. and Pac ...	Oct. 18	Apr. 29, 1849	600	2, 400	30, 000	
Ind. and N. W..	Sept. 10	Apr. 2, 1849	300	2, 500	25, 000	
Pacific Ocean ..	July 18	May 10, 1850	650	1, 800	......	
Ind. and N. W..	Aug. 11	June 9, 1849	1, 450	30	......	Sent home 6,128 pounds bone.
....do	Aug. 11	....	......	......	......	Lost in Columbia River, August 25, 1848; had on board 1,400 whale; nothing saved; sent home 6,900 bone.
Pacific Ocean ..	Nov. 17	July 18, 1850	1, 600	......	......	
N. W. Coast....	June 20	May 2, 1849	25	3, 700	30, 000	Bought from New Bedford 1846; sent home 150 sperm, 16,000 pounds bone.
Pacific Ocean ..	Nov. 14	May 8, 1850	1, 705	75	......	Wilson Barnes, fourth mate, died October, 1847; Captain Luce killed by a whale 1848.
Indian Ocean ..	Aug. 7	June 10, 1852	118	343	4, 700	Added 1846 from New Bedford; sent home 490 whale, 6,750 pounds bone.
South Atlantic.	Sept. 12	Apr. 8, 1849	15	25	......	Added 1846; sold 1849.
Atlantic	Apr. 29	Sept. 9, 1847	450	......	......	Added 1846, from Wareham.
....do	Aug. 15	—— —, 1848	575	......	......	
....do	June 4	June 3, 1848	300	......	......	Sent home 65 barrels 1846; added 1846.
....do	Aug. 12	Sept. 9, 1848	1, 045	150	......	
Indian Ocean .	Aug. 18	Nov. 24, 1846	50	......	......	Captain Southworth drowned by the upsetting of his boat October, 1846; the Lagrange returned dismasted by a gale; added 1846.
Atlantic	May 11	June 27, 1848	250	......	......	
....do	....	Oct. 26, 1847	110	......	......	
Pac. and N. W.	Sept. 1	Apr. 23, 1848	120	2, 480	25, 000	

which to credit with oil and bone sent home. A portion of this probably belongs to the Triton, 2d.

Table showing returns of whaling-vessels

Name of vessel.	Class.	Tonnage.	Captain.	Managing owner or agent.
1846.				
Sippican, Mass.				
Cossack	Bark	256	—— Dexter	S. C. Luce
Quito	Brig	140	—— Chase	J. S. Bates
Westport, Mass.				
Janet	Bark	194	—— Davis	Henry Wilcox
President	...do	167	—— Hicks	Andrew Hicks
Th. Winslow	...do	126	—— Stanton	Thomas W. Mayhew
Theo. Chase	...do	168	—— Ball	Henry Willcox
U. States	...do	217	—— Smith	Andrew Hicks
Nantucket, Mass.				
Alabama	Ship	340	Benjamin Coggeshall	John H. Shaw
Alpha	...do	345	Joseph W. Folger	Hadwen & Barney
Atlantic	...do	321	James Coleman	R. F. Gardner
Columbia	...do	329	Joseph C. Chase	C. G. & H. Coffin
Hero	...do	313	Sylvanus Swain	Joseph Starbuck
James Loper	...do	348	William S. Whippey	Levi Starbuck
Maria	...do	365	George A. Coffin	J. W. Barrett & Sons
Napoleon	...do	360	Stephen B. Gibbs	...do
Narragansett	...do	398	John B. Rogers	Christopher Wyer
Ontario	...do	354	John Horn	J. W. Barrett & Sons
Rose	...do	349	William Miller	Simeon Starbuck
Susan	...do	349	Charles B. Ray	Aaron Mitchell
Sophia	Schooner	170	—— Swain	J. Cook, jr., & Co
Three Brothers	Ship	384	Joseph Mitchell, 2d	G. & M. Starbuck & Co.
Two Brothers	Schooner	70	—— Hatch	J. Cook, jr., & Co
Young Hero	Ship	340	William B. Swain	J. Starbuck
Edgartown, Mass.				
Splendid	Ship	392	—— Baylies	Abm. Osborne
Newport, R. I.				
Damon	Bark	195	—— Davenport	Silas H. Cotterell
Mechanic	Ship	335	Oliver Potter	R. P. Lee
Provincetown, Mass.				
Bell Isle	Schooner	104		Parker Cook
Cadmus	Brig	130	—— Soper	Samuel Soper
Council	Schooner	100		Samuel Cook
Edwin	...do	100	—— Nickerson	R. L. Thatcher
Fairy	Bark	186		Ebenezer Cook
Franklin	Brig	172	—— Tillson	Samuel Soper
Gem	...do	162		Timothy P. Johnson
Grand Island	Schooner	100	—— Cook	Samuel Cook
John Adams	...do	110		R. L. Thatcher
Louisa	...do	98		Samuel Cook
Medford	...do	105	—— Cook	Parker Cook
Pacific	Brig	130	—— Perry	D. Small
Parker Cook	Bark	135	—— Smith	Parker Cook
Phenix	Brig	150	—— Small	Abm. Small
Rienzi	Schooner	115		A. Cook
Rienzi	Brig	101	Samuel Small	James Small

sailing from American ports—Continued.

Whaling-ground.	Date—		Result of voyage.			Remarks.
	Of sailing.	Of arrival.	Sperm-oil.	Whale-oil.	Whalebone.	
			Bbls.	*Bbls.*	*Lbs.*	
Pacific Ocean	Sept. 29	June 26, 1850	50	1,500	9,000	Sent home 129 sperm, 4,000 pounds bone; sold to New Bedford 1850.
Atlantic	June 14	Nov. 11, 1847	270	100	......	Sold to Nantucket 1848.
Indian Ocean	July 31	June 18, 1848	160	......	......	Added 1846.
South Seas	Aug. —	Oct. 15, 1847	250	......	......	Condemned and broken up at Westport 1848.
South Atlantic	July 31	Sept. 9, 1847	170	......	......	Returned in consequence of a defective foremast.
....do	May 6	May 4, 1848	30	......	......	Sailed March 18; returned April 6, having lost her five boats and davits, and sustained other damage, in a gale; sent home 200 barrels 1846.
Indian Ocean	June 11	Oct. 18, 1849	830	70	......	Second mate died from a wound received in cutting in ——; sent home 125 sperm.
Pacific Ocean	May 26	Sept. 26, 1850	1,454	......	......	Built 1846, at Medford.
....do	July 2	Apr. 24, 1850	1,182	180	3,000	Reuben Coleman, second mate, died August 29, 1849.
....do	Sept. 13	Dec. 2, 1849	2,081	......	......	Sent home 85 barrels sperm.
....do	Aug. 7	June 12, 1850	1,689	183	......	
....do	Nov. 2	Nov. 15, 1846	......	......	......	Returned leaking; was rebottomed and sailed in 1847.
....do	Dec. —	May 10, 1851	1,261	40	......	
....do	Sept. 20	June 27, 1850	896	13	......	Crew all deserted in California 1849; Capt. Coffin left the ship at Talcahuano, sick.
....do	Dec. 31	May 15, 1851	1,609	......	......	Captain Gibbs came home sick; sold 90 sperm on voyage.
....do	Aug. 9	Apr. 1, 1851	2,286	......	......	Sold some oil on the voyage.
....do	July 10	Apr. 30, ——	1,205	179	......	
....do	Nov. 7	......	......	......	......	Took about 900 barrels of sperm, went to California, and was sold.
....do	Nov. 16	Aug. 16, 1851	744	......	......	Sold 120 sperm.
Atlantic	June 20	Oct. 20, 1847	130	......	......	Added 1846; built at Baltimore 1839.
Pacific Ocean	July 7	July 15, 1851	1,330	170	......	
Atlantic	Dec. 17	Oct. —, 1846	70	......	......	Added 1846; built at Newcastle, Me., 1829.
Pacific Ocean	July 12	June 17, 1850	2,144	158	......	Captain Swain left the ship sick.
Pac. and N. W.	Aug. 17	Apr. 1, 1849	100	3,000	15,000	Withdrawn for California 1849.
Ind. and Pac	Oct. 6	......	......	......	......	Lost on a reef near Gallipagos Islands, June 28, 1847.
Pacific Ocean	Nov. 11	May 19, 1851	145	1,635	12,200	Sent home 438 sperm, 19,165 pounds bone.
Atlantic	Apr. 18	Apr. 18, 1846	.....	25	......	The Belle Isle sailed again in April and returned Oct. 7, 1846, with 90 barrels sperm.
....do	Mar. 19	Nov. 15, 1846	40	......	......	
....do	Apr. 16	Oct. 25, 1846	80	20	......	Added 1845.
....do	Mar. 23	Sept. 13, 1846	195	25	......	
......	......	Aug. 11, 1846	610	40	......	
Atlantic	Sept. 8	June 23, 1848	250	......	......	
....do	......	Sept. 17, 1847	280	......	......	
....do	June 26	Aug. —, 1846	40	30	......	Added 1845; withdrawn 1847.
......	......	Sept. 13, 1846	285	15	......	
Atlantic	......	Oct. —, 1846	207	......	......	
....do	Aug. —	Sept. 25, 1847	150	......	......	
....do	July 25	May 26, 1847	40	......	......	Sold 1847.
South Atlantic	Oct. 23	May —, 1848	250	......	......	
Atlantic	July 28	Oct. 13, 1847	180	......	......	
....do	......	Oct. 4, 1846	250	......	......	
....do	April 3	......	......	......	......	Totally wrecked at sea September 16, 1846. Of the brig's company, twenty-one all told, only the second mate and four men survived and were taken from the wreck, after the most extreme suffering, by ship Minerva, of New Bedford.

Table showing returns of whaling-vessels

Name of vessel.	Class.	Tonnage.	Captain.	Managing owner or agent.
1846.				
Provincetown, Mass.—Continued.				
Sam'l Cook	Brig	140	—— Cook	
Samuel and Thomas	Bark	191	—— Swift	Samuel Soper
Tarquin	Schooner	100		H. Sparks
Plymouth, Mass.				
Exchange	Schooner	99	—— Hopkins	Richard W. Holmes
Maracaibo	Brig	93		Atwood L. Drew
Wareham, Mass.				
Inga	Brig	160	—— Cudworth	M. S. F. Tobey
Boston, Mass.				
Ontario	Schooner	100	—— Prior	
Fall River, Mass.				
Gold Hunter	Ship	281	—— Marvel	Nathan Durfee
Rowena	do	404	—— Adams	do
Providence, R. I.				
South America	Ship	616	R. N. Sowle	Pearce & Bullock
Bristol, R. I.				
Troy	Brig	156	—— Easterbrooks	Samuel Church
Warren, R. I.				
Bowditch	Ship	399	—— Borden	S. P. Child
Covington	do	351	—— Devol	Mauran & Fessenden
Portsmouth	do	520	—— Munroe	Burr & Smith
Powhattan	Bark	237	—— Mayhew	do
Barnstable, Mass.				
March	Brig	90	Seth Weeks	Silas Baker
Somerset, Mass.				
Pilgrim	Bark	137	—— Pettis	George B. Hood
Mystic, Conn.				
Bingham	Ship	375	—— Scholfield	Charles Mallory
Vermont	Bark	292	—— Bailey	do
Bridgeport, Conn.				
Hamilton	Ship	359	—— Wade	Sherwood Sterling
New London, Conn.				
Armata	Ship	413	—— Fitch	Abner Bassett
Benj. Morgan	do	407	—— Bellows	Perkins & Smith
Clement	Bark	279	—— Lane	Miner, Lawrence & Co.
Columbus	Brig	159	—— Forsyth	Williams & Barnes
Columbus	Ship	344	—— Buchanan	Lyman Allyn
Dove	Bark	151	—— Douglas	Williams & Haven
Exile	Schooner	83	—— Church	Stoddard & Learned
Flora	Bark	338	—— Potter	N. & W. W. Billings
Franklin	Schooner	119	—— Butler	Perkins & Smith
Georgia	Ship	344	—— Hull	Thomas Fitch, 2d
Hannibal	do	441	—— Brown	Benjamin Brown
Jason	do	335	—— Morgan	Stoddard & Learned
McLellan	do	366	—— Slate	Perkins & Smith
Phœnix	do	404	—— Higgins	N. & W. W. Billings
Sarah Lavinia	Schooner	114	—— Fuller	B. Brown
Vesper	Ship	321	—— Clark	Williams & Barnes

sailing from American ports—Continued.

Whaling-ground.	Date— Of sailing.	Date— Of arrival.	Result of voyage. Sperm-oil.	Result of voyage. Whale-oil.	Result of voyage. Whalebone.	Remarks.
			Bbls.	*Bbls.*	*Lbs.*	
Atlantic	Mar. 9	Oct. —, 1846	220	.....	.....	Brig Sam'l Cook added 1846.
....do	Sept 11	Apr. 13, 1848	410	.....	.....	Sold to Mattapoisett 1850.
....do	....	....	.....	.....	.....	Withdrawn 1846; no report.
Atlantic	Apr. —	....	.....	.....	.....	Lost on Island of Margarita 1847.
....do	Oct. 12	....	.....	.....	.....	Totally wrecked October 19, 1846; second mate and two of the crew washed overboard and drowned.
Atlantic	Aug. 10	Dec. 23, 1847	350	.....	.....	Returned in consequence of a leak; sold 1848.
North Atlantic	Dec. 14	Sept. 10, 1847	250	20	.....	
Pacific Ocean	Oct. 24	Apr. 9, 1849	500	1,500	.....	Withdrawn for California 1849.
Northwest	Aug. 29	Apr. 23, 1849	40	3,280	15,000	Do.
Pacific Ocean	Nov. 4	Jan. 13, 1849	200	5,300	23,000	Went into California trade 1849; sent home 25,000 pounds bone; sold to New Bedford 1851.
Atlantic	Aug. 26	....	.....	.....	.....	Put into St. Catharines in distress May, 1847, and was condemned; had taken three barrels blackfish.
N. W. Coast	Nov. 29	Apr. 23, 1849	75	3,025	23,000	Added 1846.
....do	Aug. 24	Apr. 4, 1849	450	2,300	16,000	
....do	Feb. 4	June 5, 1849	160	4,500	19,000	Bought from New York 1845; sent home 19,000 pounds bone.
Pacific Ocean	Feb. 1	Mar. 9, 1849	360	.....	.....	Added 1845; formerly a merchantman; withdrawn for California 1849.
Atlantic	June 4	Aug. 21, 1847	250	30	.....	Formerly a schooner; altered to a hermaphrodite brig 1846; sold to Yarmouth 1847.
South Seas	Aug. 19	May 1, 1848	400	.....	.....	
N. W. Coast	July 2	....	.....	....	.....	Sent home 6,100 pounds bone; withdrawn at Honolulu for California trade 1848.
Indian Ocean	July 14	....	.....	.....	.....	Lost on Islands of St. Paul's 1847.
South Seas	Aug. —	....	.....	.....	.....	Condemned at Hong Kong 1849.
Indian & N. W	July 24	Apr. 2, 1849	40	2,760	28,000	
Chili & N. W.	June 25	May 16, 1848	70	2,830	29,000	
Indian & N. W	July 15	May 6, 1849	400	2,000	8,000	
South Atlantic	June 3	May 15, 1848	250	50	.....	
Indian & N. W.	July 2	May 3, 1849	50	1,750	15,000	Sent home 70 barrels 1846; withdrawn 1849.
South Atlantic	Nov. 4	June 10, 1849	850	.....	.....	
Desolation Isld.	Apr. 9	May —, 1848	.....	330	.....	
Coast of Chili	June 4	May 4, 1849	20	800	20,000	
South Seas	July 28	July 19, 1847	50	400	.....	
Chili & N. W	June 23	May 5, 1848	25	2,300	20,000	
Falkland Islds	July 23	June 14, 1849	.....	4,000	.....	
Desolation Isld.	Apr. 9	May 20, 1848	.....	2,600	16,000	
Davis Straits	Apr. 8	Sept. 17, 1846	.....	140	.....	Added 1846; resumption of Davis Strait fishery; part of the officers and crew of the McLellan were English.
Indian Ocean	Aug. 6	Sept. 2, 1850	830	70	.....	
Falkland Islds.	July 23	June 13, 1849	.....	30	.....	Added 1846; withdrawn for California 1849.
N. W. Coast	Sept. 15	June 1, 1849	250	2,800	32,000	

Table showing returns of whaling-vessels

Name of vessel.	Class.	Tonnage.	Captain.	Managing owner or agent.
1846.				
New London, Conn.—Continued.				
Wm. C. Nye	Ship	389	—— Church	N. & W. W. Billings
Stonington, Conn.				
Betsy Williams	Ship	400	Palmer Hall	C. P. Williams
Caledonia	do	446	—— Barber	do
Calumet	do	347	—— Skinner	do
Mercury	do	305	—— Pendleton	Pendleton & Trumbull
Newark	do	323	B. T. Pendleton	John F. Trumbull
Tybee	do	299	—— Dukens	do
Sag Harbor, L. I.				
Ann	Ship	299	—— Curry	Mulford & Howell
Crescent	do	340	—— Westfall	Post & Sherry
Citizen	do	464	—— Lansing	Mulford & Sleight
Fanny	do	391	—— Edwards	N. & G. Howell
Josephine	do	397	—— Hedges	Post & Sherry
John Wells	do	366	—— French	Thomas Brown
Nimrod	Bark	280	—— Jennings	Charles T. Dering
Noble	do	273	—— Howes	do
Portland	Ship	292	—— Corwin	S. & B. Huntting & Co
Romulus	do	233	—— Cartwright	Ezekiel Mulford
Thames	do	414	James Bishop	T. Brown
Timor	do	280	—— Edwards	Huntting Cooper
Wm. Tell	do	370	—— Glover	T. Brown
Greenport, N. Y.				
Philip 1st	Ship	293	—— Case	Ireland, Wells & Carpenter.
Washington	do	236	—— Corwin	Wiggins & Parsons
Cold Spring, N. Y.				
Alice	Bark	281	—— Woolley	John H. Jones
Monmouth	do	273	—— Haley	do
Richmond	Ship	437	—— Winters	do
Holmes' Hole.				
Pocahontas	Ship	341	—— Cottle	Thomas Bradley
1847.				
New Bedford, Mass.				
Abigail	Ship	310	—— Young	Pope & Morgan
Alto	Bark	236	E. F. Lakeman	Richmond & Wood
Brighton	Ship	354	—— West	C. R. Tucker & Co
Bramin	Bark	245	—— Butts	Gideon Allen
Barth. Gosnold	Ship	356	—— Taber	I. Howland, jr., & Co
Cambria	do	362	—— Harding	James Arnold
Canton, 2d	do	280	—— Taber	C. R. Tucker & Co
Corinthian	do	401	—— Armington	George Howland
Columbus	Bark	313	—— Davis	William R. Rodman
Champion	Ship	336	—— Parker	J. D. Thompson
Draco	Bark	257	J. V. Cox	Jona. Bourne, jr
Dartmouth	Ship	336	—— Osborn	I. Howland, jr., & Co
Draper	do	291	—— Lawton	Joseph Dunbar & Co
Dragon	Bark		S. E. Cook	
Dryade	do	263	S. C, Fisher	S. Thomas & Co.
Emma	do	246	—— Hussey	Rodney French
Elizabeth	Ship	339	M. Baker	T. & A. R. Nye
Endeavour	Bark	252	—— Hamblin	C. R. Tucker & Co

sailing from American ports—Continued.

Whaling-ground.	Date—		Result of voyage.			Remarks.
	Of sailing.	Of arrival.	Sperm-oil.	Whale-oil.	Whalebone.	
			Bbls.	*Bbls.*	*Lbs.*	
Chili & N. W..	Apr. 30	Feb. 10, 1851	90	2,900	25,000	Sold to New Bedford 1851; Captain Church died 1848.
N. W. Coast....	Nov. 11	Feb. 1, 1849	250	2,650	30,000	New 1846.
....do	July 3	Apr. 25, 1848	350	2,150	......	Sent home 40 barrels 1846.
Pacific Ocean .	Sept. 29	May 24, 1849	80	2,600	27,000	Withdrawn 1849.
Coast of Chili..	June 10	Mar. 30, 1848	65	2,200	20,000	
N. W. Coast....	Aug. 22	Mar. 11, 1849	40	2,100	12,000	
....do	Sept. 14	May 4, 1849	50	2,200	12,000	Sent home 12,000 pounds bone.
Coast of Chili..	Aug. 27	June 10, 1850	40	2,300	7,000	
N. Z. & N. W..	July 28	June 4, 1849	44	2,200	12,000	
Pac. & N. W...	Sept. 19	Feb. 1, 1849	700	2,900	18,000	
Chili & N. W..	Aug. 5	Mar. 10, 1849	80	2,900	14,000	Sold for California 1849.
Pacific Ocean..	Oct. 15	Aug. 28, 1849	60	2,400	......	Sold to New Bedford 1849; sent home 16,000 pounds bone.
N. W. Coast....	Aug. 12	July 20, 1849	140	2,160	8,000	Sold to New Bedford 1849.
Crozettes	Nov. 11	June 30, 1848	250	600	5,000	
S. A. & Indian.	Aug. 24	June 10, 1848	300	900	8,000	
Chili & N. W ..	Aug. 1	July 15, 1848	40	1,650	12,000	Withdrawn for California 1849.
Japan..........	Sept. 29	....	......	......	......	Wrecked and condemned at Honolulu, December, 1849; sent home 26,765 pounds bone.
Chili & N. W ..	Sept. 3	....	......	......	......	Captain Bishop came home sick 1848; sold at San Francisco 1849, with 1,800 barrels whale; sent home 14,000 pounds bone.
....do	July 28	July 26, 1849	80	1,650	9,000	
Pacific Ocean..	Oct. 7	June 21, 1848	300	1,300	12,000	
N. W. Coast....	July —	May 27, 1848	30	1,270	11,000	
....do	Aug. —	June 26, 1848	250	1,600	16,000	
South Seas.....	Sept. 3	Apr. 27, 1849	......	1,900	16,000	
....do	Mar. 13	Aug. 8, 1850	......	1,600	......	Sent home 300 sperm, 2,432 pounds bone.
N. W. Coast....	July 21	....	......	......	......	Sent home 99 sperm, 430 whale, 13,500 bone; lost in Behring's Straits 1848 with 3,500 barrels oil. Captain Winters died on passage home.
South Pacific ..	Oct. 5	Mar. 21, 1850	400	1,600	16,000	
Pacific Ocean..	Oct. 27	May 29, 1852	381	39	1,300	Sent home 140 sperm.
Indian Ocean..	Sept. 14	Aug. 16, 1851	1,595	......	......	
....do	Aug. 11	May 3, 1850	......	1,558	19,100	Sent home 2,420 bone
Pacific Ocean..	Nov. 30	July 14, 1851	178	1,554	18,700	
Indian Ocean..	June 28	Apr. 9, 1851	1,796	435	......	Third mate, John M. Austin, died at sea July, 1850; sent home 75 barrels sperm.
Pacific Ocean..	Jan. 12	Mar. 24, 1851	1,140	1,946	......	Sent home 9,800 pounds bone.
Indian & Pac ..	Oct. 4	Feb. 23, 1851	425	1,095	9,100	
Pacific Ocean..	Oct. 9	Jan. 5, 1851	868	56	......	
....do	July 2	Oct. 4, 1850	1,527	......	......	Sent home 65 sperm.
Indian & N. W.	Aug. 5	Apr. 8, 1850	307	2,619	23,300	Sent home 46 sperm and 11,000 pounds bone.
Indian & Pac ..	Aug. 21	Nov. 30, 1850	1,382	......	......	
N. W. Coast....	Nov. 16	....	......	......	......	Returned March 30, 1848; captain sick.
South Seas.....	Dec. 20	Apr. 1, 1851	868	235	800	
....	....	....	......	......	......	Lost at Cape de Verdes 1847.
Pacific Ocean..	Aug. 19	....	......	......	......	Sold at San Francisco 1851; sent home 81 sperm.
Indian Ocean...	May 19	Sept. 17, 1851	691	......	......	Sent home 52 sperm.
Pacific Ocean..	Oct. 26	June 25, 1851	1,720	325	......	
Indian Ocean..	July 21	Aug. 3, 1851	630	285	......	

Table showing returns of whaling-vessels

Name of vessel.	Class.	Tonnage.	Captain.	Managing owner or agent.
1847.				
New Bedford, Mass.—Continued.				
Enterprise	Ship	291	—— Little	Robert Gibbs
Emerald	do	359	—— Munkley	J. Dunbar & Co
Equator	Bark	263	F. H. Mathews	O. & G. O. Crocker
Exchange	do	180	—— Reynolds	Thomas Knowles & Co
Fenelon	Ship	328	E. P. Mosher	B. B. Howard
Fortune	Bark	291	E. Woodbridge	Gilbert Hatheway
Frances	Ship	348	E. Gardner	J. Arnold
George	do	273	D. Clark	J. A. Parker & Son
Gideon Howland	do	379	William Cash	I. Howland, jr., & Co
Golconda	do	331	—— Brush	George Howland
Good Return	do	376	—— Cook	H. Taber & Co
Gov. Troup	do	430	—— Coggeshall	E. C. Jones
Harvest	Bark	263	Thomas Bailey	Swift & Allen
Herald, 2d	Ship	303	—— Macomber	T. & A. R. Nye
Hercules, 2d	do	290	L. B. Imbert	D. R. Greene & Co
Hope, 2d	do	295	—— Christian	Wilcox & Richmond
Hope	Bark	186	S. Brayton	William Watkins
Huntress	Ship	391	—— Shearman	Robert Gibbs
Iris	do	311	William Weeks	E. C. Jones
John Coggeshall	do	338	—— West	Edward M. Robinson
John Howland	do	377	—— Leary	J. & J. Howland
John & Edward	do	318	—— Coggeshall	Wilcox & Richmond
Julian	do	356	—— Taber	Hathaway & Luce
Junior	do	378	—— Tinkham	D. R. Greene & Co
Lafayette	do	260	—— Lawrence	Edw. W. Howland
Le Baron	Bark	170	—— Chadwick	Lorenzo Pierce
Liverpool	Ship	300	—— Tripp	Abraham Barker
Logan	do	302	—— Nickerson	I. Howland, jr., & Co
Liverpool, 2d	do	428	—— West	Thomas Willcox
Morea	do	330	R. T. Wyatt	B. B. Howard
Maria Theresa	do	330	—— Swift	T. & A. R. Nye
Mary	do	287	T. J. Corey	I. Howland, jr., & Co
Milton	do	388	—— Smith	H. Taber & Co
Marcella	Bark	210	—— Worth	C. R. Tucker & Co
Margaret Scott	Ship	307	—— Luce	R. French
Midas	do	326	D. P. Eldridge	J. B. Wood & Co
Minerva	do	408	Jason Seabury	William Gifford
Minerva	Bark	195	—— Perry	William O. Brownell
Messenger	Ship	291	A. E. Arthur	J. R. Thornton
Montpelier	do	320	—— Young	J. R. Thornton
Moctezuma	do	436	—— Tower	West & Paine
Marcia	do	315	—— Ellison	E. W. Howland
Olympia	do	296	—— Woodward	Ashley & Philips
Otranto	Bark	150	—— Winslow	Cranston Willcox
Phœnix	Ship	423	—— McCleave	John A. Parker
Pioneer	Bark	231	—— Hathaway	J. D. Thompson
Roscoe	Ship	362	—— McCleave	Andrew Robeson
Rodman	do	371	—— Allyne	C. W. Morgan
Roman	do	375	S. Wilbur	E. C. Jones
Roman, 2d	do	350	—— Blackmer	A. Barker
Sally Anne	do	312	J. B. Brooks	D. R. Greene & Co
St. George	do	408	—— Hawes	A. Barker
Stephania	do	315	W. N. Bourne	J. Bourne
Two Brothers	do	288	—— Jenney	D. R. Greene & Co

sailing from American ports—Continued.

Whaling-ground.	Date— Of sailing.	Date— Of arrival.	Result of voyage. Sperm-oil.	Result of voyage. Whale-oil.	Result of voyage. Whalebone.	Remarks.
			Bbls.	*Bbls.*	*Lbs.*	
Indian & N. W.	Aug. 2	June 15, 1849	85	1,114	6,000	
Pacific Ocean..	Oct. 27	June 13, 1851	1,518	......	......	
....do	Sept. 4	....	......	......	......	No report.
....do	May 4	May 2, 1849	468	4	......	Bought from Warren 1847.
Indian & N. W.	Aug. 3	....	......	......	......	Condemned and sold at St. Catharine's 1848.
....do	Aug. 5	June 6, 1850	......	2,430	......	Sent home 29,000 pounds bone.
Pacific Ocean..	Oct. 4	June 29, 1850	823	......	......	Captain Gardner returned sick 1846.
....do	Nov. 30	Aug. 1, 1853	1	817	12,400	Sent home 404 whale.
Indian & N. W.	July 17	Apr. 8, 1850	180	3,133	34,500	
Pacific Ocean..	Aug. 25	Apr. 2, 1851	1,148	43	......	Captain Brush came home sick 1850.
N. W. Coast....	Dec. 9	Jan. 29, 1850	519	2,742	15,600	Sent home 9,979 pounds bone.
Pacific & N. W.	Aug. 26	May 8, 1850	34	3,161	35,700	Sent home 458 barrels sperm and 17,000 pounds bone.
Indian & Pac ..	Dec. 4	July 18, 1850	384	1,493	19,700	Added 1847; second mate and boat's crew lost April 22, 1850.
Pacific Ocean..	Nov. 5	May 6, 1851	117	2,471	......	
....do	July 27	....	......	......	......	Lost off Navigator's Islands, April 17, 1850; sent home 166 sperm.
....do	Sept. 1	May 8, 1851	745	64	......	
Indian Ocean ..	Oct. 26	May 9, 1850	1,177	......	......	
Pac. & N. W ...	Oct. 4	May 8, 1850	135	2,675	21,400	Sent home 11,500 pounds bone.
Indian Ocean ..	June 24	Jan. 2, 1850	1,541	324	1,300	
N. W. Coast....	Nov. 20	June 10, 1850	423	700	9,300	Bought from Newport 1847; Captain West left the ship and went to California; sent to California 1850; sold to Fairhaven 1852.
Pacific Ocean ..	Nov. 2	July 21, 1851	1,824	15	......	
Indian Ocean ..	May 25	Dec. 18, 1850	594	164	......	Sent home 67 sperm.
....do	June 23	May 8, 1851	92	2,530	28,900	Captain Taber left at Honolulu 1850; sent home 2,318 bone.
South Seas.....	Dec. 15	Mar. 15, 1850	32	2,518	29,500	
Coast Peru.....	Dec. 27	....	......	......	......	Lost on Gallipagos Islands, June, 1850; oil (600 sperm 200 whale) saved by Nauticon, of Nantucket.
Indian Ocean ..	Apr. 28	....	......	......	......	Added 1846 from Newport; lost 1851; sent home 117 sperm; sold 130 sperm at Sydney.
Ind. & N. W ...	June 16	June 2, 1850	69	2,062	17,500	Sent home 550 whale, 39,898 pounds bone.
Pacific Ocean ..	Nov. 11	May 3, 1851	146	1,056	9,800	
Ind. & N. W ...	Oct. 3	Apr. 12, 1851	27	4,043	......	Sent home 500 whale, 34,793 pounds bone.
N. W. Coast....	Oct. 12	June 12, 1850	40	2,880	24,000	
....do	Nov. 26	Mar. 22, 1851	117	2,389	......	Sent home 82 sperm, 338 whale, 37,200 pounds bone.
Pacific Ocean ..	July 21	Apr. 8, 1850	481	772	2,000	
....do	Sept. 1	July 15, 1851	2,594	10	......	
Atlantic & Ind.	Apr. 5	Apr. 18, 1850	613	......	......	
N. W. Coast....	Nov. 20	May 13, 1851	70	2,540	18,600	Sent home 16,728 pounds bone.
Pac. & N. W ...	Aug. 19	June 3, 1850	166	1,593	......	Sent home 15,685 pounds bone.
Ind. & N. W ...	July 20	Jan. 13, 1850	220	2,656	16,800	Sent home 50 sperm, 20,000 pounds bone.
Pacific Ocean ..	June 9	....	......	......	......	Voyage broken up by crew deserting to California; run as a packet from Valparaiso to San Francisco; sold in California; sent home 51 sperm.
....do	July 27	Sept. 8, 1851	1,010	22	......	Sent home 79 sperm.
Pac. & N. W ...	Oct. 9	Apr. 18, 1850	304	2,495	25,400	
....do	Aug. 16	Mar. 25, 1851	93	2,943	25,400	Sent home 10,000 pounds bone.
N. W. Coast....	July 29	May 11, 1850	314	2,219	31,900	
Pacific Ocean ..	Aug. 19	June 21, 1851	1,148	3	......	Sent home 90 sperm.
Indian Ocean ..	Jan. 17	Apr. 30, 1849	420	......	......	Sold to go to California 1849.
Pacific Ocean ..	Aug. 3	May 27, 1851	729	1,774	......	Sent home 97 sperm, 19,420 pounds bone.
Indian Ocean ..	June 29	Apr. 26, 1851	102	1,630	27,300	
Pacific Ocean ..	Oct. 7	June 2, 1851	1,826	......	......	Sent home 90 sperm.
....do	Nov. 5	May 10, 1851	276	2,519	26,600	
....do	Nov. 18	Aug. 8, 1851	2,335	52	......	
N. W. Coast	Oct. 20	Apr. 12, 1850	361	2,812	34,500	
Ind. & Pacific..	June 3	Sept. 11, 1850	782	742	......	Sent home 94 sperm.
Pac. & N. W ...	Sept. 9	Apr. 5, 1850	497	2,422	13,500	Sent home 17,026 pounds bone.
Indian Ocean ..	Sept. 15	Oct. 22, 1850	229	1,191	6,800	
Ind. & Pacific..	Sept. 1	Mar. 31, 1851	801	903	......	Sent home 140 sperm, 16,500 pounds bone

Table showing returns of whaling-vessels

Name of vessel.	Class.	Tonnage.	Captain.	Managing owner or agent.
1847.				
New Bedford, Mass.—Continued.				
Virginia	Ship	346	—— Manter	Hathaway & Luce
Washington	...do	344	S. D. Fisher	J. Bourne, jr
Zephyr	...do	361	—— Shearman	Alex. Gibbs
Fairhaven, Mass.				
Albion	Ship	326	—— Hathaway	E. Sawin
Erie	...do	451	—— Norton	Nathan Church
Gen. Scott	...do	333	—— Fisher	L. C. Tripp
Heroine	...do	337	Thomas Wall	N. Church
Herald	...do	262	—— Terry	Seth A. Mitchell
James Monroe	...do	424	—— Bowman	F. R. Whitwell
London Packet	...do	335	Jabez B. Howland	Gibbs & Jenney
Marcus	...do	286	—— Osborn	Lemuel Tripp
Omega	...do	305	—— Morey	N. Church
Popmunnet	Bark	184	—— Eldridge	I. F. Terry
Sarah Frances	Ship	301	—— Wood	E. Sawin
Sylph	...do	336	—— Gardner	Edmund Allen
William Rotch	...do	290	—— Kempton	Fish & Huttleston
Mattapoisett, Mass.				
Cachelot	Bark	230	—— Luther	Wilson Barstow
Helen	Brig	120	—— Jenney	R. L. Barstow
Lagrange	Bark	170	—— Dornin	E. Willis
Solon	Brig	129	J. W. Bolles	Samuel Sturtevant, jr
Willis	Bark	164	—— Taber	R. L. Barstow
Westport, Mass.				
Barclay	Bark	167	—— King	Alex. H. Corey
Champion	...do	209	—— Gardner	Andrew Hicks
Dr. Franklin	...do	171	—— Hazard	Job Davis
Leonidas	Brig	128	—— Cornell	John L. Anthony
Mattapoisett	...do	150	—— Briggs	Freeman Lawrence
Mexico	...do	130	—— Macomber	Gideon Davis
Platina	Ship	266	—— Gifford	Andrew Hicks
President	Bark	167	—— Worth	...do
Rajah	...do	250	—— West	Henry Willcox
Nantucket, Mass.				
Barclay	Ship	301	Eben Baker	John H. Shaw
Constitution	...do	318	Obed Bunker	C. G. & H. Coffin
Henry Clay	...do	385	Samuel P. Skinner	Christopher Wyer
Hero	...do	313	Sylvanus Swain	Joseph Starbuck
Kirkwood	Brig	201	Charles Alley	J. Cook, jr., & Co
Mary	Ship	369	William B. Harris	Edward Perry
Peru	Bark	257	Consider Fisher	R. F. Gardner
Planter	Ship	340	Isaac B. Hussey	...do
President	...do	293	Joseph Marshall	J. Starbuck
Rambler	...do	318	James H. Haughton	F. C. Sanford
Spartan	...do	333	Crom. Morselander	Daniel Jones
Two Brothers	Schooner	70	—— Carey	J. Cook, jr., & Co
Washington	Ship	308	Stephen Bailey	
Edgartown, Mass.				
Almira	Ship	362	—— Coffin	Abm. Osborne

sailing from American ports—Continued.

Whaling-ground.	Date— Of sailing.	Date— Of arrival.	Result of voyage. Sperm-oil.	Result of voyage. Whale-oil.	Result of voyage. Whalebone.	Remarks.
			Bbls.	*Bbls.*	*Lbs.*	
Pacific Ocean ..	Aug. 18	Aug. 6, 1851	1,589	125	......	First mate, Mr. Luce, died at Callao, May, 1849.
Pac. & N. W ...	Oct. 12	May 28, 1850	348	1,790	1,400	Sent home 15,000 pounds bone.
Ind. & Pacific ..	Oct. 21	June 1, 1851	719	194	1,800	
Indian Ocean ..	Aug. 30	Mar. 27, 1851	300	1,900	20,000	
Ind. & N. W ..	Sept. 1	Apr. 11, 1850	150	3,200	21,000	Sent home 116 sperm, 22,500 pounds bone.
Pacific Ocean ..	July 14	May 8, 1851	727	1,352	18,600	Sent home 8 casks sperm.
... do	Nov. 18	May 28, 1851	......	2,685	......	Sent home 434 sperm, 16,000 bone.
Indian Ocean	Nov. 11	....	......	......	......	Sent home 27 whale, 25,497 bone; shipped oil to London; sold at Honolulu, March, 1854.
Pacific Ocean ..	Oct. 30	....	......	......	......	Sold at San Francisco 1849.
South Seas	Oct. 11	....	......	......	......	Condemned at Sydney 1850; refitted and sailed whaling from there.
Pacific Ocean ..	Oct. 14	Sept. 1, 1850	700	800	......	
Ind. & Pacific ..	Jan. 6	July 6, 1850	600	1,600	23,000	
Pacific Ocean ..	Nov. 26	....	......	......	......	Crew all deserted save one in California; added 1847, from Sippican.
....do	Dec. 22	....	......	......	......	
....do	July 8	May 22, 1850	30	400	4,000	Added 1847; sent home 1,474 sperm.
....do	Sept. 30	Aug. 18, 1851	748	577	10,000	Bought from New Bedford, 1847.
Pacific Ocean ..	Aug. 4	Sept. 2, 1851	......	......	......	No report.
Atlantic	June 8	Sept. 30, 1847	90	......	......	Added 1847.
Pacific Ocean ..	Feb. 5	Apr. 6, 1849	230	......	......	Sent home 6,414 pounds bone.
Atlantic	Dec. 21	July 29, 1849	80	......	......	Sold to Westport 1849.
....do	Dec. 4	Sept. 29, 1848	500	......	......	
Atlantic	May 27	Dec. 31, 1848	450	......	......	Sent home 131 sperm.
Atl. & Pacific ..	Jan. 22	Nov. 7, 1848	300	50	......	
Indian Ocean ..	June 24	Feb. 2, 1849	700	......	......	
Atlantic	Nov. 5	May 10, 1850	400	......	......	Sailed from Fall River 1847; sold to Westport, 1848.
....do	Apr. 15	Dec. 10, 1848	200	......	......	Bought from Mattapoisett
....do	Mar. —	June 21, 1848	300	......	......	
Pacific Ocean ..	July 29	May 28, 1850	600	275	......	Added 1847.
Atlantic	Nov. 18	Oct. —, 1848	75	......	......	
Ind. & Pacific ..	Oct. 30	June 10, 1851	224	1,702	14,400	
Pacific Ocean ..	Oct. 29	Oct. 15, 1851	1,150	......	......	
....do	Sept. 5	Apr. 23, 1852	555	90	......	Mr. Prince, third mate, died at sea; sold and sent home about 50 barrels.
....do	Oct. 27	....	......	......	......	Condemned at Rio Janeiro.
....do	Apr. 2	July 7, 1851	852	......	......	Sold 50 barrels sperm.
....do	Oct. 19	....	......	......	......	Bought from Baltimore 1847; built 1843; third mate killed 1849; Captain Alley died at Panama, and the brig was sold there.
....do	Oct. 17	Sept. 21, 1851	717	30	......	Sold 30 barrels sperm.
....do	Aug. 21	Dec. 27, 1850	750	150	......	Sold 60 barrels blackfish.
....do	July 5	July 12, 1851	1,095	530	......	Sent home 8 casks sperm; Captain Hussey shipped on board brig Wm. Penn, of San Francisco, and was killed in a mutiny November 6, 1852.
....do	Sept. 1	Dec. 9, 1850	1,369	20	......	Got ashore on Gallipagos Islands and came home damaged.
....do	Dec. 5	July 28, 1851	1,837	8	......	Sold 125 barrels sperm; second mate killed by a whale December, 1847.
....do	{ Oct. 6 Nov. 21 }	 June 21, 1851	868	......	......	{ Returned to Edgartown, damaged in gale, and refitted. }
South Atlantic.	June 19	Nov. 15, 1847	50	......	......	Returned in consequence of illness of captain.
Pacific Ocean ..	Oct. 30	....	......	......	......	Condemned at Oahu in 1849.
Pacific Ocean ..	July 29	Mar. 20, 1851	1,000	1,500	18,000	

Table showing returns of whaling-vessels

Name of vessel.	Class.	Tonnage.	Captain.	Managing owner or agent.
1847.				
Edgartown, Mass.—Continued.				
Vineyard	Ship	381	—— Coon	Benjamin Worth
Vesta	Brig	156	—— Mayhew	do
Holmes's Hole, Mass.				
Malta	Bark	150	—— Cromwell	Thomas Barrows
Ocmulgee	Ship	458	—— Manter	Thomas Bradley
Provincetown, Mass.				
Belle Isle	Schooner	104	—— Cook	Parker Cook
Cadmus	Brig	130	—— Nickerson	Samuel Soper
Council	Schooner	100	—— Genn	Howe & Lord
Edwin	do	100	—— Nickerson	R. L. Thatcher
Fairy	Bark	186	—— Cook	Ebenezer Cook
John Adams	Schooner	110	—— Turner	R. L. Thatcher
Louisa	do	98		Samuel Cook
Rienzi	do	115	—— Young	A. Cook
Samuel Cook	Brig	140		
Wareham, Mass.				
G. Washington	Ship	374	—— Gibbs	S. C. Gibbs
Fall River, Mass.				
Leonidas	Brig	128	—— Cornell	Nathan Durfee
Providence, R. I.				
Cassander	Ship	299	—— Winslow	Nathaniel F. Potter
Richmond	Bark	343	E. A. Swift	Pearce & Bullock
Warren, R. I.				
Boy	Ship	252	Obed Luce	John R. Wheaton
Franklin	Bark	240	—— Barton	Samuel Barton
Warren	Ship	383	—— Evans	Joseph Smith
Yarmouth, Mass.				
March	Brig	90	—— Wood	Silas Baker
Mystic, Conn.				
Antarctic	Ship		—— Kenney	
Alibree	Bark	378	—— Hull	I. & W. P. Randall
Congress	do	280	—— Taylor	do
Coriolanus	Ship	268	—— Maginly	Charles Mallory
Leander	Bark	213	—— Brerieton	do
Cold Spring, N. Y.				
Huntsville	Ship	523	—— Smith	John H. Jones
New London, Conn.				
Alert	Ship	398	—— Green	Williams & Haven
Atlas	Schooner	81	—— Lyon	Perkins & Smith
Blk. Warrior	Bark	231	—— Babcock	Williams & Haven
Bengal	Ship	304	—— Hempsted	Thomas Fitch, 2d
Chas. Carroll	do	412	—— Long	Perkins & Smith
Candace	do	310	—— Hempsted	Williams & Haven
Corinthian	do	505	—— Slate	Perkins & Smith

sailing from American ports—Continued.

Whaling-ground.	Date—		Result of voyage.			Remarks.
	Of sailing.	Of arrival.	Sperm-oil.	Whale-oil.	Whalebone.	
			Bbls.	*Bbls.*	*Lbs.*	
Pacific Ocean ..	Oct. 30	May 7, 1850	2, 000	150	......	
Atlantic	Apr. 12	Oct. 6, 1848	300	....	......	Sent home 95 sperm; withdrawn 1848.
Pacific Ocean ..	Sept. 2	Apr. 8, 1850	900	......	......	
N. W. Coast....	Sept. 2	Apr. 21, 1850	60	3, 000	30, 000	
North Atlantic	Feb. 11	Aug. 26, 1847	300	......	......	
Atlantic	Feb. 1	Sept. 24, 1847	240	......	......	
North Atlantic.	Mar. 13	July 14, 1847	120	8	......	Sailed again September 6, 1847, for Straits Belle Isle; returned July 4, 1848, with 90 barrels sperm.
Atlantic	....	May —, 1848	140	......	......	Withdrawn 1848.
....do	....	Oct. 12, 1848	415	......	......	
....do	Apr. 13	Oct. 22, 1847	100	60	......	
....do	Mar. 28	Oct. 25, 1847	110	......	......	
....do	Feb. 17	Aug. 15, 1847	210	10	......	
....do	Apr. 1	May 13, 1848	200	10	......	
N. W. Coast....	Nov. 17	Mar. 17, 1850	200	2, 800	34, 000	Lost 100 barrels whale in a heavy gale on the passage home.
Atlantic	Nov. 5	....	......	......	.....	Sold to Westport 1848, and returned to that port.
Pacific Ocean ..	Nov. 16	....	......	......	.....	Burned at sea June 10, 1848. Crew landed at St. Martha Grande after being 10 days in their boats without provisions, during which time two died; sent home 1,500 pounds bone.
N. W. Coast....	July 10	Feb. 11, 1850	60	3, 400	20, 000	Sold for California 1850; sent home 99 sperm, 14,000 bone.
Pacific Ocean ..	Dec. 19	July 31, 1852	205	....	....	Captain Luce and 5 men massacred by natives of Mackill's Island January, 1851; sold to Bristol for Cuba trade, 1852; sold to Boston 1853; shipped oil to London.
....do	Dec. 22	June 26, 1848	900	300	....	
N. W. Coast....	Nov. 29	May 8, 1851	168	2, 789	29, 100	Withdrawn 1852.
Atlantic	Oct. 23	Aug. 21, 1847	250	30	....	Bought from Barnstable 1847; sailed again October 23, 1847, and arrived at New Bedford October 21, 1848, with 30 barrels sperm.
....	Aug. 16	....	......	......	......	Lost at Fayal September 23, 1847.
N. W. Coast....	June 24	Apr. 25, 1849	300	3, 000	30, 000	
Indian Ocean ..	July 1	July 27, 1849	......	800	7, 000	
Crozettes	Sept. 6	July 7, 1849	25	1, 675	13, 000	
....do	Sept. 29	Mar. 29, 1850	250	500	4, 000	Thomas White, second mate, died September 30, 1849.
South Pacific...	Sept. 30	Apr. 21, 1849	.....	4, 200	50, 000	
Indian and N. W	Aug. 3	Feb. 15, 1850	80	3, 400	4, 000	Sent home 52 sperm, 18,680 pounds bone.
Desolation Isld	Aug, 11	May 2, 1849	......	200	......	Added 1847.
Indian Ocean ..	June 2	Aug. 20, 1849	15	1, 600	......	Sent home 9 casks sperm, 14,500 pounds bone.
....do	June 2	Mar. 16, 1850	......	2, 300	25, 000	Sent home 11,000 pounds bone.
Desolation Isld.	July 21	June 3, 1849	......	3, 600	......	Withdrawn for California 1849.
Indian Ocean ..	July 13	Apr. 27, 1849	......	2, 100	21, 000	
Desolation Isld.	Sept. 23	June 26, 1849	......	3, 700	......	Bought from Bristol 1847.

Table showing returns of whaling-vessels

Name of vessel.	Class.	Tonnage.	Captain.	Managing owner or agent.
1847.				
New London, Conn.—Continued.				
Dromo	Ship	306	——— Steele	T. Fitch, 2d
Electra	do	348	——— Brown	Williams & Barnes
Friends	do	403	——— Howard	Benjamin Brown
Franklin	Schooner	119	——— Norie	Perkins & Smith
Geo. & Mary	Ship	356	——— Middleton	Lyman Allyn
Hibernia	do	551	——— Smith	T. Fitch, 2d
H'y Thompson	do	315	——— Holm	Frink, Chew & Co
India	do	433	——— Miller	Williams & Haven
Indian Chief	do	401	——— Bailey	Frink, Chew & Co
Jefferson	do	396	——— Gray	William P. Benjamin
John & Elizabeth	do	296	——— Chappell	Williams & Haven
Julius Cæsar	do	347	——— Morgan	Stoddard & Learned
Lark	Bark	288	——— Kelley	Perkins & Smith
Mogul	Ship	395	——— Huntley	Williams & Barnes
McLellan	do	376	——— Perkins	Perkins & Smith
Merrimack	do	414	——— Destin	Williams & Haven
Neptune	do	285	——— Holt	do
N. America	Bark	388	——— Bolles	do
Pembroke	do	199	——— Potter	Miner, Lawrence & Co
Tenedos	do	245	——— Comstock	Joseph Lawrence
Venice	do	353	——— Harris	Weaver, Rogers & Co
Stonington, Conn.				
Charles Phelps	Ship	362	——— Burch	Charles P. Williams
Eugene	d	297	——— Brown	do
Mary & Susan	do	392	——— Pendleton	do
Newburyport	do	341	——— Lester	Pendleton & Trumbull
United States	do	244	——— Barnum	John F. Trumbull
Sag Harbor, N. Y.				
Acasta	Bark	286	——— Harlow	John Budd
Arabella	Ship	367	——— Ludlow	N. & G. Howell
Cadmus	Bark	307	——— Smith	Mulford & Sleight
Concordia	do	265	——— Hedges	Thomas Brown
Franklin	Ship	391	Mercator Cooper	Huntting Cooper
Gem	Bark	326	——— Worth	do
Illinois	Ship	413	——— Jaggar	John Budd
Jefferson	do	435	——— Smith	T. Brown
Levant	do	382	——— Lowen	Tiffany & Halsey
Marcus	Bark	283	——— Babcock	N. & G. Howell
Ontario	Ship	368	——— Brown	S. & B. Huntting & Co
Panama	do	465	——— Hallock	N. & G. Howell
Phenix	do	314	——— Green	Cook & Green
Superior	Bark	275	——— Royce	Post & Sherry
Tuscany	Ship	299	S. W. Edwards	John Budd
Greenport, N. Y.				
Caroline	Ship	252	——— Babcock	Ireland, Wells & Carpenter.
Italy	do	299	——— Weld	David G. Floyd
Lucy Ann	do	309	——— Brown	Wiggins, Parsons & Cook
Neva	do	362	——— Case	Ireland, Wells & Carpenter.
Roanoke	Bark	252	——— Baldwin	Wiggins & Parsons

sailing from American ports—Continued.

Whaling-ground.	Date— Of sailing.	Of arrival.	Result of voyage. Sperm-oil.	Whale-oil.	Whalebone.	Remarks.
			Bbls.	*Bbls.*	*Lbs.*	
N. W. Coast ...	Oct. 9	May 31, 1850	......	1,600	3,500	Sent home 11,500 pounds bone.
Indian and N. W	July 20	Mar. 23, 1850	......	2,300	22,000	Sent home 1,100 whale, 18,500 pounds bone.
Pacific Ocean ..	July 14	May 7, 1849	......	2,300	3,000	Sent home 141 sperm, 18,630 pounds bone.
Crozettes	Aug. 24	Aug. —, 1849	......	25	......	
Indian and N. W	Aug. 14	Apr. 8, 1850	130	2,250	16,000	
Patagonia	Nov. 5	....	......	......	......	Sold to New Bedford 1849; no report.
Indian and N. W	July 31	June 16, 1850	100	2,300	......	Sent home 23,500 pounds bone.
....do	June 23	Mar. 29, 1850	200	4,000	25,000	Sent home 27,990 bone.
N. W. Coast	Nov. 18	Feb. 15, 1851	75	3,100	18,000	Sailed October 21; was damaged by a gale on the 26th and returned; sailed again 18th November; sent home 17,500 pounds bone.
Indian and N. W	Aug. 19	Mar. 31, 1849	......	2,700	27,000	Sent home 85 sperm.
....do	July 7	May 7, 1850	150	2,000	18,000	Sent home 7 casks sperm.
Indian Ocean ..	Aug. 12	June 13, 1849	50	2,200	18,000	
....do	Oct. 9	June 16, 1850	450	1,700	14,000	Bought from New York 1847.
Indian and N. W	June 7	May 8, 1851	83	3,732	28,500	Sent home 19,350 pounds bone.
Davis Straits ..	Mar. 5	Oct. 5, 1847	......	1,111	15,000	Brought 845 seal-skins.
N. W. Coast	Oct. 9	....	50	3,300	23,000	
Indian Ocean ..	July 21	Jan. 28, 1850	100	2,000	10,000	Sent home 13,000 bone.
Chili and N. W	Aug. 11	Mar. 23, 1849	70	2,600	26,000	
Indian Ocean ..	July 14	....	......	......	......	Lost 1851.
Indian and Pac	Aug. 12	June 21, 1850	16	1,500	3,000	Sent home 100 sperm, 9,800 bone
Indian and N. W	June 15	May 13, 1849	50	2,600	18,000	Sent home 16,500 pounds bone.
....do	June 12	Jan. 13, 1850	270	2,700	33,000	Sent home 15 casks sperm.
Chili and N. W	July 12	Apr. 7, 1850	100	2,300	25,000	
N. W. Coast	Oct. 23	Mar. 23, 1850	40	3,200	45,000	
Indian and N. W	Sept. 14	Apr. 18, 1850	......	2,700	34,000	
Atlantic and In	Dec. 4	May 3, 1849	......	2,075	1,200	
Indian Ocean ..	Oct. 14	Aug. 22, 1849	155	525	4,000	Withdrawn 1850; returned in consequence of the illness of Captain Harlow; second mate killed by a whale December, 1847.
Pacific Ocean ..	Aug. 10	July 9, 1849	50	2,000	10,500	Sold to New Bedford 1849.
Indian Ocean ..	Sept. 30	June 24, 1849	80	1,720	9,000	Sent home 4,000 pounds bone.
South Atlantic.	July 13	July 9, 1849	350	600	5,500	Sent home 39 sperm.
N. W. Coast	July 21	....	......	......	......	Lost on coast of Brazil June 7, 1850; had 3,300 whale; saved about 2,300; sent home 60 sperm.
....do	Oct. 9	....	......	......	......	Totally lost with her cargo near Suwarrow Island December, 1848; had 170 sperm, 2,800 whale, 27,000 bone.
....do	Oct. 29	Mar. 31, 1850	60	2,800	14,000	Sent home 13,562 pounds bone; sold to New Bedford 1850.
....do	July 29	May 28, 1850	......	3,200	9,000	Sent home 25,193 pounds bone.
....do	Oct. 13	Mar. 26, 1851	......	3,500	8,000	Sent home 7,500 pounds bone.
South Atlantic.	July 21	....	......	......	......	Condemned at Honolulu November, 1850.
N. W. Coast ...	Oct. 11	Feb. 5, 1850	......	3,000	10,000	Sold to New Bedford 1850.
....do	Sept. 15	Mar. 25, 1850	......	3,800	30,000	Withdrawn 1850; condemned at Valparaiso 1851.
....do	Oct. 22	May 31, 1849	80	2,400	20,000	Sold to Boston 1849.
South Atlantic.	July 14	May 5, 1849	......	1,700	......	Sent home 22,936 pounds bone.
Indian Ocean ..	Aug. 12	Apr. 28, 1851	56	2,788	17,400	Sent home 96 sperm, 21,750 pounds bone; Captain Edwards died October 29, 1849.
Indian Ocean ..	Dec. 4	June 4, 1850	500	800	6,000	George Babcock, first mate, died September 18, 1849.
N. W. Coast ...	Aug. 17	Apr. 7, 1849	200	2,400	30,000	Sent home 53 sperm.
....do	Aug. 21	July 8, 1849	120	2,280	22,000	Sent home 20,290 pounds bone; sailed 1849, and was condemned at Rio Janeiro 1850.
....do	Aug. 17	May 3, 1851	88	2,783	25,700	Sent home 32 sperm, 12,000 bone.
....do	Aug. 25	July 12, 1849	250	350	3,000	

Table showing returns of whaling-vessels

Name of vessel.	Class.	Tonnage.	Captain.	Managing owner or agent.
1848.				
New Bedford, Mass.				
Abm. H. Howland	Ship	414	—— Fisher	Abm. H. Howland
Abm. Barker	do	400	Á. R. Barker	Abm. Barker
Addison	do	426	—— Lawrence	Isaac B. Richmond
Alexander	do	421	—— Black	J. A. Parker
America	do	418	—— Adams	I. Howland, jr., & Co.
America	Bark	257	—— Tucker	C. R. Tucker & Co.
Archer	Ship	322	—— Smith	Edward W. Howland
Arnolda	do	350	R. Wood	J. B. Wood & Co.
Brunswick	do	29[illegible]	—— Johnson	Barton Ricketson
Chandler Price	do	44[illegible]	—— Taber	Pope & Morgan
Copia	do	315	—— Taber	Lemuel Kollock
Condor	do	349	J. Allen.	Pope & Morgan
Cornelia	Bark	216	—— Devoll	L. Kollock
Charleston Packet	do	184	—— Lewis	Thomas Knowles & Co.
Chili	Ship	291	—— Dexter	B. B. Howard
Cowper	do	301	—— Cole	do
Dartmouth	do	336	—— Pierce	I. Howland, jr. & Co.
Dunbarton	Bark	199	M. Mayhew.	I. B. Richmond
Envoy.	do	392	W. T. Walker	William C. Brownell
Emigrant	do	180	Bartholomew West	Russell Maxfield
Florida	Ship	330	—— Weeks	E. C. Jones
Frances Henrietta	do	407	—— Clough	Samuel W. Rodman
George and Susan	do	356	—— Wight	George Howland
George Porter	Bark	285	—— Ellis	William Watkins
Geo. Washington	do	242	—— Baker	Charles Hitch
Gratitude	Ship	337	P. S. Wilcox	Swift & Allen
Hector	do	380	Peter Smith	William J. Rotch
Henry Kneeland	do	304	G. H. Clark	B. B. Howard
Hydaspe	do	31[illegible]	—— Tallman	J. B. Wood & Co.
India	do	366	—— Swift	A. H. Howland
Inga	Brig	160	—— Barnes	Ingalls & Lucas
Isaac Howland	Ship	399	—— West	I. Howland, jr., & Co.
Isabella	do	411	—— Brayton	L. P. Ashmead
James Allen	do	355	—— Smith	Gideon Allen
Java	do	278	—— Stanton	George Howland
James	do	321	—— Cornell	T. & A. R. Nye
James Maury	do	395	—— Whelden	Charles R. Tucker & Co
Jeannette	do	340	—— West	I. B. Richmond
John	do	308	—— Anderson	Frederick Parker
Kutusoff	do	415	—— Slocum	J. Dunbar & Co.
Lancaster	do	383	—— Almy	T. & A. R. Nye
London Packet	do	280		A. H. Howland

sailing from American ports—Continued.

Whaling-ground.	Date—		Result of voyage.			Remarks.
	Of sailing.	Of arrival.	Sperm-oil.	Whale-oil.	Whalebone.	
			Bbls.	*Bbls.*	*Lbs.*	
Kamschatka...	Aug. 9	Mar. 19, 1851	137	3, 226	37, 300	Sent home 200 barrels oil and 6,197 pounds bone.
Ind. and Pacific	July 1	June 11, 1850	45	2, 809	......	
Pacific Ocean ..	Aug. 17	June 10, 1852	1, 965	25	......	
Ind. and Pacific	May 23	Mar. 25, 1851	26	2, 767	18, 200	Captain Black died at sea November 25, 1848. Sent home 307 barrels oil and about 13,500 pounds bone.
N. W. Coast....	Oct. 23	Apr. 26, 1851	430	3, 620	56, 400	
Pacific Ocean ..	Feb. 2	May 28, 1851	297	1, 002	9, 000	
....do	May 17	May 1, 1852	2, 133	......	......	Sent home 160 sperm.
....do	July 1	Mar. 12, 1852	1, 910	67	....	
South Seas.....	Nov. 17	May 9, 1851	186	1, 959	30, 000	Sold to Dartmouth 1851.
N. W. Coast...	July 3	Jan. 14, 1851	256	3, 682	21, 700	Sent home 34,283 pounds bone.
....do	July 3	June 2, 1852	125	585	8, 700	Captain Taber came home in the Julian 1851; sent home 2,056 whale, 18,700 bone.
Ind. and Pacific	June 23	May 3, 1850	70	2, 628	39, 500	
Indian Ocean ..	Sept. 11	July 18, 1850	920	....	....	
......do	Aug. 3	Dec. 11, 1850	434	......	....	
Ind. and Pacific	Aug. 31	Apr. 9, 1852	No	oil.	....	Sent home 400 whale.
N. W. Coast....	Nov. 11	Mar. 22, 1851	198	3, 627	25, 800	Sent home 29,600 pounds bone.
....do	June 1	Mar. 21, 1851	......	3, 047	25, 400	Sailed early in season; went as far as Pernambuco and returned; captain sick; shipped to London from Hong-Kong 180 sperm, 11,600 pounds bone.
Pacific Ocean ..	Sept. 5	June 24, 1850	261	......	......	Bought from Mattapoisett 1848.
N. W. Coast....	July 12	....	......	....	......	Bought from Providence 1847; built 1826; sold at San Francisco 1851; took on voyage 5,300 whale, 75,000 pounds bone.
Indian Ocean ..	June 1	....	....	......	......	Bought from Bristol 1848; found in 1849 bottom up; crew never heard from; sent home 20 sperm.
....do	Nov. 7	Dec. 21, 1850	990	550	3, 000	
N. W. Coast....	Aug. 29	Jan. 17, 1851	304	2, 814	19, 200	Sent home 21,582 pounds bone.
Pacific Ocean ..	Oct. 26	May 11, 1852	943	1, 036	17, 300	
Indian Ocean ..	Mar. 29	....	......	......	....	Wrecked and condemned at Mahe 1850; oil (700 sperm) sent home.
....do	June 21	June 30, 1851	928	......	......	Enlarged 1848; built at New Bedford 1832.
South Seas.....	Dec. 5	May 6, 1851	171	2, 829	37, 600	
Ind. and Pacific	June 13	Aug. 9, 1852	2, 278	......	......	Dropped anchor but four times on voyage.
....do	July 19	May 4, 1851	......	2, 620	29, 000	Sent home 36 sperm.
Pacific Ocean ..	Dec. 13	Mar. 17, 1852	1, 365	......	....	
N. W. Coast....	Aug. 9	May 9, 1851	76	3, 272	....	Sent home 273 sperm, 1,015 whale, 76,500 pounds bone.
Indian Ocean ..	May 9	....	......	....	......	Added 1848; cut off at Pleasant Island December, 1852. Captain Barnes and most of the crew murdered by the natives. Sold 150 sperm at Hobart Town.
N. W. Coast...	June 30	Mar. 26, 1851	97	3, 260	.....	Shipped 180 sperm, 600 whale, to London, from Hong-Kong. Sent home 37,417 pounds bone.
Pacific Ocean ..	Sept. 13	....	....	.....	......	Lost on island of Chiloe January 31, 1850; Captain Brayton died immediately after the wreck.
N. W. Coast...	Dec. 28	Feb. 17, 1851	130	3, 025	1, 800	Sold 100 whale at Lahaina; sent home 44,000 bone.
Pacific Ocean ..	Aug. 22	Mar. 6, 1852	558	114	2, 100	First mate, Nathan Manter, killed by a whale December 4, 1850.
....do.	Aug. 23	Aug. 1, 1851	55	1, 876	......	Sent home on the voyage 500 sperm, 27,000 pounds bone.
N. W. Coast....	Nov. 1	June 25, 1851	85	1, 924	26, 500	Sold 1,600 barrels whale at Bahia, and took part load of sugar for New York; sent home 450 bone.
....do	Nov. 7	Oct. 14, 1850	214	2, 707	......	
Pacific Ocean ..	Sept. 28	Nov. 4, 1851	900	1, 330	.....	Sent home 28,407 bone.
N. W. Coast....	July 6	May 7, 1851	168	3, 035	34, 600	
Indian Ocean ..	Nov. 2	Mar. 15, 1851	368	2, 168	25, 550	Sailed early in year under Captain Cornell; returned September 30. Captain badly injured by a man falling from aloft and striking him on the back.
....	....	....	.....	.....	.....	Lost at sea near Cape de Verdes January 28, 1849; four of the crew lost.

Table showing returns of whaling-vessels

Name of vessel.	Class.	Tonnage.	Captain.	Managing owner or agent.
1848.				
New Bedford, Mass.—Continued.				
Lalla-Rookh	Ship	323	—— Gardner	J. A. Parker & Son
L. C. Richmond	do	341	C. S. Norton	J. B. Wood & Co.
Marengo	do	426	—— Devoll	Jona. Bourne, jr.
Mobile	do	263	George B. Long	E. C. Jones
Majestic	do	297	—— Hall	Thomas & Dow
Mars	Bark	270	—— Borden	C. R. Tucker & Co.
Metacom	Ship	360	—— Shockley	J. B. Wood & Co.
Menkar	do	371	—— Norton	Philip Anthony
Mexican	do	226	—— Cudworth	C. R. Tucker & Co.
Minerva Smyth	do	335	—— Childs	I. Howland, jr., & Co.
Mercury	do	340	—— West	do
Massachusetts	do	364	—— Chase	O. & G. O. Crocker
Minerva, 2d	do	291	O. Smalley	T. Knowles & Co.
Niger	do	437	—— Gray	Hathaway & Luce
New Bedford	do	351	—— Hamblin	I. Howland, jr., & Co.
Nimrod	do	340	—— Sherman	B. Ricketson
Nye	do	211	—— Francis	T. & A. R. Nye
Navy	do	356	—— Norton	J. B. Wood & Co.
Ohio	do	383	—— Norton	E. W. Howland
Orozimbo	do	588	—— Bartlett	B. Ricketson
Pacific	do	385	—— Hoxie	J. Perry
Ploughboy	do	391	—— Phelon	O. N. Swift
Parachute	do	331	—— Fisher	B. B. Howard
Rhine	Bark	174	—— Downs	E. C. Jones
Sappho	do	320	—— Cushman	O. & E. W. Seabury
Seine	Ship	281	Frederick Slocum	R. French
Statira	Bark	346	—— Coon	Hathaway & Luce
South Carolina	Ship	302	—— Corey	J. D. Thompson
Valparaiso	Bark	402	—— Cleveland	Hathaway & Luce
William and Eliza	Ship	321	—— Allen	Henry Taber & Co.
W. Hamilton	do	463	H. Shockley	I. Howland, jr., & Co.
Fairhaven, Mass.				
Acushnet	Ship	359	—— Bradley	Bradford, Fuller & Co.
Adeline Gibbs	do	354	—— Weeks	Gibbs & Jenney
Amazon	do	318	—— Daggett	Nathan Church
Bruce	Bark	148	—— Fuller	M. O. Bradford
Clifford Wayne	Ship	305	—— Wady	E. Sawin
Hesper	Bark	262	—— Slocum	Jenney & Tripp
Jos. Maxwell	Ship	302	E. T. Howland	F. R. Whitwell
Kingston	do	312	—— Luscomb	N. Church
Lydia	do	353	—— Worth	Sheffield Reed
Martha	do	298	—— Skinner	N. Church
Martha, 2d	do	301	—— Stewart	Atkins Adams
Phipe Delanoye	do	383	—— Morse	Warren Delano
Sharon	do	354	—— Bonney	Gibbs & Jenney
South Boston	do	339	—— Sowle	E. Sawin
Falmouth, Mass.				
Awashonks	Ship	342	—— Smith	Oliver C. Swift
Hobomok	do	414	Roland R. Jones	Elijah Swift
Mattapoisett, Mass.				
America	Brig	148	—— Lambert	R. L. Barstow
Annawan	do	159	—— Taber	Seth Freeman
Helen	do	120	—— Cushing	R. L. Barstow
Sarah	Ship	370	—— Purrington	Joseph Meigs
Sarah	Bark	171	—— Mayhew	Wilson Barstow

sailing from American ports—Continued.

Whaling-ground.	Date.		Result of voyage.			Remarks.
	Of sailing.	Of arrival.	Sperm-oil.	Whale-oil.	Whalebone.	
			Bbls.	*Bbls.*	*Lbs.*	
Pacific Ocean ..	Sept. 21	....	......	1, 853	......	First mate, Mr. McNulty, drowned at Tahiti August, 1850. Shipped 800 sperm to London from Hobart Town. Lost.
....do	July 15	Mar. 26, 1851	775	1, 814	26, 400	Sent home 120 whale.
N. W. Coast....	Aug. 1	May 16, 1851	158	4, 080	......	Sent home 150 sperm, 290 whale, 15,480 pounds bone.
....	....	....	......	......	......	Lost at sea September 23, 1848; Captain Long, first mate, and eight men, washed overboard and drowned.
N. W. Coast....	Nov. 1	Apr. 25, 1851	55	2, 618	30, 400	Sent home 400 whale, 18,256 pounds bone.
Pacific Ocean ..	Aug. 27	Mar. 16, 1852	912	61	......	
Pac. and N. W.	July 15	Apr. 24, 1850	293	1, 974	......	
....do	Sept. 5	May 8, 1851	......	2, 320	32, 900	
Atlantic	May 31	....	......	......	......	Bought from New York 1848; lost in Arctic 1851. Sent home 55 sperm.
Pacific Ocean ..	Oct. 5	Apr. 18, 1852	639	73	2, 100	
....do	June 1	Sept. 1, 1852	1, 350	70	.....	
....do	Aug. 17	Nov. 1, 1851	673	......	......	Fourth mate, William Henson, killed by a whale August 28, 1848.
Pac. and N. W.	June 26	Apr. 22, 1851	914	1, 562	18, 000	
Pacific Ocean ..	June 21	June 8, 1852	1, 687	310	......	Captain Gray left ship 1851, sick.
....do	May 27	Sept. 2, 1850	506	246	......	Sent home 70 sperm.
....do	Sept. 22	July 1, 1851	46	2, 579	......	Sent home 250 sperm, 33,000 pounds bone.
Atlantic	Sept. 11	Feb. 7, 1850	1, 315	12	......	Sent home 214 sperm.
N. W. Coast....	Aug. 10	Mar. 21, 1851	217	2, 903	29, 900	Sent home 20,880 pounds bone.
....do	Oct. 18	Mar. 31, 1851	184	2, 908	......	Sent home 275 whale, 22,736 pounds bone.
....do	Nov. 28	Mar. 22, 1851	96	4, 199	......	Sold 600 whale at Lahaina; sent home 22,590 bone.
Pacific Ocean ..	Nov. 11	July 22, 1852	367	3	400	Sold 140 sperm at Maui.
....do	June 16	....	......	......	......	Lost near Tombez 1849; saved 200 barrels of oil.
....do	June 8	Mar. 30, 1851	......	2, 571	31, 400	Sent home 59 sperm.
....do	July 16	....	......	......	......	Sold 180 sperm at Valparaiso. No report.
....do	July 21	Jan. 17, 1852	1, 077	860	......	Bought from Salem 1848.
Indian and Pac.	June 6	Mar. 15, 1850	69	1, 971	19, 000	
Pacific Ocean ..	Nov. 28	Mar. 17, 1853	1, 948	34	......	
Indian Ocean ..	Aug. 22	Jan. 17, 1851	105	1, 351	8, 100	
Pacific Ocean ..	June 27	June 10, 1852	1, 218	53	......	
....do	Nov. 26	Oct. 4, 1852	1, 461	23	......	
Indian & N. W.	June 17	Feb. 20, 1850	197	3, 570	31, 000	
Pacific Ocean ..	Aug. 31	....	......	......	......	Lost on St. Lawrence Island August 16, 1851. Had 1,300 whale; saved 250.
New Zealand ..	Nov. 16	July 16, 1853	2, 107	8	......	A. N. Briggs, first mate, died June, 1849.
Pacific Ocean ..	Aug. 19	June 10, 1852	991	8	......	
Indian Ocean ..	May 20	May 14, 1851	498	......	......	
South Seas.....	Jan. 4	May 19, 1851	1, 439	......	......	
Indian Ocean ..	Nov. 6	June 26, 1853	333	207	......	
Pacific Ocean ..	June 27	Apr. 2, 1852	1, 098	......	......	
....do	Dec. 16	Dec. 4, 1848	30	......	......	Returned in consequence of sickness of captain. Sold 1850.
P. O. & N. W...	Aug. 16	July 1, 1851	875	1, 190	18, 800	
Pacific Ocean ..	Nov. 27	Sept. 11, 1852	1, 347	......	......	
Indian Ocean ..	May 25	Sept. 8, 1851	1, 552	......	......	
Pacific Ocean ..	June 28	May 25, 1852	518	230	4, 300	Built 1848.
....do	July 25	July 31, 1852	1, 431	......	......	Captain Bonney came home sick 1850. Sent home 100 sperm.
P. O. & N. W...	Sept. 5	Jan. 28, 1851	300	2, 600	11, 000	
Pacific Ocean ..	Oct. 25	Apr. 5, 1851	......	2, 600	......	Mr. Slater, second mate, lost overboard August, 1849. Sent home 14,300 bone.
Indian and Pac.	Aug. 12	Apr. 28, 1853	669	604	7, 400	Captain Jones died 1850. Sent home 75 sperm.
Atlantic	May 8	Sept. 2, 1849	500	......	......	
....do	Oct. —	Jan. 27, 1850	550	......	......	
....do	May 13	Sept. 9, 1848	950	150	......	
Pac. and N. W.	Aug. 15	Mar. 21, 1851	250	2, 600	15, 000	
Atlantic	Oct. 9	July 2, 1850	700	50	......	The 50 barrels were humpback.

Table showing the returns of whaling-vessels

Name of vessel.	Class.	Tonnage.	Captain.	Managing owner or agent.
1848.				
Westport, Mass.				
Catherwood	Brig	199	—— Stanton	Thomas W. Mayhew
Janet	Bark	194	—— Hosmer	Henry Wilcox
Harbinger	Ship	262	—— Fisher	Alexander H. Corey
Mexico	Brig	130	—— Whites	Henry Willcox
Th. Winslow	do	126	—— Mayhew	Thomas W. Mayhew
Theo. Chase	Bark	168	—— Macomber	H. Willcox
Nantucket, Mass.				
Catawba	Ship	335	Obed Swain, 2d	C. G. & H. Coffin
Charles Carroll	do	376	Josiah C. Long	W. C. Swain
Christopher Mitchell	do	387	Thomas Sullivan	C. Mitchell & Co
Daniel Webster	do	336	Henry C. Bunker	Benjamin Coffin
Empire	do	403	William Upham	G. & M. Starbuck & Co.
Harvest	do	360	William H. Tice	Rand & Paddock
Henry	do	346	Benjamin A. Coleman	Perry & Gardner
Laura	Schooner		—— Pratt	
Lexington	Ship	399	David Bunker, 2d	Field & Sanford
Massachusetts	do	360	Seth Nickerson, jr	Zenas Adams
Nauticon	do	372	Charles A. Veeder	G. & M. Starbuck & Co.
Norman	do	338	John J. Gardner	do
Peruvian	do	334	George B. Folger	Frederick Arthur
Phœnix	do	323	Perry Winslow	Thomas Macy
Quito	Brig	140	John C. Brock	J. Cook, jr., & Co
Richard Mitchell	Ship	386	Robert McCleave	Field & Sanford
Sophia	Schooner	170	William Baldwin	J. Cook, jr., & Co
Zenas Coffin	Ship	338	Charles G. Arthur	C. G. & H. Coffin
Provincetown, Mass.				
Belle Isle	Schooner	104	—— Cook	Parker Cook
Cadmus	Brig	130	—— Soper	Samuel Soper
John Adams	Schooner	110	—— Freeman	R. L. Thatcher
Louisa	do	98	—— Young	Samuel Cook
Medford	do	105	—— Dyer	Parker Cook
Rienzi	do	115		A. Cook
Edgartown, Mass.				
Alfred Tyler	Bark	225	—— Luce	Alex. P. Weeks
Champion	Ship	399	—— Codd	Benjamin Worth
Mary	do	343	—— Crocker	Ab'm Osborne
Pavillion	Brig	120	—— Adams	Calvin C. Adams
Fall River, Mass.				
Sol Saltus	Ship	316	—— Stafford	Nathan Durfee
Chilmark, Mass.				
Rodman	Brig	83	—— Tilton	
Warren, R. I.				
Dromo	Bark	267	—— Daggett	Charles T. Child
Franklin	do	240	—— Barton	Samuel Barton
Hector	do	225	—— Cutler	R. B. Johnson
Lafayette	Ship	341	—— Barton	Coffin & Gardner
Luminary	do	432	—— Norton	Joseph Smith
Millinoket	Bark	186	—— Martin	R. B. Johnson
Niantic	Ship	452	—— Cleveland	Burr & Smith

sailing from American ports—Continued.

Whaling-ground.	Date— Of sailing.	Date— Of arrival.	Result of voyage. Sperm-oil.	Result of voyage. Whale-oil.	Result of voyage. Whalebone.	Remarks.
			Bbls.	*Bbls.*	*Lbs.*	
Indian Ocean	Apr. 3	Sept. 1, 1850	600			Sent home 394 sperm.
Pacific Ocean	Nov. 7	Dec. 31, 1851	475			Sold 150 sperm at Lahaina.
....do	May 15	July 25, 1851	1,000			Third mate, Peleg M. Brownell, drowned August, 1850.
Atlantic	Oct. 28	June 30, 1850	250			
....do	June 4	Apr. 1, 1849	170			Sold 150 whale at Bahia.
....do	Aug. 2	June 22, 1849	800			
Pacific Ocean	Apr. 24	June 16, 1852	1,415	29		
....do	Dec. 2	Dec. 29, 1852	1,050	93		Sold 35 sperm, 200 whale. Sold in California 1853.
....do	Dec. 11	—— —, 1852	2,023			Sold to New Bedford.
....do	May 19	May 17, 1852	230	660	2,500	Captain Bunker came home sick.
....do	Jan. 2	June 7, 1852	1,847			Sold to New Bedford.
....do	Oct. 27	Mar. 20, 1853	1,446	7		Sailed September 23; returned dismasted. Sold 150 sperm, 50 whale.
....do	July 15	Aug. 10, 1853	900			
Atlantic		Sept. 3, 1848	40			
Pacific Ocean	Nov. 10	Jan. 22, 1853	743	229		Sent home 3,400 pounds bone.
....do	Nov. 16	Apr. 22, 1851	97	2,412	38,000	
....do	Sept. 12	Mar. 27, 1853	1,100	145	1,400	Sold 200 barrels whale; sent home 3,200 pounds bone. Built 1848 at Mattapoisett; sold to New Bedford 1853.
... do	Aug. 8					Went to California—voyage broken up.
....do	July 16	Aug. 10, 1852	534	70		Sold 30 barrels sperm, 40 blackfish.
....do	Nov. 7	Feb. 3, 1853	1,158	10		
....do	May 10					Added 1848 from Sippican. Sent home some sperm-oil; went to California and was sold.
....do	Aug. 31	Aug. 31, 1852	1,745	53		Sold to New Bedford 1853.
....do	June 15					Sent home some oil, and was sold in California.
....do	Nov. 9	July 12, 1853	478	11		
North Atlantic	Mar. —	Aug. 27, 1848	380			
Atlantic	Feb. 17	Sept. 15, 1848	200			
....do	Apr. 10	Aug. 4, 1848	270	10		
....do	Mar. 7	Sept. 27, 1848	180			
....do	May 12	Oct. 19, 1848	280	10		
....do	Apr. 12	Sept. 29, 1848	280			
Pacific Ocean	Nov. 27	May 7, 1853	300	1,200	1,000	Sent home 67 sperm, 86 whale, 800 bone.
Pac. & N. W	Aug. 16	Apr. 25, 1851	100	2.600	25,000	Sent home 6,660 pounds bone.
....do	Aug. 3	Nov. 8, 1851	1,915			
Atlantic	May 23					Sent home 68 sperm; condemned at Bermudas 1853.
Indian Ocean	Sept. 9					Took 600 barrels sperm and whale; was condemned at Sydney August, 1850; afterward went whaling from there; finally lost on the Feejee Islands 1852.
Atlantic	May 4	Sept. 4, 1849	60	30		Withdrawn for California 1849.
Indian Ocean	Oct. 11	Aug. 29, 1853	615	120		
Pacific Ocean	Dec. 22	June 10, 1852	632			Sold to New Bedford 1852; sent home 300 sperm.
Indian Ocean	May 3	Apr. 22, 1850	1,000			Sent home 91 sperm.
Pacific Ocean	Dec. 9	May 3, 1852	947			Sold to New Bedford 1852; repaired and renamed Gazelle.
N. W. Coast	Sept. 30	May 17, 1852	93	2,254	5,600	Withdrawn for merchant service 1852; sold to Providence 1853.
Indian Ocean	Dec. 9	Jan. 27, 1852	862			Added 1848.
N. W. Coast	Sept. 16					Bought from Sag Harbor 1847; sold at San Francisco 1849.

Table showing returns of whaling-vessels

Name of vessel.	Class.	Tonnage.	Captain.	Managing owner or agent.
1848.				
Newport, R. I.				
Margaret	Ship	375	—— Fales	J. S. Munroe
Wm. Lee	do	311	—— Lee	do
Lynn, Mass.				
Com. Preble	Ship	323	—— Lamphier	Andrews Breed
Somerset, Mass.				
Pilgrim	Bark	137	—— Clark	George B. Hood
Mystic, Conn.				
Hellespont	Ship	346	—— Manwarring	I. & W. P. Randall
Hudson	do	36[illegible]	—— Clift	Geo. W. Ashley & Co
Meteor	do	325	—— Kenney	I. & W. P. Randall
Robin Hood	do	395	—— Baker	Charles Mallory
Romulus	do	365	C. Hull	do
Shepherdess	do	274	—— Benjamin	I. & W. P. Randall
Washington	Schooner	190	—— Oat	G. W. Ashley & Co.
Stonington, Conn.				
Cabinet	Ship	305	—— Hathaway	John F. Trumbull
Cavalier	Bark	295	—— Barber	Charles P. Williams
Mercury	Ship	305	—— Pendleton	F. Pendleton
Prudent	Bark	398	—— Nash	C. P. Williams
Tiger	Ship	311	—— Brewster	J. F. Trumbull
Cold Spring, Conn.				
N. P. Tallmadge	Ship	370	—— Mulford	John H. Jones
Splendid	do	473	—— Fordham	do
Tuscarora	do	379	—— Leek	do
Greenport, N. Y.				
Delta	Ship	314		Ireland, Wells & Carpenter.
Nile	do	403		do
Philip 1st	do	293	—— Woodruff	do
Washington	do	236		Wiggins & Parsons
New London, Conn.				
Benj. Morgan	Ship	407	—— Chappel	Perkins & Smith
Brooklyn	do	360	—— Jeff ey	do
Clematis	do	311	—— Bellows	Williams & Barnes
Columbus	Brig	159	—— Andrews	do
Catharine	do	384	—— Green	Thomas Fitch, 2d
Dover	do	430	—— Jeffrey	Benjamin F. Brown
Exile	Schooner	83	—— Butler	E. V. Stoddard
Gen. Williams	Ship	446	—— Forsyth	Williams & Barnes
Garland	Schooner			
Gen. Scott	Bark	360	—— Harris	Weaver, Rogers & Co.
Isaac Hicks	Ship	495	—— Rice	Miner, Lawrence & Co.
Montezuma	do	424	—— Benjamin	Williams & Barnes
New England	do	368	—— Wilcox	Miner, Lawrence & Co.
Peruvian	do	388	—— Brown	E. V. Stoddard
Superior	do	406	—— Sloan	B. F. Brown
Sag Harbor, N. Y.				
Columbia	Bark	285	—— Sweeney	John Rudd
Eliz. Frith	do	355	—— Winters	Post & Sherry
Henry	Ship	333	—— Lowen	Huntting Cooper
Nimrod	Bark	280	—— Huntting	Charles T. Dering

sailing from American ports—Continued.

Whaling-ground.	Date—Of sailing.	Date—Of arrival.	Result of voyage.—Sperm-oil.	Result of voyage.—Whale-oil.	Result of voyage.—Whalebone.	Remarks.
			Bbls.	*Bbls.*	*Lbs.*	
Indian & N. W	June 17	....	......	......	......	Added 1848 from New Bedford; lost on Society Islands February 27, 1850; had 2,400 whale; two of the crew lost; oil, about 1,800 barrels, sent home.
Pacific Ocean ..	Mar. 22	Nov. 10, 1851	1, 117	130	......	
Indian Ocean ..	Sept. 26	Apr. 26, 1851	120	2, 600	25, 000	
Indian Ocean ..	Aug. 7	May 3, 1849	140	......	......	Sold for California 1849.
Kamschatka ...	Sept. 6	Apr. 8, 1851	20	2. 760	15, 000	
Falkland Islds .	Nov. 3	Feb. 26, 1852	......	2, 382	18, 000	Bought from Sag Harbor 1848.
N. W. Coast....	Apr. 22	Apr. 28, 1851	......	2, 553	24, 700	
....do	Oct. 6	Mar. 10, 1849	800	......	......	The Robin Hood took her oil from the wreck of the freight-ship Carmelita, and was proceeding on her voyage, but sprung a leak and returned.
....do	Aug. 27	Jan. 19, 1851	10	3, 200	......	
....do	Aug. 1	Jan. 28, 1851	......	2, 300	12, 000	Sent home 17,500 pounds bone.
Falkland Islds .	Nov. 3	Feb. 26, 1852	......	10	......	Added 1848.
N. W. Coast....	Aug. 9	May 2, 1851	143	2, 444	21, 700	
....do	Oct. 7	Apr. 1, 1851	250	2, 400	15, 000	
....do	July 21	....	......	......	......	Burned at Honolulu, with about 1,200 barrels of oil, November, 1849.
Chili & N. W ..	June 6	June 3, 1850	40	2, 000	30, 000	
N. W. Coast....	June 29	May 7, 1851	41	2, 629	21, 000	Sent home 17,000 pounds bone.
N. W. Coast....	Sept. 26	Mar. 26, 1851	......	2, 700	......	Built 1836.
....do	Oct. 28	Mar. 15, 1851	......	3, 400	38, 000	
Indian & Pacific	Aug. 3	....	......	......	......	Condemned at Sydney March, 1851; had 2,000 whale; shipped it to London.
....	Oct. —	June 3, 1851	267	1, 334	5, 800	
N. W. Coast....	Sept. —	Mar. 22, 1851	......	3, 000	......	
....do	Sept. 1	Mar. 27, 1851	110	2, 200	22, 000	Sent home 22,656 pounds bone.
....	Sept. —	May 12, 1851	17	1, 636	22, 000	Sent home 3,000 pounds bone; sold to Sag Harbor 1851.
Chili & N. W ..	July 26	Apr. 8, 1851	28	3, 325	8, 300	Sent home 32 sperm.
....do	July 10	May 7, 1851	3	3, 440	......	Sent home 135 sperm.
N. W. Coast....	Oct. 5	Mar. 21, 1851	75	2, 400	17, 000	Sent home 13,600 pounds bone.
Atl. & Ind	July 6	....	......	350	......	Mate died 1850; condemned at Johanna September, 1850.
Ind. & N. W ...	Aug. 10	Mar. 28, 1850	250	2, 300	25, 000	
Chili & N. W ..	July 5	Mar. 23, 1851	50	3, 550	......	
Desolation Isld	Aug. 14	July 3, 1852	......	260	......	
N. W. Coast....	Aug. 1	May 17, 1851	283	3, 314	......	Sent home 335 sperm, 32,000 bone.
....	......	....	......	......	......	Garland lost on Desolation 1848.
Ind. & N. W ...	July 5	Mar. 22, 1851	......	2, 800	22, 000	
Chili & N. W ..	Aug. 1	May 8, 1851	35	3, 700	34, 000	
S. A. & N. W ..	Aug. 17	Feb. 17, 1850	400	3, 000	......	Added 1848; sent home 43 sperm.
Ind. & N. W ...	Aug. 16	Feb. 12, 1851	......	3, 150	20, 000	
Desolation Isld	Aug. 14	Aug. 8, 1850	......	2, 900	6, 000	1,300 barrels were elephant.
Ind. & N. W ...	May 21	Apr. 4, 1851	71	1, 787	29, 700	
N. W. Coast ...	Oct. 12	May 17, 1851	......	2, 237	14, 500	
....do	July 13	May 13, 1850	95	2, 700	35, 000	Sent home 160 sperm; withdrawn 1850.
....do	July 10	Sept. 13, 1850	190	210	3, 000	Sold for California 1850.
South Atlantic.	Sept. 5	Sept. 2, 1850	120	1, 050	3, 000	Sent home 100 sperm, 5,000 pounds bone.

Table showing returns of whaling-vessels

Name of vessel.	Class.	Tonnage.	Captain.	Managing owner or agent.
1848.				
Sag Harbor, N. Y.—Continued.				
Noble	Bark	273	—— Glover	Charles T. Dering
Ontario, 2d	Ship	489	—— Paine	Post & Sherry
Washington	...do	340	—— Drake	Huntting Cooper
Wm. Tell	...do	370	—— Taber	Thomas Brown
New Suffolk,				
Gentleman	Bark	227		Ira B. Tuthill
1849.				
New Bedford, Mass.				
Arabella	Ship	367	Wm. Maxfield	Chas. R. Tucker & Co
Balæna	...do	301	—— Dexter	J. & J. Howland
Benj. Tucker	...do	349	—— Wood	C. R. Tucker & Co
Brandt	...do	310	—— Honeywell	Alexander Gibbs
Callao	...do	324	—— Sisson	Henry Taber & Co
California	...do	398	—— Adams	I. Howland, jr., & Co
Caroline	...do	364	—— Plaskett	William Gifford
Charles Drew	...do	344	—— Carey	...do
Canton Packet	...do	274	—— Howland	I. H. Bartlett & Son
C. W. Morgan	...do	351	—— Sampson	Edward M. Robinson
Charles	...do	290	—— Manchester	Lemuel Kollock
Chase	Bark	153	—— Ricketson	Barton Ricketson
Cicero	Ship	252	—— Fox	Lemuel Kollock
Cortes	...do	382	—— Cromwell	George Howland
Cherokee	Bark	261	—— Cleveland	Hathaway & Luce
Congress	Ship	339	—— Mendall	Edward C. Jones
Desdemona	...do	295	John A. Beckerman	T. & A. R. Nye
Edward	Bark	274	—— Luce	Thomas Knowles & Co
Emma C. Jones	Ship	347	Charles Little	E. C. Jones
Emily Morgan	...do	368	—— Ewer	William J. Rotch
Enterprise	...do	291	—— Swift	Charles Hitch
Euphrates	...do	365	—— Crosby	E. W. Howland
Eagle	...do	336	—— Potter	J. Perry
Exchange	Bark	180	—— Hazard	Thos. Knowles & Co
Falcon	Ship	273	—— Smith	...do
Formosa	...do	450	—— Swift	O. N. Swift
Franklin	Bark	273	—— Lake	John P. West
Fabius	Ship	432	Peleg S. Wing	C. R. Tucker & Co
Garland	...do	243	John N. Smith	Rodney French
Herald	...do	274	—— Stevens	E. W. Howland
Hercules	...do	335	—— Fisher	J. Perry
Hecla	Bark	207	—— Besse	T. Knowles & Co
Hibernia	Ship	327	—— Baker	Robert Gibbs
Houqua	...do	339	—— Brown	Alex. Gibbs
J. E. Donnell	Bark	343	—— Bennett	Swift & Allen
Lewis	Ship	308	—— Clement	I. H. Bartlett & Son
Mary Frazier	...do	288	—— Hagerty	A. H. Howland
Maria	Bark	202	—— Movers	Sam'l W. Rodman
Milo	Ship	398	—— Sowle	E. C. Jones
Montezuma	Bark	195	—— Allen	James Slocum
Mount Vernon	Ship	352	—— Willis	D. R. Greene & Co

sailing from American ports—Continued.

Whaling-ground.	Date— Of sailing.	Of arrival.	Result of voyage. Sperm-oil.	Whale-oil.	Whalebone.	Remarks.
			Bbls.	*Bbls.*	*Lbs.*	
South Atlantic.	Sept. 12	May 13, 1850	40	1, 245	6, 000	Sent home 5,000 pounds bone.
N. W. Coast....	Aug. 7	Apr. 30, 1850	30	2, 700	30, 000	
Chili & N. W ..	June 3	May 3, 1850	60	2, 000	20, 000	
N. W. Coast....	Sept. 1	Mar. 30, 1851	80	2, 720	25, 000	
....	Aug. 8	Nov. 12, 1849	300	300	2, 500	
Japan Sea......	Dec. 30	....	......	......	......	Bought from Sag Harbor 1849; sailed October 17; returned December 6, leaking 2,000 strokes in 24 hours; lost in ice near East Cape 1851.
Pacific Ocean ..	Sept. 1	June 23, 1853	1, 509	6	......	
N. W. Coast....	July 18	June 1, 1851	170	2, 339	......	Sent home about 20,000 pounds bone.
Indian Ocean ..	Nov. 20	Sept. 12, 1852	1, 088	141	1, 200	
Pacific Ocean ..	Oct. 16	May 16, 1852	649	1, 577	......	Sent home 100 whale.
North Pacific ..	Aug. 15	Mar. 15, 1851	47	2, 995	44, 500	
Pacific Ocean ..	Aug. 1	Apr. 16, 1852	75	1, 800	16, 000	Sold 150 sperm, 300 whale; sent home 30,298 bone.
North Pacific ..	Nov. 17	....	......	......	......	Lost at Honolulu October 22, 1850; had 1,300 whale, 10,000 pounds bone; saved 600 barrels whale; sent home 11,600 bone.
New Zealand ..	Dec. 28	July 4, 1853	135	1, 584	21, 000	Sent home 134 sperm, 282 whale, 11,830 bone.
Pacific Ocean..	June 5	May 27, 1853	1, 121	......	......	
....do	July 25	May 8, 1853	840	716	14, 400	Sold 240 whale at Valparaiso.
Atlantic	Apr. 18	....	......	......	......	Lost 1851; sent home 160 sperm.
Indian Ocean ..	Sept. 13	Apr. 20, 1853	......	291	......	Captain Fox came home sick 1852; Captain Churchill died at Honolulu October 30, 1852; shipped 440 sperm, 80 whale, 1,000 bone to London from Hobart Town; sent home 198 whale, 4,898 bone.
Pacific Ocean..	July 29	Mar. 15, 1851	91	2, 737	44, 000	Sent home 8,800 bone.
South Seas.....	July 24	June 19, 1851	68	1, 908	200	Sent home 20,700 bone.
Indian Ocean ..	May 27	June 16, 1851	1, 002	1, 149	9, 000	Sent home 100 sperm.
Pacific Ocean..	Aug. 11	July 29, 1852	1, 766	......	......	Sent home 126 sperm.
....do	June 30	June 20, 1853	900	......	......	Sent home 60 sperm.
Indian Ocean ..	Oct. 30	June 22, 1852	608	1, 583	3, 400	Built at Fairhaven 1849; sent home 70 sperm, 9,000 pounds bone.
Pacific Ocean..	Oct. 23	Apr. 13, 1854	1, 892	......	......	
Japan Sea......	Oct. 4	Apr. 22, 1851	69	2, 107	13, 800	
Pacific Ocean..	July 25	Mar. 21, 1851	......	2, 757	40, 300	Sent home 26 sperm; 10,000 pounds bone.
....do	June 5	July 1, 1853	1, 700	......	......	
Atlantic	June 12	Apr. 29, 1850	......	......	......	Captain Hazard died at St. Thomas April, 1850. No oil.
Indian Ocean ..	Oct. 5	Apr. 30, 1852	44	2, 327	20[illegible]	Sent home 40 sperm, 200 whale, 40,000 bone.
Japan	Sept. 1	....	......	......	......	Lost near Woosung February 15, 1850.
Pacific Ocean..	Nov. 27	May 30, 1853	802	51	......	
Japan	June 16	Feb. 14, 1851	57	2, 613	38, 800	
Pacific Ocean..	June 19	Sept. 4, 1853	73	......	......	Voyage abandoned; went into California trade temporarily.
....do	May 15	July 31, 1852	1, 305	12	......	Sent home 169 sperm.
....do	Oct. 3	July 3, 1853	242	1, 747	28, 800	Sent home 194 sperm, 120 whale, 3,471 bone.
Atlantic & Pac	May 29	Dec. 6, 1852	1, 006	10	......	Added 1848; sent home 220 sperm.
Indian Ocean ..	Oct. 2	Apr. 5, 1853	329	1, 450	5, 400	Sent home 31,000 bone.
North Pacific..	Sept. 8	....	......	......	......	Lost in Arctic July, 1851, near Cape Oliver; had 2,700 barrels of oil; saved 1,100.
....do	June 19	May 28, 1851	193	2, 492	41, 200	
New Zealand ..	May 15	Jan. 7, 1853	1, 263	......	......	
Pacific Ocean..	Oct. 31	Apr. 29, 1853	177	2, 289	18, 500	
Indian Ocean ..	Nov. 5	Aug. 15, 1852	330	8	......	Seized by natives of Johanna Islands; Captain Movers imprisoned; afterward released.
....do	Aug. 16	July 20, 1851	331	2, 826	......	Sent home 32,400 bone.
....do	Dec. 28	Aug. 24, 1851	796	......	......	
Pacific Ocean..	Sept. 5	May 18, 1852	276	1, 756	4, 600	Bought from Nantucket 1848; sent home 999 whale, 36,533 bone; sold 50 whale at Maui.

Table showing returns of whaling-vessels

Name of vessel.	Class.	Tonnage.	Captain.	Managing owner or agent.
1849.				
New Bedford, Mass.—Continued.				
Mt. Wallaston	Bark	325	—— Barker	Abraham Barker
Newton	do	283	—— Watson	Jona. Bourne, jr
Ocean	Ship	349	—— Driggs	J. R. Thornton
Paulina	Bark	271	—— Tatch	Swift & Allen
Peri	do	191	—— Russell	R. French
Phocion	Ship	266	—— Nichols	J. R. Thornton
Pantheon	Bark	271	—— Worth	J. Bourne, jr
Persia	do	240	—— Hazell	L. Kollock
Rebecca Simms	Ship	400	—— Jernegan	W. R. Rodman
Roscoe	Bark	235	—— Gorham	J. Bourne, jr
Robert Edwards	Ship	356	—— Burgess	J. & J. Howland
Rousseau	do	306	—— Taber	Geo. Howland
Saratoga	do	542	—— Harding	Abraham Ashley
Swift	do	321	—— Vincent	Thos. S. Hathaway
Smyrna	Bark	219	—— Tobey	Richmond & Wood
St. Peter	Ship	267	—— Almy	J. B. Wood & Co
Susan	Bark	261	—— Howland	A. H. Howland
Superior	do	275	—— Luce	J. B. Wood & Co
Triton, 2d	Ship	315	—— Sands	C. R. Tucker & Co
Uncas	do	413	—— Edwards	A. H. Howland
Waverly	do	327	—— Neill	I. Howland, jr., & Co
Young Phenix	do	377	Isaac B. Thompkins	John A. Parker & Son
Fairhaven, Mass.				
Ansel Gibbs	Ship	319	—— Worth	Gibbs & Jenney
Arab	do	336	—— Braley	E. Sawin
Columbus	do	382	—— Crowell	Gibbs & Jenney
George	do	360	—— Marston	Reuben Fish
Java	do	294	—— Thompson	Atkins Adams
John A. Robb	do	273	—— Wimpenny	L. C. Tripp
Leonidas	do	243	—— Gifford	Jenney & Tripp
Oregon	do	339	—— Wimpenny	L. C. Tripp
Sam. Robertson	do	421	—— Washburn	I. F. Terry
Mattapoisett, Mass.				
Elizabeth	Bark	219	—— Flanders	R. L. Barstow
Willis	do	164	—— Taber	do
Westport, Mass.				
Barclay	Bark	167	—— King	Alexander H. Corey
Champion	do	209	—— Gardner	Andrew Hicks
Dr. Franklin	do	171	—— Gifford	Job Davis
Mattapoisett	do	150	—— Wing	Freeman Lawrence
President	do	180	—— Sowle	A. Hicks
Theo. Chase	do	168	Pardon Macomber	Henry Wilcox
U. States	do	217	—— Perkins	A. Hicks
Dartmouth, Mass.				
Gov. Hopkins	Ship	111	—— Baker	A. R. Tucker
Nantucket, Mass.				
Edward Carey	Ship	350	Roland Phinney	C. G. & H. Coffin
Ganges	do	315	Thomas Coffin, 2d	Barker Burnell
Mariner	do	349	Albert S. Ray	Matthew Crosby

sailing from American ports—Continued.

Whaling-ground.	Date— Of sailing.	Of arrival.	Result of voyage. Sperm-oil.	Whale-oil.	Whalebone.	Remarks.
			Bbls.	*Bbls.*	*Lbs.*	
Japan	Oct. 12	Apr. 16, 1853	19	1,484	10,500	Sent home 14,015 bone.
Pacific Ocean	July 16	June 22, 1851	87	2,019	30,400	
....do	July 7	Apr. 15, 1853	1,270	49		Fourth mate, Michael Taylor, died 1852.
Indian Ocean	Dec. 2	May 19, 1853	807	30		Bought from Boston 1849.
....do	May 7	Oct. 13, 1851	635			Sent home 49 sperm.
....do	Nov. 17	Sept. 1, 1852	1,390	248		Built at New York 1807; sold and broken up after this voyage; was of a "remarkably bad model."
Indian & Pac.	Oct. 31	July 16, 1853	1,092			
Pacific Ocean {	May 26	July 26, 1849	136			} Sailed May 26; returned July 26, captain sick; sailed again and was condemned in 1852 at Callao; sent home 91 sperm.
	Aug. 4					
....do	Oct. 16	June 20, 1853	1,817			
Indian Ocean	May 15	July 20, 1853	635			
Pacific Ocean	June 1	May 28, 1853	1,344	210		Sent home 63 sperm.
....do	May 9	June 2, 1853	886	185		Sent home 201 sperm.
North Pacific	Sept. 5	May 26, 1852	209	3,607	21,900	Sent home 364 whale, 58,500 bone; cargo sold for $124,000.
New Zealand	June 25	Nov. 26, 1852	1,991			Sent home 110 sperm.
Pacific Ocean	Dec. 27	Sept. 30, 1853	870			
Indian Ocean	Oct. 17	Oct. 10, 1852	1.042	97		
Pacific Ocean	July 24	July 26, 1853	1,131	22		
....do	Nov. 29	Feb. 8, 1853	1,118	31		Added 1849.
North Pacific	Nov. 23	June 25, 1851	205	1,824		
....do	July 20	Mar. 21, 1851	93	3,127	37,200	Sent home 8,800 bone.
Japan	July 9	Apr. 25, 1851	157	2,295	34,100	
Indian Ocean	May 8	Mar. 14, 1853	1,460			Sent home 54 sperm.
Indian Ocean	Nov. 28	Sept. 11, 1853	1,004			Sent home 300 sperm.
....do	Nov. 21	Sept. 15, 1853	1,058			Sent home 200 sperm, 700 whale.
North Pacific	Nov. 14	July 1, 1851	262	2,501	20,400	Sent home 13,750 pounds bone.
....do	June 27	May 16, 1851	41	2,264		
Pacific Ocean	Oct. 27	July 29, 1853	900	31		Charles Cushing, third mate, and one man drowned at Tombez 1852.
....do	Oct. 23	July 1, 1853	693	85		
Indian Ocean	Oct. 18					Condemned at Mauritius 1851; had 575 sperm, 75 hump; shipped it to London.
Pacific Ocean	July 5	July 6, 1853	465			Sent home 37 sperm.
North Pacific	Aug. 25	Apr. 22, 1852	95	2,600	13,000	Second mate died 1850; sent home 500 whale, 30,882 bone.
Atlantic	Apr. 27	Sept. 25, 1850	820			Sent home 240 sperm.
....do		June 3, 1850	660	40		40 barrels were humpback.
Atlantic	June 1	Sept. 1, 1850	600			
Atl. and Pacific	Apr. 13	Aug. 4, 1853	539			Sent home 218 sperm.
Atlantic	May 20	Jan. 18, 1851	400			
....do	June 7	Aug. 22, 1850	550			
....do	May 26	Aug. 22, 1850	500	45		Built 1849 at Mattapoisett; sent home 203 sperm.
....do	Aug. 23					Missing.
Indian Ocean	Dec. 21	Sept. 3, 1852	905			
Atlantic	May 17	Aug. 2, 1850	33	7		
Pacific Ocean	Oct. 8	Nov. 12, 1853	1,133	50		
....do	Sept. 12	July 20, 1853	1,813			
....do	May 20					Returned July 30, with Captain Ray sick and first mate hurt by falling from aloft; sailed again August 5 under Captain David U. Coffin; took 837 barrels sperm, and was condemned at Payta; refitted from Payta under name of "Sophia Somontes."

Table showing returns of whaling-vessels

Name of vessel.	Class.	Tonnage.	Captain.	Managing owner or agent.
1849.				
Nantucket, Mass.—Continued.				
Navigator	Ship	333	George Palmer	M. Crosby
Omega	do	363	Charles C. Russell	Joseph Starbuck
Potomac	do	356	Charles Grant	I. & P. Macy
Tyleston	Brig	111	Reuben F. Starbuck	
Fall River, Mass.				
Caravan	Ship	330	—— Dimon	J. W. Lindsey
Falmouth, Mass.				
Com. Morris	Ship	350	Lewis H. Lawrence	Oliver C. Swift
Provincetown, Mass.				
Allstrum	Schooner		—— Genn	
Belle Isle	do	104		
Council	do	100		
Cadmus	Brig	130	—— Nickerson	Samuel Soper
Chanticleer	Schooner			
E. R. Cook	do			
Fairy	Bark	186	—— Soper	Ebenezer Cook
Jane Howes	Brig		—— Nickerson	
John Adams	Schooner	110		R. L. Thatcher
Lewis Bruce	Brig		—— Young	
Louisa	Schooner	98	—— Cook	Samuel Cook
Medford	do	105	—— Ryer	Parker Cook
Parker Cook	Bark	135	—— Cook	do
Rienzi	Schooner	115	—— Snow	A. Cook
Robert Raikes	do	110	—— Swift	Ephraim Cook
Sam. Cook	Brig	140	—— Atson	
Shylock	do		—— Hersey	
Beverly, Mass.				
Gem	Brig	162	—— Small	F. W. Choate
Quincy, Mass.				
Curacoa	Brig		—— Prior	
Yarmouth, Mass.				
March	Brig	90	—— Weeks	Silas Baker
Warren, R. I.				
Benj. Rush	Ship	385	—— Swan	S. P. Child and Jas. Coffin
Bowditch	do	399	—— Waldron	S. P. Child
Covington	do	351	—— Devoll	do
Hoogley	do	292	—— Morse	John R. Wheaton
Mary Frances	do	311	—— Smith	S. P. Smith
Stonington, Conn.				
B. Williams	Ship	400	—— Hancox	C. P. Williams
Cincinnati	do	457	—— Williams	F. Pendleton & Co
George	Bark	251	—— Pendleton	C. P. Williams
Newark	Ship	323	—— Dickens	J. F. Trumbull
Philetus	Bark	278	—— Stevens	John F. Trumbull
Tybee	Ship	299	—— Barber	J. F. Trumbull
United States	do	244	—— Barnum	do
Lynn, Mass.				
William Badger	Ship	337	—— Perkins	Andrews Breed
Providence, R. I.				
Lion	Ship	298	—— Nichols	Lloyd Bowers
Mystic, Conn.				
Æronaut	Ship	265	—— Guyn	Charles Mallory
Coriolanus	do	268	—— Maginly	do
Robin Hood	do	395	—— Baker	do

sailing from American ports—Continued.

Whaling-ground.	Date—Of sailing.	Date—Of arrival.	Result of voyage.—Sperm-oil.	Result of voyage.—Whale-oil.	Result of voyage.—Whalebone.	Remarks.
			Bbls.	*Bbls.*	*Lbs.*	
Pacific Ocean ..	Aug. 27	June 19, 1854	837	......	......	
....do	June 5	Oct. 3, 1853	696	......	......	
....do	Aug. 7	May 10, 1853	1,976	25	......	Sold and sent home 60 barrels.
Atlantic	Apr. 7	July 27, 1850	30	80	......	
Pacific Ocean ..	Nov. 3	May 11, 1852	......	2,525	15,000	Sent home 400 whale, 30,569 pounds bone.
Pacific Ocean ..	Aug. 13	Aug. 19, 1853	1,860	......	......	
Atlantic	Mar. 6	Sept. 22, 1849	150	......	......	
....	....	Oct. 16, 1849	240	......	......	
....	....	Sept. —, 1849	......	160	......	
Atlantic	Mar. 20	Sept. 11, 1849	160	......	......	
....do	....	July —, 1849	210	......	......	
....do	....	Aug. —, 1849	......	50	......	
....do	Jan. 15	....	......	......	......	Withdrawn 1850.
South Atlantic.	Jan. 16	Sept. 13, 1849	210	......	......	
Atlantic	Apr. —	Sept. 13, 1849	60	20	......	
....do	Apr. 11	Sept. 28, 1849	200	......	......	
....do	Apr. 11	Oct. 30, 1849	160	......	......	
....do	Feb. 6	Sept. 30, 1849	100	......	......	
....do	Apr. 18	Nov. 9, 1849	285	......	......	
....do	Mar. 20	Sept. 6, 1849	100	......	......	
....do	May 23	Sept. 17, 1850	110	......	......	
....do	Feb. 9	Oct. 16, 1850	325	......	......	
....do	Apr. 12	Oct. 16, 1850	215	......	......	
Atlantic	Apr. 14	Oct. 21, 1850	60	......	......	Sent home 240 sperm.
Atlantic	May 14	Sept. 29, 1849	......	4	......	Withdrawn 1850.
Atlantic	Apr. 10	Aug. 4, 1850	70	30	......	The 30 barrels were blackfish; sold 1850.
Pacific Ocean ..	Sept. 5	June 10, 1852	520	1,244	......	Sent home 15 sperm, 22,370 pounds bone.
Japan..........	Sept. 18	Apr. 23, 1852	81	2,460	17,000	
N. W. Coast....	July 25	Mar. 7, 1852	108	1,728	7,800	Sent home 1,000 whale, 32,915 pounds bone.
Pacific Ocean ..	Aug. 16	July 18, 1853	113	1,012	8,900	
....do	Jan. 6	May 27, 1852	859	......	......	Added 1848.
Indian Ocean ..	June 20	Apr. 6, 1851	400	2,300	35,000	
N. W. Coast....	Aug. 22	Apr. 2, 1852	147	2,528	3,800	Sent home 18,500 pounds bone.
....do	Oct. 16	Aug. 7, 1851	221	1,631	......	Sent home 21,500 pounds bone.
....do	Aug. 1	Aug. 3, 1851	79	1,758	......	Sent home 21,669 pounds bone.
Indian Ocean ..	Jan. 1	....	......	......	......	Condemned at Mauritius October, 1850.
N. W. Coast....	Oct. 15	Apr. 26, 1851	124	1,869	31,000	
Crozette Island	June 18	May 24, 1851	......	845	......	
Indian Ocean ..	Sept. 15	May 11, 1853	1,484	......	......	Sold 1853.
Pacific Ocean ..	Dec. 2	Oct. 23, 1853	1,876	......	......	
Indian Ocean ..	June 23	May 31, 1852	59	1,971	......	Sent home 31,000 pounds bone.
....do	Oct. 12	May 3, 1851	152	1,632	25,000	
Ind. and N. P ..	July 11	Mar. 27, 1851	......	3,263	44,200	

Table showing returns of whaling-vessels

Name of vessel.	Class.	Tonnage.	Captain.	Managing owner or agent.
1849.				
New London, Conn.				
Armata	Ship	413	C. Strong Holt	Williams & Barnes
Atlas	Schooner	81	—— Lyon	Perkins & Smith
Black Warrior	Bark	231	—— Babcock	Williams & Haven
Candace	do	310	—— Walker	do
Clement	do	279	—— Lane	Miner, Lawrence & Co.
Corinthian	Ship	505	—— Slate	Perkins & Smith
Charles Carroll	do	412	—— Chapel	do
Dove	Bark	151	—— Forsyth	Williams & Haven
Franklin	Schooner	119	—— Noorie	Perkins & Smith
Hannibal	Ship	441	—— Gray	Benjamin Brown Sons
Jefferson	do	396	—— Skinner	Miner, Lawrence & Co.
Julius Cæsar	do	347	—— Morgan	E. V. Stoddard
McLellan	do	376	—— Chappell	Perkins & Smith
N. America	Bark	388	—— Pendleton	Williams & Haven
Venice	do	353	—— Harris	Weaver, Rogers & Co.
Vesper	Ship	321	—— Fournier	Williams & Barnes
Greenport, L. I.				
Bayard	Ship	339	—— Graham	Ireland, Wells & Carpenter.
Italy	do	299	—— Weld	David G. Floyd
Sag Harbor, L. I.				
Concordia	Bark	265	—— French	Thomas Brown
Timor	do	280	—— Baker	Huntting Cooper
Cold Spring, N. Y.				
Alice	Bark	281	—— Smith	John H. Jones
Huntsville	Ship	523	—— Smith	do
Sheffield	do	579	—— Roys	do
1850.				
New Bedford, Mass.				
Abraham Barker	Ship	400	—— Norton	Abraham Barker
Adeline	do	329	—— Carr	I. Howland, jr. & Co.
America, 2d	do	464	Charles P. Seabury	William O. Brownell
Amethyst	do	359	—— Howes	John A. Parker & Son
Ann Alexander	do	253	—— Deblois	George Howland
Andrews	Bark	303	James L. Nye	William P. Howland
Bevis	do	214	A. Snell	Benjamin B. Howard
Barclay	Ship	281	—— Taber	Henry Taber & Co.
Brighton	do	354	—— Weaver	James D. Thompson
Braganza	do	470	W. Devoll	William G. E. Pope
Canton	do	409	J. Allen	Perry & Tillinghast
Chas. Frederick	do	317	—— Haskins	J. A. Parker & Son
China	do	370	R. C. Reynard	William Philips
City	do	351	Henry Eldridge	Abm. H. Howland
Courier	do	381	C. Howland	O. & G. O. Crocker
Clarice	Bark	237	—— Gifford	Edward C. Jones
Condor	Ship	349	—— Kempton	C. W. Morgan
Cornelia	Bark	210	—— Devoll	Lemuel Kollock
Coral	Ship	370	E. P. Sherman	Gideon Allen
Columbus	Bark	313	—— Carr	William R. Rodman
Champion	Ship	336	Joseph Bailey	J. D. Thompson
Cossack	Bark	256	—— Slocum	Charles Hitch
Dunbarton	do	199	—— Davis	Isaac B. Richmond

sailing from American ports—Continued.

Whaling-ground.	Date—Of sailing.	Date—Of arrival.	Result of voyage. Sperm-oil.	Result of voyage. Whale-oil.	Result of voyage. Whalebone.	Remarks.
			Bbls.	*Bbls.*	*Lbs.*	
N. W. Coast....	Oct. 2	....	......	......	......	Lost on a reef near Cape North July 15, 1851; shipped home 200 sperm, 4,500 whale.
Desolation Isld.	Sept. 1	Apr. 22, 1851	......	220	......	
Ind. and N. P ..	Oct. 11	May 10, 1851	48	1,584	......	Sent home 28,131 pounds bone.
....do	July 17	Mar. 15, 1851	25	2,100	21,000	
N. W. Coast....	July 11	May 10, 1851	81	1,877	27,200	
Desolation Isld.	Sept. 7	Apr. 27, 1851	18	2,871	11,000	
North Pacific ..	....	Mar. 23, 1854	......	784	12,800	Sent home 3,315 whale, 37,049 bone.
Indian Ocean ..	Aug. 15	Nov. 6, 1851	797	5	......	
Desolation Isld.	Sept. 7	May 10, 1851	17	183	......	
Ind. and N. P ..	Sept. 6	Mar. 21, 1851	100	3,400	45,000	
N. W. Coast....	Aug. 22	Mar. 23, 1851	170	2,630	......	Sent home 27,000 pounds bone.
Desolation, &c.	Sept. 7	May 10, 1851	......	2,470	14,200	
Davis Straits ..	Mar. 3	Oct. 16, 1849	......	600	12,000	
Ind. and N. P ..	June 20	Mar. 26, 1851	......	2,700	28,000	
....do	Aug. 7	Mar. 26, 1851	......	2,900	40,000	
N. W. Coast....	Aug. 28	Mar. 23, 1851	330	2,670	......	
Pacific Ocean ..	Aug. 21	Apr. 20, 1853	......	1,604	20,800	Sent home 450 whale, 20,719 bone.
N. W. Coast....	Aug. —	May 14, 1851	......	2,577	38,100	Added 1848.
South Atlantic.	Oct. 12	June 4, 1854	......	691	......	Sent home 50 sperm, 577 whale, 5,350 bone.
North Pacific ..	Oct. 12	Oct. 11, 1852	125	1,475	15,000	Sent home 90 sperm, 11,994 pounds bone.
Arctic	Sept. —	Mar. 23, 1851	......	2,800	25,000	Sent home 21,214 bone.
Behring Straits	Oct. 26	Mar. 21, 1851	......	3,350	45,000	
Whaling & Cal.	Aug. 17	Jan. 24, 1854	......	2,532	36,900	Shipped 1,600 whale, 22,000 pounds bone, to London from Sydney.
North Pacific ..	Sept. 10	Mar. 14, 1853	56	2,306	22,000	Sold 80 barrels whale; sent home 62 barrels sperm, 417 whale.
....do	Sept. 21	June 13, 1853	......	894	15,500	Sent home about 10,000 pounds bone.
....do	Sept. 10	....	......	......	......	Added 1850; formerly in California trade; crushed by the ice in Anadir Sea 1851.
Pacific Ocean ..	Sept. 28	June 18, 1854	2,308	......	......	
....do	June 1	....	......	......	......	Lost 1851; sunk by a whale; sent home 115 sperm.
....do	June 3	May 3, 1853	908	......	......	Built 1850; Captain Nye and two men killed by a whale December 29, 1852; sold 80 sperm at Callao.
Indian Ocean ..	June 4	May 25, 1853	931	......	......	Bought from Boston 1850.
Atl. and Ind ...	May 11	Apr. 22, 1852	544	......	......	Sent home 450 sperm.
North Pacific ..	Oct. 9	June 1, 1854	......	791	4,000	Sold to Dartmouth 1855; sent home 158 sperm, 947 whale, 17,996 pounds bone.
....do	Sept. 10	Apr. 22, 1854	40	1,714	5,000	Sent home 158 sperm, 947 whale, 4,351 pounds bone.
....do	Oct. 1	Apr. 1, 1852	149	2,946	600	
Pacific Ocean ..	Aug. 22	....	......	......	......	Lost 1854.
North Pacific ..	Sept. 24	Mar. 3, 1852	342	2,222	26,700	
....do	Oct. 1	Mar. 13, 1853	78	1,800	10,000	Built 1850; sent home 18,329 bone.
Pacific Ocean ..	Oct. 7	July 16, 1856	615	26	......	Sent home 621 sperm.
Indian Ocean ..	Jan. 2	Apr. 28, 1853	665	......	......	
North Pacific ..	Sept. 21	May 22, 1853	254	1,563	11,100	Sent home 74 sperm, 173 whale, 17,600 bone.
Indian Ocean ..	Nov. 20	Aug. 26, 1853	547	270	2,200	
North Pacific ..	Sept. 10	Apr. 6, 1854	12	2,627	23,300	Sent home 5,893 pounds bone.
Pacific Ocean..	Dec. 4	Sept. 27, 1854	340	......	......	Sent home 600 barrels sperm.
North Pacific ..	June 18	Mar. 24, 1853	34	1,001	16,000	Captain Bailey died at Hong-Kong February 27, 1852; sent home 175 whale, 3,500 pounds bone.
....do	Oct. 8	May 10, 1853	56	1,153	12,900	Bought from Sippican 1850; sent home 5,800 pounds bone.
Pacific Ocean ..	July 25	Oct. 24, 1852	152	5	......	Sent home 360 sperm.

Table showing returns of whaling-vessels

Name of vessel.	Class.	Tonnage.	Captain.	Managing owner or agent.
1850.				
New Bedford, Mass.—Continued.				
Exchange	Bark	180	George W. Stewart	Thomas Knowles & Co.
Fortune	do	291	—— Hathaway	Gilbert Hatheway
Frances	Ship	348	W. Swain, jr	Henry Taber & Co
Franklin	do	333	—— Lamb	William P. Howland
Gen. Pike	do	313	N. P. Baker	William Gifford
Geo. Howland	do	374	—— Cromwell	George Howland
Gideon Howland	do	379	—— Jernegan	I. Howland, jr., & Co
Gladiator	do	650	James K. Turner	do
Globe	do	479	Asa Taber	George Hussey
Globe	Bark	215	—— Handy	Ingalls & Lucas
Gov. Troup	Ship	430	F. Coggeshall	Edw. C. Jones
Harrison	do	371	—— Hathaway	Gilbert Hathaway
Harvest	Bark	263	—— Almy	Swift & Allen
Hope	do	186	C. H. Robbins	William Watkins
Huntress	Ship	391	George Gibbs	Robert Gibbs
Illinois	do	413	A. Covell	Wood & Nye
Iris	do	311	—— Sherman	E. C. Jones
Junius	Bark	198	—— Kendrick	do
Jasper	do	223	—— Rotch	Alex. Gibbs
Jeannette	Ship	340	—— West	Isaac B. Richmond
John Wells	do	366	—— Cross	T. Knowles & Co
Joseph Meigs	do	356	George Allen	George Hussey
Junior	do	378	S. Tinkham	D. R. Greene & Co
Lagoda	do	341	—— Tobey	Jona. Bourne, jr.
Leonidas	do	231	B. S. Clark	Russell Maxfield
Levi Starbuck	do	376	W. M. Ellison	Edw. W. Howland
Liverpool	do	306	Henry P. Barker	Abm. Barker
Louisiana	do	300	Walter Taber	T. & A. R. Nye
Louisa	Bark	316	R. T. Wyatt	Swift & Allen
Morea	Ship	330	—— Kelley	B. B. Howard
March	Brig	90	—— Reynolds	William P. Howland
Mary	Ship	287	—— Henry	I. Howland, jr., & Co
Mercator	Bark	246	—— Macomber	John A. Parker
Metacom	Ship	360	—— Bonney	J. B. Wood & Co
Marcella	Bark	210	Pardon C. Winslow	C. R. Tucker & Co
Midas	Ship	326	E. Woodbridge	J. B. Wood & Co
Minerva	do	408	G. Hazard	William Gifford
Montpelier	do	320	M. G. Tucker	John R. Thornton
Montreal	do	547	Frederick Fish	C. R. Tucker & Co
Monongahela	do	497	Jason Seabury	O. & E. W. Seabury
Marcia	do	315	I. Wing	Edw. W. Howland

sailing from American ports—Continued.

Whaling-ground.	Date— Of sailing.	Date— Of arrival.	Result of voyage. Sperm-oil.	Result of voyage. Whale-oil.	Result of voyage. Whalebone.	Remarks.
			Bbls.	*Bbls.*	*Lbs.*	
Atlantic	May 18	....	......	......	......	A missing vessel; her fate was never known.
North Pacific	Oct. 19	May 18, 1854	102	2,125	24,000	Captain Hathaway died at Petro Paulovski June, 1852; sold 100 sperm, 400 whale, at Valparaiso; sent home 8,308 pounds bone.
....do	Sept. 4	....	......	......	......	Sent home 133 sperm, 844 whale, 18,878 bone; lost on Mangea Island 1853.
....do	July 15	July 16, 1853	124	2,049	......	Sent home 366 whale, 25,992 bone.
....do	June 13	July 18, 1853	84	2,425	25,400	Sent home 82 sperm, 6,993 bone.
Pacific Ocean	Aug. 20	Oct. 29, 1852	218	70	......	Seized by convicts at Gallipagos Islands; recaptured by a Swedish frigate; sent home 25 sperm.
North Pacific	Sept. 4	Mar. 10, 1853	8	3,133	32,000	
....do	Aug. 15	Apr. 7, 1854	......	3,200	39,700	Bought from New York 1850; formerly New York and London packet; took in all 6,200 whale, 95,000 bone; withdrawn 1854.
....do	Nov. 16	....	......	......	......	Lost on East Cape (Behring Straits) August, 1851.
Pacific Ocean	Sept. 9	Jan. 2, 1855	250	650	.....	Bought from New York 1850.
North Pacific	Aug. 15	May 7, 1853	797	2,058	24,800	Sent home 16 sperm.
....do	Dec. 12	Apr. 20, 1854	177	2,543	......	Sent home 11,300 bone.
....do	Oct. 1	May 1, 1854	......	697	11,000	Sent home 315 whale, 18,360 bone.
Indian Ocean	Aug. 17	May 7, 1853	996	......	......	Sent home 200 sperm.
North Pacific	Aug. 10	....	......	......	......	Lost on Kaiaghiusky Island (Kamschatka) April 25, 1852; the crew suffered severely from cold; sent home 63 sperm, 585 whale, 10,800 bone.
....do	Aug. 15	May 20, 1853	31	2,657	32,900	Bought from Sag Harbor 1850; sent home 8,352 bone.
Indian Ocean	May 8	Mar. 16, 1853	1,291	373	3,400	
....do	Aug. 5	....	......	......	......	Lost in Mozambique Channel October 21, 1851; sent home 108 sperm.
Pacific Ocean	Feb. 26	....	......	......	......	Condemned at New Zealand September, 1853; oil (850 sperm) shipped to London.
North Pacific	Nov. 21	Apr. 20, 1854	......	902	11,700	Sent home 20 sperm, 506 whale, 49,300 bone.
....do	June 18	Apr. 25, 1854	317	1,639	25,000	Bought from Sag Harbor 1849; sent home 175 sperm, 34,874 bone.
Pacific Ocean	Oct. 22	Aug. 2, 1854	1,258	16	......	Formerly in merchant-service; added 1850; sent home 225 sperm.
North Pacific	July 1	July 10, 1853	64	959	16,600	Captain Tinkham died at sea November 27, 1850; sent home 251 whale, 2,000 bone.
....do	July 1	Apr. 21, 1853	38	2,413	34,500	Sent home 309 sperm, 400 whale, 5,670 bone.
Pacific Ocean	Oct. 1	June 9, 1854	850	37	......	
North Pacific	Oct. 21	July 10, 1853	175	1,508	21,000	Bought from Nantucket 1850; sent home 35 sperm, 6,408 bone.
....do	Oct. 5	May 27, 1853	19	1,909	22,200	Sent home 243 sperm, 717 whale, 6,117 bone.
Pacific Ocean	Aug. 15	May 18, 1853	1,158	29	......	Bought from New York 1850.
North Pacific	Nov. 20	May 12, 1853	221	1,157	16,300	Bought from Baltimore 1850.
....do	Oct. 2	June 7, 1853	69	1,128	20,100	Second mate killed by a whale 1852; sent home 60 sperm, 973 whale.
Atlantic	Sept. 25	Sept. 20, 1851	65	8	......	Sailed September 16; returned September 20; captain sick; sailed again September 25; added 1850; sold to Mattapoisett 1852.
Indian Ocean	June 20	Apr. 2, 1852	39	1,932	40,800	First mate, William B. Eaton, died April 26, 1853.
Atl. and Ind	July 6	Sept. 9, 1852	416	7	.....	Sent home 450 sperm, 588 bone.
North Pacific	July 1	May 9, 1853	185	1,148	12,400	Mate and boat's crew lost; fast to a whale.
Indian Ocean	June 12	Dec. 6, 1852	416	50	500	Captain Winslow died at Johanna July 11, 1852.
North Pacific	Oct. 3	Mar. 30, 1853	......	2,060	21.500	Sent home 4,647 bone.
....do	Aug. 20	Mar. 19, 1853	60	2,224	32,000	Sent home 270 sperm, 250 whale, 8,300 bone.
....do	Aug. 3	May 22, 1853	75	2,250	23,700	Sent home 55 sperm, 538 whale, 13,680 bone.
....do	July 15	Mar. 30, 1853	195	3,823	31,700	Bought from Boston 1850; sent home 209 sperm, 1,026 whale, 45,959 bone; total value of cargo, $136,023.19.
....do	Oct. 1	....	......	......	......	Bought from Philadelphia 1850; supposed to have been lost in the Arctic with all on board 1853; sent home 83 sperm, 36,200 bone.
....do	Aug. 20	June 21, 1853	428	1,282	12,100	Shipped 3,834 pounds bone to London.

Table showing returns of whaling-vessels

Name of vessel.	Class.	Tonnage.	Captain.	Managing owner or agent.
1850.				
New Bedford, Mass.—Continued.				
Martha	Bark	271	—— Chase	Swift & Allen
Nassau	Ship	408	J. W. White	Jireh Perry
New Bedford	do	351	—— Gray	I. Howland, jr., & Co.
Ohio	Bark	237	—— Sawtelle	Cook & Snow
Oliver Crocker	Ship	350	William B. Cash	James B. Wood & Co.
Ontario	do	368	Frederick Slocum	David B. Kempton
Osceola	Brig	158	—— Maxam	William C. N. Swift
Roman, 2d	Ship	350	—— Tripp	Abm. Barker
Roscius	do	300	J. Winslow	William P. Howland
Sally Anne	do	312	S. H. Andrews	D. R. Greene & Co
St. George	do	408	W. Hawes	A. Barker
Seine	do	281	—— Landra	Rodney French
Stephania	do	315	—— Terry	Jona. Bourne
Tamerlane	do	357	—— Shockley	T. Knowles & Co
Trident	do	449	—— Taber	J. A. Parker & Son
Triton	do	300	—— Fish	I. Howland, jr., & Co
Wm. Hamilton	do	463	H. Shockley	do
Wm. Thompson	do	495	—— Jernegan	J. Perry
Washington	do	344	Martin Palmer	J. Bourne, jr
Fairhaven, Mass.				
Arab	Bark	276	—— Snell	I. F. Terry
Arctic	Ship	431	C. W. Gellett	Edmund Allen
Atkins Adams	do	330	—— Fish	William G. Blackler
Erie	do	451	—— Blackmer	Nathan Church
Favorite	Bark	293	E. Pierce	F. R. Whitwell
Harvest	do	314	—— Spooner	Jabez Delano, jr
Lagrange	do	280	—— Hammond	William G. Blackler
Marcus	Ship	286	—— Sherman	Lemuel Tripp
Mary Ann	do	335	—— Dallman	L. C. Tripp
Omega	do	305	—— Fisher	N. Church
Pacific	do	314	—— Alden	Reuben Fish
Sylph	do	336	F. M. Gardner	E. Allen
William Wirt	do	387	—— Fisher	Warren Delano
Mattapoisett, Mass.				
America	Brig	148	—— West	R. L. Barstow
Annawan	do	159	—— Phinney	Seth Freeman
Elizabeth	Bark	219	—— Dexter	R. L. Barstow
Lagrange	do	170	—— Flanders	do
Sarah	do	171	—— Mayhew	Wilson Barstow
Samuel and Thomas	do	191	—— Lambert	R. L. Barstow
Willis	do	164	—— Briggs	do
Westport, Mass.				
Barclay	Bark	167	—— Tripp	Alexander H. Corey
Gov. Carver	do	185	—— Hosmer	Henry Wilcox
Leonidas	Brig	128	—— Cornell	John L. Anthony
Mexico	do	130	—— Whitues	H. Wilcox
Platina	Bark	266	—— Lee	Andrew Hicks
President	do	180	—— Sowle	do
Solon	Brig	129	—— Smith	Henry Smith
Th. Winslow	Bark	136	—— Chase	Thomas W. Mayhew

sailing from American ports—Continued.

Whaling-ground.	Date— Of sailing.	Date— Of arrival.	Result of voyage. Sperm-oil.	Result of voyage. Whale-oil.	Result of voyage. Whalebone.	Remarks.
			Bbls.	*Bbls.*	*Lbs.*	
New Zealand ..	May 18	Nov. 20, 1853	1, 616	......	......	Bought from Newport 1849; second mate killed by a whale July, 1853; shipped 75 whale, 700 pounds bone to London from Hobart Town; sent home 83 whale, 108 sperm.
North Pacific ..	Aug. 5	May 22, 1853	148	2, 612	35, 800	Sent home 22 sperm.
Pacific Ocean ..	Oct. 10	....	......	......	......	Lost on Fox Islands June, 1851; four of her crew lost.
....do	Oct. 1	July 10, 1854	1, 405	38	......	Bought from Philadelphia 1850.
....do	Aug. 12	July 6, 1854	979	......	......	Built 1850 at Mattapoisett.
North Pacific ..	Sept. 4	Apr. 21, 1854	......	573	11, 000	Bought from Sag Harbor 1850; sent home 275 sperm, 588 whale, 35,000 bone.
Atlantic	Sept. 5	Oct. 1, 1853	187	17	......	Bought from Boston 1850; sent home 30 sperm.
North Pacific ..	Aug. 1	May 11, 1854	336	1, 501	7, 400	
Pacific Ocean ..	June 3	Jan. 2, 1854	928	925	16, 000	Sent home 325 sperm on the voyage.
North Pacific ..	Nov. 20	May 8, 1853	218	1, 446	18, 600	Sent home 4,096 bone.
....do	Sept. 4	May 18, 1853	360	1, 812	18, 900	Sent home 137 sperm, 84 whale.
....do	Aug. 10	May 21, 1853	......	1, 429	18, 000	Sent home 662 whale, 14,400 bone.
....do	Nov. 27	Apr. 4, 1854	69	594	8, 300	Sent home 993 whale, 13,549 bone.
....do	Oct. 28	Apr. 24, 1854	......	1, 517	32, 000	Owned in Savannah, Georgia; sent home 368 sperm, 1,177 whale, 13,150 bone.
....do	Oct. 21	Apr. 24, 1854	65	3, 292	......	Sent home 22,369 bone.
....do	Aug. 22	June 30, 1853	1, 600	50	......	Sent home 650 whale, 9,918 bone.
....do	June 20	May 1, 1854	......	339	3, 900	Captain Shockley came home sick 1851; sent home 80 sperm, 1,440 whale, 38,212 bone.
....do	July 30	Mar. 3, 1853	88	2, 557	35, 800	Sent home 54 sperm, 317 whale.
....do	Oct. 15	Mar. 17, 1853	195	2, 524	......	Sent home 25,329 bone.
Indian Ocean ..	Aug. 7	Apr. 7, 1853	......	1, 735	29, 000	Sent home 32 sperm, 900 whale, 12,000 bone.
North Pacific ..	Dec. 10	Apr. 8, 1854	80	970	16, 800	Built at Mattapoisett 1850; sent home 1,624 whale, 28,093 bone.
Pacific Ocean..	Sept. 30	Aug. 21, 1854	1, 367	......	......	
North Pacific ..	Oct. 1	July 16, 1853	80	2, 920	40, 000	
....do	June 15	June 19, 1853	84	2, 211	31, 900	Sent home 300 sperm, 4,484 whale, 41,000 bone.
....do	Dec. 10	July 17, 1853	69	1, 905	......	
Pacific Ocean..	Dec. 10	Nov. 16, 1853	556	......	......	
North Pacific ..	Nov. 9	....	......	......	......	Lost in the ice near East Cape September, 1853; saved 900 barrels oil; sent home 12,000 bone.
....do	Oct. 29	May 14, 1854	98	1, 057	3, 500	Sent home 85 sperm, 382 whale, 21,992 bone.
....do	Oct. 12	May 22, 1854	159	1, 192	7, 000	Sent home 121 sperm, 970 whale, 5,936 bone.
....do	June 14	Jan. 21, 1851	115	......	......	Returned in consequence of illness of Captain Alden.
Pacific Ocean..	Sept. 12	....	......	......	......	Sent home 536 sperm, 150 whale; lost on Isle of Sol January 9, 1854.
....do	Oct. 15	May 21, 1853	243	2, 326	19, 800	Sold to New Bedford, 1853; sent home 79 sperm.
Atlantic	Apr. 10	Sept. 19, 1851	305	2	......	
....do	May —	Oct. 7, 1851	360	6	......	
....do	Dec. 22	Dec. 7, 1852	140	64	......	
....do	Apr. 16	Aug. 25, 1851	510	18	......	
....do	Aug. 20	Aug. 9, 1852	422	150	1, 500	
....do	July 18	June 11, 1852	449	22	......	Added 1850, from Provincetown.
....do	Aug. 7	Oct. 1, 1851	321	7	......	
Atlantic	Dec. 4	May 26, 1852	330	8	......	
....do	June 12	Aug. 24, 1851	602	......	......	Added, 1850, from Fairhaven.
Indian Ocean ..	July 2	Sept. 20, 1851	400	30	......	The 30 barrels were blackfish.
Atlantic	Oct. 7	Oct. 4, 1852	244	20	......	Sent home 100 barrels oil.
Pacific Ocean..	July 15	July 10, 1853	1, 011	......	......	
Atlantic	Oct. 30	Sept. 19, 1851	405	12	......	
....do	May 2	Sept. 2, 1851	141	25	......	Bought from Mattapoisett 1849.
....do	July 2	Apr. 28, 1852	31	3	......	Sent home 225 sperm.

Table showing returns of whaling-vessels

Name of vessel.	Class.	Tonnage.	Captain.	Managing owner or agent.
1850.				
Edgartown, Mass.				
Vineyard	Ship	381	Edwin Coffin	Benjamin Worth
Nantucket, Mass.				
Alpha	Ship	345	Joseph Congdon	Hadwen & Barney
American	...do	329	Frederick W. Luce	R. F. Gardner
Apphia Maria	...do	260	Hiram Folger	John H. Shaw
Atlantic	...do	321	Zenas M. Coleman	R. F. Gardner
Columbia	...do	329	William Cash	C. G. & H. Coffin
Enterprise	...do	413	Charles B. Swain, 2d	E. W. Gardner
Maria	...do	365	David Baker	J. W. Barrett & Sons
Mohawk	...do	350	Oliver C. Swain	I. & P. Macy
Monticello	...do	365	John M. Folger	J. H. Shaw
Nantucket	...do	350	Richard C. Gibbs	H. G. O. Dunham
Ontario	...do	354	Obed Cathcart	J. W. Barrett & Sons
Paragon	Bark	309	Thomas Nelson	H. G. O. Dunham
Tyleston	Brig	111	Shadrach Gifford	Zenas Adams
Young Hero	Ship	304	Samuel C. Wyer	G. & M. Starbuck
Dartmouth, Mass.				
Gov. Hopkins	Ship	111	——— Briggs	A. R. Tucker
Provincetown, Mass.				
A. Nickerson	Schooner	108	——— Sparks	J. H. Hilliard
Belle Isle	...do	104	——— Turner	Ebenezer Cook
C. Allstrum	...do	106	——— Snow	John Adams
Cadmus	...do	115	——— Soper	Samuel Soper
Chanticleer	...do	87	——— Cook	Samuel Cook
Council	...do	100	——— Higgins	H. P. Higgins
E. Nickerson	Brig	131	——— Nickerson	Enoch Nickerson
Franklin	...do	172	——— Soper	Samuel Soper
Harriet Neal	Schooner	123	——— Bush	R. L. Thatcher
H. N. Williams	...do	108	——— Young	Philip Cook
Jane Howes	Brig	109	——— Young	J. E. Bowley
John Adams	Schooner	104	——— Freeman	John Adams
Lewis Bruce	Brig	113	——— Young	B. Allstrum
Louisa	Schooner	109	——— Young	S. Cook
Medford	Brig	107	——— Dyer	Ephraim Cook
Parker Cook	Bark	135	——— Cook	...do
R. E. Cook	Schooner	80	——— Cook	John Dunlap
Rienzi	...do	109	——— Iverson	J. E. Bowley
Sam'l Cook	Brig	120	——— Handy	S. Cook
Shylock	Schooner	115	——— Hersey	Nathaniel Holmes
Spartan	Bark	190	——— Cook	Stephen Nickerson
Union	Schooner	90	——— Smith	Jonathan Nickerson
Vesta	...do	98	——— Rich	Philip S. Rich
Virginia	...do	115	——— Morton	Winsor Snow
Walter Ervin	...do	130	——— Nickerson	Atkins Nickerson
Walter K	...do	114	——— Tillson	Henry Cook
Willis Putnam	...do	100	——— Foster	E. L. Smith
Holmes' Hole, Mass.				
Malta	Bark	150	——— Daggett	Thomas Barrows
Ocmulgee	Ship	458	——— Cottle	Thomas Bradley
Pocahontas	...do	341	——— Dias	...do

sailing from American ports—Continued.

Whaling-ground.	Date— Of sailing.	Date— Of arrival.	Result of voyage. Sperm-oil.	Result of voyage. Whale-oil.	Result of voyage. Whalebone.	Remarks.
			Bbls.	*Bbls.*	*Lbs.*	
North Pacific ..	Nov. 29	Mar. 14, 1853	650	2, 150	......	Sent home 112 sperm, 11,173 pounds bone.
Pacific Ocean ..	Aug. 17	July 25, 1854	1, 627	......	......	
....do	Aug. 17	July 16, 1853	306	22	......	Sold to Edgartown.
....do	July 25	Aug. 24, 1854	340	282	......	Bought from Portsmouth, N. H.; built 1846.
....do	July 7	Nov. 10, 1853	1, 330	......	......	Sent home 90 barrels sperm.
....do	Oct. 13	May 28, 1854	......	1, 634	19, 400	The bone with the oil sent home on the voyage brought $22,000.
North Pacific ..	July 10	May 28, 1854	674	1, 194	10, 000	Captain Swain left the ship at Talcahuano. Sent home 15,630 bone.
Pacific Ocean ..	Sept. 15	....	1, 326	30	......	Captain Baker came home sick. Condemned at Rio Janeiro September 1854.
North Pacific ..	May 29	Apr. 20, 1854	1, 890	70	......	Built 1850 at Medford.
Pacific Ocean ..	Sept. 10	Sept. 6, 1853	604	1, 004	......	Sold 80 barrels whale.
....do	June 8	Aug. 31, 1854	1, 022	63	......	Sent home 769 sperm, 100 whale.
....do	Sept. 12	....	700	......	......	Condemned at Tahiti; oil shipped to England.
....do	Nov. 22	....	......		......	Built 1850 at Medford; sent home and sold 210 sperm; lost March 20, 1853, on Strong's Island.
Atlantic	Sept. 2	May 4, 1851	22	......	......	Edward Narbeth, first mate, died.
Pacific Ocean .	Nov. 4	June 27, 1855	1, 275	......	......	
Atlantic	Aug. 15	May 28, 1851	48	14	......	The 14 barrels were blackfish.
Atlantic	Apr. 9	Oct. 17, 1850	41	......	......	Added 1850.
....do	Apr. 10	Oct. 19, 1850	145	......	......	
....do	Apr. 30	July 20, 1851	30	20	......	Added 1850; withdrawn 1852.
Sts. of Belleisle	June 4	Sept. 9, 1851	70	......	......	Withdrawn 1852.
Atlantic	May 15	Sept. 1, 1850	145	35	......	Added 1850.
Sts. of Belleisle	May 23	Sept. 18, 1850	......	50	......	Blackfish.
Atlantic	Apr. 23	Oct. 27, 1850	225	......	......	Added 1850; sailed again December 27, 1850; returned August 17, 1851, with 360 barrels sperm, 100 barrels whale.
....do	Mar. 13	Oct. 27, 1850	115	......	......	Sailed again December 20, 1850; returned September 26, 1851, with 245 sperm, 60 whale.
....do	Apr. 17	Oct. 27, 1850	60	......	......	Added 1850; sailed again December 25, 1850; returned October 18, 1851, with 75 barrels sperm.
....do	Apr. 17	Sept. 22, 1850	240	......	......	Added 1850.
....do	Apr. 3	Sept. 18, 1850	160	......	......	Added 1850.
North Atlantic	Feb. 25	Sept. 2, 1850	75	......	......	
Atlantic	Apr. 8	Oct. 27, 1850	70	......	......	Added 1850.
....do	Apr. 30	Nov. 1, 1851	40	......	......	
....do	Apr. 10	June 26, 1851	154	25	......	Withdrawn 1852.
....do	Apr. 17	Nov. 3, 1851	350	......	......	Added 1850.
....do	Apr. 10	Aug. 13, 1850	130	......	......	Added 1850.
North Atlantic	Feb. 25	Oct. 24, 1850	240	......	......	
Atlantic	Apr. 17	Nov. 1, 1850	140	......	......	
....do	Apr. 17	Oct. 18, 1850	90	......	......	Added 1850.
....do	Mar. 25	Dec. 28, 1850	560	......	......	Added 1850.
....do	May 1	Oct. 1, 1850	110	......	......	Added 1850.
....do	June 8	Sept. 18, 1850	......	80	......	Added 1850; humpback; withdrawn 1851.
....do	June 16	Nov. 27, 1850	240	......	......	
....do	Apr. 23	Sept. 19, 1850	315	......	......	Added 1850.
....do	Apr. 20	Nov. 20, 1850	200	......	......	Added 1850.
North Atlantic	Apr. 20	Nov. 6, 1850	......	......	......	Added 1850; clean.
Pacific Ocean ..	July 18	May 6, 1852	......	Clean	......	Sold 1852; sent home 263 sperm.
North Pacific ..	Sept. 20	Apr. 4, 1854	105	2, 320	......	Sent home 68 sperm, 707 whale, 4,900 bone.
Pacific Ocean ..	July 10	May 7, 1853	320	1, 720	1, 000	Sent home 16,998 bone.

Table showing returns of whaling-vessels

Name of vessel.	Class.	Tonnage.	Captain.	Managing owner or agent.
1850.				
Boston, Mass.				
Rothschild	Bark	261	—— Small	Philip A. Locke
Beverly, Mass.				
B. Franklin	Brig	164	—— Brown	F. W. Choate
Truro, Mass.				
Eschol	Brig	143	—— Smith	Richard Sevens
Wareham, Mass.				
G. Washington	Ship	374	Benjamin F. Gibbs	S. C. Gibbs
Warren, R. I.				
Dolphin	Bark	325	—— Cutter	R. B. Johnson
Hector	do	225	—— Cole	do
Wm. Henry	do	180	J. H. Jolls	S. P. Child
Newport, R. I.				
Helen Augusta	Ship	530	Nathaniel Fales, jr	J. S. Munroe
Providence, R. I.				
Ocean	Ship	567	E. A. Swift	Edward Pearce
Mystic, Conn.				
Leander	Bark	213	B. Glover	Charles Mallory
New London, Conn.				
Alert	Ships	398	—— Bolles	Williams & Haven
Bengal	do	304	—— Phillips	Thomas Fitch, 2d
Catharine	do	384	—— Hull	do
Dromo	do	306	—— Starr	do
Electra	do	348	—— Clark	Williams & Barnes
Friends	do	403	—— Low	Benjamin Brown Sons
George and Mary	do	356	—— Greene	Lyman Allyn
Hy. Thompson	do	315	—— Holme	Frink, Chew & Co
India	do	433	—— Miller	Williams & Haven
John and Elizabeth	do	296	—— Chappell	do
Lark	Bark	388	—— Kelley	Perkins & Smith
Merrimack	Ship	414	—— Destin	Williams & Haven
McLellan	do	376	—— Perkins	Perkins & Smith
Neptune	do	285	—— Allen	Williams & Haven
North Star	do	399	Robert Brown	Williams & Barnes
Peruvian	do	388	—— Brown	E. V. Stoddard
Phœnix	do	404	—— Brewster	Miner Lawrence & Co
Tenedos	Bark	245	—— Middleton	do
W. T. Wheaton	do	437	James Green	James Green

sailing from American ports—Continued.

Whaling-ground.	Date— Of sailing.	Date— Of arrival.	Result of voyage. Sperm-oil.	Result of voyage. Whale-oil.	Result of voyage. Whalebone.	Remarks.
			Bbls.	*Bbls.*	*Lbs.*	
N. and S. Atl ..	June 6	Apr. 24, 1851	300	......	......	Added 1850.
Atlantic	Dec. 14	Nov. 17, 1850	350	......	......	Added 1850; sailed again December 14, 1850; returned April 27, 1852, with 500 sperm, 2 whale.
Atlantic	Mar. 13	Nov. 5, 1850	130	......	......	Added 1849.
North Pacific ..	Aug. 7	Apr. 24, 1853	......	2, 513	27, 700	Sent home 172 sperm, 13,683 bone.
Indian Ocean ..	Nov. 15	Sept. 5, 1853	259	1	......	Built 1850 at Somerset.
....do	Aug. 5	Nov. 22, 1852	600	......	......	
....do	July 8	Feb. 2, 1854	441	......	......	Added 1850.
North Pacific ..	Dec. 10	May 1, 1854	......	1, 080	......	Sent home 10,286 bone; bought from New York 1850.
North Pacific ..	Aug. 6	May 10, 1853	......	4, 200	54, 000	Added 1850; sold to Warren 1853; sent home 306 sperm, 28,250 bone.
South Atlantic.	July 5	July 31, 1852	408	311	1, 900	Captain Glover came home sick 1851; sent home 100 sperm.
North Pacific ..	June 18	May 21, 1853	205	2, 402	27, 800	Sent home 14,500 pounds bone.
Ind. and N. P ..	Sept. 25	Mar. 24, 1856	14	931	......	Sent home 1,533 whale, 10,500 bone; shipped some oil to London; rebuilt in 1856, and named Northwest.
North Pacific ..	July 9	Apr. 20, 1854	82	751	8, 500	Sent home 4,341 whale, 45,829 bone.
Ind. and N. P ..	Oct. 3	May 2, 1854	......	223	3, 000	Sent home 110 sperm, 1,878 whale, 40,216 pounds bone.
North Pacific ..	June 1	Mar. 30, 1854	40	1, 052	17, 600	Sent home 211 sperm, 3,363 whale, 51,638 bone.
....do	July 25	....	......	......	......	Sent home on voyage 90 sperm, 1,200 whale, 26,145 bone; sold 500 whale; loaded with guano at Chincha Islands.
....do	July 20	Apr. 4, 1853	......	1, 970	28, 500	Sent home 1,300 whale; shipped some oil to London.
Ind. and Pac ...	Oct. 22	....	......	......	......	Lost in the ice near Diomede Island July 15, 1851.
North Pacific ..	Aug. 28	Apr. 13, 1854	......	2, 261	36, 200	Sent home some bone; shipped some oil to London.
....do	July 20	June 2, 1855	......	830	......	Sent home 495 whale, 12,000 bone.
Indian Ocean ..	Aug. 15	May 8, 1853	140	1, 528	24, 000	Sent home 527 whale.
Ind. and Pac ...	Oct. 17	July 7, 1853	280	2, 983	49, 000	
Davis's Strait ..	Mar. 7	Oct. 22, 1850	......	450	7, 000	
Ind. and N. P ..	May 7	....	......	......	......	Shipped oil to London; withdrawn 1857; sold and broken up at Sandwich Islands; sent home 235 sperm, 3,101 whale, 12,925 bone.
North Pacific ..	July 30	June 5, 1855	......	660	8, 200	Sent home 2,007 whale, 22,497 bone; bought from Philadelphia 1850.
Desolation Isld	Sept. 11	July 21, 1852	15	2, 947	9, 100	
Ind. and Pac ...	Nov. 7	May 24, 1853	30	2, 150	21, 500	Sent home 60 sperm.
North Pacific ..	Sept. 3	Apr. 19, 1853	1, 856	......	......	Sent home 32,292 pounds bone.
....do	Sept. 4	....	......	......	......	Bought from Warren 1850; fourth mate died July, 1852; sold at Honolulu 1853; sent home 82 sperm, 2,658 whale, 15,000 bone; lost March 29, 1855, 60 miles south of San Francisco; sold 1,000 whale and some sperm at San Francisco.

Table showing returns of whaling-vessels

Name of vessel.	Class.	Tonnage.	Captain.	Managing owner or agent.
1850.				
Stonington, Conn.				
Byron	Bark	170	—— Wilcox	John F. Trumbull
Charles Phelps	Ship	362	—— Burch	C. P. Williams
Eugene	do	297	—— Pendleton	do
Fellowes	do	268	—— Pendleton	do
Mary and Susan	do	392	—— Brown	do
Newburyport	do	341	—— Lester	J. F. Trumbull
Prudent	Bark	298	—— Nash	C. P. Williams
Greenport, L. I.				
Caroline	Ship	252	Hedges Babcock	Ireland, Wells & Carpenter.
Pioneer	Bark	235	—— Weeks	David G. Floyd
Roanoke	do	252	—— Hand	Parsons & Brown
Sag Harbor, L. I.				
Ann	Bark	299	J. Steen	Thomas Brown
Charlotte	Brig	230	—— Winters	William R. Post
Jefferson	Ship	435	—— Huntting	T. Brown
Odd Fellow	Bark	239	—— Hedges	do
Ontario	Ship	489	—— Brown	W. R. Post
Washington	do	340	—— Rose	Huntting Cooper
New Suffolk.				
Gentleman	Bark	227	—— Cartwright	Ira B. Tuthill
1851.				
New Bedford, Mass.				
Abm. H. Howland	Ship	414	P. Pease	Abra. H. Howland
Alexander	do	421	J. Ryan	John A. Parker
Alexander Coffin	do	381	—— Purrington	Jonathan Bourne, jr
Alice Frazier	Bark	406	D. H. Taber	Lemuel Kollock
Alice Mandell	Ship	425	P. S. Wing	Charles R. Tucker & Co
Alto	Bark	236	—— Carr	Richmond & Wood
Alfred Gibbs	Ship	425	Isaac H. Jenney	Wood & Nye
America	do	418	L. Fisher	I. Howland, jr., & Co
America	Bark	257	Abner West	Jos. A. Beauvais
Anadir	do	615	J. H. Swift	Swift & Perry
Atlantic	do	367	—— Luce	Hathaway & Luce
Baltic	do	390	Jethro B. Brooks	Randall & Stead
Barnstable	Ship	373	R. M. Corn	William F. Dow
Benj. Tucker	do	340	B. R. Sands	Charles R. Tucker & Co.
Bramin	do	245	—— Childs	Gideon Allen
Bartholomew Gosnold	do	356	C. B. Heustis	I. Howland, jr., & Co
Cambria	do	362	J. Cottle	James B. Wood & Co.
California	do	398	D. D. Wood	I. Howland, jr., & Co.
Canada	do	545	Thomas West	Barton Ricketson
Canton, 2d	do	280	—— Folger	C. R. Tucker & Co
Chandler Price	do	441	J. Taber	William G. E. Pope

sailing from American ports—Continued.

Whaling-ground.	Date— Of sailing.	Date— Of arrival.	Result of voyage. Sperm-oil.	Result of voyage. Whale-oil.	Result of voyage. Whalebone.	Remarks.
			Bbls.	*Bbls.*	*Lbs.*	
Patagonia......	May 25	Feb. 26, 1852	......	249	18, 000	
North Pacific ..	Oct. 1	Jan. 22, 1853	326	2, 600	32, 000	
....do	Oct. 5	Apr. 28, 1853	......	2, 007	27, 600	Sent home 7,500 pounds bone.
....do	Sept. 21	....	......	......	......	Sent home 3,500 bone; condemned at Honolulu December 5, 1853.
....do	Oct. 1	May 24, 1854	90	1, 000	1, 600	Sent home 9,309 bone.
....do	Aug. 8	Mar. 21, 1853	......	2, 126	25, 500	Third mate, William Hancox, and boat's crew lost October 13, 1854; sent home 150 sperm, 22,000 pounds bone.
N. W. Coast....	Oct. 8	May 31, 1855	......	1, 107	16, 800	Sent home 20,700 pounds bone, 2,419 whale; sold to Greenport 1855.
South Atlantic.	Aug. 7	July 9, 1852	920	75	......	
....do	Jan. 19	Sept. 9, 1851	290	60	550	Added 1849.
....do	June 4	Apr. 5, 1853	224	1, 080	7, 500	Sent home 40 sperm, 100 whale.
North Pacific ..	Oct. 9	Apr. 7, 1853	32	739	7, 500	Sent home 150 whale.
South Pacific ..	July 25	May 28, 1852	307	2	......	Added 1850; sent home 316 sperm.
Arctic Ocean ..	Nov. 17	Mar. 24, 1853	24	2, 872	39, 000	Sent home 600 whale, 18,000 pounds bone.
South Atlantic	July 26	June 2, 1852	401	320	1, 900	Added 1850.
North Pacific ..	Sept. 4	....	......	......	......	Captain Brown killed while "cutting in" 1853; sent home 230 whale.
....do	Sept. 4	....	......	......	......	Lost on Pitt's Island 1851; sent home 10,000 pounds bone.
....	June —	May 20, 1852	......	1, 385	10, 500	Sold to Sag Harbor 1852.
North Pacific ..	Aug. 18	....	......	......	......	Sent home 45 sperm, 1,858 whale, 17,100 bone; lost at Honolulu December, 1852.
....do	June 11	Apr. 19, 1855	......	2, 359	17, 100	Sold 50 whale at Honolulu; sent home 600 whale, 17,500 bone.
....do	Nov. 13	May 19, 1854	76	2, 272	6, 000	From California trade; restored 1851; sent home 28,337 bone.
....do	Sept. 10	Sept. 4, 1855	136	......	12, 000	Bought from Boston 1851; built 1848; sent home 831 whale, 14,081 bone; sold 1,100 whale at Melbourne.
....do	Sept. 10	Apr. 10, 1855	85	1, 729	4, 900	Added 1851; sent home 31,969 bone.
Atl. and Indian	Sept. 8	Feb. 22, 1854	1, 508	......	......	Sent home 63 sperm.
North Pacific ..	Nov. 13	July 20, 1854	206	1, 634	......	Built at Bath, Me., 1851; sent home 46 sperm, 130 whale, 19,227 bone.
....do	June 25	June 21, 1854	127	2, 024	8, 200	Sent home 18,000 bone; withdrawn 1854.
Atlantic	July 24	Oct. 2, 1852	400	2	......	
North Pacific ..	Jan. 2	Mar. 16, 1854	......	2, 498	18, 800	Formerly United States store-ship Erie; bought from New York 1850; withdrawn 1854; sent home 500 whale, 28,000 bone.
Atlantic, &c ...	Oct. 31	July 17, 1854	1, 097	196	600	Built at New Bedford 1851; sent home 444 sperm.
North Pacific ..	Nov. 16	Mar. 24, 1855	107	1, 654	11, 000	Bought from Providence 1851; sold 97 whale at Honolulu; sent home 400 sperm, 600 whale, 24 043 bone.
Pacific Ocean..	May 6	Aug. 4, 1855	824	257	......	Bought from Boston 1851; sent home 110 sperm.
North Pacific ..	Nov. 5	May 30, 1855	124	833	8, 300	Sent home 664 whale, 15,858 bone.
....do	Sept. 9	....	......	......	......	Lost in Arctic September 25, 1852.
Pacific Ocean ..	July 15	Apr. 20, 1854	148	2, 435	......	Sent home 23,124 bone.
North Pacific ..	Sept. 3	May 10, 1854	182	1, 596	11, 500	Sent home 900 whale, 32,300 bone.
....do	Oct. 22	May 24, 1854	136	2, 110	8, 800	Sent home 17,200 bone.
....do	Oct. 1	Apr. 9, 1855	......	1, 200	8, 000	Added 1851; sent home 910 whale, 13,227 bone.
Pacific Ocean ..	July 31	June 20, 1855	1, 171	2	......	Sold part of her cargo at Sydney.
North Pacific ..	July 25	May 1, 1854	......	3, 297	33, 700	Sent home 25 sperm, 500 whale, 29,730 bone.

Table showing returns of whaling-vessels

Name of vessel.	Class.	Tonnage.	Captain.	Managing owner or agent.
1851.				
New Bedford, Mass.—Continued.				
Citizen	Ship	464	Thomas A. Norton	I. Howland, jr., & Co.
Corinthian	...do	401	A. Stewart	George Howland
Coul's Howland	...do	431	S. W. Crosby	Edward W. Howland
Cachelot	Bark	230	—— Hosmer	I. H. Bartlett & Son
Cortes	Ship	382	P. Cromwell	G. Howland
Cherokee	Bark	261	P. Smith	Hathaway & Luce
Charleston Packet	...do	184	H. Lewis	Thomas Knowles & Co.
Congress	Ship	339	—— Mendall	Edward C. Jones
Cowper	...do	391	N. C. Fisher	Benjamin B. Howard
Congaree	...do	321	M. Malloy	Thomas Wilcox
Draco	Bark	257	George Kimball	J. Bourne, jr
Dartmouth	Ship	336	—— Manchester	I. Howland, jr., & Co.
Dominga	Bark	230	—— Tripp	John L. Anthony
Draper	Ship	291	G. Coffin	Henry F. Thomas
Emma	Bark	246	Jeremiah Austin	Rodney French
Elisha Dunbar	...do	257	Benjamin Ellis	W. & G. D. Watkins
Eliza Adams	Ship	403	—— Smith	E. C. Jones
Elizabeth	...do	329	—— Baker	T. & A. R. Nye
Endeavour	Bark	252	Jacob Howland	Abraham Ashley, 2d
Enterprise	Ship	291	H. Jernegan	Charles Hitch
Eugenia	Bark	356	William Wood	Swift & Allen
Euphrates	Ship	365	Thomas M. Peakes	E. W. Howland
Europa	...do	380	—— Weeks	E. C. Jones
Emerald	...do	359	J. Munkley	Henry F. Thomas
Florida	...do	330	J. C. Little	E. C. Jones
Frances Henrietta	...do	407	George Swain	Samuel W. Rodman
Fabius	...do	432	J. S. Smith	C. R. Tucker & Co
Garland	...do	243	J. King	R. French
Geo. Washington	...do	609	—— Edwards	I. Howland, jr., & Co.
Geo. Washington	Bark	242	W. O. Harps	C. Hitch
Golconda	Ship	331	F. Dougherty	G. Howland
Good Return	...do	376	B. F. Wing	H. Taber & Co
Gratitude	...do	337	—— Cornell	Swift & Allen
Gypsy	Bark	356	—— Mickell	I. Howland, jr., & Co.
Helen Snow	...do	300	Shubael Brayton	Cook & Snow
Herald, 2d	Ship	303	H. A. Slocum	T. & A. R. Nye
Henry Kneeland	...do	304	W. H. Vinal	B. B. Howard
Hibernia, 2d	...do	551	—— Jeffrey	Seth H. Ingalls
Hillman	...do	383	Chris. Cook	H. Taber & Co
Hope, 2d	...do	295	—— Gifford	Wilcox & Richmond
Hunter	...do	453	John S. Holt	J. Bourne, jr
India	...do	366	F. E. Stranburg	A. H. Howland
Ionia	Bark	234	—— Coggeshall	Cranston Wilcox
Isaac Howland	Ship	399	—— West	I. Howland, jr., & Co

sailing from American ports—Continued.

Whaling-ground.	Date—		Result of voyage.			Remarks.
	Of sailing.	Of arrival.	Sperm-oil.	Whale-oil.	Whalebone.	
			Bbls.	*Bbls.*	*Lbs.*	
North Pacific ..	Oct. 29	....	.....	.....	....	Formerly in California trade; added 1851; lost 300 miles north of East Cape October 14, 1853; 6 of the crew lost, and 1 died subsequently; sent home 69 sperm.
Pacific Ocean ..	June 4	June 11, 1854	210	539	1,900	Sent home 3,125 bone.
North Pacific ..	Aug. 19	Apr. 6, 1854	109	2,357	15,200	Built at New Bedford 1851; sent home 326 whale, 32,007 bone.
Atlantic	Dec. 10	Apr. 17, 1854	454	150	600	
Pacific Ocean ..	June 26	Apr. 12, 1853	48	2,576	41,100	Sent home 64 sperm.
....do	Aug. 19	Apr. 27, 1855	.....	1,108	14,900	Sent home 8,249 bone.
Indian Ocean ..	Apr. 19	July 10, 1853	275	6	.....	
....do	Dec. 3	May 8, 1854	153	807	6,100	
North Pacific ..	Sept. 10	May 6, 1855	.....	3,217	20,200	Sent home 221 whale, 22,400 bone.
Pacific Ocean ..	May 8	May 6, 1855	1,176	7	......	
Indian Ocean ..	May 22	Apr. 13, 1854	1,188	......	......	
North Pacific ..	Sept. 1	Mar. 23, 1854	206	2,827	......	Sent home 20,100 bone.
Atlantic	Nov. 20	June 3, 1854	43	363	1,300	Added 1851; built 1831; bought from Boston.
North Pacific ..	Oct. 14	Apr. 27, 1855	215	1,403	16,400	Sailed September 2; returned leaking 1,200 strokes in 24 hours.
Pacific Ocean.	Dec. 11	....	.....	.....	.....	Burned by the crew at Paita October 15, 1853, with 650 barrels of oil on board.
Indian Ocean..	June 19	May 9, 1854	1,113	......	......	Built at Mattapoisett 1851.
North Pacific ..	Nov. 3	Sept. 23, 1854	184	1,220	14,000	Added 1851; sent home 457 sperm, 1,400 whale, 12,624 bone; sold 130 sperm at Valparaiso.
Pacific Ocean ..	Nov. 11	June 9, 1855	2,060	....	.....	
South Seas....	Oct. 26	June 1, 1854	80	1,789	.....	First mate, Mr. Johnson, killed by a whale 1853; sent home 156 sperm.
North Pacific ..	July 26	Apr. 5, 1854	8	1,664	16,000	Captain Jernegan died at sea September 26, 1853; sent home 116 sperm, 380 whale, 15,223 bone.
Pacific Ocean ..	May 26	July 5, 1855	318	135	......	Bought from New York 1851; sent home 765 sperm, 143 whale.
North Pacific ..	July 1	July 6, 1854	512	1,738	6,000	Sent home 10,446 bone.
....do	Oct. 14	Mar. 1, 1854	62	2,636	20,200	Built at Mattapoisett 1851; sent home 85 whale, 5,620 bone.
Pacific Ocean ..	Nov. 16	July 3, 1856	553	......	......	Sent home 350 sperm; Captain Munkley died May 8, 1856.
Ind. and Pac...	May 19	May 26, 1853	242	2,149	.....	Sent home 21 sperm, 11,000 bone.
North Pacific ..	June 17	Apr. 28, 1855	......	470	1,700	Sent home 120 sperm, 1,288 whale, 25,600 bone.
....do	July 14	Mar. 13, 1854	32	1,488	19,500	Sent home 952 whale.
Atlantic	May 6	Sept. 9, 1853	73	.....	.....	
North Pacific ..	Nov. 4	May 31, 1855	52	2,505	800	George Washington made one whaling voyage from New London; bought from New York 1851; built at New Bedford for a Liverpool packet 1832; sent home 50,420 bone; took in all 7,000 whale and 75 sperm; an extraordinary voyage.
Atl. and Ind...	Nov. 6	Dec. 3, 1853	54	3	.....	Sent home 258 sperm; Second Mate A. B. Smith died March, 1853.
North Pacific ..	July 31	Apr. 11, 1855	9	1,035	12,100	Sent home 12,418 bone.
....do	Sept. 2	Apr. 6, 1855	......	2,825	22,800	Sent home 223 sperm, 1,440 whale, 26,431 bone.
....do	Aug. 14	June 24, 1854	60	2,031	5,600	Sent home 19,000 bone.
Indian Ocean ..	Dec. 2	Sept. 17, 1855	1,640	......	......	Built at Fairhaven 1851.
....do	July 17	May 12, 1854	667	......	....	Built at Bath, Me., 1851; second mate, Mr. Lumm, died at sea June 15, 1853.
North Pacific ..	July 21	Mar. 31, 1855	......	1,387	6,000	Sent home 120 sperm, 18,777 bone.
....do	Aug. 16	Apr. 5, 1854	222	2.314	16,200	Sent home 19,203 bone.
....do	Dec. 4	Apr. 18, 1855	2	1,511	21,300	Added 1851; withdrawn 1855.
....do	July 11	Mar. 17, 1854	.....	2,540	29,500	Built at New Bedford 1851; sent home 30,790 bone.
Pacific Ocean..	Nov. 1	Apr. 12, 1857	965	30	......	Sent home 1,235 sperm.
North Pacific..	Oct. 29	Mar. 15, 1854	77	1,740	15,400	Built at Gardiner, Me., 1851; sent home 93 sperm, 825 whale, and 16,410 bone.
....do	Aug. 20	Apr. 29, 1855	......	1,234	9,000	Boat's crew lost at Rorotonga December 20, 1854; sent home 21,233 pounds bone.
Indian Ocean ..	Sept. 20	Oct. 18, 1854	1,122	......	......	Bought from New York 1851.
North Pacific..	July 23	Apr. 24, 1854	59	2,771	31,300	Sent home 1,874 whale and 24,750 bone.

Table showing returns of whaling-vessels

Name of vessel.	Class.	Tonnage.	Captain.	Managing owner or agent.
1851.				
New Bedford, Mass.—Continued.				
James Allen	Ship	355	A. Newcomb	G. Allen
James Andrews	Bark	275	H. Beetle	C. Hitch
James Edward	Ship	434	R. Luce, jr	George F. Barker
Janus	do	321	J. Cornell	T. & A. R. Nye
James Maury	do	395	—— Whelden	C. R. Tucker & Co
John Howland	do	377	—— Childs	James H. Howland
John and Edward	do	318	G. H. Cathcart	Wilcox & Richmond
Julian	do	356	—— Cleveland	Hathaway & Luce
J. E. Donnell	Bark	343	William Earl	Swift & Allen
Kutusoff	Ship	415	—— Pierce	H. F. Thomas
Lancaster	do	383	E. C. Almy	T. & A. R. Nye
Lexington	Bark	201	—— Tilton	B. B. Howard
Liverpool, 2d	Ship	428	W. J. Swift	T. Wilcox
Logan	do	302	A. Tucker	I. Howland, jr., & Co
L. C. Richmond	do	341	D. Cochran	J. B. Wood & Co
Magnolia	do	396	G. L. Cox	William G. E. Pope
Manuel Ortiz	Bark	351	C. H. Cole	Weston Howland
Marengo	Ship	426	—— Devoll	J. Bourne, jr
Maria Theresa	do	330	J. Taylor	T. & A. R. Nye
Mary and Martha	do	317	—— Slocum	B. Ricketson
Majestic	do	297	T. Percival	S. Thomas & Co
Menkar	do	371	Joseph Pease	Philip Anthony
Milton	do	388	—— Jones	H. Taber & Co
Milwood	Bark	254	T. R. Pease	G. Allen
Margaret Scott	Ship	307	B. C. Eldridge	R. French
Massachusetts	do	364	J. E. Bennett	W. F. Dow
Milo	do	401	George H. Sowle	C. C. Jones
Minerva, 2d	do	291	—— Reynolds	T. Knowles & Co
Messenger	do	291	—— Baker	J. R. Thornton
Moctezuma	do	436	W. E. Tower	John P. West
Martha, 2d	Bark	360	G. S. Tooker	W. O. Brownell
Natchez	Ship	523	Worthen Hall	S. Thomas & Co
Nautilus	do	372	Alexander Seabury	G. Allen
Newton	Bark	283	—— Sherman	J. Bourne, jr
Nimrod	Ship	340	N. C. Cary	W. Gifford
Navy	do	356	J. W. Norton	J. B. Wood & Co
Nye	Bark	211	D. Baker	Abner R. Tucker
Ohio	Ship	383	—— Norton	Ed. W. Howland
Olympia	do	296	James Russell	William Phillips
Orozimbo	do	588	—— Johnson	B. Ricketson
Osceola	Bark	158	—— King	William C. N. Swift
Ospray	do	236	T. Macomber	Swift & Allen
Peri	do	205	—— Higgins	R. French
Phœnix	Ship	423	—— Bellows	J. A. Parker
Pioneer	Bark	231	F. Billings	J. D. Thompson
Parachute	Ship	331	William A. Barton	B. B. Howard

sailing from American ports—Continued.

Whaling-ground.	Date—		Result of voyage.			Remarks.
	Of sailing.	Of arrival.	Sperm-oil.	Whale-oil.	Whalebone.	
			Bbls.	*Bbls.*	*Lbs.*	
Ind. and Pacific.	May 14	Mar. 18, 1855	1,561	......	......	
Atl. and Indian.	June 2	Nov. 4, 1853	400	16	......	Bought from New York 1851; built 1847; sent home 331 sperm.
North Pacific..	Sept. 11	....	......	......	......	Added 1851; sent home on voyage 170 sperm, 530 whale, 15,000 pounds bone; sold 350 whale; lost 1854.
....do	Nov. 4	Apr. 21, 1854	120	1,090	19,700	Sent home 1,038 whale; sold 170 sperm at Lahaina.
....do	Oct. 21	Sept. 26, 1855	21	1,844	11,600	Sent home 10 sperm and 160 whale.
Pacific Ocean ..	Nov. 17	June 10, 1854	55	2,385	24,000	Sent home 10,213 pounds bone.
North Pacific..	May 21	July 24, 1854	65	981	17,500	Sold 110 whale at Talcahuano; sent home 267 sperm and 10 blackfish.
....do	Nov. 24	June 16, 1854	163	2,636	......	Sent home 30,104 pounds bone.
....do	Aug. 28	May 7, 1853	112	2,286	38,800	
....do	Sept. 9	May 3, 1855	......	1,412	2,100	Second mate, George W. Clark, died 1853; sent home 1,350 sperm and 39,066 bone.
....do	July 2	May 14, 1854	40	1,101	9,500	Sent home 70 sperm and 693 whale.
Atlantic	Apr. 3	Oct. 29, 1852	129	......	......	Bought from Providence 1850.
North Pacific..	Nov. 18	....	......	......	......	Sent home 375 whale and 35,000 bone; wrecked in Behring Straits July 20, 1853; got into St. Lawrence Bay and was condemned and sold.
....do	Aug. 12	June 10, 1854	200	1,808	......	Sent home 180 sperm.
....do	July 1	July 8, 1854	219	1,692	11,900	Sent home 225 sperm, 266 whale, and 28,044 pounds bone.
....do	Sept. 19	May 12, 1854	144	1,632	24,300	Added 1851; sent home 1,983 whale and 25,600 pounds bone.
Pacific Ocean ..	July 5	May 1, 1854	19	2,029	......	Bought from New York 1851; nearly new; sent home 995 whale and 25,470 bone.
North Pacific..	Nov. 22	Apr. 24, 1855	......	1,579	23,500	Sent home 17,253 pounds bone.
....do	June 28	Apr. 8, 1854	......	1,818	28,300	Sent home 23,700 pounds bone.
....do	Nov. 27	Apr. 11, 1855	75	1,133	10,500	Added 1851; sent home 31 whale and 3,665 bone; sold to Boston 1855; condemned and broken up at Buenos Ayres 1859.
....do	July 2	Apr. 20, 1853	......	1,607	21,400	
....do	Aug. 18	Apr. 6, 1854	41	2,525	14,100	Sent home 200 whale and 24,700 bone.
Pacific Ocean ..	Nov. 1	Apr. 6, 1856	2,050	......	......	
Atl. and Indian.	May 21	June 27, 1854	311	138	500	Sent home 136 sperm.
North Pacific..	Sept. 26	May 6, 1855	......	182	3,500	Sent home 171 sperm.
....do	Dec. 4	June 5, 1856	186	1,240	19,000	Sent home 104 sperm, 2,039 whale, and 34,988 pounds bone.
....do	Nov. 9	May 27, 1855	50	2,789	33,800	Sent home 12 sperm, 84 whale, and 24,800 pounds bone.
....do	June 18	May 4, 1855	1	1,093	10,600	Sent home 4,939 pounds bone.
Pacific Ocean ..	Nov. 1	Mar. 17, 1855	890	......	......	
North Pacific..	July 19	Feb. 18, 1854	237	2,923	18,600	Sent home 35,433 pounds bone.
....do	Aug. 6	May 11, 1854	7	2,794	27,000	A condemned slaver; bought from New York 1850; sent home 600 whale and 32 510 pounds bone.
....do	Oct. 4	Apr. 24, 1855	251	2,681	15,500	Bought from New York 1851; formerly in China trade; sent home 750 whale and 22,950 pounds bone.
Pacific Ocean ..	July 8	Apr. 24, 1855	872	19	......	Built at Fairhaven 1851; second mate, John Smith, drowned in a gale August, 1852; sent home 265 sperm and 6 blackfish.
North Pacific..	Sept. 1	Apr. 8, 1854	61	1,978	10,600	
....do	Sept. 13	Mar. 26, 1854	55	2,250	......	Capt. Cary came home sick 1852; sent home 50 sperm, 50 whale, and 27,983 bone.
....do	Oct. 2	Apr. 7, 1855	151	1,400	5,600	Sent home about 500 whale.
Atlantic	Apr. 10	Aug. 13, 1853	294	19	......	
North Pacific..	Oct. 9	May 28, 1853	133	2,307	34,700	Added 1850.
....do	Aug. 23	Apr. 21, 1855	38	628	3,400	Sent home 17,600 pounds bone.
....do	Aug. 15	May 10, 1854	......	1,620	23,200	Sent home 24,115 pounds bone.
Atlantic	July 7	Oct. 1, 1853	187	17	......	Sent home 114 sperm.
Indian Ocean ..	June 4	Oct. 1, 1854	545	......	......	Formerly a brig; bought from Baltimore 1851.
Atlantic	Dec. 9	Oct. 15, 1853	180	......	......	Sent home 49 sperm.
North Pacific..	Aug. 6	Mar. 23, 1854	......	3,211	34,100	Sent home 40 sperm, 439 whale, and 29,600 pounds bone.
Atlantic, &c ...	June 24	Apr. 8, 1854	49	735	7,100	Sent home 14,600 bone; withdrawn 1854.
North Pacific..	Oct. 8	June 2, 1855	52	1,649	10,000	Sent home 14,891 pounds bone.

Table showing returns of whaling-vessels

Name of vessel.	Class.	Tonnage.	Captain.	Managing owner or agent.
1851.				
New Bedford, Mass.—Continued.				
Richmond	Bark	185	Henry Bonney	E. W. Howland
Roscoe	Ship	362	William C. Hayden	A. Robeson
Robert Morison	Bark	310	Richard Norton	T. Knowles & Co
Robert Pulsford	Ship	406	A. J. Corey	Edmund Maxfield
Rodman	...do	371	W. R. Allyn	C. W. Morgan
Roman	...do	375	M. Cuminskey	E. C. Jones
Sarah Sheafe	Bark	400	Thomas Wall	Cranston Wilcox
Scotland	Ship	384	G. A. Smith	O. & E. W. Seabury
Sea Flower	Bark	150	J. W. Bolles	Charles Almy
Stafford	...do	206	Hiram Francis	T. & A. R. Nye
Sophia Thornton	Ship	425	—— Young	J. R. Thornton
South America	...do	616	W. T. Walker	W. O. Brownell
South Carolina	...do	306	—— Alexander	J. D. Thompson
Thomas Nye	...do	460	J. C. Almy	T. & A. R. Nye
Triton, 2d	...do	315	—— Maynard	C. R. Tucker & Co
Tropic Bird	Bark	220	—— Stanton	W. P. Howland
Two Brothers	Ship	288	E. Nichols	Wood & Nye
Uncas	...do	413	—— James	A. H. Howland
Vernon	Bark	307	—— Little	Charles Hitch
Virginia	...do	346	O. P. Seabury	Hathaway & Luce
Waverly	Ship	327	Eph. W. Kempton	David B. Kempton
Wave	Bark	200	Charles Downs	T. Knowles & Co
William C. Nye	Ship	389	—— Adams	C. R. Tucker & Co
Zephyr	...do	361	Thomas M. Gardner	Alexander Gibbs
Fairhaven, Mass.				
Albion	Ship	326	—— Soule	E. Sawin
Bruce	Bark	172	—— Dyer	James Tripp, 2d
Clifford Wayne	Ship	305	—— Davis	E. Sawin
Columbus	...do	382	—— Crowell	Gibbs & Jenney
E. L. B. Jenney	...do	380	—— Marsh	...do
Florida	...do	524	Isaiah West	Fish, Robinson & Co
General Scott	...do	333	—— Fisher	L. C. Tripp
George	...do	360	—— Marston	Reuben Fish
Heroine	...do	337	T. M. Pease	Nathan Church
Lively	Schooner	104	—— Pierce	Fish & Robinson
Lydia	Ship	351	Henry F. Worth	F. R. Whitwell
Navigator	...do	416	—— Fish	William G. Blackler
Niagara	...do	538	Benjamin Clough	N. Church

sailing from American ports—Continued.

Whaling-ground.	Date—		Result of voyage.			Remarks.
	Of sailing.	Of arrival.	Sperm-oil.	Whale-oil.	Whalebone.	
			Bbls.	*Bbls.*	*Lbs.*	
Atl. and Indian.	Sept. 8	Oct. 13, 1853	......	......	......	Formerly a brig; rerigged 1851; voyage broken up by desertions of the crew, and she returned with freight.
Pacific Ocean ..	Aug. 8	Apr. 8, 1855	1, 505	......	......	Sent home 60 sperm, 907 whale, and 19,500 pounds bone.
North Pacific..	Oct. 16	May 1, 1854	16	1, 102	11, 000	Bought from New York 1851; built at Philadelphia, 1832; sent home 147 sperm, 897 whale, and 19,152 pounds bone.
....do	June 10	....	......	......	......	Bought from Boston 1851; lost on Christmas Island, February 16, 1853.
....do	Oct. 15	May 24, 1855	102	1, 163	11, 500	First mate, Mr. Clark, died at sea, 1852; sent home 125 sperm, 1,656 whale, and 18,153 pounds bone.
Pacific Ocean..	Dec. 21	Sept. 1, 1855	381	1, 765	12, 400	Second mate, C. L. Thomas, killed by a whale 1852; sent home 161 sperm, 144 whale, and 20,400 pounds bone.
North Pacific..	Dec. 4	Apr. 24, 1855	......	1, 056	6, 100	Bought from New York 1851; sent home 750 whale and 13,000 pounds bone.
... do	June 22	Apr. 25, 1854	58	2, 877	......	Bought from Nantucket 1851.
Atlantic	May 15	May 8, 1853	50	19	......	Formerly a brig; rerigged 1851.
... do	July 8	May 26, 1854	667	49	......	Bought from Kingston 1851; built 1849; sent home 127 sperm.
North Pacific..	July 11	Mar. 18, 1855	30	2, 270	31, 600	Built at Bath, Me., 1851; sent home 160 sperm, 959 whale, and 17,208 bone.
... do	Dec. 24	Apr. 22, 1855	......	2, 552	37, 500	Bought from Providence 1851; sent home 20 sperm, 1,961 whale, and 25,035 bone.
....do	Apr. 29	....	......	......	......	Lost 1852; sent home 80 sperm.
Indian, &c	Sept. 4	June 28, 1854	260	2, 404	1, 000	Built at Fairhaven 1851; sent home 257 sperm, 318 whale, and 7,449 pounds bone.
North Pacific..	Sept. 28	May 22, 1854	......	289	......	
Atlantic	Apr. 19	Sept. 28, 1853	242	88	800	Built 1851; sent home 80 sperm.
Pacific Ocean ..	May 22	Mar. 16, 1854	660	1, 187	......	Sent home 137 sperm and 25 whale.
North Pacific..	July 18	May 25, 1854	363	1, 778	14, 300	Sent home 16 075 pounds bone.
....do	Oct. 9	July 20, 1854	......	2, 052	16, 100	Added 1851 from New York; sent home 25 sperm and 22,675 pounds bone.
Pacific Ocean ..	Dec. 16	Apr. 22, 1855	......	697	10, 800	
North Pacific..	July 17	June 19, 1854	23	1, 307	3, 000	Sent home 10,260 pounds bone.
Atl. and Indian.	July 17	Mar. 25, 1854	448	62	800	Bought from New York 1851.
North Pacific..	Aug. 21	May 29, 1854	1	1, 550	18, 500	Bought from New London 1851; built at Mattapoisett 1832; sent home 220 sperm and 261 whale.
Pacific Ocean ..	Aug. 5	July 28, 1855	883	5	......	Sent home 580 sperm.
North Pacific..	Sept. 9	Apr. 20, 1854	370	1, 831	1, 000	
Atlantic, &c ...	July 11	Apr. 20, 1854	200	75	......	
Pacific Ocean ..	Sept. 25	June 1, 1855	1, 278	......	......	
North Pacific..	Oct. 29	June 19, 1854	103	2, 344	24, 700	Sent home 12,321 pounds bone; did not sail again; sold and broken up, 1858.
Pacific Ocean ..	Sept. 9	May 12, 1856	2, 688	......	......	Sent home 1,800 sperm.
North Pacific..	June 2	Apr. 20, 1854	28	2, 760	25, 000	Sent home 16,250 pounds bone.
Pacific Ocean ..	Oct. 1	May 30, 1855	30	1, 434	10, 700	Sent home 19,000 pounds bone.
North Pacific..	Sept. 9	....	......	......	......	Condemned and broken up at Honolulu 1857.
....do	Sept. 3	....	......	......	......	Oil—900 barrels—shipped home; fitted from Honolulu; second mate, C. Fuller and five men washed overboard and drowned in a severe gale 1852; badly burned in September, and injured by gale; condemned at Honolulu December 1852.
Atlantic	July 26					Wrecked at sea; added 1851.
North Pacific..	Nov. 9	Mar. 12, 1854	......	1, 513	8, 400	Sent home 950 whale and 38,000 bone.
....do	Sept. 15	Apr. 20, 1854	......	2, 310	17, 000	Sent home 32,877 bone; bought from Boston; built 1839; sold to Boston 1855, for merchant-service.
....do	Oct. 9	Feb. 17, 1854	62	3, 063	16, 000	Built at Fairhaven 1851; sent home 1,850 whale and 47,498 pounds bone; sold 160 whale at Valparaiso.

Table showing returns of whaling-vessels

Name of vessel.	Class.	Tonnage.	Captain.	Managing owner or agent.
1851.				
Fairhaven, Mass.—Continued.				
Northern Light	Ship	513	William Stott	Edmund Allen
Pacific	do	314	—— Pease	R. Fish
South Boston	do	339	—— Williams	E. Sawin
William and Henry	do	261	—— Mayhew	I. F. Terry
Zone	do	365	Avery F. Parker	Levi Jenney, jr
Dartmouth, Mass.				
A. R. Tucker	Bark	220	Thomas Bailey	Abner R. Tucker
Brunswick	Ship	295	—— Wing	do
Gov. Hopkins	Brig	111	—— Taylor	do
Westport, Mass.				
Catherwood	Brig	199	—— Allen	Thomas W. Mayhew
D. Franklin	Bark	171	—— Gifford	Job Davis
Gov. Carver	do	180	—— West	Henry Wilcox
Greyhound	do	249	—— Wing	do
Harbinger	Ship	262	—— Cornell	Alexander H. Corey
Leonidas	Brig	128	—— Cornell	C. A. Church
Mattapoisett	Bark	150	—— Manchester	H. Wilcox
President	do	180	—— Cook	Andrew Hicks
Rajah	do	250	—— Fisher	H. Wilcox
Sea Fox	Brig	250	—— Spooner	A. Hicks
Sea Queen	do	263	Joseph Marshall	do
Mattapoisett, Mass.				
Cachelot	Bark	230	—— Hosmer	Wilson Barstow
Lagrange	do	170	—— Jenney	R. L. Barstow
Massasoit	do	206	—— Haskins	
Oscar	do	369	—— Dexter	S. K. Eaton
R. L. Barstow	do	208	—— Taber	R. L. Barstow
Sarah	Ship	370	Ezra Smalley	Loring Meigs
Sun	Bark	183	—— Flanders	R. L. Barstow
Edgartown, Mass.				
Almira	Ship	362	—— Jenks	Abraham Osborne
Champion	do	399	—— Ripley	Benjamin Worth
Splendid	do	392	—— Fisher	A. Osborne
Nantucket, Mass.				
Alabama	Ship	340	Benjamin Coggeshall	John H. Shaw
Citizen	do	360	Richard C. Bailey	C. G. & H. Coffin
Edward	do	339	Edward P. Mosher	Edward Field
Hero	do	313	Jos. McCleave	G. & M. Starbuck & Co
James Loper	do	348	William S. Whippey	Obed Starbuck
Massachusetts	do	360	Seth Nickerson	Zenas L. Adams
Napoleon	do	360	William Holley	J. W. Barrett & Sons
Narragansett	do	398	James Coleman	Z. L. Adams

sailing from American ports—Continued.

Whaling-ground.	Date— Of sailing.	Of arrival.	Result of voyage. Sperm-oil.	Whale-oil.	Whalebone.	Remarks.
			Bbls.	*Bbls.*	*Lbs.*	
North Pacific..	Nov. 18	Apr. 14, 1855	......	2, 360	28, 000	Built at Mattapoisett 1851; first mate, Mr. Baker, and three men drowned in Ochotsk Sea September, 1852; —— mate, Isaac Briggs, died August, 1853; sent home 1,400 whale and some bone.
Pacific Ocean ..	Feb. 19	May 18, 1854	94	865	1, 800	Sent home 266 sperm and 44,298 bone.
North Pacific..	July 15	Apr. 3, 1854	58	2, 417	11, 000	Sent home 522 sperm, 3,088 whale, and 30,000 pounds bone.
Pacific Ocean ..	Dec. 3	Aug. 19, 1855	715	......	......	Sent home 194 sperm; added 1851.
....do	June 19	May 5, 1855	96	1, 056	15, 000	Captain Parker came home sick 1853; sent home 104 sperm, 900 whale, and 15,946 bone; added 1851; formerly of Nantucket.
Atlantic	June 2	Sept. 24, 1853	332	275	......	Built at Dartmouth 1851; sent home 433 sperm and 6,700 pounds bone.
North Pacific..	Nov. 5	May 9, 1853	53	1, 595	25, 800	Bought from New Bedford 1851,
Atlantic	June 30	....	......	......	......	Lost on coast of Brazil February 10, 1853; saved 150 barrels sperm; sent home 50 whale.
Atlantic	Jan. 8	June 3, 1853	561	6	......	
....do	May 9	Mar. 14, 1853	270	......	......	
Atl. and Indian.	Dec. 4	Mar. 17, 1854	350	192	500	
....do	July 28	Nov. 8, 1853	836	4	......	Built 1851.
Pacific Ocean ..	Dec. 21	....	......	......	......	Sent home 231 sperm; condemned at Paita October 5, 1855.
Atlantic	Dec. 11	Sept. 20, 1854	431	20	......	Sent home 72 sperm.
....do	Jan. 2	Sept. 22, 1851	380	10	......	
....do	Nov. 11	Sept. 19, 1851	405	12	......	
North Pacific..	Sept. 11	Apr. 27, 1855	......	......	600	Sent home 1,000 whale, 17,400 bone; sailed under Captain Wickerson, who came home sick 1851; sold to New Bedford 1856.
Atlantic	May 12	Sept. 29, 1853	403	......	.....	Added 1851.
Pacific Ocean ..	Oct. 15	Apr. 26, 1855	1, 082	......	......	Sent home 412 sperm; built at Mattapoisett 1851.
Atlantic	Dec. 10	....	......	......	......	Sold to New Bedford 1853; returned under that port.
....do	Oct. 23	Apr. 21, 1852	31	309	......	Condemned 1855.
....do	Apr. 19	Sept. 15, 1852	325	......	......	Bought from Boston 1851.
North Pacific..	Nov. 1	Aug. 21, 1854	280	1, 091	1, 900	Captain Dexter killed by a whale January 1, 1854. Sent home 16,404 bone.
Atlantic	June 21	Sept. 5, 1853	536	20	......	Built 1851. Second mate died 1851.
North Pacific..	July 16	Apr. 22, 1855	40	1, 218	15, 000	Captain Smalley died January 2, 1852. Sent home 1,388 whale, 18,500 bone.
Atlantic	June 28	May 20, 1853	441	5	......	Formerly a packet between New Bedford and the South; added 1851.
Pacific Ocean ..	June 11	Mar. 5, 1855	100	2, 252	28, 000	Sent home 180 sperm, 500 whale, 16,000 bone.
...do	Sept. 8	Apr. 16, 1853	100	2, 000	30, 000	
North Pacific..	Oct. 1	May 1, 1854	112	1, 853	......	Added 1851; sent home 15,400 bone.
Pacific Ocean ..	June 10	Jan. 24, 1855	1, 794	......	......	Captain Coggeshall left the ship sick, and died at home, November, 1854.
North Pacific..	Oct. 28	June 27, 1855	351	1, 597	16, 121	
....do	July 23	July 27, 1854	......	......	......	Sent home 17,236 bone; bought from New Bedford. Captain Mosher took 900 barrels of oil, went to Sydney and sold it. Capt. E. E. Austin was sent to bring the ship home.
Pacific Ocean ..	Nov. 1	May 31, 1855	810	23	8, 300	
North Pacific..	Sept. 6	Apr. 9, 1855	15	1, 559	15, 700	Sent home 400 sperm, 800 whale, 15,000 bone.
....do	Sept. 20	Mar. 12, 1853	276	2, 585	40, 300	
Pacific Ocean ..	July 13	July 20, 1854	492	1, 263	......	Sold to New Bedford.
....do	July 6	May 31, 1855	1, 757	......	......	

Table showing returns of whaling-vessel

Name of vessel.	Class.	Tonnage.	Captain.	Managing owner or agent.
1851.				
Nantucket, Mass.—Continued.				
Norman	Ship	338	Joseph C. Chase	G. & M. Starbuck
Oneco	Schooner	90	Peter C. Raymond	
Palmyra	do	100	Benjamin Raymond	E. W. Perry
Peru	Bark	257	Charles E. Starbuck	David Thain
President	Ship	293	William C. Folger, 2d	Joseph Starbuck
Rambler	do	318	John Porter	Frederick W. Paddock
Spartan	do	333	James Wyer	D. Thain
Susan	do	349	Veranus Smith	do
Three Brothers	do	384	Joseph Adams	G. & M. Starbuck & Co.
Tyleston	Brig	111	Edward Swain	E. W. Gardner
Falmouth, Mass.				
Awashonks	Ship	342	—— Lawrence	Oliver C. Swift
Provincetown, Mass.				
A. Nickerson	Schooner	108	—— Cornell	J. H. Hilliard
Alexander	do		—— Young	B. Allstrum
Antarctic	do		—— Howard	J. E. Bowley
Belle Isle	do	104	—— Nye	Ebenezer Cook
Chanticleer	do	87	—— Young	Samuel Cook
Council	do	100	—— Genn	H. P. Higgins
Hanover	do		—— Holmes	T. Hilliard
H. N. Williams	do	108	—— Young	Philip Cook
Jane Howes	Brig	109	—— Nickerson	J. E. Bowley
John Adams	Schooner	104	—— Freeman	John Adams
Lewis Bruce	Brig	113	—— Young	B. Allstrum
Preston	Schooner		—— Handy	Samuel Cook
R. E. Cook	do	80	—— Cook	John Dunlap
Rienzi	do	109	—— Joseph	J. E. Bowley
Rob't Raikes	do	110	—— Swift	Ephraim Cook
Sam'l Cook	Brig	126	—— Cook	S. Cook
Sea Shell	Schooner		—— Cook	E. Cook
Shylock	do	115	—— Hersey	Nathaniel Holmes
Spartan	Bark	190	—— Cook	Stephen Nickerson
Union	Schooner	90	—— Nickerson	Jonathan Nickerson
Virginia	do	115	—— Morton	Winsor Snow
Walter Ervin	do	130		Atkins Nickerson
Walter K	do	114	—— Tillson	Henry Cook
Willis Putnam	do	100	—— Genn	E. L. Smith
Orleans, Mass.				
Esther	Brig	136	—— Macy	Winsor Snow
Virginia	Schooner	115	—— Morton	do
Holmes' Hole, Mass.				
Warren	Ship	461	—— Smith	Thomas Bradley
Sandwich, Mass.				
Amelia	Schooner	127	—— Hoxie	W. F. Lapham
Ocean	Brig	165	—— Wright	do
Lynn, Mass.				
Com. Preble	Ship	323	—— Lampher	Andrews Breed
Beverly, Mass.				
Gem	Brig	162	—— Ryder	F. W. Choate
N. D. Chase	Bark	242	—— Miller	do

sailing from American ports—Continued.

Whaling-ground.	Date— Of sailing.	Of arrival.	Result of voyage. Sperm-oil.	Whale-oil.	Whalebone.	Remarks.
			Bbls.	*Bbls.*	*Lbs.*	
Pacific Ocean ..	Oct. 21	Aug. 4, 1855	20	1,180	......	
Atlantic	May 10	Oct. 15, 1851	89	......	......	
....do	July 5	Aug. 10, 1852	67	......	......	Sent home 30 sperm; built at Plymouth 1839.
Pacific Ocean ..	July 16	May 31, 1855	664	......	......	Sent home 1,080 sperm; sold 200 blackfish.
....do	July 21	May 23, 1855	600	50	......	Sold to New Bedford 1855.
....do	Oct. 23	....	......	......	......	Condemned at Upola 1855.
....do	Oct. 26	Nov. 14, 1853	630	1,570	......	Bought the whale-oil at Navigator Islands of ship York.
....do	Dec. 5	....	......	......	......	Lost going into the Arctic, off Company Island, April 26, 1853; had 400 sperm.
North Pacific..	Oct. 15	Mar. 17, 1854	18½	2,285	26,300	Sent home 100 sperm, 1,050 whale.
Atlantic	June 18	Dec. 29, 1852	4	2	......	
North Pacific..	Aug. 12	July 25, 1854	513	1,828	......	First mate, Mr. Jones, killed by a whale 1853. Sent home 243 whale.
Atlantic	May 22	Oct. 29, 1851	110	......	......	Withdrawn 1852; lost on Manatilla reef July 16, 1852.
....do	Mar. 31	Sept. 28, 1851	45	......	......	Added 1851.
....do	May 26	Oct. 23, 1851	60	......	......	Do.
....do	Apr. 14	....	......	......	......	Run into by steamship William Penn and sunk; four men lost 1851.
North Atlantic	Mar. 25	Sept. 20, 1851	150	......	......	
Atlantic	Apr. 29	Dec. 7, 1851	25	......	......	Withdrawn 1852.
....do	May 20	Oct. 18, 1851	160	......	......	Added 1851.
....do	Apr. 3	Nov. 10, 1851	65	......	......	
....do	May 15	Oct. 15, 1851	95	......	......	
....do	Apr. 21	Oct. 16, 1851	150	......	......	
....do	Mar. 1	Sept. 29, 1851	270	......	......	
....do	May 21	Sept. 12, 1851	80	......	......	Added 1851.
....do	Jan. 7	Aug. 9, 1851	......	12	......	Blackfish.
....do	Apr. 14	Oct. 10, 1851	115	......	......	
....do	May 19	Jan. 28, 1852	......	8	......	Added 1850; withdrawn 1852.
....do	Apr. —	Oct. 26, 1851	50	......	......	
....do	May 20	Aug. 15, 1851	40	20	......	Added 1851; the 20 barrels were blackfish; withdrawn 1852.
....do	Apr. 30	Oct. 22, 1851	10	2	......	
....do	Apr. 14	Sept. 16, 1852	250	......	......	
....do	May —	June 10, 1852	60	......	......	
....do	May 19	....	......	......	......	Transferred to Orleans.
....do	....	Dec. 1, 1851	160	2	......	
....do	Apr. 29	Jan. 15, 1852	200	......	......	
....do	May 16	July 3, 1852	50	......	......	Nine men died on the voyage. Withdrawn 1853.
Atlantic	July 31	May 24, 1852	60	20	......	Formerly of Salem; wrecked near Chatham; bought by Cape Cod Whaling Company and fitted.
....do	May 19	Dec. 31, 1851	210	......	......	Added 1850.
North Pacific..	July 30	Apr. 27, 1855	43	1,330	12,000	Added 1851; badly burned by the crew 1852; sold to New Bedford 1855; sent home 12,700 bone.
Atlantic	July 3	Feb. 25, 1852	115	1	......	
North Atlantic	Mar. 29	Jan. 24, 1852	......	14	......	Added 1851.
Indian Ocean ..	Aug. 21	June 15, 1853	172	2,150	28,000	
Atlantic	Apr. 7	Nov. 24, 1851	250	......	......	Sailed once and returned leaking 8,000 strokes per hour.
Indian Ocean ..	Sept. 26	Oct. 19, 1852	420	......	......	Added 1851.

Table showing returns of whaling-vessels

Name of vessel.	Class.	Tonnage.	Captain.	Managing owner or agent.
1851.				
New London, Conn.				
Atlas	Schooner	81	—— Whipple	Perkins & Smith
Black Warrior	Bark	231	—— Bartlett	Williams & Haven
Benj. Morgan	Ship	407	—— Chappell	Perkins & Smith
Brooklyn	do	360	—— Newry	do
Candace	Bark	310	—— Walker	Williams & Haven
Clematis	Ship	311	—— Benjamin	Williams & Barnes
Clement	Bark	279	—— Lane	Miner, Lawrence & Co.
Corinthian	Ship	505	—— Rogers	Perkins & Smith
Columbus	Bark	344	—— Harris	Chester & Harris
Dove	do	151	—— Rose	Wiliiams & Haven
Dover	Ship	430	—— Havens	Benjamin Brown's Sons
Franklin	Schooner	119	—— Williams	Perkins & Smith
Gen. Williams	Ship	446	—— Forseth	Williams & Barnes
Gen. Scott	Bark	360	—— Smith	Weaver, Rogers & Co.
Hannibal	Ship	441	—— Lester	Benjamin Brown's Sons
Indian Chief	do	401	—— Bailey	Frink & Prentis
Isaac Hicks	do	495	—— Skinner	Miner, Lawrence & Co.
Jefferson	do	396	—— Williams	do
John E. Smith	Schooner	119	—— Babcock	E. V. Stoddard
Julius Cæsar	Ship	347	—— Morgan	do
Marcia	Schooner	128	—— Church	do
McLellan	Ship	376	—— Quail	Perkins & Smith
Mogul	do	395	—— Fitch	William & Barnes
Montezuma	do	424	—— Benjamin	do
N. America	Bark	388	—— Mason	Williams & Haven
New England	Ship	368	—— Pendleton	Miner, Lawrence & Co.
Superior	do	406	—— Babcock	Benjamin Brown's Sons
Venice	Bark	353	—— Harris	Weaver, Rogers & Co.
Vesper	Ship	321	—— House	Williams & Barnes
Fall River, Mass.				
Ærial	Bark	225	Charles Petty	John S. Cotton
Warren, R. I.				
Sea	Ship	807	—— Sowle	S. P. Child
Smithfield	Bark	164	—— Coit	R. B. Johnson
Warren	Ship	383	—— Heath	Joseph Smith
Newport, R. I.				
Antelope	Bark	340	Oliver Potter	Macy & Clark
Mechanic	Ship	335	J. C. Corey	Peleg Clark
Boston, Mass.				
Afton	Bark	242	—— Cannon	Oliver Locke
Rothschild	do	261	—— Small	Philip A. Locke
September	Brig	115	—— Farwell	Francis Fluker
Salem, Mass.				
Margaretta	Bark	230	—— Prior	Benjamin Webb
Mystic, Conn.				
Coriolanus	Ship	268	—— Grinnell	Charles Mallory

sailing from American ports—Continued.

Whaling-ground.	Date— Of sailing.	Of arrival.	Result of voyage. Sperm-oil.	Whale-oil.	Whalebone.	Remarks.
			Bbls.	*Bbls.*	*Lbs.*	
Desolation Isld	Aug. 12	June 14, 1856	......	115	......	
North Pacific..	July 15	....	......	......	......	Sent home 1,710 whale; shipped 212 sperm, 116 whale, to London; sold at Honolulu December 19, 1854.
....do	Oct. 7	Sept. 5, 1856	50	1, 626	13, 900	Sent home 85 sperm, 2,944 whale, 12,600 bone.
....do	July 11	Apr. 30, 1856	......	1, 342	13, 300	Sent home 3,151 whale, 27,700 bone.
....do	July 2	May 2, 1853	......	2, 075	30, 400	Sent home 57 whale.
....do	July 2	May 8, 1853	61	2, 395	37, 900	
....do	July 29	May 2, 1854	......	1,517	......	Sold to Provincetown 1854.
Desolation Isld	Aug. 19	June 24, 1853	......	3, 058	10, 000	Added 1851.
North Pacific..	Sept. 24	May 2, 1854	27	562	3,000	Sent home 40 sperm, 783 whale, 22,000 bone.
Indian Ocean ..	Dec. 16	June 27, 1854	524	15	......	
North Pacific..	Sept. 4	May 19, 1855	......	1, 212	16, 000	Sent home 40 sperm, 2,415 whale, and 12,998 pounds of bone.
Desolation Isld	July 29	June 17, 1856	......	133	......	
North Pacific..	Sept. 16	Apr. 5, 1854	73	3, 936	11, 500	
....do	July 2	Apr. 20, 1854	21	1, 921	7, 400	Sent home 18,300 bone; sold to Fairhaven 1855.
....do	June 24	Apr. 4, 1854	97	1, 678	......	Sent home 20,000 pounds of bone.
....do	July 26	Apr. 1, 1855	1	2, 303	23, 800	Captain Bailey came home sick 1853; Mr. Barker, first mate, murdered by one of the crew—a Kanaka—1852; sent home 8,500 pounds of bone.
....do	Sept. 11	Apr. 6, 1855	......	2, 165	16, 200	Sent home 40 sperm, 1,700 whale, and 48,670 pounds of bone.
Ind. and Arctic.	June 2	Feb. 9, 1853	68	2, 600	......	Sent home 41,284 pounds of bone.
Desolation Isld	Aug. 4	June 26, 1854	......	205	1, 400	Added 1851.
....do	Aug. 18	June 4, 1853	......	2, 391	10, 500	Do.
....do	Aug. 4	May 6, 1853	......	639	......	
Davis's Strait..	Feb. 8	Oct. 28, 1851	......	258	4, 900	Sailed again in 1852 and was lost in Davis's Strait.
North Pacific..	Aug. 6	June 25, 1853	26	2, 154	39, 800	Sent home 24,570 bone; sold 400 whale at Pernambuco.
....do	July 15	May 27, 1854	133	2, 444	600	
Ind. and Pacific	June 3	Apr. 20, 1855	61	860	12, 500	Sent home 40 sperm, 508 whale, 15,772 bone.
North Pacific..	Aug. 21	Mar. 29, 1854	......	1, 111	7, 200	Sent home 108 sperm, 518 whale, 25,252 bone.
....do	Oct. 4	....	......	......	......	Lost 1852 in the Arctic; had 600 whale, saved 200.
....do	Aug. 12	June 9, 1854	206	2, 266	31, 100	Sent home 5,500 bone.
....do	June 10	Apr. 19, 1855	3	1, 975	28, 300	Captain House was killed by a whale; Mr. Burch, who assumed command, died at Honolulu November 27, 1852; sent home 14,983 pounds of bone.
Atlantic	May 12	June 1, 1852	310	......	......	Added 1851.
North Pacific..	Nov. 17	Apr. 7, 1855	54	4, 721	19, 200	Bought from New York 1851; the largest whaler in service; sold 1855.
Atl. and Indian.	June 4	Apr. 22, 1853	456	......	......	Added 1851.
North Pacific..	Nov. 19	....	......	......	......	Burned July 10, 1852, in Anadir Sea.
Pacific Ocean ..	Nov. 19	May 31, 1855	50	339	6, 000	Added 1851; sent home 250 sperm, 500 whale.
North Pacific..	Aug. 16	Apr. 7, 1855	22	1, 189	......	Sold to New Bedford 1855; sent home 3,818 pounds of bone.
Indian Ocean ..	Sept. 18	May 17, 1853	......	10	......	Added 1851; withdrawn 1853; sent home 135 sperm.
Atlantic	June 1	June 15, 1852	277	......	......	
North Atlantic	Feb. 21	June 2, 1852	150	......	......	Added 1851.
Atlantic	May 3	July 26, 1852	320	37	......	Added 1851.
North Pacific..	Aug. 7	May 27, 1853	99	1, 860	24, 300	

Table showing returns of whaling-vessels

Name of vessel.	Class.	Tonnage.	Captain.	Managing owner or agent.
1851.				
Mystic, Conn.—Continued.				
Hellespont	Ship	346	—— Manwarring	Randall, Smith & Ashly.
Meteor	do	325	—— Jeffrey	do
Robin Hood	do	395	—— McGinley	C. Mallory
Romulus	do	365	—— Baker	do
Shepherdess	Bark	274	—— Watrous	Randall, Smith & Ashly.
Stonington, Conn.				
B. Williams	Ship	400	—— Pendleton	C. P. Williams
Cabinet	do	305	—— Noyes	John F. Trumbull
Cavalier	Bark	295	—— Freeman	C. P. Williams
George	do	251	—— Stevens	do
Newark	Ship	323	—— Dickens	J. F. Trumbull
S. H. Waterman	do	480	—— Hall	C. P. Williams
Sarah E. Spear	Bark	150	—— Keene	J. F. Trumbull
Tiger	Ship	311	—— Gavit	do
Tybee	do	299	—— Barber	do
United States	Bark	244	—— Wilcox	do
Greenport, N. Y.				
Delta	do	314	—— Weeks	Ireland, Wells & Carpenter.
Italy	Ship	299	—— Rowley	David G. Floyd
Neva	do	362	—— Case	Ireland, Wells & Carpenter.
Nile	do	403	—— Conklin	do
Pioneer	Bark	235	—— Baldwin	D. G. Floyd
Philip, 1st	do	293	—— Sisson	Ireland, Wells & Carpenter.
Sag Harbor, N. Y.				
Black Eagle	do	311	Jeremiah Ludlow	Thomas Brown
Columbia	do	285	—— Hallock	John Budd
Emerald	Ship	518	—— Jaggar	do
Levant	do	382	Mercator Cooper	Huntting Cooper
Mary Gardner	do	316	David Smith	Gilbert H. Cooper
Nimrod	Bark	280	—— Green	Charles T. Dering
Noble	do	273	—— Nicholl	do
Tuscany	Ship	299	—— Halsey	John Budd
Washington	Bark	236	—— Edwards	T. Brown
William Tell	Ship	370	—— Taber	do
Cold Spring, N. Y.				
Alice	Bark	281	—— White	John H. Jones
Huntsville	Ship	523	—— Smith	do
Monmouth	Bark	273	—— Ludlow	do
N. P. Tallmadge	Ship	370	—— Edwards	do
Splendid	do	473	—— Smith	do
Truro, Mass.				
Eschol	Brig	143	—— Smith	Richard Sevens

Two vessels sailed from San Francisco—the Nile and the Russell. The data in regard to San Francisco and Provincetown are extremely hard to get at; vessels are reported arriving, with no date of sailing, and sailing, with no date of arrival; and the product is often wholly ignorod in the reports. The Nile arrived September 30, 1851, with 500 whale.

sailing from American ports—Continued.

Whaling-ground.	Date—		Result of voyage.			Remarks.
	Of sailing.	Of arrival.	Sperm-oil.	Whale-oil.	Whalebone.	
			Bbls.	*Bbls.*	*Lbs.*	
North Pacific..	Sept. 1	....	......	......	......	Condemned 1855; sent home 190 sperm and 9,317 pounds of bone.
....do	Nov. 8	Mar. 23, 1856	47	1,000	22,000	Sent home 1,829 whale and 20,633 bone; one of "Stone Fleet No. 1."
....do	Sept. 13	Mar. 24, 1854	373	2,897	14,500	
....do	Aug. 16	May 11, 1854	108	1,600	12,300	
....do	Sept. 8	May 23, 1853	147	1,950	26,600	
North Pacific..	July 23	Apr. 20, 1854	......	2,959	30,000	Sent home 255 whale and 1,000 bone; sold to New Bedford 1854.
Arctic	Sept. 2	Apr. 3, 1854	250	2,375	36,000	Withdrawn 1855; sold to New York.
North Pacific..	Aug. 11	May 8, 1855	38	1,188	7,800	Withdrawn 1855; sold to New Bedford; sent home 5,246 pounds of bone.
....do.	Oct. 2	....	......	......	......	Condemned at Honolulu 1854; sent home 1,775 whale and 25,881 pounds of bone.
....do	Nov. 19	Apr. 9, 1855	......	1,380	15,000	Withdrawn 1855; sold to New Bedford; sent home 341 whale and 16,500 bone.
....do	Nov. 3	Apr. 8, 1855	......	2,640	25,000	Sent home 3,997 bone; added 1851; withdrawn 1855.
Pacific Ocean ..	Aug. 6	Sept. 18, 1852	......	Clean	......	Added 1851.
North Pacific..	Sept. 19	May 21, 1853	133	1,363	21,200	
....do	Oct. 6	May 31, 1855	80	1,288	13,000	Sent home 700 whale and 15,000 bone.
Pacific Ocean ..	Aug. 6	June 5, 1852	52	1,535	800	
Arctic	Aug. 1	....	......	......	......	Sent home 585 whale and 20,218 bone; sold to New London 1856.
....do	Aug. 2	May 10, 1854	25	2,600	12,000	Sent home 12,600 pounds of bone.
....do	Oct. 1	June 12, 1854	46	2,351	13,500	Sent home 365 whale and 18,750 bone.
....do	Sept. 1	Apr. 19, 1855	16	2,305	14,100	Broken up 1857; sent home 300 sperm and 29,592 pounds of bone.
South Atlantic	Oct. 31	May 15, 1855	250	550	3,500	
Arctic	July 14	Apr. 6, 1854	......	2,231	......	
Arctic	July 24	Apr. 5, 1854	......	718	......	Built 1851; sent home 85 whale, 20,098 bone.
North Pacific..	Aug. 2	Apr. 27, 1855	......	1,409	14,000	Sent home 7,885 pounds of bone.
....do	Aug. 19	May 12, 1855	55	2,471	14,300	Added 1851; built 1835; was a Havre packet 15 years; sent home 35,720 bone.
....do	Aug. 7	....	......	......	......	Sent home 12,560 bone; lost 1855.
South Atlantic.	July 24	Oct. 7, 1852	25	300	......	Built 1851; Captain Smith died August, 1852; ship returned in consequence.
....do	July 7	Aug. 10, 1853	690	290	1,200	Sent home 40 sperm.
....do	June 5	Aug. 6, 1853	291	600	3,500	
North Pacific..	Oct. 1	Apr. 22, 1854	......	1,600	1,200	Sent home 920 whale.
....do	Oct. 14	May 28, 1853	129	1,787	21,400	Bought from Greenport 1851.
....do	Sept. 20	Apr. 22, 1854	......	1,341	......	
North Pacific.	Oct. 6	Apr. 13, 1854	33	1,186	7,100	
....do	Dec. 4	Apr. 7, 1854	22	2,589	29,000	Sent home 370 whale and 1,700 bone.
Atl. and Indian.	Aug. 28	May 3, 1854	345	1,380	11,700	
North Pacific..	Oct. 3	Apr. 26, 1855	......	1,435	14,000	Sent home 10,960 bone; sold 1855.
....do	Oct. 15	Apr. 12, 1853	......	2,359	34,200	
Atlantic	Feb. 8	Nov. 10, 1851	175	8	......	

Table showing returns of whaling-vessels

Name of vessel.	Class.	Tonnage.	Captain.	Managing owner or agent.
1852.				
New Bedford, Mass.				
Abigail	Ship	310	Francis D. Drew	Wm. G. E. Pope
Active	Bark	333	Thomas Morrison	Cook & Snow
Addison	Ship	426	George H. Cash	Isaac B. Richmond
Alfred	Schooner	184	Philander Gifford	Wm. G. E. Pope
Anaconda	Bark	383	Thos. H. Lawrence	I. B. Richmond
Antarctic	Ship	319	Ebenezer Bradbury, jr.	Wm. P. Howland
Archer	Ship	322	G. C. Macomber	Edward W. Howland
Arnolda	do	360	Edward Harding	Jas. B. Wood & Co
Barclay	do	281	Asaph P. Taber	Henry Taber & Co
Callao	do	324	Hiram Baker	do
Caroline	do	364	Geo. W. Gifford	William Gifford
Carolina	do	395	Wanton H. Gray	S. Thomas & Co
Catalpa	Bark	260	Josiah Hamblin	I. Howland, jr., & Co
Canton	Ship	409	Andrew J. Wing	E. Perry & W. C. N. Swift
China	do	370	Willis Howes	William Phillips
Chili	do	291	Matt. Anderson	Benj. B. Howard
Cleora	Bark	263	James L. Smith	Charles Hitch & Son
Cleone	Ship	373	W. H. Sherman	Edmund Maxfield
Congress, 2d	do	376	R. M. Hathaway	Gideon Allen
Copia	do	315	Chas. H. Newell	Lemuel Kollock
Daniel wood	do	345	Jos. R. Tallman	J. B. Wood & Co
Desdemona	do	295	John Ellis	T. & A. R. Nye
Dunbarton	Bark	199	Humphrey Hathaway	I. B. Richmond
Emma C. Jones	Ship	347	Weston Jenney	Edward C. Jones
Empire	do	403	Jas. L. Henry	Abraham Barker
Falcon	do	273	Joseph Gardner	Thos. Knowles & Co
Fanny	Bark	391	D. B. Nye, jr	Swift & Allen
Gay Head	Ship	389	Richard D. Wood	J. B. Wood & Co
Geo. Howland	do	374	David C. Wight	G. & M. Howland
George and Susan	do	356	Joseph S. Jenckes	do
Hector	do	380	Henry D. Norton	William J. Rotch
Herald	do	274	George C. Rule	E. W. Howland
Hydaspe	do	313	Russel E. Snow	J. B. Wood & Co
Isabella	Bark	315	Orrick Smalley	T. Knowles & Co
Java	Ship	278	John R. Lawrence	G. & M. Howland
Jireh Perry	do	435	George Lawrence, jr	Perry & Swift
John	do	308	Otis Tilton	Frederick Parker
John A. Parker	Bark	342	Wm. L. Taber	Henry F. Thomas
Joseph Butler	do	193	——— Mayhew	I. Howland, jr., & Co
Kathleen	do	312	——— Allen	James H. Slocum
Kensington	Ship	357	Shubael Clark	David B. Kempton
Lafayette	Bark	341	Charles E. Allen	I. H. Bartlett & Son
Laetitia	do	275	Silas Alden	F. & G. R. Taber
Lancer	Ship	395	Edward F. Lakeman	Richmond & Wood
Malta	Bark	151	Philip Smith	B. B. Howard

sailing from American ports—Continued.

Whaling-ground.	Date—		Result of voyage.			Remarks.
	Of sailing.	Of arrival.	Sperm-oil.	Whale-oil.	Whalebone.	
			Bbls.	*Bbls.*	*Lbs.*	
North Pacific ..	Aug. 24	Apr. 28, 1856	296	1, 309	21, 000	Sent home 29,000 bone.
Indian Ocean ..	June 1	Mar. 4, 1856	633	1, 058	700	Bought from Baltimore 1852; sent home 84 sperm, 11,298 bone.
Pacific Ocean ..	Sept. 20	July 14, 1856	855	522	......	
Atlantic	June 12	Aug. 28, 1853	73	13	......	Sent home 85 sperm.
Pacific Ocean ..	Nov. 24	Aug. 11, 1856	1, 480	8	......	Built at Baltimore; added 1852.
....do	May 3	....	......	......	......	First mate, Edward Howland, lost overboard 1852; lost near Chatham Islands 1853; Mr. Macy, first mate, and one man lost; sent home 15 sperm.
....do	Oct. 5	May 30, 1856	1, 635	......	......	Sent home 292 sperm.
....do	July 19	Sept. 26, 1855	429	1, 913	......	Sent home 23 sperm.
Atlantic	July 7	Apr. 20, 1854	587	365	2, 400	Sent home 141 sperm.
North Pacific ..	July 27	May 27, 1855	94	2, 005	26, 100	Sent home 108 sperm, 1,584 whale, 1,800 bone.
....do	Aug 3	Mar. 8, 1856	12	1, 690	8, 200	Sent home 159 sperm, 11,100 bone.
....do	Dec. 14	July 12, 1856	202	250	4, 000	Bought from New York 1852.
Atlantic & Ind.	Aug. 12	Apr. 11, 1856	806	21	......	Formerly a freighter; built 1844; added 1852.
North Pacific ..	Aug. 10	....	......	......	......	Lost on a reef in Pacific Ocean with cargo of 1,300 barrels whale.
....do	June 22	May 29, 1856	54	1, 660	10, 600	
Pacific Ocean ..	July 13	....	395	848	......	Sent home 643 whale.
....do	May 18	Mar. 31, 1855	1, 243	......	......	Bought from Boston 1852; sent home 131 sperm.
North Pacific ..	Aug. 17	May 28, 1855	50	2, 160	30, 500	Built at Mattapoisett 1847; bought from Yarmouth 1852.
Atlantic & Ind.	May 20	Apr. 10, 1855	......	1, 822	19, 000	Bought from New York 1851; built at New York 1831; rebuilt 1840; sent home 35 sperm, 1,000 whale.
North Pacific ..	Oct. 13	May 28, 1855	......	952	9, 000	Condemned at New Bedford 1855; sent home 550 whale, 10,557 bone.
Pacific Ocean ..	Dec. 21	May 22, 1856	114	1, 029	13, 900	Built at Mattapoisett 1852; sent home 150 sperm, 1,250 whale, 10,000 bone.
....do	Oct. 25	July 6, 1855	1, 466	......	......	
....do	Dec. 25	May 26, 1854	121	168	700	Captain Hathaway died at St. Helena March 15, 1854.
Atlantic & Ind.	July 7	Aug. 15, 1854	1, 004	1, 209	3, 500	Sent home 190 sperm.
North Pacific ..	Aug. 4	Mar. 15, 1856	......	2, 012	......	Bought from Nantucket 1852; sent home 2,514 whale, 23,511 bone.
Pacific Ocean ..	July 25	June 2, 1855	116	528	2, 400	Sent home 15 sperm, 3,701 bone.
....do	Oct. 5	May 19, 1856	......	2, 075	22, 000	Bought from Nantucket 1852; sent home 9 sperm, 1,323 whale, 7,470 bone.
....do	Sept. 23	June 28, 1856	1, 502	......	......	Built at Mattapoisett 1852.
....do	Nov. 28	May 8, 1857	606	1, 171	......	Sent home 57 sperm, 3,000 bone; seized by convicts at Gallipagos Islands; recaptured by a Swedish frigate.
....do	Oct. 4	May 23, 1857	......	356	......	Sent home 716 sperm.
....do	Dec. 18	July 2, 1856	365	......	......	Sent home 731 sperm.
....do	Nov. 30	Sept. 13, 1856	646	26	......	Sent home about 150 sperm, 150 whale.
....do	July 13	May 5, 1856	752	54	......	Sent home 335 sperm.
....do	June 1	July 28, 1855	232	1, 346	7, 900	Bought from New York 1852; sent home 108 sperm, 15,269 bone.
....do	Sept. 1	Nov. 2, 1855	140	1, 414	......	Sent home 225 sperm, 17,000 bone.
....do	July 4	June 16, 1856	183	183	1, 400	Built at Newburyport 1851; sent home 1,440 sperm.
....do	May 18	....	......	......	......	Crew mutinied; killed captain, first and second mates, and several of the crew.
....do	Oct. 25	June 23, 1857	557	20	......	Built at Mattapoisett 1852; sent home 901 sperm.
Atlantic	May 4	May 26, 1854	675	143	1, 200	Bought from Nantucket 1852; sent home 291 sperm.
Indian Ocean ..	May 4	Feb. 17, 1855	491	892	6, 000	Bought from New York 1851; sent home 490 sperm, 300 whale.
Pacific Ocean ..	Oct. 11	July 25, 1857	1, 385	80	500	Bought from Baltimore 1852.
....do	Dec. 25	Oct. 19, 1856	552	......	......	First mate taken out of his boat by a line and drowned; bought from Warren 1852.
....do	May 17	Aug. 24, 1854	598	13	......	Bought from Baltimore 1852; sent home 458 sperm.
Indian Ocean ..	June 15	May 11, 1856	2, 101	......	......	Built at Newburyport 1852.
Atlantic	June 10	Apr. 21, 1854	67	......	......	Added 1852.

Table showing returns of whaling-vessels

Name of vessel.	Class.	Tonnage.	Captain.	Managing owner or agent.
1852.				
New Bedford, Mass.—Continued.				
Maria	Bark	202	Chas. C. Mooers	Samuel W. Rodman
Mars	do	270	G. P. Harrison	C. R. Tucker & Co
Mary Wilder	Ship	213	Jas. F. Cleveland	Charles Almy
March	Brig	89	—— Reynolds	William P. Howland
Mary	Ship	287	Wm. L. Slocum	I. Howland, jr., & Co
Mercator	Bark	246	Wm. R. Norton	J. A. Parker
Mercury	Ship	340	Francis L. Dimon	I. Howland, jr., & Co
Minerva Smyth	do	335	Austin Smith	do
Montezuma	Bark	196	Chas. W. Kempton	Jas. H. Slocum
Montgomery	do	248	William Cushing	Daniel Perry
Mount Vernon	Ship	352	Ebenezer F. Nye	D. R. Greene & Co
Niger	do	437	N. M. Jernegan	Hathaway & Luce
Orray Taft	Bark	176	—— Hamlin	Allen Lucas
Osceola, 2d	do	197	C. M. Skiff	J. & W. R. Wing
Osceola, 3d	do	200	E. H. Chisole	Cranston Wilcox
Pacific	Ship	385	James R. Allen	Pardon Tillinghast
Polar Star	do	475	Joseph Holley	C. R. Tucker & Co
Rainbow	do	474	H. M. Plasket	William. Gifford
Rambler	do	399	James M. Willis	F. & G. R. Taber
San Francisco	Bark	268	Harvey Phillips	William Phillips
Sappho	do	320	Jabez B. Howland	O. & E. W. Seabury
Saratoga	Ship	542	Ephraim Harding	Abraham Ashley, 2d
Silas Richards	do	454	P. S. Wilcox	Swift & Allen
St. Peter	Bark	267	Thos. G. Young	C. R. Tucker & Co
Thomas Dickason	Ship	454	Asa Taber	Alex. Gibbs
Undine	Bark	216	William Merry	T. Knowles & Co
Valparaiso	do	402	S. R. Tilton	Hathaway & Luce
Vigilant	do	282	John S. Deblois	W. & G. D. Watkins
William and Eliza	Ship	321	Ezra Pickens	H. Taber & Co
Winslow	Bark	263	D. P. Eldridge	Wm. H. Reynard
Fairhaven, Mass.				
Amazon	Ship	318	Edw'd H. Barber	Nathan Church
Joseph Maxwell	do	302	John H. Wady	F. R. Whitwell
John Coggeshall	do	338	John O. Norton	Reuben Fish
Martha	do	298	—— Meader	N. Church
Martha, 2d	do	301	—— Stewart	William G. Blackler
Ph'pe Delanoye	do	383	David G. Pierce	Warren Delano
Sam. Robertson	do	421	William Washburn	I. F. Terry
Tahmiroo	do	371	George F. Neil	Fish, Robinson & Co
William Rotch	do	290	C. Morslander	Reuben Fish
Winthrop	Bark	218	W. Woodward	Dexter Jenney
Wolga	do	285	Joseph Dimmick	Levi Jenney, jr
Dartmouth, Mass.				
H. H. Crapo	Bark	199	Spooner Jenking	Abner R. Tucker

sailing from American ports—Continued.

Whaling-ground.	Date—		Result of voyage.			Remarks.
	Of sailing.	Of arrival.	Sperm-oil.	Whale-oil.	Whalebone.	
			Bbls.	*Bbls.*	*Lbs.*	
Pacific Ocean ..	Dec. 14	Apr. 6, 1856	699	......	......	
Indian Ocean ..	July 21	Oct. 18, 1855	1,125	468	4,600	
Pacific Ocean ..	Sept. 20	May 28, 1854	974	2	......	Added 1852.
Atlantic	May 3	Dec. 14, 1852	......	4	......	
Indian Ocean ..	July 22	June 10, 1854	305	224	1,300	
Pacific Ocean ..	Oct. 28	....	......	......	......	Sent home 310 sperm and whale.
North Pacific ..	Nov. 13	Apr. 10, 1855	......	1,979	18,100	
Pacific Ocean ..	July 15	Mar. 21, 1855	1,047	1,348	13,000	Sent home 95 sperm.
Indian Ocean ..	May 25	Mar. 22, 1855	500	......	......	Sailed under Captain Abner Tripp; returned in consequence of his death.
Pacific Ocean ..	June 10	June 21, 1855	100	36	......	Bought from Nantucket 1852; built 1845.
North Pacific ..	July 28	May 4, 1855	11	1,756	19,600	Sent home 257 sperm; bought from New York.
Pacific Ocean ..	Oct. 14	Mar. 24, 1856	470	1,575	8,600	Sent home 19,140 bone.
Atlantic	May 6	Aug. 31, 1854	20	2	......	Formerly a brig; bought from Providence 1852; sent home 72 sperm.
....do	July 5	July 9, 1854	215	485	4,200	Bought from Mattapoisett 1852; built a brig in 1847; rerigged 1852; sent home 155 sperm.
....do	June 29	Apr. 20, 1854	67	......	......	Formerly a brig in southern lumber trade; built 1847; added and rerigged 1852; sent home 100 sperm.
Pacific Ocean ..	Oct. 5	Apr. 7, 1855	......	2,025	20,500	
North Pacific ..	Oct. 11	June 11, 1856	131	540	7,200	Built at Mattapoisett 1852; sent home 68 sperm, 728 whale, 6,749 bone.
....do	Oct. 26	June 2, 1856	48	960	8,000	Built at Fairhaven 1852; sent home 789 whale; 13,800 bone.
Pacific Ocean ..	Oct. 4	June 10, 1856	95	2,934	16,300	Bought from Boston 1852; sent home 91 sperm, 908 whale, 12,120 bone.
Atlantic	Dec. 14	Nov. 11, 1854	78	413	500	Bought from New York 1852; built 1849.
Pacific Ocean ..	June 1	June 22, 1855	580	7	......	Captain Howland died at Paita October 25, 1853.
North Pacific ..	Dec. 14	June 21, 1856	90	3,179	......	Sent home 36,200 bone.
South Pacific ..	May 18	....	......	......	......	Bought from Baltimore 1851; formerly a whaler from Sag Harbor; lost in Shanta Bay July 12, 1854; saved 800 whale, 14,000 bone; had sent home 325 sperm, 1,900 whale, 35,000 bone.
Indian Ocean ..	Dec. 22	....	......	......	......	Lost on Chatham Island 1855; sent home 274 sperm, 409 whale, 63,000 bone.
North Pacific ..	June 26	Apr. 26, 1856	100	1,375	13,100	Added 1852; sent home 298 sperm, 143 whale, 11,693 bone.
Indian Ocean ..	Oct. 28	....	......	......	......	Bought from New York 1852; missing.
Pacific & N. W.	Oct. 14	May 19, 1856	535	768	1,400	Sent home 373 sperm and whale and 9,631 bone.
Pacific Ocean ..	June 29	July 9, 1855	202	1,060	......	Added 1852; sent home 135 sperm, 12,100 bone.
Indian Ocean ..	Dec. 18	May 27, 1856	1,287	......	......	
Atlantic	May 22	June 6, 1855	227	......	......	Formerly in merchant-service; added 1852; sent home 297 sperm, 250 whale.
North Pacific ..	Sept. 29	July 27, 1856	21	1,984	......	Sent home 30,600 bone.
Pacific Ocean ..	Sept. 8	May 7, 1855	1,210	......	......	
North Pacific ..	Oct. 25	May 3, 1855	.....	2,401	......	Bought from New Bedford 1852; sent home 112 whale, 12,900 bone.
Pacific Ocean ..	Dec. 14	July 20, 1857	870	28	......	
Indian Ocean ..	May 19	Nov. 16, 1857	1,607	......	......	
Pacific Ocean ..	Sept. 6	Sept. 28, 1855	225	873	......	Sent home 211 sperm, 523 whale, 15,568 bone.
North Pacific ..	Aug. 18	Apr. 5, 1856	86	3,000	10,000	Sent home 56 sperm, 117 whale.
....do	June 29	Apr. 6, 1856	......	1,172	......	Sent home 120 sperm, 11,000 bone.
Pacific Ocean ..	Jan. 3	May 22, 1856	335	......	......	Bought from Boston 1852; sold to New Bedford 1856.
Atlantic	Jan. 1	Apr. 25, 1855	852	73	......	Bought from Bristol 1851.
Indian Ocean ..	Oct. 25	June 9, 1855	386	......	......	
Pacific Ocean ..	Aug. 13	May 1, 1854	869	8	......	Built 1852; sent home 98 sperm.

Table showing returns of whaling-vessels

Name of vessel.	Class.	Tonnage.	Captain.	Managing owner or agent.
1852.				
Westport, Mass.				
Elizabeth	Bark	270	Edward G. Sowle	Andrew Hicks
George and Mary	do	165	George Manchester	Rescom Macomber
Janet	do	194	John H. Ricketson	Henry Wilcox
Mattapoisett	do	150	Benjamin C. Wing	do
Sacramento	do	218	James W. Sowle	Alex. H. Corey
Solon	do	129	Joseph E. Smith	Henry Smith
T. Winslow	do	136	Allen Hart	John Hicks
U. States	do	217	Reuben C. Hicks	A. Hicks
Mattapoisett, Mass.				
America	Brig	148	—— Clark	R. L. Barstow
Annawan	do	159	—— Phinney	Seth Freeman
Clara Bell	Bark	295	Daniel Flanders	R. L. Barstow
Excellent	Brig	70	Benjamin Smith	John T. Atsatt
Massasoit	Bark	206	Amos Haskins	Caleb King, jr
Sarah	do	179	Bartlett Mayhew	Wilson Barstow
Samuel and Thomas	do	191	Ephraim Poole	R. L. Barstow
Willis	do	164	—— Briggs	do
Newport, R. I.				
George	Bark	220	—— Dexter	Josiah S. Munroe
William Lee	Ship	311	L. Gruninger	do
New London, Conn.				
Corea	Ship	365	—— Cranskie	Frink & Prentis
Delaware	do	299	C. Strong Holt	Williams & Barnes
Exile	Schooner	83	—— Butler	E. V. Stoddard
H. Brewer	Bark	293	—— Brown	Perkins & Smith
Iris	do	245	—— Rice	Frink & Prentis
N. S. Perkins	Ship	309	—— Allyn	
Pearl	Bark	195	—— Forsyth	Williams & Haven
Peruvian	Ship	388	—— Morgan	E. V. Stoddard
Topaz	Brig	138	—— Anthony	Benj. Brown's Sons
Stonington, Conn.				
Byron	Bark	170	—— Holt	John F. Trumbull
Cincinnati	Ship	457	—— Williams	F. Pendleton & Co
Flying Cloud	Schooner	100	—— Wilcox	J. F. Trumbull
Sarah E. Spear	Bark	150	—— Pendleton	do
United States	do	244	—— Wilcox	do
Greenport, N. Y.				
Caroline	Ship	252	J. M. Case	Wells & Carpenter
Pioneer	Brig	235	H. A. Babcock	David G. Floyd
Mystic, Conn.				
Æronaut	Ship	265	—— Eldridge	Charles Mallory
Hudson	do	368	—— Clift	Geo. W. Ashbey & Co
Leander	Bark	213	—— Holmes	C. Mallory
Lion	Schooner	150	—— Clark	do
Washington	do	190	—— Eldridge	G. W. Ashbey & Co
Sag Harbor, N. Y.				
Charlotte	Brig	230	—— Halsey	William R. Post
Gentleman	Bark	227	—— Cartwright	Gilbert H. Cooper
Mary Gardner	do	316	—— Lowen	do
Odd Fellow	do	239	—— Young	Thomas Brown

sailing from American ports—Continued.

Whaling-ground.	Date— Of sailing.	Date— Of arrival.	Result of voyage. Sperm-oil.	Result of voyage. Whale-oil.	Result of voyage. Whalebone.	Remarks.
			Bbls.	*Bbls.*	*Lbs.*	
Atlantic	July 17	Aug. 19, 1854	213	216	600	Added 1852.
....do	June 23	Apr. 3, 1854	101	15		Built 1852, at Dartmouth.
....do	June 18	July 26, 1854	340	......	......	
....do	May 30	Sept. 6, 1853	117	......	......	
Indian Ocean	July 22	July 27, 1854	472	......	......	Added 1852, from Providence; second mate, T. Allen, killed by a whale August, 1852.
Atlantic	July 9	Oct. 15, 1853	115	40	......	
....do	June 14	Aug. 14, 1853	151	25	......	
Atlantic & Ind.	Nov. 11	Apr. 11, 1856	631	8	......	Sent home 13 sperm.
Atlantic	Apr. 27	Sept. 19, 1853	222	7	......	
....do	May 4	Oct. 29, 1853	134	4	......	
Atlantic & Ind.	Aug. 7	June 27, 1855	794	91	2,000	Built 1852 at Mattapoisett.
Atlantic	June 10	June 27, 1853	30	6	......	Added 1852; sent home 17 sperm.
....do	Nov. 20	July 24, 1853	60	......	......	
....do	Dec. 6	Dec. 3, 1853	393	......	......	
....do	Sept. 5	Sept. 1, 1854	389	11	......	
....do	May 3	Apr. 21, 1854	363	24	......	
Indian Ocean	Sept. 29	May 15, 1854	......	......	......	Added 1852; Captain Dexter died April 18, 1853; no oil reported.
Indian & Pacific	Feb. 14	May 38, 1856	700	......	......	Illegally detained in Tombez three months.
North Pacific	....	Apr. 19, 1853	......	1,652	37,000	Added 1852.
....do	July 14	May 8, 1857	......	1,116	......	Added 1852; sent home 1,750 whale, 62,200 bone.
Desolation Isld	Aug. 18	June 12, 1859	......	212	......	
....do	Sept. 29	July 15, 1854	137	1,748	6,400	Added 1852; built 1850 at Robinson, Me.
South Atlantic	Oct. 7	July 15, 1856	32	700	......	Added 1852; sent home 900 whale, 8,000 bone.
North Pacific	Sept. 22	Mar. 18, 1857	......	1,296	......	Built 1852; sent home 328 whale, 21,045 bone.
Atlantic & Ind	Mar. 10	Apr. 8, 1854	47	388	2,900	Added 1852; sent home 369 sperm, 50 whale, 1,400 bone.
Desolation Isld.	Aug. 19	July 6, 1854	43	1,946	4,300	
Atlantic	June 23	....	......	......	......	Wrecked and condemned at Falkland Islands April, 1853; oil, 95 barrels, saved; added 1852.
South Atlantic	June 1	Nov. 13, 1853	......	680	4,000	Withdrawn 1855; sold to New Bedford.
Indian Ocean	Aug. 24	May 7, 1856	......	1,382	17,000	
Patagonia	July 20	May 7, 1853	......	40	......	Added 1852 from Rockland; built 1851.
S. Shetland I	Sept. 27	May 18, 1853	......	530	......	Elephant.
Patagonia	July 20	May 10, 1853	......	2,029	......	
South Atlantic	Aug. 19	Aug. 5, 1854	700	300	......	
....do	Oct. 15	Sept. 3, 1852	150	......	......	Sold to New Bedford 1855.
S. Shetland I	Aug. 9	May 22, 1853	......	1,188	......	
Patagonia	July 10	May 18, 1854	......	220	1,500	Hudson seized at Falkland Islands with schooner Washington, her tender, by an English vessel; released by United States ship Germantown; sold to Fairhaven 1855.
South Atlantic	Sept. 16	Apr. 13, 1854	56	1,144	8,500	
S. Shetland I	Aug. 18	July —, 1853	......	......	......	Added 1852; no report of oil.
Patagonia	July 12	May 12, 1854	......	......	......	No report of oil.
South Atlantic	July 21	June 21, 1854	134	204	......	Captain Halsey left in 1853, sick.
North Pacific	Aug. 30	Apr. 24, 1856	39	134	3,000	Added 1852 from New Suffolk; withdrawn 1856; sent home 7,000 bone.
....do	Nov. 27	May 15, 1856	......	1,207	18,600	Sent home 247 whale, 12,740 bone.
South Atlantic	Aug. 2	Mar. 16, 1854	137	1,190	9,200	

Table showing returns of whaling-vessels

Name of vessel.	Class.	Tonnage.	Captain.	Managing owner or agent.
1852.				
San Francisco, Cal.				
Aquetnet	Ship	300	—— Taylor	Chas. H. Todd
Columbia	Schooner	110	—— Phillips	Martin Phillips
Emily Farnham	Ship	216	—— Miller	Brigham & Reynolds
Emperor	Schooner	110	—— Minor	J. B. Minor
Mary Helen	Brig	160	—— Scammon	Harrington & Ludlow
Nile	Ship	320	Otis Webb	Moore & Folger
Russell	Bark	301	—— Cootey	do
Zoroaster	Brig	159	—— Thomas	Webb & Harris
Sippican, Mass.				
Altamaha	Schooner	119	Chas. B. Hammond	Stephen C. Luce
Holmes' Hole, Mass.				
Helen Augusta	Bark	270	—— West	Thomas Bradley
Nantucket, Mass.				
Barclay	Ship	301	David Cottle	John H. Shaw
Catawba	do	335	Obed Swain, 2d	
Constitution	do	318	Joseph Winslow	C. G. & H. Coffin
Daniel Webster	do	336	Henry Starbuck	Zenas L. Adams
Gazelle	do	340	William Upham	G. & M. Starbuck & Co.
Homer	Brig	140	Joseph Fisher	Kelley, Coffin & Co.
Mary	Ship	369	Benjamin C. Sayer	Edward W. Perry
Memnon	do	430	James H. Haughton	E. Field & F. C. Sanford
Oneco	Schooner	90	Alex. G. Brown	E. G. Kelley
Palmyra	do	105	Abraham Swain	Matthew Crosby, jr.
Peruvian	Ship	334	Edward B. Hussey, jr.	Robert F. Gardner
Planter	do	340	Henry Pease	E. W. Perry
Richard Mitchell	do	386	Thad. C. Defriez	Field & Sanford
Edgartown, Mass.				
Ellen	Bark	232	James E. Huxford	Wm. H. Munroe
Mary	Ship	343	Gustavus A. Baylies	Abraham Osborn
Sarah	Bark	286		
Walter Scott	Ship	369	—— Collins	Benjamin Worth
Sandwich, Mass.				
Amelia	Schooner	127	Abraham Hoxie	W. F. Lapham
Ocean	Brig	165	—— Chadwick	do
Provincetown, Mass.				
Alleghany	Schooner		—— Cook	
Alexander	do	75		B. Allstrum
Antarctic	do	136	—— Snow	J. E. Bowley
Chanticleer	do	87	—— Cook	Samuel Cook
E. Nickerson	Brig	131	—— Ryder	Enoch Nickerson
F. Bunchinia	Bark	200	Francis B. Tuck	Enas Nickerson
Franklin	do	172	—— Soper	Samuel Soper
Hanover	Schooner	114	—— Holmes	T. Hilliard
Harriet Neal	do	125	—— Rider	R. L. Thatcher
H. N. Williams	do	108	—— Joseph	Philip Cook
Jane Howes	Brig	109	—— Doyle	J. E. Bowley
John Adams	Schooner	104	Reuben Freeman	John Adams
Lewis Bruce	Brig	113	—— Young	B. Allstrum
Louisa	Schooner	109	—— Handy	S. Cook
Parker Cook	Bark	135	—— Cook	Ephraim Cook
Phenix	Brig	120	—— Puffer	
Preston	Schooner	75	—— Handy	S. Cook

sailing from American ports—Continued.

Whaling-ground.	Date— Of sailing.	Date— Of arrival.	Result of voyage. Sperm-oil.	Result of voyage. Whale-oil.	Result of voyage. Whalebone.	Remarks.
			Bbls.	*Bbls.*	*Lbs.*	
Arctic	Apr. 3	Oct. 31, 1852		500		
Ceros Island	Apr. 1	Aug. 11, 1852		200		Elephant.
N. W Coast	Apr. 15					No report.
Ceros Island	Apr. 1					No report.
Elephanting	Apr. 1	Aug. 26, 1852		350		Elephant.
Pacific & Arctic	Jan. 25	Oct. 30, 1852		1,800		
....do	Jan. 19	Sept. 21, 1852		1,500		
Gulf of Cal	May 1	Aug. 18, 1853	275	100		The 100 barrels were elephant-oil.
Atlantic	July —	Aug. 15, 1853	60	40		Added 1852; withdrawn 1853.
South Atlantic	June 23	Mar. 12, 1854	320	870	3,000	Added 1852 from New Bedford; built 1849; sent home 377 sperm, 510 whale, 2,400 bone.
Pacific Ocean	July 13					Condemned at Tahiti 1856; oil shipped home by schooner Heloise and lost near Rio.
....do	Dec. 25	May 31, 1857	789			Sent home 417 barrels sperm; Broken up 1856.
....do	Sept. 2	July 14, 1856	1,600	130		
....do	Aug. 28	July 15, 1856	750			Sold to New Bedford.
....do	Dec. 15	June 1, 1857	1,060			Built 1852 at Mattapoisett; Captain Upham died on the voyage; sold to New Bedford.
Atlantic	June 6	Sept. 12, 1854	165	25		Built 1848 at Woolwich, Me.
Pacific Ocean	Aug. 5	May 11, 1856	300	1,200		
....do	Oct. 2					Built 1852 at Newburyport; sent home 443 barrels sperm; burned at Payta October, 1854.
Atlantic	May 20	June 21, 1853	Clean			
....do	Sept. 26	Aug. 22, 1853	60	30		
Indian Ocean	Dec. 6	Oct. 19, 1856	1,000			Broken up at New Bedford 1857.
Pacific Ocean	May 19	Aug. 7, 1856	1,300	100		Was taken upon the marine railway at Brant Point, Nantucket, and the hull repaired; burned there in 1859.
....do	Dec. 22	July 14, 1856	734			Sent home 350 barrels sperm; sold to Edgartown.
Sooloo Sea	June 1	Apr. 20, 1856	835	382	6,300	Added 1852 from New York; built 1848; sent home 30 sperm.
Pacific Ocean	June 8	Apr. 28, 1856	77	1,857	14,100	Added 1852.
						Condemned at Callao 1852.
North Pacific	Jan. 28	Aug. 10, 1855	168	628	4,500	Added 1851.
Atlantic	June 10	Mar. 19, 1853	129	4		
....do	Feb. 26	Feb. 15, 1853	250			Formerly a Boston and Baltimore packet; added 1851.
Atlantic	May 16	Sept. 14, 1852		150		Added 1852.
....do	Apr. —	Aug. 6, 1852	160			
....do	Jan. 12	Oct. 20, 1852	240	50		
....do	Mar. 27	Sept. 25, 1852	120			
....do	Jan. 12	Oct. 2, 1852	175	100		
....do	May 20	May 9, 1854	520	29		Built 1852; sent home 220 barrels humpback.
....do	Jan. 27	Oct. 29, 1852	230	8		Withdrawn 1853.
....do	May 22	Oct. 14, 1852	240			
....do	Mar. 22	Sept. 11, 1852	175			
....do	Feb. 1	Jan. 15, 1854	81	7		
....do	Mar. 24	Apr. 6, 1853	60			
....do	Apr. 26	Sept. 3, 1852	205			
....do	Apr. 2	Nov. 2, 1852	170			Sold to Orleans 1853.
....do	May 14	Sept. 10, 1852		250		
....do	Apr. 26	Nov. 12, 1853	115			
....do	June 29	Jan. 10, 1854	202			Added 1852.
....do	May 5	Sept. 16, 1852	120			

Table showing returns of whaling-vessels

Name of vessel.	Class.	Tonnage.	Captain.	Managing owner or agent.
1852.				
Provincetown, Mass.—Continued.				
R. E. Cook	Schooner	80	—— Nickerson	John Dunlap
Rienzi	...do	109	—— Katon	J. E. Bowley
S. R. Soper	...do	130	—— Soper	S. Soper
Sam'l Cook	Brig	126	—— Smith	S. Cook
Shylock	Schooner	115	—— Green	Nathaniel Holmes
Union	...do	90	—— Genn	Jonathan Nickerson
Walter Erwin	...do	130	—— Nickerson	Atkins Nickerson
Walter K	...do	114	—— Tilson	Henry Cook
Orleans, Mass.				
Corvo	Bark	175	William Martin	Thomas A. Snow
Esther	Brig	136	—— Hopkins	Heman Smith
Virginia	Schooner	115	—— Pettengill	...do
Truro, Mass.				
Eschol	Brig	143	—— Smith	Richard Stevens
Germ	...do	171	—— Ryan	...do
Beverly, Mass.				
B. Franklin	Bark	164	—— Brown	F. W. Choate
Gem	Brig	162	—— Cook	...do
N. D. Chase	Bark	242	—— Chase	...do
Boston, Mass.				
Rothschild	Bark	261	—— Small	Philip A. Locke
September	Brig	115	—— Heath	Francis Fluker
Fall River, Mass.				
Ærial	Bark	225	—— Baker	John S. Cotton
Caravan	Ship	330	—— Bragg	Wm. Lindsey
D. M. Hall	Bark	263	—— Manchester	John S. Cotton
Salem, Mass.				
Margaretta	Bark	230	—— Holmes	Benjamin Webb
Warren, R. I.				
Belle	Bark	286	—— Borden	S.P. Child
Benjamin Rush	Ship	385	—— Munroe	...do
Bowditch	...do	399	—— Waldron	...do
Covington	Bark	351	—— Newman	C. T. Child
Florence	...do	326	Charles Barton	R. B. Johnson
Mary Frances	...do	311	—— Smith	S. P. Child
Millinoket	...do	180	—— Worth	R. B. Johnson
1853.				
New Bedford, Mass.				
Adeline	Ship	329	Joseph Brotherson	C. R. Tucker & Co
Abm. Barker	...do	400	Abm. Barker, jr	Abraham Barker
Afton	Bark	249	James Archer	F. & G. R. Taber
Alfred	Schooner	184	R. W. Dexter	William G. E. Pope
America	Bark	257	Abner West	Jos. A. Beauvais
Andrews	...do	303	Obed Smith	William P. Howland
Brandt	Ship	310	Henry M. Bonney	Alexander Gibbs
Balæna	...do	301	John S. Dorman	J. & J. Howland
Bevis	Bark	214	Seth D. McFarlin	Benjamin B. Howard
Canton Packet	Ship	274	Gilb. B. Borden	I. H. Bartlett & Son
Chas. W. Morgan	...do	351	Tristram P. Ripley	I. Howland, jr., & Co
Charles	...do	290	John Manter	L. Kollock & Son
Champion	...do	336	William B. Waterman	James D. Thompson
Charleston Packet	Bark	184	Benjamin F. Ellis	Thomas Knowles & Co
Chris. Mitchell	Ship	387	Frederick Slocum	David B. Kempton

sailing from American ports—Continued.

Whaling-ground.	Date—		Result of voyage.			Remarks.
	Of sailing.	Of arrival.	Sperm-oil.	Whale-oil.	Whalebone.	
			Bbls.	*Bbls.*	*Lbs.*	
Atlantic	Apr. 30	Aug. 8, 1852	150			
do	Apr. 16	Oct. 14, 1852	170			
do	Apr. 16	Dec. 20, 1852	85			Added 1852.
do	May 26	Aug. 29, 1853	154			
do	Mar. 12	Dec. 8, 1852	10			Withdrawn 1853.
do	June 8	Sept. 9, 1852		160		
do	Mar. 22	Jan. 11, 1853	150			
do	Apr. 29	June 27, 1853	74			Also 15 barrels blackfish.
Atlantic	May 19	Oct. 27, 1853	360			Added 1852 from New York.
do	June 28	July 30, 1853	70	25		
do	Apr. 24	Sept. 10, 1852	275			
Atlantic	June —	Oct. 20, 1853	70			
do	Apr. 26					Bought from Boston 1852; condemned at Saint Thomas November 4, 1852.
Atlantic	June 15	Sept. 21, 1853	250	50		
do	Feb. 16	Apr. 28, 1853	300			
do	Dec. 18	Oct. 30, 1854	260			Added 1851.
Atlantic	Aug. 14	Aug. 8, 1854	291	4		Sold to Orleans 1854.
do	July 8	June 18, 1853	120	150		Sold to Orleans 1853.
Atlantic	July 13	Sept. 12, 1853	80	41		Sent home 31 sperm.
North Pacific	Sept. 22	Apr. 14, 1856		1,944	11,600	Sold to New Bedford 1856; sent home 20,303 bone.
Indian Ocean	June 8	Sept. 23, 1852	140	2		Added 1852; sailed again October 27, 1852; returned September 5, 1853, with 259 sperm and 1 whale.
Atlantic	Sept. 17	Dec. 8, 1853	180	30		
Pacific Ocean	Aug. 15	Mar. 24, 1856	114	498		Built at Warren 1852; sent home 5,600 bone.
N. W. Coast	Oct. 13	June 16, 1853	50	40		Put into New Bedford; Captain Munroe and three men killed by a whale February 24, 1853; crew discouraged.
North Pacific	Aug. 19	May 20, 1856		2,524	16,500	Sent home 22,050 bone.
do	July 20	Apr. 14, 1856	32	1,538	2,700	Sent home 25 sperm, 206 whale, 20,000 bone.
Indian Ocean	Sept. 22	June 5, 1855	1,118	100		Added 1852.
Pacific Ocean	Sept. 19	June 25, 1856	804			
Indian Ocean	May 24	Apr. 29, 1855	240			Third mate died at sea 1852; sold to New Bedford 1855.
Pacific Ocean	Aug. 29	July 12, 1856	33	1,674	14,400	Sent home 1,236 whale, 31,320 bone.
North Pacific	July 20	May 6, 1857	138	430	5,100	
Atlantic	Aug. 9	May 5, 1856	336	67		Bought from Boston 1853.
do	Nov. 5	Apr. 7, 1855	86	40		Sold to Boston for a Fayal packet 1855.
do	May 7	Sept. 22, 1854	309	61		Sold to Mattapoisett 1855.
Pacific Ocean	June 20	Mar. 25, 1858	530			Sent home 200 sperm.
						Lost on Gallipagos Islands 1853.
do	Sept. 16	May 13, 1858	970			Sent home 473 sperm.
Indian Ocean	July 27	May 27, 1856	642	5		
North Pacific	Nov. 7	Apr. 24, 1857	17	1,401	13,300	Sent home 400 sperm, 542 whale, 11,500 bone.
do	Sept. 20	Apr. 27, 1856	268	1,958	12,000	Sent home 10,700 bone.
Pacific Ocean	Sept. 1					Lost 1855.
do	Sept. 22	July 3, 1855	511	1,841	27,000	Sent home 90 sperm.
Indian Ocean	Sept. 16					Condemned at Mahe 1853.
North Pacific	July 5	Apr. 14, 1856	129	2,633	14,600	Bought from Nantucket 1853; sent home 12,000 bone.

Table showing returns of whaling-vessels

Name of vessel.	Class.	Tonnage.	Captain.	Managing owner or agent.
1853.				
New Bedford, Mass.—Continued.				
Cicero	Ship	252	Fobes W. Manchester	L. Kollock & Son
City	...do	351	S. Henry Gifford	Abm. H. Howland
Clarice	Bark	237	Peleg W. Gifford	Edward C. Jones
Condor	Ship	349	Stephen Kempton	Charles W. Morgan
Cortes	...do	382	Charles F. Stetson	G. & M. Howland
Cornelia	Bark	219	Reuben W. Crapo	L. Kollock & Son
Cossack	...do	256	Ansel Tripp	Charles Hitch & Son
Edward	...do	274	Abner Smith	T. Knowles & Co
Eagle	Ship	336	——— Cannon	Swift & Perry
Eliza F. Mason	...do	582	Nathaniel M. Jernegan	I. Howland, jr., & Co
Florida	...do	330	Joseph C. Little	Edward C. Jones
Franklin	Bark	273	Roland T. Packard	Isaac M. West
Franklin, 2d	...do	219	Samuel Lee	Francis Post
Franklin	Ship	333	Josiah Richmond	William P. Howland
Garland	...do	243	William C. Parsons	Rodney French
Gen. Pike	...do	313	Henry Tew	William Gifford
George	...do	280	Jonathan Jenney	John A. Parker
Gideon Howland	...do	379	Charles R. Bryant	I. Howland, jr., & Co
Gov. Troup	...do	430	Anthony Milton	E. C. Jones
Hecla	Bark	207	Henry T. Gifford	T. Knowles & Co
Hercules	...do	335	Joshua W. Potter	Perry & Swift
Hibernia	Ship	327	John M. Honeywell	Robert Gibbs
Hope	Bark	186	Crary Waite	W. & G. D. Watkins
Illinois	Ship	413	George A. Covell	Wood & Nye
Iris	...do	311	John C. Weeks	E. C. Jones
James Andrews	Bark	275	Benjamin Kelley	Charles Hitch & Son
James Arnold	Ship	393	Thomas Sullivan	Henry Taber & Co
Jireh Swift	...do	454	William Earl	Swift & Allen
John Dawson	Bark	237	Samuel H. Crowell	J. & W. R. Wing
Joshua Bragdon	...do	270	Benjamin Swain	Lawrence Grinnell
Junior	Ship	378	S. H. Andrews	D. R. Greene & Co
J. E. Donnell	Bark	343	John Charry	Swift & Allen
Keoka	...do	250	John G. Howland	James H. Slocum
King Fisher	Ship	425	Martin Palmer	J. Bourne, jr
Lagoda	...do	341	Benjamin B. Lamphier	...do
Lapwing	...do	432	William Weeks	E. C. Jones
Levi Starbuck	...do	376	William Jernegan	E. W. Howland
Lewis	...do	308	Charles A. Bonney	Chapman & Bonney
Lexington	Bark	201	Hilliard Mayhew	B. B. Howard
Liverpool	Ship	306	Henry P. Barker	Abm. Barker
Louisiana	...do	297	Jeremiah C. Norton	T. & A. R. Nye
Louisa	Bark	316	Daniel B. Green	Swift & Allen
Majestic	Ship	297	Thomas Percival	S. Thomas & Co
Marcella	Bark	210	Benjamin S. Morton	C. R. Tucker & Co
Marcia	Ship	315	Isaac H. Wing	E. W. Howland
Mary Frazier	...do	288	James S. Hazard	Benjamin F. Howland
Mary Ann	Bark	214	A. H. Macomber	J. A. Parker
Metacom	Ship	360	E. H. Woodbridge	J. B. Wood & Co
Midas	...do	326	Ezra T. Howland	...do

sailing from American ports—Continued.

Whaling-ground.	Date— Of sailing.	Date— Of arrival.	Result of voyage. Sperm-oil.	Result of voyage. Whale-oil.	Result of voyage. Whalebone.	Remarks.
			Bbls.	*Bbls.*	*Lbs.*	
Pacific Ocean..	July 7	Apr. 14, 1856	82	643	6, 300	Sent home 6,140 bone.
....do	June 20	....	......	......	......	Lost in Saghalien Bay, September 7, 1854.
....do	Oct. 16	June 2, 1857	1, 270	11	.....	
North Pacific ..	Sept. 16	May 19, 1856	169	1, 694	700	Sent home 40 whale.
....do	Sept. 13	Feb. 22, 1857	691	1, 834	11, 200	Sent home 14,000 bone.
South Atlantic.	Oct. 24	May 7, 1857	93	590	1, 800	Sent home 403 sperm, 205 whale, 2,500 bone.
North Pacific ..	Aug. 1	Apr. 24, 1857	76	1, 279	9, 300	Sent home 7,170 bone.
....do	Oct. 6	May 11, 1856	25	1, 982	15, 000	Sent home 10,361 bone.
....do	Oct. 12	Apr. 5, 1856	......	1, 964	24, 200	Sent home 350 whale, 6,500 bone.
....do	Dec. 2	Apr. 10, 1857	2	1, 122	16, 80[illegible]	Bought from Baltimore 1853; built 1851; fired by crew and considerably burned 1855; sent home 20 sperm, 997 whale, 12,300 bone.
....do	Oct. 15	Sept. 4, 1856	312	1, 938	.....	Sent home 7,659 bone.
Pacific Ocean..	Sept. 1	Sept. 16, 1857	724	......	......	Sent home 406 sperm, 14,790 bone.
....do	June 25	July 8, 1857	214	19	......	Bought from Warren 1852; sent home 331 sperm.
North Pacific ..	Sept. 5	May 6, 1857	210	1, 610	7, 700	
Pacific Ocean..	Nov. 16	Apr. 10, 1858	627	74	......	Sent home 405 sperm.
North Pacific ..	Nov. 17	June 15, 1856	152	1, 154	5, 400	Sent home 8,580 bone; Captain Tew died May 11, 1856.
Atlantic & Ind.	Sept. 20	Aug. 2, 1857	42	937	.....	Sent home 54 sperm, 9,000 bone.
North Pacific ..	Sept. 2	May 7, 1857	......	1, 278	5, 500	Sent home 84 sperm, 1,026 whale, 20,000 bone.
....do	Aug. 2	Mar. 16, 1856	......	3, 301	......	Sent home 14,000 bone.
Indian Ocean ..	Apr. 21	Nov. 16, 1855	192	......	.....	
North Pacific ..	Dec. 1	May 30, 1857	1, 845	.....	.....	
Atlantic & Ind	June 7	Aug. 8, 1857	199	537	.....	Sent home 45 whale, 12,000 bone.
Indian Ocean ..	Aug. 16	May 4, 1856	905	.....	......	Sent home 1,209 sperm.
North Pacific ..	Oct. 18	July 2, 1857	212	668	5, 100	
Indian Ocean ..	June 16	June 9, 1854	62	......	......	Sent home 27 sperm,
North Pacific ..	Dec. 13	Oct. 8, 1857	......	1, 189	......	Sent home 450 whale, 3,000 bone; Captain Kelley was hurt in Marguerita Bay.
Pacific Ocean ..	May 3	Nov. 29, 1856	2, 550	63	500	Built 1852.
North Pacific ..	Sept. 6	May 5, 1857	45	1, 746	2, 900	Built at Dartmouth 1853. Sent home 973 whale, 12,000 bone.
Atlantic & Pac	May 2	....	......	......	......	Added 1853.
Pacific Ocean ..	Oct. 29	Aug. 2, 1867	314	46	......	Added 1853; sent home 875 sperm, 561 whale.
North Pacific ..	Sept. 17	May 16, 1857	......	469	5, 000	Sent home 20,100 bone.
....do	Aug. 30	Apr. 11, 1857	......	2, 536	7, 700	Sent home 20,481 bone; sold to Fairhaven and broken up 1857.
Pacific Ocean..	Oct. 29	May 7, 1857	147	26	......	Formerly a merchantman; added 1853; sold to Westport 1857.
North Pacific ..	Sept. 22	....	......	......	......	Sent home 402 whale, 19,100 bone; built at Gardiner, Me., 1853; sailed once and returned badly damaged, having been run into by a New York ship; lost on Company's Island May 13, 1855; had 500 sperm, 1,200 whale.
....do	Nov. 3	May 25, 1856	.....	1, 683	23, 000	Captain Lamphier drowned by the upsetting of his boat at Shantoe Islands October 9, 1855; sent home 149 sperm, 825 whale, 12,500 bone.
Atlantic & Ind.	Aug. 11	Feb. 27, 1856	2, 100	175	......	Built at Mattapoisett 1853.
North Pacific ..	Oct 12	Apr. 30, 1857	......	2, 302	9, 600	Sent home 390 sperm, 50 whale, 22,865 bone.
....do	Aug. 15	May 6, 1857	8	2, 267	......	Added 1853; sent home 520 whale, 38,600 bone.
Indian Ocean ..	Apr. 19	Nov. 14, 1854	52	28	......	Sent home 321 sperm.
North Pacific ..	Oct. 12	June 3, 1857	72	1, 270	3, 300	Sent home 300 whale, 10,000 bone; sold to Dartmouth 1857.
Pacific Ocean ..	July 9	Sept. 8, 1857	1, 000	......	.....	
North Pacific ..	Aug. 2	July 12, 1856	157	1, 543	19, 200	Sent home 580 whale, 10,000 bone.
....do	July 20	Apr. 15, 1857	107	1, 370	......	Sent home 8,100 bone.
Pacific Ocean..	Nov. 23	July 11, 1856	234	......	......	Sent home 63 sperm.
North Pacific ..	Nov. 29	May 7, 1857	240	1, 861	3, 900	Sent home 13,000 bone.
....do	Oct. 29	June 19, 1856	153	1, 702	24, 300	Sent home 1,090 sperm, 18,800 bone.
Atlantic	May 9	May 20, 1856	455	39	......	Formerly a brig; bought from New York and rerigged 1852; sent home 310 sperm; sold 1856 to Mattapoisett.
North Pacific ..	Aug. 9	May 6, 1857	2	1, 052	11, 300	Sent home 477 whale, 28,300 bone.
Pacific Ocean..	July 27	Mar. 21, 1857	549	740	250	Sent home 7, 740 bone.

Table showing returns of whaling-vessels

Name of vessel.	Class.	Tonnage.	Captain.	Managing owner or agent.
1853.				
New Bedford, Mass.—Continued.				
Miantonomi	Ship	427	William W. Clement	Swift & Allen
Minerva	do	408	Peter Pease	William Gifford
Montpelier	do	320	Job Macomber	J. R. Thornton
Montreal	do	543	S. L. Gray	C. R. Tucker & Co.
Morea	do	330	Thomas B. Peabody	B. B. Howard
Morning Star	Bark	305	William Cleveland	S. Thomas & Co.
Mt. Wollaston	Ship	325	William R. Potter	Wood & Nye
Nassau	do	408	H. C. Murdock	Perry & Swift
Nauticon	do	372	William H. Luce	A. H. Howland
Nye	Bark	211	—— Howland	Abner R. Tucker
Ocean	Ship	349	William C. Fuller	J. R. Thornton
Ohio	do	383	John Barrett	E. W. Howland
Othello	do	424	John A. Beckerman	T. & A. R. Nye
Pantheon	do	271	Gardner Hazard	Lorenzo Pierce
Pauline	Bark	271	J. E. Stanton	Swift & Allen
Petrel	Ship	350	Moses G. Tucker	J. R. Thornton
Reindeer	do	450	Peter Cromwell	E. W. Howland
Rebecca Sims	do	400	Samuel B. Gavitt	William R. Rodman
Robert Edwards	do	356	John A. Kelley	J. & J. Howland
Roscoe, 2d	Bark	235	Asa R. Gifford	J. Bourne, jr
Rousseau	Ship	306	Charles S. Pope	G. & M. Howland
Sally Anne	do	312	Jabez S. Hathaway	D. R. Greene & Co
Sea Breeze	Bark	493	—— Cushman	O. & E. W. Seabury
Sea Flower	do	150	E. G. Cudworth	Charles Almy
Sea Gull	Ship	455	Charles Nichols	J. R. Thornton
Seine	do	281	Amb. S. Landra	Rodney French
Smyrna	Bark	219	George Bliss	Richmond & Wood
Statira	do	348	James Burdett	William Hathaway, jr
St. George	Ship	408	Joseph Dias, jr	Abm. Barker
Superior	Bark	275	Charles L. Norton	James B. Wood & Co
Sea Breeze	do	493	—— Smith	O. & E. W. Seabury
Susan	do	261	Jos. K. Green	A. H. Howland
Swift	Ship	321	Frederick Vincent	Thomas S. Hathaway
Triton	do	300	John B. Dornin	I. Howland, jr., & Co.
Tropic Bird	Bark	220	Alfred C. Davis	William P. Howland
Washington	Ship	344	Richard Holley	J. Bourne, jr
Wm. Badger	do	334	Jason L. Braley	B. B. Howard
Wm. Thompson	do	495	James W. White	Perry & Swift
William Wirt	do	387	Edward R. Ashley	Edmund Maxfield
Young Hector	do	411	Peter G. Smith	W. P. Howland
Young Phenix	do	377	Charles Tobey	J. A. Parker

sailing from American ports—Continued.

Whaling-ground.	Date—		Result of voyage.			Remarks.
	Of sailing.	Of arrival.	Sperm-oil.	Whale-oil.	Whalebone.	
			Bbls.	*Bbls.*	*Lbs.*	
Pacific Ocean ..	July 27	....	.....	......	......	Added 1853; built in North Carolina 1850; lost on Island of Ascension November 18, 1854; saved 100 sperm.
North Pacific ..	Sept. 20	Apr. 7, 1856	.....	1,864	15,800	
....do	Sept. 6	....	.....	......	......	Sent home 243 sperm, 1,200 whale, 25,150 bone; condemned and broken up at Honolulu March 5, 1857; oil (630 barrels) shipped home.
....do	Sept. 1	Apr. 7, 1857	.....	2,377	16,500	Sent home 100 sperm, 12,000 whale, 35,399 bone.
....do	Oct. 13	May 1, 1856	43	1,953	22,600	Sent home 35 sperm, 225 whale, 8,000 bone.
Pacific Ocean ..	Nov. 10	May 18, 1857	712	......	......	Built at Dartmouth 1853; sent home 791 sperm; Mr. Lestes, fourth mate, died March, 1855.
....do	Dec. 21	June 27, 1857	1,051	1,214	2,700	Sent home 9,500 bone.
North Pacific ..	Oct. 9	July 14, 1856	91	2,210	18,200	Sent home 15,400 bone.
....do	Oct. 13	....	.....	......	......	Bought from Nantucket 1853; returned once badly damaged in a gale; David A. Little, second mate, died September, 1854; lost in Honolulu harbor November 24, 1856; cargo (2,300 barrels oil and 10,000 pounds bone) saved and sent home; sent home also about 15,000 bone.
Atlantic	Dec. 16	....	.....	......	......	
Pacific Ocean ..	May 27	June 29, 1856	1,563	......	......	Sent home 403 sperm.
North Pacific ..	Nov. 10	May 6, 1857	237	2,595	......	Sent home 245 sperm, 23,075 bone.
Pacific Ocean ..	Aug. 11	June 15, 1858	1,599	1	......	Built 1853 at Fairhaven; sent home 237 sperm.
....do	Nov. 24	....	.....	......	......	Sent home 54 sperm, 130 whale, 11,594 bone; burned by crew at Nukahiva March 25, 1856; saved 300 sperm.
Indian Ocean ..	Sept. 20	May 30, 1857	446	71	......	Sent home 792 sperm.
North Pacific ..	Oct. 4	June 23, 1857	63	1,055	5,900	Built at Mattapoisett 1853; sent home 14 sperm, 970 whale, 16,193 bone.
....do	Oct. 4	Feb. 14, 1856	60	2,212	......	Built at Mattapoisett 1853;(?) sent home on voyage 250 sperm, 20,000 pounds bone, and sold and sent home 275 whale.
....do	Dec. 2	June 9, 1857	.....	920	11,300	Sent home 1,250 whale, 10,000 bone; sold to Fairhaven 1857.
....do	Sept. 6	July 24, 1857	761	17	......	Sent home 624 sperm.
....do	Nov. 17	July 24, 1856	142	1,448	5,600	
....do	Oct. 17	July 5, 1857	29	794	5,900	Sent home 121 sperm, 6,426 bone.
Pacific Ocean ..	July 9	....	.....	......	......	Lost on Friendly Islands April 2, 1854.
....do	Dec. 5	June 30, 1856	711	1,046	......	Sent home 243 sperm, 7,000 bone.
Atlantic	June 7	Sept. 2, 1857	81	11	......	
Pacific Ocean ..	June 9	Aug. 26, 1857	2,025	10	......	Built at Fairhaven 1853.
North Pacific ..	Oct. 18	Aug. 28, 1858	65	925	1,500	Sent home 250 whale, 12,800 bone.
Indian Ocean ..	Dec. 9	Sept. 9, 1857	701	......	......	
Pacific Ocean ..	Aug. 31	Aug. 8, 1857	1,037	33	......	Sent home 85 sperm.
North Pacific ..	Sept. 10	May 6, 1857	2	1,100	9,900	Sent home 76 sperm, 1,058 whale, 9,450 bone.
Pacific Ocean ..	May 18	Mar. 16, 1857	795	272	......	Sent home 4,200 bone.
....do	Sept. 1	Nov. 25, 1853	26	......	......	Built 1853; returned in consequence of illness of Captain Smith.
....do	Nov. 17	June 25, 1856	1,154	137	......	
....do	June 18	Dec. 2, 1856	1,425	......	......	Sent home 724 sperm.
....do	Aug. 29	Feb. 23, 1857	836	......	......	Sent home 541 sperm.
Atlantic & Ind.	Nov. 1	Apr. 27, 1855	720	66	......	
North Pacific ..	Aug. 22	Mar. 24, 1857	55	1,802	15,200	Sent home 18 sperm, 880 whale, 21,833 bone.
Indian Ocean ..	Sept. 17	June 3, 1857	.....	135	3,000	Bought from Lynn 1853; sent home 100 sperm, 425 whale, 5,000 bone.
North Pacific ..	Nov. 2	May 6, 1857	164	3,350	11,500	Sent home 31,553 bone.
....do	Oct. 2	May 10, 1856	97	2,486	22,900	Bought from Fairhaven 1853; third mate, James Clark, drowned October 6, 1853; sold and sent home 80 sperm, 400 whale, 23,000 pounds bone.
Pacific Ocean ..	Oct. 4	June 3, 1857	1,770	......	......	Built 1853.
North Pacific ..	Aug. 16	Apr. 7, 1857	.....	1,257	19,700	Sent home 696 sperm and whale, 27,549 bone

Table showing returns of whaling-vessels

Name of vessel.	Class.	Tonnage.	Captain.	Managing owner or agent.
1853.				
Fairhaven, Mass.				
Adeline Gibbs	Ship	351	G. P. Pomeroy	Gibbs & Jenney
Arab	do	336	Edwin Grinnell	Ezekiel Sawin
Arab	Bark	276	Asa E. Copeland	I. F. Ferry
Belle	do	320	Ichabod Handy	Edmund Allen
Erie	Ship	451	Jared Jernegan	Nathan Church
Favorite	Bark	293	Shubael S. Spooner	F. R. Whitwell
Harvest	do	314	Obadiah B. Spencer	Jabez Delano, jr
Iowa	do	265	Stephen Merrihew	Levi Jenney, jr
John A. Robb	do	273	William H. Skinner	L. C. Tripp
Oregon	Ship	339	Henry Eldridge	do
Sharon	do	354	John Church	Gibbs & Jenney
Speedwell	do	496	Benjamin F. Gibbs	Stephen C. Gibbs
Syren Queen	do	461	Ira Lakey	Gibbs & Jenney
Dartmouth, Mass.				
A. R. Tucker	Bark	218	Joseph C. Smith	Abner R. Tucker
Brunswick	Ship	295	Henry P. Butler	do
Nye	Bark	211	Frederick S. Howland	Tucker & Cummings
Westport, Mass.				
Barclay	Bark	186	Weston S. Tripp	Alexander H. Corey
Catherwood	do	199	Ingraham D. Oliver	C. A. Church
Champion	do	209	John S. Gardner	Andrew Hicks
D. Franklin	do	171	David S. Russell	Job Davis
Mattapoisett	do	150	Leander Smith	Henry Wilcox
Mexico	Brig	130	Job Collins	do
Platina	Bark	266	David E. Allen	A. Hicks
President	do	180	Horace Young	do
Sea Fox	do	246	Stephen H. Comery	do
T. Winslow	do	136	Davis A. Blake	John Hicks
Edgartown, Mass.				
Alfred Tyler	Bark	225	—— Ripley	John A. Baylies
American	Ship	329	—— Jernegan	do
Champion	do	399	—— Pease	Benjamin Worth
Europa	do	400	John H. Pease	Abraham Osborne
Monterey	Schooner	100	Consider Fisher	
Vineyard	Ship	381	—— Fisher	B. Worth
Wareham, Mass.				
G. Washington	Ship	374	Granville S. Allen	Stephen C. Gibbs
Sandwich, Mass.				
Amelia	Brig	127	Elijah A. Chadwick	W. F. Lapham
Ocean	do	165	—— Chadwick	do
Provincetown, Mass.				
Alleghany	Schooner	..		B. Allstrum
Alexander	do	75		J. E. Bowley
Antarctic	do	136	—— Snow	Samuel Cook
Chanticleer	do	87	—— Cook	Enoch Nickerson
E. Nickerson	do	131	—— Soper	Samuel Soper
Franklin	Bark	172	O. W. Allerton	
Hanover	Schooner	114	—— Holmes	T. Hilliard
Harriet Neal	do	125	—— Cook	R. L. Thatcher
H. N. Williams	do	108	—— Fisher	Philip Cook

sailing from American ports—Continued.

Whaling-ground.	Date— Of sailing.	Of arrival.	Result of voyage. Sperm-oil.	Whale-oil.	Whalebone.	Remarks.
			Bbls.	*Bbls.*	*Lbs.*	
North Pacific ..	Sept. 12	May 10, 1857	150	2, 066	......	Sent home 563 whale, 29,800 pounds bone.
Pacific Ocean ..	Dec. 9	May 30, 1857	40	1, 471	14, 100	
North Pacific ..	Oct. 3	May 9, 1857	......	623	......	Sent home 812 whale, 1,397 pounds bone.
Pacific Ocean ..	Jan. 7	Aug. 21, 1857	605	......	......	Sent home 387 sperm, 593 cocoa-oil.
North Pacific ..	Sept. 1	Mar. 8, 1857	......	3, 011	10, 600	Sent home 70 whale, 24,297 pounds bone.
....do	Nov. 10	May 30, 1857	100	856	4, 500	Sent home 639 whale, 12,000 pounds bone.
....do	Oct. 29	May 6, 1857	105	1, 046	10, 000	Captain Spencer came home sick 1857.
Atl. and Pac...	May 27	Apr. 27, 1856	353	175	1, 300	Bought from Baltimore 1853; built 1843; sent home 40 sperm.
Pacific Ocean ..	Oct. 28	June 23, 1857	370	......	......	Sent home 620 sperm.
North Pacific ..	Sept. 16	May 31, 1857	220	595	......	Sent home 1,550 pounds bone.
Pacific Ocean ..	Jan. 6	Sept. 6, 1856	772	......	......	Sent home 983 sperm.
North Pacific ..	Nov. 16	Apr. 9, 1857	62	1, 854	10, 800	Built at Fairhaven 1853; sent home 334 whale, 18,360 pounds bone.
....do	Oct. 29	Apr. 15, 1858	......	1, 100	16, 100	Built at Mattapoisett 1853; Captain Lakey took command of Arctic 1855; sent home 2,814 whale, 38,489 pounds bone.
Pacific Ocean ..	Nov. 16	June 21, 1857	344	49	......	Sent home 431 sperm.
North Pacific ..	July 28	July 14, 1856	......	690	5, 800	Third mate, Mr. Randall, drowned in a gale October, 1852; sent home 575 whale, 14,000 pounds bone.
Atlantic	Dec. 16	Mar. 26, 1856	783	664	2, 600	Sent home 75 sperm, 2,600 pounds bone.
Atlantic	Jan. 8	Aug. 21, 1854	466	40	......	
....do	Aug. 29	....	......	......	......	Lost on Gallipagos Islands Nov. 18, 1855.
Pacific Ocean ..	Nov. 15	Apr. 16, 1857	828	......	......	
Atlantic	June 16	Mar. 7, 1855	407	22	......	
....do	.... Nov. 10	Sept. 6, 1853	117	......	......	Sailed again Nov. 10, 1853; returned Sept. 4, 1854, with 259 sperm, 18 whale.
....do	Jan. 31	....	......	......	......	Condemned at Saint Thomas Mar. 25, 1854.
Indian Ocean ..	Oct. 6	Feb. 21, 1857	909	......	......	
Pacific Ocean ..	Nov. 29	Aug. 21, 1853	334	2	......	Captain Young left ship 1856.
....do	Nov. 28	June 1, 1858	615	32	......	Sent home 200 sperm.
Atlantic	Dec. 2	June 6, 1855	135	10	......	Sent home 21 sperm.
North Pacific ..	Aug. 31	May 13, 1857	10	550	......	Sent home 11,000 pounds bone; renamed Eureka in 1857.
....do	Oct. 13	Apr. 16, 1857	138	1, 135	6, 600	Added 1853; sent home 540 whale, 9,500 pounds bone.
....do	Sept. 9	May 20, 1856	......	1, 857	16, 700	Sent home 10,440 pounds bone.
....do	Oct. 4	June 12, 1857	131	896	11, 800	Bought from Salem 1853; sent home 37 sperm, 98 whale, 30,000 pounds bone.
Atlantic	May 2	June 24, 1853	......	60	......	Monterey formerly in fishing business; added 1853; sailed again 1853; returned August 16, 1854, with 102 sperm, 8 whale.
North Pacific ..	July 16	Apr. 7, 1856	281	2, 064	26, 200	Sent home 13 sperm.
North Pacific ..	Aug. 22	....	......	......	......	Sent home 252 sperm, 5,601 pounds bone.
Atlantic	May 11	Sept. 2, 1856	......	Clean	......	Formerly a schooner; rig changed 1853; sold.
....do	May 11	Apr. 25, 1856	380	140	1, 000	
Atlantic	May —	Sept. 4, 1853	......	200	......	
....do	May —	Sept. 15, 1853	108	......	......	
....do	Mar. 19	July 24, 1854	135	10	......	
....do	May 10	Sept. 19, 1853	135	15	......	
....do	Mar. 8	Sept. 25, 1853	145	100	......	
....do	....	....	......	......	......	Lost on Isle of Sal, Cape de Verdes; saved 140 barrels whale.
....do	May 22	Oct. 21, 1853	50	6	......	
....do	Mar. 9	June 24, 1854	90	......	......	
....do	Apr. 19	Jan. 15, 1854	80	7	......	

Table showing returns of whaling-vessels

Name of vessel.	Class.	Tonnage.	Captain.	Managing owner or agent.
1853.				
Provincetown, Mass.—Continued.				
John Adams	Schooner	104	—— Burke	John Adams
Louisa	do	109	—— Rider	S. Cook
Medford	do	105		
Montezuma	do	100	—— Freeman	
Mountain Spring	do	86	—— Young	J. E. Bowley
Preston	do	75	—— Smith	S. Cook
Richard	do	100	—— Young	
R. E. Cook	do	80	—— Higgins	John Dunlap
Rienzi	do	109	—— Katon	J. E. Bowley
S. R. Soper	do	130	—— Soper	Samuel Soper
Seychelle	Ship			
Spartan	Bark	190	—— Cook	Stephen Nickerson
Union	Schooner	90	—— Genn	Jonathan Nickerson
Walter Ervin	do	130	—— Nickerson	Atkins Nickerson
Walter K	do	114	—— Heath	Henry Cook
Waldron Holmes	do	90	—— Young	Alstrum & Holmes
Orleans, Mass.				
Lewis Bruce	Brig	113	Reuben Freeman	Leander Crosby
September	do	115	—— Allerton	Heman Smith
Virginian	Schooner	115	—— Pettengill	do
Gloucester, Mass.				
Flying Arrow	Schooner	110	—— Cornell	Merchent & Wells
Beverly, Mass.				
B. Franklin	Bark	164	—— Johnson	F. W. Choate
Eben Dodge	do	221	—— Osborn	do
Gem	Brig	162	—— Cook	do
Lady Suffolk	Bark	210	—— Miller	do
Lynn, Mass.				
Com. Preble	Bark	323	Samuel M. Prentice	Andrews Breed
Mattapoisett, Mass.				
Elizabeth	Bark	219	Asa Hoxie	R. L. Barstow
March	Brig	89	M. Adams	do
Sun	Bark	184	—— Tatch	do
Sippican, Mass.				
Admiral Blake	Schooner	120	Benjamin B. Handy	B. B. Handy
Holmes's Hole, Mass.				
Pocahontas	Ship	341	—— Butler	Thomas Bradley
Falmouth, Mass.				
Com. Morris	Ship	355	Lewis H. Lawrence	Oliver C. Swift
Hobomok	do	414	—— Childs	do
Nantucket, Mass.				
Game Cock	Schooner		William Patterson	
Ganges	Ship	315	John B. Nickerson	Meader & Easton
Harvest	do	360	Benjamin F. Riddell	Rand & Paddack
Henry	do	346	David Bunker, 2d	Perry & Gardner
Hamilton	Schooner		James McGuire	
Lexington	Ship	399	Peter C. Brock	Perry & McCleave
Massachusetts	do	360	Horace Nickerson	Zenas L. Adams

sailing from American ports—Continued.

Whaling-ground.	Date— Of sailing.	Of arrival.	Result of voyage. Sperm-oil.	Whale-oil.	Whalebone.	Remarks.
			Bbls.	*Bbls.*	*Lbs.*	
Atlantic	May —	Sept. 19, 1853	243	......	......	Put into Newport Sept. 17, dismasted.
....do	Apr. 11	Oct. 20, 1853	75	......	......	
....do	May 16	Jan. 20, 1854	20	......	......	Added 1853.
....do	May —	Sept. 20, 1853	30	17	......	Added 1853.
....do	Apr. 20	Sept. 20, 1853	15	20	......	New 1853.
....do	Feb. 18	Sept. 17, 1853	25	......	......	
....do	Apr. 11	July 25, 1854	124	3	......	Added 1853.
....do ...... {	Apr. 22	Apr. 23, 1853	......	10	...... }	{The R. E. Cook sailed again in 1853 or 1854; returned July 28, 1856, with 220 barrels of whale.
	May —	Sept. 19, 1853	35	......	...... }	
....do	Apr. 27	Oct. 20, 1853	15	......	......	
....do	Feb. 25	Aug. 22, 1853	150	100	......	
....do	Apr. 22	Apr. 22, 1853	......	30	......	Sailed again April 25 and seen next day returning with two small whales, about 15 barrels each.
....do	Apr. 19	Aug. 15, 1854	191	6	......	Sent home 58 sperm.
....do	June 10	Sept. 2, 1853	......	140	......	
....do	Apr. 27	Jan. 4, 1854	150	......	......	
....do	July 15	June 27, 1853	74	......	......	Withdrawn 1853.
....do	May 10	Sept. 14, 1853	117	......	......	Built 1853.
Atlantic	May 7	Oct. 22, 1853	15	82	......	Bought from Provincetown 1853.
... do	Aug. 24	May 2, 1854	......	......	......	Added 1853; had 25 sperm at last report.
....do	Mar. 7	Oct. 5, 1853	100	......	......	
Atlantic	Feb. 19	Aug. 29, 1854	82	......	......	Built at Essex in 1853; withdrawn 1854.
South Atlantic.	Oct. 13	June 10, 1855	54	......	......	Sent home 22 sperm.
Indian Ocean ..	July 15	Oct. 28, 1855	253	8	......	Added 1852 from merchant-service, nearly new.
Atlantic	June 7	Apr. 23, 1854	88	......	......	Withdrawn 1855.
Atl. and Ind ...	Aug. 19	July 29, 1853	65	......	......	Bought from Boston 1853; returned on account of a defective mast; sailed again; Captain Miller died at sea Nov. 12, 1853; sent home 36 sperm.
Pacific Ocean ..	Oct. 7	May 10, 1857	108	2, 550	17, 200	Sent home 220 whale, 44,400 pounds bone; sold 1857 and withdrawn.
Pacific Ocean ..	June 21	......	......	......	......	Sent home 883 sperm; condemned at Talcahuano March, 1856.
Atlantic	June 8	Aug. 29, 1854	183	46	......	Bought from New Bedford 1853.
Atlantic & Ind.	Oct. 14	Sept. 8, 1855	380	......	......	Sent home 147 sperm.
Atlantic	May 20	Oct. 5, 1853	140	6	......	Added 1853.
Pacific Ocean ..	July 26	May 31, 1857	40	885	6, 000	Sent home 100 sperm, 150 whale, 28,800 bone; sold to New Bedford 1857.
Pacific Ocean ..	Dec. 7	Oct. 17, 1858	1, 098	......	......	
North Pacific ..	Sept. 30	Aug. 2, 1856	307	2, 477	18, 400	Sent home 4,700 pounds bone.
Atlantic	June 20	July 24, 1853	Clean	......	......	Made two voyages between these dates.
Pacific Ocean ..	Oct. 19	......	......	......	......	Condemned at Talcahuano June, 1858.
....do	Aug. 9	Nov. 10, 1857	495	770	......	Sent home 100 sperm, 450 whale, 22,537 pounds bone; sold to New Bedford.
....do	Oct. 18	......	......	......	......	Sent home 446 sperm, 42 whale, 576 pounds bone; condemned at Talcahuano 1858.
Atlantic	Apr. 8	Sept. 15, 1853	......	101	......	Made five voyages between these dates; built at New York 1844.
Atl. and Pacific	May 21	June 25, 1856	310	1, 637	......	Sold 20 whale; sent home 19,952 bone.
North Pacific ..	Aug. 16	June 20, 1856	30	1, 500	......	Sent home 15,500 pounds bone.

Table showing returns of whaling-vessels

Name of vessel.	Class.	Tonnage.	Captain.	Managing owner or agent.
1853.				
Nantucket, Mass.—Continued.				
Monticello	Ship	368	Eben Baker	John H. Shaw
Oneco	Schooner	....	Alexander Brown	
Omega	Ship	363	William T. Hawes	G. & M. Starbuck & Co.
Phœnix	do	323	Israel Morey	Gardner & McCleave
Potomac	do	356	Enoch Ackley	I. & P. Macy
Tyleston	Brig	111	William H. Tice	E. W. Gardner
William P. Dolliver	Schooner	....	David Patterson	
Zenas Coffin	Ship	368	J. R. Rose	C. G. & H. Coffin
Fall River, Mass.				
A. Houghton	Bark	326	John Marble	Brown & Durfee
Aerial	do	225	—— Borden	John S. Cotton
D. M. Hall	do	263	—— Pratt	do
Cold Spring, N. Y.				
Splendid	Ship	473	—— Smith	John H. Jones
Warren, R. I.				
Benjamin Rush	Ship	385	—— Hotchkiss	S. P. Child
Brutus	do	470	—— Swift	R. B. Johnson
Dromo	Bark	267	—— Thompson	Charles T. Child
Hector	do	225	—— Johnson	R. B. Johnson
Hoogley	Ship	292	—— Cole	William L. Baker
Ocean	do	567	—— Norton	R. B. Johnson
Sea Shell	Bark	331	William Martin	do
Smithfield	do	164	—— Cornell	do
New London, Conn.				
Alert	Bark	398	—— Church	Williams & Haven
Amaret	Brig	...	—— Buddington	Perkins & Smith
Candace	Bark	310	—— Star	Williams & Haven
Clematis	Ship	311	—— Benjamin	Williams & Barnes
Corinthian	do	505	—— Rogers	Perkins & Smith
George & Mary	do	356	—— Walker	Williams & Haven
Georgiana	Brig	...	—— Buddington	Perkins & Smith
Jefferson	Ship	396	—— Williams	Miner, Lawrence & Co.
Julius Cæsar	do	347	—— Babcock	E. V. Stoddard
Lark	Bark	388	—— Kiblon	Perkins & Smith
Marcia	Schooner	128	—— Church	E. V. Stoddard
Mechanic	do	...	—— Edwards	Perkins & Smith
Mogul	Ship	395	—— Clark	Williams & Barnes
Phœnix	do	404	—— Pendleton	Miner, Lawrence & Co.
Tenedos	Bark	245	—— Norey	do
Stonington, Conn.				
Charles Phelps	Ship	362	—— Layton	C. P. Williams

sailing from American ports—Continued.

Whaling-ground.	Date— Of sailing.	Date— Of arrival.	Result of voyage. Sperm-oil.	Result of voyage. Whale-oil.	Result of voyage. Whalebone.	Remarks.
			Bbls.	*Bbls.*	*Lbs.*	
Pacific Ocean ..	Nov. 15	Jan. 15, 1858	1,182	......	......	Sold to New London 1859.
Atlantic	Aug. 4	Sept. 6, 1853	......	......	......	No report.
North Pacific ..	Dec. 8	May 7, 1857	100	1,900	......	Sold to Edgartown; sent home 11,056 bone.
....do	July 19	May 13, 1856	72	975	......	Sent home 90 sperm, 1,000 whale, 10,800 pounds bone.
Pacific Ocean ..	Oct. 27	Sept. 17, 1857	875	......	......	Captain Ackley died on the voyage; sent home 300 sperm; one of the "stone fleet" sunk off Charleston harbor.
....do	Oct. 30	....	......	......	......	Encountered gales off Cape Horn; returned to Pernambuco and was condemned; took no oil.
Atlantic	Apr. 19	Sept. 21, 1853	......	186	......	W. P. D. bought from New Bedford; built 1852; made four voyages between those dates.
North Pacific ..	Nov. 17	Feb. 15, 1857	80	2,515	......	Sold to New York; sent home $15,000 worth of oil and bone.
Atlantic	June 27	Feb. 14, 1857	700	803	......	Built at Robbinston, Me., 1853; sent home 1,400 pounds bone.
Indian Ocean ..	Dec. 13	Nov. 4, 1856	......	30	......	Sent home 326 sperm; sold, 1857, to Newport.
....do	Oct. 7	....	......	......	......	Sold at Papeete 1855.
North Pacific ..	Oct. —	Apr. 4, 1856	......	2,096	12,000	Sent home 1,050 whale.
North Pacific ..	Aug. 9	May 23, 1856	......	917	13,500	
N. W. Coast....	Dec. 1	Apr. 18, 1856	......	2,460	29,300	Bought from New York 1853; sent home 508 whale, 17,910 pounds bone.
Mobile..........	Nov. 21	May 2, 1854	......	223	3,000	
Indian Ocean ..	Apr. 30	Feb. 11, 1856	494	......	......	
Ind. and Pacific	Nov. 17	May 31, 1857	10	1,593	......	Sent home 350 whale, 22,690 pounds bone; sold to Boston 1859.
North Pacific ..	Oct. 18	July 31, 1857	......	1,208	6,900	Bought from Providence 1853; sent home 27 whale, 6,900 pounds bone; sold to New Haven 1858.
Indian Ocean ..	Jan. 1	June 3, 1856	1,203	......	......	Built at Warren 1852.
Atlantic	June 21	Aug. 29, 1855	275	......	......	
Desolation Isl'd	Oct. 7	June 18, 1856	....	3,374	7,400	
Davis's Strait..	July 13	Aug. 29, 1854	....	369	8,000	Added 1853.
North Pacific ..	June 21	....	....	......	......	Sent home 500 whale, 8,000 pounds bone; condemned 1855.
Pacific Ocean ..	Aug. 30	Aug. 12, 1856	83	2,374	10,300	
Desolation Isl'd	Nov. 15	June 9, 1856	......	3,208	8,600	Sent home 13,337 pounds bone.
Pacific Ocean ..	Aug. 18	June 3, 1857	219	939	12,300	Sent home 40 sperm, 560 whale, 26,000 bone.
Davis's Strait..	July 13	Oct. 9, 1854	......	890	16,000	Bought 1853.
North Pacific ..	Aug. 1	....	......	......	......	Lost on Cape Elizabeth, Saghalien Islands, 1855; saved 300 barrels of oil; sent home 800 whale, 11,000 pounds bone.
Desolation Isl'd	Sept. 3	Apr. 7, 1856	......	1,565	4,100	
Pacific Ocean ..	Sept. 21	Apr. 12, 1857	1	1,451	......	Sent home 2,154 whale.
Desolation Isl'd	Aug. 2	June 16, 1856	....	218	....	
....do	Oct. 26	....	......	......	......	Added 1853; tender to Corinthian; carried into New South Wales in October, 1856, in distress, the captain and two of the crew having been washed overboard in a gale.
North Pacific ..	Sept. 30	May 18, 1857	45	903	550	Sent home 539 whale, 14,000 pounds bone; broken up 1858.
....do	Oct. 13	May 18, 1857	90	1,377	19,650	Sent home 94 sperm, 2,234 whale, 35,298 bone.
South Pacific ..	Aug. 31	May 20, 1856	55	1,138	7,800	
North Pacific ..	July 12	Aug. 4, 1859	......	1,153	......	Sent home 20 sperm, 3,660 whale, 48,604 pounds bone; sold to New London on voyage; sold to the United States for a storeship; sold to New Bedford 1865.

Table showing returns of whaling-vessels

Name of vessel.	Class.	Tonnage.	Captain.	Managing owner or agent.
1853.				
Stonington, Conn.—Continued.				
Eugene	Bark	297	—— Pendleton	C. P. Williams
Flying Cloud	Schooner	100	—— Hidden	John F. Trumbull
Newburyport	Ship	341	—— Lester	do
Sarah E. Spear	do	150	—— Kane	do
Tiger	do	311	—— Lax	do
United States	Bark	244	—— Wilcox	do
Greenport, N. Y.				
Armida	Schooner			
Bayard	Ship	339	—— Graham	Wells & Carpenter
Oregon	Bark	224	—— Terry	do
Mystic, Conn.				
Aeronaut	Ship	265	—— Eldridge	Charles Mallory
Coriolanus	do	268	—— Guynn	do
Lion	Schooner	150	G. H. Buckminster	do
Shepherdess	Bark	274	—— Watrous	Randall, Smith & Ashbey
Wilmington	Schooner	100	—— Gilderdale	C. Mallory
Sag Harbor, N. Y.				
Ann	Bark	299	—— Hedges	Thomas Brown
Jefferson	Ship	435	—— Hunting	do
Noble	Bark	273	—— Nicoll	Charles T. Dering
Nimrod	do	280	—— Green	do
Parana	Brig	209	—— Smith	T. Brown
Timor	Ship	280	—— Rogers	Huntting Cooper
Washington	do	340	—— Brown	do
San Francisco, Cal.				
Aquetnet	Ship	300		Charles H. Todd & Co
Equator	Bark	263	—— Russell	
H. Thompson	do		—— Glover	
Jupiter	Schooner	90		Eldridge & Pousland
Nile	Brig	320		More & Folger
R. Adams	Bark	271	—— Andrews	William Bailey
Venezuela	Brig		—— Russell	
1854.				
New Bedford, Mass.				
Alex. Coffin	Ship	381	Isaiah Purrington	Jona. Bourne, jr
Alto	Bark	236	Angler Snell	Richmond & Wood
Alfred Gibbs	Ship	425	—— Nichols	Wood & Nye
Amethyst	do	359	William F. Jones	Frederick Parker
Atlantic	Bark	367	William J. Wyer	William Hathaway
Barclay	Ship	281	And. J. Fuller	Henry Taber & Co
Bartholemew Gosnold	do	356	John Fisher	I. Howland, jr., & Co
Betsy Williams	do	400	Jeremiah Austin	F. & G. R. Taber
Braganza	do	470	—— Jackson	William G. E. Pope
Cachelot	Bark	230	Thomas J Lee	Abraham Ashley, 2d
Cambria	Ship	362	—— Pease	James B. Wood & Co
California	do	398	W. B. Manchester	I. Howland, jr., & Co
Chandler Price	do	441	John Curn	W. G. E. Pope
Congress	do	339	Reuben Kelley	Edward C. Jones
Corinthian	do	401	Thomas N. Russell	G. & M. Howland

sailing from American ports—Continued.

Whaling-ground.	Date— Of sailing.	Date— Of arrival.	Result of voyage. Sperm-oil.	Result of voyage. Whale-oil.	Result of voyage. Whalebone.	Remarks.
			Bbls.	*Bbls.*	*Lbs.*	
North Pacific ..	Oct. 6	June 1, 1857	103	900	13, 500	Sold to New Bedford and broken up 1858.
S. Shetland Isl's	July 28	....	......	......	......	
North Pacific ..	Sept. 29	May 20, 1856	90	1, 570	21, 000	Sent home 1,000 whale.
S. Shetland Isl's	July 28	....	......	......	......	
N. W. Coast....	July 14	June 29, 1856	......	903	12, 000	Sent home 37 sperm, 1,036 whale, 13,000 pounds bone; withdrawn 1858; sold.
S. Shetland Isl's	July 28	July —, 1854	......	......	......	Transferred to Honolulu; no report of oil.
....	......	....	......	......	......	Made short voyages, and brought blubber home to be tried out.
Arctic Ocean ..	Aug. 11	....	......	......	......	Bayard sent home 155 sperm, 608 whale, 9,200 pounds bone.
South Atlantic	June 2	Aug. 19, 1854	302	276	1, 300	Added 1853; built at Hallowell, Me., 1848; sailed under Captain Babcock, who came home sick, 1853.
S. Shetland Isl's	July 28	July 13, 1854	......	490	......	
North Pacific ..	Oct. 2	Aug. 15, 1856	39	1, 708	12, 600	
S. Shetland Isl's	July 28	....	......	......	......	Lost on English Bank March 22, 1854.
North Pacific ..	Sept. 2	May 11, 1856	.....	1, 570	700	Sent home 870 whale, 32,248 pounds bone.
S. Shetland Isl's	July 28	....	......	......	......	Added 1853; no report.
South Atlantic	July 15	July 1, 1855	193	105	......	
North Pacific ..	Oct. 26	Mar. 19, 1857	......	3, 400	....	Sent home 1,647 pounds bone.
South Atlantic	Nov. 15	Sept. 2, 1855	240	703	4, 000	
....do	Nov. 26	Nov. 3, 1855	22	840	4, 200	Sold 1855.
....do	June 16	June 15, 1854	29	662	1, 200	Bought 1853.
North Pacific ..	June 7	May 24, 1856	324	1, 541	9, 600	Sent home 50 sperm, 800 whale, 10,222 bone.
....do	Sept. 2	May 23, 1855	......	519	11, 500	Sent home 5,371 bone; withdrawn 1855.
Pacific Ocean ..	Dec. 25	....	......	......	......	
....do	Feb. —	Nov. 17, 1853	......	700	......	
....do	Apr. 8	Sept. 28, 1853	......	140	......	
....	....	Nov. 6, 1853	......	180	......	Elephant.
Pacific Ocean ..	Apr. —	....	......	......	......	No report.
....	Nov. —	Apr. 2, 1854	200	50	......	
Pacific Ocean ..	Apr. 4	....	......	......	......	No report.
North Pacific..	Sept. 21	....	......	......	......	Sent home 150 sperm, 1,709 whale, and 20,500 bone; lost in Ochotsk Sea 1856.
Indian Ocean ..	June 4	Apr. 8, 1857	842	4	......	
Pacific Ocean..	Nov. 1	July 22, 1858	1, 860	11	......	Sent home 95 whale.
....do	Oct. 10	Apr. 26, 1859	1, 484	......	......	Sold and withdrawn 1859; sold at San Francisco 1860.
....do	Oct. 14	May 28, 1859	1, 170	......	......	
Atl. and Indian	Aug. 1	Aug. 24, 1857	410	1, 016	2, 100	Withdrawn 1859.
North Pacific..	Nov. 1	May 3, 1858	38	1, 144	12, 000	Four men lost while fast to a whale June 11, 1856; sent home 216 sperm, 939 whale, and 19,330 bone.
Pacific Ocean..	June 19	July 22, 1858	2	874	800	Bought from Stonington 1854; sent home 169 sperm; withdrawn 1858 for guano trade; sold 1861 to New York.
North Pacific..	Sept. 11	May 7, 1859	16	538	600	Sent home 13,722 bone.
Pacific Ocean..	Aug. 2	June 20, 1857	952	20	......	Bought from Mattapoisett 1853; sent home 22 sperm.
North Pacific..	Sept. 16	Apr. 29, 1858	......	1, 708	14, 300	Sent home 229 sperm, 930 whale, and 10,800 bone.
....do	Nov. 2	Apr. 23, 1858	54	1, 814	14, 900	Sent home 83 sperm, 985 whale, and 11,381 bone.
....do	Sept. 11	May 30, 1857	27	1, 615	......	Captain Curn died at sea April 26, 1856; sent home 11,600 bone.
Atl. and Indian	Aug. 21	Sept. 11, 1856	1, 438	1, 082	......	
North Pacific..	Oct. 11	Apr. 6, 1858	......	1, 842	16, 300	

Table showing returns of whaling-vessels

Name of vessel.	Class.	Tonnage.	Captain.	Managing owner or agent.
1854.				
New Bedford, Mass.—Continued.				
Cowls Howland	Ship	431	John A. Luce	Edward W. Howland
Coral	do	370	Charles L. Manchester	Gideon Allen
Dartmouth	Bark	336	Nathan B. Heath	Weston Howland
Dominga	do	230	—— Phinney	do
Draco	do	257	Charles P. Worth	J. Bourne, jr
Dunbarton	do	199	Joseph P. Nye	Isaac B. Richmond
Elisha Dunbar	do	257	James L. Lincoln	W. & G. D. Watkins
Eliza Adams	Ship	403	Jona. C. Hawes	E. C. Jones
E. Swift	Bark	420	Josiah E. Chase	Swift & Allen
Emily Morgan	Ship	368	Joseph B. Chase	William J. Rotch
Endeavour	Bark	252	Israel Horsley	A. Ashley, 2d
Enterprise	Ship	291	—— Russell	C. Hitch & Son
Euphrates	do	365	Charles B. Killmer	E. W. Howland
Europa	do	380	William H. Vinal	E. C. Jones
Fabius	do	432	Lyman Wing	C. R. Tucker & Co
Fortune	Bark	291	Henry W. Beetle	James Beetle
Geo. Washington	do	242	William O. Harps	C. Hitch & Son
Gratitude	do	337	John B. Cornell	Swift & Allen
Harrison	Ship	371	Samuel T. Braley	Edmund Maxfield
Harvest	Bark	263	F. H. Winslow	Lorenzo Pierce
Henry Kneeland	Ship	304	Jonathan Whalon	Benjamin B. Howard
Helen Snow	Bark	299	Reuben D. Weeks	Cook & Snow
Hillman	Ship	383	Christopher Cook	H. Taber & Co
Hunter	do	453	James W. Monroe	Jona. Bourne, jr
Ionia	Bark	234	David B. Randall	C. Wilcox
Iris	Ship	311	Edward S. Devoll	E. C. Jones
Isaac Howland	do	399	Reuben R. Hobbs	I. Howland, jr., & Co
Janus	do	321	Hudson Winslow	T. & A. R. Nye
Jeannette	do	340	John C. Peirce	I. B. Richmond
John Howland	do	377	Alex. G. Taylor	James H. Howland
John Wells	do	366	Alden Besse	T. Knowles & Co
Joseph Butler	Bark	193	Arthur F. White	I. Howland, jr., & Co
Joseph Meigs	Ship	356	—— Coffin	Kelley & Swift
Julian	do	356	Jacob L. Cleaveland	William Hathaway, jr
Lætitia	Bark	275	Randall Himes	—— & G. R. Taber
Lancaster	Ship	383	William Carver	T. & A. R. Nye
Leonidas	do	231	Samuel C. Oliver	Russell Maxfield
Lexington	Bark	201	Philip Smith	B. B. Howard
Logan	Ship	302	Moses Wells	I. Howland, jr., & Co
L. C. Richmond	do	341	David Cochran	J. B. Wood & Co
Magnolia	do	396	G. L. Cox	W. G. E. Pope
Malta	Bark	151	Godfrey King	B. B. Howard
Manuel Ortez	do	351	Gilb. B. Heustis	Weston Howland
Maria Theresa	Ship	330	William Davis, jr	T. & A. R. Nye
Martha	Bark	271	Francis Smith	Swift & Allen
Martha, 2d	do	360	David R. Drake	William O. Brownell
Mary Wilder	Ship	213	Pres. N. Luce	Charles Almy
Mary	do	287	Silas Cottle	I. Howland, jr., & Co
Matthew Luce	Bark	410	James Coon	William Hathaway, jr
Menkar	Ship	371	Thomas R. Broomfield	Philip Anthony

sailing from American ports—Continued.

Whaling-ground.	Date—Of sailing.	Date—Of arrival.	Result of voyage.—Sperm-oil.	Result of voyage.—Whale-oil.	Result of voyage.—Whalebone.	Remarks.
			Bbls.	*Bbls.*	*Lbs.*	
North Pacific..	Aug. 15	May 2, 1858	78	1,713	10,886	Sent home 290 sperm and 308 whale.
....do	Sept. 4	May 12, 1858	58	1,007	6,900	Sent home 95 sperm and 920 whale.
....do	Nov. 19	Aug. 22, 1858	29	1,550	4,300	Sent home 70 sperm, 160 whale, and 2,000 bone.
Pacific Ocean..	Sept. 12	Aug. 22, 1858	541	82	......	Sent home 185 sperm.
Indian Ocean ..	June 22	Oct. 16, 1857	1,068	141	800	Sent home 91 sperm.
Atlantic	July 1	Oct. 28, 1855	199	162	1,400	
Indian Ocean ..	Nov. 14	Mar. 26, 1858	902	30	......	Sent home 33 sperm.
North Pacific..	Oct. 18	May 1, 1857	138	2,737	31,700	
Pacific Ocean..	Nov. 28	Oct. 19, 1858	1,481	......	......	Built at Fairhaven 1854; sent home 100 sperm.
....do	Nov. 1	July 6, 1859	676	......	......	
....do	Nov. 1	July 8, 1857	46	1,050	......	Sent home 13,800 bone.
North Pacific..	Sept. 11	....	......	......	......	Lost on Company's Island May 13, 1855.
....do	Oct. 27	May 2, 1857	123	1,423	20,100	Sent home 50 sperm, 1,000 whale, and 14,846 bone.
Pacific Ocean..	July 20	Apr. 17, 1856	280	2,408	1,800	Sent home 55 sperm.
North Pacific..	July 27	Mar. 17, 1857	45	2,255	17,500	Sent home 36 sperm and 21,500 bone.
....do	Aug. 9	May 4, 1856	128	1,775	23,900	
Indian Ocean ..	May 17	June 25, 1857	80	797	3,000	Sent home 104 sperm.
North Pacific..	Sept. 4	June 3, 1858	32	994	2,800	
....do	July 13	Sept. 16, 1857	1,227	1	......	
Pacific Ocean..	Nov. 14	May 20, 1859	955	8	....	
Japan	Sept. 4	May 22, 1857	177	1,447	3,800	
Pacific Ocean..	Sept. 26	Aug. 30, 1857	887	6	......	Sent home 381 sperm.
North Pacific..	Oct. 3	Feb. 14, 1857	197	2,349	......	Sent home 19,000 bone.
Indian Ocean ..	Dec. 11	Nov. 24, 1858	741	394	1,500	
... do	Dec. 3	Aug. 30, 1857	476	......	....	
....do	Aug. 23	....	......	......	......	Lost at Port Gregory, New Holland, June 29, 1855.
Pacific Ocean..	Dec. 7	June 26, 1859	953	......	......	Sent home 439 sperm.
North Pacific..	Aug. 13	Apr. 22, 1858	.....	1,178	......	Sent home 58 sperm, 1,673 whale, and 7,500 bone.
....do	Aug. 24	Apr. 29, 1858	233	1,873	......	Sent home 6,300 bone.
....do	Nov. 8	Apr. 11, 1858	37	858	......	Sent home 800 whale and 18,328 bone.
....do	July 18	Apr. 8, 1857	.....	1,955	15,600	Sent home 342 sperm, 297 whale, and 21,406 bone.
Pacific Ocean..	Sept. 29	....	.....	......	......	Sent home 1,445 sperm; condemned at Manila June 16, 1859.
North Pacific..	Oct. 19	Apr. 4, 1858	......	1,041	1,700	Sent home 20 sperm and 8,300 bone.
....do	Oct. 17	Apr. 22, 1858	......	2,232	9,600	Sent home 69 sperm and 464 whale.
Atlantic	Nov. 19	Apr. 5, 1857	240	......	......	Sent home 300 sperm.
North Pacific..	Aug. 22	Apr. 23, 1858	.....	331	......	Sent home 102 sperm, 970 whale, and 15,523 bone.
Pacific Ocean..	Oct. 10	July 19, 1858	230	13	.....	Sent home 197 sperm.
Indian Ocean ..	Dec. 19	....	......	.....	......	Condemned at Mauritius September, 1856; shipped oil (about 250 sperm) to London.
North Pacific..	July 27	....	......	......	......	Sent home 87 sperm; lost on Sandy Island Reef January 26, 1855; four men lost; survivors landed on Feejee Islands after much suffering.
....do	Nov. 1	Aug. 1, 1857	47	2,027	......	Sent home 100 whale and 7,915 bone.
....do	Oct. 21	May 22, 1858	......	656	8,200	Sent home 56 sperm, 1,365 whale, and 18,700 bone.
Indian Ocean ..	July 13	Sept. 13, 1856	179	11	.....	Sent home 193 sperm.
North Pacific..	Sept. 2	May 30, 1857	195	1,047	......	Sent home 6,470 bone.
....do	Oct. 24	July 6, 1857	......	1,752	18,500	Sent home 18 sperm, 308 whale, and 13,568 bone.
Pacific Ocean..	May 21	May 20, 1858	695	......	......	
North Pacific..	July 6	May 29, 1857	85	1,811	13,400	Sent home 14,000 bone.
Pacific Ocean..	July 27	Apr. 7, 1857	956	......	......	Sent home 22 sperm.
....do	Oct. 2	Aug. 30, 1856	668	169	1,400	Boat stove while fast to a whale; Captain Cottle and one man drowned; other four picked up next day by Maria Theresa; sent home 4,400 bone.
....do	July 18	May 31, 1858	1,960	10	300	Built at Mattapoisett 1854; sent home 109 sperm.
North Pacific..	Aug. 8	....	......	......	......	Third mate, Henry Ives, drowned 1854, wrecked on New Zealand; condemned at Hobart Town March, 1858; shipped cargo (1,100 oil and 6,000 pounds bone) to London.

Table showing returns of whaling-vessels

Name of vessel.	Class.	Tonnage.	Captain.	Managing owner or agent.
1854.				
New Bedford, Mass.—Continued.				
Milwood	Bark	254	Joseph D. Silvea	Gideon Allen
Moctezuma	Ship	436	Daniel Tinker	Simeon N. West
Newton	Bark	283	George Sherman	J. Bourne, jr
Nimrod	Ship	34(	Neh. P. Baker	W. Gifford
Ohio	Bark	237	Daniel Baker	Cook & Snow
Oliver Crocker	Ship	352	Robert McCleave	J. B. Wood & Co
Ontario	...do	489	George S. Tooker	W. O. Brownell
Onward	...do	461	James A. Norton	E. W. Howland
Orozimbo	...do	58(	Lafayette Rowley	D. R. Green & Co
Orray Taft	Bark	176	Peleg Cornell	Allen Lucas
Osceola	...do	15(	George H. Macomber	Perry & Swift
Osceola, 2d	...do	197	Charles A. Hosmer	J. & W. R. Wing
Osceola, 3d	...do	200	John D. Sampson	C. Wilcox
Ospray	...do	236	—— Fisher	Swift & Allen
Peri	...do	205	Elihu Russell	Rodney French
Pioneer	...do	231	Thomas F. Lambert	J. D. Thompson
Richmond	...do	180	Richmond Mancheste	L. Kollock & Son
Robt. Morrison	...do	307	Josiah C. Pease	T. Knowles & Co
Roman, 2d	Ship	350	Seth M. Blackmer	Abm. Barker
Roscius	...do	300	Calvin Dexter	William P. Howland
Scotland	...do	384	George A. Smith	O. & E. W. Seabury
Sea Flower	Bark	150	H. B. Macomber	C. Almy
Stafford	...do	206	Hiram Francis	T. & A. R. Nye
Stephania	Ship	315	Matthew Fisher	J. Bourne, jr
Tamerlane	...do	357	Josh. B. Winslow	T. Knowles & Co
Triton, 2d	...do	315	George White	C. R. Tucker & Co
Thomas Nye	...do	461	John C. Smith	T. & A. R. Nye
Two Brothers	...do	288	John D. Childs	Wood & Nye
Twilight	...do	386	Isaac B. Thompkins	William Phillips
Uncas	...do	413	Clark W. James	A. H. Howland
Union	Bark	424	Zaccheus Macy	Chapman & Bonney
Vernon	...do	307	H. B. Gardner	C. Hitch & Son
Waverly	Ship	327	Charles B. West	David B. Kempton
Wave	Bark	197	William B. Stanton	T. Knowles & Co
William C. Nye	Ship	389	John M. Sowle	C. R. Tucker & Co
Fairhaven, Mass.				
Albion	Ship	326	John F. Hinds	Ezekiel Sawin
Ansel Gibbs	...do	319	Charles Stetson	Gibbs & Jenney
Arctic	...do	431	William H. Phillips	Edmund Allen
Atkins Adams	...do	330	George Wilson	William G. Blackler
Bruce	Bark	172	Thomas Nelson	Jenney & Tripp
Florida	Ship	523	Thomas W. Williams	Fish, Robinson & Co
Hesper	...do	262	Dennis Stevens	Dexter Jenney
Java	...do	292	Jarvis Wood	W. G. Blackler
Lagrange	Bark	280	William W. Thomas	...do
Lydia	Ship	351	John W. Leonard	F. R. Whitwell
Mary Ann	...do	335	Thomas Dallman	L. C. Tripp
Omega	...do	305	Merrill W. Sanborn	Nathan Church
Pacific	...do	314	Moses Snell	Reuben Fish
South Boston	...do	339	Edward F. Randolph	E. Sawin
Dartmouth, Mass.				
B. Cummings	Bark	391	Spooner Jenkins	Tucker & Cummings

sailing from American ports—Continued.

Whaling-ground.	Date— Of sailing.	Date— Of arrival.	Result of voyage. Sperm-oil.	Result of voyage. Whale-oil.	Result of voyage. Whalebone.	Remarks.
			Bbls.	*Bbls.*	*Lbs.*	
Indian Ocean ..	July 27	July 26, 1857	120	969	2,000	Sent home 17,200 bone.
North Pacific..	July 22	June 9, 1857	65	2,487	14,900	First mate, Abm. Spooner, taken out of his boat by a line June 20, 1855; sent home 45 sperm, 700 whale, and 26,160 bone.
....do	Oct. 15	....	......		......	Sent home 140 sperm, 600 whale, and 16,200 bone; stove by ice in Ochotsk 1857.
....do	Aug. 19	May 30, 1857	17	1,337	9,900	Sent home 308 sperm, 453 whale, and 17,884 bone.
Pacific Ocean..	Nov. 15	June 1, 1858	863	180	......	
Indian Ocean ..	Sept. 21	Sept. 30, 1858	1,917	......	......	Sent home 500 sperm.
North Pacific..	Nov. 3	Apr. 4, 1858	95	2,753	29,800	Added 1854; sent home 32 sperm, 1,175 whale, and 61,355 bone.
....do	Oct. 17	May 30, 1858	28	1,377	8,150	Built at Mattapoisett 1854.
....do	Oct. 13	June 23, 1857	301	2,225	19,200	Built 1803; sent home 1,061 whale.
Atlantic	Nov. 20	Aug. 25, 1856	540	62	......	
....do	June 14	Oct. 1, 1856	198	171	400	Sent home 702 sperm.
Atl. and Indian	Aug. 22	Apr. 11, 1857	448	497	800	
Pacific Ocean..	June 2	June 3, 1856	146	......	......	
... do	Nov. 23	Aug. 1, 1857	640	209	......	Sent home 752 sperm.
Indian Ocean ..	June 9	May 26, 1857	1,048	52	500	Sent home 22 sperm.
...do	June 27	Apr. 9, 1858	389	801	6,000	
Pacific Ocean..	June 1	May 31, 1857	676	50	......	Sent home 27 sperm.
North Pacific..	Aug. 15	May 11, 1857	102	1,661	21,600	Sent home 50 sperm.
....do	Aug. 16	May 15, 1857	18	1,934	28,700	Sent home 100 sperm, 448 whale, and 11,000 bone.
Pacific Ocean..	June 1	June 24, 1858	1,229	6	.....	Sent home 411 sperm.
North Pacific..	Aug. 16	May 6, 1857	162	2,945	15,500	
Atlantic	Nov. 19	May 16, 1856	131	......	......	Sent home 145 sperm.
Atl. and Indian	Aug. 21	June 23, 1857	235	280	......	Sent home 353 sperm.
Indian Ocean ..	Aug. 2	Feb. 9, 1857	438	1,040	10,300	
North Pacific..	Oct. 1	June 1, 1858	3	2,658	15,000	Sent home 760 whale.
....do	Sept. 26	June 5, 1858	165	1,853	.....	Sent home 10,058 bone.
....do	Sept. 1	Apr. 25, 1857	60	2,743	23,700	Sent home 65 sperm and 14,100 bone.
South Pacific ..	June 14	July 18, 1858	383	262	......	Sent home 28 sperm and 2,355 bone.
Indian Ocean ..	July 20	Apr. 6, 1858	1,330	127	1,000	Built at Fairhaven 1853.
North Pacific..	Oct. 16	June 24, 1857	193	1,932	9,500	
Atlantic	May 23	Aug. 4, 1855	......	6	......	
North Pacific..	Oct. 8	....	......	......	......	Sent home 2,269 whale and 7,000 bone; sold to Honolulu November 30, 1857.
....do	Nov. 8	May 1, 1858	85	1,115	......	Sent home 104 whale and 12,788 bone.
Indian Ocean ..	May 28	Apr. 20, 1856	376	4	....	Sent home 85 sperm.
North Pacific..	Oct. 17	June 13, 1857	394	1,641	8,800	
North Pacific .	Nov. 8	May 3, 1857	......	1,357	......	Sold to New York 1863 for merchant service.
....do	Dec. 20	Apr. 17, 1859	1,470			Sent home 473 whale.
....do	July 27	May 20, 1856	805	1,440	......	Captain Phillips took command of Syren Queen 1855.
Pacific Ocean..	Dec. 9	July 19, 1858	1,580	350	......	
....do	June 28	....	......	......	......	Wrecked and condemned at Zanzibar June 17, 1856; bought by parties in Providence.
North Pacific ..	Oct. 11	Apr. 6, 1858	......	2,463	9,700	Sent home 150 sperm, 356 whale, 18,316 bone.
Pacific Ocean ..	July 27	July 23, 1858	590	48	......	Sent home 438 sperm.
North Pacific ..	Apr. 19	May 11, 1857	50	2,100	1,500	Sent home 63 sperm, 70 whale, 800 bone; transferred to New Bedford and altered to a bark 1857.
Pacific Ocean .	May 21	Apr. 15, 1857	1,426	150	....	Sent home 86 sperm; sold to New Bedford 1857.
North Pacific ..	Oct. 14	May 21, 1858	119	329	4,800	Sent home 400 whale.
Pacific Ocean .	Sept. 16	Apr. 1, 1858	1,520	......		
North Pacific ..	Aug. 31	May 11, 1857	.....	1,588	10,900	First mate, D. R. Remson, died June 6, 1853; sent home 16,600 bone.
....do	Sept. 21	Feb. 21, 1857	65	836	......	Sent home 85 sperm, 13,107 bone; sold to New Bedford 1858.
....do	Nov. 4	May 21, 1858	154	1,232	16,000	Sent home 837 whale, 7,341 bone.
Pacific Ocean	Nov. 14	June 26, 1859	1,424	3	......	Built 1854; sent home 200 sperm.

Table showing returns of whaling-vessels

Name of vessel.	Class.	Tonnage.	Captain.	Managing owner or agent.
1854.				
Dartmouth, Mass.—Continued.				
Cape H. Pigeon	Ship	300	William H. Almy	William Potter
H. H. Crapo	Bark	19	Archelaus Baker, jr	Tucker & Cummings
Westport, Mass.				
Elizabeth	Bark	270	Dennis Cook	Andrew Hicks
George and Mary	do	165	George L. Manchester	Rescom Macomber
Gov. Carver	do	180	Orvin B. Higgins	Henry Wilcox
Grayhound	do	249	Frederick A. Wing	do
Leonidas	Brig	128	Fred. M. Crossman	C. A. Church
Sacramento	Bark	218	Otis S. Snow	Alex. H. Corey
Solon	do	129	—— Smith	Henry Smith
Mattapoisett, Mass.				
America	Brig	148	Cyrus Fisher	R. L. Barstow
Annawan	do	159	James M. Clark	Josiah Holmes, jr
Excellent	do	70	Leonard West	R. L. Barstow
Massasoit	Bark	206	E. B. Handy	Caleb King, jr
Oscar	do	369	Franklin Cross	J. Holmes, jr., & Bro
R. L. Barstow	do	203	Warren Luce	R. L. Barstow
Sarah	do	179	Job E. Rounseville	Atsatt & Sturtevant
Sippican, Mass.				
Adm'l Blake	Schooner	120	Benjamin B. Handy	B. B. Handy
Altamaha	do	119	Charles Hammond	Stephen C. Luce
Holmes' Hole, Mass.				
Helen Augusta	Bark	270	—— West	Thomas Bradley
Ocmulgee	Ship	458	—— West	do
Nantucket, Mass.				
Atlantic	Ship	321	Zenas M Coleman	Robert F. Gardner
Columbia	do	329	Hiram Folger	John H. Shaw
Edward Carey	do	353	Perry Winslow	C. G. & H. Coffin
Enterprise	do	413	John Brown	E. W. Gardner
Hamilton	Schooner	...	Hiram Bailey	
Mohawk	Ship	350	Charles Grant	I. & P. Macy
Palmyra	Schooner	100	Benjamin Raymond	Thomas Potter
Spartan	Ship	333	Elihu F. Turner	David Thain
Three Brothers	Ship	384	Charles E. Cleaveland	G. & M. Starbuck & Co.
William P. Dolliver*	Schooner	90	Nathan Manter; Hiram Bailey	
Edgartown, Mass.				
Navigator	Ship	350	—— Fisher	John A. Baylies
Splendid	do	392	—— Smith	Abraham Osborne
Falmouth, Mass.				
Awashonks	Bark	342	—— Tobey	Oliver C. Swift
Sandwich, Mass.				
Amelia	Brig	127	Nathaniel Hamlen	W. F. Lapham
Ocean	do	165	Josh. T. Chadwick	do
Provincetown, Mass.				
Alleghany	Schooner	95	—— Cook	E. & E. K. Cook
Alexander	do	75	—— Cornell	B. Allstrum

* Several other schooners sailed

sailing from American ports—Continued.

Whaling-ground.	Date— Of sailing.	Date— Of arrival.	Result of voyage. Sperm-oil.	Result of voyage. Whale-oil.	Result of voyage. Whalebone.	Remarks.
			Bbls.	*Bbls.*	*Lbs.*	
Indian Ocean	June 12	July 28, 1858	1,150	150		Built 1854; sent home 330 sperm.
....do	June 12					Lost at sea January 19, 1857, with a full cargo of sperm oil; the captain and one man—the sole survivors—were rescued by the English steamer England.
Indian Ocean	Oct. 1	May 7, 1857	365			
Atlantic	July 2	Aug. 30, 1855	123			
Pacific Ocean	Nov. 17	June 9, 1857	764	11		
....do	July 2	Nov. 17, 1856	266	71	500	
Atlantic	Mar. 5	July 10, 1855	82	44		Sent home 160 sperm.
Ind. and Pac.	Nov. 10	Apr. 16, 1857	337	69		Sent home 125 sperm.
Atl. and Ind	Apr. 6	Apr. 15, 1856	113	180		
Atlantic	May 28					Condemned at Teneriffe July, 1855; oil (50 barrels) sent home.
....do	May 22	Sept. 4 1855	290			Sent home 84 sperm.
....do	May 13	Aug. 15, 1855	142	1		
Pacific Ocean	Apr. 11	Dec. 20, 1857	726			Sent home 26 sperm.
....do	Nov. 28	Apr. 30, 1857		1,757		Set on fire and considerably damaged 1855, at Honolulu; sent home 23 sperm, 380 whale, 31,600 bone.
Atlantic	May 12	May 16, 1856	409	276		
....do	May 2	Oct. 4, 1855	262	143		Sent home 25 sperm.
Atlantic	May 12	Sept. 8, 1854	156	10		Sent home 100 sperm; value of cargo $11,000.
...do	May 12	Nov. 14, 1854	40			
Atlantic	May 24	Mar. 25, 1856	215	890	2,000	Sent home 3,000 bone.
Atl. and Ind	Sept. 14	May 2, 1857	185	2,308	8,500	Sent home 11,572 bone; sold to Edgartown 1857.
Pacific Ocean	June 13	Apr. 17, 1858	1,038			Sent home 260 sperm; sold 10 sperm.
....do	Dec. 9	May 24, 1859	1,040			
....do	May 22	Aug. 8, 1858	665			Sent home 570 sperm.
North Pacific	Dec. 16	May 5, 1858	213	2,500		Second mate, Charles H. Ellis, killed by the falling of a block December, 1855; sold to New Bedford; broken up 1858; sent home 23,000 bone.
Atlantic	Apr. 25	July 26, 1854		136		
Pacific Ocean	Aug. 13	Aug. 23, 1858	1,746			
North Atlantic	May 11	Aug. 7, 1855	100	22		Sold to Mattapoisett.
Pacific Ocean	July 3	June 21, 1858	1,600			
....do	July 10	Apr. 20, 1859		6,000		Sent home 179 sperm, 31,000 bone; largest quantity ever brought into Nantucket.
Atlantic {	Apr. 26	June 26, 1854	18	97		
	Dec. 17		32	284		
North Pacific	Oct. 5	June 19, 1858	80	1,500	3,700	First mate, Jonathan V. Smith, died 1855; sent home 200 whale.
....do	Nov. 2	June 2, 1858		850		Sent home 243 sperm, 520 whale, 10,400 bone.
North Pacific	Nov. 23	Nov. 27, 1858	1,227			Sold to New Bedford 1860.
Atlantic	July 27	Sept. 6, 1855		265		
....do	May 4	Apr. 25, 1856	380	140	1,000	
Atlantic	May 12	Sept. —, 1854	228			
....do	May 30	Nov. 3, 1854	35			

this year, but returned clean.

Table showing returns of whaling-vessels

Name of vessel.	Class.	Tonnage.	Captain.	Managing owner or agent.
1854.				
Provincetown, Mass.—Continued.				
Antarctic	Schooner	136	—— Costa	J. E. & G. Bowley
Chanticleer	...do	87	—— Young	Samuel Cook
E. Nickerson	...do	132	—— Freeman	Samuel Soper
John Adams	...do	99	—— Birch	John Adams
Louisa	...do	97	—— Tilson	S. Cook
Montezuma	...do	92	—— Freeman	—— Freeman
M. Spring	...do	86	—— Young	J. E. & G. Bowley
M. King	...do	86	—— Petingill	Thatcher, Cook & Co
Parker Cook	Bark	130	—— Cook	E. & E. K. Cook
Rienzi	Schooner	108	—— Long	J. E. & G. Bowley
S. R. Soper	...do	130	—— Soper	S. Soper
Union	...do	97	—— Genu	Jonathan Nickerson
W. Holmes	...do	89	—— Young	—— Young
Walter Irvin	...do	133	—— Nickerson	S. Soper
Orleans, Mass.				
Esther	Brig	135	—— Lamson	Heman Smith
Lewis Bruce	...do	113	—— Freeman	Leander Crosby
Rothschild	Bark	261	O. W. Allerton	Heman Smith
September	Brig	115	Nathaniel Ryder	...do
Virginian	Schooner	114	John Smith, jr	...do
Wm. Martin	...do	134	—— Martin	...do
Beverly, Mass.				
Eben Dodge	Bark	221	—— Osborn	F. W. Choate
Lady Suffolk	...do	210	—— Robertson	...do
N. D. Chase	...do	242	—— Hussey	...do
Salem, Mass.				
Messenger	Bark	216	—— Holmes	Benjamin Webb
Newport, R. I.				
George	Bark	220	—— Spooner	Josiah S. Munroe
Helen Augusta	Ship	536	—— Marble	...do
Providence, R. I.				
Lion	Ship	298	—— Hardwick	Lloyd Bowers
Warren, R. I.				
Dolphin	Bark	325	—— Cutler	R. B. Johnson
Dromo	...do	267	—— Taber	Charles T. Child
New London, Conn.				
Amaret	Brig	91	—— Whipple	Perkins & Smith
Catharine	Ship	384	—— Hull	Thomas Fitch, 2d
Charles Carroll	...do	412	—— Parsons	Perkins & Smith
Columbus	Bark	344	—— Huntley	George Huntley
Dove	...do	151	—— Rose	Williams & Haven
Electra	Ship	348	—— Brown	Williams & Barnes
Friends	...do	403	—— Brown	Benjamin Brown's Sons
Gen. Williams	...do	446	—— Miller	Williams & Barnes
H. Brewer	Bark	293	—— Smith	Perkins & Smith
India	Ship	433	—— Allen	Williams & Haven
Montezuma	...do	424	—— Forsyth	Williams & Barnes
New England	Bark	368	—— Smith	Minor Lawrence & Co
Pearl	...do	195	—— Forsyth	Williams & Haven
Ripple	...do	234	—— Morgan	E. V. Stoddard
Venice	...do	353	—— Lester	Weaver, Rogers & Co
Cold Spring, N. Y.				
Alice	Bark	281	—— Penney	John H. Jones

sailing from American ports—Continued.

Whaling-ground.	Date— Of sailing.	Date— Of arrival.	Result of voyage. Sperm-oil.	Result of voyage. Whale-oil.	Result of voyage. Whalebone.	Remarks.
			Bbls.	*Bbls.*	*Lbs.*	
Atlantic	....	July 24, 1854	135	10	......	
....do	May 19	Sept. 13, 1854	......	252	......	
.... do	Sept. —	June 16, 1854	......	455	......	
North Atlantic	Apr. 19	Sept. 16, 1854	158	......	......	
Atlantic	May 22	Nov. 7, 1854	......	32	.....	
....do	May 21	Sept. 5, 1854	159	6	......	
....do	Jan. 8	Aug. 15, 1854	31	......	......	
....do	June 8	Sept. 11, 1854	34	......	......	
....do	May 20	Oct. 4, 1855	364	......	......	
....do	May 14	Sept. 24, 1854	49	......	......	
North Atlantic	Mar. 1	Aug. 28, 1854	175	......	......	
Atlantic	June 18	Aug. 30, 1854	......	179	......	Sold to New Bedford 1854.
....do	May 24	Sept. 16, 1854	62	......	......	Withdrawn 1855.
....do	Apr. 21	Oct. 19, 1854	248	4	......	
Atlantic	Jan. 6	....	......	......	......	
....do	Apr. 24	Oct. —, 1854	19	......	......	
....do	Dec. 8	Aug. 20, 1855	90	190	......	Bought from Boston 1854.
....do	July 17	....	......	......	......	Bought from Boston 1853; missing; had a crew of 16 officers and men.
North Atlantic	Apr. 19	....	......	......	......	Missing; had a crew of 22 officers and men.
Atlantic	July 13	Sept. 26, 1855	190	100	......	
South Pacific ..	Nov. 28	Oct. 23, 1856	215	......	......	Sold to New Bedford 1856; sent home 65 sperm.
Atlantic	Oct. 12	Apr. 23, 1856	125	20	......	
South Atlantic.	Dec. 21	Dec. 28, 1856	......	15	......	Sent home 25 sperm.
Atlantic	June 14	Aug. 30, 1856	231	219	1,200	Withdrawn 1856.
Atlantic	Aug. 25	....	......	......	......	Condemned at St. Helena December 26, 1856.
North Pacific ..	Nov. 28	....	......	......	......	Burned by crew at Munganui, New Zealand, 1856; built 1847.
Pacific Ocean ..	July 17	....	......	......	......	Lost near Sydney November 30, 1856, with 500 sperm; was built at Wickford 1821, and rebuilt 1846; Providence's last whaler.
Indian Ocean ..	May 17	Jan. 17, 1858	770	48	......	
....do	Aug. 16	Oct. 28, 1856	175	1,400	5,300	Withdrawn 1857.
Davis's Straits.	Sept. 7	Aug. 12, 1855	......	Clean	......	Arrived on Labrador late, and was frozen into the ice from October, 1854, to July, 1855.
North Pacific ..	Nov. 21	Nov. 22, 1855	126	1,500	7,000	
....do	June 28	June 1, 1858	9	1,330	......	Sent home 1,228 whale.
Indian Ocean ..	Oct. 12	May 21, 1856	115	1,593	11,800	
South Atlantic	Sept. 7	May 10, 1857	158	9	......	Sent home 75 sperm, 110 whale.
Ind. & N. P ..	June 7	Apr. 11, 1857	35	2,611	......	Sent home 26,125 bone.
North Pacific ..	July 1	June 29, 1857	121	710	6,150	Withdrawn 1859.
....do	Sept. 12	Apr. 15, 1858	......	650	600	Sent home 2,055 whale.
Desolation	Aug. 19	....	......	......	......	Condemned at St. Helena February 19, 1857.
Honolulu	July 13	July 28, 1858	....	1,370	......	Sent home 1,840 whale, 57,769 bone; withdrawn 1858.
North Pacific ..	Oct. 22	June 22, 1857	266	1,930	11,300	Sent home 13,500 bone.
Pacific Ocean ..	Aug. 23	May 30, 1857	144	1,500	10,000	
Indian Ocean...	May 23	Apr. 19, 1856	33	2	....	
Atlantic	June 5	Mar. 21, 1856	59	1,012	8,800	Sent home 450 whale, 5,000 pounds bone.
North Pacific ..	Oct. 11	May 17, 1858	......	2,065	24,100	Withdrawn 1859; sold to Calcutta 1863.
North Pacific ..	Oct. 31	Apr. 24, 1858	25	1,333	21,000	Sent home 1,457 whale, 22,397 pounds bone.

Table showing returns of whaling-vessels

Name of vessel.	Class.	Tonnage.	Captain.	Managing owner or agent.
1854.				
Cold Spring, N. Y.—Continued.				
Huntsville	Ship	523	—— Grant	John H. Jones
Monmouth	Bark	273	—— Eldridge	do
Sheffield	Ship	579	—— Green	do
Stonington, Conn.				
Tekoa	Schooner	145	—— Keene	John F. Trumbull
United States	Bark	244	—— Holt	do
Greenport, N. Y.				
Caroline	Bark	252	—— Case	Wells & Carpenter
Italy	Ship	299	—— Weld	David G. Floyd
Neva	do	362	—— Hand	Wells & Carpenter
Oregon	Bark	224	—— Babcock	do
Philip, 1st	do	293	—— Sisson	do
Roanoke	do	252	—— Wade	do
Mystic, Conn.				
Leander	Bark	213	—— Kimball	Charles Mallory
Robin Hood	Ship	395	—— McGenley	do
Romulus	do	365	—— Baker	do
Sag Harbor, N. Y.				
Black Eagle	Bark	311	—— Edwards	Thomas Brown
Montauk	Ship	512	—— French	John Budd
Odd Fellow	Bark	230	—— Goodale	T. Brown
Parana	Brig	209	—— Smith	do
Tuscany	Ship	299	—— White	J. Budd
William Tell	do	370	—— Smith	T. Brown
San Francisco, Cal.				
Charles Carroll	Ship	376	—— Hunting	More, Folger & Dow
Cynosure	Schooner	..	—— Gregory	Wood & Co
Emeline	do	..	—— Osborn	Blanchard & Connor
Nonpariel	Brig	130	—— Sayre	Moore & Folger
R. Adams	Bark	271	—— Andrews	William Bailey
1855.				
New Bedford, Mass.				
Alexander	Ship	421	—— Dougherty	Swift & Perry
Alice Frazier	Bark	406	C. M. Newell	L. Kollock & Son
Alice Mandell	Ship	413	John S. Dennis	C. R. Tucker & Co
Arnolda	do	360	Andrew S. Sarvent	James B. Wood & Co
Baltic	Bark	395	L. B. Brownson	Alexander Gibbs
Barnstable	Ship	373	Nehemiah C. Fisher	David B. Kempton
Benjamin Tucker	do	349	Albert D. Barber	C. R. Tucker & Co
Byron	Bark	179	William E. Tower	Zeno Kelley

* No oil reported,

sailing from American ports—Continued.

Whaling-ground.	Date— Of sailing.	Date— Of arrival.	Result of voyage. Sperm-oil.	Result of voyage. Whale-oil.	Result of voyage. Whalebone.	Remarks.
			Bbls.	*Bbls.*	*Lbs.*	
North Pacific ..	Oct. 15	May 6, 1858	......	651	......	Sent home 1,457 whale, 32,035 pounds bone; sold to New York October, 1858.
South Atlantic.	Nov. 28	June 2, 1857	201	371	3,100	
Arctic Ocean ..	Sept. 12	May 4, 1859	......	900	......	Sold to Boston 1860; sent home 1,191 whale, 44,495 pounds bone.
South Atlantic	Mar. 24	....	......	......	......	Withdrawn 1855.
North Pacific ..	Nov. 21	....	......	......	......	Sent home 59 sperm, 1,546 whale; condemned at Honolulu January, 1857, and broken up.
South Atlantic	Dec. 6	Apr. 19, 1857	104	318	2,500	
Arctic Ocean ..	Sept. 26	....	......	......	......	Sent home 135 sperm, 3,072 whale, 23,800 pounds bone; condemned at Honolulu January, 1857; fitted from Honolulu and condemned again in December, 1858.
North Pacific ..	Aug. 30	Mar. 18, 1857	......	2,505	1,900	Withdrawn 1859.
South Atlantic.	Nov. 1	July 15, 1856	525	100	......	
North Pacific ..	July 17	Apr. 24, 1858	......	1,225	......	Built at Rochester, Mass., 1825; new topped 1853; picked up a dismasted Japanese junk with 27 people on board; carried her into Loo Choo; sold to New London 1858; sent home 1,453 whale, 21,337 pounds bone.
South Atlantic	Oct. 10	Mar. 18, 1857	488	351	......	
Indian Ocean...	Aug. 9	Apr. 4, 1856	35	373	3,000	
Japan Sea	Oct. 4	Aug. 2, 1857	179	1,982	......	Sent home 75 sperm, 32,000 pounds bone.
....do	Oct. 4	May 30, 1857	301	1,958	8,500	
Arctic Ocean ..	Nov. 4	Aug. 16, 1858	(*)	(*)	(*)	Built 1851; sent home 75 sperm, 872 whale, 1,360 bone; sold to New Bedford 1859.
North Pacific ..	Sept. 5	June 26, 1859	......	630	......	Sold to Boston 1860; sent home 70 sperm, 700 whale, 11,604 pounds bone.
South Atlantic	July —	May 29, 1856	222	796	900	
Patagonia, &c..	Aug. 12	Mar. 24, 1856	79	359	100	
Arctic Ocean ..	Sept. 20	....	......	......	......	Withdrawn 1855.
North Pacific ..	Aug. 24	May 6, 1857	150	1,400	14,000	Sent home 1,490 whale.
North Pacific ..	Nov. 28	....	......	......	......	No report.
Pacific Ocean.	Dec. 4	....	......	......	......	No report.
... do	Dec. 6	May 10, 1855	190	......	......	Sperm and elephant.
... do	Dec. 30	Oct. 14, 1855	150	150	......	Part blackfish.
... do	Sept. 12	Apr. 1, 1855	200	50	......	
Indian Ocean..	Sept. 3	....	......	......	......	Lost on coast of New Zealand, January 3, 1858; had 1,300 sperm; saved a part.
North Pacific ..	Oct. 31	May 9, 1859	4	990	5,400	Sent home 245 sperm, 12,500 pounds bone.
....do	Aug. 10	....	......	......	......	Sent home 282 sperm, 598 whale, 11,230 bone; lost on Prate Shoals, China Sea, March, 1857; two men lost.
....do	Nov. 12	Apr. 26, 1859	24	1,303	11,200	Sent home 1,190 whale, 59,100 pounds bone.
....do	Sept. 26	May 23, 1859	52	2,365	15,000	Captain Brownson came home 1858; sent home 38 sperm, 407 whale, 4,400 pounds bone; sold and withdrawn 1859; lost 1859.
....do	Oct. 31	May 4, 1859	55	1,472	3,500	Sent home 203 sperm, 470 whale, 11,400 bone.
....do	Nov. 22	June 1, 1859	190	1,520	2,200	Dismasted in a gale 1856; refitted at Honolulu at an expense of over $8,000; sent home 810 whale, 19,400 pounds bone.
Pacific Ocean ..	Aug. 27	Mar. 9, 1861	495	77	650	Bought from Stonington 1855; Captain Tower died at sea October, 1856.

only freight.

Table showing returns of whaling-vessels

Name of vessel.	Class.	Tonnage.	Captain.	Managing owner or agent.
1855.				
New Bedford, Mass.—Continued.				
Callao	Ship	324	Alden B. Howland	Henry Taber & Co
Canton	do	280	S. E. Cook	C. R. Tucker & Co
Cavalier	Bark	295	E. Nickerson	James D. Thompson
Champion	Ship	336	Nathaniel P. Gray	do
Cherokee	Bark	261	Philander Smith	William Hathaway, jr
Cleora	do	263	Shubael H. Norton	Charles Hitch & Son
Cleone	do	373	John E. Simmons	Edmund Maxfield
Columbus	do	313	Joseph S. Taylor	William R. Rodman
Congress, 2d	Ship	376	F. E. Stranburg	Gideon Allen
Congaree	Bark	321	James T. Eldridge	Thomas Wilcox
Cowper	Ship	391	Aaron Dean	Benjamin B. Howard
Desdemona	do	295	Thomas H. Smith	T. & A. R. Nye
Draper	do	291	William P. Sanford	Henry F. Thomas
Dunbarton	Bark	199	Joseph P. Nye	Isaac B. Richmond
E. Corning	do	325	Francis O. Rotch	Alexander Gibbs
Elizabeth	Ship	329	Obed Pierce	T. & A. R. Nye
Emma C. Jones	do	347	Weston Jenney	Edward C. Jones
Emily	Bark	333	Augustus Hale	Charles Almy
Eugenia	do	356	William Cottle	Swift & Allen
Falcon	Ship	273	Shubael C. Norton	Thomas Knowles & Co
Francis Henrietta	Bark	407	F. D. Drew	William G. E. Pope
Geo. Washington	Ship	609	Pardon C. Edwards	I. Howland, jr., & Co
Globe	Bark	215	Alexander A. Tripp	Allen Lucas
Golconda	Ship	331	Philip Howland	G. & M. Howland
Good Return	do	376	Benjamin F. Wing	Henry Taber & Co
Henry Taber	Bark	355	Prince W. Ewer	do
Herald, 2d	Ship	303	Henry H. Slocum	T. & A. R. Nye
India	do	366	Timothy Howland	Charles Taber
Isabella	Bark	315	J. Lyon	T. Knowles & Co
James Allen	Ship	355	William Devoll	G. Allen
James Edward	do	434	Freeman H. Smith	Abraham Barker
James	Schooner	78	Zenas F. Eldridge	Luther S. Chase
James Maury	Ship	395	E. L. Curry	C. R. Tucker & Co
J. D. Thompson	Bark	432	William B. Waterman	James D. Thompson
Java	do	295	Augustus Lawrence	G. & M. Howland
John Dawson	do	237	Amos C. Baker	J. & W. R. Wing
John and Edward	Ship	318	F. C. Smith	Wilcox & Richmond
Kathleen	Bark	312	William Almy	James H. Slocum
Kutusoff	Ship	415	Andrew J. Wing	H. F. Thomas
Marengo	do	420	James T. Skinner	Jona. Bourne, jr
Margaret Scott	Bark	307	Jacob A. Howland	Rodney French
Marion	do	328	Alfred C. Davis	William P. Howland
Mercury	do	340	William C. Hayden	I. Howland, jr., & Co
Messenger	Ship	291	Isaac H. Jenney	John R. Thornton
Millinoket	Bark	180	—— Taber	Benjamin F. Howland

sailing from American ports—Continued.

Whaling-ground.	Date— Of sailing.	Date— Of arrival.	Result of voyage. Sperm-oil.	Result of voyage. Whale-oil.	Result of voyage. Whalebone.	Remarks.
			Bbls.	*Bbls.*	*Lbs.*	
Pacific Ocean ..	Oct. 3	June 11, 1858	163	1,433	10,500	Sent home 6,300 pounds bone.
....do	Sept. 5	Sept. 17, 1858	1,237	175	1,300	Sent home 13 sperm.
Atl. and Indian.	Sept. 29	May 16, 1858	192	961	......	Bought from Stonington 1855; Captain Nickerson came home sick 1855.
Pacific Ocean ..	Oct. 11	Apr. 30, 1858	85	1,470	8,000	Sent home 300 whale, 28,700 pounds bone.
Indian Ocean...	Nov. 1	Mar. 21, 1860	153	565	250	Sent home 2,600 pounds bone.
Indian and Pac	June 19	Apr. 29, 1858	1,378	......	......	Sent home 135 sperm.
North Pacific ..	Aug. 16	Apr. 11, 1858	145	2,255	1,200	Altered from a ship 1855; sent home 222 sperm, 308 whale, 14,184 pounds bone.
Pacific Ocean ..	Mar. 7	Mar. 6, 1859	1,319	202	......	Sent home 599 sperm.
North Pacific ..	Oct. 31	Apr. 3, 1858	70	1,668	20,000	Sailed July 27 for Davis's Strait; returned September 25 badly stove by a block of ice near Northumberland Inlet; sent home 774 whale, 16,100 pounds bone.
Pacific Ocean ..	Sept. 3	June 1, 1859	982	1,057	......	
North Pacific ..	Oct. 6	May 30, 1859	117	2,072	12,600	Sent home 30 whale, 15,314 pounds bone; sold for freighting 1859.
Pacific Ocean ..	Nov. 7	May 9, 1860	1,662	1	......	
North Pacific ..	Aug. 14	Mar. 24, 1859	56	1,941	13,000	Sent home 80 sperm, 793 whale, 15,500 bone.
Atlantic	Nov. 14	Aug. 22, 1858	237	20	......	Sent home 160 sperm; withdrawn 1859.
Atl. and Indian.	Aug. 25	June 4, 1860	660	6	......	Bought from New York 1855; sent home 650 sperm.
Pacific Ocean ..	Oct. 11	Oct. 7, 1859	1,335	......	......	Sent home 370 sperm.
South Atlantic	May 29	June 1, 1858	811	1,371	7,000	Sent home 45 sperm.
Pacific Ocean ..	Oct. 18	Sept. 6, 1857	471	3	......	Formerly in merchant-service; added 1855.
....do	Nov. 6	May 17, 1859	1,351	215	......	
South Pacific ..	Aug. 11	July 27, 1859	35	619	1,100	Second mate, Matthew Towne, killed by falling from aloft December, 1855; sent home 3,800 pounds bone.
North Pacific ..	Oct. 3	June 19, 1860	18	684	......	Sent home 4,279 whale, 43,849 pounds bone; sold to the United States 1861; one of "Stone Fleet," No. 1.
... do	Oct. 9	....	.....	......	......	Burned at Talcahuano March 16, 1856, by crew.
Atl. & Indian ..	Aug. 15	May 13, 1858	295	142	......	Sent home 360 sperm, 140 whale.
Indian Ocean ..	June 21	June 30, 1859	1,467	120	......	Sent home 105 sperm.
North Pacific ..	Oct. 9	Apr. 18, 1858	179	2,983	2,000	Sent home 42 sperm, 460 whale, 17,400 pounds bone.
Pacific Ocean ..	July 24	July 23, 1859	1,214	17	......	Built 1855; sent home 544 sperm.
Indian Ocean ..	Aug. 13	July 30, 1858	1,020	282	3,000	
Ind. & Pacific.	July 18	June 17, 1858	963	1,250	6,200	Sent home 35,000 pounds bone.
Pacific Ocean ..	Sept. 4	May 18, 1859	61	1,499	13,700	Sent home 177 sperm, 320 whale, 3,900 bone.
Indian Ocean ..	June 7	June 25, 1859	1,558	247	1,400	
North Pacific ..	Nov. 16	....	.....	......	......	Added 1855; shipped 30 sperm, 300 whale, 3,000 pounds bone, to London; Captain Smith died at Mauritius May 20, 1856; abandoned and sold at Mauritius 1857.
Atlantic	May 24	Aug. 25, 1855	.....	9	.....	Sold to Sippican 1856.
North Pacific ..	Nov. 29	May 5, 1859	102	1,628	2,200	Sent home 108 sperm, 840 whale, 22,177 pounds bone.
....do	Sept. 18	Apr. 3, 1858	76	2,324	1,800	Built 1855; sent home 82 sperm, 275 whale, 36,500 pounds bone.
Pacific Ocean ..	Dec. 5	June 26, 1860	21	1,346	10,000	Altered from a ship 1855; Captain Lawrence died at Valparaiso May 2, 1856; sent home 565 sperm, 881 whale, 30,664 pounds bone.
Atl. & Indian ..	Oct. 3	May 6, 1859	577	......	......	
Indian Ocean ..	Jan. 8	Dec. 10, 1858	50	1,900	......	Sent home 143 sperm, 80 whale, 10,870 pounds bone; withdrawn 1859.
Atl. & Indian ..	Sept. 12	July 3, 1857	388	63	......	Sent home 162 sperm, 167 whale.
North Pacific ..	Nov. 14	Apr. 6, 1860	......	1,445	13,013	Sent home 21,852 pounds bone; withdrawn 1860; condemned at Rio Janeiro 1861.
Indian Ocean ..	Oct. 10	Apr. 16, 1859	......	1,486	......	Sent home 40 sperm, 544 whale, 19,000 bone; altered from a ship 1855; sent home 60 sperm.
Pacific Ocean ..	Aug. 2	July 24, 1857	82	2,742	8,200	
....do	Oct. 8	Apr. 19, 1859	1,188	49	......	Added 1855; sent home 27 sperm, 108 whale.
... do	Oct. 4	Apr. 27, 1859	459	......	......	Sent home 387 sperm.
Indian Ocean ..	Aug. 14	Mar. 31, 1859	260	1,330	8,800	
Pacific Ocean ..	Aug. 6	Sept. 21, 1858	115	2	......	Bought from Warren 1855; sent home 394 sperm.

Table showing returns of whaling-vessels

Name of vessel.	Class.	Tonnage.	Captain.	Managing owner or agent.
1855.				
New Bedford, Mass.—Continued.				
Milo	Ship	401	George H. Sowle	E. C. Jones
Minerva Smyth	do	335	John Bowles	I. Howland, jr., & Co.
Minerva, 2d	do	291	Calvin Swain	T. Knowles & Co
Montezuma	Bark	196	—— Baxter	James H. Slocum
Montgomery	do	248	William B. Chapman	Swift & Allen
Mount Vernon	Ship	352	E. F. Nye	David R. Greene & Co
Napoleon	do	360	James A. Crowell	Charles Almy
Natchez	do	524	Dexter Bellows	S. Thomas & Co
Nautilus	do	374	Charles C. Swain	G. Allen
Navy	do	356	Daniel D. Wood	J. B. Wood & Co
Newark	do	323	James L. Smith	C. Hitch & Son
Olympia	do	296	John Ryan, jr	William Phillips
Pacific	Bark	385	John W. Sherman	Swift & Perry
Pamelia	do	300	Edward Coggeshall	William H. Reynard
Parachute	Ship	331	Andrew J. Cory	B. B. Howard
Phœnix	do	423	Horace Nickerson	Philip Anthony
Plover	do	330	Charles M. Skiff	W. & G. D. Watkins
President	do	293	George H. Allen	Richmond & Wood
Rodman	Bark	371	Elisha Babcock	C. W. Morgan
Roman	Ship	375	Zeb. A. Devoll	E. C. Jones
Roscoe	Bark	362	Alfred M. Coffin	And. Robeson
San Francisco	do	268	Elisha G. Cudworth	William Phillips
Sappho	do	320	Alexander Seabury	O. & E. W. Seabury
Sarah Sheafe	do	402	Henry C. Tobey	William H. Reynard
Seconet	Ship	400	J. F. Cleaveland	Charles Almy
Sophia Thornton	do	424	James Nichols	J. R. Thornton
So. America	Bark	606	Wash. T. Walker	W. O. Brownell
Stella	do	338	R. W. Hathaway	Cook & Snow
Trident	Ship	449	Marcus W. Taber	Frederick Parker
Tropic Bird	Bark	220	Cyrus E. Clark, jr	William P. Howland
Union	do	124	R. F. Ellis	Chapman & Bonney
Vigilant	do	283	Joseph McCleave	W. & G. D. Watkins
Virginia	do	346	Thomas M. Peakes	William Hathaway, jr
Warren	do	461	Preserved S. Wilcox	William Wilcox
Wavelet	do	300	George Swain	Lawrence Grinnell
Wm. Hamilton	Ship	463	D. P. West	I. Howland, jr., & Co
Winslow	Bark	263	William Watson	W. H. Reynard
Zephyr	Ship	361	James W. Ferril	Alexander Gibbs

sailing from American ports—Continued.

Whaling-ground.	Date—		Result of voyage.			Remarks.
	Of sailing.	Of arrival.	Sperm-oil.	Whale-oil.	Whalebone.	
			Bbls.	*Bbls.*	*Lbs.*	
North Pacific ..	Nov. 5	June 25, 1859	1,002	1,864	1,900	Sent home 17,141 pounds bone.
Indian Ocean ..	June 5	May 26, 1858	235	2,070	1,700	Sent home 65 sperm, 122 pounds bone.
Pacific Ocean ..	Oct. 22	Sept. 27, 1859	1,375	......	......	
Indian Ocean ..	June 5	Aug. 23, 1858	339	99	......	
Pacific Ocean ..	Aug. 23	June 18, 1858	385	1	......	Built 1845; third mate and boat's crew lost November 19, 1856, fast to a whale.
North Pacific ..	Sept. 1	....	......	......	......	Stove by ice and sunk in Ochotsk June 15, 1856; saved 230 sperm, 40 whale.
Pacific Ocean ..	Jan. 17	July 23, 1858	1,090	......	......	Bought from Nantucket, 1854; sent home 519 sperm.
....do	Aug. 15	....	......	......	......	Sent home 48 sperm, 487 whale, 6,500 pounds bone; lost in Potter's Bay, (Ochotsk,) October 7, 1856.
....do	July 26	June 27, 1859	916	107	......	Sent home 455 sperm, 32 whale.
North Pacific ..	Aug. 1	May 21, 1859	166	1,769	7,700	Sent home 145 sperm, 580 whale, 19,200 pounds bone.
Pacific Ocean ..	Oct. 15	June 10, 1859	1,553	......	......	Bought from Stonington, 1855.
North Pacific ..	Aug. 15	July 5, 1859	140	1,321	6,200	Sent home 600 whale, 20,600 pounds bone; sold and withdrawn, 1859.
Indian Ocean ..	July 24	Mar. 20, 1859	934	......	......	
....do	June 4	Aug. 22, 1858	1,344	......	......	Added 1855; sent home 38 sperm.
Pacific Ocean ..	Aug. 7	May 10, 1859	94	1,802	17,300	Sent home 1,340 whale.
Ind. & Pacific..	July 1	May 24, 1859	......	......	......	Sent home 255 sperm, 395 whale, 19,400 pounds bone; no oil on board; withdrawn, 1861, for merchant service.
Pacific Ocean ..	Aug. 28	Feb. 27, 1857	171	......	......	Built 1855.
....do	Oct. 4	June 1, 1859	1,189	......	......	Bought from Nantucket, 1855.
North Pacific ..	Sept. 10	July 13, 1859	1,780	620	700	
....do	Nov. 16	June 9, 1859	......	1,648	15,000	Sent home 1,749 whale.
Pacific Ocean ..	Aug. 1	July 27, 1859	869	......	......	Altered from a ship, 1855; sent home 588 sperm.
Atlantic	Mar. 12	Nov. 19, 1856	196	723	......	Sent home 80 sperm.
Pacific Ocean ..	Aug. 18	May 28, 1859	670	660	300	Sent home 6 sperm, 170 whale, 4,800 bone.
....do	Sept. 19	May 28, 1859	......	1,431	600	Took a bowhead whale, yielding 100 barrels oil, 2,000 pounds bone; sent home 958 whale, 20,617 pounds bone; sold and withdrawn, 1859; sold to Boston, and condemned at Baltimore, 1861.
....do	Sept. 6	July 28, 1860	1,570	......	......	Built at Fairhaven, 1855; sent home 129 sperm.
South Pacific ..	June 27	Aug. 7, 1859	1,250	60	......	Sent home 385 sperm, 1,300 pounds bone.
Pacific Ocean ..	Oct. 3	May 5, 1859	......	2,200	1,300	Captain Walker came home, 1858; sent home 138 sperm, 799 whale, 37,543 pounds bone; sold and withdrawn, 1860; one of "Stone Fleet" No. 1.
....do	Nov. 6	Apr. 1, 1860	759	677	......	Bought from New York, 1855; built 1848; sent home 676 sperm, 105 humpback.
Indian Ocean ..	Jan. 14	May 8, 1859	82	2,014	......	Sailed November 23, 1854; returned in December, leaky; sent home 260 sperm, 460 whale, 16,578 pounds bone.
Atlantic	June 4	Dec. 14, 1856	136	23	......	Sent home 50 sperm.
....do	Aug. 31	July 8, 1857	30	138	......	Formerly a schooner; added, 1854, from Provincetown; sold to Mattapoisett, 1857.
Pacific Ocean ..	Nov. 16	May 28, 1859	10	530	5,400	Sent home 400 sperm on voyage; third mate, Charles Swartwout, and four men lost by running on to a loose whale while fast to another, and the boat upsetting.
....do	Aug. 15	June 19, 1860	826	49	......	
Ind. & Pacific..	Oct. 4	May 8, 1860	......	415	......	Sent home 1,181 whale, 13,652 bone; added 1855, from Holmes's Hole; third mate, Watson Burpee, lost overboard October 17, 1855; withdrawn 1860; finally condemned at St. Catharine's, March, 1861.
Pacific Ocean ..	Oct. 9	....	......	......	......	Bought from New London, 1855; built 1853; sent home 2,714 whale, 34,153 pounds bone; sold at San Francisco, 1860.
North Pacific ..	Sept. 11	....	......	......	......	Sailed June 19; returned July 16; Captain hurt; sent home a small quantity of oil; lost off coast of Chili January 27, 1856.
Indian Ocean ..	Aug. 21	....	......	......	......	Sent home 369 sperm; lost on a reef near Honolulu, March 17, 1858.
Pacific Ocean ..	Dec. 14	Aug. 5, 1859	887	1	......	

Table showing returns of whaling-vessels

Name of vessel.	Class.	Tonnage.	Captain.	Managing owner or agent.
1855.				
Fairhaven, Mass.				
Clifford Wayne	Ship	305	William H. Swain	Ezekiel Swain
General Scott	do	333	Isaac Daggett	L. C. Tripp
Gen. Scott	Bark	360	Benjamin Clough	Nathan Church
Hudson	Ship	368	David Marston	Jenney & Tripp
Japan	do	487	Francis L. Dimon	William G. Blackler
Joseph Maxwell	Bark	302	And. P. Jenney	F. R. Whitwell
John Coggeshall	Ship	338	Phineas Fish	Reuben Fish
Northern Light	do	513	E. A. Chapel	Edmund Allen
Phipe Delanoye	do	383	Thomas M. Gardner	Warren Delano
William and Henry	do	261	Isaac Grinnell	I. F. Terry
Winthrop	Bark	218	Issacher H. Akin	Dexter Jenney
Wolga	do	285	William H. Crowell	Jenney & Tripp
Zone	do	365	Moses R. Fish	do
Dartmouth, Mass.				
Brighton	Bark	354	Abner Tucker	Tucker & Cummings
Charles and Edward	Ship	150	William H. Salter	William Potter, 2d
Elliot C. Cowdin	do	280	Thomas S. Bailey	Tucker & Cummings
Westport, Mass.				
Barclay	Bark	180	Weston S. Tripp	Alexander H. Corey
D. Franklin	do	171	Leander Smith	Job Davis
George and Mary	do	165	Samuel B. Devoll	Rescom Macomber
Janet	do	194	Henry S. West	Henry Wilcox
Leonidas	Brig	128	Asa Grinnell	C. A. Church
Mattapoisett	Bark	150	James M. Sowle	H. Wilcox
Mermaid	do	330	Gorham B. Howes	Andrew Hicks
Sea Queen	do	261	James H. Houghton	do
T. Winslow	do	136	George F. Davoll	John Hicks
Mattapoisett, Mass.				
America	Bark	257	—— West	R. L. Barstow
Annawan	Brig	159	Fred. P. Cornell	J. Holmes, jr. & Bro
Clara Bell	Bark	295	Charles H. Robbins	R. L. Barstow
Excellent	Brig	70	Calvin C. Adams	do
March	Brig	89	Henry Lewis	do
Sarah	Ship	370	Stephen Swift	Loring Meigs
Sarah	Bark	179	Job P. Rounesville	Attsatt & Sturtevant
Sm'l & Thomas	do	191	—— Briggs	R. L. Barstow
Willis	do	164	James King	do
Nantucket, Mass.				
Alabama	Bark	340	Thomas Coffin, 2d	John H. Shaw
Alpha	Ship	345	William H. Haswell	Hadwen & Barney
Apphia Maria	Bark	260	Charles H. Chase	J. H. Shaw
Citizen	Ship	360	William Cash	C. G. & H. Coffin
Hamilton	Schooner	75	—— Sheffield	J. B. Macy
Homer	Brig	140	Lewis B. Imbert	E. G. Kelley
James Loper	Ship	348	Obed Ramsdell	Obed Starbuck
Nantucket	do	351	Richard C. Gibbs	Perry & Dunham

sailing from American ports—Continued.

Whaling-ground.	Date— Of sailing.	Date— Of arrival.	Result of voyage. Sperm-oil.	Result of voyage. Whale-oil.	Result of voyage. Whalebone.	Remarks.
			Bbls.	*Bbls.*	*Lbs.*	
Pacific Ocean ..	Nov. 20	June 10, 1860	731	......	......	Sent home 77 sperm, 43 whale.
....do	Oct. 11	Dec. 20, 1859	1,434	7	......	Sent home 234 sperm, 80 whale.
Indian Ocean ..	Sept. 4	July 20, 1858	488	1,608	......	Bought from New London, 1855; sent home 14,700 pounds bone.
North Pacific ..	Nov. 26	Apr. 25, 1859	50	1,975	17,400	Bought from Mystic, 1855; sent home 150 sperm, 1,005 whale, 9,700 pounds bone.
Pacific Ocean ..	Nov. 8	Apr. 16, 1859	33	860	......	Built at Fairhaven, 1855; sent home 124 sperm, 1,850 whale, 28,349 pounds bone; sold to New Bedford 1859.
....do	Nov. 3	Aug. 7, 1858	1,495	16	......	Altered from a ship.
Ind. & Pacific ..	July 17	May 9, 1859	55	1,149	......	Captain Fish died 1856; sent home 57 sperm, 12,700 pounds bone; sold to New Bedford 1860.
North Pacific ..	Oct. 10	June 19, 1860	......	900	12,000	Sent home 25 sperm, 2,752 whale, 37,401 pounds bone; sold to New Bedford 1861.
Pacific Ocean ..	Dec. 25	July 25, 1860	1,000	300	......	Withdrawn for merchant service, 1860.
....do	Dec. 3	May 29, 1859	175	920	8,850	Sent home 59 sperm, 293 whale, 4,086 bone.
....do	Aug. 11	Oct. 29, 1858	760	77	600	
Indian Ocean ..	Aug. 18	May 28, 1859	24	643	3,500	Sent home 503 whale, 1,800 pounds bone; sold to Boston 1859.
Pacific Ocean ..	Sept. 4	May 9, 1858	1,384	......	......	
Indian Ocean ..	June 5	....	......	......	......	Bought from New Bedford 1855; Elijah R. Gifford, first mate, killed by a whale December 19, 1855; condemned at Sydney May 14, 1859; sent home 620 sperm, 477 whale, 5,831 pounds bone.
Atlantic	June 13	Aug. 6, 1856	244	45	......	Sent home 25 sperm; added 1855.
Pacific Ocean ..	Oct. 9	Mar. 3, 1860	911	90	......	Sent home 59 sperm; added 1855; sold to New Bedford 1860.
Atlantic	May 7	....	......	......	......	Lost on Cape Antonio March 18, 1856.
....do	May 30	Sept. 6, 1856	200	75	......	
....do	Oct. 24	Aug. 6, 1857	280	23	......	
Indian Ocean .	May 10	May 21, 1858	249	287	4,500	
Atlantic	Aug. 22	May 1, 1857	209	50	......	Sent home 150 sperm.
....do	Oct. 23	Apr. 11, 1857	570	4	......	
Pacific Ocean ..	Aug. 6	June 19, 1860	1,215	7	......	Built 1855; sent home 471 sperm.
....do	July 19	July 11, 1858	1,111	......	......	
Atlantic	July 17	July 7, 1857	161	10	......	Sent home 250 sperm.
Atlantic	Sept. 28	Aug. 24, 1858	576	151	300	Bought from New Bedford 1855; sold 1856.
....do	Dec. 18	July 25, 1857	302	31	......	Sent home 176 sperm.
....do	Aug. 20	May 4, 1858	971	10	......	Sent home 1,900 bone.
....do	Oct. 29	Aug. 9, 1857	......	Clean	......	Her last voyage; she went ashore and broke up in a gale in March, 1860; sent home 270 sperm.
....do	June 21	Aug. 12, 1856	247	29	......	Sent home 35 sperm.
Pacific Ocean .	Oct. 15	May 8, 1859	32	620	7,500	Sent home 225 sperm, 2,004 whale, 28,300 bone.
Atlantic	Dec. 4	June 2, 1858	425	28	......	
Indian & Pacific	Feb. 21	Apr. 29, 1858	121	274	......	Sent home 127 sperm.
Pacific Ocean .	May 25	Oct. 2, 1856	323	63	......	Sent home 266 sperm.
Pacific Ocean ..	June 27	Sept. 28, 1859	1,151	......	......	Returned September 1, leaking; sailed again September 24; sent home 54 sperm.
....do	July 9	July 29, 1859	1,281	......	......	
....do	May 23	....	......	......	......	Condemned at Valparaiso March, 1859.
....do	Oct. 29	July 4, 1859	2,012	130	......	Sent home 900 bone; sold to New York.
Atlantic	Nov. 23	No report...	......	......	......	
....do	Aug. 12	Oct. 30, 1856	107	20	......	
Pacific Ocean ..	Sept. 18	Aug. 14, 1860	928	64	......	Sold to New York.
....do	June 14	....	......	......	......	Lost on Nashawena, homeward bound; had 736 sperm, 794 whale; sent home 240 sperm, 320 whale, 3,000 pounds bone.

Table showing returns of whaling-vessels

Name of vessel.	Class.	Tonnage.	Captain.	Managing owner or agent.
1855.				
Nantucket, Mass.—Continued.				
Narragansett	Ship	398	George W. Gardner	Zenas L. Adams
Norman	do	338	Charles C. Ray	G. & M. Starbuck
Ocean Rover	do	417	Charles A. Veeder	G. & M. Starbuck & Co.
Peru	Bark	259	Frederick A. Easton	Z. L. Adams
Watchman	Schooner	140	Hiram Bailey	J. B. Macy
William P. Dolliver	do	90	James Maguire	do
Young Hero	Ship	340	Valentine C. Long	G. & M. Starbuck
Edgartown, Mass.				
Almira	Ship	362	—— Crosby	Abraham Osborn
Monterey	Schooner	80	Wimpenney	Ira Darrow
Walter Scott	Ship	369	—— Collins	Benjamin Worth
Washington	Schooner	140	—— Fisher	John A. Baylies
Holmes's Hole, Mass.				
Eliza Jane	Schooner	130	—— West	Thomas Bradley
Pavilion	Brig	150	—— Adams	do
Sippican, Mass.				
Adm'l Blake	Schooner	120	Benjamin B. Handy	Benjamin B. Handy
Altamaha	do	119	Consider Fisher	Stephen C. Luce
Sandwich, Mass.				
Amelia	Brig	127	David S. Russell	W. F. Lapham
Provincetown, Mass.				
Alleghany	Schooner	95	—— Cook	Daniel C. Cook
Alexander	do	75	—— Snow	Johnson & Cook
Chanticleer	do	87	—— Young	Samuel Cook
E. Nickerson	do	132	—— Freeman	Samuel Soper
F. Bunchinia	Bark	200	—— Tuck	E. Nickerson
John Adams	Schooner	99	—— Birch	John Adams
Louisa	do	97	—— Cook	S. Cook
Montezuma	do	92	—— Kilborn	T. & S. Hilliard
M. Spring	do	86	—— Young	J. E. & G. Bowley
M. King	do	86	—— Pettengill	Johnson & Cook
Olive Clark	do	95	—— Tuck	S. Soper
Richard	do	92	—— Young	Philip Cook
Rienzi	do	108	—— Caton	J. E. & G. Bowley
Samuel Cook	Brig	126	—— Genn	S. Cook
S. R. Soper	Schooner	130	{ —— Soper —— Needham }	S. Soper
Spartan	Bark	188	—— Cook	Stephen Nickerson
Union	Schooner	97	—— Genn	Jonathan Nickerson
Walter Irvin	do	133	—— Paine	S. Soper
Orleans, Mass.				
Lewis Bruce	Brig	135	—— Ryder	Heman Smith
Medford	do	108	—— Lamson	do
Rothschild	Bark	261	—— Allerton	do
Beverly, Mass.				
B. Franklin	Bark	164	—— Brown	F. W. Choate
Warren, R. I.				
Florence	Bark	326	—— Champlin	R. B. Johnson
Smithfield	do	164	—— McCleave	do
Wm. Henry	do	186	—— Coit	Charles T. Child

sailing from American ports—Continued.

Whaling-ground.	Date— Of sailing.	Date— Of arrival.	Result of voyage. Sperm-oil.	Result of voyage. Whale-oil.	Result of voyage. Whalebone.	Remarks
			Bbls.	*Bbls.*	*Lbs.*	
Pacific Ocean ..	Nov. 22	May 20, 1860	83[illegible]	.....	.....	
....do	Oct. 16	May 12, 1860	97[illegible]	.....	.....	
....do	July 11	Oct. 26, 1858	1,721	....	.....	Built 1855; sold to the Spanish government.
....do	Oct. 4	Aug. 1, 1859	820	.....	.....	Sent home 73 whale.
Atlantic	Nov. 30	July 14, 1856	.....	530	.....	Built at Manchester 1853. Captain Bailey was drowned at Bona Vista May 31, 1856.
....do	Nov. 8	....	....	.....	.....	
North Pacific ..	Oct. 8	....	.....	.....	.....	Burned at Sandwich Islands 1858.
Pacific Ocean ..	Aug. 21	May 6, 1858	342	2,000	3,700	
Atlantic	May 15	....	.....	.....	.....	Sent home 12,000 bone; sold at Talcahuano February, 1858; sent home 192 sperm, 103 whale.
North Pacific ..	Nov. 26	June 11, 1859	181	506	500	Sent home 12,000 bone.
Atlantic	Oct. 11	July 28, 1856	34	11	.....	Added 1855.
Atlantic	Aug. 25	Oct. 31, 1856	2[illegible]	....	.....	Added 1855; withdrawn 1856.
....do	Oct. 27	Apr. 10, 1858	280	....	.....	Added 1855; sent home 163 sperm.
Atlantic	May 12	Aug. 31, 1855	20[illegible]	12	.....	Took, in all, 240 sperm, 8 blackfish; worth $13,510.
....do	May 10	Nov. 12, 1855	7[illegible]	....	....	
Atlantic	Oct. 16	Sept. 2, 1856	.....	.....	....	Returned clean; sold to Mattapoisett 1856.
Atlantic	May 15	Sept. 3, 1855	.....	164	.....	
....do	Apr. 6	May 6, 1856	40	164	.....	
....do	May 11	Sept. 1, 1855	......	16[illegible]	.....	
....do	Aug. 24	June 22, 1856	17[illegible]	325	.....	
Indian Ocean ...	July 17	Sept. 16, 1856	204	520	4,000	Sent home 217 sperm; added 1855.
Atlantic	Apr. 24	Oct. 25, 1856	59	.....	.....	
....do	May 15	Oct. 6, 1855	......	58	.....	Withdrawn 1856.
....do ...... {	May 11	Sept. 3, 1855	110	.....	.....	
	....	Apr. 19, 1856	84	8	.....	
....do	May 1	....	.....	.....	....	Capsized in Cintra Bay 1855; Captain Young and two men saved, thirteen lost.
....do	Apr. 14	Aug. 31, 1855	29	3	.....	
....do	Apr. 25	Apr. 12, 1856	.....	250	.....	Added 1855.
....do	May 18	Oct. 3, 1855	.....	.....	....	No report.
....do	Apr. 17	Nov. 22, 1855	170	.....	.....	
....do	May 8	Sept. 14, 1855	....	80	.....	Added 1855; withdrawn 1856.
....do ...... {	Apr. 3	Sept. 2, 1855	227	4	.....	
	Oct. 16	Sept. 11, 1856	42	152	....	
Ind. & Atlantic	June 11	Sept. 6, 1857	450	450	4,000	
Atlantic	Nov. 9	Sept. 26, 1855	.....	150	.....	
....do	Nov. 9	Sept. 16, 1856	40	150	.....	
Atlantic	Apr. 21	Apr. 25, 1856	....	313	2,800	Sent home 50 sperm.
....do	Mar. 20	July 3, 1856	155	4	.....	Added 1855; sent home 50 sperm.
....do	Sept. 12	Sept. 30, 1856	325	380	.....	
Atlantic	Aug. 15	Aug. 28, 1856	16	169	.....	Sold to Fall River 1856.
Pacific Ocean ..	Nov. 13	....	.....	.....	.....	Captain Champlin died in Japan Sea 1858; sent home 200 sperm, 300 whale, 3,675 bone; condemned at Honolulu 1859.
Atlantic & Ind.	Oct. 26	....	.....	.....	.....	Condemned at Pernambuco December 1855.
....do	May 10	July 21, 1857	432			

Table showing returns of whaling-vessels

Name of vessel.	Class.	Tonnage.	Captain.	Managing owner or agent.
1855.				
Newport, R. I.				
Antelope	Bark	340	Oliver Potter	S. W. Macy
Mechanic	do	335	T. J. Corey	Oliver Read
New London, Conn.				
Corea	Ship	365	—— Fish	Frink & Prentis
Georgiana	Brig	190	—— Buddington	Perkins & Smith
George Henry	Bark	303	James Buddington	do
Hannibal	Ship	441	—— Royce	Benj. Brown's Sons
John & Elizabeth	do	206	—— Destin	Williams & Haven
John E. Smith	Schooner	119	—— Fisher	R. H. Chappell
Laurens	Ship	420	—— Smith	Perkins & Smith
N. America	Bark	385	—— Lyons	Williams & Haven
North Star	Ship	399	—— Fish	Williams and Barnes
Peruvian	do	388	Lucius L. Butler	E. V. Stoddard
Pioneer	Bark	235	—— Morgan	do
Vesper	Ship	321	—— Hempstead	Williams & Barnes
Zoe	Brig	197	—— Royce	Thomas Fitch, 2d
Greenport, N. Y.				
Kanawha	Bark	269	—— Terry	Wells & Carpenter
Prudent	do	298	—— Hamilton	David G. Floyd
Sag Harbor, N. Y.				
Ann	Bark	299	—— Hamilton	Thomas Brown
Concordia	do	265	—— McCorkle	do
Emerald	Ship	518	—— Hallock	John Budd
Noble	Bark	273	—— Jennings	Gilbert H. Cooper
Washington	do	236	—— Babcock	T. Brown
San Francisco, Cal.				
Eagle	Schooner		—— Dubois	
Francis	Brig		—— Chester	G. B. Post & Co
Herald	Ship	262	—— Derrick	Benjamin F. Hardy
Hopewell	Schooner		—— Reynolds	
Leonore	Ship	370	—— Scammon	Tubbs & Co
Nonpareil	Brig	133	—— Andrews	Moore & Folger
R. Adams	Bark	271	—— Andrews	William Bailey
S. McFarland	Brig	142	—— Miller	J. G. Wallace
Mystic, Conn.				
Aeronaut	Ship	265		Charles Mallory
1856.				
New Bedford, Mass.				
Abigail	Ship	310	Rufus N. Smith	William G. E. Pope
Active	Bark	333	William Wood	Cook & Snow
Adeline	Ship	329	Asa Taber	C. R. Tucker & Co
Addison	do	426	Samuel Lawrence	Isaac B. Richmond
Afton	Bark	249	James M. Clark	F. & G. R. Taber
Anaconda	do	383	Samuel T. Crenner	I. B. Richmond
Archer	Ship	322	Matthew L. Smith	Edward W. Howland

sailing from American ports—Continued.

Whaling-ground.	Date— Of sailing.	Date— Of arrival.	Result of voyage. Sperm-oil.	Result of voyage. Whale-oil.	Result of voyage. Whale-bone.	Remarks.
			Bbls.	*Bbls.*	*Lbs.*	
Pacific Ocean ..	Oct. 4	June 10, 1859	381	52	700	Sold to New Bedford 1859.
North Pacific..	Nov. 27	Apr. 12, 1860	360	530	.....	Sold 1860; one of "stone fleet," No. 2; sunk 1861.
North Pacific..	Aug. 18	June 26, 1859	.....	1,237	.....	Added 1855; sent home 1,120 whale, 24,900 bone. One of "stone fleet," No. 1.
Davis's Strait..	Apr. 11	Sept. 27, 1856	.....	.....	.....	Returned clean; lost 14 men from scurvy; wintering in Frobisher's Straits.
....do	May 29	Dec. 20, 1855	.....	184	.....	Added 1855; fell in with the abandoned English discovery ship Resolute and carried her into New London.
Spitzbergen Sea	May 21	Mar. 21, 1856	.....	28	.....	First American vessel sailing for this sea.
Indian Ocean ..	Sept. 11	June 11, 1856	.....	518	5,110	
Atlantic	Sept. 18	June 21, 1856	.....	365	3,000	Added 1855.
Desolation Isld	Sept. 17	May 8, 1857	.....	4,324	.....	Do.
Atlantic	Aug. 7	June 18, 1858	.....	1,534	1,790	
Pacific Ocean .	Sept. 11	....	.....	.....	.....	Lost on Bedout Island, New Holland, July 12, 1856.
South Atlantic	May 15	Apr. 7, 1856	....	88	500	
Desolation Isld	Oct. 4	June 13, 1857	55	1,448	1,000	Added 1855.
Indian Ocean...	July 19	June 20, 1858	129	2,540	1,200	
Desolation Isld	Oct. 26	Apr. 4, 1857	11	1,074	.....	Added 1855; sent home 225 elephant.
Atlantic & Ind	Nov. 6	Apr. 30, 1860	35	890	900	Bought from New York 1855; built 1847; sold 1860; Greenport's last whaler.
Atlantic	Dec. 29	May 18, 1859	128	2,000	11,000	Second mate killed by natives of Easter Island 1856; added 1855, from Stonington; sold 1859; sent home 742 whale, 6,700 bone.
Indian Ocean ..	Dec. 7	....	.....	....	.....	Sent home 280 sperm, 720 whale, 6,000 bone; condemned at St. Helena February 25, 1858.
South Atlantic.	Oct. 25	Oct. 10, 1858	38	1,030	6,400	
North Pacific..	Oct. 26	May 9, 1859	.....	570	.....	Sent home 112 sperm, 412 whale, 8,100 bone.
South Atlantic	Nov. 9	July 9, 1857	950	250	1,200	One of "stone fleet," No. 2; sunk 1862
....do	Aug. 5	Dec. 4, 1858	279	780	1,000	Sent home 160 sperm, 466 whale, 3,000 bone.
Pacific Ocean ..	Aug. 26	July 25, 1856	.....	.....	.....	No report.
....do	Jan. 11	....	.....	.....	.....	Do.
North Pacific..	Jan. 9	....	.....	.....	.....	Do.
Pacific Ocean ..	Dec. 19	....	.....	.....	.....	Do.
....do	Dec. 3	July 25, 1856	60	500	.....	
....do	Dec. 13	Aug. 15, 1857	24	10	.....	
....do	Apr. 28	....	.....	.....	.....	Do.
....do	Dec. 27	....	550	.....	.....	Last reported at Panama November 2, 1856.
....	....	....	.....	.....	....	Lost 1856.
North Pacific..	Aug. 25	Aug. 18, 1860	504	703	630	Sent home 1,600 pounds bone.
Pacific Ocean ..	June 3	July 9, 1860	807	91	.....	Sent home 786 sperm, 33 whale.
North Pacific..	Oct. 22	June 25, 1860	182	900	4,100	Sent home 321 whale, 11,000 pounds bone.
Pacific Ocean ..	Nov. 25	June 14, 1860	.....	665	.....	Sold 60 sperm, 1,717 whale, 10,282 bone.
Atl. and Indian	May 26	Aug. 28, 1858	765	.....	.....	Sent home 120 sperm.
Pacific Ocean ..	Oct. 2	Aug. 14, 1860	1,341	.....	.....	Sent home 265 sperm.
....do	Oct. 7	Apr. 13, 1861	1,357	.....	.....	Mr. Corbin, first mate, died from injuries received from a whale August, 1860; sold to the United States 1861; sunk off Charleston—one of the "stone fleet."

Table showing returns of whaling-vessels

Name of vessel.	Class.	Tonnage.	Captain.	Managing owner or agent.
1856.				
New Bedford, Mass.—Continued.				
Bevis	Bark	214	David G. Pierce	John A. Macomber
Caroline	Ship	364	George W. Gifford	William Gifford
Carolina	do	395	—— Harding	S. Thomas & Co.
Catalpa	Bark	260	William F. Snow	I. Howland, jr., & Co.
Canada	Ship	545	Barton Ricketson	Gideon Allen & Son
Caravan	do	330	James G. Bragg	William O. Brownell
Chas. W. Morgan	do	351	Thomas N. Fisher	I. Howland, jr., & Co.
China	do	370	John W. Thompson	William Phillips & Son
Chili	do	291	Benjamin S. Clark	Azel Howard
Chris. Mitchell	do	387	Edward Manchester	David B. Kempton
Cicero	do	252	Charles Courtney	L. Kollock & Son
Condor	do	349	Samuel H. Whiteside	W. G. E. Pope
Contest	do	441	Jeremiah Ludlow	I. Howland, jr., & Co
Courier	do	381	Frederick W. Coffin	O. & G. O. Crocker
Courser	Bark	327	S. H. Gifford	B. Franklin Howland
Daniel Wood	Ship	345	Thomas Morrison	Jas. B. Wood & Co
Eagle	Bark	336	John McNelly	Swift & Perry
Eben Dodge	do	221	John W. Norton	B. F. Howland
Edward	do	274	William B. Stanton	Thomas Knowles & Co.
Eliza	do	366	Joseph H. Cornell.	Cornell & Penniman
Empire	Ship	403	Stephen G. Russell	George F. Parker
Europa	do	380	Edward B. Phinney	Edward C. Jones
Fanny	Bark	39	Benjamin L. Boadry	Swift & Allen
Florida	Ship	339	Coddington P. Fish	E. C. Jones
Fortune	Bark	291	Matthew Anderson	James Beetle
Gay Head	Ship	389	William Lowen	Jas. B. Wood & Co.
Gen. Pike	do	313	James Russell	William Gifford
Gov. Troup	do	430	Anthony Milton	E. C. Jones
Gypsy	do	360	Austin Smith	I. Howland, jr., & Co.
Hecla	Bark	207	Orrick Smalley	T. Knowles & Co.
Hector	Ship	380	Amos A. Chase	William J. Rotch
Helen Mar	Bark	367	Henry F. Worth	L. Kollock & Son
Hiawatha	Ship	381	John Ellis	T. & A. R. Nye
Hope	Bark	186	Shubael F. Brayton	Zeno Kelley
Huntress	do	383	William Allen	Cook & Snow
Hydaspe	Ship	313	Pardon Taber	J. B. Wood & Co
Jireh Perry	do	435	George H. Cannon	Swift & Perry

sailing from American ports—Continued.

Whaling-ground.	Date— Of sailing.	Of arrival.	Result of voyage. Sperm-oil.	Whale-oil.	Whalebone.	Remarks.
			Bbls.	*Bbls.*	*Lbs.*	
Pacific Ocean ..	Aug. 5	....	......	......	......	Sent home 54 sperm; lost on Point Mangle, New Granada, July 20, 1857.
Ind. and Pacific	Aug. 5	....	......	......	......	Built at Dartmouth 1843; sent home 95 sperm, 882 whale, 6,039 pounds bone; lost on Minerva Shoals May 24, 1859; one man lost.
Pacific Ocean ..	Oct. 3	Apr. 13, 1861	40	597	5, 400	Sailed under command of James Gray, who came home sick 1856; sent home 1,185 whale, 11,644 pounds bone; withdrawn 1861.
....do	June 20	June 19, 1860	824	5	......	Sent home 274 sperm; sold and withdrawn 1860; sold to San Francisco 1862.
North Pacific..	Oct. 16	....	......	......	......	Sent home 50 sperm; lost on coast of Brazil on account of intemperance of Brazilian officials; subsequently paid for by Brazilian government.
....do	Aug. 25	....	......	......	......	Bought from Fall River 1856; sent home 45 sperm, 569 whale, 5,869 pounds bone; condemned at Montevideo March, 1860.
....do	Sept. 15	Apr. 16, 1859	118	822	13, 800	Sent home 108 sperm, 978 whale, 14,900 bone.
... do	Oct. 15	June 26, 1859	37	1, 375	16, 200	Sent home 195 sperm, 844 whale.
Indian Ocean ..	July 31	June 8, 1860	704	128	......	Sent home 67 sperm.
North Pacific..	Aug. 16	May 17, 1860	97	1, 670	9, 400	Sent home 55 sperm, 473 whale, 14,000 pounds bone; withdrawn for merchant-service 1861; sold to San Francisco 1861.
... do	Aug. 12	May 16, 1860	.....	485	4, 600	Sent home 226 sperm, 598 whale, 8,900 bone.
....do	Aug. 7	....	.....	......	......	Sent home 73 sperm, 2,779 whale, 35,621 pounds bone; condemned at Honolulu December, 1858.
... do	Oct. 24	Apr. 12, 1860	......	1, 803	8, 850	Built at Mattapoisett 1856; sent home 1,920 whale, 24,176 pounds bone.
Pacific Ocean .	Oct. 4	July 2, 1861	733	......	......	Sent home 535 sperm; one of the "stone-fleet No. 1."
... do	Feb. 19	June 26, 1860	406	332	.....	Built 1855; sent home 147 sperm.
North Pacific.	Oct. 2	Apr. 12, 1860	.....	617	6, 200	Sent home 1,290 whale, 23,593 pounds bone.
Pacific Ocean ..	Oct. 22	Mar. 28, 1861	930	......	.....	Altered from a ship 1856.
Atlantic	May 15	Aug. 18, 1858	303	90	......	Bought from Beverly 1856; sent home 170 sperm.
Pacific Ocean ..	July 8	Apr. 24, 1860	741	55	......	
North Pacific.	Nov. 13	June 13, 1860	145	955	5, 400	Built at Mattapoisett 1856; sent home 146 sperm, 890 whale, 11,800 pounds bone.
....do	Aug. 11	May 9, 1860	35	967	7, 600	Sent home 1,412 whale, 8,424 pounds bone.
Ind. and Pacific	June 24	Apr. 30, 1860	885	680	......	Sent home 59 sperm, 1,800 pounds bone.
North Pacific.	July 19	Apr. 30, 1860	.....	1, 179	....	Sent home 52 sperm, 800 whale, 31,648 pounds bone.
....do	Oct. 16	Apr. 25, 1859	......	1, 605	10, 000	Sent home 32 sperm, 919 whale, 13,597 bone.
....do	Oct. 22	1860 or 1861	......	......	......	Sent home 1,850 whale, 17,700 pounds bone; one of "stone-fleet" No. 1.
....do	Oct. 20	Aug. 28, 1860	89	1, 176	985	First mate, John C. Clark, taken out of boat by a whale; his body was recovered after hauling in 150 fathoms of line; sent home 8 sperm, 728 whale, 19,053 bone.
....do	Sept. 9	Mar. 12, 1859	113	1, 956	5, 100	Sent home 759 whale, 5,900 pounds bone.
... do	Aug. 27	Apr. 16, 1859	......	1, 430	11, 000	Sent home 305 sperm, 907 whale, 16,600 bone.
Indian Ocean ..	May 15	Oct. 31, 1856	23	6	.....	Left Captain Smith sick at Fayal; sent home 98 sperm.
Pacific Ocean ..	June 3	June 2, 1859	562	80	......	Sent home 632 sperm.
....do	Nov. 17	July 19, 1860	894	....	......	Sent home 910 sperm; captured by a rebel privateer subsequently.
....do	Jan. 15	Mar. 17, 1861	65	1, 261	8, 500	Built 1855; sent home 239 sperm, 490 whale, 16,497 pounds bone; sold to Boston 1862.
....do	Oct. 11	Mar. 26, 1861	1, 246	......	......	Built at New Bedford 1856; sent home 250 sperm; sold to Boston 1862, for merchant-service.
Indian Ocean ..	Aug. 21	June 1, 1859	312	2	......	
Atl. and Indian	Aug. 11	July 19, 1857	161	4	......	Built at Mattapoisett 1856; sent home 290 sperm, 240 whale, 2,000 pounds bone.
Ind. and Pacific	Aug. 14	June 19, 1859	1, 319	322	......	Sent home 177 sperm.
North Pacific ..	Sept. 2	May 27, 1860	75	1, 127	7, 200	Second mate, Jabez Webb, killed by a whale March 21, 1860; sent home 54 sperm, 1,084 whale, 7,216 pounds bone.

Table showing returns of whaling-vessels

Name of vessel.	Class.	Tonnage.	Captain.	Managing owner or agent.
1856.				
New Bedford, Mass.—Continued.				
Josephine	Ship	446	James R. Allen	Swift & Perry
Kingfisher	Bark	451	Martin Palmer	Jona. Bourne, jr
Lafayette	do	341	George G. Ray	I. H. Bartlett & Sons
Lagoda	Ship	341	John D. Willard	J. Bourne, jr
Lancer	do	395	Aaron C. Cushman	Richmond & Wood
Lapwing	do	432	Michael Cumiskey	E. C. Jones
Louisa	Bark	316	William R. Hathaway	Swift & Allen
Malta	do	151	Ingraham D. Oliver	Benjamin B. Howard
Maria	do	202	Joseph Abbott	Thomas R. Rodman
Marcella	do	210	William T. West	C. R. Tucker & Co
Massachusetts	do	364	Daniel B. Greene	Swift & Allen
Mars	do	270	Gerardus P. Harrison	C. R. Tucker & Co
Mary Frazier	Ship	288	John Rounds	B. F. Howland
Mary	do	287	John R. Sands	I. Howland, jr., & Co
Merlin	Bark	348	John S. Deblois	W. & G. D. Watkins
Milton	Ship	388	Charles Halsey	Henry Taber & Co
Minerva	do	408	Charles H. Gifford	William Gifford
Montezuma	Bark	196	Dennis D. Baxter	James H. Slocum
Morea	Ship	330	Beriah C. Manchester	Azel Howard
Morning Light	do	361	—— Norton	S. Thomas & Co
Nassau	do	408	Henry Murdock	Swift & Perry
Niger	do	437	Nathan M. Jernegan	William Hathaway, jr
Ocean	do	349	Ezra Gifford	John R. Thornton
Ocean Wave	Bark	380	Hiram Baker	H. Taber & Co
Orray Taft	do	176	John C. Clark	Allen Lucas
Osceola, 3d	do	200	John P. Carr	Cranston Wilcox
Polar Star	Ship	475	Hiram Weeks	C. R. Tucker & Co
President	Bark	189	Seth D. McFarlin	Edmund Maxfield
Rajah	do	250	Ansel N. Stewart	do
Rainbow	Ship	474	Benjamin H. Halsey	W. Gifford
Rapid	do	505	David P. West	I. Howland, jr., & Co
Rambler	do	399	James W. Willis	F. & G. R. Taber
Reindeer	do	450	Edward R. Ashley	Edward W. Howland
Roscoe, 2d	Bark	235	Nathan H. Mendell	J. Bourne, jr
Saratoga	Ship	542	Frederick Slocum	Abraham Ashley
Sea Breeze	Bark	473	Benjamin F. Jones	O. & E. W. Seabury
Sea Flower	do	150	Sylvanus Cleaveland	Charles Almy
Silver Cloud	do	451	Edward Coggeshall	Russell Maxfield

sailing from American ports—Continued.

Whaling-ground.	Date—		Result of voyage.			Remarks.
	Of sailing.	Of arrival.	Sperm-oil.	Whale-oil.	Whalebone.	
			Bbls.	*Bbls.*	*Lbs.*	
Pacific Ocean ..	July 15	Apr. 24, 1859	63	1, 880	16, 900	Built 1856 at Fairhaven; sent home 94 sperm, 1,494 whale, 21,000 pounds bone.
North Pacific ..	Sept. 27	May 8, 1860	......	821	......	Built at New Bedford 1856; Captain Palmer taken down by a foul line and lost May 20, 1859; sent home 2,525 whale, 43,914 pounds bone; sold to United States for a blockader 1861.
Pacific Ocean ..	Dec. 18	May 13, 1861	950	......	......	Sent home 300 sperm.
....do	July 17	June 27, 1860	165	1, 280	11, 500	Sent home 893 whale; 15,436 pounds bone.
....do	Aug. 4	June 3, 1860	1, 539	7	......	Captain Cushman died November 23, 1856; sent home 54 sperm.
Indian Ocean ..	June 3	Nov. 4, 1859	1, 700	850	......	Sent home 18 sperm, 6,000 pounds bone.
North Pacific..	Sept. 23	May 9, 1860	58	379	4, 800	Sent home 104 sperm, 831 whale, 18,500 bone.
Atlantic	Oct. 22	....	......	......	......	Sent home 80 sperm; condemned and sold at Fayal August 27, 1857.
Ind. and Pacific	Sept. 1	Aug. 11, 1859	684	......	......	
Atl. and Indian	Sept. 16	June 18, 1858	293	233	......	Sent home 1,200 pounds bone.
North Pacific..	Nov. 20	June 26, 1860	130	1, 547	12, 000	Altered from a ship 1856; sent home 50 sperm, 1 400 whale, 26,176 pounds bone.
Indian Ocean ..	June 10	Apr. 13, 1860	423	428	1, 700	Sent home 238 sperm, 84 whale, 300 bone.
North Pacific..	Sept. 23	June 10, 1860	166	1, 213	8, 600	Sent home 93 sperm, 985 whale, 8,838 bone.
Pacific Ocean ..	Nov. 2	May 27, 1859	344	914	2, 200	Sold and broken up 1860.
....do	June 25	June 19, 1859	1, 506	31	......	Built at Mattapoisett 1856; took 2,000 sperm all told.
....do	Sept. 10	Mar. 22, 1860	22	2, 043	14, 200	Sent home 95 sperm, 883 whale, 22,826 bone.
....do	July 10	Apr. 14, 1860	27	925	......	Built at Charlestown 1816; sent home 10 sperm, 949 whale, 28,618 pounds bone; sold and withdrawn 1860.
....do	June 8	Aug. 23, 1858	339	99	......	Sent home 59 sperm.
North Pacific..	Sept. 2	....	......	......	......	Sent home 790 sperm, 1,558 whale, 22,600 pounds bone; condemned at Honolulu November 13, 1859.
Pacific Ocean ..	June 4	July 9, 1859	300	1, 039	500	Built at South Dartmouth 1856; sent home 229 sperm, 650 whale, 2,100 pounds bone.
North Pacific..	Nov. 17	May 10, 1860	......	1, 642	7, 800	Sent home 127 sperm, 610 whale, 28,870 bone.
Pacific Ocean ..	Sept. 2	Aug. 14, 1860	1, 535	10	500	Sent home 97 sperm.
....do	Oct. 22	Aug. 11, 1859	2, 101	......	......	
North Pacific..	Oct. 28	....	......	......	......	Built 1856, at New Bedford; sent home 180 sperm, 350 whale, 7,000 pounds bone; lost on Elbow Island October 12, 1859.
Atlantic	Nov. 20	July 16, 1858	372	42	......	Sent home 71 sperm.
Atl. and Indian	July 29	Sept. 11, 1858	497	17	......	
North Pacific..	Aug. 26	July 18, 1860	261	1, 392	......	Sent home 297 sperm, 350 whale, 18,888 bone.
Indian Ocean ..	Nov. 3	Apr. 19, 1859	621	5	......	Bought from Westport 1856; sent home 425 sperm, 37 whale.
Atl. and Indian	June 6	....	......	......	......	Bought from Westport 1856; lost off Tech-antar 1858; Captain Stewart, mate, and 11 men lost; sent home 9 sperm, 35 whale.
North Pacific..	Oct. 11	Apr. 18, 1859	122	1, 802	2, 000	Sent home 18 sperm, 904 whale, 26,522 bone.
....do	Oct. 1	....	......	......	......	Built at Fairhaven 1856; had a series of reverses in 1860—was fired by the crew, struck on a sunken rock, and run into the Jeannette; condemned 1860; sent home 1,512 whale, 15,600 pounds bone.
....do	Oct. 15	June 27, 1860	......	2, 325	6, 300	Sent home 195 whale, 18,853 pounds bone; sold to Boston 1860.
....do	Oct. 15	Mar. 24, 1860	2	1, 995	12, 000	Sent home 45 sperm, 2,353 whale, 14,213 bone.
Ind. and Pacific	Sept. 18	May 4, 1859	282	220	1, 500	Sold and withdrawn 1859.
North Pacific..	Nov. 3	June 1, 1860	110	1, 926	10, 000	E. W. Kempton, first mate, died at Lahaina November, 1857; sent home 80 sperm, 500 whale, 17,914 bone; withdrawn 1860; sold at Barcelona 1863.
Pacific Ocean ..	Oct. 1	Mar. 2, 1861	1, 475	50	......	Second mate, George W. Reed, drowned March, 1857; sent home 182 sperm, 1,450 whale.
Atlantic	June 5	Sept. 2, 1857	81	11	......	Sent home 121 sperm; sold to Providence 1858.
North Pacific..	Nov. 12	Aug. 14, 1860	840	1, 475	......	Bought from Boston 1856; sent home 305 sperm, 537 whale, 22,352 pounds bone; sold to New York 1862, for China trade.

Table showing returns of whaling-vessels

Name of vessel.	Class.	Tonnage.	Captain.	Managing owner or agent.
1856.				
New Bedford, Mass.—Continued.				
Sunbeam	Bark	360	Samuel H. Cromwell	J. & W. R. Wing
Susan	do	261	Joseph K. Green	Abraham H. Howland
Swallow	Ship	439	Herman N. Stewart	William O. Blackler
Thos. Dickason	do	454	Henry D. Plaskett	Alexander Gibbs
Thomas Pope	do	323	Robert P. Reynard	William Phillips & Son
Valparaiso	Bark	402	S. R. Tilton	William Hathaway, jr.
Wave	do	197	Leonard W. Hill	Thomas Knowles & Co.
William & Eliza	Ship	321	Charles A. Crocker	H. Taber & Co.
William Rotch	do	290	William M. Ellison	E. W. Howland
William Wirt	do	387	Abraham Osborn, jr.	E. Maxfield
Dartmouth, Mass.				
Brunswick	Ship	295	Henry P. Butler	Tucker & Cummings
Charles & Edward	do	150	William H. Salter	William Potter, 2d
Matilda Sears	Bark	300	Peleg S. Wing	do
Nyo	do	211	Fred. S. Howland	Tucker & Cummings
Westport Point, Mass.				
Aurora	Bark	351	Joseph Marshall	Andrew Hicks
D. Franklin	do	171	David S. Russell	Job Davis
Kate Cory	Schooner	130	George L. Manchester	Alex. H. Cory
Solon	Bark	127	William Childs	Henry Smith
United States	do	217	Warren Woodward	A. Hicks
Sippican, Mass.				
Admiral Blake	Schooner	120	Jared Blankenship	Peleg Blankenship
Altamaha	do	119	—— Fisher	Stephen C. Luce
James	do	80	Benjamin B. Handy	B. B. Handy
Sandwich, Mass.				
Ocean	Bark	165	Henry G. Smith	W. F. Lapham
Fairhaven, Mass.				
Alfred	Schooner	180	Lucius L. Butler	I. F. Terry
Amazon	Bark	318	Robert Eldridge	Nathan Church
Arctic	Ship	431	Charles A. Evans	Edmund Allen
E. L. B. Jenney	Bark	383	William Marsh	Gibbs & Jenney
Iowa	do	265	Charles C. Mooers	Jenney & Tripp
Martha, 2d	Ship	301	Timothy C. Spaulding	William G. Blackler
Samuel Robertson	do	421	Daniel S. Babcock	I. F. Terry
Sharon	do	354	Lillibridge B. King	Gibbs & Jenney

sailing from American ports—Continued.

Whaling-ground.	Date—		Result of voyage.			Remarks.
	Of sailing.	Of arrival.	Sperm-oil.	Whale-oil.	Whalebone.	
			Bbls.	*Bbls.*	*Lbs.*	
Ind. and Pacific	July 21	Apr. 13, 1860	1,514	......	......	Built at Mattapoisett 1856.
Pacific Ocean ..	Nov. 10	....	....	......	......	Lost at Esmeraldas, S. A., June 20, 1857; saved 250 sperm; the sixth vessel lost by A. H. Howland in 8 years.
Indian Ocean ..	Oct. 9	Dec. 22, 1860	600	800	......	Built at Fairhaven 1856.
North Pacific..	Nov. 2	June 18, 1860	28	376	4,700	Sent home 1.803 whale, 28,531 pounds bone.
Pacific Ocean ..	June 10	June 10, 1859	1,439	199	......	Built 1856 at Mattapoisett; sent home 437 sperm, 30 whale.
....do	Sept. 16	Apr. 30, 1861	1,202	110	......	Sent home 200 sperm; one of "stone-fleet" No. 2; sunk 1862.
....do	Aug. 15	June 30, 1860	177	10	......	Sailed July 29; returned August 10, with a defective mainmast.
Indian Ocean ..	July 22	....	....	.....	......	Built in 1805 at New Bedford; sent home 270 sperm; lost on Fortuna Island August 19, 1859; oil (450 sperm) saved.
Atl. and Indian	July 8	May 20, 1860	120	588	4,000	Bought from Fairhaven 1856; sent home 129 sperm, 44 whale, 4,298 pounds bone; withdrawn 1864; after went whaling from Honolulu; lost in Arctic 1871.
North Pacific..	Sept. 12	Apr. 12, 1860	10	1,787	4,800	Sent home 511 whale, 13,466 pounds bone; sold to New York 1862.
Indian Ocean ..	Oct. 9	Sept. 19, 1859	677	589	.....	
Atlantic	Oct. 21	May 15, 1858	140	20	......	
Indian Ocean ..	June 17	Aug. 9, 1860	1,051	197	......	Built 185[illegible] at Dartmouth; sent home 100 sperm, 175 whale, 2,000 pounds bone.
Atlantic	May 19	Aug. 22, 1858	12	......	......	Sent home 400 sperm; Captain Howland came home sick 1857.
Pacific Ocean ..	Nov. 10	July 12, 1861	1,505	.....	......	Built at Dartmouth 1856.
Atlantic	Nov. 11	Aug. 1, 1859	95	275	.....	Sold to New Bedford 1861.
....do	May 20	May 13, 1857	149	36	.....	Built at Westport 1856.
... do	June 16	June 20, 1858	140	100	....	Sent home 27 sperm.
Ind. and Pacific	June 23	....	....	......	....	Wrecked and abandoned at sea May 1, 1860, with 550 sperm on board; had sent home 175 sperm.
Atlantic	May 13	Sept. 14, 1856	100	32	....	
....do	May 22	Aug. 31, 1858	193	150	....	Sent home 99 sperm.
....do	May 20	Aug. 31, 1856	193	.....	.....	Bought from New Bedford 1856; took, in all, 220 sperm, worth $10,000.
Atlantic	June 26	July 20, 1857	....	Clean	....	
Desolat'n Island	Aug. 16	....	....	....	....	Bought from Boston 1856; formerly of New Bedford; lost on Hurd's Island December 29, 1856; tender to Sam. Robertson.
Indian Ocean ..	Oct. 15	June 7, 1860	10	1,522	7,000	Altered from a ship 1856; sent home 276 sperm, 10,685 pounds bone; one of the "stone-fleet" sunk off Charleston 1861.
Pacific Ocean ..	July 23	....	....	....	.....	Captain Evans was drowned off New Zealand 1857; his successor, ——— Beekman, came home 1858; sent home 2,128 whale, 28,568 pounds bone; withdrawn 1861; sold to New York; lost in Arctic 1876.
....do	Nov. 11	....	....	....	....	Altered from a ship 1856; sent home 900 sperm; condemned at Sydney January, 1862; sold oil (1,100 sperm) there.
... do	Oct. 19	Aug. 25, 1859	342	647	......	Sold to New York 1859.
Indian Ocean ..	May 20	Apr. 1, 1860	1,001	189	......	Sold 1860.
Desolat'n Island	Aug. 23	Oct. 17, 1858	....	3,399	....	John Faustin, third mate, and three men drowned while chasing whales September, 1857; first ship from New Bedford district to Hurd's Island; elephant-oil; withdrawn for freighting 1859; condemned at Pernambuco June, 1863.
Pacific Ocean ..	Nov. 26	Aug. 16, 1861	.....	1,616	....	Sold to Boston 1861; sent home 591 whale, 21,504 pounds bone; finally condemned at Sydney January 18, 1863.

Table showing returns of whaling-vessels

Name of vessel.	Class.	Tonnage.	Captain.	Managing owner or agent.
1856.				
Fairhaven, Mass.—Continued.				
South Seaman	Ship	497	Thomas A. Norton	E. Allen
Tahmaroo	Ship	371	Jas. B. Robinson	Fish & Robinson
Mattapoisett, Mass.				
Amelia	Brig	127	Charles W. Kempton	L. Meigs & Co
Elvira	...do	131	Stephen Merrihew	......do
Mary Ann	Bark	214	Joseph R. Taber	R. L. Barstow
March	Brig	89	Henry Lewis	......do
Palmyra	Schooner	100	Benjamin Smith	L. Meigs
R. L. Barstow	Bark	203	—— Devoll	R. L. Barstow
Sun	...do	184	Ephraim Poole	......do
Nantucket, Mass.				
Hero	Ship	313	William Holway	G. & M. Starbuck & Co
Homer	Brig	140	James L. Fisher	E. G. Kelley
Hamilton	Schooner	....	David Patterson	
Islander	Bark	347	Charles E. Starbuck	Matthew Crosby
Lexington	Ship	399	James Fisher	Edward W. Perry
Mary	...do	369	John C. Brock	......do
Massachusetts	...do	360	Thomas Chatfield	Zenas L. Adams
Phœnix	Bark	323	J. Hinckley	Gardner & McLeave
Sea Ranger	...do	370	Henry W. Davis	Samuel C. Wyer
Watchman	Schooner	140	Charles W. Hussey	J. B. Macy
Wm. P. Dolliver	...do	86	James McGuire ....do James Russell	....do
Edgartown, Mass.				
Champion	Ship	400	—— Coffin	Benjamin Worth
Delaware	Schooner	132	James McGuire	Henry Pease
Ellen	Bark	232	—— Slocum	Henry Colt
Louisa Sears	..do	180	Edward Mayhew	Abraham Osborn
Mary	Ship	343	—— Jenks	......do
Richard Mitchell	..do	386	James Huxford	Henry Colt
Rose Pool	Bark	285	Alex. P. Fisher	Joseph Holley
Vineyard	...do	381	—— Caswell	Benjamin Worth
Washington	Schooner	140	—— Blankenship	John A. Baylies
Holmes's Hole, Mass.				
Helen Augusta	Bark	270	—— Worth	Thomas Bradley
Falmouth, Mass.				
Hobomok	Ship	414	—— Marchant	Oliver C. Swift

sailing from American ports—Continued.

Whaling-ground.	Date— Of sailing.	Date— Of arrival.	Result of voyage. Sperm-oil.	Result of voyage. Whale-oil.	Result of voyage. Whalebone.	Remarks.
			Bbls.	*Bbls.*	*Lbs.*	
Pacific Ocean ..	Aug. 26	....	.....	.....	.....	Built at Mattapoisett 1856; sent home 70 sperm, 3,560 whale, and 21,027 pounds bone; lost on French Frigate Shoal March 13, 1859.
North Pacific ..	Aug. 5	Feb. 21, 1860	43	1,290	2,600	Took, in all, 275 sperm, 2,300 whale, 17,700 pounds bone; sold to New Bedford 1860; the Tahmaroo was afterward sold at Fayal, 1861.
Atlantic	Dec. 19	June 19, 1858	100	87	....	Bought from Sandwich 1856; fired into and boarded by English steamer Lex on the coast of Africa, 1857.
....do	July 24	....	.....	.....	.....	Bought from Boston 1856; condemned at Saint Thomas April 21, 1859.
Indian Ocean ..	Sept. 4	Sept. 24, 1858	676	103	.....	Bought from New Bedford 1856; sent home 27 sperm.
Atlantic	Nov. 13	Sept. 7, 1857	142	6	.....	
....do	June 24	Nov. 9, 1857	193	....	.....	Bought from Nantucket 1856; sent home 60 sperm.
....do	Aug. 19	Aug. 30, 1858	704	115	.....	
....do	Apr. 20	Oct. 18, 1857	375	229	.....	Sent home 157 sperm.
Pacific Ocean ..	Oct. 11	July 11, 1860	1,150	250	.....	
Atlantic	Nov. 20	Sept. 9, 1857	77	54	....	
....do	July 21	Aug. —, 1856	.....	40	.....	
Pacific Ocean .	Aug. 19	June 9, 1861	800	.....	.....	Built at Fairhaven 1856.
....do	Sept. 19	....	.....	....	.....	Sent home 82 sperm, 628 whale, 12,385 bone; lost on Strong's Island 1859; saved 100 barrels sperm.
....do	Sept. 9	Apr. 29, 1861	1,170	.....	.....	Sold to New York and fitted for California.
....do	Sept. 28	Oct. 14, 1860	.....	1,540	.....	Sent home 43,000 pounds bone; sold to San Francisco 1861.
North Pacific ..	Oct. 19	....	.....	.....	.....	Captain Hinckley came home sick; sent home 150 sperm, 1,075 whale; lost on Elbow Island, Ochotsk Sea.
Pacific Ocean ..	Sept. 16	Oct. 14, 1860	1,713	51	.....	Built at Mattapoisett 1856; sold to Providence; afterward bought for New Bedford.
Atlantic	Sept. 23	Aug. 26, 1858	44	386	1,350	Obtained 4 barrels of ambergris, which sold for $10,000.
	June 24	Aug. 15, 1856	.....	55		
....do	Aug. 20	Aug. 25, 1856	.....	Clean	....	Added 1856.
	Oct. 30	Oct. 20, 1857	2[illegible]	66		
North Pacific.	Oct. 5	Mar. 21, 1860	17[illegible]	1,140	2,000	
Atlantic	Nov. 7	....	.....	.....	.....	Bought from Provincetown 1856; lost in a white squall.
Ind. and Pacific	Aug. 14	Nov. 25, 1859	425	515	.....	Sent home 121 sperm.
Atl. and Indian	Oct. 30	Aug. 17, 1858	417	302	.....	Bought from Plymouth 1856; built 1847 a brig; Captain Mayhew died at Saint Helena April 25, 1857.
North Pacific ..	Aug. 6	Apr. 3, 1860	23	1,[illegible]89	4,600	Sent home 254 sperm, 427 whale, 21,199 bone.
Ind. and Pacific	Nov. 19	May 9, 1860	50[illegible]	2,175	1,900	Bought from Nantucket 1856; sent home 4,700 pounds bone; sold to New Bedford for merchant service 1861; sold to Bremen 1863.
Ind. and Pac ...	July 21	July 20, 1860	222	808	.....	Bought from Boston 1856; sent home 102 sperm, 100 whale, 4,528 bone.
North Pacific ..	Aug. 6	May 23, 1859	119	1,496	9,500	Sent home 165 sperm, 19,500 bone.
Atlantic	Sept. 3	Sept. 9, 1857	90	64	.....	
Atlantic	June 19	Dec. 6, 1858	71	910	1,200	Sent home 27 sperm.
Pacific Ocean ..	Nov. 21	Mar. 21, 1860	30	1,572	10,500	Sent home 74 sperm, 491 whale, 17,859 bone; sold to New Bedford 1860; sold to New York for merchant service 1863; renamed Live Oak.

Table showing returns of whaling-vessels

Name of vessel.	Class.	Tonnage.	Captain.	Managing owner or agent.
1856.				
Provincetown, Mass.				
Acorn	Bark	215	—— Puffer	Nickerson & Tuck
Alleghany	Schooner	95		Daniel C. Cook
Alexander	do	75	—— Cook	Johnson & Cook
Antarctic	do	136	—— Costa	J. E. & G. Bowley
Chanticleer	do	87	—— Young	Samuel Cook
E. Nickerson	do	132	—— Freeman	Samuel Soper
Eschol	Brig	143	—— Nickerson	Hannum & Co
F. Bunchinia	Bark	200	—— Tuck	Nickerson & Tuck
John Adams	Schooner	99	{ —— Burch —— Doyle }	John Adams
J. H. Duvall	Bark	200	—— Young	J. E. & G. Bowley
Montezuma	Schooner	92	—— Chapman	T. & S. Hilliard
M. King	do	86		Johnson & Cook
Olive Clark	do	95	—— Martyne	S. Soper
Parker Cook	Bark	130	—— Cook	E. & E. K. Cook
Richard	Schooner	92		Philip Cook
Rienzi	do	105	—— Katon	J. E. & G. Bowley
Union	do	97		Jonathan Nickerson
V. Doane	do	99	—— Cook	H. & S. Cook & Co
Walter Irvin	do	133	—— Holmes	S. Soper
Orleans, Mass.				
Lewis Bruce	Brig	135		Heman Smith
Medford	do	108	—— Snow	do
Wm. Martin	Schooner	134	—— Martin	do
Beverly, Mass.				
Lady Suffolk	Bark	210	—— Robertson	F. W. Choate
Fall River, Mass.				
B. Franklin	Bark	164	—— Brown	
Warren, R. I.				
Belle	Bark	286	—— Smith	S. P. Child
Benjamin Rush	Ship	385	—— Wyatt	do
Bowditch	do	399	—— Martin	R. B. Johnson
Brutus	do	470	—— Henry	do
Covington	Bark	351	—— Newman	Charles T. Child
Hector	do	225	—— Johnson	R. B. Johnson
Sea Shell	do	331	—— Ware	do
Xanthe	do	325	Charles Barton	do
Newport, R. I.				
William Lee	Bark	311	W. L. Slocum	Josiah S. Munroe
New London, Conn.				
Agate	Brig	187	—— Allen	C. A. Williams & Co
Alert	Bark	398	—— Church	E. V. Stoddard
Amaret	Brig	91	—— Quaile	Perkins & Smith
Atlantic	Schooner	130	—— Brown	do
Atlas	do	81	—— Starr	do
Benj. Morgan	Ship	407	—— Sisson	do

sailing from American ports—Continued.

Whaling-ground.	Date—		Result of voyage.			Remarks.
	Of sailing.	Of arrival.	Sperm-oil.	Whale-oil.	Whalebone.	
			Bbls.	*Bbls.*	*Lbs.*	
Atl. and Ind	July 25	June 12, 1859	595			Added 1856.
Atlantic		Aug. 26, 1856		220		
North Atlantic	June 10	Aug. 26, 1856	10	130		
Atlantic	Sept. 12	Sept. 3, 1857	210			
North Atlantic	May 12	Aug. 26, 1856		264		
Atlantic	Aug. 18	Aug. 4, 1857	65	200	1,800	Sent home 54 sperm.
....do	Apr. 28	Jan. 1, 1857	130			Bought from Newburyport 1855.
Atl. and Ind	Dec. 26	Aug. 30, 1858	95	125	600	Sent home 800 pounds bone.
Atlantic	Apr. 23	Oct. 3, 1856	164			
North Atlantic	Nov. 22	Mar. —, 1858	90			
Indian Ocean	Nov. 27	Apr. 28, 1860	504	683	4,300	Bought from Boston, 1856.
		Sept. 5, 1857	7	150		
Atlantic	Nov. 12	Dec. 28, 1856	57			
....do	Apr. 28	June 16, 1857		130		Sailed again in 1856, or early in 1857; arrived May 24, 1858, 25 sperm, 200 whale.
....do	June 6	May 23, 1857		105		
....do	May 28	Oct. 6, 1857	300	60		
		Oct. 9, 1856		90		
North Atlantic	May 12	Apr. 17, 1857	101	52		Sent home 45 sperm.
Atlantic	Apr. 28	Dec. 28, 1856		60		
N. Atlantic {	May 20	Sept. 6, 1856	131			} Added 1856.
	Dec. 27	Aug. 22, 1857	100	120		
Atlantic	Nov. 17	Jan. —, 1858		50		
Atlantic	June 26	May 23, 1857	58	28		
....do	Aug. 18	Sept. 7, 1857	55	285	2,100	
....do	Jan. 30	Sept. 28, 1856		192	800	
North Atlantic	Dec. 26	Aug. 24, 1858	225	96		
North Atlantic	May 30	Oct. 19, 1857	346	30		Sent home 72 sperm.
Atlantic	Nov. 28	June 19, 1858	151	134		Bought from Beverly 1856.
Pacific Ocean	May 21	May 8, 1859	975			Sold to New York 1859.
North Pacific	Oct. 28					Sent home 6 sperm, 1,014 whale, 12,344 bone; went into guano trade; sold to Honolulu 1860.
Pacific Ocean	Nov. 18					Sent home 32 sperm, 2,523 whale, 20,602 bone; went into guano trade; sold to Honolulu 1860.
North Pacific	Sept. 15	Apr. 4, 1860		1,020	13,000	Sent home 22 sperm, 3,639 whale, 50,436 bone; sold to New York 1860; thence to New Bedford same year.
....do	Aug. 16	May 8, 1860		640	9,000	Sent home 38 sperm, 463 whale, 6,687 bone.
Ind. and Pac	June 27	May 28, 1859	420			Sold to Boston 1859; was built at Warren 1842.
Pacific Ocean	Oct. 23	Oct. 4, 1860	848			Withdrawn for China trade 1862.
Ind. and Pac	Aug. 14	Jan. 11, 1860	1,019			Built at Warren 1856; sold to New York 1860.
Pacific Ocean	Sept. 17	May 17, 1860	510	425		Withdrawn 1860; one of "stone fleet," No. 2; sunk 1862.
Arctic Ocean	Apr. 6					Added 1856; sent home 1,443 whale, 24,000 bone, 13,000 pounds walrus teeth; sold at Honolulu 1860; broken up 1861.
Desolat'n Island	July 23	May 31, 1858		3,615	500	
Davis's Strait	May 21	—— —, 1857		190	2,200	Added 1856.
Desolat'n Island	July 19	Jan. 12, 1857	2			Lost at Desolation Island 1858.
....do	July 31					
North Pacific	Oct. 23	May 8, 1860	54	904	800	Sent home 30 sperm, 1,450 whale, 17,703 bone; withdrawn, 1860; sold to New York 1861; used for United States store-ship; broken up 1866.

Table showing returns of whaling-vessels

Name of vessel.	Class.	Tonnage.	Captain.	Managing owner or agent.
1856.				
New London, Conn.—Continued.				
Brooklyn	Ship	30	—— Rose	Perkins & Smith
Clematis	do	311	—— Watrous	Williams & Barns
Corinthian	do	505	—— Rogers	Perkins & Smith
Columbus	Bark	344	—— Ward	George Huntley
Dover	Ship	430	—— Jeffrey	Benjamin Brown's Sons
Dromo	do	306	—— May	Thomas Fitch, 2d
E. R. Sawyer	Schooner	126	—— Kimball	E. V. Stoddard
George Henry	Bark	303	—— Buddington	Perkins & Smith
Hannibal	Ship	441	C. B. Chappell	B. Brown's Sons
Indian Chief	do	401	—— Huntley	George Huntley
Iris	Bark	245	—— Bolles	Frink & Prentiss
Isaac Hicks	Ship	495	—— Norie	Lawrence & Co
John & Elizabeth	do	296	—— Eldridge	Williams & Haven
John E. Smith	Schooner	119	—— Anderson	R. H. Chappell
Julius Cesar	Ship	347	—— Bartlett	E. V. Stoddard
Marcia	Schooner	128	—— Fowler	R. H. Chappell
North West	Ship	304	—— Rogers	Thomas Fitch, 2d
Pacific	Schooner	161	—— Ward	Lawrence & Co
Pearl	Bark	195	—— Jeffrey	Williams & Haven
Peruvian	Ship	388	—— Chadwick	E. V. Stoddard
Restless	Bark	191	—— Middleton	Thomas Fitch, 2d
Ripple	do	234	—— Morgan	E. V. Stoddard
Sea Witch	Schooner	109	—— Reed	W. A. Reed
Silver Cloud	do	140	—— Fisher	R. H. Chappell
Tenedos	Bark	245	—— King	Lawrence & Co
Stonington, Conn.				
Cincinnati	Ship	457	—— Williams	Stanton & Pendleton
Newburyport	Bark	341	—— Crandall	J. E. Smith & Co
Tybee	do	299	—— Freeman	do
Greenport, N. Y.				
Oregon	Bark	224	—— Case	Wells & Carpenter
Mystic, Conn.				
Coriolanus	Ship	268	—— Nash	Charles Mallory
Leander	Bark	213	—— Chester	do
Shepherdess	do	274	—— Watrous	Randall, Smith & Ashbey
Sag Harbor, N. Y.				
Columbia	Bark	285	—— White	John Budd
Mary Gardner	do	316	—— Nicoll	W. & H. G. Cooper
Nimrod	do	280	—— Green	do
Odd Fellow	do	239	—— Goodale	Thomas Brown
Parana	Brig	209	—— Royce	do
Susan	Schooner	134	Edwin Smith	J. E. & E. Smith
S. S. Learned	do	116	—— Taber	H. & S. French
Timor	Ship	280	—— White	Huntting Cooper
W. F. Safford	Brig	174	—— Royce	T. Brown

sailing from American ports—Continued.

Whaling-ground.	Date—Of sailing.	Date—Of arrival.	Result of voyage.—Sperm-oil.	Result of voyage.—Whale-oil.	Result of voyage.—Whalebone.	Remarks.
			Bbls.	*Bbls.*	*Lbs.*	
Pacific Ocean..	Sept. 6	May 5, 1859	264	1,240	......	Sent home 11,500 bone; sold to Boston 1859.
....do	Oct. 8	Aug. 7, 1859	35	2,400	6,000	
Desolat'n Island	July 9	Apr. 10, 1858	......	3,482	436	Withdrawn for South American trade 1859.
Atlantic & Ind.	July 10	....	......	......	......	Sent home 57 sperm, 523 whale, 5,000 bone; lost in Shanta Bay August 10, 1858.
....do	July 26	May 7, 1859	45	1,800	700	Sent home 21,280 bone; sold to Boston 1860.
Pacific Ocean..	Sept. 16	May 27, 1860	106	215	3,400	Added 1856; sent home 70 sperm, 880 whale, 9,084 bone; withdrawn and sold 1860; wrecked at Bliss's Island January, 1862.
Desolat'n Island	Aug. 13	Apr. 10, 1858	......	512	......	Bought from Boston 1856.
Davis's Strait..	May 21	Sept. 17, 1857	......	416	......	
Pacific Ocean..	Nov. 6	Nov. 23, 1859	......	1,880	24,600	Sent home 356 whale, 6,500 bone.
S. A. & Indian.	Sept. 29	....	......	......	......	Stove by ice and lost in Arctic August 25, 1857; third mate and boat's crew lost.
Pacific Ocean..	Oct. 29	May 5, 1859	535	665	5,500	Sent home 23 sperm, 1,076 bone; sold to Boston 1859.
Desolat'n Island	July 19	June 2, 1858	......	4,275	600	Withdrawn and sold for merchant-service 1862.
North Pacific..	July 24	....	......	......	......	Sent home 38 sperm, 1,770 whale, 12,000 bone; condemned and broken up at Honolulu November, 1858.
Atlantic	July 14	Aug. 17, 1857	8	......	......	
S. A. & Ind	Oct. 11	May 28, 1859	311	1,598	5,600	Sold and broken up 1859.
South Atlantic	Aug. 21	....	......	......	......	Lost at Prince Rupert's Bay December 29, 1856; saved 30 sperm, 12 whale.
S. A. & Indian..	Oct. 4	....	......	......	......	Formerly the Bengal; rebuilt and renamed 1856; sold at Mauritius April 6, 1863; sent home 4,000 bone.
Desola'n Island	July 12	May 12, 1858	......	991	......	Added 1856.
Atlantic & Ind	May 27	Dec. 7, 1858	2	499	......	
S. A. & Indian..	June 4	June 28, 1857	184	186	650	
....do	June 25	....	......	......	......	Added 1856; sent home 72 sperm; missing; supposed to be lost with all on board.
South Atlantic	May 13	June 14, 1857	332	240	1,550	
North Atlantic	Apr 10	Sept. 30, 1856	......	50	......	Added 1856; withdrawn 1857.
	Nov. 4	July 19, 1857	......	130	600	
....do	Oct. 26	....	......	......	......	Added 1856; wrecked at sea September 25, 1862.
S. Shetlands ...	Aug. 7	May 12, 1860	22	706	7,000	Sent home 16 sperm, 986 whale, 21,406 bone; one of "stone fleet," No. 1.
Ochotsk	Oct. 21	Mar. 26, 1860	......	600	7,000	Sent home 1,140 whale, 11,880 bone; sold to New York 1860.
....do	Aug. 22	Apr. 25, 1859	115	2,105	17,000	Sent home 4,800 bone; sold to Boston 1860; one of "stone fleet," No. 2.
....do	Oct. 20	June 12, 1860	72	628	8,000	Sent home 40 sperm, 1,653 whale, 21,252 bone; sold to New York 1860.
Atlantic	Sept. 4	May 7, 1859	257	591	250	Sold to Fairhaven for West India trade 1859.
Indian Ocean..	Nov. 5	May 28, 1859	244	1,350	1,700	Sent home 13 sperm.
Atlantic & Ind.	May 20	June 29, 1857	......	916	6,000	
North Pacific..	Sept. 3	May 9, 1860	250	630	4,000	Sent home 227 sperm, 400 whale; sold to Boston 1860.
Pacific Ocean..	Apr. 25	May 31, 1858	143	960	5,700	Sent home 100 sperm.
Atlantic & Ind	July 17	May 31, 1859	510	51	......	Sent home 320 sperm.
S. A. & Indian.	June 9	Sept. 17, 1858	316	162	1,000	
South Atlantic	Aug. 13	July 6, 1858	253	211	600	
Straits of Lutka	June 9	Sept. 8, 1857	......	450	4,900	Sent home 380 sperm.
Falk. Islands ..	July 28	June 1, 1857	375	......	......	Bought from Harwich 1856.
Sts. of Belleisle.	June 24	Apr. 8, 1858	......	30	100	Added 1856; chartered by United States Government for light-house service 1857.
Pacific Ocean..	Aug. 13	May 4, 1859	......	400	4,000	Sent home 142 sperm, 628 whale, 8,022 bone; one of "stone fleet," No. 1.
Spitzbergen ...	May 5	....	......	......	......	Added 1856; withdrawn 1860.

Table showing returns of whaling-vessels

Name of vessel.	Class.	Tonnage.	Captain.	Managing owner or agent.
1856.				
San Francisco, Cal.				
Charles Carroll	Ship	376	——— Hunting	Moore & Folger
Cynosure	Schooner	94	——— Edwards	Wood & Co
Eagle	do	75	——— Claxton	G. B. Post & Co
Emeline	do	75	——— Moore	Blanchard & Conner
Francis	Brig	114	——— Poole	G. B. Post & Co
Henry	Schooner		——— Reynolds	J. W. Growley
Leverett	Brig	147	——— Brooks	W. R. Roberts
May Flower	Ship	350	——— Gardner	Robert B. Swain & Co
S. McFarland	Brig	142	——— Osborne	J. G. Wallace
Cold Spring, N. Y.				
Splendid	Ship	473	——— Pierson	S. A. & W. E. Jones
1857.				
New Bedford, Mass.				
Abraham Barker	Ship	400	George W. Slocum	Abraham Barker
Alto	Bark	236	Thomas H. Lawrence	Richmond & Pierce
America	Ship	418	Charles R. Bryant	I. Howland, jr., & Co
Cachelot	Bark	230	William H. Perry	Abraham Ashley, 2d
Canton Packet	Ship	274	Charles E. Allen	I. H. Bartlett & Sons
Chandler Price	do	441	Crayton P. Holcomb	William G. E. Pope
Clarice	Bark	237	Frederick W. Brown	Edward C. Jones
Congress	Ship	339	——— Hamblin	do
Cortes	do	382	E. F. Lakeman	Geo. & Matt. Howland
Cornelia	Bark	219	Caleb Spooner	L. Kollock & Son
Cossack	do	256	John C. Haskins	Charles Hitch & Son
Eliza F. Mason	Ship	582	Richard P. Smith	I. Howland, jr., & Co
Eliza Adams	do	403	Reuben T. Thomas	E. C. Jones
Emerald	Bark	350	Abraham W. Peirce	Henry F. Thomas
Emily	do	333	Presbury N. Luce	Charles Almy
Endeavour	do	252	Richard Wilson	Abraham Ashley, 2d
Euphrates	Ship	365	William H. Heath	Edward W. Howland
Fabius	do	452	George A. Smith	C. R. Tucker & Co
Franklin	do	333	Josiah Richmond	William P. Howland
Franklin, 2d	Bark	219	John S. Howland	William Wilcox
Gazelle	Ship	340	Michael Baker, 3d	T. & A. R. Nye
George Howland	do	374	G. P. Pomeroy	G. & M. Howland
George	Bark	280	Joseph D. Silva	Gideon Allen & Son
George and Susan	Ship	356	Robert Jones	G. & M. Howland
Gideon Howland	do	379	James M. Williams	I. Howland, jr., & Co
Gypsy	Bark	360	Frederick W. Mantor	do
Helen Snow	do	299	Ebenezer F. Nye	Cook & Snow

sailing from American ports—Continued.

Whaling-ground.	Date.		Result of voyage.			Remarks.
	Of sailing.	Of arrival.	Sperm-oil.	Whale-oil.	Whalebone.	
			Bbls.	*Bbls.*	*Lbs.*	
North Pacific	Jan. 8	Nov. 8, 1856	......	750	......	Condemned 1857.
Pacific Ocean	Mar. 24	Nov. 13, 1856	......	350	......	
....do	Aug. 30	Apr. 27, 1857	......	450	......	
....do	Jan. 4	....	......	......	......	No report.
....do	May 26	May 2, 1857	......	425	......	Sailed in 1857 and was lost in Magdalena Bay.
....do	Aug. 9	....	......	......	......	Withdrawn 1857.
....do	July 28	....	......	......	......	
....do	May 28	Sept. 15, 1857	250	......	......	
....do	June 26	....	......	......	......	Sent East 600 whale.
North Pacific	Sept. 15	Apr. 27, 1860	......	1,049	21,000	Sold to Boston 1860.
Indian Ocean	Aug. 17	Mar. 24, 1861	219	1,792	7,100	Sent home 9,729 bone; sold to New York 1862, for merchant service.
Pacific Ocean	June 29	May 2, 1862	492	3	......	Sent home 642 sperm, 193 whale, 2,400 bone; sold to Fairhaven 1862.
North Pacific	Oct. 14	May 2, 1861	......	1,324	13,200	Carried a steam whaleboat as an experiment, but it was not used; was temporarily in merchant service; one of "stone fleet," No. 2; sunk 1862; sent home 160 sperm, 284 whale, 19,552 bone.
Pacific Ocean	Sept. 2	....	......	......	......	Captain Perry was replaced by Captain Wilson; sold at Valparaiso May 8, 1861.
....do	June 9	May 19, 1861	1,934	......	......	Sent home 50 sperm.
North Pacific	Sept. 29	May 20, 1862	2	1,835	3,850	Sent home 70 sperm, 321 whale, 17,677 bone; withdrawn 1862.
Pacific Ocean	Oct. 10	May 23, 1862	386	17	......	Sent home 300 sperm, 25 whale.
Indian Ocean	Jan. 1	May 31, 1859	479	1,919	12,000	
....do	July 3	....	......	......	......	Sent home 30 sperm; burned at Cape Crusade with 300 barrels of oil by the crew, March, 1858.
....do	July 12	Aug. 26, 1860	636	27	......	Sent home 300 sperm.
Ind. & Pacific	Aug. 20	Mar. 28, 1861	79	477	......	Sent home 2,452 bone; one of the "stone fleet;" sunk off Charleston, 1861.
North Pacific	Oct. 2	Apr. 14, 1861	......	1,710	8,900	Sent home 87 sperm, 195 whale, 15,858 bone; withdrawn 1861 for merchantman; sold at Hong Kong 1863.
....do	Sept. 30	May 8, 1861	70	1,976	......	Sent home 1,373 whale, 3 cocoanut, 45,500 bone.
Ind. & Pacific	July 15	Aug. 31, 1861	67	2,550	......	Sent home 144 sperm, 1,349 whale, 33,522 bone; sold to Honolulu 1862; name changed to Kamehameha III.
Pacific Ocean	Oct. 17	May 8, 1861	814	......	......	Withdrawn 1861 for merchant service.
North Pacific	Oct. 14	May 6, 1860	......	953	9,600	Sailed October 1; returned leaking, 4,500 strokes in 24 hours; sent home 779 sperm, 14,354 bone.
....do	Oct. 15	Apr. 6, 1861	......	1,707	13,500	Sent home 44 sperm, 423 whale, 15,196 bone.
....do	Aug. 4	Apr. 18, 1862	167	2,304	12,050	Sent home 115 sperm, 703 whale, 15,602 bone.
Ind. & Pacific	Aug. 18	....	......	......	......	Sent home 200 sperm, 300 whale, 2,520 bone; lost at Strong's Island April 12, 1859; saved 70 sperm out of 700.
Pacific Ocean	Sept. 29	....	......	......	......	Sent home 996 sperm; condemned and sold at Valparaiso February 15, 1861.
....do	Aug. 18	June 9, 1862	1,358	5	......	Bought from Nantucket 1857; sent home 204 sperm.
North Pacific	Oct. 14	July 11, 1861	......	2,226	......	Sent home 58 sperm, 902 whale, 19,216 bone.
....do	Nov. 14	Nov. 29, 1861	375	401	......	Altered from a ship 1857; sent home 58 sperm, [illegible]58 whale, 5,530 bone.
....do	Sept. 7	Apr. 29, 1861	376	2,070	......	Sent home 21,281 bone.
....do	Aug. 11	Apr. 8, 1861	110	1,016	2,500	Sent home 87 sperm, 1,066 whale, 16,000 bone; sold to New York 1862 for merchant service.
....do	July 2	June 28, 1861	65	759	1,400	Sent home 437 whale, 7,000 bone.
....do	Oct. 20	June 13, 1861	386	815	......	Sent home 370 sperm, 598 whale, 15,848 bone.

Table showing returns of whaling-vessels

Name of vessel.	Class.	Tonnage.	Captain.	Managing owner or agent.
1857.				
New Bedford, Mass.—Continued.				
Herald	Ship	274	George H. Cash	E. W. Howland
Hercules	Bark	335	George Athearn	Swift & Perry
Hibernia	Ship	327	William Booker	Jona. Bourne, jr.
Hibernia, 2d	Ship	551	Pardon C. Edwards	I. Howland, jr., & Co.
Hillman	..do	383	Joseph C. Little	Henry Taber & Co.
Hope	..do	295	Leonard S. Gifford	Wilcox & Richmond
Huntress	Bark	383	William Allen	Cook & Snow
James Arnold	Ship	393	Thomas Sullivan	H. Taber & Co.
Java, 2d	Bark	292	George W. Raynor	William G. Blackler
Jireh Swift	..do	454	William Earl	Swift & Allen
John A. Parker	..do	342	Benjamin Swain	Henry F. Thomas
John Wells	..do	366	E. H. Woodbridge	Thomas Knowles & Co.
Joshua Bragdon	..do	270	William Bates, jr	Charles S. Randall
Junior	Ship	378	Archibald Mellen	David R. Greene & Co.
Kathleen	Bark	312	John Marble	J. & W. R. Wing
Kensington	Ship	357	Charles F. Stetson	David B. Kempton
Lætitia	Bark	275	Joseph Stowell	F. & G. R. Taber
Lagrange	..do	280	Thomas Golding	W. G. Blackler
Levi Starbuck	Ship	376	William Jernegan	E. W. Howland
Lewis	..do	308	George F. Neil	Chapman & Bonney
L. C. Richmond	..do	341	Thomas B Hathaway	James B. Wood & Co.
Manuel Ortez	Bark	351	James S. Hazard	Weston Howland
Majestic	Ship	297	Job Macomber	S. Thomas & Co.
Marcia	..do	315	Randall Billings	E. W. Howland
Margaret Scott	Bark	300	Oliver S. Cleaveland	Rodney French
Maria Theresa	Ship	330	Henry J. Coop	T. & A. R. Nye
Mary & Susan	..do	409	——— Stewart	C. Knowles & Co.
Mary Wilder	..do	213	Abner P. Barker	Charles Almy
Metacom	..do	360	John F. Hinds	James B. Wood & Co.
Midas	Bark	326	Joseph R. Tallman	..do
Milwood	..do	254	Lawrence Gruninger	Gid. Allen & Son
Moctezuma	Ship	436	Joseph Tinker	Simeon N. West
Montreal	..do	543	Nathaniel W. Sowle	C. R. Tucker & Co.
Morning Star	Bark	305	Henry D. Norton	S. Thomas & Co.
Nimrod	Ship	340	Willis Howes	William Gifford
Ohio	..do	383	John Barrett	E. W. Howland

sailing from American ports—Continued.

Whaling-ground.	Date—Of sailing.	Date—Of arrival.	Result of voyage.—Sperm-oil.	Result of voyage.—Whale-oil.	Result of voyage.—Whalebone.	Remarks.
			Bbls.	*Bbls.*	*Lbs.*	
Pacific Ocean ..	July 15	June 14, 1861	1,299	2	......	Sent home 40 sperm; one of the "stone fleet;" sunk off Charleston 1861.
North Pacific..	Sept. 1	June 8, 1861	186	1,486	12,700	Sent home 758 whale, 16,995 bone.
....do	Oct. 10	May 7, 1862	74	2,802	......	Sent home 47 sperm, 284 whale, 1,714 bone; sold and withdrawn.
North Pacific ..	June 18	May 7, 1861	......	2,300	......	Added 1857; sent home 56 sperm, 613 whale, 30,371 pounds bone; withdrawn 1861.
....do	July 7	July 25, 1861	235	1,279	2,350	Sent home 256 sperm, 272 whale, 15,513 bone.
Pacific Ocean ..	Sept. 7	....	......	......	......	Sold 575 gallons sperm at Talcahuano and 115 barrels sperm at Sydney; sent home 101 sperm, 14 whale; lost on Brampton Shoals October, 1863, with 750 sperm and 200 cocoanut.
Indian Ocean ..	Sept. 27	Sept. 13, 1861	684	313	......	Sailed once and returned with 14 of her crew in irons for mutiny; sent home 363 sperm, 450 whale, 8,300 bone; sold to Boston 1862 for China trade.
Pacific Ocean ..	Aug. 18	Nov. 4, 1861	2,503	......	......	Sent home 98 sperm.
North Pacific..	Oct. 22	Apr. 12, 1860	145	1,446	17,000	Formerly ship; bought from Fairhaven and rerigged 1857; sent home 42 sperm.
....do	July 15	Aug. 15, 1861	61	1,407	3,200	Altered from a ship 1857; sent home 460 sperm, 1,031 whale, 23,158 pounds bone.
Pacific Ocean ..	Dec. 2	Aug. 10, 1862	532	23	......	Sent home 992 sperm; sold to Sydney 1862 for a whaler.
North Pacific..	Oct. 6	May 10, 1861	......	1,017	1,900	Altered from a ship 1857; sent home 169 sperm, 618 whale; 10,261 pounds bone.
Pacific Ocean ..	Oct. 1	May 8, 1861	920	......	......	
North Pacific..	July 21	Aug. 20, 1858	....	Clean	.....	
S. A. and Ind ..	Aug. 25	Apr. 13, 1860	968	430	......	
Indian Ocean ..	Oct. 20	Aug. 27, 1861	255	1,629	6,800	Sent home 233 sperm, 8,116 pounds bone; one of the "stone fleet;" sunk off Charleston 1861.
Pacific Ocean ..	June 12	June 26, 1860	684	18	......	Sent home 580 sperm.
... do	Aug. 31	....	......	......	......	Bought from Fairhaven 1857; sent home 708 sperm, 13 whale; condemned at Pernambuco July, 1861.
North Pacific..	Nov. 3	Sept. 17, 1861	....	871	2,750	Sent home 313 sperm, 625 whale, 14,900 bone.
Indian Ocean ..	July 21	Apr. 14, 1861	....	......	......	Sent home 37 sperm, 6,400 pounds bone; one of "stone fleet" No. 1.
North Pacific..	Oct. 20	July 17, 1861	....	1,941	......	Sent home 33 sperm, 653 whale, 7,788 pounds bone; one of the "stone fleet;" sunk off Charleston 1861.
....do	Oct. 5	June 10, 1860	110	1,403	11,938	Sent home 460 whale, 13,000 pounds bone; sold to New York 1861.
....do	July 25	May 24, 1861	......	195	1,100	Sent home 72 sperm, 840 whale, 7,422 bone; one of "stone fleet" No. 2; sunk 1862.
... do	Aug. 25	May 16, 1861	....	1,686	9,000	Sent home 252 sperm, 460 whale, 18,123 pounds bone; sold to Boston 1862.
Atl. and Ind...	Sept. 16	July 4, 1861	175	......	......	Sent home 221 sperm, 739 whale, 4,416 pounds bone; condemned as a slaver, and sold to United States for blockading fleet No. 2.
North Pacific..	Oct. 13	May 26, 1861	65	227	3,400	Sent home 9,250 pounds bone; one of the "stone fleet;" sunk off Charleston 1861.
....do	July 15	May 11, 1860	39	1,862	1,400	Built at New Bedford 1857; sent home 903 whale, 44,971 pounds bone.
Pacific Ocean ..	June 16	June 18, 1860	953	......	.....	
North Pacific..	July 16	....	......	......	......	Sent home 110 sperm, 199 whale, 12,142 pounds bone; lost on Tutuilla, Navigator's Islands, December, 1860; saved and sold 700 barrels oil.
....do	July 7	Apr. 1, 1860	124	353	4,000	Altered from a ship 1857; Captain Tallman died at Ayan August 5, 1859; sent home 106 sperm, 192 whale, 4,333 bone.
Indian Ocean ..	Sept. 3	Dec. 14, 1861	600	......	......	
North Pacific..	Oct. 9	Apr. 11, 1861	......	1,518	14,500	Sent home 62 sperm, 3,668 pounds bone; sold to New York 1862.
... do	Nov. 11	May 20, 1862	83	2,928	17,000	Sent home 434 whale, 15,154 pounds bone; sold to New York 1862.
Pacific Ocean ..	July 21	June 26, 1862	465	......	......	Sent home 630 sperm, 1,800 pounds bone.
North Pacific..	Sept. 18	July 14, 1861	30	1,040	......	Sent home 11 sperm, 576 whale, 25,643 bone.
....do	Nov. 11	Apr. 8, 1861	145	2,491	......	Sent home 75 sperm, 610 whale, 23,463 bone.

Table showing returns of whaling-vessels

Name of vessel.	Class.	Tonnage.	Captain.	Managing owner or agent.
1857.				
New Bedford, Mass.—Continued.				
Oneida	Ship	420	Frederick Vincent	Thomas S. Hathaway
Orozimbo	do	588	Francis Pease	D. R. Green & Co
Osceola	Bark	158	—— Webb	Charles S. Randall
Osceola, 2d	do	197	Joshua T. Chadwick	J. & W. R. Wing
Ospray	do	236	James E. Stanton	Swift & Allen
Paulina	do	271	John Steen	do
Peri	do	205	George H. Macomber	Rodney French
Pocahontas	Ship	341	John S. Dennis	
Petrel	do	350	William C. Fuller	John R. Thornton
Richmond	Bark	180	Edward B. Hussey	Cook & Snow
Rob't Morrison	do	307	Benjamtn W. Tilton	T. Knowles & Co
Robert Edwards	Ship	356	Jarvis Wood	James H. Howland
Roman, 2d	do	350	Abraham Dehart	Abm. Barker
Rousseau	do	306	Paul Green	G. & M. Howland
San Francisco	Bark	268	—— Perry	William Phillips & Son
Scotland	Ship	384	Joshua Weeks, jr	O. & E. W. Seabury
Stafford	Bark	206	Charles B. Hosmer	T. & A. R. Nye
Statira	do	346	Richard G. Luce	William Hathaway, jr
Stephania	Ship	315	Matthew Fisher	Jona. Bourne, jr
St. George	do	408	Josiah C. Pease	Abm. Barker
Superior	Bark	275	Richard D. Wood	James B. Wood & Co
Swift	Ship	321	Francis S. Worth	Thomas S. Hathaway
Thomas Nye	do	461	Richard Holley	T. & A. R. Nye
Triton	Bark	300	John B. Dornin	I. Howland, jr., & Co
Tropic Bird	do	320	Godfrey King	William P. Howland
Uncas	Ship	413	William H. Luce	Abm. H. Howland
Washington	do	344	Josiah Purrington	J. Bourne, jr
William Badger	do	334	William Maxfield	Benjamin B. Howard
William C. Nye	do	389	John M. Soule	C. R. Tucker & Co
*William Thompson	do	495	Peter E. Childs	Swift & Perry
Young Hector	do	411	Charles H. Hager	William P. Howland
Young Phenix	do	377	William Shockley	William Phillips & Son
Dartmouth, Mass.				
A. R. Tucker	Bark	218	Oren Higgins	Tucker & Cummings
Liverpool	do	306	Joseph C. Smith	do
Westport, Mass.				
Champion	Bark	209	Edward G. Sowle	Andrew Hicks
Gov. Carver	do	180	John A. Beebe	Henry Wilcox

sailing from American ports—Continued.

Whaling-ground.	Date— Of sailing.	Date— Of arrival.	Result of voyage. Sperm-oil.	Result of voyage. Whale-oil.	Result of voyage. Whalebone.	Remarks.
			Bbls.	*Bbls.*	*Lbs.*	
Pacific Ocean..	Oct. 22	Dec. 7, 1861	1,550	......	......	Sent home 708 sperm, 634 whale, 8,876 pounds bone; added 1857, from merchant-service; withdrawn 1862, for merchant-service; captured and burned by the Florida 1863.
North Pacific..	Oct. 30	Apr. 5, 1860	......	425	3,900	Sailed September 22; returned October 12, leaking 2,000 strokes in 24 hours; James Rogers, 1st mate, and 2 men drowned while fast to a whale by a foul line, 1858; sold and withdrawn 1860.
Atlantic	Apr. 15	......	......	......	......	Sent home 203 sperm; sold 4,200 gallons whale at Pernambuco; condemned at Pernambuco April, 1859.
....do	June 23	Nov. 14, 1859	96	985	......	Sent home 75 sperm.
Pacific Ocean..	Oct. 10	July 30, 1862	396	......	......	Sent home 452 sperm.
....do	Oct. 1	......	......	......	......	Sent home 50 sperm, 1,550 whale, 11,108 pounds bone; lost at Lahaina November 14, 1860; had 400 barrels oil, mostly saved.
Atl. and Ind...	July 13	Nov. 20, 1859	393	662	2,500	
......	......	......	......	......	......	Bought from Holmes' Hole 1857; lost at Cape de Verdes October 29, 1857.
Pacific Ocean..	Aug. 31	May 20, 1862	1,409	91	......	Withdrawn 1864; sent home 100 sperm.
Atl. and Ind...	Oct. 1	Mar. 24, 1860	156	134	600	Sent home 23 sperm, 161 whale, 18,000 pounds bone; withdrawn 1860, for freighting.
North Pacific.	Aug. —	Apr. 12, 1861	139	1,353	6,300	Sent home 76 sperm, 483 whale, 19,673 bone.
... do	Nov. 4	May 23, 1862	95	1,231	4,750	Sent home 108 sperm, 125 whale, 8,800 bone.
....do	Aug. 24	May 15, 1861	76	589	800	Sent home 5,750 pounds bone; withdrawn for merchant-service 1861; sold to the United States for a storeship 1861.
Ochotsk	Sept. 23	June 16, 1862	31	1,760	......	Sent home 7,170 pounds bone.
Atlantic	May 13	May 17, 1859	370	230	......	Sent home 75 sperm.
North Pacific..	Aug. 19	May 1, 1860	17	2,151	15,500	Sent home 80 sperm, 685 whale, 16,113 pounds bone; sold to New York 1861.
Atl. and Ind...	Oct. 3	Aug. 18, 1860	547	......	......	
....do	Oct. 30	Sept. 24, 1860	134	2,203	9,150	Withdrawn 1861; lost on coast of Ireland January, 1862.
Indian Ocean..	July 18	Apr. 24, 1860	462	1,363	450	Sent home 54 sperm, 9,600 pounds bone.
North Pacific..	Sept. 22	Mar. 24, 1861	323	1,076	7,400	Sent home 240 whale, 9,525 pounds bone; withdrawn and sold 1861.
Pacific Ocean..	June 24	......	......	......	......	Burned by natives of Solomon Islands, and all but 6 of the crew massacred, September, 1860; sent home 200 sperm, 628 whale, 3,225 pounds bone.
....do	June 30	Dec. 9, 1861	1,200	......	......	Sent home 181 sperm.
North Pacific..	Oct. 1	Apr. 6, 1861	......	2,329	8,700	Sent home 196 sperm, 325 whale, 22,816 pounds bone; sold to Boston 1862.
Pacific Ocean..	July 11	June 27, 1860	939	......	......	Altered from a ship 1857; sent home 240 sperm, 43 whale, 7,100 pounds bone.
Atlantic	Apr. 11	Dec. 3, 1859	179	333	......	Sent home 102 sperm.
North Pacific..	Sept. 21	June 17, 1861	175	602	4,500	Sold for merchant-service 1862.
... do	Aug. 5	Apr. 28, 1861	25	1,572	7,900	Sent home 76 sperm, 485 whale, 13,747 bone.
Indian Ocean..	Oct. 5	May 7, 1861	451	438	3,250	Withdrawn for merchant-service 1861; sold to the United States for a storeship 1861.
North Pacific.	Oct. 30	Apr. 18, 1861	68	1,106	14,400	Sent home 1,650 whale, 28,522 bone; sold to San Francisco 1862, for a whaler; withdrawn 1861, for merchant-service; William C. Nye captured and burned by Shenandoah 1865.
....do	Aug. 4	Sept. 6, 1860	251	2,502	......	Sent home 88 sperm, 30,957 pounds bone.
Pacific Ocean..	Sept. 1	July 29, 1861	1,164	9	......	Sent home 29 sperm; withdrawn for merchant-service 1861.
North Pacific..	July 21	Mar. 22, 1860	819	1,636	......	Took, in all, 1,150 sperm, 2,400 whale, 18,000 pounds bone.
Indian Ocean..	Oct. 1	Mar. 31, 1861	456	3	......	Sent home 323 sperm.
Atl. and Ind...	Oct. 10	Oct. 28, 1858	343	......	......	Altered from a ship 1857; bought from New Bedford.
Atlantic	Sept. 21	Aug. 7, 1859	254	7	......	
Indian Ocean..	Sept. 9	June 28, 1860	783	......	......	

Table showing returns of whaling-vessels

Name of vessel.	Class.	Tonnage.	Captain.	Managing owner or agent.
1857.				
Westport, Mass.—Continued.				
Greyhound	Bark	249	George G. Cathcart	Henry Wilcox
Kate Cory	Schooner	130	Weston S. Tripp	Alex. H. Cory
Keoka	Bark	250	Asa Grinnell	C. A. Church
Leonidas	Brig	128	Rescom Borden	do
Mattapoisett	Bark	150	George L. Manchester	H. Wilcox
Platina	do	266	David E. Allen	A. Hicks
Thos. Winslow	do	136	Thomas G. Reed	John Hicks
Sippican, Mass.				
Admiral Blake	Schooner	120	Jared Blankenship	P. Blankenship
Altamaha	do	119	—— Fisher	Stephen C. Luce
Hopeton	Brig	145	Obed Delano	Obed Delano
James	Schooner	80	Benjamin B. Handy; Zenas F. Eldridge	Benjamin B. Handy
Roswell King	do	134	Pardon Tripp	Peleg Blankenship
Wareham, Mass.				
G. Washington	Ship	374	Elihu S. Brightmen	Stephen C. Gibbs
Sandwich, Mass.				
Ocean	Bark	165	Peleg Cornell	W. F. Lapham
Fairhaven, Mass.				
Adeline Gibbs	Ship	351	Sumner Withington	Gibbs & Jenney
Arab	do	336	Edwin Grinnell	Ezekiel Sawin
Belle	Bark	320	Roswell Brown	Edmund Allen
Erie	Ship	451	Jared Jernegan, 2d	Nathan Church
Favorite	Bark	292	Henry T. Smith	F. R. Whitwell
Harvest	do	314	John Charry	John Howard
John A. Robb	do	273	Archelaus Baker, jr	L. C. Tripp
Martha	Ship	298	Calvin Manchester	N. Church
Omega	do	305	Jonathan Whalon	do
Oregon	do	393	Charles Tobey	L. C. Tripp
Oriole	Bark	404	Thomas Mickel	Jenney & Tripp
Oxford	Schooner	130	—— Mayhew	I. F. Terry
Rebecca Sims	Ship	400	William T. Hawes	Jenny & Tripp
Speedwell	do	496	Benjamin F. Gibbs	Stephen C. Gibbs
Mattapoisett, Mass.				
Annawan	Brig	159	Charles F. Keith	J. Holmes, jr., & Bro
Brewster	Ship	225	Grary B. Waite	do
Oscar	Bark	369	Thomas C. Landers	do

sailing from American ports—Continued.

Whaling-ground.	Date—Of sailing.	Date—Of arrival.	Result of voyage.—Sperm-oil.	Result of voyage.—Whale-oil.	Result of voyage.—Whalebone.	Remarks.
			Bbls.	*Bbls.*	*Lbs.*	
Pacific Ocean ..	May 8	Oct. 6, 1861	471	2	....	Sent home 226 sperm.
Atlantic	July 9	Aug. 24, 1858	248	23	....	
....do	Sept. 9	Oct. 16, 1860	474	580	......	Bought from New Bedford 1857; sold to New Bedford 1861, to go to California.
....do	June 18	Aug. 22, 1858	3	3	......	Sent home 230 sperm.
....do	July 30	July 9, 1859	224	23	......	
Indian Ocean ..	June 9	Apr. 15, 1860	1,115	3	......	Sent home 180 sperm.
Atlantic	Aug. 10	Sept. 3, 1859	39	9	....	Sent home 161 sperm, 100 whale; transferred to New Bedford 1860.
Atlantic	May 7	Oct. 24, 1857	135	......	....	Sent home 220 sperm.
....do	July 31	Apr. 15, 1857	63	53	......	
....do	June 16	Apr. 16, 1859	206	37	......	Formerly a schooner; added and altered 1857.
....do	May 18	Sept. 5, 1857	111	15	.....	
	Oct. 21	Aug. 27, 1858	25	25	......	
....do	May 21	Aug. 2, 1858	210	67	.....	Formerly a coaster; added 1857; sold to Fairhaven 1860.
North Pacific ..	Oct. 1	May 18, 1861	25	900	8,000	Sent home 40 sperm, 169 whale, 5,595 pounds bone; sold to Honolulu 1861.
Atlantic	Sept. 29	June 25, 1859	408	47	......	Returned once, the crew having mutinied. Sent home 130 sperm.
North Pacific ..	Oct. 1	Mar. 28, 1861	27	517	3,950	Sent 25 sperm, 330 whale, 7,164 bone.
....do.	Nov. 3	May 21, 1862	106	1,160	10,000	Sent home 142 sperm, 1,392 whale, 30,295 bone; sold to Boston 1862.
Pacific Ocean ..	Oct. 22	May 20, 1862	1,303	6	.....	Sold to parties in Bridgewater for merchant-service 1862.
North Pacific ..	Aug. 3	Feb. 28, 1861	16	2,992	6,700	Sent home 9 sperm, 27,000 bone; sold to New Bedford 1862; withdrawn.
....do	Nov. 11	Apr. 7, 1861	52	564	....	Libelled at Monganui, N. Z., 1860, for a misdemeanor by one of the crew, and voyage ruined.
....do	Aug. 18	July 12, 1861	74	413	3,000	One of the "stone fleet;" sunk off Charleston 1861.
....do	Oct. 21	May 16, 1861	1,516	94	......	Sold to Sag Harbor 1861.
Pacific Ocean ..	Nov. 14	June 5, 1861	116	1,504	4,900	Daniel Donnavan, first mate, knocked overboard by a whale and drowned 1858; sent home 12,576 bone; sold to Boston 1862.
North Pacific ..	Sept. 9	July 19, 1861	150	850	900	Sold to New York for freighting 1861.
....do	Oct. 8	May 25, 1861	286	813	1,200	Sent home 126 sperm, 680 whale, 10,308 bone; sold to Bremen 1862, to be fitted by a branch establishment at Honolulu for whaling.
Indian Ocean ..	July 8	Sept. 11, 1861	1,800	......	.....	Built at Fairhaven 1857; sold to New Bedford 1862.
Desolat'n Island	July 17	Apr. 11, 1860	.....	580	......	Bought from New London 1857; built 1849; took place of Alfred as tender to Samuel Robertson; withdrawn 1860.
North Pacific ..	Nov. 17	Apr. 14, 1861	89	1,291	10,700	Bought from New Bedford 1857; sent home 56 sperm, 305 whale, 4,706 bone; one of the "stone fleet;" sunk off Charleston 1861.
....do	Sept. 1	....	.....	......	......	Charles H. Sprague, second mate, killed by a whale November 20, 1857; lost in Scammon's Lagoon, Lower California, February, 1861; the wreck was sold to Honolulu; sent home 215 sperm, 425 whale, 26,793 bone.
Atlantic	Oct. 12	Aug. 4, 1859	376	58	......	Sent home 87 sperm.
Indian Ocean...	May 11	Aug. 28, 1860	1,057	......	......	Added 1856; sent home 83 sperm.
North Pacific ..	Sept. 29	Mar. 25, 1861	155	1,500	8,000	Sent home 25 sperm, 600 whale, 17,078 bone; sold to New Bedford and withdrawn 1861.

Table showing returns of whaling-vessels

Name of vessel.	Class.	Tonnage.	Captain.	Managing owner or agent.
1857.				
Mattapoisett, Mass.—Continued.				
Union	Bark	124	David Dexter	R. L. Barstow
Willis	do	164	James King	do
Nantucket, Mass.				
Catawba	Ship	335	Israel Morey	McCleave & Macy
Constitution	do	400	Joseph Winslow	C. G. & H. Coffin
Eliza Jane	Schooner	130	William T. Swain	McCleave & Macy
Nautilus	Bark	220	Edwin M. Hardwick	Zenas L. Adams
Edgartown, Mass.				
American	Bark	329	—— Pease	John A. Baylies
E. A. Luce	Schooner	132	—— Ripley	Joseph Holley
Europa	Ship	400	—— Manter	Abraham Osborn
Eureka	Bark	225	Thomas M. Pease	J. A. Baylies
Ocmulgee	Ship	458	—— Greene	A. Osborn
Omega	do	363	—— Sanborn	Benjamin Worth
Provincetown, Mass.				
Alleghany	Schooner	95		Daniel C. Cook
Alexander	do	75	—— Nickerson	Johnson & Cook
Chanticleer	do	87	—— Dyer	Samuel Cook
Emporium	do	80		D. C. Cook
E. Nickerson	do	132	John Pettengill	Samuel Soper
Eschol	Brig	143	—— Miller	Robert M. Miller
Estella	Schooner	94	—— Chapman	J. E. & G. Bowley
Montezuma	do	92	—— Chapman	T. & S. Hilliard
N. J. Knights	do	95		D. Connell
Oread	do	90	—— Banister	E. S. Smith & Co
Panama	Brig	125		John Adams
R. E. Cook	Schooner	80	—— Genn	R. & E. Cook
Richard	do	92	—— Young	Philip Cook
Rienzi	do	108	—— Milliken	J. E. & G. Bowley
S. R. Soper	do	130		Samuel Soper
Thriver	do	95	—— Small	S. Small
Union	do	97		Jonathan Nickerson
V. Doane	do	99	—— Cook	H. & S. Cook & Co
V. H. Hill	do	155	—— Freeman	J. E. & G. Bowley
Orleans, Mass.				
Lewis Bruce	Brig	135	—— Nickerson	Heman Smith
Rothschild	Bark	261	—— Holman	do
Beverly, Mass.				
Lady Suffolk	Bark	210	—— Robertson	F. W. Choate
N. D. Chase	do	242	—— Ryder	do
Salem, Mass.				
Messenger	Ship	216	—— Holmes	Benjamin Webb
New London, Conn.				
Amaret	Brig	91	—— Quayle	Perkins & Smith
Atlantic	Schooner	130	—— Rathbone	do
Architect	Bark	400	—— Fish	do

sailing from American ports—Continued.

Whaling-ground.	Date— Of sailing.	Date— Of arrival.	Result of voyage. Sperm-oil.	Result of voyage. Whale-oil.	Result of voyage. Whalebone.	Remarks.
			Bbls.	*Bbls.*	*Lbs.*	
Atlantic	Nov. 4	Sept. 11, 1861	190	8	......	Sent home 56 sperm; bought from New Bedford 1857.
....do	June 3	Sept. 21, 1858	293	19	......	Sent home 268 sperm.
South Atlantic	Sept. 3	Apr. 19, 1859	24	2, 827	......	Sold to New York.
Pacific Ocean	Sept. 18	July 1, 1863	1, 600	......	......	Built at Mystic 1857; sold to New York 1863.
South Atlantic	Aug. 15	Apr. 9, 1859	......	550	......	Added 1857; sold to New Bedford; tender to ship Catawba.
Indian Ocean	June 22	....	......	......	......	Bought from Boston 1857; sent home 80 sperm; lost at Port Dauphin.
Ind. and Pacific	Aug. 4	Apr. 17, 1861	......	335	4, 900	Sent home 36 sperm, 390 whale, 366 bone; one of the "stone fleet;" sunk off Charleston 1861.
Pacific Ocean	July 2	....	......	......	......	Added 1857; sent home 25 sperm, 11 whale; withdrawn 1860.
North Pacific	Sept. 17	July 27, 1862	563	1, 845	1, 200	Sent home 170 sperm, 6,562 bone.
Indian Ocean	Oct. 21	May 19, 1861	......	540	......	Formerly the Alfred Tyler; sold to Boston 1861.
North Pacific	Nov. 11	Apr. 18, 1861	276	2, 622	......	Bought from Holmes's Hole 1857; sent home 62 sperm, 21,736 bone.
....do	Oct. 14	Apr. 9, 1861	......	1, 658	250	Sent home 1,039 whale, 48,864 bone; bought from Nantucket 1857; sold to Boston for freighting 1862.
....	....	Jan. 9, 1858	......	178	......	
North Atlantic	May 1	Sept. 6, 1857	......	225	......	
....do	Apr. 29	Sept. 14, 1857	......	200	......	
....do	....	Aug. 27, 1857	......	80	......	Added 1857.
....do	....	....	......	......	......	A missing vessel; captain had wife and two children with him.
....do	May 5	May 19, 1858	200	140	300	Sold to Beverly 1858.
Atlantic	May 6	Sept. 14, 1857	.....	160	......	Added 1857.
....	....	Dec. 2, 1858	50	......	......	
....	....	Sept. 6, 1857	......	180	......	Do.
North Atlantic	Dec. 19	Aug. 12, 1858	12	230	......	Added 1857; built at Essex 1853.
Atlantic	....	Nov. 17, 1857	415	......	......	Added 1857; sent home 107 sperm.
....do	Feb. 25	Sept. 5, 1857	......	130	......	Added 1856.
North Atlantic	May 6	Aug. 27, 1857	......	210	......	
Atlantic	June 16	June 16. 1857	......	20	......	
....	....	Aug. 28, 1858	156	30	......	
....	....	July 25, 1857	200	130	......	
Atlantic	May 23	June 12, 1859	380	......	......	Added 1857.
....do	May 22	....	......	......	......	Withdrawn 1859.
....do	Dec. 22	July 28, 1858	140	100	......	
South Atlantic	May 23	Sept. 15, 1858	230	120	......	Added 1857; sent home 98 sperm.
Atlantic	July 6	May 26, 1858	125	......	......	
....do	Jan. 6	Sept. 16, 1858	46	64	......	
....do	Dec. 23	June 4, 1859	250	......	......	Built 1851; sent home 90 sperm.
Indian Ocean	June 8	Oct. 13, 1859	140	575	5, 500	Built 1848; sent home 280 barrels whale and 3,000 pounds bone.
Atlantic	Apr. 29	Aug. 25, 1859	362	114	......	Added 1857; sent home 35 sperm.
Davis's Strait	Sept. 7	Sept. 21, 1858	......	267	5, 700	Frozen into the ice 8 months; took first whale July 1, and by July 22 was full.
Desolation Isld.	July 9	July 28, 1858	......	283	......	Withdrawn 1859.
North Pacific	Aug. 25	....	......	......	......	Bought from New York 1857; built at Rockland, Me., 1854; sent home 1,552 whale and 17,396 bone; withdrawn 1859.

Table showing returns of whaling-vessels

Name of vessel.	Class.	Tonnage.	Captain.	Managing owner or agent.
1857.				
New London, Conn.—Continued.				
Delta	Ship	314		
Delaware	do	299	—— Kenworthy	Williams & Barnes
Dove	Bark	151	—— Church	Williams & Haven
Electra	Ship	348	—— Brown	Williams & Barnes
Franklin	Schooner	119	—— Holt	Perkins & Smith
Fortune	Bark	291	—— Comstock	C. A. Williams & Co
Frances Palmer	do	303	—— Green	do
George and Mary	Ship	356	—— Walker	Williams & Haven
Georgiana	Brig	190	—— Buddington	Perkins & Smith
J. E. Comstock	Ship	75	—— Smith	Thomas Fitch
John E. Smith	Schooner	119	—— Forsyth	Richard H. Chapell
Lark	Bark	388	—— Perkins	Perkins & Smith
Laurens	Ship	420	—— Morgan	do
Mary Powell	Schooner	240	—— Nash	Lawrence & Co
Merrimac	Bark	414	—— Rice	C. A. Williams & Co
Montezuma	Ship	424	—— Homan	Williams & Barnes
N. S. Perkins	do	309	—— Kiblon	Perkins & Smith
New England	Bark	368	—— Hempstead	Lawrence & Co
Peruvian	Ship	388	—— Rose	E. V. Stoddard
Phœnix	do	404	—— Hempstead	George Huntley
Pioneer	Bark	235	—— Brown	E. V. Stoddard
Ripple	do	234	—— Chadwick	do
R. B. Coleman	Schooner	115	—— Jerome	do
Tempest	Bark	330	—— Allen	Frink & Prentiss
Zoe	do	196	—— Rogers	T. Fitch
Fall River, Mass.				
A. Houghton	Bark	326	—— Robinson	Brown & Durfee
B. Franklin	do	164	—— Brown	John B. Reed
Warren, R. I.				
Dromo	Bark	267	—— Cole	C. T. Child
Mary Frances	do	311	—— Rule	S. P. Child
William Wilson	Ship	375	George Taber	Charles T. Child
Stonington, Conn.				
Tekoa	Schooner	143	—— Anthony	J. E. Smith & Co
Greenport, N. Y.				
Caroline	Bark	252	—— Pontus	Wells & Carpenter
Roanoke	do	252	—— Wade	do
Sag Harbor, N. Y.				
Augusta	Bark	390	James M. Tabor	W. & G. H. Cooper
Excel	do	375	—— Winters	Wade & Brown

sailing from American ports—Continued.

Whaling-ground.	Date—		Result of voyage.			Remarks.
	Of sailing.	Of arrival.	Sperm-oil.	Whale-oil.	Whalebone.	
			Bbls.	*Bbls.*	*Lbs.*	
......	......	......	......	......	......	Sent home 385 whale and 6,425 bone; lost 1857; bought from Greenport same year.
Indian & Pac ..	June 30	......	......	......	......	Oliver Rogers, third mate, and 2 men killed by a whale; lost on Ballenas Bar, Lower California, 1860; sent home 130 sperm, 2,308 whale, and 24,369 bone.
South Atlantic.	June 13	May 12, 1858	94	......	......	
North Pacific ..	June 11	Apr. 30, 1859	......	2,305	1,500	Sent home 20,427 bone.
Atlantic & Ind.	Oct. 9	Mar. 23, 1859	......	15	......	
......	......	June 6, 1861	......	692	1,400	Fortune sent home 563 whale and 3,356 pounds bone.
North Pacific ..	Mar. 18	......	......	......	......	Formerly a packet between San Francisco and the Sandwich Islands; fitted from Honolulu; sold to Honolulu 1858; sent home 480 whale and 3,000 bone.
Indian & Pac ..	Oct. 1	......	......	......	......	Sent home 50 sperm, 1,297 whale, and 6,255 bone; lost in the ice in Ochotsk Sea June 9, 1860.
Davis's Strait ..	Apr. 11	Dec. 20, 1857	......	443	6,500	
Desolation Isld.	May 30	......	......	......	......	Added 1857; sold to Warren 1859.
North Atlantic	Sept. 1	Sept. 5, 1858	......	42	800	Sent home 120 whale and 1,260 bone; withdrawn 1858.
Pacific Ocean ..	July 1	Dec. 12, 1860	......	600	......	Sent home 1,303 whale and 7,097 bone.
Desolation Isld.	Aug. 4	Aug. 16, 1858	......	4,196	......	Elephant-oil.
Indian Ocean ..	June 8	May 17, 1858	......	1,558	......	Added 1857.
North Pacific ..	July 20	......	......	......	......	Added 1857; sent home 22,444 bone; condemned at Honolulu December, 1858.
....do	Sept. 29	Aug. 22, 1861	41	2,348	13,300	Sent home 89 sperm and 25,272 bone; one of "stone fleet" No. 2; sunk 1862.
Ochotsk	May 25	......	......	......	......	Sent home 283 sperm and 217 whale.
North Pacific ..	Sept. 7	Nov. 4, 1861	......	1,492	......	Sent home 11,991 bone; one of "stone fleet" No. 2; sunk 1862.
South Atlantic.	Aug. 21	July 12, 1858	71	108	700	
Pacific Ocean ..	Oct. 29	July 10, 1861	......	1,275	......	Sent home 990 whale and 5,560 bone; one of the "stone fleet;" sunk off Charleston 1861.
Desolation Isld.	July 9	July 10, 1859	......	1,498	......	Sent home 900 elephant.
Indian & Pac ..	Sept. 1	......	......	......	......	Sent home 297 sperm, 2,474 whale, and 10,046 bone.
Desolation Isld.	June 25	......	......	......	......	Added 1857; out of the business 1859.
Pacific Ocean ..	May 21	Apr. 11, 1861	......	765	6,450	Added 1857; sent home 1,491 whale and 13,023 bone.
Desolation Isld.	June 10	Apr. 15, 1859	......	1,030	......	Sent home 250 elephant; sold to Honolulu 1859.
Pacific Ocean ..	July 7	May 27, 1861	825	......	......	Sent home 648 sperm; sold to Newport 1861 for California trade.
Atlantic	Nov. 7	June 19, 1858	151	134	......	
North Pacific ..	Nov. 14	Apr. 12, 1861	......	390	......	
Indian Ocean ..	Feb. 27	Apr. 4, 1861	265	295		Sent home about 90 sperm and 225 whale; withdrawn 1861.
....do	Oct. 3	Jan. 4, 1861	512	1,452	3,100	Built at Warren 1857; sent home 115 sperm and 1,497 whale and elephant; withdrawn temporarily 1861; sold to New York 1861.
South Atlantic.	Oct. 1	May 28, 1859	......	260	......	
North Pacific ..	July 15	......	......	......	......	Sent home 600 whale and 5,890 bone; condemned at Honolulu September 11, 1859.
Indian & Pac ..	June 12	Feb. 25, 1860	185	375	......	Sold to Boston 1860.
Pacific Ocean..	July 24	Jan. 19, 1861	30	286	700	Formerly a brig; packet between Savannah and New York; added and altered 1857; sent home 282 whale and 1,011 bone; sold to Greenport 1861.
South Atlantic.	July 27	May 28, 1859	......	1,420	10,000	Formerly a brig; added and altered 1857.

Table showing returns of whaling-vessels

Name of vessel.	Class.	Tonnage.	Captain.	Managing owner or agent.
1857.				
Sag Harbor, N. Y.—Continued.				
Jefferson	Ship	435	—— Huntting	Wade & Brown
Noble	Bark	273	—— Jennings	W. & G. H. Cooper
Parana	Brig	209	—— Royce	Wade & Brown
Susan	Schooner	134	—— Smith	J. E. & E. Smith
Union	Bark	300	Jeremiah Hedges	Wade & Brown
William Tell	Ship	370	—— Austin	do
Cold Spring, N. Y.				
Monmouth	Bark	273	—— Ormsby	John H. Jones
San Francisco, Cal.				
Boston	Brig	181	—— Scammon	Tubbs & Co
Carib	Bark	205	—— Reynolds	Joseph W. Gawley
Francis	Brig	114	—— Andrews	J. C. Hewlett
Sarah Warren	Bark		Jared F. Poole	do
Mystic, Conn.				
Cornelia	Ship		—— Eldridge	
1858.				
New Bedford, Mass.				
Afton	Bark	249	Francis Allen	F. and G. R. Taber
Andrews	do	303	Jeremiah C. Norton	William P. Howland
Balæna	Ship	301	John S. Dorman	James H. Howland
Bart Gosnold	do	356	George H. Clark	I. Howland, jr., & Co
Callao	Bark	324	—— Fuller	Henry Taber & Co
Cambria	Ship	362	Henry Pease, jr	James B. Wood & Co
Camilla	Bark	429	Samuel M. Prentice	Swift & Allen
California	Ship	398	Charles West	I. Howland, jr., & Co
Canton	do	280	George White	C. R. Tucker & Co
Cleora	Bark	263	George R. Himes	Charles Hitch & Son
Cleone	do	373	John E. Simmons	Edmund Maxfield
China	do	370	Andrew J. Fuller	
Congress, 2d	Ship	376	Francis E. Stranburg	Gideon Allen & Son
Corinthian	do	401	Valentine Lewis	Geo. & Matt. Howland
Coral	Bark	370	Benjamin H. Sisson	G. Allen & Son
Daniel Webster	Ship	336	Dexter Bellows	S. Thomas & Co
Dartmouth	Bark	336	James H. Haughton	Weston Howland
Dominga	do	230	Thomas I. Lee	do
Draco	do	257	Charles P. Worth	Jonathan Bourne, jr
Eben Dodge	do	221	William Lewis	B. Franklin Howland
Elisha Dunbar	do	257	James L. Lincoln	W. & G. D. Watkins
Emma C. Jones	Ship	347	Jonathan C. Hawes	Edward C. Jones
Franklin	Bark	273	W. H. Gifford	Isaac M. West
Globe	do	215	Alexander A. Tripp	Allen Lucas
Good Return	Ship	376	Elial T. Fish	H. Taber & Co
Gratitude	Bark	337	William Davis, jr	Swift & Allen
Harrison	Ship	371	John Dennis	E. Maxfield
Henry Kneeland	do	304	Benjamin Kelley	Benjamin B. Howard
India	do	366	Richard Flanders	B. F. Howland
Ionia	Bark	234	—— Russell	Cranston Wilcox
J. D. Thompson	do	432	William B. Waterman	James D. Thompson

sailing from American ports—Continued.

Whaling-ground.	Date— Of sailing.	Date— Of arrival.	Result of voyage. Sperm-oil.	Result of voyage. Whale-oil.	Result of voyage. Whalebone.	Remarks.
			Bbls.	*Bbls.*	*Lbs.*	
North Pacific ..	Sept. 9	Apr. 15, 1861	159	720	5,000	Sent home 79 sperm, 1,361 whale, and 12,922 bone; broken up 1861.
S. A. & Indian	Nov. 3	June 26, 1859	582	537	4,000	
Straits of Lutke	Nov. 2	Sept. 20, 1859	60	......	......	Sent home 200 whale and 600 bone.
Falklands	Dec. 12	Feb. 25, 1860	65	285	......	
South Atlantic.	Sept. 9	May 8, 1861	......	460	3,000	Bought from New York 1857; built 1849; sent home 44 sperm, 629 whale, and 3,900 bone.
North Pacific ..	Sept. 9	....	......	......	......	Sent home 126 whale and 1,800 bone; lost on East Cape July 14, 1859.
South Atlantic.	Aug. 22	....	......	......	......	Sent home 50 sperm and 17,056 bone; sold at Valparaiso 1862.
Coast California	July 1	May 14, 1858	......	740	......	
Pacific Ocean.	May 9	—— —, 1858	......	......	......	Added 1857; no report.
Coast California	June 26	....	......	......	......	Lost in Margaritta Bay 1858.
....do	Aug. 9	May 23, 1858	......	235	......	Formerly in Oregon trade; added 1857.
....	......	June 6, 1858	......	1,092	......	
Pacific Ocean ..	Nov. 15	Aug. 9, 1862	186	2	......	Sent home 552 sperm; sold to New York 1862.
....do	May 20	Sept. 16, 1862	267	......	......	Sent home 48 sperm.
....do	Oct. 5	July 26, 1863	220	......	......	Sent home 525 sperm; sold to Sag Harbor 1863.
North Pacific ..	Sept. 15	May 27, 1862	229	1,111	3,750	Sent home 140 sperm, 7,006 pounds bone.
Pacific Ocean ..	Aug. 25	July 20, 1862	197	1,333	......	Sent home 17 sperm, 210 whale, 10,062 bone.
North Pacific ..	Oct. 5	Mar. 25, 1862	515	1,476	650	Sent home 131 whale, 32,450 pounds bone; sold 1862 on foreign account.
....do	May 10	May 17, 1862	438	1,660	......	Built at Fairhaven 1857; sent home 712 sperm, 1,051 whale, 34,900 pounds bone.
....do.	Aug. 25	June 6, 1862	87	632	3,200	The California was built at New Bedford 1842; sent home 185 sperm, 1,360 whale, 16,081 pounds bone.
Indian Ocean ..	Dec. 1	Aug. 2, 1862	1,630	......	......	
Indian and Pac.	June 23	....	......	......	......	Captain Hines died at sea, October 31, 1858; sent home 45 sperm.
North Pacific ..	Oct. 5	Aug. 4, 1862	......	1,904	......	Sent home 382 whale, 19,663 pounds bone.
....	......	—— —, 1859	......	......	......	Altered from a ship 1858; no report.
North Pacific ..	Aug. 5	Aug. 2, 1862	130	1,127	7,000	
... do	Oct. 5	June 7, 1862	239	2,376	19,200	Sent home 35 sperm, 12,081 pounds bone.
....do	Oct. 19	Mar. 12, 1863	......	2,100	......	Altered from a ship 1858; sent home 94 whale, 21,500 pounds bone.
Cum Inlet.....	June 11	Nov 23, 1859	50	1,316	18,000	Bought from Nantucket 1857.
Pacific Ocean ..	Dec. 1	....	......	......	......	Condemned and sold at Tahiti, March, 1863.
....do	Oct. 19	....	......	......	......	Sent home 425 sperm; condemned at Paita, January 1, 1862; repaired at Paita.
Indian Ocean ..	Apr. 22	Apr. 24, 1862	925	534	3,600	
Pacific Ocean ..	Nov. 2	Sept. 20, 1861	275	......	......	Sent home 517 sperm.
Indian Ocean ..	Aug. 10	May 17, 1862	715	......	......	Sent home 70 sperm.
Atl'tic and Pac	Aug. 10	Aug. 28, 1860	120	1,100	2,200	
Pacific Ocean ..	May 31	June 23, 1861	1,285	......	......	Sold to New York 1862.
Atlantic	Aug. 11	May 8, 1861	954	177	......	
North Pacific ..	Oct. 5	Apr. 23, 1862	......	1,381	9,700	Sent home 18 sperm, 1,800 pounds bone; sold out of the service 1862.
....do	Aug. 25	Apr. 22, 1862	213	1,946	13,800	Sent home 289 sperm, 500 whale, 16,278 bone.
Atl'tic and Ind.	May 17	....	......	......	......	Sent home 152 sperm, 894 whale, 5,200 bone; sold at Honolulu 1861.
Indian and Pac	June 9	May 29, 1862	107	1,732	14,500	Sent home 18 sperm, 1,081 whale, 15,388 bone.
Indian Ocean ..	Aug. 25	Nov. 4, 1861	310	655	4,500	One of "stone fleet," No. 2; sunk 1861.
Pacific Ocean ..	May 4	Nov. 4, 1861	299	618	4,750	Sent home 170 sperm.
North Pacific ..	Aug. 31	Aug. 21, 1861	247	1,500	8,100	Captain Waterman died August 25, 1859; sent home 7,600 pounds bone; sold to New London 1863.

Table showing returns of whaling-vessels

Name of vessel.	Class.	Tonnage.	Captain.	Managing owner or agent.
1858.				
New Bedford, Mass.—Continued.				
Janus	Ship	321	John C. Smith	T. & A. R. Nye
Jeannette	do	340	Hudson Winslow	Isaac B. Richmond
John Howland	do	377	Alexander Whelden	James H. Howland
John P. West	Bark	420	Daniel Tinker, jr	Simeon N. West
Joseph Grinnell	Bark	46[illegible]	William W. Thomas	William G. Blackler
Joseph Meigs	Ship	356	Leonard S. Mitchell	Abraham H. Howland
Julian	do	356	Samuel P. Winegar	William Hathaway, jr
Junior	do	378	Lafayette Rowley	David R. Greene & Co
Lancaster	do	383	Thomas N. Russell	T. & A. R. Nye
Leonidas	Bark	231	Albert J. Aldrich	Russell Maxfield
Louisiana	Ship	297	John A. Kelley	T. & A. R. Nye
Magnolia	do	396	Severino D. Pierce	William G. E. Pope
Marcella	Bark	210	Benjamin Ellis	C. R. Tucker & Co
Martha	do	271	John P. Cornell	Swift & Allen
Martha, 2d	do	360	Barnard H. Daily	William O. Brownell
Mary Ann	do	214	——— Macy	Robert B. Greene
Minerva Smyth	Ship	335	Abner Smith	I. Howland, jr., & Co
Montezuma	Bark	196	Shubael S. Spooner	J. & W. R. Wing
Montgomery	do	248	Reuben N. Crapo	Swift & Allen
Mt. Wollaston	Ship	325	John A. Coffin	Wood & Nye
Napoleon	do	360	Thomas Dallman	Charles Almy
Ohio	Bark	237	David Baker	Loune Snow
Oliver Crocker	Ship	352	David Cochran	J. B. Wood & Co
Ontario	Bark	489	Josiah Foster	W. O. Brownell
Onward	Ship	461	William H. Allen	Edward W. Brownell
Orray Taft	Bark	176	Micajah C. Fisher	Allen Lucas
Othello	Ship	424	Charles B. Killmer	T. & A. R. Nye
Pacific, 2d	Bark	314	William Cleaveland	William H. Reynard
Pioneer	do	231	Henry P. Barker	J. D. Thompson
Plover	Ship	330	Augustus N. Perkins	W. & G. D. Watkins
Roscius	Bark	300	Frederick S. Howland	William P. Howland
Sea Gull	Ship	455	Charles Nichols	John R. Thornton
Tamerlane	Bark	357	Joshua B. Winslow	Thomas Knowles & Co
Two Brothers	do	288	Joshua B. Davis	Wood & Nye
Twilight	Ship	386	Sylvester Hathaway	William Phillips & Son
Wm. Gifford	Bark	320	Nehemiah P. Baker	William Gifford
Fairhaven, Mass.				
Arab	Bark	276	William Washburn	I. F. Terry
Atkins Adams	do	330	William Wilson	William G. Blackler

sailing from American ports—Continued.

Whaling-ground.	Date— Of sailing.	Date— Of arrival.	Result of voyage. Sperm-oil.	Result of voyage. Whale-oil.	Result of voyage. Whalebone.	Remarks.
			Bbls.	*Bbls.*	*Lbs.*	
North Pacific ..	Oct. 9	May 20, 1862	28[illegible]	1, 34[illegible]	8, 600	
....do	Oct. 7	Aug. 8, 1862	13[illegible]	1, 762	2, 100	Sent home 14,200 pounds bone; sold to New York 1862.
....do	Oct. 12	Sept. 6, 1863	....	2, 200	......	Captain Whelden came home sick April, 1863; Benjamin F. Pierce, first mate, killed by a whale February 23, 1863; sent home 3,532 whale, 64,468 bone.
....do	May 24	May 20, 1863	20	1, 500	9, 000	Built at New Bedford 1857; John Lynch, second mate, died at Honolulu, January 12, 1862; sent home 68 sperm, 1,857 whale, 32,141 pounds bone.
Pacific Ocean ..	June 24	May 20, 1863	1, 050	.....	......	Built at Fairhaven 1858; sent home 216 sperm.
....do	June 16	Sept. 6, 1861	37[illegible]	.....	.....	Sold to New York 1862.
North Pacific ..	Sept. 30	June 13, 1862	38	921	12, 800	Sent home 50 sperm, 2,400 pounds bone; sold to New York 1862.
....do	Oct. 7	Oct. 21, 1862	490	681	......	Sent home 157 sperm, 6,166 pounds bone; sold to New York 1862.
....do	Oct. 26	....	.....	......	......	Sent home 264 sperm, 600 whale, 6,952 bone; condemned at Saint Thomas 1861.
Atlantic	Sept. 15	Apr. 25, 1861	7[illegible]	370	......	Altered from a ship 1858; sent home 156 sperm; one of the "stone fleet;" sunk off Charleston 1861.
Pacific Ocean ..	Aug. 3	Oct. 11, 1863	900	.....	......	Sent home 500 sperm.
North Pacific ..	July 27	....	.....	.....	......	Condemned at Sydney 1862; sold oil (230 sperm, 2,400 whale) at Sydney; sent home 100 sperm, 31,675 pounds bone.
Indian Ocean .	Aug. 17	July 27, 1861	575	.....	......	
Pacific Ocean .	Sept. 14	July 18, 1863	....	900	......	Sent home 47 sperm, 1,419 whale, 5,700 bone.
North Pacific ..	July 13	July 13, 1862	100	1, 522	9, 9[illegible]0	Sent home 172 sperm, 199 whale, 24,179 pounds bone.
Pacific Ocean ..	Dec. 16	Oct. 26, 1862	731	......	.....	Sold to New York 1863.
Atl'tic and Ind	Nov. 24	Apr. 22, 1862	58[illegible]	726	3, 300	Sold to Boston 1863 for merchant-service; sent home 234 whale, 2,000 pounds bone.
....do	Oct. 19	... .	.....	......	......	Missing; last seen off Gulf Stream in a gale 1859.
Pacific Ocean ..	July 20	Oct. 17, 1862	384	.....	......	Sent home 734 sperm, 88 whale; sold to New York 1862.
... do	June 2	Sept. 18, 1862	1, 307	39	......	Sent home 37 sperm.
....do	Dec. 24	July 6, 1862	1, 371	26	......	
... do	Oct. 4	Aug. 20, 1862	1, 11[illegible]	36	....	
North Pacific ..	Oct. 26	Feb. 28, 1863	300	1, 200	1, 20[illegible]	Sent home 93 sperm, 1,399 whale, 17,086 pounds bone.
....do	Oct. 26	July 23, 1862	32	1, 717	......	Altered from a ship 1858; sent home 347 whale, 7,844 pounds bone.
....do	Oct. 5	July 5, 1862	175	1, 854	......	Took on voyage 170 sperm, 6,350 whale, 63,000 pounds bone.
Atlantic	Sept. 1	Oct. 11, 1863	....	600	9, 000	Sent home 449 sperm.
North Pacific ..	Aug. 17	Mar. 12, 1863	60	1, 500	2, 800	Built at Fairhaven 1855; sent home 56 sperm, 1,812 whale, 11,172 pounds bone; sold to Boston for China trade 1860.
Pacific Ocean ..	Oct. 5	May 10, 1863	800	.....	......	Bought from Fairhaven 1858.
Indian and Pac	Aug. 10	July 31, 1861	140	160	1 500	
Indian Ocean ..	June 22	June 8, 1862	919	1	......	Sent home 44 sperm.
Atlantic ,......	Sept. 10	Aug. 2, 1861	1, 069	746	1, 500	Altered from a ship 1858; sent home 450 pounds bone.
Pacific Ocean ..	May 28	May 21, 1863	1, 750	.....	.....	Sent home 36 sperm; sold to Boston 1864, for merchant-service.
North Pacific .	Oct. 23	July 20, 1862	113	1, 547	10, 900	Altered from a ship 1858; sent home 292 sperm, 594 whale, 11,185 pounds bone.
Pacific Ocean ..	Nov. 3	June 30, 1863	1, 030	......	......	Altered from a ship 1858; sent home 473 sperm; sold and withdrawn 1864.
....do	Oct. 12	....	.....	.....	......	Lost at island of Hivaoa June 1, 1859; had trouble with the natives, but were protected by a missionary residing there.
North Pacific ..	Aug. 31	Feb. 28, 1863	300	1, 000	[illegible]	Built at Dartmouth 1858; sent home 329 sperm, 11,230 pounds bone.
Atl. and Ind ...	Sept. 14	Apr. 23, 1860	.....	2, 000	1, 000	Had schooner Oxford for a tender.
Pacific Ocean ..	Oct. 8	June 16, 1863	.....	6	......	Altered from a ship 1858; sold to New York 1863; sent home 275 sperm.

36

Table showing returns of whaling-vessels

Name of vessel.	Class.	Tonnage.	Captain.	Managing owner or agent.
1858.				
Fairhaven, Mass.—Continued.				
Florida	Ship	523	Thomas W. Williams	Fish, Robinson & Co.
General Scott	Bark	360	James R. Huntting	Nathan Church
Mary Ann	Ship	335	Lemuel M. Potter.	L. C. Tripp
South Boston	do	339	Edward F. Randolph	Ezekiel Sawin
Zone	Bark	365	James G. Frazer	Jenney & Tripp
Mattapoisett, Mass.				
Amelia	Brig	127	Charles W. Kempton	Loring Meigs & Co
Clara Bell	Bark	295	Timothy H. Fisher	R. L. Barstow
Elvira	Brig	131	Shubael P. Edwards	L. Meigs & Co
Mary Ann	Bark	214	Thomas H. Macy	R. L. Barstow
Massasoit	do	235	Thomas Percival	L. Meigs & Co
March	Brig	89	Henry Lewis	R. L. Barstow
Palmyra	Schooner	100	Benjamin Smith	L. Meigs & Co
Sarah	Bark	179	Job P. Rounseville	Atsatt & Sturtevant
Sun	do	184	Daniel Flanders	R. L. Barstow
Holmes' Hole, Mass.				
Pavilion	Brig	150	—— Adams	Thomas Bradley
Sippican, Mass.				
Admiral Blake	Schooner	120	Jared Blankenship	Peleg Blankenship
Retrieve	do	100	William C. Hathaway	Benjamin B. Handy
Beverly, Mass.				
Eschol	Brig	143	Foster Brown	F. W. Choate
Dartmouth, Mass.				
Cape Horn Pigeon	Ship	300	Reuben G. Weeks	William Potter, 2d
Charles and Edward	do	150	Frederick P. Cornell	do
Liverpool	do	306	Charles D. Davenport	Tucker & Cummings
Nye	Bark	211	William Childs	do
Westport, Mass.				
Elizabeth	Bark	270	Hiram Francis	Andrew Hicks
George and Mary	do	165	Allen W. Pierce	Rescom Macomber
Kate Cory	Brig	132	Weston S. Tripp	Alexander H. Cory
Leonidas	do	128	Samuel B. Devoll	C. A. Church
Sacramento	Bark	218	Thaddeus Defriez	A. H. Cory
Sea Fox	do	246	Peleg W. Gifford	A. Hicks
Sea Queen	do	261	Thomas Burdett	do
Solon	do	129	Joseph E. Smith	Henry Smith
Fall River, Mass.				
B. Franklin	Bark	164	George E. Brown	John B. Reed
Edgartown, Mass.				
Almira	Ship	372	—— Smith	Abraham Osborn
Navigator	do	350	Jared Fisher, jr	John A. Baylies
Splendid	do	392	Shubael Norton	A. Osborn
Washington	Schooner	140	—— Fisher	William H. Munro

sailing from American ports—Continued.

Whaling-ground.	Date— Of sailing.	Date— Of arrival.	Result of voyage. Sperm-oil.	Result of voyage. Whale-oil.	Result of voyage. Whalebone.	Remarks.
			Bbls.	*Bbls.*	*Lbs.*	
North Pacific ..	Sept. 7	....	......	....	......	Sold at San Francisco 1861; oil and bone shipped home.
....do	Oct. 20	May 20, 1862	87	1,500	2,800	Sold 1862 to Boston; sent home 102 sperm, 9,158 bone.
Pacific Ocean ..	Nov. 27	June 29, 1863	1,350	.....	.....	Sold to Quebec 1864.
North Pacific ..	Oct. 8	....	....	......	.....	Asa Hoxie, first mate, drowned while fast to a whale in March, 1862; sent home 1,590 whale, 6,843 pounds bone; condemned at Honolulu 1862.
Pacific Ocean ..	Aug. 19	June 27, 1862	807	138	......	Captain Frazier died June, 1861; sent home 311 sperm, 700 pounds bone; sold to New York 1862.
Atlantic	July 20	Sept. 27, 1859	120	60	......	Sent home 142 sperm.
Pacific Ocean ..	June 24	Oct. 9, 1864	509	......	.....	Boat's crew lost while fast to a whale December, 1863; sent home 950 sperm on voyage; sold for merchant-service 1864.
Atlantic	May 15	....	......	......	......	Sent home 31 sperm; condemned 1859 at Saint Thomas.
Pacific Ocean ..	Dec. 16	June 29, 1863	1,350	......	......	Sent home 300 sperm.
Atlantic	May 22	Jan. 29, 1862	6	770	......	Sent home 103 sperm, 328 whale, 4,200 lbs. bone; sold to Boston 1862.
....do	May 26	June 11, 1859	99	4	......	Sent home 362 sperm.
....do	Apr. 1	Oct. 2, 1860	99	2	......	Sold to New Bedford 1861; sent home 80 sperm.
....do	Sept. 28	Sept. 12, 1860	260	25	......	Sent home 35 sperm.
....do	Oct. 6	July 30, 1860	306	23	......	Sent home 150 sperm; sold to New Bedford 1860.
Atlantic	July 9	Aug. 7, 1860	302	54	......	Sent home 42 sperm; sold to Fairhaven in 1860.
Atlantic	Apr. 29	July 13, 1859	34	44	......	Sent home 81 sperm.
....do	May 13	Aug. 23, 1858	148	5	....	Bought from Gloucester 1858.
....	Nov. 11	June 1, 1859	150	430	......	Bought from Provincetown 1858.
Pacific Ocean ..	Oct. 5	June 26, 1862	344	27	......	Sent home 183 sperm.
Atlantic	June 17	Aug. 7, 1860	198	54	......	
....do	Nov. 25	....	.....	......	.....	Sent home 90 sperm; sold to New York 1860.
....do	Sept. 28	Aug. 17, 1860	507	543	2,434	Sold to New Bedford 1860.
Atlantic	May 16	Sept. 22, 1860	874	......	......	Sent home 300 sperm; sold to New Bedford 1860.
....do	May 4	Nov. 14, 1862	225	....	......	Sent home 110 sperm, 9,000 pounds bone.
....do	Dec. 9	Aug. 20, 1860	151	2	......	Altered from a schooner 1858.
... do	Nov. 9	Aug. 13, 1860	151	6	......	Sent home 71 sperm.
Pacific Ocean ..	May 27	June 16, 1863	680	....	......	Sent home 461 sperm; sold to Dartmouth 1864, thence to New York.
Indian Ocean ..	Aug. 2	Sept. 9, 1861	840	......	......	Sent home 87 sperm.
Pacific Ocean .	Oct. 21	Aug. 8, 1862	810	......	......	Sailed September 17; returned October 9 damaged by a gale.
Atlantic	July 29	Mar. 27, 1860	262	18		Sold to New Bedford 1860.
Atlantic	Nov. 18	Sept. 24, 1860	367	50	......	
Indian Ocean ..	Aug. 23	May 25, 1861	1,021	354	......	Sent home 114 sperm.
Ind. and Pac ...	Oct. 23	July 27, 1862	317	47	......	Sent home 265 sperm; sold to Boston 1862.
....do	Dec. 13	May 5, 1862	1,530	262	......	Sailed earlier in the season; put into Norfolk, Va., November 1, dismasted.
Atlantic	May 19	Aug. 11, 1859	170	37	......	Sent home 46 sperm.

Table showing returns of whaling-vessels

Name of vessel.	Class.	Tonnage.	Captain.	Managing owner or agent.
1858.				
Warren, R. I.				
Dolphin	Bark	325	—— Norie	R. B. Johnson
Nantucket, Mass.				
Atlantic	Ship	321	Zenas M. Coleman	Zenas L. Adams
Edward Carey	do	353	Francis M. Gardner	G. & M. Starbuck & Co.
Homer	Brig	140	George Haggerty	McCleave & Macy
Key West	Schooner		James McGuire	
Spartan	Ship	333	Obed R. Bunker	Gardner & Chase
Watchman*	Schooner	140	Charles W. Hussey	J. B. Macy
Provincetown, Mass.				
Alleghany	Schooner	95	—— Young	Daniel C. Cook
Alexander	do	75	—— Dunham	Johnson & Cook
Antarctic	do	136	—— Young	J. E. & G. Bowley
Chanticleer	do	87		Samuel Cook
Emporium	do	80	—— Cook	D. C. Cook
Estella	do	94	—— Chapman	J. E. & G. Bowley
John Adams	do	99	—— Cook	John Adams
Metropolis	do		—— Graham	
N. J. Knights	do	95	—— Sparks	D. Connell
Olive Clark	do	95		Samuel Soper
Oneco	Ship		—— Harwich	
Oread	do	90	—— Farwell	E. S. Smith & Co
Panama	Brig	125	—— Rich	J. Adams
Richard	Schooner	92	—— Holmes	Philip Cook
R. E. Cook	do	80	—— Cornell	R. & E. Cook
S. R. Soper	do	130		Samuel Soper
Spartan	Bark	188	—— Cook	Stephen Nickerson
V. H. Hill	Schooner	155	—— Cornell	J. E. & G. Bowley
Walter Irvin	do	133	—— Small	S. Soper
W. Holmes	do		—— Holmes	
Orleans, Mass.				
Medford	Brig	108	—— Snow	Calvin Snow
New London, Conn.				
Alert	Bark	398	—— Parsons	E. V. Stoddard
Catharine	Ship	384	—— Hempstead	Thomas Fitch
E. R. Sawyer	Schooner	126	—— Whipple	E. V. Stoddard
Gen. Williams	Ship	446	S. W. Fisk	Williams & Barns
Georgiana	Brig	190	—— Buddington	Williams & Haven
Isaac Hicks	Ship	495	—— Bolles	Lawrence & Co
Mary Powell	Schooner	240	—— Nash	do
North America	Bark	388	—— Morgan	Williams & Haven
Nile	Ship	322	George Destin	do
Pacific	Schooner	161	—— Smith	Lawrence & Co
Peruvian	Ship	388	—— Long	E. V. Stoddard
Philip 1st	Bark	293	—— Hempstead	George Huntley
Silver Cloud	Schooner	140	—— Billings	Richard H. Chapell
Vesper	Ship	321	—— Bailey	Williams & Barns
Mystic, Conn.				
Cornelia	Schooner	197	—— Buddington	Charles Mallory

*Four other schooners sailed, but returned clean.

sailing from American ports—Continued.

Whaling-ground.	Date— Of sailing.	Date— Of arrival.	Result of voyage. Sperm-oil.	Result of voyage. Whale-oil.	Result of voyage. Whalebone.	Remarks.
			Bbls.	*Bbls.*	*Lbs.*	
Hurd's Island..	Sept. 30	....	......	......	......	Built at Warren 1850; lost on coast of Patagonia 1859.
Pacific Ocean ..	Aug. 2	Aug. 23, 1862	1,316	......	......	Sold to New York.
....do	Oct. 20	....	......	......	......	Sold in San Francisco; fitted for a whaler from there, and was captured and burned by the Shenandoah; sent home 1,500 bone.
South Atlantic.	July 6	Oct. 4, 1859	......	325	......	Sold to Fairhaven.
Nant. Shoals ...	July 7	July 25, 1858	......	14	......	
Pacific Ocean ..	Oct. 19	Aug. 23, 1863	643	557	......	Sold to New Bedford.
Atlantic	....	....	......	563	......	
North Atlantic	Apr. 10	Sept. 10, 1858	......	147	......	
....do	Apr. 22	Aug. 27, 1858	12	175	......	
....do	Apr. 19	Aug. 16, 1859	30	100	......	Sent home 30 sperm.
....	....	Sept. 20, 1858	......	214	......	
North Atlantic	May 3	Oct. 2, 1858	....	128	......	
....do	Apr. 19	Aug. 24, 1858	12	90	......	
....do	Apr. 15	Apr. —, 1859	89	....	......	
....do	Apr. 22	....	......	......	......	No report.
....do	May 4	Sept. 10, 1858	......	218	......	
....	....	Sept. 14, 1858	......	140	......	Sailed again September 30; Soper, master; no report; withdrawn 1858.
North Atlantic	May 5	....	....	......	......	No report.
....do	Nov. 7	June 26, 1859	285	......	......	Sent home 100 sperm.
....do	Apr. 8	July 25, 1859	185	....	......	Sent home 69 sperm.
....do	Apr. 29	Sept. 7, 1858	......	196	......	
Atlantic	....	Aug. 6, 1858	115	100	......	
... do	Jan. 8	Dec. —, 1858	115	30	......	
South Atlantic	June 4	July 11, 1860	441	94	......	Sent home 76 sperm.
Atlantic	Nov. 6	Oct. 12, 1859	240	150	......	
....do	Jan. 9	Oct. 4, 1858	119	104	......	
North Atlantic	Apr. 23	....	......	......	......	No report; withdrawn 1859.
....do	Mar. 3	July 16, 1859	25	224	......	Sent home 119 sperm; sold 1860.
Hurd's Island..	June 29	May 14, 1860	......	3,537	2,900	
Indian Ocean ..	Nov. 24	....	......	......	......	Sailed October 19; returned November 8, dismasted; sent home 3,916 whale, 13,700 bone; captured and burned by the Shenandoah in Behring's Straits, June, 1865.
Hurd's Island..	June 10	May 16, 1860	......	388	......	
North Pacific ..	Oct. 5	July 12, 1861	......	3,945	16,700	Sent home 63 sperm, 12,265 bone.
Davis Straits ..	June 1	Dec. 9, 1859	......	847	15,000	Sailed for $9,000; cargo worth $21,000.
Hurd's Island..	July 20	Apr. 30, 1861	......	4,000	2,900	
....do	June 28	....	......	......	......	Lost at Hurd's Island October 21, 1859, with 400 barrels of oil; had landed 1,000 barrels; built at Belleville, N. J., 1848.
Indian Ocean ..	Sept. 20	....	......	......	......	Condemned and sold at Hobart Town April, 1861.
North Pacific ..	May 4	Apr. —, 1869	......	500	.....	Sent home 98 sperm, 4,406 whale, 42,671 bone; the longest whaling voyage on record; had 11 different captains; was captured by the Shenandoah in 1865 and bonded for $45,000.
Hurd's Island..	July 7	Apr. 16, 1861	......	651	......	
North Pacific ..	Aug. 12	Sept. 16, 1859	52	223	1,200	Broken up 1859.
....do	Sept. 8	....	......	.....	.....	Bought from Greenport 1858; sold to Honolulu 1861.
Desolation Isl'd	June 10	Nov. 17, 1859	14	516	......	
North Pacific ..	Aug. 10	....	......	......	......	Sent home 42 sperm, 800 whale; condemned and sold at Honolulu April 1, 1861.
Hurd's Island..	July 14	May 12, 1860	......	1,317	600	Sent home 400 elephant-oil.

Table showing returns of whaling-vessels

Name of vessel.	Class.	Tonnage.	Captain.	Managing owner or agent.
1858.				
Mystic, Conn.—Continued.				
Frank	Schooner	200	—— Chester	Charles Mallory
Leander	Bark	213	—— Chester	do
Robin Hood	Ship	395	—— McGinley	do
Romulus	do	365	—— Turner	do
New Haven, Conn.				
Ocean	Ship	567	W. W. Clark	Amos F. Barnes
Sag Harbor, N. Y.				
Nimrod	Bark	280	—— Green	W. & G. H. Cooper
Odd Fellow	do	239	—— Rose	Wade & Brown
S. S. Learned	Schooner	116	—— Goodbee	H. & S. French
San Francisco, Cal.				
Carib	Bark	205	—— Reynolds	Jos. W. Gawley
Ocean Bird	Ship		—— Scammons	
Sarah Warren	Bark		—— Poole	J. C. Hewlett
1859.				
New Bedford, Mass.				
Alice Frazier	Bark	406	Washingt'n T. Walker	L. Kollock & Son
Alfred Gibbs	Ship	425	Edward Nichols	Wood & Nye
Atlantic	do		Francis J. Silvea	
Arnolda	do	360	James A. Crowell	James B. Wood & Co
Benjamin Tucker	do	349	Samuel E. Cooke	C. R. Tucker & Co
Braganza	Bark	470	—— Turner	William O. Brownell
Cavalier	do	295	Nathaniel P. Gray	James D. Thompson
C. W. Morgan	Ship	351	James A. Hamilton	I. Howland, jr., & Co
China	do	370	Sylvester Hathaway	William Phillips & Son
Cleora	Bark	263	Isaachar H. Akin	Charles Hitch & Son
Columbus	do	313	Edwin A. Luce	John P Knowles, 2d
Congress	Ship	339	John A. Castino	Edward C. Jones
Congaree	Bark	321	Weston J. Swift	Thomas Wilcox
Cornelius Howland	Ship	431	Francis Dougherty	Edward W. Howland
Elizabeth	do	329	Perry Winslow	Thomas Nye, jr
E. Swift	Bark	425	Josiah E. Chase	Swift & Allen
Emily Morgan	Ship	368	Samuel H. Whiteside	William J. Rotch
Eugenia	Bark	356	Solomon F. Hamblin	Swift & Allen
Falcon	do	273	Bartlett Mayhew, 2d	Thomas Knowles & Co
Florida	Ship	330	Coddington P. Fish	E. C. Jones
Gen. Pike	Bark	313	John P. Fisher	William Gifford
Golconda	do	331	Joseph R. Green	George & M. Howland
Gov. Troup	Ship	430	Reuben Kelley	E. C. Jones

sailing from American ports—Continued.

Whaling-ground.	Date— Of sailing.	Date— Of arrival.	Result of voyage. Sperm-oil.	Result of voyage. Whale-oil.	Result of voyage. Whalebone.	Remarks.
			Bbls.	*Bbls.*	*Lbs.*	
Desolation Isl'd	June 18					Added 1858; struck an iceberg and was lost at Desolation Island February, 1859; mate, Charles Francis, lost also.
S. A. and Ind...	June 11					Sent home 475 whale; 3,000 bone; condemned at Pernambuco January 3, 1860.
Indian Ocean...	May 25	Sept. 17, 1861	21	791		Sent home 9,391 bone; one of the "stone fleet;" sunk off Charleston 1861.
Desolation Isl'd	June 3	May 9, 1860		2,538		Sold to New York 1860.
Pacific Ocean ..	Aug. 7					Bought from Warren 1858; sent home 64 sperm, 1,103 whale, 1,652 bone; sold at San Francisco for merchant-service.
Atl. & Indian ..	Dec. 1					Condemned at Sydney November 25, 1860; oil sold.
....do	Sept. 29	Mar. 6, 1861	350	600		
North Atlantic	June 7	Nov. 21, 1858	1	291		Returned 1858.
Pacific Ocean ..	May 17					No report; sailed 1859; Easton, captain; returned 1860, with 600 whale.
....do	......	Apr. 27, 1860		1,200		
Coast California	June 10					No report.
North Pacific ..	Sept. 22					Third mate, Mr. Littlefield, died from an accident May, 1861; lost in the Ochotsk January, 1860.
Pacific Ocean ..	Nov. 2	Jan. 25, 1864	857	95	600	Sent home 500 sperm.
....						
North Pacific ..	Aug. 16	July 17, 1863	800			Sent home 174 sperm.
Indian Ocean ..	Aug. 2					Captain Cook was killed by a whale October 26, 1860.
Pacific Ocean ..	Nov. 2					Altered from a ship 1859; took on voyage 685 sperm, 3,950 whale, 24,000 bone; condemned at Honolulu October, 1862; fitted as a whaler from that port under the Oldensburg flag.
....do	May 12					Sent home 255 sperm.
North Pacific ..	Oct. 4	May 12, 1863	135	1,800		Sent home 2,280 whale, 23,834 bone.
Pacific Ocean ..	Dec. 3	July 14, 1864	682			Sent home 425 sperm.
Indian Ocean ..	May 10					Condemned at Mauritius July, 1862.
Pacific Ocean ..	Aug. 10					Sent home 75 sperm.
Indian Ocean ..	Aug. 10	May 4, 1863	900	350		Sent home 125 sperm, 3,000 bone.
Pacific Ocean ..	Oct. 19					Sent home 200 sperm; condemned and sold at Valparaiso July, 1863.
....do	Apr. 20	Mar. 26, 1863	1,200	250		Sent home 267 sperm.
....do	Dec. 9	Apr. 24, 1864	570			Sent home 100 sperm; sold to New York 1864 for merchant-service.
....do	May 3	Sept. 18, 1863	900	80	1,800	Sent home 456 sperm.
North Pacific ..	Nov. 17	Apr. 18, 1863		2,000	20,000	Fourth mate died 1860; crew refused duty at Honolulu and were discharged by the consul; sent home 1,611 whale, 24,467 bone.
Pacific Ocean ..	Oct. 6	July 10, 1864	961			Sent home 55 sperm.
Atlantic	Oct. 5	May 23, 1862	460			Altered from a ship 1859
North Pacific ..	July 26	Apr. 9, 1863	4	2,200	600	Sent home 338 sperm, 1,096 whale, 38,186 bone.
....do	Sept. 6	Jan. 30, 1863	450	2,000	6,000	Altered from a ship 1859; took, in all, 450 sperm, 2,000 whale, 18,000 bone—valued at $100,000.
Pacific Ocean ..	Oct. 15					Altered from a ship in 1859; sent home 460 sperm; captured and burned by the Florida July 8, 1864, with 140 sperm of her own, and about 1,100 barrels sperm and 600 barrels whale on freight.
Indian Ocean ..	June 23	Oct. 5, 1862	635	540	2,000	The larger part of the crew mutinied and deserted at St. Catharine's; sent home 240 sperm.

Table showing returns of whaling-vessels

Name of vessel.	Class.	Tonnage.	Captain.	Managing owner or agent.
1859.				
New Bedford, Mass.—Continued.				
Harvest	Ship	360	Wilbour Manchester	Charles E. Hawes
Harvest	Bark	263	David R. Gifford	Lorenzo Pierce
Hecla	..do	207	Eben Nickerson	T. Knowles & Co
Henry Taber	..do	355	David G. Kirby	Henry Taber & Co
Herald, 2d	Ship	303	William S. Beebe	T. Nye, jr
Hope	Bark	186	Seth McFarlan	Zeno Kelley
Hudson	Ship	368	Moses R. Fish	Thomas Nye, jr
Hunter	..do	453	Alden Besse	Jonathan Bourne, jr
Hydaspe	..do	313	Charles S. Pope	J. B. Wood & Co
Illinois	..do	413	William R. Potter	Wood & Nye
Isaac Howland	..do	399	Thomas Long	I. Howland, jr., & Co
Isabella	Bark	315	Moses G. Tucker	T. Knowles & Co
James Allen	..do	355	Wm. D. Van Wyke	Gid. Allen & Son
James Maury	Ship	395	Lyman Wing	C. R. Tucker & Co
Japan	..do	487	Charles Grant	William G. Blackler
John Dawson	Bark	237	John W. Cornell	J. & W. R. Wing
Josephine	Ship	446	James L. Chapman	Swift & Perry
Marengo	..do	426	Frederick A. Weld	Jonathan Bourne, jr
Maria	Bark	202	Wm. B. Thompson	Thomas R. Rodman
Marion	..do	328	Clothier Pierce	William P. Howland
Matthew Luce	..do	410	——— Cleaveland	William Hathaway, jr
Mercury	Ship	340	Edward F. Lakeman	I. Howland, jr., & Co
Messenger	Bark	291	John W. Gifford	John R. Thornton
Millinoket	..do	180	Charles A. M. Taber	B. Franklin Howland
Milo	Ship	401	Thomas E. Fordham	E. C. Jones
Morning Light	..do	361	Hervey E. Luce	S. Thomas & Co
Nautilus	Bark	374	Charles G. Swain	G. Allen & Son
Navy	Ship	356	Andrew S. Sarvent	J. B. Wood & Co
Newark	Bark	323	Nathan S. Smith	C. Hitch & Son
Ocean	Ship	390	Ezra Gifford	J. R. Thornton
Osceola, 2d	Bark	197	John E. Barker	J. & W. R. Wing
Osceola, 3d	..do	200	Otis F. Hamblin	Cranston Wilcox
Pacific	..do	385	Jacob A. Howland	Swift & Perry
Pacific, 2d	..do	314	Joseph C. Smith	William H. Reynard
Pamelia	..do	300	Henry A. Slocum	..do
Parachute	Ship	331	Timothy Howland	Edmund Maxfield
President	Bark	293	William J. Macy	Richmond & Richardson
President, 2d	..do	189	Isaac Wordell	E. Maxfield
Rainbow	Ship	474	James Nichols	William Gifford

sailing from American ports—Continued.

Whaling-ground.	Date— Of sailing.	Date— Of arrival.	Result of voyage. Sperm-oil.	Result of voyage. Whale-oil.	Result of voyage. Whalebone.	Remarks.
			Bbls.	*Bbls.*	*Lbs.*	
Pacific Ocean ..	May 5	....	.....	.....	......	Added 1859; sent home 1,375 whale, 3,600 bone; put under Hawaiian flag 1862; captured and burned by the Shenandoah; paid for by the English government.
Indian Ocean ..	Aug. 23	....	.....	.....	......	Sent home 360 sperm; condemned at Mauritius 1861.
Pacific Ocean ..	Aug. 4	May 29, 1863	400	.....	......	Captain Nickerson died of heart disease March 4, 1861; sent home 695 sperm, 519 bone.
....do	Oct. 25	June 28, 1864	772	......	.....	Charles Floyd, first mate, drowned 1863; boat stove while fast to a whale.
....do	May 10	Aug. 30, 1863	650	......	......	Captain Beebe came home sick 1861; sent home 115 sperm.
Indian Ocean...	Aug. 1	....	.....	.....	......	Lost at island of Coetiva 1862; saved 200 barrels oil.
Pacific Ocean ..	July 6	Mar. 26, 1863	1,550	.....	......	Sold to Honolulu 1863; name changed to Hae Hawaii.
....do	June 8	Aug. 30, 1863	1,865	635	......	Sent home 177 sperm.
....do	Nov. 5	....	.....	.....	......	Sent home 738 sperm; condemned at Talcahuano 1863; named changed to Narcissa and went whaling from Talcahuano.
....do	Oct. 20	Oct. 25, 1863	1,000	1,000	8,000	
North Pacific ..	Dec. 31	Apr. 15, 1864	.....	698	.....	Sent home 40 sperm, 12,443 bone.
Pacific Ocean ..	Aug. 2	May 27, 1863	2[illegible]	2,500	12,000	
Indian Ocean ..	Oct. 4	Feb. 5, 1865	660	454	......	Altered from a ship 1859; Captain Van Wyke left at Callao sick 1864.
....do	Sept. 6	Sept. 15, 1862	79[illegible]	2,321	5,550	Sent home 12,000 bone.
Pacific Ocean .	May 31	May 19, 1863	1,200	.....	.....	Added 1859 from Fairhaven; sent home 499 sperm; sold to Boston 1863.
Atl. & Indian ..	July 16	Nov. 3, 1861	617	.....	......	Sent home 380 sperm.
North Pacific ..	July 14	July 27, 1862	295	2,319	......	First mate, Mr. Stevens, and boat's crew taken down by a whale December 30, 1859, off New Holland; sent home 425 sperm, 96 whale, 10,740 bone.
Indian Ocean ..	Aug. 12	Apr. 22, 1863	.....	3,100	8,780	Sent home 30 sperm.
Pacific Ocean ..	Sept. 29	....	.....	....	......	Condemned at Talcahuano 1863; used as a coaler till 1866, then fitted again for a whaler; sent home 840 sperm.
Atl. & Indian ..	June 7	May 14, 1863	1,300	30	......	Sent home 322 sperm.
Pacific Ocean ..	May 18	May 22, 1863	1,200	.....	......	Manuel Frates, fourth mate, killed by a whale August, 1862; sent home 260 sperm; sold to Boston for China trade 1865.
Indian Ocean ..	June 28	Oct. 21, 1862	1,083	6	......	
...do	June 7	....	.....	.....	......	Altered from a ship 1859.
Atl. & Indian ..	May 3	May 24, 1862	153	.....	......	Sent home 230 sperm; sold to Dartmouth 1862.
North Pacific ..	Nov. 15	May 24, 1863	175	1,800	6,000	Sent home 88 sperm, 1,546 whale, 28,500 bone.
Pacific Ocean ..	Sept. 22	May 20, 1862	638	1,012	2,100	Sent home 80 sperm, 9,000 bone; sold to Boston 1862.
....do	Nov. 1	July 13, 1864	1,003	48	......	Altered from a ship 1859.
North Pacific ..	Aug. 10	Apr. 18, 1864	265	1,938	21,950	Sent home 269 sperm, 1,025 whale, 10,700 bone.
Indian Ocean ..	Oct. 19	....	.....	.....	......	Lost on Sandal Wood Island (Malay Archipelago) April 7, 1863; crew in boats 9 days and 10 nights, with but little bread and water; sent home 76 sperm.
Pacific Ocean ..	Nov. 29	Oct. 28, 1863	220	.....	......	Sold to Edgartown 1864.
Indian Ocean ..	Dec. 20	Mar. 26, 1863	920	.....	.....	Sent home 650 sperm.
Pacific Ocean ..	Jan. 2	June 20, 1862	890	..	....	
Indian Ocean ..	June 15	June 7, 1862	107	2,420	3,000	Sent home 106 sperm, 1,040 whale, 17,932 bone.
....do	May 10	....	....	.....	.....	Sent home 123 sperm; sold to Sag Harbor 1864.
....do	May 4	May 4, 1862	975	57	....	Sent home 190 sperm, 1,000 bone; withdrawn 1862.
Ind. and Pacific	Nov. 11	....	.....	.....	......	Lost near Papeete June 10, 1864; saved 880 sperm out of 1,225.
Pacific Ocean ..	Oct. 10	June 18, 1864	978	.....	......	Altered from a ship 1859; sent home 319 sperm.
Atl. & Indian ..	June 13	May 10, 1862	185	......	......	
Pacific Ocean ..	Nov. 12	June 10, 1864	1,200	......	......	

Table showing returns of whaling-vessels

Name of vessel.	Class.	Tonnage.	Captain.	Managing owner or agent.
1859.				
New Bedford, Mass.—Continued.				
Rodman	Bark	371	William Whitton, jr	William G. E. Pope
Roman	Ship	370	John C. Hamblin	E. C. Jones
Roscoe	Bark	362	William H. Almy	Loum Snow
San Francisco	do	268	Daniel F. Worth	William Phillips & Son.
Seine	do	281	John S. Smith	Rodney French
Smyrna	do	219	Isaac P. Webb	Charles S. Randall
Thomas Pope	Ship	323	Charles H. Robbins	William G. E. Pope
Trident	do	449	Elisha H. Fisher	Frederick Parker
Vigilant	Bark	282	Frederick P. Cole	W. & G. D. Watkins
Waverly	do	327	William H. Vinal	David B. Kempton
Zephyr	Ship	361	Joseph S. Taylor	Thomas Nye, jr
Fairhaven, Mass.				
Emerald	Schooner	101	Thomas F. Lambert	Damon & Judd
Hesper	Ship	262	Joseph Hamblin, jr	Dexter Jenney
Hudson	do	368	Moses R. Fish	Jenney & Tripp
Joseph Maxwell	do	302	Andrew B. Jenney	F. R. Whitwell
Winthrop	Bark	218	William P. Weeks	Albert Sawin
Mattapoisett, Mass.				
America	Bark	257	John A. Luce	R. L. Barstow
Annawan	do	159	Charles F. Keith	J. Holmes, jr., & Bro
Ocean Rover	Ship	314	James M. Clark	do
R. L. Barstow	Bark	203	—— Michell	R. L. Barstow
Sarah	Ship	370	Henry P. Butler	L. Meigs
Samuel & Thomas	Bark	191	Asa Hoxie	R. L. Barstow
Willis	do	164	James King	do
Sippican, Mass.				
Altamaha	Schooner	119	John C. Clark	Stephen C. Luce
Hopeton	Brig	145	Otis S. Snow	Obed Delano
James	Schooner	80	Benjamin B. Handy	Benjamin B. Handy
Retrieve	do	100	William C. Hathaway	do
Roswell King	do	134	Pardon Tripp	Peleg Blankenship
Sandwich, Mass.				
Ocean	Bark	165	Peleg Cornell	W. F. Lapham
Falmouth, Mass.				
Com. Morris	Ship	355	Silas Jones	Oliver C. Swift
Holmes's Hole, Mass.				
America	Bark	257	—— Luce	Thomas Bradley
Helen Augusta	do	270	—— West	do
Beverly, Mass.				
Eschol	Brig	143	—— Hoxie	F. W. Choate
Lady Suffolk	Bark	210	—— Robertson	do
Dartmouth, Mass.				
Benj Cummings	Bark	391	David Briggs	Tucker & Cummings
Brunswick	Ship	295	Varenus Baker	do

sailing from American ports—Continued.

Whaling-ground.	Date— Of sailing.	Date— Of arrival.	Result of voyage. Sperm-oil.	Result of voyage. Whale-oil.	Result of voyage. Whalebone.	Remarks.
			Bbls.	*Bbls.*	*Lbs.*	
Pacific Ocean ..	Nov. 17	....	.....	....	.....	Sent home 1,550 sperm, 250 whale; sold at Mauritius 1863.
Indian Ocean ..	Aug. 22	May 9, 1863	1, 500	750	.....	Sent home 74 sperm.
Pacific Ocean ..	Nov. 8	Apr. 12, 1860	79	6	.....	Captain Almy and 7 men (part of two boats' crews) killed by a whale 1859.
Atlantic	Aug. 1	....	.....	.....	.....	Foundered at sea off Montauk Point February 24, 1862; sent home 2,000 bone.
Pacific Ocean ..	May 13	May 4, 1862	220	1	500	
Atlantic	Sept. 3	June 11, 1863	35	.....	.....	Sent home 435 sperm, 421 whale, 4,400 bone.
Indian Ocean ..	July 20	June 21, 1863	650	.....	.....	Sent home 312 sperm; sold to New York 1863, for African trade.
Pacific Ocean..	Dec. 21	June 7, 1864	1, 110	.....	.....	Sent home 320 sperm.
... do	Aug. 23	June 18, 1864	427	549	.....	Sent home 435 sperm.
Ind. and Pacific	Apr. 26	May 4, 1863	1, 550	750	1, 200	Altered from a ship; sent home 326 sperm, 5, 040 bone.
Indian Ocean ..	Nov. 21	....	.....	.....	.....	Condemned at Mauritius 1863; shipped oil (900 sperm) to London.
Atlantic	May 2	Aug. 19, 1860	150	10	.....	Added 1859; sent home 200 sperm.
Pacific Ocean..	June 5	....	.....	.....	.....	Sailed January 31; returned February 22, leaking 300 strokes per hour; sent home 951 sperm; condemned at Paita 1864.
....do	July 6	....	.....	.....	.....	Sent home 180 sperm; transferred to New Bedford 1862.
Indian Ocean..	Aug. 27	May 13, 1863	860	.....	.....	Sent home 42 sperm.
....do	July 26	Sept. 29, 1862	290	48	.....	Sent home 30 sperm; sold to Boston for merchant service 1863.
Indian Ocean ..	Dec. 27	....	.....	.....	.....	Sold to Holmes's Hole 1861.
Atlantic	Nov. 17	June 27, 1862	230	1	.....	Altered from a brig 1859; sold to New Bedford 1862; sent home 50 sperm.
Atlantic & Ind.	May 26	....	.....	.....	.....	Built at Mattapoisett 1859; captured and burned by the Alabama, with 900 barrels of oil, 1862; sent home 240 sperm, 250 whale, 2,000 bone.
Atlantic	May 20	Aug. 28, 1861	297	9	.....	Sold to New Bedford 1861; sold thence to Nantucket 1862.
Indian Ocean ..	Dec. 22	June 19, 1864	201	.....	.....	Transferred to New Bedford 1861.
Atlantic	Sept. 3	June 29, 1863	160	.....	.....	Sold to New Bedford 1863; sent home 400 sperm.
... do	June 2	Sept. 12, 1860	384	40	.....	
Atlantic	June 29	July 24, 1860	151	13	.....	
....do	June 2	Aug. 29, 1860	255	7	.....	Sent home 40 sperm.
....do	May 2	Sept. 16, 1859	163	6	.....	
....do	May 2	Sept. 11, 1859	53	1	.....	
....do	Apr. 26	Aug. 19, 1860	85	40	.....	Sent home 56 sperm.
Atlantic	Sept. 12	Aug. 25, 1861	447	3	.....	Sent home 214 sperm.
Pacific Ocean ..	July 13	June 19, 1864	931	232	1, 700	Sent home 50 sperm; sold to New Bedford 1864.
Indian Ocean..	Dec. 13	May 9, 1862	705	.....	.....	
Atlantic	May 25	June 8, 1861	500	.....	.....	Withdrawn for merchant service 1861; sent home 106 sperm.
Atlantic	July 14	Sept. 12, 1860	110	.....	.....	Bought from Provincetown 1858.
....do	Aug. 24	Aug. 30, 1860	260	120	.....	Withdrawn; sold to Salem.
Pacific Ocean..	Sept. 12	Aug. 3, 1866	.....	101	.....	Sent home 387 sperm, 518 whale, 4,000 bone; sold to New Bedford 1866.
Indian Ocean ..	Nov. 27	Aug. 19, 1862	537	103	800	Sold to New Bedford 1862.

Table showing returns of whaling-vessels

Name of vessel.	Class.	Tonnage.	Captain.	Managing owner or agent.
1859.				
Westport, Mass.				
Champion	Bark	209	—— Coggeshall	Andrew Hicks
Janet	...do	194	George G. Coffin	Henry Wilcox
Edgartown, Mass.				
Louisa Sears	Bark	180	George P. Fisher	Abraham Osborn
Vineyard	Ship	381	—— Caswell	Benjamin Worth
Walter Scott	...do	369	—— Baxter	...do
Washington	Schooner	140	—— Ripley	William H. Munro
Nantucket, Mass.				
Mohawk	Ship	350	George H. Swain	I. & P. Macy
Peru	Bark	257	Elihu F. Turner	Zenas L. Adams
Three Brothers	Ship	384	Calvin Swain	G. & W. Starbuck
Watchman	Schooner	140	Charles W. Hussey	J. B. Macy
Provincetown, Mass.				
Acorn	Bark	215	—— Nickerson	Nickerson & Tuck
Alleghany	Schooner	95	—— Cook	Daniel C. Cook
Alexander	...do	75	—— Nickerson	Johnson & Cook
Chanticleer	...do	87	—— Small	Samuel Cook
Emporium	...do	80	—— Cook	
Estella	...do	94		
F. Bunchinia	Bark	200	—— Tuck	Nickerson & Tuck
John Adams	Schooner	99		John Adams
Montezuma	...do	92	—— Chapman	T. & S. Hilliard
N. J. Knights	...do	95	—— Soarks	D. Connell
Oread	...do	90	—— Farwell	E. S. Smith & Co
R. E. Cook	...do	80	—— Freeman	R. & E. Cook
Richard	...do	92		David Conwell
Rienzi	...do	108	—— Milliken	J. E. & G. Bowley
S. R. Soper	...do	130	—— Soper	Samuel Soper
Thriver	...do	95	Leonard Small	S. Small
V. Doane	...do	99	—— Cook	H. and S. Cook & Co
Walter Irvin	...do	133	—— Small	Samuel Soper
Orleans, Mass.				
Lewis Bruce	Brig	135	—— Cook	Heman Smith
Rothschild	Bark	261	—— Allerton	...do
William Martin	Schooner	134	—— Martin	...do
New London, Conn.				
Amaret	Brig	91	—— Quayle	Williams & Haven
Charles Carroll	Ship	412	—— Smith	Frink & Prentis
Clematis	...do	311	—— Watrous	Williams & Barns
Dove	Bark	151	—— Smith	Richard H. Chappell
Electra	Ship	348	—— Brown	Williams & Barns
Exile	Schooner	83	Alex. Tillinghast	E. V. Stoddard
Franklin	...do	119	—— Church	R. R. Chappell
Northwest	Ship	304	William Dunbar	Thomas Fitch
Pearl	Bark	195	—— Bartlett	Williams & Haven
Sag Harbor, N. Y.				
Columbia	Bark	285	—— McCorkle	John Budd
Concordia	...do	265	—— Hamilton	Wade & Brown
Excel	...do	375	—— Loper	...do
Mary Gardner	...do	316	—— Jennings	W. & G. H. Cooper

sailing from American ports—Continued.

Whaling-ground.	Date—		Result of voyage.			Remarks.
	Of sailing.	Of arrival.	Sperm-oil.	Whale-oil.	Whalebone.	
			Bbls.	*Bbls.*	*Lbs.*	
Indian Ocean ..	Oct. 6	June 20, 1863	370	......	......	Sold and withdrawn for merchant-service 1863.
Atlantic	July 14	May 9, 1863	800	......	......	Sent home 35 sperm.
Atlantic	Apr. 13	....	......	......	......	Sent home 100 sperm, 67 whale; lost in Fayal Harbor September 7, 1860.
North Pacific ..	Sept. 25	May 27, 1862	156	2,304	10,600	Sent home 16,866 bone.
....do	Dec. 11	....	......	......	......	Sent home 52 sperm, 1,000 bone; condemned at Honolulu June, 1861.
Atlantic	Oct. 5	Aug. 4, 1861	......	12	......	Sold to New York 1862; sent home 176 sperm.
Pacific Ocean ..	May 12	June 29, 1863	1,000	......	......	Sold to New York.
....do	Sept. 25	May 7, 1863	1,360	12	......	Sold to New London.
....do	....	Apr. 2, 1865	925	250	......	Sold to New Bedford.
Atlantic	Sept. 6	Sept. 25, 1860	65	430	......	
Atlantic	Dec. 13	Aug. 26, 1861	89	70	......	
....do	May 17	Sept. 12, 1859	......	115	......	
....do	May 17	Sept. 10, 1859	......	110	......	
North Atlantic	Mar. 28	Sept. 18, 1859	......	134	......	
Atlantic	May 24	Sept. 12, 1859	......	65	......	
....do	May —	Sept. 12, 1859	196	......	......	
....do	May 16	Dec. 1, 1860	540	60	......	Sent home 160 sperm.
....do	May —	Jan. —, 1861	125	20	......	
N. Atlantic .. {	May 24	Sept. 20, 1859	65	......	......	
	Nov. 28	Aug. 26, 1862	190	......	......	
....do	Feb. —	July 15, 1859	205	103	......	
....do	Aug. 19	Sept. 9, 1860	183	14	......	
Atlantic	May 16	Aug. 9, 1860	168	47	......	
....	....	Sept. 20, 1859	......	139	......	Lost on island of Nevis April 7, 1860; saved 125 sperm.
North Atlantic.	Mar. 2	June 16, 1860	15	......	......	
Atlantic	Mar. 16	Aug. 19, 1859	300	......	......	
North Atlantic.	Aug. 19	....	......	......	......	Captain Small, second mate, and two men died January, 1862; sold to Beverly 1862; sent home 261 sperm.
....do	Feb. 11	July 16, 1859	144	108	......	Added 1859.
....do	Feb. 15	June 9, 1860	215	81	......	
Atlantic	May 30	Aug. 28, 1860	128	10	......	Sent home 50 sperm.
....do	Jan. 8	Sept. 29, 1859	340	340	......	
... do	May 17	Sept. 10, 1860	58	60	......	Sent home 210 sperm.
Cumberland Sts	Apr. 13	....	......	......	......	Lost in Cumberland Straits September 27, 1860; the Amaret formed a part of the Kane Expedition.
Davis's Strait ..	May 14	....	......	......	......	Wrecked in Mozambique Channel; condemned at Mata 1862; sent home 1,000 barrels of oil.
Indian Ocean ..	Oct. 11	....	......	......	......	Lost at Solomon Islands September, 1861; second mate, Benjamin Small, died 1861.
Desolat'n Isl'd.	Aug. 11	July 15, 1861	......	933	......	One of the "stone fleet," No. 2.
North Pacific ..	Aug. 16	Mar. 26, 1862	80	1,590	13,850	Sent home 1,390 whale, 21,716 bone.
Desolat'n Isl'd	Sept. 1	....	......	......	......	No report.
... do	July 15	June 4, 1862	474	500	......	
Indian Ocean ..	Sept. 1	....	......	......	......	
Ind. and Pacific	Oct. 17	Sept. 12, 1862	194	6	......	
South Atlantic.	Aug. 1	Apr. 16, 1862	712	131	......	Sent home 930 bone; sold to New York 1862.
Atlantic	May 23	May 8, 1862	109	938	1,000	Sent home 2,400 bone.
Coast of Pat ...	July 1	May 26, 1861	68	940	3,500	
Atlantic	Oct. 31	June 20, 1861	845	459	3,000	Was chased two hours off Bermudas by rebel privateer on passage home.

Table showing returns of whaling-vessels

Name of vessel.	Class.	Tonnage.	Captain.	Managing owner or agent.
1859.				
Sag Harbor, N. Y.—Continued.				
Myra	Brig	150	—— Havens	W. & G. H. Cooper
Noble	Bark	27[illegible]	—— Fowler	do
S. S. Learned	Ship	110	—— Eldridge	H. & S. French
Susan	Schooner	134	—— King.	do
Washington	Bark	236	—— Babcock	Wade & Brown
Stonington, Conn.				
Tekoa	Schooner	143	—— Stivers	J. E. Smith & Co
1860.				
New Bedford, Mass.				
Active	Bark	333	Davis Blake	Loum Snow
Adeline	Ship	329	Albert D. Barber	Charles R. Tucker & Co.
Addison	Bark	426	John C. Peirce	Isaac B. Richmond
Anaconda	do	38[illegible]	John H. Paun	do
Antelope	do	340	—— Wrisley	S. Thomas & Co
Atlantic	do	367	William H. Sherman	William Hathaway, jr
Awashonks	do	342	John Marble	J. & W. R. Wing
Brutus	Ship	....	E. S. Davoll	
Barnstable	Bark	373	L. B. Brownson	David B. Kempton
Black Eagle	do	311	Charles E. Allen	S. Thomas & Co.
Cherokee	do	261	James H. McKenzie	W. Hathaway, jr
Cicero	Ship	252	John R. Stivers	L. Snow
Contest	do	441	Elijah B. Morgan	I. Howland, jr., & Co.
Courser	Bark	327	John M. Hammett	B. Franklin Howland
Daniel Webster	Ship	336	—— Allen	S. Thomas & Co.
Daniel Wood	do	345	Josiah Richmond	James B. Wood & Co.
Desdemona	do	295	Franklin Bates, jr	Thomas Nye, jr
Draper	do	291	Charles W. Parker	Charles E. Hawes
E. Corning	Bark	325	Charles Stetson	William C. N. Swift
Edward	do	274	Orrick Smalley	Thomas Knowles & Co.
Eliza	do	366	William Devoll	Cornell & Penniman
Elliot C. Cowdin	Ship	280	William Cleaveland	Tucker & Cummings
Emma C. Jones	do	347	Gorham B. Howes	Edward C. Jones
Empire	do	403	John A. Macomber	Henry Taber & Co
Endeavour	Bark	252	Owen Fisher	Abraham Ashley, 2d
Fanny	do	391	George W. Bliven	Swift & Allen
Gay Head	Ship	389	Lewis H. Lawrence	J. B. Wood & Co
Java	Bark	295	Edward B. Phinney	G. & M. Howland
Java, 2d	do	292	T. C. Spaulding	William G. Blackler
Jireh Perry	Ship	435	Wanton H. Sherman	Swift & Perry
John Coggeshall	do	338	Aaron Dean	B. B. Howard
Kathleen	Bark	312	Charles C. Movers	J. & W. R. Wing
Kingfisher	do	451	Elisha Russell	Jona. Bourne, jr
Lætitia	do	275	Joseph Stowell	George R. Taber
Lagoda	Ship	341	Z. A. Devoll	J. Bourne, jr
Lancer	do	395	George H. Allen	Joshua Richmond

sailing from American ports—Continued.

Whaling-ground.	Date—		Result of voyage.			Remarks.
	Of sailing.	Of arrival.	Sperm-oil.	Whale-oil.	Whalebone.	
			Bbls.	*Bbls.*	*Lbs.*	
South Atlantic.	June 20	Oct. 16, 1860	220	.....	.....	Added 1859.
....do	Sept. 1	Aug. 19, 1861	468	51	500	
....do	Apr. 20	....	.....	.....	.....	Sent home 60 sperm; condemned at St. Catharine's 1862.
Atlantic	May 23	....	.....	.....	.....	
South Atlantic.	May 2	May 6, 1862	552	605	4, 000	Sold to New York 1862.
Atlantic	July 7	July 25, 1860	31	46	.....	
Pacific Ocean ..	Nov. 21	May 22, 1865	2	83	750	Sent home 865 sperm.
North Pacific ..	Sept. 19	May 7, 1865	28	1, 084	6, 000	Sent home 15 sperm, 2,250 whale, 18,500 bone.
Ind. and Pacific	Aug. 28	Apr. 22, 1867	......	525	4, 000	Altered from a ship 1860; sent home 238 sperm, 460 whale, 13,650 bone; withdrawn 1867 for freighting; lost.
Pacific Ocean ..	Nov. 17	Sept. 8, 1864	1, 006	50	.....	Withdrawn 1864.
Davis's Strait..	Mar. 15	Oct. 12, 1863	......	1, 500	24, 000	Sent home 50 sperm.
Pacific Ocean..	May 1	May 4, 1864	211	10	.....	Sent home 335 sperm.
Indian Ocean ..	Sept. 6	Apr. 4, 1862	148	100	550	Bought from Falmouth 1860; Captain Marble died October 22, 1861.
....	Aug. —	....	....	....	.....	Brutus bought from Warren 1860.
Pacific Ocean..	May 22	Apr. 28, 1864	65	1, 407	.....	Barnstable sent home 14 700 bone; altered from a ship 1860; sold to New York 1864 for merchant service.
Davis's Strait..	May 20	Nov. 3, 1861	......	1, 122	17, 800	Built 1851; bought from Sag Harbor 1859; Walter Smith, third mate, died at sea 1860.
Indian Ocean ..	Oct. 10	Nov. 22, 1864	900	378	3, 500	
Pacific Ocean..	Oct. 9	May 25, 1865	70	320	3, 800	Sent home 116 sperm, 1,333 whale, 8,800 bone.
Atlantic	June 21	Apr. 25, 1861	......	354	.....	Sent home 161 sperm, 2 256 bone.
Pacific Ocean ..	Aug. 14	June 9, 1864	159	.....	.....	First mate, Mr. Thomas, died December 18, 1860; Captain Hammett came home sick 1862; sent home 228 sperm.
Davis's Strait..	Mar. 21	Jan. 5, 1863	......	......	6, 500	Put into Aberdeen, Scotland, on account of the rebellion; sent home 2,500 bone; George Bessel, second mate, and two men died of scurvy 1862.
Pacific Ocean ..	June 12	July 28, 1864	808	318	.....	Sent home 420 sperm, 3,000 bone.
....do	July 17	Mar. 15, 1865	450	.....	.....	Sent home 113 sperm.
Indian Ocean ..	May 8	July 10, 1864	705	100	450	Sent home 186 sperm; sold to Boston 1864.
Pacific Ocean..	Nov. 15	May 24, 1866	7	...	.....	Sent home 737 sperm.
....do	July 2	June 27, 1864	14	48	.....	Sent home 448 sperm.
....do	Oct. 2	Dec. 30, 1864	950	.....	.....	
....do	May 22	May 4, 1864	1, 097	13	.....	Bought from Dartmouth 1860; sent home 213 sperm; sold to New York 1864 for merchant service.
....do	Nov. 19	Apr. 24, 1866	14	387	5, 600	Sent home 1,286 sperm.
....do	Nov. 1	....	... ..	.....	.....	Lost on Chatham Island April 15, 1862; saved 500 sperm; sent home 111 sperm.
....do	Oct. 30	Aug. 28, 1864	460	177	.....	
North Pacific ..	June 13	Apr. 14, 1864	112	2, 348	28, 550	Sent home 455 sperm, 1,680 whale, 28,400 bone.
Pacific Ocean ..	Oct. 2	Apr. 12, 1865	......	1, 051	15, 300	Sent home 631 sperm, 700 bone.
Indian Ocean ..	Sept. 6	May 28, 1864	1, 292	284	1, 700	
....do	June 27	Apr. 13, 1864	1, 040	104	.....	
Pacific Ocean ..	Sept. 13	June 18, 1864	471	955	2, 850	Sent home 274 sperm, 219 whale, 9,000 bone.
....do	June 9	May 2, 1864	33	924	6, 700	Bought 1860 from Fairhaven; sent home 131 sperm, 1,100 whale, 13,300 bone; sold to New York 1864.
Indian Ocean ..	June 19	Apr. 13, 1864	1, 258	25	......	Sent home 214 sperm.
Atlantic	June 1	Mar. 30, 1861	214	11	......	
Pacific Ocean ..	Oct. 19	May 4, 1864	600	.....	......	Sent home 400 sperm.
....do	Aug. 27	Apr. 18, 1864	94	2, 164	......	Sent home 162 sperm, 25,400 bone.
....do	Aug. 25	Nov. 20, 1864	936	......	......	Sent home 763 sperm.

Table showing returns of whaling-vessels

Name of vessel.	Class.	Tonnage.	Captain.	Managing owner or agent.
1860.				
New Bedford, Mass.—Continued.				
Lapwing	Ship	432	George H. Soule	E. C. Jones
Massachusetts	Bark	364	Daniel B. Greene	Swift & Allen
Mars	do	270	Abner P. Barker	Gifford & Cummings
Mary Frazier	Ship	288	Job Hathaway	B. F. Howland
Mary & Susan	do	409	Philip Howland	T. Knowles & Co
Mary Wilder	do	213	Sylvanus Cleaveland	Charles Almy
Mary	Bark	287	Warren Woodward	William O. Brownell
Merlin	do	348	John S. Deblois	W. & G. D. Watkins
Milton	Ship	388	Charles Halsey	H. Taber & Co
Minerva	Bark	291	Edward Penniman	Thomas Knowles & Co
Nassau	Ship	408	E. P. Herendeen	Swift & Perry
Nye	Bark	211	Joseph B. Barker	Tucker & Cummings
Peri	do	205	John W. Norton	Rodney French
Polar Star	Ship	475	Daniel D. Wood	C. R. Tucker & Co
Reindeer	do	450	George W. Raynor	E. W. Howland
Roscoe	Bark	362	George H. Macomber	L. Snow
Sappho	do	320	Edward B. Coffin	O. & D. W. Seabury
Scotland	Ship	384	Humphrey W. Seabury	do
Solon	Bark	129	Joseph E. Smith	J. R. Thornton
Sophia Thornton	Ship	424	William P. Briggs	T. Nye, jr
Stafford	Bark	206	Obed Pierce	William Hathaway, jr
Stella	do	338	Frederick Hussey	L. Snow
Stephania	Ship	315	James M. Witherell	J. Bourne, jr
Sunbeam	Bark	366	Samuel H. Cromwell	J. & W. R. Wing
Sun	do	184	Thomas Smith	Gifford & Cummings
Tahmaroo	Ship	371	Jabez S. Hathaway	Jabez Hathaway
Thomas Dickason	do	454	James Stewart	G. & M. Howland
T. Winslow	Bark	136	Joseph H. Fisher	John Hicks
Triton	do	300	Roland T. Packard	I. Howland, jr., & Co
Tropic Bird	do	220	Jos. L Dimmick	William P. Howland
Wave	do	197	Leonard Courtney	T. Knowles & Co
Young Phœnix	Ship	377	Benjamin F. Wing	William Phillips & Son
Fairhaven, Mass.				
Ansel Gibbs	Ship	319	Henry G. Chapel	Gibbs & Jenney
Arab	Bark	276	Joseph P. Nye	Damon & Judd
Emerald	Schooner	101	E. G. Cudworth	do
General Scott	Bark	360	James T. Eldridge	L. C. Tripp
Homer	Brig	....	John A. Benson	
Lydia	Ship	351	Elisha Babcock	Jenney & Tripp
Northern Light	do	513	Edward A. Chapel	Edmund Allen
Pavillion	Brig	150	George H. Cannon	Damon & Judd

sailing from American ports—Continued.

Whaling-ground.	Date— Of sailing.	Date— Of arrival.	Result of voyage. Sperm-oil.	Result of voyage. Whale-oil.	Result of voyage. Whalebone.	Remarks.
			Bbls.	*Bbls.*	*Lbs.*	
Indian Ocean ..	June 14	....	.....	.....	....	Sold at Mauritius 1863; renamed W. A. Farnsworth; returned to whaling under the Hawaiian flag, 1876; sent home 847 sperm.
North Pacific ..	Sept. 4	May 12, 1865	....	472	.....	Sent home 152 sperm, 904 whale, 28,950 bone.
Pacific Ocean ..	Oct. 2	July 2, 1865	851	1	.....	Sent home 90 sperm.
Indian Ocean ..	Aug. 1	Apr. 23, 1865	487	....	.....	Sent home 75 sperm, 1,600 bone; shipped 1,000 sperm to London.
Pacific Ocean ..	Aug. 7	May 28, 1864	1,380	.....	.....	Sent home 489 sperm.
....do	Aug. 8	May 10, 1864	250	.....	.....	Sent home 25 sperm; sold to New York 1864.
Indian Ocean ..	Nov. 1	Aug. 5, 1863	460	.....	.....	Sent home 195 sperm; altered from a ship 1860; Captain Woodward died 1861.
Pacific Ocean ..	June 12	Aug. 2, 1863	900	...	.....	Sent home 561 sperm.
North Pacific ..	Sept. 6	Apr. 6, 1865	......	2,209	.....	Sent home 2,413 whale, 63,200 bone.
Pacific Ocean ..	May 15	Apr. 27, 1864	1,866	.....	.....	Altered from a ship 1860; sent home 116 sperm.
Indian Ocean ..	Oct. 2	Apr. 21, 1863	100	500	8,000	
Atlantic	Oct. 2	....	.....	.....	.....	Bought from Dartmouth 1860; captured and burned by the Alabama 1863.
Indian Ocean ..	May 2	....	....	.....	.....	Sold at Mauritius 1863.
North Pacific ..	Sept. 6	....	.....	.....	.....	Sent home 98 sperm; lost on Kamschatka May 28, 1861; first mate, James Wilson, and boat's crew lost in landing.
....do	Oct. 2	Feb. 27, 1864	......	1,845	31,500	Was attacked by natives in the Arctic 1862; sent home 123 sperm, 3,648 whale, 31,100 bone.
Indian Ocean ..	May 15	Nov. 23, 1864	1,083	395	.....	Sent home 251 sperm, 800 bone.
Pacific Ocean ..	May 3	July 18, 1863	1,450	12	.....	Sent home 21 sperm.
....do	May 22	Dec. 1, 1860	239	7	.....	
Atlantic	May 21	May 7, 1862	20	31	.....	Bought from Westport 1860; sent home 125 sperm.
Pacific Ocean ..	Apr. 28	Sept. 10, 1864	1,256	18	.....	Sent home 68 sperm, 800 bone.
....do	Oct. 16	Sept. 10, 1864	210	.....	.....	Sent home 460 sperm.
....do	May 31	July 6, 1864	737	15	.....	Sent home 325 sperm.
Indian Ocean ..	Aug. 16	Apr. 17, 1864	783	1,034	150	Sent home 25 sperm, 9,300 bone.
Pacific Ocean ..	Oct. 22	June 15, 1864	889	.....	.....	John D. Thompson, first mate, and one man drowned while fast to a whale, 1860; Captain Cromwell came home sick 1861; sent home 107 sparm.
New Zealand ..	Nov. 13	....	......	......	.....	Bought from Mattapoisett 1860; sent home 570 sperm; condemned at Bay of Islands August, 1863.
Atlantic	July 3	....	......	......	.....	Bought from Fairhaven 1860; sent home 37 sperm.
North Pacific ..	Oct. 16	July 12, 1865	54	658	.....	Latham C. Ryder, first mate, died at Honolulu January 11, 1862; sent home 2,230 whale, 21,000 bone.
Atlantic	Apr. 24	July 2, 1862	148	.....	.....	Transferred from Westport 1859; sent home 137 sperm.
Pacific Ocean ..	Oct. 10	Apr. 23, 1865	257	......	.....	
Atlantic	Apr. 16	Oct. 3, 1861	124	9	.....	Sent home 821 sperm.
....do	July 24	Sept. 23, 1862	257	......	.....	Sent home 275 sperm.
Indian Ocean ..	Oct. 2	Nov. 19, 1863	1,200	800	.....	Sent home 140 sperm, 8,000 bone.
Davis's Strait ..	Apr. 11	Nov. 11, 1861	......	500	9,000	Sold to New Bedford 1861.
Atlantic	June 1	Sept. 6, 1861	278	1	.....	Sold to New London 1862 to replace the Alert.
....do	Sept. 5	Nov. 4, 1861	96	6	.....	Sent home 75 sperm; sold to Sippican 1862.
Pacific Ocean ..	Sept. 4	June 23, 1865	3	45	.....	Sent home 142 sperm; returned with all her original officers, an unusual circumstance.
....	....	....	....	.....	.....	Bought from Nantucket 1859; lost at Terceira September 7, 1860; sent home 100 sperm.
Pacific Ocean ..	May 16	May 17, 1864	754	709	600	Sent home 298 sperm; Lydia sold to New London 1864.
Davis's Strait ..	July 21	Oct. 11, 1861	......	1,104	21,000	Second mate, I. M. Larrabee, died April 20, 1861.
Atlantic	Nov. 22	May 15, 1863	65	.....	.....	Bought from Holmes' Hole, 1860; sent home 180 sperm.

Table showing returns of whaling-vessels

Name of vessel.	Class.	Tonnage.	Captain.	Managing owner or agent.
1860.				
Fairhaven, Mass.—Continued.				
Syren Queen	Ship	461	C. B. Chapel	Gibbs & Jenney
William and Henry	do	261	William C. Parsons	I. F. Terry
Mattapoisett, Mass.				
Amelia	Brig	127	Charles W. Kempton	L. Meigs
Brewster	Ship	220	John A. Beebe	J. Holmes, jr., & Brother
March	Brig	89	Henry Lewis	R. L. Barstow
Union	Bark	124	David Dexter	do
Dartmouth, Mass.				
Charles and Edward	Ship	150	William D. Gifford	William Potter, 2d
Matilda Sears	Bark	300	Edward J. Howland	do
Beverly, Mass.				
Eschol	Brig	143	—— Robertson	F. W. Choate
N. D. Chase	Bark	242	—— Hamlin	do
Sippican or Marion, Mass.				
Admiral Blake	Schooner	120	William C. Hathaway	Peleg Blankenship
Hopeton	Brig	145	Edwin A. Perry	Obed. Delano
James	Schooner	80	Benj. B. Handy	Benj. B. Handy
Retrieve	do	100	Zenas F. Eldridge	do
Salem, Mass.				
Messenger	Ship	216	—— Holmes	Benjamin Webb
Westport, Mass.				
George and Mary	Bark	165	Allen W. Pierce	Rescom Macomber
Gov. Carver	do	180	John W. Sherman	Henry Wilcox
Leonidas	Brig	128	James L. Skiff	C. A. Church
Mattapoisett	Bark	150	Benjamin Gifford	Henry Smith
Mermaid	do	330	George W. Jenks	Andrew Hicks
Platina	do	266	David E. Allen	do
Fall River, Mass.				
B. Franklin	Bark	164	—— Brown	John B. Reed
Warren, R. I.				
Covington	Bark	351	—— Jenks	Charles T. Child
Edgartown, Mass.				
Champion	Ship	400	—— Worth	Benjamin Worth
Rose Pool	Bark	285	—— Fisher	Joseph Holley
Nantucket, Mass.				
Alabama	Bark	340	Alfred M. Coffin	George Starbuck
Alpha	Ship	345	William H. Caswell	Geo. & Wm. Starbuck
Columbia	do	329	Joseph Abbott	Robert F. Gardner
Hero	do	313	Edward B. Hussey, jr	G. & M. Starbuck & Co.
Norman	do	338	Richard C. Gibbs	do
Watchman	Schooner	140	Charles W. Hussey	J. B. Macy

sailing from American ports—Continued.

Whaling-ground.	Date— Of sailing.	Date— Of arrival.	Result of voyage. Sperm-oil.	Result of voyage. Whale-oil.	Result of voyage. Whalebone.	Remarks.
			Bbls.	*Bbls.*	*Lbs.*	
Davis's Strait..	June 13	Oct. 11, 1861	......	665	15, 700	Lost five men by scurvy; sold to Sydney, N. S. W., for merchant service 1861.
Pacific Ocean ..	Apr. 24	Mar. 10, 1864	296	......	......	Sent home 561 sperm.
Atlantic	Apr. 3	Sept. 9, 1861	152	33	......	Sailed once and returned, leaking 500 strokes an hour; sent home 120 sperm; withdrawn 1861; finally wrecked and abandoned 1863.
Indian Ocean ..	Oct. 13	June 30, 1863	970	......	......	Sold to New Bedford 1863.
Atlantic	May 28	No report ...	......	......	......	
....do	May 15	Sept. 11, 1861	191	......	......	
Pacific Ocean ..	Sept. 18	....	......	......	......	Sent home 1,175 sperm, 70 whale; sold at Talcahuano 1865 to sail under the Chilian flag.
....do	Nov. 1	Nov. 11, 1864	500	525	......	Sent home 4,200 bone.
Atlantic	Oct. 6	May 5, 1862	238	40	......	
Atl. and Pacific	Apr. 18	Sept. 21, 1861	4	70	......	Sent home 79 sperm; sold to Liverpool, Nova Scotia, 1861.
Atlantic	Apr. 6	Sept. 20, 1860	182	2	......	
....do	Oct. 9	Nov. 25, 1861	140	10	......	Sold for merchant service 1862.
....do	Apr. 30	Aug. 29, 1860	103	......	......	
....do	Apr. 30	Sept. 6, 1860	118	......	......	
Atlantic	Apr. 18	July 17, 1861	330	16	......	Sold to Boston 1861; Salem's last whaler; one of "stone fleet," No. 2; sunk 1861.
Atlantic	Nov. 19	Aug. 16, 1863	321	2	......	Sold to Boston 1863 for merchant service.
Indian Ocean ..	Nov. 21	May 23, 1863	670	......	......	
Atlantic	Nov. 12	May 2, 1863	130	70	......	Sent home 188 sperm; sold to N. Bedford 1863.
... do	May 29	Feb. 16, 1862	328	10	......	
Pacific Ocean .	Oct. 4	Sept. 21, 1864	760	3	......	Sent home 48 sperm; shipped 200 sperm to London.
Indian Ocean ..	Aug. 16	Dec. 8, 1863	800	20	......	
Atlantic	Nov. 20	Oct. 30, 1862	15	......	......	Sent home 300 sperm; sold to New Bedford 1862; Fall River's last whaler.
Pacific Ocean ..	Nov. 7	....	......	......	......	Sent home 904 sperm, 144 whale, 2,700 bone; captured and burned by the Shenandoah in Behring Strait June, 1865; Warren's last whaler.
North Pacific ..	Oct. 26	Apr. 18, 1864	153	1, 525	15, 650	Sent home 113 sperm 8,900 bone.
Indian Ocean ..	Sept. 27	Aug. 25, 1863	1, 200	100	......	Sold to Boston 1863 for merchant service.
Pacific Ocean ..	May 6	....	......	......	......	Sent home 4,000 gallons sperm-oil; lost on Chatham Islands.
....do	Apr. 26	....	......	......	......	Took 1,000 barrels sperm; sold at San Francisco.
....do	Apr. 30	....	......	......	......	Captain Abbott died at sea September 5, 1861; condemned at Upola.
....do	Sept. 30	....	......	......	......	Lost in Algoa Bay, New Holland, 1861.
....do	Aug. 20	May 3, 1865	1, 200	......	......	Sold to New Bedford.
Atlantic	Nov. 30	Oct. 13, 1861	20	400	......	Sold to Provincetown.

Table showing returns of whaling-vessels

Name of vessel.	Class.	Tonnage.	Captain.	Managing owner or agent.
1860.				
Provincetown, Mass.				
Alleghany	Schooner	95	—— Cook	Daniel C. Cook
Alexander	do	75		Johnson & Cook
Antarctic	do	136		J. E. & G. Bowley
Chanticleer	do	87	—— Young	Samuel Cook
Civilian	Bark		—— Burch	
Emporium	Schooner	80	{ —— Cook —— Curran }	D. C. Cook
Estella	do	94	—— Freeman	J. E. & G. Bowley
J. H. Duvall	Bark	200	—— Tribble	do
Mermaid	Ship	158	Robert Soper, jr	S. R. Soper
N. J. Knights	Schooner	95	—— Sparks	D. Connell
S. R. Soper	do	130	—— Holmes	Samuel Soper
Spartan	Bark	18[illegible]	—— Cook	Stephen Nickerson
V. Doane	Schooner	99	—— Young	H. & S. Cook & Co
V. H. Hill	do	157	—— Freeman	J. E. & G. Bowley
Walter Irvin	do	133	—— Atkins	Samuel Soper
Weather Gage	do	105	—— Small	H. & S. Cook & Co
Orleans, Mass.				
Lewis Bruce	Brig	135	—— Cornell	Heman Smith
Rothschild	Bark	261	—— Allerton	do
New London, Mass.				
Alert	Bark	398	—— Parsons	E. V. Stoddard
Charles Colgate	Schooner	250	—— Nash	Lawrence & Co
E. R. Sawyer	do	120	—— Lyon	E. V. Stoddard
Geo. Henry	Bark	303	Sidney O. Buddington	Williams & Haven
Georgiana	Brig	190	—— Tyson	do
Hannibal	Ship	441	—— Rogers	Benj. F. Brown
Monticello	Bark	356	—— Church	Richard H. Chapell
Pioneer	do	235	—— Lester	Williams & Haven
Silver Cloud	Schooner	140	—— Billings	R. H. Chapell
Stonington, Conn.				
Tekoa	Schooner	143	—— Williams	J. E. Smith & Co.
Mystic, Conn.				
Coriolanus	Ship	268	—— Fish	Charles Malloy
Cornelia	Schooner	197	—— Chester	do
Sag Harbor, N. Y.				
Parana	Brig	209	—— Green	H. & S. French
Susan	Schooner	134	—— King	do
1861.				
New Bedford, Mass.				
A. R. Tucker	Bark	218	Asa Grinnell	J. & W. R. Wing
Adeline Gibbs	Ship	351	Henry W. Davis	Jonathan Bourne, jr
Antelope	Bark	340	George Taber	S. Thomas & Co
Benjamin Tucker	Ship	349	William Childs	C. R. Tucker & Co
Chili	do	291	Godfrey King	Azel Howard
Contest	do	441	Thomas H. Norton	I. Howland, jr., & Co
Cornelia	Bark	219	Ephraim Poole	John P. Knowles, 2d
Dr. Franklin	do	171	Beriah C. Manchester	Cobb & Manchester

sailing from American ports—Continued.

Whaling-ground.	Date—		Result of voyage.			Remarks.
	Of sailing.	Of arrival.	Sperm-oil.	Whale-oil.	Whalebone.	
			Bbls.	*Bbls.*	*Lbs.*	
Atlantic	Jan. 8	July 26, 1860	160	140		
		June 14, 1860	210	5		
		Oct. 19, 1860	320	8		
North Atlantic	Apr. 25	Sept. 3, 1860	67	15		
Atlantic	May 26	Sept. 4, 1862	740			Added 1860; sent home 280 sperm.
....do	Feb. 7	Aug. 22, 1860	61	5		
	Dec. 28	June 23, 1861	206	10		
....do	May 5	Sept. 12, 1861	120	25		
....do	July 17					Sold at Bombay; renamed Hannah Maria, and sailed under the English flag.
....do	Dec. 28					Added 1860; built at East Boston 1860; captured and burned by rebel privateer Calhoun 1861.
....do	Jan. 3	Aug. 14, 1860	84	130		
North Atlantic	Jan. 13	Nov. 12, 1860	208			
Atlantic	July 17	Aug. 11, 1863	150	100		
....do	Feb. 7	Aug. 28, 1860	120	20		
North Atlantic	Jan. 2	Aug. 25, 1860	321	9		
Atlantic	Dec. 28	Dec. 7, 1861	267	12		
North Atlantic	Jan. 2	Aug. 14, 1860	81	136		Added 1859.
Atlantic	Nov. 16	July 13, 1862	45			Transferred to Boston 1862.
....do	Jan. 20	Aug. 28, 1861	30	706		Sent home 110 sperm; transferred to Boston 1862.
Hurd's Island	July 24	July 12, 1862		3,190	1,850	
Desolation Isld.	June 4	May 20, 1862		1,289		Added 1860.
....do	June 27	July 2, 1862		493		
Davis's Strait	May 29	Sept. 13, 1862		564	10,100	
....do	May 1	Oct. 7, 1861		695	14,700	
....do	Mar. 21					Sent home 8,000 bone; abandoned in Cumberland Inlet October, 1861.
Indian Ocean	Sept. 4	July 30, 1861	18	153		Bought from Nantucket 1859.
Cumber'd Inlet	June 1	Oct. 22, 1861		10		Captain Lester died June 15, 1860.
Desolation Isld.	June 13					Probably lost with all on board 1862; had sent home 700 barrels of elephant-oil.
South Atlantic	Nov. 13	Jan. 20, 1861				Arrived at New York; sold to Fairhaven 1861.
Indian Ocean	July 10					Sent home 18 sperm, 75 whale; condemned at Mauritius November, 1861.
Hurd's Island	June 16	June 17, 1862		968		Sold to New London 1862.
Atlantic	May 16	July 2, 1862	110			Sent home 295 sperm, 200 whale, 1,800 bone; altered to a bark 1862.
....do	May 7	Aug. 7, 1861	341	176		
....do	May 29	May 4, 1864	55			Sent home 376 sperm.
Pacific Ocean	Oct. 2	Apr. 24, 1866	90	41	350	
Hudson's Bay	Oct. 31	Oct. 12, 1863		1,500	24,000	
Atlantic	May 8					Sent home 151 sperm; captured and burned by the Alabama, with 450 bbls. of oil, 1862.
Atl. and Ind.	May 21	Apr. 27, 1864	334	94		Sent home 266 sperm; sold and broken up 1864.
....do	May 30	Aug. 5, 1864	208	691	950	Sailed under Captain Morgan; returned because he died suddenly of heart disease, March 4, 1861; sent home 283 sperm and 5,000 bone; sold to New London, 1864, for Valparaiso.
Atlantic	May 5	Apr. 29, 1864	320	592	200	Sent home 120 sperm.
Atl. and Ind.	Nov. 11					Bought from Westport 1861; sent home 250 sperm and 150 whale; sold at Talcahuano 1864, to fit under the Chilian flag; name changed to Mathieu & Branas.

Table showing returns of whaling-vessels

Name of vessel.	Class.	Tonnage.	Captain.	Managing owner or agent.
1861.				
New Bedford, Mass.—Continued.				
Eben Dodge	Bark	221	Gideon C. Hoxie	B. Franklin Howland
George & Susan	Ship	356	N. M. Jernegan	George and M. Howland
Hector	...do	380	Amos A. Chase	William J. Rotch
John Wells	...do	366	Matthew Fisher	Thomas Knowles & Co
Joshua Bragdon	Bark	270	—— Spooner	Charles S. Randall
Lafayette	Ship	311	Obed Sherman	I. H. Bartlett & Sons
Louisa	Bark	316	John Steen	Swift & Allen
Majestic	Ship	297	Alex. A. Tripp	S. Thomas & Co
Midas	Bark	326	Henry A. Howland	James B. Wood & Co
Niger	Ship	437	Francis J. Allen	William Hathaway, jr
Nimrod	Bark	340	Alfred C. Davis	William Gifford
Northern Light	Ship	513	Jacob Taber	Jonathan Bourne, jr
Palmyra	Schooner	100	E. S. Davoll	A. H. Potter & Co
Robert Morrison	Bark	307	Crary B. Waite	Thomas Knowles & Co
Roscius	...do	300	John M. Honeywell	William P. Howland
Sea Breeze	...do	473	Joshua Weeks, jr	Otis Seabury
Swallow	Ship	439	Frederick Slocum	William G. Blackler
Tropic Bird	Bark	220	Charles H. Hagar	W. P. Howland
Washington	...do	344	John D. Willard	J. Bourne, jr
Fairhaven, Mass.				
Arab	Bark	276	Joseph P. Nye	Damon & Judd
Kingfisher	Schooner	120	Thomas W. Lambert	C. H. Tripp
Oxford	...do	130	Otis B. Snow	I. F. Terry
Roswell King	...do	134	Busel Tripp	Fisk, Robinson & Co
Tekoa	...do	143	John A. Benson	Damon & Judd
Mattapoisett, Mass.				
Sarah	Bark	179	James King	J. R. & W. L. Taber
Willis	...do	164	Bradford B. Briggs	H. N. Barstow
Sippican, Mass.				
Admiral Blake	Schooner	120	William C. Hathaway	Peleg Blankenship
Altamaha	...do	119	Benjamin B. Handy	Stephen C. Luce
James	...do	80	Allen D. Rider	Benjamin B. Handy
Retrieve	...do	100	Zenas T. Eldridge	...do
Westport, Mass.				
Aurora	Ship	351	John Church	Andrew Hicks
Elizabeth	Bark	270	Hiram Francis	...do
Kate Cory	Brig	132	Stephen Flanders	Alexander H. Cory
Sea Fox	Bark	246	John Horan	A. Hicks
Warren, R. I.				
Dromo	Bark	267	—— Ray	Charles T. Child
Edgartown, Mass.				
Ellen	Bark	232	—— Marchant	William H. Munroe

sailing from American ports—Continued.

Whaling-ground.	Date—		Result of voyage.			Remarks.
	Of sailing.	Of arrival.	Sperm-oil.	Whale-oil.	Whalebone.	
			Bbls.	*Bbls.*	*Lbs.*	
Atl. and Pacific	Nov. 25	....	......	......	......	Captured and burned by the Sumter December 7, 1861.
Pacific Ocean	Aug. 28	Aug. 25, 1864	176	1,258	7,850	Sent home 1,028 sperm and 2,150 bone; built at Dartmouth 1809.
Atl. and Pacific	May 22	....	......	......	......	Sent home 260 sperm, 140 whale, and 1,850 bone; captured and burned by the Shenandoah, at Ascension, 1865; value $31,000, and oil.
Atl. and Ind	June 26	....	......	......	......	Sold 570 sperm and 120 whale at Sydney.
Atlantic	June 17	Oct. 5, 1864	276	10	......	Captain William Childs took Captain Spooner's place 1863; sent home 344 sperm; sold to New York for merchant-service 1864.
....do	May 29	Dec. 4, 1861	213	......	......	
....do	July 3	Nov. 23, 1864	540	5	......	Sent home 460 sperm, 640 whale, 5,000 bone.
....do	June 12	Nov. 26, 1861	158	......	......	
Pacific Ocean	May 15	Aug. 28, 1865	229	3	......	Sent home 327 sperm.
....do	May 21	May 21, 1865	454	3	......	Captain Allen died at sea June 9, 1864; sent home 170 sperm; sent also 128 sperm by Golconda; burned by the Florida.
Atl. and Ind	Aug. 26	Dec. 28, 1862	359	......	......	Altered from a ship 1861.
Hudson's Bay	Nov. 18	Oct. 17, 1862	......	1,295	19,900	Bought from Fairhaven 1861; sent home 70 sperm.
Atlantic	Apr. 25	....	......	......	......	Bought from Mattapoisett 1861; sent home 120 sperm; withdrawn 1862 for a coaster.
Indian Ocean	June 5	Aug. 21, 1864	1,019	......	......	Sent home 120 sperm.
Atlantic	Oct. 8	Dec. 27, 1862	448	8	......	Sent home 100 sperm; took a sperm whale which made 153 barrels.
Pacific Ocean	Oct. 1	Nov. 13, 1864	325	120	1,250	Sent home 635 sperm and 60 whale.
....do	May 1	Apr. 23, 1865	1,509	......	......	
Atlantic	Oct. 30	Nov. 26, 1863	125	......	......	Sent home 120 sperm.
Ind. and Pac	July 22	May 26, 1865	136	1,075	5,100	Sent home 250 sperm, 400 whale, 8,960 bone.
Atlantic	Oct. 16	Sept. 24, 1862	447	......	......	Sold to New London to replace Alert.
....do	July 30	....	......	......	......	Added 1861; sent home 104 sperm; captured and burned by the Alabama 1863.
....do	June 5	Aug. 22, 1862	125	10	......	Altered to a brig 1862.
....do	May 8	Aug. 14, 1863	17	6	......	Sent home 100 sperm; bought from Sippican 1860.
....do	July 11	May 28, 1863	......	6	......	Bought from Stonington 1861; sent home 110 sperm.
Atlantic	May 9	Oct. 8, 1862	156	......	......	Sent home 153 sperm.
....do	June 9	Sept. 18, 1862	146	176	......	
Atlantic	May 9	Sept. 27, 1861	135	......	......	
....do	May 21	....	......	......	......	Burned at sea by the rebel cruisers.
....do	May 16	Aug. 29, 1861	125	4	......	
....do	May 16	....	......	......	......	Sent home 109 sperm; condemned at Fayal 1861.
Pacific Ocean	Nov. 20	Aug. 7, 1865	150	363	......	Altered from a bark 1861; Edwin A. Sherman, third mate, died January, 1863, from injuries received from a whale; sold to New B dford 1865; sent home 825 sperm and 6,700 bone.
Atlantic	May 13	Oct. 5, 1863	440	......	......	Sent home 350 sperm.
....do	Apr. 20	Apr. 18, 1862	305	12	......	
Pacific Ocean	Nov. 4	Oct. 19, 1864	961			
Pacific Ocean	Nov. 5	....	......	......	......	Sent home 280 sperm; condemned at Paita 1864.
Atl. and Ind	Jan. 5	....	......	......	....	Sent home 99 sperm; condemned at Barbadoes 1863.

Table showing returns of whaling-vessels

Name of vessel.	Class.	Tonnage.	Captain.	Managing owner or agent.
1861.				
Edgartown, Mass.—Continued.				
Mary	Ship	343	—— Morrison	Abraham Osborn
Nantucket, Mass.				
Samuel Chase	Schooner	65	James McGuire	
New London, Conn.				
Atlantic	Schooner			
Provincetown, Mass.				
Alleghany	Schooner	95	—— Cook	Daniel C. Cook
Alexander	do	75	—— Rich	Johnson & Cook
Antarctic	do	136	—— Cornell	J. E. & G. Bowley
Arizona	do	115	—— Cook	Stephen Cook
Courser	do	120	—— Young	H. & S. Cook & Co
E. H. Hatfield	do	125	—— Cook	E. & E. K. Cook
E. Gerry	do			
Emporium	do	80	—— Caton	D. C. Cook
F. Bunchinia	Bark	200	—— Rich	Nickerson & Tuck
G. W. Lewis	Schooner	110	—— Holmes	—— Taylor
John Adams	do	99	Joseph Caton	John Adams
N. J. Knights	do	95	—— Sparks	D. Connell
Oread	do	98	—— Young	E. S. Smith & Co
Panama	Ship	..	George Pow	
Quickstep	Schooner	119	—— Cook	E. & E. K. Cook
R. E. Cook	do	80	—— Tilson	R. & E. Cook
Rienzi	do	108	—— Goodspeed	J. E. & G. Bowley
S. R. Soper	do	130	—— Abbott	Samuel Soper
V. Doane	do	99	—— Cook	H. & S. Cook & Co.
V. H. Hill	do	155	—— Freeman	J. E. & G. Bowley
Watchman	do	140		
Weather Gage	do	105	—— Small	H. & S. Cook & Co.
Orleans, Mass.				
William Martin	Schooner	134	—— Martin	Heman Smith
Sag Harbor, N. Y.				
Excel	Bark	375	—— Rose	O. R. Wade
John A. Robb	do	273	—— Jennings	
Myra	Brig	150	Jacob Havens	W. & G. H. Cooper
Odd Fellow	Bark	239	—— Weld	Wade & Brown
Susan	Brig	134	—— King	H. & S French
Union	Bark	30[illegible]	—— Ludlow	O. R. Wade
Bark Carib, 205 tons, Captain Fay, (San Francisco,) sailed April 18, 1861, for the Arctic; no further report.				
1862.				
New Bedford, Mass.				
Abigail	Ship	310	Ebenezer F. Nye	Loum Snow
Ansel Gibbs	do	319	William Washburn	Jonathan Bourne, jr
Awashonks	Bark	34[illegible]	Peleg S. Wing	J. & W. R. Wing
Bartholemew Gosnold	Ship	350	John Bolles	I. Howland, jr., & Co.
Black Eagle	Bark	311	Charles E. Allen	S. Thomas & Co.
Brunswick	Ship	295	Alden T. Potter	J. & W. R. Wing

sailing from American ports—Continued.

Whaling-ground.	Date—		Result of voyage.			Remarks.
	Of sailing.	Of arrival.	Sperm-oil.	Whale-oil.	Whalebone.	
			Bbls.	*Bbls.*	*Lbs.*	
Indian Ocean ..	June 19	July 26, 1865	656	......	......	
Shoals	....	....	......	125	......	Made five trips, humpbacking; sold to Dartmouth.
....	....	Sept. 18, 1861	50	......	......	
Atlantic	Jan. 1	Aug. 20, 1861	4	140	......	
....do	Mar. 12	Sept. 22, 1861	170	3	......	
....do	Mar. 28	Sept. 4, 1862	194	57	......	
....do	Jan. 22	Aug. 14, 1861	38	145	......	Bought from Salisbury 1860; built 1858.
North Atlantic.	May 10	Oct. 4, 1861	......	Clean	......	
....	....	May 21, 1862	181	239	......	Built 1861; sent home 50 sperm.
....	....	Sept. 10, 1861	156	......	......	
Atlantic	Aug. 15	July 10, 1862	109	14	......	
....do	....	Sept. 23, 1862	372	480	......	Sent home 119 sperm.
....do	....	Sept. 1, 1863	90	10	......	Sent home 29 sperm.
....do	Feb. 5	....	......	......	......	Captured and burned by rebel privateer Calhoun 1861.
....do	Jan. 1	July 23, 1861	61	182	......	Reported also in September with 60 sperm, 180 whale.
....do	Jan. 1	Aug. 5, 1861	130	116	......	
....	....	....	......	......	......	Captured and burned by rebel privateer Calhoun 1861.
Atlantic	Jan. 9	Aug. 25, 1864	300	135	......	Sent home 285 sperm, 60 whale.
....do	Mar. 25	Aug. 14, 1861	138	5	......	
....do	Mar. 25	....	......	......	......	Captured and burned by a rebel privateer 1863.
....do	....	Nov. —, 1862	75	......	......	
....do	Jan. 1	Aug. 8, 1861	146	152	......	
....do	Feb. 7	Sept. 11, 1862	131	134	......	
....	....	Oct. 13, 1861	20	360	......	
Atlantic	Jan. 1	Aug. 14, 1861	144	149	......	
Atlantic	Jan. 22	Sept. 6, 1861	336	27	......	Transferred to Boston 1862.
Atl. and Indian	July 22	....	......	......	......	Sent home 147 sperm; condemned 1863.
Atlantic	Oct. 15	Apr. 27, 1863	400	700	3, 000	
South Atlantic	June 14	Apr. 20, 1863	240	......	......	Added 1861.
Atl. and Indian	Aug. 23	Mar. 13, 1864	555	335	2, 600	
Atlantic	Oct. 14	July 13, 1863	150	150	......	Sold to New York 1863.
Atl. and Indian	Nov. 15	June 4, 1864	558	170	1, 100	
North Pacific ..	July 31	....	......	......	......	Sent home 355 sperm, 1,548 whale, 6,100 bone; captured and burned by the Shenandoah 1865, in Ochotsk; value, $30,000 and catchings; Captain Nye immediately manned two boats and started to warn the rest of the fleet.
Hudson's Bay ..	Apr. 15	Oct. 11, 1863	......	1, 000	17, 580	Bought from Fairhaven 1861; sent home 20 sperm.
Atlantic	May 28	Aug. 1, 1865	207	239	1, 050	Sent home 277 sperm, 500 bone.
Indian Ocean ..	Sept. 16	Apr. 16, 1866	......	566	3, 750	Sent home 43 sperm, 1,080 whale, 14,700 bone.
Cumber'd Inlet	May 5	Sept. 24, 1863	......	1, 650	30, 000	
North Pacific ..	Oct. 15	....	......	......	......	Bought from Dartmouth 1862; captured and burned by the Shenandoah in Behring Strait June, 1865; sent home 30 sperm, 1,230 whale, 5,000 bone.

Table showing returns of whaling-vessels

Name of vessel.	Class.	Tonnage.	Captain.	Managing owner or agent.
1862.				
New Bedford, Mass.—Continued.				
Callao	Bark	324	Frederick S. Howland	Henry Taber & Co
Camilla	do	429	Reuben T. Thomas	Swift & Allen
California	Ship	398	Charles E. Cleaveland	I. Howland, jr., & Co
Canton	do	280	Archelaus Baker, jr	C. R. Tucker & Co
Canton Packet	do	274	Obed Freeman	I. H. Bartlett & Sons
Cleone	Bark	273	—— Maxfield	Edmund Maxfield
Corinthian	Ship	401	Valentine Lewis	Geo. & Matt. Howland
Dolphin	Schooner	97	Wash. T. Walker	W. T. Walker
Draco	Bark	257	John R. Lawrence	Jonathan Bourne, jr
Eagle	do	336	James R. Allen	Swift & Perry
Elisha Dunbar	do	....	David R. Gifford	....
Euphrates	Ship	365	Thomas B. Hathaway	Edward W. Howland
Europa	do	380	Anthony Milton	Edward C. Jones
Fabius	do	432	Daniel B. Wood	C. R. Tucker & Co
Falcon	do	273	Richard Flanders	Thomas Knowles & Co
Gazelle	do	340	Daniel F. Worth	Thomas Nye, jr
George Howland	do	374	Robert Jones	G. & M. Howland
George	do	280	Joseph D. Silva	Gideon Allen & Son
Globe	Bark	215	Alexander A. Tripp	Charles Tucker
Governor Troup	Ship	430	E. R. Ashley	E. C. Jones
Gratitude	Bark	337	Lewis N. Herendeen	Swift & Allen
Gypsey	do	360	Orlando G. Robinson	I. Howland, jr., & Co
Helen Snow	do	299	Joseph S. Adams	Loum Snow
Henry Kneeland	Ship	304	John M. Soule	Benjamin B. Howard
Hercules	Bark	335	John G. Dexter	Swift & Perry
Hillman	Ship	383	S. W. Fisk	H. Taber & Co
James Arnold	do	393	David H. Bartlett	do
James	do	321	Joseph H. Cornell	Thomas Nye, jr
Jireh Swift	Bark	454	Thomas W. Williams	Swift & Allen
John Dawson	do	237	John W. Cornell	J. & W. R. Wing
Lafayette	do	357	William Lewis	I. H. Bartlett & Sons
Levi Starbuck	Ship	..	Thomas Mellen	....
Marcella	Bark	210	Alfred K. Crosby	C. R. Tucker & Co
Martha, 2d	do	360	Barnard H. Dailey	William O. Brownell
Milwood	do	254	Rich W. Hathaway	G. Allen & Son
Morning Star	do	305	Hervey E. Luce	S. Thomas & Co

sailing from American ports—Continued.

Whaling-ground.	Date— Of sailing.	Date— Of arrival.	Result of voyage. Sperm-oil.	Result of voyage. Whale-oil.	Result of voyage. Whalebone.	Remarks.
			Bbls.	*Bbls.*	*Lbs.*	
Atlantic	Sept. 2	Aug. 30, 1865	296	301	1,550	Sent home 550 sperm, 710 whale, 5,000 bone.
North Pacific	Dec. 23	Apr. 11, 1867		700		Sent home 75 sperm, 3,256 whale, 41,500 bone.
....do	Aug. 25	Apr. 11, 1866		1,198	17,150	James B. Wood, first mate, died January 1, 1866; sent home 80 sperm, 1,020 whale, 11,900 bone.
Indian Ocean	Dec. 28	Apr. 7, 1866	1,415	81		
Atlantic	Apr. 30	Nov. 27, 1862	311	2		
....do	Sept. 9	Nov. 21, 1863	160			Sent home 92 sperm.
North Pacific	Aug. 30	Apr. 20, 1866	374	1,620	18,750	Sent home 215 sperm, 1,973 whale, 53,100 bone.
Atlantic	May 20					Formerly in Havana trade; added 1862; No further report.
Atl. and Indian	June 19	Oct. 8, 1865	313			Sent home 900 sperm.
Atlantic	June 17	Oct. 7, 1864	138	900		Silas B. Plato, second mate, and boat's crew lost while fast to a whale December 29, 1863; sent home 632 sperm, 5,800 bone.
	Aug. —					Captured and burned by the Alabama 1862.
North Pacific	Aug. 5					Captured and burned by the Shenandoah off Cape Thaddeus 1865; value, $32,000 and oil; sent home 1,883 whale, 19,400 bone.
....do	July 1	Sept. 16, 1867	90	230		Sent home 178 sperm, 1,599 whale, 25,200 bone.
....do	Oct. 16					Sent home 285 sperm, 1,193 whale, 19,500 bone; lost on Solidad reef, coast of California, January 27, 1865.
Atlantic	July 8	June 17, 1865	197	722		
Indian Ocean	Aug. 25	Apr. 20, 1866	906	290	1,650	
Pacific Ocean	June 4	Apr. 16, 1866		1,035	11,800	Sent home 364 sperm, 2,950 whale, 36,996 bone.
....do	June 3	May 27, 1864	3	5		Sent home 612 sperm.
Atlantic	June 10	Aug. 31, 1864	23	4		Sent home 834 sperm, 120 whale, 600 bone.
North Pacific	Dec. 2	June 4, 1867	40	400	5,000	Sent home 53 sperm, 2,206 whale, 28,800 bone.
Pacific Ocean	June 19					Sent home 410 sperm, 600 whale; struck an iceberg and lost in Arctic July 2, 1865.
....do	May 28					Sent home 174 sperm, 670 whale, 9,200 bone; captured and burned by the Shenandoah in Behring Strait June, 1865; sent 505 whale by Golconda, (burned by the Florida.)
....do	Oct. 9	May 13, 1867	175	600	10,000	Captain Adams died in the Arctic August 20, 1864; sent home 210 sperm, 729 whale, 15,300 bone.
North Pacific	Aug. 11					Sent home 419 whale, 5,200 bone; lost in the ice in the Arctic July, 1864.
....do	Sept. 2	May 8, 1865	222	605	5,800	Sent home 126 sperm, 2,073 whale, 19,800 bone.
....do	Oct. 28					Captain Fisk died February 28, 1864; sent home 20 sperm, 1,942 whale, 6,300 bone; captured and burned by the Shenandoah in Behring Strait June, 1865.
Atlantic	June 12	Dec. 19, 1863	380			Sent home 95 sperm.
....do	July 15	Oct. 29, 1865	829	401		Sent home 350 sperm, 300 whale, 6,362 bone.
North Pacific	Sept. 2					Sent home 25 sperm, 1,540 whale, 20,950 bone; captured and burned by the Shenandoah June 22, 1865; value, $40,000 and catchings; had 400 whale.
Atlantic	May 12	June 18, 1864	270			Sent home 548 sperm.
....do	May 20					Sent home 235 sperm; captured and burned by the Alabama 1863, with 184 sperm.
	Oct. —					Captured and burned by the Alabama five days out; value, $32,000.
Atlantic	May 14	Oct. 27, 1864	99			Sent home 684 sperm.
North Pacific	Oct. 1					Captain Dailey died at sea April, 1864; captured and burned by the Shenandoah in Behring Strait June, 1865; sent home 171 sperm, 1,113 whale, 22,477 bone.
Atlantic	July 1	Sept. 26, 1863	100			Sent home 204 sperm.
....do	Aug. 7	Apr. 21, 1863	90			Sent home 112 sperm.

Table showing returns of whaling-vessels

Name of vessel.	Class.	Tonnage.	Captain.	Managing owner or agent.
1862.				
New Bedford, Mass.—Continued.				
Mount Wollaston	Ship	325	James M. Willis	Wood & Nye
Ohio	...do	383	Matthew L. Smith	E. W. Howland
Ohio	Bark	237	Daniel Flanders	Loum Snow
Orray Taft	...do	176	George E. Tyson	George Homer & Co
Osceola	Ship			
Osceola, 3d	Bark	200	Michael S. Hogan	Cranston Wilcox
Pacific	...do	385	Jetur Rose	Swift & Perry
Pioneer	...do	231	Henry R. Plaskett	J. D. Thompson
Plover	...do	330	George N. Macy	W. & G. D. Watkins
President, 2d	...do	189	Benjamin Gifford	E. Maxfield
Seine	...do	281	Edwin A. Luce	J. P. Knowles, 2d
Solon	...do	129	Daniel B. Baxter	J. & W. R. Wing
Swift	Ship	321	Francis S. Worth	Thomas S. Hathaway
Tamerlane	...do	357	N. P. Gray	T. Knowles & Co
T. Winslow	Bark	136	E. G. Cudworth	John Hicks
Union	...do	124	—— Dexter	J. P. Knowles, 2d
Virginia	...do		Shadrach R. Tilton	
Wave	...do	197	M. C. Fisher	T. Knowles & Co
Fairhaven, Mass.				
Alto	Bark	236	Joseph D. Nye	Damon & Judd
Erie	Ship			
Oxford	Brig			
Mattapoisett, Mass.				
Willis	Bark	164	B. B. Briggs	H. N. Barstow
Dartmouth, Mass.				
Cape Horn Pigeon	Ship	300	Daniel Sherman	William Potter, 2d
Sippican, Mass.				
Admiral Blake	Schooner	120	William C. Hathaway	Peleg Blankenship
Attamaha	...do	119	Rufus Gray	Stephen C. Luce
Emerald	...do	101	Zenas F. Eldridge	Benjamin B. Handy
Hopeton	Brig	145	Benjamin B. Handy	Obed Delano
James	Schooner	80	Allen D. Ryder	Benjamin B. Handy
Westport, Mass.				
Greyhound	Bark	249	James M. Sowle	Henry Wilcox
Kate Cory	Brig	132	Stephen Flanders	Alexander H. Cory
Mattapoisett	Bark	150	George W. Beebe	Henry Smith
Sea Queen	...do	261	Peleg W. Gifford	Andrew Hicks
Provincetown, Mass.				
Abby H. Brown	Schooner	131	—— Higgins	E. & E. K. Cook
Acorn	Bark	215	—— Allerton	Nickerson & Tuck
Allegbany	Schooner	95	—— Cook	Daniel C. Cook
Alexander	...do	75	—— Rich	Johnson & Cook
Arizona	...do	115	—— Cook	Stephen Cook
C. L. Sparks	...do	128	—— Sparks	D. Conwell
Courser	...do	120	Silas S. Young	H. & S. Cook & Co
E. B. Conwell	...do	132	—— Kilburn	D. Conwell
E. Gerry	...do	104	—— Small	C. A. Homan
E. H. Hatfield	...do	125	—— Cook	E. & E. K. Cook
Ellen Rizpah	...do	100	—— Smith	Stephen Cook & Co
Estella	...do	94	—— Snow	J. E. & G. Bowley
G. W. Lewis	...do	110	—— Holmes	—— Taylor

sailing from American ports—Continued.

Whaling-ground.	Date—		Result of voyage.			Remarks.
	Of sailing.	Of arrival.	Sperm-oil.	Whale-oil.	Whalebone.	
			Bbls.	*Bbls.*	*Lbs.*	
North Pacific ..	Nov. 24	June 13, 1867	140	700	12,000	Sent home 1,040 whale, 22,800 bone.
Pacific Ocean ..	June 17	June 19, 1866	1,334	12	.....	
Atl. and Indian	Oct. 4	Dec. 11, 1864	....	5	.....	Sent home 220 sperm, 300 whale.
Cumber'd Inlet.	Apr. 27	Oct. 25, 1867	.....	225	3,000	
....	....	....	.....	.....	.....	Captured and burned by the Alabama 1862.
Pacific Ocean ..	Aug. 5	July 14, 1865	....	Clean	....	Sent home 210 sperm, 375 whale, 4,900 bone.
North Pacific ..	Nov. 4	May 11, 1865	.....	817	.....	Sent home 83 sperm, 1,780 whale, 49,500 bone.
Atlantic	Apr. 20	Nov. 6, 1864	176	.....	.....	Sent home 15 sperm.
South Pacific ..	Oct. 15	....	.....	.....	.....	Altered from a ship 1862; sent home 800 bone; lost on a reef north of Fejee Islands August 5, 1864; saved 265 sperm, 55 whale.
Atlantic	June 16	Oct. 6, 1864	85	.....	....	Sent home 657 sperm.
Pacific Ocean ..	July 8	June 11, 1865	661	2	.....	Sent home 211 sperm.
Atlantic	June 12	Oct. 19, 1863	60	.....	.....	Sent home 140 sperm.
Pacific Ocean ..	Oct. 12	....	.....	.....	.....	Sent home 25 sperm; lost off Rorotonga July 15, 1863.
North Pacific .	Aug. 26	Apr. 11, 1865	83	1,194	1,400	Sent home 700 whale, 14,670 bone.
Atlantic	July 28	Oct. 5, 1863	15	.....	....	
... do	Apr. 23	Sept. 6, 1863	25	....	.....	Sent home 226 sperm.
....	Aug. —	....	.....	....	....	Captured and burned by the Alabama 1862.
Atlantic	Oct. 26	Sept. 4, 1864	92	.....	.....	Sent home 370 sperm.
Atlantic	Nov. 10	Sept. 15, 1864	228	2	.....	Bought from New Bedford 1862; sent home 319 sperm.
....	....	....	.....	.....	.....	Dismasted and abandoned off Cape Horn August, 1862.
....	....	....	.....	.....	.....	Altered from a schooner; sailed 1862 or 1863; no report.
Atlantic	Nov. 24	Sept. 15, 1864	50	.....	700	Sent home 303 sperm, 195 whale; sold to New Bedford 1865; Mattapoisett's last whaler.
Pacific Ocean ..	Sept. 15	Apr. 9, 1866	....	723	12,800	Sent home 325 sperm, 675 whale, 15,100 bone.
Atlantic	May 12	Oct. 18, 1862	10	5	.....	
....do	May 12	....	.....	.....	.....	Captured and burned by the Alabama 1862.
... do	May 20	Oct. 21, 1862	35	5	.....	Bought from Fairhaven 1862.
... do	May 20	Oct. 18, 1862	138	.....	.....	Withdrawn 1862.
....do	May 14	Sept. 6, 1862	62	7	.....	
Atlantic	June 20	Oct. 16, 1864	350	.....	.....	Sent home 343 sperm.
....do	June 26	....	.....	.....	.....	Sent home 126 sperm; captured and burned by the Alabama 1863.
....do	May 20	Apr. 14, 1864	75	20	.....	Sent home 110 sperm.
Indian Ocean ..	Sept. 18	Apr. 27, 1866	1,063	.....	.....	
Atlantic	Jan. 29	Aug. 18, 1863	190	110	.....	Added 1862.
....do	Apr. 13	Apr. 16, 1862	.....	.....	.....	Put into Gloucester leaking 650 strokes per hour; sold to Boston on voyage.
....do	Jan. 11	Sept. 23, 1862	68	71	.....	
....	....	May —, 1863	.....	.....	.....	No report.
Atlantic	Jan. 11	Aug. 19, 1862	182	157	.....	
....do	....	June 18, 1863	75	225	.....	Added 1862.
....do	....	....	.....	.....	.....	Captured and burned by the Alabama 1862.
....do	Jan. —	Aug. 28, 1862	245	38	.....	Added 1862.
....do	....	Apr. —, 1863	50	.....	.....	
....do	Aug. 12	Oct. —, 1863	....	.....	.....	No report.
....do	Aug. 11	Aug. 11, 1863	50	30	.....	Added 1862; built at Essex 1856.
....do	....	Mar. —, 1863	100	.....	.....	
....do	....	Sept. 1, 1863	90	10	.....	

Table showing returns of whaling-vessels

Name of vessel.	Class.	Tonnage.	Captain.	Managing owner or agent.
1862.				
Provincetown, Mass.—Continued.				
Montezuma	Schooner	92	—— Curren	T. & S. Hilliard
N. J. Knights	do	95		D. Conwell
Oread	do	98	—— Young	E. S. Smith & Co
R. E. Cook	do	80		R. & E. Cook
Rising Sun	do	108	—— Young	E. S. Smith & Co
V. Doane	do	99		H. & S. Cook & Co.
Union	do	97		
Walter Irvin	do	138		Samuel Soper
Watchman	do	140		
Weather Gage	do	105	Samuel C. Small	H. & S. Cook & Co.
Boston, Mass.				
Acorn	Bark	215	—— Allerton	John Tyler
Rothschild	do	261	—— Dimmick	Heman Smith
Sarah E. Lewis	Schooner	140	—— Farwell	do
William Martin	do	134	—— Martin	do
Sandwich, Mass.				
Ocean	Bark	165	Peleg Cornell	W. F. Lapham
Holmes' Hole, Mass.				
America	Bark	257	—— Luce	Thomas Bradley
Salem, Mass.				
Falcon	Brig	159	—— Holmes	J. C. Osgood
Beverly, Mass.				
Eschol	Brig	143	—— Robertson	F. W. Choate
Thriver	Schooner	95	—— Holman	do
New London, Conn.				
Alert	Bark	398	Edwin Church	Richard H. Chapell
Arab	do	276		do
Electra	Ship	348	Oliver Sisson	Williams & Barns
E. R. Sawyer	Schooner	126	—— Rogers	R. H. Chapell
Gen. Williams	Ship	419	—— Benjamin	Williams & Barns
Georgianna	Brig	190	—— Rogers	Williams & Haven
Monticello	Bark	356	—— Chapell	R. H. Chapell
Pacific	Schooner	161	—— Turner	Lawrence & Co
Pearl	Bark	195	—— Bush	Williams & Haven
Pioneer	do	235	—— Chapell	do
Edgartown, Mass.				
Europa	Ship	400	—— Crosby	Abraham Osborn
Ocmulgee	do			
Splendid	do	392	James B. Huxford	Abraham Osborn
Vineyard	do	381	—— Caswell	Benjamin Worth
Nantucket, Mass.				
Islander	Ship	347	William Cash	Zenas L. Adams
Rainbow	do	80	James Maguire Robert F. Kent	Joseph B. Macy

sailing from American ports—Continued.

Whaling-ground.	Date—Of sailing.	Date—Of arrival.	Result of voyage. Sperm-oil.	Result of voyage. Whale-oil.	Result of voyage. Whalebone.	Remarks.
			Bbls.	*Bbls.*	*Lbs.*	
Atlantic	Jan. —	Aug. 26, 1862	126	168	.....	
....do	....	Sept. 11, 1862	122	167	.....	
....do .... {	Mar. 5	Sept. 18, 1862	64	42	} ...	Withdrawn 1864.
	Dec. 2	Aug. 20, 1863	115	.....		
....do	....	....	......	.....	.....	
....do	Jan. 28	Nov. 22, 1862	217	5	.....	Added 1862.
....do	....	July 23, 1863	......	200	.....	
....	....	Nov. 12, 1862	109	22	.....	Added 1862.
Atlantic	....	Nov. 13, 1862	182	10	....	
....do	....	Apr. —, 1863	.....	100	....	
....do	....	....	.....	.....	.....	Captured and burned by the Alabama 1862.
Atlantic	Apr. 13	Aug. 31, 1863	250	50	.....	Bought from Provincetown 1862; sent home 29 sperm; withdrawn 1863 for merchant-service.
....do	May 7	... .	.....	.....	.....	Transferred from Orleans 1862; sent home 300 sperm, 100 whale; condemned at Inagua March, 1864.
....do	Aug. 11	Aug. 6, 1864	150	2	.....	Added 1862; sent home 43 sperm.
....do	Apr. 18	Nov. 5, 1862	207	.....	.....	
Atlantic	May 6	No report ...	......	......	.....	Sent home 291 sperm; sold to Sag Harbor 1864.
Atlantic	Sept. 10	May 4, 1865	620	....	.....	Sold to New Bedford 1865 to be broken up; Holmes' Hole's last whaler.
Atlantic	May 19	July 26, 1863	200	40	.....	Built at Hanover 1862; sent home 218 sperm.
Atlantic	June 9	Sept. 7, 1863	210	....	.....	Sent home 102 sperm.
North Atlantic	Aug. 19	May 27, 1865	10	3	.....	Bought from Provincetown 1862; sent home 218 sperm.
....	....	....	.....	......	.....	Captured and burned by the Alabama 1862.
Hurd's Island..	Dec. 23	June 8, 1864	.....	2,241	.....	Bought from New Bedford 1862 to replace the Alert.
Pacific Ocean ..	Aug. 5	....	.....	......	.....	Lost on Nunivack Island July 14, 1863.
Hurd's Island..	July 24	May 25, 1864	.....	556	.....	
Pacific Ocean ..	Oct. 4	....	.....	......	.....	Captured and burned by the Shenandoah in Behring Strait June, 1865; sent home 150 whale, 1,500 bone.
Cumber'd Inlet	May 9	Nov. 3, 1863	......	319	4,700	
Pacific Ocean ..	July 3	Oct. 6, 1864	5	1,117	19,700	
Desolation Isld	June 17	....	.....	.....	.....	Lost at Hurd's Island February 1, 1864.
Pacific Ocean ..	Nov. 1	....	.....	.....	.....	Sent home 1,483 whale, 5,600 bone; captured and burned by the Shenandoah April, 1865, off Ascension.
Hudson's Bay ..	May 24	Oct. 13, 1863	18	561	9,000	
North Pacific ..	Nov. 1	Apr. 7, 1866	......	1,358	11,400	Sent home 250 sperm, 2,950 whale, 31,800 bone.
....	....	....	......	......	......	Captured and burned by the Alabama 1862; value, $51,750.
Indian Ocean ..	Aug. 11	Apr. 11, 1867	......	1,300	20,000	Captain Huxford came home in 1863 sick; sent home 340 sperm, 358 whale.
North Pacific ..	Nov. 5	Aug. 17, 1866	407	925	14,600	Sent home 850 whale, 12,100 bone.
Pacific Ocean ..	June 13	July 13, 1865	2,400	560	.....	Sent home 1,800 pounds bone; sold to New Bedford.
Atlantic .... {	May 8	July 3, 1862	35	56	.....	
	Nov. 17	June 23, 1863	29	......	.....	

Table showing returns of whaling-vessels

Name of vessel.	Class.	Tonnage.	Captain.	Managing owner or agent.
1862.				
Nantucket, Mass.—Continued.				
R. L. Barstow	Bark	200	Charles W. Hussey	Joseph B. Macy
1863.				
New Bedford, Mass.				
Andrews	Bark	303	Silas G. Baker	Jona. Bourne, jr
Annawan	...do	159	John S. Howland	Edmund Maxfield
Arnolda	Ship	360	William T. Hawes	James B. Wood & Co
Benj. Franklin	Bark	164	Samuel T. Braley	E. Maxfield
Brewster	...do	220	John A. Beebe	J. & W. R. Wing
Canton Packet	...do	274	Charles E. Allen	I. H. Bartlett & Sons
Chas. W. Morgan	Ship	351	Thomas C. Landers	J. & W. R. Wing
Clarice	Bark	237	David R. Gifford	Edward C. Jones
Congress, 2d	...do	376	Frs. E. Stranburg	Gideon Allen & Son
Cornelius Howland	Ship	431	——— Homan	Edward W. Howland
Coral	...do	370	Jared S. Crandall	G. Allen & Son
Daniel Webster	...do	336	Merrill W. Sanborn	S. Thomas & Co
Eliza Adams	...do	403	Coddington P. Fish	E. C. Jones
E. Swift	Bark	425	Reuben Pontius	Swift & Allen
Emily Morgan	Ship	368	George Athearn	J. & W. R. Wing
Glendower	Schooner	112	Nehemiah West	Nehemiah West
Hecla	Bark	207	Barzillai Luce	Thomas Knowles & Co
Hunter	Ship	453	Asa S. Tobey	Jona. Bourne, jr
Isabella	Bark	315	Hudson Winslow	T. Knowles & Co
John P. West	...do	420	Daniel J. Tinker	Simeon N. West
Josephine	Ship	446	James L. Chapman	Swift & Perry
Martha	Bark	271	William W. Thomas	Swift & Allen
Mary	Ship	287	Edwin P. Thompson	William O. Brownell
Mercury	Bark	340	George S. Tooker	...do
Merlin	...do	348	David Baker	William Watkins
Milo	Ship	401	Jona. C. Hawes	E. C. Jones
Nassau	...do	408	Samuel Greene	Swift & Perry
Nimrod	Bark	340	James M. Clark	William Gifford
Northern Light	Ship	513	Jacob Taber	Jona. Bourne, jr
Oliver Crocker	Bark	352	Clothier Pierce, jr	James B. Wood & Co
Ontario	...do	489	William M. Barnes	William O. Brownell

sailing from American ports—Continued.

Whaling-ground.	Date— Of sailing.	Date— Of arrival.	Result of voyage. Sperm-oil.	Result of voyage. Whale-oil.	Result of voyage. Whalebone.	Remarks.
			Bbls.	*Bbls.*	*Lbs.*	
Atlantic	May 9	July 26, 1865	360	556	.....	
Hudson's Bay	Apr. 29	Oct. 25, 1864	.....	1,046	17,150	
Atlantic	Apr. 8	May 5, 1865	121	45	.....	Bought from Mattapoisett 1862; returned once, damaged by a gale; sent home 210 sperm.
North Pacific	Dec. 1	Apr. 8, 1866	.....	800	13,000	Sent home 46 sperm, 1,836 whale, 20,000 pounds bone.
Atlantic	May 4	Sept. 11, 1865	233	.....	.....	Bought from Fall River 1862; sent home 340 sperm and 55 whale.
Indian Ocean	Oct. 17	Nov. 28, 1865	1,135	.....	.....	Bought from Mattapoisett 1863; sent home 30 sperm.
North Pacific	Dec. 3	.....	.....	.....	.....	Sent home 230 sperm, 1,480 whale, and 21,500 bone; lost April 3, 1867, in a typhoon off Japan; five men lost at same time; struck on Cape Syra and broke in two in ten minutes.
....do	Dec. 1	June 12, 1867	125	270	.....	Sent home 824 whale and 13,200 bone.
Indian Ocean	Apr. 30	Apr. 10, 1866	1,078	65	500	
North Pacific	June 3	.....	.....	.....	.....	Altered from a ship 1863; Captain Stranburg died 1865; captured and burned by the Shenandoah in Behring Strait June, 1865.
....do	Nov. 4	Apr. 21, 1867	15	2,000	20,000	Sent home 158 sperm, 3,798 whale, and 50,800 pounds bone.
....do	Nov. 25	May 11, 1867	40	400	5,000	Sent home 2,273 whale and 35,000 bone.
Hudson's Bay	Apr. 21	Oct. 27, 1864	.....	636	9,700	
North Pacific	Oct. 20	Apr. 22, 1867	30	700	10,000	Captain Fish came home sick 1866; sent home 206 sperm, 1,215 whale, and 8,450 pounds bone.
....do	Nov. 12	Apr. 14, 1868	.....	867	.....	Sent home 170 sperm, 2,183 whale, and 12,100 pounds bone.
....do	July 7	June 13, 1868	207	700	.....	Sent home 770 sperm, 1,890 whale, and 10,200 pounds bone.
Atlantic	June 5	.....	.....	.....	.....	Bought from Surry, Me., 1862.
Pacific Ocean	Oct. 25	May 29, 1867	140	.....	.....	Sent home 972 sperm and 11 blackfish.
....do	Oct. 20	May 21, 1865	191	1,694	.....	Sent home 10,400 pounds bone.
North Pacific	Sept. 29	.....	.....	.....	.....	Captured and burned by the Shenandoah in Behring Strait June, 1865; sent home 160 sperm, 480 whale, and 7,180 bone.
....do	Dec. 9	Apr. 14, 1868	32	1,187	14,856	Captain Tinker came home 1867; sent home 409 sperm, 1,508 whale, and 28,000 bone.
....do	Apr. 14	June 12, 1867	95	1,200	.....	Sent home 12 sperm, 3,180 whale, and 45,700 pounds bone.
....do	Dec. 7	May 16, 1868	87	185	.....	Sent home 25 sperm, 731 whale, and 14,800 pounds bone.
....do	Dec. 16	.....	.....	.....	.....	Lost in North East Harbor, Ochotsk, 1864.
....do	July 20	May 25, 1867	35	550	.....	Sent home 70 sperm, 900 whale, and 44,250 pounds bone.
....do	Dec. 1	May 9, 1868	40	550	.....	Sent home 90 sperm, 2,013 whale, and 13,110 pounds bone.
....do	Nov. 26	May 7, 1869	223	.....	.....	Captured and bonded by the Shenandoah for $46,000 1865; sold out 1872; sent home 2,431 whale and 9,780 pounds bone.
....do	Dec. 3	.....	.....	.....	.....	Captured and burned by the Shenandoah June, 1865, in Behring Strait; sent home 209 sperm, 683 whale, and 8,100 bone.
Indian Ocean	Apr. 15	.....	.....	.....	.....	Sent home 171 sperm, 220 whale, and 3,800 bone; captured and burned by the Shenandoah in Behring Strait June, 1865.
Hudson's Bay	Apr. 29	Oct. 24, 1864	18	1,270	20,900	
North Pacific	Oct. 28	Mar. 12, 1864	.....	6	.....	Altered from a ship 1863; sent home 170 sperm; returned having left Captain Pierce sick at Falklands.
....do	July 2	.....	.....	.....	.....	Collided with the Helen Mar September 27, 1866, and somewhat damaged; the crew refusing duty, she was abandoned with 1,050 whale; sent home 590 sperm, 1,150 whale, and 18,000 pounds bone.

Table showing returns of whaling-vessels

Name of vessel.	Class.	Tonnage.	Captain.	Managing owner or agent.
1863.				
New Bedford, Mass.—Continued.				
Onward	Ship	461	William H. Allen	E. W. Howland
Oriole	Bark	404	Jared Jernegan	E. C. Jones
Ocean	Ship			
Osceola, 2d	Bark	197	Zenas E. Bourne	J. & W. R. Wing
Ospray	do	236	Reuben W. Crapo	Swift & Allen
Robert Edwards	Ship	356	Caleb O. Hamblen	E. C. Jones
Roscius	Bark	300	—— Honeywell	W. P. Howland
Rousseau	do	306	Frederick A. Smith	G. & M. Howland
Samuel and Thomas	do	191	William Lewis	David B. Kempton
Sappho	do	320	Edward B. Coffin	Otis Seabury
Smyrna	do	219	Reuben Kelley	C. Hitch & Son
Solon	do	129	Charles B. Barstow	J. & W. R. Wing
Union	do	124	Amos C. Baker	J. P. Knowles 2d
Waverly	do	327	Richard Holley	D. B. Kempton
Wm. Gifford	do	320	John P. Fisher	William Gifford
Wm. Thompson	Ship	495	Jacob A. Howland	William C. N. Swift
Fairhaven, Mass.				
Favorite	Bark	298	Thomas G. Young	F. R. Whitwell
Joseph Maxwell	Ship	302	Ariel Chase	do
Pavilion	Brig	150	Ichabod Handy	Damon & Judd
Tekoa	Schooner	143	Valentine C. Long	do
Mattapoisett, Mass.				
Sarah	Bark	179	Elihu B. Handy	J. R. & W. L. Taber
Sippican, Mass.				
Admiral Blake	Schooner	120	William C. Hathaway	Peleg Blankenship
Emerald	do	101	Zenas F. Eldridge	Benjamin B. Handy
James	do	80	George H. Keen	do
Sunbeam	do	...	Benjamin B. Handy	
Nantucket, Mass.				
Rainbow	Schooner	80	R. F. Kent	Joseph B. Macy
Provincetown, Mass.				
Alleghany	Schooner	95	—— Nickerson	Daniel C. Cook
Alexander	do	75	—— Rich	Johnson & Cook
Antarctic	do	136	—— Cornell	J. E. & G. Bowley
Arizona	do	115	—— Cook	Stephen Cook
Civilian	do	201	—— Burch	S. R. Soper
E. B. Conwell	do	132	—— Kilburn	D. Conwell
E. Gerry	do	104	—— Small	C. A. Homan
E. H. Hatfield	do	125	—— Small	E. & E. K. Cook
Emporium	do	80	—— Leach	D. C. Cook
Estella	do	94	—— Snow	J. E. & G. Bowley

sailing from American ports—Continued.

Whaling-ground.	Date—		Result of voyage.			Remarks.
	Of sailing.	Of arrival.	Sperm-oil.	Whale-oil.	Whalebone.	
			Bbls.	*Bbls.*	*Lbs.*	
North Pacific..	June 2	Apr. 10, 1866	180	1,200	.....	Made a great voyage, took, in all, 180 sperm, 5,650 whale, and 62,100 pounds bone.
....do	June 3	Sept. 2, 1866	443	4	......	Bought from Fairhaven 1862; sent home 264 sperm and 688 whale.
....	....	....	......	......	....	Captured and burned by the Alabama in '63.
Indian Ocean ..	Apr. 30	Apr. 2, 1866	.....	1,085	18,050	Sent home 500 sperm.
Atlantic	June 2	Nov. 13, 1864	534	20	......	Sent home 600 sperm.
Indian Ocean ..	Aug. 5	Apr. 14, 1867	950	930	......	
Atlantic	Mar. 27	Dec. 19, 1863	300	......	......	Sent home 380 sperm.
Indian Ocean ..	Mar. 25	July 14, 1866	1,014	.....	.....	
Pacific Ocean ..	Dec. 19	Jan. 18, 1866	489	209	......	Bought from Mattapoisett 1863; shipped 5,724 gallons whale by Golconda; burned by Florida.
....do	Oct. 4	June 9, 1866	1,163	231	......	Shipped 6,874 gallons whale by Golconda; burned by the Florida; sent home 280 sperm.
Atl. and Indian.	Dec. 3	....	......	......	......	Burned by the crew at St. Helena, with 350 whale on board; was built at Duxbury, Mass., 1822.
Atlantic	Oct. 23	June 24, 1865	117	351	1,600	Sent home 163 sperm and 300 whale.
....do	Oct. 9	Oct. 10, 1864	100	.....	......	Sent home 100 sperm.
North Pacific..	Nov. 25	....	......	......	......	Mr. Holt, third mate, and boat's crew lost, fast to a whale. 1865; captured and burned by the Shenandoah in Behring Strait June, 1865; sent home 455 whale and 8,300 pounds bone.
....do	Nov. 25	May 20, 1868	......	447	1,337	Sent home 228 sperm, 1,710 whale, and 14,150 bone; shipped 5,484 gallons sperm by Golconda; burned by the Florida.
Hudson's Bay..	Mar. 17	Dec. 19, 1863	350	100	1,200	
North Pacific..	May 16	....	.....	......	......	Sent home 240 whale and 4,500 bone; taken and burned by the Shenandoah June, 1865, in Behring Strait; the Favorite was built at Boston about 1812, launched 1815.
....do	Dec. 16	July 1, 1868	86	540	8,000	Stephen Bradley, 2d mate, drowned at Honolula April, 1866; sent home 180 sperm, 900 whale, and 16,650 pounds bone; sold to New Bedford 1868.
Hudson's Bay..	June 15	....	......	......	......	Lost in Hudson's Bay, crushed by ice, 1863; seven men lost; survivors suffered severely from cold and exposure.
Atlantic	June 29	Nov. 20, 1863	100	6	......	
Atlantic	May 11	Nov. 23, 1864	21	5	......	Sent home 427 sperm; sold to New Bedford 1865.
Atlantic	May 14	Oct. 9, 1863	105	8	......	
....do	May 25	Oct. 17, 1863	115	....	......	Bought from Fairhaven 1862.
....do	May 9	Aug. 27, 1863	47	15	......	Withdrawn 1863; lost on Fortune Island February 11, 1864, loaded with salt.
....do	May 26	Aug. 17, 1863	45	5	......	Sold to Plymouth 1863, for mackerel fishing.
Atlantic	July —	Sept. —, 1863	Clean	......	......	
Atlantic	Feb. 14	Sept. 30, 1863	15	40	......	
....do	May 23	Jan. —, 1864	70	......	......	
....do	May 26	Sept. 15, 1864	252	19	......	
....do	Feb. 3	Aug. 7, 1864	200	240	1,000	Sent home 80 sperm.
....do	Mar. 19	Sept. 15, 1864	340	60	......	Sent home 163 sperm; withdrawn 1864.
....do	Mar. 2	Aug. 31, 1864	55	25	......	
....do	May 1	Aug. 18, 1863	120	114	......	Sent home 42 sperm and 82 whale.
....do	Nov. 25	Oct. 31, 1864	185	54	......	Sent home 223 sperm and 70 hump.
....do	Jan. 14	Aug. 30, 1863	100	......	......	
....do	Apr. 8	Jan. —, 1865	45	65	......	

Table showing returns of whaling-vessels

Name of vessel.	Class.	Tonnage.	Captain.	Managing owner or agent.
1863.				
Provincetown, Mass.—Continued.				
F. Bunchinia	Bark	200	—— Goodspeed	J. E. & G. Bowley
Montezuma	Schooner	92	—— Curren	Freeman & Hilliard
N. J. Knights	...do	95	—— Dyer	D. Conwell
R. E. Cook	...do	80	—— Cook	Jesse Cook
Rising Sun	...do	108	—— Young	E. S. Smith & Co.
Union	...do	97	—— Nickerson / —— Smith	S. Freeman
V. Doane	...do	99	—— Dyer	H. & S. Cook & Co
V. H. Hill	...do	155	—— Freeman	J. E. & G Bowley
Walter Irvin	...do	138		Samuel Soper
Watchman	...do	140	—— Tillson	Jesse Cook
Boston, Mass.				
Lewis Bruce	Brig	135	—— Kilburn	Heman Smith
Wm. Martin	Schooner	134	—— —— / —— Currier	...do
Salem, Mass.				
Falcon	Brig	159	—— Holmes	J. C. Osgood
Beverly, Mass.				
Eschol	Brig	143	—— Robertson	F. W. Choate
New London, Conn.				
Actor	Schooner	90	—— Spicer	S. Chapman
Charles Colgate	...do	250	—— Rogers	Lawrence & Co.
Franklin	...do	119	—— Buddington	Richard H. Chapell
Geo. Henry	Bark	303	C. B. Chapell	Williams & Haven
Isabella	Brig	192	—— Parsons	R. H. Chapell
J. D. Thompson	Bark	432	—— Brown	Williams & Barns
Sag Harbor, N. Y.				
J. A. Robb	Bark	273	—— Greene	H. & S. French
Myra	Brig	150	—— Babcock	...do
1864.				
New Bedford, Mass.				
A. R. Tucker	Bark	218	Issachar H. Aikin	J. & W. R. Wing
Ansel Gibbs	Ship	319	C. B. Kilmer	Jona. Bourne, jr.
Antelope	Bark	340	George E. Tyson	S. Thomas & Co.
Black Eagle	...do	311	Edwin W. White	...do
Cleone	...do	373	Hervey E. Luce	Edmund Maxfield
C. C. Comstock	Schooner	95	Nehemiah West	Nehemiah West
Congress	Ship	339	John A. Castino	Edward C. Jones
Cornelia	Bark	219	Warren Luce	John P. Knowles, 2d
Edward	...do	274	Charles Worth	Thomas Knowles & Co.
Endeavour	...do	252	—— Wilson	Lorenzo Pierce
Fanny	...do	391	James R. Huntting	Swift & Allen
Florida	Ship	330	Thomas E. Fordham	E. C. Jones
Gen. Pike	Bark	313	Shadrach R. Tilton	William Gifford

sailing from American ports—Continued.

Whaling-ground.	Date— Of sailing.	Date— Of arrival.	Result of voyage. Sperm-oil.	Result of voyage. Whale-oil.	Result of voyage. Whalebone.	Remarks.
			Bbls.	*Bbls.*	*Lbs.*	
Atlantic	May 18	Sept. 15, 1864	35	150	.....	Built at New London; sold 1864 to Charleston.
....do	Apr. 1	Aug. 18, 1863	135	......	.....	
....do	Jan. 14	July 23, 1863	......	230	1,000	
....do	May 20	Aug. 31, 1863	22	85	.....	
....do	Apr. 3	June 10, 1864	18	290	.....	
....do	Apr. 3	Sept. 24, 1863	100	30	.....	
	Dec. 4	Sept. 17, 1865	148	20	.....	
....do	Jan. 20	July 23, 1863	......	200	.....	
....do	Apr. 8	Apr. —, 1865	75	185	.....	
....	....	Aug. 19, 1863	175	......	.....	
Atlantic	May 1	Aug. 21, 1864	55	240	300	Sent home 100 sperm.
Atlantic	Jan. 30	....	......	......	.....	Transferred from Orleans, 1862.
....do	May 27	Aug. 30, 1863	155	5	.....	Transferred from Orleans, 1862.
	Nov. 11	June 20, 1864	16	440	.....	
Atlantic	Aug. 31	Sept. 30, 1864	90	20	.....	Sent home 80 sperm.
Atlantic	Oct. 29	May 13, 1865	17	100	.....	
Cumberland St.	June 15	Oct. 25, 1863	......	151	2,150	Withdrawn 1864.
Desolat'n Isl'd	May 23	Apr. 9, 1865	......	1,265	.....	
Frobisher Strait	June 24	Sept. 8, 1864	......	341	5,800	
Hudson Bay ...	Mar. 19	....	......	......	.....	Lost in Hudson's Bay 1863.
....do	June 6	Oct. 4, 1864	......	502	7,250	
North Pacific..	May 26	Mar. 19, 1868	......	1,656	23,100	Bought from New Bedford 1863; Mr. Kenworthy, first mate, and boat's crew lost while fast to a whale; sent home 4,493 whale, 41,600 pounds bone.
South Atlantic.	Aug. 3	Apr. 8, 1866	210	165	2,500	Shipped 230 sperm, 470 whale to Liverpool from Port Stanley; sent home 3,100 bone.
....do	Oct. 5	Apr. 18, 1866	......	310	1,500	Sent home 70 sperm, 192 whale.
Atlantic	June 6	Nov. 3, 1865	299	241	.....	Sent home 810 sperm, 216 whale, 2,300 bone.
Hudson's Bay..	Mar. 15	Oct. 1, 1865	......	885	12,900	
....do	Apr. 30	....	......	......	.....	Lost in Cumberland Inlet 1866; sent home 375 whale, 1,500 pounds bone.
....do	May 7	Oct. 1, 1865	......	781	12,400	
Atl. and Pacific.	May 24	June 13, 1868	721	55	.....	Sent home 823 sperm, 172 whale, 3,898 bone.
Atlantic	Dec. 1	....	......	......	.....	Bought from Edgartown 1864; formerly of ———; sent home 29 sperm; lost at Pernambuco January 19, 1866.
North Pacific..	May 31	....	......	......	.....	Sent home 370 sperm, 1,900 whale, 26,500 bone; stove by ice and abandoned in Anadir Sea May 13, 1867.
Atlantic	June 10	Nov. 1, 1865	52	......	.....	Sent home 421 sperm.
Atl. and Pacific.	Aug. 2	....	......	......	.....	Captured and burned by the Shenandoah 1865; value $30,000 and oil.
North Pacific..	Oct. 26	May 15, 1868	......	266	.....	Sent home 715 whale, 3,600 bone; sold to New York 1868; sold to Boston 1871, and broken up; built at Salem 1803.
...do	Sept. 1	Apr. 24, 1869	76	1,040	.....	W. J. Huntting, first mate, died in Arctic July, 1867; sent home 322 sperm, 2,992 whale, and about 57,400 pounds bone.
....do	July 11	Sept. 20, 1868	159	653	3,730	Sent home 91 sperm, 1,035 whale, 44 950 bone.
....do	May 17	....	......	......	.....	Captain Tilton died February 25, 1865; captured in Behring Strait in June, 1865, by the Shenandoah, 220 captured whalemen put on board and the vessel bonded; sent home 484 sperm, 720 whale.

Table showing returns of whaling-vessels

Name of vessel.	Class.	Tonnage.	Captain.	Managing owner or agent.
1864.				
New Bedford, Mass.—Continued.				
George	Bark	280	James E. Stanton	Gideon Allen & Son
Glacier	Schooner	262	George Taber	S. Thomas & Co.
Herald	Ship	303	Benjamin B. Handy	I. H. Bartlett & Sons
Henry Taber	Bark	355	David H. Bartlett	Henry Taber & Co.
Illinois	Ship	413	Joshua Davis	Wood & Nye
Isaac Howland	do	399	Jeremiah Ludlow	C. R. Tucker & Co
James Arnold	do	393	Jacob L. Cleaveland	H. Taber & Co.
James Maury	do	395	S. L. Gray	C. R. Tucker & Co
Java	Bark	295	Manuel Enos	G. & M. Howland
Java, 2d	do	292	Nathan S. Smith	Charles Hitch & Son
Jireh Perry	Ship	435	Benjamin H. Halsey	Swift & Perry
John Dawson	Bark	237	James Cottle, jr	J. & W. R. Wing
John Howland	do	377	Alexander Whelden	James H. Howland
Kathleen	do	312	Charles H. Robbins	J. & W. R. Wing
Lætitia	do	275	Joseph Stowell	do
Lagoda	do	341	Charles W. Fisher	Jona. Bourne, jr
Leonidas	do	128	Francis M. Cottle	David B. Kempton
Louisiana	Ship	297	William H. Haskins	Thomas Nye, jr
Mary and Susan	Bark	409	Philip Howland	Thomas Knowles & Co
Minerva Smyth	Ship	335	Obed Sherman	J. H. Bartlett & Sons
Minerva	Bark	291	Edward Penniman	Thomas Knowles & Co
Milwood	do	254	James O. Aveline	Gid. Allen & Son
Morning Star	do	305	Charles E. Allen	S. Thomas & Co.
Napoleon	do	360	William C. Fuller	Charles Tucker
Northern Light	Ship	513	Benjamin Clough	Jona. Bourne, jr
Oliver Crocker	Bark	352	John A. Lapham	James B. Wood & Co
Orray Taft	do	176	George J. Parker	S. Thomas & Co.
Roscius	do	300	John M. Honeywell	William P. Howland
Roman	Ship	370	John C. Hamblen	E. C. Jones
Sophia Thornton	do	424	Moses G. Tucker	John R. Thornton
Spartan	do	333	Leonard B. Brownson	David B. Kempton
Stella	Bark	338	Seth M. Blackmer	Loum Snow
Stephania	do	315	James G. Sinclair	Jona. Bourne, jr
Sunbeam	do	366	D. C. Barrett	J. & W. R. Wing
Thomas Winslow	do	132	John Grinnell	John Hicks
Tropic Bird	do	220	Charles H. Hagar	William P. Howland
Wm. Thompson	Ship	495	F. C. Smith	William C. N. Swift
Young Phœnix	do	377	Tristram P. Ripley	William Phillips & Son
Fairhaven, Mass.				
Alto	Bark	236	Joseph P. Nye	Damon & Judd

sailing from American ports—Continued.

Whaling-ground.	Date— Of sailing.	Date— Of arrival.	Result of voyage. Sperm-oil.	Result of voyage. Whale-oil.	Result of voyage. Whalebone.	Remarks.
			Bbls.	*Bbls.*	*Lbs.*	
Atlantic	June 21	Aug. 25, 1865	132	.....	......	
Hudson's Bay	June 21	Nov. 13, 1865	18	328	5,500	Built at Fairhaven 1864.
Atlantic	Apr. 19	Dec. 19, 1864	110	.....	......	
....do	Sept. 3	Dec. 7, 1865	118	236	......	Sent home 110 whale, 2,800 pounds bone.
Pacific Ocean	Sept. 26	July 25, 1869	.....	1,550	......	Sent home 139 sperm, 2,265 whale, 64,450 pounds bone.
North Pacific	Oct. 19	....	.....	.....	......	Captured and burned by the Shenandoah in Behring Strait June, 1865.
Atlantic	May 28	Nov. 2, 1865	494	10	300	Sent home 215 sperm.
North Pacific	June 1	May 18, 1868	151	691	......	Captain Gray died at Guam March 24, 1865; captured by the Shenandoah in Behring Strait June, 1865; bonded because Captain Gray's widow was on board; sent home 110 sperm, 965 whale, 26,333 bone.
Ind. and Pac	Aug. 25	Apr. 25, 1869	112	667	5,144	Sent home 1,075 whale, 13,500 bone.
Indian Ocean	Sept. 1	Oct. 13, 1867	1,600	70	......	Sent home 700 pounds bone.
North Pacific	July 27	Mar. 26, 1868	81	1,147	......	Captain Halsey came home sick 1866; Captain Green came home 1867; sent home 269 sperm, 1,558 whale, 39,379 bone.
Atlantic	July 19	Nov. 18, 1866	252	.....	......	Sent home 565 sperm.
North Pacific	June 25	May 29, 1871	.....	1,800	......	Altered from a ship 1864; Captain Whelden came home sick 1865; sent home 228 sperm, 6,689 whale, 48,472 pounds bone.
Indian Ocean	June 25	May 23, 1867	200	200	......	Sent home 880 sperm, 1,250 bone; Captain Robbins came home sick 1865.
Pacific Ocean	Aug. 25	June 25, 1868	1,307	30	......	Sent home 241 sperm.
....do	July 25	May 23, 1868	163	1,092	18,821	Sent home 88 sperm, 1,727 whale, 37,108 bone.
Atlantic	May 28	Aug. 18, 1865	21	42	......	Altered from a brig 1864; bought from Westport 1863; sent home 155 sperm.
Indian Ocean	Apr. 25	....	.....	.....	......	Lost in Kotzebue Sound July 9, 1865; oil saved; sent home 147 sperm, 21 whale.
Pacific Ocean	Aug. 30	July 3, 1867	850	.....	......	Captain Howland died at sea November 11, 1866; sent home 917 sperm, 94 whale, and 600 bone.
Atlantic	Mar. 15	Dec. 6, 1864	272	7	....	Returned to whaling 1864.
North Pacific	Oct. 12	Apr. 12, 1868	6	1,314	22,671	Fourth mate drowned at New Zealand 1866.
Hudson's Bay	Apr. 24	Oct. 28, 1864	100	.....	......	Sent home 227 sperm, 2,082 whale, and 39,200 bone.
..do	May 14	Oct. 14, 1865	...	1,170	17,900	
Atl. and Pacific	May 31	Sept. 8, 1867	1,300	150	1,400	Sent home 151 sperm and 800 bone.
North Pacific	Dec. 8	Aug. 5, 1867	1,350	450	......	Sent home 14,200 bone.
....do	Apr. 19	Apr. 6, 1868	.....	674	......	Captain Lapham died at Plover Bay August 29, 1867; sent home 407 sperm, 2,438 whale, and 46,411 bone.
Hudson's Bay	Apr. 9	Oct. 6, 1865	.....	472	7,250	
Atlantic	Mar. 1	Sept. 10, 1864	99	1	......	Returned on account of illness of Captain Honeywell; sent home 270 sperm.
Pacific Ocean	July 14	Apr. 27, 1868	158	1,006	9,060	Sent home 588 sperm and 2,284 whale.
North Pacific	Dec. 5	....	.....	.....	......	Captured and burned by the Shenandoah 1865; value, $48,000 and catchings.
....do	Nov. 23	Oct. 29, 1865	241	.....	......	Bought from Nantucket 1864; sent home 312 sperm.
Atlantic	Aug. 10	May 8, 1866	428	225	......	Sent home 1,280 bone.
Pacific Ocean	June 22	....	....	.....	......	Albert H. Wright, fourth mate, died July 4, 1866; sent home 41 sperm, 720 whale, and 13,750 bone; put into Sydney in distress and was condemned April, 1868; refitted, renamed Onward, and sailed under English flag.
North Pacific	Nov. 2	Apr. 27, 1868	203	669	8,028	Sent home 167 sperm, 806 whale, and 7,400 bone.
Atlantic	Mar. 15	July 23, 1865	23	309	1,450	Sent home 150 sperm.
....do	Jan. 4	May 21, 1865	83	25	......	Sent home 200 sperm.
North Pacific	June 25	....	.....	.....	......	Sent home 316 sperm; captured and burned by the Shenandoah off Cape Thaddeus 1865; value, $56,000 and catchings.
Ind. and Pac	May 14	Mar. 21, 1866	1,025	465	2,600	Shipped 400 whale to London from Cape Town; sent home 455 sperm, 224 whale, and 4,070 bone.
Atlantic	Nov. 19	Oct. 24, 1866	154	.....	......	Sent home 14 sperm and 2 whale; sold to New Bedford 1867.

Table showing returns of whaling-vessels

Name of vessel.	Class.	Tonnage.	Captain.	Managing owner or agent.
1864.				
Fairhaven, Mass.—Continued.				
Oxford	Brig	130	John Charry	Damon & Judd
Tekoa	...do	143	John R. Taber	...do
William and Henry	Ship	261	Charles F. Stetson	Isaiah F. Terry
Sippican, Mass.				
Admiral Blake	Schooner	120	William C. Hathaway	A. J. Hadley
Emerald	...do	101	Zenas F. Eldridge	...do
Westport, Mass.				
Elizabeth	Bark	270	Hiram Francis	Andrew Hicks
Gov. Carver	..do	180	Thomas H. Macy	Henry Wilcox
Janet	...do	194	Stephen Flanders	...do
Mattapoisett	..do	150	Weston M. Tripp	Henry Smith
Platina	...do	266	Otis F. Hamblen	A. Hicks
Edgartown, Mass.				
Almira	Ship	372	——— Osborn	Abraham Osborn
Nantucket, Mass.				
Rainbow	Schooner	80	Zenas M. Coleman	J. B. Macy
Provincetown, Mass.				
A. H. Brown	Schooner	131	——— Higgins	E. & E. K. Cook
Alleghany	...do	95	——— Rich	Daniel C. Cook
Alexander	...do	75	——— Nickerson	Johnson & Cook
E. B. Conwell	...do	132	——— Marshall	David Conwell
E. Gerry	...do	104	——— Remington	A. Small
Ellen Rizpah	...do	100	——— Smith	Stephen Cook & Co
Emporium	...do	86	——— Dyer	D. C. Cook
G. W. Lewis	...do	110	——— Holmes	——— Taylor
Montezuma	...do	92	——— Leach	Freeman & Hilliard
N. J. Knights	...do	95	——— Dyer	D. Conwell
Quickstep	...do	119	——— Ryder	E. & E. K. Cook
Sassacus	...do	160	——— Cook	...do
V. Doane	...do	99	——— Freeman	H. & S. Cook & Co
Walter Irvin	...do	138	——— Atkins	Samuel Soper
Boston, Mass.				
S. N. Smith	Schooner	150	——— Martin	Heman Smith
Wm. Martin	...do	134	——— Cook	...do
Mattapoisett, Mass.				
Sarah	Bark	179	Elisha B. Handy	J. R. & W. L. Taber
New London, Conn.				
Arab	Bark	276	——— Church	Richard H. Chappell
Cornelia	Schooner	197	James T. Skinner	S. Hobson & Son
Era	...do	188	——— Bellows	Moses Darrow
E. R. Sawyer	...do	126	——— Rogers	R. H. Chappell
Geo. and Mary	Bark	165	Charles Jeffrey	Williams & Barns
Georgiana	Brig	190	——— Keeney	Williams & Haven
Helen F	Schooner	108	——— Chapell	R. H. Chapell
Isabel	...do	95	——— King	S. Chapman
Leader	...do	81	——— Newbury	Williams & Haven
Lydia	Bark	351	——— Turner	Lawrence & Co

sailing from American ports—Continued.

Whaling-ground.	Date— Of sailing.	Date— Of arrival.	Result of voyage. Sperm-oil.	Result of voyage. Whale-oil.	Result of voyage. Whalebone.	Remarks.
			Bbls.	*Bbls.*	*Lbs.*	
Hudson's Bay..	May 5	May 31, 1865	20	25	.....	Sailed once and returned April 16, leaking 1,000 strokes per hour; Captain Charry was presented with an elegant sextant by the British government, for rescuing the crew of English bark Joana burned at sea; sent home 50 whale and 795 bone.
Atlantic	Jan. 23	Sept. 29, 1865	32	38	.....	
North Pacific..	Nov. 23	May 25, 1868	126	994	8,420	Sent home 607 whale and 9,350 bone.
Atlantic	Apr. 29	Oct. 12, 1864	155	9	.....	
....do	May 20	....	.....	.....	.....	Supposed to have foundered at sea with all on board.
Atlantic	Feb. 3	Aug. 9, 1864	62	9	....	Sent home 250 sperm.
	Aug. 18	Nov. 11, 1864	33	.....	....	
Atl. and Indian	May 20	Sept. 1, 1867	180	.....	.....	Sent home 325 sperm.
Atlantic	June 15	Aug. 14, 1866	669	272	500	Sent home 130 sperm.
... do	Oct. 3	Aug. 5, 1866	360	22	.....	Sent home 120 sperm and 30 blackfish.
....do	Jan. 20	Mar. 14, 1867	931	.....	.....	Sent home 130 sperm and 793 whale.
North Pacific..	Aug. 8	Oct. 4, 1868	.....	1,310	.....	Sent home 184 sperm, 1,661 whale, and 70,000 bone.
Atlantic	May 4	Sept. 12, 1864	80	20	.....	Sold to Dartmouth.
Atlantic	Feb. 10	July 9, 1865	120	349	1,350	Sent home 107 sperm.
....do	Feb. 10	Aug. 29, 1864	85	102	.....	
....do	Jan. 24	Sept. 28, 1864	60	80	.....	
....do	Oct. 10	Aug. 2, 1866	63	25	.....	Sailed under Captain Kilburn, who died at Isle of Sal, January 19, 1865; sent home 40 sperm and 180 whale.
....do	Oct. 4	July 24, 1865	30	32	.....	Sent home 80 sperm.
....do	Oct. 4	Aug. 13, 1864	63	227	1,300	
....do	Oct. 17	Aug. 7, 1864	103	140	.....	
....do	Feb. 20	July 8, 1865	71	110	.....	
....do	Jan. 24	Aug. 21, 1864	79	.....	.....	
....do	Jan. 2	Jan. —, 1865	20	80	.....	
....do	Oct. 25	Aug. 22, 1865	224	198	850	
....do	July 12	Sept. 23, 1865	162	3	.....	Added 1864; sent nome 66 sperm and 190 whale.
....do	Mar. 1	Aug. 9, 1865	136	119	500	
....do	May 4	Aug. 23, 1865	138	.....	400	
Atlantic	June 30	Sept. 9, 1865	190	100	.....	Added 1864; sent home 84 sperm.
....do	Aug. 10	Aug. 12, 1865	80	270	1,100	
Atlantic	July 15	Nov. 23, 1864	21	5	....	
Hurd's Island..	Aug. 4	June 23, 1865	53	1,692	....	
Hudson's Bay..	May 9	Oct. 11, 1865	.....	300	4,200	Added 1864; sold to Groton 1866.
Cum. Inlet.....	Aug. 31	Sept. 20, 1864	.....	.....	.....	Bought from Boston 1864.
Hurd's Island..	July 14	....	.....	.....	.....	Te nder to the Roman; lost September 17, 1866, on Hurd's Island.
Hudson's Bay..	June 4	Oct. 10, 1865	.....	180	2,800	Bought from Gloucester 1864; formerly of Westport.
Cum. Inlet....	Apr. 13	Oct. 10, 1865	.....	766	15,250	
Hudson's Bay..	June 30	Sept. 18, 1865	.....	Clean	.....	Added 1864.
....do	June 8	Oct. 28, 1864	.....	Clean	.....	Do.
Greenland	May 28	Sept. 11, 1865	.....	287	5,000	
Hurd's Island..	Aug. 18	May 17, 1865	.....	1,734	.....	Bought from Fairhaven 1864

Table showing returns of whaling-vessels

Name of vessel.	Class.	Tonnage.	Captain.	Managing owner or agent.
1864.				
New London, Conn.—Continued.				
Monticello	Bark	356	—— Chapell	R. H. Chapell
Peru	do	259	—— Hempstead	Williams & Haven
Pioneer	do	235	Ebenezer Morgan	do
Roswell King	do	134	—— Church	R. H. Chapell
S. B. Howes	do	101	—— Spicer	Williams & Haven
Somerset	do	201	—— Ward	Lawrence & Co
Sag Harbor, N. Y.				
Balæna	Bark	301	—— Jennings	H. & S. French
Concordia	do	265	—— Rogers	O. R. Wade
Ocean	do	165	Davis C. Osborn	Davis C Osborn
Pacific	do	314	{ —— Pierson —— Huntting }	H. & S. French
Union	do	300	—— Hedges	O. R. Wade
1865.				
New Bedford, Mass.				
A. R. Tucker	Bark	218	Asa Grinnell	J. & W. R. Wing
Active	do	333	O. G. Robinson	Loum Snow & Son
Adeline	Ship	329	John M. Soule	C. R. Tucker & Co
Alfred Gibbs	do	425	Edward E. Jennings	Dennis Wood
Alpha	do	345	—— Lawton	Edward W. Howland
Andrews	Bark	303	Tim. C. Packard	Jonathan Bourne, jr
Annawan	do	159	M. C. Fisher	Edmund Maxfield
Atlantic	do	367	Benj. F. Wing	J. & W. R. Wing
Aurora	do	351	James O. Aveline	Swift & Allen
Awashonks	do	342	Ariel Norton	J. & W. R. Wing
Callao	do	324	Roswell Brown	Henry Taber & Co
Cherokee	do	261	Henry Eldridge	William Hathaway, jr
China	do	370	Charles H. Gifford	Wm. Phillips & Son
Cicero	do	252	John H. Paun	L. Snow & Son
Com. Morris	Ship	355	Jacob A. Howland	Swift & Perry
Courser	Bark	381	Joseph Hamblen, jr	Charles Tucker
Daniel Webster	Ship	336	Benjamin Kelley	S. Thomas & Co
Daniel Wood	Bark	345	Josiah Richmond	James B. Wood & Co
Desdemona	do	295	E. B. Phinney	G. & M. Howland
Eagle	do	336	Jas. H. McKenzie	Swift & Perry
Eliza	do	366	James M. Witherell	J. Bourne, jr
Eugenia	do	356	John Steen	Swift & Allen
Falcon	do	273	Francis Dougherty	Thos Knowles & Co
Gayhead	Ship	389	William H. Kelley	J. B. Wood & Co
George	Bark	280	William L. Davis	Gideon Allen & Son

sailing from American ports—Continued.

Whaling-ground.	Date— Of sailing.	Date— Of arrival.	Result of voyage. Sperm-oil.	Result of voyage. Whale-oil.	Result of voyage. Whalebone.	Remarks.
			Bbls.	*Bbls.*	*Lbs.*	
Hudson's Bay..	June 30	Sept. 21, 1865	......	271	3,900	
Pacific Ocean..	May 28	May 8, 1869	......	......	......	Added 1864; Charles N. Marsh, third mate, died at Honolulu December 2, 1866; sent home 567 sperm, 1,660 whale, and 19,560 bone.
Hudson's Bay..	June 4	Sept. 18, 1865	......	1,391	22,650	Made best voyage on record; sold at $35,800; cargo worth $150,000.
Desol'n Island.	Aug. 23	Apr. 30, 1867	11	703	645	Sent home 1,100 whale and elephant and 4,000 bone; added 1864.
Greenland	Apr. 19	Oct. 5, 1865	......	199	3,000	Bought from Boston 1864.
Desol'n Island.	June 4	....	......	......	......	Bought from Baltimore 1864; lost on Desolation Island August 26, 1864.
Atlantic	May 20	May 25, 1867	350	600	1,400	Bought from New Bedford 1863; sent home 122 sperm, 183 whale, and 3,600 bone.
Hudson's Bay..	June 3	Oct. 7, 1865	......	70	900	
Pacific Ocean..	May 29	Apr. 16, 1866	185	30	......	Bought from Sandwich 1864.
South Atlantic	July 26	Nov. 11, 1864	20	......	......	Bought from New Bedford 1864; Captain
Atlantic	Nov. 28	No report ..	......	......	......	Pierson died at Pernambuco Oct., 1864.
South Atlantic	Aug. 22	Aug. 10, 1867	300	300	......	Sent home 275 sperm; withdrawn for freighting 1868.
Atlantic	Dec. 4	Oct. 7, 1868	318	4	......	Sent home 176 sperm, 200 whale, 1,900 bone.
North Pacific ..	Nov. 8	Sept. 6, 1871	152	1,052	......	Mr. Taber, first mate, and boat's crew lost while fast to a whale July, 1866; Captain Robinson came home 1868; sent home 126 sperm, 2,092 whale, 35,130 bone.
... do	Aug. 29	July 26, 1869	320	600	......	Sent home 164 sperm, 449 whale, 17,535 bone.
Pacific Ocean ..	June 26	Sept. 7, 1869	670	......	......	Sent home 679 sperm, 972 bone.
North Pacific ..	Dec. 9	Apr. 18, 1868	......	566	9,790	Bought from Nantucket 1865; sold and broken up 1872; sent home 807 whale.
Hudson's Bay ..	Apr. 1	Apr. 25, 1866	......	1,038	16,600	
Atlantic	June 14	July 21, 1867	340	......	......	Sent home 214 sperm, 22 whale.
Indian Ocean ..	Oct. 3	Apr. 12, 1868	736	1,037	7,490	Sent home 40 sperm 675 whale, 6,000 bone.
North Pacific ..	Nov. 14	Apr. 23, 1871	243	1,286	......	Bought from Westport 1865; Captain Aveline came home sick 1868; sent home 360 sperm 2,293 whale, 33,685 bone; sold to Salem 1871.
....do	Oct. 11	June 3, 1870	30	696	10,237	Sent home 358 sperm, 2,040 whale, 24,550 bone.
Atlantic	Nov. 15	Oct. 11, 1870	853	1	......	Jos. B. Baker, first mate, drowned while fast to a whale March 18, 1866; sent home 592 sperm, 87 whale, 900 bone.
Indian Ocean ..	Sept. 11	June 10, 1869	200	436	643	Sent home 459 sperm, 400 whale, 4,125 bone; sold to New York 1872.
Atl. & Indian ..	May 13	Apr. 22, 1868	937	600	3,201	Altered from a ship 1865; sent home 415 sperm, 450 whale, 3,350 bone.
North Pacific ..	Oct. 17	Sept. 3, 1869	60	280	......	Sent home 212 sperm, 212 whale, 17,106 bone.
Atlantic	May 10	Dec. 10, 1867	850	70	......	Bought from Falmouth 1864; sent home 1,810 sperm, 30 whale.
North Pacific ..	Oct. 17	Sept. 12, 1869	315	120	......	Sent home 226 sperm, 400 whale, 9,223 bone; towed into Newport dismasted by a gale, homeward bound.
Hudson's Bay..	May 20	Nov. 14, 1866	......	703	11,500	
North Pacific ..	May 16	....	......	......	......	Altered from a ship 1865; sent home 304 sperm, 595 whale, 10,500 bone; lost on French Frigate Shoal April 14, 1867.
Indian Ocean ..	Sept. 5	June 1, 1869	698	20	200	Altered from a ship 1865.
North Pacific ..	June 7	....	......	......	......	Sent home 3,100 whale, 40,000 bone; lost on Sea Horse Island (Ochotsk) September 30, 1869, with 1,600 whale, 25,000 bone.
Pacific Ocean ..	July 1	Apr. 23, 1869	1,005	446	4,776	Sent home 105 sperm.
Atlantic	June 6	Apr. 22, 1869	151	500	......	Sent home 257 sperm, 1,234 whale, 2,300 bone.
....do	Aug. 1	Sept. 16, 1867	250	500	......	Sent home 1,600 bone.
North Pacific ..	July 11	Apr. 25, 1870	......	1,200	17,000	Sent home 648 sperm, 2,879 whale, 44,346 bone.
....do	Oct. 24	July 6, 1869	5	492	......	Sent home 455 sperm, 191 whale, 12,831 bone.

Table showing returns of whaling-vessels

Name of vessel.	Class.	Tonnage.	Captain.	Managing owner or agent.
1865.				
New Bedford, Mass.—Continued.				
George & Susan	Bark	356	Samuel F. Davis	G. & M. Howland
Globe	do	215	Alex'r A. Trip	C. Tucker
Herald	Ship	303	——— Gillis	I. H. Bartlett & Sons
Hunter	do	355	Alden Besse	J. Bourne, jr
Islander	Bark	347	Richard Holley	David B. Kempton
James Allen	do	355	Eben Pierce	G. Allen & Son
James	Ship	321	F. C. Smith	Swift & Perry
John Wells	Bark	366	Aaron Dean	William O. Brownell
Lancer	Ship	395	William J. Macy	Joshua Richmond
Leonidas	Bark	128	Eben Cook	David B. Kempton
Louisa	do	316	Reuben W. Crapo	Swift & Allen
Lydia	do	351	Thos. B. Hathaway	Edmund Maxfield
Marcella	do	210	Henry B. Chase	Chas. R. Tucker & Co
Massachusetts	do	364	Nathan B. Wilcox	Swift & Allen
Mars	do	270	George Gray	Gifford & Cummings
Mary Frazier	do	288	William Allen; Andrew J. Fuller	Chas. Tucker
Midas	do	326	David R. Drake	Wm. O. Brownell
Milton	Ship	388	Charles Grant	Henry Taber & Co
Minerva Smyth	do	335	Obed Sherman	I. H. Bartlett & Sons
Milwood	Bark	254	Isaac Allen	G. Allen & Son
Nautilus	do	374	George W. Bliven	do
Navy	do	356	William Davis	James B. Wood & Co
Norman	do	338	Peter E. Childs	Chas. S. Randall
Ocean	Ship	349	Albert D. Barber	John R. Thornton
Ohio	Bark	237	James W. Staplewood	L. Snow & Son
Osceola, 3d	do	200	Peleg Cornell	Jacob B. Hadley
Ospray	do	236	Peter Gartland	Swift & Allen
Pacific	do	385	James R. Allen	Swift & Perry
Petrel	Schooner	90	John S. Howland	Chas. Thatcher & Co
President	Bark	293	Edmond Kelley	Taber, Read & Co
President, 2d	do	189	Benjamin D. Gifford	Edmund Maxfield
Rainbow	Ship	474	Nehemiah Baker	Wm. Gifford
Reindeer	do	450	George W. Raynor	Edward W. Howland
Robt. Morrison	Bark	307	Charles P. Worth	T. Knowles & Co
Roscius	do	300	Ezra W. Crapo	Wm. Penn Howland
Roscoe	do	362	Geo. H. Macomber	L. Snow & Son
Sarah	do	179	Aaron C. Baker	John P. Knowles, 2d
Sea Breeze	do	473	Jas. A. Hamilton	Jona. Bourne, jr
Seine	do	281	Abner Smith	J. P. Knowles, 2d
Solon	Bark	129	John M. Shaw	J. & W. R. Wing
Spartan	Ship	333	Daniel W. Gifford	David B. Kempton
St. George	do	408	George H. Soule	Taber, Read & Co
Stafford	Bark	206	Chas. B. Barstow	J. & W. R. Wing

sailing from American ports—Continued.

Whaling-ground.	Date— Of sailing.	Date— Of arrival.	Result of voyage. Sperm-oil.	Result of voyage. Whale-oil.	Result of voyage. Whalebone.	Remarks.
			Bbls.	*Bbls.*	*Lbs.*	
Atl. & Indian	June 1	Aug. 2, 1868	639	909	1,322	Altered from a ship 1865; sent home 486 sperm, 427 whale, 2 300 bone.
Atlantic	June 14	July 29, 1868	300	10	......	Sent home 496 sperm.
....do	Apr. 19	Nov. 12, 1866	115	2	......	Sailed under Captain Honeywell, who came home sick 1865; sent home 316 sperm.
....do	Aug. 31	Oct. 22, 1867	400	1,400	5,000	Sent home 110 sperm, 145 whale.
North Pacific	Nov. 11	June 12, 1869	279	274	2,200	Bought from Nantucket 1865; sent home 417 sperm, 2,083 whale, 35.715 bone.
....do	Aug. 24	June 7, 1870	70	947	13,132	Sent home 135 sperm, 1,836 whale, 25,480 bone.
....do	Dec. 6	June 8, 1871	65	347	......	George G. Faville, fourth mate, killed by a whale December 27, 1867; Captain Jas. M. Green, who took Captain Smith's place, died 1870; sent home 731 sperm, 2,161 whale, 6 221 bone.
North Pacific	Sept. 20	Aug. 13, 1869	345	1,000	......	Added 1865; sent home 294 sperm, 2,220 whale, 47,715 bone.
Atl. & Indian	May 21	Sept. 5, 1868	1,030	1	......	
Atlantic	Sept. 21	July 8, 1867	180	270	1,000	Sent home 95 sperm, 36 whale.
....do	June 13	Nov. 2, 1868	470	......	......	Sent home 318 sperm, 36 whale.
North Pacific	Nov. 2	May 1, 1869	......	766	......	Added 1865; sent home 33 sperm, 504 whale, 16,898 bone.
Atlantic	Apr. 25	Apr. 13, 1867	85	5	......	
North Pacific	Aug. 15	May 10, 1870	39	1,025	16,050	Sent home 153 sperm, 4,056 whale, and about 11,000 bone.
Pacific Ocean	Oct. 29	Aug. 13, 1868	1,030	62	......	Sent home 956 sperm.
Atlantic {	June 23	Sept. 1, 1865	76	......	......	
	Sept. 7	Aug. 1, 1867	350	250	2,000	
North Pacific	Nov. 1	Mar. 24, 1869	38	1,302	10,480	Sent home 104 sperm, 1,561 whale, 15,016 bone.
Pacific Ocean	Aug. 15	June 29, 1869	1,330	......	......	Sent home 1,568 sperm.
Atlantic	Apr. 24	Dec. 10, 1865	140	......	......	
Hudson's Bay	Apr. 19	Nov. 7, 1866	37	923	14,500	
North Pacific	June 13	July 5, 1869	92	1,000	10,000	Sent home 346 sperm, 1,833 whale, 31,974 bone.
....do	Nov. 20	June 12, 1869	107	176	1,585	Altered from a ship 1865; sent home 136 sperm, 1,080 whale, 18,818 bone.
....do	Oct. 12	May 26, 1871	74	376	1,495	Bought from Nantucket 1865; Captain Childs came home 1867; sent home 457 sperm, 2,200 whale, 41,957 bone.
....do	Nov. 15	June 23, 1869	387	16	......	Sent home 25 sperm, 725 whale, 22,112 bone.
Atlantic	May 16	Apr. 18, 1868	365	......	......	Sent home 555 sperm, 588 whale, 9,050 bone.
....do	Sept. 4	Aug. 14, 1866	312	2	......	Sent home 158 sperm, 70 whale.
....do	May 2	Oct. 27, 1867	175	......	......	Sent home 619 sperm, 90 whale, 600 bone.
....do	June 13	Oct. 13, 1867	300	650	2,000	Sent home 152 sperm, 400 whale, 2,900 bone.
....do	Oct. 22	July 23, 1866	28	138	450	Added 1865.
North Pacific	July 11	Apr. 8, 1869	16	471	......	Sent home 208 sperm, 1,817 whale, 42,351 bone.
Atlantic	Mar. 20	Nov. 13, 1865	100	......	......	
North Pacific	Sept. 12	Apr. 20, 1870	91	1,177	13,040	Sent home 262 sperm, 441 whale, 1,000 bone.
....do	June 13	Apr. 20, 1869	100	1,613	24,270	Sent home 3, 92 whale, 56,767 bone.
Atl. & Indian	July 6	June 1, 1868	692	378	440	Sent home 65 sperm, 500 bone.
Atlantic	Apr. 1	Sept. 15, 1866	122	21	......	Sent home 97 sperm.
North Pacific	July 11	June 10, 1870	1,450	8	......	Sent home 554 sperm, 1,128 whale, 1,550 bone.
Atlantic	May 1	July 29, 1867	180	......	......	Bought from Mattapoisett 1865; sent home 192 sperm.
North Pacific	Oct. 18	Apr. 11, 1871	......	1,340	17,531	Abram Cuffee, first mate, and Stillman Smith, fourth mate, died 1866; Captain Hamilton's term of shipment expired 1868, and Captain Chas Fisher took his place; sent home 5,658 whale, 54,805 bone.
....do	Nov. 2	May 7, 1870	209	30	......	Sent home 280 whale, 1,165 bone.
Atlantic	July 18	....	......	......	......	Took on voyage 210 sperm, 50 whale; wrecked and condemned at Barbadoes June 1866.
South Atlantic	Dec. 12	July 27, 1868	287	......	......	Sailed once and returned with captain sick; sent home 386 sperm, 100 whale, 400 bone.
North Pacific	Oct. 29	Sept. 10, 1869	420	270	3,200	Formerly in South American trade; added 1865; sent home 148 sperm, 2,046 whale, 34,322 bone.
Atlantic	Nov. 20	Oct. 18, 1867	240	......	......	Sent home 175 sperm, 48 whale.

Table showing returns of whaling-vessels

Name of vessel.	Class.	Tonnage.	Captain.	Managing owner or agent.
1865.				
New Bedford, Mass.—Continued.				
Swallow	Ship	439	William Weeks	William Watkins
Tamerlane	Bark	357	Joshua B. Winslow	T. Knowles & Co
Thomas Dickason	Ship	454	Nathaniel Jernegan	G. & M. Howland
Thomas Winslow	Bark	136	John Grinnell	John Hicks
Three Brothers	Ship	384	Jacob Taber	C. R. Tucker & Co
Trident	Bark	449	Jetur R. Rose	Swift & Perry
Triton	do	300	John W. Cornell	J. & W. R. Wing
Tropic Bird	do	220	Lemuel P. Adams	W. P. Howland
Union	do	124	Abner Smith	J. P. Knowles, 2d
Vigilant	do	282	William Childs	W. Watkins
Washington	do	344	Silas G. Baker	J. Bourne, jr
Wave	do	197	Elisha B. Handy	T. Knowles & Co
Willis	do	164	Bradford C. Briggs	Andrew H. Potter
Fairhaven, Mass.				
General Scott	Ship	333	William Washburn	Tripp & Terry
Oxford	Brig	130	Nathan Briggs	Damon & Judd
President	Schooner	60	S. B. Bourne	F. R. Whitwell, jr
Tekoa	Brig	143	Jos. D. Benjamin	Damon & Judd
Dartmouth, Mass.				
Matilda Sears	Bark	303	William D. Gifford	William Potter, 2d
Sippican, Mass.				
Admiral Blake	Schooner	120	Wm. C. Hathaway; Arthur H. Hammond	A. J. Hadley
Herald	Brig	178	John A. Kelley	Henry M. Allen
Westport, Mass.				
Elizabeth	Bark	270	Hiram Francis	Andrew Hicks
Greyhound	do	249	John E. Barker	Henry Wilcox
Mermaid	do	330	John Horan	Andrew Hicks
Sea Fox	do	246	David E. Allen	do
Edgartown, Mass.				
Champion	Ship	400	—— Worth	Grafton N. Collins
Nantucket, Mass.				
E. H. Adams	Schooner	107	Zenas M. Coleman	Freeman E. Adams
R. L. Barstow	Bark	182	Charles W. Hussey	Jos. B. Macy
Provincetown, Mass.				
A. H. Brown	Schooner	131		E. & E. K. Cook
Alleghany	do	95	—— Dyer	Daniel C. Cook
Alexander	do	75	—— Carlow	Johnson & Cook
Antarctic	do	136	—— Cornell; —— Hill	J. E. & G. Bowley
Arizona	do	115	—— Cook	Stephen Cook
C. H. Cook	do	149	do	do
E. H. Hatfield	do	125	—— Rich	E. & E. K. Cook
Ellen Rizpah	do	100	—— Smith	Stephen Cook & Co
Emporium	do	80	—— Chandler	Daniel C. Cook

sailing from American ports—Continued.

Whaling-ground.	Date—		Result of voyage.			Remarks.
	Of sailing.	Of arrival.	Sperm-oil.	Whale-oil.	Whalebone.	
			Bbls.	*Bbls.*	*Lbs.*	
Indian Ocean ..	Sept. 9	Oct. 19, 1868	1,632	1	232	Charles F. Brown, second mate, drowned while fast to a whale December 25, 1865.
North Pacific ..	Aug. 23	May 30, 1869	116	1,448	3,892	Sent home 341 sperm, 90 whale, 9,575 bone.
....do	Oct. 21	July 15, 1869	270	1,150	3,000	Sent home 442 sperm, 1,018 whale, 30,993 bone.
Atlantic	Oct. 25	Apr. 23, 1867	40	210	500	Sent home 133 sperm, 37 whale, 450 bone.
North Pacific ..	Sept. 22	Aug. 9, 1869	100	1,800	20,000	Bought from Nantucket 1865; sent home 280 sperm, 2,316 whale, 49,911 bone.
....do	Nov. 16	June 10, 1871	.....	2,000	.....	Altered from a ship 1865; sent home 81 sperm, 4 074 whale, 36,789 bone.
Atlantic	June 12	May 31, 1868	139	.....	.....	Sent home 984 sperm.
....do	June 23	Nov. 11, 1866	255	.....	.....	Sent home 153 sperm.
....do	May 12	July 14, 1865	59	13	.....	Sailed again in August under Captain John Dimmick and was lost off Western Islands September 27, 1865.
....do	May 4	Oct. 13, 1837	175	275	1,400	Sent home 236 sperm.
North Pacific ..	Aug. 12	....	.....	.....	.....	Sent home 245 sperm, 1,590 whale. 21,619 bone; condemned at San Francisco August, 1868.
Atlantic	May 18	Oct. 22, 1866	465	3	.....	Sent home 115 sperm.
....do	Aug. 15	....	.....	.....	.....	Bought from Mattapoisett 1865; badly strained by cutting in in rough weather; condemned at Fayal 1866; sent home 408 sperm, 180 whale, 800 bone.
North Pacific ..	Oct. 18	Oct. 5, 1869	239	1,480	.....	Sent home 75 sperm, 915 whale, 37,577 bone.
Atlantic	June 26	Dec. 4, 1865	.....	220	5,500	
....do	Nov. 6	....	.....	.....	.....	Bought from New Bedford 1865; formerly a coaster; no report.
....do	Nov. 15	Sept. 29, 1866	176	98	.....	
Pacific Ocean ..	May 15	Apr. 8, 1869	365	72	.....	Sent home 1,103 sperm, 42 whale, 8,000 bone.
Atlantic ..... {	May 2	Aug. 21, 1865	285	2	.....	
	Dec. 28	Nov. 4, 1866	130	150	.....	
....do	Oct. 24	Aug. 9, 1866	237	277	.....	Added 1865 from the merchant service.
....do	Mar. 13	Nov. 4, 1865	260	3	.....	Sent home 20 sperm.
Atl. & Indian .	May 24	Oct. 26, 1867	490	160	.....	
....do	Aug. 28	....	.....	.....	.....	Mr. Perry, second mate, drowned while fast to a whale November, 1866.
Indian Ocean ..	May 24	May 2, 1867	980	.....	.....	Sent home 65 sperm.
North Pacific ..	Aug. 8	May 12, 1869	38	1,084	9,080	Sent home 41 sperm, 1,412 whale, 13,627 bone.
Atlantic	Apr. 18	Sept. 30, 1865	230	.....	.....	
....do	Nov. 19	Sept. 20, 1868	400	400	.....	
....do	Oct. 8	——— 1866	.....	.....	.....	No report.
....do	Feb. 1	Aug. 3, 1865	110	150	.....	
....do	Feb. 16	Aug. 27, 1865	46	110	450	Sailed again December 2; arrived September 5, 1866; 25 sperm.
....do .... {	May 23	Aug. 21, 1865	240	48	.... }	Sent home 145 sperm, 95 whale.
	Sept. 26	July 24, 1867	25	40	.... }	
....do	Jan. 18	Aug. 27, 1865	102	33	100	Sailed again December 17, and July 30, 1867; 80 sperm.
....do	May 30	Aug. 25, 1865	249	102	493	Added 1865; sent home 260 sperm.
....do	Feb. 1	Aug. 31, 1865	160	186	800	Sailed again December 2, arrived October 24, 1866; 85 sperm.
....do	Jan. 12	July 15, 1865	39	162	600	
....do	Jan. 30	Aug. 3, 1865	102	98	450	

Table showing returns of whaling-vessels

Name of vessel.	Class.	Tonnage.	Captain.	Managing owner or agent.
1865.				
Provincetown, Mass.—Continued.				
Estella	Schooner	94	—— Snow	J. E. & G. Bowley
Mary Curren	do	146	—— Curren	Freeman & Hilliard
M. E. Simmons	do	160	—— Taylor	E. & E. K. Cook
Montezuma	do	92	—— Leach	Freeman & Hilliard
M. J. Knights	do	96	—— Dyer	David Conwell
Quickstep	do	119	—— Thompson	E. & E. K. Cook
Rising Sun	do	108	{ —— Young —— Clark }	E. S. Smith & Co
Sassacus	do	160	—— Ryder	E. & E. K. Cook
S. R. Soper	do	130		Samuel Cook
T. R. Hughlett				
V. Doane	Schooner	99	—— Dyer	H. & S. Cook & Co
V. H. Hill	do	155	—— Small	J. E. & G. Bowley
Walter Irvin	do	138	—— Atkins	Samuel Soper
Watchman	do	140	—— Tillson	Jesse Cook
Boston, Mass.				
Louisa A	Schooner	122	—— Freeman	Heman Smith
S. E. Lewis	do	140	{ —— Farwell —— Caton }	do
S. N. Smith	do	150		do
Wm. Martin	do	134	—— Senter	do
Salem, Mass.				
Falcon	Brig	159	—— Holmes	John C. Osgood
Para	Schooner	135	—— Hussey	do
Beverly, Mass.				
Eschol	Brig	143	Bugbee	F. W. Choate
Thriver	Schooner	95	—— Wood	do
New London, Conn.				
Arab	Bark	276	—— Church	Richard H. Chapell
Cornelia	Schooner		James Carbury	
Chas. Colgate	do	250	—— Turner	Lawrence & Co.
Era	do	188	—— Bellows	Moses Darrow
Franklin	do	119	—— Buddington	R. H. Chappell
Golden West	do	144	Simeon Church	Lawrence & Co
Isabella	Brig	192	—— Chappell	R. H. Chappell
Monticello	Bark	356	—— Comstock	do
S. B. Howes	Schooner	101	—— Spicer	Williams & Haven
Sag Harbor, N. Y.				
Odd Fellow	Bark	239	—— Weld	O. R. Wade
Pacific	do	314	—— French	H. & S. French
San Francisco, Cal.				
C. E. Forte	Schooner		—— Hazard	
1866.				
New Bedford, Mass.				
Abm. Barker	Bark	380	Andrew T. Potter	J. & W. R. Wing
Adeline Gibbs	do	327	Elisha Babcock	Jona. Bourne, jr.
Andrews	do	277	James B. Huxford	do
Ansel Gibbs	do	303	C. B. Kilmer	do
Armadillo	Schooner	82	Charles H. Hager	D. R. Greene & Co

sailing from American ports—Continued.

Whaling-ground.	Date— Of sailing.	Of arrival.	Result of voyage. Sperm-oil.	Whale-oil.	Whalebone.	Remarks.
			Bbls.	*Bbls.*	*Lbs.*	
Atlantic	Jan. 25	Aug. 25, 1865	90	171	650	
....do	Feb. 20	May 24, 1866		31[illegible]		Added 1865; sent home 507 sperm.
....do	Feb. 10	July 17, 1866	51	252		Added 1865; sent home 280 sperm.
....do	Feb. 6	Aug. 14, 1866	230	90		
....do	Jan. 25	Aug. 14, 1865	180	75	400	Sailed again December 29.
....do	Oct. 31	Sept. 18, 1866	80	275		
....do {	Jan. 5	Aug. 14, 1865	129	155	600	
	Oct. 4	Aug. 10, 1866	40	249		
....do	Dec. 10	Aug. 21, 1867	120	45		Sent home 60 sperm, 175 humpback.
....do	May 4	Aug. 28, 1866	318	35		Sent home 64 sperm.
						Added 1865; withdrawn same year; no report.
Atlantic	Jan. 24	Aug. 9, 1865	136	109	500	
....do	May 26	Aug. 10, 1866	160	90		
....do	Dec. 13	Sept. 19, 1866	130	12		Sent home 35 sperm, 60 whale.
....do	Jan. 24	Aug. 26, 1865	154	112	450	
Atlantic	July 17	Sept. 8, 1867	220			Added 1865; sent home 112 sperm, 175 whale.
....do {	Jan. 27	Aug. 3, 1865	120	100		Sent home 131 sperm; brought in also 40 pounds of ambergris.
	Oct. 2	June 9, 1867	70			
....do	Nov. 25	Sept. 2, 1867	240			
....do	Dec. 21	Sept. 12, 1866	203	18		
Atlantic	Jan. 11	Oct. 5, 1866	127	31		Sent home 288 sperm, 105 hump, 470 bone.
....do	Oct. 3	Oct. 20, 1867		140		Added 1865; sent home 200 humpback.
Atlantic	July 15	Sept. 4, 1866	168	21		Sent home 149 sperm.
....do	June 20	Oct. 5, 1865	45			Sailed again; ——— Wood, captain, November 15 and August 15, 1866; 131 sperm, 103 whale.
Hurd's Island	Aug. 9	June 6, 1866	35	2,064	3,900	Sold to New Bedford 1867.
						No report.
Hurd's Island	June 5	May 28, 1867		1,100		Sent home 850 elephant; added 1864.
Greenland	May 17	Nov. 9, 1866		236	2,900	
Hudson's Bay	Apr. 25	Sept. 17, 1866		534	8,9[illegible]0	
Desolation Isld.	Nov. 30	May 25, 1868		651	500	Bought from Baltimore 1865; sent home 1,400 elephant.
Baffin's Bay	Mar. 7	Nov. 9, 1866		584	10,500	
North Pacific	Nov. 18					Sent home 50 sperm, 2,411 whale; shipped 8,309 bone to Bremen; lost in the Arctic 1871.
Labrador	Oct. 26	Oct. 9, 1867		300	6,000	
Atlantic	July 7	June 13, 1868	315			James M. Ward, first mate, died at Fayal, September 1, 1867; sent home 70 sperm, 457 whale, 2,700 bone; sold to New London 1869.
Pacific Ocean	Aug. 14					Lost at Behring's Island July 30, 1866; third mate and five men arrived at Hakodadi, after being two months in an open boat.
Coast Cal		Apr. 18, 1866		1,000		
Pacific Ocean	June 19	May 24, 1870	1,852	53		Bought from New York 1865; sent home 1,021 sperm, 913 bone.
Indian Ocean	July 10	May 12, 1870	1,413	685		Sent home 150 sperm, 2 whale, 4,000 bone.
Atlantic	Oct. 17	May 2, 1867	90	3		
Hudson's Bay	May 1	Oct. 9, 1867		320	6,000	
Atlantic	July 18					Added 1866; lost at St. Eustatia March 25, 1867.

Table showing returns of whaling-vessels

Name of vessel.	Class.	Tonnage.	Captain.	Managing owner or agent.
1866.				
New Bedford, Mass.—Continued.				
Barth. Gosnold	Ship	365	Charles Nichols	Charles R. Tucker & Co
B. Cummings	Bark	305	Charles Halsey	Taber, Gordon & Co
Benj. Franklin	do	122	Samuel T. Braley	Edmund Maxfield
Black Eagle	do	229	Edwin W. White	S. Thomas & Co
Brewster	do	170	Issachar Aikin	J. & W. R. Wing
California	Ship	367	Daniel B. Wood	C. R. Tucker & Co
Canton	do	239	Joshua G. Lapham	do
Clarice	Bark	183	John G. Morrison	Edward C. Jones
Contest	Ship	341	James Coon	Swift & Perry
Corinthian	do	390	Valentine Lewis	G. & M. Howland
Cornelia	Bark	203	Ephraim Poole	John P. Knowles, 2d
Draco	do	258	—— Braley	J. Bourne, jr
E. Corning	do	225	George Taber	Swift & Perry
Ellen Morrison	do	150	Presbury A. Luce	Thomas Knowles & Co
Emma C. Jones	Ship	307	Ezra Gifford	E. C. Jones
Gazelle	do	273	David R. Gifford	do
Geo. Howland	do	361	James H. Knowles	G. & M. Howland
Glacier	Schooner	177	Edwin A. Potter	S. Thomas & Co
Greyhound	Bark	215	L. W. H. Gifford	Charles Tucker
Hamilton	do	137	Edwin R. Osgood	Zenas L. Adams
Helen Mar	do	358	—— Herendeen	Swift & Allen
Henry Taber	do	396	Frederick S. Howland	Taber, Gordon & Co
Hercules	do	511	Isaac C. Howland	Swift & Perry
Hibernia	Ship	256	Jeremiah Ludlow	C. R. Tucker & Co
James Arnold	do	346	Thomas Sullivan	Taber, Gordon & Co
John Carver	Bark	319	Henry F. Worth	T. Knowles & Co
Laconia	do	158	Charles W. Parker	John P. Knowles, 2d
Marengo	Ship	478	Joseph C. Little	William O. Brownell
Minerva Smyth	do	310	Timothy Howland	I. H. Bartlett & Sons
Morning Star	Bark	238	Charles E. Allen	S. Thomas & Co
Niger	Ship	412	Jacob L. Cleaveland	William Hathaway, jr
Ohio	do	363	Lewis H. Lawrence	Edward W. Howland
Oriole	Bark	280	Henry S. Hayes	E. C. Jones
Orray Taft	do	134	George J. Parker	S. Thomas & Co
Osceola, 2d	do	159	John M. Shaw	J. & W. R. Wing
Osceola, 3d	do	140	Martin Malloy	Jacob B. Hadley
Osmanli	do	292	Moses K. Fish	Charles S. Randall
Petrel	do	257	Francis S. Worth	T. Knowles & Co
Petrel	Schooner	59	John M. Honeywell	Charles Thatcher & Co
Pioneer	Bark	228	—— Hoxie	James D. Thompson
President, 2d	do	123	Benjamin Gifford	Edmund Maxfield

sailing from American ports—Continued.

Whaling-ground.	Date— Of sailing.	Date— Of arrival.	Result of voyage. Sperm-oil.	Result of voyage. Whale-oil.	Result of voyage. Whalebone.	Remarks.
			Bbls.	*Bbls.*	*Lbs.*	
Pacific Ocean ..	June 10	July 8, 1870	1,456	47	.....	Sent home 716 sperm.
North Pacific ..	Sept. 27	Apr. 30, 1871	.....	1,100	15,000	Bought from Dartmouth, 1866; sent home 456 sperm, 1,209 whale, 15,246 bone.
Atlantic	May 8	....	.....	.....	.....	Second mate, Richard Flanders, died 1868; sent home 150 sperm; lost near Zanzibar Sept. 8, 1867.
Hudson's Bay ..	Apr. 20	Sept. 24, 1867	75	200	3,000	
Atlantic	May 1	....	.....	.....	.....	
North Pacific ..	Aug. 1	Apr. 22, 1871	52	1,352	15,000	Sent home 371 sperm, 2,065 whale, 37,285 bone.
Indian Ocean ..	Oct. 2	July 9, 1870	1,339	.....	.....	Sent home 70 sperm.
....do	July 12	Aug. 10, 1870	1,002	.....	.....	Sold to Edgartown 1871; sent home 30 sperm.
Pacific Ocean ..	May 15	Oct. 11, 1868	463	7	.....	Built at Mattapoisett 1866; sent home 295 sperm.
North Pacific ..	Nov. 6	....	.....	.....	.....	Lost on Blossom Shoals August 30, 1868, with 1,100 whale, 20,000 bone; sent home 563 whale, 16,696 bone.
Atlantic	May 1	Sept. 9, 1868	152	.....	203	Sent home 283 sperm, 236 whale.
....do	Apr. 7	July 15, 1868	496	.....	.....	
Indian Ocean ..	July 10	Mar. 12, 1869	560	300	2,280	Sent home 280 sperm, 625 whale, 4,000 bone.
Pacific Ocean ..	Oct. 3	June 15, 1870	172	.....	.....	Bought from New Haven 1866; built at Baltimore 1850; sent home 400 sperm.
... do	June 9	May 23, 1870	1,591	.....	.....	E. J. Howland, first mate, killed by a whale August 6, 1866; sent home 877 sperm.
Indian Ocean ..	Aug. 15	Apr. 20, 1870	1,285	3	.....	Sent home 315 sperm.
North Pacific ..	Aug. 7	May 2, 1870	70	1,195	14,852	Sent home 84 sperm, 2,627 whale, 35,564 bone.
Hudson's Bay	Apr. 10	Oct. 8, 1867	20	200	.....	
Pacific Ocean ..	Oct. 27	July 5, 1871	514	4	.....	Bought from New York 1866; built at Kingston, Mass., 1850; sold to New York 1872; sent home 540 sperm.
....do	June 5	....	.....	.....	.....	Added 1866; Captain Osgood came home sick 1867; sent home 440 sperm; condemned at ——— ———, 1869; refitted and renamed Maggie Hill.
North Pacific ..	Apr. 18	May 12, 1870	.....	630	11,050	Bought from Boston 1865; sent home 200 sperm; 2,295 whale.
Atlantic	June 15	June 11, 1868	131	.....	.....	Sent home 416 sperm, 2,083 whale, 5,785 bone.
North Pacific ..	July 17	Apr. 30, 1871	.....	1,595	.....	Sent home 261 sperm, 3,100 bone.
....do	May 3	....	.....	.....	.....	Bought from New York 1866; stove by ice and lost in Arctic, 1870; had sent home 790 sperm; 2,800 whale, 35,000 bone; had on board 500 whale and 5,000 bone.
Pacific Ocean ..	May 29	Aug. 11, 1869	1,350	.....	.....	Sent home 1,629 sperm.
North Pacific ..	Nov. 13	June 10, 1870	.....	785	13,876	Bought from New York 1866; Captain Worth came home sick 1869; sent home 69 sperm, 750 whale, 9,100 bone.
Atlantic	June 2	Sept. 20, 1868	102	.....	.....	Bought from Boston 1866; sent home 305 sperm.
North Pacific ..	Oct. 17	Apr. 23, 1871	191	1,029	.....	Sent home 822 sperm, 1,270 whale, 31,248 bone.
Atl. and Ind ...	June 19	May 22, 1870	700	338	2,633	Sent home 1,075 sperm, 1,580 whale; broken up 1870.
Hudson's Bay ..	Apr. 18	Oct. 31, 1867	.....	650	12,000	
North Pacific .	May 29	June 2, 1870	866	533	1,362	Sent home 513 sperm, 265 whale, 4,395 bone.
....do	Aug. 7	May 24, 1871	130	1,510	16,700	
....do	June 26	Apr. 27, 1870	.....	1,188	14,361	Sent home 176 sperm; 1,819 whale, 29,777 bone.
Hudson's Bay ..	May 8	Oct. 25, 1867	.....	225	3,000	
Pacific Ocean ..	Oct. 31	May 12, 1870	605	34	.....	Captain Shaw came home sick 1869; sent home some oil and bone.
Atlantic	Sept. 17	Oct. 4, 1868	132	.....	.....	Sent home 982 sperm, 35 whale.
....do	May 29	Sept. 7, 1868	525	330	.....	Bought from Boston 1866; sent home 255 sperm.
Pacific Ocean ..	Nov. 5	Oct. 16, 1870	297	2	.....	Returned to whaling 1866; sent home 700 sperm.
Atlantic	Aug. 7	Nov. 16, 1866	133	9	.....	Gone three months and nine days; value of cargo about $11,000.
Hudson's Bay ..	Apr. 19	Sept. 12, 1867	.....	500	8,000	
Atlantic	Apr. 10	Apr. 15, 1867	65	4	.....	Sent home 353 sperm.

Table showing returns of whaling-vessels

Name of vessel.	Class.	Tonnage.	Captain.	Managing owner or agent.
1866.				
New Bedford, Mass.—Continued.				
Progress	Bark	358	James Dowden	W. O. Brownell
Roscius	...do	302	Ezra W. Crapo	William Penn Howland
Rousseau	...do	305	James Hyland	G. & M. Howland
Sam'l and Thomas	...do	132	Samuel H. Cromwell	David B. Kempton
Sappho	...do	263	James T. Handy	Otis Seabury
Sea Ranger	...do	273	William Lewis	I. H. Bartlett & Sons
Stamboul	...do	260	Reuben Kelley	Charles Hitch & Son
Stella	...do	270	Ebenezer F. Nye	Loum Snow & Son
Xantho	...do	325	John A. Beebe	J. & W. R. Wing
Fairhaven, Mass.				
Ellen Rodman	Schooner	73	Thomas F. Lambert	George F. Wing
George J. Jones	...do	126	John R. Taber	James I. Church
John Hathaway	Brig	....	William H. Haskins	
Oxford	...do	91	Nathan Briggs	Damon & Judd
Selah	Bark	166	Heman N. Stewart	Benjamin H. Chase
Tekoa	Brig	99	William G. Morton	Damon & Judd
Dartmouth, Mass.				
C. Horn Pigeon	Ship	212	Charles H. Robbins	William Potter, 2d
Rainbow	Schooner	48	Robert D. Eldridge	......do
Marion, Mass.*				
Herald	Brig	148	John A. Kelley	Henry M. Allen
Wm. Wilson	Schooner	92	William C. Hathaway	A. J. Hadley
Westport, Mass.				
Elizabeth	Bark	203	Hiram Francis	Andrew Hicks
Janet	...do	154	Alonzo J. Marvin	Henry Wilcox
Mattapoisett	...do	150	Alfred C. Davis	Henry Smith
Sea Queen	...do	195	Charles C. Movers	A. Hicks
Edgartown, Mass.				
Europa	Ship	392	Thomas Mellen	C. B. Marchant
Mary	...do	373	George A. Smith	William H. Munroe
Vineyard	...do	349	—— Smith	Grafton N. Collins
Nantucket, Mass.				
Amy	Bark	232	Joseph Winslow	Joseph B. Macy
B. Concord	...do	234	Edward McCleave	Freeman E. Adams
E. H. Adams	Schooner	107	Zenas M. Coleman	......do
M. Wrightington	Bark	132	Elihu F. Turner	......do

* Name changed

sailing from American ports—Continued.

Whaling-ground.	Date— Of sailing.	Date— Of arrival.	Result of voyage. Sperm-oil.	Result of voyage. Whale-oil.	Result of voyage. Whalebone.	Remarks.
			Bbls.	*Bbls.*	*Lbs.*	
North Pacific ..	May 29	May 8, 1870	......	1, 096	.....	Formerly the Charles Phelps of Stonington; added, rebuilt, and renamed 1866; sent home 1,420 whale, 39,692 bone.
Atlantic	Nov. 5	....	......	......	......	Condemned at Barbadoes, March, 1867.
Pacific Ocean ..	Oct. 4	June 15, 1870	1, 471	......	......	
Atl. and Pac...	June 12	....	......	......	......	Thomas Parker, third mate, killed by falling from aloft, September, 1866; Captain Cromwell came home sick 1867; sold at Talcahuano 1869; continued whaling from that port; sent home 943 sperm, 2 whale.
Pacific Ocean ..	Oct. 1	July 5, 1870	1, 263	9	......	Sent home 460 sperm, 600 bone.
....do	July 17	June 25, 1869	1, 096	......	......	Added 1866; formerly of Nantucket; sent home 650 sperm.
Atlantic	May 15	June 25, 1869	144	1, 046	6, 389	Bought from Boston 1865; sent home 260 sperm, 650 whale, 4,700 bone.
North Pacific ..	July 10	....	......	......	......	Lost on Foggy Island, Gulf of California, August 11, 1867; 2 men lost; sent home 6 blackfish.
Atl. and Ind ...	Nov. 17	Nov. 28, 1869	1, 455	.....	.....	Bought from New York, 1866; formerly of Warren, R. I.
Atlantic	May 3	Sept. 13, 1866	116	3	......	Bought from New Bedford 1865.
....do	June 28	Feb. 19, 1869	100	.....	.....	Bought from Dennis 1866; sent home 179 sperm.
....	June —	....	......	......	......	Bought from Newport 1866; condemned at St. Thomas 1866.
Cumberland I..	May 1	Sept. 22, 1867	.....	280	8, 000	
Atl. and Ind ...	May 29	May 25, 1869	25	......	......	Bought from Boston 1866; built 1849; sent home 352 sperm, 80 whale, 700 bone.
Atlantic	Nov. 14	Aug. 17, 1867	34	.....	......	Sent home 85 whale.
Atl. and Ind ...	May 30	May 24, 1869	395	87	620	Sailed under Capt. Charles H. Robbins, who came home sick, 1866; sent home 1,002 sperm, 82 whale, 500 bone.
Atlantic	Dec. 13	Aug. 17, 1867	35	3	......	
Atlantic	Dec. 12	Sept. 27, 1868	112	20	......	Sailed once and returned on account of damage to boats and crew by a whale.
....do	May 18	Aug. 28, 1866	220	......	......	Bought from Plymouth 1866.
Atlantic	Jan. 31	Aug. 18, 1867	100	100	......	Sent home 80 sperm.
....do	Dec. 21	June 16, 1869	391	140	700	Sent home 204 sperm.
....do	Nov. 13	Aug. 25, 1868	362	30	......	
Indian Ocean ..	July 3	Sept. 5, 1869	910	......	......	Sent home 87 sperm.
North Pacific ..	Aug. 29	Aug. 17, 1872	148	230	4, 000	Sent home 1,408 sperm, 2,870 whale, 35,293 bone.
....do	Sept. 22	....	......	......	......	Sent home 1,100 sperm, 990 whale, 15,115 bone; lost in the Arctic 1871.
....do	Oct. 25	Apr. 23, 1871	93	1, 418	17, 502	Sent home 334 sperm, 2,049 whale, 26,792 bone; sold to New Bedford and withdrawn 1872.
Pacific Ocean..	May 30	....	1, 450	50	......	Bought from Boston 1866; sold to Boston 1871.
....do	Nov. 6	....	......	......	......	Sent home 723 bone; Mr. Munroe, first mate, killed by falling from aloft January, 1871; sold at Talcahuano for whaling.
Atl. and Ind ...	May 8	Sept. 26, 1866	203	......	......	Mate James H. Bunker killed by a whale; altered to a brig 1867.
Pacific Ocean ..	July 2	....	......	......	......	Bought from Fall River 1866; sold at Talcahuano.

from Sippican 1866.

Table showing returns of whaling-vessels

Name of vessel.	Class.	Tonnage.	Captain.	Managing owner or agent.
1866.				
Wellfleet, Mass.				
Edith May	Schooner	135	—— Gross	R. R. Freeman
Provincetown, Mass.				
A. H. Brown	Schooner	131	N. Y. Higgins	E. & E. K. Cook & Co
Alleghany	do	95	—— Dyer	Daniel C. Cook
A. L. Putnam	do	178	—— Handy	H. & S. Cook & Co
Alcyone	do	130	—— Hudson	E. & E. K. Cook & Co
A. Clifford	do	118	—— Dyer	H. & S. Cook & Co
Allegro	do	76	—— Ryder	James Rich
Ada M. Dyer	do	119	Isaac A. Dyer	Alfred Cook
B. T. Crocker	do	118	—— Chandler	John Atwood & Co
Cetacean	do	123	Nathaniel Atwood	A. T. Williams
C. H. Cook	do	149	—— Cook	Stephen Cook
C. L. Sparks	do	130	H. Sparks	David Conwell
E. Gerry	do	104	—— Dunham John S. Smith	A. Small A. T. Williams
Ellen Rizpah	do	100	—— Taylor	Stephen Cook & Co
Emporium	do	80	—— Young	Daniel C. Cook
E. P. Howard	do	83	—— Hudson	E. & E. K. Cook
Estella	do	94	—— Snow	J. E. & G. Bowley
G. W. Lewis	do	110	—— Carlow	C. H. Rich
H. M. Simmons	do	146	—— Cook	Stephen Cook
J. Taylor	do	174	—— Smith	J. Atwood, jr, & Co
John A. Lewis	do	117	Lewis L. Chapman	B. A. Lewis & Co
L. P. Simmons	do	119	—— Cornell —— Atkins	J. E. & G. Bowley
Mary G. Curren	do	143	—— Farwell	Freeman & Hilliard
M. E. Simmons	do	160	—— Parsons	E. & E. K. Cook & Co
Montezuma	do	92	—— Nye	Freeman & Hilliard
N. J. Knights	do	95	—— Dyer	David Conwell
Olive Clark	do	98	—— Sparks	do
Quickstep	do	119	—— Taylor	E. & E. K. Cook & Co
Rising Sun	do	108	—— Clark	E. S. Smith & Co
Union	do	97	—— Nickerson	P. N. Freeman
V. Doane	do	99	—— Atkins	H. & S. Cook & Co
Watchman	do	140	—— Stid	Isaiah Gifford
W. A. Grozier	do	168	Moses Young	E. S. Smith & Co
Winged Racer	do	100	Xenophon Rich	David Conwell
Boston, Mass.				
A. Pickering	Bark	223	—— Jenks	Thomas L. Jenks
E. B. Phillips	do	144	—— Ellerton	Joshua E. Bowley
Geo. Brown	Schooner	105	—— Crenner	Lewis & Folger
Heman Smith	Brig	123	—— Martin	Heman Smith
St. Elizabeth	Bark	144	—— Ellerton	Joshua E. Bowley
Wm. Martin	Schooner	92	—— Senter	Heman Smith
Salem, Mass.				
Falcon	Brig	159	—— Macy	John C. Osgood
Wm. H. Shailer	Bark	175	—— Marshall	do
Newburyport, Mass.				
Georgia	Schooner	127	Eben Bradbury	Sumner, Swazy & Co

sailing from American ports—Continued.

Whaling-ground.	Date—Of sailing.	Date—Of arrival.	Result of voyage.—Sperm-oil.	Result of voyage.—Whale-oil.	Result of voyage.—Whalebone.	Remarks.
			Bbls.	*Bbls.*	*Lbs.*	
Atlantic	Feb. 26	Sept. 6, 1867	230	......	.....	Added 1866; sent home 80 sperm.
Atlantic	Feb. 5	July 31, 1867	180	10	.....	Sent home 87 sperm.
....do	Jan. 31	Aug. 22, 1866	85	120	.....	
....do	June 7	Oct. 27, 1867	160	70	.....	Added 1866; sent home 60 sperm.
... do	June 10	Sept. 5, 1867	160	......	......	Added 1866.
... do	Feb. 6	Sept. 1, 1866	106	140	......	
....do	June 3	Aug. 28, 1866	83	......	......	Added 1866; withdrawn 1866.
....do	Jan. 31	Sept. 1, 1866	158	140	.....	Built at Essex, Mass., 1865.
....do	Feb. 1	July 4, 1866	......	117	......	Added 1866; sent home 40 sperm; sailed again December 25; withdrawn 1868.
....do	Jan. 27	Aug. 29, 1866	241	125	......	Built at Essex, Mass., 1865.
... do	Jan. 17	Aug. 10, 1867	100	......	.....	Sent home 224 sperm, 8 blackfish.
....do	May 14	Aug. 10, 1867	100	50	.....	Added 1866; sent home 130 sperm, 15 blackfish.
....do	Feb. 13	July 4, 1866	.....	97	.....	
....do	Aug. 14	Aug. 13, 1867	......	200	......	
....do	Feb. 6	July 22, 1866	169	130	......	Sailed again December 25; ——— Nickerson, captain; arriued August 19, 1867; 70 sperm, 165 whale.
....do	Jan. 31	Aug. 24, 1866	50	100	......	
... do	Feb. 13	May 28, 1866	.....	64	.....	Added 1866; withdrawn 1866.
....do	Jan. 22	Aug. 24, 1866	45	175	.....	
....do	Jan. 22	Aug. 27, 1866	70	140	.....	Sailed again December 13, arrived August 10, 1867; 80 sperm, 60 whale.
....do	Feb. —	Oct. 15, 1867	400	......	......	Sent home 120 sperm; added 1866.
....do	Feb. 28	June 28, 1867	30	120	.....	Sent home 45 sperm, 60 whale; added 1866.
....do	Feb. 5	Nov. 27, 1866	138	......	.....	Built at Ipswich, Mass., 1865.
....do .... {	Apr. 26	Sept. 1, 1866	240	15	... }	Added 1866.
	Oct. 24	Sept. 30, 1867	......	110	... }	
....do	July 3	June 2, 1867	25	......	......	
Desolation Isl'd	Aug. 16	May 31, 1868	.....	809	......	Sent home 850 elephant.
Atlantic	Dec. 19	July 29, 1867	160	35	......	
....do ...... {	Jan. 6	Aug. 22, 1866	90	125	.....	
	Nov. 26	Sept. 13, 1867	100	20	......	
....do	May 20	Aug. 28, 1866	50	......	......	Added 1866.
....do	Nov. 24	Sept. 8, 1867	200	200	......	
....do	Dec. 19	Sept. 8, 1867	260	......	.....	
....do .... {	Jan. 13	Oct. 10, 1866	70	80	... }	Sold to Fairhaven 1866.
	Nov. 18	Sept. 14, 1867	50	......	... }	
....do	Feb. 13	Aug. 22, 1866	68	70	....	
....do	Jan. 11	Aug. 30, 1866	75	90	......	
....do	Jan. 6	Aug. 15, 1867	30	......	......	Built at Kennebunkport, Me., 1866; sent home 121 sperm.
....do	May 1	Sept. 19, 1866	130	......	......	Bought from Wellfleet 1865.
Pacific Ocean.	Apr. 26	....	......	......	......	Added 1866; W. S. Maxfield, first mate, died April, 1868; sent home 513 sperm, 8 whale.
Atlantic	Mar. 9	Oct. 29, 1867	30	10	......	
....do	Feb. 17	....	......	......	......	Sold to New London 1868; added 1866; wrecked and sold at Bermudas September, 1868.
....do	July 28	Sept. 20, 1868	170	20	......	Added 1866; sent home 138 sperm.
....do	Mar. 9	....	......	......	......	Added 1866; William Lewis, first mate, drowned at Fayal 1866; condemned.
....do	Nov. 24	Aug. 27, 1867	225	......	......	
Atlantic	Nov. 26	Apr. 21, 1868	......	6	......	
....do	Oct. 17	Oct. 13, 1867	100	......	......	Added 1866; formerly in African trade.
Atlantic	Oct. 31	Sept. 21, 1868	138	4	......	Whaling company formed 1866 and Georgia bought; sold to Brewer, Me., 1869.

Table showing returns of whaling-vessels

Name of vessel.	Class.	Tonnage.	Captain.	Managing owner or agent.
1866.				
Beverly, Mass.				
Thriver	Schooner	95	—— Woods	F. W. Choate
New London, Conn.				
Acoro Barns	Bark	296	Charles Jeffrey	Williams & Barnes
Geo. and Mary	do	105	Horace M. Newbury	do
Georgiana	Brig	128	—— Spicer	Williams & Haven
Helen F	Schooner	108	—— Smith	do
Leader	do	57	George W. Bailey	do
Pioneer	Bark	212	Ebenezer Morgan	do
Quickstep	Schooner	105	—— Chester	Williams & Barns
Roman	do	350	—— Church	Richard H. Chapell
S. B. Howes	do	101	—— Keeney	Williams & Haven
U. D	do	77	—— Buddington	S. Chapman
Groton, Conn.				
Cornelia	Schooner	148	Lorenzo B. Baker	Ebenezer Morgan
Sag Harbor, N. Y.				
Concordia	Bark	217	—— Skinner	O. R. Wade
J. A. Robb	do	244	—— Green	H. & S. French
Myra	Brig	116	—— Babcock	do
Ocean	Bark	239	—— Weld	do
New York, N. Y.				
Minnesota	Ship	243	Sidney L. Pierce	Lorenzo Pierce
1867.				
New Bedford, Mass.				
Alaska	Bark	340	Shubael H. Norton	Jonathan Bourne, jr
Albion	do	328	Albert A. Thomas	Nathaniel T. Gifford
Alto	do	200	Elias H. White	Charles H. Gifford
Andrews	do	277	Tim. C. Packard	J. Bourne, jr
Annawan	do	108	Edward K. Russell	Edmund Maxfield
Ansel Gibbs	do	303	James B. Huxford	J. Bourne, jr
Arab	do	278	Frederick P. Cole	William T. Smith
Arnolda	Ship	340	James A. Crowell	James B. Wood & Co
Avola	Bark	230	Zenas E. Bourne	John P. Knowles, 2d
Camilla	do	328	Benj. F. Jones	Swift & Allen
Catalpa	do	202	Obed Pierce	N. T. Gifford
C. W. Morgan	do	314	George Athearn	J. & W. R. Wing
Concordia	do	368	Robert Jones	G. & M. Howland
Corn'ls Howland	Ship	333	John A. Luce B. F. Homan	Edward W. Howland
Daniel Webster	do	3[illegible]7	George F. Marvin	William O. Brownell
D. N. Richards	Schooner	92	Elisha D. Russell	William Penn Howland.
Edw'd Everett	Bark	187	Joseph D. Silva	Gideon Allen & Son

sailing from American ports—Continued.

Whaling-ground.	Date—Of sailing.	Date—Of arrival.	Result of voyage.—Sperm-oil.	Result of voyage.—Whale-oil.	Result of voyage.—Whalebone.	Remarks.
			Bbls.	*Bbls.*	*Lbs.*	
Atlantic	Oct. 31	Aug. 14, 1867	20	170	......	Sold to Boston 1867.
Ind. and Pacific	June 6	Apr. 24, 1871	......	850	11, 500	Built at New London 1866; sent home 65 sperm, 1,939 whale, 27,745 bone.
Hudson's Bay..	Apr. 18	Sept, 14, 1867	......	500	10, 000	
Cumberl'd Inlet	July 12	Nov. 29, 1867	......	800	16, 000	
. . do	July 16	Nov. 10, 1867	......	50	......	
Atlantic	Dec. 25	No report....	......	......	......	
Davis's Strait..	Apr. 28	Nov. 14, 1866	.....	340	5, 300	Rebuilt 1865; originally built at Charlestown, Mass., for a Government transport; first steam whaler from United States.
Cumberl'd Inlet	June 28	Sept. 14, 1868	.....	362	6, 600	Added 1866.
Desolation Isld.	Aug. 22	June 2, 1867	19	1, 684	815	Added 1866; formerly of New Bedford bought from United States.
Cumberl'd Inlet	June 28	Oct. 9, 1866	.....	249	5, 600	
Davis's Strait..	June 6	Sept. 26, 1866	.....	Clean	.....	Added 1866; sold to Fairhaven 1867.
Hudson's Bay..	Apr. 18	Oct. 31, 1867	.....	200	......	Bought from New London 1866.
Hudson's Bay..	May 11	Sept. 13, 1867	.....	440	7, 300	
South Atlantic	July 24	....	.....	....	......	Sold at St. Helena March 1868.
Atlantic	May 28	Dec. 30, 1867	.....	....	......	Sent home 80 sperm; no other report.
South Atlantic.	Aug. 9	....	.....	....	......	Lost 1867.
Atlantic	May 29	May 16, 1868	321	....	......	Bought 1866; built at Philadelphia 1849; fitted from New Bedford; Captain Pierce came home sick 1867; sent home 40 sperm.
Pacific Ocean ..	Aug. 21	Apr. 19, 1871	.....	751	10, 161	Built 1867; sent home 987 sperm.
....do	Dec. 25	....	.....	....	......	Bought as a ship from New York 1867; formerly of Fairhaven; built at Haverhill; sold to Auckland, N. Z., as the nucleus of a whaling company there; sent home 287 sperm.
....do	June 7	....	.....	....	......	Bought from Fairhaven 1867; sent home 595 sperm; lost on reef near Falkland Islands 1870, with 515 sperm, 475 whale.
Hudson's Bay..	May 20	....	.....	....	......	Lost at Harrison's Point, Cumberland Inlet, November 14, 1867.
Atlantic	Oct. 1	May 3, 1870	142	.....	......	Sent home 288 sperm.
....do	Oct. 23	Apr. 23, 1868	200	....	......	
Pacific Ocean ..	June 25	....	.....	....	......	Bought from New London 1867; sent home 1,354 sperm, 673 whale; condemned at ——— 1871.
....do	June 25	June 18, 1871	972	....	......	Sent home 62 sperm.
Indian Ocean ..	Aug. 22	Oct. 13, 1870	773	5	......	Bought from Boston 1867; built at Waldoborough, Me., 1841; Sent home 55 sperm.
Pacific Ocean ..	July 16	July 5, 1871	1, 277	....	......	Sent home 1,009 sperm.
....do	May 8	May 27, 1871	233	....	....	Added 1866 from New York; formerly a whaler; sent home 430 sperm; sold to Gloucester 1873.
....do	July 17	Aug. 16, 1871	567	1	......	Sent home 325 sperm, 525 whale, 3,000 bone.
North Pacific ..	Dec. 7	....	......	.....	.....	Added 1867; sent home 164 sperm, 3,563 whale, 34,965 bone; lost in the Arctic 1871.
Atlantic	May 7	Sept. 28, 1867	140	......	......	Sent home 100 whale.
North Pacific ..	Nov. 12	May 7, 1871	93	1, 590	19, 350	Sent home 24 sperm, 2,555 whale, 43,326 bone.
....do	May 20	May 2, 1872	77	310	......	Sent home 161 sperm, 3,175 whale, 45,635 bone.
Atlantic	June 1	Nov. 5, 1868	25	0	......	Bought from Sandwich 1867; sent home 85 sperm.
Indian Ocean ..	June 8	....	......	....	......	Bought from Boston 1867; built at Medford 1863; sent home 1,699 sperm, 20 whale.

Table showing returns of whaling-vessels

Name of vessel.	Class.	Tonnage.	Captain.	Managing owner or agent.
1867.				
New Bedford, Mass.—Continued.				
Eliza Adams	Ship	408	Caleb O. Hamblen	Taber, Gordon & Co
Europa	...do	323	John G. Nye	Edward C. Jones
Falcon	Bark	285	Charles Allen	Thos. Knowles & Co
Hadley	...do	163	B. B. Briggs	Andrew H. Potter
Hecla	...do	160	Elisha B. Handy	T. Knowles & Co
Helen Snow	...do	215	Thos. G. Campbell	Loum Snow & Son
Herald	Ship	300	Seth Nickerson	Zenas L. Adams
Hunter	Bark	355	Josiah E. Chase	J. Bourne, jr
Ionia	...do	291	John O. Norton	Edmund Maxfield
Java, 2d	...do	290	Chas. H. S. Kempton	Charles Hitch & Son
John Dawson	...do	173	Asaph S. Wicks	J. & W. R. Wing
J. W. Dodge	Schooner	83	John M. Honeywell Edwin N. Clark	Charles Thatcher & Co.
Josephine	Ship	363	Bernard Cogan	Swift & Perry
Kathleen	Bark	206	James Cottle	J. & W. R. Wing
Leonidas	...do	98	Eben Cook	David B. Kempton
Marcella	...do	161	Charles West	C. R. Tucker & Co
Mary Frazier	...do	301	Thos. F. Caswell	C. Tucker
Mary and Susan	...do	327	A. O. Herendeen	T. Knowles & Co
Milwood	...do	216	Isaac Allen	G. Allen & Son
Mt. Wollaston	Ship	325	Edward B. Coffin	Otis Seabury
Northern Light	Bark	385	Michael Baker, 3d	J. Bourne, jr
Onward	Ship	339	E. C. Pulver	Edward W. Howland
Orlando	Bark	190	James M. Clark	C. Hitch & Son
Pacific	...do	341	William Allen	Swift & Perry
Petrel	Schooner	59	Benj. B. Morris Loring Braley	Charles Thatcher & Co
President, 2d	Bark	123	James M. Soule	Edmund Maxfield
Robert Edwards	Ship	336	Stephen Flanders	Taber, Read & Co
Sarah	Bark	128	Alex. Newcomb	J. P. Knowles, 2d
Stafford	...do	156	Dan'l L. Ricketson	J. & W. R. Wing
Starlight	Brig	141	Frederick Slocum	Charles S. Randall
Thomas Winslow	Bark	97	Elihu Russell	John Hicks
Tropic Bird	...do	145	Lemuel D. Adams	Wm. Penn Howland
Vigilant	...do	2[illegible]5	Archelaus Baker	William Watkins
Wave	...do	150	Elisha Cannon 2d	T. Knowles & Co
Young Phenix	Ship	355	Daniel Sherman	William Phillips & Son
Fairhaven, Mass.				
A. Lawrence	Brig	160	David Marston	James I. Church
Ellen Rodman	Schooner	73	Thomas F. Lambert	George F. Wing
John Randolph	...do	83	—— Coggeshall	Dexter Jenney
Oxford	Brig	91	Amos C. Baker	Damon & Judd
Star Castle	...do	116	Henry Clay	...do
U. D	Schooner	77	Joseph P. Nye	...do
Wash. Freeman	...do	96	Benj. G. Stowell Jonathan Jenney	Obed F. Hitch

sailing from American ports—Continued.

Whaling-ground.	Date— Of sailing.	Date— Of arrival.	Result of voyage. Sperm-oil.	Result of voyage. Whale-oil.	Result of voyage. Whalebone.	Remarks.
			Bbls.	*Bbls.*	*Lbs.*	
Pacific Ocean	July 22	Jan. 20, 1871	1,509	361	1,115	Took on voyage 2,000 sperm, 1,400 whale, 11,000 bone.
Indian Ocean	Oct. 23	July 13, 1871	320	1,183	....	F. Armstrong, third mate, died September 1868; fourth mate drowned 1869.
Pacific Ocean	Oct. 23	Sept. 16, 1871	358	4	.....	Sent home 393 sperm, 5 whale
Atlantic	May 16	May 24, 1870	32	....	.....	Added 1867; sent home 192 sperm.
....do	July 9	July 29, 1869	200	1[illegible]	.....	Sent home 286 sperm.
North Pacific	Aug. 31	Apr. 19, 1871	12[illegible]	99[illegible]	.....	Sent home 277 sperm, 2,089 whale, 37,710 bone.
Atlantic	Apr. 30	Apr. 25, 1869	947	71	....	Got 70 pounds ambergris, worth $97.50 per pound.
Pacific Ocean	Dec. 4	July 19, 1871	1,821	.....	.....	Sent home 620 sperm, 36 whale.
....do	May 2	July 1, 1871	353	1,07[illegible]	....	Bought from Salem 1866; built at Duxbury 1848; sold to New York 1872; sent home 317 sperm, 1,200 bone.
Indian Ocean	Dec. 10	Jan. 12, 1872	99[illegible]	.....	.....	Part of the crew mutinied, killed third mate, (J. W. Jones,) beat and tied up first mate and escaped, while Captain Kempton was on shore.
Atlantic	Apr. 20	Apr. 7, 1870	950	.....	....	Sent home 50 sperm.
....do	Apr. 14	June 27, 1867	......	3	...	Added 1866.
	July 9	Apr. 17, 1868	.....	Clear	....	
North Pacific	Sept. 3	Apr. 20, 1871	......	2,10[illegible]	....	Sent home 360 sperm, 2,625 whale, 10,700 bone.
Indian Ocean	July 2	July 26, 1871	88[illegible]	.....	.....	Sent home 639 sperm.
Atlantic	Aug. 14	July 23, 1869	160	3[illegible]	....	Sent home 120 sperm.
....do	May 30	Oct. 4, 1869	208	3[illegible]	....	Sent home 294 sperm, 84 whale, 800 bone.
Pacific Ocean	Oct. 8	Mar. 12, 1871	435	4	....	John George, third mate, and boat's crew drowned while fast to a whale, December 26, 1868; sent home 629 sperm, 6 whale.
....do	Sept. 10	May 30, 1870	1,244	......	.. ...	
Hudson's Bay	Apr. 2	Nov. 13, 1868	......	37[illegible]	3,88[illegible]	Sent home 10 sperm.
Pacific Ocean	Aug. 15	Aug. 9, 1871	1,138	......	....	Benjamin Pease, second mate, lost overboard 1868; sent home 60 sperm.
....do	Oct. 15	Aug. 2, 1871	1,104	21[illegible]	.....	Sent home 644 sperm, 235 whale, 2,293 bone.
North Pacific	Oct. 1	Apr. 6, 1871	[illegible]	1,58[illegible]	20,70[illegible]	Sent home 1,076 whale, 40,921 bone.
Indian Ocean	Apr. 10	May 6, 1870	857	10	....	Bought from Philadelphia 1866.
Atlantic	Nov. 6	July 15, 1868	597	30	.....	
....do	Apr. 3	Sept. 13, 1867	100	......	....	
	Nov. 5	June 25, 1868	......	Clean	.....	
....do	May 23	Sept. 4, 1868	285	11	....	
....do	June 26	Oct. 10, 1869	240	730	....	Sent home 733 sperm, 4,450 bone.
....do	Sept. 25	Oct. 28, 1870	230	33	....	First mate, Mr. Lambert, died November 6 1867; sent home 89 sperm.
....do	Nov. 27	Sept. 11, 1870	932	7	....	
....do	May 6	May 21, 1870	16[illegible]	412	....	Bought 1866; built in Nova Scotia 18[illegible]0; Captain Slocum came home sick 1868; sent home 451 sperm.
....do	June 4	....	....	....	....	Lost at sea September 8, 1869, latitude 38° 50′ north, longitude 71° 40′ west; seven lives lost; had 150 sperm; Captain Russell was 69 years old.
....do	Jan. 8	Oct. 28, 1868	128	......	......	Sent home 172 sperm, 13 whale.
Indian Ocean	Nov. 27	Apr. 27, 1870	1,47[illegible]	2	....	
Atlantic	May 6	Apr. 25, 1869	137	8	..	Sent home 573 sperm.
Indian Ocean	Nov. 12	Apr. 22, 1871	860	73	67[illegible]	Sent home 758 sperm, 705 whale, 4,500 bone.
Atlantic	June 10	May 13, 1869	209	......	......	Bought from Boston 1867; sent home 40 sperm.
... do	Apr. 12	Sept. 23, 1868	30	9	.....	Sent home 65 sperm.
....do	Oct. 10	Aug. 4, 1869	40	10	.....	Added 1876 from Edgartown; withdrawn 1870; sent home 112 sperm.
....do	Oct. 15	June 14, 1868	75	.....	......	
....do	May 13	....	......	.....	......	Sent home 1,020 sperm, 150 humpback; bought from New London 1867; lost 1869.
....do	June 5	Oct. 13, 1868	37	......	.....	Bought from Provincetown, 1867.
... do	May 13	Aug. 18, 1867	110	.....	....	Bought from Wellfleet 1867; sent home 25 sperm.
	Aug. 28	Sept. 17, 1868	200	10	....	

Table showing returns of whaling-vessels

Name of vessel.	Class.	Tonnage.	Captain.	Managing owner or agent.
1867.				
Dartmouth, Mass.				
Rainbow	Schooner	48	H. B. Macomber	William Potter, 2d
Marion, Mass.				
Admiral Blake	Schooner	84	Arthur H. Hammond	Henry M. Allen
Cohannet	do	83	Wm. C. Hathaway	A. J. Hadley
Wm. Wilson	do	92	Judah Hathaway	do
Westport, Mass.				
Andrew Hicks	Bark	303	Otis F. Hamblen	A. Hicks
Elizabeth	do	203	T. C. Spaulding	do
Gov. Carver	do	128	Jason W. Gifford	Henry Wilcox
Platina	do	214	Amos A. Chase	Andrew Hicks
Sea Fog	do	166	Joseph W. Lavers	do
Edgartown, Mass.				
Linda Stewart	Bark	236	Frederick Smith	William H. Munroe
Splendid	Ship	369	—— Jernegan	do
Tisbury, Mass.				
M. Taylor	Brig	117	Thomas Foster	J. M. Taber
Nantucket, Mass.				
Abby Bradford	Schooner	114	John Murray	Joseph B Macy
E. H. Adams	Brig	107	Zenas M. Coleman	Freeman E. Adams
Oak	Bark	167	Joshua Chadwick	do
Provincetown, Mass.				
A. H. Brown	Schooner	131	—— Elwell	Thomas Hilliard
A. L. Putnam	do	178	—— Dyer	H. & S. Cook & Co
Alcyone	do	130	—— Brown	E. & E. K. Cook & Co
Alleghany	do	95	—— Graham	Daniel C. Cook
Alexander	do	75	—— Hopkins	P. N. Freeman
Antarctic	do	136	—— Hill	J. E. & G. Bowley
Arizona	do	115	—— Goodspeed	Stephen Cook
A. Clifford	do	118	—— Dyer	H. & S. Cook & Co
Albert Clarence	do	135	—— Small	J. Freeman
Ada M. Dyer	do	119	—— Dyer	Alfred Cook
Alice B. Dyer	do	129	James S. Dyer	David Conwell
Carrie Jones	do	130	—— Cornell	J. E. & G. Bowley
Cetacean	do	116	—— Atwood	Union Wharf Co
C. H. Cook	do	149	—— Gelett	S. Cook
C. L. Sparks	do	130	—— Roberts	David Conwell
D. C. Smith	do	67	—— Kenney	John Atwood
E. B. Conwell	do	132	—— Cannon	D. Conwell
E. H. Hatfield	do	125	—— Keith	E. & E. K. Cook & Co
Emma F. Lewis	do	120	George W. Powe	B. A. Lewis & Co
Emporium	do	80	{ —— Cook —— Downer }	D. C. Cook
Estella	do	94	—— Snow	J. E. & G. Bowley
Etta G. Fogg	do	120	—— Thompson	E. & E. K. Cook
Express	do	85	{ —— Cook —— Atkins }	do
G. H. Phillips	do	130	—— Taylor	S. Cook
J. H. Collins	do	93	Ira B. Atkins	David A. Small

sailing from American ports—Continued.

Whaling-ground.	Date—		Result of voyage.			Remarks.
	Of sailing.	Of arrival.	Sperm-oil.	Whale-oil.	Whalebone.	
			Bbls.	*Bbls.*	*Lbs.*	
Atlantic	Sept. 9	May 1, 1868	20	......	......	Bought from Nantucket 1866.
Atlantic	May 10	Apr. 23, 1868	212	32	......	Sent home 55 sperm.
....do	May 13	Aug. 14, 1867	220	......	......	Bought from Boston 1866; gone three months; value of cargo $13,000.
....do	May 10	Aug. 28, 1867	185	15	......	Brought also 8 pounds of ambergris.
Pacific Ocean ..	Sept. 11	May 14, 1872	225	730	......	Built 1867; sent home 843 sperm, 4 whale.
Indian Ocean ..	Dec. 18	June 13, 1870	927	10	......	Took 208 pounds ambergris, worth $94 per pound, and sent it to London; sold to Boston 1872.
....do	Dec. 25	......	......	......	......	Sent home 670 sperm; condemned and sold at Mauritius 1869.
Pacific Ocean ..	May 23	June 13, 1871	270	209	......	Sent home 812 sperm.
Indian Ocean ..	July 10	......	......	......	......	Sent home 259 sperm.
Indian Ocean ..	May 15	Apr. 7, 1870	578	......	......	Bought from New York 1867; built at Dorchester, Md., 1862; sent home 257 sperm; sold to Tisbury 1871.
North Pacific ..	Oct. 2	May 17, 1872	981	......	......	Sent home 1,100 sperm; sold to New Zealand 1873 for whaling thence.
Atlantic	May 11	Sept. 20, 1868	208	......	......	Bought from Dennis 1866; formerly a schooner; sent home 116 sperm.
Atlantic	Apr. 30	Sept. 1, 1868	404	5	......	
....do	May 1	Sept. 26, 1868	170	......	......	
Atlantic & Ind.	June 11	Sept. 20, 1869	570	15	......	
Atlantic	Oct. 30	Aug. 19, 1869	280	80	......	Sent home 45 sperm; withdrawn 1869.
....do	Dec. 26	July 30, 1868	13	34	1,000	
....do	Oct. 15	Aug. 24, 1868	153	133	......	
....do	Feb. 7	Aug. 12, 1867	130	170	......	
....do	Feb. 18	Aug. 13, 1867	20	6	......	Withdrawn 1868; sold to New Bedford 1869.
....do	Nov. 14	July 30, 1869	20	50	......	
....do	Dec. 21	July 10, 1869	180	190	......	
....do	Jan. 3	Aug. 18, 1867	90	200	......	
	Dec. 26	Sept. 3, 1868	73	132	......	
....do	Feb. 18	Aug. 19, 1868	90	145	......	Added 1866; sent home 45 sperm.
....do	Jan. 3	Sept. 12, 1867	70	200	......	
	Dec. 26	Sept. 3, 1868	155	220	......	
....do	Jan. 31	July 7, 1867	......	200	......	Sailed again August 6; arrived July 24, 1868; 70 sperm; built 1866; added 1867; withdrawn 1868; sent home 60 sperm.
....do	May 15	Aug. 10, 1868	69	12	......	
....do	Mar. 20	Aug. 15, 1868	40	5	......	Sent home 190 sperm.
....do	Oct. 22	May 18, 1868	184	......	......	
....do	Nov. 5	July 31, 1868	380	......	......	
....do	May 16	Aug. 20, 1867	......	10	......	Added 1867; withdrawn 1869.
	Dec. 11	Aug. 30, 1868	39	3	......	
....do	Jan. 3	Aug. 1, 1868	150	10	......	
....do	Jan. 22	Sept. 15, 1868	75	......	......	Sent home 133 sperm.
....do	Jan. 22	Oct. 9, 1867	220	60	......	Built at Ipswich 1866.
....do	Jan. 3	June 22, 1867	75	145	......	Sold to West Indies 1868; sailed from thence whaling under a Provincetown captain.
	Dec. 30	Sept. 17, 1868	31	29	......	
....do	Jan. 25	June 16, 1867	......	8	......	Second mate, Edwin Dunham, lost overboard 1867; also lost four men, boats, &c.
	July 22	Aug. 22, 1868	14	139	......	
....do	May 11	......	......	......	......	Added 1867; supposed to be lost with all on board.
....do	Mar. 29	Aug. 10, 1867	50	......	......	Added 1867.
	Dec. 18	Sept. 1, 1868	32	166	......	
....do	June 4	Sept. 5, 1868	177	78	......	Added 1867; sent home 225 sperm.
... do	Feb. 4	Aug. 12, 1867	90	110	......	Built 1866.
	Dec. 18	Aug. 26, 1868	91	114	......	

Table showing returns of whaling-vessels

Name of vessel.	Class.	Tonnage.	Captain.	Managing owner or agent.
1867.				
Provincetown, Mass.—Continued.				
J. Taylor	Schooner	174	Atkins Smith	J. Atwood, jr. & Co
John A. Lewis	do	117	—— Chapman	B. A. Lewis & Co
Joseph Lindsey	do	95	—— Ryder	James Rich
Mary D. Leach	do	138	W. A. Leach	Union Wharf Co
Mary G. Curren	do	143	—— Fisher	Freeman & Hilliard
Montezuma	do	92	—— Nye	do
N. J. Knights	do	95	—— Dyer	D. Conwell
N. F. Putnam	do	...	—— Tilson	H. & S. Cook
O. M. Remington	do	138	William Remington	Union Wharf Company
Olive Clark	do	98	—— Sparks —— Dyer	D. Conwell
Quickstep	do	119	—— Nickerson	E. & E. K. Cook & Co
Rising Sun	do	108	—— Freeman	Atkins Nickerson
S. A. Paine	do	..	—— Curran	Freeman & Hilliard
S. R. Soper	do	130	—— Burch	Robert Soper
V. Doane	do	99	—— Young	H. & S. Cook & Co
V. H. Hill	Brig	155	—— Freeman	J. E. & G. Bowley
Walter Irvin	Schooner	158	—— Atkins	Amos Nickerson
Winged Racer	do	100	—— Rich	D. Conwell
Willie Irving	do	115	—— White	C. H. Cook
Watchman	do	140	—— Stid James E. Cook	Isaiah Gifford
W. A. Grozier	do	168	—— Young	Atk. Nickerson
Wellfleet, Mass.				
Edith May	Schooner	135	—— Gross	R. R. Freeman
Boston, Mass.				
Louisa A	Schooner	122	—— Senter	Heman Smith
Money Hill	do	100	—— Abbott	Robert Soper & Son
Rosa Baker	Brig	108	—— Stetson	H. Smith
S. E. Lewis	Schooner	96	—— Smith	do
Thriver	do	69	—— Swain	Robert Soper & Son
Wm. Martin	do	92	—— Bourne	H. Smith
Salem, Mass.				
Para	Brig	135	—— Worth	John C. Osgood
Said bin Sultan	Bark	235	James W. Holmes	do
Wm. H. Shailer	do	175	—— Marshall	do
Beverly, Mass.				
Eschol	Brig	143	—— Cottle	F. W. Choate
Newburyport, Mass.				
Hannah Grant	Schooner	71	—— Robbins	Sumner, Swasey & Co
Life Boat	do	88	Joseph H. Caton	do
New London, Conn.				
Chas. Colgate	Schooner	250	—— Bolles	Lawrence & Co
Emma Jane	do	86		Richard H. Chapell
Era	do	188	—— Tyson	Williams & Barns
Franklin	do	119	—— Buddington	R. H. Chapell
Isabella	Brig	192	—— Bailey	do
Perry	Bark	150	Stephen Bolles	Williams & Barns
Pioneer	Ship			

sailing from American ports—Continued.

Whaling-ground.	Date— Of sailing.	Date— Of arrival.	Result of voyage. Sperm-oil.	Result of voyage. Whale-oil.	Result of voyage. Whalebone.	Remarks.
			Bbls.	*Bbls.*	*Lbs.*	
Atlantic	Aug. 20	Aug. 24, 1869	150	.....	.....	Withdrawn 1869.
....do	Mar. 15	July 30, 1868	80	.....	.....	Sent home 72 sperm.
....do	Mar. 25	Aug. 15, 1867	25	.....	....	Added 1866; withdrawn 1868.
	Oct. 2	Sept. 8, 1868	8[illegible]	100	....	
....do	Mar. 15	Aug. 31, 1868	60	10	.....	Added 1867; sent home 362 sperm.
....do	June 18	Nov. 27, 1867	50	.....	.....	Sailed under Captain Jos. Farwell, who died May 14, 1867.
....do	Oct. 30	Sept. 15, 1868	170	10	.....	
....do	Dec. 21	Sept. 17, 1868	100	32	.....	
....do	May 31	Aug. 6, 1868	90	.....	.....	Added 1867; sent home 70 sperm.
....do	May 16	....	....	.....	.....	Built 1867; sent home 448 sperm.
....do	May 13	Aug. 12, 1867	....	15	.....	
	Dec. 26	Sept. 17, 1868	75	130	.....	
....do	Nov. 24	Aug. 28, 1869	105	175	.....	Sent home 68 sperm.
....do	Dec. 11	Aug. 28, 1868	177	90	.....	
....do	Apr. 18	Sept. 21, 1869	180	180	.....	Added 1867; sent home 114 sperm.
....do	Apr. 18	Aug. 19, 1818	.....	Clean	.....	Sent home 160 sperm.
....do	Jan. 3	Aug. 26, 1867	35	1[illegible]0	.....	
....do	May 11	Oct. 5, 1868	290	20	.....	
....do	Feb. 25	Sept. 20, 1868	30	94	.....	Altered from a schooner 1867.
....do	Feb. 2	July 31, 1867	.....	.....	.....	
....do	Jan. 25	....	.....	.....	.....	Added 1866; supposed to have foundered near George's Bank, and all on board lost, 1867; sent home 160 sperm.
....do	Jan. 25	Aug. 15, 1867	40	....	....	
	Sept. 12	Aug. 6, 1868	80	110	....	
....do	Oct. 10	Sept. 5, 1869	190	200	.....	Sent home 239 sperm.
Atlantic	Dec. 11	Sept. 26, 1869	260	85	.....	Sent home 85 sperm; withdrawn 1870.
Atlantic	Dec. 18	July 9, 1870	50	200	.....	Sent home 271 sperm; withdrawn 1871.
....do	May 6	....	.....	.....	.....	Added 1867; supposed to have been lost with all on board.
....do	July 9	July 24, 1869	170	.....	.....	Built 1867; sent home 324 sperm.
....do	Oct. 22	Sept. 10, 1869	225	.....	.....	Sent home 76 sperm.
....do	Nov. 9	Nov. 22, 1868	.....	8	.....	Bought from Beverly 1867.
....do	Nov. 12	Sept. 3, 1868	17[illegible]	.....	.....	
Indian Ocean ..	Dec. 17	May 16, 1871	760	.....	.....	Altered from a schooner 1867; built at Wilmington, Del., 1861; sold to Boston 1871; sent home 116 sperm.
Atl'tic and Pac.	June 13	June 13, 1871	294	149	.....	Bought from Boston 1867; built at Newburyport 1861; sent home 410 sperm; sold to Boston 1872; Salem's last whaler.
Atlantic	Dec. 26	....	.....	.....	.....	Sent home 243 sperm, 20 whale; condemned and sold at Rio Janeiro Nov. 6, 1869.
Atlantic	Apr. 26	Sept. 12, 1868	190	4	.....	Put into New Bedford April 30; damaged by collision with British ship Isabella; sent home 60 sperm.
Atlantic	Apr. 10	Sept. 5, 1868	64	13	.....	Added 1867; built on the Merrimac 1847.
....do	Mar. 6	Aug. 26, 1868	20	31	.....	Added 1866; sent home 35 sperm.
Hurd's Island..	June 22	May 4, 1869	.....	1,150	1,200	
Desolat'n Island	July 6	Apr. 26, 1872	.....	97	1,10[illegible]	Bought from Baltimore 1867; built at Baltimore 1855, to replace the E. R. Sawyer.
Cumber'ld Inlet	Apr. 11	Aug. 27, 1868	.....	837	13,400	Added 1866; third mate, H. Griswold, died May, 1868.
....do	May 2	Sept. 10, 1868	.....	393	6,600	
Hudson's Bay.	May 25	Sept. 14, 1868	.....	668	8,700	
Atlantic	June 1	July 21, 1870	366	10	.....	Formerly of the United States Navy; bought 1867; sold to Edgartown 1874.
....	Mar. 20	Apr. 29, 1867	.....	.....	.....	Returned d maged by a gale; sunk in ice in Hudson's Strait July 6, 1867.

Table showing returns of whaling-vessels

Name of vessel.	Class.	Tonnage.	Captain.	Managing owner or agent.
1867.				
New London, Conn.—Continued.				
Roman	Ship	350	—— Church	R. H. Chapell
Roswell King	Schooner	134	R. H. Glass	do
Sag Harbor, N. Y.				
Balæna	Bark	215	—— Jennings	H. & S. French
Highland Mary	do	209	—— French	do
New York, N. Y.				
Addison	Bark	426	Peleg Cornell	Lorenzo Peirce
1868.				
New Bedford, Mass.				
A. R. Tucker	Bark	129	Charles B. Barstow	J. & W. R. Wing
Ansel Gibbs	do	303	Elnathan B. Fisher	Jonathan Bourne, jr
Atlantic	do	291	Henry R. Craw	J. & W. R. Wing
Black Eagle	do	229	B. Swain, jr	Andrew H. Potter
China	do	367	Charles H. Gifford	William Phillips & Son
Cleone	do	347	Hervey E. Luce	Edmund Maxfield
Com. Morris	Ship	338	Jacob A. Howland	Swift & Perry
Contest	do	341	James L. Chapman	do
Cornelia	Bark	203	Edward P. Shiverick	John P. Knowles, 2d
Coral	do	361	James E. Potter	Taber, Gordon & Co
D. N. Richards	Schooner	92	Isaac P. Webb	William P. Howland
Draco	Bark	258	Andrew M. Braley	J. Bourne, jr
E. Swift	do	327	George W. Bliven	Swift & Allen
Emily Morgan	do	365	Benjamin Dexter	J. & W. R. Wing
Geo. and Susan	do	343	James W. Stapleford	G. & M. Howland
Glacier	do	195	Benjamin Gifford	A. H. Potter
Gov. Troup	Ship	407	John A. Castino	Edward C. Jones
Henry Taber	Bark	296	Tim. C. Packard	Taber, Gordon & Co
Irving	Schooner	106	George Fox	W. P. Howland
James Maury	Bark	432	John C. Smith	Charles R. Tucker & Co.
Jireh Perry	Ship	316	George F. Smith	Swift & Perry
J. W. Dodge	Schooner	83	John M. Honeywell	Abraham Delano
John P. West	Bark	353	Calvin Manchester	Simeon N. West
Joseph Maxwell	do	263	George Cowie	Taber, Read & Co
Laconia	do	158	John A. Luce	J. P. Knowles, 2d
Lætitia	do	208	Joseph Stowell	J. & W. R. Wing
Lagoda	do	371	—— Swift	Jonathan Bourne, jr
Martha	do	[illegible]	Peter Gartland	Swift & Allen
Merlin	do	246	David E. Allen	William Watkins
Minerva	do	337	Hezekiah Allen	T. Knowles & Co

sailing from American ports—Continued.

Whaling-ground.	Date— Of sailing.	Date— Of arrival.	Result of voyage. Sperm-oil.	Result of voyage. Whale-oil.	Result of voyage. Whalebone.	Remarks.
			Bbls.	*Bbls.*	*Lbs.*	
Hurd's Island..	Aug. 12	June 6, 1868	19	1,926	....	
....do	July 13	May 19, 1870	......	602	3,22	Sent home 1,550 whale and elephant.
Indian Ocean ..	Oct. 13	Oct. 21, 1870	50	......	.....	Joseph Menday, third mate, and three men, drowned at Tristan d'Acunha, November, 1868; sent home 550 sperm; sold to New Bedford 1871.
Atlantic	July 3	....	......	......	.....	Formerly named Michael, under the Portuguese flag; then the Parana, sailing from Sag Harbor; then was an English brig; added again to Sag Harbor 1866; the crew, except the second and third mate and one boat-steerer, deserted at Saint Catharine's 1868; condemned at Panama; refitted and named Sallie French 1868; sent home 180 sperm, 400 whale, 2,200 pounds bone.
Atlantic	July 4	Oct. 25, 1868	257	......	.....	Added 1867; sent home 290 sperm.
Atlantic	Nov. 12	Sept. 14, 1870	147	.....	.....	Sent home 108 sperm.
Hudson's Bay..	June 3	Sept. 26, 1869	......	650	10,100	
Indian Ocean ..	May 12	May 13, 1872	1,075	150	.....	Sent home 203 sperm, 340 whale, 2,500 bone.
Pacific Ocean ..	July 8	June 30, 1872	458	9	305	Sent home 542 sperm, 503 whale; sold to Beverly 1873, for freighting.
Indian Ocean ..	Oct. 6	Aug. 30, 1871	975	1,198	7,460	Sent home 530 whale, 4,100 pounds bone.
Pacific Ocean ..	Oct. 6	Aug. 3, 1872	451	1,015	......	Sent home 476 sperm, 85 whale, 685 pounds bone; sold to New York for merchant-service.
Atlantic	May 12	Dec. 3, 1869	759	43	.....	Sent home 164 sperm.
Pacific Ocean ..	Dec. 15	May 18, 1870	184	1,120	4,235	
....do	Nov. 16	Aug. 4, 1871	1,135	.....	.....	Sent home 256 sperm, 36 humpback.
North Pacific ..	Sept. 9	July 19, 1872	1,309	567	.....	Sent home 524 sperm, 1,421 whale, 5,000 pounds bone.
Atlantic	Dec. 3	....	.....	......	.....	Sent home 92 sperm, 104 whale; put into Norfolk disabled; withdrawn 1870.
....do	Oct. 17	Nov. 7, 1871	690	327	.....	Sent home 88 sperm.
North Pacific ..	July 21	....	.....	......	.....	Sent home 80 sperm; 911 whale, 15,300 pounds bone; lost in the Arctic 1871.
....do	Nov. 10	....	.....	......	.....	Altered from a ship 1868; sent home 351 sperm, 1,354 whale, 1,747 bone; lost in the Arctic 1871.
Atlantic	Oct. 20	June 13, 1871	219	328	.....	
....do	May 12	Sept. 21, 1870	245	.....	.....	Altered from a schooner 1868; sent home 273 sperm.
Indian Ocean ..	June 16	May 10, 1872	1,324	455	......	Sold to Boston 1872.
North Pacific ..	Oct. 23	....	.....	......	.....	Sent home 1,978 whale, 35,903 pounds bone; lost in the Arctic 1871.
Atlantic	June 10	May 13, 1870	.....	Clean	.....	Formerly the Hattie Hunt; built in the Provinces 1866; bought and renamed 1868; sent home 80 sperm, two blackfish.
Indian Ocean ..	Aug. 27	June 4, 1872	1,420	958	......	Altered from a ship 1868; sent home 410 sperm, 80 whale, 500 pounds bone; sold to New York 1873.
Atlantic	May 12	Aug. 28, 1871	273	695	3,149	Sent home 207 sperm.
....do	May 22	....	.....	......	.....	Sent home 146 sperm; sold to Gloucester 1869.
Indian Ocean ..	July 11	June 2, 1871	735	800	3,350	Sent home 2,000 pounds bone.
....do	Sept. 1	Oct. 5, 1871	983	141	......	Bought from Fairhaven 1868; sent home 700 pounds bone.
....do	Oct. 15	May 28, 1871	506	.....	.....	
Pacific Ocean ..	Sept. 22	May 29, 1872	400	500	.....	Sent home 218 sperm, 369 whale.
... do	July 25	June 1, 1873	516	516	.....	Sent home 249 sperm, 2,459 whale, 24,659 pounds bone.
....do	June 16	July 1, 1872	846	54	.....	Sent home 422 sperm, 40 whale.
Indian Ocean ..	June 23	Apr. 3, 1872	1,147	.....	.....	
North Pacific ..	July 7	May 12, 1873	....	2,639	.....	Sent home 339 sperm, 1,573 whale, 12,715 pounds bone; abandoned in the Arctic 1871.

Table showing returns of whaling-vessels

Name of vessel.	Class.	Tonnage.	Captain.	Managing owner or agent.
1868.				
New Bedford, Mass.—Continued.				
Morning Star	Bark	238	George H. Allen	Charles Hitch & Son
Napoleon	do	322	William C. Fuller	Charles Tucker
Ohio	do	205	J. R. Jenney	Loum Snow & Son
Oliver Crocker	do	305	James H. Fisher	James B. Wood & Co
Osceola, 3d	do	140	H. J. Hogan	J. & W. R. Wing
Osmanli	do	292	James M. Williams	Jacob B. Hadley
Ospray	do	173	Andrew R. Hyer	Swift & Allen
Pacific	do	341	James B. Huxford	Swift & Perry
Palmetto	do	215	James B. Robinson	C. R. Tucker & Co
Petrel	Schooner	61	Loring Braley	C. Thatcher & Co
Robt. Morrison	Bark	314	Henry A. Slocum	T. Knowles & Co
Roman	do	358	Jared Jernegan	W. Watkins
Sunbeam	do	255	Thomas N. Fisher	J. & W. R. Wing
Triton	do	264	Moses L. Snell	do
Tropic Bird	do	145	Edgar W. Crapo	W. P. Howland
Wm. Gifford	do	241	Charles A. Veeder	Charles H. Gifford
Fairhaven, Mass.				
Oxford	Brig	91	Nathan Briggs	Damon & Judd
U. D	Schooner	77	Ambrose H. Bates	do
Union	do	66	Owen Fisher	Dexter Jenney
Wash. Freeman	do	96	Loring Braley	Obed F. Hitch
Marion, Mass.				
Admiral Blake	Schooner	84	Arthur H. Hammond	Henry M. Allen
Cohannet	do	83	William C. Hathaway	A. J. Hadley
Express	do	80	—— Handy	Benjamin B. Handy
Graduate	do	58	Allen D. Ryder	H. M. Allen
Herald	Brig	148	John A. Kelley	do
Pocahontas	do	200	Micajah C. Fisher	do
Wm. Wilson	Schooner	92	—— Hathaway	A. J. Hadley
Dartmouth, Mass.				
Rainbow	Schooner	48	Thomas J. Cannon	William Porter, 2d
Westport, Mass.				
Greyhound	Bark	163	John M. Allen	Henry Wilcox
Tisbury, Mass.				
Mercy Taylor	Brig	117	Thomas Foster	J. M. Taber
Nantucket, Mass.				
Bohio	Bark	197	Henry W. Davis	Joseph B. Macy
R. L. Barstow	do	182	William Jernegan	do
Provincetown, Mass.				
A. L. Putnam	Schooner	123	—— Smith	H. & S. Cook & Co
Alcyone	do	92	—— Baldwin	E. & E. K. Cook & Co
Alleghania	do	70	—— Graham	Daniel C. Cook
A. Clifford	do	85	—— Dyer	H. & S. Cook & Co

sailing from American ports—Continued.

Whaling-ground.	Date—Of sailing.	Date—Of arrival.	Result of voyage.—Sperm-oil.	Result of voyage.—Whale-oil.	Result of voyage.—Whalebone.	Remarks.
			Bbls.	*Bbls.*	*Lbs.*	
Pacific Ocean ..	July 1	Aug. 16, 1872	1,074	......	......	Sent home 472 sperm.
....do	June 1	June 11, 1872	1,380	957	......	Sent home 92 sperm, 110 whale, and 570 bone.
Atlantic	July 14	July 8, 1871	350	285	1,477	Sent home 1,109 sperm, 1,273 whale, and 30,581 bone.
North Pacific..	July 1	....	......	......	......	Lost in the Arctic 1871; sent home 433 sperm, 1,953 whale, and 27,320 bone.
Atlantic	Dec. 2	Nov. 25, 1870	125	......	......	Sent home 455 sperm.
Indian Ocean ..	Oct. 6	July 14, 1871	234	711	2,788	Sent home 337 sperm and 675 whale.
Atlantic	May 5	Apr. 30, 1871	303	373	......	Sent home 498 sperm and 320 humpback.
....do	Oct. 20	Apr. 28, 1869	64	1	......	W. S. Church, first mate, died from wound received from a bomb lance Nov. 6, 1869.
Pacific Ocean..	June 10	June 19, 1872	358	561	......	Bought from New York 1868; sent home 119 sperm and 256 whale.
Atlantic	July 13	Oct. 7, 1868	56	1	......	
Indian Ocean ..	July 21	July 15, 1871	443	131	1,239	Sold to Edgartown 1871.
North Pacific..	Oct. 29	....	......	......	......	Altered from a ship 1868; sent home 379 sperm, 2,232 whale, and 30,763 bone; lost in the Arctic 1871.
Pacific Ocean ..	June 4	Aug. 28, 1871	1,390	......	......	
Atlantic	July 21	Nov. 6, 1871	118	1,082	696	Sent home 137 sperm, 200 whale, and 1,100 bone.
....do	Nov. 23	Oct. 17, 1870	21	8	......	Sent home 280 sperm; sold and withdrawn 1871.
Pacific Ocean..	Aug. 1	Feb. 7, 1873	886	35	......	Withdrawn 1873.
Cumberl'd Inlet	July 20	....	......	......	......	Lost in Cumberland Inlet 1869.
Atlantic	Nov. 6	....	......	......	......	Sent home 190 sperm; condemned and sold at Barbadoes, January, 1870.
....do	Sept. 17	Sept. 26, 1869	90	......	......	Bought from Provincetown 1868; sold to New Bedford 1870.
....do	Nov. 23	Sept. 30, 1870	21	312	......	Sent home 137 sperm; sold to Thomaston, Me., for freighting 1871.
Atlantic	Dec. 3	Mar. 13, 1871	......	361	760	Sent home 50 sperm and 221 whale; withdrawn for freighting 1871.
... do	May 12	Oct. 8, 1868	......	7	......	
....do	May 20	Oct. 12, 1868	17	3	......	Added 1868.
....do	May 12	Sept. 21, 1868	51	......	......	Do.
....do	Dec. 18	July 27, 1870	270	......	......	Sent home 48 sperm, 442 whale, and 1,748 bone; withdrawn for merchant-service 1871.
....do	July 16	....	......	......	......	Bought from New Bedford 1868; condemned at Barbadoes, October, 1870; sent home 150 sperm.
....do	May 22	Aug. 28, 1868	162	......	......	
Atlantic	May 15	Sept. 25, 1868	75	......	......	
Atlantic	May 27	May 15, 1871	634	40	400	
Atlantic	Dec. 3	Aug. 3, 1870	250	150	......	Sent home 180 sperm and 238 whale; sold to New York 1871.
Pacific Ocean ..	July 12	....	......	......	......	Bought from New York 1868; sold at Callao, January, 1872.
....do	Dec. 19	....	430	650	......	Sold at Callao, February, 1873.
Atlantic	Aug. 17	Sept. 9, 1869	45	50	......	Withdrawn 1869.
Indian Ocean ..	Oct. 20	June 8, 1871	238	......	......	Sent home 235 sperm; withdrawn 1871.
Atlantic	Jan. 24	Aug. 28, 1868	145	6	......	
....do	Dec. 21	Sept. —, 1870	73	236	......	Withdrawn 1870.

Table showing returns of whaling-vessels

Name of vessel.	Class.	Tonnage.	Captain.	Managing owner or agent.
1868.				
Provincetown, Mass.—Continued.				
Albert Clarence	Schooner	101	—— Bourne	J. Freeman
Allie B. Dyer	do		Orlando J. Tripp	
Ada M. Dyer	do	87	—— Dyer	Alfred Cook
B. F. Sparks	do	92	—— Cook	Stephen Cook
Carrie W. Clark	do	116	William Clark, jr	Atkins Nickerson
C. H. Cook	do	114	—— Crowell	Stephen Cook
Chas. A. Higgins	do	118	N. Y. Higgins	Union Wharf Company
D. A. Small	Brig	119	Josiah Ryder	David A. Small
E. B. Conwell	Schooner	91	—— Cann	David Conwell
E. Gerry	do	71	—— Emery	Union Wharf Company
Ellen Rizpah	do	67	—— White	Stephen Cook
Emma F. Lewis	do	85	—— Powe	B. A. Lewis & Co
Estella	do	70	—— Higgins	J. E. & G. Bowley
Express	do	70	—— Merithew	E. & E. K. Cook
G. W. Lewis	do	65	—— Stid	Joshua Lewis
Grace Lothrop		141	John S. Smith	Union Wharf Company
H. M. Simmons	Schooner	116	—— Cook	Stephen Cook
John A. Lewis	do	80	—— Chapman	B. A. Lewis & Co
Lizzie J. Bigelow	Brig	130	Josiah Cook	do
L. P. Simmons	Schooner	90	—— Dunham	J. E. & G. Bowley
Mary E. Nason	do	108	H. Sparks	D. Conwell
Mary G. Curren	do	102	—— Fisher	Freeman & Hilliard
M. E. Simmons	do	105	—— Gellett	E. & E. K. Cook & Co
N. F. Putnam	do	87	—— Dyer	H. & S. Cook
Olive Clark	do	64	—— Atkins	D. Conwell
Sassacus	do	110	—— Freeman	E. & E. K. Cook & Co
S. R. Soper	do	88	—— Eldridge	Robert Soper
V. Doane	do	63	—— Young	H. & S. Cook
Winged Racer	do	80	—— Rich —— Graham	D. Conwell
Boston, Mass.				
Carrie Jones	Schooner	97	—— Cornell	
F. H. Moore	Brig	107	—— Wood	Robert Soper & Son
S. N. Smith	Schooner	108	—— Rounseville	Heman Smith
Thriver	do	69	—— Cook	R. Soper & Son
Wm. Martin	do	92	—— Fisher	H. Smith
Salem, Mass.				
Falcon	Brig	126	—— Richmond	John C. Osgood
Newburyport, Mass.				
Georgia	Schooner	127	—— Bradbury	Sumner, Swasey & Co
Life Boat	do	88	—— Caton	do
Groton, Conn.				
Cornelia	Schooner	148	—— Baker	Ebenezer Morgan
New London, Conn.				
E. B. Phillips	Bark	144	C. B. Chapell	Williams & Haven
George and Mary	do	105	—— Newbury	Williams & Barns
Georgiana	Brig	128	A. J. Parsons	Williams & Haven
Golden West	Schooner	144	—— Church	Lawrence & Co

sailing from American ports—Continued.

Whaling-ground.	Date—Of sailing.	Date—Of arrival.	Result of voyage.—Sperm-oil.	Result of voyage.—Whale-oil.	Result of voyage.—Whalebone.	Remarks.
			Bbls.	*Bbls.*	*Lbs.*	
Atlantic	Nov. 28	Nov. 4, 1870	107	......	......	Withdrawn 1870.
....do	Aug. 4	No report	......	......	......	Withdrawn 1871; sent home 70 sperm.
....do	Dec. 21	Sept. 14, 1869	......	185	......	
....do	July 3	....	......	......	......	Added 1868; sent home 150 sperm and 300 whale; wrecked on Gay Head 1869.
....do	May 5	June 18, 1869	129	356	......	Built at East Boston 1868; sent home 350 sperm.
....do	June 3	Oct. 25, 1868	140	......	......	
....do	June 15	Aug. 27, 1870	80	200	......	Built at Duxbury 1868; sent home 56 sperm; withdrawn 1870.
....do	Dec. 21	Sept. —, 1870	206	1	......	Built at Provincetown 1868.
....do	Oct. 6	Sept. 2, 1869	220	......	......	
....do	Mar. 19	July 10, 1869	......	170	......	Sent home 53 sperm.
....do	Jan. 17	Sept. 15, 1868	77	58	......	
	Dec. —	Sept. 9, 1869	20	180	......	
....do	Apr. 29	Sept. 17, 1869	110	30	......	Sent home 90 humpback; withdrawn 1869.
....do	Nov. 14	Aug. 5, 1870	33	34	......	Sold out 1870.
....do	Oct. 27	July 26, 1870	19	28	......	Withdrawn 1870.
....do	May 27	Aug. 31, 1869	85	95	......	Withdrawn 1870; sent home 18 sperm.
....do	June 10	July 26, 1870	71	87	......	Built at Duxbury in 1868; sent home 203 sperm; withdrawn 1870.
....do	June 19	Aug. 31, 1870	31	300	......	Sent home 190 whale; withdrawn 1870.
....do	Nov. 13	June 2, 1870	......	184	......	Withdrawn for the cod-fishery 1870.
....do	July 11	Nov. —, 1871	150	......	......	Built at Hanover in 1868; sent home 20 sperm; withdrawn 1871.
....do	May 20	July 20, 1870	53	123	......	Withdrawn 1870; sold to New York 1872.
Pacific Ocean	June 1	May 11, 1871	80	300	......	First whaler for the Pacific from Provincetown; withdrawn 1871; sent home 75 sperm; 430 humpback.
Atlantic	May 27	Oct. 4, 1869	230	......	......	
....do	July 23	Oct. 4, 1869	138	11	......	
....do	Nov. 12	July 27, 1869	130	300	......	
....do	Dec. —	June 25, 1869	......	159	......	Withdrawn 1870.
....do	Jan. 18	June 2, 1869	......	300	......	Sent home 410 sperm; 82 whale.
....do	Sept. 28	....	......	......	......	Sent home 90 sperm; lost on Bird Island May 25, 1870; had 150 sperm; saved 120.
....do	Jan. 16	Sept. 4, 1868	35	184	......	Withdrawn for mackerel-fishery 1868.
....do	Jan. 24	Sept. 6, 1868	50	40	....	Withdrawn 1869.
	Dec. —	Sept. 14, 1869	......	100	....	
Atlantic	Oct. 1	Sept. 9, 1869	275	......	......	Added 1868.
....do	May 5	Aug. 29, 1870	180	27	......	Added 1868; sent home 48 sperm.
....do	Feb. 29	....	......	......	......	Lost August 28, 1869; the captain's wife, 2 children, first and second mates, boatsteerers, and 13 of the crew lost; had 180 sperm; sent home 65 sperm.
....do	Nov. 2	Aug. 29, 1869	100	100	......	
....do	Dec. 3	Oct. 13, 1869	170	......	......	
Atlantic	June 9	May 9, 1871	471	4	......	Sent home 25 sperm; sold to Boston 1871.
Atlantic	Nov. 23	Sept. 28, 1869	93	......	......	Sold to Brewer, Me., 1869.
....do	Dec. 21	Aug. 6, 1870	127	166	......	Withdrawn 1870.
Cum. Inlet	May 26	Sept. 23, 1869	......	143	1,765	Withdrawn 1870; Groton out of the business.
Indian Ocean	Aug. 22	May 16, 1871	163	273	......	Bought from Boston 1868; Captain Chapell died at St. Helena October 20, 1870; sent home 219 sperm; shipped 2,000 gallons sperm to London from St. John's, N. F.; sold to Boston 1874.
Cum. Inlet	May 16	Sept. 17, 1869	......	450	8,000	
....do	Aug. 5	....	......	......	......	Supposed to be lost, with all on board, 1868.
Desolation Isld.	June 30	Apr. 18, 1871	......	724	......	Sent home 125 elephant.

Table showing returns of whaling-vessels

Name of vessel.	Class.	Tonnage.	Captain.	Managing owner or agent.
1868.				
New London, Conn.—Continued.				
Helen F	Schooner	108	—— Spicer	Williams & Haven
J. D. Thompson	Bark	432	—— Allen	Williams & Barns
Roman	Ship	350	—— Church	Richard H. Chapell
S. B. Howes	Schooner	101	—— Avery	Williams & Haven
Sag Harbor, N. Y.				
Concordia	Bark	217	—— Dunbar	O. R. Wade
Myra	Brig	116	—— Babcock	H. & S. French
New York, N. Y.				
A. B. Cook	Brig	155	Wells S. Field	I. McKim Cook
Endeavour	Bark	252	Henry P. Taber	Lorenzo Peirce
Minnesota	do	243	Clothier Peirce	do
Ocean Steed	do	258	G. B. Borden	do
San Francisco, Cal.				
Florida	Ship	470	—— Fraser	Sherwood & Co
1869.				
New Bedford, Mass.				
Adeline	Ship	353	Alonzo J. Marvin	C. R. Tucker & Co
Annie Ann	Bark	220	John C. Pierce	John W. Pierce
Ansel Gibbs	do	303	Charles Stetson	Jonathan Bourne, jr
Desdemona	do	236	Samuel F. Davis	G. & M. Howland
Edward Everett	do	187	Hubert A. White	Gideon Allen & Son
E. Corning	do	225	John W. Cornell	Swift & Perry
Eliza	do	296	John C. Diamond	J. Bourne, jr
Eugenia	do	315	Daniel B. Nye	Swift & Allen
Fanny	do	391	Lewis W. Williams	do
Florida	Ship	...	N. P. Gray	
George	Bark	259	Abraham Osborn	Gideon Allen & Son
Globe	do	200	Alexander A. Tripp	Charles Tucker
Hecla	do	160	Frederick H. Smith	Thomas Knowles & Co
Herald	do	300	John R. Sturgis	Zenas L. Adams
James Arnold	Ship	346	William P. Briggs	Taber, Gordon & Co
Java	Bark	295	Benjamin Manter	G. & M. Howland
John Wells	do	357	Aaron Dean	William O. Brownell
Lancer	do	295	William J. Macy	Joshua Richmond & Son
Leonidas	do	98	A. L. Stickney	David B. Kempton
Live Oak	do	448	John A. Beckerman	Charles S. Randall
Louisa	do	303	George W. Slocum	Swift & Allen
Lydia	do	329	Lysander W. Gifford	Edmund Maxfield
Marcella	do	166	Owen H. Tilton	C. R. Tucker & Co
Mars	do	256	—— Allen	Gifford & Cummings
Mercury	do	311	Tristram P. Ripley	William Phillips & Son
Midas	do	313	Charles Hamill	W. O. Brownell
Milton	Ship	373	Thomas Wilson	Taber, Gordon & Co

sailing from American ports—Continued.

Whaling-ground.	Date— Of sailing.	Date— Of arrival.	Result of voyage. Sperm-oil.	Result of voyage. Whale-oil.	Result of voyage. Whalebone.	Remarks.
			Bbls.	*Bbls.*	*Lbs.*	
Cum. Inlet.....	June 20	Out, 1877....	......	......	......	Had taken at last report 1,450 whale, 13,600 pounds bone.
North Pacific ..	June 13	....	......	......	......	Sent home 82 sperm, 2,774 whale, 31,829 pounds bone; lost in the Arctic 1871.
Desolation Isld.	Aug. 13	May 18, 1869	......	1,617	693	
Cum. Inlet.....	June 20	Nov. 6, 1869	Clean	......	......	
Cum. Inlet.....	Apr. 20	Oct. 7, 1869	116	200	2,930	Sent home 121 sperm; sold to New London 1870.
Pacific Ocean ..	Aug. 24	Apr. 25, 1871	235	310	......	Sent home 325 sperm; 339 whale.
Pacific Ocean ..	Aug. 5	....	......	......	......	Belongs to parties in Panama; fitted from New Bedford 1868; sailed under American flag; lost on Point Mangales, June 11, 1873; sent home 700 sperm, 450 whale.
....do	Nov. 14	Oct. 2, 1870	760	475	......	Bought from New Bedford 1868.
Indian Ocean ..	June 25	June 13, 1872	1,030	130	......	Third mate, Mr. Greene, died Nov. 9, 1869; sent home 146 sperm; withdrawn 1873.
Atlantic	Apr. 27	Nov. 28, 1869	428	17	......	Added 1868 from New Bedford; transferred to New Bedford 1870; took, in all, 1,170 sperm, 20 whale.
North Pacific ..	Dec. 7	Nov. 7, 1869	45	1,600	20,000	Sailed 1870 for the Arctic; lost there 1871.
Pacific Ocean ..	Sept. 21	July 1, 1874	792	746	......	Sent home 570 sperm, 1,500 pounds bone; sold to Manchester, Mass., 1874.
....do	June 24	....	......	......	......	Added 1869; sent home 495 sperm; condemned at Mauritius in November, 1871.
Atlantic	Oct. 20	May 12, 1870	109	......	......	
....do	July 6	Aug. 1, 1872	1,022	9	......	Sent home 150 whale, 800 pounds bone.
Pacific Ocean ..	Nov. 4	May 12, 1873	311	521	......	
Atlantic	Apr. 19	Sept. 4, 1870	461	......	......	Sent home 264 sperm.
Pacific Ocean ..	Aug. 14	Sept. 24, 1873	624	162	......	Joseph Caton, second mate, killed while cutting in 1871.
North Pacific ..	Sept. 14	....	......	......	......	Sent home 175 sperm, 390 whale, 6,563 lbs. bone; lost in the Arctic 1871.
....do	July 21	....	......	......	......	Lost in the Arctic 1871.
....	May —	....	......	......	......	Condemned at Mauritius, September, 1869; sent home 658 whale.
Pacific Ocean ..	Aug. 10	....	......	......	......	Lost in the Arctic 1871.
Atlantic	Mar. 6	May 20, 1872	115	875	......	Sent home 533 sperm; sold to Gloucester 1872.
Indian Ocean ..	Aug. 31	....	......	......	......	Sent home 8 sperm; lost on Bird Island Dec. 29, 1870; had 530 sperm, saved 28.
....	Aug. 14	Aug. 23, 1872	1,180	80	300	Altered from a ship 1869; sold to London 1873.
Pacific Ocean ..	Oct. 12	Dec. 4, 1873	600	860	......	Sent home 370 sperm, 712 whale, 3,462 bone.
Atlantic	June 9	June 30, 1872	418	513	1,678	Sent home 146 sperm.
North Pacific ..	Nov. 9	....	......	......	......	Sent home 1,208 whale, 17,148 pounds bone; lost in the Arctic 1871.
Indian Ocean ..	Apr. 22	Apr. 25, 1873	1,560	38	150	Sent home 83 sperm; sold to Mount Sinai, Long Island, 1874.
Atlantic	Oct. 2	June 15, 1872	95	288	......	Sent home 105 sperm, 108 whale.
Indian Ocean ..	June 22	June 6, 1874	105	1,257	......	Transferred from the merchant-service in 1869; formerly the Hobomok; sent home 1,071 sperm, 1,515 whale; sold to St. Johns, N. B., for merchant-service, 1874.
....do	May 4	June 23, 1874	55	1,138	......	Sent home 1,170 sperm, 757 whale, 25,352 pounds bone.
Pacific Ocean ..	July 14	Aug. 1, 1873	288	360	......	William Michael, fourth mate, died Nov., 1871; sent home 803 whale, 1,638 bone.
Atlantic	Nov. 25	June 28, 1873	531	384	......	Sent home 317 sperm.
Pacific Ocean ..	Jan. 3	May 19, 1873	1,440	70	600	Sent home 479 sperm.
Indian Ocean ..	May 26	Nov. 1, 1872	1,031	481	1,028	Sent home 269 sperm, 4 whale.
North Pacific ..	June 22	June 8, 1874	39	531	......	Sent home 446 sperm, 2,868 whale, 42,975 pounds bone.
Pacific Ocean ..	Oct. 21	June 11, 1873	790	950	......	Mr. Porter, second mate, killed by a whale October 5, 1872; sent home 1,159 sperm, 29 whale, 407 pounds bone.

Table showing returns of whaling-vessels

Name of vessel.	Class.	Tonnage.	Captain.	Managing owner or agent.
1869.				
New Bedford, Mass.—Continued.				
Milwood	Bark	216	Edwin W. White	G. Allen & Son
Nautilus	do	277	George A. Smith	do
Navy	do	385	George F. Bouldry	James B. Wood & Co
Orray Taft	do	134	M. V. B. Howland	Andrew H. Potter
Pacific	do	341	William Allen	Swift & Perry
Pioneer	do	228	James S. Hazard	Nathaniel T. Gifford
President	do	257	E. C. Almy	Taber, Read & Co
President, 2d	do	123	George M. Seabury	Edmund Maxfield
Sea Ranger	do	273	Charles E. Allen	I. H. Bartlett & Sons
Seneca	do	328	Edmund Kelley	Loum Snow & Son
Spartan	do	333	Edwin R. Osgood	David B. Kempton
Stamboul	do	260	William H. Mitchell	Charles Hitch & Son
Swallow	do	326	Willard W. Ryder	William Watkins
Tamerlane	do	372	Thomas E. Fordham	T. Knowles & Co
Thomas Dickason	do	461	Valentine Lewis	G. & M. Howland
Three Brothers	Ship	357	James M. Witherell	C. R. Tucker & Co
Wave	Bark	150	B. A. Briggs	T. Knowles & Co
Fairhaven, Mass.				
A. Lawrence	Bark	160	Hiram J. Cleveland	James I. Church
Crowninshield	do	257	John P. Praro	Terry & Chase
Ellen Rodman	Schooner	73	Jonathan Jenney	Tucker Damon, jr
Selah	Bark	166	G. B. Howes	Benjamin H. Chase
Marion, Mass.				
Cohannet	Schooner	83	Obed Delano	A. J. Hadley
Express	do	80	Benjamin B. Handy	Benjamin B. Handy
Graduate	do	58	Rufus L. Savery	Henry M. Allen
Wm. Wilson	do	92	William C. Hathaway	A. J. Hadley
Dartmouth, Mass.				
Cape Horn Pigeon	Bark	212	G. I. F. Hazard	William Potter, 2d
Matilda Sears	do	231	William D. Gifford	do
Rainbow	Schooner	48	Thomas J. Cannon	do
Westport, Mass.				
Janet	Bark	154	George N. Macy	Henry Wilcox
Mattapoisett	do	110	Weston S. Tripp	Henry Smith
Mermaid	do	27[illegible]	John Horan	Andrew Hicks
Sea Fox	do	166	Samuel T. Braley	do
Edgartown, Mass.				
Almira	Ship	310	—— Marchant	Samuel Osborn, jr
Champion	do	367	—— Pease	Grafton N. Collins
Nantucket, Mass.				
Abby Bradford	Schooner	114	John Murray	Joseph B. Macy
E. H. Adams	Brig	107	Zenas M. Coleman	Freeman E. Adams
Oak	Bark	167	William B. Thompson	do

sailing from American ports—Continued.

Whaling-ground.	Date—Of sailing.	Date—Of arrival.	Result of voyage.—Sperm-oil.	Result of voyage.—Whale-oil.	Result of voyage.—Whalebone.	Remarks.
			Bbls.	*Bbls.*	*Lbs.*	
Cum. Inlet....	Apr. 6	Oct. 6, 1870	.....	99	15, 900	Sent home 220 sperm.
Pacific Ocean ..	Oct. 6	May 22, 1874	.....	562	6, 850	Sent home 154 sperm, 2,205 whale, 7,200 pounds bone.
North Pacific ..	Oct. 7	....	.....	......	......	Sent home 433 sperm, 702 whale, 10,579 lbs. bone; lost in the Arctic 1871.
Atlantic	May 19	May 20, 1872	642	......	.....	
....do	May 25	Aug. 9, 1870	713	10	.....	
....do	Aug. 6	Dec. 1, 1872	306	179	900	Held by United States consul at Mauritius several months; released 1872; sent home 232 sperm.
Atlantic & Ind.	Aug. 11	Aug. 31, 1872	636	657	2, 660	Sent home 387 sperm, 135 whale, 2,500 bone.
Atlantic	Apr. 13	Sept. 15, 1871	378	......	......	Sent home 43 sperm.
Pacific Ocean ..	Oct. 19	May 17, 1874	754	176	......	Sent home 456 sperm.
North Pacific ..	Oct. 16	....	.....	.....	.....	Bought from Baltimore 1869; sent home 82 sperm, 1,251 whale; lost in the Arctic 1871.
Pacific Ocean ..	July 10	Apr. 28, 1872	820	.....	.....	
Indian Ocean ..	Aug. 31	June 1, 1873	619	148	737	Sent home 50 sperm, 350 whale, 2,500 bone.
....do	June 29	June 29, 1873	1, 257	133	.....	Altered from a ship 1869; sent home 1,100 pounds bone; sold to Boston 1873, for merchant-service.
Pacific Ocean ..	July 20	June 5, 1873	406	568	......	Sent home 348 sperm; 3,500 pounds bone.
North Pacific ..	Nov. 2	....	.....	......	......	Altered from a ship 1869; sent home 102 sperm, 1.056 whale, 18,047 pounds bone; lost in the A ctic 1871.
Pacific Ocean ..	Oct. 12	Aug. 18, 1873	1, 561	8	......	Sold to New York 1873.
Atlantic	June 1	Dec. 1, 1870	......	524	....	Sent home 348 sperm.
Atlantic	June 29	Apr. 25, 1872	113	7	......	Withdrawn 1872 for freighting; sent home 355 sperm; sold to New Bedford 1874.
Pacific Ocean ..	May 10	....	......	......	......	Bought from Boston 1869; sent home 719 sperm; condemned and sold at Bermudas August 28, 1873; oil (600 sperm and 100 whale) shipped home; Captain Praro received Order of the Rose from Emperor of Brazil for saving crew of Brazilian brig Damao.
Atlantic	Oct. 20	Sept. 27, 1870	191	5	.....	
Pacific Ocean ..	July 28	....	.....	.....	......	Sent home 833 sperm, 6 whale; condemned and sold at Panama June 6, 1873.
Atlantic	May 18	Sept. 19, 1869	85	6	.....	
....do	May 19	June 15, 1870	80	......	......	Sent home 44 sperm; sold to Provincetown 1871.
....do	May 18	....	.....	......	......	Lost at sea 1869; 5 men lost.
....do	May 18	Oct. 3, 1869	85	......	......	
Atlantic	June 29	July 11, 1872	916	90	868	Captain Hazard came home 1871; sent home 330 sperm, 500 bone.
Pacific Ocean ..	Aug. 2	June 11, 1873	752	39	......	Sent home 5[illegible]0 sperm; 664 whale.
Atlantic	May 4	Aug. 13 1870	Clean	......	......	Withdrawn for mackerel-fishery 1871.
Indian Ocean ..	Nov. 6	May 13, 1873	501	......	......	Sold to New Bedford 1874.
Atlantic	Apr. 22	Nov. 2, 1870	212	7	......	
Indian Ocean ..	July 3	June 1, 1873	1, 170	......	......	
....do	Nov. 25	Feb. 14, 1871	32	......	......	
North Pacific ..	Aug. 5	....	.....	......	......	Sent home 185 sperm; stove by ice and lost in Arctic 1870; had on board 400 whale.
....do	Aug. 14	....	.....	......	......	Sent home 37 sperm, 934 whale, 365 pounds bone; lost in the Arctic 1871.
Atlantic	May 1[illegible]	Oct. 24, 1869	500	10	......	Sold to New Bedford.
....do	Mar. 31	June 14, 1870	550	10	......	Do.
Pacific Ocean ..	Nov. 16	....	......	......	......	Sold at Panama 1872; sent home 60 sperm 450 whale; Nantucket's last whaler.

Table showing returns of whaling-vessels

Name of vessel.	Class.	Tonnage.	Captain.	Managing owner or agent.
1869.				
Provincetown, Mass.				
Agate	Schooner	81	—— Atkins	W. A. Atkins
Alexander	do	75	—— Ryder	Judah Gifford
Alleghania	do	70	—— Fisher	Daniel C. Cook
Arizona	do	79	—— Bell	Stephen Cook
Allie B. Dyer	do	87	—— Tripp	David Conwell
Carrie W. Clark	do	116	—— Dyer	Atkins Nickerson
Cetacean	do	81	—— Atkins	Union Wharf Company
C. H. Cook	do	114	—— Cowell	Stephen Cook
C. L. Sparks	do	96	—— Roberts	D. Conwell
Eleanor B. Conwell	do	91	—— Cannon	do
E. H. Hatfield	do	89	—— Burch	E. & E. K. Cook & Co
G. H. Phillips	do	107	—— Taylor	S. Cook
J. H. Collins	do	50	—— Ryder	David A. Small
Mary D. Leach	do	119	—— Atwood	Elisha M. Dyer
Montezuma	do	60	—— Nye	Freeman & Hilliard
N. F. Putnam	do	87	—— Atkins	H. & S. Cook & Co
N. J. Knight	do	70	—— Dyer	D. Conwell
O. M. Remington	do	139		Elisha M. Dyer
Rising Sun	do	69	—— Freeman	Atkins Nickerson
Sassacus	do	110	—— Leach	E. & E. K. Cook & Co
V. H. Hill	Brig	126	—— Freeman	J. E. & G. Bowley
Walter Irvin	Schooner	90	—— Lair	Amos Nickerson
Watchman	do	84	—— Snow	Isaiah Gifford
Boston, Mass.				
Carrie Jones	Schooner	97	—— Cornell	E. H. Atwood
Heman Smith	Brig	123	—— Martin	Heman Smith
Rosa Baker	do	108	—— Gifford	do
Sarah E. Lewis	Schooner	96	—— Payne	do
Thriver	do	69	—— Cook	Robert Soper & Son
Newburyport, Mass.				
Hannah Grant	Schooner	71	—— Chadwick	Sumner, Swasey & Co
Beverly, Mass.				
Eschol	Brig	143	—— Cottle	F. W. Choate
New London, Conn.				
Charles Colgate	Schooner	250	—— Norie	Lawrence & Co
Era	do	188	—— Tyson	Williams & Barns
Francis Allyn	do	107	R. H. Glass	Richard H. Chapell
Franklin	do	119	—— Chapell	do
Isabella	Brig	192	—— Bailey	do
Odd Fellow	Bark	239		
Quickstep	Schooner	105	—— Allen	Williams & Barns
Roman	Ship	350	—— Williams	R. A. Chapell
New York, N. Y.				
Addison	Bark	385	Peleg Cornell	Lorenzo Peirce
San Francisco, Cal				
Florida	Ship	470	—— Frazer	Sherwood & Co
Menschikoff	do	223		Hutchinson, Kohl & Co
Massachusetts	do	351	—— Cooty	Moore & Co
Victoria	Brig	149	—— Redfield	
1870.				
New Bedford, Mass.				
Addison	Bark	385	James G. Sinclair	Lorenzo Peirce

sailing from American ports—Continued.

Whaling-ground.	Date—		Result of voyage.			Remarks.
	Of sailing.	Of arrival.	Sperm-oil.	Whale-oil.	Whalebone.	
			Bbls.	*Bbls.*	*Lbs.*	
Atlantic	Feb. 8	July 15, 1870	96	136	....	Added 1868; sent home 167 humpback.
....do	May 24	Aug. 24, 1869	....	80	.....	Added 1869; withdrawn 1870.
....do	Jan. 15	Sept. 1, 1869	40	100	.....	
....do	Dec. 14	Sept. 9, 1870	182	69	.....	
....do	Apr. 16	Aug. 27, 1870	132	224	.....	
....do	July 31	Aug. 5, 1870	350	40	.....	Sent home 70 sperm; withdrawn 1870.
....do	Jan. 6	Sept. 1, 1870	30	130	.....	Sent home 100 humpback; withdrawn 1870.
....do	Apr. 5	July 30, 1870	30	5	.....	Sent home 45 sperm; withdrawn 1870.
....do	Mar. 16	Sept. 1, 1870	174	176	.....	
....do	Nov. 30	Aug. 25, 1871	35	4	.....	Sent home 122 sperm; withdrawn 1872.
....do	Apr. 29	Aug. 27, 1870	225	15	.....	Sent home 24 sperm; withdrawn 1870.
....do	Jan. 6	July 1, 1870	49	382	.....	Sent home 30 sperm; 140 humpback.
....do	Jan. 19	Aug. 24, 1869	30	40	.....	Withdrawn 1869.
....do	Jan. 19	Sept. 25, 1870	120	......	.....	Withdrawn 1870; sent home 62 sperm.
....do ...... {	Jan. 20	Sept. 19, 1869	140	30	.....	
	Nov. 9	Sept 19, 1870	....	140	.....	
....do	....	No report ..	....	......	.....	Withdrawn 1870.
....do	Mar. 15	Sept. —, 1870	50	150	.....	Withdrawn 1871; sent home 8 sperm, 80 whale.
....do	Nov. 1	Sept. 2, 1869	250	40	.....	
....do	Jan. 6	Sept. 14, 1869	60	100	.....	
....do	June 24	Sept. 30, 1869	23	......	.....	Withdrawn 1870.
....do	May 10	Oct. 14, 1870	75	......	.....	Do.
....do	Feb. 24	Sept. 1, 1870	337	2	.....	Sold to New York 1871.
....do	Jan. 7	Sept. 9, 1869	....	150	.....	Witndrawn 1870.
Atlantic	Dec. —	Aug. 30, 1870	125	......	.....	Withdrawn 1870.
....do	Aug. 28	Oct. 10, 1870	500	30	.....	
....do	Oct. 1	Aug. 25, 1871	263	......	....	Sent home 70 sperm.
....do	Dec. 24	June 24, 1871	50	55	.....	Sent home 39 sperm.
....do	Dec. 29	Aug. 29, 1869	100	100	....	
Atlantic	Apr. 28	Aug. 31, 1870	54	14	.....	Sent home 47 sperm; withdrawn 1870; Newburyport out of the business.
Atlantic	May 7	Sept. 30, 1870	100	......	....	
Desolation Isl'd	June 13	Apr. 18, 1871	....	1, 114	......	
Cum. Inlet	May 11	Oct. 5, 1870	....	533	5, 400	H. Griswold, first mate, died 1869.
Indian Ocean ..	Aug. 21	Apr. 27, 1870	....	780	......	Built at Duxbury 1869.
Cum. Inlet	May 18	Oct. 5, 1870	....	473	8, 418	
....do	Apr. 14	Oct. 15, 1870	....	527	6, 587	
....	....	....	....	.....	......	Bought from Sag Harbor 1869; lost at Little Placentea August, 1869.
Cum. Inlet	May 18	....	.....	....	....	Lost 1870.
Desolation Isl'd	June 25	May 23, 1870	39	2, 188	1, 681	
Atlantic	Apr. 22	....	....	.....	.....	Transferred to New Bedford 1870, which see.
Pacific Ocean ..	Dec. 11	Nov. 5, 1870	.....	1, 900	30, 000	
....do	....	Nov. 3, 1870	....	800	15, 000	
....do	Dec. 23	Nov. 3, 1870	....	1, 050	8, 500	
....do	....	....	.....	.....	.....	Added 1869; lost in the Arctic 1871.
Pacific Ocean ..	May 20	Apr. 19, 1874	96	639	3, 550	Transferred from New York 1870; built at Philadelphia 1816; withdrawn 1874; lost on Fayal, freighting, 1875; sent home 180 sperm, 550 pounds bone.

Table showing returns of whaling-vessels

Name of vessel.	Class.	Tonnage.	Captain.	Managing owner or agent.
1870.				
New Bedford, Mass.—Continued.				
Adeline Gibbs	Bark	327	Jacob L. Cleaveland. Fred'k J. Forman	Jonathan Bourne, jr.
Alfred Gibbs	do	347	Edward E. Jennings	Dennis Wood
Ansel Gibbs	do	303	Elnathan B. Fisher	J. Bourne, jr
Avola	do	230	Zenas E. Bourne	John P. Knowles, 2d
Awashonks	do	380	Ariel Norton	J. & W. R. Wing
Canton	Ship	239	J. G. Lapham	Charles R. Tucker & Co
Cicero	Bark	226	Henry Clay	Loum Snow & Son
Commodore Morris	Ship	338	Gilbert B. Borden	Swift & Perry
Contest	do	341	Leander C. Owen	do
Gazelle	Bark	273	David R. Gifford	Edward C. Jones
Gay Head	Ship	300	William H. Kelley	James B. Wood & Co.
George Howland	Bark	361	James K. Knowles	G. & M. Howland
Hadley	do	163	John M. Soule	Andrew H. Potter
Irving	Schooner	106	Charles F. Crapo	William P. Howland
John Carver	Bark	319	Jacob L. Howland	Thomas Knowles & Co.
John Dawson	do	173	Asaph S. Wicks	J. & W. R. Wing
Massachusetts	do	356	West Mitchell	Swift & Allen
Mary and Susan	do	327	A. O. Herendeen	T. Knowles & Co
Niger	Ship	412	Charles Grant	Taber, Gordon & Co
Ocean Steed	Bark	258	Elisha E. Russell	L. Peirce
Oriole	do	280	H. S. Hayes	E. C. Jones
Orlando	do	190	Horace Montross	Charles Hitch & Sons
Osceola, 2d	do	158	Jonathan Chase	J. & W. R. Wing
Pacific	do	341	George Taber	Swift & Perry
Petrel	Schooner	61	John W. Sherman	Josiah W. Bonney
Progress	Bark	358	James Dowden	William O. Brownell
Rainbow	do	351	George Gray	Charles H. Gifford
Reindeer	Ship	332	B. F. Loveland	Edward W. Howland
Roscoe	Bark	313	Edward D. Lewis	Loum Snow & Co
Robert Edwards	Ship		Thomas F. Pease	
Rousseau	Bark	305	James Hyland	G. & M. Howland
Stafford	do	156	George W. J. Moulton	J. & W. R. Wing
Starlight	Brig	141	Reuben W. Crapo	Charles S. Randall
Union	Schooner	66	Owen Fisher	Hiram Webb
Vigilant	Bark	215	Otis F. Thatcher	William Watkins
Xantho	do	206	James W. Lavers	J. & W. R. Wing
Fairhaven, Mass.				
Ellen Rodman	Schooner	73	Jonathan Jenney	Tucker Damon, jr
George J. Jones	do	126	Jaser M. Ears	do
William and Henry	Bark	234	Daniel B. Green	Isaiah F. Terry
Marion, Mass.				
Cohannet	Schooner	83	James T. Wittet	Amos J. Hadley
William Wilson	do	92	—— Hathaway	do

sailing from American ports—Continued.

Whaling-ground.	Date—		Result of voyage.			Remarks.
	Of sailing.	Of arrival.	Sperm-oil.	Whale-oil.	Whalebone.	
			Bbls.	*Bbls.*	*Lbs.*	
Indian Ocean	Sept. 1 Oct. 19	Sept. 26, 1870 May 22, 1875	600	200	......	Captain Cleaveland died, and the vessel was damaged in a gale.
Pacific Ocean ..	May 25	July 20, 1873	819	209	......	Sent home 567 sperm, 1,700 pounds bone; sold to New York 1873.
Hudson's Bay ..	June 21	Oct. 6, 1871	......	1,340	22,040	
Pacific and Ind.	Dec. 7	Feb. 13, 1874	986	15	......	Sent home 494 sperm.
North Pacific ..	Oct. 19	....	......	......	......	Lost in the Arctic 1871.
Indian Ocean ..	Oct. 19	Sept. 22, 1874	991	4	......	
Atlantic	May 9	Oct. 24, 1873	284	85	......	J. F. Mandousa, third mate, dropped dead in his boat while fast to a whale 1870; sent home 691 sperm, 290 whale, 1,300 bone.
....do	Apr. 27	May 24, 1873	610	......	......	Sent home 1,215 sperm.
North Pacific ..	July 19	....	......	......	......	Sent home 97 sperm; lost in the Arctic 1871.
Indian Ocean ..	Oct. 26	June 2, 1874	954	......	......	Captain Gifford died August 26, 1873, at sea; sent home 25 sperm.
North Pacific ..	Oct. 26	....	......	......	......	Lost in the Arctic 1871.
....do	Sept. 29	....	......	......	......	Do.
Pacific Ocean ..	Sept. 27	July 20, 1874	247	444	......	
Atlantic	May 28	Oct. 2, 1871	......	301	5,204	Withdrawn 1872.
Pacific Ocean ..	Aug. 23	July 2, 1874	1,081	4	......	Robert Saulsbury, fourth mate, died at Valparaiso May, 1873; sent home 437 sperm.
Indian Ocean ..	July 6	Oct. 7, 1872	691	4	......	Sent home 278 sperm, 10 whale.
North Pacific ..	July 19	....	......	......	......	Sent home 184 sperm; lost in the Arctic 1871.
Pacific Ocean ..	Aug. 6	June 4, 1874	975	6	......	Sent home 721 sperm.
....do	Nov. 10	Aug. 10, 1874	481	1,346	......	Added 1870; formerly a freighter; C. W. Swain, second mate, drowned by a foul line while fast to a whale, May 7, 1872; sent home 870 sperm, 825 whale, 2,124 bone.
Atlantic	May 4	....	......	......	......	Transferred from New York 1870; sent home 594 sperm; sold to San Francisco 1873.
North Pacific ..	Nov. 7	....	......	......	......	Sent home 93 sperm; stove by ice in the Arctic 1871.
Sooloo Sea	June 28	Oct. 6, 1873	1,192	1	......	Sent home 171 sperm; sold to Port Jefferson for freighting 1873.
Pacific Ocean ..	Aug. 1	....	......	......	......	Sent home 718 sperm; condemned at Mahe October, 1872.
Indian Ocean ..	Oct. 5	June 19, 1873	930	70	......	
Atlantic	June 1	Oct. 11, 1871	119	......	......	
North Pacific ..	Oct. 19	May 10, 1875	434	3,225	......	Captain Dowden left at San Francisco; Captain Eldridge, formerly of Cherokee, took command; sent home 39,836 bone.
Pacific Ocean ..	Nov. 1	Sept. 1, 1874	287	419	......	Mr. Garrity, fourth mate, murdered by one of the crew May, 1873; sent home 309 sperm, 837 pounds bone.
North Pacific ..	Oct. 4	....	......	......	......	Sent home 154 sperm; lost in the Arctic September, 1871.
Pacific Ocean ..	Nov. 1	....	......	......	......	Sent home 470 sperm, 319 elephant; crushed by ice in the Arctic August 19, 1872; had 800 sperm.
....	May —	....	......	......	......	Burned at sea July 24, 1870; fired by the crew.
Pacific Ocean ..	Oct. 26	May 2, 1875	1,130	650	2,500	Captain Hyland came home sick 1871.
Indian Ocean ..	Oct. 21	May 5, 1873	860	141	1,707	Sent home 242 sperm, 58 whale.
Atlantic	July 6	Aug. 12, 1873	128	......	......	Sent home 630 sperm, 372 whale; sold to Bangor, Me., for the African trade, 1873.
....do	May 21	Aug. 11, 1871	39	135	......	Added 1870 from Fairhaven; sent home 129 sperm.
Indian Ocean ..	Oct. 25	Aug. 24, 1874	992	146	......	Sent home 506 sperm, 1,040 whale.
....do	May 4	....	......	......	......	Sent home 230 sperm, 800 bone; lost off Celebes July, 1871.
Atlantic	Nov. 4	Sept. 14, 1872	83	......	......	Sent home 230 sperm.
....do	June 7	Aug. 6, 1871	109	135	......	Added 1870; sent home 30 sperm.
....do	May 12	....	......	......	......	Sent home 414 sperm; condemned at Fayal November, 1871.
Atlantic	May 17	Sept. 24, 1870	......	8	......	
....do	May 17	Sept. 23, 1870	173	......	......	

Table showing returns of whaling-vessels

Name of vessel.	Class.	Tonnage.	Captain.	Managing owner or agent.
1870.				
Westport, Mass.				
Sea Queen	Bark	195	Edward E. Hicks	Andrew Hicks
Provincetown, Mass.				
Alleghania	Schooner	70	——— Snow	Daniel C. Cook
Antarctic	...do	101	——— Cornell	J. E. & G. Bowley
Ada M. Dyer	...do	87	——— Dyer	Alfred Cook
B. F. Sparks	...do	92	——— Goodspeed	Stephen Cook
C. L. Sparks	...do	96	——— Atwood	David Conwell
Elbridge Gerry	...do	71	——— Fisher	Union Wharf Co
Ellen Rizpah	...do	67	——— White	S. Cook
Gage H. Phillips	...do	107	——— Cook	...do
Gracie M. Parker	...do	82	——— Dyer	Alfred Cook
Mary G. Curren	...do	102	——— Nye	Freeman & Hilliard
M. E. Simmons	...do	105	——— Taylor	E. & E. K. Cook & Co
Montezuma	...do	60	——— Leach	Freeman & Hilliard
O. M. Remington	...do	139	——— Remington	Elisha M. Dyer
Quickstep	...do	94	——— Gillette	E. & E. K. Cook & Co
Rising Sun	...do	69	——— Freeman	Atkins Nickerson
Sassacus	...do	110	——— Nickerson	E. & E. K. Cook & Co
S. A. Paine	...do	139	——— William Curren	Freeman & Hilliard
William A. Grosier	...do	117	——— Young	A. Nickerson
Boston, Mass.				
F. H. Moore	Brig	107	——— Eldridge	Robert Soper & Son
Heman Smith	...do	123	——— Senter	Heman Smith
Thriver	Schooner	69	——— Cook	R. Soper & Son
New London, Conn.				
Flying Fish	Schooner	75	Alfred Turner	Lawrence & Co
Francis Allyn	...do	107	——— Smith	Williams, Haven & Co
George and Mary	Bark	105	——— Palmer	Williams & Barns
Peru	...do	259	——— Glass	Williams, Haven & Co
Roman	Ship	350	——— Williams	...do
Roswell King	Schooner	134	——— Fuller	...do
S. B. Howes	...do	101	——— Gardner	...do
Trinity	Bark	417	——— Rogers	Lawrence & Co
San Francisco, Cal.				
C. E. Foote	Schooner	156	——— Hazard	E. Higgins & Co
Carlotta	Bark	480	——— Smith	Hutchison, Kohl & Co
Massachusetts	Ship	351	——— Cooty	Moore & Co
Menshikoff	Bark	223	——— Chapman	Hutchinson, Kohl & Co
Page	Schooner	110	——— Holcomb	Taylor & Bendel
1871.				
New Bedford, Mass.				
A. R. Tucker	Bark	129	D. L. Ricketson	J. & W. R. Wing
Abm. Barker	...do	380	Alden T. Potter	...do
Active	...do	291	Thomas G. Campbell	Loum Snow & Son
Alaska	...do	340	Charles W. Fisher	Jona. Bourne, jr
Annawan	...do	108	Jason W. Gifford	Azel Howard
Ansel Gibbs	...do	303	Thomas McPherson	J. Bourne, jr
Barth. Gosnold	...do	365	James M. Willis	Charles R. Tucker & Co.
Benj. Cummings	...do	305	Roswell Brown	Taber, Gordon & Co
Callao	...do	299	Ferdinand Lee	...do
Camilla	...do	328	E. C. Pulver	Swift & Allen

sailing from American ports—Continued.

Whaling-ground.	Date— Of sailing.	Date— Of arrival.	Result of voyage. Sperm-oil.	Result of voyage. Whale-oil.	Result of voyage. Whalebone.	Remarks.
			Bbls.	*Bbls.*	*Lbs.*	
Pacific Ocean ..	Nov. 22	Apr. 15, 1873	1,231	......	......	
Atlantic	Feb. 7	Sept. 9, 1870	30	15	......	Withdrawn 1871.
....do	May 12	Sept. 6, 1871	206	50	......	Sent home 72 sperm.
....do	Jan. 11	Sept. 5, 1870	11	189	......	Sent home 100 whale.
....do	Jan. 11	June 27, 1870	10	124	......	
....do	Dec. 24	Nov. 23, 1871	149	21	......	
....do	Feb. 12	June 21, 1871	30	170	......	Sent home 250 sperm, 18 whale; withdrawn 1871.
....do	Jan. 8	Aug. 28, 1870	148	151	......	
....do	Oct. 24	June 11, 1873	109	60	......	Sent home 180 sperm, 352 whale, 700 hump.
....do	Jan. 11	Sept. 1, 1873	163	182	......	Built at Essex 1869; added 1869; sent home 100 whale.
....do	Jan. 29	Aug. 25, 1871	123	......	......	Withdrawn 1871.
....do	Apr. 23	Sept. 16, 1871	135	36	......	Sent home 220 sperm, 200 whale.
....do	Feb. 22	Sept. 25, 1870	73	2	......	
....do	May 16	Aug. 9, 1871	120	325	......	Sent home 315 sperm; withdrawn 1871.
....do	Feb. 26	Sept. 19, 1870	21	180	......	
....do	Jan. 4	Sept. 1, 1870	70	130	......	
....do	Feb. 12	Aug. 31, 1870	65	50	......	
....do	Jan. 11	July 29, 1871	151	229	......	Withdrawn 1871.
A. and Ind	Apr. 26	June 6, 1872	556	66	......	Sent home 50 sperm.
Atlantic	Oct. —	Oct. 16, 1872	142	316	......	Sent home 295 sperm, 323 whale.
....do	Dec. 7	Oct. 4, 1872	540	40	......	
....do	Jan. 3	Aug. 22, 1870	38	69	......	Sailed again soon after, and was lost at Aux Cayes February 3, 1873; sent home 45 sperm, 150 whale.
South Atlantic	July 5	Apr. 18, 1871	Clean	......	......	Bought from Gloucester 1870.
....do	June 30	June 6, 1872	19	395	......	
Cumberl'd Inlet	May 3	Nov. 20, 1871	......	425	5,000	Sold to New Bedford 1873.
South Atlantic	July 9	June 1, 1871	18	771	......	Do.
Hurd's Island ..	June 22	May 3, 1871	......	1,500	......	
Desolation Isl'd	June 29	Apr. 26, 1873	......	633	......	Sent home 1,750 whale and elephant, 5,000 bone.
Hudson's Bay ..	July 7	....	......	......	......	Lost in Cumberland Inlet 1873.
Atlantic	July 23	Apr. 21, 1871	......	210	......	Added 1870; formerly a freighter.
Pacific Ocean ..	Oct. 7	June 30, 1872	......	263	......	Withdrawn 1872.
....do	Dec. 31	....	......	......	......	Added 1870; lost in the Arctic Ocean 1871.
....do	Dec. 22	....	......	......	......	Lost at Scammon's Lagoon Feb. 6, 1871.
....do	Dec. 10	Aug. 14, 1872	320	......	......	Menshikoff withdrawn 1872.
....do	Apr. 27	—— —, 1872	......	......	......	Added 1870; withdrawn 1872; no report.
Indian Ocean ..	May 2	Oct. 18, 1874	220	......	......	Sent home 344 sperm.
Pacific Ocean ..	May 16	Sept. 21, 1875	1,450	2,050	......	
North Pacific ..	Nov. 11	....	......	......	......	Sent home 395 sperm, 1,079 whale, 22,215 pounds bone; condemned at Yokohama, April 25, 1874.
Pacific Ocean ..	June 28	Oct. 4, 1875	1,850	1,700	15,500	
Atlantic	May 23	May 16, 1873	40	108	755	Sent home 202 sperm; sold to Fairhaven, 1873.
Hudson's Bay ..	Dec. 13	....	......	......	......	Lost on Marble Island, Hudson's Bay, October 19, 1872; had 530 whale, 10,000 pounds bone; saved 3,500 pounds bone. Fifteen of the crew died of scurvy.
North Pacific ..	Nov. 2	Mar. 30, 1876	950	1,200	12,500	
Pacific Ocean ..	June 20	Sept. 5, 1875	1,400	......	......	
....do	July 15	Sept. 21, 1875	410	760	......	
North Pacific ..	Dec. 6	....	......	......	......	Abandoned in the Arctic, 1876: had on board 190 sperm, 300 whale, 5,000 pounds bone; sent home 75 sperm, 3,850 whale, 45,778 pounds bone.

Table showing returns of whaling-vessels

Name of vessel.	Class.	Tonnage.	Captain.	Managing owner or agent.
1871.				
New Bedford, Mass.—Continued.				
Charles W. Morgan	Bark	314	John M. Pinkham	J. & W. R. Wing
Cornelia	...do	203	Leroy S. Lewis	John P. Knowles, 2d
Courser	...do	259	Elias H. White	I. H. Bartlett
Emma C. Jones	Ship	307	Ezra Gifford	William Watkins
Europa	...do	323	J. H. McKenzie	Charles Tucker
George and Susan	Bark	343	Andrew R. Beyer	G. & M. Howland
Glacier	...do	195	Edwin A. Potter	Andrew H. Potter
Helen Mar	...do	324	William H. Koon	Swift & Allen
Helen Snow	...do	215	George H. Macomber	L. Snow & Son
Hercules	...do	311	Archelaus Baker	Swift & Perry
Hunter	...do	355	Charles L. Holt	J. Bourne, jr
Islander	...do	240	John C. Hamlin	I. H. Bartlett & Sons
Jireh Perry	Ship	316	Leander C. Owen	Swift & Perry
John P. West	Bark	353	Calvin Manchester	Simeon N. West
Josephine	Ship	363	George F. Long	Swift & Allen
Kathleen	Bark	206	Samuel R. Howland	J. & W. R. Wing
Laconia	...do	158	John A. Kelley	J. P. Knowles, 2d
Marengo	Ship	478	William M. Barnes	William O. Brownell
Mary Frazier	Bark	301	John G. Nye	Charles Tucker
Milwood	...do	216	Sanford S. Milner	Gid. Allen & Son
Northern Light	...do	385	Gilbert L. Smith	J. Bourne, jr
Osmanli	...do	292	James M. Williams	Charles S. Randall
Ospray	...do	173	M. V. B. Millard	Swift & Allen
Petrel	...do	257	Frederick H. Smith	T. Knowles & Co
Petrel	Schooner	61	Philip H. Reed	Philip H. Reed
Sarah	Bark	128	Thomas Foster	J. P. Knowles, 2d
Sea Breeze	...do	323	R. D. Wicks	J. Bourne, jr
Sunbeam	...do	255	Joseph W. Lavers	J. & W. R. Wing
Trident	...do	432	Jacob A. Howland	Swift & Perry
Wave	...do	150	B. A. Briggs	T. Knowles & Co
Young Phœnix	Ship	355	—— Fuller	William Phillips & Son
Fairhaven, Mass.				
General Scott	Bark	315	—— Taber	Tripp & Terry
Marion, Mass.				
Cohannet	Schooner	83	Loring Braley	Andrew J. Hadley
William Wilson	...do	92	—— Hathaway	...do
Westport, Mass.				
Mattapoisett	Bark	110	Orlando J. Tripp	Henry Smith
Platina	...do	214	Amos A. Chase	Andrew Hicks
Sea Fox	...do	166	William W. Eldridge	...do
Edgartown, Mass.				
Clarice	Bark	183	—— Marchant	Samuel Osborn, jr
Provincetown, Mass.				
Agate	Schooner	81	—— Atkins	W. A. Atkins
Arizona	...do	79	—— Higgins	Stephen Cook
Ada M. Dyer	...do	87	—— Dyer	Alfred Cook
B. F. Sparks	...do	92	—— Bell	S. Cook

sailing from American ports—Continued.

Whaling-ground.	Date—		Result of voyage.			Remarks.
	Of sailing.	Of arrival.	Sperm-oil.	Whale-oil.	Whalebone.	
			Bbls.	*Bbls.*	*Lbs.*	
Indian Ocean ..	Sept. 26	Oct. 31, 1874	1, 340	242	......	Sent home 109 sperm, 1,600 pounds bone.
Pacific Ocean ..	Oct. 10	....	......	......	......	Condemned at Paita March, 1873; sent home 278 sperm, 498 humpback.
....do	July 19	....	......	......	......	Run down by steamship Ytata October 26, 1873; cut down and abandoned with 200 sperm, 350 whale; sent home 170 sperm, 350 whale.
....do	July 11	Nov. 6, 1874	2, 137	3	......	Sent home 415 sperm.
North Pacific ..	Dec. 14	Apr. 17, 1876	50	4, 200	32, 386	Belongs to Dartmouth parties.
Atlantic	Aug. 21	May 2, 1874	647	1, 019	......	Sent home 572 sperm, 141 whale, 540 bone.
Cum. Inlet	July 9	Sept. 26, 1873	......	75	1, 600	Sold to Wiscasset, Me., 1873.
North Pacific ..	Sept. 26	Apr. 15, 1876	340	3, 850	36, 085	
Pacific Ocean ..	Oct. 17	....	......	......	......	Sent home 169 sperm; damaged by ice in the Arctic, August 19, 1872, and abandoned; afterward found, taken into San Francisco, and sold to pay salvage; sailed one voyage from San Francisco then under Russian flag.
Indian Ocean ..	Aug. 23	Aug. 4, 1875	1, 410	965	......	
Pacific Ocean ..	Sept. 27	July 14, 1875	2, 700	1, 100	......	
Indian Ocean ..	July 25	....	......	......	......	Sent home 695 sperm; sold at Albany, New Holland, March, 1873.
North Pacific ..	Dec. 21	Apr. 1, 1875	715	4, 550	72, 000	
Indian Ocean ..	Sept. 9	Oct. 3, 1874	402	1, 752	7, 400	Sent home 37 sperm, 4,700 pounds bone.
North Pacific ..	Sept. 26	May 22, 1875	540	4, 175	53, 500	
Indian Ocean ..	Oct. 16	Apr. 30, 1875	1, 450	......	......	
Atlantic	June 20	Nov. 3, 1872	101	1	......	Sent home 95 sperm.
North Pacific ..	June 27	....	......	......	......	Sent home 230 sperm, 2,302 whale, 29,300 pounds bone; sold at San Francisco 1874; lost in the Arctic 1876.
Pacific Ocean ..	Nov. 7	Aug. 25, 1876	770	1, 500	1, 200	Sold to Edgartown 1876.
Cum. Inlet	Apr. 25	....	......	......	......	Sent home 20 sperm; lost on Black Lead Island, November 13, 1871; saved 140 whale; built in 1806.
North Pacific ..	Oct. 10	Out 1877.....	......	......	......	Had taken at last report 430 sperm 4,850 whale, 57,489 pounds bone.
Indian Ocean ..	Oct. 4	June 15, 1875	535	1, 235	......	
Pacific Ocean ..	July 27	July 13, 1874	......	156	......	Captain Millard came home sick 1872; sent home 655 sperm, 465 humpback.
Indian Ocean ..	July 20	May 1, 1874	1, 338	69	400	Sent home 74 sperm.
Atlantic	Dec. 30	Sept. 1, 1872	11	112	......	
....do	May 24	May 12, 1873	185	311	......	Sent home 696 sperm, 208 whale, 1,080 bone.
North Pacific ..	Aug. 3	May 10, 1875	60	940	8, 300	
Indian Ocean ..	Dec. 4	Dec. 6, 1875	560	......	......	
North Pacific ..	Sept. 6	....	......	......	......	Sent home 397 sperm, 1,640 whale, 21,000 pounds bone; lost at Panama 1873.
Atlantic	May 9	July 21, 1873	336	......	......	Sent home 416 sperm, 7 whale.
Indian Ocean ..	Oct. 3	June 14, 1875	340	400	1, 000	Sailed under Capt. Silas G. Baker, who came home 1871.
Pacific Ocean ..	June 20	Apr. 1, 1875	650	650	......	George S. Harris, third mate, died February 12, 1873.
Atlantic	June 13	Sept. 17, 1871	150	......	......	
....do	May 24	Sept. 13, 1871	175	......	......	
Atlantic	June 21	Sept. 1, 1872	438	38	......	Sent home 115 sperm.
Pacific Ocean ..	Nov. 6	June 25, 1875	1, 605	865	......	
Indian Ocean ..	Apr. 18	June 6, 1874	355	267	......	Mr. Crocker, first mate, killed by a whale, December 12, 1873; sold to New Bedford 1874.
Atlantic	Oct. 5	Sept. 4, 1875	1, 040	......	......	Bought from New Bedford 1871; out 1875.
Atlantic	Jan. —	Sept. 24, 1871	106	100	......	
....do	Jan. —	Aug. 30, 1871	......	70	......	
....do	Feb. 20	Sept. 11, 1871	42	210	......	
....do	Jan. —	Sept. 29, 1871	215	186	......	

Table showing returns of whaling-vessels

Name of vessel.	Class.	Tonnage.	Captain.	Managing owner or agent.
1871.				
Provincetown, Mass.—Continued.				
D. A. Small	Brig	119	—— Lair	David A. Small
Ellen Rizpah	Schooner	67	—— White	S. Cook
Gracie M. Parker	...do	82	—— Dyer	A. Cook
Montezuma	...do	60	—— Leach	Freeman & Hilliard
Quickstep	...do	94	—— Birch	E. & E. K. Cook & Co
Rising Sun	...do	69	—— Marshall	Atkins Nickerson
Boston, Mass.				
Rosa Baker	Brig	108	—— Gifford	Heman Smith
Sarah E. Lewis	Bark	96	—— Cannon	...do
Beverly, Mass.				
Eschol	Brig	143	—— Williams	F. W. Choate
New London, Conn.				
Charles Colgate	Schooner	250	—— Norrie	Lawrence & Co
Concordia	Bark	217	—— Chipman	Williams, Haven & Co
Francis Allyn	Schooner	107	—— Glass	...do
Franklin	...do	119	—— Holmes	...do
Golden West	...do	144	—— Rogers	Lawrence & Co
Isabella	Brig	192	—— Keeney	Williams, Haven & Co
Peru	Bark	259	—— Gilderdale	...do
Roman	Ship	350	—— Williams	...do
Sag Harbor, N. Y.				
Myra	Brig	116	—— Babcock	H. & S. French
San Francisco, Cal.				
Mannella	Brig	128	—— Herendeen	Wright & Bowne
1872.				
New Bedford, Mass.				
Abbie Bradford	Schooner	115	Robt. P. Gifford	Jonathan Bourne, jr
Arnolda	Bark	340	Geo. F. Bouldry	James B. Wood & Co
Atlantic	...do	291	James F. Brown	J. & W. R. Wing
California	Ship	367	Josiah E. Chase	Chas. R. Tucker & Co
China	Bark	367	David P. Gifford	Wm. Phillips & Son
Coral	...do	361	George B. Marvin	Taber, Gordon & Co
Draco	...do	258	M. L. Snell	J. Bourne, jr
Eliza Adams	Ship	408	Caleb O. Hamblin	Taber, Gordon & Co
E. H. Adams	Brig	107	Hiram J. Cleveland	William Lewis
Falcon	Bark	285	Hezekiah Allen	Thos. Knowles & Co
Illinois	...do	409	—— Fraser	I. H. Bartlett & Sons
James Allen	...do	349	W. H. Kelley	Gideon Allen & Son
Janus	Ship	276	J. R. Jenney	Swift & Perry
Java	Bark	309	Edmund Kelley	G. & M. Howland
Java, 2d	...do	290	James H. Fisher	Chas. Hitch & Son
John Dawson	...do	173	Caleb Babcock	J. & W. R. Wing
John Howland	...do	377	Fred'k P. Cole	William O. Brownell
Joseph Maxwell	...do	263	Stephen Hickmott	Taber, Read & Co

sailing from American ports—Continued.

Whaling-ground.	Date—Of sailing.	Date—Of arrival.	Result of voyage. Sperm-oil.	Result of voyage. Whale-oil.	Result of voyage. Whalebone.	Remarks.
			Bbls.	*Bbls.*	*Lbs.*	
Atlantic	Jan. 4	June 11, 1873	188	235	570	Sent home 160 sperm, 425 whale.
....do	Feb. —	Sept. 8, 1871	78	61	......	
....do	Feb. 20	Sept. 7, 1871	75	240	......	
....do	Feb. 17	Aug. 30, 1871	60	25	......	Towed into Vineyard Haven; dismantled in a gale, August 16.
....do	Apr. —	Sept. 2, 1872	95	6	......	Sent home 206 sperm.
....do	Mar. 23	Nov. 23, 1871	70	10	......	
Atlantic	Nov. 28	Apr. 13, 1874	71	5	......	Sent home 505 sperm.
....do	....	Sept. 11, 1872	109	158	......	
Atlantic	May 20	Aug. 14, 1872	150	......	......	Sent home 149 sperm.
Desolation Isl'd	June 27	Apr. 11, 1873	......	987	......	Sent home 850 elephant.
Cum. Inlet.....	Apr. 25	Nov. 9, 1871	......	......	......	Nothing but freight; broken up, 1873; bought from Sag Harbor, 1870.
Atlantic	July 22	June 6, 1872	19	395	......	
....do	Aug. 26	June 9, 1872	......	Clean	......	
....do	Aug. 7	May 14, 1872	......	40[illegible]	......	
Cum. Inlet.....	May 31	Oct. 28, 1872	......	228	......	
Atlantic	Aug. 17	June 14, 1872	......	187	......	Boat's crew lost by boat capsizing, March 2, 1872; withdrawn and sold, 1874.
Desolation Isl'd	June 26	June 9, 1872	21	1,518	......	
Atlantic	July 17	....	......	......	......	Sent home 430 sperm, 590 whale, 700 pounds bone; condemned at Barbadoes, December 14, 1874; Sag Harbor's last whaler.
Pacific Ocean ..	Feb. 4	....	......	......	......	No report; lost at Scammon's Lagoon, Lower California.
Hudson's Bay..	May 28	Sept. 7, 1873	......	878	13,131	Bought from Nantucket 1872; H. B. Martin, second mate, died January, 1873.
North Pacific..	Jan. 2	May 1, 1876	620	1,175	16,200	
Pacific Ocean ..	June 25	June 8, 1876	670	540	......	
New Zealand ..	Aug. 7	Aug. 17, 1876	2,600	200	1,500	
Indian Ocean ..	June 5	....	......	......	......	Sent home 428 sperm, 1,170 whale, 8,000 bone; condemned.
Pacific Ocean ..	Dec. 4	Out 1877.....	......	......	......	Had taken at last report 630 sperm, 1,320 whale.
Atlantic	May 1	May 1, 1875	1,390	45[illegible]	......	
Pacific Ocean ..	June 10	July 26, 1876	2,215	18[illegible]	1,100	Mr. Soverino, second mate, died March, '75.
Atlantic	June 18	Aug. 10, 1874	326	...	......	Sent home 272 sperm.
....do	May 14	Aug. 5, 1875	1,205	300	......	
North Pacific..	Jan. 9	....	......	......	......	Added 1871; collided with the Marengo and sunk in the Arctic April 18, 1876; sent home 587 whale, 26,590 bone.
....do	Jan. 3	....	......	......	......	First mate John N. Norton and boat's crew lost 1874, taken down by a whale; abandoned in the Arctic 1876; sent home 150 sperm, 5,100 whale, 79,500 bone; had 1,600 whale, 10,000 bone on board.
Atlantic	May 28	May 21, 1875	1,650	1,150	3,572	
North Pacific..	Oct. 3	Out 1877.....	......	......	......	Captain Kelley came home sick 1873; had taken at last report 330 sperm 3,200 whale, 30,340 bone.
....do	Oct. 2	....	......	......	......	Abandoned in the Arctic 1876; had 800 whale, 3,000 bone; sent home 520 sperm, 2,050 whale, 20,000 bone.
Indian Ocean ..	Nov. 26	Sept. 14, 1875	1,000	10	......	
....do	June 4	Out 1877.....	......	......	......	Had taken at last report 1,150 sperm, 2,000 whale.
North Pacific..	Jan. 16	....	......	......	......	Sent home 1,203 whale, 24,000 bone; condemned and sold at Honolulu December 2, 1874.

Table showing returns of whaling-vessels

Name of vessel.	Class.	Tonnage.	Captain.	Managing owner or agent.
1872.				
New Bedford, Mass.—Continued.				
Lætitia	Bark	208	Henry T. Craw	J. & W. R. Wing
Martha	do	235	James E. Stanton	Swift & Allen
Merlin	do	246	Albert A. Thomas	William Watkins
Mt. Wollaston	do	325	West Mitchell	Swift & Allen
Ohio	do	205	——— Howland	Loum Snow & Co
Onward	do	339	H. S. Hayes	G. & M. Howland
Orray Taft	do	134	George J. Parker	Andrew H. Potter
Palmetto	do	215	Sylvanus D. Robinson	C. R. Tucker & Co
Petrel	Schooner	61	Lemuel P. Adams	Philip H. Reed
President, 2d	Bark	123	Geo. W. Seabury	Edmund Maxfield
Seine	do	234	Edw'd P. Shiverick	John P. Knowles, 2d
Spartan	do	294	Benjamin Gifford	David B. Kempton
St. George	Ship	392	James H. Knowles	G. & M. Howland
Triton	Bark	264	John Heppingstone	J. & W. R. Wing
Union	Schooner	66	Owen Fisher	Hiram Webb
Fairhaven, Mass.				
Ellen Rodman	Schooner	73	Jacob Anderson	Tucker Damon, jr
Geo. J. Jones	Brig	128	Jos. D. Silva	do
Marion, Mass.				
Admiral Blake	Schooner	84	Wm. C. Hathaway	Andrew J. Hadley
Cohannet	do	83	Loring Braley	do
Wm. Wilson	do	92	Edward Cluny	do
Dartmouth, Mass.				
Cape Horn Pigeon	Bark	212	George O. Baker	William Potter, 2d
Westport, Mass.				
A. Hicks	Bark	303	Timothy Howland	Andrew Hicks
Greyhound	do	163	John M. Allen	Henry Smith
Provincetown, Mass.				
Agate	Schooner	81	——— Atkins	W. A. Atkins
Alcyone	do	92	——— Ewell	E. & E. K. Cook & Co
Antarctic	do	101	——— Cornell	J. E. & G. Bowley
Arizona	do	79	——— Nickerson	Stephen Cook
Ada M. Dyer	do	87	——— Dyer	Alfred Cook
B. F. Sparks	do	92	——— Bell	S. Cook
C. L. Sparks	do	96	——— Sparks	David Conwell
E. H. Hatfield	do	89	——— Freeman	E. & E. K. Cook & Co
Elbridge Gerry	do	71	——— Fisher	Union Wharf Co
Ellen Rizpah	do	67	——— White	S. Cook
Gracie M. Parker	do	82	——— Dyer	A. Cook
John Atwood	do	..	——— Fisher	E. E. Small
M. E. Simmons	do	105	——— Taylor	E. & E. K. Cook & Co
Montezuma	do	60	——— Leach	Freeman & Hilliard
N. J. Knights	do	70	——— Freeman	D. Conwell
Rising Sun	do	69	——— Marshall	Atkins Nickerson
New London, Conn.				
Acors Barns	Bark	296	——— Allen	Williams & Barns
Emma Jane	Schooner	86	——— Swain	Williams, Haven & Co
Florence	do	56	——— Athearn	do
Flying Fish	do	75	——— Church	Lawrence & Co
Francis Allyn	do	107	——— Glass	Williams, Haven & Co
Franklin	do	119	——— Buddington	do
Golden West	do	144	——— Rogers	Lawrence & Co

sailing from American ports—Continued.

Whaling-ground.	Date—		Result of voyage.			Remarks.
	Of sailing.	Of arrival.	Sperm-oil.	Whale-oil.	Whalebone.	
			Bbls.	*Bbls.*	*Lbs.*	
Atlantic	July 18	Aug. 18, 1875	1,500	......	......	
Pacific Ocean ..	Oct. 5	....	......	......	......	Condemned at Bay of Islands November 20, 1874; sent home 494 sperm, 365 whale.
New Zealand ..	July 2	June 19, 1876	1,920	......	......	
North Pacific..	July 9	....	......	......	......	Abandoned in the Arctic 1876; sent home 250 sperm, 2,235 whale, 29,000 bone.
Atlantic	May 28	Oct. 19, 1875	1,600	60	533	
Pacific Ocean ..	June 25	....	......	......	......	Abandoned in the Arctic 1876; had 1,400 whale, 14,000 bone; sent home 645 sperm, 856 whale, 47,200 bone.
Hudson's Bay..	July 2	....	......	......	......	Lost on Marble Island, (Hudson's Bay,) September 14, 1872.
Atlantic	Oct. 2	Sept. 4, 1875	1,350	......	......	
... do	Oct. 21	July 22, 1873	......	Clean	......	
....do	May 3	Sept. 20, 1874	409	18	......	Sent home 540 sperm, 10 blackfish.
Pacific Ocean..	June 3	July 1, 1875	1,610	......	......	
Atlantic	May 22	May 5, 1873	705	......	......	
North Pacific..	June 4	....	......	......	......	Abandoned in the Arctic 1876; had 1,400 whale, 1,800 bone; sent home 295 sperm, 4,100 whale, 36,390 bone.
....do	Jan. 8	June 6, 1876	255	2,700	43,000	
Atlantic	May 13	Sept. 21, 1872	87	......	......	
Atlantic	Oct. 9	Sept. 1, 1873	73	......	......	
....do	May 28	....	......	......	......	Sent home 278 sperm; condemned at Barbadoes April 1873.
Atlantic	May 22	Sept. 22, 1873	24	11	......	Added 1872.
... do .... {	Jan. 30	Aug. 31, 1872	260	20	......	
	Dec. 4	Sept. —, 1873	158	2	......	Sold to Fairhaven 1874.
....do	May 27	June 15, 1873	22	5	285	Sent home 200 sperm.
Pacific Ocean ..	Aug. 8	May 11, 1876	1,070	3,200	......	
Atlantic	July 23	Sept. 14, 1876	1,760	......	......	E. N. Briggs, first mate, drowned by a foul line 1872.
Indian Ocean ..	June 25	Oct. 18, 1875	1,620	500	......	
Atlantic	Jan. 31	Sept. 2, 1872	93	221	......	
....do	Feb. 22	Oct. 7, 1872	101	236	......	Returned 1872.
....do	Apr. 23	Sept. 14, 1872	128	28	......	
....do	Jan. 25	Sept. 6, 1872	......	221	......	
....do	Jan. 25	Sept. 13, 1872	57	190	......	Withdrawn 1872.
....do	Feb. 7	Sept. 25, 1872	75	254	......	
....do	May 6	Aug. 28, 1873	107	169	1,468	Sent home 175 sperm.
....do	Apr. 11	Oct. 5, 1872	143	......	......	Replaced 1872; sailed again in 1872, arrived September 16, 1873; 137 sperm.
....do	Mar. 16	Sept. 25, 1872	47	72	......	Returned 1872.
Atlantic	Feb. 22	July 16, 1872	112	214	......	
....do	Jan. 25	Aug. 7, 1872	105	323	......	
Hudson's Bay..	May 29	Oct. 8, 1872	......	180	3,128	Formerly a freighter; added 1872; withdrawn 1872.
Atlantic	Feb. 22	Sept. 1, 1873	163	156	......	Sent home 150 sperm, 250 whale.
....do	June 18	Sept. 18, 1873	85	3	......	Sent home 105 whale; withdrawn 1874.
....do	Feb. 29	Sept. 14, 1872	59	115	......	Returned 1872.
....do	Jan. 30	Sept. 21, 1872	58	80	......	
North Pacific..	Jan. 18	—— —, 1874	235	1,130	22,740	Sold at San Francisco to New Bedford, 1875.
Hurd's Island..	June 27	Out, 1877	......	......	......	Had at last report 800 whale.
Atlantic	Aug. 6	1875 or 1876	......	......	......	Added 1872; no report.
....do	Aug. 10	Apr. 15, 1874	......	53	......	
....do	Aug. 20	May 10, 1873	......	32	......	
....do	Aug. 5	May 13, 1873	27	60	......	
....do	Aug. 15	Apr. 6, 1873	......	Clean	......	

Table showing returns of whaling-vessels

Name of vessel.	Class.	Tonnage.	Captain.	Managing owner or agent.
1872.				
New London, Conn.—Continued.				
Nile	Ship	293	—— Williams	Williams, Haven & Co.
Roman	do	350	—— Turner	do
New York, N. Y.				
Lizzie P. Simmons	Schooner	89	—— Potts	Lewis J. Phillips
1873.				
New Bedford, Mass.				
Annawan	Bark	...	Geo. W. Bassett	
Com. Morris	do	338	George F. Winslow	Swift & Perry
Desdemona	do	230	Sam'l F. Davis	G. & M. Howland
Edward Everett	do	187	Joseph D. Silva	Gideon Allen & Son
Lagoda	do	371	Edward D. Lewis	Jonathan Bourne, jr
Marcella	do	166	John R. Sturgiss	Chas. R. Tucker & Co
Mercury	do	311	Chas. H. Gifford	William Phillips & Son
Milton	Ship	373	William C. Fuller	Taber, Gordon & Co
Morning Star	Bark	238	James E. Potter	Joshua C. Hitch
Pacific	do	341	Gilbert B. Borden	Swift & Perry
Pioneer	do	228	Alex. A. Tripp	G. Allen & Son
Sarah	do	128	Thomas Foster	John P. Knowles, 2d
Stafford	do	156	Edward A. King	Jos. & Wm. R. Wing
Tamerlane	do	372	Geo. W. J. Moulton	Thos. Knowles & Co
Union	Schooner	66	Philip H. Reed	Philip H. Reed
Dartmouth, Mass.				
Matilda Sears	Bark	231	Charles Childs	William Potter, 2d
Westport, Mass.				
Mattapoisett	Bark	110	Orlando J. Tripp	Henry Smith
Mermaid	do	273	Edward E. Hicks	Andrew Hicks
Sea Queen	do	195	David E. Allen	do
Provincetown, Mass.				
Agate	Schooner	81	—— Atkins	W. A. Atkins
Alcyone	do	92	—— Ewell	E. & E. K. Cook & Co
Antarctic	do	101	—— Cornell	J. E. & J. Bowley
Arizona	do	79	—— White	Stephen Cook
B. F. Sparks	do	92	—— Bell	do
E. H. Hatfield	do	89	—— Kickcornell	E. & E. K. Cook & Co
Elbridge Gerry	do	71	—— Fisher	Union Wharf Co
Ellen Rizpah	do	67	—— Atkins	S. Cook
Gracie M. Parker	do	82	—— Dyer	Alfred Cook
N. J. Knights	do	70	—— Foster	David Conwell
Quickstep	do	94	—— Burch	E. & E. K. Cook & Co
Rising Sun	do	69	—— Taylor	Thomas S. Taylor
Sassacus	do	...		
Wm. A. Grozier	do	117	—— Roberts	William A. Atkins
Boston, Mass.				
F. H. Moore	Brig	107	—— Soper	Robert Soper & Son
Heman Smith	do	123	Chas. B. Barstow	Heman Smith
Sarah E. Lewis	Schooner	96	Geo. H. Cannon	do
Beverly, Mass.				
Eschol	Brig	143	—— Williams	F. W. Choate
New London, Conn.				
Charles Colgate	Schooner	250	—— Sisson	Lawrence & Co
Flying Fish	do	75	—— Church	do
Francis Allyn	do	107	—— Glass	Williams, Haven & Co

sailing from American ports—Continued.

Whaling-ground.	Date— Of sailing.	Date— Of arrival.	Result of voyage. Sperm-oil.	Result of voyage. Whale-oil.	Result of voyage. Whalebone.	Remarks.
			Bbls.	*Bbls.*	*Lbs.*	
Atlantic	Sept. 3	May 5, 1873	76	303		
Desolation Isld	July 16	Mar. 31, 1873		1,225		
Atlantic	July 25	May 8, 1873		Clean		Bought from Provincetown 1872; fitted from New London.
						Lost near Bermudas July 8, 1873; five men lost.
Atlantic	July 29	Sept. 24, 1876	2,930			
do	June 3	Apr. 29, 1876	1,600	875		
do	July 21	Aug. 12, 1875	890	23		
Pacific Ocean	July 21	Out, 1877				Had taken at last report 1,130 sperm, 290 whale, 1,450 bone.
Indian Ocean	Nov. 11	May 2, 1876	1,050			
do	May 13	Nov. 6, 1876	1,260	500	1,200	
Pacific Ocean	Oct. 8	Oct. 24, 1876	2,360	200	1,363	
do	Nov. 13	Out, 1877				Captain Potter died June 30, 1875; had taken at last report 1,135 sperm.
Atlantic	Oct. 1	Nov. 5, 1876	1,670			
do	July 8	Sept. 20, 1874	851			Sent home.
do	Aug. 5	May 2, 1876	1,035	780		
Indian Ocean	June 30	May 24, 1876	880	230		
Atlantic	Aug. 6	Out, 1877				Had taken at last report 1,200 sperm; 300 whale.
do	Apr. 10	Sept. 26, 1873	170			
Pacific Ocean	July 22	Out, 1877				Had taken at last report 800 sperm, 670 whale.
Atlantic	June 10	Sept. 21, 1874	337			Sent home 102 sperm.
Indian Ocean	Aug. 28	Apr. 16, 1876	1,825			
do	June 20	Aug. 20, 1875	1,210	80		
Atlantic	Feb. 5	Sept. 15, 1873	37	86		
do	Feb. 20	Sept. 24, 1873	171	158		
do	Feb. 20	Sept. 16, 1873	117	45		
do	Feb. 20	Sept. 9, 1873	125	258		
do	Feb. 20	Sept. 26, 1873	357			
do	Dec. 30	Sept. 23, 1874	242			Sailed again in 1873 or 1874, arrived September 7, 1875, with 250 sperm.
do	Feb. 20	Sept. 10, 1873	121	191		Withdrawn 1874.
do	Feb. 20	Aug. 12, 1873	105	207		
do	Feb. 20	Sept. 2, 1873	138	202		
do	Feb. 20	Sept. 14, 1873	32	210		
do	May 5	Aug. 20, 1874	175	22		Sent home 63 sperm.
do	Feb. 20	Aug. 30, 1873	123	245	1,436	
						Sassacus lost at Cape Negro, (Nova Scotia,) August 24, 1873.
do	May 12	Aug. 17, 1874	487			Replaced 1873; sent home 180 sperm.
Atlantic	May —	Aug. 6, 1875	625			
do	May 29	Sept. 24, 1874	187	11		Sent home 200 sperm.
do	May 14	Sept. 17, 1874	222	5		Sent home 151 sperm.
Atlantic	May 20					Condemned at Barbadoes 1874; Beverly's last whaler.
Hurd's Island	June 18	Apr. 27, 1875		900	400	
South Shetland	July 23	Apr. 15, 1874		53		
do	July 25	June 14, 1875		Clean		

Table showing returns of whaling-vessels

Name of vessel.	Class.	Tonnage.	Captain.	Managing owner or agent.
1873.				
New London, Conn.—Continued.				
Franklin	Schooner	119	—— Chester	Williams, Haven & Co.
Golden West	...do	144	—— Williams	Lawrence & Co
Isabella	Brig	192		Williams, Haven & Co.
Roman	Ship	350	—— Swain	...do
Roswell King	Schooner	134	—— Fuller	...do
New York, N. Y.				
L. P. Simmons	Schooner	89	—— Potts	Lewis J. Phillips
San Francisco, Cal.				
Florence	Bark	245	—— Williams	Williams, Haven & Co.
1874.				
New Bedford, Mass.				
A. R. Tucker	Bark	129	Amos C. Baker	Jos. & Wm. R. Wing
Abbie Bradford	Schooner	115	Elnathan B. Fisher	Jonathan Bourne, jr
Avola	Bark	230	Zenas E. Bourne	John P. Knowles, 2d
Canton	...do	239	Peleg L. Sherman	Charles R. Tucker & Co
Cicero	...do	226	Edward Penniman	J. P. Knowles, 2d
Cornelius Howland	Ship	333	B. Franklin Homan	Swift & Perry
Eliza	Bark	296	John M. Dimond	J. Bourne, jr
E. H. Adams	Brig	107	William C. Brownell	William Lewis
George & Susan	Bark	343	Andrew R. Heyer	Geo. & Matt. Howland
Hadley	...do	163	Hiram J. Cleveland	William Lewis
Janet	...do	154		Antone Thomas
James Arnold	Ship	346	Thomas H. Wilson	Taber, Gordon & Co
Louisa	Bark	303	Martin V. B. Millard	Swift & Allen
Lydia	...do	329	John P. Praro	Baylies & Cannon
Mars	...do	256	—— Allen	Gifford & Cummings
Mary & Susan	...do	327	James T. Handy	Thos. Knowles & Co
Mattapoisett	...do	110	Jonathan Chase	Abbot P. Smith
Napoleon	...do	322	Jared Jernegan	J. Bourne, jr
Nautilus	...do	277	Theodore A. Lake	Gideon Allen & Son
Niger	Ship	412	Thomas A. Hallett	Taber, Gordon & Co.
Ocean	Bark	288	Isaac D. Pease	I. H. Bartlett & Sons
Ospray	...do	173	Reuben W. Crapo	Swift & Allen
Petrel	...do	257	Charles S. Downs	T. Knowles & Co
Petrel	Schooner	61	Michael A. Baker	Philip H. Reed
President	Bark	257	Robert F. Gifford	J. Bourne, jr
Sea Ranger	...do	273	John W. Cornell	I. H. Bartlett & Sons
Stamboul	...do	260	Horace Montross	Joshua C. Hitch
Union	Schooner	66	Philip H. Reed	Philip H. Reed
Vigilant	Bark	215	William D. Gifford	William Watkins
Wave	...do	150	B. A. Briggs	T. Knowles & Co.
Fairhaven, Mass.				
Ellen Rodman	Schooner	73	Joseph S. Gelett	Tucker Damon, jr
Marion, Mass.				
Adm'l Blake	Schooner	84	William C. Hathaway	Andrew J. Hadley
William Wilson	...do	92	Loring Brailey	...do

sailing from American ports—Continued.

Whaling-ground.	Date— Of sailing.	Date— Of arrival.	Result of voyage. Sperm-oil.	Result of voyage. Whale-oil.	Result of voyage. Whalebone.	Remarks.
			Bbls.	*Bbls.*	*Lbs.*	
South Shetland.	July 22	May 13, 1874	......	267	......	
....do	July 24	Apr. 20, 1874	31	112	......	
Cumberl'd Inlet	June 26	Sept. 2, 1873	....	Clean	......	
Hurd's Island..	May 17	Apr. 17, 1874	....	1,441	2,314	
....do	Aug. 5	Apr. 29, 1875	30	750	1,800	
South Shetland.	Aug. 2	May 7, 1875	Clean	......	......	Belonged to New London.
Pacific Ocean ..	Dec. 24	Nov. 12, 1874	80	200	......	Added 1872.
Atlantic	Nov. 26	Oct. 25, 1876	800	......	......	
Hudson's Bay..	May 12	Sept. 14, 1875	60	650	12,000	First mate and boat's crew lost in the ice September 5, 1874.
Indian Ocean ..	July 16	Out, 1877	......	......	......	Had taken at last report 800 sperm.
....do	Dec. 8	Out, 1877	......	......	......	Had taken at last report 900 sperm, 10 whale.
Atlantic	May 9	Dec. 6, 1875	250	300	......	
North Pacific ..	Aug. 4	....	......	......	......	Abandoned in the Arctic 1876; had 1,400 whale, 8,000 bone; sent home 600 sperm, 1,220 whale, 10,000 bone.
Pacific Ocean ..	May 28	Out, 1877	......	......	......	Had taken at last report 150 sperm.
Atlantic	Oct. 1	Aug. 15, 1876	330	10	......	
....do	Sept. 17	Out, 1877	......	......	......	Had taken at last report 1,250 sperm, 1,250 whale.
....do	Oct. 29	Out, 1877	......	......	......	Had taken at last report 740 sperm, 15 whale.
....	....	Nov. 27, 1874	172	......	......	Bought from Westport 1874.
Pacific Ocean ..	June 3	Out, 1877	......	......	......	Had taken at last report 1,400 sperm.
Atlantic	Aug. 11	Out, 1877	......	......	......	Had taken at last report 640 sperm, 900 whale, 545 bone.
Pacific Ocean ..	June 18	Out, 1877	......	......	......	Had taken at last report 1,150 sperm.
....do	July 1	Out, 1877	......	......	......	Had taken at last report 1,275 sperm, 75 whale.
....do	Aug. 11	Out, 1877	......	......	......	Had taken at last report 1,750 sperm.
Atlantic	Oct. 14	July 3, 1876	400	200	......	Bought from Westport 1874.
....do	July 13	Out, 1877	......	......	......	Had taken at last report 940 sperm.
Pacific Ocean..	Aug. 25	Out, 1877	......	......	......	Had taken at last report 1,720 sperm.
....do	Oct. 17	Out, 1877	......	......	......	Had taken at last report 1,400 sperm, 500 whale.
Atlantic	July 21	Out, 1877	......	......	......	Had taken at last report 1,350 sperm.
....do	Nov. 10	Oct. 26, 1876	880	......	......	
Indian Ocean ..	July 7	Out, 1877	......	......	......	Had taken at last report 1,000 sperm, 200 whale, 1,629 bone.
Atlantic	May 9	Sept. 7, 1875	125	......	......	
Hudson's Bay..	June 9	Sept. 16, 1875	......	500	8,000	
Atlantic	July 1	Sept. 27, 1875	1,650	......	......	
Pacific Ocean ..	May 27	Out, 1877	......	......	......	T. F. Morse, third mate, killed by a whale June, 1874; had at last report 1,100 sperm.
Atlantic	May 19	May 9, 1875	180	10	......	
Pacific Ocean ..	Nov. 3	Out, 1877	......	......	......	Had at last report 660 sperm, 475 whale.
Atlantic	May 19	Oct. 5, 1876	750	......	......	
Atlantic ..... {	Apr. 21	Sept. 3, 1874	85	......	......	
	Sept. 21	Sept. 17, 1875	170	136	......	
Atlantic ..... {	May 22	Oct. 6, 1874	78	......	......	
	Oct. 27	Apr. 17, 1875	85	5	......	
....do .... {	June 11	Oct. 9, 1874	188	......	......	
	Dec. 2	Sept. 16, 1875	185	35	......	

Table showing returns of whaling-vessels

Name of vessel.	Class.	Tonnage.	Captain.	Managing owner or agent.
1874.				
Edgartown, Mass.				
Perry	Bark	150	George W. Bassett	Samuel Osborn, jr
Provincetown, Mass.				
Agate	Schooner	81	—— Atkins	W. A. Atkins
Alcyone	do	92	—— Fisher	E. & E. K. Cooke & Co
Antarctic	do	101	—— Bell	W. A. Atkins
Arizona	do	79	—— White	Stephen Cook
B. F. Sparks	do	92	—— Ewell	do
Charles Thompson	do	152	—— Leach	S. S. Swift
C. L. Sparks	do	96	—— Sparks	David Conwell
Ellen Rizpah	do	67	—— Atkins	S. Cook
Gracie M. Parker	do	82	—— Dyer	Alfred Cook
M. E. Simmons	do	103	—— Rich	E. & E. K. Cook & Co
N. J. Knights	do	70	—— Foster	D. Conwell
Rising Sun	do	69	—— Taylor	Thomas S. Taylor
Boston, Mass.				
E. B. Phillips	Bark	144	Joseph F. Francis	John Medina
Rosa Baker	Brig	108	Joseph Thompson	Heman Smith
Wm. Martin	Schooner	92	—— Martin	do
New London, Conn.				
Franklin	Schooner	119	—— Buddington	Williams, Haven & Co
Golden West	do	144	—— Williams	Lawrence & Co
Nile	Ship	293	—— Spicer	Williams, Haven & Co
Roman	do	350	—— Rogers	do
New York, N. Y.				
Oak	Bark	152	—— Gifford	Henry Shuber
1875.				
New Bedford, Mass.				
Abm. Barker	Bark	380	Otis F. Thacher	Jos. & Wm. R. Wing
Abbott Lawrence	Brig	160	Elisha H. Russell	William Lewis
Acors Barns	Bark	296	—— Hickmott	I. H. Bartlett & Sons
Adeline Gibbs	do	327	M. L. Snell	Jonathan Bourne, jr
Benj. Cummings	do	305	Roswell Brown	Taber, Gordon & Co
Callao	do	299	Henry T. Craw	do
Catalpa	do	202	George S. Anthony	John T. Richardson
Charles W. Morgan	do	314	John M. Tinkham	J. & W. R. Wing
Draco	do	258	Henry M. Peaks	J. Bourne, jr
Edward Everett	do	187	Rufus W. Gifford	Gideon Allen & Son
Emma C. Jones	Ship	307	Sylv. B. Potter	William Watkins
Falcon	Bark	285	Alonzo O. Herendeen	Thos. Knowles & Co
Gazelle	do	273	Andrew J. Mosher	Swift & Allen
General Scott	do	315	Charles H. Robbinse	J. T. Richardson
George & Mary	do	105	George H. Cannon	J. Bourne, jr
Golden City	Schooner	89	Henry Clay	Henry Clay
Greyhound	Bark	163	Timothy C. Allen	Abbott P. Smith
Hercules	do	311	Jireh Sherman	Swift & Perry

sailing from American ports—Continued.

Whaling-ground.	Date— Of sailing.	Of arrival.	Result of voyage. Sperm-oil.	Whale-oil.	Whalebone.	Remarks.
			Bbls.	*Bbls.*	*Lbs.*	
Atlantic	Aug. 12	Out, 1877				Bought from New London 1874; had taken at last report 650 sperm.
Atlantic	Feb. 12	Sept. 24, 1874	134	150		
....do	Jan. 24	Sept. 10, 1874		275		
....do	Mar. 30	Oct. 7, 1874	315			
....do	Feb. 28	Sept. 10, 1874	100	101		
....do	June 22	Aug. 9, 1875	285	140		
....do	May 28	Oct. 14, 1874	34	8		Added 1874; sent home 145 sperm, 20 whale; sailed again 1874 or 1875; returned September 21, 1875, with 315 sperm, 10 whale.
....do	Apr. 14	Sept. 15, 1875	230	100		
....do	Feb. 28	Aug. 20, 1874	114	197		
....do	Mar. 2	Sept. 13, 1874	148	222		
....do	Mar. 2	Sept. 6, 1874	19	266		
....do	Feb. 12	Sept. 9, 1874	92	83		
....do	Feb. —	Sept. 19, 1874	140	210		
Atlantic	July 28	July 30, 1876	450			Added 1874 from New London.
....do	May 22	May 2, 1875	270	15		
....do	June 5	Oct. 4, 1874	56			Added 1874.
	Nov. 13	Sept. 21, 1875	320	15		
Atlantic	July 15	Apr. 29, 1875	160			Sold to New Bedford 1875.
....do	July 18	May 4, 1875		50		
Cum. Inlet	June 15	Dec. 9, 1874		800	8,000	
Desolation Isld	June 22	May 13, 1876	50	1,300		Sold to New Bedford 1876.
Pacific Ocean	Dec. 22	Out, 1877				Had taken at last report 300 sperm, 1,500 whale.
Pacific Ocean	Oct. 26	Out, 1877				Had at last report 230 sperm, 80 whale.
Atlantic	Apr. 20	Out, 1877				Bought from Fairhaven 1874; had at last report 320 sperm.
North Pacific	Mar. 27					Bought from New London 1875; abandoned in the Arctic 1876; sent home 130 sperm, 1,650 whale, 13,450 bone; had on board 900 bone.
Atlantic	Aug. 9	Out, 1877				Had taken at last report 360 sperm, 600 whale.
Pacific Ocean	Nov. 17					Lost on the island of Fogo December 20, 1875.
Indian Ocean	Nov. 30	Out, 1877				Had taken at last report 300 sperm.
Atlantic	Apr. 29	Aug. 24, 1876	250			Returned to whaling; fitted ostensibly for whaling, but was owned by parties who dispatched her to Australia, where she rescued the Fenian prisoners
....do	Apr. 23	Out, 1877				Had taken at last report 375 sperm.
....do	July 1	Out, 1877				Had taken at last report 180 sperm, 700 whale.
	Oct. 5					Lost in a gale 5 days out.
Pacific Ocean	June 1	Out, 1877				Had taken at last report 980 sperm.
....do	Oct. 26	Out, 1877				Had taken at last report 450 sperm.
....do	June 29	Out, 1877				Had taken at last report 470 sperm, 90 whale, 729 bone.
Indian Ocean	July 7	Out, 1877				Had taken at last report 600 sperm.
Atlantic	May 4	Out, 1877				Had taken at last report 250 sperm; bought from New London 1874.
....do	Dec. 9	Sept. 29, 1876	440	40		Bought from Boston.
Indian Ocean	Nov. 30	Out, 1877				Had taken at last report 400 sperm, 1,000 bone.
....do	Oct. 19	Out, 1877				Had taken at last report 400 sperm.

Table showing returns of whaling-vessels

Name of vessel.	Class.	Tonnage.	Captain.	Managing owner or agent.
1875.				
New Bedford, Mass.—Continued.				
Hope On	Bark	191	Michael A. Baker	J. T. Richardson
Hunter	do	355	Charles L. Holt	J. Bourne, jr
Janet	do	154	Peter Gartland	William Lewis
Janus	do	276	Warren Gifford	Swift & Perry
Jireh Perry	Ship	316	Amos A. Chace	do
John Carver	Bark	319	Aaron Dean	T. Knowles & Co
John Dawson	do	173	Caleb Babcock	J. & W. R. Wing
John P. West	do	353	Calvin Manchester	Simeon N. West
Josephine	do	363	Charles Hamill	Swift & Perry
Kathleen	do	206	S. R. Howland	J. & W. R. Wing
Lætitia	do	208	George F. Church	do
Lancer	do	295	James Dowden	William Lewis
Linda Stewart	do	336	Benjamin I. Wilson	do
Midas	do	313	Josh. G. Lapham	Joshua C. Hitch
Norman	do	316	Thomas G. Campbell	Loum Snow, jr
Ohio 2d	do	363	Fred. H. Smith	Swift & Perry
Osmanli	do	292	Abraham Osborn	Gifford & Cummins
Palmetto	do	215	Edmund H. Bolles	Chas. R. Tucker & Co
Peru	do	259	Jasper M. Ears	John McCullough
Pioneer	do	228	Alexander R. Tripp	G. Allen & Son
Petrel	Schooner	61	Philip H. Reed	Philip H. Reed
Platina	Bark	214	Walter F. Howland	C. R. Tucker & Co
President	do	257	Alfred C. Davis	Jonathan Bourne, jr
President 2d	do	123	William J. Robinson	C. R. Tucker & Co
Rainbow	do	351	Bernard Cogan	I. H. Bartlett & Sons
Rousseau	do	305	Eber C. Almy	G. & M. Howland
Sappho	do	263	James H. Edick	William Lewis
Sarah B. Hale	do	183	Holder Slocum	G. Allen & Son
Sea Breeze	do	323	William M. Barnes	J. Bourne, jr
Sea Fox	do	166	Otis F. Hamblin	J. P. Knowles, 2d
Seine	do	234	—— White	do
Spartan	do	294	Orlando J. Tripp	Charles H. Gifford
Three Brothers	do	357	Leander J. Owen	I. H. Bartlett & Sons
Union	Schooner	66	—— Barstow	Philip H. Reed
Young Phœnix	Ship	355	David L. Gifford	Wm. Phillips & Son
Fairhaven, Mass.				
Cohannet	Schooner	83	Owen Fisher	
Marion, Mass.				
Admiral Blake	Schooner	84	W. C. Hathaway	Andrew J. Hadley
Westport, Mass.				
Sea Queen	Bark	195	Hezekiah Allen	Andrew Hicks
Edgartown, Mass.				
Clarice	Bark	183	—— Marchant	Samuel Osborn, jr
Provincetown, Mass.				
Agate	Schooner	81	—— Atkins	W. A. Atkins

sailing from American ports—Continued.

Whaling-ground.	Date— Of sailing.	Date— Of arrival.	Result of voyage. Sperm-oil.	Result of voyage. Whale-oil.	Result of voyage. Whalebone.	Remarks.
			Bbls.	*Bbls.*	*Lbs.*	
Atlantic	Nov. 24	Out, 1877				Formerly a schooner; added from Boston and rerigged; had taken at last report 160 sperm, 375 whale.
Pacific Ocean	Sept. 20	Out, 1877				Had taken at last report 630 sperm, 95 whale.
Atlantic	Apr. 14	Nov. 4, 1876	750			
....do	July 20	Jan. 1, 1877	580	3,200		
Indian Ocean	Sept. 27	Out, 1877				Had taken at last report 625 sperm.
Pacific Ocean	June 1	Out, 1877				Captain Dean died of heart disease July 28, 1876; had taken at last report 250 sperm, 80 whale.
Indian Ocean	Nov. 25	Out, 1877				Had taken at last report 260 sperm.
Pacific Ocean	May 4	Out, 1877				Had taken at last report 1,050 sperm.
North Pacific	Aug. 24					Abandoned in the Arctic 1876; had 1,400 whale, 10,000 bone; sent home 190 sperm.
Indian Ocean	July 19	Out, 1877				Had taken at last report 440 sperm.
....do	Oct. 11	Out, 1877				Had taken at last report 450 sperm.
Atlantic	June 15	Out, 1877				Had taken at last report 645 sperm.
....do	July 7	Out, 1877				Had taken at last report 966 sperm.
....do	Oct. 26	Out, 1877				Had taken at last report 190 sperm.
North Pacific	Oct. 9	Out, 1877				Had taken at last report 160 sperm, 500 whale.
Atlantic	July 6	Out, 1877				Had taken at last report 970 sperm.
Pacific Ocean	July 20	Out, 1877				Had taken at last report 170 sperm, 220 whale, 1,800 bone.
Atlantic	Nov. 24	Out, 1877				Had taken at last report 750 sperm.
....do	Apr. 15	Out, 1877				Had taken at last report 600 sperm; bought from New London 1874.
....do	Apr. 10	Out, 1877				Had taken at last report 700 sperm.
....do		Sept. 16, 1876	120			
Indian Ocean	Oct. 28	Out, 1877				Had taken at last report 250 sperm.
Atlantic	Nov. 17	June 14, 1876	60			Returned leaking.
....do	Apr. 29	Out, 1877				Had taken at last report 700 sperm.
North Pacific	Jan. 21	Out, 1877				Captain Cogan came home 1875; had taken at last report 185 sperm, 1,550 whale, 32,300 bone.
Atlantic	July 14	Out, 1877				Had taken at last report 170 sperm, 250 whale.
....do	Dec. 1	Out, 1877				Had taken at last report 560 sperm.
....do	Apr. 27	Out, 1877				Bought from Portland, Me., 1874; had taken at last report 400 sperm.
Pacific Ocean	Oct. 2	Out, 1877				Had taken at last report 175 sperm, 375 whale
....do	June 1	Out, 1877				Bought from Westport 1874; had taken at last report 750 sperm, 80 whale.
Atlantic	July 30	Oct. 22, 1876	575	25		
....do	May 12					Condemned at St. Michaels November 6, 1876; sent home 380 sperm.
North Pacific	Oct. 12	Out, 1877				Had taken at last report 30 sperm, 1,700 whale, 14,920 bone.
Atlantic	June 8	Sept. 12, 1876	67	7		
Indian Ocean	July 8	Out, 1877				Had taken at last report 75 sperm, 425 whale.
Atlantic	May 1	Nov. 16, 1875	14			Bought from Marion 1874.
Atlantic	May 26	Oct. 4, 1875	195	10		Sailed again in 1875; arrived March 31, 1876, with 80 sperm, 20 whale.
Atlantic	Oct. 25	Out, 1877				Had taken at last report 130 sperm.
Atlantic	Nov. 3	Out, 1877				Had taken at last report 530 sperm.
Atlantic	Mar. 25	Aug. 2, 1876	310	100		

Table showing returns of whaling-vessels

Name of vessel.	Class.	Tonnage.	Captain.	Managing owner or agent.
1875.				
Provincetown, Mass.—Continued.				
Alcyone	Schooner	92	—— Fisher	E. & E. K. Cook & Co
Antarctic	do	101	—— Bell	W. A. Atkins
Arizona	do	92	—— White	Stephen Cook
D. A. Small	Brig	119	William Curren	William Curran
Edward Lee	Schooner	110	Asaph Atkins	Asaph Atkins
E. H. Hatfield	do	89	—— Kickcornell	E. & E. K. Cook & Co
Ellen Rizpah	do	67	—— Dunham	S. Cook
Gage H. Phillips	do	107	—— Cook	do
Lottie E. Cook	do	82	Israel A. Dyer	William A. Atkins
M. E. Simmons	do	105	—— Rich	E. & E. K. Cook & Co
Quickstep	do	94	—— Higgins	do
Rising Sun	do	69	—— Taylor	Thomas S. Taylor
Wm. A. Grozier	do	117	—— Roberts	W. A. Atkins
Boston, Mass.				
F. H. Moore	Brig	107	Robert Soper	Frederick Davis
Louisa A	Schooner	122	George E. Senter	Heman Smith
Rosa Baker	Brig	108	Joseph Thompson	do
Sarah E. Lewis	Schooner	96	—— Cook	do
New London, Conn.				
Charles Colgate	Schooner	250	—— Sisson	Lawrence & Co
Flying Fish	do	75	—— Neal	do
Francis Allyn	do	107	—— Glass	Haven, Williams & Co
Golden West	do	144	—— Williams	Lawrence & Co
Isabella	Brig	192	—— Palmer	Haven, Williams & Co
L. P. Simmons	Schooner	89	—— Buddington	do
Nile	Ship	293	—— Spicer	do
Roswell King	Schooner	134	—— Fuller	do
San Francisco, Cal.				
Florence	Bark	245		Thomas W. Williams
1876.				
New Bedford, Mass.				
Abbie Bradford	Schooner	115	E. B. Fisher	Jonathan Bourne
A. Houghton	Bark	219	James G. Sinclair	John T. Richardson
Alaska	do	347	Charles M. Fisher	Jonathan Bourne
A. R. Tucker	do	145	Amos C. Baker	J. & W. R. Wing
Arnolda	do	340	Isaac C. Howland	Loum Snow, jr
Amelia	Schooner	95	—— Braley	William N. Church
Atlantic	Bark	291	Benjamin F. Wing	Jos. & Wm. R. Wing
Bartholemew Gosnold	do	365	Sylv. D. Robinson	Charles R. Tucker & Co
Bounding Billow	do	262	Harvey E. Luce	Gifford & Cummings
California	Ship	367	George F. Brightman	Chas. R. Tucker & Co
Cicero	Bark	226	Thomas Foster	John P. Knowles, 2d
Cleone	do	346	James E. Stanton	Swift & Allen
Desdemona	do	236	Francis W. Vincent	Geo. & Mat. Howland
E. B. Phillips	do	144	Joseph F. Francis	John McCullough
Eliza Adams	Ship	408	John W. Cornell	Taber, Gordon & Co
E. H. Adams	Brig	107	Leonard E. West	William Lewis
Europa	Bark	323	Edward Penniman	Swift & Perry
Franklin	Schooner	77	David B. Sprague	William Lewis
Helen Mar	Bark	324	George E. Bauldry	Swift & Allen
John & Winthrop	do	338	Edward P. Shiverick	John P. Knowles, 2d
Laconia	do	157	Rufus W. Gifford	William Lewis
Marcella	do	166	Frederick P. Tripp	Chas. R. Tucker & Co
Mattapoisett	do	110	Welcome J. Lawton	Abbott P. Smith
Mercury	do	311	J. Franklin Brooks	William Phillips & Son
Merlin	do	246	John R. Sturgis	Chas. R. Tucker & Co
Minnesota	Ship	243	David E. Allen	William Lewis

sailing from American ports—Continued.

Whaling-ground.	Date— Of sailing.	Date— Of arrival.	Result of voyage. Sperm-oil.	Result of voyage. Whale-oil.	Result of voyage. Whalebone.	Remarks.
			Bbls.	*Bbls.*	*Lbs.*	
Atlantic	Apr. 10	Oct. 4, 1875	20	......	......	
....do	Mar. 25	Oct. 21, 1875	100	......	......	
....do	Mar. 19	Sept. 22, 1875	160	......	......	
....do	Mar. 25	Aug. 16, 1876	300	......	......	Returned to whaling 1875.
....	Mar. 11	Sept. 27, 1875	90	......	......	Bought from Newburyport 1874.
Atlantic	Jan. 23	Sept. 4, 1876	190	......	......	
....do	Mar. 19	Sept. 21, 1875	......	220	......	
....do	Jan. 8	Sept. 7, 1875	......	450	......	Resumed 1875; sailed again in December; last reported with 75 sperm.
....do	Mar. 19	Sept. 21, 1875	20	190	......	Bought 1874.
....do	Mar. 30	Sept. 26, 1875	170	......	......	
....do ...... {	Jan. 23	Sept. 24, 1875	100	......	......	
	Dec. 18	Sept. 22, 1876	75	15	......	
....do	Mar. 27	Sept. 22, 1875	159	60	......	
....do	Mar. 25	Aug. 20, 1876	680	30	......	
Atlantic	Oct. 12	Out, 1877	......	......	......	Had taken at last report 600 sperm.
....do ...... {	....	Sept. 23, 1875	160	......	......	} Replaced 1875.
	Dec. 1	Oct. 4, 1876	290	......	......	
....do	June 22	Sept. 14, 1876	450	......	......	
....do	Oct. 11	Sept. 22, 1876	135	......	......	
Desolation Isld.	June 15	Out, 1877	......	......	......	Last reported with 240 whale.
....do	July 7	Apr. 2, 1876	......	200	......	
Atlantic	July 27	Out, 1877	......	......	......	David Gavitt, second mate, lost at sea 1876.
Desolation Isld.	June 30	—— —, 1876	......	......	......	
Cum. Inlet	June 8	Out, 1877	......	......	......	Had at last report 250 whale, 4,000 bone.
Atlantic	July 13	Apr. 1, 1876	......	500	......	
Cum. Inlet	May 4	Jan. 11, 1876	......	380	5,000	
Desolation Isld	June 29	Out, 1877	......	......	......	Had at last report 300 whale.
Pacific Ocean ..	Mar. 31	Nov. 3, 1875	......	1,250	......	
Atlantic	May 4	Out, 1877	......	......	......	
Hudson's Bay ..	May 23	Out, 1877	......	......	......	Rebuilt by the United States during the rebellion.
Pacific Ocean ..	June 1	Out, 1877	......	......	......	Had taken at last report 280 sperm.
Atlantic	Dec. 12	Out, 1877	......	......	......	
....do	July 6	Out, 1877	......	......	......	
....do	Dec. 27	Out, 1877	......	......	......	Had taken at last report 60 sperm.
Indian Ocean ..	Aug. 8	Out, 1877	......	......	......	Had taken at last report 12 sperm.
Atlantic	May 23	Out, 1877	......	......	......	Had taken at last report 300 sperm.
Pacific Ocean ..	Sept. 13	Out, 1877	......	......	......	Built at Chelsea 1854; had taken at last report 20 sperm.
....do	Nov. 8	Out, 1877	......	......	......	
Atlantic	Sept. 6	Out, 1877	......	......	......	Had taken at last report 100 sperm.
North Pacific ..	May 23	Out, 1877	......	......	......	Captain Stanton came home sick 1876; returned to whaling 1876; had taken at last report 130 sperm.
Atlantic	July 20	Out, 1877	......	......	......	Had taken at last report 20 sperm.
....do	Nov. 1	Out, 1877	......	......	......	Bought from Boston.
....do	Sept. 6	Out, 1877	......	......	......	Had taken at last report 125 sperm.
....do	Oct. 3	Out, 1877	......	......	......	
Pacific Ocean ..	Sept. 12	Out, 1877	......	......	......	Had taken at last report 150 sperm.
Atlantic	Aug. 29	Out, 1877	......	......	......	Bought from New London.
North Pacific ..	July 6	Out, 1877	......	......	......	
Pacific Ocean ..	July 19	Out, 1877	......	......	......	Had taken at last report 12 sperm.
Indian Ocean ..	May 30	Out, 1877	......	......	......	Had taken at last report 160 sperm.
....do	Aug. 1	Out, 1877	......	......	......	
Atlantic	Aug. 7	Out, 1877	......	......	......	Had taken at last report 60 sperm.
North Pacific ..	Dec. 14	Out, 1877	......	......	......	
Indian Ocean ..	Nov. 27	Out, 1877	......	......	......	
....do	July 11	Out, 1877	......	......	......	Returned to whaling 1876.

Table showing returns of whaling-vessels

Name of vessel.	Class.	Tonnage.	Captain.	Managing owner or agent.
1876.				
New Bedford, Mass.—Continued.				
Ohio	Bark	205	William B. Ellis	Loum Snow, jr
Pedro Varela	Schooner	89	Anthony P. Brenton	Gideon Allen & Son
Petrel	...do	61	James Avery	Philip H. Reed
President	Bark	257	Thomas F. Pease	Jonathan Bourne
Pacific	...do	341	Charles R. Smethers	Swift & Perry
Progress	...do	358	William T. Hawes	I. H. Bartlett & Sons
Sarah	...do	128	Joseph D. Silva	John P. Knowles, 2d
Sea Ranger	...do	273	Stephen Flanders	I. H. Bartlett & Sons
Seine	...do	234	Henry Clay	John P. Knowles, 2d
Stafford	...do	156	Edward A. King	Jos. & Wm. R. Wing
Sunbeam	...do	255	Benjamin Gifford	...do
Swallow	...do	326	Thomas L. Ellis	Swift & Perry
Triton	...do	264	Charles F. Keith	J. & W. R. Wing
Thomas Pope	...do	231	Joseph W. Lavers	William Lewis
Tropic Bird	...do	145	Owen H. Tilton	...do
Varnum H. Hill	Brig	126	Dennis D. Baxter	John McCullough
Wave	Bark	150	James H. Hammond	Thomas Knowles & Co
Fairhaven, Mass.				
Cohannet	Schooner	83	Edgar W. Crapo	Jeremiah H. Pease
Ellen Rodman	...do	73	Charles H. Wilbur	Tucker Damon, jr
Marion, Mass.				
Admiral Blake	Schooner	84	William C. Hathaway	Andrew J. Hadley
William Wilson	...do	92	Loring Braley; Charles B. Barstow	...do
Dartmouth, Mass.				
Cape Horn Pigeon	Bark	212	George O. Baker	William Potter, 2d
Westport, Mass.				
A. Hicks	Bark	303	Edward E. Hicks	Andrew Hicks
Mermaid	...do	273	George E. Allen	...do
Edgartown, Mass.				
Mary Frazier	Bark	301	—— Dexter	Samuel Osborn, jr
Provincetown, Mass.				
Alcyone	Schooner	92	—— Fisher	E. & E. K. Cook & Co
Antarctic	...do	101	—— Bell	William A. Atkins
Arizona	...do	79	—— White	Stephen Cook
B. F. Sparks	...do	92	—— Ewell	...do
Carrie W. Clark	...do	116	—— Burch	Central Wharf Company
Charles Thompson	...do	152	—— Leach	S. S. Swift
C. L. Sparks	...do	96	—— Sparks	David Conwell
Edward Lee	...do	110	—— Atkins	Asaph Atkins
E. H. Hatfield	...do	89	—— Kirkcornell	E. & E. K. Cook & Co
Ellen Rizpah	...do	67	—— Dunham	Stephen Cook
Gracie M. Parker	...do	82	—— Dyer	Alfred Cook
H. M. Simmons	...do	116	—— Atkins	William A. Atkins
Lottie E. Cook	...do	82	—— Dyer	...do
M. E. Simmons	...do	105	—— Rich	E. & E. K. Cook & Co
N. J. Knights	...do	70	—— Foster	David Conwell
Quickstep	...do	94	—— Manly	E. & E. K. Cook & Co
Rising Sun	...do	69	—— Taylor	Thomas S. Taylor
Boston, Mass.				
Heman Smith	Brig	122	John J. Cook	Heman Smith
William Martin	Schooner	93	William Martin	...do
Sarah E. Lewis	...do	96	—— Cook	...do
New London, Conn.				
Florence	Schooner	56	—— Miner	Haven, Williams & Co

sailing from American ports—Continued.

Whaling-ground.	Date—		Result of voyage.			Remarks.
	Of sailing.	Of arrival.	Sperm-oil.	Whale-oil.	Whalebone.	
			Bbls.	*Bbls.*	*Lbs.*	
Atlantic	May 9	Out, 1877				Had taken at last report 100 sperm.
....do	Nov. 6	Out, 1877				
....do	Nov. 16	Out, 1877				Had taken at last report 35 sperm.
....do	July 26	Out, 1877				Had taken at last report 30 sperm.
North Pacific	Dec. 13	Out, 1877				
....do	Nov. 16	Out, 1877				
Atlantic	June 20	Out, 1877				Had taken at last report 215 sperm.
....do	July 6	Out, 1877				Had at last report 30 sperm.
....do	Nov. 9	Out, 1877				Had at last report 115 sperm.
....do	July 17	Out, 1877				Had at last report 75 sperm.
....do	May 2	Out, 1877				Had at last report 430 sperm.
....do	Apr. 18	Out, 1877				Returned to whaling; had at last report 420 sperm.
....do	Aug. 26	Out, 1877				Had taken at last report 140 sperm.
North Pacific	Dec. 7	Out, 1877				
Atlantic	May 2	Out, 1877				Had taken at last report 280 sperm.
....do	Sept. 7	Out, 1877				Bought from Provincetown.
....do	Nov. 15	Out, 1877				
Atlantic {	May 2	Sept. 22, 1876	75			
	Nov. 14	Out, 1877				
....do	Dec. 1	Out, 1877				
Atlantic	May 16	Oct. 8, 1876	90			Sailed again in December.
....do {	Mar. 27	Sept. 14, 1876	100			} Had at last report 60 sperm.
	Nov. 27	Out, 1877				
Pacific Ocean	Sept. 6	Out, 1877				Had taken at last report 25 sperm.
Indian Ocean	Oct. 18	Out, 1877				
....do	June 20	Out, 1877				Had taken at last report 365 sperm.
Atlantic	Oct. 25	Out, 1877				
Atlantic	Apr. 20	Out, 1877				Had taken at last report 340 sperm.
....do	Jan. 22	Sept. 26, 1876	115	80		
....do	Jan. 24	Sept. 15, 1876	80	20		
....do	May 11	Out, 1877				Had taken at last report 160 sperm.
....do	Mar. —	Out, 1877				Had taken at last report 230 sperm.
....do	Jan. 24	Out, 1877				Had taken at last report 150 sperm, 20 whale.
....do	May 1	Out, 1877				Had taken at last report 190 sperm.
....do	Jan. 24	Sept. 16, 1876		180		
....do	Jan. 22	Aug. 29, 1876				Sailed again in December.
....do	Jan. 24	July 30, 1876	110	200		
....do	Feb. 21	Sept. 4, 1876	165	200		
....do	Apr. 20	Out, 1877				Had taken at last report 150 sperm.
....do	Jan. 24	Sept. 15, 1876	75	200		
....do	Feb. 21	Sept. 15, 1876	150	200		
....do	Jan. 8	Aug. 25, 1876	160	125		
....do	Nov. 11	Out, 1877				Had taken at last report 25 sperm.
....do	Feb. 18	Sept. 12, 1876	100	200		
Atlantic	May 12	Out, 1877				Last reported with 150 sperm, 10 whale.
....do	May 8	Oct. 2, 1876	225			
....do	Dec. 18	Out, 1877				
Atlantic	July 22	Out, 1877				

Table showing returns of whaling-vessels

Name of vessel.	Class.	Tonnage.	Captain.	Managing owner or agent.
1876.				
New London, Conn.—Continued.				
Flying Fish	Schooner	75	—— Holmes	Lawrence & Co
Golden West	do	144	—— Williams	do
L. P. Simmons	do	89	—— Buddington	Haven, Williams & Co
Nile	Ship	293	—— Spicer	do
Trinity	Bark	317	—— Rogers	Lawrence & Co
San Francisco, Cal.				
Clara Bell	Bark	196	—— Williams	Richard T. Howland
Florence	do	245	—— Williams	Thomas W. Williams

sailing from American ports—Continued.

Whaling-ground.	Date—		Result of voyage.			Remarks.
	Of sailing.	Of arrival.	Sperm-oil.	Whale-oil.	Whalebone.	
			Bbls.	*Bbls.*	*Lbs.*	
Atlantic	June 29	Out, 1877				
....do	Aug. 9	Out, 1877				
....do	June 27	Out, 1877				
Cum. Inlet	June 24	Nov. 17, 1876		550	6,500	
Atlantic	July 1	Out, 1877				
Pacific Ocean	Apr. 18					Abandoned in the Arctic 1876; had 650 whale.
North Pacific	Mar. 3	Oct. 22, 1876		700		Sailed again November 29.

J.—*Recorded summary of importation of oil and bone, and total value computed for each year, commencing January 1, 1804, and ending December 31, 1876, with gross valuation for the whole period.*

NOTE.—From 1804 to 1817 it would appear by the table of exports that much oil and bone was imported which is not credited to any port. Assuming the exportation of whale-oil for that period at one-third of the importation, and the exportation of bone at two-thirds of the importation, it is necessary to add to the former 9,226,834 gallons, and to the latter 206,551 pounds.

Year.	Gallons sperm-oil.	Average price per gallon.	Gallons whale-oil.	Average price per gallon.	Pounds whalebone.	Average price per pound.	Total value.
1804 ..	297,045	$1 40*	221,057	$0 50*	46,690	$0 08*	$530,126 70
1805 ..	412,492	96*	612,895	50*	13,131	10*	703,752 92
1806 ..	378,788	80	741,951	50	86,544	07*	680,103 48
1807 ..	356,548	1 00	934,259	50	72,784	07*	828,771 88
1808 ..	362,471	80	567,095	44	49,970	07*	543,016 50
1809 ..	443,709	60	587,664	44	17,092	08*	525,164 92
1810 ..	572,271	75	585,869	40	41,437	08*	666,865 81
1811 ..	844,200	1 25	304,825	40	43,200	09*	1,180,494 96
1812 ..	429,692	1 00	191,079	50	6,266	10*	529,120 00
1813 ..	111,289	1 25*	80,860	50	9,901	10*	180,167 85
1814 ..	108,486	1 25*	2,573	1 40	....	....	140,167 80
1815 ..	48,510	1 00	4,347	83	....	....	71,522 01
1816 ..	237,479	1 12½	294,525	65	796	12*	458,700 08
1817 ..	1,028,475	72	581,836	60*	19,444	12*	1,091,576 88
1818 ..	586,688	90	608,013	50	65,446	10*	838,570 30
1819 ..	671,674	83	1,204,308	35	83,843	10*	987,381 52
1820 ..	1,093,302	93½	1,409,846	35*	78,879	10*	1,523,571 37
1821 ..	1,357,618	67½	1,213,506	33*	62,893	12*	1,324,396 29
1822 ..	1,351,350	65	1,619,951	32	50,799	12*	1,402,857 70
1823 ..	2,938,351	43	1,697,440	32*	103,404	13*	1,820,114 25
1824 ..	3,091,064	45½	1,833,237	30*	133,472	13*	1,973,756 58
1825 ..	1,924,303	70½	1,666,413	32*	152,534	15*	1,912,765 87
1826 ..	919,800	75	1,108,233	30*	79,368	16*	1,035,018 78
1827 ..	2,958,480	72½	1,119,037	30*	106,255	18*	2,499,735 00
1828 ..	2,475,176	62½	1,591,790	26	137,323	25	1,995,181 15
1829 ..	2,350,152	61½	2,256,502	26	563,654	25	2,172,947 50
1830 ..	3,482,042	65½	2,831,315	39	514,991	20	3,487,949 56
1831 ..	3,636,738	71	3,609,774	30	279,279	17	4,139,790 61
1832 ..	2,299,563	85	5,703,894	23½	442,881	13	3,352,618 17
1833 ..	3,289,765	85	5,153,148	26	266,432	13	4,170,754 89
1834 ..	3,891,573	72½	4,144,833	27½	343,324	21	4,033,317 55
1835 ..	5,181,529	84	3,950,289	39	965,192	21	6,095,787 35
1836 ..	4,200,021	89	4,301,892	44	1,028,773	25	5,888,044 42
1837 ..	5,329,138	82½	6,389,995	35	1,753,104	20	6,983,657 90
1838 ..	4,076,100	86	7,204,365	32	2,200,000	20	6,250,842 80
1839 ..	4,408,866	1 05	7,040,975	36	2,000,000	18	7,524,060 30
1840 ..	4,928,017	1 00	6,408,391	30	2,000,000	19	7,230,534 30
1841 ..	4,956,304	94	6,459,516	32	2,000,000	20	7,125,970 88
1842 ..	3,256,155	73	4,876,232	34	1,500,000	23	4,379,812 03
1843 ..	5,260,027	63	6,511,900	34	2,127,270	36	6,293,680 21
1844 .	4,239,711	90⅘	8,254,481	36 7-12	2,532,445	40	7,875,970 38
1845 ..	4,967,550	88	11,593,483	33	3,195,054	34	9,283,611 75
1846 ..	3,155,481	87⅞	6,589,737	33¾	3,252,939	34	6,203,115 43
1847 ..	3,803,719	1 00¾	9,864,225	36	3,341,680	31	8,419,288 49
1848 ..	3,401,274	1 00	8,840,663	33	2,003,000	25	6,819,442 78
1849 ..	3,179,736	1 08⅞	7,827,498	39 11-12	2,281,100	21⅞	7,069,953 74
1850 ..	2,926,098	1 20 7-10	6,319,152	49 1-10	2,869,200	32 2-5	7,564,124 72
1851 ..	3,137,116	1 27¼	10,347,214	45 5-16	3,916,500	34½	10,031,744 05
1852 ..	2,484,468	1 23¾	2,652,647	68¼	1,259,900	50 5-6	5,565,409 89
1853 ..	3,246,925	1 24¾	8,193,591	58 1-6	5,652,300	34½	10,766,521 20
1854 ..	2,315,924	1 48¾	10,074,866	59⅝	3,445,200	39 1-5	10,802,594 20
1855 ..	2,288,443	1 77 2-10	5,796,472	71 3-10	2,707,500	45¼	9,413,148 93
1856 ..	2,549,642	1 62	6,233,535	79½	2,592,700	58	9,589,846 36
1857 ..	2,470,860	1 28⅓	7,274,641	73¼	2,058,850	96¾	10,491,548 90
1858 ..	2,581,142	1 21	5,740,025	54	1,571,200	92¼	7,672,227 31
1859 ..	2,879,352	1 36¼	5,997,946	48½	1,923,850	88	8,525,108 91
1860 ..	2,306,934	1 41½	4,410,158	49½	1,337,650	80 1-5	6,520,135 12
1861 ..	2,171,358	1 31½	4,212,085	44½	1,038,450	66	5,415,090 59
1862 ..	1,752,692	1 42¾	3,165,057	59⅓	763,500	88	5,051,781 64
1863 ..	2,049,232	1 61	1,983,681	95¼	488,750	1 53	5,936,507 17
1864 .	2,027,718	1 89½	2,263,685	1 28	760,450	1 80⅔	8,113,922 07
1865 ..	1,047,123	2 25½	2,401,497	1 45	619,350	1 71⅔	6,906,650 51
1866 ..	1,154,885	2 55	2,340,513	1 21	920,375	1 37	7,037,891 23
1867 ..	1,368,139	2 27	2,812,603	73⅔	1,001,397	1 17¾	6,356,772 51
1868 ..	1,485,981	1 92	2,065,613	82	900,850	1 02½	5,470,157 43
1869 ..	1,509,984	1 81⅓	2,677,846	1 01¾	603,603	1 23	6,205,244 32
1870 ..	1,738,265	1 36⅔	2,289,767	67½	708,365	85	4,529,126 02

* Assumed value.

J.—*Recorded summary of importation of oil and bone, &c.*—Concluded.

Year.	Gallons sperm-oil.	Average price per gallon.	Gallons whale-oil.	Average price per gallon.	Pounds whalebone.	Average price per pound.	Total value.
1871..	1,308,321	1 31	2,367,288	64	600,655	77	3,691,469 18
1872..	1,423,832	1 45¼	973,684	65½	193,793	1 28½	2,954,783 00
1873..	1,324,669	1 47½	1,260,441	62¼	206,396	1 08⅓	2,962,106 96
1874..	1,014,395	1 59	1,190,133	60½	345,560	1 10	2,713,034 51
1875..	1,342,435	1 60½	1,089,711	65¼	372,303	1 20 3-5	3,314,800 24
1876..	1,254,047	1 40½	1,039,815	56	150,628	1 96	2,639,463 31
......	(†)	....	9,226,834	59	206,517	9	5,462,418 59
Total.	161,452,702	....	266,996,217	....	75,268,361	....	331,947,480 51

† Deficit, as per note at head of table.

NOTE.—Scammon estimates that sperm whales will average 25 and right whales 60 barrels of oil, and of the former 10 and of the latter 20 per cent. of those killed are lost. Upon that basis the above amounts of oil would represent the slaughter of 225,521 sperm, and 193,522 right whales.

K.—*Synopsis of importation, by ports, from* 1804 *to* 1877.

NOTE.—These returns, up to 1838, excepting in the cases of Nantucket, Sag Harbor, and New London, are made up mainly from the newspaper reports of the voyages, an occasional estimate being made when there was no report of oil.

Port of departure.	Nature and number of vessels returning.			Importation.			Tonnage.		
	Ships and barks.	Brigs and schooners.	Total.	Sperm-oil.	Whale-oil.	Bone.	Ships and barks.	Brigs and schooners.	Total.
1804.				*Bbls.*	*Bbls.*	*Lbs.*			
Hudson, N. Y.	1	1	2		1,400				
Nantucket, Mass.	13	7	20	7,395	6,718	46,690			
New Bedford, Mass	13	10	*23	2,035	14,600				
Sag Harbor, N. Y	3		3		3,309				
Total	30	18	48	9,430	7,018	46,690			
1805.									
Hudson, N. Y	2		2	2,500					
Nantucket, Mass.	9	2	11	7,493	4,507	13,131			
New Bedford, Mass	11	5	16	3,100	11,300				
Sag Harbor, N. Y.	4		4		3,650				
Total	26	7	33	13,093	19,457	13,131			
1806.									
Nantucket, Mass	24		24	10,785	15,954	86,544			
New Bedford, Mass	1		1	1,200					
New London, Conn	1		1		800				
Sag Harbor, N. Y	5		5	40	6,800				
Total	31		31	12,025	23,554	86,544			
1807.									
Nantucket, Mass.			†	11,249	13,959	72,784			
New Bedford, Mass	5	1	6		6,700				
New London, Conn.	3		3		1,600				
Sag Harbor, N. Y	6		6	70	7,400				
Total	14	1	15	11,319	29,659	72,784			
1808.									
Greenwich, R. I.	1		1		1,000				
Nantucket, Mass.	15	2	17	7,707	10,503	49,970			
New Bedford, Mass	5	3	8	3,800	3,800				
New London, Conn.	3		3		1,500				
Sag Harbor, N. Y	2		2		1,200				
Total	26	5	31	11,507	18,003	49,970			

1809.									
Greenwich, R. I	1		1		1, 200				
Nantucket, Mass	11	4	15	9, 336	7, 256	17, 092			
New Bedford, Mass	3	4	7	4, 750	2, 000				
New London, Conn	3		3		2, 500				
Sag Harbor, N. Y	4		4		5, 700				
Total	22	8	30	14, 086	18, 656	17, 092			
1810.									
Greenwich, R. I	1		1		1, 200				
Nantucket, Mass	17		17	7, 247	7, 929	41, 437			
New Bedford, Mass	13		13	10, 920	4, 500				
Sag Harbor, N. Y	6		6		4, 970				
Total	37		37	18, 167	18, 599	41, 437			
1811.									
Greenwich, R. I					1, 000				
Nantucket, Mass	18	1	19	22, 100	6, 377	43, 200			
New Bedford, Mass	4		4	4, 700	1, 500				
Sag Harbor, N. Y	1		1		800				
Total	23	1	24	26, 800	9, 677	43, 200			
1812.									
Nantucket, Mass	12		12	7, 591	2, 230	6, 266			
New Bedford, Mass	6		6	6, 000	1, 000				
Sag Harbor, N. Y	2		2	50	2, 836				
Total	20		20	13, 641	6, 066	6, 266			
1813.									
Nantucket, Mass	2		2	1, 133	2, 567	9, 901			
New Bedford, Mass	2		2	2, 400					
Total	4		4	3, 533	2, 567	9, 901			
1814.									
Nantucket, Mass	1		1	1, 644	83				
New Bedford, Mass	1		1	1, 800					
Total	2		2	3, 444	83				
1815.									
Nantucket, Mass		15	15	920	138				
New Bedford, Mass		2	2	620					
Total		17	17	1, 540	138				

* Up to 1815 New Bedford includes Fairhaven, Westport, and Dartmouth. † Unknown.

K.—*Synopsis of importation, by ports, from 1804 to 1877*—Continued.

Port of departure.	Nature and number of vessels returning.			Importation.			Tonnage.		
	Ships and barks.	Brigs and schooners.	Total.	Sperm-oil.	Whale-oil.	Bone.	Ships and barks.	Brigs and schooners.	Total.
1816.				*Bbls.*	*Bbls.*	*Lbs.*			
Fairhaven, Mass	1	5	6	635	1, 400				
Holmes' Hole, Mass		1	1	250					
Mattapoisett, Mass		1	1	160					
Nantucket, Mass	10	8	18	2, 232	2, 700	796			
New Bedford, Mass	1	6	7	1, 350	1, 500				
Sag Harbor, N. Y	3		3	80	3, 250				
Wareham, Mass		1	1	100					
Westport, Mass		1	1		500				
Other ports				*2, 792					
Total	15	23	38	7, 539	9, 350	796			
1817.									
Boston, Mass	1	1	2		2, 000				
Hudson, N. Y	2		2	2, 000					
Nantucket, Mass	25	13	38	22, 214	5, 771	19, 444			
New Bedford, Mass	8	5	13	7, 490	7, 800				
Sag Harbor, N. Y	2		2		2, 900				
Other ports				946					
Total	38	19	57	32, 650	18, 471	19, 444			
1818.									
Edgartown, Mass	1		1	1, 500					
Nantucket, Mass	17	9	26	14, 874	13, 426	65, 446			
New Bedford, Mass	1	2	3	2, 250	1, [illegible]00				
Sag Harbor, N. Y	4		4		4, 876				
Total	23	11	34	18, 625	19, 302	65, 446			
1819.									
Boston, Mass		1	1		1, 150				
Fair Haven, Mass	1		1		1, 500				
Nantucket, Mass	16	4	20	18, 522	11, 511	62, 403			
New Bedford, Mass	9	4	13		17, 880				
Sag Harbor, N. Y	5		5	459	6, 191	21, 440			
Westport, Mass		1	1	300					
Other ports				2, 042					
Total	31	10	41	21, 323	38, 232	83, 843			

1820.									
Edgartown, Mass	1		1	1, 250					
Hudson, N. Y	1	2	3	100	1, 500				
Mattapoisett, Mass		1	1	250					
Nantucket, Mass	17	12	29	16, 911	11, 736	59, 794			
New Bedford, Mass	19	9	28	8, 680	21, 580	17, 045			
New London, Conn	3		3	78	1, 731	2, 040			
Philadelphia, Pa	1		1		350				
Sag Harbor, N. Y	6		6	547	7, 860				
Westport, Mass		5	5	580					
Other ports				6, 312					
Total	48	29	77	34, 708	44, 757	78, 879			
1821.									
Boston, Mass	1		1		1, 400				
Edgartown, Mass	1	3	4	1, 800					
Fair Haven, Mass	3		3	2, 200	800				
Falmouth, Mass		1	1	300					
Hudson, N. Y	1		1		1, 050				
Nantucket, Mass	19	14	33	22, 915	8, 632	38, 092			
New Bedford, Mass	16	13	29	12, 680	15, 070				
New London, Conn	3		3	105	2, 323	2, 375			
Provincetown, Mass		11	11	2, 290					
Sag Harbor, N. Y	6		6	389	8, 649	22, 426			
Salem, Mass	1	1	2	150	600				
Westport, Mass		11	11	270					
Total	51	54	105	43, 099	38, 524	62, 893			
1822.									
Boston, Mass		4	4	480	220				
Dartmouth, Mass		1	1		500				
Fair Haven, Mass	4		4		4, 700				
Falmouth, Mass		1	1	150					
Hudson, N. Y	2	1	3		2, 800				
Marblehead, Mass		1	1	100					
Nantucket, Mass	19	10	29	27, 401	5, 407	3, 197			
New Bedford, Mass	19	6	25	12, 305	20, 705	13, 174			
New Haven, Conn	1		1		700				
New London, Conn	1	4	5	194	4, 528	2, 260			
Newport, R. I	1	1	2		1, 200				
Provincetown, Mass		8	8	890					
Sag Harbor, N. Y	9		9	630	10, 367	32, 168			
Salem, Mass		1	1		100				
Stonington, Conn		1	1		200				
Westport, Mass		6	6	750					
Total	56	45	101	42, 900	51, 427	50, 799			

* Probably nearly, if not quite, all the sperm-oil credited to "other ports" belongs to New Bedford, Mass.

K.—*Synopsis of importation, by ports, from* 1804 *to* 1877—Continued.

Port of departure.	Nature and number of vessels returning.			Importation.			Tonnage.		
	Ships and barks.	Brigs and schooners.	Total.	Sperm-oil.	Whale-oil.	Bone.	Ships and barks.	Brigs and schooners.	Total.
1823.				*Bbls.*	*Bbls.*	*Lbs.*			
Boston, Mass	2	4	6	1,320	2,900				
Edgartown, Mass	3		3	4,750					
Fairhaven, Mass	5		5	3,800	4,750				
Hudson, N. Y	5		5	5,870	750				
Mattapoisett, Mass		1	1	100					
Nantucket, Mass	25	4	29	36,063	3,808	20,243			
New Bedford, Mass	26	13	39	29,843	23,736	14,068			
New Haven, Conn.	1		1	1,800	200				
New London, Conn	4	2	6	2,318	6,712	23,293			
Newport, R. I	3		3	4,000	1,300				
Providence, R. I		2	2	200					
Provincetown, Mass		2	2	300					
Sag Harbor, N. Y	8		8	1,842	9,731	45,800			
Tiverton, R. I		1	1	75					
Westport, Mass		3	3	1,000					
Total	82	32	114	93,281	53,887	103,404			
1824.									
Boston, Mass	2	1	3	4,560					
Edgartown, Mass	1		1	2,300					
Fairhaven, Mass	4		4	1,850	5,300				
Falmouth, Mass	1		1	2,000					
Hudson, N. Y	3		3	6,400					
Nantucket, Mass	25	4	29	41,230	4,322	22,062			
New Bedford, Mass	35	3	38	29,100	32,969	9,314			
New London, Conn	3	2	5	1,924	4,996	32,535			
Newport, R. I	3		3	4,200					
Plymouth, Mass	1		1	2,000	1,450				
Sag Harbor, N. Y	7		7	335	9,161	69,561			
Warren, R. I	1		1	1,800					
Westport, Mass		2	2	430					
Total	86	12	98	98,129	58,198	133,472			
1825.									
Boston, Mass	1		1	1,500					
Edgartown, Mass	2		2	3,[illegible]50					
Fairhaven, Mass	3		3	1,200	3,400				
Nantucket, Mass	22	1	23	31,780	7,194	39,596			
New Bedford, Mass	18	5	23	13,659	23,178	38,365			

New Haven, Conn	1		1	1,800	220				
New London, Conn	4		4	2,276	5,483	No record			
Newport, R. I	1		1		1,800				
Plymouth, Mass	1		1	2,000					
Perth Amboy, N. J	1		1		1,500				
Sag Harbor, N. Y	7		7	1,724	9,927	73,173			
Stonington, Conn	1		1	1,800	200	1,400			
Westport, Mass		1	1	200					
Total	62	7	69	61,089	52,902	152,534			
1826.									
Boston, Mass	1		1		1,000				
Dartmouth, Mass		1	1	350					
Edgartown, Mass	1	1	2	2,700					
Fairhaven, Mass	4		4	450	4,300				
Nantucket, Mass	12		12	16,334	2,402	16,002			
New Bedford, Mass	12	4	16	5,723	18,220	11,389			
New London, Conn	2		2	88	2,804				
Newport, R. I	1		1	2,000					
Sag Harbor, N. Y	6		6	625	6,456	51,977			
Westport, Mass		2	2	930					
Total	39	8	47	29,200	35,182	79,368			
1827.									
Dartmouth, Mass		1	1	450					
Edgartown, Mass	1		1	2,200					
Fairhaven, Mass	3	1	4	270	5,150				
Falmouth, Mass	1		1	2,100					
Hudson, N. Y	1		1	2,300					
Mattapoisett, Mass		1	1	150	15				
Nantucket, Mass	14	3	17	27,970	583	5,152			
New Bedford, Mass	32	4	36	47,127	18,186	47,785			
New London, Conn	5		5	6,166	3,375				
Newport, R. I	6		6	2,082	6,716	53,318			
New York, N. Y	1		1		1,500				
Plymouth, Mass	1		1	2,300					
Westport, Mass		4	4	805					
Total	65	14	79	93,920	35,525	106,255			
1828.									
Boston, Mass	1		1		700				
Dartmouth, Mass		1	1	160					
Edgartown, Mass	2		2	3,900					
Fairhaven, Mass	4	4	8	2,830	3,650				
Mattapoisett, Mass		4	4	710					
Nantucket, Mass	21	3	24	43,174	1,033	8,662			
New Bedford, Mass	29	9	38	22,208	26,438	32,191			
New London, Conn	3		3	168	5,435				
Newport, R. I	1	1	2	2,450					

K.—*Synopsis of importation, by ports, from* 1804 *to* 1877—Continued.

Port of departure.	Nature and number of vessels returning.			Importation.			Tonnage.		
	Ships and barks.	Brigs and schooners.	Total.	Sperm-oil.	Whale-oil.	Bone.	Ships and barks.	Brigs and schooners.	Total.
1828—Continued.				*Bbls.*	*Bbls.*	*Lbs.*			
New York, N. Y		2	2		2,000				
Sag Harbor, N. Y	8		8	346	10,977	96,470			
Warren, R. I	1		1	2,211					
Westport, Mass		2	2	420					
Total	70	26	96	78,577	50,533	137,323			
1829.									
Bristol, R. I	2		2		2,100	700			
Dartmouth, Mass		1	1	300					
Edgartown, Mass	1	2	3	465					
Fairhaven, Mass	5	3	8	3,700	4,250	25,000			
Mattapoisett, Mass		3	3	270	40				
Nantucket, Mass	25		25	33,493	8,576	76,808			
New Bedford, Mass	30	5	35	30,277	26,130	211,631			
New London, Conn	9		9	2,205	11,325	108,592			
New York, N. Y	2		2		2,000				
Plymouth, Mass	1		1	2,500					
Sag Harbor, N. Y	9		9	268	15,939	140,923			
Stonington, Conn	1		1		1,200				
Westport, Mass		4	4	1,130	75				
Total	85	18	103	74,608	71,635	563,654			
1830.									
Bristol, R. I	4		4	2,292	3,200				
Dartmouth, Mass		1	1	250					
Edgartown, Mass	2		2	3,980					
Fairhaven, Mass	9	2	11	3,062	11,093	57,300			
Falmouth, Mass	1		1	1,700					
Mattapoisett, Mass		1	1	70					
Nantucket, Mass	20		20	36,013	7,758	67,508			
New Bedford, Mass	40	6	46	40,513	35,271	280,438			
New London, Conn	14		14	9,792	15,248				
Newport, R. I	1		1	2,800					
New York, N. Y	2		2	2,000	1,500				
Plymouth, Mass	1		1	2,350					
Sag Harbor, N. Y	10		10	3,464	13,189	109,745			
Stonington, Conn	1		1		1,600				
Warren, R. I	1		1		1,000				

Westport, Mass	1	5	6	2, 255	24				
Total	107	15	122	110, 541	89, 883	514, 991			
1831.									
Bristol, R. I	4		4	5, 300	3, 400				
Edenton, N. C		1	1	50					
Edgartown, Mass	1	1	2	3, 035					
Fairhaven, Mass	4		4	2, 370	6, 430				
Falmouth, Mass	1		1	3, 468					
Hudson, N. Y	1		1	123	2, 200	1, 600			
Lynn, Mass	1		1		1, 500				
Mattapoisett, Mass	1	2	3	110	1, 790				
Nantucket, Mass	21		21	41, 289	8, 568	83, 206			
New Bedford, Mass	45	2	47	45, 833	49, 186	21, 200			
New London, Conn	14		14	5, 487	19, 402				
Provincetown, Mass		2	2	270					
Sag Harbor, N. Y	13		13	1, 577	20, 735	172, 073			
Stonington, Conn	1		1	20	185	1, 200			
Warren, R. I	4		4	5, 900	1, 200				
Westport, Mass		4	4	620					
Total	111	12	123	115, 452	114, 596	279, 279			
1832.									
Boston, Mass	1		1		1, 500				
Bristol, R. I	3		3		4, 15[illegible]	15, 800			
Fairhaven, Mass	11		11	5, 550	18, 650	1, 300			
Hudson, N. Y	2		2		3, 500				
Lynn, Mass	2		2		2, 400				
Mattapoisett, Mass	2	2	4	430	2, 950				
Nantucket, Mass	24	1	25	30, 888	16, 364	155, 379			
New Bedford, Mass	48	2	50	23, 705	72, 735	24, 200			
New London, Conn	12		12	703	21, 375	20, 000			
Newport, R. I	2		2	4, 900					
Plymouth, Mass	1		1	2, 500					
Sag Harbor, N. Y	14		14	848	25, 831	217, 602			
Salem, Mass	1		1	100	1, 500				
Stonington, Conn	1		1	148	1, 721	8, 600			
Truro, Mass	2	1	3		3, 500				
Warren, R. I	3		3	1, 650	3, 700				
Westport, Mass	2	2	4	1, 580	1, 200				
Total	131	8	139	73, 002	181, 076	442, 881			
1833.									
Boston, Mass	1	1	2	320	2				
Bristol, R. I	3		3		4, 500	10, 000			
Edgartown, Mass	1		1	1, 600					
Fairhaven, Mass	12		12	3, 133	18, 410	20, 000			
Falmouth, Mass	1		1	2, 600					
Fall River, Mass	1		1		1, 000				

K.—*Synopsis of importation, by ports, from* 1804 *to* 1877—Continued.

Port of departure.	Nature and number of vessels returning.			Importation.			Tonnage.		
	Ships and barks.	Brigs and schooners.	Total.	Sperm-oil.	Whale-oil.	Bone.	Ships and barks.	Brigs and schooners.	Total.
1833—Continued.				*Bbls.*	*Bbls.*	*Lbs.*			
Greenport, N. Y	1		1		1, 400				
Hudson, N. Y	5		5	4, 820	5, 180	18, 900			
Lynn, Mass	3		3		3, 000	5, 000			
Mattapoisett, Mass	2	1	3		2, 275				
Mystic, Conn	1		1		550				
Nantucket, Mass	21	5	26	29, 511	5, 422	49, 429			
New Bedford, Mass	52	4	56	43, 775	62, 750				
Newburgh, N. Y	1		1	140	1, 060				
New London, Conn	17		17	8, 503	22, 395				
Newport, R. I	2		2	3, 400					
New York, N. Y	1		1	1, 700					
Sag Harbor, N. Y	14		14	4, 145	21, 578	163, 103			
Salem, Mass	1		1		1, 200				
Stonington, Conn	3	1	4	400	7, 000				
Warren, R. I	4		4	400	5, 870				
Westport, Mass		3	3	590					
Total	147	15	162	104, 437	163, 592	266, 432			
1834.									
Bridgeport, Conn	1		1		1, 500				
Bristol, R. I	1		1	1, 800					
Edgartown, Mass	2		2	5, 800					
Fairhaven, Mass	16		16	12, 953	12, 601	51, 500			
Falmouth, Mass	2		2	860					
Fall River, Mass	1		1		1, 200				
Gloucester, Mass	2		2	400	1, 500				
Greenport, N. Y	2		2	500	3, 800	1, 800			
Hudson, N. Y	2		2	1, 650	1, 000				
Lynn, Mass	2		2		2, 600				
Mattapoisett, Mass	2	1	3	550	1, 500				
Nantucket, Mass	16	17	33	20, 517	4, 747	37, 137			
New Bedford, Mass	53	3	56	57, 688	41, 419	16, 000			
New London, Conn	9	3	12	4, 565	12, 930	3, 200			
New York, N. Y	5	2	7	565	9, 950	31, 400			
Plymouth, Mass	3		3	2, 900	2, 800				
Portsmouth, N. H	1		1	450	1, 550				
Provincetown, Mass		1	1	400					
Sag Harbor, N. Y	17		17	6, 537	24, 288	188, 387			
Salem, Mass	1		1		1, 200				
Stonington, Conn	1	1	2	97	2, 447	13, 900			

Warren, R. I	6		6	4, 930	4, 550				
Westport, Mass		2	2	380					
Total	145	30	175	123, 542	131, 582	*343, 324			
1835.									
Bridgeport, Conn	1		1		800				
Bristol, R. I	4	2	6	8, 600					
Dartmouth, Mass	1		1	40	1, 400				
Edgartown, Mass	1		1	3, 100					
Fairhaven, Mass	10		10	4, 597	13, 590	29, 000			
Falmouth, Mass	2		2	4, 600					
Fall River, Mass	2		2	2, 000	1, 850				
Greenport, N. Y	2		2		3, 700				
Hudson, N. Y	3		3	3, 100	1, 620				
Lynn, Mass	3		3	150	3, 500				
Mattapoisett, Mass	4	2	6	3, 215	3, 845	6, 000			
Mystic, Conn	1		1	170	130				
Nantucket, Mass	26	4	30	38, 824	4, 497				
New Bedford, Mass	53		53	66, 792	30, 488	90, 000			
Newburyport, Mass	1		1		2, 100				
Norwich, Conn	1		1	270	700				
New London, Conn	13	1	14	11, 866	14, 041	66, 000			
Newport, R. I	3		3	1, 925	2, 900	9, 000			
New York, N. Y	2		2	57	2, 493				
Newburgh, N. Y	3		3	30	3, 500	11, 000			
Poughkeepsie, N. Y	1		1	500					
Portsmouth, N. H	2		2	250	2, 100	7, 000			
Plymouth, Mass	1		1	1, 000					
Provincetown, Mass		1	1	470					
Sag Harbor, N. Y	17		17	2, 367	25, 402	211, 882			
Salem, Mass	4	1	5	2, 700	2, 300				
Stonington, Conn	1	1	2	100	1, 800				
Wareham, Mass	1		1	2, 950					
Warren, R. I	4		4	3, 250	2, 650				
Westport, Mass	1	2	3	1, 570					
Not recorded						535, 310			
Total	168	14	182	164, 493	125, 406	965, 192			
1836.									
Bridgeport, Conn	1		1		1, 800				
Bristol, R. I	6		6	4, 630	3, 800				
Dorchester, Mass	1		1	500	1, 250				
Dartmouth, Mass	2		2	450	2, 100				
Edgartown, Mass	1	1	2	2, 530	60				
Fairhaven, Mass	12		12	6, 175	14, 314				
Falmouth, Mass	5		5	5, 790					
Gloucester, Mass	1		1	550	1, 600				

* There is no record of the imports of bone except for the ports of Nantucket and Sag Harbor, up to 1835, except an occasional report; up to that time the footing is wha was actually reported.

K.—*Synopsis of importation, by ports, from 1804 to 1877*—Continued.

Port of departure.	Nature and number of vessels returning.			Importation.			Tonnage.		
	Ships and barks.	Brigs and schooners.	Total.	Sperm-oil.	Whale-oil.	Bone.	Ships and barks.	Brigs and schooners.	Total.
1836—Continued.				*Bbls.*	*Bbls.*	*Lbs.*			
Greenport, N. Y	1		1	150	1,650				
Hudson, N. Y	4		4	5,190	700				
Lynn, Mass	2		2	450	2,500				
Mattapoisett, Mass		5	5	1,100	50				
Mystic, Conn	3		3	480	6,800				
Nantucket, Mass	17	3	20	35,157	2,188				
New Bedford, Mass	48	5	53	39,654	38,243	32,000			
New London, Conn	12	1	13	3,198	18,663				
Newport R. I	2		2	2,270	1,130	14,000			
New York, N. Y	1	1	2	1,450	500				
Plymouth, Mass	1		1	300	1,300				
Providence, R. I	1		1	60	1,440				
Poughkeepsie, N. Y	1		1	800	2,000				
Provincetown, Mass		3	3	885					
Portsmouth, N. H	3		3	4,900					
Sag Harbor, N. Y	20		20	3,445	25,063	197,960			
Salem, Mass	4		4	5,700					
Stonington, Conn	3	1	4	1,500	4,800				
Warren, R. I	7		7	5,040	4,610				
Westport, Mass		3	3	980	7				
Not recorded						784,813			
Total	159	23	182	133,334	136,568	1,028,773			
1837.									
Bristol, R. I	4	2	6	4,833	1,820				
Bridgeport, Conn	2		2	250	3,800				
Dartmouth, Mass	3		3	550	3,370				
Dorchester, Mass	2		2	2,000	1,200				
Edgartown, Mass	3	1	4	5,000					
East Haddam, Conn		1	1	450					
Fairhaven, Mass	14		14	14,956	13,565	5,500			
Falmouth, Mass	2		2	760	400				
Fall River, Mass	1	1	2	239	1,240				
Greenport, N. Y	3		3	100	4,450				
Hudson, N. Y	4		4	4,62[illegible]	1,125				
Holmes' Hole, Mass	1		1	180	1,920				
Lynn, Mass	3		3	470	3,800				
Mattapoisett, Mass	1	2	3	258	1,235				
Mystic, Conn	1		1	400	1,200				

Nantucket, Mass	22	3	25	35, 056	4, 569				
New Bedford, Mass	48	5	53	56, 831	63, 683	242, 316			
Newburyport, Mass	3		3	4, 700	4, 500				
New London, Conn	17	1	18	8, 469	26, 774				
Newport, R. I	4	1	5	3, 532	3, 412				
New York, N. Y	5		5	350	4, 850				
Poughkeepsie, N. Y	2		2	1, 300	2, 900	3, 000			
Providence, R. I	1		1	200	1, 200				
Plymouth, Mass	1		1	150	2, 250				
Provincetown, Mass		2	2	550					
Portsmouth, N. H	1		1	170	1, 830				
Sag Harbor, N. Y	23		23	8, 634	31, 784	236, 757			
Salem, Mass	6	5	11	3, 000	4, 120				
Stonington, Conn	4		4	470	7, 300				
Wilmington, Del	2		2	1, 300	1, 400				
Warren, R. I	5	3	8	5, 050	3, 120				
Wiscasset, Me	1		1	2, 800					
Westport, Mass	2	1	3	1, 517	40				
Port not recorded						1, 265, 531			
Total	184	28	212	169, 179	202, 857	1, 753, 104			
1838.									
Bristol, R. I	6		6	1, 900	5, 900				
Boston, Mass	1	2	3	1, 400	1, 950				
Edgartown, Mass	1		1	470	2, 500				
Nantucket, Mass	13	3	16	21, 730	6, 200				
New Bedford, Mass*	81	11	92	77, 600	84, 100				
New London, Conn	20	4	24	4, 400	34, 000				
Newport, R. I	5	1	6	4, 000	6, 200				
New York, N. Y†	7	1	8	6, 250	7, 000				
Sag Harbor, N. Y	24		24	1, 860	37, 600				
Salem, Mass	3	1	4	1, 000	4, 750				
Warren, R. I	7		7	2, 500	9, 700				
Other ports	21	11	32	6, 290	28, 810				
Total	189	34	223	129, 400	228, 710	‡2, 200, 000			
1839.									
Bristol, R. I	4	2	6	4, 100	5, 450		5	1	1, 782
Bridgeport, Conn	2		2		3, 250		3		913
Boston, Mass§	5	4	9	4, 230	7, 600			1	125
Dartmouth, Mass							3		874
Dorchester, Mass							2		581
Edgartown, Mass	3		3	4, 800	1, 600		8		2, 659
Fairhaven, Mass							43	1	13, 274
Falmouth, Mass	6		6	5, 250	3, 800		8		2, 490
Fall River, Mass	3	2	5	2, 490	3, 900		4	3	1, 604
Greenport, N. Y	3	1	4	905	4, 750		4	1	1, 414
Holmes' Hole, Mass							3	1	1, 180

* Including Fairhaven. † Including ports on North River. ‡ Estimated. § Including Dorchester.

K.—*Synopsis of importation, by ports, from* 1804 *to* 1877—Continued.

Port of departure.	Nature and number of vessels returning.			Importation.			Tonnage.		
	Ships and barks.	Brigs and schooners.	Total.	Sperm-oil.	Whale-oil.	Bone.	Ships and barks.	Brigs and schooners.	Total.
1839—Continued.				*Bbls.*	*Bbls.*	*Lbs.*			
Hudson, N. Y							8		2,902
Jamesport, N. Y							1		236
Lynn, Mass							4		1,269
Mystic, Conn							5	3	1,797
Nantucket, Mass	16	2	18	23,140	7,550		77	4	27,364
New Bedford, Mass	68	7	75	61,695	72,890		169	8	56,118
Newburyport, Mass							3		1,099
New Suffolk, N. Y							1		274
New London, Conn*	18	4	22	4,500	31,690		30	9	11,447
Newport, R. I	3	1	4	2,506	3,153		9	2	3,152
Newark, N. J							1		366
New York, N. Y†	12		12	6,035	16,430		3		710
Portland, Me							1		388
Plymouth, Mass							3		910
Poughkeepsie, N. Y							6		2,043
Providence, R. I							3		1,086
Portsmouth, N. H							1		348
Provincetown, Mass								1	172
Rochester, Mass		6	6	2,530			5	10	2,615
Sag Harbor, N. Y	20		20	2,773	26,580		31		10,605
Salem, Mass	8		8	4,630	6,670		14		4,265
Stonington, Conn	4		4	300	9,500		7	5	2,912
Wareham, Mass							2	2	904
Wiscasset, Me							1		380
Warren, R. I	7	1	8	4,020	6,630		18	3	6,075
Wilmington, Del	3		3	1,600	4,900		5		1,578
Westport, Mass	4	4	8	3,220	80		5	4	1,443
Other ports	4		4	1,150	7,100				
Total	193	34	227	139,964	223,523	‡2,000,000	496	59	169,354
1840.									
Bristol, R. I	2	2	4	2,035	1,225		5	1	
Boston, Mass§	6	4	10	6,420	8,600		2		
Bridgeport, Conn	2		2	590	2,910		3		
Cold Spring, N. Y							2		
Dartmouth, Mass							3		
Dorchester, Mass							2		
Edgartown, Mass	3		3	3,380	2,300		8		
Fairhaven, Mass	3		3	3,150	1,300		43	1	
Falmouth, Mass							8		

Fall River, Mass							5	2	
Greenport, N. Y	3	1	4	410	2, 790		4	1	
Hudson, N. Y							8		
Holmes' Hole, Mass							3	1	
Jamesport, N. Y							1		
Lynn, Mass							3		
Mattapoisett, Mass							6	2	
Mystic, Conn							5	2	
Nantucket, Mass	22	3	25	43, 330	2, 275		77	1	
New Bedford, Mass ‖	70	12	82	63, 465	75, 411		167	7	
Newburyport, Mass							3		
New Suffolk, N. Y							1		
New London, Conn*	19	4	23	5, 145	38, 320		38	2	
Newport, R. I	3		3	4, 850	200		9	1	
New York, N. Y ¶	8	1	9	4, 600	11, 600		3		
Newark, N. J							1		
Plymouth, Mass							3		
Portsmouth, N. H							1		
Portland, Me							1		
Providence, R. I							3		
Poughkeepsie, N. Y							6		
Provincetown, Mass		3	3	1, 950					
Rochester, Mass		4	4	1, 395	30				
Sag Harbor, N. Y	15		15	2, 730	27, 320		31		
Salem, Mass	6		6	4, 330	8, 120		14		
Sippican, Mass							2	4	
Stonington, Conn	2	3	5	1, 200	6, 450		7	2	
Wiscasset, Me							1		
Wareham, Mass	1	2	3	1, 080	1, 500		2	1	
Warren, R. I	5		5	2, 110	10, 285		16	3	
Wilmington, Del							5		
Westport, Mass	3	3	6	2, 255	25		5	4	
Other ports	2	6	8	2, 020	2, 780				
Total	175	48	223	156, 445	203, 441	**2, 000, 000	507	35	136, 927
1841.									
Bristol, R. I	3	3	6	2, 930	175		5	1	
Bridgeport, Conn	2		2	400	3, 760		3		
Boston, Mass	2	5	7	6, 216	1, 000		1	1	
Cold Spring, N. Y	2		2		4, 250		2		
Dartmouth, Mass	1		1	2, 200			3		
Dorchester, Mass							2		
Edgartown, Mass	2	1	3	3, 169	50		8	1	
Fairhaven, Mass	13		13	8, 280	18, 450		45		
Falmouth, Mass	1		1	1, 300	379		7		
Fall River, Mass	2		2	950	900		4	2	
Greenport, N. Y	4		4	1, 000	6, 602		3	1	
Hudson, N. Y	1		1	300	2, 300		8		

* Including Mystic. † Including ports on the North River. ‡ Estimated. § Including Lynn, Newburyport, and Plymouth. ‖ Including Fairhaven.
¶ Including whaling ports on North River. **Assumed.

K.—*Synopsis of importation, by ports, from* 1804 *to* 1877—Continued.

Port of departure.	Nature and number of vessels returning.			Importation.			Tonnage.		
	Ships and barks.	Brigs and schooners.	Total.	Sperm-oil.	Whale-oil.	Bone.	Ships and barks.	Brigs and schooners.	Total.
1841—Continued.				*Bbls.*	*Bbls.*	*Lbs.*			
Holmes' Hole, Mass	1		1	500	1, 200		3	1	
Jamesport, N. Y	1		1	150	1, 550		1		
Lynn, Mass							2		
Mattapoisett, Mass*	2	6	8	2, 280	70		2	6	
Mystic, Conn	1	1	2	600	1, 600		5	2	
Nantucket, Mass	21	3	24	39, 891	3, 508		80	3	
New Bedford, Mass	48	9	57	54, 860	49, 555		168	11	
Newburyport, Mass	1		1	400	400		2		
New Suffolk, N. Y	1		1	260	1, 200		1		
New London, Conn	15	3	18	4, 115	27, 890		28	8	
Newport, R. I	1	2	3	2, 297	25		8	2	
Newark, N. J	1		1	40	2, 460		1		
New York, N. Y	1		1		1, 000				
Plymouth, Mass		4	4	500	13		3	3	
Poughkeepsie, N. Y	1		1	500	2, 000		6		
Providence, R. I	3		3	1, 670	7, 350		3		
Portland, Me	1		1	300	12, 800		1		
Provincetown, Mass		6	6	1, 025	40			3	
Portsmouth, N. H							1		
Sag Harbor, N. Y	22	1	23	5, 310	48, 620		30		
Salem, Mass	1		1	275	1, 300		12		
Somerset, Mass								1	
Sippican, Mass							4	4	
Stonington, Conn	3		3	1, 500	5, 660		8	2	
Wiscasset, Me	1		1	900	1, 200		1		
Wareham, Mass		3	3	1, 430	220		2	3	
Warren, R. I	5	1	6	3, 115	5, 300		16	2	
Wilmington, Del	4		4	5, 500	2, 300		5		
Westport, Mass	3	3	6	3, 180			6	4	
Total	171	51	222	157, 343	205, 064	†2, 000, 000	490	63	157, 405
1842.									
Bath, Me							1		
Bristol, R. I	1	2	3	590			9	2	
Bridgeport, Conn	2		2	230	3, 470		3		
Boston, Mass‡	3		3	2, 965	2, 412		2	3	
Bucksport, Me		1	1	110				1	
Cold Spring, N. Y	1		1		1, 850		2		
Dartmouth, Mass	1		1	1, 150	800		2		
Duxbury, Mass							1		

Edgartown, Mass	2	3	5	2, 167	18		8	5	
Fairhaven, Mass	14		14	14, 580	13, 100		49		
Falmouth, Mass	1		1	300			7		
Freetown, Mass							1		
Fall River, Mass	2	1	3	2, 350	1, 100		5	2	
Greenport, N. Y	1		1	580	600		4	1	
Hudson, N. Y							2		
Holmes' Hole, Mass	1		1	800	2, 200		3		
Jamesport, N. Y§							1		
Lynn, Mass							2		
Mattapoisett, Mass	3	5	8	3, 070	250		5	5	
Mystic, Conn	3		3	775	5, 926		8	1	
Nantucket, Mass	14	2	16	27, 654	1, 519		86	2	
New Bedford, Mass	59	4	63	70, 909	51, 112		204	7	
Newburyport, Mass							2		
Newark, N. J							1	1	
New London, Conn	15	6	21	4, 013	27, 799		43	5	
New Suffolk, N. Y							1		
Newport, R. I	2	2	4	3, 960	850		9	3	
New York, N. Y‖	3		3	1, 720	6, 550		2		
Poughkeepsie, N. Y							4		
Plymouth, Mass		4	4	496	28		3	6	
Portsmouth, N. H	1		1	470	1, 830		1		
Providence, R. I							8		
Provincetown, Mass	1	7	8	1, 570	80		2	14	
Quincy, Mass								1	
Sag Harbor, N. Y	11		11	3, 190	21, 330		42	2	
Salem, Mass	6		6	7, 450	120		12		
Somerset, Mass		1	1	230			1	1	
Sippican, Mass		2	2	340	20		5	3	
Stonington, Conn	3	1	4	850	6, 500		15	1	
Wareham, Mass	1	3	4	1, 240	2, 200		3	4	
Warren, R. I	2	2	4	1, 800	258		20	2	
Wilmington, Del							3		
Westport, Mass	6	3	9	2, 690	60		10	5	
On freight at different ports				5, 121	2, 819				
Total	159	49	208	103, 370	154, 801	¶1, 500, 000	592	77	152, 518
1843.									
Bath, Me	1		1	300					
Bridgeport, Conn	1		1	300	2, 100	**21, 000	3		913
Boston, Mass	2	6	8	4, 984	170	1, 700	3		551
Bristol, R. I	2	1	3	620			6	2	2, 116
Cold Spring, N. Y	2		2	150	3, 250	32, 500	4		1, 436
Dartmouth, Mass							1		387
Duxbury, Mass							1		206
Edgartown, Mass	3	1	4	6, 460	110	1, 100	7	3	2, 936
Fairhaven, Mass	14		14	14, 157	11, 707	117, 070	45		14, 350

* Including Sippican. † Assumed, at an average of 10 pounds to the barrel of oil. ‡ Including Lynn. § Generally included with Greenport or Sag Harbor. ‖ Including all the North River ports. ¶ Assumed. ** This amount of bone is predicated on an average of 10 pounds of bone to the barrel of oil.

K.—*Synopsis of importation, by ports, from 1804 to 1877*—Continued.

Port of departure.	Nature and number of vessels returning.			Importation.			Tonnage.		
	Ships and barks.	Brigs and schooners.	Total.	Sperm-oil.	Whale-oil.	Bone.	Ships and barks.	Brigs and schooners.	Total.
1843—Continued.				*Bbls.*	*Bbls.*	*Lbs.*			
Falmouth, Mass	4		4	5,709	820	8,200	5		1,826
Fall River, Mass	2	1	3	780	4,015	40,150	5	2	1,988
Freetown, Mass							1		349
Greenport, N. Y	5		5	860	9,100	91,000	8		2,363
Holmes' Hole, Mass	2		2	1,600	1,700	17,000	3		1,037
Hudson, N. Y							2		643
Lynn, Mass							2		583
Mattapoisett, Mass	3	1	4	1,644	331	3,310	5	5	1,9[illegible]8
Mystic, Conn	3		3	340	4,560	45,600	9		2,647
Nantucket, Mass	18	2	20	30,280	1,563	15,630	64	2	26,668
New Bedford, Mass	53	3	56	61,066	40,922	409,220	214	5	69,703
Newburyport, Mass	1		1	600	1,300	13,000	1		414
New Suffolk, N. Y							1		274
New London, Conn	20		20	4,243	36,850	368,500	50	1	*17,684
Newport, R. I	1	1	2	2,050	50		9	3	3,324
Newark, N. J							1		366
New York, N. Y	2		2	3,155	2,900	29,000	3		1,092
Portsmouth, N. H							1		348
Providence, R. I	2		2	340	3,260	32,600	8		2,998
Poughkeepsie, N. Y	3		3	1,770	5,700	57,000	1		343
Provincetown, Mass	2	11	13	4,370	975	9,750	3	14	2,354
Plymouth, Mass		3	3	390	55	550	3	4	1,409
Sag Harbor, N. Y	25	1	26	4,390	49,180	491,800	49		17,598
Salem, Mass	2		2	800	1,800	18,000	6		1,876
Somerset, Mass	2		2	442	567	5,670	2		369
Sippican, Mass	2	2	4	1,132	1,446	14,460	5	2	1,335
Stonington, Conn	7		7	2,415	12,345	123,[illegible]50	19		†5,616
Wareham, Mass		2	2	1,105			4		1,366
Warren, R. I	11		11	7,740	9,910	99,100	19		5,964
Wilmington, Del							3		1,033
Westport, Mass	3	3	6	2,802	41		7	4	1,982
Sent home in merchantmen						60,000			
Total	197	38	235	166,985	206,727	2,137,270	595	49	200,484
1844.									
Bridgeport, Conn	2		2	180	3,720	33,000	3		972
Boston, Mass	1	2	3	1,960	200	200,000	1		174
Bristol, R. I	3	1	4	1,500	1,400	14,000	5	1	1,743
Cold Spring, N. Y							7		2,736

Dartmouth, Mass							1		387
Duxbury, Mass	1		1	200	1,300	7,000	1		206
Edgartown, Mass	3	1	4	2,340	4,709	40,000	9	2	3,191
Fair Haven, Mass	11		11	9,667	12,176	131,000	45		14,470
Falmouth, Mass	1		1	2,200	200		4	1	1,570
Freetown, Mass	1		1	150	850	8,500	2		634
Fall River, Mass							5	2	1,988
Greenport, N. Y	3		3	100	4,000	30,500	10		2,852
Hudson, N. Y	1		1	400	2,400	24,000	1		274
Holmes' Hole, Mass							3		1,137
Lynn, Mass	1		1	100	1,400	11,000	2		583
Mattapoisett, Mass	4	3	7	3,002	4,544	21,600	4	5	1,634
Mystic, Conn	4		4	415	7,485	65,250	12		3,584
Nantucket, Mass	19	2	21	31,290	4,461	39,000	75	2	26,234
New Bedford, Mass	76		76	54,509	102,992	978,592	234	5	76,784
Newburyport, Mass	1		1	260	2,750	22,000	1		414
Newark, N. J	1		1	650	1,950	19,000			
New London, Conn	18	5	23	2,296	39,816	298,400	65	6	24,011
Newport, R. I	3	2	5	3,880	1,125	11,000	10	1	3,157
New Suffolk, N. Y							2		501
New York, N. Y	1	1	2	1,193	880	39,643	2		676
Portsmouth, N. H							1		378
Providence, R. I	4		4	3,050	7,000	71,000	9		3,248
Plymouth, Mass	1	2	3	310	35		2	3	999
Provincetown, Mass	1	16	17	3,351	656		2	17	2,534
Poughkeepsie, N. Y	1		1	700	1,600	13,000			
Sag Harbor, N. Y	14		14	2,010	31,500	272,400	60		21,842
Salem, Mass	2		2	3,300			5		1,584
Somerset, Mass		1	1	350			2		368
Sippican, Mass	1		1	600			3	1	787
Stonington, Conn	7		7	845	14,840	103,800	24		7,285
Wareham, Mass	1	2	3	2,442	70		4	2	1,366
Warren, R. I	4		4	1,970	4,670	28,000	20		6,608
Wilmington, Del	2		2	1,700	2,500	43,800	1		328
Westport, Mass	6	1	7	2,674	818	6,960	8	3	2,066
Total	199	39	238	134,594	262,047	2,532,445	643	52	218,655
1845.									
Boston, Mass	4	7	‡11	5,283	3,030	487,100	1	2	375
Bristol, R. I	1		1	1,000			5	1	1,743
Cold Spring, N. Y	2		2	200	4,818	87,490	8		3,315
Dartmouth, Mass	1		1	1,400	200		1		387
Edgartown, Mass	3	1	4	1,719	1,816	14,000	8	2	3,017
Fairhaven, Mass	15		15	15,381	16,659	148,100	48		15,391
Falmouth, Mass	2	1	3	2,800	140	22,000	4		1,470
Fall River, Mass	2	2	4	1,646	3,050	44,600	5	2	1,908
Greenport, N. Y	6		6	578	7,824	62,887	11		3,255

* Not including schooners Betty, (125 tons) Franklin, (119 tons.) nor Hand, (tender, 86 tons,) nor sloop Shaw Perkins.

† Not including brig Enterprise, 95 tons, sealer.

‡ Three ships and barks, six brigs and schooners, were freighters.

K.—*Synopsis of importation, by ports, from* 1804 *to* 1877—Continued.

Port of departure.	Nature and number of vessels returning.			Importation.			Tonnage.		
	Ships and barks.	Brigs and schooners.	Total.	Sperm-oil.	Whale-oil.	Bone.	Ships and barks.	Brigs and schooners.	Total.
1845—Continued.				*Bbls.*	*Bbls.*	*Lbs.*			
Holmes' Hole, Mass	1		1	201	2, 239	23, 300	3	1	1, 287
Hudson, N. Y	1		1	800	800	8, 000			
Lynn, Mass	1		1	150	1, 650	15, 000	3		980
Mattapoisett, Mass	1	2	3	831	240		5	5	1, 864
Mystic, Conn	4		4	712	7, 271	51, 400	18		5, 521
Nantucket, Mass	29	2	31	45, 864	6, 280	46, 100	73	1	25, 564
New Bedford, Mass	66	2	68	52, 022	83, 724	1, 006, 007	252	4	82, 633
Lew London, Conn	21		21	1, 411	52, 576	469, 700	69	8	26, 513
Newport, R. I	2	2	4				10	2	3, 099
New York, N. Y	2	1	*3	714	2, 550	24, 000	1		495
New Suffolk, N. Y	1		1	108	398	6, 669	2		501
Providence, R. I	2		2	750	3, 450	30, 000	9		3, 341
Plymouth, Mass	1	2	3	1, 390			3	1	999
Provincetown, Mass	1	13	14	2, 545	730		3	20	3, 001
Portsmouth, N. H	1		1	2, 000			1		348
Sag Harbor, N. Y	22		22	2, 624	43, 784	475, 186	63		23, 103
Salem, Mass	2		2	3, 300	800	6, 000	2		660
Sippican, Mass	2	1	3	1, 216	540	3, 000	3	2	910
Stonington, Conn	9		9	1, 941	15, 362	115, 625	26		8, 076
Wareham, Mass	1	2	3	943	1, 991	16, 800	4	2	1, 366
Warren, R. I	5		5	2, 511	7, 284	7, 300	25		8, 218
Wilmington, Del	1		1	300	250	2, 000			
Westport, Mass	3	4	7	2, 780	488		8	3	2, 066
Total	215	42	257	157, 700	272, 809	3, 195, 054	680	51	233, 149
1846.									
Bristol, R. I	2	1	3	977	3, 601	14, 600	5	1	1, 743
Bridgeport, Conn	1		1	130	2, 500	7, 500	3		972
Boston, Mass	2	4	6	2, 573	60	40, 000		1	100
Barnstable, Mass								1	90
Cold Spring, N. Y	3		3	366	7, 125	36, 457	8		3, 315
Dartmouth, Mass							1	1	498
Edgartown, Mass	1	1	2	731	2, 010	19, 000	7	2	2, 842
Fairhaven, Mass	12		12	12, 049	15, 475	101, 449	48		15, 410
Falmouth, Mass							4		1, 470
Fall River, Mass	2		2	369	4, 070	24, 266	5	2	1, 989
Freetown, Mass							2		634
Greenport, N. Y	2		2	120	3, 106	30, 574	11		3, 255
Holmes' Hole, Mass	1		1	1, 062	1, 020	9, 400	3	1	1, 287

Lynn, Mass							3		980
Mattapoisett, Mass	4	3	7	1,809	1,517	24,000	7	4	2,297
Mystic, Conn	2		2	78	4,130	40,400	17		5,263
Nantucket, Mass	11	2	13	16,979	1,731	14,000	72	3	25,436
New Bedford, Mass	59	3	62	38,380	80,812	456,900	251	3	82,701
New Suffolk, N. Y							2		501
New London, Conn	13	3	16	1,307	27,441	183,450	69	8	26,515
Newport, R. I	3	1	4	1,584	230	1,200	8	2	2,554
New York, N. Y	3		3†	448	363	680,000	1		495
Portsmouth, N. H							1		348
Providence, R. I	2		2	140	5,096	34,000	8		2,942
Plymouth, Mass	2	1	3	2,455	8		1	1	274
Provincetown, Mass	1	17	18	4,672	282		3	15	2,406
Sag Harbor, N. Y	14		14	1,220	29,295	205,018	62		22,679
Salem, Mass							2		660
Somerset, Mass	1		1	109	18		1		137
Sippican, Mass	1	1	2	374	1,515	6,600	3	2	910
Stonington, Conn	5		5	1,055	9,169	71,900	27		8,476
Wareham, Mass		1	1	672			3	1	1,023
Warren, R. I	6		6	2,324	6,633	20,200	23		7,656
Westport, Mass	5	2	7	2,918	71		9	4	2,410
Sent home from outward bound, condemned, &c				4,953	1,705	976,000			
Total	159	41	200	160,174	209,198	3,252,939	670	51	1,230,218
1847.‡									
Barnstable, Mass		1	1	238	8			1	90
Bridgeport, Conn	1		1	230	1,365	4,000§	2		709
Boston, Mass		1	1	3,859		445,100		1	100
Bristol, R. I	1		1	272	130		1		222
Cold Spring, N. Y	1		1	201	2,797	31,458	8		3,315
Dartmouth, Mass								1	111
Edgartown, Mass	3	1	4	2,440	3,939	39,900	6	2	2,408
Fairhaven, Mass	13		13	12,032	11,280	91,700	50		15,977
Freetown, Mass							1		285
Fall River, Mass		1	1	188	28		5	1	1,743
Greenport, N. Y	5		5	633	9,880	80,422	11		3,252
Holmes' Hole, Mass	1	1	2	629	2,902	32,700	2	1	949
Lynn, Mass	1		1	75	1,575	8,000	2		720
Mattapoisett, Mass	2	3	5	1,369	574	3,600	6	5	2,079
Mystic, Conn	7		7	840	11,414	59,600	15		4,680
Nantucket, Mass	14	2	16	23,387	2,021	8,600	68	3	24,070
New Bedford, Mass	78	1	79	56,437	98,735	1,568,200	247	1	80,946
New London, Conn	34	2	36	4,755	76,340	382,500	56	7	23,054
Newport, R. I	2		2	1,743	1,148		6		1,826
New York, N. Y	1		1	68	1,742	2,000			
New Suffolk, N. Y							1		227
Providence, R. I	4		4	514	8,854	127,500	6		2,228
Plymouth, Mass							1		175
Provincetown, Mass	1	10	11	2,020	20		2	13	1,988

* Two of these were freighters. † Freighters. ‡ Eight merchantmen arrived with freight also; the freight is enumerated, the vessels not. § Mostly freight.

K.—*Synopsis of importation, by ports, from* 1804 *to* 1877—Continued.

Port of departure.	Nature and number of vessels returning.			Importation.			Tonnage.		
	Ships and barks.	Brigs and schooners.	Total.	Sperm-oil.	Whale-oil.	Bone.	Ships and barks.	Brigs and schooners.	Total.
1847—Continued.				*Bbls.*	*Bbls.*	*Lbs.*			
Portsmouth, N. H							1		348
Sag Harbor, N. Y	26		26	3, 257	51, 599	279, 900	50		17, 823
Salem, Mass							2		660
Somerset, Mass							1		137
Sippican, Mass	1	1	2	488	104		2	1	603
Stonington, Conn	9		9	705	18, 460	146, 900	25		7, 795
Wareham, Mass	1	1	2	1, 049	1, 644	5, 900	2	1	804
Warren, R. I	3		3	1, 441	5, 106	10, 900	21		7, 071
Westport, Mass	3	2	5	1, 883	1, 485	13, 400	10	4	2, 676
Total	212	27	239	120, 753	313, 150	3, 341, 680	610	42	209, 071
1848.									
Bristol, R. I	1		1	700	100		1		222
Bridgeport, Conn							2		709
Boston, Mass	3	3	6	2, 300	1, 747				
Cold Spring, N. Y	3		3	351	4, 220	8, 300	8		3, 315
Dartmouth, Mass								1	111
Edgartown, Mass	3	1	4	1, 798	4, 107	28, 400	6	2	2, 408
Fairhaven, Mass	10		10	4, 096	13, 102	61, 200	49		15, 805
Falmouth, Mass	2		2	2, 670	2, 226	8, 200	3		1, 106
Fall River, Mass	1		1	150	2, 000	20, 000	5		1, 615
Greenport, N. Y	5		5	636	8, 731	74, 000	10		3, 059
Holmes' Hole, Mass							3		949
Lynn, Mass	1		1	171	1, 643		2		720
Mattapoisett, Mass	5	1	6	2, 625	2, 639	2, 800	6	4	1, 880
Mystic, Conn	5		5	677	11, 484	72, 000	15	1	4, 897
Nantucket, Mass	16		16	22, 362	7, 479	27, 500	66	3	23, 477
New Bedford, Mass	75		75	48, 827	115, 436	621, 900	247	3	81, 075
New Suffolk, N. Y	1		1	249	162	1, 300	1		227
New London, Conn	20	2	22	3, 606	54, 115	408, 000	48	5	17, 880
Newport, R. I	1		1	1, 006			6		1, 984
New York, N. Y	1	2	3	300	500	410, 000			
Plymouth, Mass	1		1	550			1		175
Providence, R. I							4		1, 458
Provincetown, Mass	1	11	12	3, 149	37		1	9	1, 260
Portsmouth, N. H	1		1	566					
Sag Harbor, N. Y	14		14	2, 271	27, 700	146, 500	41		14, 658
Salem, Mass	1		1	588	1, 413	8, 100	1		398
Somerset, Mass	1		1	310			1		137

Sippican, Mass	1		1	450			1			256
Stonington, Conn	7		7	1, 755	11, 654	50, 500	21			6, 414
Wareham, Mass	1		1	624	10	54, 300	1			374
Warren, R. I	7		7	3, 571	10, 058		20			6, 647
Westport, Mass	5	2	7	1, 588	93		11		4	2, 804
Yarmouth, Mass		1	1	30					1	90
Total	193	23	216	107, 976	280, 656	2, 003, 000	581		33	196, 110
1849.										
Bridgeport, Conn	1		1	354	2, 702	27, 300				
Beverly, Mass									1	162
Boston, Mass	3	1	4	1, 360	3, 445	202, 300				
Cold Spring, N. Y	3		3	299	8, 697	68, 600	7			2, 878
Dartmouth, Mass		1	1	8	28				1	111
Edgartown, Mass	1		1	118	2, 742	18, 800	5		1	1, 860
Fairhaven, Mass	13		13	10, 806	18, 998	150, 100	46			14, 735
Falmouth, Mass	1		1	2, 060	115		3			1, 106
Fall River, Mass	4		4	856	8, 049	140, 600	2			646
Greenport, N. Y	4		4	587	7, 487	78, 400	10			3, 059
Holmes' Hole, Mass							3			949
Lynn, Mass	1		1	383	1, 580		2			720
Mattapoisett, Mass	1	2	3	780	19		6		3	1, 760
Mystic, Conn	5		5	1, 509	6, 747	51, 100	10		1	3, 384
Nantucket, Mass	13		13	17, 887	6, 461	68, 200	58		4	20, 831
New Bedford, Mass	63	1	64	46, 338	72, 961	797, 300	236		2	77, 138
Newburyport, Mass	1		1				1			227
New Suffolk, N. Y				242	314	1, 200				
New London, Conn	17	3	20	1, 949	38, 030	301, 100	42		5	15, 909
Newport, R. I	1		1	1, 055			4			1, 382
New York, N. Y	1	1	2	195	1, 655					
Providence, R. I	2		2	2, 317	4, 542	30, 200	3			842
Provincetown, Mass	2	15	17	2, 924	277		1		9	1, 260
Quincy, Mass		1	1		4				1	100
Sag Harbor, N. Y	16		16	1, 797	37, 579	186, 400	23			7, 935
Somerset, Mass	1		1	140			1			137
Sippican, Mass							1			256
Stonington, Conn	8		8	1, 628	15, 334	97, 500	19			5, 877
Wareham, Mass							1			374
Warren, R. I	6		6	2, 384	10, 626	61, 500	15			4, 939
Westport, Mass	3	1	4	2, 518	100	500	11		4	2, 817
Yarmouth, Mass									1	90
Total	171	26	197	100, 494	248, 492	2, 281, 100	510		33	171, 484
1850.										
Beverly, Mass		2	2	368					2	326
Boston, Mass	7	1	8	3, 845	786	3, 700	1			261
Cold Spring, N. Y	1		1	776	763		7			2, 878
Dartmouth, Mass		1	1	266	7				1	111
Edgartown, Mass	1		1	2, 164	184	1, 700	5		1	1, 860
Fairhaven, Mass	10		10	8, 812	10, 559	477, 900	45			14, 430

K.—*Synopsis of importation, by ports, from 1804 to 1877*—Continued.

Port of departure.	Nature and number of vessels returning.			Importation.			Tonnage.		
	Ships and barks.	Brigs and schooners.	Total.	Sperm-oil.	Whale-oil.	Bone.	Ships and barks.	Brigs and schooners.	Total.
1850—Continued.				*Bbls.*	*Bbls.*	*Lbs.*			
Falmouth, Mass							3		1, 106
Fall River, Mass							2		646
Greenport, N. Y	1		1	505	828	4, 900	9	1	2, 985
Holmes' Hole, Mass	3		3	1, 208	4, 960	56, 800	3		949
Lynn, Mass							2		720
Mattapoisett, Mass	3	1	4	2, 689	81		7	2	1, 822
Mystic, Conn	2		2	251	1, 588	3, 000	9	1	3, 009
Nantucket, Mass	12	1	13	17, 989	1, 328	133, 000	53	2	18, 697
New Bedford, Mass	64		64	39, 298	91, 627	1, 081, 500	245	4	81, 442
New Suffolk, N. Y							1		227
New London, Conn	17		17	2, 349	36, 545	203, 000	44	4	16, 586
Newport, R. I							4		1, 543
New York, N. Y	1	3	4	2, 054	1, 310	460, 000			
Orleans, Mass		1	1	240				1	115
Providence, R. I	2		2	112	3, 368	23, 600	2		865
Provincetown, Mass	1	22	23	3, 205	501		2	25	3, 095
Sag Harbor, N. Y	11	1	12	718	26, 438	193, 100	14	1	4, 758
Sippican, Mass	1		1	43	1, 453	9, 300			
Stonington, Conn	7		7	900	15, 226	179, 600	17		5, 391
Truro, Mass		1	1	140				1	143
Wareham, Mass	1		1	250	2, 719	38, 100	1		374
Warren, R. I	1		1	1, 035			15		4, 669
Westport, Mass	5	2	7	3, 607	324		11	5	2, 963
Yarmouth, Mass		1	1	68	13				
Total	151	37	188	92, 892	200, 608	2, 869, 200	502	51	171, 971
1851.									
Beverly, Mass		1	1	250			1	2	568
Boston, Mass*	6	6	12	6, 842	280	9, 300	2	1	618
Cold Spring, N. Y	4		4	217	11, 591	130, 000	6		2, 499
Dartmouth, Mass		1	1	48	14		2	1	626
Edgartown, Mass	3		3	2, 874	3, 840	44, 000	8	1	2, 877
Fairhaven, Mass	13		13	9, 480	15, 385	97, 100	49	1	16, 490
Falmouth, Mass	1		1		2, 719	24, 300	3		1, 106
Fall River, Mass							2		555
Greenport, N. Y	7		7	839	13, 487	115, 100	8	1	2, 749
Holmes' Hole, Mass							4		1, 410
Lynn, Mass	1		1	135	2, 740	28, 700	2		720
Mattapoisett, Mass	3	2	5	1, 747	2, 581	12, 000	11	2	2, 788
Mystic, Conn	6		6	183	15, 757	168, 800	9	1	3, 009

Nantucket, Mass	13	2	15	16, 601	3, 385	38, 000	52	4	18, 472
New Bedford, Mass	89	5	94	45, 150	155, 711	2, 349, 900	278	4	94, 642
New London, Conn	26	2	28	2, 914	67, 508	609, 000	43	5	16, 273
Newport, R. I	2	....	2	1, 262	1, 765	12, 200	5	....	1, 883
New Suffolk, N. Y	....	....	....	....	....	....	1	....	227
New York, N. Y*	2	3	5	2, 042	....	42, 400	....	....	....
Orleans, Mass	....	1	1	210	....	....	....	2	251
Providence, R. I	....	....	....	....	....	....	2	....	865
Provincetown, Mass	1	24	25	2, 911	229	....	2	28	3, 359
Philadelphia, Pa.†	....	1	1	60	....	....	....	....	....
Sag Harbor, N. Y	4	....	4	133	11, 066	67, 200	17	1	5, 856
Salem, Mass	....	....	....	....	....	....	1	....	230
Sandwich, Mass	....	....	....	....	....	....	....	2	292
Stonington, Conn	8	....	8	1, 310	15, 859	125, 000	18	....	5, 743
Truro, Mass	....	1	1	175	8	....	....	1	143
Wareham, Mass*	....	....	....	....	....	....	1	....	374
Warren, R. I	1	....	1	168	2, 789	29, 100	17	....	5, 640
Westport, Mass	7	2	9	4, 040	1, 769	4, 400	14	5	3, 725
Total	197	51	248	99, 591	328, 483	3, 916, 500	558	62	193, 990
1852.									
Beverly, Mass	2	....	2	920	2	....	1	2	568
Boston, Mass*	6	2	8	4, 979	211	....	2	1	618
Cold Spring, N. Y	....	....	....	....	....	....	7	....	2, 919
Dartmouth, Mass	....	....	....	....	....	....	3	1	825
Edgartown, Mass	....	....	....	....	....	....	8	1	2, 823
Fairhaven, Mass	8	....	8	6, 242	4, 001	38, 600	49	....	16, 542
Falmouth, Mass	....	....	....	....	....	....	3	....	1, 106
Fall River, Mass	3	....	3	481	2, 527	15, 000	3	....	818
Greenport, N. Y	1	1	2	1, 070	75	....	8	1	2, 749
H lmes' Hole, Mass	....	1	1	....	....	....	4	....	1, 530
Lynn, Mass	....	....	....	....	....	....	2	....	720
Mattapoisett, Mass	4	....	4	1, 396	236	1, 500	12	3	3, 153
Mystic, Conn	3	1	4	467	4, 674	19, 900	9	2	3, 159
Nantucket, Mass	8	7	15	10, 869	1, 238	2, 500	52	4	18, 484
New Bedford, Mass	54	5	59	40, 313	42, 352	925, 600	307	4	104, 006
New London, Conn	3	1	4	492	8, 441	178, 600	47	6	17, 335
Newport, R. I	....	....	....	....	....	....	5	....	1, 742
New York, N. Y*	6	1	7	426	4, 156	12, 200	....	....	....
New Suffolk, N. Y	1	....	1	....	1, 385	10, 500	....	....	....
Orleans, Mass	....	2	2	335	20	....	1	2	426
Providence, R. I	....	....	....	....	....	....	2	....	865
Provincetown, Mass	2	20	22	2, 810	741	....	3	24	3, 198
Sag Harbor, N. Y	2	2	4	1, 021	2, 077	18, 700	18	1	6, 083
Salem, Mass	1	....	1	320	30	....	1	....	230
Sandwich, Mass	....	2	2	115	15	....	....	2	292
Sippican, Mass	....	....	....	....	....	....	....	1	119
Stonington, Conn	3	1	4	199	4, 313	6, 400	18	1	5, 843
Truro, Mass	....	....	....	....	....	....	....	1	143

* Of these part were freighters. † Freighter.

K.—*Synopsis of importation, by ports, from 1804 to 1877*—Continued.

Port of departure.	Nature and number of vessels returning.			Importation.			Tonnage.		
	Ships and barks.	Brigs and schooners.	Total.	Sperm-oil.	Whale-oil.	Bone.	Ships and barks.	Brigs and schooners.	Total.
1852—Continued.				*Bbls.*	*Bbls.*	*Lbs.*			
Wareham, Mass							1		374
Warren, R. I	10		10	4, 907	7, 686	30, 400	16		5, 257
Westport, Mass	2	2	4	1, 510	31		17	5	4, 360
Total	119	48	167	78, 872	84, 211	1, 259, 900	599	62	206, 287
1853.									
Baltimore, Md	1		1		842				
Beverly, Mass	2	1	3	615	50		3	2	999
Boston, Mass	6	2	8	4, 469	560		1		261
Cold Spring, N. Y	1		1		2, 359	51, 200	7		2, 919
Dartmouth, Mass	2		2	385	1, 870	25, 800	3		714
Edgartown, Mass						31, 000	10		3, 402
Fairhaven, Mass	13		13	8, 083	14, 172	188, 700	49		16, 754
Falmouth, Mass	2		2	2, 660	600	9, 000	3		1, 106
Fall River, Mass	2		2	360	280		4		1, 144
Gloucester, Mass								1	110
Greenport, N. Y	2		2	224	2, 684	28, 300	9	1	2, 973
Holmes' Hole, Mass		1	1	320	1, 720	1, 000	4		1, 530
Lynn, Mass	2		2	1, 656	2, 120	28, 000	1		323
Mattapoisett, Mass	4	3	7	1, 816	42	4, 900	11	4	3, 013
Mystic, Conn	3		3	246	4, 998	50, 900	9	3	3, 259
Nantucket, Mass	15	4	19	19, 232	7, 598	43, 700	44	3	15, 571
New Bedford, Mass	89	2	91	44, 923	118, 672	2, 835, 800	316	2	107, 512
New London, Conn	18	3	21	1, 107	45, 990	1, 881, 200	46	9	17, 308
Newport, R. I							5		1, 742
New York, N. Y	4	4	8	992	20, 275	177, 900			
Orleans, Mass	1	2	3	530	25		1	4	654
Providence, R. I	2		2	1, 963	4, 527	54, 000	1		298
Provincetown, Mass	1	21	22	1, 761	603		3	24	3, 065
Sag Harbor, N. Y	5		5	1, 366	6, 338	74, 600	18	2	6, 292
Salem, Mass	1		1	180	30		1		230
Sandwich, Mass		3	3	439	14			2	292
Sippican, Mass		2	2	200	40			2	239
Stonington, Conn	6	3	9	561	14, 142	110, 300	18	1	5, 843
Truro, Mass		1	1	70				1	143
Wareham, Mass	1		1	136	2, 513	46, 700	1		374
Warren, R. I	5		5	3, 173	1, 548	9, 300	17		5, 969
Westport, Mass	10	1	11	4, 610	92		17	5	4, 360
Total	198	53	251	103, 077	260, 114	5, 652, 300	602	66	208, 399

1854.									
Beverly, Mass	2	2	4	643			3	2	999
Boston, Mass	6		6	3,911	74	21,800			
Cold Spring, N. Y	4		4	400	7,687	84,700	7		2,919
Dartmouth, Mass	1		1	869	8		6		1,616
Edgartown, Mass	1	1	2	214	1,861		11	1	3,832
Fairhaven, Mass	13		13	2,881	21,507	274,000	45		15,202
Falmouth, Mass	1		1	513	1,828		3		1,106
Fall River, Mass							4		1,144
Gloucester, Mass		1	1	82				1	110
Greenport, N. Y	5		5	1,197	7,773	29,200	9	1	2,973
Holmes' Hole, Mass	2		2	425	3,190	3,000	4		1,530
Lynn, Mass							1		323
Mattapoisett, Mass	4	1	5	1,329	2,182	9,400	11	4	3,013
Mystic, Conn	5		5	537	6,351	36,800	8	3	2,451
Nantucket, Mass	9	3	12	8,900	9,314	73,900	41	2	14,337
New Bedford, Mass	113		113	42,924	175,336	1,669,200	312	2	105,459
New London, Conn	20	3	23	1,610	42,705	250,200	44	8	16,329
Newport, R. I	2		2		3,430		5		1,742
New York, N. Y	8		8	3,517	19,453	893,800			
Orleans, Mass		1	1	32	420		1	4	738
Providence, R. I							1		298
Provincetown, Mass	1	22	23	2,708	1,041		2	16	1,988
Sag Harbor, N. Y	6	2	8	300	6,979	22,500	18	1	6,085
Salem, Mass							1		216
Sandwich, Mass		2	2	377	62			2	292
Sippican, Mass		2	2	196	10			2	239
Stonington, Conn	3		3	460	8,145	70,600	13	1	4,508
Wareham, Mass							1		374
Warren, R. I	1		1	441			16		5,289
Westport, Mass	6	1	7	2,230	481	1,100	17	4	4,230
Total	213	41	254	76,696	319,837	3,445,200	584	54	199,842
1855.									
Beverly, Mass	2		2	307	8		4		837
Boston, Mass	3	1	4	926	5,666	15,000			
Cold Spring, N. Y	1		1		1,435	14,000	5		2,129
Dartmouth, Mass							8	1	2,400
Edgartown, Mass	2		2	268	2,880	32,500	11	2	3,972
Fairhaven, Mass	11		11	7,551	9,775	86,600	48		16,417
Falmouth, Mass							3		1,106
Fall River, Mass							4		1,144
Greenport, N. Y	2		2	266	2,855	17,600	11		3,305
Holmes' Hole, Mass	1		1	59	2,079	182,000	3	2	1,349
Lynn, Mass							1		323
Mattapoisett, Mass	5	1	6	1,908	2,543	45,500	11	4	3,100
Mystic, Conn							7		2,165
Nantucket, Mass	9	3	12	9,852	5,067	59,700	40	2	14,136
New Bedford, Mass	76	2	78	42,987	102,968	1,460,500	319	1	107,702
New London, Conn	10	2	12	171	19,978	372,500	45	9	13,651
Newport, R. I	2		2	72	2,654	81,500	5		1,742

K.—*Synopsis of importation, by ports, from* 1804 *to* 1877—Continued.

Port of departure.	Nature and number of vessels returning.			Importation.			Tonnage.		
	Ships and barks.	Brigs and schooners.	Total.	Sperm-oil.	Whale-oil.	Bone.	Ships and barks.	Brigs and schooners.	Total.
1855—Continued.				*Bbls.*	*Bbls.*	*Lbs.*			
New York, N. Y	1	2	3	1, 696	140	....	....	....	....
Orleans, Mass	1	1	2	280	450	....	1	3	616
Providence, R. I	....	....	....	....	....	....	1	....	298
Provincetown, Mass	2	12	14	1, 290	1, 062	5, 000	3	17	2, 319
Sag Harbor, N. Y	6	....	6	846	6, 580	60, 000	15	1	5, 064
Salem, Mass	1	....	1	42	....	....	1	....	216
Sandwich, Mass	....	1	1	....	265	....	....	2	292
Sippican, Mass	....	2	2	277	12	....	....	2	239
Stonington, Conn	5	....	5	246	9, 911	111, 800	7	....	2, 311
Wareham, Mass	....	....	....	....	....	....	1	....	374
Warren, R. I	4	....	4	1, 687	5, 821	161, 800	14	....	4, 696
Westport, Mass	5	1	6	1, 918	1, 866	600	17	4	4, 298
Total	149	28	177	72, 649	184, 015	2, 707, 500	585	50	199, 141
1856.									
Beverly, Mass	3	....	3	141	144	....	2	....	452
Boston, Mass	7	....	7	379	342	28, 500	....	....	....
Cold Spring, N. Y	1	....	1	....	2, 596	27, 000	5	....	2, 129
Dartmouth, Mass	2	1	3	1, 027	1, 399	8, 400	10	....	2, 700
Edgartown, Mass	4	1	5	1, 227	6, 171	104, 300	14	3	4, 955
Fairhaven, Mass	8	....	8	5, 696	9, 648	26, 300	47	1	16, 656
Falmouth, Mass	1	....	1	307	2, 477	13, 400	3	....	1, 106
Fall River, Mass	2	....	2	30	1, 944	11, 600	3	....	715
Greenport, N. Y	1	....	1	675	150	4, 000	9	....	2, 652
Holmes' Hole, Mass	1	1	2	238	890	2, 000	3	1	1, 219
Lynn, Mass	....	....	....	....	....	....	1	....	323
Mattapoisett, Mass	2	1	3	979	368	....	12	6	3, 530
Mystic, Conn	4	....	4	121	5, 146	69, 000	6	....	1, 840
Nantucket, Mass	9	4	13	6, 015	7, 354	57, 500	38	3	13, 620
New Bedford, Mass	78	1	79	52, 885	81, 783	1, 087, 600	329	....	111, 364
New London, Conn	18	7	25	961	31, 808	249, 900	50	15	18, 999
Newport, R. I	1	....	1	700	....	....	4	....	1, 206
New York, N. Y	7	1	8	2, 083	18, 997	691, 200	....	....	....
Orleans, Mass	1	3	4	480	889	3, 600	1	3	616
Providence, R. I	....	....	....	....	....	....	1	....	298
Provincetown, Mass	1	13	14	889	2, 806	4, 000	5	17	2, 735
Sag Harbor, N. Y	4	1	5	664	4, 097	32, 200	14	4	5, 261
Salem, Mass	1	....	1	231	219	1, 200	....	....	....
Sandwich, Mass	....	2	2	380	140	1, 000	....	1	165

Sippican, Mass		2	2	293	32			3	319
Stonington, Conn	3		3	220	6, 307	54, 500	6		1, 949
Wareham, Mass							1		374
Warren, R. I	9		9	3, 073	11, 909	109, 000	15		5, 043
Westport, Mass	5		5	1, 247	334	1, 500	14	5	3, 983
Total	173	38	211	80, 941	197, 890	2, 592, 700	593	62	204, 209
1857.									
Beverly, Mass	1		1	346	40		2		452
Boston, Mass	3		3	131	104	10, 000			
Cold Spring, N. Y	1		1	201	371	3, 100	5		2, 129
Dartmouth, Mass	1		1	344	49	2, 100	10		2, 807
Edgartown, Mass	3	1	4	880	3, 331	18, 400	16	3	5, 776
Fairhaven, Mass	15		15	5, 500	17, 417	103, 200	47	1	16, 840
Falmouth, Mass							3		1, 106
Fall River, Mass	1		1	700	800		2		490
Gloucester, Mass		1	1	20	20				
Greenport, N. Y	3		3	592	3, 299	5, 600	7		1, 950
Holmes' Hole, Mass	2		2	225	3, 930	14, 500	1	1	420
Lynn, Mass	1		1	108	2, 550	17, 200			
Mattapoisett, Mass	3	4	7	2, 012	2, 143	20, 700	13	6	3, 654
Mystic, Conn	2		2	480	4, 856	14, 500	6		1, 840
Nantucket, Mass	6	2	8	3, 456	5, 736	20, 300	36	4	13, 073
New Bedford, Mass	103	2	105	48, 108	127, 362	1, 350, 850	324		110, 267
New Haven, Conn	1		1	58					
New London, Conn	19	5	24	3, 619	28, 683	89, 600	47	16	18, 535
Newport, R. I							3		986
New York, N. Y	5		5	1, 866	11, 263	306, 300			
Orleans, Mass		2	2	113	313	2, 100	1	3	638
Providence, R. I	1		1	358	5				
Provincetown, Mass	2	18	20	1, 981	2, 712	5, 800	5	23	3, 337
Philadelphia, Pa		2	2	94					
Sag Harbor, N. Y	2	2	4	1, 100	5, 875	20, 100	17	3	6, 139
Salem, Mass							1		216
Sandwich, Mass							1		165
Sippican, Mass		3	3	309	68			5	598
Stonington, Conn	1		1	103	2, 050	17, 800	5		1, 705
Wareham, Mass	1		1	408	1, 609	3, 000	1		374
Warren, R. I	3		3	563	5, 959	33, 700	16		5, 418
Westport, Mass	8	2	10	4, 765	396		18	2	4, 233
Total	188	44	232	78, 440	230, 941	2, 058, 850	587	67	203, 148
1858.									
Beverly, Mass							2	1	595
Boston, Mass	5	1	*6	340	1, 466	25, 300			
Cold Spring, N. Y	2		2	25	3, 984	21, 000	4		1, 606
Dartmouth, Mass	4		4	1, 801	250		10		2, 807
Edgartown, Mass	4		4	2, 024	4, 827	9, 400	16	2	5, 696
Fairhaven, Mass	13		13	8, 553	15, 745	84, 500	45	1	16, 144

* All freighters.

K.—*Synopsis of importation, by ports, from 1804 to 1877*—Continued.

Port of departure.	Nature and number of vessels returning.			Importation.			Tonnage.		
	Ships and barks.	Brigs and schooners.	Total.	Sperm-oil.	Whale-oil.	Bone.	Ships and barks.	Brigs and schooners.	Total.
1858—Continued.				*Bbls.*	*Bbls.*	*Lbs.*			
Falmouth, Mass	2	....	2	3, 130	....	....	3	....	1, 106
Fall River, Mass	1	....	1	151	134	....	2	....	490
Greenport, N. Y	1	....	1	....	1, 225	....	4	....	1, 657
Holmes' Hole, Mass	1	*2	3	351	910	700	1	1	420
Mattapoisett, Mass	6	1	7	2, 936	777	300	13	6	3, 654
Mystic, Conn	1	....	1	....	1, 092	....	6	1	2, 040
Nantucket, Mass	7	1	8	7, 945	2, 684	5, 100	30	3	11, 037
New Bedford, Mass	77	3	†80	46, 218	103, 105	1, 184, 900	316	....	107, 931
New Haven, Conn	....	....	....	....	....	....	1	....	567
New London, Conn	19	4	‡23	1, 830	38, 120	116, 100	43	13	16, 755
Newport, R. I	....	....	....	....	....	....	3	....	986
New York, N. Y	6	3	§9	....	120	90, 200	....	....	....
Orleans, Mass	....	2	2	309	188	....	1	3	638
Provincetown, Mass	1	19	20	1, 289	2, 655	1, 500	5	21	3, 099
Sag Harbor, N. Y	7	2	9	1, 321	4, 200	15, 000	16	4	5, 956
Salem, Mass	....	....	....	....	....	....	1	....	216
Sandwich, Mass	....	....	....	....	....	....	1	....	165
Sippican, Mass	....	4	4	576	248	....	....	6	698
Stonington, Conn	....	....	....	....	....	....	4	....	1, 394
Wareham, Mass	....	....	....	....	....	....	1	....	374
Warren, R. I	1	....	1	776	48	12, 700	15	....	4, 851
Westport, Mass	4	1	5	2, 366	445	4, 500	18	2	4, 233
Total	162	43	205	81, 941	182, 223	1, 571, 200	561	64	195, 115
1859.									
Beverly, Mass	2	1	3	540	1, 025	5, 500	2	1	595
Boston, Mass‖	5	1	6	1, 299	200	1, 800	....	....	....
Cold Spring, N. Y	1	....	1	....	2, 900	....	4	....	1, 606
Dartmouth, Mass	2	....	2	2, 379	592	....	9	....	2, 453
Edgartown, Mass	3	1	4	895	2, 554	10, 000	16	2	5, 696
Fairhaven, Mass	9	....	9	3, 583	6, 201	29, 750	40	3	14, 417
Falmouth, Mass‖	....	....	....	....	....	....	3	....	1, 106
Fall River, Mass	....	....	....	....	....	....	2	....	490
Greenport, N. Y	1	1	2	385	2, 623	11, 650	2	....	521
Holmes' Hole, Mass	....	....	....	....	....	....	1	1	420
Mattapoisett, Mass	3	1	4	974	1, 303	7, 500	14	5	3, 837
Mystic, Conn	1	....	1	244	1, 350	1, 700	5	1	1, 712
Nantucket, Mass	9	2	11	6, 340	6, 850	15, 000	20	1	7, 244
New Bedford, Mass‖	86	3	89	64, 327	121, 522	1, 608, 250	301	....	103, 564

New Haven, Conn							1		567
New London, Conn‖	19	1	20	1, 489	29, 483	188, 000	33	10	12, 825
Newport, R. I	1		1	381	52	700	2		646
New York, N. Y‖	10	2	12	722	5, 307	9, 000			
Orleans, Mass		2	2	365	564			3	638
Providence, R. I	1		1	293					
Provincetown, Mass		16	16	2, 625	1, 349		4	22	3, 075
Sag Harbor, N. Y	7		7	1, 152	3, 608	18, 000	15	4	5, 425
Salem, Mass	1		1	362	114		1		216
Sandwich, Mass	1		1	408	47		1		165
Sippican, Mass		4	4	456	88			6	698
Stonington, Conn	3		3	115	2, 365	17, 000	3	1	1, 240
Wareham, Mass							1		374
Warren, R. I	2		2	1, 395			10	1	3, 286
Westport, Mass	3		3	679	314		18	2	4, 233
Total	170	35	205	91, 408	190, 411	1, 923, 850	508	63	177, 049
1860.									
Beverly, Mass	1	1	2	249	160		1	1	385
Boston, Mass‖	3	1	4	390	150	1, 300			
Cold Spring, N. Y	1		1		1, 716	21, 000	2		554
Dartmouth, Mass	2		2	1, 447	251		6		1, 656
Edgartown, Mass	4		4	915	5, 212	8, 500	15	1	5, 384
Fairhaven, Mass	7	1	8	3, 669	7, 976	10, 600	36	3	13, 051
Falmouth, Mass	1		1	30	1, 572	10, 500	1		350
Fall River, Mass	1		1	367	50		2		490
Greenport, N. Y	2		2	220	1, 265	900			
Holmes' Hole, Mass		1	1	318	54		1		270
Mattapoisett, Mass	4	1	5	2, 106	64	1, 850	13	5	3, 653
Mystic, Conn	3		3	250	4, 480	4, 600	2	1	860
Nantucket, Mass	5	1	6	5, 316	749	10, 000	17	1	6, 157
New Bedford, Mass‖	85	3	83	43, 716	90, 450	1, 112, 600	291		98, 760
New Haven, Conn							1		567
New London, Conn	8	1	9	623	13, 040	93, 200	29	9	11, 245
Newport, R. I	2		2	870	955				
New York, N. Y‖	10	5	15	821	5, 329	20, 700			
Orleans, Mass		2	2	186	70		1	2	530
Provincetown, Mass	3	16	19	3, 698	1, 447	4, 300	5	21	3, 250
Sag Harbor, N. Y	1	1	2	285	430		14	3	4, 739
Salem, Mass							1		216
Sandwich, Mass							1		165
Sippican, Mass		5	5	898	133			5	564
Stonington, Conn	2	1	3	103	1, 274	15, 600		1	143
Wareham, Mass							1		374
Warren, R. I	4		4	1, 867	2, 460	22, 000	4		1, 632
Westport, Mass	8	1	9	5, 364	618		15	2	3, 751
Total	157	41	198	73, 708	140, 005	1, 337, 650	459	55	158, 746

* One freighter. † Ten freighters. ‡ Four freighters. § All freighters. ‖ Including freight; New York and Boston arrivals were all freighters.

K.—*Synopsis of importation, by ports, from 1804 to 1877*—Continued.

Port of departure.	Nature and number of vessels returning.			Importation.			Tonnage.		
	Ships and barks.	Brigs and schooners.	Total.	Sperm-oil.	Whale-oil.	Bone.	Ships and barks.	Brigs and schooners.	Total.
1861.				*Bbls.*	*Bbls.*	*Lbs.*			
Beverly, Mass	1		1	4	70			1	143
Boston, Mass	4		4	1,084	133				
Cold Spring, N. Y							2		554
Dartmouth, Mass							5		1,438
Edgartown, Mass	5	1	6	1,860	5,821	5,150	11	1	4,075
Fairhaven, Mass	14	1	15	4,565	13,217	86,300	23	6	8,386
Falmouth, Mass							1		350
Fall River, Mass	1		1	1,054		7,100	1		164
Holmes' Hole, Mass	1		1	500			1		257
Mattapoisett, Mass	3	1	4	795	1,542	800	8	1	1,819
Mystic, Conn	1		1	621	2,291			1	197
Nantucket, Mass	1	1	2	920	360		13		4,619
New Bedford, Mass	83	2	85	47,404	72,134	724,434	259	1	86,971
New Haven, Conn							1		567
New London, Conn	12	2	14	179	17,809	76,750	15	6	6,491
New York, N. Y	11	1	12	634	9,190	67,500			
Orleans, Mass	1	1	2	366	733		1	2	530
Provincetown, Mass	1	12	13	1,725	1,049		5	23	3,499
Sag Harbor, N. Y	7	1	8	2,414	3,692	15,700	6	5	2,520
Salem, Mass	1		1	330	16				
Sandwich, Mass	1		1	447	3		1		165
Sippican, Mass		3	3	400	14			4	464
Wareham, Mass	1		1	25	900	8,000			
Warren, R. I	4		4	777	2,137	5,300	3		946
Westport, Mass	3		3	3,198	2		13	2	3,330
Total	156	26	182	68,932	133,717	1,038,450	369	53	125,465
1862.									
Beverly, Mass		1	1	335	40			2	238
Boston, Mass	*5	2	7	1,612	3,657		2	3	885
Cold Spring, N. Y	1		1	80	2,123	1,100			
Dartmouth, Mass	2		2	881	130	800	4		1,143
Edgartown, Mass	4		4	2,247	4,579	11,800	8		2,764
Fairhaven, Mass	6	1	7	3,486	4,048	12,800	13	5	4,570
Falmouth, Mass							1		350
Fall River, Mass	1		1	15					
Holmes' Hole, Mass	1		1	705			1		257
Mattapoisett, Mass	4		4	538	947		5		1,022
Mystic, Conn		1	1		968				

Nantucket, Mass	1	2	3	1,069	87		12	1	4,175
New Bedford, Mass	†65	3	68	36,529	61,056	297,600	219	1	73,061
New Haven, Conn							1		567
New London, Conn	4	4	8	1,034	8,225	26,300	12	4	4,627
New York, N. Y	‡11		11	538	11,301	408,100			
Provincetown, Mass	2	13	15	3,042	1,604		4	26	3,660
Sag Harbor, N. Y	3	1	4	1,483	1,674	5,000	5	4	1,999
Salem, Mass								1	159
Sandwich, Mass							1		165
Sippican, Mass		4	4	245	17			3	301
Warren, R. I							2		615
Westport, Mass	3	1	4	1,802	22		13	2	3,330
Total	113	33	146	55,641	100,478	763,500	303	52	103,888
1863.									
Beverly, Mass		1	1	210				2	238
Boston, Mass	§6	6	12	4,916	5,637	88,900	1	2	535
Dartmouth, Mass							4		1,141
Edgartown, Mass	1		1	1,170	100	900	6	1	2,383
Fairhaven, Mass	2	4	6	3,356	1,137	7,800	7	2	2,389
Falmouth, Mass							1		355
Holmes' Hole, Mass							1		257
Mattapoisett, Mass	2		2	1,573	7		3		638
Nantucket, Mass	4	1	5	3,823	557	4,950	9	1	3,173
New Bedford, Mass	‖65	1	66	42,458	43,191	307,950	195	2	64,815
New London, Conn	2	¶2	4	23	2,148	35,550	10	9	4,571
New York, N. Y	9	1	**10	969	7,351	37,600			
Provincetown, Mass	1	15	16	1,290	1,730		2	23	2,969
Sag Harbor, N. Y	1	2	3	885	855	5,100	6		1,528
Salem, Mass		1	1	200	40			1	159
Sippican, Mass		4	4	308	26			3	301
Warren, R. I							2		618
Westport, Mass	6		6	3,874	195		11		2,715
Total	99	38	137	65,055	62,974	488,750	258	46	88,785
1864.									
Beverly, Mass								2	238
Boston, Mass	††7	6	13	3,894	9,611	159,000		3	424
Dartmouth, Mass	1		1	500	525		4		1,118
Edgartown, Mass	1		1	153	1,525	15,650	6		2,288
Fairhaven, Mass	3		3	1,278	711	600	5	2	1,703
Falmouth, Mass	1		1	931	232	1,700			
Holmes' Hole, Mass							1		257
Mattapoisett, Mass	5		5	881	4	700	2		343
Nantucket, Mass		1	1	78	18		6	1	2,037
New Bedford, Mass	‡‡77		77	48,172	35,883	224,250	173	2	58,041

* Two ships and barks and 3 brigs and schooners were freighters. † Ships and barks, all freighters. ‡ All freighters. § Three of the ships and barks and 2 brigs and schooners were freighters. ‖ Five of these ships and barks were freighters. ¶ The brigs and schooners were freighters. ** All freighters. †† All but two brigs and schooners were freighters; each voyage represents an arrival. ‡‡ Five were freighters

K.—*Synopsis of importation, by ports, from 1804 to 1877*—Continued.

Port of departure.	Nature and number of vessels returning.			Importation.			Tonnage.		
	Ships and barks.	Brigs and schooners.	Total.	Sperm-oil.	Whale-oil.	Bone.	Ships and barks.	Brigs and schooners.	Total.
1864—Continued.				*Bbls.*	*Bbls.*	*Lbs.*			
New London, Conn	*2	4	6	915	8, 091	149, 600	11	13	5, 376
New York, N. Y	†14	6	20	2, 101	12, 955	202, 650			
Provincetown, Mass	1	13	14	1 850	1, 742	2, 600		23	2, 630
Sag Harbor, N. Y	3		3	1, 133	505	3, 700	8		2, 007
Salem, Mass		1	1	90	20			1	159
Sippican, Mass		1	1	155	9			2	221
Warren, R. I							1		351
Westport, Mass	4		4	2, 241	32		10		2, 497
Total	119	32	151	64, 372	71, 863	760, 450	227	49	79, 690
1865.									
Beverly, Mass		3	3	67	101			2	238
Boston, Mass	8	4	‡12	2, 479	3, 383	94, 250		4	418
Dartmouth, Mass							3		901
Edgartown, Mass	1		1	687			6		2, 288
Fairhaven, Mass	1	3	4	269	328	7, 500	4	4	1, 437
Holmes' Hole, Mass	1		1	620					
Nantucket, Mass	4	1	5	3, 488	842	3, 100	1	1	289
New Bedford, Mass	57		§57	21, 292	51, 693	376, 450	161	3	50, 403
New London, Conn	5	5	10	53	8, 569	56, 800	8	12	4, 153
New York, N. Y	10	11	21	828	8, 643	71, 800			
Provincetown, Mass		21	21	2, 752	2, 238	8, 550		33	4, 020
Sag Harbor, N. Y	1		1		70	900	7	1	2, 007
Salem, Mass								2	294
Sippican, Mass		1	1	285	2			2	232
Westport, Mass	2		2	422	369		9		1, 856
Total	90	49	139	33, 242	76, 238	619, 350	199	64	68, 536
1866.									
Beverly, Mass		2	2	289	124			2	238
Boston, Mass	11	5	¶16	4, 183	4, 231	114, 050	2	6	1, 013
Dartmouth, Mass	2		2	673	956	15, 400	2	1	491
Edgartown, Mass	2		2	407	2, 596		6		2, 245
Fairhaven, Mass	1	2	3	446	101	26, 000	5	4	1, 669
Groton, Conn								1	148
Marion,‖ Mass		3	3					4	407
Nantucket, Mass		1	1	199			4	2	1, 055
New Bedford, Mass	38	2	**40	21, 345	44, 513	392, 100	176	5	53, 798
Newburyport, Mass								2	215

New London, Conn	2	4	††6	35	5, 190	41, 950	9	13	4, 337
New York, N. Y	24	11	†35	2, 832	12, 261	326, 375	1		243
Provincetown, Mass		31	31	3, 053	3, 073			46	5, 551
Sag Harbor, N. Y	2	1	3	395	505	4, 000	7		1, 534
Salem, Mass		1	1	127	31		1	2	436
Sippican, Mass				587	427				
Tisbury, Mass								1	117
Wellfleet, Mass								1	135
Westport, Mass	3		3	2, 092	294	500	9		1, 710
Total	85	63	148	36, 663	74, 302	920, 375	222	90	75, 342
1867.									
Beverly, Mass		1	1	25				1	143
Boston, Mass	6	5	‡‡11	4, 310	689	1, 087	2	9	1, 290
Dartmouth, Mass		1	1	35	3		2	1	491
Edgartown, Mass	1		1		1, 155	21, 350	7		2, 458
Fairhaven, Mass		2	2	100	284	7, 800	4	9	1, 965
Groton, Conn		1	1		200	2, 600		1	148
Marion, Mass		2	2	401	8			4	407
Nantucket, Mass							5	2	1, 154
New Bedford, Mass	55	7	62	24, 552	72, 108	731, 146	176	5	52, 652
Newburyport, Mass								3	286
New London, Conn	2	5	7	30	5, 746	30, 371	8	11	3, 825
New York, N. Y	21	12	‖‖33	6, 752	4, 493	193, 088	2		628
Provincetown, Mass		38	38	3, 475	2, 887	3, 135		54	4, 775
Sag Harbor, N. Y	3		3	801	1, 310	8, 900	5	2	1, 540
Salem, Mass	1	1	2	112	140	1, 000	2	2	671
Tisbury, Mass								1	117
Wellfleet, Mass		1	1	225	2			1	135
Westport, Mass	5		5	2, 615	264	920	10		1, 909
Total	94	76	170	43, 433	89, 289	1, 001, 397	223	106	74, 544
1868.									
Beverly, Mass		1	1	190	4			1	143
Boston, Mass	3	5	¶¶8	2, 724	432		1	9	1, 145
Dartmouth, Mass		2	2	95			2	1	4[illegible]1
Edgartown, Mass					1, 310		7		2, 396
Fairhaven, Mass	2	4	6	656	2, 077	17, 118	3	9	1, 603
Groton, Conn								1	148
Marion, Mass		6	6	554	62			7	745
Nantucket, Mass	1	2	3	597	229		6	2	1, 351
New Bedford, Mass	53	16	†††69	31, 841	49, 939	667, 507	173	5	50, 628
Newburyport, Mass		3	3	222	48			3	286
New London, Conn	2	5	7	66	7, 761	61, 700	9	11	3, 969
New York, N. Y	21	14	†53	6, 646	2, 153	154, 525	4	1	1, 293

* Two vessels were freighters. † All freighters. ‡ All these, save 3 schooners, were freighters. § Six of these were freighters. ‖ Name changed from Sippican 1866. ¶ All freighters except one schooner. ** Eight ships and barks were freighters. †† One schooner was a freighter. ‡‡ Of these all the ships and barks and one schooner were freighters. §§ Of these 12 of the ships and barks and 5 schooners were freighters. ‖‖ All freighters but one. ¶¶ All but 3 (brigs and schooners) freighters. ††† Eight ships and barks and 3 brigs and schooners were freighters.

K.—*Synopsis of importation, by ports, from* 1804 *to* 1877—Continued.

Port of departure.	Nature and number of vessels returning.			Importation.			Tonnage.		
	Ships and barks.	Brigs and schooners.	Total.	Sperm-oil.	Whale-oil.	Bone.	Ships and barks.	Brigs and schooners.	Total.
1868—Continued.				*Bbls.*	*Bbls.*	*Lbs.*			
Provincetown, Mass		24	24	2,698	1,524			54	5,079
Sag Harbor, N. Y	1		1	315			3	2	996
Salem, Mass		1	1		6		2	2	671
San Francisco, Cal							3	3	1,414
Tisbury, Mass		1	1	208				1	117
Wellfleet, Mass								1	135
Westport, Mass	1		1	362	30		10		1,909
Total	84	84	168	47,174	65,575	900,850	223	113	74,519
1869.									
Beverly, Mass								1	143
Boston, Mass	7	6	*13	4,548	291	4,400		8	814
Dartmouth, Mass							2	1	491
Edgartown, Mass	1		1	38	1,084	9,080	7		2,396
Fairhaven, Mass	2	5	7	839	1,490		4	7	1,653
Groton, Conn								1	148
Marion, Mass		2	2	170	6			6	687
Nantucket, Mass							6	2	1,351
New Bedford, Mass	53	6	†59	32,673	54,566	471,495	172	4	50,775
Newburyport, Mass		1	1	93				3	286
New London, Conn	2	1	‡3	21	8,883	17,992	9	11	3,948
New York, N. Y	28	15	§43	6,451	13,223	76,370	4	1	1,293
Provincetown, Mass		29	29	2,798	3,526			49	4,612
Sag Harbor, N. Y	1		1		200	2,930	2	2	757
Salem, Mass							1	2	496
San Francisco, Cal	1		1	45	1,657	21,336	2	3	1,254
Tisbury, Mass								1	117
Wellfleet, Mass		1	1	260	85			1	135
Westport, Mass							9		1,781
Total	95	66	161	47,936	85,011	603,603	218	103	73,137
1870.									
Beverly, Mass		1	1	100				1	143
Boston, Mass				4,301	1,246			7	717
Dartmouth, Mass							2	1	491
Edgartown, Mass				578			6		2,086
Fairhaven, Mass		2	2	212	317		4	4	1,427
Marion, Mass		4	4	523	8			5	487

Nantucket, Mass	1	2	3	503	10		5	1	1, 112
New Bedford, Mass	56	3	‖59	42, 886	49, 563	‖569, 861	171	5	50, 213
Newburyport, Mass		2	2	181	180				
New London, Conn				595	10, 382	25, 309	11	11	4, 552
New York, N. Y	26	4	¶30	1, 812	5, 757	47, 195	2	1	650
Provincetown, Mass		33	33	2, 580	3, 058			27	2, 545
Sag Harbor, N. Y	1		1	450			1	2	540
Salem, Mass							1	2	496
San Francisco, Cal	5	1	**6		4, 013	66, 000	4	4	2, 015
Tisbury, Mass		1	1	250	150			1	117
Westport, Mass	2		2	212	7		9		1, 781
Total	91	53	144	55, 183	72, 691	708, 365	216	72	69, 372
1871.									
Beverly, Mass								1	143
Boston, Mass	4	8	††12	4, 162	628			6	595
Dartmouth, Mass							2		443
Edgartown, Mass	1		1	93	1, 418	17, 502	4		1, 293
Fairhaven, Mass		1	1	109	135		3	3	1, 097
Marion, Mass		3	3	325	361	760		2	175
Nantucket, Mass							3		531
New Bedford, Mas	53	3	‡‡56	30, 654	55, 710	‡‡560, 993	138	5	40, 045
New London, Conn	7	2	9	181	8, 459	18, 500	9	10	3, 576
New York, N. Y	17	3	§§20	1, 920	6, 260	2, 500	1	1	398
Provincetown, Mass		17	17	2, 024	1, 827			16	1, 447
Sag Harbor, N. Y		1	1	235	310			2	325
Salem, Mass	1	2	3	1, 231	4		1		235
San Francisco, Cal							1	3	617
Westport, Mass	3		3	600	40	400	9		1, 781
Total	86	40	126	41, 534	75, 152	600, 655	171	49	52, 701
1872.									
Beverly, Mass		1	1	150				1	143
Boston, Mass	3	7	‖‖10	2, 409	807			5	503
Dartmouth, Mass	1		1				2		443
Edgartown, Mass	2		2	1, 611	1, 428	6, 600	3		944
Fairhaven, Mass		2	2	196	7		3	2	937
Marion, Mass		1	1					3	259
Nantucket, Mass							1		182
New Bedford, Mass	30	3	‖‖33	33, 021	15, 573	177, 868	125	5	36, 686
New London, Conn	2	5	¶¶7	40	5, 672	8, 000	9	11	3, 603
New York, N. Y	28	3	§§31	4, 644	5, 441	1, 325	1	2	487
Provincetown, Mass		13	13	1, 378	1, 379			19	1, 661
Sag Harbor, N. Y								2	325

* Eight freighters. † Twelve freighters. ‡ Two freighters. § Forty-two freighters. ‖ Ten ships and barks and 4 brigs and schooners were freighters; 66,000 pounds of bone came by railroad from San Francisco. ¶ All but 1 bark were freighters. ** Two ships and barks were freighters. †† All but 1 schooner freighters. ‡‡ Four ships and barks freighters; a large amount of bone came by rail from San Francisco. §§ All freighters. ‖‖ All but three freighters. ¶¶ Two ships and barks, and one schooner freighters. *** One schooner freighter.

K.—*Synopsis of importation, by ports, from 1804 to 1877*—Continued.

Port of departure.	Nature and number of vessels returning.			Importation.			Tonnage.		
	Ships and barks.	Brigs and schooners.	Total.	Sperm-oil.	Whale-oil.	Bone.	Ships and barks.	Brigs and schooners.	Total.
1872—Continued.				*Bbls.*	*Bbls.*	*Lbs.*			
San Francisco, Cal	3	1	4	320			1		245
Westport, Mass	2		2	1, 432	768		8		1, 578
Total	71	36	107	45, 201	31, 075	193, 793	153	50	47, 996
1873.									
Beverly, Mass								1	143
Boston, Mass	4	3	*7	4, 483	10			4	434
Cold Spring, N. Y							2		443
Dartmouth, Mass	1		1						
Edgartown, Mass							1		183
Fairhaven, Mass		1	1	73			1	1	388
Marion, Mass		3	3	158	2			3	259
New Bedford, Mass	32	7	†39	30, 229	25, 757	150, 598	109	4	32, 556
New London, Conn	2	4	6	103	3, 442	2, 212	8	10	3, 285
New York, N. Y	25	2	*27	4, 807	9, 284	53, 000		1	89
Provincetown, Mass		15	15	1, 699	1, 519	586		17	1, 472
Sag Harbor, N. Y								1	116
San Francisco, Cal							1		245
Westport, Mass	1		1	501			8		1, 578
Total	65	35	100	42, 053	40, 014	206, 396	130	42	41, 191
1874.									
Boston, Mass	6	6	‡12	3, 058	974	8, 609	1	5	670
Dartmouth, Mass							2		443
Edgartown, Mass							2		333
Fairhaven, Mass		1	1	85			1	2	471
Marion, Mass		2	2	266				2	176
New Bedford, Mass	31	1	§32	25, 480	26, 340	§321, 637	102	5	29, 541
New London, Conn	2	3	5	59	3, 684	15, 314	4	10	2, 627
New York, N. Y	21	1	*22	1, 863	5, 652		1	1	241
Provincetown, Mass		13	13	1, 392	1, 132			18	1, 722
Sag Harbor, N. Y								1	116
San Francisco, Cal	1		1				1		245
Westport, Mass	1		1				5		1, 148
Total	62	27	89	32, 203	37, 782	345, 560	119	44	37, 733

1875.‖									
Boston, Mass	7	6	13	3, 106	417		1	6	792
Dartmouth, Mass							2		443
Edgartown, Mass	1		1	148			2		333
Fairhaven, Mass	1	2	3	617	620			2	156
Marion, Mass		2	2	218	37			2	176
New Bedford, Mass	41	12	53	34, 430	25, 067	359, 973	110	6	31, 691
New London, Conn		4	4		2, 002	1, 860	3	11	2, 320
New York, N. Y	13	2	15	2, 112	4, 185	425	1		152
Provincetown, Mass		10	10	1, 671	1, 066			19	1, 804
San Francisco, Cal	2		2	315	1, 200	10, 045	1		245
Westport, Mass							3		771
Total	65	38	103	42, 617	35, 594	372, 303	123	46	38, 883
1876.¶									
Boston, Mass	4	3	7	3, 013				6	648
Dartmouth, Mass							2		443
Edgartown, Mass							3		634
Fairhaven, Mass		1	1	71				2	156
Marion, Mass		2	2	173	22			2	176
New Bedford, Mass	37	18	55	30, 234	20, 535	93, 484	108	10	30, 465
New London, Conn	3	2	5	50	4, 374	24, 744	2	10	1, 851
New York, N. Y	23	2	25	5, 156	6, 640	22, 000	1		152
Provincetown, Mass		7	7	1, 114	764			21	2, 027
San Francisco, Cal	2		2		675	10, 400	2		505
Westport, Mass							3		771
Total	69	35	104	39, 811	33, 010	150, 628	121	51	37, 828

* All freighters. † Six ships and barks, and three schooners were freighters. ‡ Five ships and barks, and one schooner freighters. § Five ships and barks freighters; 285,275 pounds of bone arrived by rail from San Francisco. ‖ All the New York vessels, and a part of those at Boston and New Bedford, were freighters. Of late years many whalers belonging to Westport, Marion, Dartmouth, Provincetown, and Boston have discharged at New Bedford, and the cargoes are credited to that port. ¶ All the New York vessels, most of those at Boston and part of those at New Bedford and San Francisco, were freighters.

L.—*Table of exports from the United States—the products of the whale fishery.*

[Compiled from Pitkin's Statistics and Reports of the Treasurer of the United States.]

Year.	Spermaceti-oil.	Value.	Whale and other fish oils.	Value.	Whalebone.	Value.	Spermaceti-candles.	Value.	Sperma-ceti.	Value.	Gross value.
	Gallons.		*Gallons.*		*Pounds.*		*Pounds.*		*Pounds.*		
1791	134, 595	....	447, 323	....	124, 829	....	182, 400	....	....	....	....
1792	436, 423	....	119, 733	....	154, 407	....	157, 520	....	....	....	....
1793	512, 780	....	78, 524	....	202, 620	....	235, 600	....	....	....	....
1794	1, 000, 208	....	55, 053	....	354, 617	....	214, 960	....	....	....	....
1795	810, 524	....	64, 335	....	410, 664	....	240, 720	....	....	....	....
1796	1, 176, 650	....	59, 797	....	308, 314	....	221, 903	....	....	....	....
1797	582, 425	....	38, 221	....	452, 127	....	130, 438	....	....	....	....
1798	128, 758	....	700, 040	....	62, 805	....	144, 149	....	....	....	....
1799	114, 264	....	420, 949	....	89, 552	....	240, 301	....	....	....	....
1800	221, 762	....	204, 468	....	32, 636	....	181, 321	....	....	....	....
1801	91, 684	....	215, 522	....	23, 106	....	290, 666	....	....	....	....
1802	28, 470	....	379, 976	....	80, 334	....	135, 627	....	....	....	....
1803	46, 984	*$175, 000	550, 535	*$280, 000	96, 802	....	238, 034	....	....	....	$455, 000
1804	5, 550	70, 000	646, 505	310, 000	134, 006	....	127, 602	....	....	....	380, 000
1805	72, 624	163, 000	626, 089	315, 000	21, 335	....	180, 535	....	....	....	478, 000
1806	42, 785	182, 000	826, 233	418, 000	50, 594	....	294, 789	....	....	....	600, 000
1807	44, 339	130, 000	932, 797	476, 000	104, 635	....	172, 132	....	....	....	606, 000
1808	612	33, 000	198, 019	88, 000	8, 660	....	45, 130	....	....	....	121, 000
1809	51, 071	136, 000	421, 282	169, 000	8, 825	....	214, 444	....	....	....	305, 000
1810	63, 910	132, 000	544, 734	222, 000	42, 843	....	187, 190	....	....	....	354, 000
1811	136, 249	273, 000	186, 661	78, 000	30, 346	....	257, 094	....	....	....	351, 000
1812	63, 216	141, 000	106, 369	56, 000	8, 128	....	157, 596	....	....	....	197, 000
1813	....	....	4, 979	2, 500	....	....	26, 522	$10, 500	....	....	13, 000
1814	....	....	837	1, 000	....	....	21, 154	9, 000	....	....	10, 000
1815	....	143, 000	....	57, 000	....	....	....	....	....	....	200, 000
September 30, 1815, to October 1, 1816	2, 756	59, 000	177, 810	116, 000	....	....	116, 916	....	....	....	175, 000
September 30, 1816, to October 1, 1817	11, 300	11, 300	460, 888	230, 444	3, 668	$734	201, 939	100, 970	....	....	343, 448
September 30, 1817, to October 1, 1818	208, 467	156, 350	986, 252	493, 126	9, 300	1, 581	305, 142	137, 314	....	....	788, 371
September 30, 1818, to October 1, 1819	75, 360	55, 520	860, 112	430, 056	8, 038	804	169, 919	76, 463	....	....	562, 843
September 30, 1819, to October 1, 1820	9, 307	6, 980	1, 262, 094	631, 047	25, 202	5, 040	267, 177	106, 871	....	....	749, 938
September 30, 1820, to October 1, 1821	7, 250	5, 340	1, 068, 025	348, 991	16, 349	1, 489	424, 952	169, 777	....	....	525, 597
September 30, 1821, to October 1, 1822	7, 610	6, 060	990, 325	311, 415	....	....	399, 925	151, 226	....	....	468, 701
September 30, 1822, to October 1, 1823	18, 333	8, 972	1, 453, 126	415, 713	86, 474	16, 402	749, 973	212, 337	....	....	653, 424
September 30, 1823, to October 1, 1824	23, 578	10, 500	1, 251, 836	296, 708	60, 693	9, 306	598, 181	157, 772	....	....	474, 286
September 30, 1824, to October 1, 1825	30, 548	17, 679	1, 072, 615	250, 200	212, 062	46, 225	617, 072	202, 188	....	....	516, 292
September 30, 1825, to October 1, 1826	35, 528	23, 517	652, 401	183, 343	188, 709	53, 502	836, 280	288, 104	....	....	548, 466
September 30, 1826, to October 1, 1827	78, 661	48, 220	481, 180	142, 648	241, 085	80, 956	1, 003, 658	316, 061	....	....	587, 885
September 30, 1827, to October 1, 1828	297, 276	190, 669	488, 468	140, 279	120, 128	40, 991	904, 597	255, 378	....	....	627, 317
September 30, 1828, to October 1, 1829	140, 241	92, 554	1, 237, 962	358, 822	464, 225	136, 341	1, 055, 906	261, 315	....	....	849, 032
September 30, 1829, to October 1, 1830	58, 814	38, 618	1, 833, 196	568, 326	404, 919	112, 357	1, 032, 941	249, 292	....	....	968, 593
September 30, 1830, to October 1, 1831	78, 159	53, 526	1, 637, 534	554, 440	565, 926	133, 842	847, 384	217, 830	....	....	959, 638
September 30, 1831, to October 1, 1832	48, 212	38, 161	3, 605, 913	1, 009, 728	1, 044, 227	186, 595	859, 886	267, 333	....	....	1, 501, 817

September 30, 1832, to October 1, 1833	50, 392	42, 589	3, 298, 872	924, 810	1, 203, 176	185, 329	905, 318	259, 451	....	....	1, 412, 179
September 30, 1833, to October 1, 1834	60, 935	50, 048	2, 614, 814	740, 619	873, 983	169, 434	851, 556	257, 718	....	....	1, 217, 819
September 30, 1834, to October 1, 1835	63, 127	52, 531	2, 217, 321	773, 486	270, 977	55, 954	920, 746	284, 019	....	....	1, 165, 990
September 30, 1835, to October 1, 1836	115, 142	119, 787	2, 362, 325	1, 049, 466	731, 500	187, 008	1, 018, 540	341, 907	....	....	1, 698, 168
September 30, 1836, to October 1, 1837	177, 004	151, 875	3, 624, 001	1, 271, 545	1, 129, 509	223, 682	892, 852	294, 510	....	....	1, 941, 612
September 30, 1837, to October 1, 1838	166, 805	137, 809	4, 824, 376	1, 556, 775	1, 634, 570	321, 458	1, 074, 569	340, 531	....	....	2, 356, 573
September 30, 1838, to October 1, 1839	86, 047	85, 015	1, 482, 908	515, 484	1, 445, 098	288, 790	466, 896	178, 142	....	....	1, 067, 431
September 30, 1839, to October 1, 1840	434, 608	430, 490	4, 520, 878	1, 404, 984	1, 892, 259	310, 379	853, 938	332, 353	....	....	2, 478, 206
September 30, 1840, to October 1, 1841	349, 393	343, 300	4, 094, 924	1, 260, 660	1, 271, 363	259, 148	599, 657	231, 960	....	....	2, 095, 068
September 30, 1841, to October 1, 1842	287, 761	233, 114	3, 909, 728	1, 315, 411	918, 280	225, 382	986, 010	318, 997	....	....	2, 092, 904
October 1, 1842, to July 1, 1843	476, 688	310, 768	2, 479, 916	803, 774	898, 773	257, 481	965, 073	243, 308	....	....	1, 615, 331
July, 1843, to July, 1844	451, 317	344, 930	4, 104, 504	1, 464, 968	1, 149, 607	463, 096	606, 454	180, 492	....	....	2, 453, 486
July, 1844, to July, 1845	1, 054, 301	975, 195	4, 505, 662	1, 520, 363	2, 034, 019	762, 642	812, 879	236, 917	....	....	3, 495, 117
July, 1845, to July, 1846	772, 019	697, 570	2, 652, 874	946, 298	1, 697, 892	583, 870	1, 083, 839	295, 606	....	....	2, 523, 344
July, 1846, to July, 1847	795, 792	738, 456	3, 189, 562	1, 070, 659	2, 031, 137	671, 601	705, 150	191, 467	....	....	2, 672, 183
July, 1847, to July, 1848	206, 431	208, 832	1, 607, 038	552, 388	1, 054, 379	314, 107	598, 452	186, 839	....	....	1, 262, 166
July, 1848, to July, 1849	526, 817	572, 763	2, 783, 480	965, 597	1, 198, 250	337, 714	503, 911	159, 403	....	....	2, 035, 477
July, 1849, to July, 1850	730, 743	788, 794	1, 470, 197	672, 640	1, 981, 231	646, 483	742, 528	260, 107	....	....	2, 368, 024
July, 1850, to July, 1851	905, 778	1, 044, 967	2, 004, 886	882, 485	2, 281, 931	689, 662	538, 549	195, 916	....	....	2, 813, 030
July, 1851, to July, 1852	644, 765	809, 274	892, 309	440, 287	1, 184, 156	436, 673	397, 398	143, 098	....	....	1, 829, 332
July, 1852, to July, 1853	1, 131, 098	1, 418, 845	321, 989	223, 247	2, 825, 069	1, 063, 705	343, 992	112, 600	....	....	2, 818, 397
July, 1853, to July, 1854	847, 535	1, 105, 907	718, 842	490, 426	2, 156, 864	817, 817	255, 825	77, 991	....	....	2, 492, 141
July, 1854, to July, 1855	958, 744	1, 593, 832	705, 492	485, 505	1, 944, 809	781, 680	489, 326	136, 463	177, 354	$45, 411	3, 042, 891
July, 1855, to July, 1856	540, 784	977, 005	646, 694	526, 338	1, 982, 800	1, 036, 647	149, 514	48, 449	51, 876	16, 408	2, 604, 847
July, 1856, to July, 1857	819, 081	1, 216, 888	414, 466	363, 665	2, 042, 390	1, 307, 322	104, 576	35, 121	80, 987	34, 917	2, 957, 913
July, 1857, to July, 1858	896, 923	1, 097, 505	840, 127	597, 107	1, 103, 301	1, 105, 223	†168, 897	†66, 012	....	....	2, 865, 847
July, 1858, to July, 1859	1, 341, 025	1, 737, 734	996, 341	598, 762	1, 380, 465	1, 233, 539	†126, 229	†46, 278	....	....	3, 616, 313
July, 1859, to July, 1860	1, 335, 736	1, 789, 089	939, 872	537, 547	1, 068, 895	896, 293	†157, 783	†51, 829	....	....	3, 274, 758
July, 1860, to July, 1861	1, 518, 457	2, 110, 823	1, 009, 468	581, 264	979, 231	736, 552	456, 408	143, 907	....	....	3, 572, 546
July, 1861, to July, 1862	739, 477	962, 603	2, 599, 316	1, 280, 697	796, 384	556, 795	‡280, 526	‡64, 481	....	....	2, 864, 576
July, 1862, to July, 1863	1, 034, 794	1, 569, 287	2, 055, 511	1, 483, 593	603, 186	575, 733	‡229, 472	‡76, 946	....	....	3, 705, 559
July, 1863, to July, 1864	851, 066	1, 298, 058	416, 405	438, 957	548, 099	793, 562	‡280, 478	‡60, 951	343, 651	123, 657	2, 715, 185
July, 1864, to July, 1865	700, 186	1, 511, 323	644, 547	816, 494	313, 912	493, 316	‡22, 024	‡8, 045	202, 138	85, 017	§2, 914, 195
July, 1865, to July, 1866	510, 978	1, 180, 381	177, 509	205, 250	486, 370	656, 188	‖3, 477	‖1, 654	188, 322	31, 938	2, 075, 411
July, 1866, to July, 1867	570, 894	1, 482, 570	426, 882	319, 840	618, 363	653, 253	‖31, 668	‖8, 069	46, 047	15, 270	2, 479, 002
July, 1867, to July, 1868	662, 570	1, 379, 814	706, 534	507, 476	696, 064	587, 303	‖30, 891	‖7, 248	301, 132	121, 089	2, 602, 930
July 1, 1868, to July 1, 1869	717, 172	1, 361, 388	94, 361	81, 860	405, 396	384, 435	....	....	....	....	1, 827, 683
July 1, 1869, to July 1, 1870	499, 797	794, 432	310, 878	228, 278	386, 728	343, 937	....	....	82, 520	27, 172	1, 393, 819
July 1, 1870, to July 1, 1871	539, 582	692, 469	862, 434	452, 937	353, 742	251, 562	....	....	157, 263	42, 170	1, 439, 138
July 1, 1871, to July 1, 1872	693, 674	979, 682	1, 171, 646	552, 756	172, 889	137, 855	....	....	190, 736	56, 996	1, 727, 289
July 1, 1872, to July 1, 1873	756, 306	1, 095, 831	288, 263	154, 243	324, 653	329, 214	....	....	197, 671	55, 815	1, 635, 103
July 1, 1873, to July 1, 1874	529, 903	827, 991	573, 775	290, 750	114, 530	115, 098	....	....	304, 865	78, 346	1, 302, 185
July 1, 1874, to July 1, 1875	491, 130	847, 014	895, 907	413, 411	251, 572	291, 165	....	....	238, 641	61, 725	1, 613, 315
July 1, 1875, to July 1, 1876	892, 762	1, 366, 246	1, 067, 515	436, 072	154, 500	215, 327	....	....	141, 157	35, 915	2, 053, 560
......	566, 263	797, 601	926, 407	390, 513	71, 708	160, 666	....	....	153, 552	41, 027	1, 389, 867
Totals	35, 399, 785	41, 733, 451	105, 800, 474	41, 533, 473	54, 967, 200	23, 740, 245	33, 395, 056	9, 068, 516	2, 857, 912	872, 873	116, 948, 558

* From 1803 to 1817 the values of sperm oil and candles are aggregated, as also are those of whale oil and bone.
† Spermaceti and spermaceti-candles are aggregated in reports for this year.
‡ Including paraffine.
§ Also "whale-foots," worth $6,290.
‖ Including wax.

M.—*Table of tonnage of vessels engaged in the whale fishery.*

[From the Report of the Secretary of the Treasury, 1817.]

Year.	Tonnage.	Year.	Tonnage.	Year.	Tonnage.
1794	4, 139	1802	580	1809	573
1795	3, 163	1803	1, 143	1810	339
1796	2, 364	1804	323	1811	54
1797	1, 104	1805	898	1812	942
1798	763	1806	729	1813	789
1799	592	1807	907	1814	562
1800	652	1808	724	1815	1, 230
1801	736				

Special table of tonnage of vessels engaged in the whale fishery.

[From the Report of the Secretary of the Treasury, 1854.*]

Year.	Registered.	Enrolled.	Year.	Registered.	Enrolled.
1818	16, 135	615	1829	57, 284	....
1819	31, 700	686	1830	38, 912	793
1820	35, 391	1, 054	1831	82, 316	482
1821	26, 071	1, 924	1832	72, 869	378
1822	45, 449	3, 134	1833	101, 158	478
1823	39, 918	585	1834	108, 060	364
1824	33, 166	180	1835	97, 640	....
1825	35, 379	....	1836	144, 681	1, 573
1826	41, 757	227	1837	127, 242	1, 895
1827	45, 653	329	1838	119, 630	5, 230
1828	54, 621	180			

Special table of the whaling interest of New Bedford and Fairhaven.

[From Hazard's Register.]

Year.	Barks and ships.	Tons.	Year.	Barks and ships.	Tons.
1820	94	27, 475	1834	171	54, 488
1830	116	35, 209	1835	178	56, 530
1831	146	45, 102	1836	208	64, 260
1832	150	50, 068	1837	205	62, 812
1833	178	56, 352	1838	213	63, 982

*These tables are hardly accurate enough to show the extent of the business. Thus, at the close of 1815, Nantucket had at least 8,300 tons of shipping engaged in whaling; New Bedford district, 2,200; Hudson, N. Y., 250; Sag Harbor, N. Y., 750—in all, about 11,500 tons In 1818 there were at least 18,000 tons.

TABLE OF CONTENTS.

* The latitude is misprinted in the note.

ERRATA.

Page 322. Include both entries to Imogene of Provincetown in one.

Page 377. Reverse the notes to the Sharon and the Oregon, of Fairhaven.

Page 411. Note to Albion, Fairhaven, should be credited to Belle, of the same port, on pages 412, 413.

Page 505. Note to Morea should belong to Morning Star.

INDEX TO VOYAGES BY VESSELS' NAMES.

* Signifies that a marginal note accompanies the record of the vessel.

HUDSON, N. Y.:

American Hero, *ship*, 192, 194.
Alexander Mansfield, *ship*, 288, 304, 320, 342.*
America, *ship*, 304, 342, 360.*

LYNN, MASS.:

Atlas, *ship*, 284, 292, 296, 306, 318.*

MARBLEHEAD, MASS.:

Atlas, *ship*, 300.

MARION, OR SIPPICAN, MASS.:

Altamaha, *schooner*, 498,* 518, 530, 538, 570, 582, 588,*
Admiral Blake, *schooner*, 508,* 518,* 530,* 538, 562, 578, 582, 588, 594, 600, 606, 620, 626,* 644,* 648, 652, 656.

MATTAPOISETT, OR ROCHESTER, CONN.:

Annawan, *brig*, 326, 336, 346.*
Annawan, (2d,) *brig*, 378,* 402, 414, 436, 454, 470, 496, 518, 528, 552; *bark*, 570.*
America, *brig*, 436,* 454, 470, 496, 518.*
America, *bark*, 528,* 570.* (See Holmes's Hole.)
Amelia, *brig*, 540,* 562, 578.*

MYSTIC, CONN.:

Æronaut, *ship*, 312, 330,* 350, 372, 406, 432, 464, 496, 512, 532.*
Atlantic, *ship*, 420.*
Alibree, *bark*, 420,* 448.
Antarctic, *ship*, 448.*

NANTUCKET, MASS.:

Asia, *ship*, 186.
Africa, *ship*, 186.
Amazon, *ship*, 186, 188, (2 places.)
Alliance, *ship*, 186, 187,* 192, (2 places,) 194, 196, 198, 200, 202, 204, 206, 210, 212.
Atlas, *ship*, 198, 206, 208, 212, 216, 222, 230.*
Alligator, *ship*, 200, 202, 206, 210.*
Aurora, *brig*, 200.
Aurora, *ship*, 202.
Alert, *brig*, 206, 216,* 222, 230, 242.
Adolphus, *sloop*, 206.
Amphibious, *schooner*, 218.*
Antoinette, *schooner*, 218.* (Probably a small sealing-schooner.)
Aurora, *ship*, 228,* 246, 260, 278, 298, 336, 376, 426.
Ark, *ship*, 228.*
Atlantic, *ship*, 228,* 242, 254, 356, 438, 518, (2 places.)
Ann, *schooner*, 236.
Alexander, *ship*, 236, 250, 260, 284.*
Ann, *ship*, 260,* 278, 298, 336.*
American, *ship*, 264,* 278, 308, 346, 376, 426, 472.*
Atlantic, *ship*, 264, 270, 290, 326, 400, 472, 564.*
Alexander Coffin, *ship*, 290,* 326, 366.* (See New Bedford.)
Alpha, *ship*, 308,* 346, 390,* 438,* 472, 528, 578.*
Amazon, *sloop*, 308.
Alabama, *ship*, 438,* 484,* 528,* 578.*
Apphia Maria, *ship*, 472,* 528.*
Abby Bradford, *schooner*, 620, 632.* (See New Bedford.)
Amy, *bark*, 612.*

NEW BEDFORD, MASS.:

Atlantic, ——, 190, (2 places.)
Ann, *ship*, 192, 196, 200, 206, 214, 372.
Abby, *brig*, 198, 200, (2 places,) 202.
Acushnet, *ship*, 206.
Augustus, *ship*, 226,* 230.
Alliance, *brig*, 230,* 232, 238.
Ann Alexander, *ship*, 232, 236, 242, 248, 250, 254, 258, 260, 266, 288, 322, 332, 342, 372, 420, 466.*
Abigail, *ship*, 238, 254, 270, 280, 314, 352,* 396, 442, 492, 532, 584.*
Alliance, *ship*, 242.*
Amazon, *brig*, 254.
America, *brig*, 254,* 258, 266.

MATTAPOISETT, OR ROCHESTER, MASS.:
Brewster, *ship*, 552,* 578.* (See New Bedford.)

MYSTIC, CONN.:
Bingham, *ship*, 294, 312,* 360, 372, 394, 440.*
Blackstone, *ship*, 312, 322, 340, 360, 382, 406, 432.*

NANTUCKET, MASS.:
Britannia, 186, 188.
Beaver, *ship*, 186, 187, 188, 192, (2 places.)
Boston Packet, 190.
Brothers, *ship*, 192, 198, 206, (2 places,) 208, 212, 214, 216, 222, 230, 246.*
Betsey, *sloop*, 196.
Bluebell, *schooner*, 196.
Boston, *ship*, 198, 202, 206, 210, 212, 216, 218, 224, 230, 242.*
Betsey, *schooner*, 198, 200, 212.
Belvidere, *ship*, 198, 202, 206.
Belvidere, *brig*, 216, 218.
Betsey, *brig*, 218, 222, 224.
Boniff, *brig*, 218.*
Barclay, *ship*, 228,* 242, 250, 254, 258, 278, 284, 290, 318, 356, 400, 446, 498.*
Belvidere, *schooner*, 242.
Baltic, *ship*, 264,* 284, 318, 356.*
B. Colcord, *bark*, 612.*
Bohio, *bark*, 626.*

NEW BEDFORD, MASS.:
Betsey, *schooner*, 188, 194, 202.
Beaver, 190, (2 places,) 193, 194.
Berkeley, *ship*, (probably the Barclay, which see,) 192.
Barclay, *ship*, 194, 196,* 197, 198,* 200, 206, 210, 214, 218, 226, 238, 250, 260, 280,* 306, 344, 362, 396,* 408, 466, 492, 512.*
Bedford, *ship*, 194.
Balæna, *ship*, 226,* 238, 250, 254, 266, 274, 306, 332, 372, 420, 460, 500, 558.* (See Sag Harbor.)
Bourbon, *ship*, 242,* 248.*
Benezet, *brig*, 248.
Braganza, *ship*, 274, 306, 362, 396, 434, 466, 512; *bark*, 566.*
Brandt, *ship*, 274, 280, 288, 296, 314, 332, 344, 352, 396, 434, 460, 500.*
Bramin, *bark*, 280, 288, 324, 362, 372,* 420, 442, 476.*
Brighton, *ship*, 280,* 314, 386, 408, 442, 466.*
Benezet, *bark*, 296. (See Fairhaven.)
Benjamin Tucker, *ship*, 352, 396, 434, 460, 476, 522,* 566,* 580.*
Bogota, *brig*, 362,* 386.*
Brunswick, *ship*, 396, 434, 452,* 584.* (See Dartmouth and Providence.)
Bevis, *bark*, 466,* 500, 534.*
Bartholomew Gosnold, *ship*, 408,* 442,* 476, 512,* 558, 584, 610; *bark*, 638, 654. (From Falmouth.)
Baltic, *bark*, 476,* 522.*
Barnstable, *ship*, 476,* 522; *bark*, 574.*
Brutus, *ship*, 574.* (From Warren.)
Betsey Williams, *ship*, 512.*
Byron, *bark*, 522.*
Black Eagle, *bark*, 574,* 584, 596, 610, 624.* (From Sag Harbor.)
Benjamin Franklin, *bark*, 592,* 610.* (From Fall River.)
Brewster, *bark*, 592,* 610. (From Mattapoisett.)
Benjamin Cummings, *bark*, 610,* 638, 650.* (From Dartmouth.)
Bounding Billow, *bark*, 654.*

NEW LONDON, CONN.:
Boston, *ship*, 294,* 302, 320, 338, 358, 368, 378.*
Bingham, *ship*, 310, 328, 348.*
Betsey, *brig*, 294.
Betsey, *schooner*, 368, 394, 416.
Black Warrior, *ship*, 394,* 430, 448, 466, 488.*
Benjamin Morgan, *ship*, 404, 440, 458, 488, 542.*
Bengal, *ship*, 416,* 448, 474.* (From Salem; see ship Northwest.)
Brooklyn, *ship*, 430, 458, 488, 544.*

NEWPORT, R. I.:
Benjamin D. Wolf, *schooner*, 362.

FAIRHAVEN, MASS.—Continued.

Charleston Packet, *brig*, 256, 258, 268.
Charles Drew, *ship*, 282, 290, 308, 346.* (See New Bedford.)
Cadmus, *ship*, 282, 308, 346, 376.*
Clifford Wayne, *ship*, 326, 336, 376, 412, 454, 482, 528.
Cohannet, *schooner*, 652,* 656. (From Marion.)
Crowninshield, *schooner*, 632.*

FALL RIVER, MASS.:

Caravan, *ship*, 428,* 464, 500.* (See New Bedford.)

FALMOUTH, MASS.:

Commodore Morris, *ship*, 384, 424,* 464, 508, 570* (See New Bedford.)

GREENPORT, N. Y.:

Caroline, *ship*, 404, 432, 450,* 476, 496, 522, 556.*

GROTON, CONN.:

Cornelia, *schooner*, 616,* 628.* (From New London.)

LYNN, MASS.:

Clay, *ship*, 306, 310, 318. (See Salem.)
Commodore Preble, *ship*, 310, 330, 338, 348, 368, 392, 428, 458, 486, 508.*

MATTAPOISETT, OR ROCHESTER, MASS.:

Caduceus, *brig*, 326.*
Chase, *brig*, 356.*
Cossack, *bark*, 366. (See Marion.)
Cachelot, *ship*, 424,* 446, 484.* (See New Bedford.)
Clara Bell, *bark*, 496,* 528, 562.*

MARION, OR SIPPICAN, MASS.:

Cossack, *bark*, 402, 438.* (From Mattapoisett.) (See New Bedford.)
Cohannet, *schooner*, 620,* 626, 632, 636, 640, 644.* (See Fairhaven.)

MYSTIC, CONN.:

Congress, *bark*, 394, 420, 448.
Coriolanus, *ship*, 420,* 448, 464, 488, 512, 544, 580.*
Cornelia, *schooner*, 558, 564, 580.* (See New London.)

NANTUCKET, MASS.:

Columbia, ——, 186, 188.
Cato, *ship*, 190, 192, 196, 198, 204.
Commerce, *ship*, 190, 194,* 198, 202, 204.
Cæsar, *ship*, 192,* 194.
Criterion, *ship*, 198, 202, 206, (2 places,) 208, 216, 222, 230, 250,* 264,* 270.*
Chili, *ship*, 204, 206, 208.*
Chili, *ship*, 228,* 246.*
Charles, *ship*, 214, 216,* 224, 230.*
Charles, *schooner*, 216.
Charles, *brig*, 218, 222.*
Cordelia, *sloop*, 224.
Crown Prince, *schooner*, 230.
Columbus, *ship*, 230,* 278, 284, 290, 318, 356.* (See New London.)
Constitution, *ship*, 236,* 250, 258,* 260, 284, 290, 298, 318, 356, 390,* 446,* 498.* (Note to Catawba: Last part wrongly credited.)
Cyrus, *ship*, 236, 254, 264,* 290, 326, 366, 426.*
Clarkson, *ship*, 258,* 278, 308, 344, 390.*
Congress, *ship*, 258,* 270,* 278, 290, 318, 356.* (See New Bedford.)
Catharine, *ship*, 284,* 318, 356.* (See New London.)
Charles Carroll, *ship*, 290,* 326, 366, 412, 456.* (See San Francisco.)
Charles and Henry, *ship*, 290,* 326, 366, 426.*
Christopher Mitchell, *ship*, 308, 346, 376,* 426,* 456.* (See New Bedford.)
Catawba, *ship*, 326,* 366, 400, 456, 498, 554.*
Comet, *schooner*, 356.
Columbia, *ship*, 376,* 438, 472, 518, 578.*
Citizen, *ship*, 412,* 484, 528.*
Constitution, *ship*, 554.*

NEWBURYPORT, MASS.:

Chance, *brig*, 180.

MARION, OR SIPPICAN, MASS.:

Emerald, *schooner*, 588, 594, 600.* (From Fairhaven.)
Express, *schooner*, 626,* 632.* (See Provincetown.)

MYSTIC, CONN.:

Eleanor, *ship*, 432.*

NEW YORK, N. Y.:

Eliza Barker, *ship*, 234, 236. (See Hudson.)
Elizabeth, *brig*, 350.
Endeavour, *bark*, 630.* (From New Bedford.)

NANTUCKET, MASS.:

Eagle, *ship*, 194, 202, 224, 236, 254, 264, 284, 290, 298,* 318.*
Eliza, *ship*, 198, 200, 204, 208.
Essex, *ship*, 202, 204, 208, 212, 216, 222, 228.*
Eliza, *brig*, 202, 206.
Edward, *ship*, 204, 222.
Experiment, *sloop*, 216, 220, 222.
Edward, *brig*, 216, 224, 260.
Equator, *ship*, 224,* 236, 246.* (See New Bedford.)
Eagle, *brig*, 224.
Eagle 2d, *ship*, 228.*
Enterprise, *ship*, 242,* 258, 270, 290,* 326, 366, 426, 472,* 518.*
Elizabeth Starbuck, *ship*, 308,* 376, 426.
Edward Carey, *ship*, 376,* 426, 462, 518, 564.*
Empire, *ship*, 400,* 456.* (See New Bedford.)
Edward, *ship*, 484.* (From New Bedford.)
Eliza Jane, *schooner*, 554.*
Eunice H. Adams, *schooner*, 606, 612;* *brig*, 620, 632.* (See New Bedford.)

NEW BEDFORD, MASS.:

Eliza, 188, 190.
Edward, *ship*, 196, (2 places,) 202, 208.
Exchange, *ship*, 198, 200,* 202.
Elizabeth, *sloop*, 218, 220, 222.
Experiment, *sloop*, 220.
Eliza Barker, *schooner*, 232, 238, 242.
Elizabeth, *schooner*, 232.
Elizabeth, *brig*, 238, 242, 248, 252, 258.
Elizabeth, *ship*, 242.*
Emily, *brig*, 258, 266.
Empire, *ship*, 262.
Endeavour, *ship*, 276, 280, 288, 296, 314, 334,* 374, 396, 422, 442, 478,* 514, 546;* *bark*, 574, 596.* (See New York.)
Emerald, *ship*, 272, 276, 280, 288, 296, 306, 314, 352, 396, 444, 478;* *bark*, 546.*
Euphrates, *ship*, 262, 276, 296, 334, 386,* 434, 460, 478, 514, 546, 586.*
Eagle, *ship*, 262, 272,* 276, 288, 296, 334, 365,* 460, 502; *bark*, 534,* 586,* 602.*
Equator, *ship*, 258,* 266, 280; *bark*, 296, 324, 354, 396, 444. (From Nantucket.) (See San Francisco.)
Enterprise, *ship*, 248, 266, 272, 280, 306, 344, 386, 408, 444, 460, 478,* 514.*
Emily Morgan, *ship*, 296,* 334, 386, 434, 460, 514, 566,* 592, 624.*
Eliza Adams, *ship*, 314, 478, 514, 546, 592,* 618, 642,* 654. (See Fairhaven.)
Elizabeth, *bark*, 314,* 340.* (See Dartmouth.)
Emma, *bark*, 354, 386, 408, 442, 478.*
Elizabeth, *ship*, 374, 408,* 442, 478, 524, 566.*
Emeline, *brig*, 374.*
Edward, *ship*, 420.* (From Hudson.) (See Nantucket.)
Edward, *bark*, 434, 460, 502, 534, 596.*
Exchange, *bark*, 444,* 460,* 468.*
Envoy, *bark*, 452.* (From Providence.)
Emigrant, *bark*, 452.* (From Bristol.)
Emma C. Jones, *ship*, 460,* 492, 524, 558, 574, 610,* 640, 650.
Elisha Dunbar, *ship*, 478,* 514, 558, 586.*
Eugenia, *bark*, 478,* 524, 566, 602.
Europa, *ship*, 478,* 514, 534, 586, 618,* 640,* 654.
Empire, *ship*, 492,* 534, 574.* (From Nantucket.)
Eliza F. Mason, *ship*, 502,* 546.*
Elizabeth Swift, *bark*, 514,* 566, 592, 624.*
Erastus Corning, *bark*, 524,* 630.
Emily, *bark*, 524,* 546.*

SAG HARBOR, N. Y.:
Fair Helen, *ship*, 224, 230, 234,* 240, 246, 248, 252, 256, 258, 264.
Franklin, *ship*, 294, 304, 340, 360; *bark*, 382, 418, 450.*
Fanny, *ship*, 328, 340,* 348, 360, 382, 406, 442. (Probably sold to New Bedford.)
France, *ship*, 340, 348, 382, 406.*

SALEM, MASS.:
Franklin, *schooner*, 328, 338.*
Falcon, *brig*, 590,* 596, 608, 614, 628.*

SAN FRANCISCO, CAL.:
Francis, *brig*, 532, 546,* 558.*
Florida, *ship*, 630,* 634.
Florence, *bark*, 648,* 654.

STONINGTON, CONN.:
Frances, *ship*, 294.
Fellowes, *ship*, 394, 430, 476.*
Flying Cloud, *schooner*, 496,* 512.

WARREN, R. I.:
Franklin, *bark*, 330, 352, 370, 402, 448, 456.* (See New Bedford.)
Florence, *bark*, 500,* 530.*

G.

BEVERLY, MASS.:
Gem, *brig*, 464, 486,* 500, 508.* (From Provincetown.)

BOSTON, MASS.:
George, *ship*, 234.
George Brown, *schooner*, 614.*

BRISTOL, R. I.:
Governor Fenner, *ship*, 286, 310.*
General Jackson, *ship*, 292, 330, 392.*
Ganges, *ship*, 270, 292, 330.* (See Fall River.)
Governor Hopkins, *brig*, 310, 330, 338, 352, 358, 370, 380, 392. (See Dartmouth.)
Golconda, *ship*, 320.* (See New Bedford.)

DARTMOUTH, MASS.:
Grand Turk, *ship*, 330, 350. (See New Bedford.)
Governor Hopkins, *brig*, 436;* *ship*, 462, 472, 484.* (Probably from Bristol.)

EDGARTOWN, MASS.:
George and Martha, *ship*, 388.
George and Mary, *ship*, 316, 358.* (See New London.)
Gold Hunter, *brig*, 316, 326.*

FALL RIVER, MASS.:
Gold Hunter, *ship*, 292, 298, 314, 320, 338, 358, 380, 402, 440.*
Ganges, *ship*, 358.* (From Bristol.)

FAIRHAVEN, MASS.:
George, *ship*, 326, 346, 376, 412, 436, 462, 482.*. (Probably from Nantucket.)
General Scott, *ship*, 356, 400, 446, 482, 528, 606, 640.*
General Scott, *bark*, 528,* 562,* 576.* (From New London.)
George J. Jones, *schooner*, 612,* 636,* 644.*

FALMOUTH, MASS.:
George Washington, *bark*, 322,* 336, 348, 368.*

HUDSON, N. Y.:
George Clinton, *ship*, 312.*
General Scott, *ship*, 218.*

MARION, OR SIPPICAN, MASS.:
Graduate, *schooner*, 626,* 632.*

MATTAPOISETT, OR ROCHESTER, MASS:
Gideon Barstow, *ship*, 292, 326, 346.*

MYSTIC, CONN.:
Governor Endicott, *ship*, 350,* 360.*
Globe, *ship*, 432.*

NEW LONDON, CONN.—Continued.
Garland, *schooner*, 416,* 458.*
General Scott, *ship*, 430;* *bark*, 458, 488.* (See Fairhaven.)
George Washington, *ship*, 430.*
Georgiana, *brig*, 510,* 532,* 566, 564,* 580, 590, 600, 616, 628.*
George Henry, *bark*, 532,* 544, 580, 596.*
George and Mary, *bark*, 600,* 616, 628, 638.* (See New Bedford.)
Golden West, *schooner*, 608,* 628, 642, 644, 648, 650, 654, 658.

NEWBURYPORT, MASS.:
Georgia, *schooner*, 614,* 628.*

NEW SUFFOLK, N. Y.:
Gentleman, *bark*, 418,* 432, 460, 476.* (See Sag Harbor.)

PHILADELPHIA, PA.:
Governor Hawkins, *ship*, 228.*
George and Albert, *ship*, 254.*

PROVINCETOWN, MASS.:
General Jackson, *schooner*, 246.
Gem, *brig*, 378,* 402, 414, 428, 438. (See Beverly.)
Grand Island, *schooner*, 428,* 438.*
G. W. Lewis, *schooner*, 584, 588, 600, 614, 628.*
Gage H. Phillips, *schooner*, 620,* 634, 636, 654.*
Grace Lathrop, *schooner*, 628.*
Gracie M. Parker, *schooner*, 638,* 642, 644, 646, 650, 656.

STONINGTON, CONN.:
George, *bark*, 322, 348; *ship*, 384, 406, 430, 464, 490.*

SAG HARBOR, N. Y.:
Governor Clinton, *ship*, 224, 294, 304.*
General Scott, *brig*, 246, 248.
Gem, *ship*, 312, 318, 328, 340, 360, 370, 382, 396, 406, 432, 450.*
Gentleman, *bark*, 496.* (From New Suffolk.)

SALEM, MASS.:
General Knox, *ship*, 234.

TRURO, MASS.:
Gem, *brig*, 500.*

WAREHAM, MASS.:
George Washington, ——, 292,* 330, 372, 414, 448,* 476, 506, 552.*

WARREN, R. I.:
Galen, *ship*, 302, 310, 352, 394.*

WESTPORT, MASS.:
Governor Carver, *bark*, 470,* 484, 518, 550, 578, 600, 620.*
Greyhound, *bark*, 484,* 518, 552, 588, 606, 626, 644.
George and Mary, *bark*, 496,* 518, 528, 562, 578.*

H.

BOSTON, MASS.:
Hope, *ship*, 190, 238,* 256.
Heman Smith, *brig*, 614,* 634, 638, 646, 656.

BRIDGEPORT, CONN.:
Hamilton, *bark*, 322, 330, 342, 350, 360, 382, 406,* 440.*
Harvest, *bark*, 342, 350, 360, 370, 420.* (See New Bedford.)

COLD SPRING, N. Y.:
Huntsville, *ship*, 416,* 448, 466, 490, 522.*

DARTMOUTH, MASS.:
Hero, *sloop*, 180.
H. H. Crapo, *bark*, 494,* 518.*

DORCHESTER, MASS.:
Herald, *ship*, 310, 342.* (See Stonington.)

I.

J.

NEW BEDFORD, MASS.—Continued.
John A. Parker, *bark*, 492,* 548.*
Joseph Butler, *bark*, 492,* 514.*
James Arnold, *ship*, 502,* 548, 586, 598, 610, 630, 648.
Jireh Swift, *ship*, 502;* *bark*, 548,* 586.*
John Dawson, *bark*, 502,* 524, 568, 586, 598, 618, 636, 642, 652.
Joshua Bragdon, *bark*, 502,* 548, 582.*
James, *schooner*, 524.* (Sold to Sippican, Marion.)
J. D. Thompson, *bark*, 524,* 558.* (See New London.)
Josephine, *ship*, 536,* 568,* 592, 618, 640, 652.* (From Sag Harbor.)
Java 2d, *bark*, 548,* 574, 598, 618,* 642.* (From Fairhaven.)
John P. West, *bark*, 560,* 592,* 624, 640.
Joseph Grinnell, *bark*, 560.*
Japan, *ship*, 568.* (From Fairhaven.)
John Carver, *bark*, 610,* 636,* 652.*
J. W. Dodge, *schooner*, 618,* 624.*
Joseph Maxwell, *bark*, 624,* 642.* (From Fairhaven.)
Janet, *bark*, 648, 652. (From Westport.)
John J. Winthrop, *bark*, 654.

NEW YORK, N. Y.:
Josephus, ——, 188.
Julia, *brig*, 320.

NEWPORT, R. I.:
James Munroe, *sloop*, 240.
John Coggeshall, *ship*, 286,* 322, 362, 404.* (See New Bedford.)

NEW LONDON, CONN.:
Jones, *ship*, 244, 250, 252, 256, 258, 264, 270, 272, 280, 294, 312, 320, 340, 358, 378.*
John and Edward, *ship*, 270, 272, 280, 312,* 320, 340,* 348.* (See New Bedford.)
Julius Cæsar, *ship*, 286, 294, 312, 320, 328, 340, 348, 358, 368, 378, 404, 418, 450, 466. 488, 510, 544.*
Jason, *bark*, 286,* 320, 328, 340, 358, 378, 394, 418, 440.
John and Elizabeth, *ship*, 328, 348, 368, 394, 418, 450, 474, 532, 544.*
Jefferson, *ship*, 418,* 432, 450, 466, 488, 510.* (From Wilmington.)
John E. Smith, *schooner*, 488,* 532,* 544, 556.*
J. E. Comstock, *schooner*, 556.*
J. D. Thompson, *bark*, 596,* 630.* (From New Bedford.)

PLYMOUTH, MASS.:
James Munroe, *brig*, 342, 352, 372, 380, 392.*

PROVINCETOWN, MASS.:
John B. Dods, *brig*, 378, 392, 402, 414.
Joshua Brown, *schooner*, 392, 414,* 428.
Jane Howes, *brig*, 428,* 464, 472, 486, 498.
John Adams, *schooner*, 428, 438, 448, 456, 464, 472, 486, 498, 508,* 520, 530, 542, 564, 572, 584.*
J. H. Duvall, *bark*, 542,* 580.*
J. Taylor, *schooner*, 614, 622.*
John A. Lewis, *schooner*, 614,* 622, 628.*
J. H. Collins, *schooner*, 620,* 634.*
Joseph Lindsey, *schooner*, 622.*
John Atwood, *schooner*, 644.*

SAG HARBOR, N. Y.:
Jefferson, *ship*, 210, 450, 476, 512, 558.*
Julius Cæsar, *ship*, 234, 240.
John Jay, *ship*, 396,* 432.
Josephine, *ship*, 406,* 442.* (See New Bedford.)
John Wells, *ship*, 418,* 442.* (From Newark. See New Bedford.)

SALEM, MASS.:
James Maury, *ship*, 302,* 338, 384.* (See New Bedford.)

SOMERSET, MASS.:
Jane, *bark*, 380, 404.*

SAN FRANCISCO, CAL.:
Jupiter, *schooner*, 512.

---

† Probably should be Newport.

SAG HARBOR, N. Y.:
- Lucy, *brig*, 180,* 184, 190.
- Lavinia, *ship*, 210.
- Levant, *ship*, 418,* 450, 490.*
- Laurens, *bark*, 432.* (See New London.)

WARREN, R. I.:
- Luminary, *ship*, 302, 338, 370, 414,* 456.*
- Lafayette, *ship*, 394, 428, 456.* (See New Bedford.)

WAREHAM, MASS.:
- Levant, *bark*, 390.*

WESTPORT, MASS.:
- Leader, *bark*, 370. (From New Bedford.)
- Leonidas, *brig*, 446,* 470, 484, 518, 528, 552, 562, 578.* (See New Bedford.)

WILMINGTON, DEL.:
- Lucy Ann, *ship*, 320, 342, 360, 384.* (See Greenport.)

M.

BOSTON, MASS.:
- Mars, *schooner*, 188.
- Margaret, *brig*, 342.*
- Maine, *brig*, 386, 392,* 402.*
- Money Hill, *schooner*, 622.*

BALTIMORE, MD.:
- Monticello, *schooner*, 306.

BRISTOL, R. I.:
- Moro Castle, *brig*, 392.*

BARNSTABLE, MASS.:
- March, *brig*, 440.* (See Yarmouth.)

COLD SPRING, N. Y.:
- Monmouth, *bark*, 382, 396, 406, 442, 490, 522, 558.* (From Sag Harbor.)

DARTMOUTH, MASS.:
- Matilda Sears, *bark*, 538,* 578, 606, 632, 646.

EDGARTOWN, MASS.:
- Meridian, *ship*, 268,* 288, 308.*
- May Ann, *ship*, 272.*
- Mary, *ship*, 326,* 346, 384, 412,* 456, 498,* 540, 584, 612.*
- Milton, *bark*, 412.*
- Monterey, *schooner*, 506,* 530.*
- Mary Frazier, *bark*, 656. (From New Bedford.)

FAIRHAVEN, MASS.:
- Mentor, *brig*, 262,* 268, 272.
- Maine, *ship*, 272, 276,* 290, 308, 324, 346, 366, 388, 436.*
- Marcus, *ship*, 276, 298, 336, 366, 412,* 446, 470.*
- Marcia, *ship*, 290, 298, 316, 336, 346, 356, 376. (See New Bedford.)
- Martha, *ship*, 326, 346, 376, 424, 454, 494, 552.*
- Martha 2d, *ship*, 326, 346, 366, 412, 454, 494, 538.*
- Mary Ann, *ship*, 346, 388, 436, 470, 516, 562.*

FALL RIVER, MASS.:
- Montezuma, *brig*, 372.

GLOUCESTER, MASS.:
- Mount Wollaston, *ship*, 300, 310.

HOLMES'S HOLE, MASS.:
- Macon, *ship*, 362, 388.*
- Malta, *brig*, 426,* 448; *bark*, 472.*

HUDSON, N. Y.:
- Meteor, *ship*, 278,* 306.
- Martha, *ship*, 288, 304,* 350, 360, 384.* (See New York and Sag Harbor.)

NEW BEDFORD, MASS.—Continued.

Milo, *ship*, 276, 316,* 344,* 398, 434, 460, 480, 526, 568, 592.*
Mayflower, *ship*, 282, 306, 354, 374,* 410.* (See San Francisco.)
Magnolia, *ship*, 282, 306, 344, 388, 422,* 480, 514, 560.*
Mentor, *brig*, 282.* (From Westport.)
Milton, *ship*, 288, 324, 354, 388, 410, 444, 480, 536, 576, 604, 630, 646.
Messenger, *ship*, 288, 316, 334, 354,* 374, 398, 444, 480, 524; *bark*, 568.
Mary Ann, *brig*, 288; *bark*, 298.
Mary, *ship*, 288.*
Moss, *ship*, 298, 334,* 364.*
Mary, *ship*, 324, 344, 354, 388, 410, 444, 468,* 494, 514,* 536; *bark*, 576,* 592.*
Minerva, *ship*, 324, 334,* 354, 388, 410, 444, 468, 504, 536.*
Mount Vernon, *ship*, 324, 334, 364, 398, 434.
Massachusetts, *ship*, 324,* 364, 410, 454,* 480; *bark*, 536,* 576, 604, 636.*
Marcella, *bark*, 324, 364, 388, 410,* 444, 468,* 502, 536, 560, 586, 604, 618, 630, 646, 654.
Montpelier, *ship*, 354, 388, 410, 444, 468, 504.*
Mobile, *ship*, 364, 410, 454.*
Margaret Scott, *ship*, 374,* 410, 444, 480; *bark*, 524,* 548.*
Mars, *bark*, 374,* 422, 454, 494, 536, 576, 604, 630, 648.
Moctezuma, *ship*, 374, 410, 444, 480, 516,* 548.*
Metacom, *ship*, 374, 422, 454, 468,* 502, 548.* (From Warren.)
Majestic, *ship*, 388,* 410, 454, 480, 502, 548,* 582.
Mary Frazier, *bark*, 388,* 460, 502, 536, 576, 604, 618,* 640.* (See Edgartown.)
Morea, *ship*, 410,* 444, 468,* 504, 536.*
Marcia, *ship*, 410,* 444, 468, 502, 548.* (From Fairhaven.)
Marengo, *ship*, 422, 454, 480, 524, 568, 610, 640.*
Menkar, *ship*, 422,* 454, 480, 514.* (From Newport.)
Minerva 2d, *ship*, 422, 454, 480, 526; *bark*, 576,* 598,* 624.*
Mount Wollaston, *ship*, 422, 462, 504, 560, 588, 618,* 644.* (From Salem.)
Montezuma, *bark*, 434,* 460, 494,* 526, 536, 560.* (From Wareham.)
Mexican, *ship*, 454.*
Mount Vernon, *ship*, 460,* 498,* 526.* (From Nantucket.)
March, *brig*, 468,* 494. (See Mattapoisett.)
Montreal, *ship*, 468,* 504, 548.*
Monongahela, *ship*, 468.*
Martha, *bark*, 470,* 514, 560, 592, 624, 644.* (From Newport.)
Manuel Ortez, *bark*, 480,* 514, 548.*
Mary and Martha, *ship*, 480.* (From Plymouth.)
Martha 2d, *ship*, 480,* 514, 560, 586.*
Malta, *ship*, 492,* 514, 536.*
Mary Wilder, *ship*, 494,* 514, 548, 576.*
Montgomery, *bark*, 494,* 526,* 560.*
Mary Ann, *bark*, 502,* 560.* (See Mattapoisett.)
Miantonomi, *ship*, 504.*
Morning Star, *bark*, 504,* 548, 586, 598, 610, 626, 646.*
Matthew Luce, *bark*, 514,* 568.*
Marion, *bark*, 524,* 568.
Millinoket, *bark*, 524, 568.* (From Warren.)
Merlin, *bark*, 536,* 576, 592, 624, 644, 654.
Morning Light, *ship*, 536,* 568.*
Mary and Susan, *ship*, 548,* 576, 598,* 618, 636, 648.
Mattapoisett, *bark*, 684,* 654. (From Westport.)
Minnesota, *ship*, 654.* (See New York.)

NEW LONDON, CONN.:

Mary, *brig*, 234, 240.
Mary Ann, *brig*, 234, 240.
Manchester Packet, *ship*, 270, 272, 280, 294, 302.*
Mentor, *ship*, 280, 286, 294,* 328, 358, 378, 404, 430.*
Montgomery, *schooner*, 294, 304.
McDonough, *schooner*, 294, 348.
Montezuma, *ship*, 378, 418,* 458,* 488, 520, 556.*
Mogul, *ship*, 394, 418, 450, 488, 510.
Merrimack, *ship*, 418,* 450, 474; *bark*, 556*. (From Newburyport.)
Morrison, *ship*, 418.*
McClellan, *ship*, 440,* 450, 466, 474, 488.*
Marcia, *schooner*, 488, 510, 544.*
Mechanic, *schooner*, 510.*
Mary Powell, *schooner*, 556,* 564.*
Monticello, *bark*, 580,* 590, 602, 608.* (From Nantucket.)

SAG HARBOR, N. Y.:

Neptune, *ship*, 264, 280, 286, 294, 304, 312, 318, 328, 340, 360, 382, 406, 432.
Nimrod, *ship*, 280, 286, 294, 304, 312, 318, 328,* 340, 350, 360, 370, 382, 396; *bark*, 418, 442, 458, 490, 512,* 544, 566.*
Noble, *bark*, 340, 418,* 442, 460, 490, 512, 532,* 558, 574.
Niantic, *bark*, 418.* (See Warren.)

SALEM, MASS.:

Nancy, *brig*, 236.

SAN FRANCISCO, CAL.:

Nile, *ship*, 490, (see Note,) 498, 512. (From New Bedford.)
Nonpareil, *brig*, 522, 532.

STONINGTON, CONN.:

Newark, *ship*, 384, 416, 442, 464, 490.* (From Poughkeepsie.) (See New Bedford.)
Newburyport, *bark*, 416,* 450, 476,* 512, 544.*

WAREHAM, MASS.:

Nabby, *schooner*, 190.

WARREN, R. I.:

North America, *ship*, 274, 302, 310, 320, 338, 358,* 394.*
Niantic, *ship*, 456.* (From Sag Harbor.)

WILMINGTON, DEL.:

North America, *ship*, 332, 350.*

BOSTON, MASS.:

Onslow, *brig*, 250.
Ontario, *schooner*, 434, 440.

EDGARTOWN, MASS.:

Ocmulgee, *ship*, 554,* 590.* (From Holmes's Hole.)
Omega, *ship*, 554.* (From Nantucket.)

FAIRHAVEN, MASS.:

Oregon, *ship*, 258, 272, 284, 308.*
Oregon, *ship*, 376, 424, 462, 506, 552.*
Oscar, *ship*, 290.
Omega, *ship*, 366, 400, 446, 470, 516,* 552.
Oriole, *bark*, 552. (See New Bedford.)
Oxford, *schooner*, 552,* 582;* *brig*, 588,* 600,* 606, 612, 618, 626.*

FALL RIVER, MASS.:

Otranto, *bark*, 380.*

GREENPORT, N. Y.:

Oregon, *bark*, 512,* 522, 544.*

HOLMES'S HOLE, MASS.:

Ocmulgee, *ship*, 412,* 448, 472, 518.* (See Edgartown.)

HUDSON, N. Y.:

Oswego, *ship*, 194.

MATTAPOISETT, OR ROCHESTER, MASS.:

Orion, *brig*, 234, 292, 322, 326, 336, 346, 356.* (See New Bedford.)
Oscar, *bark*, 484,* 518.* (From Sag Harbor.)
Ocean Rover, *ship*, 570.*

NANTUCKET, MASS.:

Olive, *ship*, 206, 216.
Ocean, *brig*, 212.*
Orange, *sloop*, 212.
Ontario, *ship*, 232,* 250, 260, 266.* 290, 326, 366, 400,* 438, 472.*
Oliver H. Perry, *schooner*, 232, 236, 242.
Oeno, *ship*, 236, 250.*
Ocean, *ship*, 242, 254, 266, 290, 326, 366.* (See New Bedford.)
Otter, *brig*, 258, 260.*
Orion, *ship*, 258,* 270, 300,* 326, 376, 426.*

SAG HARBOR, N. Y.—Continued.
Ocean, *sloop*, 246, 248.
O. C. Raymond, *ship*, 382.*
Ontario 2d, *ship*, 406,* 432, 460, 476.*
Ohio, *ship*, 418.*
Oscar, *ship*, 420,* 432.* (See Mattapoisett.)
Odd Fellow, *bark*, 476,* 496, 522, 544, 566, 584, 608.* (See New London.)
Ocean, *bark*, 602,* 616.* (From Sandwich.)

SANDWICH, MASS.:
Ocean, *brig*, 486,* 498,* 506, 518; *bark*, 538, 570, 590.* (See Sag Harbor.)

SAN FRANCISCO, CAL.:
Ocean Bird, *ship*, 566.

WARREN, R. I.:
Ocean, *ship*, 510.* (From Providence.) (See New Haven.)

P.

BOSTON, MASS.:
Peace and Plenty, *schooner*, 180.
Peacock, *brig*, 180.
Polly, *sloop*, 180.
Penelope, ——, 182.
Polly, *schooner*, 192,* 194.
Paulina, *schooner*, 192.*
Potomack, *ship*, 222.*
Palladium, *ship*, 238.
President, *schooner*, 244. (Probably of Provincetown.)

EDGARTOWN, MASS.:
President, *schooner*, 256.
Pavilion, *brig*, 384,* 400, 426, 456.*
Planter, *brig*, 238, 264, 272, 280.*
Palmer, *schooner*, 238.
Perry, *bark*, 650.* (From New London.)

FAIRHAVEN, MASS.:
Pindus, *bark*, 230, 234,* 238, 244, 256, 258,* 278, 284, 290, 298, 308, 346, 366.*
Pactolus, *ship*, 290, 326.*
Pacific, *ship*, 346;* *bark*, 366,* 400, 424, 470.* (See New Bedford.)
Popmunnett, *bark*, 446. (From Sippican.) (Marion.)
Phillipe Delanoye, *ship*, 450,* 494, 528.*
Pavilion, *brig*, 576,* 594.* (From Holmes's Hole.)
President, *schooner*, 606.*

FALL RIVER, MASS.:
Pantheon, *ship*, 320;* *bark*, 358, 392, 428.
Panama, *ship*, 358,* 380,* 392.*
Pleiades, *bark*, 372,* 424. (See Wareham.)

FALMOUTH, MASS.:
Pocahontas, *ship*, 240,* 254, 264, 286.
Popmunnett, *bark*, 330,* 336, 348, 362.*

GREENPORT, N. Y.:
Potosi, *ship*, 274. (See Sag Harbor.)
Philip 1st, *ship*, 418,* 442, 458, 490, 522.* (See New London.)
Pioneer, *bark*, 476,* 490, 496.* (See New Bedford.)
Prudent, *bark*, 532.* (From Stonington.)

GLOUCESTER, MASS.:
Polly, ——, 184, 190.*

HOLMES'S HOLE, MASS.:
Pocahontas, *ship*, 348, 368, 412, 442, 472, 508.* (See New Bedford.)
Pavilion, *brig*, 530,* 562.* (See Fairhaven.)

MARION, OR SIPPICAN, MASS.:
Popmunnett, *brig*, 372, 390, 402, 424.* (See Fairhaven.)
Pocahontas, *brig*, 626.*

NEW BEDFORD, MASS.—Continued.

Pacific 2d, *bark*, 560,* 568. (From Fairhaven.) (See Sag Harbor.)
Palmyra, *schooner*, 582.* (From Mattapoisett.)
Petrel, *schooner*, 604,* 610,* 618, 626, 636, 640, 644, 648, 652, 656.
Progress, *bark*, 612,* 636,* 656. (Formerly the Charles Phelps, of Stonington.)
Palmetto, *bark*, 626,* 644, 652.
Peru, *bark*, 652.* (From New London,)
Platina, *bark*, 652. (From Westport.)
Pedro Varela, *schooner*, 656.

NEW LONDON, CONN.:

Pizarro, *brig*, 234, 240, 244, 250.
Phœnix, *ship*, 264, 280, 312, 340, 348, 378, 394, 418, 440, 474, 510, 556.*
Palladium, *ship*, 294, 320, 340, 358, 378, 404, 430.
Philetus, *bark*, 320. (Probably of Stonington; which see.)
Pembroke, *ship*, 340, 368,* 378; *bark*, 394, 404, 430, 450.*
Pacific, *schooner*, 358, 378.
Peruvian, *ship*, 378, 404, 430, 458, 474, 496, 532, 544, 556, 564.
Pearl, *bark*, 496,* 520, 544, 572, 590.*
Pioneer, *bark*, 532,* 556, 580,* 590, 602,* 616,* 622.*
Pacific, *schooner*, 544,* 564, 590.*
Philip 1st, *bark*, 564.* (From Greenport.)
Peru, *bark*, 602,* 638,* 642.* (See New Bedford.)
Perry, *bark*, 622.* (See Edgartown.)

NEWBURG, N. Y.:

Portland, *ship*, 296,* 304, 342.* (See New York and Sag Harbor.)

NEWPORT, R. I.:

Pocahontas, *schooner*, 338; *brig*, 352, 362, 368, 380, 404,* 416.*

NEW YORK, N. Y.:

Portland, *ship*, 320. (Of Newburg; which see.)

PROVINCETOWN, OR CAPE COD, MASS.:

Patty, ——, 186. (Probably a brig or schooner.)
President, *schooner*, 240.
Phenix, *brig*, 372, 378, 392, 402, 428, 438, 498.
Pacific, *brig*, 392,* 402, 414, 438.
Parker Cook, *brig*, 428; *bark*, 438, 464, 472, 498, 520, 542.
Preston, *schooner*, 486,* 498, 508.
Panama, *brig*, 554,* 564, 584.*

PORTSMOUTH, N. H.:

Pocahontas, *ship*, 292, 328.*
Plato, *ship*, 314.

SAG HARBOR, N. Y.:

Phenix, *ship*, 280, 286, 294, 304, 312, 328, 350,* 370, 396, 420, 450.*
Potosi, *ship*, 280, 286.* (See Greenport.)
Panama, *ship*, 350, 382, 420, 450.* (From Nantucket.)
Portland, *ship*, 360,* 382, 396, 420, 442.* (From Newburgh.)
Plymouth, *ship*, 432.*
Parana, *brig*, 512,* 522, 544, 558, 580.*
Pacific, *bark*, 602,* 608.* (From New Bedford.)

SALEM, MASS.:

Polly, *brig*, 234.
Pallas, *bark*, 292.
Palestine, *bark*, 318, 358.*
Para, *schooner*, 608;* *brig*, 622.

STONINGTON, CONN.

Philetus, ——, 322, 340,* 360, 384, 406, 430, 464.* (See New London.)
Prudent, *bark*, 416,* 458, 476.* (See Greenport.)

SAN FRANCISCO, CAL.:

Page, *schooner*, 638.*

SOMERSET, MASS.:

Pilgrim, *brig*, 360,* 380, 392, 404; *bark*, 416, 440, 458.*

S.

NEW BEDFORD, MASS.—Continued.
Stamboul, *bark*, 612,* 632, 648.*
Starlight, *brig*, 618,* 636.*
Seneca, *bark*, 632.*
Sarah B. Hale, *bark*, 652.*
Sea Fox, *bark*, 652.* (From Westport.)

NEW LONDON, CONN.:
Stonington, *ship*, 240,* 252, 264, 280, 286, 304, 340, 358, 368, 394, 404.
Superior, *ship*, 264, 280, 304,* 340, 348, 368, 396, 404, 418, 458, 488.*
Sun, *schooner*, 304.
Shaw Perkins, *sloop*, 368,* 396, 418.*
Somerset, *brig*, 378.*
Sarah Lavinia, *schooner*, 440.*
Sea Witch, *schooner*, 544.*
Silver Cloud, *schooner*, 544,* 564, 580.*
S. B. Howes, *schooner*, 602, 608, 616, 630, 638.*
Somerset, *bark*, 602.*

NEWPORT, R. I.:
Sailor's Return, *schooner*, 352.*
Sea Bird, *brig*, 380,* 394.*

NEW YORK, N. Y.:
Shibboleth, *bark*, 330,* 350.*
Scituate, *schooner*, 342.*
Sabina, *ship*, 384.* (See Sag Harbor.)
Sarah, *ship*, 404.* (See Nantucket.)

ORLEANS, MASS.:
September, *schooner*, 508,* 520.* (From Boston.)

PROVINCETOWN, MASS.:
Sophronia, *schooner*, 236, 238, 246, 250.
Seventh Son, *schooner*, 246.
Spartan, *bark*, 378, 392, 414, 428,* 472,* 486, 508, 530, 564, 580.
Samuel and Thomas, *brig*, 378,* 392, 402, 414, 440.* (See Mattapoisett.)
Stranger, *schooner*, 414, 428.*
Samuel Cook, *brig*, 440,* 448, 464, 472, 486, 500, 530.*
Shylock, *brig*, 464, 472,* 486, 500.*
Sea Shell, *schooner*, (probably Seychelle,) 486,* 508.
S. R. Soper, *schooner*, 500,* 508, 520, 530, 554, 564, 572, 580, 584, 608, 622, 628.*
Sassacus, *schooner*, 600,* 608, 628, 634,* 638, 646.
S. A. Paine, *schooner*, 622,* 638.*

PERTH AMBOY, N. J.:
Susquehanna, *ship*, 252.

PORTSMOUTH, R. I.:
Sarah Atkins, *sloop*, 264.

POUGHKEEPSIE, N. Y.:
Siroc, *ship*, 304.*

PORTLAND, ME.:
Science, *ship*, 314, 352.

PROVIDENCE, R. I.:
South America, *ship*, 402,* 440.* (See New Bedford.)

SAG HARBOR, N. Y.:
Superior, *bark*, 396, 406, 432, 450. (From Wilmington.) (See New Bedford.)
Silas Richards, *ship*, 382, 420.* (See New Bedford.)
Salem, *ship*, 420.*
Saint Lawrence, *ship*, 420.*
Sabina, *ship*, 420.* (From New York.)
Susan, *schooner*, 544,* 558, 574,* 580;* *brig*, 584.*
S. S. Learned, *schooner*, 544,* 566,* 574.*

SALEM, MASS.:
Samuel Wright, *ship*, 302, 328, 358.*
Sapphire, *ship*, 328, 358.*
Statesman, *bark*, 328, 350, 392.*
Said bin Sultan, *bark*, 622.*

NANTUCKET, MASS.—Continued.

Tarquin, *ship*, 218,* (see foot-note,) 222, 228,* 242.*
Three Sons, *brig*, 218.*
Two Brothers, *ship*, 226, 236.*
Thomas 2d, *ship*, 228, 236, 250.
Thule, *ship*, 292,* 326, 346, 390.*
Three Brothers, *ship*, 300, 336, 376, 438, 486, 518,* 572.* (See New Bedford.)
Tyleston, *schooner*, 356;* *brig*, 376, 390, 400, 426, 464, 472,* 486, 510.*
Telescope, *schooner*, 356.
Two Brothers, *schooner*, 412, 438,* 446.*

NEW BEDFORD, MASS.:

Tryall, ——, 188.
Triton, *ship*, 200, 202, 204, 206, 208, 226, 238,* 252, 256, 262, 268, 282, 306, 344, 388, 436,* (see foot-note,) 470, 504; *bark*, 550,* 576, 606, 626, 644, 656.
Thacher, *schooner*, 208,* 210. (Probably the William Thacher; which see.)
Timoleon, *ship*, 230,* 232, 238, 244,* 248, 252,* 258, 268,* 282, 316, 354,* 398,* 424.*
Traveller, *brig*, 232. (See Westport.)
Telemachus, *schooner*, 244. (See Fairhaven.)
Trident, *ship*, 268, 282, 306, 344, 398, 436,* 470, 526,* 570; *bark*, 606,* 640.*
Two Brothers, *ship*, 282, 290, 298, 306, 316, 334, 344. 364, 374, 410, 444, 482, 516; *bark*, 560.*
Tobacco Plant, *ship*, 282, 290, 306, 344, 388, 436.*
Tuscaloosa, *ship*, 316,* 344,* 364, 410.*
Two Sisters, *brig*, 398.* (From Mattapoisett.)
Tacitus, *ship*, 410.*
Triton 2d, *ship*, 436,* 462, 482, 516. (From Plymouth.)
Tamerlane, *ship*, 470,* 516; *bark*, 560,* 588, 606, 632, 646.
Thomas Nye, *ship*, 482,* 516, 550.*
Tropic Bird, *bark*, 482,* 504, 526, 550, 576, 582, 598, 606, 618, 626,* 656.
Thomas Dickason, *ship*, 494,* 538, 576,* 606; *bark*, 632.* (From Sag Harbor.)
Twilight, *ship*, 516,* 560.*
Thomas Pope, *ship*, 538,* 570,* 656.
Tahmaroo, *ship*, 576.* (From Fairhaven.)
Thomas Winslow, *bark*, 576,* 588, 598, 606, 618.* (From Westport.)
Three Brothers, *ship*, 606,* 632,* 652. (From Nantucket.)

NEW LONDON, CONN.:

Thames, *brig*, 244, 250.
Tuscarora, *ship*, 294, 304, 312, 320, 328.* (See Cold Spring.)
Tenedos, *bark*, 368,* 396, 418,* 450, 474, 510, 544.*
Topaz, *brig*, 496.*
Tempest, *bark*, 556.*
Trinity, *bark*, 638,* 658.

NEW HAVEN, CONN.:

Thames, *brig*, 244.

PLYMOUTH, MASS.:

Triton, *ship*, 300,* 306,* 318,* 330, 358, 402.* (See New Bedford.)

PORTSMOUTH, N. H.;

Triton, *ship*, 314, 322.

PROVINCETOWN, MASS.:

Tarquin, *schooner*, 428,* 440.*
Thriver, *schooner*, 554,* 572.* (See Beverly.)
T. R. Hughlett, *schooner*, 608.

SAG HARBOR, N. Y.:

Thomas Nelson, *ship*, 226, 230.
Thorn, *ship*, 240, 246, 248, 252, 260, 264, 268, 274, 280, 286, 294, 312, 320, 328, 340, 350.*
Thames, *ship*, 260, 264, 268, 274, 280, 286, 304, 312, 320, 328, 340.*
Telegraph, *ship*, 286, 312.*
Triad, *ship*, 286.*
Thomas Dickason, *ship*, 340, 360, 382, 420.* (See New Bedford.)
Thames, *ship*, 360, 382, 406, 442.*
Timor, *ship*, 396,* 420, 442, 466, 512, 544.*
Tuscany, *ship*, 396,* 432, 450,* 490, 522.*

W.

NEW BEDFORD, MASS.—Continued.
Warren, *bark*, 526.* (From Holmes's Hole.)
Wavelet, *bark*, 526.*
William Gifford, *bark*, 560,* 594,* 626.*
Willis, *bark*, 606.* (From Mattapoisett.)

NEW LONDON, CONN.:
Wabash, *ship*, 270, 272, 280, 286, 294, 304.*
White Oak, *bark*, 378,* 406.* (From New York.)
William C. Nye, *ship*, 378, 406, 442. (See New Bedford.)
William T. Wheaton, *bark*, 474.*

NEWPORT, R. I.:
William Lee, *ship*, 332, 368, 416, 458, 496,* 542.*

ORLEANS, MASS.:
William Martin, *schooner*, 520, 542, 572, 584.* (See Boston.)

PROVINCETOWN, MASS.:
Walter Irving, *schooner*, 472,* 486, 500, 508, 520, 530, 542, 564, 572, 580, 596, 600, 608, 622, 634.*
Walter K., *schooner*, 472,* 486, 500, 508.*
Willis Putnam, *schooner*, 472,* 486.*
Waldron Holmes, *schooner*, 508,* 520, 564.*
Weather Gage, *schooner*, 580,* 584, 590.*
Watchman, *schooner*, 584, 590, 596, 608, 614, 622, 634.* (From Nantucket.)
William A. Grozier, *schooner*, 614,* 622, 638, 646,* 654.
Winged Racer, *schooner*, 614,* 622, 628.*
Willie Irving, *schooner*, 622.*

SAG HARBOR, N. Y.:
Washington, *ship*, 208, 210, 294, 304, 312, 320, 328, 350, 360, 382,* 406, 432, 460, 476,* 512.*
Warren, *ship*, 208, 210, 218.*
Wickford, *brig*, 382.*
Wiscasset, *ship*, 382, 420.* (From Wiscasset.)
William Tell, *ship*, 406,* 442, 460, 490, 522, 558.* (From New York.)
Washington, *bark*, 490,* 532, 574.* (From Greenport.)
W. F. Safford, *brig*, 544.*

SALEM, MASS.:
William H. Shailer, *bark*, 614,* 622.*

STONINGTON, CONN.:
Warsaw, *ship*, 416.*

WARREN, R. I.:
Warren, *ship*, 286, 310, 338, 370, 402, 448,* 488.*
William Baker, *ship*, 310, 320, 330, 352, 358, 382, 402.*
William Henry, *bark*, 474,* 530.
William Wilson, *ship*, 556.*

WELLFLEET, MASS.:
Wellfleet, ——, 182.

WISCASSET, ME.:
Wiscasset, *ship*, 314, 352.* (See Sag Harbor.)

X.

NEW BEDFORD, MASS.:
Xantho, *bark*, 612,* 636.* (Formerly of Warren.)

SAG HARBOR, N. Y.:
Xenophon, *ship*, 286, 320, 340, 350, 370.*

WARREN, R. I.:
Xantho, *bark*, 542.* (See New Bedford.)

Y.

EDGARTOWN, MASS.:
York, *ship*, 384, 412.*

GENERAL INDEX.

LIST OF ILLUSTRATIONS.

*The figures of whales and of apparatus used in the whale-fisheries are taken from the important and remarkably interesting volume entitled "The Marine Mammals of the Northwestern Coast of North America described and illustrated; together with an account of the American Whale-Fishery." By Charles M. Scammon, Captain United States Revenue Marine. San Francisco: John H. Carmany & Co. New York: G. P. Putnam & Sons. 1874. 4to. 27 plates.

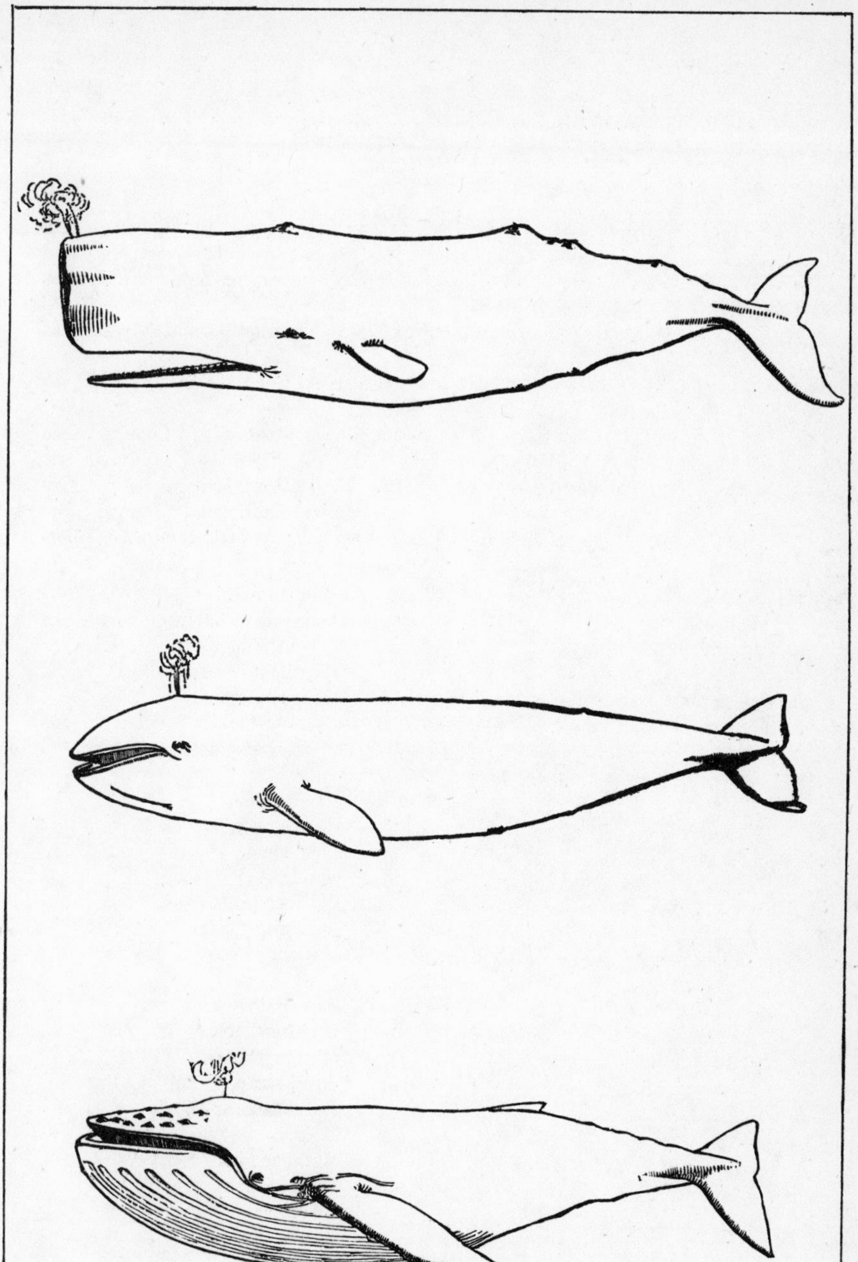

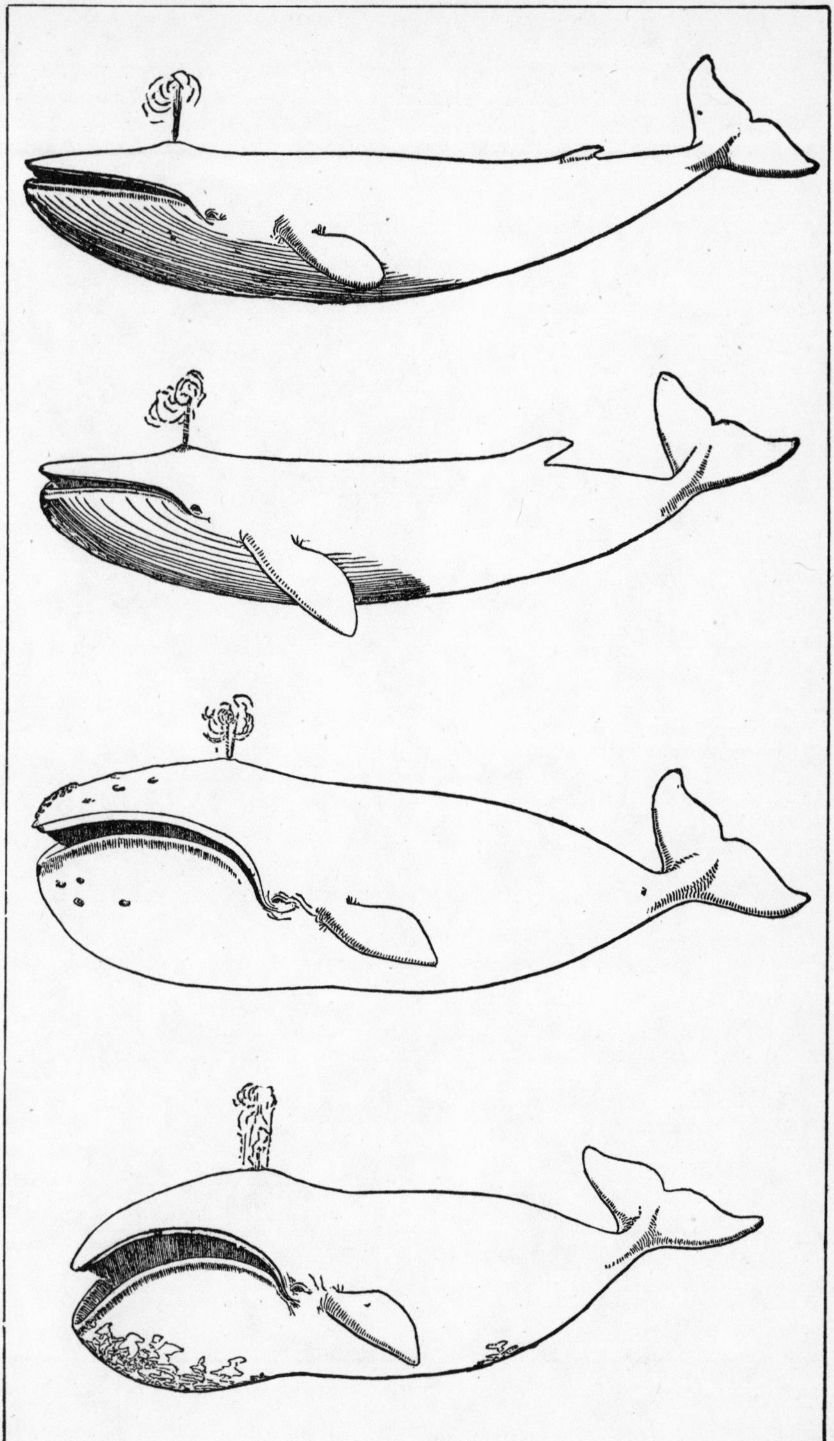

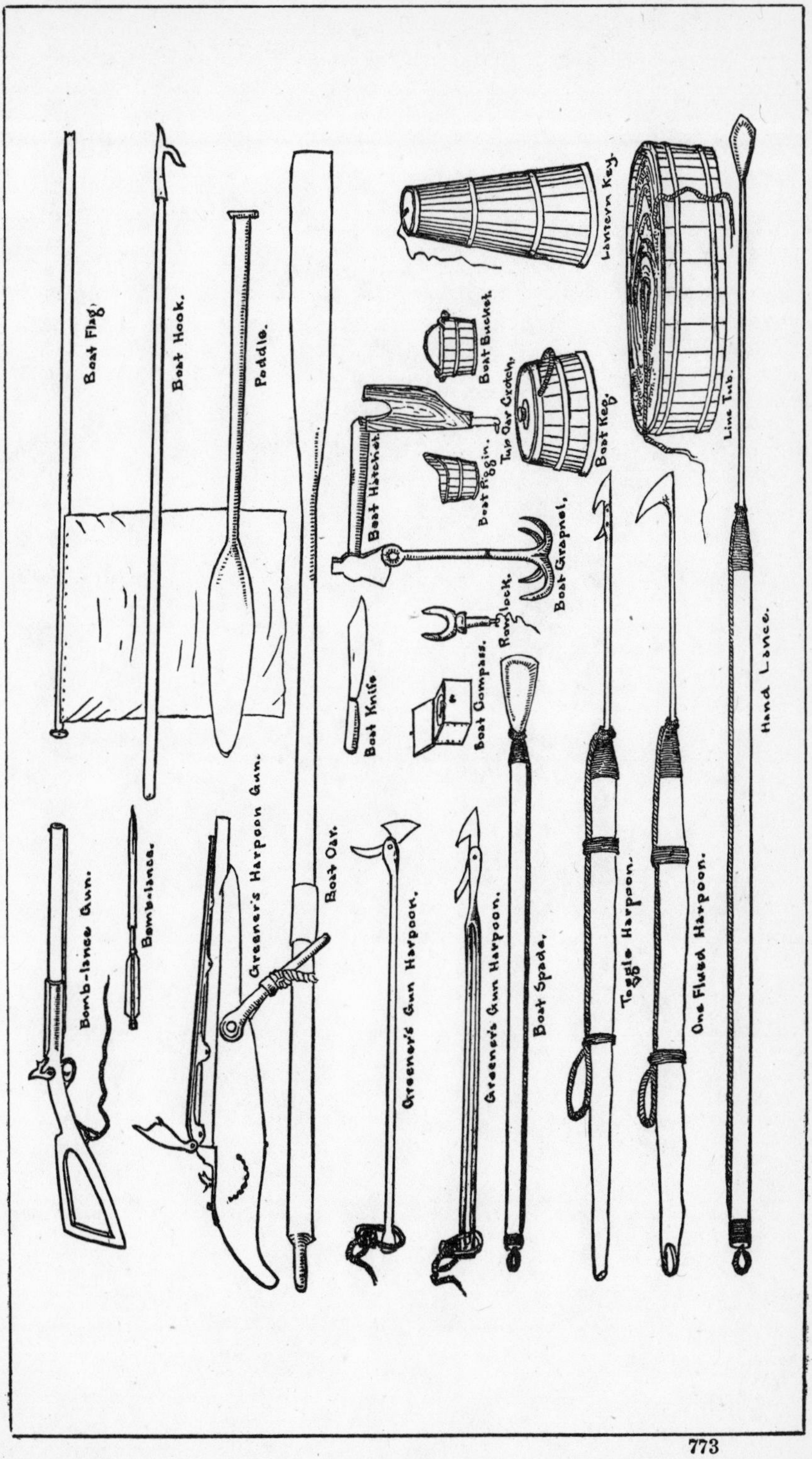

Boat Flag.
Boat Hook.
Paddle.
Boat Oar.
Lantern Keg.
Line Tub.
Boat Bucket.
Tub Oar Crotch.
Boat Keg.
Boat Piggin.
Boat Hatchet.
Boat Grapnel.
Rowlock.
Boat Knife.
Boat Compass.
Hand Lance.
Bomb-lance Gun.
Bomb-lance.
Greener's Harpoon Gun.
Greener's Gun Harpoon.
Greener's Gun Harpoon.
Boat Spade.
Toggle Harpoon.
One Flued Harpoon.

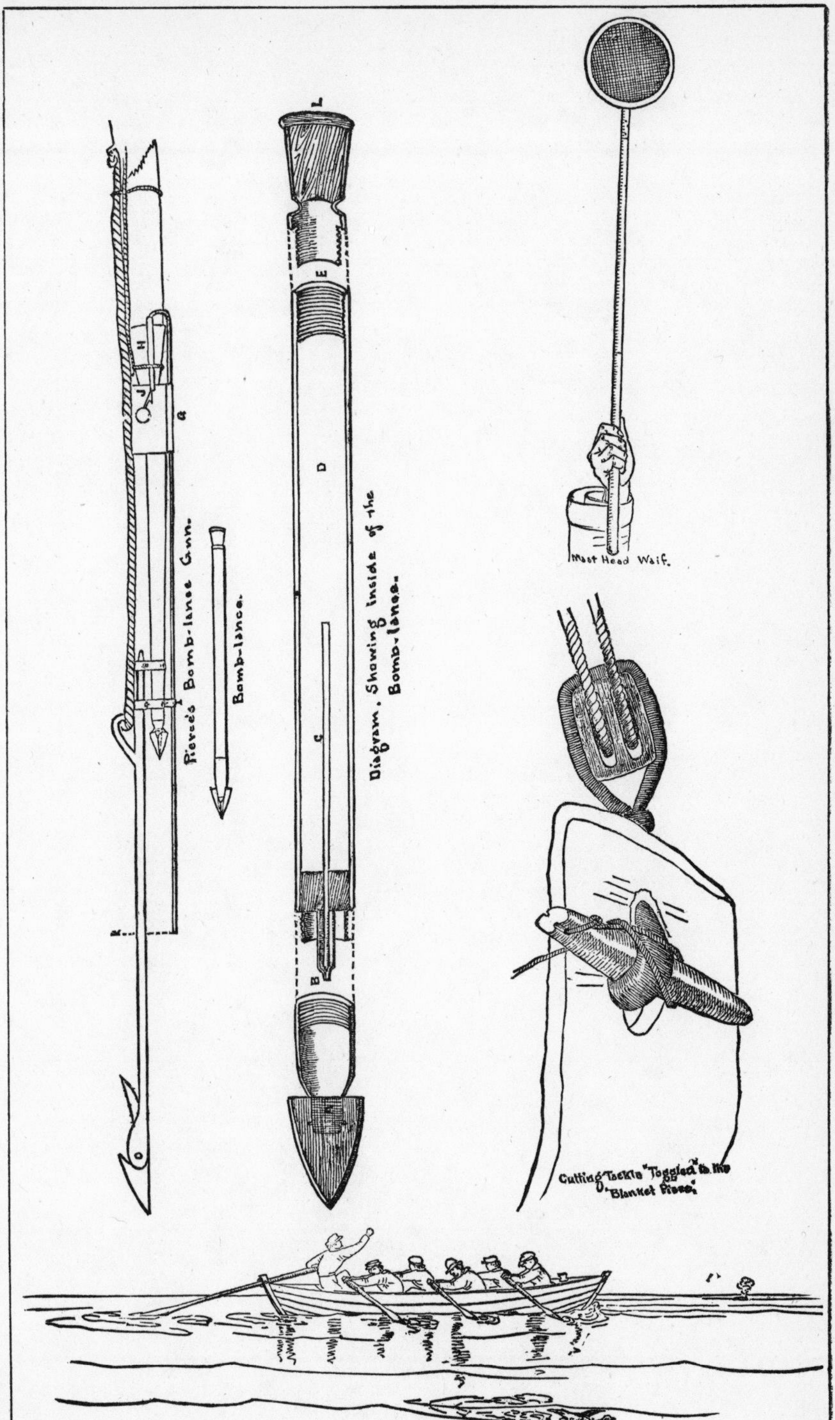
Pierce's Bomb-lance Gun.
Bomb-lance.
Diagram, Showing inside of the Bomb-lance.
Mast Head Waif.
Cutting Tackle "Toggled" to the "Blanket Piece."
The Whale Boat

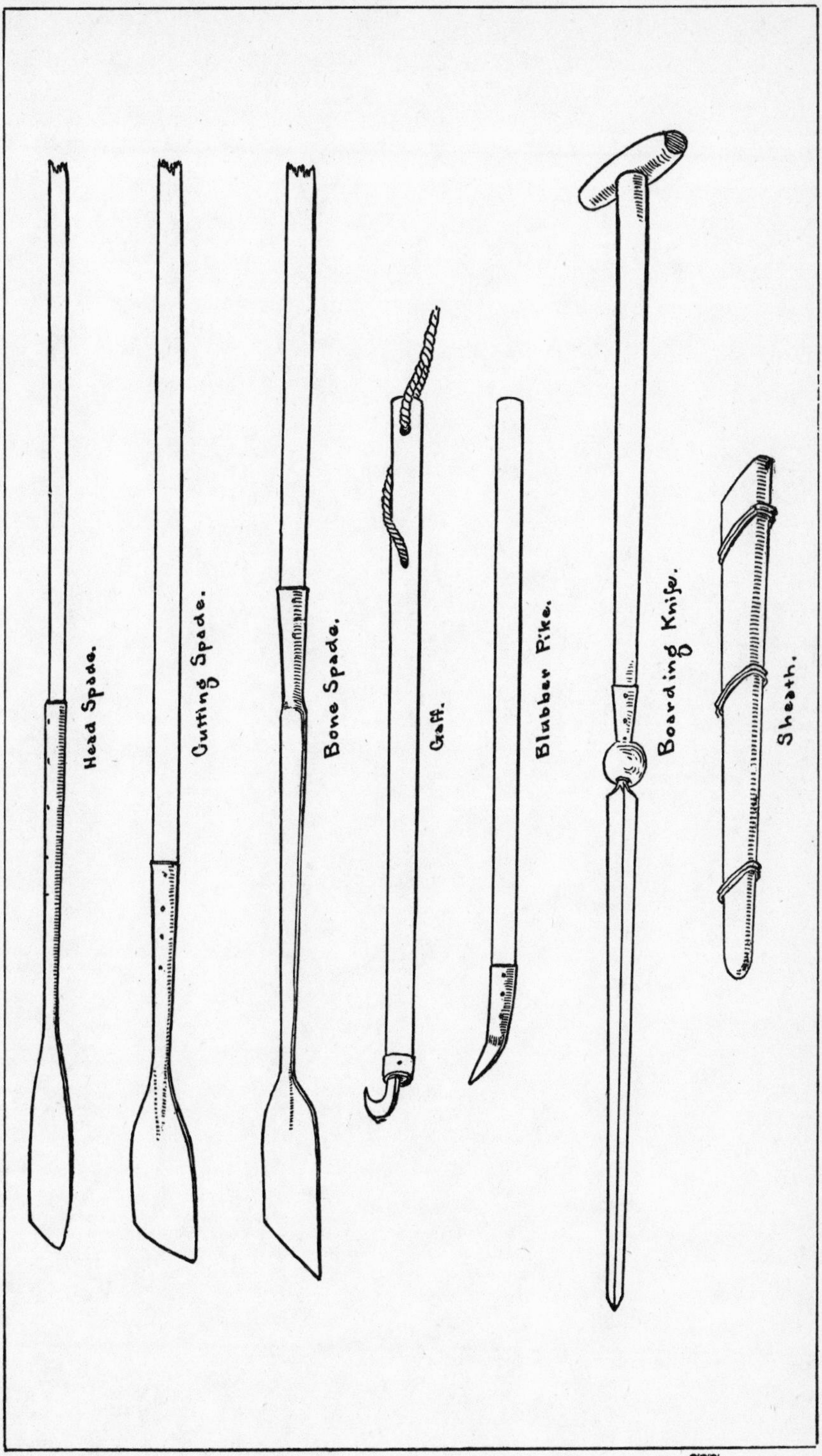
Head Spade.
Cutting Spade.
Bone Spade.
Gaff.
Blubber Pike.
Boarding Knife.
Sheath.

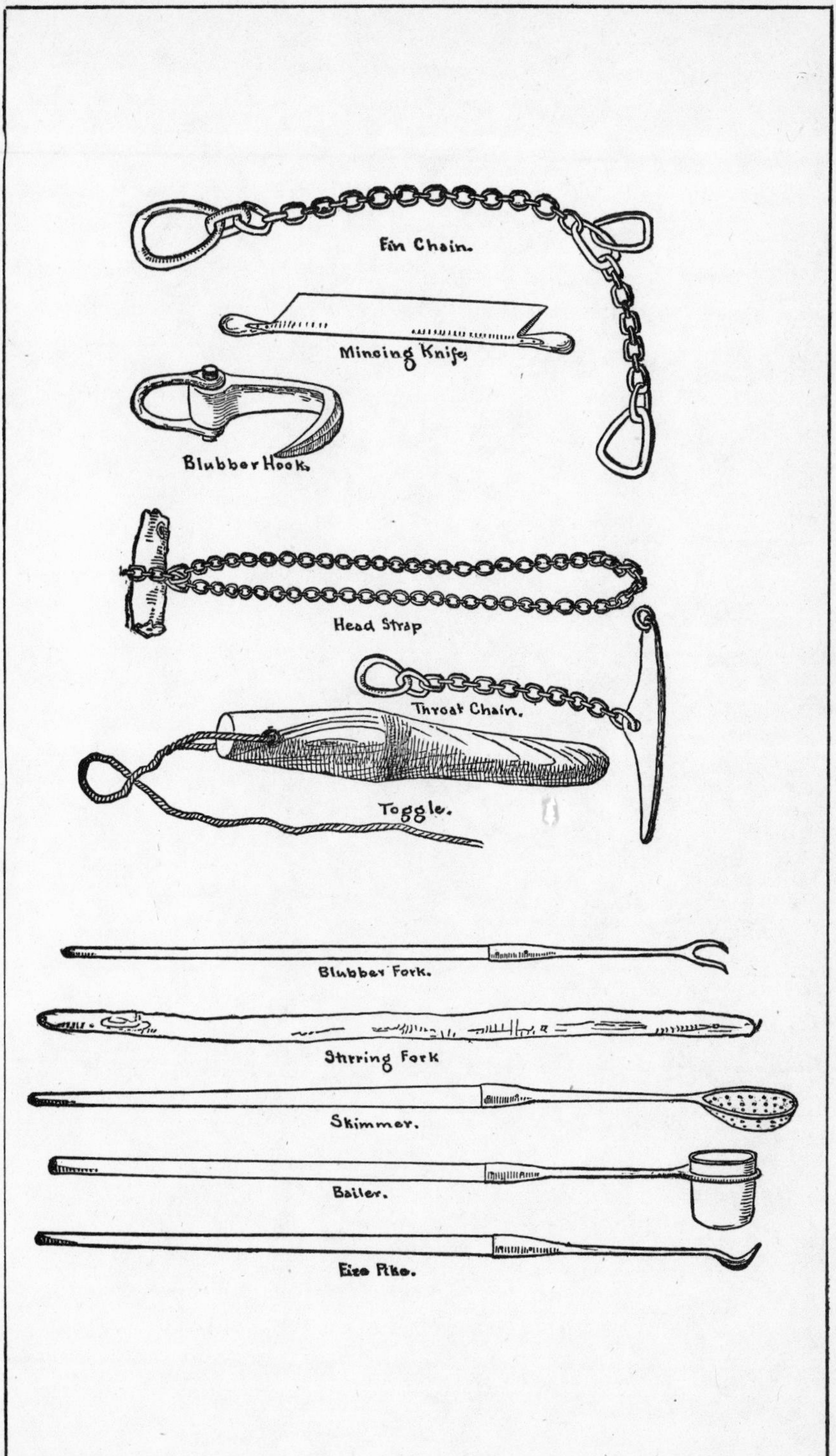
Fin Chain.
Mincing Knife.
Blubber Hook.
Head Strap
Throat Chain.
Toggle.
Blubber Fork.
Stirring Fork
Skimmer.
Bailer.
Fire Pike.